GREEK ISLAND HOPPING

2004

Written and researched by

Frewin Poffley

Thomas Cook
Publishing

Published by Thomas Cook Publishing,
a division of Thomas Cook Tour Operations Limited
PO Box 227, Units 15-16, The Thomas Cook Business Park,
Coningsby Road, Peterborough, PE3 8SB, United Kingdom

E-mail: books@thomascook.com
Advertising sales: 01733 (+44 1733) 416477

Distributed in the USA by The Globe Pequot Press
PO Box 480, Guilford, Connecticut 06437

Text & Artwork: © 2004 Frewin Poffley

ISBN   1-841573-74-4

Published annually
ISSN   1362-0002

Whilst every care has been taken in compiling this publication using
the most up-to-date information available at the time of going to press,
neither the author nor Thomas Cook Tour Operations Limited as publishers
can accept any liability arising from errors or omissions in the text or
maps, however caused. Readers should note especially that timings and
fares of many Mediterranean ferry services are fixed only shortly before
the beginning of the season and are often subject to change without
notice. It is therefore strongly advised that all such information should
be checked before beginning any journey on one of the services listed in
this publication. The views and opinions expressed in this book are not
necessarily those of Thomas Cook Tour Operations Limited or those of the
Thomas Cook UK Limited group of companies.

Repro and imagesetting by PDQ Digital Media Solutions Limited, Bungay, Suffolk, UK

Printed and bound in Italy by Legoprint S.P.A.

Drawn ⌐ & typeset by Frewin Poffley/Thingumajigolo Productions

Contents

How to Use this Book

While everybody has heard of Greek island hopping, if you have yet to try it, the notion of booking a flight to Greece and then wandering between islands one has only vaguely heard of (complete with funny names written in an even more unintelligible looking alphabet) can seem a rather daunting prospect. In fact, once you understand how the Greek ferry system works and how respective islands are linked together, you will find that it is remarkably easy.

That said, those who go Greek island hopping (be they novice or a seasoned veteran) can never be said to be lacking a challenge. For Greece is a country apart. Thanks to good international ferry links and a very competitive domestic ferry system (to say nothing of small intimate islands touched by 4,000 years of history and populated with friendly islanders long used to speaking English), it offers the best island hopping in the Med. But there are problems, not least of which is Greece's inability to publish ferry timetables despite having a large fleet that carries 10 million passengers each year. Protected by cabotage laws that prevented foreign competition until late 2002 (it is unclear if foreign operators will appear in 2004) ferry companies chop and change boats and services seemingly at random (though in fact most boats use similar routes each summer), with the result that the majority of tourists stick to a few well-trodden routes while guide books to the Greek islands concentrate on the islands while glossing over the means of travelling between them.

This book attempts to address this imbalance and give you the facts you need to move around with ease. In addition to the more usual sightseeing information, it contains a synopsis of the ferry network around the Greek islands (as well as Aegean and other international services in the Mediterranean east of Venice). As a result, it is very much oriented towards showing you *how* to get around as well as telling you what you will find when you get there. It has been designed to answer the questions:

'Where can I go to?'

'How can I get there?'

'What will I find there?'

'Where can I hop to from there?'

In this guide chapters are determined by the main ferry routes. These are followed by a **Port Table** section showing typical High Season departures from the Islands and Mainland Ports covered in the book. At the back of the guide is a **Reference** section containing ferry company information (including a ferry colour key), a **Useful Greek** section and the **Index.**

For ease of use chapters are divided into three sections:

1

Overview & Itinerary

The initial — 'Where can I go to?' — section of each chapter is intended to give you a clear idea of the geographical area covered by the chapter and the best means of tackling the islands and ports within it. On the title page itself you will find a map showing the main ferry route linking the islands, along with approximate sailing times between them (using regular ferries) and the island name in Greek (in the form — usually the accusative case — that you are most likely to encounter it on ship destination boards and ticket agency timetables). This is followed by a brief description of the characteristics of the group, a map of the area covered, and a model itinerary showing a practical way of tackling the islands in the chain. The itinerary also identifies the best home or 'base' port in the group should you wish to use one island as a springboard to viewing the rest.

2

Ferry Services

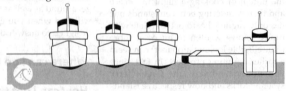

The second — 'How can I get there?' — section is devoted to the ferries that link the islands within each group. (Where a ferry's itinerary includes islands and ports split between several lines-cum-chapters it is described in the chapter in which it plays the most important role.) Each boat's previous High Season route is mapped, and the accompanying text lists the owning company, year of build (and rebuild, if any), and gross registered tonnage (GRT). In addition, there are comments on each ferry's history, reliability and likely changes in 2004. This will give you the means to interpret local advertising and assess the merits or otherwise of the individual boats.

You should find that all ferries are covered bar the four or five last-minute arrivals that turn up out of the blue each summer. Usually these new arrivals are not too much of a problem since they tend to either line up in competition with an existing service or simply replace it.

More of a handicap are the periodic fleet reshuffles which can result in up to four or five boats swapping (and adapting) itineraries and giving the appearance of far more substantive change than there really is.

3

Islands
& Ports

The third — 'What will I find there?' — section consists of a mini A—Z of the Islands and Ports found within the chapter area. All islands, mainland ports and the major sights are briefly described. The 60-odd islands large enough to warrant a ferry link also have an accompanying map showing typical High Season *weekday* bus and beach boat services, along with town maps identifying the important landmarks and places to stay.

Port
Tables

The greatest difficulty in moving around the Greek islands is not knowing the frequency of connections between specific ports. This section of the guide is designed to clue you in on the 'hopping' potential of each port and the ships sailing from them. The Port Tables show *typical* High Season ferry departure times as well as offering **Connections Maps** showing High Season frequency of service to other ports of call.

Working within the constraints imposed by much last minute summer scheduling by Greek ferry operators, this Port Table section of the book is **not** intended to be a timetable, but a guide that you can usefully employ to hop freely between islands and ports or to adjacent islands from your holiday base. The tables — showing services operating in 2003 (updated with the latest information where available) — are intended to give you the means of determining what is happening and the likely options available when you arrive at any port during 2004, and (given the constraints outlined on p. 32) through to 2005.

Planning
an Itinerary

Flexibility is the key to a successful island hopping holiday. Publilius Syrus' natty apophthegm *'It is a bad plan that admits of no modification'* was surely stylused with Greek island hopping in mind. Pre-planning an itinerary around the islands is perfectly practical, provided a number of points are borne in mind:

**Decide where you
would like to go, but leave
the details until you get to Greece**

Armed with a book like this in the pre-holiday enthusiasm it is very easy to over-plan. It is far better to make a hit list of the four or five islands you simply must get to and then a list of those you would also like to see, and thereafter keep your plans reasonably fluid; you can add precise boats and times when you get to your first port of call and establish which are running.

Build a two-week itinerary along the lines of 'on Tuesday we'll arrive at the port at 14.20, giving us a free 20 minutes to sup a pint of ouzo before catching the 14.45 boat', and the chances are you will come unstuck sooner rather than later. You would also end up extremely drunk. Greece is a casual country so an 'on the Tuesday afternoon or evening we'll catch a ferry' approach will be far more successful.

**Build itineraries
using 'Daily' connections**

When pre-planning, use the Port Table Connections maps (in the timetable section at the back of this book) and try to keep as many *6–7 days per week* links in your itinerary as possible, even if this means deviating from your preferred route.

Example: Rhodes to Nissiros. The Rhodes Connections map below shows that a link exists 2–3 days a week. Closer examination of the Port Table and Ferry description reveals that the primary boat (the C/F *Nissos Kalimnos*) operating this route has broken down in the past. The wise island hopper will note the possibility of using this service if it happens to be running when they get to Rhodes, but when pre-planning will reckon on travelling via Kos — which has

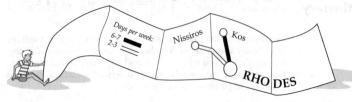

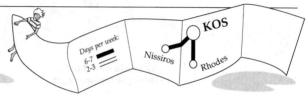

a daily link with both Rhodes and Nissiros (see above). The rule of thumb therefore is that *2–3 days per week* links should always be treated with suspicion: don't build an itinerary that *depends* on them — unless that link comes early enough in your holiday to make alternative plans. Similarly, if the Port Tables show that a route exists courtesy of a single boat, it pays to be aware of the vulnerability of the link to change.

**Always arrive at a
port with an Alternative Plan**

At some point in the average two-week island hopping holiday you will find yourself left high and dry on a quay waiting for a boat that for some reason or other fails to turn up. Life is far more relaxed if you have already pre-planned for such an eventuality and can blithely shrug your shoulders and say 'okay we'll do this instead…' The 'this' options usually come down to a later alternative boat, a change of route, and/or the afternoon on the nearest decent beach.

**Build in a 2-day
'delay' into your itinerary**

One of the great attractions of island hopping is that every island is different and sooner or later you will be washed up on the shores of the one the Gods made for you, tempting you to linger longer than intended. Build this into your calculations: it will also provide you with an extra safety net should weather, a fully booked ferry or lightning strike disrupt your plans.

**Allow plenty of time
to catch your return flight**

Always arrange an easily accessible final/return port of call and *allow at least one clear day spare* to ensure that you don't miss your return ferry or flight away from civilization. This is something that cannot be emphasized enough. If you are starting from a poorly connected airport give yourself two clear days: in short, always play safe — there is usually somewhere to play near your starting point so this needn't damage your holiday. If you are moving between chains (e.g. starting from the Dodecanese and moving into one of the Cycladic Lines) save the visits to islands near your return destination for the end of your holiday so that your final hops are both short and easy.

When you've used this book ...

... help us update

Greek Island Hopping is field-researched each year before being updated. Nevertheless, there will always be instances where up-to-date information was not obtainable at the time of research, and we welcome reports and comments from guide users.

Similarly, we aim to make the guide as practical and useful as possible to island hoppers and are grateful for any comments, criticisms and suggestions for improving future editions.

A free copy of the next edition of the guide, or of any other Thomas Cook publication, will be sent to all readers whose information or ideas are incorporated in future editions. Please address all contributions to:

The Editor, Greek Island Hopping,
Thomas Cook Publishing,
PO Box 227, Peterborough, PE3 8SB,
United Kingdom.

Or fax us on: 01733 416688
International: +44 1733 416688
E-mail: FrewinPoffley@greekislandhopping.com

Symbols, Maps & Tables

Symbols — see front cover flap

Times — see back cover flap

Street Maps

The majority of Greek island towns do not have street names (buildings are numbered instead). The best way of using the maps in this book is to navigate via landmarks (e.g. churches & hotels)

Scale

The maps in this book use the metric system used in Greece. To convert to yards and miles:
1 metre = 1.09 yards
1 kilometre = 0.62 miles

Map Legend

┝┼┼┼┼┤	Railway			Cliff / Steep Slope
┝─☐─┤	Railway Station			Map Cross-Section
─○─	Metro Station			Waterlogged Land
═══	Street / Path			
┉┉┉	Staircase / Muletrack			Pedestrianized Street
∷∷∷	Dirt Road			
	Building			Bridge
	Archway			City / Castle Wall
	Park / Woodland			Ruins
	Beach			Ruins (roofed over)
	Rocks			Line of Lost Walls
	Sports Field / Playground			Cemetery
	Fountain / Pool			Windmills

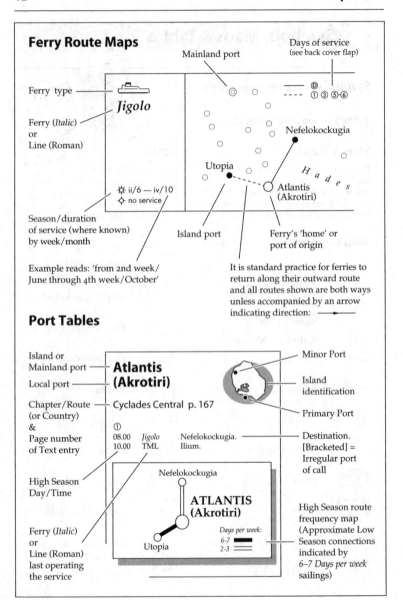

Ferry Route Maps

Days of service
(see back cover flap)

Mainland port

Ferry type

Jigolo

Ferry (*Italic*)
or
Line (Roman)

Nefelokockugia

Utopia

Atlantis
(Akrotiri)

☼ ii/6 — iv/10
◇ no service

Season/duration
of service (where known)
by week/month

Island port

Ferry's 'home' or
port of origin

Example reads: 'from 2nd week/
June through 4th week/October'

It is standard practice for ferries to
return along their outward route
and all routes shown are both ways
unless accompanied by an arrow
indicating direction: ⟶

Port Tables

Island or
Mainland port

Local port

Chapter/Route
(or Country)
&
Page number
of Text entry

High Season
Day/Time

Ferry (*Italic*)
or
Line (Roman)
last operating
the service

Atlantis
(Akrotiri)

Cyclades Central p. 167

①
08.00   *Jigolo*   Nefelokockugia.
10.00   TML   Ilium.

Nefelokockugia

**ATLANTIS
(Akrotiri)**

Days per week:
6-7
2-3

Utopia

Minor Port

Island
identification

Primary Port

Destination.
[Bracketed] =
Irregular port
of call

High Season route
frequency map
(Approximate Low
Season connections
indicated by
6–7 Days per week
sailings)

Island Bus & Beach Boat Maps

Island name/s
(former name
shown in light
face).

Town, Village
or Hamlet
(Importance
indicated by
the size of
the text)

Symbols
(from L to R):

International
Ferry Connection

Base Port

Camping

Rooms available

Air, Rail, Bus
connecting
service

Upland Areas   Bus Station/s on accompanying Town Street Map

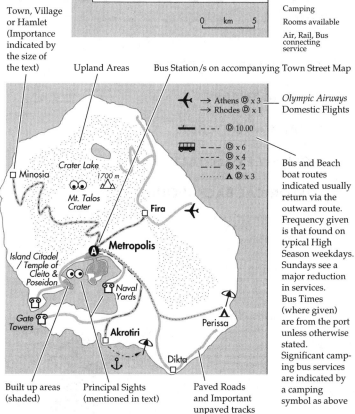

→ Athens ⑩ x 3
→ Rhodes ⑩ x 1

Olympic Airways
Domestic Flights

---·--- ⑩ 10.00

--- ⑩ x 6
--- ⑩ x 4
-·-·- ⑩ x 2
········ ▲ ⑩ x 3

Bus and Beach
boat routes
indicated usually
return via the
outward route.
Frequency given
is that found on
typical High
Season weekdays.
Sundays see a
major reduction
in services.
Bus Times
(where given)
are from the port
unless otherwise
stated.
Significant camp-
ing bus services
are indicated by
a camping
symbol as above

Built up areas
(shaded)

Principal Sights
(mentioned in text)

Paved Roads
and Important
unpaved tracks

All maps in this guide are orientated with North at the top of the page unless otherwise indicated.

INTRODUCTION

- **GREEK ISLAND HOPPING**
- **GETTING THERE**
- **FERRIES AND TICKETS**
- **HOLIDAY ESSENTIALS**
- **HISTORICAL BACKGROUND**

SIGHTSEEING ISLES

CYCLADES NORTH	DELOS
CYCLADES CENTRAL	SANTORINI NAXOS ANTIPAROS
CRETE	IRAKLION
DODEC-ANESE	RHODES KOS PATMOS
ARGO-SARONIC	AEGINA
NORTH AEGEAN	THESSALONIKA KAVALA CHIOS SAMOS SAMOTHRACE
EASTERN LINES	CHIOS SAMOS (PITHAGORIO)
IONIAN	CORFU

NIGHTLIFE ISLES

CYCLADES NORTH	MYKONOS
CYCLADES CENTRAL	IOS SANTORINI PAROS
CYCLADES WEST	SIFNOS
NORTH AEGEAN	SKIATHOS THASSOS
IONIAN	CORFU LEFKADA ZAKINTHOS
DODEC-ANESE	KOS RHODES
EASTERN LINES	SAMOS (PITHAGORIO)
ARGO-SARONIC	SPETSES

BEACH ISLANDS

CYCLADES NORTH	MYKONOS ANDROS
CYCLADES CENTRAL	IOS NAXOS PAROS SANTORINI
CYCLADES EAST	KOUFONISSIA
NORTH AEGEAN	SKIATHOS SKYROS THASSOS
IONIAN	CORFU ZAKINTHOS LEFKADA
DODEC-ANESE	KOS KARPATHOS RHODES LIPSI PATMOS
EASTERN LINES	LESBOS
ARGO-SARONIC	AEGINA
CYCLADES WEST	SERIFOS SIFNOS

WINDMILL ISLES

CYCLADES NORTH	MYKONOS
CYCLADES CENTRAL	IOS SANTO ANTIPARO PAROS
CYCLADES WEST	SERIFOS KIMOLOS
EASTERN CYCLADES	ASTIPALEA

QUIET ISLANDS

CYCLADES WEST	FOLEGANDROS SERIFOS SIFNOS
CYCLADES NORTH	KEA ANDROS KYTHNOS
CYCLADES CENTRAL	ANTIPAROS
NORTH AEGEAN	LIMNOS SKYROS SAMOTHRACE ALONISSOS
DODEC-ANESE	NISSIROS TILOS
IONIAN	ITHACA MEGANISI
CYCLADES EAST	ALL OF THEM !

PICTURESQUE 'CHORA' ISLANDS

CYCLADES NORTH	MYKONOS
CYCLADES CENTRAL	IOS SANTORINI PAROS
EASTERN LINES	LESBOS
NORTH AEGEAN	SKYROS
CYCLADES WEST	SERIFOS SIKINOS FOLEGANDROS
EASTERN CYCLADES	ASTIPALEA AMORGOS ANAFI

IDEAL ISLANDS
FOR MAROONING YOUR PARTNER ON WHEN THEY ARE BEING PARTICULARLY IRRITATING

CYCLADES CENTRAL	ANAFI
NORTH AEGEAN	AGIOS EFSTRATIOS
CRETE & EASTERN CYCLADES	GAVDOS
ARGO-SARONIC	ANTIKITHERA

Greek Island Hopping

Guidebooks to Greece are apt to intimidate any would-be island hopper by observing that the country has some 1,425 islands, of which 166 are inhabited. In practice, life is much simpler: Greece has 78 islands connected by regular ferry or hydrofoil, with another 40-odd islets visited by tour or beach boats (the remaining 48 'inhabited' islands being occupied by odd monks, goat herds and the occasional shipping billionaire). You can therefore get to some 120 islands using commercial boats.

Of course, apart from the growing number of island hopping fans devoting holidays toward the goal of doing them all, in the eyes of most tourists not all these islands are *worth* a visit; but which you add to, or cross off, your list rather depends on your vision of the ideal Greek island. Herein lies the fascination of the islands, for the mix of history and geography is different on every one. It is almost as if the Olympian Gods had taken turns at trying their hands at different combinations and then laid the results down side by side to compare each in turn. Any temptation to linger is tempered by curiosity as to what one is likely to find at the next island down the line.

The Greek islands fall into six named groups. The most popular are the Cyclades. With 26 ferry-linked small islands, this is the group that naturally comes to mind when thinking of island hopping. Following close on behind are the 17 Dodecanese islands running down the Turkish coast. The other groups have less mass appeal and fewer islands, but are growing in popularity. The most frequently visited are the closely bunched Saronic Gulf islands (running south of Athens) as all can be 'done' by day-trippers from the capital, while the widely scattered Eastern and Northern Aegean

islands have much to offer if you have more than a fortnight at your disposal. The Ionian islands, distinguished by being the only group to lie outside the Aegean, are poorly connected with the rest of the ferry system but also have their fans.

If you are new to island hopping the first — and most important — thing that you need to appreciate is that the Greek ferry system is not actually geared to moving tourists between islands within any one group, but primarily exists to ferry local Greeks between the islands and Athens (over a third of the population of Greece lives in Athens and many are economic migrants from the islands, returning periodically to their family homes). This is why there is so little timetable information in the islands — the locals are not interested in moving to other islands on the line.

The ferry network that has developed as a result is best imagined as a wheel, with the 'hub' being Athens (via its ports of Piraeus and Rafina), from which radiate ten 'spokes' or chains of islands, along which ferries regularly steam up and down — usually running 24- or 48-hour return trips from Piraeus. Cross-chain services that enable you to jump between islands on different chains without returning to Athens also exist, but are far fewer in number. It is therefore easy to island hop between the islands along a particular chain or line, but hopping over to an island on another can, on occasions, be quite difficult.

The frequency of boats down each line is very tourist-dependent. The standard Low Season daily sailing between the popular islands and the capital can mushroom up to six or more once the summer crowds start arriving. The smaller, less touristed, islands tend to retain an annual twice-weekly subsidized lifeline ferry link with the capital regardless of season, with a smaller rise in the numbers of visiting summer boats.

The first decision that any island hopper therefore needs to make is which 'spoke' or chain of islands they wish to visit. This is an important decision as the islands collected in each chain combine to offer very different experiences (individual chains also vary greatly in the opportunities on offer to cross over to another chain). This guide attempts to make this task easier by grouping the Greek islands into chapters according to their regular ferry-linked chain or line (rather than the formal group to which they belong).

The chapter summaries on the next three pages and the chain/chapter map on p. 19 should help you quickly sort out which is the best chain for you. Brief descriptions of the general characteristics of each chain are followed by short sections giving:

1. The Main Islands
These are listed in their normal order of call when sailing from Piraeus.

2. High Season Cross Lines
Crossing between 'spokes' or chains can be difficult at times (though the degree of difficulty varies with the seasons). This section seeks to highlight those islands most likely to be offering the best chance to cross over to another chain. Note: other islands will also offer irregular cross-line connections via ferries, hydrofoils or tourist boats.

3. Computer Ticket Traps
This year sees the sixth year of operation for the new computer ticket booking system for passengers using all large ferries (see p. 38). Partially in operation since 1997, it has resulted in some island hoppers finding that they couldn't travel for a day or two because of fully booked ferries.

This list tries to identify those islands and times when high demand for tickets is likely to cause problems in High Season (though it would be unwise to assume that it is infallible!). Apart from the Easter holiday (when most Greeks attempt to return to their home island), computer tickets shouldn't cause you too many problems.

Easily the most popular line in Greece (regularly attracting over 40% of island hopping tourists), the Cyclades Central links four very popular islands that offer everything from nightlife to nudist beaches. The chain is characterized by being overcrowded in High Season. Out of the High Season peak period of mid-July to mid-August they remain busy, but not oppressively so.

Main Islands
Paros, Naxos, Ios, Santorini.

High Season Cross Lines
Paros — Mykonos (Cyclades North)
Paros — Sifnos (Cyclades West)
Paros — Kos (Dodecanese)
Paros — Samos (Eastern Lines)
Paros — Skiathos, Thessalonika
                              (Northern Aegean)
Naxos — Mykonos (Cyclades North)
Naxos — Amorgos (Cyclades East)
Ios — Sikinos, Folegandros (Cyclades West)
Santorini — Sikinos, Folegandros
                              (Cyclades West)
Santorini — Iraklion (Crete)
Santorini — Skiathos, Thessalonika
                              (Northern Aegean)

Computer Ticket Traps
Frequency of boats should ensure that missing one shouldn't delay you too much. Overnight boats to Athens fill up fast in August, so you should obtain tickets for these as soon as you know when you are travelling.

A much visited group thanks to over-popular Mykonos, which shares the same characteristics as the islands on the Cyclades Central Line. The other islands are relatively quiet, most visitors being Greeks. Another feature common to the islands in this chain in High Season is the very strong *meltemi* wind that rushes south down the Aegean; this chain acts as something of a wind break for the rest of the Cyclades. Daily ferries run to these islands from both Piraeus and Rafina.

Main Islands
Syros, Tinos, Mykonos, Andros.

High Season Cross Lines
Mykonos — Paros, Naxos, Ios, Santorini
(Cyclades Central)
Mykonos — Ikaria, Samos (Eastern Lines)
Mykonos — Skiathos, Thessalonika
(Northern Aegean)
Mykonos — Amorgos (Cyclades East)

Computer Ticket Traps
The holy island of Tinos is subjected to an invasion of Greeks in the week of the 15th of August, when ferries are booked solid. Ferries to Tinos on Saturdays and from Tinos on Sundays are also sure to be full. Mykonos is the only other island where you could have problems; links to Paros and Athens can fill to capacity in High Season.

4.

Cyclades West............................... p. 224

A collection of relatively quiet islands increasing in popularity. Most have some nightlife and at least one good beach. Ferry links with other lines are relatively poor, but catamarans have opened up extra connections in the last couple of years.

Main Islands
Kea, Kythnos, Serifos, Sifnos, Kimolos, Milos, Folegandros, Sikinos.

High Season Cross Lines
Serifos — Paros (Cyclades Central)
Folegandros — Ios, Santorini
(Cyclades Central)
Sikinos — Ios, Santorini (Cyclades Central)
Milos — Agios Nikolaos, Sitia (Crete)

Computer Ticket Traps
Kea, Kythnos and Serifos are so close to Athens that they see large numbers of Greek visitors at weekends. Ferries to all are likely to be fully booked Friday evenings to Sundays.

5.

Cyclades East............................... p. 262

The quietest of the Cyclades lines, and also a sub-line running out of Naxos. The islands are

the least spoilt in the Cyclades, but ferry links are erratic, hampering easy hopping.

Main Islands
Amorgos, Iraklia, Schinoussa, Koufonissia, Astipalea, Anafi.

High Season Cross Lines
Amorgos — Naxos, Paros (Cyclades Central)
Amorgos — Mykonos (Cyclades North)
Astipalea — Kalimnos (Dodecanese)
Anafi — Santorini (Cyclades Central)

Computer Ticket Traps
Space limitations on the small, local ferry running from Amorgos to Mykonos could result in High Season ticket rationing.

6.

Crete .... p. 288

A popular starting point for island hopping holidays, Crete sees daily overnight non-stop ferries from Piraeus (making it an 'empty' — i.e. island-free — spoke from Athens). Crete is also the termination point for a number of ferries running down other lines. The island has something to suit all tastes, with a highly developed resort-packed north coast and a scenic hinterland and south coast.

High Season Cross Lines
Iraklion — Santorini, Paros (Cyclades Central)
Iraklion — Mykonos (Cyclades North)
Iraklion — Rhodes (Dodecanese)
Iraklion — Skiathos, Thessalonika
(Northern Aegean)
Agios Nikolaos — Milos (Cyclades West)
Sitia — Milos (Cyclades West)

Computer Ticket Traps
Rhodes and Thessalonika-bound ferries often fill up to capacity in High Season: much depends on the number of ferry sailings.

7.

Dodecanese Lines........................ p. 320

Attracting 25% of island hoppers, the Dodecanese islands offer a popular contrast with the Cyclades. They feel slightly less Greek, but have much more variety and sightseeing, with some of the best nightlife and beaches. The longest chain in the Greek islands, links are reasonable, though links with other chains are limited. The islands south of Rhodes are poorly connected to the rest of the group.

Main Islands
Patmos, Leros, Kalimnos, Kos, Nissiros, Tilos, Symi, Rhodes, Kastelorizo, Chalki, Karpathos, Kassos.

High Season Cross Lines
Rhodes — Sitia, Agios Nikolaos, Iraklion (Crete)
Rhodes — Paros, Santorini (Cyclades Central)
Kos — Paros (Cyclades Central)
Kalimnos — Astipalea (Cyclades East)
Patmos — Samos (Eastern Lines)

Computer Ticket Traps
Midday ferries running either way between Athens and Rhodes tend to be filled to bursting in High Season and should be booked as soon as possible.

8.

Eastern Lines .... p. 396

A quiet line: most visitors tend to be one-stop visitors as the islands are too large and out of the way to be popular with island hoppers. Piraeus ferries run to Ikaria and Samos or to Chios and Lesbos, with small ferries connecting the two sections of the chain.

Main Islands
(a) Ikaria, Samos. (b) Chios, Lesbos.

High Season Cross Lines
Lesbos — Limnos, Kavala, Alexandroupolis
                                    (Northern Aegean)
Samos — Paros (Cyclades Central)
Samos — Patmos, Kalimnos (Dodecanese)
Ikaria — Paros (Cyclades Central)
Ikaria — Mykonos (Cyclades North)

Computer Ticket Traps
None known.

9.

Northern Aegean .... p. 432

A quiet and very poorly linked line, the small Sporades sub-chain (Skiathos, Skopelos and Alonissos) sees more island hoppers than

the rest of the group put together and can be easily reached via ferries from the Cyclades. The North Aegean islands offer a nice mix of quiet beaches and well-wooded interiors.

Main Islands
Skiathos, Skopelos, Alonissos, Skyros, Limnos, Thassos, Samothrace.

High Season Cross Lines
Limnos — Lesbos, Chios (Eastern Lines)
Skiathos — Paros, Santorini (Cyclades Central)
Skiathos — Iraklion (Crete)
Skiathos — Mykonos (Cyclades North)

Computer Ticket Traps
Limnos—Athens ferries fill up very early: in early August you can get trapped on Limnos for several days if you are not careful.

10.

Argo-Saronic Lines .... p. 478

A group of largely small wooded islands close to Athens and the Peloponnese. The chain is best tackled day-tripping from Athens.

Main Islands
Aegina, Angistri, Poros, Hydra, Spetses, Kithera.

High Season Cross Lines
None. You will have to return to Athens or continue south to Crete.

Computer Ticket Traps
None known.

11.

Ionian Lines .... p. 512

Despite being a chain of large wooded islands with good beaches, this is the least popular group with island hoppers as links are poor (usually requiring a hop to the mainland).

Main Islands
Corfu/Kerkyra, Paxi/Paxos, Lefkada/Lefkas, Ithaca, Kefalonia, Zakinthos/Zante

High Season Cross Lines
None. Buses to Athens from most islands.

Computer Ticket Traps
None known.

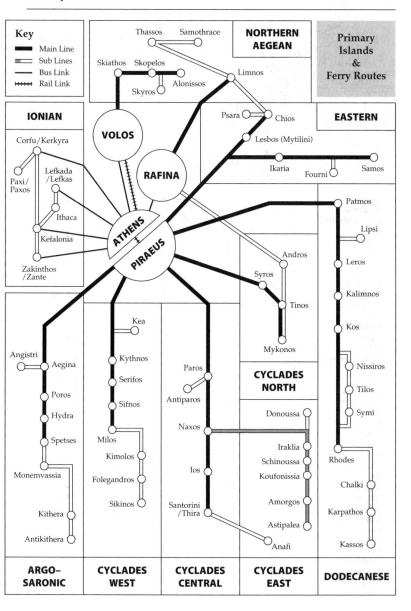

Key
- Main Line
- Sub Lines
- Bus Link
- Rail Link

Primary
Islands
&
Ferry Routes

NORTHERN AEGEAN

Thassos Samothrace
Skiathos Skopelos
Skyros Alonissos
Limnos

IONIAN

Corfu/Kerkyra
Paxi/Paxos
Lefkada/Lefkas
Ithaca
Kefalonia
Zakinthos/Zante

VOLOS

RAFINA

ATHENS

PIRAEUS

Psara Chios
Lesbos (Mytilini)
Ikaria Fourni Samos

EASTERN

Patmos
Lipsi
Leros
Kalimnos
Kos
Nissiros
Tilos
Symi
Rhodes
Chalki
Karpathos
Kassos

Andros
Syros
Tinos
Mykonos

CYCLADES NORTH

Kea
Kythnos
Serifos
Sifnos
Milos
Kimolos
Folegandros
Sikinos

Paros
Antiparos
Naxos
Ios
Santorini/Thira
Anafi

Donoussa
Iraklia
Schinoussa
Koufonissia
Amorgos
Astipalea

Angistri
Aegina
Poros
Hydra
Spetses
Monemvassia
Kithera
Antikithera

ARGO–SARONIC **CYCLADES WEST** **CYCLADES CENTRAL** **CYCLADES EAST** **DODECANESE**

Island Ratings

Having established which island group you want to visit, the next question you need to address is which islands within the group are likely to have most appeal. Rating the Greek islands is necessarily a very subjective exercise. Not only are an island's merits (or otherwise) conditioned by whether

ISLAND RATINGS

	Main Town	Landscape	Tree Cover	Sightseeing	Nightlife	Eating	Peace & Quiet	Beaches	Nudism	Tourism Level	Summary (out of 5)
Aegina	7	4	4	8	7	7	4	4	2	7	●●●●
Agathonisi	0	1	0	0	0	2	10	0	0	1	●
Agios Efstratios	1	3	0	0	0	0	10	4	6	0	
Alonissos	3	6	8	1	2	5	5	5	4	3	●●●●
Amorgos	8	9	3	6	3	6	8	5	5	4	●●●●●●
Anafi	4	4	0	2	0	2	8	5	3	1	●
Andros	4	6	4	1	1	5	6	6	3	3	●●●
Angistri	2	3	7	0	1	3	4	2	0	5	●●
Antikithera	0	2	3	0	0	0	10	1	0	0	
Antiparos	6	4	2	4	5	5	6	7	10	6	●●●●
Antipaxi	2	4	4	0	0	3	6	6	4	3	●●
Arki	0	2	1	0	0	0	10	3	0	1	
Astipalea	8	5	2	6	4	5	7	4	1	2	●●●●●●
Chalki	7	3	0	1	2	6	6	3	0	5	●●●
Chios	4	7	6	5	3	7	5	3	2	3	●●●
Corfu / Kerkyra	6	6	6	8	10	6	2	9	4	10	●●●
Crete	5	10	6	10	9	7	8	8	5	9	●●●●
Delos	0	4	0	9	0	0	6	1	0	5	●●●●●
Donoussa	2	5	2	0	0	3	8	4	0	2	●
Elafonissos	6	5	1	0	0	6	10	7	5	2	●●
Evia	1	7	5	3	1	5	7	4	0	4	●
Folegandros	9	5	1	2	1	7	8	3	2	4	●●●●●●
Fourni	4	4	1	0	0	6	10	5	0	1	●●●●
Gavdos	1	5	2	1	0	0	10	3	0	0	●
Hydra	7	4	0	2	7	7	4	1	0	10	●●
Ikaria	2	9	4	1	3	4	6	5	3	3	●
Ios	7	5	1	1	10	2	3	9	8	10	●●●●
Iraklia	2	3	2	0	0	4	7	4	1	2	●●
Ithaca	4	8	4	2	1	6	7	2	0	2	●●●
Kalimnos	3	6	3	3	4	5	3	6	2	6	●●
Karpathos	4	9	3	5	2	6	6	6	3	3	●●●
Kassos	2	4	0	1	0	2	9	3	0	1	●
Kastelorizo	6	5	3	4	0	5	9	0	0	2	●●●●
Kea	5	4	3	6	2	6	6	4	1	5	●●●
Kefalonia	1	8	5	3	2	7	6	7	3	5	●●
Kimolos	5	5	1	2	2	5	10	5	2	2	●●●●
Kithera	6	7	3	3	2	6	9	6	1	1	●●●●

your priorities are beaches and nightlife or peace and quiet, but many islands are apt to leave very different impressions at different times of the year. Ios is a classic example of this: quiet and dreamy in the Low Season, it becomes *the* party island in August, usually attracting very negative reviews in consequence.

Nevertheless, it is possible to give some indication of an island's likely appeal, and the table below should help in this respect. Ratings are given out of ten (*the* place to go if you want this), with zero representing 'forget it'. Summaries are given out of five. Those islands rating less than one are better avoided.

THE TOP 14	Main Town	Landscape	Tree Cover	Sightseeing	Nightlife	Eating	Peace & Quiet	Beaches	Nudism	Tourism Level	Summary (out of 5)
Kos	6	3	2	8	10	3	1	8	4	10	●●●
Koufonissia	3	4	0	1	1	6	10	6	0	2	●●●
Kythnos	2	3	1	1	0	1	8	4	0	1	●
Lefkada / Lefkas	7	7	4	4	5	4	4	6	2	6	●●●
Leros	5	5	2	1	2	5	6	4	0	3	●●●
Lesbos	5	7	3	4	3	7	6	7	3	3	●●
Limnos	6	6	2	6	3	4	8	7	2	1	●●●●
Lipsi	4	2	1	1	0	5	9	5	3	3	●●
Milos	6	8	2	6	3	6	7	6	1	4	●●●●●
Mykonos	10	4	0	6	10	8	2	10	10	8	●●●●●●
Naxos	10	8	6	6	7	7	5	10	9	10	●●●●●●
Nissiros	6	9	4	6	1	4	8	2	0	3	●●●
Oinousses	1	2	3	0	0	2	9	4	0	1	●
Paros	6	5	3	4	9	4	2	8	6	10	●●●
Patmos	8	6	1	6	4	5	7	5	2	7	●●●●●
Paxi / Paxos	5	6	5	2	6	5	6	2	0	8	●●●
Poros	4	4	5	2	6	5	3	2	0	8	●
Psara	3	5	0	1	0	4	10	4	0	1	●
Rhodes	8	7	4	10	10	6	1	8	3	10	●●●●●
Salamina / Salamis	0	2	0	1	0	0	2	0	0	0	
Samos	3	7	7	6	4	5	5	8	2	6	●●●●
Samothrace	4	8	5	4	0	6	9	3	1	2	●●
Santorini / Thira	10	10	0	10	8	5	2	4	1	10	●●●●●
Schinoussa	1	3	1	0	1	5	9	5	0	2	●
Serifos	6	6	1	1	2	5	6	7	2	4	●●●
Sifnos	7	7	3	5	5	7	6	6	0	6	●●●
Sikinos	5	4	2	2	0	3	10	3	0	1	●●●
Skiathos	7	6	8	5	8	6	3	9	10	9	●●●●
Skopelos	7	7	7	3	5	5	3	5	8	6	●●●
Skyros	8	5	5	2	1	4	9	4	3	3	●●●●
Spetses	3	4	6	1	7	4	4	3	0	8	●●
Symi	8	5	3	4	5	6	5	4	1	6	●●●●
Syros	5	1	2	2	3	4	4	3	0	4	●●
Thassos	8	9	8	7	6	7	7	10	7	5	●●●●●●
Tilos	4	7	2	3	3	5	9	5	4	2	●●●●
Tinos	6	7	4	5	3	4	4	3	0	8	●●●
Zakinthos / Zante	3	8	7	3	10	5	3	9	3	8	●●●

Getting There

Part of the key to a successful holiday is getting your documentation, money supply, and entry and exit to and from Greece right. Attention to these details will help acquire the peace of mind needed for carefree island hopping. This can be also encouraged by taking further precautions: i.e. leave someone an idea of your likely itinerary (along with photocopies of all documents), and start out with a clear idea of what you would do if you are one of the unlucky few to hit trouble.

Passports and Visas

Personal documentation is a subject easily dealt with as no visa is required for EU nationals or nationals of Australia, Canada, New Zealand, and the USA for visits to most of the countries on the shores of the Eastern Mediterranean for up to three months, though some countries (such as

Embassies in Athens

Opening Hours:

Australia	37 D. Soutsou	☎ (210) 645 0404	①-⑤ 09.00–13.00
Austria	26 L. Alexandras	821 1036	
Belgium	3 Sekeri	361 7886–7	
Canada	4 Ioannou Gennadiou	723 9511	①-⑤ 09.00–13.00
Cyprus	16 Herodotou	723 7883	
Czech Republic	6 G. Seferis	671 3755	
Denmark	11 Vassilissis Sofias	360 8315	
Finland	1 Eratosthenous & V. Kon.	701 0444	
France	7 Vassilissis Sofias	361 1663–5	①-⑤ 09.00–11.00
Germany	10 Vassilissis Sofias	369 41	
Hungary	16 Kalvou	671 4889	
Ireland	7 Leoforos Vasileos	723 2771–2	
Israel	1 Marathonodromou	671 9530–1	
Italy	2 Sekeri	361 1723	①-⑤ 09.00–11.00
Japan	2–4 L. Messoghion	775 8101–3	
Netherlands	5–7 L. Vas. Konstantinou	723 9701–4	
New Zealand	268 Kifissias Halandri	687 4700	①-⑤ 09.00–13.00
Norway	7 L. Vas. Konstantinou	724 6173–4	
South Africa	60 Kifissias Maroussi	610 6645	
Spain	29 Vassilissis Sofias	721 4885	
Sweden	7 L. Vas. Konstantinou	729 0421	
Switzerland	2 Iassiou	723 0364–6	
UK	1 Ploutarchou	727 2600	①-⑤ 08.00–13.30
USA	91 Vassilissis Sofias	721 2951–9	①-⑤ 08.30–17.00

Thessalonika Consulates

UK	8 Venizelou, Eleftheria Sq.	☎ (2310) 278 006	①-⑤ 09.00–14.00
USA	59 Nikis St.	☎ (2310) 266 121	①-⑤ 09.00–12.00

Other UK Consulates

Corfu	2 Alexandras	☎ (26610) 30055, 37995
Rhodes	23 25th Martiou	☎ (22410) 27247, 27306

Turkey) have a small visa/entry charge. Since 1993 EU nationals with ID cards have not been required to carry passports within the EU. As the UK has no ID card scheme, UK nationals must continue to travel with a passport. All nationals are recommended to carry passports as they are often required when cashing traveller's cheques or exchanging money in Greece. Passports are always required when taking day excursions to Turkey.

National Tourist Organisation of Greece

One valuable source of information worth tapping before you go to Greece is the Greek tourist service (⊕ www.gnto.gr). Usually known by the initials NTOG (or GNTO) outside the country and EOT within Greece, their offices provide advice and information on all aspects of the country. Within Greece there are branches in most of the large tourist towns (see the town maps in this book) and at larger airports. Overseas there are branches in most major countries, including:

UK
4 Conduit Street, London, W1R 0DJ
☎ (0207) 734 5997

USA
645 Fifth Ave, New York, NY 10022
☎ (212) 421 5777

168 North Michigan Ave, Chicago, IL
☎ (312) 782 1084

611 West 6th St, Los Angeles, CA
☎ (213) 626 6696

Australia
51 Pitt Street, Sydney, NSW2000
☎ (02) 241 1663

Canada
1300 Bay Street, Main Level, Toronto
☎ (416) 968 2220

Money

While it is desirable to have some hard cash always to hand, the safest way of hanging onto your money is to take the bulk in travellers cheques (Thomas Cook Master-

Card Travellers Cheque 24-hour UK emergency number: ☎ +44 1733 502 995). American Express (emergency number: ☎ +44 1273 696933) are also well represented in the

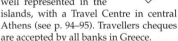

islands, with a Travel Centre in central Athens (see p. 94–95). Travellers cheques are accepted by all banks in Greece.

Outside banking hours, currency and cheques can be exchanged at ticket agencies (albeit at a worse rate of exchange). Every year tourists arrive armed with cash cards only to discover that ATMs are either not working, won't accept their cards, or — though this is now quite rare — aren't around at all. You should therefore ensure that you have access to some cash via other means. However you choose to take your funds, don't keep them all in one place (this way, if you are robbed you will still have something to fall back on).

In January 2002 Greece replaced the Drachma with the Euro. The new banknotes come in 500, 200, 100, 50, 20, 10 and 5 Euro denominations (each is a different size and colour); there are also 2 and 1 Euro coins, along with 50, 20, 10, 5, 2 and 1 cent pieces. At the time of going to press the tourist exchange rate of the Euro to the UK Pound Sterling was €1.42, to the US dollar, €0.87.

Travelling to Greece

How you get to Greece is going to be largely determined by the nature of your holiday. If you want to maximize your time in the islands the best way is to fly (see overleaf), possibly plugging into the Greek domestic air system (see p. 27). If you are doing the European tour then rail (see p. 29) or a combination of train and ferry (the whole of Chapter 13 is devoted to international ferry services) is the most popular route. International bus services have also been popular in the past. Having declined with the Balkan wars, they are beginning to make a comeback.

Flights to Greece

The great majority of visitors to Greece now choose to arrive and depart by air; the market is dominated by a mix of short-haul charter flights (most from Europe) and long-haul regular services focusing on countries with significant ethnic Greek immigrant populations (the two largest being the USA and Australia).

European Charter Flights

Cheap charter flights from Europe are the most popular (and cheapest) way for island hoppers to get to Greece. Because they are 'piggy-backing' on holiday flights, travellers opting to fly this way have to accept certain limitations. The most important of these are that once booked, these flights cannot be changed, and most require you to return a fortnight later (though with a bit of effort you can find operators who will offer you a 28-day return flight only ticket). Once you are in Greece there is a further dangerous potential pitfall: because charter tickets are cheap concessionary tickets aimed at encouraging tourism to Greece, it is a usual condition of issue that you do not stay overnight out of the country. This is particularly relevant should you be tempted to take one of the day-tripper boats or ferries to Turkey. You are likely to be denied your flight home should you — for any reason — be forced to stay overnight there.

Despite recent cut-backs in the number of charter holiday on offer, even in High Season it is possible to visit a Thomas Cook Flight Centre or other travel agent and pick up a last-minute return charter flight ticket from around UK£190/US$250. At other times of the year you can do even better with some tickets costing under UK£100/US$150.

Apart from flights to Athens, there are UK and European connections to 17 Greek airports. However, most are of limited use to the would-be ferry user. On an island hopping holiday the arrival/departure point is an important consideration, since you will have to plan your movements with a view to getting back there.

Of the various destinations available, **Athens** remains the safest in this respect, since its port of Piraeus is accessible on a daily basis from most islands in the Aegean. Naturally, the Cycladic islands of **Mykonos** and **Santorini** are also good starting points (though flights to both are apt to be more expensive than elsewhere) and Crete has a useful and popular airport at **Iraklion** (and to a lesser extent **Chania**) as well. Other regional airports tend to restrict the wider island hopping options available, though the Dodecanese island chain is well served with frequent flights to **Kos** and **Rhodes** — both islands with regular connections with the Cyclades (albeit with long 12-hour sailing times).

Other destinations are often better avoided if you are only in Greece for a fortnight as they do not connect as well into the ferry system and you could end up spending half your holiday worrying about getting back in time for your return flight. **Samos** and **Skiathos** are the best placed of these and worth considering if you are not planning to venture too far, but **Kavala (Keramoti)** and **Thessalonika** can be hard to return to quickly and shouldn't be considered unless you are planning to pick up a return flight elsewhere.

The isolated Ionian group is better served by aircraft than ferries, with charter flights to **Corfu**, **Kefalonia**, **Lefkada (Preveza)** and **Zante**, the first two of which offer starting points for viable small-scale island hopping holidays. Finally, a small number of charter flights also operate to **Patras (Araxos)** and poorly connected **Karpathos** and **Limnos**, but these are not served by all tour operators.

One-way Student/Youth Charter Flights also operate from the UK and other European destinations. These offer the possibility of staying in Greece over the one-month regular charter flight limit,

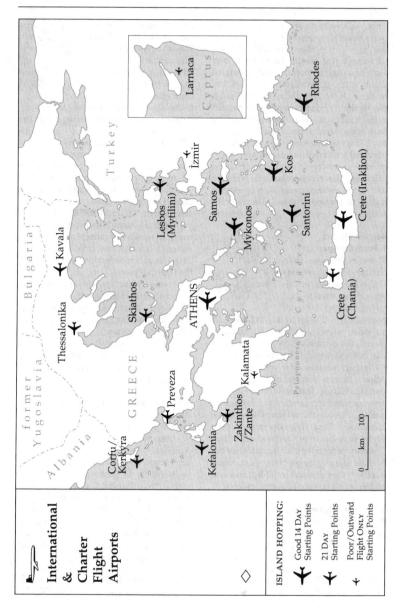

since you can buy a one-way return ticket (ferry ticket agencies in Greece also widely sell the 'return' portion of these flight deals) — though you should take care to buy early or avoid the popular end-of-August flights when seat availability declines dramatically. If you are holidaying on a 2-week charter flight ticket it cannot be emphasized enough that you should always plan to be back at your arrival point at least one clear day before your return flight, otherwise a ferry strike, bad weather, or an over-booked or missing ferry could result in your having to buy an expensive regular flight home via one of the three airports with scheduled flights to Europe (Athens, Thessalonika and Corfu).

Regular Flights
1. From Europe:

More expensive than charter flights, regular flights are worth considering if you want to start and finish at different points or if you want to stay in Greece for an odd or extended period. In such circumstances the extra odd £100/US$160 on the cost of a charter flight can be justified.

Olympic Airways offer daily flights to Athens from a number of European airports (including Heathrow). *British Airways* also operate from London to Greece with daily flights to Athens (from Gatwick and Heathrow). *Easyjet* also operate cut-price flights from Luton to Athens and Skiathos. The only potential pitfall in opting for one of these flights is the problem of last minute booking; they do tend to fill up, and late-comers can't be sure of getting tickets.

2. From North America:

The numbers wishing to travel direct between North America and Greece are well down compared with European levels: as a result the only direct flights to Greece are to Athens (as yet there are no direct North America—Greek island flights) and prices are quite high. The Greek national carrier,

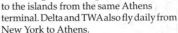

Olympic Airways flies out of New York (JFK), Boston, Toronto and Montreal. The airline has one great advantage over other carriers in being able to offer connecting domestic flights to the islands from the same Athens terminal. Delta and TWA also fly daily from New York to Athens.

Regular flight return tickets often cost in excess of US$1,200 during the summer months; as a result many travellers fly to Western Europe and then make their way to Greece (via a local flight or rail ticket) from there. Low Season fares are more reasonable (usually around US$800). If Greece is your desired North American flight destination (a number of carriers offer flights to Athens via East Coast or West European cities) there are several ways of reducing the financial pain:

1. Book early (tickets sold well in advance attract slightly cheaper fares).

2. Buy a discounted regular or charter flight ticket (taking care to check just exactly what you are getting).

3. Under-24s can pick up cheaper special APEX tickets that can be valid for as long as a year (though travel in High Season is not encouraged).

2. From Australia & New Zealand:

Although the total number of visitors to Greece from the southern hemisphere is substantially lower than from North America, there is demand thanks to the large number of Greek expatriots living in Australia. In past years *Olympic Airways* offered Athens flights to Brisbane, Melbourne and Sydney, but in the post-September 11 world links have been greatly curtailed (*Olympic Airways* now head no further than Bangkok). This has left the skies open for *Thai Airways, Singapore Airlines* and *Gulf Air* to clean up with their connecting services.

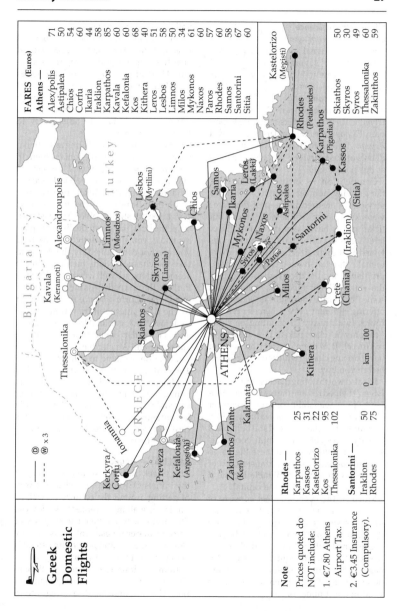

Greek Domestic Flights

FARES (Euros)

Athens —

Alex/polis	71
Astipalea	50
Chios	54
Corfu	60
Ikaria	44
Iraklion	58
Karpathos	85
Kavala	60
Kefalonia	60
Kos	68
Kithera	40
Leros	51
Lesbos	58
Limnos	50
Milos	34
Mykonos	61
Naxos	60
Paros	57
Rhodes	60
Samos	58
Santorini	67
Sitia	60

Skiathos	50
Skyros	30
Syros	49
Thessalonika	60
Zakinthos	59

Note

Prices quoted do NOT include:

1. €7.80 Athens Airport Tax.

2. €3.45 Insurance (Compulsory).

Rhodes —

Karpathos	25
Kassos	31
Kastelorizo	22
Kos	95
Thessalonika	102

Santorini —

Iraklion	50
Rhodes	75

Flights Within Greece

Greece has a very well developed internal air service. After several years of deregulation in which a number of small airlines have come and

gone, island links are now the preserve of *Olympic Airways* (and its associated company *Olympic Aviation*) and its smaller rival *Aegean Airlines*. Both have web sites with details of their services (you will find links at this book's site).

Competition — including that from the growing number of high speed ferry services — ensured in the past that fares were kept down to tolerable levels, but ticket prices have been rising rapidly of late thanks to a combination of higher tolls levied by the new Athens airport, the drive to make the state-owned *Olympic Airways* profitable, and the rise in aviation costs in the wake of September 11. There is also some ticket price confusion as *Olympic* are offering different price schemes on some routes (with heavy discounting on some Economy 'L' class tickets that are *bought in Greece*). It is therefore worth checking ticket pricing closely with your ticket agent before you buy.

It is also worth noting that ticket price rises haven't helped resolve the traditional problem of poor availability of aircraft seats for all the popular islands (particularly in July and August) — these should still be booked as early as possible. Last minute booking is still possible though, and these flights do offer the option of a quick transfer, and of course a potentially invaluable lifeline if you need to rush back to the capital.

Much of the domestic fleet consists of light aircraft, so you have to take care not to exceed the 15 kilo baggage allowance (this can be a problem if you are buying a combined international and domestic ticket: international flights attract a higher baggage allowance). All domestic seats are non-smoking. Prices given overleaf were valid in the summer of 2003.

Rail Links — International

Thanks to the many sightseeing options and its geographical position, Greece is a natural objective for many trans-Europe rail travellers. There are two traditional rail routes from Europe: the first (and most popular) is via ferry from Italy, the second is through Eastern Europe and the Balkans.

1: London—Milan—Brindisi: ferry to Patras, and train to Athens.

Offers the option of visiting additional islands by stopping in the Ionian chain. In 2002 three lines — Superfast, Blue Star and HML Ferries — offered free 'Deck' accommodation to InterRail ticket holders (Zone G) on their Brindisi—Patras ferries (note: port taxes are still payable). You just turn up at the boat; but given the limited space available, you should arrive *very* early. If you are not constrained by the desire to take the cheapest route, then other more scenic options are well worth considering. Perhaps the best of these is the combination of a Patras/Corfu—Venice ferry followed by the daily afternoon train from Venice — across the Austrian Alps — to Munich and its regular connections with Paris, Hamburg and Amsterdam.

2: London overland to Athens.

The civil war in what was Yugoslavia has made the traditional Adriatic route via Venice and Belgrade impracticable. In order to avoid the areas of conflict travellers now have to journey via Romania. See the *Thomas Cook European Timetable* for advice on the current situation.

Rail Links — Aegean

The Greek railway system (known by the initials OSE) offers the cheapest way of getting around the country as well as (mules or walking excepted) the slowest. The network has suffered from years of chronic under-investment. This is now slowly changing, and new rolling stock is being introduced. Sadly, throwing stones at train windows is a national pastime in Greece, and many cars show evidence of this. The interminable delays that are to

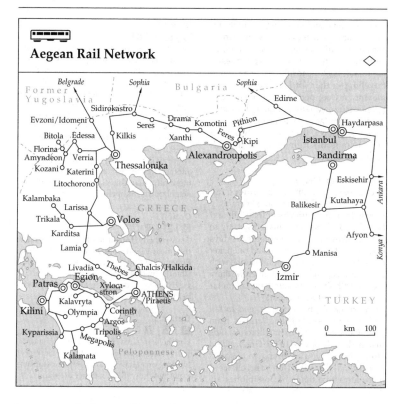

Aegean Rail Network

be encountered when travelling are also a serious disincentive. Most of the system is single track; so trains have to keep stopping to allow oncoming trains to clear the line (it is not unknown for flies to travel down a carriage by hopping in and out of windows as a train crawls along). Timetables are often as much theoretical as factual — the Thessalonika—Larissa/Volos service has been known to leave up to an hour before its stated departure time — and the trains are invariably crowded. Intercity trains are somewhat better, but fewer in number.

In an effort to drum up more tourist custom the OSE have introduced three rail passes. The most useful is the *Vergina*

Flexipass. This is for periods of 3, 5 or 10 days' travel, and the pass includes other features to increase its appeal (these include accommodation, and a city tour of Athens and a one-day cruise to Aegina, Poros and Hydra).

The second pass is the *Greek Flexipass*. This offers 1st class rail travel for 3 or 5 days. The final pass is the *Greek Flexipass Rail'n Fly* which offers a combination of rail travel and coupons for *Olympic Airways* domestic flights to the islands. This sounds a good idea, though it isn't clear how these coupons can be honoured if a flight is fully booked (as many are): clarify this aspect of your travel plans before buying this pass.

If you are on a wide-ranging island hopping holiday then these passes are worth considering. In any event the rail system, for all its many faults, is useful, and provides an invaluable back-up to missing ferries when travelling in the Northern Aegean, or in moving between ports on the Peloponnese. Likewise, the equally antiquated Turkish rail link from İzmir up to İstanbul offers a back-up option to the increasingly limited number of ferries running up the Turkish Aegean coast.

One Stop Island Hopping

The appeal of travelling across Europe and hopping on to a Greek island is seemingly very great if the numbers of InterRail and Eurail card users doing this is anything to go by. However, time is a problem since days spent island hopping are wasted rail ticket days. The ideal island is therefore one with good connections to the mainland. Many mainland holiday makers have a similar desire to 'do' a Greek island.

Unfortunately, both groups tend to fall foul of the rip-off '3-Island' cruises from Piraeus to Aegina, Hydra and Poros, islands that are largely devoid of the Greek island atmosphere. If you are prepared to spend a night on the island of your choice a more attractive range of possibilities are open to you:

Option 1
1) 2 +) 4 ?
Rail travellers arriving in Greece via Eastern Europe tend to head straight for Athens and then worry about finding a boat once there. Escape the crowds by abandoning your train corridor at Larissa. Frequent connections to Volos will see you a mere three hours from Skiathos — one of the most attractive Greek islands. Daily sea links with Thessalonika mean that you can jump from there as well or return to Eastern Europe without retracing your rail journey. Day trips from Athens are another way to visit; but the island deserves more time than this. Save a day for hops to neighbouring Skopelos and Alonissos.

Option 2
3) 5) 7
As everybody stops off at Athens it is inevitable that most island hoppers tend to start from Piraeus and that means a wide choice of possible destinations. Paros is the easiest island to get to. A second day can be spent on Santorini before hopping back to Piraeus.

Option 3
5) 6) 7
For those in a real hurry: Athens then on to Patras stopping over on Corfu for a day before heading on to Italy. Again a popular stopping point with travellers in either direction.

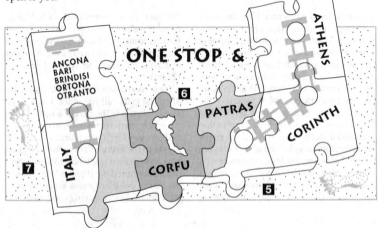

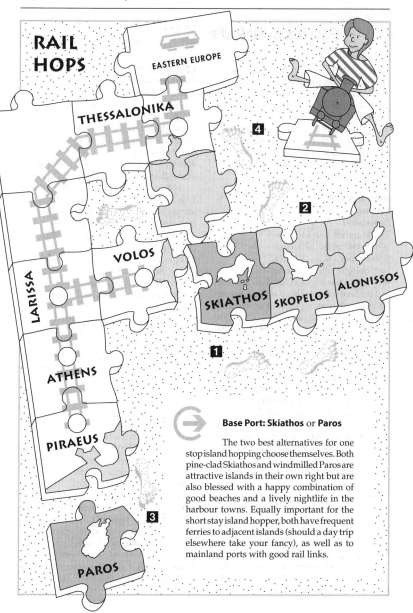

RAIL HOPS

EASTERN EUROPE

THESSALONIKA

4

2

VOLOS

LARISSA

SKIATHOS   SKOPELOS   ALONISSOS

1

ATHENS

PIRAEUS

Base Port: Skiathos or **Paros**

The two best alternatives for one stop island hopping choose themselves. Both pine-clad Skiathos and windmilled Paros are attractive islands in their own right but are also blessed with a happy combination of good beaches and a lively nightlife in the harbour towns. Equally important for the short stay island hopper, both have frequent ferries to adjacent islands (should a day trip elsewhere take your fancy), as well as to mainland ports with good rail links.

3

PAROS

Ferries & Tickets

Having established which group of islands you want to visit and how you intend travelling to Greece, the next thing you need to take on board are the differences between High and Low Season, ferry, hydrofoil and tour boat types, and the vagaries of the Greek ferry ticket system, as these all have a substantial impact on the ease with which you can move around the island chains.

HIGH SEASON
Late June—Late September

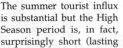

The summer tourist influx is substantial but the High Season period is, in fact, surprisingly short (lasting only 12–14 weeks, from late June through to late September, with the High Season tourist peak running for four weeks from the last week in July to the end of the third week in August). One result of this is that the accompanying high level of ferry services is a relatively short-term phenomenon. Unfortunately, as Greek ferry operators do not arrange their schedules until just before the season starts it is impossible to provide definitive timetables in advance of the summer season. That said, the majority of summer services either remain the same or undergo only minor modification, so that despite the almost total lack of availability of even the scantiest pre-season information, it is possible to give a reasonable report of probable activity.

Given previous years' experience you can expect to find between 60–80% of the High Season sailings or an equivalent running in 2004. In some instances names of boats or days they run particular itineraries will have changed as companies swap boats around in fleet reorganizations, and sailing times might have been brought forward or put back an hour or two.

LOW SEASON
October—Early June

There is a lot to be said for travelling out of the popular High Season period, particularly during the months immediately either side of it, but there is a penalty to be paid, as ferry activity is at a reduced level, with considerable fluctuations in the times of services — and indeed the ferries running them. Low Season Port Tables are not provided simply because in most instances travelling between the islands is merely a matter of catching the single boat every 24/48 hours running up or down the major chains (a rough guide to the likely links available is to take the Port Table Connections Maps and ignore all but the *6–7 days per week* links).

Times are much more dependent on sea conditions, as is the likelihood of any of the smaller boats running, with hydrofoil and catamaran services barely extant at all. June and October are particularly awkward months to describe simply because services are either expanding during the former, or running down in the latter.

During the Low Season reliability also declines. This is partly due to poorer sea conditions (as late as the end of May you can encounter storms that will leave ships port-bound for 24 hours), but economic factors also come into play.

Ferry companies are granted licences by the Greek government provided they (i) operate on an annual basis, and (ii) regularly visit the less popular islands. The result is that boats run very profitably for four months of the year and at a loss for the remainder. Even though the operators are able to minimize their losses by running a reduced winter service, it is very tempting to have a ferry suffer a 'mechanical' failure from time to time, thereby reducing them further.

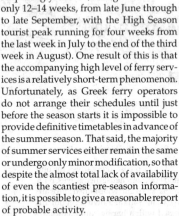

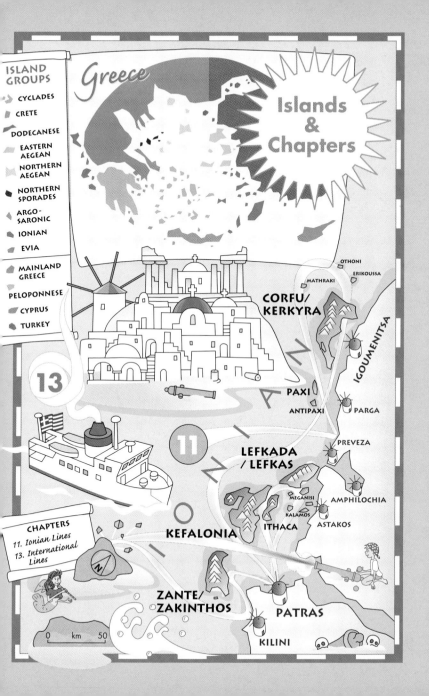

ISLAND GROUPS
CYCLADES
CRETE
DODECANESE
EASTERN AEGEAN
NORTHERN AEGEAN
NORTHERN SPORADES
ARGO-SARONIC
IONIAN
EVIA
MAINLAND GREECE
PELOPONNESE
CYPRUS
TURKEY

Greece

Islands & Chapters

13

11

OTHONI
ERIKOUSSA
MATHRAKI

CORFU/KERKYRA

IGOUMENITSA

PAXI
ANTIPAXI
PARGA

PREVEZA

LEFKADA / LEFKAS

MEGANISI
AMPHILOCHIA
KALAMOS
ITHACA
ASTAKOS

KEFALONIA

ZANTE/ZAKINTHOS

PATRAS

KILINI

CHAPTERS
11. Ionian Lines
13. International Lines

0   km   50

N

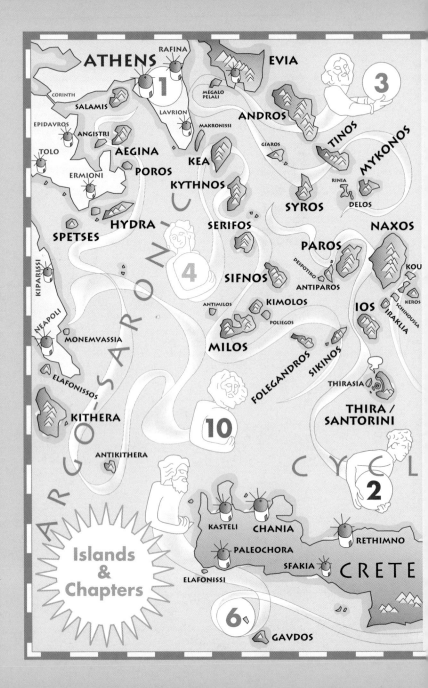

ATHENS
RAFINA
EVIA
1
CORINTH
SALAMIS
MEGALO PELALI
3
EPIDAVROS
ANGISTRI
LAVRION
ANDROS
TOLO
AEGINA
MAKRONISSI
TINOS
MYKONOS
ERMIONI
POROS
KEA
GIAROS
RINIA
KYTHNOS
DELOS
SYROS
HYDRA
SERIFOS
NAXOS
SPETSES
PAROS
KOU
4
DESPOTIKO
KIPARISSI
SIFNOS
ANTIPAROS
KEROS
NEAPOLI
ANTIMILOS
KIMOLOS
IOS
SCHINOUSSA
IRAKLIA
MONEMVASSIA
POLIEGOS
ELAFONISSOS
MILOS
SIKINOS
THIRASIA
FOLEGANDROS
10
THIRA /
SANTORINI
KITHERA
2
ANTIKITHERA
CYCL
Islands
&
Chapters
KASTELI
CHANIA
RETHIMNO
PALEOCHORA
ELAFONISSI
SFAKIA
CRETE
6
GAVDOS

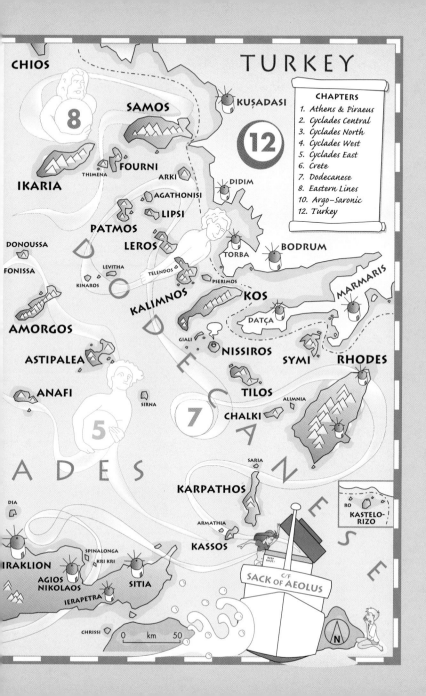

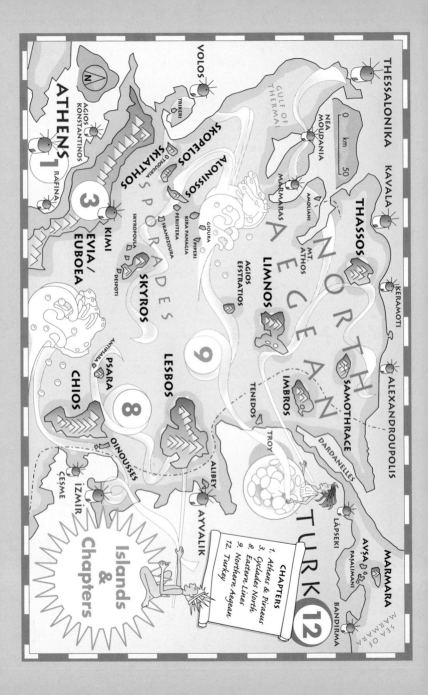

Islands & Chapters

THESSALONIKA
KAVALA
IKERAMOTI
THASSOS
ALEXANDROUPOLIS
VOLOS
TRIKERI
GULF OF THERMAI
NEA MOUDANIA
MARMARAS
AMOLIANI
MT. ATHOS
AGIOS KONSTANTINOS
ATHENS **1**
RAFINA
SKOPELOS
SKIATHOS
3
D.TSOUGRIA
ALONISSOS
S P O R A D E S
GIOURA
VIPERI
KIRA PANAGIA
PERISTERA
SKANDZOURA
SKYROPOULA
DESPOTI
EVIA / EUBOEA
KIMI
SKYROS
ANTIPSARA
PSARA
CHIOS
8
OINOUSSES
ÇEŞME
İZMIR
LESBOS
ALIBEY
AYVALIK
AGIOS EFSTRATIOS
LIMNOS
9
N O R T H   A E G E A N
SAMOTHRACE
IMBROS
TENEDOS
TROY
DARDANELLES
LAPSEKI
MARMARA
AVŞA
PAŞALIMANI
BANDIRMA
T U R K **12**
S E A   O F   M A R M A R A

0   km   50

N

CHAPTERS
1. Athens & Piraeus
3. Cyclades North.
8. Eastern Lines.
9. Northern Aegean
12. Turkey

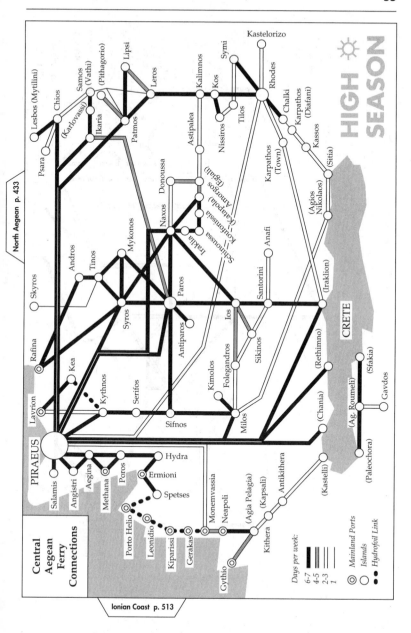

North Aegean p. 433

HIGH SEASON

Kastelorizo

Lesbos (Mytilini)

Chios

Psara

Samos (Vathi) (Pithagorio)

(Karlovassi)

Ikaria

Lipsi

Leros

Patmos

Kalimnos

Kos

Symi

Rhodes

Chalki

Karpathos (Diafani)

Kassos

Astipalea

Nissiros

Tilos

Karpathos (Town)

Karpathos (Sitia)

(Agios Nikolaos)

Donoussa

Amorgos (Katapola)

Koufonissia

Schinoussa

Iraklia

Anafi

Naxos

Andros

Tinos

Mykonos

Skyros

Paros

Ios

Santorini

(Iraklion)

Syros

Antiparos

Sikinos

(Rethimno)

Rafina

Kea

Serifos

Kimolos

Folegandros

(Chania)

CRETE

(Sfakia)

Lavrion

Kythnos

Milos

(Ag. Roumeli)

Gavdos

PIRAEUS

Sifnos

(Paleochora)

Salamis

Angistri

Aegina

Methana

Poros

Hydra

Ermioni

Spetses

Monemvassia

Neapoli

(Agia Pelagia)

(Kapsali)

Antikithera

(Kastelli)

Porto Helio

Leonidio

Kiparissi

Gerakas

Kithera

Cythio

Central Aegean Ferry Connections

Ionian Coast p. 513

Days per week:
6-7
4-5
2-3
1

◉ Mainland Ports
○ Islands
•••• Hydrofoil Link

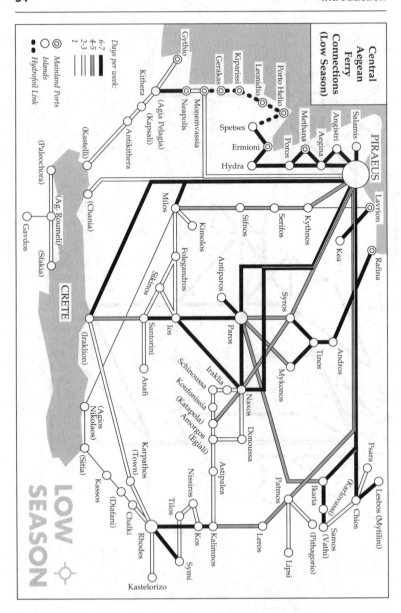

Car Ferries

Of the 120-odd larger car ferries licensed to operate in Greek waters, some 60 are engaged on international

routes, with the rest operating to the islands. International ferries are on a par with those operating cross-Channel services and are significantly better than most of their domestic counterparts. Accommodation options range from cabins, lounges with aircraft-style seats (Pullman class) and basic deck-class facilities (i.e. saloons and open decks).

Most of the large Greek domestic ferries operate out of Piraeus, providing either a daily service (returning overnight) or (if venturing further afield) running a thrice-weekly service. These services tend to be reliable (this means to within 2–3 hours of their scheduled arrival time), the most likely cause of disruption coming from odd one-day strikes. Even so, these are normally confined to Piraeus departures/arrivals rather than ferries already at sea. Normally there are a few days' warning of a strike, though unless you hear of it on the grapevine the chances are that you will only find out when you go to buy your ticket.

Conditions on domestic ships vary widely, and the gap between the best and the worst is growing. At the top end are brand-new high speed ferries which charge double the regular ferry fare, but which get you to your destination in half the time and in some style. Regular ferries are often over 25 years old and showing it.

All ferries have their name in English on the bow and in Greek on the stern. Class distinctions are somewhat arbitrary, with facilities classed as 'deck' on the better ships classified as 2nd or 'tourist' on the less good. Classes are segregated pretty strictly on board most vessels. Unfortunately, there is no similar distinction made between smoking and non-smoking areas

(the latter being totally unknown). On the high speed ferries you are usually expected to sit at the seat numbered on your ticket. Regular ferries allow you to sit where you will (hence the rush for saloon seats on overnight trips).

With a 'deck' ticket you can expect the seating to be divided equally between interior saloons (complete with TVs) and the outside upper decks (where plastic-moulded bench-style seats welded to the deck are the norm). Those travelling 2nd class will find cabin accommodation is also on offer (prices are on a par with C-class hotel rates). Food and drink facilities vary from tired cafeterias to franchise-operated sandwich and burger bars. All drinks and foodstuffs are much more expensive than those ashore.

If you want more detailed ferry information (previous names, capacity, lengths etc.) you will find most listed in Geoffrey Hamer's *Trip Out in Southern Europe* (available from 'Trip Out', PO Box 1287, London, W4 3LG, UK: £5.50). A second excellent, if rather dated, source of information (and photos) is John May's *Greek Ferries* (Ferry Publications, PO Box 9, Narberth, Pembrokeshire, UK: £9.99).

Landing-Craft Ferries

In sheltered waters where car ferries are needed on short haul routes (usually mainland to island links) small 'Landing-Craft' type vessels predominate. The large ferry operators don't have an interest in these local craft, which can carry anything from four to forty vehicles. Passengers are accommodated in the cabin decks at the stern of the ship. These vessels only offer deck-class seats. The bigger boats have a bar. Usually running all year round, High Season sees occasional problems over the limited space available. In many cases, passenger tickets are normally bought on board, on or after departure.

Catamarans

The last decade has seen half a dozen of these vessels arrive in the Aegean, several with car-carrying facilities. Offering a very fast, air-conditioned ride in flat seas and — with the smaller boats — a slow, stomach-churning roll in anything else, they remain summer boats. In the past they have not been viewed with favour by the Greek government as they were seen to siphon off ferry profits in the High Season, but now their numbers are growing steadily. Fares are normally on a par with hydrofoils (this makes these craft comparatively expensive on longer runs: e.g. Piraeus to Paros), but their speed ensures their popularity, and in High Season you often have to book ahead.

Hydrofoils

Known throughout Greece as 'Dolphins' (i.e. *Delphini*), there are now some 30 of these craft operating in Greek waters. Travelling at twice the speed of the average ferry, they each carry around 140 passengers. Very much fair-weather craft, they require reasonably calm sea conditions and so tend to confine visits to islands in more sheltered waters. Consequently services are greatly reduced out of High Season. Rarely operating in the winter or out of daylight hours (their hulls are not strong enough to cope with chance collisions with large pieces of flotsam), they are a fast — if noisy — way of rattling around the Aegean.

All these boats are fitted out with air-craft-style seats divided between bow, central and rear cabins. The rear cabins (complete with WCs) sometimes have a bar where the crew socialize. As a rule, the further back you go the less bumpy the ride: an important consideration given that these

boats often bring out the worst among those inclined to seasickness. Between the central and small rear cabins there is usually a tiny open deck area over the engine. Here you can stand and admire the view — provided you can cope with the noise, the petrol fumes and (when underway) the 'riding a kicking mule' sensation and occasional cascades of surf. Easily the best seats on a hydrofoil lie at the stern: here there is a small open deck complete with a popular seat offering the smoothest ride and panoramic views.

With tickets costing the equivalent of a 2nd class ferry ticket, it is rare for hydrofoil companies to compete against each other: the market just isn't strong enough. As a result, the standard of service is rather patchy. *Hellas Flying Dolphins* is the largest line in Greece and has a good reputation (though a number of its hydrofoils are looking pretty old), offering well thought-out timetables published for the year, and a good record for reliability and continuity of services between years.

Other lines tend to operate in less hospitable areas and are less consistent, with timetables that are only available for the month in hand, if at all, and major variations in their itineraries and schedules each year. In short, you can assume that *Hellas Flying Dolphins* boats will be operating, but the Port Table entries for other lines are best treated as 'optimistic' projections of what might be around!

Passenger Boats

Increasingly operated as purely tourist excursion boats, these craft range from small-car-ferry-sized vessels to converted fishing boats known as caïques. Less strike-prone than the large ferries, their main bane are the seas whipped up by the *meltemi* wind in the summer months and the generally more volatile conditions during the rest of the year. They do, however, provide a useful adjunct to the larger boats, though you will encounter wide disparities in fares depending on their 'ferry' or 'tourist boat' status (the latter can be used for one-way island hopping if you are prepared to pay for a return ticket). Some larger 'passenger' boats can also accommodate 2 or 3 cars, or more commonly, motorbikes.

Ticket Agents

In the absence of any central ferry ticket-issuing or information authority, ticket agents are to be found at every port, usually occupying offices in buildings near the quay or along the sea front; they also frequently offer exchange facilities (albeit at a higher rate of commission), room finding services, and, occasionally, unsecured luggage deposit facilities to ticket purchasers. Hours are variable (an attractive feature if you need to change money or cheques out of banking hours) and are often determined by the arrival times of the boats. In Greece most agencies will open up for a short time to sell tickets during the night if a boat is due; however, you cannot count on this, and with the advent of computer ticketing (taking away the option of being able to buy tickets on board ferries) the wisest course of action is to make a habit of buying your ticket from an agent during office hours.

Ticket agents are the only people who seem to thrive on the apparent chaos of the ferry system. Many would argue that they are largely responsible for it. Inevitably they are very keen to relieve you of your money and you should enter an agency with eyes open. The vast majority of passengers do, however, use them without any difficulty. When dealing with an agent bear in mind that:

1. It is rare for a ticket agent to sell tickets for all the vessels calling at a port. The schedules they advertise are therefore incomplete and many will lie blatantly in order to get custom by telling you that their boat is the

fastest, next, or the only one available. One common dodge is to say a boat is 'full' when they have sold their allocation of tickets — a rival agent nearby could well be able to sell you one.

2. As fares are regulated by the government there is no difference in the prices ticket agents are able to charge. Any agent's claim that their deck-class tickets are cheaper is rubbish. Another dodge is to advertise prices omitting the port tax and VAT to entice the unwary inside.

3. Outright attempts to sell tourists something they don't want are rare, but do occur, either by selling a higher class ticket than the basic 'deck' fare, or selling the customer a return ticket without saying so. In very rare instances tourists have been sold tickets for a boat that has just departed.

You can prevent most of these problems by checking that the class, ferry's name, and departure time are on the ticket. Of course, the easiest way of avoiding problems is to establish which ferry you want before you approach the agent and then simply ask for a ticket for that boat.

International Tickets

International ferry travel in the Eastern Mediterranean is comparatively expensive. This is due to the longer distances involved, the much higher port taxes international boats attract (currently around £5 / US$8 per person and also per vehicle), and partly because in some instances you are obliged to buy a bunk or aircraft-type seating as a minimum rather than a deck ticket. Various discounts are available, depending on the operator. These range from a Student discount (20%), Return ticket discount (5%) — usually advertised as a 10% discount, but in fact only given on the cost of the return part of the ticket — Group concessions (usually 15% for nine or more), as well as reduced Low Season fares. In addition a number of lines operating to Greece offer 'Stop-over' tickets allowing you to break the journey along the way (though they are quick to point out that during the High

Season re-embarkation on a particular boat cannot be guaranteed). However, it is rare for you to be able to travel between two ports in the same country using international boats except as a designated 'stop over' on an international ticket. Fares also tend to be structured on a country-to-country basis so, for example, if you travel from Greece to Cyprus, the ticket will usually cost the same if you start from Piraeus or a port en route such as Rhodes.

Greek Domestic Tickets
1. Tickets
Until 1998 it was possible to buy tickets from quayside vendors or on the ferry itself as well as from regular ticket agents. This inevitably led to safety problems as there was no check on the numbers boarding a ferry. Ferry operators were happy to turn a blind eye to this as the odd thousand passengers over official capacity didn't hurt revenues, besides sparing them the expense of buying additional vessels to cover the shortfall in capacity during the short High Season period.

Things changed in 1995 after a couple of highly publicized incidents of chronic overloading: first, when the C/F *Marina*'s captain received a five-month prison sentence for sailing during the Easter rush with 2,700 passengers aboard (her licensed capacity is 1,447); second, when the C/F *Express Olympia* (licensed capacity 1,200) had her captain arrested at Piraeus on the 31st of July for trying to sail with 2,725 passengers on board. These incidents called into question ferry safety standards in Greece besides attracting damaging international publicity, with the result that a Presidential Decree was issued, requiring ferry operators to bring in a computer ticket system. This is now in place and as a result:
1. Passengers can no longer board a ferry without a valid ticket (at all large ports the Port Police are now checking passengers have valid tickets before they board). You should therefore buy a ticket before you arrive at the quay.

2. At the height of the High Season travellers should no longer expect to be able to just jump on the next boat to their desired destination: boats can be more easily booked up as agents no longer have an allocated number of tickets to sell, but can go on selling until the boat is full. This opens up the serious possibility that at the height of the summer some island hoppers could face delays (and possibly miss flights home) as a result.

In High Season it is therefore highly advisable to buy the ticket for both the next stage and the final stage of your journey as soon as you have decided what they will be (particularly if your hop would be via a catamaran or involve a weekend journey to or from Piraeus). This will also give you the maximum available time to consider your other options should your chosen ferry be full.

2. Ticket Types & Fares
As the Greek ferry scene becomes increasingly deregulated the old rigid structure of fares and boat types is breaking down. In the past the Greek government set a standard fare for each port-to-port connection and ferry operators were obliged to keep to this. Today, fares are still controlled by the state, but there are a number of price points for each connection depending on the type and speed of vessel. Fare discounting — something unheard of in the past — also appeared in 2003.

There are now three fare price points for each route:
1. Regular Ferry — now the preserve of the old slow boats. This is the cheapest option (typical fares are listed opposite).
2. Fast Ferries (invariably new, and some 20% faster than old regular ferries).
3. High Speed Vessels — primarily catamarans and hydrofoils, but this category also includes a number of 'High Speed' ferries that travel at speeds of over 30 knots.
With all the above, basic 'Deck' fares are set by the government, but operators can charge what they like for higher classes.

Domestic Tickets

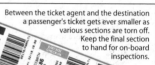

With the exception of a few landing-craft type ferries and tourist excursion boats, all ferries, catamarans and hydrofoils now use a standardized computer ticket that carries a passenger name. The only differences between tickets are the use of company logos. On some islands a harbour tax slip (usually amounting to around €0.50) is also stapled to the ticket.

Between the ticket agent and the destination a passenger's ticket gets ever smaller as various sections are torn off. Keep the final section to hand for on-board inspections.

Domestic Inter-Island 'Deck' Fares (Euros)

	12.00	17.20	17.50	20.50	24.20	31.00	26.20	28.30	35.00	•	Rhodes
	Kos	5.30	7.60	10.40	15.00	16.10	18.50	21.20	27.00	•	Kos
		Kalimnos	7.00	9.40	14.20	13.50	17.90	21.50	25.80	•	Kalimnos
			Leros	5.90	12.80	•	17.50	19.50	26.60	•	Leros
				Patmos	10.60	14.20	15.70	18.00	27.20	•	Patmos
	Thessalonika				Samos	15.30	10.90	15.20	24.60	•	Samos
Skiathos	16.00	Skiathos				Paros	•	•	•	•	Paros
Amorgos	•	•	Amorgos				Chios	12.10	19.60	27.30	Chios
Tinos	34.00	20.40	11.60	Tinos				Lesbos	16.20	23.60	Lesbos
Mykonos	35.00	21.00	11.30	4.40	Mykonos				Limnos	13.70	Limnos
Syros	30.70	19.60	12.80	4.00	5.50	Syros				Kavala	
Naxos	32.50	24.40	8.80	6.90	6.60	7.70	Naxos				
Paros	33.30	23.10	10.10	6.80	6.50	7.00	6.50	Paros			
Ios	34.70	26.50	15.90	12.00	11.80	13.70	10.50	8.70	Ios		
Santorini /Thira	35.80	30.00	16.50	14.90	12.70	14.80	10.70	10.80	6.60	Thira	
Crete (Iraklion)	44.20	36.10	•	22.90	21.50	20.20	18.60	17.70	15.60	13.20	

Piraeus–Island Fares (Euros)		
(Including port taxes and 8% VAT)		
PIRAEUS to:	Deck	C/M or H/F
Aegina	4.00	8.40
Amorgos	17.20	•
Anafi	22.80	•
Angistri	5.40	9.50
Astipalea	23.20	•
Chalki	32.70	•
Chios	19.50	•
Crete (Agios Nikolaos)	25.30	•
Crete (Chania)	22.70	•
Crete (Iraklion)	27.50	•
Crete (Rethimno)	23.10	•
Donoussa	16.50	•
Epidavros	6.00	13.00
Folegandros	17.00	•
Fourni	19.80	•
Hydra	8.00	16.00
Ikaria	18.60	•
Ios	18.00	•
Iraklia	16.30	•
Kalimnos	24.00	•
Karpathos	27.00	•
Kassos	26.90	•
Kastelorizo	37.20	•
Kea	•	17.40
Kimolos	15.30	30.40
Kithera	17.90	36.30
Kos	25.80	•
Koufonissia	15.70	•
Kythnos	10.50	20.40
Leros	21.90	•
Lesbos (Mytilini)	24.20	•
Milos	16.90	33.30
Monemvassia	•	31.50
Mykonos	17.50	34.40
Naxos	17.30	34.10
Neapoli	•	34.80
Nissiros	25.30	•
Paros	17.30	34.10
Patmos	21.10	•
Poros	7.25	14.20
Rhodes	30.70	•
Samos (Vathi)	22.50	•
Santorini / Thira	20.20	40.50
Schinoussa	17.00	•
Serifos	15.20	25.80
Sifnos	14.80	29.00
Sikinos	19.90	•
Spetses	11.00	22.20
Symi	30.10	•
Syros	15.00	29.40
Tilos	27.70	•
Tinos	16.10	29.40

Tickets for regular ferries remain the most cost effective travel option. In 2003 *G.A. Ferries* even reduced this minimum fare by 15% during part of the High Season in attempt to make its older boats more attractive. There are three classes on the larger vessels: 1st (Luxury), 2nd (Tourist), and 3rd (Deck or Economy). Deck tickets are the norm and unless you state otherwise you can expect to be sold one. On the older boats **Class numbers** are indicated on ship signs using a letter and apostrophe numbering system derived from the Classical Greek alphabet. The 'class' (ΘΕΣΙΣ/ΘΕΣΗ) is thus written accordingly: A'= 1st, B'= 2nd, and Γ'= 3rd.

It is standard practice to issue one-way rather than return tickets, though the latter are available (at a saving of 10–15% of the cost of two single fares) provided you don't mind the inconvenience of being locked into using the same line's boats for your return. Groups of 10 or more also can get discounted tickets, and students can occasionally get discounts by waving their student cards at agents.

The average regular ferry 'Deck' fare, when hopping to the next island down the line, is about €9; children between 4 and 10 travel half-fare. Car rates average 4 or 6 times the cost of a deck ticket, depending on whether the length of the vehicle exceeds 4.5 m. Motorcycle rates also go according to size. For a sub-250cc machine the fare is similar to a deck ticket; larger machines are up to double that. However, bicycles are usually allowed free passage, regardless of the type of vessel.

Fast ferries command a higher 'Deck' fare. Economy tickets for *Blue Star Ferries* carry this premium (the legitimate justification being that their boats are 20% faster than regular ferries). The price differential between the two is sufficiently low that it is worth paying the extra few Euros to travel on these faster and more comfortable boats. Ticket agents seem to be in two minds as to how to class these intermediate boats: some consider them to be just more pricey regular ferries, others call them high speed boats.

Tickets for high speed ferries and catamarans are slightly different — though with computerized ticketing they look the same. Fares are usually double the regular ferry fare on all routes (this can make these tickets very expensive on longer outings such as Piraeus to Rhodes). Your seat number is also far more important: with 'deck' tickets on regular ferries the number doesn't entitle you to sit in a specific seat, but on the high speed boats it does, and you will normally be expected to find and sit in your numbered seat. This practice tends to be enforced far more rigorously when the boat is full. At other times some passengers opt to disregard the seat numbers (they will be the ones having arguments with boarding passengers waving tickets in their hands, and insisting on sitting in their numbered seat).

In the past it has not been the practice to buy ferry tickets for journeys unrelated to your starting point (e.g. one couldn't buy a ticket for travel from Paros to Naxos from an agent on Santorini); this was largely because agents on one island haven't had sufficient information about sailing times from other islands. This has now changed with the advent of computer ticketing, and it is worth booking ahead with these popular high speed boats in High Season. During the rest of the year they can be a great way to travel — and sometimes not overly expensive: NEL offered a 50% discount on tickets for its boats during May 2003.

Excursion boats are not bound by government price regulation and usually charge about twice the regular ferry fare, often because you are buying a round trip (you don't have to use the return leg of your ticket if you use them for island hopping).

Greek Island Ferry Passes are the subject of regular e-mail enquiries to this book's website. Sadly, there are now no passes available in Greece: so there is no option but to buy tickets as you go. This isn't that much of a big deal as ticket prices are ridiculously low compared to those in other European countries. In past years there was a ferry pass on sale in Athens, but the scheme — operated by *Hellas Flying Dolphins* — only covered their boats and those of *G.A. Ferries* (whom *HFD* part own) and didn't save you much. The pass was only ever bought by impoverished backpackers, and one suspects that as the above companies now have a near monopoly on the cheaper, slower, regular ferries on many routes, they have concluded that they would get these customers anyway.

Paying for tickets can be interesting. In Greece it is expected that you will pay for passenger ferry tickets in cash: credit cards are usually only accepted when buying international tickets. The tickets are not transferable to other lines and are only refundable if a ferry fails to arrive. In such instances, standing inside the office of the agent who sold you the ticket until they refund your money is the most effective way of getting it back.

Sources of Ferry Information

Current information on international services can be gleaned from the *Thomas Cook European Timetable* and the *Thomas Cook Overseas Timetable*. A few international operators also have their timetables on websites (see p. 653–654).

Greece is an awkward country when it comes to obtaining timetables on the ground. In order to get the maximum information you will need to consult several sources:

(1). **The National Tourist Organisation of Greece** (addresses on p. 23). Until 2002 overseas branches gave out domestic ferry timetables in the form of the booklet *Greek Travel Routes* (a summer timetable compiled each May) or photocopies of the timetables published in a monthly Greek trade-only publication: *Greek Travel Pages*. Neither was available last year, and it is unclear if

Greek Travel Routes will be available in the summer of 2004 (it isn't looking likely). The information contained in both is identical (though it is not over-easy to consult as ferries and routes are identified by a code system). A second problem is that operators buy and move ferries during the summer, so inaccuracies creep in. In an effort to overcome this problem, the *Greek Travel Pages* has a website (⊕ www.gtpnet.com) that gives point-to-point timetables that are updated on a weekly basis.

(2). **In Greece** you will find most ticket agents only display information for their port or island. However, they will have a copy of the *Greek Travel Pages* that you can ask to see. Many also have a second — less good — timetable: *Hellenic Travelling*. In rare instances you might also come across variants of these timetables on sale. The Cyclades section of *Greek Travel Routes/Pages* is sold as a timetable called *Cyclades* (+ the month): price €2, and the *Hellenic Travelling* variant (which covers the whole of Greece) is called *Domestic Sea Lines* (€6). Both publications are published monthly from June to September.

(3). **In Athens** there are additional sources of information. Foremost among these are the National Tourist Organisation of Greece (known locally as the EOT) ferry departure sheets — available from the central Athens (see p. 95) and airport tourist information centres . These contain a list (in English) of the domestic ferry departures from Piraeus (excluding hydrofoils and Saronic Gulf boats). As these are added to on a daily basis, the EOT officer will ask you which day you are travelling and just give you that sheet (so you have to ask for a full week's worth if you are trying to get an overall picture of things). Rafina departures are listed on a separate sheet.

If you don't want to venture into Athens or want information on other mainland port departures you can always do what the locals do and resort to the city newspapers. The best of these is a business daily:

H NAYTEMΠOPIKH

which has Piraeus departures for the following week as well as limited information about departures from other mainland ports. If you are prepared to struggle with the Greek alphabet, it is worth the €1 price, and is on sale at most newspaper kiosks and newsagents.

(4). **On the islands** available information is usually confined to departure times for the island you are on. Sometimes company timetables are available and EOT offices (see individual island entries) also distribute lists of local ferry times. Some agents make up photocopy ferry timetables, to augment the billboards to be found outside all agencies advertising boats and current times (these are usually in both English and Greek capitals). In the last resort you can always try the Port Police, who are guaranteed to have a complete list of the day's sailings as well as someone who can't speak English.

Check out the latest **ferry safety** info at greekislandhopping.com

Ferry Safety
The Greek island world suffered a severe shock on the night of 26 September 2000 when the C/F *Express Samina* (formerly the *Golden Vergina*), an old, decrepit ferry just months way from compulsory retirement, hit a well-known rocky islet — topped with a navigation light that is visible 12 km away — while approaching Paros, and sank with the loss of 80 lives. The captain and several of the crew were arrested and charged with manslaughter amid allegations that at the time of the collision they were watching a soccer match on TV instead of manning their positions on the ship's bridge.

Many of the 450 survivors complained of the failure of the crew to help passengers find life-jackets and evacuate the ship, and reported that vital safety equipment wasn't working.

After years of deference towards the powerful ferry-operator lobby, the Greek government was stung into action by public anger. Within a week of the disaster it suspended the licences of almost half the large domestic ferries for failing safety inspections. Operators were given 20 days to sort out the problems or face losing the licences permanently.

Unfortunately, while this initial response looked impressive, it failed to address the fundamental problems of the domestic ferry fleet, as the suspended ferries failed fire safety-checks (fire wasn't an issue in the *Express Samina* tragedy). The Greek government has since brought in various measures in an effort to improve safety standards, and the number of boats over 25 years old is declining — in part thanks to the policy of allowing new faster boats to charge higher ticket prices.

Most of the safety problems — usually engine room fires — that occur with island ferries are age-related. Greece has a concession which allows it to operate ferries until they are 34 years old, while the rest of the EU retires them at 27. This state of affairs ensures that older boats in the domestic fleet have often been sold on to local operators because they can't be operated elsewhere in Europe. As island hoppers often depend on these vessels, some comments on the safety record of Greek ferries are worth making.

The most encouraging thing one can say is that Greece has the largest ferry fleet in Europe (over 40% of the EU total) and, until the *Express Samina*, had a good safety record. Moreover, the arrival of some 20 new ferries in a mere 18 months (and the ferry musical chairs that is following) is seeing the poorer boats disappear from the most popular routes. If you are concerned about safety then stick to these newer — usually high-speed — boats and avoid travelling on old boats to remoter islands.

Statistically, the chances of being involved in an incident are minuscule. Without going over the top about safety, on boarding a ferry it is always worthwhile taking a couple of minutes to consider what you would do if you have to leave in a hurry. Look around for the life-jackets, and, if you are inside, establish the location of the nearest exit points (if they are doors then check that they are unlocked). If you are travelling at night, have a torch handy.

On a day-to-day level, more mundane dangers pose the greater threat:

1. In order to facilitate rapid ferry turn-around, passenger embarkation/ disembarkation is normally via the stern car door. Passengers are often 'invited' down on to the car deck before the ferry has docked, and are usually left standing among the vehicles while the mooring lines are secured. Vehicles are rarely lashed to the car-deck — if the ferry was to collide with the quay or another boat, things could get very unpleasant.

2. Once mooring ropes are secured, and the stern door lowered, ferries keep their vulnerable stern away from the quay by maintaining 'slow forward' propulsion to keep their mooring ropes taut. The door is apt to slide along the quay while passengers are stepping on or off — occasionally trapping feet in the process. When you are caught in a pushing crowd of locals, moving vehicles and backpackers this can become a major hazard.

3. The lowering/raising cables on the doors of older ferries should also be treated with caution. Get a backpack snagged on one of those and as likely as not you'll end up in the water next to those turning propellers.

4. On small ferries it is not uncommon to find that you can get into areas to which one would not expect to have access: e.g. the bow deck (complete with capstans, winches etc.). Anyone travelling with children should check that areas containing kiddie-crushing kit are inaccessible before they are allowed to run free.

Holiday Essentials

Accommodation

Arguably the most challenging part of island hopping is finding accommodation once you arrive. But then this is part of the challenge of this sort of independent holiday. Generalizations on bed availability and price are difficult to make since much depends on when and where you arrive. But in High Season, whatever you are planning to do, it doesn't hurt to take a sleeping bag along so you can decamp to the local campsite should your luck be really out. That said, it is *very* rare to find island hoppers *forced* to resort to roughing it on one of the local beaches.

All types of accommodation are graded by the Greek government (via the NTOG /EOT). Unfortunately, an increasing number of establishments are operating without a licence, or doing their best to evade regulation by understating the number of rooms on offer, or proclaiming themselves to have a higher grade listing than their official one (thus enabling them to charge higher prices). A survey of 25 hotels on Santorini in 1994 showed that all had unlisted rooms and three no operating licence. Other islands produced similar statistics. As a result, some of the hotels mapped in this guide are shown without a class rating, and all those that are shown are given their listed class.

Prices also vary greatly between accommodation in the same class group, a reflection of the hoteliers' ability to levy additional charges and supplements (e.g. if you stay under three nights you can be charged an extra 10%). Breakfast sometimes must be paid for whether wanted or not. Regardless of where you stay, you should therefore try to ascertain exactly what your total bill will be when you check in. It also

never hurts to ask to see a room before you agree to take it. If you encounter any problems don't hesitate to call in the tourist police (usually the threat is enough to resolve disputes!). It is standard practice for all types of accommodation to hold onto your passport while you are in residence (see 'Scams', p. 56).

The accommodation options in Greece are divided between hotels, pensions, rooms in private houses, the odd youth hostel and numerous campsites.

1. Hotels:

These are categorized by the Greek government into six classes, ranging from 'L' (Luxury), followed by 'A' through to 'E'. Prices are very good value by West European standards. Island hoppers usually find that most A to C category hotels are booked en bloc by package tour operators (though if you go in and ask they often have booked, but unoccupied, rooms available). D and E category hotels rely much more on independent clientele.

A-Class:

Singles: €90–250

Doubles: €130–3000

Top quality rooms with prices to match. You can be virtually certain of finding air-conditioning, en suite bathrooms with unlimited hot water, TVs in all rooms and full restaurant facilities within the building. On the down side, A-class hotels are comparatively rare on all but the major tourist islands and are usually inconveniently placed out of town so that they can take advantage of a nearby beach.

B-Class:

Singles: €65–135

Doubles: €90–170

Basically cut-down A-class hotels, B-class establishments are more common on the islands. They usually have en suite bathrooms and hot water, but TVs and air-conditioning are less common. Prices are often as high as A-class hotels. Former government-run quality hotels known as 'Xenias' usually fall into this category.

C-Class:
Singles: €45–100
Doubles: €60–135
Mid-range hotels offering reasonable rooms. Fairly common all over Greece, they are often the top dollar hotels of twenty years ago. En suite bathrooms are uncommon. No air-conditioning or restaurant facilities.

D-Class:
Singles: €30–55
Doubles: €40–65
Once you reach this level then shared bathrooms become the norm (most bedrooms have a sink — minus plug, of course). Buildings tend to be much older; usually being converted turn-of-the-century mansions. Popular with backpackers and local Greeks, they offer good basic accommodation, usually close to town centres and ports.

E-Class:
Singles: €20–45
Doubles: €25–50
Bottom of the range and very variable. At their best E-class hotels are excellent family-run establishments offering attractive clean rooms; at their very worst you will find saucers of rat poison on the landings. Hot water is rare and WCs are usually of the hole-in-the-floor type. Room keys will usually open half the doors in the building. In popular locations hoteliers offer backpackers roof space for a small sum.

Pensions:
Now the popular choice with island hoppers, pensions offer quality rooms at a reasonable price. Like hotels they are graded, but confusingly the grades are A to C and are rated one grade lower than the hotel equivalent (i.e. a B-class pension offers comparable rooms to a C-class hotel).

Clean rooms, usually sharing a bathroom, and with a refrigerator thrown in. Hot water is usually solar-generated, so is only available in the evenings. Friendly and helpful pension owners usually live in the building.

2. Rooms (Domatia):
Mainly on offer in High Season, rooms in private houses sup up the thousands of independent travellers who haven't hotel accommodation and who don't want to camp. Morning ferries at most islands will be met by eager householders thrusting placards at you as you disembark, adorned with photographs of the room on offer and a price that makes a good starting point for negotiation. Other establishments simply have signs up advertising rooms and await the masses to come knocking on their door (the rooms marked on the town maps in this guide usually display a sign of some kind).

Conditions vary despite government regulation. Officially checked out *domatia* are slightly more expensive and have an EOT plaque on the door:
This is a fair guarantee of quality, as are the rooms advertised as 'Apartments', which in the main are simply pricier rooms with an en suite bathroom and a refrigerator (though at the upper end of the scale you will find cooking and laundry facilities as well).

If you opt to take advantage of a quayside offer of a room establish exactly what you are getting while haggling over the price: e.g. Where *exactly* is it? (ask them to show you on the map). Is the price for one or two people? (get them to write it down to avoid future arguments). Has the room a private bathroom, shower, hot water?

Many ticket agencies also have lists of rooms and hotels and will push you in the direction of a bed. As with hotel accommodation, room availability does tend to dry up during the day and evening arrivals could have problems.

3. Youth Hostels:

Facilities are basic (i.e. grimy) but usually adequate for the needs of the night. Unlike the rest of Europe, Youth Hostels are something of a rarity in Greece outside the big mainland cities. YHA cards are rarely necessary, but are worth taking if you already have one to hand (though few youth hostels in Greece are recognized as the genuine article by official YHAs elsewhere in Europe). Only three islands have hostels: Crete (7), Santorini (4) and Corfu (2). All offer the cheapest, and therefore popular, 'roofed' option.

4. Campsites:

Most islands boast at least one campsite; the popular islands usually have three or four. Camping is very popular with island hoppers as it not only offers the cheapest accommodation option, but a guaranteed place to stay in High Season. Competition between sites is intense and most have mini-buses that meet arriving ferries. As with hotels, prices are regulated. Sites are divided up into A, B and C classes. As a rough rule of thumb, trailer-park-type sites are usually A-class, while the silent majority are B-class; it is only with the former that the price differential is apparent (most charge around €5 per person and €3 per tent in High Season).

Of more relevance are the differing High and Low Season rates: sites are apt to change these without informing campers of the transition (bar a notice advertising rates at reception). As a result, every July some get caught out by the size of their bill. There is no recognized High Season start date, so sites up prices when they can. A limited number of island sites are signatories to *Camping Club* schemes, which offer 10%+ discounts to campers visiting other sites in each scheme (see individual site entries).

Site conditions vary according to the proximity to the port (the nearer, the poorer) and the amount of competition. The time of year can also make a vast difference. Most sites have some tree cover, a mini-market selling basics, and toilet and shower blocks (be prepared for shower doors that don't lock, and salt water at some sites). Where competition is particularly fierce, sites often offer discos and swimming pools as well.

Other characteristics shared by all sites are the bone-hard ground (short, strong tent pegs are strongly recommended) and bamboo roofed areas for the large number of 'sleeping bag Sloanes'. Laundry and cooking areas (though the latter activity is rare), safety deposit facilities for valuables, and notice-boards for campers' messages are also common to all.

Outside of the main sites there is a fair amount of freelance camping — though this is technically illegal in Greece and has been diminishing in popularity of late. Islands without official sites take a relaxed view of freelancers, and usually have a quiet beach where freelance camping is tolerated.

5. Sleeping on Ferries:

A good way of maximizing your island hopping opportunities, as well as saving on your accommodation bill, is to take overnight ferries wherever possible. All large ferries offer cabin facilities, though on the popular routes and at the peak season period early pre-booking is a necessity, as cabins are very popular with travelling Greeks. The price of a night in a cabin obviously varies according to the length of your journey. In most cases a ticket will cost just under double the price of a deck ticket. Travelling on a simple deck ticket is also very popular despite the uncomfortable conditions. In High Season sun-decks

and lounges become impromptu dormitories, though the former get quite wet and the latter become stuffy floating smoke holes.

Banks & Post Offices

Greek **banks** are open 08.00–13.00 Mondays to Fridays. On some of the small islands the bank doubles up with the post office, though banking hours remain the same. Through-the-wall cash machines are now arriving in Greece in numbers and all the major islands have at least one. However, if you are relying on cash cards you are likely to encounter problems on the very small islands as ATMs are still a rarity.

Most islands now have banks — usually a branch of the main bank: the National Bank of Greece. Other banks are rarer, the Agricultural Bank and the Ionian Bank being the most common. Regardless of name, the banks usually offer significantly better rates of exchange than you will find at ticket agents (who also almost always offer money-changing facilities).

Post Offices (easily identified by their yellow signs showing a horn) are unlike banks in one important respect — there is sure to be one on every island. Regular hours are 07.30–13.30 Mondays to Fridays (though local times vary). Post offices also serve a residual banking role on some smaller islands. As a rule, traveller's cheques can't be cashed in post offices, but on islands too small to have a bank they usually cash them in addition to selling stamps. Postage stamps can also be purchased from street kiosks and newsagents — with a 10% mark-up. Most post offices offer fax machines in addition to the usual *poste restante* and parcel services. It is normal in Greece to inspect the contents of parcels going abroad (though these days this usually means outside the EU) before accepting them, so don't seal them up in advance.

Beaches

One of the great attractions of the Greek islands is the abundance of excellent beaches, many conveniently placed near the main towns and ports. Most islands can boast at least one sand beach, and many are blessed with many — the best usually lying on the more protected south or west coasts (the majority of north coast beaches are pebble). A large number of Greek beaches enjoy Blue Flag status (a widely recognized endorsement of cleanliness), though this is no guarantee that they are as clean as they should be: abuse has occurred — notably at Lindos on Rhodes (see p. 382).

Although for the most part free and easy (going topless is the norm unless the beach is right in the centre of town), on several islands, where the town strand is the only good beach within easy distance, the EOT have turned them into pay beaches (entry usually costs around €2). They are always crowded, but are kept clean and have showers.

Nudism is very popular in Greece even though it is technically illegal except on very rare licensed beaches. In an attempt to keep popular beaches clothed many islands designate one beach for nudists — these are marked 'FKK' (for 'Freikörperkultur') in this guide — though this isn't going to be much of a legal defence if the police feel like having a crackdown. This happened a few years ago on Anafi, when the island policeman received considerable publicity after he took to disappearing behind a bush on the camping beach. This in itself was harmless enough (most people disappear behind a bush at some point in their lives), but in this case he did it in order to jump out and arrest young female nudists. The Greek press called him a 'hero', though there are other, less flattering, nouns that come to mind. Rare incidents like this aside, in practice, provided you are discreet, you are unlikely to be troubled by gawpers or the police. To some extent where you can go nude depends on the time of year: in High Season you usually have to venture further afield as the more accessible beaches get crowded out with beachwear fans.

Bus Services

Greek bus services fall into two types: intercity and local. Intercity buses usually require you to buy a ticket in advance from the bus station.

This will have a time and seat number on it and you will be expected to travel on the particular bus departing at that time and to start the journey in the appropriate seat (the number is on the back of your seat). Timetables are strictly adhered to. Prices are low (reckon on paying €0.25 per km on journeys over 10 km, €0.30 per km on shorter rides), and the system is extensive, taking in all the major towns around the country. Buses on intercity routes (e.g. Thessalonika—Athens) can get booked solid on weekends and holidays, but by and large you can expect to catch your desired bus. On journeys over two hours the bus will make a 10 minute pit stop (invariably at a restaurant or shop owned by a relative of the driver).

Local, and most island, buses are very different affairs, since you normally pay on the bus and most are so crowded that you are usually doing well to find a seat at all. The majority of island buses are operated as one-vehicle family businesses. Dad will drive while one of the kids weaves their way through the masses collecting the fares. Timetables are usually fairly strictly adhered to, though this isn't quite as good as it sounds as they change much more frequently. It is also very unwise to expect to find bus services operating on Sundays outside tourist areas.

Further problems are posed by the local nature of island buses: they are geared to moving the islanders — not tourists — around. Parties of tourists all settling a €0.90 fare with a €20 note are almost made to feel unwelcome. Services tend to finish at the end of the working day and this is often not compatible with the tourist who likes his or her nightlife. Re-routing is also a problem; it is a sad fact of life that given the choice between driving down a road and an earth track, island bus drivers are irresistibly drawn to the latter. Out of High Season school days add another imponderable to timetables, as buses tour the remoter villages twice a day collecting and delivering the kids.

Electricity

Greece's electrical system runs at 220 volts, with most sockets taking standard two-pin continental style plugs (most UK and US devices will

require adaptors). Each Greek island has its own generation plant (usually whining away on the next bay but one from the main town).

Employment Opportunities

There are a number of employment options open at the student end of the market if you are looking to finance an island hopping holiday with casual work. These include the famous ones (notably the donkey dropping collectors on Hydra and the disco dancers employed on Ios to make the outfits seem busy). Most opportunities, however, are more mundane and are to be found in doing jobs the locals either wouldn't want to do (many are too busy polishing their Range Rovers to find time to serve customers) or wouldn't want their daughters to do: i.e. cleaning and bar work.

Rates of pay are lousy — hence the rapid turnover in staff. These start at €15 per night for bar work, and, if you are lucky, up to €15 per day with a supermarket job. Payment in kind is also sometimes offered: free camping is given by some sites in exchange for a few hours on the quay pulling campers as they come off the ferries.

Campsite notice boards occasionally carry advertisements for girls wanted to work in Athens during the winter. What they have to do, and with whom, is never made clear.

Environment

The development of mass tourism has had a major environmental impact on the Greek islands over the last 20 years. Add to this the wider problems faced by the almost landlocked Mediterranean, and you have undeniable problems. The only solace is that, as yet, the islands have exhibited a surprising resilience; most beaches are cleaner than their counterparts in the Western Med (three-quarters of Mediterranean pollution comes from France, Spain and Italy), and the marine damage is, for the most part, indiscernible to the tourist — barring the damage to a small number of species (see p. 62).

Of course, there are spots where things are very bad. Athens is the main casualty, with serious air and marine pollution. The waters of the adjacent Saronic Gulf are very badly damaged and have seen a fall in the number of species of marine fauna from 170 in 1960 to 30 in 1994. Near Piraeus the sea is almost dead: no health-minded Athenian will swim within 15 km of the capital. Things are worse elsewhere. The Turkish city of İzmir pours half a million cubic metres of untreated sewage into the Aegean each year, while the northern Adriatic regularly sees tides of a yellow mucus-like foam on its shorelines. The situation can only deteriorate: problems aren't being addressed and the renewal of sea water in the Mediterranean by exchange with the Atlantic (via the Strait of Gibraltar) takes some 150 years.

The European Union has also been responsible for major terrestrial changes. Most islands have been eligible for grants to improve their previously scenic dirt road and donkey path networks. A secondary consequence of EU membership has been the relaxing of the restrictions on the ownership of holiday homes by non-Greek nationals in the islands. As the barriers come down so many new buildings are going up.

Food & Drink

Greek cuisine enjoys a rather chequered reputation. At its best it can be very enjoyable and healthy (there are very low rates of heart disease in this part of the world), but there is no disguising the fact that many Greek restaurants fail to do more than provide an acceptable minimum, with a selection of dishes that can only be described as limited (chicken, grilled steak and fish dishes predominating). The general standard of Greek cuisine hasn't been helped by the regular practice of cooking the meal well before eating, the theory being that lukewarm food is better for the digestion. Large quantities of olive oil are also added to 'lube the tubes'. Sadly, the invention of the microwave has only served to further encourage this practice.

All this said, there is plenty of good food around; the trick in finding it is to look for the tavernas and restaurants that are attracting a local clientele: Greeks enjoy good food as much as anyone else, and their patronage is a fair indication that this is *the* place to eat hereabouts. In many cases these aren't the most glamorous-looking establishments in town, which are often the sole preserve of the tourist (not to mention seasonal staff: this is apt to make restaurant recommendations very unreliable at times).

This doesn't necessarily mean that they are bad. Thanks to the large number of expatriate Greeks returning from the USA and Australia to set up catering establishments in Greece, the number of foreign food outlets is steadily rising on the popular islands. US-style pizzerias are now opening on some of the most unlikely islands (one of the latest is at Katapola on Amorgos), and increasingly exotic eating places are adding further culinary colour to the scene.

Paros and Ios now have Chinese restaurants, Mykonos a Thai (all looking rather incongruous amidst their whitewashed chora surroundings). At the worst end of the scale, package-tour dominated Kos even has a Mexican restaurant that requires its customers to wear sombreros. **Fast Food** burger chains are to be found on all the more heavily touristed islands, the best being a local operation called *Goody's*. Branches of *McDonald's* were confined to the cities until 2003 when branches appeared on Kos and Skiathos.

While Greek food is relatively cheap (you can get a reasonable meal and beer in a restaurant for around €9), those on a tight budget doing the islands on the cheap will find they can economize by living out of supermarkets. A local grocery store is a standard feature of all island settlements. Except on the islands that see very few tourists, most sell all the essentials. Common to all islands is the much underrated local fast food. Sold from small shops and bars it consists of an Arabic bread-style roll (**Pita**) filled either with **Gyros** (spit-cooked layers of meat—usually pork) or **Souvlaki** (kebab), with tomatoes, onions and yoghurt. For a hungry island hopper a plateful of Souvlaki Pita can be a fast-track stairway to heaven, but as with tavernas and restaurants, it pays to look to see where the locals are congregating for they are the ones who really know where to go for the real thing; poor tourist outlets are apt to add handfuls of french fries to the mélange (thus saving on the amount of meat in the pita).

The other great mainstay of the island culinary scene is the ubiquitous **Greek salad**. Known as *choriatiki*, it is made up of sliced tomatoes, onions, peppers and cucumbers, topped with *feta* (goat's cheese) and the odd decorative olive. It is often produced as a side dish to the main course in tavernas. **Main courses** tend to be uninspiring. The most common offerings are spiced meat-balls (*keftedes*), mousaka, and roast chicken.

Seafood is regularly on offer in the islands, though it is now quite expensive

as a result of over-fishing; the strings of *chtapodi* (octopus) hung out to dry outside tavernas have traditionally been one of the more photogenic culinary sights. Somewhat less attractive is the sight of the little critters being clobbered until their pips squeak in order to soften them up to the point of being nicely chewy. If this doesn't appeal, you can always eat tender-fried baby squid (*kalamarakia*) instead. **Shellfish** is also very popular. Crayfish (*astakos*) and lobster (*kalogeros*) are commonly found on menus. Of the fish proper, the most sought-after dishes are grilled mullet (*bouni/barbounia*) and bream (*lithrini*). The small fish of the day's catch are often baked in tomato sauce — a dish known as *bourthéto*.

Vegetarians will find that the Greek practice of ordering vegetable dishes for both first and main courses ensures that most restaurants will be able to serve up something vaguely palatable. As dairy products are not widely used in Greek cooking it is also perfectly possible to follow a vegan diet in the islands.

Many islands now have patisseries offering fancy cakes and pastries. These include traditional Greek fare, notably **cheese pies** (*tiropitta*) served piping hot. Island bakeries also sell these and breakfast **doughnuts**, alongside freshly baked bread in the tourist season. Many also now stock soft canned drinks, ice cream and refrigerated chocolate bars (forget about buying chocolate that isn't) as well.

The usual brands of **soft drinks** are all widely available, though shop prices are half what you are charged elsewhere. **Mineral water** is the staple backpacker's day-time drink. On many of the islands it is claimed that you can drink the tap water, but this isn't to be recommended given that summer shortages often result in supplies being heavily adulterated with sea water. Many islands also produce wines, with heavy reds predominating, along with another speciality: *retsina* — a dubious pine-barrel 'wine' that doubles up wondrously as turpentine in a pinch.

Greek

One of the most immediate (and often intimidating) problems new visitors to Greece expect to encounter is the apparently strange Greek language with its alien-looking alphabet. Such worries are all but groundless these days. Greece has been on the tourist map for so long that Greek phrase books are now to be numbered among the 'non-essential' items (though they are widely on sale in Greece).

In fact, you can be sure of finding someone who can speak English in all the tourist facilities, if only because the language is compulsory in schools, and each summer the country is full of Greek-expatriate families from the USA, Canada and Australia (it isn't usually even necessary to ask the locals if they can speak English). Reading the Greek alphabet on signs and maps is a different matter. Fortunately most road and other tourist-related signs are in both Greek and English, as are most ferry timetables outside ticket agencies. The only exceptions to this are the less touristed islands of the Northern Aegean and the Turkish coast, where German is now the de facto lingua franca (reflecting the nationality of the majority of visitors). Even though you don't need any Greek, any efforts to speak it are appreciated, and a few basic phrases are given on p. 660 along with a summary of the letters and their English equivalents.

Precise transliteration between Greek and English letter forms is difficult, as in some instances equivalents are lacking. For example: the Greek for 'Saint' Agiou can be variously transcribed as Agiou, Ag., Ayios or Aghios. It is also not uncommon to find non-Greek names used alongside their older Greek counterparts. Hence the Cretan town of Agios Nikolaos is known by island bus drivers as 'San' Nikolaos (a hangover from the days of Venetian control of the island). 'Santorini' is another example of a later Venetian name coexisting with an earlier one: 'Thira'. Both are commonly used but refer to the same island. Just to make life really interesting 'Thira' can also be transcribed as 'Phira' or even 'Fira', and like a lot of Greek islands both the island and its principal town have the same name. This all sounds horribly confusing but it isn't really a major problem provided you look at any unfamiliar name with an eye to the possibility that it could be a variation on the name you are looking for. Thus: Cos = Kos, Lesbos = Lesvos, Siros = Syros, etc. Where an island is commonly known by two names or by a name in a form which does not correspond particularly closely to the form used in Greece (e.g. Rhodes is always referred to locally as 'Rodos', Crete = 'Kriti'), both names are given on island maps.

To aid recognition on each chapter title page you will find the names of the major ports covered by the chapter in Greek. For the most part they are shown in the accusative form as they appear on ticket agency timetables and ship destination boards: e.g. Paros = ΠΑΡΟΣ (nominative) is shown in its more commonly encountered accusative form: ΠΑΡΟ.

As a further aid to the language you will find below an old school rhyme (even though it doesn't) used to drum the Greek alphabet into the minds of countless poor kids:

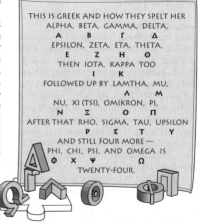

THIS IS GREEK AND HOW THEY SPELT HER
ALPHA, BETA, GAMMA, DELTA,
A   B   Γ   Δ
EPSILON, ZETA, ETA, THETA,
E   Z   H   Θ
THEN IOTA, KAPPA TOO
I   K
FOLLOWED UP BY LAMTHA, MU,
Λ   M
NU, XI (TSI), OMIKRON, PI,
N   Ξ   O   Π
AFTER THAT RHO, SIGMA, TAU, UPSILON
P   Σ   T   Y
AND STILL FOUR MORE —
PHI, CHI, PSI, AND OMEGA IS
Φ   X   Ψ   Ω
TWENTY-FOUR.

Health & Insurance

The countries along the northern shore of the Mediterranean maintain reasonable levels of sanitation and no inoculations are mandatory. However, vaccination against tetanus, typhoid, hepatitis A and polio is a good idea. Minor ailments are often treated by pharmacists, who have a wider remit than in many other countries. All the large islands have 'cottage' hospitals, though most are primitive by West European standards (you should get all injuries treated checked by your own doctor as soon as you get home). These are backed up by at least one doctor on all the islands served by regular ferry and an emergency air ambulance service. Reciprocal arrangements for UK NHS patients exist with most countries, but the widely mentioned E111 form is of limited value and no substitute for proper insurance.

Full medical insurance (including emergency flight home) is very strongly recommended. Amongst the easiest to obtain is the Thomas Cook Travel Insurance Package. This offers comprehensive medical insurance (including the all-important cover for accidents on mopeds 125cc and under) and is available from all Thomas Cook Retail travel shops in the UK. Note: most insurance policies do not provide cover for injury in high-risk activities such as bungee jumping.

Luggage Deposits

Most large islands have luggage deposit facilities that charge between €2 and €6 a day and staple a numbered ticket to each bag (to redeem it you produce the counterfoil). Ticket agents have also got into the act (see p. 37). These are useful but should be treated with caution: look to see if any check is being made on who is removing bags as they rarely ticket them (and never leave passports or money in your pack). If they don't, be aware that if your bag goes missing it is possible that your insurer will not be willing to recognize your claim as your bag will be deemed 'unsecured'.

Maps & Guides

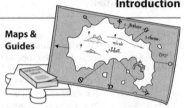

Greece has attracted guide-writers since Pausanias put stylus to scroll in Roman times — so much so, that most guidebook series include the country. If you want to take an additional volume along you will be spoilt for choice. However, most are re-researched every second or third year. This tends to be a weakness as the Greek islands are changing rapidly: it pays to look at the edition date and reckon that the contents date from a year earlier. Inside Greece it is hard to find big name guides outside of Athens, and those that are on sale have a hefty price mark-up. Locally produced island guides (in a form of English) are on sale on most islands.

The Greek islands also have a place in the history of cartography, featuring in one of the earliest printed atlases: the *Isolario* of Benedetto Bordone. Published in 1528, it carried woodcut maps based on old books of sailing directions known as 'island books'. The example above is of Mykonos (orientated with Jerusalem at the top).

Almost all the islands have modern maps on sale — most are about €1.50. To date, their quality has not been high (e.g. minor tracks often end up depicted as major highways). Salvation is now at hand, however, with the arrival of a new series — the *ROAD EDITIONS*. Sporting dark blue covers, they are easily the best road and island walking maps around. Unfortunately only 21 islands had been published by 2003 — though more will be in print in 2004. The lack of good town street maps has prompted the publication of many of the maps in this book. Locally, the most interesting on sale are the colourful *Sky Maps* (though these can be deceptive, as they show only those businesses that pay to advertise in them).

Moped & Car Hire

In recent years the islands have seen a dramatic increase in moped hire. Prices are low (reckon on €10 per day rental for a low powered machine). Unfortunately, with their increased popularity has come a large rise in the number of tourist deaths and injuries. The former are running at over a hundred a year; the latter are too numerous to count. Many of these are the result of inexperienced and ill-equipped riders attempting too much on poor roads using poorly maintained bikes. Before succumbing to the temptation to go roaring off into the sunset you should consider the possibility that that sunset could be more final than picturesque.

Even if you are an experienced rider, there are a number of points worth noting. First, insurance: does your holiday insurance cover all the potential risks you run riding a moped or motorbike without a helmet (these can't always be hired along with the moped as few bother with them in Greece)? Secondly, before handing over your day's rental money and your passport (a guarantee that you will bring the machine back) you should: (1) check the condition of the machine, (2) ascertain who is liable for what if it breaks down, (3) check how much fuel you are getting (reputable outlets can often be distinguished by fuel in the tank). Once you have your machine, accept its limitations; most are not powerful enough to negotiate steeper hills and many island roads are all pot-holes.

All the above points also apply to car hire (see p. 382). This can be expensive if you pay by the day, but longer deals are good value: Reckon on paying €150 per week, €80 for 3 days (including tax and insurance), for a Jeep or beach buggy. In order to hire a car (and some mopeds) you will also need a driving licence. A Green Card insurance warranty is also recommended.

Newspapers & Books

Most major European papers are available on all but the remotest of the islands — usually via a stationery shop or street kiosk. On the majority of islands they appear a day after publication. In central Athens they are available on the evening of the day they are published. In High Season it pays to arrive early if you want the more popular titles. The difficulty is determining when 'early' is, for it varies according to an island's links with Athens or the nearest island with a direct airport link to Western Europe. On Paros, for example, it is early afternoon as the newspapers are carried on the morning ferries from Piraeus.

Prices are high: expect to pay double the home country published price. Most newsagents also have a pricey supply of pulp fiction, as well as locally produced maps and guides.

Nightlife

One of the most charming aspects of Greek island life is the traditional evening promenade around the centre of town. Nights in Greece are the time for the locals to bask in the cooler temperatures and catch up with the gossip. As a result, even the most uninspiring of towns exude an air of companionable bustle that lasts from dusk to 10 or 11 pm. Tavernas take in the lingerers who want to chat (those near the ports also serve as a temporary home for those waiting for night ferries).

Most islands also boast at least one disco where you can touch a few more hands in the dance of life. Discos and bars usually stay open until 3 am. Thereafter the streets are often filled with slowly dispersing crowds of the slightly inebriated. This can be a problem time in some parts as a lack of manpower means that there is little of a police presence to curb the excesses of the more exuberant revellers.

Photography

Popular makes of film are available on all but the smallest Greek islands. However, if your requirements are in anyway exotic (e.g. brands like Kodachrome 64) you can be certain of encountering considerable difficulty replenishing supplies. The cost of film (generally around 25% more than UK prices) also varies wildly from centre to centre. An extreme example of this is the fact that it is actually cheaper to buy a return ticket to Aegina to buy some brands than it is to buy them at Piraeus. If you want to view the results of your endeavours sooner rather than later you will find that all the popular islands now have at least one 1-hour film processing outlet in the centre of town.

If you want something more than the usual holiday snaps then you should consider using a polarizing filter to combat the brilliant sunlight that bathes the islands. A second constraint on a photographer's prowess are the signs prohibiting photography in military areas. This is particularly true on parts of Kos (and other islands and ports along the Turkish coast) and Crete (home to a major NATO base). Given local sensibilities on this subject it is best to work on the assumption that it is unwise to snap naval craft or personnel no matter where you are.

Police

Greece has three types of police in addition to the usual customs and traffic officials: the regular police, the tourist police and the port police. The islands have a varying number of each depending on their population size. Small or very popular islands have extra officials drafted in to help cope with the tourist season. Islands with a population of under 400 usually have one permanent official who wears all three hats.

The regular **Police** (identified by a regular police-style blue uniform and peaked cap) have a station on most islands. For the greater part of the year they don't have a lot to do given the very low crime rate among islanders (it is difficult to get away with crime on an island where everyone knows everyone else). For this reason they are relatively few in number and have little opportunity to practise and develop such detection skills as they may possess. Things of course change in the summer when they are faced with a procession of foreigners who have had a couple of dozen beers too many, their possessions stolen (usually by other holiday makers), or worse (see p. 63). Sad to say it, but the reaction to tourists beating at their doors is often óne of polite indifference. If you are reporting a crime, the chances are it will be solely for insurance purposes; the probability of the police recovering lost items is very low. It therefore pays to be extra vigilant when it comes to looking after your property. If you are one of the very few who hit serious trouble, then it is advisable to contact your nearest consulate before the police, if practicable.

The **Tourist Police** are not to be confused with the regular police (despite having an all but identical uniform: this makes it easier for small island officials to do a quick change act). As their name implies, their function is to look after tourists and ensure that outlets serving them (i.e. hotels, pensions, restaurants, shops, taxis, etc.) are conforming to official regulations. In common with the NTOG/EOT and occasional island tourist offices they also provide maps, island information, travel and accommodation details. If you ever have difficulty finding a bed or end up embroiled in an argument with a local over a bill, then the tourist police should be your first port of call (often the mere threat of bringing them in is enough to resolve arguments): they are generally very helpful, can speak some English (of sorts) and are disposed to be on the tourist's 'side' if there is a just cause for complaint. They can also perform a valuable liaison role if you need to visit the regular police (their offices are often to be found in the same building); so much so, that it is worth taking most problems to them first. Unfortunately, they generally only have officials on islands with a large summer tourist population. Some of these islands (e.g. Santorini) also use summer volunteers as tourist wardens. Armed with a khaki uniform and a smile, they point the masses in which ever direction they are seeking to go.

The third — and most visible — police are the **Port Police**. Decked out in a natty all-white naval officer-like uniform, their sole responsibility is the supervision of the island and mainland ports. Armed with whistles (that are blown constantly) they attempt to keep tourists and locals alike from boarding ferries before those passengers that wish to disembark have done so, as well as keeping both out of the road of cars and lorries attempting to use the same exit/boarding door. They tend to be a fairly frustrated lot as no one takes a blind bit of notice of them as a rule.

On the busier islands quayside passenger sheds have been installed to make the port police's job easier as they enable foot passengers to be corralled behind a locked gate at the end of the shed until the port police deign to release them with a key. On smaller islands they don't bother resorting to such stratagems and just roll up (often on a moped) 20 minutes or so before the ferry turns up; armed with ship-to-shore radios, they *know* exactly when a ferry is going to arrive. If you have been waiting several hours for an overdue ferry a port policeman is always a very welcome sight.

The port police are usually stationed in a separate building from the regular police.

More often than not it is within a couple of hundred metres of the ferry quay and sometimes has a board outside listing the day's ferry departures (sadly, only ever in Greek). Usually Port Policemen are not in the least bit interested in helping you to find a room, or anything else for that matter, so don't waste your time asking (many are imported just for the High Season) — though they are approachable enough if you want regular ferry information. Much depends on the size of the island (the smaller the better).

Public Holidays

As a rule, public/ bank holidays tend to have much more impact on bus rather than ferry services within Greece. Plans to travel on religious holidays should allow for the possibility that services will be reduced or suspended. The Greek Orthodox church still exerts a powerful influence, and ferries are sometimes diverted to carry pilgrims to the shrine of the moment (Tinos on August 15 being a good example of this). If you are planning an Easter break in the islands, you should expect to find ferries very busy. In Greece, Easter is the most important holiday of the year, and a great many islanders working in Athens or elsewhere on the mainland try to get back to their island homes to spend the holiday period with their families.

Public holidays in 2004:

January 1	New Year's Day
January 6	Epiphany
February 23	Shrove Monday
March 25	Independence Day
April 9, 12	Easter
May 1	Labour Day
June 15, 16	Feast of the Holy Spirit
August 15	The Feast of the Assumption of the Virgin Mary
October 28	Ohi Day
December 25, 26	Christmas

Religion

Thanks to the Greek Orthodox church religion continues to play an important part in Greek society. The result is a profusion of churches and a veneration of things religious no longer seen in Western Europe. This even extends to little old ladies giving up their bus seats to priests just out of theological college — something which might not seem so surprising until you try to get on a ferry alongside them, for the little old ladies in black — the notorious black widows — are the original Hell's Grannies of Monty Python fame, kicking and shoving their way aboard with grim determination that refuses to admit defeat. Much of their anger can be put down to the convention that requires them to wear black for years on end. Widowers in Greece get off more lightly, wearing a black armband for a year.

Given this strict observance of the traditional dress code, it isn't perhaps too surprising to find that islanders get very upset when tourists attempt to enter churches in shorts or beachwear. Properly dressed (i.e. with torso and legs covered) tourists are made to feel very welcome.

Thanks to a tradition which expects every family to build its own chapel, small room-sized chapels abound on the Greek Islands. Roman Catholic communities are also to be found on some — a remnant from the days of Venetian or Italian rule. Thanks to the population exchanges that followed the Helleno-Turkish war of 1919–22 Islam has all but disappeared from the islands.

Athens and a number of island towns still contain mosques sporting increasingly dilapidated minarets, but without exception they have been taken out of use as places of worship and converted into museums or warehouses. This process has

been reversed in the former Greek towns along the Turkish coast. Religious tolerance is a casualty of politics in this part of the world.

Scams

The large number of tourists (particularly in Athens) has, sad to say it, produced some sharp practices by an unscrupulous few. These are the most common scams:

1. Short-changing

Examples here applied to Drachma notes, but no doubt Euro versions will be tried and tested by the time you get to Greece.

1: the tourist pays a taxi-driver (airport taxis love this one) or waiter with a large-value bank note and by a sleight of hand it is handed back with the protest that it is only a small note. *Always* check the size of notes when paying a bill. You can avoid the problem arising by holding the note up before handing it over and saying 'I only have a xxx Euro note'. If you do get done, vigorously stand your ground and suggest a visit to the Police: this response is usually sufficient to remedy the situation.

Version 2: the tourist hands over a large bank note and is given change for a smaller one. Again, the same response to Version 1 is the best way of resolving things.

2. The Passport Trick

Some hotel and room owners charge tourists who have checked in, found the room unsatisfactory and checked out again a fee for the return of their passport. You can avoid this by keeping your passport until you have checked the room. If you do get caught don't hand over any cash: instead call in the tourist police.

3. Bar Tricks

Two bar tricks are common enough to be worth mentioning. The first is the adding of meths or some other tasteless additive to spirits in resort bars (with dire consequences for the drinker a few hours latter). The second is the occasional habit of charging bar/disco entrance fees which can be offset against your first drink. It is only when you get inside that you discover that prices are much higher than elsewhere. Ask about bar prices when buying your ticket.

Seasickness

If you fall victim to seasickness it is more likely as not that it will be thanks to the vessel you are on rather than changes in sea conditions. The Mediterranean is calm compared to the English Channel. Obviously it can get rough — particularly in the Aegean when the *meltemi* wind rushes down from the north — but as a rule on most ferries you are hard put to distinguish any sea movement. Catamarans and hydrofoils can be a different matter.

Seasickness is caused by the inability of the brain to correlate conflicting information from the eye and ear. The eye perceives the vessel as being a static object while the balance mechanism of the ear is telling the brain that the body is travelling up, down, and all over the place. The easiest way of resolving this cerebral conflict is to: (1) go up on deck where you can keep the horizon, rather than the ship, as the visual static point of reference, thus allowing the brain to accurately interpret the balance information being received from the ear; (2) take up a position in the centre of the vessel about two-thirds the length of the ship from the bow. This will be the optimum point of least vertical and horizontal movement (ferries are designed stern-heavy to ensure that their screws and rudder remain in the water) and is akin to being at the top — rather than the bottom — of a pendulum; (3) eat before you sail and keep nibbling during the journey to keep the stomach occupied.

A number of over-the-counter anti-seasickness drugs can be obtained locally in Greece. *Dramamine* is the most widely available but like many of these drugs it is apt to cause drowsiness; for this reason alone it is better to get motion sickness drugs before you travel so that you can be advised as to possible reactions. Alternatives such as adhesive patches, Ginger Root Capsules (the herbalist remedy) and Sea Bands (wrist-bands that rely on Nei-Kuan acupressure point techniques) aren't usually available in Greece.

Shopping

Regular shopping hours in Greece are 08.00–13.30/15.00 Monday to Saturday and 17.30–20.30 on Tuesday, Thursday and Friday. In lucrative tourist towns an open-all-hours (even Sundays) regime is adopted in High Season, but city centre shopping closes down. Pharmacies in the towns open in the evenings on a rota basis: a sign in Greek on the door will tell you which one if you can read it. Street kiosks are usually open from 08.00–23.00 — so liquid refreshments, snacks and English-language newspapers (one day late) are always readily available.

Each island chain has its own specialities (the Cyclades have reproduction Cycladic idols, the Dodecanese duty-free liquor). Leather goods, reproduction statuary, bronzes and ceramics by the score and sponges are common to all. Other islands are noted for individual goods: e.g. the pistachio nuts of Aegina. Popular islands are 'blessed' with pricey gold and clothing boutiques. An incongruous (given the temperatures) and less attractive feature of the more up-market islands are the fur shops now driven to extinction elsewhere.

Sightseeing

Most archeological sites and museums in Greece are regulated by the EOT (the local branch of the Greek National Tourist Board). Opening hours for sites vary, but most operate something akin to a 08.30–15.00 timetable, Tuesdays to Sundays, and are closed on Mondays. Major archaeological sites in Athens and elsewhere usually stay open until at least 18.00 in High Season. You can expect to pay to enter archaeological sites and museums in Greece. Ticket prices are around €3 to enter a museum, €5 for any of the major sites. ISIC-carrying students usually get a 50% discount, and in some instances

gain free admission. In past years Sundays have seen free entry for all visitors to sites, but many (including the popular sites in Athens) are now charging between 1 April—31 October.

On archaeological sites, tourists are increasingly prohibited from entering individual buildings, or standing on mosaics (to prevent wear and tear): each usually has strategically sited wardens armed with forbidding whistles, to bring those who step beyond the boundary ropes back into line; as a result a visit to the Athenian Acropolis or Olympia is apt to sound like a school sports day. Site guides are usually on sale at ticket kiosks. Ruins and exhibits are usually labelled in Greek and English, but this can vary if other countries have been extensively involved with a site's excavation (e.g. signs on Delos are in French).

Taxis
Island taxis perform a valuable back-up role to the buses; on some islands (e.g. Leros) they have all but replaced them. All are metered, but it is common for the driver to forget to switch the meter on. Other common practices are similarly weighted against the passenger: it is normal for each passenger to pay the full fare and individual items of baggage also usually attract a small charge. In view of this, you should always endeavour to establish how much the journey will cost before you get going. Finally, don't be too surprised to find locals (who don't pay) grabbing a lift if they know your driver.

Telephones
The Greek telephone system has seen a radical change over the last few years thanks to the widespread introduction of the telephone card. Phonecards have become the way to make both domestic and international calls. They are on sale from street kiosks and the communal telephone offices to be found in every port and town. Easily spotted by the grey satellite dish that adorns the roof, they are advertised by the

initials OTE (ask for the 'Otay'). Usually open from 07.00–13.00 most contain 6 to 8 booths equipped with meters; you make your call and then pay afterwards at the supervisor's desk.

Until the arrival of phonecards the OTE was a natural meeting point and one of the hubs of island life. These days it is usually empty apart from a few staff trying to sell mobile phones. Phonecard prices in 2003 were €3, €10, and €15 — depending on the number of units (high-value cards are only available from OTEs). The cost of making calls in Greece is quite low, and even the €3 card is good for a couple of international calls.

Phonecards aside, the Greek telephone system is pretty antiquated. Connections are often hard to make within Greece as most go via undersea cable and you can spend a happy twenty minutes redialling. Phone calls can also be made from the confectionery and tobacco kiosks found in main town streets and from some ticket agencies (in both instances you will have to pay roughly 10% more for your call).

International calls (via satellite) are less of a problem (if you need the International operator dial 161). When phoning from Greece, Cyprus and Italy prefix your home number (after removing any initial '0' in the area code) with:

Australia	0061
Austria	0043
Belgium	0032
Canada	001
Denmark	0045
France	0033
Germany	0049
Ireland	00353
Italy	0039
Netherlands	0031
New Zealand	0064
Spain	0034
Switzerland	0041
UK	0044
USA	001

Time

Greece and the Eastern Mediterranean countries are — apart from a few days during the change-over period to and from summer time in March and October — 1 hour ahead of most European countries, 2 hours ahead of UK GMT/Summer Time, 7 hours ahead of North America Eastern Standard Time, and 10 hours ahead of Pacific Standard Time.

Walking in the Islands

The Greek islands offer some very attractive hiking territory, and a fair few island hoppers choose to hop between islands and then walk the rest of the way. The combination of a wide variety of spectacular Aegean scenery and convenient size (many islands are ideal for day-trip walking excursions) can be irresistible. The fact that walking an island is an excellent way to get to know it — while avoiding any evidence of mass tourism — also often comes into play.

The best time for hiking is between Easter and October, though this period encompasses a wide variety of conditions. The early spring is arguably the most attractive, as one is walking through hillsides dotted with wild flowers. The downside is that one can never be terribly sure about the weather, and the sea is far too cold for comfortable swimming.

May and June see the end of the flower season and are the most popular months for serious hiking, as the sea temperatures are rising and the air temperatures aren't too excessive. September and October are similarly blessed, but the autumnal end-of-tourist-season atmosphere in the towns can be a problem.

High Season tends to be far too hot for comfortable long-distance walking: unless you can be cooled by the strong *meltemi* winds, you will find it very hard going from 11.00 to 17.00 — given the lack of shade on most islands. If you want to do some serious walking at this time of the year then you should seriously consider visiting islands north of the Cyclades and

Dodecanese which tend to have plenty of tree cover.

Hiking is not a pastime that appeals to Greeks: the notion of walking anywhere in the sun if you can avoid it is a bizarre concept to people living hereabouts. You should therefore assume that you will have to bring all equipment with you, as you are unlikely to find it on sale locally. It doesn't need to be very specialized: the standard items are a day-pack, good walking shoes, a whistle and water bottle. Long trousers can be helpful if the paths you are negotiating meander through scrubby vegetation. The final prerequisite is a sunhat capable of remaining on one's head in the windy conditions that are normal in this part of the world.

Conventional hiking maps don't really exist for the islands (though some, e.g. the Northern Sporades, do have excellent maps aimed at walkers). The new *ROAD EDITIONS* maps (see p. 52) are also very good as they have most paths marked. Unfortunately the ready availability of EU road-building grants means that many of the old donkey trails ('*monopatia*') are now being bulldozed into roads, and cartographers are struggling vainly to keep up with the changes.

One big plus is that an increasing number of islands have on sale local walking guides (see the 'Walking' page on this book's website). These vary considerably in style and form, but the writers in most cases are well versed in their subject and often live on the islands in question. Particularly good examples are mentioned in the relevant island entry in this book.

Given the growing popularity of the islands as a walking holiday destination, it is surprising that stand-alone guidebooks on this subject are rare. The best one now in print is *Walking the Aegean Islands* by Dieter Graf. Available in Greece, it describes some 48 hikes on 20 Cycladian islands.

What to take

When Phileas Fogg went around the world in 79 days he packed only 2 shirts and 3 pairs of stockings. Admittedly this was backed up with a manservant complete with a carpet bag containing £20,000, but this minor item aside, you could do worse than follow his example and pack as little as you can get away with: the big disadvantage of island hopping is that you have to carry all your luggage with you — so it pays to pack the absolute minimum.

Luckily, Greece in the summer is warm and dry enough for most people to comfortably get by with their beachwear and a couple of changes of clothes (girls in sarongs are becoming a common sight). Add to this sundry items determined by your interests in life (those keen on monasteries or churches tend to take more formal clothing, while most young male Italians go for designer sun-glasses and five bottles of aftershave lotion), and this is quite enough to be going on with. Some other ideas that are worth considering (in no particular order):

A good **novel**: all island-hopping holidays involve a certain amount of guaranteed waiting around on harbour quays for boats — a novel will do a lot to reduce any tedium. **Backgammon** is also a popular ferry-waiting pastime. Card games, however, tend to be far less successful thanks to the strong summer winds.

A **pullover** and **windcheater**: ferries are a good way of keeping cool during the day, but a very poor way of keeping warm at night. Deck-class passengers travelling on outside decks (or waiting on quaysides) will soon regret not having some kind of wind-proof clothing.

Sleeping bags are also commonly seen accoutrements, and a good insurance policy in High Season should you not be able to find a room (as you can make tracks for the nearest campsite). The nights ashore are so mild that it is often only the more amorous (and moany) campers who bother bringing a tent.

Foam mats and **airbeds** are also very popular with deck-class passengers wanting to sleep or lie out on deck. If you are overnighting on a ferry deck they are invaluable, as decks get too wet to place sleeping bags on them unprotected. Both mats and airbeds are available in Greece at a price, along with the cheap straw roll-up beach mats used by almost everyone.

A second useful accoutrement for heavy travellers is an **inflatable neck-pillow**. Those with more cash to hand can buy these as part of an 'Airline comfort kit' (these usually include a lightweight blanket, and sometimes an inflatable back-pillow as well). **Earplugs** are occasionally desirable on some campsites, and if you want to stand on the noisy outside decks of hydrofoils. A **can opener** is invaluable if you are eating out of local supermarkets (even small grocery shops carry odd tins from the Heinz range, and Kellogg's cereals).

Student cards: if you have one, make sure that you take it, as it will get you significant discounts on tours and site entry charges. On some archaeological sites they can even get you free entry. Luxury items are better brought with you than purchased in Greece. Cosmetics, contact lens solutions (the choice is limited outside Athens) and medicines are all notably more expensive than in the UK.

Unusual makes of **film** should be brought with you. Regular film is often more expensive, but as keeping your luggage weight down is a priority, this sort of item can be bought as you travel. Computer-related kit can be hard to find outside Athens.

You should also assume that you will need to carry **lavatory paper** and **mosquito repellent** (there are more mossies than tourists in Greece — take care to look out for a repellent with a high 'Deet' content) and a **sink plug** wherever you go. Finally, if you want to avoid backpack check-in hassle at Athens airport, a rucksack bag is a must.

When to go

The Eastern Mediterranean has a similar climate to Southern California: hot dry summers, warm wet winters and around 3250 hours of sunshine a year. Within the Aegean there are also significant climatic variations, with the north — not surprisingly — being a couple of degrees cooler than average, Rhodes and Crete a degree above the average, and the centre and west being appreciably drier than the east. This latter feature is in part due to the Cyclades, which form a rain 'shadow', thanks to a ring of hilly islands (notably Kea, Kythnos, Serifos, Santorini, Ios, Sikinos, Folegandros, Anafi and Amorgos) obscuring rain-bearing clouds. Though there has been little apparent change in climate since prehistoric times, extensive deforestation on the islands has also contributed to the dryness of the region.

Although most island hoppers visit during July and August, the nicest time to visit Greece is in April and May when the wild flowers are out, but then the weather can't always be guaranteed. September and October also have their fans, but at some point the first autumn storms arrive, and when the weather first breaks these can be positively vicious. It also rains roughly one day per month between early June and mid-September in the Northern Aegean and the Ionian islands, but rarely in July and August south of Athens.

August is the hottest month of the year, with average daytime temperatures around 26° C. July follows a degree behind but boasts a higher sea temperature. How hot you end up will depend largely on where you are: Athens in August is pretty terrible, along with much of the mainland. Fortunately, the majority of the islands (the main exceptions are the Ionian and Saronic Gulf groups) are spared over-high temperatures thanks to the summer *meltemi* wind and sea breezes.

The *meltemi* (a cooling north wind caused by summer low pressure over Asia) normally starts up in mid-morning and blows into the evening. It can be a surprise if you are not prepared for it: the central Aegean from mid-June to October is *very* windy (see overleaf). This is great for windsurfers (of which there are many), but can leave beach lovers in sandblasted shock. Tinos, Mykonos and Paros regularly 'enjoy' over 20 days in July and August with winds over 4 on the Beaufort Scale, and 12 days when winds go over 6. (The Beaufort Scale is used to categorize wind speeds and their influence on the sea: 4 is a point where paper gets blown around and waves have small white caps; 6 is the point where telephone wires whistle, umbrellas blow inside out and large waves form, preventing smaller boats and hydrofoils from operating). The Dodecanese, Eastern Aegean and Saronic Gulf islands escape this phenomenon and tend to be much more steamy and humid in consequence.

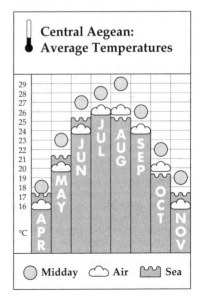

**Central Aegean:
Average Temperatures**

○ Midday ☁ Air ▨ Sea

☾ Central Aegean: Wind Averages

Days:	Calm	Breezy	Windy
APR	12	11	7
MAY	14	11	6
JUN	11	10	9
JUL	9	10	12
AUG	7	12	12
SEP	9	12	9
OCT	9	14	8
Beaufort Scale	0 – 4	4 – 6	6 +

Wildlife

Sad to say it, the most visible wildlife to be found in Greece these days is human rather than animal (though most animals are pretty wild by the end of the tourist season), for the country is remarkably free of potential pests to tourists. Greece is lucky in having few life-threatening species.

Insects are likely to pose the biggest problem for tourists, particularly the large mosquito population that feed along every island promenade. Other terrestrial threats are something of a non-event. A small **scorpion** exists, but possesses a very indifferent sting.

Snakes play an important part in many island traditions, but are uncommon, and are only mildly poisonous (the only poisonous snake native to Greece is the common European adder/viper). If you are bitten you should always seek medical help. In the case of small children an anti-venom serum is usually administered. Note: this could necessitate an emergency medical flight to the mainland: bites are so rare that few islands seem to carry stocks of the anti-venom serum. Likewise, bites from dogs should also be checked out, as rabies is also known in this part of the world.

Marine wildlife is responsible for many of the more painful encounters with nature. The rockier island coasts are home to some painful **Sea Urchins** and **Conger Eels** that regularly inflict minor damage. A more serious threat is posed by the **Dragon Fish** (or 'Drakena'), which has poisonous spikes on its spine and gills. It is to be found hidden just off sandy beaches where it burrows under the surface awaiting its prey. Most injuries are incurred while paddling. The symptoms are sharp pain followed by numbness: local doctors are equipped with a serum that will counter the crippling swelling that will otherwise occur over the following days: don't be deceived into believing that the numbness is the extent of the problem — if you are unlucky enough to step on one, seek medical attention.

Greece is also home to a number of attractive species now in decline. Most notable of these is the small colony of **Monk Seals**. Now reckoned to be one of the twelve most endangered species in the world (estimates as to its numbers range from 750 to 300), this poor creature hangs on in its reduced breeding grounds around the small islets east of Alonissos island. **Loggerhead Turtles** on Zakinthos are rapidly going the same way thanks to tourism (see p. 544) and government neglect.

In a more enlightened action the Greek government has moved to protect the magnificently horned **Kri-kri** mountain goats of Crete. Sanctuaries have been established on a number of deserted islets around Crete (notably on the island of Dia just north of Iraklion). **Dolphins** also inhabit Greek waters. If half the passengers on a ferry sun deck suddenly rush over to one side of the ship as sure as eggs is eggs the cause will be a dolphin or a school of dolphins swimming alongside.

Women Travellers

There is an old Chinese saying that runs something like 'Ying chu you yong chee choo yee' which roughly translated means 'the difference between a dream and a nightmare is no more than the thickness of the wing of a butterfly'. The Greek islands are often deemed dream country, thanks to their all-pervasive, laid-back atmosphere. However, this appealing feature is a disadvantage when it encourages one to drop one's guard too much. Greece has long taken pride in its long-merited reputation as a 'safe' destination for women travellers, and solo women island hoppers are not uncommon. However, there appears to be a small but growing problem of assaults.

This was particularly evident in the summer of 2002, when the large package-holiday resort islands of Rhodes and Corfu experienced a spate of attacks directed at English-speaking girls. In both instances a multiple rapist struck at least six times, and at the time of this book going to press nobody had been charged. Putting this into context it has to be noted that over two million Brits visit Greece each year, so the numbers are small, but they are still very worrying, given that many assaults undoubtedly go unreported.

Part of the trouble is that the past treatment of rape victims by Greek police officers has left a lot to be desired. Even the UK Foreign Office has been moved to complain that victims have been treated unsympathetically. This is not because officials are indifferent, but more the combination of a lack of language, training and experience in dealing with victims, combined with a conservative outlook that leads them to regard scantily clad young women who party day and night with crowds of young men, both downing alcohol as fast as they can open the bottles, as asking for trouble; it is noticeable that young Greek women have yet to gain a similar degree of freedom. A further unpalatable fact that local officials are loath to recognize is that a large proportion of reported attacks are by Greek youths or men. This doesn't fit readily with the undoubted fact that, once tourists are taken out of the equation, most islands are crime-free zones.

The problem is, of course, the old Mediterranean male one of seeing Western girls as (1) loose, and (2) available. Add to this the chaste nature of most of the local girls, and it is inevitable that the unattached Greek male is going to turn the charm on when holidaying alongside zillions of foreign tourists. With a new lot of victims arriving every week, they have plenty of opportunity to practise their lines.

In view of all this, the best advice must be to enjoy yourself but take care to avoid potentially dangerous situations. Most attacks appear to take place at the big resorts and party islands. Women walking home alone in the early hours or accepting lifts from locals are particularly vulnerable. Obviously, on holiday one wants a night or two on the town; on these occasions splash out on a hotel bed near the centre, don't hang around until closing time when the streets are suddenly awash with inebriated men looking for a good time, and travel home with someone you know.

If you are attacked there are a number of things you can subsequently do:

1. Get medical help or, if that isn't available, seek help from women locally, who may lend emotional support.

2. Inform your embassy or consulate (both are very sympathetic) before you talk to the police as they can liaise on your behalf.

3. If you can't be represented by an embassy or consular official, try to go to the police with a companion — preferably someone who can speak Greek.

4. Don't be afraid to curtail your holiday; embassy officials or tour reps can arrange your early return.

5. If you haven't felt up to reporting the attack in Greece, do so when you get back home; inquiries can still be pursued.

www.greekislandhopping.com

Updates to this book are now available online ...

The website attached to this book has pages updating the information contained in this edition. Check it out either before you go to Greece, or from cyber cafés in the islands, and get the very latest information — both on the boats and the islands, and the rapidly changing ferry safety situation.

ground material — for example: a weekly updated timetable for the Athenian ports of Piraeus and Rafina.

• Hop into the future ...

Some pundits are predicting that within a decade most guidebooks will be published online. The internet offers the prospect of giving readers constantly updated, much larger guidebooks. Given the rapidly changing nature of the Greek island scene, there is an obvious case for *Greek Island Hopping* to move in this direction. We will be exploring some of the possibilities in 2004.

• Extensive Links Pages

The **Links Café** pages on the site enable you to quickly find and access the most useful Greek island and ferry related web sites. Each link is accompanied by a write-up and a rating — to help you quickly sort the wheat from the chaff.

• Additional Information

There is a limit on what can be put into any printed guidebook, so the web offers us the chance to give you extra back-

Athens

Parthenon
(East Façade)

Mosque of the Bazaar
(with the Acropolis in
the background)

Monastiraki Square
(the only good bits)

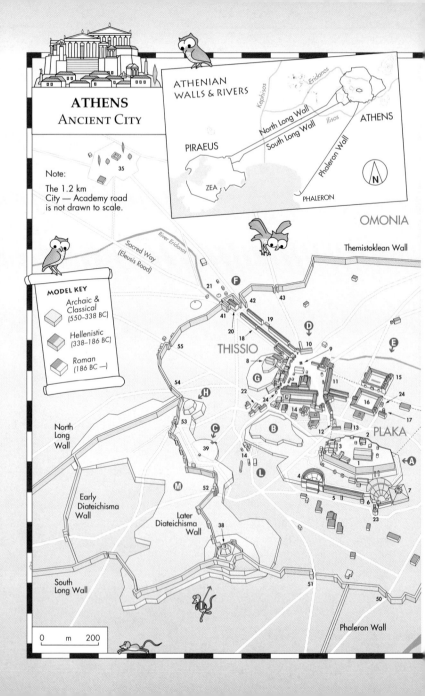

Key

- **A** Acropolis
- **B** Areopagus
- **C** Pnyx (Parliament)
- **D** Agora (Marketplace)
- **E** Roman Agora Area
- **F** Kerameikos
- **G** Kolonos Hill
- **H** Hill of the Nymphs
- **I** Mouseion Hill
- **J** Ardettos Hill
- **K** Roman 'New City'
- **L** Early City Centre
- **M** Early Residential Area

CITY LANDMARKS

1. Parthenon
2. Erechtheion
3. Propylaea
4. Odeon of Herodes Atticus
5. Stoa of Eumenes
6. Theatre of Dionysos
7. Odeon of Pericles
8. Hephaisteion
9. Altar of the Twelve Gods (City Centre)
10. Stoa Poikile
11. Stoa of Attalos
12. Eleusinion
13. Diogeneum
14. Private Houses
15. Library of Hadrian
16. Roman Agora
17. Tower of the Winds
18. Stoas lining the Panathenaic Way
19. Euboulides Monument
20. Pompeion
21. Main Cemetery
22. Classical Prison
23. Public Bath-houses
24. Public Latrines
25. Lysicrates Monument
26. Palladion
27. Arch of Hadrian
28. Temple of Kronos & Rhea
29. Olympieion
30. Delphinium
31. Temple of Tyche
32. Tomb of Herodes
33. Temple of Artemis Agrotera
34. Stadium
35. Academy (Gymnasium)
36. Lyceum (Gym)
37. Kynosarges (Gym)
38. Monument of Philopappus
39. City Parliament Platform (Pnyx)
40. Garden of Theophrastos

MODERN DISTRICTS

LIKAVITTOS

N

River Eridanos

SYNTAGMA

Hadrianic/Roman Wall

River Ilisos

CITY GATES

41. Sacred Gate
42. Dipylon Gate
43. Eriai Gate
44. Acharnian Gate
45. North-East Gate
46. Diochares Gate
47. Hippades Gate
48. Diomeian Gate
49. Itonian Gate
50. Halade Gate
51. South Gate
52. 'Dipylon above the Gates'
53. Melitides Gate
54. Demian Gate
55. Peiraic or Piraeus Gate
56. Roman Gates

Main Road
Minor Road
------- Line of the Valerian Wall

Waterfront Fishmonger
RAFINA

Main Ticket Agency Block
PIRAEUS

EXPRESS NAIAS

Rumour has it that this is what
happens to backpackers who
dare to enter the
Deck-class
saloon ...

Quayside
Breadseller

Piraeus

Historical Background

Scattered like confetti on Homer's 'wine dark' Aegean Sea, the Greek islands lie on one of the crossroads of world culture. Almost every Mediterranean civilization has left some mark, resulting in plenty of sightseeing and adding a fascinating dimension to an island hopping holiday. The islands have naturally been influenced by the major periods of Greek history, but being islands they were able to 'enjoy' a greater degree of individual historical variation, and this has added greatly to their separate identities.

Early Cycladic
4500–2000 BC

4500–3200 BC	Early Period
3200–2700 BC	Grotta–Pelos Culture
2700–2300 BC	Keros–Syros Culture
2300–2000 BC	Phylakopi I Culture

The first evidence of human activity in Greece dates from around 8500 BC. The islands appear to have been quickly populated thereafter. Most being wooded, within sight of each other, and of an ideal size for easy defence by small fishing and agrarian communities, they were natural centres of population. The Cyclades in particular flourished during the latter part of this period (3200 – 2000 BC). Removed from the outside influences of mainland cultures, they developed a distinct and unique subculture of their own.

Now known mainly through small figurines, this prehistoric Cycladic culture remains tantalizingly elusive. Even the idols carved out of white marble remain a mystery, as their function is far from clear (in this respect, echoes with the massive Easter Island figures extend beyond looks). Most have been recovered from graves (though they have also been found in settlements) and depict naked women — usually in a highly stylized form — standing with arms folded (left above right) and sometimes pregnant.

Their 'modernist' appearance has also made them very popular around the world,

with high prices and a large number of fakes typifying the market today. All this is a long way removed from the culture that created them. In the absence of evidence of political or military facets to this society, in retrospect, it looks to have existed in something like the garden of Eden. But clearly it was not all apples and Eves if the depressed, introspective posture of the occasional carved Adam is anything to go by.

Minoan
2000–1500 BC

c. 2000 BC	First sailing ships appear in the Aegean
c. 1900 BC	Palaces built on Crete
c. 1700 BC	Palaces rebuilt after earthquakes
c. 1640 BC	Santorini eruption fatally disrupts Minoan economy
c. 1450 BC	Knossos Palace destroyed

Around 2000 BC the first major power emerged in the Aegean. Named after a king whose name passed down through legend, the non-Greek Minoans were only rediscovered in the early years of the last century thanks to archaeology. Based on a commercial hegemony, the Minoan civilization, with its huge palaces, brilliant frescoes, intricate jewellery, baths, drainage systems, and above all the first writing, marked a cultural high point that was not to be regained for over a thousand years. Known only through their artifacts, the Minoans never recovered from the economically destructive volcanic eruption of Santorini c. 1640 BC. Taken over by the first Greeks, they disappeared and were forgotten even by the ancient Greeks themselves. They hovered on the edge of memory in dark legends of the sea-king Minos and his labyrinth palace, built to house his half-man, half-bull son (the Minotaur) who lived on a diet of Athenian youths, and the story of Atlantis — an island of bull-worshipping, affluent people who angered their god, who then sank their island into the sea by way of retribution.

66

Mycenaean & Dark Ages
1500–776 BC

c. 1500 BC	Mycenaeans conquer Minoan Crete
c. 1400 BC	Date of the Trojan War?
1200–1100 BC	Mycenaeans superseded by invading Dorian Greeks
1100–750 BC	Dark Ages
900 BC	State of Sparta founded
800 BC	Date of Homer?
	Greeks adopt Phoenician script
776 BC	First Olympic Games

The successors to the Minoans were the Mycenaeans. Already established on mainland Greece, they were able to rapidly take over the remnants of Minoan power when it collapsed. They also inherited the Minoans' Linear alphabet, but wrote in their own language — Greek. Much more militaristic, these Ionian Greeks rapidly built a trading empire across the Eastern Mediterranean (the odd little 10-year local difficulty over Troy aside). In later Archaic times this period was mythologized into the 'heroic' age given life by the Homeric poems, but latterly the clumsy fortified town walls surviving from this period have been dubbed 'Cyclopic', as they look to have been built by the one-eyed giants who the ancients believed lived on the earth before mankind arrived.

Mycenaean power diminished with the arrival of invading Dorian Greeks (c. 1100 BC): trade and communications fell away, leaving the islands in the thrall of a mini dark age. Painting and writing were forgotten, and communities reorganized themselves on a city state basis. This, combined with the arrival of the Phoenicians reopening the trade routes, proved to be the catalyst for change that led to a resurgence in Greek culture.

Only the cities such as Athens and Corinth had held out against the worst of the cultural decline. By the end of the period they were large enough to expand, establishing colony cities as far afield as France, while painting and writing (this time using a variation of the Phoenician alphabet) reap-

peared. In 776 BC the Olympic Games were established, an event now seen as marking Greece's coming of age.

Archaic
776–490 BC

650 BC	First tyrants take power in Greece
621 BC	Draco takes power in Athens
594 BC	Solon takes power in Athens and overhauls political system
546 BC	Tyrant Pisistratus rules Athens
530 BC	Start of Persian Wars
508 BC	Cleisthenes takes power in Athens and introduces democratic reforms
490 BC	Persians invade Greek mainland and are defeated at Marathon

During the Archaic period Greek art and architecture developed from Egyptian models of heavy pillared buildings and votive statues into the more elegant Greek forms that we know today. Very much an age of transition, these early examples of Archaic painting and statuary — with limbs and features all misproportioned — look to the modern eye like something 'done' by an exhibitor at the Royal Academy's summer exhibition, but the artists of this period increasingly acquired a mastery of technique and moved steadily towards a more realistic rendering of their subject matter. The islands were particularly prominent during this period, as their easily defended boundaries produced a number of powerful island states, with the result that from Aegina to Samos the remains of Archaic structures and statuary can be found. This greater artistic and cultural cohesion was bolstered by a succession of invasions by the dominant East Mediterranean power of the time — Persia. The first of these attacks came against the Cyclades in 499 and 490 BC. However, the victory by the Athenian-led Greek army at Marathon and then the Athenian naval victory over the Persians at Salamis saw the emergence of regional Greek political supremacy, and this brought with it a renewed political and artistic confidence that became the hallmark of the 'Classical' era.

Classical & Hellenistic
490–180 BC

480 BC	2nd Persian invasion: Battles of Thermopylae and Salamis
478 BC	Delian League established
460–457 BC	Athenian Long Walls and Acropolis rebuilding begins

443–429 BC	Pericles rules Athens
430 BC	Plague hits Athens
431–404 BC	The Peloponnesian War
404 BC	Athens defeated by Sparta
399 BC	Socrates executed
359 BC	Philip II becomes king of Macedonia
338 BC	Phillip II conquers Greece
333–327 BC	Alexander conquers Persia
323 BC	Alexander dies at Babylon
322 BC	Wars of succession
215–197 BC	Romo–Macedonian wars

The great winner in the Persian wars was the leading Greek participant, Athens. The Aegean islands, weakened by the Persian invasion, agreed to contribute to a fund to maintain a fleet under Athenian leadership to protect them from further aggression. Known as the Delian League, this alliance was used by Athens to exert de facto political control over the islands and prompted leading Greek city states (principally Sparta and Corinth) to fight the Peloponnesian War to prevent Athens emerging as the master of Greece. The islands were reduced to minor players in the scene with local art and architecture being neglected in consequence, while becoming more important as sources of revenue and marble than centres in their own right. Islands that dared to oppose Athens (notably Aegina and Milos) also suffered greatly.

Athens, meantime, having been sacked during the Persian invasion, was ripe for redevelopment and under the leadership of Pericles spent (without consent) much of the Delian League contributions on rebuilding the temples on the Acropolis. Accompanied by a spectacular literary, theatrical and philosophical cultural explosion, this was the golden age of Greek civilization.

However, Sparta's eventual defeat of Athens prevented Greek domination by one city, and the states (none of whom was powerful enough to take overall control) bickered on until Philip II gained the throne of Macedonia. This event marked the transition from the Classical to the Hellenistic periods, for he unified Greece, and his son, Alexander the Great, started off a wave of conquest that was to extend to the borders

of India. After the death of Alexander, the empire collapsed and the weakened city states and the islands reasserted their independence in the wars of succession that followed.

The Hellenistic period also left a major mark on Greek culture, though this was more of a natural progression from the symmetry of the Classical period than a radical or sudden change. Buildings and artwork became much more decorative and ornamental, while literature and schools of learning grew from the Classical foundations. Some of the islands benefited greatly from this, with Rhodes, Kos and Samos exerting greater influence in part as a result of their emergence as major centres of learning.

Roman
180 BC–395 AD

171–168 BC	Third Macedonian War
147–146 BC	Romans impose direct rule on Greece
48–31 BC	Roman civil war
120–150 AD	Period of Roman patronage in Athens under Hadrian
170 AD	Pausanias writes guide to Greece
200–300 AD	Rise of Christianity
395 AD	Alaric the Goth sacks Athens

As Greek power waned, Rome gradually came to exercise influence over the divided city states and islands, initially as an arbiter in intercity disputes, but then as a force in her own right. Having entered Greece in response to an attack by King Mithridates in 88 BC, she never really managed to leave and by 31 BC the whole of Greece had been incorporated into the Roman Empire: the islands divided between five provinces (the Adriatic islands were part of Epirus, the Dodecanese and Eastern Line islands were in Asia, Thassos was in Macedonia, Crete was joined with Libya in Cyrenica–Creta, and the remainder formed Achaea along with the Peloponnese, Evia, and the Greek mainland north of the Gulf of Corinth).

Despite the four centuries of stability that followed, the islands went into a slow but marked decline. Reduced to the edges of even provincial centres of power, they saw comparatively little new monumental building (a feature of Roman rule in other parts of the empire) and were increasingly prone to pirate attack. Athens and the islands also saw their first tourists during this period — notably the writer Pausanias (fl. c. 150 AD), who wrote an important guide (beloved by archaeologists wanting to know what specific buildings were called and looked like, and where they stood) to Greece describing the cities and their monuments.

Other tourists were more mercenary, and the Roman epoch also saw denudation in local art as many ancient treasures were carted off to embellish the cities and villas of Italy (the occasional shipwrecks that turn up filled with bronze statues are a legacy of this trade). The Greek cities suffered in another important respect; subsumed into Rome's urban culture, they were never able to emerge as major centres of political or cultural power again.

Byzantine
395–1453

527–567	Reign of Emperor Justinian
1050–1200	Sicilian Normans invade Venetians annex islands
1204	Sack of Constantinople
1210–1262	Feudal dukedoms established in Greece
1309	Knights of St. John capture Dodecanese islands
1355–1400	Turks conquer Greece
1453	Turks capture Constantinople

By 395 the Roman empire had grown so large that it became unmanageable: the practically minded Emperor Constantine divided it into two. Greece came under the control of the Eastern empire and was ruled from Byzantium (later renamed Constantinople and Istanbul), a city still viewed by many Greeks as a capital under occupation. The islands began the descent from a period of slow decline to one of total anarchy, suffering considerably in the Slavic and Saracen invasions of the 7th and 9th centuries before becoming embroiled in the general stagnation of the Byzantine empire. Depopulation followed with the destruction wrought by the Crusaders of the 1204 crusade who sacked Constantinople instead of retaking Jerusalem. The islands were part of the spoils and were divided among the plunderers, with the

Venetians taking control of Crete, and the Genoese of Chios, Lesbos and Astipalea among others. Thus when Constantinople fell to the Turks in 1453 many of the islands remained in Christian hands with widespread castle building going on — courtesy of much ancient temple demolition.

Venetian & Ottoman
1453–1830

1453–1469	Turks conquer Aegean islands
1687	Venetians capture Athens
1814	Beginnings of Greek independence movement
1815	Ionian islands come under British rule
1821–1825	Greek war of Independence
1827	Aegina becomes capital of Greece
1830	Frontiers of new Greek state established

During the succeeding centuries the Aegean islands gradually fell to Ottoman Turk rule. Some — such as Rhodes — were lost early (1522) but others under Venetian control held out until the last (Tinos) went in 1715. For the most part Turkish rule was benign. The new landlords were content to appoint governors and collect taxes. But even as the Turks were completing their conquest of the Aegean their power had begun to wane. The islands became famous either for being the victims of pirates or for becoming their haunts; for they were natural strongholds from which they could attack other islands and the increasing trade between Europe and the Levant.

The years between 1450 and 1750 marked the nadir of the islands' fortunes, with many being abandoned altogether after their populations were massacred or sold into slavery. With Christian, Turkish, Barbary Coast, and local pirates all preying on the islands, the roll call of horrors is a long one. The 1500s saw the worst of it, with Ios being devastated in 1528, and the notorious Barbarossa starting his many depredations in the Aegean by attacking Aegina in 1537, killing all the men and taking 6,000 women and children into slavery. In 1570 the Barbary pirate Kemal Reis went on a little slave-gathering expedition and removed the populations of Kithera, Skiathos and Skopelos to North Africa.

In the face of these attacks island communities did their best to protect themselves by abandoning coastal settlements in favour of defendable villages (or choras) inland. On a number of Cycladic islands these were built as stockade-like 'kastros' with the houses built on the inside of a defensive wall (these still survive on Folegandros, Kimolos and Antiparos — though in the case of the latter, it didn't prevent the islanders being massacred in 1794). Gradually, however, the more successful 'pirate' islands began to gain a degree of control via their fleets of ships which also took advantage of the growing trade opportunities to enhance their status still further by building impressively mansioned towns (e.g. Hydra, Spetses and Chios).

The arrival of foreign powers (notably the Russians who held control over a dozen islands during the 1770–74 Turkish war) also helped to stabilize the region. By the 19th century Greek nationalism was becoming a potent force, the islands coming to the fore as natural bastions from which insurgents could operate against weak Turkish rule. Less powerful islands demonstrated defiance of Turkish rule by the painting of island houses (heretofore kept an inconspicuous mud-brick brown) in the Greek national colours of white and blue (now the hallmark of the typical Cycladic town), while the more powerful islands, via their fleets, gained a notable place in Greek history in the independence struggle, being more than a match for the Turks. This, however, led to reprisals (notably the massacre of 25,000 on Chios in 1822).

Modern
1832–

1833	Prince Otto becomes King
1864	Britain cedes Ionian Islands
1913	George I assassinated
1914–1918	WW1: under Prime Minister Venizelos Greece joins Allies
1920–1923	Turkish War
1940	Greece enters WW2, joining the Allies following Metaxas's 'No!' ('Ohi') to Mussolini's demand for right of access
1941	Germans conquer Greece
1945–1949	Greek Civil War
1967–1974	Military rule of the Colonels
1974	Restoration of democracy

Independence in 1832 did not see all of modern Greece gain its freedom. The Cyclades aside, the islands remained in foreign hands, only gradually being gathered into the protective arms of the Greek state. Corfu and the Ionian islands were transferred from British control in 1864. WW1 saw the islands of the Northern Aegean come under Greek rule, while the Italians took the Dodecanese from Turkey and attempted an unsuccessful Italianization programme, only to see the islands handed over to Greece at the end of WW2.

Since independence Greece has been engaged in sporadic conflicts with Turkey, notably the war of 1920–23, when she attempted to gain control of the ancient Greek cities on Turkey's Aegean seaboard, as well as the former capital of the Byzantine empire — Constantinople (now İstanbul). The war ended disastrously for Greece, culminating with the sack of Smyrna (now İzmir) and a territorial settlement that resulted in 1½ million ethnic Greeks leaving Turkey for Greece, and some 400,000 ethnic Turks (mainly from the islands) going the other way. Relations between the two countries remain tense. Turkey has failed to recognize Greek sovereignty over the Aegean sea-bed (with its oil deposits) and the Turkish invasion of Cyprus in 1974 has done nothing to heal old wounds. But as both are members of NATO and have economies dependent on tourism they have an interest in avoiding outright hostilities. Greece's position has been bolstered by its emergence as a democracy and membership of the EU (European Union): you can expect to see EU flags everywhere.

Politically, Greece is now relatively stable after a torrid post-WW2 period which saw a civil war (1945–49) between the government and communist forces, the military dictatorship of the Colonels (1967–74) and the abolition of the monarchy (1975) — an institution only acquired by modern Greece after the Great Powers (Britain, France and Russia), who had championed her independence, installed Prince Otto of Bavaria as King in 1833 following the assassination of the country's first president.

1
ATHENS & PIRAEUS

ATHENS · PIRAEUS (GREAT HARBOUR) · (ZEA)
LAVRIO · RAFINA · SALAMIS

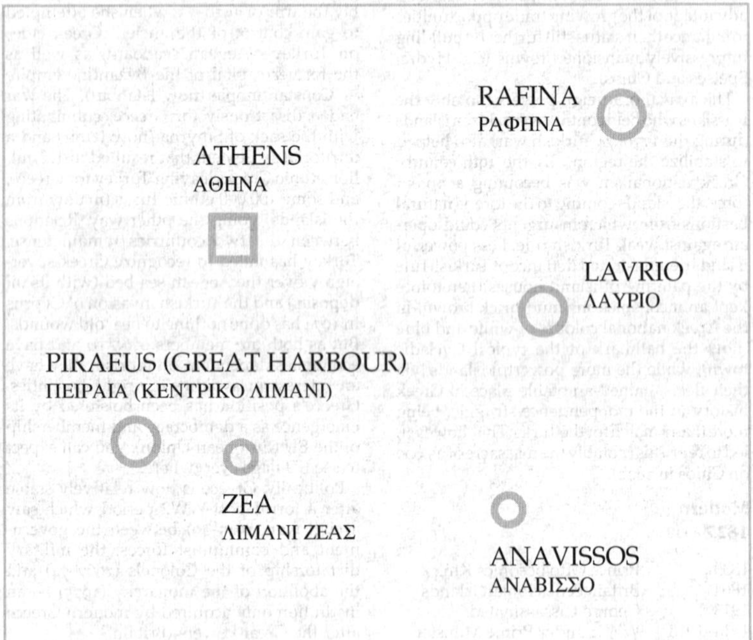

RAFINA
ΡΑΦΗΝΑ

ATHENS
ΑΘΗΝΑ

LAVRIO
ΛΑΥΡΙΟ

PIRAEUS (GREAT HARBOUR)
ΠΕΙΡΑΙΑ (ΚΕΝΤΡΙΚΟ ΛΙΜΑΝΙ)

ZEA
ΛΙΜΑΝΙ ΖΕΑΣ

ANAVISSOS
ΑΝΑΒΙΣΣΟ

SALAMIS
ΣΑΛΑΜΙΝΑ

General Features

Lying at the centre of the Eastern Mediterranean ferry web, and still the most popular charter flight entry point into Greece, Athens sees more tourists passing through than any other port of call. Unfortunately, the rise in the city's population from 12,000 in 1820 to over 4 million today has done nothing for one of the greatest cities in the world. The atmospheric and photogenic ancient heart is now surrounded by concrete urban sprawl. Significant improvements to the 'Athens experience' have come thanks to the Olympics, but a large amount of extra concrete has been added too.

Consequently, most visitors profitably fill a couple of days doing the Acropolis and centre sights and then move on fast. This chapter can thus be said to cover the 'damaged' area of Greece. Like most tourists, its gaze is firmly directed on the ancient city centre and the ports of Piraeus, Rafina and Lavrio, as well as mentioning in passing the unattractive suburb island of Salamis.

If sightseeing is not your thing (or if you want to retain the relaxed frame of mind that idling around the islands has wrought), a final day or two in or around Athens waiting for your flight home can come as something of a shock to the system, and it is worthwhile considering the alternative of flying to one of the island airports and then island hopping to the city for a long weekend from there.

ATHENS: ENVIRONS & APOLLO COAST

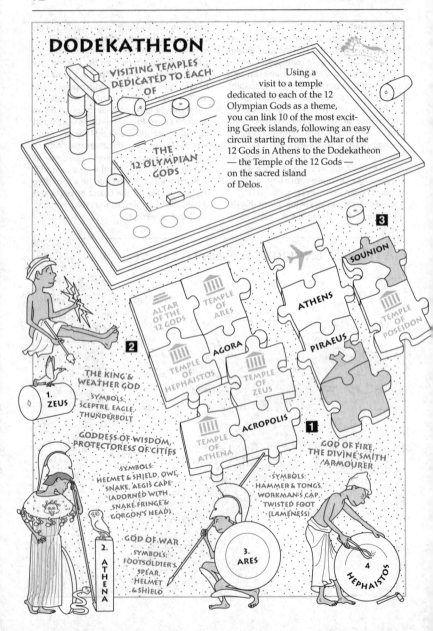

DODEKATHEON

VISITING TEMPLES DEDICATED TO EACH OF

THE 12 OLYMPIAN GODS

Using a visit to a temple dedicated to each of the 12 Olympian Gods as a theme, you can link 10 of the most exciting Greek islands, following an easy circuit starting from the Altar of the 12 Gods in Athens to the Dodekatheon — the Temple of the 12 Gods — on the sacred island of Delos.

3

SOUNION

ALTAR OF THE 12 GODS

TEMPLE OF ARES

ATHENS

TEMPLE OF POSEIDON

2

AGORA

PIRAEUS

TEMPLE OF HEPHAISTOS

TEMPLE OF ZEUS

ACROPOLIS

1

TEMPLE OF ATHENA

THE KING & WEATHER GOD

SYMBOLS: SCEPTRE, EAGLE, THUNDERBOLT

1. ZEUS

GODDESS OF WISDOM, PROTECTORESS OF CITIES

SYMBOLS: HELMET & SHIELD, OWL, SNAKE, AEGIS CAPE (ADORNED WITH SNAKE FRINGE & GORGON'S HEAD)

2. ATHENA

GOD OF WAR

SYMBOLS: FOOTSOLDIER'S SPEAR, HELMET & SHIELD

3. ARES

GOD OF FIRE, THE DIVINE SMITH/ARMOURER

SYMBOLS: HAMMER & TONGS, WORKMAN'S CAP, TWISTED FOOT (LAMENESS)

4 HEPHAISTOS

PARIS 2060 KM

QUEEN GODDESS / GODDESS OF MOTHERHOOD (WIFE OF ZEUS)

SYMBOLS: DIADEM / SCEPTRE

8. ARTEMIS

6. HERMES

7. HERA

THE MESSENGER GOD, BRINGER OF LUCK, CONDUCTOR OF SOULS

SYMBOLS: WINGED BOOTS, HERALD'S STAFF, WIDE BRIMMED HAT, CHLAMYS CLOAK

GODDESS OF VIRTUE & THE HUNT (TWIN SISTER OF APOLLO)

SYMBOLS: BOW & ARROWS / LONG HUNTING BOOTS

4 TEMPLE OF HERMES

TEMPLE OF HERA **5**

SAMOS

EPHESUS

GODDESS OF LOVE

PATMOS

TEMPLE OF ARTEMIS

KOS

6

9. APHRODITE

GOD OF THE SEA, EARTHQUAKES & HORSES

RHODES

CRETE IRAKLION

TEMPLE OF APHRODITE

SYMBOLS: DOVE / CUPID SON EROS

SYMBOLS: TRIDENT / DOLPHIN

7 GOD OF WINE & PLEASURE

SYMBOLS: IVY GROWN / BRANCH, THYRSOS, DRINKING CUP, DRUNKEN SATYRS & MAENADS PANTHER

5. POSEIDON

10. DIONYSOS

The Dodekatheon
Example Itinerary [3 Weeks]

In the Greco-Roman world many deities were worshipped but only the 12 gods with thrones in the palace above Mt. Olympus (and therefore known as the 'Olympians') had temples built to them on a wide scale. They were the national gods, transcending the political boundaries of the city states. The later Romans (whose capacity for original ideas didn't extend much beyond roads, concrete and killing people in circuses) adopted the Olympians wholesale, contenting themselves with giving them new names (with the exception of Apollo). Widely depicted in all forms of ancient art, each of the 12 Olympians had their own symbol/s to aid recognition (a fortunate circumstance as 'god spotting' will enliven many a vase-filled museum visit today). The remains of their temples also offer a light-hearted excuse for some good island hopping. The itinerary here offers an easy circuit around the islands seeking out the ghosts of the gods.

Arrival/Departure Point

Athens is the best starting point because you will encounter the only weak link in the itinerary (Samos to Patmos) early in the loop. But you can also join the circuit at Kos, Rhodes, Crete (Iraklion), Santorini or Mykonos should you so choose.

Season

This itinerary can be successfully executed at any time from June to September as it runs down the two most popular lines in the Greek ferry system — the Dodecanese and Cyclades Central lines.

1 Athens: The Acropolis

The centre of Athens offers an easy way to notch up a handful of the twelve temples without difficulty. If you join the circuit at the Thissio Metro station and walk to the north entrance of the Agora you will pass the site of the **Altar of the Twelve Gods**. It is now not clear if these included all the Olympians but the altar served as the *omphalos* (navel) of the city. The milestone for measuring distances throughout Attica, it is the logical starting point for the itinerary. Walking east around the Acropolis you will come to the largest temple ever built in Greece, the Olympieion or **Temple of Zeus**.

Zeus (Roman **Jupiter**), the king of the Olympian gods, was also the god of the sky, or weather god. He walked around with a handful of thunderbolts and was wont to give any passing nymphs a quick flash if his wife Hera was out of sight. He passed the rest of his time upon a throne of black marble set upon a pedestal of the seven rainbow colour steps, keeping a moody eye on the affairs of gods and men.

Turning west, a walk along the south side of the Acropolis will bring you to the western entrance. The Acropolis has the Parthenon as its main **Temple of Athena**.

Athena (Roman **Minerva**), the goddess of wisdom, was the most popular of the goddesses (thanks to her role as the protectress of cities). She also enjoyed a secondary role as a patroness of the feminine arts and crafts — notably spinning and weaving. She frequently appears in ancient art, usually wearing the Aegis cape (made out of snake's scales, fringed with snake's heads and sporting a Gorgon's head) showing her association with the hero Perseus, who killed the Gorgon Medusa with the goddess's help.

2 Athens: The Agora

Assuming you haven't broken your leg on the slippery marble of the Acropolis then you next head for the nearby south-east entrance of the Agora site. Walking across the Agora to the northern entrance, turn west to the mound that is all that remains of the **Temple of Ares**. Believed to be almost identical to the nearby complete temple of Hephaistos, it originally stood elsewhere only to be re-erected here during the Roman infilling of the Agora.

Ares (Roman **Mars**) was the god of war and thus not the most popular of deities. Feared rather than revered, worshippers sacrificed dogs to him. Nauseatingly handsome and usually naked, he was the paramour of Aphrodite, possibly siring her son Eros.

On the hill to the west is the **Temple of Hephaistos**. Once surrounded by artisan and craftsmen's workshops it is the most complete temple surviving in Greece.

Hephaistos (Roman **Vulcan**), the workman's god, was arguably the unhappiest deity. Not only was he once thrown (literally) out of Olympus by Hera (laming himself when he landed on the island of Limnos), he was also married to Aphrodite and thus forever hopping mad with her hopping into bed with just about everybody and then coming up with all sorts of lame excuses. He is easily identified by his tools and is often riding a mule.

3 Sounion

Athens sightseeing can be wound up with a day trip to Cape **Sounion** and the impressive **Temple of Poseidon** on the hillside overlooking the Aegean Sea. **Poseidon** (Roman **Neptune**) was another moody god, swimming around with a chip on his shoulder because he lost out to his younger brother Zeus when the three brothers divided the universe between them by lot — after defeating their father **Kronos** (Roman **Saturn**). Poseidon won the sea, Zeus the heavens, and poor old Pluto the underworld (they shared the earth). The god of the sea, earthquakes and horses, Poseidon is often only distinguishable from Zeus by his trademark trident and dolphin.

4 Piraeus to Samos

Returning to Athens, head on to Piraeus and your first island hop to the ugliest island port on the itinerary — Samos (Vathi). Buses here will take you on to Samos (Pithagorio) and the nearby Heraion — the largest Greek-built temple in Greece. Just to the east of it lie the foundations of two tiny **Temples of Hermes**. **Hermes** (Roman **Mercury**) always managed to come in as 12th man when listing the Olympians in order of importance. His natty winged boots and traveller's hat hardly encouraged respect. Temples to him were thus thin on the ground, and although he was revered as the conductor of souls to the underworld, his reputation as a trickster and cheat confined his following to the ranks of merchants, traders and thieves. Easily identified by his herald's staff he is frequently pictured taking Hera, Athena and Aphrodite to the first ever Miss Universe contest, the judgement of Paris.

The **Temple of Hera**, although only one column remains standing, is a much more substantial affair, being one of the major shrines to the goddess in Greece.

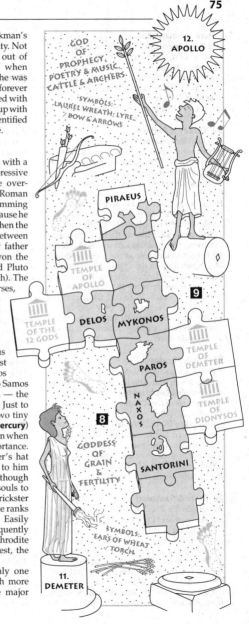

GOD OF PROPHECY, POETRY & MUSIC, CATTLE & ARCHERS

SYMBOLS: LAUREL WREATH; LYRE, BOW & ARROWS

12. APOLLO

PIRAEUS

TEMPLE OF APOLLO

TEMPLE OF THE 12 GODS

DELOS

MYKONOS

9

TEMPLE OF DEMETER

PAROS

NAXOS

8

TEMPLE OF DIONYSOS

GODDESS OF GRAIN & FERTILITY

SANTORINI

SYMBOLS: EARS OF WHEAT, TORCH.

11. DEMETER

Hera (Roman **Juno**), the queen goddess, was both the sister and wife of Zeus. They never got on, thanks to his constant attempts to ravish passing nymphs. Their life together was a litany of attempts by Hera to catch him in the act. This thwarted voyeur's symbol was a heifer but she is usually depicted with Zeus, adorned with a diadem and sceptre.

5 Turkey & Patmos

Samos (Vathi) is also the jumping-off point for day trips to Ephesus in Turkey and its **Temple of Artemis**. With one column standing it looks pretty similar to the Heraion and was built on the same massive scale. If you don't fancy visiting Turkey then pick up one of the few ferries or a tourist boat and hop down to Patmos. The monastery here was also built on the site of a temple to the goddess.

Artemis (Roman **Diana**), the beautiful virgin huntress, was goddess of all wild places, with a secondary role as the moon goddess. Having no time for the opposite sex she spent her hours protecting female chastity — along with mopping up when that failed (she was also the goddess of childbirth). Often pictured with Apollo, she used her bow and arrows to put suffering animals painlessly out of their misery — thereby acting as a sort of anti-cupid figure.

6 Kos & Rhodes

From Patmos you have very easy hops down to Kos and Rhodes. Both were home to a **Temple of Aphrodite** — though only the foundations of the Rhodes Town example are identifiable today.

Aphrodite (Roman **Venus**), the goddess of love, beauty, fertility and the sea, was very popular for obvious reasons. Usually depicted with either a dove or her winged son Eros (often depicted as a fully grown man rather than a baby-blobs style cupid).

7 Crete & Santorini

Alongside the Rhodian Temple of Aphrodite stood a temple of Dionysos. However, little of this building survives. For a better example of a temple to this god you have to do some serious island hopping on to Naxos. Easiest way is to bounce off Crete, taking one of the regular ferries from Rhodes to Crete (Iraklion). Crete was the birthplace of Zeus so there is some logic in the hop. After touring Knossos, from Iraklion you can then pick up a Cyclades

Central Line ferry stopping off at Santorini for more sightseeing before hopping on to Naxos.

8 Naxos & Paros

Naxos is home to a large Archaic temple on the small islet of Palatia just north of the ferry port. Thought to have been dedicated to either Apollo or Dionysos, visit it on the possibility that it is a **Temple of Dionysos**, since Naxos was this god's island and where he married the abandoned Ariadne.

Dionysos (Roman **Bacchus**) was the god of fun, inventing wine and orgies. Often shown accompanied by satyrs (naked bald men with horse's tails and large what-nots), nymphs or maenads (frenzied women dressed in fawn and panther skins), he started out as the god of the fruit of the trees. He was not originally one of the Olympians but gained admission when **Hestia** (Roman **Vesta**) — the old maid goddess of the hearth — stepped down in his favour.

From Naxos you have an easy hop on to Paros: the Venetian Kastro at Parikia was built on the site of a **Temple of Demeter**, its surviving wall is made up of stones from the building. **Demeter** (Roman **Ceres**) was famous for not smiling. The goddess of fertility, she was particularly associated with the crops of the soil such as grain and corn. She is often depicted holding the torch carried when she went down into the underworld (Hades) to recover her daughter Persephone, whom Zeus had ordered to be married to their brother Pluto.

9 Mykonos & Delos

From Paros you have another easy hop on to Mykonos: the starting point for excursion boats to the island of Delos — home to the foundations of an important **Temple of Apollo**. **Apollo**, the god of poetry, music and prophecy, was the most popular of the Olympian gods. He was also thought by some to be the sun god Helios. His popularity ensured that plenty of temples were erected in his name. He is often pictured as a naked and beardless youth holding a lyre.

Delos is also home to smaller temples to Aphrodite, Artemis, Demeter, and Hera, as well as the **Dodekatheon** itself. Having visited Delos and returned to Mykonos you can complete the island circuit by taking a ferry back to Piraeus for your flight home.

Athens—Mainland Port Bus Links

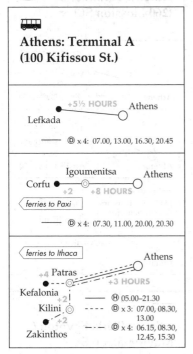

Athens: Terminal A (100 Kifissou St.)

+5½ HOURS Athens
Lefkada
——— Ⓓ x 4: 07.00, 13.00, 16.30, 20.45

Igoumenitsa Athens
Corfu ●——◎——○
  +2 +8 HOURS
⟨ ferries to Paxi ⟩
——— Ⓓ x 4: 07.30, 11.00, 20.00, 20.30

⟨ ferries to Ithaca ⟩
  Athens
+4 Patras ○
●——◎————— +3 HOURS
Kefalonia
+2 ┃ ——— Ⓗ 05.00–21.30
Kilini ◎ ———— Ⓓ x 3: 07.00, 08.30,
● +2   13.00
Zakinthos ——·— Ⓓ x 4: 06.15, 08.30,
           12.45, 15.30

Lying at the centre of the Greek bus system, Athens has a number of wider-ranging bus services of value to the island hopper. These bus routes link the capital with ports not served by Piraeus or Rafina-based ferries but which have ferry links of their own to adjacent islands. For the most part important centres in their own right, these ports have bus links from Athens timed to connect with ferries, so that buses can take passengers on to island capitals (you buy a ferry ticket along with your bus ticket). Some ferry companies also run private Athens—mainland port buses for the benefit of their passengers.

The largest bus station in Athens (Terminal A), at 100 Kifissou St., lies an inconvenient 4 km from the centre of the city, buried behind a block of semi-derelict buildings on the east side of one of the city's freeways (home to innumerable run-down scrapyards and warehouses). From the road it would be impossible to spot were it not for the constant procession of buses mysteriously disappearing down adjacent side-streets. The terminal is in fact a warehouse-like building filled with numbered bus bays and lined with confectionery stalls. Only the ticket hall is new, contrasting vividly

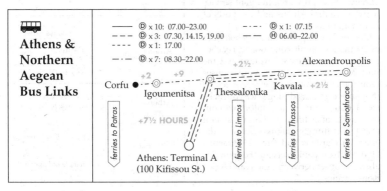

Athens & Northern Aegean Bus Links

——— Ⓓ x 10: 07.00–23.00   ——·— Ⓓ x 1: 07.15
——— Ⓓ x 3: 07.30, 14.15, 19.00   —— Ⓗ 06.00–22.00
———— Ⓓ x 1: 17.00
——·— Ⓓ x 7: 08.30–22.00

    +2½ Alexandroupolis
Corfu ●——◎————◎————
+2 +9 Igoumenitsa Thessalonika Kavala +2½
⟨ ferries to Patras ⟩ ⟨ ferries to Limnos ⟩ ⟨ ferries to Thassos ⟩ ⟨ ferries to Samothrace ⟩
+7½ HOURS
Athens: Terminal A
(100 Kifissou St.)

with the surrounding decrepitude. The terminal serves most intercity buses (including buses to Thessalonika) as well as the west coast ports (Patras and Igoumenitsa), the Ionian islands and the Peloponnese.

Terminal B at 260 Liossion St. is a much smaller and altogether friendlier affair 800 m north-west of Ag. Nikolaos metro station. A similar distance out from the centre as Terminal A, it is equally badly signposted; both are best reached via taxi. Connections from Terminal B are much more limited with port/island links confined to Evia and the Sporades. Buses from both these stations usually stop in one or two of the larger towns en route but are otherwise difficult to board from the roadside (the notable exception being the popular Patras buses — which are flagged down just north of the Corinth Canal bridge as they do not enter Corinth itself). All the important bus times are listed on NTOG/EOT bus information sheets and in the *Greek Travel Pages* (see p. 42).

The third terminus of note in Athens is near Areos Park north of the National Archaeological Museum at the junction of Platia Egyptou and Mavromateon St. (running down the west side of the park). There is no terminal building here, just a small bus parking area, along with a manned kiosk listing times and the bus stops. Buses departing from here are orange suburban variety. These provide a frequent service between central Athens and the ports of Rafina and Lavrio.

Most of the companies running boats out of Patras lay on air-conditioned coaches for passengers between Athens and the port. More expensive than regular buses (you book when buying your ferry ticket), they are worth considering since you make the 3 hour journey in comfort without the hassle of getting to the bus station (most start from Syntagma Square or the National Gardens and run via Piraeus). Hydrofoil companies serving the Sporades also offer buses between Athens and Agios Konstantinos.

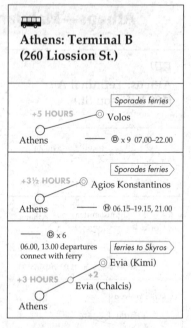

Athens: Terminal B (260 Liossion St.)

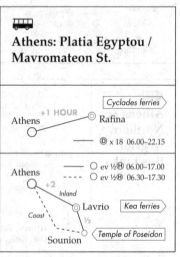

Athens: Platia Egyptou / Mavromateon St.

Athens: City Links

Getting Around

Athens has a large and overcrowded public transport system made up of buses, trolley-buses, a growing metro network and 1000 of the most uncooperative taxi drivers in Europe (who have apparently had a special pre-Olympics crash course in being nice to people). It can all seem pretty intimidating, but moving around is fairly easy.

The metro offers the most effective and quickest means of doing so — unless you want to get to an airport or intercity bus stations. For these you will have to take either an expensive taxi or resort to the Athenian bus system. The NTOG/EOT office in the city centre and at the airport provide bus timetables and route summary sheets on request.

Athens buses come in two colours: Blue (running from the centre to the suburbs) and Orange (going further afield within the province of Attica). Unlike Green inter-city buses — where tickets are bought in advance — you can buy your ticket for city buses on boarding. Larger bus stops also have ticket kiosks where you can buy tickets before boarding

(this is particularly advisable with the airport buses). Single tickets between most city centre destinations are standard (in 2003 most fares were €0.50 or €0.70 depending on distance). Between midnight and 05.00 bus and taxi fares are doubled. No matter when you travel take care to validate your ticket by putting it in the bus date punch — failure to do so can result in a heavy fine.

Athens Airport

If you are arriving in Athens by air your first encounter with the city transport system is going to be the trip from the airport to the city centre or port. This is going to be a mixed experience for most as the airport and its buses are brand new, but the new six-lane Attica Highway that will run between it and central Athens isn't due to be completed before the Olympics — resulting in over-long journey times.

The new Athens *Eleftherios Venizelos* airport opened in 2001, some 20 km outside the city at Spata (see map on p. 71). It has replaced the old airport which was located in the southern suburbs and has now closed. The new airport has one terminal building

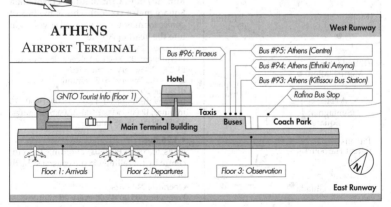

and a satellite boarding terminal (reached via an underground walkway — some 20 minutes' walking away!). The airport has all the usual facilities (including a branch of *McDonald's*), and a couple of irritating features that defy common sense. Not least of these are baggage check-in 'travelators' that can't accommodate backpacks (travellers checking in with a backpack have to take it to a special 'oversize' check-in point (no matter how small it is). The only way around this is to take your backpack in a specialist pack travel bag.

Airport Buses & Taxis

The change of airport and bus routes has also prompted the moving of bus stops in central Athens. The still-to-be-finished new highway linking the airport with the city centre also means that buses use often congested smaller roads. You should

**Athens:
Airport Buses**

- - - Ⓗ
- - - Ⓗ 06.00–21.40

(Kifissou St.
Bus Station)

Rafina

(Ethniki Amyna
Metro Station)

*El. Venizelos
Airport
Terminal*

ATHENS
(Syntagma
Square)

Piraeus
(Great Harbour)

—— Ⓗ
—·— Ⓗ
—·· — Ⓗ

Glifada

therefore build at least an hour into your journey times (more in rush hours) this side of the Olympics.

Bus tickets to the airport cost €2.90 in 2003 — regardless of the Athens, Piraeus or Rafina starting points — and (Rafina excepted) are valid for 24 hours. Taxis from Syntagma Square cost a theoretical €11 during the day and €15 between 24.00 and 05.00. The taxi driver will no doubt try and double this, and then sting you for the €0.60 toll charged at the entry to the open section of the highway, and whatever else he thinks he can get away with (dress poor, negotiate tough and make a point of being seen to carefully check the value of your bank notes before handing them over!).

There are a growing number of new express city bus services linking the airport with various points in Athens (the buses have blue and yellow stripes on a white background). Tickets are bought from the kiosk by the bus stops (when open); when kiosks are closed then on the bus. Once you are on the bus you must validate your ticket by putting it in the dating machine on the bus (travelling with an unvalidated ticket can attract a €29 fine if your grovelling skills aren't good enough). The four most useful services are:

• E95 Bus

Runs to/from **Central Athens (Syntagma Square metro station)**. This is the bus of choice for most tourists as it takes you right into the heart of Athens.
Operates: 24 hours
Frequency: 06.00–21.20 every 25 minutes.
21.20–23.35 every 30 minutes.
23.35–01.30 every 15/20 minutes.
01.30–06.30 every 30/35 minutes.
Journey time: 08.00–12.00, 15.00–19.00: 75 minutes; 12.00–15.00, 19.00–22.00: 55 minutes; 22.00–08.00: 25–35 minutes.

• E96 Bus

Runs to/from **Piraeus**, avoiding the city centre by travelling via the coastal suburb of Glifada.
Operates: 24 hours
Frequency: 05.00–19.00 every 20 minutes.

19.00–20.30 every 30 minutes.
20.30–05.00 every 40 minutes.
Journey time: 1 hour in reasonable traffic.

● E94 Bus

Runs to/from **Athens (Ethniki Amyna metro station)**. Tickets cost the same price as the more useful E95 Bus. Tourists find this bus something of a trap as the bus sign says 'Athens', but it doesn't take you right into the centre, but only to the end of the metro line.
Operates: 06.00–23.20
Frequency: 06.00–20.30 every 15 minutes.
20.30–23.20 every 25/30 minutes.
Journey time: 35–45 minutes.

● E93 Bus

Runs to/from **Athens (Kifissou/Kifisos Bus Station)**. Useful if you want to connect with buses travelling to/from the Ionian islands and other long distance bus routes.
Operates: 06.00–23.30
Frequency: 06.00–23.30 every 30 minutes.
20.30–23.20 every 25/30 minutes.

Other options include:

● E97 Bus

Runs to/from **Athens (Dafni metro station)**. The same limitations that apply to the E94 are also a feature of this bus service. More for locals than tourists.
Operates: 06.00–23.30
Frequency: 06.00–23.30 every 30 minutes.
20.30–23.20 every 25/30 minutes.

Rafina Buses (no number) are orange and cream coloured KTEL Attica services. They display a destination board in the front window, and also have signs on their sides marking them as airport buses. Tickets are only sold on the bus. At the airport the bus stop is about 25 m beyond the Athens and Piraeus bus stops. It is marked by an orange sign.
Operates: 06.00–21.20 hours
Frequency: every 40 minutes.
Journey time: 35–40 minutes.

Buses to Intercity Bus Stations

City buses run from the centre of Athens to the two main bus stations:

● **024**: Runs between the Intercity Bus Station serving Evia and Northern Greece (**Terminal B**) at Liossion St. and Amalias Ave. (entrance to the National Gardens).

● **051**: Runs between the Intercity Bus Station serving Patras and the Peloponnese (**Terminal A**) at 100 Kifissou Street and Omonia Square. The fare is €0.60.

Athens Metro

The easiest way of moving between the centre of Athens and Piraeus is via the metro system. This has been significantly upgraded recently with the building of two new lines and some impressive new stations. However, the new lines, with the exception of a few city-centre stops, are of limited use to tourists.

The original line (**Line 1**) is the most valuable: running from the city centre to Piraeus, it is largely above ground. The service is efficient, if crowded in the rush hours. The only minor problem is that many of the stations are being rebuilt and this was impacting on services in 2003 as platforms were sometimes closed — forcing passengers to double back down the line to the remaining open platform.

Lines 2 & 3 are still being extended, but the open sections are very impressive. Syntagma, Panepistimio and Acropoli stations are now attractions in their own right, as they have display cases with ancient artifacts discovered while boring the tunnels. Syntagma also has a glass wall cross-section through the levels of excavation, complete with an embedded skeleton.

Metro tickets are obtained from manned kiosks or ticket machines (these require you to select your ticket before the coin slot opens). Like bus tickets, metro tickets must be inserted in one of the date-punching machines sited at platform entrances before you are entitled to travel. The fare from the centre of Athens to Piraeus is €0.70. Note: the last train leaves Piraeus promptly at midnight — for Omonia only, and at a blistering pace (the drivers obviously have very comfortable beds).

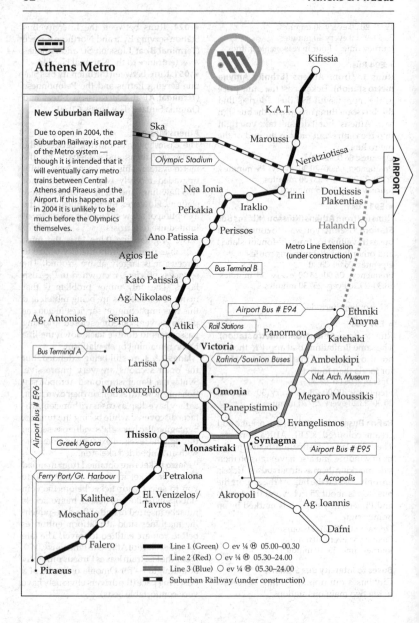

Athens Metro

New Suburban Railway

Due to open in 2004, the Suburban Railway is not part of the Metro system — though it is intended that it will eventually carry metro trains between Central Athens and Piraeus and the Airport. If this happens at all in 2004 it is unlikely to be much before the Olympics themselves.

Kifissia

K.A.T.

Maroussi

Neratziotissa

AIRPORT

Ska

Olympic Stadium

Nea Ionia

Pefkakia

Iraklio

Irini

Doukissis Plakentias

Ano Patissia

Perissos

Halandri

Agios Ele

Bus Terminal B

Metro Line Extension (under construction)

Kato Patissia

Ag. Nikolaos

Airport Bus # E94

Ethniki Amyna

Ag. Antonios

Sepolia

Atiki

Rail Stations

Panormou

Katehaki

Bus Terminal A

Victoria

Rafina/Sounion Buses

Ambelokipi

Larissa

Nat. Arch. Museum

Metaxourghio

Omonia

Megaro Moussikis

Panepistimio

Airport Bus # E96

Evangelismos

Thissio

Greek Agora

Monastiraki

Syntagma

Airport Bus # E95

Ferry Port/Gt. Harbour

Petralona

Acropolis

Kalithea

El. Venizelos/ Tavros

Akropoli

Ag. Ioannis

Moschaio

Dafni

Falero

Piraeus

Line 1 (Green) ○ ev ¼ ⊕ 05.00–00.30
Line 2 (Red) ○ ev ¼ ⊕ 05.30–24.00
Line 3 (Blue) ○ ev ¼ ⊕ 05.30–24.00
Suburban Railway (under construction)

Athens: Centre

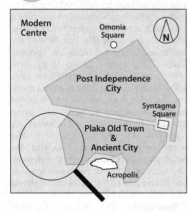

Athens

AΘHNA; pop. 4,000,001.

CODE ☎ 210
NTOG INFORMATION DESK ☎ 322 2545
TOURIST POLICE ☎ 171
POLICE ☎ 100
FIRST AID ☎ 166

Given her fantastic historical pedigree and worldwide reputation as a premier sightseeing destination, Athens is apt to inspire mixed reactions. The transition from quaint Turkish town to a city housing a quarter of Greece's population has been a very uncomfortable one, producing a glorious (if very touristy) city centre surrounded by a sea of concrete.

The Athenian conurbation is home to half of Greece's cars and 90% of the country's industry, and while the beauty of the Acropolis buildings can go to your head, so do the smog clouds (the *nephos*) that periodically force the government to ban motorists from the streets. In High Season Athens is hot and steamy, protected by the surrounding hills from the cooling summer winds that bathe the islands. However, for all this, the city offers a couple of days of

excellent sightseeing, and has good links with the islands via the ports of Piraeus and Rafina.

When visiting Athens, priority should be given to an early visit to a EOT tourist information office. This excellent service provides free city street maps along with information sheets on hotels, buses and ferry departure times for the ferry ports at Piraeus and Rafina. There are several offices in the city. The easiest to find is the desk at the airport terminal building; others include a new one in the city centre (see p.95) and at the Kifissou St. long distance bus station, and the main railway station.

Modern Centre

The centre of Athens lies some 6 km from the coast, thanks to the Acropolis. This landmark stands at the heart of the city as it has always done. The modern centre, however, is made up of three distinct districts. First is the Ancient City, now slowly making a reappearance, with a growing number of archaeological sites gradually being restored and opened to the public. The best are in the process of being united into one 'archeological park', which is due to be completed in 2005.

The second section of the modern centre lies to the north of the Acropolis, and comprises the remaining buildings and narrow winding streets of the Ottoman city (now known as Old Town or simply the 'Plaka' district). To the north of Plaka, and the part of town most visitors first encounter via the rail, bus and metro links, is the post-1832 Greek independence new centre (largely constructed in the century before 1940). When Athens was chosen — for largely sentimental reasons — as the capital of the newly independent Greece, it was little more than a minor garrison town (thanks to the heavily fortified Acropolis) with a few thousand inhabitants.

The new Bavarian-born king of Greece took advantage of the opportunity to construct a fitting West European-style capital of wide boulevards outside the old city (which was intended to be demolished, excavated, and preserved as a vast archaeological park). All went well with this scheme until the disastrous Helleno-Turkish war of 1920–22, which resulted in a flood of refugees into Athens, overwhelming the planners with their impromptu building.

As a result, the post-independence city has a centre (roughly bounded by Syntagma Square to the east, Omonia Square to the north, and Plaka to the south) which exhibits wide boulevards graced with blocks up to a dozen storeys high, while around it, defiantly ignoring the hilly terrain, chaos reigns — in the form of the encircling kilometres of concrete suburbs bisected by traffic-choked freeways.

The Post-Independence City

Often similarly jammed with traffic (thanks to the four-times-daily rush hour in Athens), the post-independence city isn't the perfect tourist destination, and has little appeal beyond the large numbers of hotels, the National Archaeological Museum, and the pleasant National Gardens to the east. Its saving grace is that the grid-iron street system makes it easy to walk between the major points via the main streets without getting too lost. The most important of these streets are **Athinas**, **Stadiou** and **Ermou** (the latter two are now home to the big city stores), which run between the three main squares.

Syntagma (Constitution) Square — the tourist 'hub' of the city and home to the Greek Parliament (complete with its famous soldier guards wearing their traditional skirts and pom-pom shoe) — is the most important and attractive of these. While it is a place tourists pass through rather than visit, it is an easy point of reference, with some greenery enlivening its otherwise empty central area. Most of the commercial activity is located on the west (Plaka) side,

where there are various food outlets and several international press stalls.

Omonia, the second largest of the big three squares, has been transformed from a very grimy traffic roundabout into something a little more appealing — thanks to a pedestrianization scheme that has divided the traffic and connected blocks on opposite sides of the square. Efforts to improve other aspects of the scene here have been less effective. Its past reputation as a meeting point for druggies and people of the night (now largely invisible) isn't being enhanced by the numbers of — seemingly unemployed — immigrant men who idle away the evenings here. This said, the atmosphere isn't particularly threatening, and there are a number of hotels (most at the poorer end of the scale) in the streets that radiate web-like from square.

Monastiraki is the smallest of the three squares, with a cute little red-brick Byzantine church in its centre. Underground work on the metro left the square looking like a building site for three years, but it is rapidly returning to its former glory, revitalized with a showcase metro station and views of the Acropolis. It also has the merit of possessing restaurants and some greenery, and ready access to the old town streets of the Plaka district on one side and the Athens flea market on the other. In addition, Monastiraki is the regular home for a number of street vendors selling fresh produce. The only incongruous note is struck by a training shoe shop which broadcasts dire in-store music to the world.

The warren of shop-filled streets between the main squares is becoming increasingly palatable thanks to an on going **pedestrianization** scheme. Quite why this particular area has been so designated is more of a mystery. Admittedly, there are a large number of stores, but this isn't a noted hotel district, and overall a mild state of grime is the order of the day (though buskers do their best to cheer things up a bit). To date this attempt to give Athens a more cosmopolitan café society feel has only been partially successful, but it is undoubtedly a considerable improvement on what went before.

One major benefit of the pedestrianization of so many city centre streets is that it is now much easier for tourists to explore the capital — such as the greener parts of the city. These include the shady **National Gardens** and the more energy-sapping **Likavittos** and Filopapou (alias Mouseion) hills with their views across the city. The Likavittos is reached via a cable car, while the Filopapou is in the centre of a pine-wood park to the south-west of the Acropolis.

Readers should be aware that, although Athens is a relatively safe capital city, visiting parks and wooded areas can be dangerous at night. In the crowd-free Low Season tourists have also been mugged at midday on Filopapou, so take care. Athenians tend to put the rise in crime levels of recent years down to the influx of illegal immigrants and refugees.

Most visitors negotiate Athens without problems, but you should be aware that the impact of 4 million tourists a year has also had an unfortunate effect on a minority of the locals. There have always been two types of Athenian: the hospitable and charming individuals on a par with most of the Greek islanders, and the other kind — who in days past ordered the death of Socrates, amongst others. Sadly, most of the descendants of the latter class have become waiters or taxi drivers. In Athens many of the taxi drivers are something else — it pays to get into a taxi before stating your desired destination: most drivers have their own patch and aren't interested in going anywhere else ('anywhere else' usually being where you want to go). Requests for the airport or Piraeus are seen as a licence to overcharge to excess. All in all, when in Athens it is wise to keep your eyes open (see also: 'Scams', p. 56).

Plaka District / Old Town

Plaka is the last remnant of pre-Greek-independence Turkish Athens, and the only part of the city with great appeal. A warren of 17th and 18th c. red-tiled town buildings mixed with earlier small Byzantine churches, small leafy squares and excavated archaeological sites, it roughly occupies the large north-east quarter of the ancient city, and is bounded by the Acropolis and Olympieion to the south and the Agora to the west. Originally, the old town extended over the Acropolis and the Agora areas as well, but the buildings were demolished between the first half of the 19th century and the 1930s.

In fact the entire Plaka district lies directly over the ancient city. There are undoubtedly important ancient sites obscured under the photogenic Plaka buildings, but their merit is recognized, and renovation mixed with piecemeal excavation (when opportunities present themselves) is now the order of the day.

The bulk of the old town — although throbbing with souvenir shops (selling items that are available at a much better price on the islands), restaurants, hotels and everything else — has a lot going for it in spite of the overblown tourist trappings. It is quite possible to forget the horror of concrete Athens while you explore the warren of streets. In addition to housing the best of the sightseeing, Plaka is also the main eating area in the city, with the bulk of the tavernas and restaurants lining or near **Adrianou** and **Kidathineon** streets. Most are on the expensive side; however, you at least have the consolation that the views are worth the added costs of a meal.

Towering over all is the Acropolis, which, floodlit at night, casts a golden glow over the crowds that safely wander in numbers into the small hours (note: single women should still be on their guard — particularly on Sundays when the whole city shuts down). Fortunately, all the principal sights are within easy walking distance of each other, and the Acropolis provides a ready point of reference should you lose your way; the streets nearest the rock rise steeply into its shadow. Syntagma Square is another ready point of reference.

The only area of the Plaka now scheduled for demolition is the thin finger of buildings that lie to the north of the Agora. Now rather dilapidated, this area (unlike the rest of Plaka) is best avoided at night. During the day it is home to the city's flea market (on Ifestou St.). For the most part it sells the worst sort of rubbish, but amid the imitation brand name clothing outlets are a couple of antique shops selling detritus from scrapped ships, and an outlet offering a million different types of beads.

If you are in Athens any length of time, you may wish to invest in a definitive street map. There are two of note: the most detailed city map is the new 'Road Editions' *Athens, Piraeus – Southern Suburbs* (€7.50). Less easy to find, but much larger in scale, is an excellent map of the Plaka district: the *Historical Map of Athens* (€4), on sale at the Agora, sounds stuffy, but is much better than any of the other maps on sale. Available in various languages, its coverage of Plaka is particularly good, with all the buildings colour-coded according to age.

▶◀

It is not much of an exaggeration to say that every street in central Athens boasts a hotel. A bed is not hard to find (the Olympics season excepted) — even at the height of the season. However, you will find that room quality is significantly lower, and prices are higher, than with a comparable class of hotel in the islands. There also seems to be a higher degree of variation in room quality in some hotels (several are not recommended here because one can't be sure of getting one of the better rooms). It is also worth noting that many D and E-class hotels don't take credit cards so check on this before you book in.

Some accommodation suggestions — working out from the centre (note: map references refer to the 4-section city centre map — see the 'Locating Hotels' section on page 91):

Plaka & Syntagma
In the perfect world the visitor to Athens should seek to stay in or near the Plaka district. Even though this is a very noisy part of town, most people don't stay in Athens long, and it is conveniently close to all the sights — so much so that you may consider it worth booking ahead to secure a room. The antiquated nature of many of the buildings means that hotels tend be small, and therefore are more likely to be full come the evening.

Top End:
• *Grand Bretagne* (☎ 333 0000) A-class; [map 4; 21-55]. The oldest hotel in Athens. Built in 1842, it is one of the poshest places in town with prices (and phone number!) to match.

• *Electra Palace* (☎ 337 0000) A-class; [map 4; 19-60]. One of the few top-end hotels in Plaka, the big plus on offer is a roof-top swimming pool with views across to the Acropolis.

• *Plaka* (☎ 322 2096) B-class; [map 3; 17-57]. One of the cheapest of the expensive hotels in a newish building.

Mid-range:
• *Adonis* (☎ 324 9737) C-class; [map 4; 20-60]. Also listed as a B-class pension, this is an attractive Plaka option — though facilities are at the lower end of the C-class scale.

• *Acropolis House* (☎ 322 2344) C-class; [map 4; 20-62]. A second Plaka hostelry also listed as a B-class pension.

• *Amazon* (☎ 323 4002) C-class; [map 4; 19-58]. Formerly listed as a B-class establishment.

• *Hermes* (☎ 323 5514) C-class; [map 4; 19-59]. Up-market C-class with refurbished rooms.

• *Aphrodite* (☎ 323 4357) C-class; [map 3; 18-59]. A quieter backstreet hotel.

• *Cecil* (☎ 321 7079) C-class; [map 3; 15-50]. A small, old fashioned 19 c. building. Atmospheric rooms are well maintained.

• *Attalos* (☎ 321 2801) C-class; [map 3; 14-51]. Although this hotel is not on the most attractive street in town, its rooms are clean: a few offering views of the Acropolis.

• *Pella Inn* (☎ 321 2229) D-class; [map 3; 12-55]. One for the desperate: poorly sited in the more dangerous, run-down part of Plaka.

• *Erechthion* (☎ 345 9606) C-class; [map 3; 8-60]. An interesting option: one the few reasonably priced hotels west of the Acropolis. Tends to fill up very quickly in High Season.

Budget:

• *Tembi* (☎ 321 3175) D-class; [map 3; 16-55]. A bit down at heel, but popular, thanks to impressive views of the Acropolis.

• *John's Place* (☎ 322 9719) E-class; [map 4; 19-59]. If you are really keen to be in Plaka and save money at the same time. Ask to see the room before you sign on.

Omonia & Metaxourghio

The district between Omonia Square and Karaiskaki Square is packed with hotels, most in the mid-range category. The weary traveller can simply exit at either Omonia or Metaxourghio metro stations and be sure of being only a block or two away from a bed. The only area that is a bit suspect is the block on the north side of Omonia: the hotels here tend to be pretty ropy, and contrast greatly with the large number of excellent mid-range hotels that line the streets to the north-west.

Top End:

• *Stanley* (☎ 524 1611) A-class; [map 1; 10-42]. One of the few top end hotels in this area of Athens with a prime location on Karaiskaki Square.

• *Minoa* (☎ 523 4622) B-class; [map 1; 12-42]. A good solid city-centre hotel. Well maintained and not over priced for its category.

• *King Jason* (☎ 523 4721) B-class; [map 1; 10-46]. Reasonable, but can be hard to find.

• *Pythagorion* (☎ 524 2811) B-class; [map 1; 13-44]. Formerly listed as C-class, this hotel's rooms fall between the two.

Mid-range:

• *Theoxenia* (☎ 380 0250) C-class; [map 1; 18-44]. An very attractive option, tucked quietly away with all facilities (internet café, bar and bakery) right outside the front door.

• *Museum* (☎ 380 5611) C-class; [map 2; 20-38]. Slightly off the beaten trail, this is another one worth considering as it is reasonably quiet yet not too far from the centre of things.

• *Exarchion* (☎ 380 0731) C-class; [map 2; 20-41]. Reasonably modern, but charges extra for air conditioned rooms.

• *Dyrades* (☎ 330 2387) C-class; [map 2; 23-39]. A hotel in the student part of town. Access via a steep hillside to put older tourists off.

• *Euripides* (☎ 321 2301) C-class; [map 1; 12-49]. A large modern hotel, reasonably well

placed. It lacks character but does have all the essentials.

Budget:

• *Youth Hostel* (☎ 524 1708); [map 1; 13-42]. The only official youth hostel in Athens.

• *Eva* (☎ 522 3079) D-class; [map 1; 11-41]. One of the better budget options.

• *Annabel* (☎ 524 5834) D-class; [map 1; 14-42]. A hotel that also styles itself as a youth hostel. Some dormitory accommodation.

• *Pindaros* (☎ 524 4229) D-class; [map 1; 15-48]. One of several closely grouped budget hotels, all of similar quality.

• *Elikon* E-class; [map 1; 17-44]. Definitely one to be avoided: saucers of rat poison periodically appear on the landings. Enough said.

Larissa Rail Station

The rail station area has several good hotels within easy reach if you prefer a rather quieter part of town (buildings here are mostly residential). This accounts for the disproportionately high number of more expensive hotels located here.

Top End:

• *Oscar Inn* (☎ 881 3211) B-class; [map 1; 10-36]. Good up-market option close to the station.

• *Balaska* (☎ 883 5211) B-class; [map 1; 12-36]. Middle-aged rooms, but not too expensive.

Mid-range:

• *Mystras* (☎ 522 7737) C-class; [map 1; 8-40]. Conveniently close to the station. A bit down at heel, with prices to match, so will appeal to budget travellers.

• *Filoxenia* (☎ 882 8611) C-class; [map 1; 15-36]. A reasonable hotel, if a bit out of the way.

Budget:

• *Rio* (☎ 522 7075) D-class; [map 1; 8-43]. A popular and cheap backpacker option.

• *San Remo* (☎ 523 3245) E-class; [map 1; 9-38]. The cheapest option close to the station.

Λ

Athens has several poor trailer sites in the outer environs that are better avoided: camping in Athens tends to be more trouble than it is worth. The best sites are a longish bus ride away along the Apollo coast near Cape Sounion, including the over-popular *Camping Sounio Beach* (☎ 2292 39358) and less appealing *Camping Varkiza* (☎ 2189 74329).

ATHENS
CITY CENTRE

1	2
3	4

Key

A Larissa Railway Station
(Eastern Europe)

B Railway Station
(Corinth, Patras & the
Peloponnese)

C Piraeus Bus Stop (Omonia)

D Bus Stop for Buses to:
Bus Terminal A
100 Kifissou St.

E Road to Bus Terminal A
100 Kifissou St. (2 km)
(Main Bus Intercity Station)

F Bus Terminal B (Evia/Kimi)
(260 Liossion St. 1.5 km NW)

G Victoria Metro Station (100 m)

H Central Market
(an Athenian Covent Garden)

I National Theatre

J Town Hall

K Municipal Art Gallery

L School of Fine Arts

M Greek Rail Head Office

N Athens Traffic Police

O Excavated Area

P Ag. Paulos Church

Q Ag. Anargiri Church

R Peristeri Road

S National Bank of Greece

T Money Exchange

U International Press

V *Kentucky Fried Chicken*

W *McDonald's*

X Supermarket

Y Bakery / Sandwich Bar

Z Pharmacy

0   m   100

Line of Ancient
City Walls

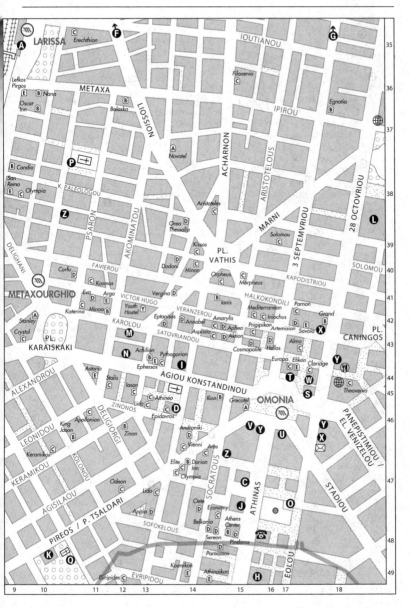

LARISSA

Erechthion C

IOUTIANOU

F

G

35

Lefkos
Pirgos

METAXA

Nana B

Oscar
Inn B

Balaska B

LIOSSION

Filoxenia
C

36

IPIROU

Egnatia
B

37

Candia B

K. PALEOLOGOU

P

San
Remo
E

Olympia C

Novotel A

ACHARNON

ARISTOTELOUS

28 OCTOVRIOU

38

Z

PSARON

AKOMINATOU

Aristofeles C

MARNI

Solomou
C

3 SEPTEMVRIOU

SOLOMOU

39

DELIGHANI

METAXOURGHIO

FAVIEROU

Orea
Thessalia D

Kissos
C

PL.
VATHIS

KAPODISTRIOU

40

Corfu D

Kosmos C

Dodoni D

Minon D

Orpheus
C

Morpheus D

Eva
D

Argo
E

VICTOR HUGO

Vergina D

Ionis B

HALKOKONDILI

Mediterranean
C

Iniochus C

Parnon
C

L

PL.
CANINGS

Stanley A

Katerina

Minoa E

Youth
Hostel Y

VERANZEROU

Eptanisos
D

Annabel D

Amarylis
C

Aphea
D

Prigipikon
C

Artemision
D

Savoia E

Grand
B

X

Crystal C

PL.
KARAISKAKI

KAROLOU

M

SATOVRIANDOU

Aspasia
C

Aktion
D

Cosmopolite C

Hellas
C

Alma
C

Europa C

Elikon
E

Claridge C

Y

YI

Theoxenia

Astoria
E

ALEXANDROU

Achilion
B

Ephessos
C

Pythagorion
C

I

AGIOU KONSTANDINOU

OMONIA

T

W

S

Stalis
C

Iason
C

Athineo C

Lido C

Ilion B

Grecotel C

44

45

LEONIDOU

KERAMIKOU

KOLONOU

DELIGIORGI

ZINONOS

King
Jason B

Apollonion
C

Zinon C

Epidavros C

D

Androniki
D

Vienni
C

Ares
D

Z

V

Y

U

PANEPISTIMIOU /
EL. VENIZELOU

46

Keramikou C

Elite B

Dorian
Inn C

Olympia C

SOCRATOUS

C

Y

X

STADIOU

47

AGISILAOU

Odeon
C

Lido C

Appia D

Oeti
D

Economy
C

J

ATHINAS

O

48

PIREOS / P. TSALDARI

K

Q

SOFOKELOUS

Belkaria
D

Sereon
D

Athens
Center
B

Pindaros
D

EOLOU

Parnassos D

Kosmikon
E

Euripides C

EVRIPIDOU

Athinaikon
E

H

49

9   10   11   12   13   14   15   16   17   18

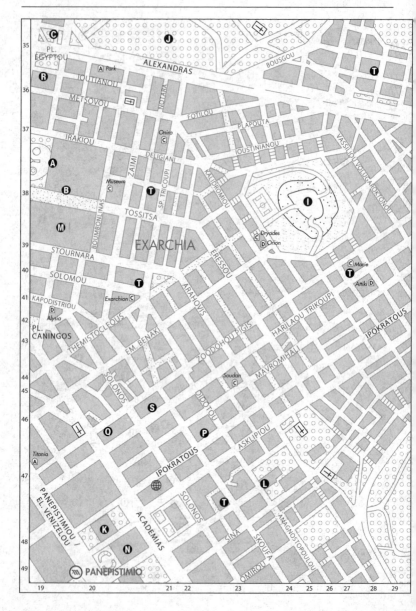

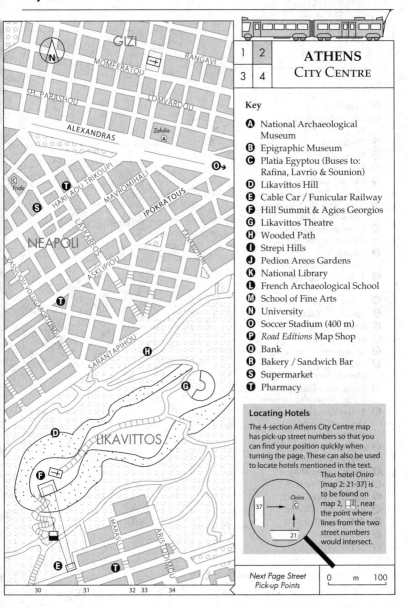

ATHENS
CITY CENTRE

| 1 | 2 |
| 3 | 4 |

Key

Ⓐ National Archaeological Museum
Ⓑ Epigraphic Museum
Ⓒ Platia Egyptou (Buses to: Rafina, Lavrio & Sounion)
Ⓓ Likavittos Hill
Ⓔ Cable Car / Funicular Railway
Ⓕ Hill Summit & Agios Georgios
Ⓖ Likavittos Theatre
Ⓗ Wooded Path
Ⓘ Strepi Hills
Ⓙ Pedion Areos Gardens
Ⓚ National Library
Ⓛ French Archaeological School
Ⓜ School of Fine Arts
Ⓝ University
Ⓞ Soccer Stadium (400 m)
Ⓟ *Road Editions* Map Shop
Ⓠ Bank
Ⓡ Bakery / Sandwich Bar
Ⓢ Supermarket
Ⓣ Pharmacy

Locating Hotels

The 4-section Athens City Centre map has pick-up street numbers so that you can find your position quickly when turning the page. These can also be used to locate hotels mentioned in the text. Thus hotel *Oniro* [map 2: 21-37] is to be found on map 2, ▢2, near the point where lines from the two street numbers would intersect.

Next Page Street Pick-up Points

0   m   100

ATHENS
City Centre

1	2
3	4

Key

A Cathedral

B Acropolis Ticket Kiosks, WCs & Drinking Water

C Parthenon

D Erechtheion

E Propylaia

F Old Acropolis Museum (closing during 2004)

G New Acropolis Museum (opening in 2004)

H Viewing Mount (with lethal, slippery marble steps)

I Areopagus (Ancient 'Senate' Hill)

J Theatre of Dionysos (Tickets & WCs)

K Agora Ticket Kiosks

L Library of Hadrian

M Roman Agora

N Roman Baths

O Monument of Lysicrates

P Pnyx (Ancient 'Parliament' Hill)

Q Mousieon / Filopapou Hill & Philopappos Monument

R Kerameikos Park (Ancient Cemetery) & Site Museum

S Gazi Cultural Park (Gas Works Museum)

T Doras Stratou Theatre

U Agia Irini Church

V Ag. Theodori Church

W Kapnikarea Church

X Old Bazaar Street

Y Flea Market

Z *McDonald's*

0 m 100	▨▨▨ Line of Ancient City Walls

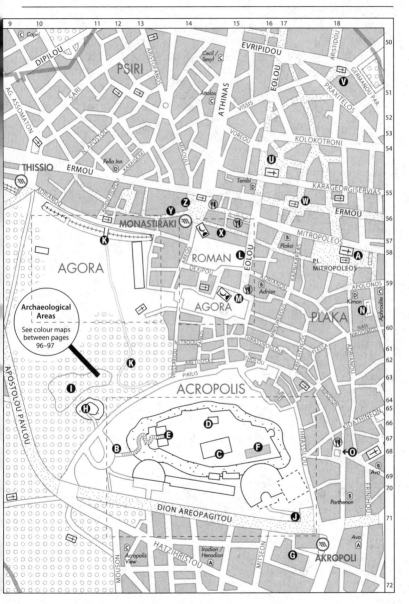

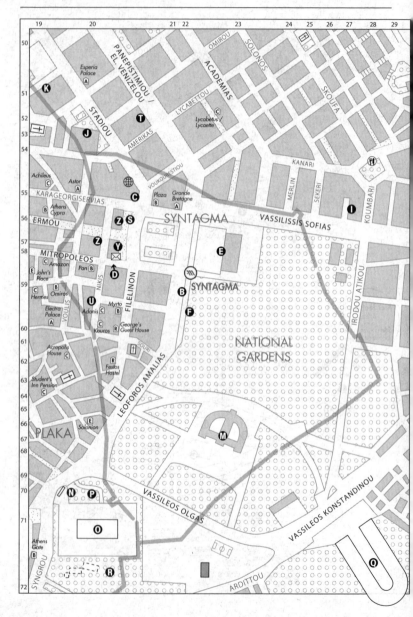

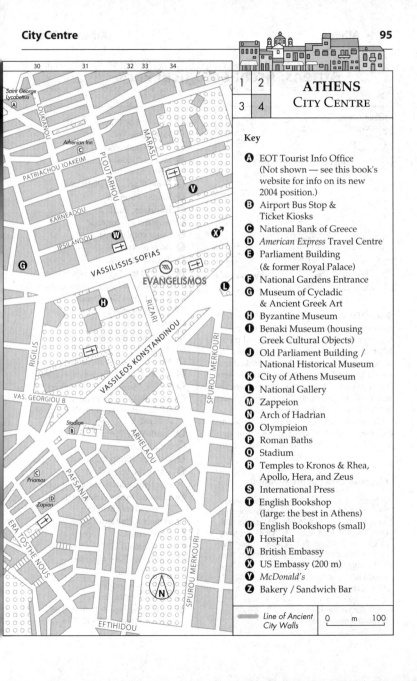

ATHENS
CITY CENTRE

Key

A EOT Tourist Info Office
(Not shown — see this book's
website for info on its new
2004 position.)
B Airport Bus Stop &
Ticket Kiosks
C National Bank of Greece
D *American Express* Travel Centre
E Parliament Building
(& former Royal Palace)
F National Gardens Entrance
G Museum of Cycladic
& Ancient Greek Art
H Byzantine Museum
I Benaki Museum (housing
Greek Cultural Objects)
J Old Parliament Building /
National Historical Museum
K City of Athens Museum
L National Gallery
M Zappeion
N Arch of Hadrian
O Olympieion
P Roman Baths
Q Stadium
R Temples to Kronos & Rhea,
Apollo, Hera, and Zeus
S International Press
T English Bookshop
(large: the best in Athens)
U English Bookshops (small)
V Hospital
W British Embassy
X US Embassy (200 m)
Y *McDonald's*
Z Bakery / Sandwich Bar

Line of Ancient   0   m   100
City Walls

⚓ Athens: Archaeological Park

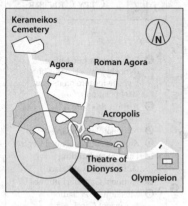

Some 150 years after the idea was first mooted Athens has collected its major sites together to make an 'archaeological park'. In practice this means that five sites near to the Acropolis have been loosely linked to it — via the pedestrianization of the streets between them. A cut-price Acropolis ticket that includes entry to all the sites (listed below) has also been introduced.

The result is a much improved sightseeing experience, particularly with the approach to the Acropolis itself; the main road south

Buy your ticket at the Acropolis

Tickets to the Acropolis (€12) now include 48-hour free entry to five other nearby sites that would otherwise cost an additional €14 if you bought entry tickets to each separately. It therefore pays to visit the Acropolis first in order to buy the multi-entry park ticket. The five sites (in addition to the Acropolis) are:

1. The Theatre of Dionysos
2. The Olympieion
3. The Agora
4. The Roman Agora
5. The Kerameikos Cemetery.

- **Ⓐ** Stoa Poikile (Painted Stoa)
- **Ⓑ** Royal Stoa
- **Ⓒ** Panathenaic Way
- **Ⓓ** Stoa of Attalos (Reconstructed) & Agora Museum
- **Ⓔ** Bema (Speaker's Platform)
- **Ⓕ** Roman Fountain
- **Ⓖ** Hadrianic Basilica
- **Ⓗ** Augustan Colonnade
- **Ⓘ** Odeon of Agrippa
- **Ⓙ** Altar of Ares
- **Ⓚ** Temple of Ares
- **Ⓛ** Altar of the Twelve Gods & Omphalos (Official Centre of the City)
- **Ⓜ** Stoa of Zeus Eleutherios
- **Ⓝ** Temple of Apollo Patroös
- **Ⓞ** Statue of Hadrian
- **Ⓟ** Hephaisteion (Temple of Hephaistos)
- **Ⓠ** Arsenal
- **Ⓡ** Metroön (Government Archives)
- **Ⓢ** Bouleuterion (City Senate House)
- **Ⓣ** Tholos (Administrative Centre)
- **Ⓤ** Monument of the Eponymonus Heroes (Founders of the Political Tribes of Athens)
- **Ⓥ** South-West Temple
- **Ⓦ** Middle Stoa
- **Ⓧ** Cobbler's Shop & Latrine
- **Ⓨ** Site of the Stratagion? (the Pentagon of Ancient Athens)
- **Ⓩ** Classical Prison & Site of the Execution of Socrates
- **Ⓕ** Heliaia (City Courthouse)
- **Ⓐ** South Stoa I
- **◎** South Stoa II
- **Ⓐ** South-East Fountain House
- **Ⓜ** Classical Mint
- **⊜** South-East Temple
- **Ⓦ** Library of Pantainos
- **Ⓞ** South-East Stoa & Path to the Roman Agora & the Wall of Valerian

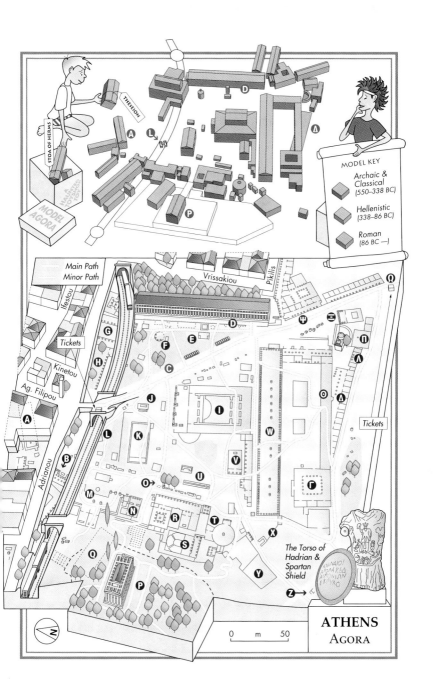

MODEL KEY

Archaic & Classical (550–338 BC)

Hellenistic (338–86 BC)

Roman (86 BC —)

STOA OF HERMS

MODEL AGORA

THESEION

Main Path

Minor Path

Ifestou

Tickets

Kinetou

Ag. Filipou

Adrianou

Vrissakiou

Pikilis

Tickets

The Torso of Hadrian & Spartan Shield

ATHENS

AGORA

0   m   50

N

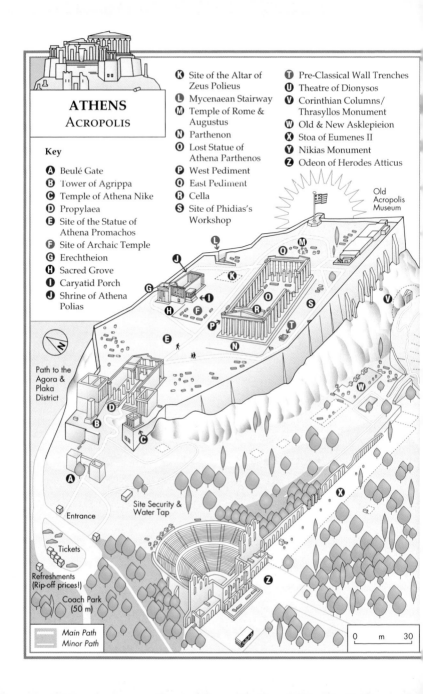

ATHENS
ACROPOLIS

Key

Ⓐ Beulé Gate
Ⓑ Tower of Agrippa
Ⓒ Temple of Athena Nike
Ⓓ Propylaea
Ⓔ Site of the Statue of Athena Promachos
Ⓕ Site of Archaic Temple
Ⓖ Erechtheion
Ⓗ Sacred Grove
Ⓘ Caryatid Porch
Ⓙ Shrine of Athena Polias

Ⓚ Site of the Altar of Zeus Polieus
Ⓛ Mycenaean Stairway
Ⓜ Temple of Rome & Augustus
Ⓝ Parthenon
Ⓞ Lost Statue of Athena Parthenos
Ⓟ West Pediment
Ⓠ East Pediment
Ⓡ Cella
Ⓢ Site of Phidias's Workshop

Ⓣ Pre-Classical Wall Trenches
Ⓤ Theatre of Dionysos
Ⓥ Corinthian Columns/ Thrasyllos Monument
Ⓦ Old & New Asklepieion
Ⓧ Stoa of Eumenes II
Ⓨ Nikias Monument
Ⓩ Odeon of Herodes Atticus

Old Acropolis Museum

Path to the Agora & Plaka District

N

Site Security & Water Tap

Entrance

Tickets

Refreshments (Rip-off prices!)

Coach Park (50 m)

Main Path
Minor Path

0   m   30

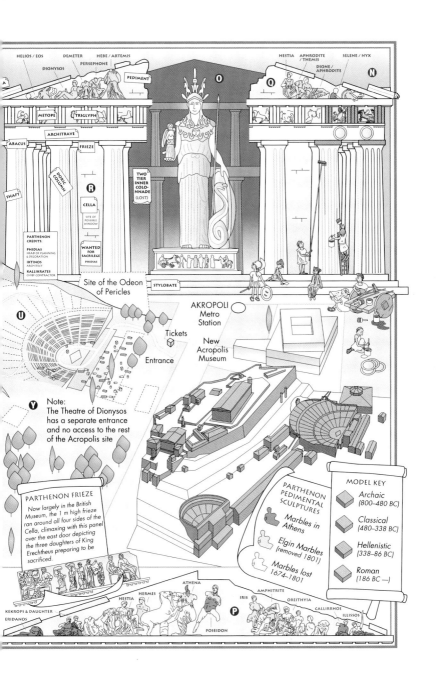

HELIOS / EOS DEMETER HEBE / ARTEMIS HESTIA APHRODITE SELENE / NYX
DIONYSOS PERSEPHONE /THEMIS DIONE / APHRODITE

PEDIMENT

O **Q** **N**

METOPE TRIGLYPH

ARCHITRAVE

ABACUS FRIEZE

DORIC COLUMN

SHAFT **R**

CELLA

SITE OF POSSIBLE WINDOW

TWO-TIER INNER COLONNADE (LOST)

PARTHENON CREDITS

PHIDIAS
HEAD OF PLANNING & DECORATION

WANTED FOR SACRILEGE
PHIDIAS

IKTINOS
ARCHITECT

KALLIKRATES
CHIEF CONTRACTOR

Site of the Odeon of Pericles

STYLOBATE

U

AKROPOLI
Metro Station

Tickets

New Acropolis Museum

Entrance

Y Note:
The Theatre of Dionysos has a separate entrance and no access to the rest of the Acropolis site

PARTHENON FRIEZE
Now largely in the British Museum, the 1 m high frieze ran around all four sides of the Cella, climaxing with this panel over the east door depicting the three daughters of King Erechtheus preparing to be sacrificed.

PARTHENON PEDIMENTAL SCULPTURES

Marbles in Athens

Elgin Marbles (removed 1801)

Marbles lost 1674–1801

MODEL KEY

Archaic (800–480 BC)

Classical (480–338 BC)

Hellenistic (338–86 BC)

Roman (186 BC —)

KEKROPS & DAUGHTER
ERIDANOS

HESTIA HERMES

ATHENA

IRIS

AMPHITRITE

OREITHYIA

CALLIRRHOE

ILLISSOS

P

POSEIDON

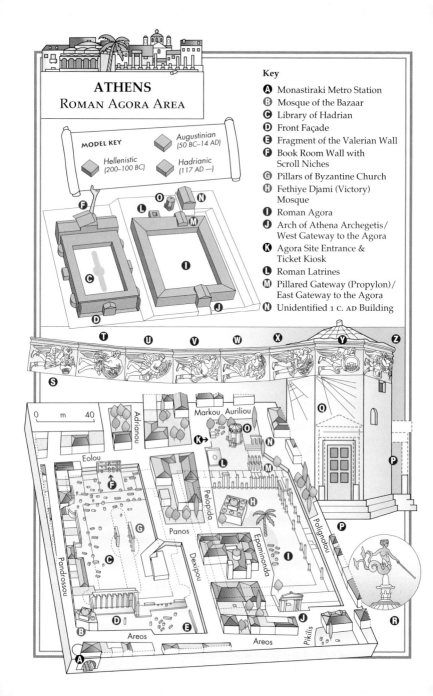

ATHENS
ROMAN AGORA AREA

MODEL KEY

Hellenistic (200–100 BC)

Augustinian (50 BC–14 AD)

Hadrianic (117 AD —)

Key

- **A** Monastiraki Metro Station
- **B** Mosque of the Bazaar
- **C** Library of Hadrian
- **D** Front Façade
- **E** Fragment of the Valerian Wall
- **F** Book Room Wall with Scroll Niches
- **G** Pillars of Byzantine Church
- **H** Fethiye Djami (Victory) Mosque
- **I** Roman Agora
- **J** Arch of Athena Archegetis / West Gateway to the Agora
- **K** Agora Site Entrance & Ticket Kiosk
- **L** Roman Latrines
- **M** Pillared Gateway (Propylon) / East Gateway to the Agora
- **N** Unidentified 1 C. AD Building

of the rock is now free of traffic and one can take in the view without danger to life and limb. Traffic fans can, however, still get some excitement out of the re-vamped 'park' as both the Olympieion and the Kerameikos Cemetery still require you to cross very busy roads.

All this is a long way from the original park concept. This involved demolishing all buildings that stood around the ancient remains and then constructing modern Athens beyond the ancient city wall line. This was partially implemented in the first half of the 19th century when the Acropolis, Agora, and Roman Agora sites were systematically cleared of the houses built amidst the ruins during the three centuries of Ottoman rule. But after the initial enthusiastic demolition, further work stopped as the business of reconstruction and preservation sapped resources. Today there are no plans for further demolition (apart from a few houses north of the Agora's disfiguring metro line).

If you plan to make full use of your ticket and visit all the sites then you should set aside a couple of days for the task. During the summer months the shade-lacking Acropolis and Olympieion are best tackled either very early or late in the day.

O The Tower of the Winds (also called the Horologion of Andronikos Cyrrhestes)

P Entrance Portico

Q Sundial Lines

R The Lost Triton Weathervane

The Winds:

S NW: **Skiron** (holds charcoal cauldron)

T W: **Zephyros** (showers lap of flowers)

U SW: **Lips** (holds stern of trireme-like ship)

V S: **Notos** (emptying an urn of raindrops)

W SE: **Euros** (mantled, with arm cloaked)

X E: **Apeliotes** (showers lap of fruit)

Y NE: **Kaikias** (holds shield of hailstones)

Z N: **Boreas** (mantled, and holding a conch)

An appreciation of the historical background to Athens is helpful when viewing the extant remains. The jumble of ruins from different periods (particularly in the Agora areas) doesn't lend itself to easy visualisation of past appearance. Sites such as the Acropolis itself and the Olympieion, which were built at one time, are much more coherent.

Athens was once the most powerful of all the Greek city states. It is best known for the work of a mere three generations in the 5 C. BC when it first stood alone as a bulwark against the massed forces of the Persian Empire (its citizens playing a crucial part in the battles of Marathon in 490 BC and Salamis in 480 BC), and then, under the leadership of Pericles and his successors, became the fountainhead of European civilization, playing host to the sudden flowering of the Greek genius that gave the western world its first theatre, greatest art and architecture, and first true history and philosophy. However, the dynamic that had set the city apart soon faded, and Athens had to settle for becoming a major centre of learning during the Hellenistic and Roman periods, then a minor town under the Turks, before emerging as the capital of Greece in the 19th century.

Thanks to the protection offered by the Acropolis, Athens has been occupied since Neolithic times. During the Mycenaean period the Acropolis was fortified, and this served the city well during the dark ages that followed, as it was able to repulse the waves of Doric Greeks pouring into Greece. By the 8 C. BC Athens had gained control of the surrounding province of Attica and emerged as one of the major art centres in Greece. This developed into a leading cultural role in the 6 C. BC under the patronage of Pisistratus, who initiated the Great Dionysia (a semi-religious eisteddfod) as part of the annual Panathenaic festival. This gave the world the first established texts of Homer, and later produced the birth of drama; most of the great plays of Greek tragedy and comedy were conceived and first performed in the city on the site of the Theatre of Dionysos.

A succession of leaders — Draco, Solon and Cleisthenes — also instituted constitutional reforms that led to Athens emerging as a champion of democracy. Rule by orators in turn prompted debate, and enquiry into words and their meanings, which in turn extended the debate to wider ideas and concepts of morality. As a result, Athens developed as a centre for the great philosophers — Socrates, Plato and Aristotle among them. Athens also emerged as a major economic power — thanks to the profits derived from the substantial silver mines at nearby Lavrio.

Athenian victories over the Persians gave the city the role of leading protector of the Greeks and, on this basis, the islands contributed funds for the maintenance of the Athenian trireme fleet. Unfortunately Athens rapidly turned these contributions into a tribute, and the islands into a de facto empire, and used the excess monies to build the Acropolis temples. Fearful of Athenian domination, the cities of Sparta and Corinth were soon embroiled in the Peloponnesian War, which Athens lost after 30 years of struggle.

Never regaining her military pre-eminence, Athens fell to Philip of Macedon in 338 BC and came under Roman control in the 2 C. BC. The city was sacked by Sulla in 86 BC, saw a brief renaissance (thanks to the patronage of Hadrian), and finally faded from the scene when it was sacked by the Herulian Goths in 267 AD. Reduced to cowering behind the small Valerian wall, Athens was a minor town in the Byzantine Empire. It was ruled by the Franks and the Venetians before the Ottoman Turks gave it three quiet centuries (their rule being briefly interrupted by the disastrous Venetian conquest of the city in 1687) prior to Greek independence in 1832.

The Ancient City & Archaeological Park Area
Considering how great a cultural and military powerhouse Athens was, the size of the ancient city comes as a surprise, for it is very small by modern standards (see map between pages 64–65). It has been calculated that the walls contained 6,000 houses for an estimated population of some 36,000. However, this figure is misleading, as a good half of the population of 'Athens' lived and worked at the Athenian port of Piraeus.

Piraeus soon developed as a city in its own right, and by the Classical period people were openly talking about the 'upper' and 'lower' cities (Athens being the former). The historian Thucydides wrote that the Athenian leader 'Themistokles thought Piraeus more useful than the upper city', and this comment reflected Piraeus's growing role as the military, business and commercial base — Athens

itself being viewed as more of the political, religious and cultural centre. This was natural enough given that Athens — represented on coins by her symbol, the owl of wisdom — was home to the traditional sites for worship (the Acropolis), law (the courts near the Agora) and learning (the three Gymnasia, including the Academy, beloved by Plato, and the recently discovered Lyceum, founded by Aristotle).

Defending this odd urban structure took some doing, particularly as Athens was primarily a maritime power (the Peloponnesian War lasted 30 years simply because Athens was dominant at sea while Sparta and her allies controlled the mainland). After the Persian sack of Athens in 480 BC, Themistokles rebuilt the city walls protecting Athens and Piraeus. Moreover, the two were connected by two walls running parallel to each other several hundred metres apart: known as the 'Long Walls', they — along with the short-lived outer Phaleron Wall — added up to a formidable defensive system that from the air would have looked like a giant dumbbell. Following the Athenian defeat in the Peloponnesian War in 404 BC, the Long Walls were demolished, only to be later rebuilt. By the Roman era they had gone, Piraeus was in decline, and the focus of Athens moved north and east, with the building of the Roman Agora and the Hadrianic Wall.

The surviving remains of the ancient city — largely within the Archaeological Park sites — are substantial, but not very representative. The Athenians built their houses and the greater part of the city walls out of adobe bricks, and over the millennia these have reverted to mud.

The park area embraces the main religious, administrative and commercial areas of the pre-Roman city, where most of the building was in stone and on an impressive scale. The reason that many of the walls and columns survive in situ is that they were sufficiently robust to form the base for medieval and later buildings. Of course while the marble stones have survived, there is little on show to give an impression of their original appearance; you would never guess that all the stonework was once painted. As for the 3,000 bronze statues observed by Roman writers: well, the National Archaeological Museum is home to the surviving odd finger or two.

The Acropolis

The greatest attraction in Athens is the Acropolis (see map between pages 96–97). The name means 'the city on the rock'. Standing some 90 m above the surrounding plain, the rock proved easily defensible, later becoming the focus of religious activity, before its defensive value again came to the fore. The buildings on the rock add up to one of the most important archaeological sites in the world. Even in their ruined state, the Parthenon and the Erechtheion remain architectural wonders, forming the nucleus of an ensemble of buildings that led the Roman writer Plutarch to say of them that 'they were created in a short time for all time … a perpetual newness blooms upon them untouched by the years, as if they held within them some everlasting breath of life and an ageless spirit intermingled in their composition'. These days this effect is diminished by the presence of three million visitors a year, but if you arrive early, you can avoid the worst of the crowds. The site is open ☺ 08.00–18.30. Coach tour guides have the right to push to the head of the ticket-kiosk queues. Tourists are not allowed to venture inside the Acropolis buildings.

The Acropolis has evidence of occupation dating back to Neolithic times, though later building has destroyed most traces. It is known that in the Mycenaean period it had a palace and saw its first major fortifications. In the Archaic period the Acropolis emerged as the religious centre of the city, with a succession of temples erected on the rock before the Persians fired them in their invasion of Greece in 480 BC. Calamitous at the time, this event cleared the way for the rebuilding programme inspired by the Athenian leader Pericles some 30 years later — just as Greek culture was bursting into full bloom; it is the ruins of these buildings that remain today.

Through the Hellenistic and Roman periods the Acropolis saw little further building, and it was only from the 7 C. AD on that the area around the temples was in-filled with other buildings, as the rock was again used as a fortress. This state of affairs continued through the period of Turkish rule (one of the early European visitors describing the Acropolis mentions that there were two streets of whitewashed houses between the Parthenon and the Erechtheion).

Once Athens became the capital of an independent Greek state, the Acropolis was rapidly converted from a fortress-town to a museum. In 1833 work began in stripping away the detritus of 2000 years (this included the removal of all houses and a 30 m tower built atop the Propylaea) to reveal the ancient buildings in all their ruined glory. However, restoration of the Classical buildings resulted in unwitting damage due to poor techniques. The worst of these was the use of iron staples in rebuilding that rusted and caused many marble blocks to split (the ancients coated the original staples with lead to prevent this process occurring). This has resulted in all the buildings requiring major attention in the last few years, and quite a lot of controversial new 'white' marble is visible. The nature of this restoration is a subject of much argument. Current rebuilding is limited to work needed to ensure the structural integrity of the monuments and all new blocks are dated to ensure there is never confusion between old and new material. All the additions are also reversible. Previous restoration has been more substantial, notably the rebuilding of the centre columns on the north façade of the Parthenon in 1933. It has been suggested that the south side be similarly 'repaired', but this is a contentious idea and has been shelved while other worries — notably the threat of acid rain damage — are discussed.

Acropolis Entrance / West Side

Modern visitors approach the Acropolis from the same side as the ancients, though the first building encountered is a late construction: ❶ the **Beulé Gate** (named after its excavator) formed part of the defensive wall constructed in the 3 C. AD. It replaced a large processional stairway constructed by the Emperor Claudius in 52 AD. Today the path winds up to the Acropolis much as it did in Classical times. After the Beulé Gate you are confronted by two bastions projecting out from the Acropolis proper. On the northern one is ❷ the distinctive **'Tower' of Agrippa** (c. 178 BC). A Hellenistic plinth 8.8 m high, it bore a succession of bronze statues (including a chariot carrying Antony and Cleopatra), and takes its name from a statue of Marcus Agrippa erected on it in 27 BC.

The south bastion is more appealing, being home to ❸ the lovely small **Athena Nike**

Temple (427–424 BC). Designed by Kallikrates, it was dismantled in 1686 by the Turks so that the bastion could be used to house cannon. Fortunately, all the stones were preserved on site and it was re-erected in 1836–42. The building has a frieze running right around it, and contained a statue of Athena with Nike (Victory). Unfortunately, the lack of tourist-retaining walls on the bastion means that it is fenced off: the steps to the Acropolis offer the best view you can get of it. Like all the Acropolis buildings, it is built of Pentelic marble. Thanks to small deposits of iron in the marble, the colour has gradually mellowed from white to a creamy yellow as the iron has gradually oxidized over the millennia.

Extending out onto the bastions are the wings of **❿** the **Propylaea** (438–432 BC): the ceremonial gateway to the Acropolis. Deemed to be the best of its kind by the ancients, it was never fully completed. The outbreak of the Peloponnesian war and Athenian defeat ensured that its decoration was never finished. Designed by Mnesikles, the building was famous for its five massive doors and painted ceiling.

The north wing was also a noted picture gallery. The building was used as a bishop's palace in the 13 C., and in the 17 C. became a magazine for the Turkish garrison, suffering severe damage when a passing lightning bolt struck. The Venetian bombardment of 1687 finished the job of demolition by putting paid to the famous ceiling. South-east of the Propylaea are the scanty foundations of a double-winged stoa, a votive shrine to **Artemis Brauronia** (the bear goddess), and nearer the Parthenon, the **Chalkotheke** or **Magazine of the Bronzes**.

The North Side

Surprisingly, the magnificent Parthenon temple was not the holy of holies on the Acropolis. It was more of a glorious ante-chamber to the true religious centre — the Erechtheion — which stands on the probable site of the Mycenaean palace. This building was guarded by a large bronze statue that stood at **❺** facing the Propylaea. Known as the **Athena Promachos**, this famous figure is long lost, but part of the stone base has been identified. The path takes you past the site where it stood, and then divides. One branch takes you along the north side of the Parthenon (the traditional approach route to this temple); the other runs northward past

foundations at **❻**. This is the site of a **Temple of Athena Polias**. Built c. 530 BC, it originally stood alongside another limestone temple — the melodiously named **Hekatompedon** — meaning 'one hundred footer' (c. 566 BC), which stood on the Parthenon site. Some time around 508 BC this building was demolished. Its incomplete successor — the **Pre-Parthenon** — was destroyed by the Persians. Its column drums were later used to close off the other entrances to the Acropolis and are still visible in the north wall when viewed from street level. After the Persian sacking, the Athenians swore never to rebuild the temples. They later got around this vow by levelling the Athena Polias temple site, and having made a gesture in this direction, proceeded to rebuild the other buildings.

Not least among these was the **Erechtheion** (c. 421–405 BC). This complex of shrines is a four-chambered building (**❼**) that conformed to an ancient and irregular plan. It was home to several ancient and venerated wooden figures — notably a statue of Athena Polias — that were removed (along with the population of Athens) to the island of Salamis during the Persian sacking. The path approaches the building running past **❽** the site of the **Sacred Grove** (which was home to the olive tree offered by Athena, when winning her contest for the patronage of the city with Poseidon) and then turns east at the **North Portico** (a shrine to Poseidon). Designed by Kallikrates, the Erechtheion is graced with delicate Ionic columns. It became a church in the 6 C. and later the harem for the Turkish commander — an idea no doubt inspired by **❾**, the **Cary-atids** — the famous maiden-column porch. All the figures are now copies: the originals are in the Acropolis Museum (barring one in the British Museum). The east portico fronted the main shrine to Athena Polias and now has a **Restored Column** (**❿**) at the north end. Added in 1981 (most postcard photos are still without it), it has attracted criticism thanks to its 'fake' weathered finish. In fact, it is an accurate copy of the original — now in the British Museum.

To the south-east of the Erechtheion stood a large stepped altar at **❿** dedicated to **Zeus Polieus**, of which little remains. Instead, the path runs east of the site past a deep well in the floor of the rock at **❿**. Known as the **Mycenaean Stairway**, it was one of two up the north side of the rock that were closed off in the Classical period (the Persians attacked the Acropolis via a second, to the north of the Erechtheion). From here the path then runs east to the flag bastion. On its way it passes the scanty remains of **◍** the tiny, round tholos **Temple of Rome and Augustus**; a late, clumsy addition (27 BC) to the Acropolis monuments, all but ignored by ancient writers.

The Parthenon

The main temple-cum-city treasury dedicated to Athena Parthenos (the Virgin Athena), the Parthenon (**◍**) dominates the Acropolis. Built between 447–432 BC, the building is remarkable for not having a straight line in it. The platform is deliberately convex to allow rainwater to drain off. The columns are also convex — a feature designed by the building's architects Iktinos and Kallikrates to correct the optical illusion that makes straight columns appear thinner in the middle. The simple Doric columns also lean in slightly — were they tall enough, their centres would meet at a point some 2.5 km above the building — as well as being abnormally tall and placed closer together than was traditional.

Tradition was also defied in the size of the building; most temples were built 6 columns wide — the Parthenon has 8. Its length was determined by a standard formula (2 x the number of width columns + 1), producing 17 columns down the sides, thus retaining regular proportions yet making it appear unusually long. The result is a building that makes all other Greek temples look small and clumsy by comparison.

Intact for over 2000 years, the Parthenon has had a chequered history. Highlights include a couple of passing rulers using it to put a finger up (among other things) at the city population by using it as a brothel. In the 6 C. it was converted into the church of St. Sophia: a change which inflicted major structural damage as the orientation of the building had to be turned 180 degrees (the main entrance was originally on the east side to allow the rising sun to shine in upon the statue of the goddess), and an apse was added to the east end.

In the Ottoman period the Parthenon became a mosque, with a minaret poking through the roof on the south-west corner.

It met its end in 1687, when a Venetian army besieged the city. On hearing that the Turks were using the Parthenon as a hiding place for their arsenal (they assumed their attackers would never bombard a former church) the Venetian commander Morosini did just that. A shell landed on the building, blowing it apart, and leaving fragments of the roof, cella and the 300 women and children sheltering inside all over the Acropolis.

In its ruined state, the Parthenon continued to suffer. Reduced to two unconnected gable ends, it was used as a quarry for a mosque that was built in the shell (described by one visitor as looking like 'an ugly cork in a beautiful bottle'). Its remaining sculptures were removed by Lord Elgin (see p. 104), and poor restoration and pollution have taken their toll since. The Parthenon is currently undergoing extensive restoration work, but this is not enough for some, who have called for the re-roofing of the building to save the foundations (protected until 1687) from increasing rainwater damage.

In its prime the Parthenon was ornately decorated, with sculpture and other decorative features brightly painted in gaudy 'Mickey Mouse' colours. As much a statement of civic pride as a temple, it housed a treasury in the room in its west end, but its main function was to house the chryselephantine (gold and ivory) statue of **Athena Parthenos (◍)**. This remarkable figure cost more than the Parthenon itself, and its designer, Phidias, his reputation and almost his life. Known now through small copies bought by ancient tourists, it stood 12 m high and represented the goddess holding a shield in her left hand and a man-sized, winged Victory in her right. Her helmet was topped by a sphinx and two griffins, and her shield was decorated with scenes from the mythical battle between the Athenians and the Amazon women.

It was this shield that brought about Phidias's downfall. His pre-eminent position as the supervisor of the Acropolis rebuilding programme brought him enemies, who took advantage of a perceived likeness in the faces of two of the figures on Athena's shield to himself and his mentor, Pericles, to have him charged with sacrilege. Forced to flee the city, he took sanctuary at Olympia and there created one of the seven wonders of the world — his chryselephantine statue of Zeus. The Athena was deemed to be the inferior of the two, though she was impressive enough, with clothing made of sheets of gold tacked onto a wooden frame. Her flesh was sculpted ivory, and her eyes, precious gems. The figure stood, facing east, before a pool of sea water (to reflect light from the door) at the back of the Parthenon's main room. In its prime it must have been overwhelming; it must have seemed as if the goddess herself was standing in the chamber. The figure survived until c. 400 AD when it was removed to Constantinople and later destroyed by fire.

The Parthenon also boasted other major art treasures that survive in part. The **Pediment Sculptures** are the most obvious of these. Now reduced to fragments in museums (those now on the building are copies), by great luck they were drawn in 1674 by Jacques Carrey, a French painter, a few years before they were damaged. ❼ the **West Pediment**, was the best preserved until 1687. Its theme was the contest between Athena and Poseidon for the patronage of the city. Sadly, when the Venetians captured Athens, Morosini decided to remove the figures as war trophies, but they were smashed in the attempt to take them down. The central **East Pediment** (❶) figures were lost in the 4 c. AD when the Parthenon was turned into a church. According to Pausanias the theme was the birth of Athena, but he gives no details. A 1–2 c. AD altar in Spain, thought to be based on this pediment, has Athena and Zeus standing in a similar pose to the main figures on the west pediment.

The other great Parthenon art treasure is the **Frieze**. Over 159 m long, it ran around the outer wall of ❿ the **Cella** (the 'building' inside the ring of columns). Long thought to depict the Panathenaic procession to the Acropolis in honour of the goddess, it is now believed by some scholars to be a representation of a myth, the sacrifice of the daughters of Erechtheus (a king of Athens). Just over half of the panels were recovered by Elgin and are in the British Museum. Along with the majority of the surviving pedimental figures, they are the most important of the 'Elgin Marbles'.

The South Side

The area to the south of the Parthenon contains a couple of oddities. Now unmarked is the site of ❾ **Phidias's Workshop**, used for the construction of the gold and ivory statue. Fragments of these materials have been found in this area. Walking along to the west

end of the Parthenon you will come to ❶ the **Pre-Classical Wall Trenches**. These pits are natural fissures in the rock inside the Acropolis walls. In the Classical period they were used as 'graves' for the damaged sculptures from the temples destroyed by the Persians (now in the Acropolis museum). Left open, with low skirting walls, they form a minor hazard. The Acropolis wall is also dangerously low, but looking over it you are able to take in the layout of the buildings lining the southern slope better than you can at street level.

Looking down from left to right, the first and largest of the south slope structures is ❶ the **Theatre of Dionysos** (c. 330 BC). Marking the spot where most of the great plays of Greek tragedy and comedy were first performed in annual competitions, the site has a separate entrance on the south-east corner of the Acropolis (⊕ 08.00–18.30; tickets €2, free entry with Acropolis ticket). In the Classical period the theatre stage and seating occupied the lower tiers and were made of wood. With the rebuilding, the seating was extended right up the slope.

Above the theatre and close under the walls stand ❶ two **Corinthian Columns** (320–310 BC). These were erected by sponsors of winning dramatic performances — the west one is known as the **Thrasyllos Monument**. Cut into the rock below is a small shrine — now the chapel of Panagia Spiliotissa. To the left of the theatre stood a major Classical hall-like building known as the **Odeon of Pericles** (little survives), while to the right are the foundations of two healing sanctuaries: ❶ the **Old Asklepieion** (c. 420 BC) and the **New Asklepieion** (c. 300 BC).

A number of minor shrines lay between these buildings and the west Acropolis slope. Running east of the theatre is ❶ the **Stoa of Eumenes II** (c. 197–159 BC), the back wall of which has survived as part of the later city wall. At its eastern end lie the foundations of ❶ the **Nikias Monument** (320–319 BC) which was demolished to build the Beulé Gate. Finally, ❷ the **Odeon of Herodes Atticus** is the best preserved building on the Acropolis slopes. Built in 160–174 AD, the inner section of its façade survived by being incorporated into the later city wall that ran around the Acropolis. The interior seating was lost, but has since been replaced to allow performances. The rooms behind the stage have also been rebuilt from the foundations.

Acropolis Museum & Elgin Marbles

During 2004 the old Acropolis Museum (buried behind the Parthenon on the Acropolis itself) is due to be replaced by a new building located at the foot of the Acropolis by Acropoli Metro Station. The new museum is scheduled to open in time for the Olympics, though the probability is that the opening will not happen much beforehand. It is also likely that there will be a period when neither is open when exhibits are moved between the two.

With the best Acropolis exhibits now divided between the British Museum and the National Archaeological Museum, the **Old Acropolis Museum** has to make do with the remains of the pre-Classical sculpture from the buildings destroyed in the Persian sack of the Acropolis, and the handful of sculptures and reliefs that escaped Lord Elgin and other collectors.

Rooms I–III: Persian Rubble Rooms

These rooms are devoted to the sculptures damaged by the Persians in 480 BC and later ceremonially buried by the Athenians. These include: **Ⓐ** the **Lioness and Calf**: the latter creature is being torn to flesh (6 c. BC); **Ⓑ** a **Gorgon's Head** (550 BC); **Ⓒ** part of a pedimental sculpture depicting **Herakles fighting the Triton**; **Ⓓ** the **Calf Bearer**, one of the most important Archaic works of art; and **Ⓔ** the **Lion Group**, also from the pediment of a temple (570–560 BC).

Room IV: Phaidimos Room

Devoted to sculptures by this artist. Primary exhibits are **Ⓕ** the **Equestrian Statue**: the torso of the oldest European equestrian statue, and **Ⓖ** the **Peplos Kore**: named after her clothing, and still bearing original paint (530 BC).

Room V: Gigantomachia Room

Lined on one side by **Ⓗ** the **Showcases**, the prime exhibit is the badly weathered frieze from the small Temple of Athena Nike. Sidecases house Archaic marble fragments, small masonry and clay sculptures. This room also contains **Ⓘ**, the **Gigantomachia**. The battle between the gods and the giants was a popular theme ; this example shows Athena fighting a giant and comes from the Archaic temple that preceded the Parthenon.

Room VI: Late Archaic Works

This room has a mixed collection of items, notably **Ⓙ**, the **Mourning Athena**, c. 460 BC (see pose of Athena on p. 72), and **Ⓚ** the **Kritios Boy**, 480 BC.

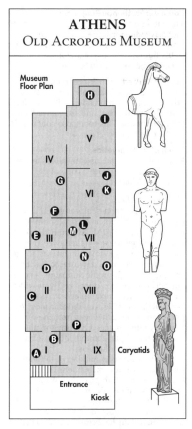

ATHENS
OLD ACROPOLIS MUSEUM

Museum
Floor Plan

Check out the
Athens **Museum** updates at
greekislandhopping.com

Opening 2004 ...

ATHENS
NEW ACROPOLIS MUSEUM

Room VII: Parthenon Fragments
This rather thin collection is dominated by ❶ the **West Pediment figure**, a male figure — possibly the river god Ilissos — and ❿ the **East Gable figure**: the torso of a woman, thought to be the moon goddess Selene.

Room VIII: Parthenon Frieze fragments
Several weathered slabs are here: ❶ the **East Frieze** depicts a procession with sacrificial animals and athletes, and ❶, shows **Youths with Amphorae**. This room also contains ❶, the **Nike Relief** (409–406 BC).

Room IX: The Caryatids
Five of the six maidens-cum-pillars are preserved here, along with a copy of the one in the British Museum.

The Elgin Marbles
The best Parthenon sculptures, along with fragments from other Acropolis buildings, are now in the British Museum thanks to Lord Elgin, whose agents removed them in 1801–4. The Greek government has sought their return over the last two decades without success via a high-profile campaign — spend any serious time in Athens and you will be sure to come across examples of it. As a result, you will find that Elgin is vilified in most local guides and (taking their lead from these) not a few international ones. Over-the-top phrases like 'looter Elgin' abound, but are hardly appropriate given the facts.

Elgin was one of a number of individuals (inspired by the revival of interest in the Classical tradition in Europe in the 18th and early 19 C.) who entered the mysterious Ottoman Empire in search of the past. Inspired by a desire to raise the standards of art and architecture in Britain, he secured the job of British Ambassador to the Ottoman court, taking with him a retinue of artists, architects and plaster moulders. Once in the Aegean he found that travellers' tales of collapsing temples thanks to neglect by the 'infidel Turk' were all too true and his ambitions grew to the point where he attempted to remove what he could (he was not the only individual doing this: almost all the most important sculpture and artifacts discovered in Greece prior to the 20 C. are now in West European museums as a result). Elgin secured a written firman directing the

Ottoman authorities who had been ruling Athens for 350 years to allow his agents to remove 'inscriptions and sculptures' from the derelict Acropolis buildings. He only narrowly beat his French counterpart to the marbles, and indeed other Parthenon sculptures are now in the Louvre and Vatican museums. The Greeks have never accepted the legitimacy of Turkish rule, and perceive these agreements as being akin to one thief passing on stolen goods to another.

Given the uniqueness of the Parthenon and its universal recognition as *the* symbol of Greece, a very strong case can be made for the return of the marbles (it is difficult to view them in London and not feel considerable qualms on this score). However, Elgin-bashers hardly help their cause by failing to acknowledge that his motives were hardly on a par with a looter's (though some of his damaging removal techniques were), or that plaster casts made by his workmen of sculptures he didn't remove show that they deteriorated significantly before their importance was recognized. In this respect, Elgin's claim that he was 'saving' the marbles was borne out by events (though the 1998 revelation that many of the marbles had been 'skinned' by overzealous cleaning by poorly supervised British Museum staff in the 1930s has somewhat eroded this).

The impact the sculptures had in London is also not readily acknowledged (beyond the fact that they bankrupted Elgin — he spent £74,240 recovering them). Widely admired (the poet Keats gazed at them for hours at a time like a 'sick eagle looking at the sky'), they have been very influential, occasionally in quite bizarre ways. Most important was their contribution to the pro-Greek romanticism sweeping Europe that led to the Great Powers' supporting Greek nationalism and the foundation of the Greek state. At the other end of the scale, London dandies made fools of themselves adopting a posture (known as the 'Grecian bend') supposedly based on the figures. However, the most delightful fall-out from Elgin's acquisitions came with the horse's head removed from the north corner of the Parthenon's east pediment. Used as the model for the standard chess-set knight, it has surely acquired an unassailable status as the most copied piece of sculpture in history.

The Agora

(See map facing p. 96.) Within easy walking distance of the Acropolis lie a number of important archaeological sites. The most important of these is the **Agora**, the ancient marketplace, to the north-west (℗ 08.00–18.30; tickets €4, free entry with Acropolis ticket). An open square during Classical times, bounded by all the major administrative buildings in the city, it was in-filled with buildings in the Hellenistic and Roman periods. Add to this 3,000 years of continuous occupation and the result is the confused jumble of foundations that one sees today. The Roman travel writer Pausanias described all the major buildings, so most of those unearthed have been identified. Problems, however, do remain. The north side of the Agora still lies under the modern city (the buildings here are dilapidated, with the sword of demolition hanging over them), hindering a comprehensive assessment of the site's history. Moreover, two important buildings — the **Theseion**, the major shrine of the city's founder, and the **Stoa of Herms** — are known to have been in the vicinity of the Agora, but remain undiscovered.

The area so far exposed has been excavated since the 1930s when the Turkish buildings covering the Agora were demolished. The metro line cutting off the northern third of the site is a legacy of the last century (1891) when its importance was unrecognized. Today the Agora is heavily planted with trees, offering a shady retreat from the hot city streets.

The North and East Sides

There are two entrances to the Agora; one on the Acropolis side, and the main entrance, sited on a bridge over the metro line. The street leading to the latter (Adrianou) offers you a glimpse of several inaccessible buildings. Most notable of these is the corner of **Ⓐ**, the **Painted Stoa** or **Stoa Poikile** (c. 460 BC), currently being excavated by students from the American School of Archaeology. Once the most famous secular building in Athens, it was a natural meeting-place for the city intelligentsia. Its reputation was based on the paintings that adorned its walls (it was the Louvre of the ancient city) and the bronze shields hung about it (captured from the Spartans at the battle of Sphakteria in 425

BC — one is now in the museum). As a result of the chattering crowds that gathered here, it became the only building to give its name to a school of philosophy, as those that followed the philosopher Zeno regularly met in the building and thus became known as 'Stoics'.

Turning to the other side of the road, you can look down on the foundations of the small, winged **Royal Stoa** (c. 500 BC) at **Ⓑ**, where the city magistrates took their oath of office. Hereafter, the road runs to the railway bridge. From the ticket kiosk on the bridge, the main path descends onto **Ⓒ** the **Panathenaic Way**. Running south-east to the Acropolis, this was the most important road in the city. It was the ceremonial route for the annual procession depicted on the Parthenon frieze. Nowadays, it runs to the south end of **Ⓓ** the **Stoa of Attalos**. Rebuilt between 1953–56 by the American excavators, it is now the **Agora Museum**. The original was a gift from the king of Pergamum c. 145 BC. It replaced an earlier row of shops and is a typical example of this type of building, with two storeys and 21 square rooms at the back that functioned as shops. A pillar with a statue of Attalos in a chariot stood in front of the stoa, with **Ⓔ** a **Bema** (a speaker's platform) directly in front of that. Nearby are the circular remains of **Ⓕ** a Roman **Fountain**. To the north stood the classical law courts, but the surviving foundations (straddled by the railway line) are of a later **Hadrianic Basilica** (**Ⓖ**) with an **Augustan Colonnade** (**Ⓗ**) running west from it.

The Central Area

The centre of the Agora was an open square during the Classical period. Now it is dominated by **Ⓘ**, the **Odeon of Agrippa**, c. 15 BC. Rebuilt several times (largely on account of the massive vaulted roof that collapsed now and again) it was later rebuilt as a vast gymnasium c. 400 AD. The most prominent feature today are the three colossal statues of tritons and giants that formed part of the entrance of the original building. The triton heads are of particular significance, as ancient sources say that they were modelled on the (now lost) pedimental sculpture of Poseidon on the Parthenon.

Just to the north of the Odeon lie the scanty remains of **Ⓙ** the **Altar of Ares** (c. 420 BC). It was here that dogs were sacrificed in honour of the god. To the west was **Ⓚ** the **Temple of Ares**, (c. 435 BC). Now no more than a low mound, it was originally very similar in design to the Hephaisteion on the hill to the west (it is thought to possibly be the work of the same architect). The building wasn't originally located here: all the surviving stones are numbered (indicating it was moved from a different site); the foundations are Roman, and some of the guttering seems to have come from the Temple of Poseidon at Sounion. The original site of the temple isn't known (suggestions range from the Roman Agora to Acharnai, outside the city), but this sort of movement wasn't uncommon in the Roman period, when many outlying shrines were abandoned because of urbanization.

North of the Temple of Ares, and now tucked against the metro line wall, lies a corner of the boundary wall that surrounded the small **❶ Altar of the Twelve Gods** (6 c. BC). Now all but lost under the track, this was one of the most important monuments in Athens. The altar was not only venerated as a place of sanctuary (particularly for the destitute) but also served as the *Omphalos* or navel of the city and the province of Attica. As such, it was the official starting point from which all distances were measured.

The West Side

Travelling west, the path then emerges at **❿**, the **Stoa of Zeus Eleutherios**, c. 430 BC, which was an early (and therefore small) stoa with projecting wings. Ornately decorated, it was the base for the official in charge of religious ceremonies and trials for murder or impiety. It is better known in literature as the favourite stoa of the philosopher Socrates. It was in this building that he was wont to argue with his fellows, taking the line that he knew nothing and then proceeding to demonstrate that those who claimed to know something 'didn't know nuffin' either. Showing up large numbers of people who thought that they were intelligent didn't exactly endear Socrates to those in power, and he was tried and executed on trumped-up sacrilege charges in 399 BC.

South of the stoa of Zeus lie the foundations of **⓫** the **Temple of Apollo Patroös** (4 c. BC). One of the oldest temples in Athens, it was destroyed and rebuilt several times. The colossal statue of Apollo (now in the Agora museum) once stood in it. On the other side of the path, and to the south, stands a replica of the torso of a **Statue of Hadrian** (**⓪**), notable for the breast-plate adorned with the delightful mix of Athena (accompanied by a snake and

owl) standing on the back of a wolf suckling Romulus and Remus.

Behind the buildings on the west side of the Agora and overlooking all is **❼** the **Hephaisteion** (449–444 BC). The best-preserved temple in Greece, it is the only temple to retain its roof substructure substantially intact (the inner cella now has a medieval roof over it). Built just before the Parthenon (but not with money raised by the islands for the Delian League: this temple hadn't a predecessor to be destroyed by the Persians), for many years it was thought to be another important temple — the Theseion (hence the metro station of that name nearby) — but this notion has now been discredited. Inside it still contains the bronze cult statues of Hephaistos and Athena. Around it are trees planted in their classical positions; the original pots were unearthed when the site was excavated. This excavation also revealed that to the north of the Hephaisteion stood **❽** the **Arsenal** of ancient Athens, now known only through post holes.

The steps leading up to the Hephaisteion also marked the boundary between the religious and secular buildings on this side of the Agora. To the south stood **❾**, the **Metroön** (430 BC); theoretically a temple dedicated to the mother of the gods, it became the repository for the government archives. It was built on the original site of **❺**, the **Bouleuterion** (5 c. BC). This was the council chamber for the city senate house, and was rebuilt a number of times during its working life, gradually increasing in size, and each time further back from the main line of buildings. This allowed the Metroön to be expanded south to **❼** the circular **Tholos** (c. 470 BC). One of the most important buildings in Athens (being the headquarters for those charged with the running of the city) it was manned 24 hours a day (and had its own kitchen). It is a controversial structure, with widely differing reconstructions being put forward (in part this is because it was rebuilt several times). In its last incarnation, it had a conical roof with diamond-shaped tiles. Opposite this collection of buildings was **⓪**, the long narrow monument of the **Eponymous Heroes**. Adorned with the statues of the founders of the political tribes of Athens, it was used to display public notices.

The South Side

The southern boundary of the Agora was dominated by a series of stoas that gradually encroached north to the point where they added to the in-filling of the Classical Agora square. Temples were also added at this later stage. They included the small **South-West Temple** at ⓥ, with an altar (of Zeus Agoraios) 30 m to the north, and a small stoa-like building to the south (used by the Athenian civil service). Behind these lie the small foundations of ⓦ the **Middle Stoa** (2 C. BC). The largest stoa to be built in Athens, it took the form of a double-aisled hall open on both sides. It was later incorporated into the 4 C. AD gymnasium along with the nearby Odeon. Abutting it to the west was ⓧ: a block of **Small Buildings** that included a cobbler's shop and a latrine, and ⓨ the **Stratagion**.

Only tentatively identified, the Stratagion was probably the Pentagon of ancient Athens, and used as both the military headquarters and home of the supreme commander. Conveniently located near the city prison, its incumbents tended to move from one to the other with alarming regularity — particularly during the Peloponnesian war when the 30-year stalemate between Athens and Sparta led to a succession of commanders being executed for failing to win the war. The Classical **Prison** (❷), just outside the Agora, was where Socrates was executed (a clay miniature of the philosopher was found on site).

South of the Middle Stoa lie the foundations of the Classical south Agora buildings. These include ❻ the **Heliaia** (C. 470 BC), the original city courthouse, and ❹ the **South Stoa I** (5 C. BC). Now overlain by ❺ the **South Stoa II** (2 C. BC), the former is of greater interest as the surviving fragment contains the foundations of the small dining rooms (the walls being no more than a dining couch and a doorway wide) that stood at the back of this stoa.

Beyond this the remains are largely Roman, consisting of: ❹ the **South-East Fountain House** (C. 470 BC); now partly overlain by a Byzantine church. The back walls also survive from ❶ the **Athens Mint** (C. 400 BC) where the famous owl coins were struck. To the east lies ❸ the **South-East Temple** (1 C. BC). This was another Roman import, the materials being taken from a Classical temple of Aphrodite at Sounion.

The other side of the Panathenaic way was also embellished in the Roman period with ❿ the **Library of Pantainos** (102 AD) and ⓘ the **South-East Stoa** (1 C. AD): yet another shopping mall on the path to the later **Wall of Valerian**, which was constructed out of the remains of Agora buildings following the Herulian sack of the city in 269 AD.

The Roman Agora

Sandwiched between 18 C. mansions in the Plaka district are the remains of several important ancient structures: notably the **Roman Agora**, the adjacent **Library of Hadrian** and the Hellenistic **Tower of the Winds** (ⓞ 08.00–18.30; tickets €2, free entry with Acropolis ticket). Unfortunately, an unsympathetic medieval street plan makes interpretation of the remains difficult, running as it does across the lines of the ancient ground plan.

The **Library of Hadrian** (2 C. AD) is usually the first building encountered thanks to the nearby Monastiraki metro station. Sadly, the library is still undergoing excavation and tourists have to make do with peering through the iron railings of the fence surrounding the site. The most prominent feature of the extant remains is the north side of the front façade. This was abnormally high, to counter the fact that the library is lower down the Acropolis slope than the adjacent market: the library was therefore made to appear the same height. The façade consists of seven columns, each of which would have been surmounted with a statue. The main peristyle court behind was, according to the Roman-era travel writer Pausanias, graced with a 'hundred splendid columns' — none of which have survived. The quad had an ornamental pool in the centre (later replaced with a 6 C. basilica, several columns from which still stand) with lecture rooms down the sides. Books took up a relatively small part of the library's space and were housed in a scroll room at the back of the building; by lucky chance, the surviving wall has the storage niches extant.

The **Roman Agora** (1 C. BC) is known to stand on the site of the Classical commercial market, but of earlier structures there is no trace. In the Roman period, it was linked to the Classical Agora via a couple of stoas running east behind the Stoa of Attalos. The surviving remains are equally diverse as those of the library; in this case consisting of a reasonable number of columns arranged as picturesquely as possible around the two surviving sides of the peristyle court. Behind them lie the foundations of a number of stoa-style shops. The gateways have survived; the main entrance is reduced to an arch standing in glorious isolation (now fenced off; access to the site is from the rear). The rear gate only exists as a series of square columns bounded by a drain on the outer side.

As you enter the Roman Agora site you are confronted by two contrasting structures. On your right are the remains of a 1 C. AD **Roman Latrine**; built to seat the masses in comfort, it offered a secluded spot to sit and chat while getting on with the business of the day. To the east stands the wonderfully preserved 2 C. BC **Tower of the Winds**. A remarkable building, cute and approachable in size, it has survived against all the odds in various guises (not least as a dervish clubhouse during the years of Turkish rule).

A marble octagon, the tower was a water-clock, sundial, and weather-vane combined, and possibly also the city planetarium. On the north-west and north-east sides were porticoed doors, while up the south side climb the remains of the clock mechanism in the form of a semicircular turret. Quite how this worked is still not really understood. Given that the ancients measured time by dividing the daylight hours into 12 (so an 'hour' was never the same length on any consecutive day) it, presumably, caused its designers a headache and a half too. The 8 cardinal winds are aligned to their respective points of the compass. Favourable winds are shown as youths; hostile winds as bearded, older figures. Each holds an appropriate object. Most are self-explanatory, with the exception of Lips (responsible for blowing an enemy fleet ashore: hence the ship's stern), and Skiron (the charcoal cauldron symbolized drought). The Roman writer Vitruvius records that the tower was topped with a bronze Triton weather-vane, holding a wand which pointed to the prevailing wind.

National Archaeological Museum

One of the great cultural treasure houses of the world, this is one attraction that should figure prominently on the itinerary of every visitor to Athens. The museum was closed for a major pre-2004 Olympics refurbishment throughout 2003. At the time of this book's going to press it is unclear if the exhibits have been reorganized as part of the renewal programme. The description here covers the pre-refurbishment layout: if there are changes, then details will be posted up on this book's website (see opposite).

Check out the Athens **Museum** updates at **greekislandhopping.com**

Among the principal exhibits are the **Minoan Frescoes** from the excavations on Santorini, the **Mask of Agamemnon** and other gold work uncovered by Schliemann at Mycenae, and **Sculpture** from all the important sites in Greece. Supposedly open ① 12.30–19.00, ②–⑤ 08.00–19.00, ⑥, ⑦ 08.30–15.00 (tickets €6), times do vary a bit, depending on the numbers of attendants who turn up (no room is left without a guard). Some rooms (usually the less important ones) are occasionally closed off for an hour or two if they can't be manned. If you really want to get the most out of a visit you should consider buying a copy of the detailed museum guide (these are on sale in Room 3, which contains the ticket kiosk, sales desk and cloakroom, where bags and cameras must be deposited).

Room 4 is the first visitors enter, and one of the most dramatic in the museum. Known as the **Mycenaean Hall**, it contains the magnificent **Mask of Agamemnon** among its impressive gold collection culled from the graves at the palace of Mycenae in the Peloponnese.

Room 5 contains Neolithic and Pre-Mycenaean artifacts, though island hoppers will find **Room 6** of more interest — known as the **Cycladic Room** as all the exhibits have been recovered from the Cyclades. The haul adds up to a pretty disparate collection. At the main entrance end are the early Cycladic figures — including the largest figurine yet discovered (see p. 269) and the better known **Harpist** (see p. 284) and **Flautist** (illustrated opposite). At the other end of the gallery you will find the **Flying-Fish Fresco** fragments recovered from Milos — though the described 'blue cloth' on the display label is now thought to be a net.

Rooms 7–8 and **11–12** are devoted to **Archaic Sculpture** (**Rooms 9–10** being devoted to smaller works). Room 9 has a number of pieces from Delos and a very Egyptianesque-looking kouros from Milos. **Room 13** contains more such figures, including the **Aristodikos** figure that gives the room its name. Used to mark graves, it is logical to find next door, in **Room 14**, a collection of **Early Classical Gravestones**.

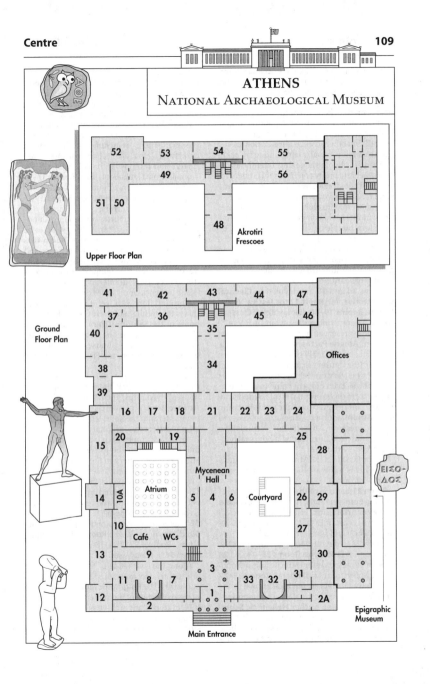

ATHENS
NATIONAL ARCHAEOLOGICAL MUSEUM

Upper Floor Plan

52 53 54 55
49 56
51 50 48 Akrotiri Frescoes

Ground Floor Plan

41 42 43 44 47
37 36 45 46
40 35
38 34 Offices
39
16 17 18 21 22 23 24
20 19 25
15 28
Mycenean Hall
14 10A Atrium
5 4 6 Courtyard 26 29
10 27
Café WCs
13 9 30
11 8 7 33 32 31
12 2A
2 3 1

EIΣO-ΔOΣ

Main Entrance

Epigraphic Museum

Room 15 is known as the **Poseidon Room**, thanks to the large bronze of the God that dominates it. Some believe the figure to be the god Zeus, but without knowing what he held in his right hand (it could have been either a trident or a thunderbolt depending on the god), we will never be sure. The figure lacks its eyeballs but otherwise has all its attributes. For this reason it is usually surrounded by packs of French schoolgirls gazing intently at the god's tackle (a pretty convincing argument for the pro-Poseidon lobby). This is one of many similar hazards you will encounter if you visit this museum with children; for not only does the National Archaeological Museum not have the Elgin marbles, it doesn't have a 'willie' or 'pecker box' either (all the statues in the British Museum were defaced by a Victorian curator worried about visiting young ladies' morals; the results are now hidden away in a large cardboard box).

Rooms 16 and **18** are devoted to **Classical Gravestones**, and **Room 17** to **Classical Votive Reliefs**. **Rooms 19–20** display **Small Classical Works**. The most interesting exhibit in Room 20 is the best-preserved miniature of the famous figure of **Athena Parthenos** that stood inside the Parthenon. Hardly of great artistic merit in itself (the figure is leaning to one side and the detail is very crudely reproduced), it has nonetheless been of great value in determining the form of the original statue. A doorway from Room 20 leads to a staircase descending to the **Atrium**, adorned with marbles recovered from a wreck off Antikithera — especially a young athlete, half-corroded by the sea, half-preserved by the mud.

On the far side of the Atrium is the museum's café. This is to be avoided if you don't care for rip-off prices.

Room 21 has one of the most impressive of the museum's exhibits, the bronze **Horse and Jockey of Artemision**. Fished out of the sea off the north coast of Evia, it captures the movement of boy and horse wonderfully.

Room 22 is devoted to sculpture from the sanctuary at **Epidavros**. **Rooms 23–24** and **28** contain 4 C. BC gravestones (including, in Room 28, the Youth from Antikithera); **Rooms 25–27** hold Votive Reliefs. **Room 29** is known as the Themis Room thanks to a statue of the goddess. **Room 30** contains further **Hellenistic Sculpture**, including the large **Poseidon of Milos** and an ugly cloaked child, known as the 'little refugee', recovered from Turkey. More fun is

a Delian statue of Aphrodite, poised in the act of spanking a cupid with a slipper. **Rooms 31–33** contain yet more Hellenistic Sculpture, and **Room 34** remnants of an Altar, and reliefs and sculptures from other sanctuaries.

Room 36 is the first housing the museum's impressive collection of bronzes. Devoted to the smaller items, it includes a well-endowed dwarf and a grizzly collection of dismembered fingers and thumbs, and a collection of tiny animals (from Deukalion's ark?). **Rooms 37–39** contain a mix of bronze figures, including some early figurines from the Acropolis, and a collection of bronze mirrors.

What you will find in the remaining ground-floor rooms is less certain as they seem to be in a state of constant 'renovation'. **Room 40** is supposed to house the Stathatos Collection and Gold Objects; **Room 41**, Clay Figurines. **Rooms 42–47** are used for **Temporary Exhibitions** (these vary from summer to summer).

The upper floor occupies only a fraction of the ground floor area, yet it includes a room that is the highlight of the museum; **Room 48**, home of the **Santorini/Thira Frescoes** (see p. 176), it has the more the famous ones lining the walls of mock-up houses. These include the **Boxing Children**, the **Fisherboys** and the Antelope frescoes.

The outer section of this room also has a number of artifacts discovered within the houses at Akrotiri, including a bed reconstructed from a plaster cast, made by pouring plaster into the holes left in the ash by the long-disintegrated original.

The other upper-floor rooms are of less interest. Home to the greatest collection of ancient Greek pottery in the world, the sheer number of artifacts makes it very difficult to give the individual pieces their just attention. The collection is divided by date and style between the various rooms: **Room 49–50**: Geometric Vases; **Room 51:** Vari Vases; **Room 52**: Heraeum of Argos and Sophilos; **Room 53**: Black-figure Vases; **Room 54**: Red-figure Vases; **Room 55**: White Background Vases, **Room 56**: 4 C. BC Vases.

Along the south side of the main building are two related museums. Nearest the main entrance is the **Epigraphic Museum**. Home to a large collection of monumental inscriptions, it is an important archive of ancient literary material. Unfortunately, unreadable letters on stones don't have much mass appeal, so this museum is always quiet.

Other Athenian Sites

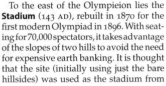

In addition to the 'big four', there are plenty of other sites worth investigating. The first port of call for Greek island fans should be the **Museum of Cycladic & Ancient Greek Art**, as its exhibits include a large collection of Cycladic idols (some showing evidence of having once had painted features).

Among the other sites east of the Acropolis is the small circular **Monument of Lysicrates** (335 BC). Three metres in diameter, it was erected to display the bronze tripod won at the Dionysia festival of that year by Lysicrates. A glorified pot-stand, it is a rare survival, and the Corinthian columns that adorn it are the oldest examples in Athens. The skimpy **Arch of Hadrian** (2 C. AD) stands nearby. Built to mark off the old city from Hadrian's Roman additions, it is adorned with inscriptions. On the Acropolis side: 'This is Athens, ancient city of Theseus'; on the reverse: 'The city of Hadrian and not of Theseus'. Built of Pentelic marble, it provides a gateway to the largest temple built in Greece.

The massive **Olympieion** (515 BC–132 AD) — the Temple of Olympian Zeus — took just under 650 years to build. Replacing an earlier temple built near the site of the plughole that Zeus opened in the earth to abate Deukalion's (the Greek Noah) flood, it was started by the tyrant Pisistratus in 515 BC but abandoned after his overthrow. It was left incomplete until work resumed in 174 BC, when Antiochos IV of Syria commissioned the Roman architect Cossutius to begin work on a modified design (the columns now on the site date from this revised building). Unfortunately Antiochos died before the building was finished, and the temple added to its record as the longest building-site in history. It even saw some of its columns removed to Rome by the general Sulla. Hadrian completed the building, adding a gold and ivory statue of himself and Zeus for good measure. Of the original 104 columns, 15 remain standing. The fallen 16th collapsed during a storm in 1852, and a 17th was demolished in 1760 by order of the Turkish governor and burnt to make lime for the construction of a mosque. It is thought that the other 4 of the 21 columns recorded standing in 1450 suffered a similar fate. The Olympieion is open ⊕ 08.00–18.30; tickets €2, free entry with Acropolis ticket).

To the east of the Olympieion lies the **Stadium** (143 AD), rebuilt in 1870 for the first modern Olympiad in 1896. With seating for 70,000 spectators, it takes advantage of the slopes of two hills to avoid the need for expensive earth banking. It is thought that the site (initially using just the bare hillsides) was used as the stadium from the 4 C. BC.

The **Hills of Athens** played a very important part in city life. Apart from the Acropolis there are two lesser hills of note. The nearby **Areopagus** was the hill of justice. Here the supreme court of the city had its home. In addition, it was reputedly used by the Amazon women, the Persians, and St. Paul during their attacks on Athens. Today, very slippery steps take you up to a good view over the Agora. A better viewing point is the **Mouseion** (alias Filopapou Hill). The spot on which the cannon that blew up the Parthenon stood (this is where the best postcard shots are taken as well), it does not have a rodent problem as its name implies. In fact, 'the hill of the Muses' (for this is what Mouseion means) was quite a mystical spot. Today, it is home to the ugly funerary **Monument of Philopappos** (114 AD), and some foundations of the **City Wall**. These run down past another hilltop viewing-point to the oddly named **Pnyx**. This was an artificial platform, built out of the side of the hill, where the Athenian democracy held its citizens' meetings. Today it plays host to *son-et-lumière* shows. The final hill of note lies at **Likavittos**. Blessed with good views of the Acropolis, it is accessed by cable car (€5).

The final major archeological site, **Kerameikos** (the name means 'potter's district'), the cemetery of Ancient Athens, is now a replica tomb-filled park, complete with bubbling brook filled with turtles and frogs (⊕ 08.00–18.30; tickets €2, free entry with Acropolis ticket). Little visited — in part because of its location — it also has the remains of two of the city gates (the **Sacred Gate** and the **Dipylon**) and the **Pompeion**, the building from where the great Panathenaic processions to the Acropolis started.

Outside Athens is one major site within easy reach. Few regret taking the 2-hour bus ride to **Sounion**, the cape on the southern tip of Attica that is home to the photogenic **Temple of Poseidon**. Built in 444–440 BC, it functioned as a landmark, guiding sailors towards Athens (it lies about 90 minutes' sailing from Piraeus).

Olympic Games: 13–29 August

Paralympic Games: 17–28 September

The Games

The Olympic games began over 2,700 years ago in 776 BC. Athletes from — often warring — city states would meet every four years at the neutral sanctuary at Olympia (some 7 hours away by bus on the eastern side of the Peloponnese). These days things are rather different, with the modern games only appearing in Greece once a century. Athens plays host in 2004: an event that will ensure that more tourists than ever will go island hopping, and that island hopping during the games becomes more difficult.

Location

The Olympics now serves some 28 sports or disciplines. The event is so large that the various competitions will be taking place at some 37 venues on 17 sites in or around **Athens**. In addition some events are taking place outside the host city.

The ones of most relevance to island hoppers are the soccer games. These are being played in the ferry port cities of **Thessalonika**, **Volos**, **Patras** and **Crete (Iraklion)**. Fortunately the amount of disruption is likely to be minimal, but there could be an unwelcome short term increase in demand for hotel accommodation.

Going or staying away?

During the games visitors to Greece are going to be divided between those heading for Athens and the rest — including many island hoppers — who are trying to avoid the city at all costs. This section of the book has advice for both groups.

1. Island hoppers going to the Games

If you are reading this book and have yet to obtain tickets then you are likely to find that it is already too late to get them (by buying directly) for the more popular events. The second important point that can't be emphasised enough is that if you haven't pre-booked your accommodation, it will be highly unlikely that you will be able to find a bed in Athens this August.

Ticket Availability

With so many sports and venues the Athens Olympics should have plenty of ticket capacity. The total number being issued is a staggering 5.3 million. The problem is that many have already been either reserved or long since sold: 2.3 million have been put aside for contractual partners of the game's sponsors, leaving 3 million for the general public. By August 2003 options on a third of these had been taken up, with high demand being reported for even the less popular sports. Local interest is highest for events with strong Greek participation: this effectively means you can forget athletics, basketball, volleyball and weightlifting as these tickets will be too hot for you to see one.

Many of the Olympic events are block booked long in advance by travel agents world wide who put together packages that include hotel accommodation. If you want to get into any of the major events then this — admittedly very expensive — route is the best way of doing so.

If you are going solo and just turning up on the day, then your options are likely to be much more limited. There should be some tickets on sale in Athens during the games, but it is difficult to say for what events. There are two **telephone hot lines** which will be offering information on ticket availability:

1. Within Greece: ☎ 80011 20042

2. Outside Greece & mobile phone users in Greece: ☎ 0030 21037 30000

Tickets started going on sale to the general public on the 12th of May 2003. Many are being sold via **web site ticket sales** pages. It also is the main avenue for selling tickets — this makes it easy to establish which events have sold out and which still have available seats (these are most likely to be obscure martial arts and marbles). The ticket selling web pages are:

1.⊕ www.athens2004.com/tickets

2.⊕ www.tickets.athens2004.com/en/

Your ability to purchase tickets using these pages varies depending on your country of residence. If you live in the EU or belong to a European Economic Area (EEA) country then you can buy online. Other nationalities are pushed in the direction of their own national Olympic committees (which are issuing tickets independently anyway). The British Olympic Committee is doing so via Sportsworld Group Plc.:

⊕ www.sportsworldathens2004.com

The US Olympic Committee is using Cartan Tours:

⊕ www.cartan.com

Ticket Prices
There are various packages on offer. At the top end are Premium Ticket Packages geared to good seats at popular events, usually with accommodation attached. Prices here can go as high as €3,000. Tickets for lesser events on sale during the games should be much cheaper. The quoted average figure is €35.

Free Street Events
If you can't get tickets to any of the indoor or stadium events then it is still possible to enjoy the street competitions. The most obvious of these is the **Marathon** (Women: Aug. 22, Men: Aug. 29). This will run along the original course first paced in 490 BC by the herald Phidippides. He ran the 26 miles to Athens to announce the defeat of the Persians at the battle of Marathon.

The second, and probably more rewarding, street event is the **Cycling Road Race** (Men: Aug. 14, Women: Aug. 15). This is taking place in Central Athens and should offer plenty to see. The route runs from Syntagma Square down to the Olympieion, around the southern side of the Acropolis, up to Kerameikos, turns east along Ermou St., north

up Athinas St. to Omonia and Egyptou Square. It then turns east along Alexandras, south-west along Ipokratous, then south-east along Academias, then around Likavittos Hill and back to Syntagma via Vassilissis Sofias St.

City Venues
Events are taking place all over Athens (if you want to find location details for specific sports visit the Olympics site at ⊕ www.athens2004.com). Inevitably most of the media attention will focus on the large prestige sites. The most obvious of these is the **OCO Main Olympic Complex** in the northern part of the city. It is home to the **Olympic Stadium**. Built some 20 years ago, the stadium seats 75,000 and is acquiring a futuristic roof glass roof. Other facilities on this site include a renovated cycling velodrome.

A second extensively refurbished arena is the **Faliro Coastal Olympic Complex**, lying just outside Piraeus. Adorned with the delightfully curvy **Peace and Friendship Stadium** (illustrated on p. 114), it is hosting the volleyball and taekwondo. Nearby is the largest of the new purpose-built facilities: the **Helliniko Olympic Complex**. Built on the site of the old Athens airport (there are still a few planes in one corner, now stranded without a runway), it is hosting odd-ball events from canoeing to fencing, along with basketball and handball. There are also new purpose built baseball and softball stadiums here.

The closer you are to the city centre the less there is going on. The most central of the new facilities is the **Goudi Olympic Complex** which is hosting the pentathlon and badminton. The only venue in the city centre is the ancient **Panathinaiko Stadium**. Rebuilt in 1896 for the first modern Olympic Games, its use is limited by its narrow horse-shoe shape, which isn't compatible with modern track and field

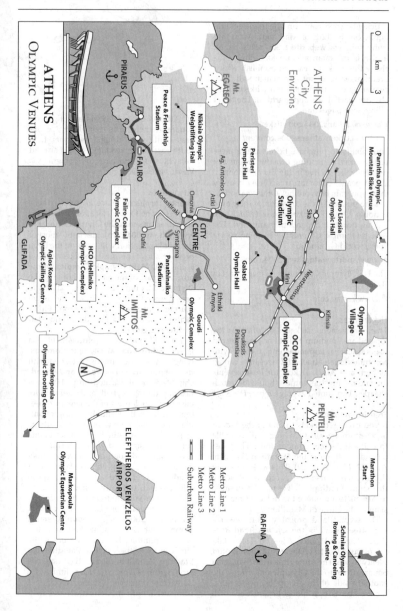

ATHENS
OLYMPIC VENUES

ATHENS
City
Environs

PIRAEUS

Peace & Friendship Stadium

Nikiaia Olympic Weightlifting Hall

Mt. EGALEO

FALIRO

Faliro Coastal Olympic Complex

HCO (Helliniko) Olympic Complex

Agios Kosmas Olympic Sailing Centre

GLIFADA

Markopoula Olympic Shooting Centre

Monastiraki

Dafni

Ag. Antonios

Attiki

Omonia

Syntagma

CITY CENTRE

Ethniki Amyna

Panathinaiko Stadium

Mt. IMITTOS

Peristeri Olympic Hall

Olympic Stadium

Galatsi Olympic Hall

Goudi Olympic Complex

Doukissis Plakentias

Ska

Nerantziotissa

Irini

Kifissia

OCO Main Olympic Complex

Mt. PENTELI

Olympic Village

Parnitha Olympic Mountain Bike Venue

Ano Liossia Olympic Hall

Marathon Start

ELEFTHERIOS VENIZELOS AIRPORT

Markopoula Olympic Equestrian Centre

N

Metro Line 1
Metro Line 2
Metro Line 3
Suburban Railway

RAFINA

Schinias Olympic Rowing & Canoeing Centre

0   km   3

events. The stadium is having to make do with hosting the finish of the marathon and the archery events.

Of the out of town facilities, the most notable is the controversial **Schinias Olympic Rowing and Canoeing Centre**. Built against a background of angry protests over environmentally sensitive marsh land, its approach roads have also damaged the site of the famous battle of Marathon. The artificial lakes failed badly during a test in August 2003 — a competition had to be abandoned due to the high *meltemi* winds which sank competing boats, so this could be one of the more interesting competitions in 2004!

Accommodation

Almost all hotels are fully booked for the Olympics period, and have been for a year or more. If you are reading this, then it is already too late to book up an A to C class hotel room during the last two weeks in August. Even the first two weeks are likely to prove problematic as news teams and journalists move into the city. There are also a number of related events in the run-up to the Olympics that will add to the accommodation pressure — notably the World Rowing Junior Championships between 6th and 9th of August and an International Archery tournament between the 9th and the 15th.

Room prices will also rise significantly in Athens during the Olympics. Typical rates are predicted to be at least 20% higher than normal at this time of the year. For info on hotel room availability (if any):

1. The Greek National Tourism Organization (EOT), 7 Tsoxa, 10564
(☎ 171; ⊕ www.gnto.gr).

2. The Hellenic Chamber of Hotels,
24 Stadiou, 105 64 (☎ 210 3310022; ⊕ http://users.otenet.gr/-grhotels).

The city authorities are trying to solve the accommodation shortfall by taking a number of measures. These include:

• **Booking Rooms on Nearby Islands** and offering day trips into the city.

• **7 Cruise Ships** have been chartered to provide extra beds. Moored at Piraeus for the duration of the games, their 7,000-odd cabins have already been sold to travel agents. The Hellenic Association of Travel and Tourism Agencies (HATTA) has info on all Greece's licensed tour operators (☎ 210 9234143; ⊕ www.hatta.gr).

• **Private Homes** are also being exploited: many Athenians leave the city for cooler parts during August and a rental scheme is being organised. The organisers hope to have over 2,000 apartments on their books come the event. Contact official housing agents at:

1. Elliniki Philoxenia
3 Artemidos, Maroussi 151 25 (☎ 210 684 9222; e-mail: gcourmouzis@mondial.gr).

2. Alpha Philoxenia 2004
43 Panepistimiou, 105 64 (☎ 210 3277400; e-mail: cpallis@alphaastikaakinita.gr).

Finally, accommodation pressure for the **Paralympics** in September shouldn't be nearly as great as the event is much smaller, and there a far fewer tourists around anyway. Athens should see a return to the 'turn up and walk straight into a room' norm.

2. Island hoppers avoiding the Games

It should be perfectly possible to island hop while the Olympics are taking place, provided of course, you avoid Athens. Even the popular ploy of flying to the capital and then heading straight for Piraeus could be risky this August. Instead:

1. Fly to an island airport (Crete, Rhodes, Kos, Santorini and Samos are all good starting points).

2. Avoid islands near Athens that will be used as day trip accommodation centres (Aegina, Paros and Mykonos are obvious candidates).

3. Avoid night ferries going to Athens.

4. Book all ferry tickets as early as you possibly can.

At the time of this book's going to press it wasn't clear to what extent ferry services are going to be disrupted by the Olympics, so publishing advice on this subject here would be premature. However, full coverage of the ferry situation (along with suggested avoidance strategies for problem areas and services) will appear on this book's website as information comes in during 2004.

Check out the
Athens **Olympics** updates at
greekislandhopping.com

⚓ Athens: Ports

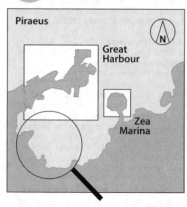

Piraeus

Great Harbour

Zea Marina

N

Piraeus
ΠΕΙΡΑΙΑΣ

CODE ☎ 210
PORT POLICE ☎ 4511 311, 4172 657
TOURIST OFFICE ☎ 4135 716

The main port of Athens for some 2,800 years, Piraeus is the hub of the modern Greek ferry system. Lying 8 km south-west of the Acropolis, it was once a city in its own right, but in the years since Greek independence it has been reduced to a suburb by the capital's urban sprawl, and a frenetic, less than pleasant place at that. In fact, it is difficult to conceive of a spot more removed from the dreamy idyllic island most tourists are in search of. This is one port of call where it pays to know in advance roughly what you are trying to do and where you are going.

Once an island itself, Piraeus is a hilly peninsula decked with anonymous, tall apartment blocks laid out in a strict grid fashion, and with harbours on each side. This is where the fun starts: for Piraeus has three harbours of note. By far the largest is the **Great Harbour**: situated on the western side, it is the departure point for all ferries,

catamarans and hydrofoils. **Zea** (otherwise known as **Zea Marina**) is the second harbour at Piraeus (500 m over the hill on the eastern side). Today it is primarily a yacht marina, but until 2002 was the departure point for Saronic Gulf hydrofoils (you will still see old maps and guides showing this). The third, **Flisvos**, is an excursion-boat port 7 km to the east of Zea: vessels departing from here are sure to be expensive and to be avoided.

The Great Harbour
Regardless of how you get to Piraeus you are likely to find yourself dumped at the north-east corner of the Great Harbour, home to the bus, metro and railway stations. The waterfront consists of a wide quay, separated by a hedge-cum-wall from the ten-lane streets behind (so clogged with traffic that in the rush hour motorbikes resort to the pavements).

Piraeus is a commercial town and this is reflected in the waterfront buildings; most of these are shipping offices or branches of banks with maritime interests. Food shops, tourist facilities and hotels are thin on the ground. For these reasons, the Great Harbour is not the ideal place to arrive at the last minute or in the small hours.

Plans are now being implemented to turn the Great Harbour into one huge passenger terminal, and all container activity has now moved elsewhere. The downside to this is that ferries can now be located much further away from the metro station, and even the improved transit facilities (in the form of free airport-style buses that run between the current terminal and the western side of the harbour — where a new passenger terminal is being constructed) don't really make up for this.

However, the focal point for most ferry travellers is still the square housing the bus station just south of the railway and metro stations (Platia Karaiskaki). In the billboard-encrusted, dilapidated block next to the Port Police building (which has a full ferry departure list posted up by the front entrance) you will find the nucleus of the **ticket agents**. Step within hailing distance of an agency door and you'll get hassle. A chorus of 'Where are you going?' rings out from the moment the agencies open at 05.00. So it helps to be both prepared (the EOT ferry information sheets are invaluable in this respect) and not over-trusting.

Likewise, you should note that although ticket agents in the islands can be very useful for changing money out of banking hours, if you use the Piraeus agencies you can be sure of being ripped off. The 'see a tourist and double the price' snack shops on the waterfront should also be treated with caution; food-hunters are better off heading for the produce stalls and supermarket that look onto the small square behind *McDonald's*.

Ferries are loosely grouped according to destination (though, irritatingly, these points are changed from time to time), and most have a regular berth — though these aren't marked. To be on the safe side you should allow yourself 45 minutes to find and board a ferry. The easiest way of doing this is to look for the funnel or hull logo, as most companies only have four or five boats. It also pays to be aware that ferries might not arrive back from their previous excursion much before their listed Piraeus departure time.

Given the limited number of access points in the wall-cum-hedge, it is advisable to walk inside this barrier when ferry hunting, for boats can be berthed anything up to 2 km around the harbour. Distant berths usually have ticket booths (complete with computer ticket-issuing facilities) somewhere nearby on the quayside.

If you do buy from one of the agents in the central ticket block (and most tourists happily do), ensure that the ferry is as direct as possible: in High Season rooms disappear fast, and arriving an hour ahead of the other

boats often makes a significant difference to what's on offer and how much you'll have to pay.

International tickets should be bought early, and ferries (when they deign to run at all) dock on the south-east side of the Great Harbour. All customs buildings are sited in this area — the poor Quay 9 shed being the most used.

⊨

Few tourists attempt to stay in Piraeus as the available accommodation is either downright horrible or inconveniently located (Piraeus isn't noted for its evening feeding or nightlife). The metro also ensures that you can still stay in Athens and catch the earliest boats.

The most obvious clutch of hotels is in the backstreets south of the metro station. They tend to be noisy, some don't take credit cards, and the occasional red light is to be seen. The best of them is arguably the *Elektra* (☎ 417 7057), just off Gouniari Street. Those who are prepared to walk will find better beds elsewhere; plush establishments shun the Great Harbour and lie on the up-market waterfront to the east of Zea Marina. These include the expensive *Kastella* (☎ 411 4735), *Cote D'Oro* (☎ 411 3744), and *Mistral* (☎ 411 7094).

Baggage Storage

If you are only in Athens for a day or so, or are taking time out while waiting for a boat, then Piraeus is arguably the best place to store baggage (**Central Athens** isn't noted for a profusion of baggage storage options, and the **Airport** houses an expensive facility that is best considered for long duration storage).

At **Piraeus** you have two storage options: the first is to use the **ticket agent** from whom you buy your ferry ticket. An increasing number of them offer free (unsecured) baggage storage facilities once you have paid up. These are usually fairly safe, but it almost goes without saying that you don't leave anything you can't afford to lose (as travel insurers aren't likely to view claims for lost baggage sympathetically if it was lost while stored in this way).

Secure luggage storage is available via a regular luggage deposit in the passenger terminal building. Costs are fixed by the number of bags and the length of time you want to store them. These are typically an expensive €4 for 5 hours.

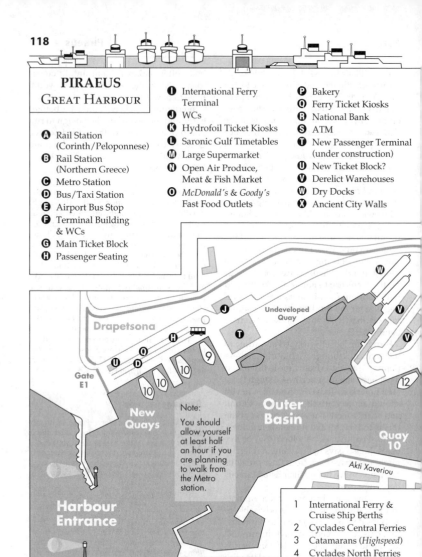

118

PIRAEUS
GREAT HARBOUR

- **A** Rail Station (Corinth/Peloponnese)
- **B** Rail Station (Northern Greece)
- **C** Metro Station
- **D** Bus/Taxi Station
- **E** Airport Bus Stop
- **F** Terminal Building & WCs
- **G** Main Ticket Block
- **H** Passenger Seating
- **I** International Ferry Terminal
- **J** WCs
- **K** Hydrofoil Ticket Kiosks
- **L** Saronic Gulf Timetables
- **M** Large Supermarket
- **N** Open Air Produce, Meat & Fish Market
- **O** *McDonald's* & *Goody's* Fast Food Outlets
- **P** Bakery
- **Q** Ferry Ticket Kiosks
- **R** National Bank
- **S** ATM
- **T** New Passenger Terminal (under construction)
- **U** New Ticket Block?
- **V** Derelict Warehouses
- **W** Dry Docks
- **X** Ancient City Walls

Drapetsona

Undeveloped Quay

Gate E1

New Quays

Note:
You should allow yourself at least half an hour if you are planning to walk from the Metro station.

Outer Basin

Quay 10

Akti Xaveriou

Harbour Entrance

Harbour Boundary

Free Harbour Bus Pick-up & Set-down Points

1 International Ferry & Cruise Ship Berths
2 Cyclades Central Ferries
3 Catamarans (*Highspeed*)
4 Cyclades North Ferries
5 Cyclades West Ferries
6 Crete Ferries (*ANEK*)
7 Crete Ferries (*Minoan*)
8 Crete Ferries (*LANE*)
9 Crete Ferries (*Blue Star*)
10 Dodecanese Ferries

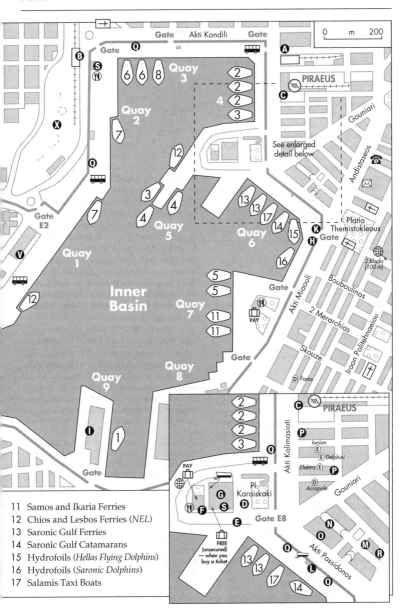

11 Samos and Ikaria Ferries
12 Chios and Lesbos Ferries (*NEL*)
13 Saronic Gulf Ferries
14 Saronic Gulf Catamarans
15 Hydrofoils (*Hellas Flying Dolphins*)
16 Hydrofoils (*Saronic Dolphins*)
17 Salamis Taxi Boats

Amidst today's grime one is apt to forget that Piraeus was once an important centre in its own right. In fact, during the 5–4 c. BC it was seen as substantially more than just the Athenian harbour-cum-naval base, becoming an embryonic sister city in all but name. Unbelievably (when one looks around today), Piraeus was also regarded as a very beautiful city — and given the proximity of Athens for comparison, the modern town has obviously lost a great deal. Part of this reputation was due to town planning; for, unlike Athens, it was entirely pre-planned. It was designed by one of the greatest of Greek city planners, Hippodamos, and boasted a grid-like street system of the kind now associated with North American cities (the streets between the Great Harbour and Zea still follow the ancient pattern). This was considered highly desirable in ancient Greece where irregular layouts based on topography were the norm.

In addition to all the regular city accoutrements (i.e. temples, public buildings and even two agoras) Piraeus was heavily fortified, with skirting walls protecting the city and harbours — you can see the fragmentary remains of one behind the quay on the west side of the Great Harbour. However, the Roman era saw a significant shift in trade routes, and with it began a period of prolonged decline — so much so, that by 1833 Piraeus had a recorded population of only 22.

Time and 19 c. building has obscured most traces of the ancient city, with few of the buildings described by Pausanias located to date. Visible remains are scanty: the best are the fragments of a Hellenistic **Odeon** west of Zea.

The remains of the famous trireme sheds (covered slipways that allowed the boats to be pulled and stored out of the water) have been found ringing Zea Harbour, but are locked away in the basements of buildings. The **Maritime Museum** (on the waterfront of Zea: open ② to ⑥ 08.30–12.30) has one on view. Archaeological finds (including several impressive bronze statues fished out of the Great Harbour) are currently housed in the **Archaeological Museum** (open ② to ⑦ 08.30–15.00). Fragments of the western wall are also visible — but not accessible — behind the quay on the west side of the Great Harbour.

Lavrio
ΛΑΥΡΙΟ; pop. 10,700.

CODE ☎ 22920
PORT POLICE ☎ 25249

To date Lavrio (or Lavrion) has been a small, commercial port famed in Classical times for its silver mines, but offering little more apart from a view of the sad island of **Makronissi** (used to detain political prisoners for much of the 20 c.) and ferry links to Kea. However, this is changing fast thanks to nearby Rafina's refusal to accept more ferry traffic. The Greek government has opted to expand Lavrio instead. It has already funded the construction of a large ferry quay, and work has begun on a new motorway link that will enable buses from the new airport at Spata to make the journey to Lavrio in around 20 minutes (local buses currently take just over 2 hours from the centre of Athens). Once all this is in place there is a distinct possibility that Lavrio will supplant Rafina as the capital's second port (ferry journey times to the Cyclades are also much shorter).

The town itself is quite attractive in a downbeat sort of way. The old centre near the harbour has a good number of red-tiled neo-classical buildings (now being rapidly converted to cafés and tavernas by locals eagerly embracing the new opportunities given to the town). All facilities are conveniently placed and centred on the wooded town square area.

Lavrio isn't geared up to cater for overnight visitors at the moment so don't build a stay into your plans. This will no doubt change as ferry activity increases, but for now the best option is the campsite at Cape Sounion (8 km).

Unlike Rafina, Lavrio offers plenty to see while you are waiting for your ferry. The town is a veritable shrine to 19 c. industrial archaeology via the old warehouses, the unique flat ore washeries, the landmark cast-iron **French Wharf**, and the museums. These include an interesting **Archaeological Museum** along with a more specialist **Mineralogical Museum** and a (19 c.) **Technological Park**.

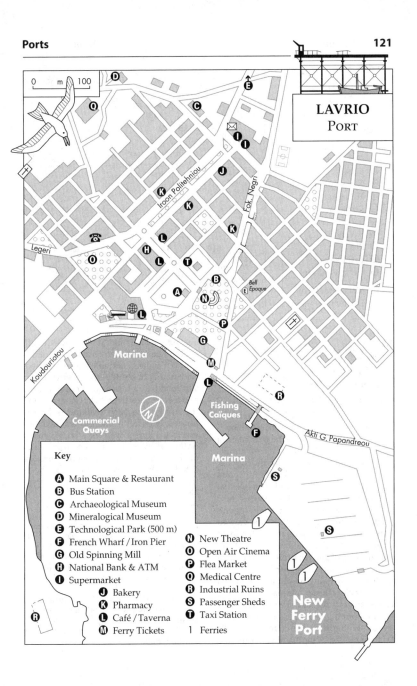

0 m 100

LAVRIO
Port

Iroon Politehniou

Fok Negri

Legeri

Koudouriotou

Marina

Bell Epoque

Commercial Quays

Fishing Caïques

Marina

Akti G. Papandreou

New Ferry Port

Key

Ⓐ Main Square & Restaurant
Ⓑ Bus Station
Ⓒ Archaeological Museum
Ⓓ Mineralogical Museum
Ⓔ Technological Park (500 m)
Ⓕ French Wharf / Iron Pier
Ⓖ Old Spinning Mill
Ⓗ National Bank & ATM
Ⓘ Supermarket
Ⓙ Bakery
Ⓚ Pharmacy
Ⓛ Café / Taverna
Ⓜ Ferry Tickets

Ⓝ New Theatre
Ⓞ Open Air Cinema
Ⓟ Flea Market
Ⓠ Medical Centre
Ⓡ Industrial Ruins
Ⓢ Passenger Sheds
Ⓣ Taxi Station

1 Ferries

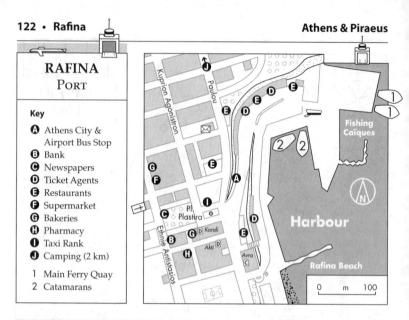

RAFINA
PORT

Key

Ⓐ Athens City &
   Airport Bus Stop
Ⓑ Bank
Ⓒ Newspapers
Ⓓ Ticket Agents
Ⓔ Restaurants
Ⓕ Supermarket
Ⓖ Bakeries
Ⓗ Pharmacy
Ⓘ Taxi Rank
Ⓙ Camping (2 km)

1 Main Ferry Quay
2 Catamarans

Rafina
ΡΑΦΗΝΑ

CODE ☎ 22940
PORT POLICE ☎ 28888

Located 27 km from the centre of Athens, Rafina (listed as 'Athens' on some island agency schedules) is a pleasant, if uninspiring, leafy suburb town on the west coast of Attica, with a reputation for fish restaurants (it is the main fishing port for the capital). The port is also the second departure point from the capital to the islands — a role that is slowly growing now that Athens' new airport (located at nearby Spata) is open.

This rise in ferry traffic is not viewed hereabouts as a blessing; in fact the town authority staged a one-day ferry strike in the summer of 2000 in protest at the prospect (hence the development of ferry facilities now going on at Lavrio). Rafina port lies below the town's main square and offers a more relaxed starting point for island hopping than Piraeus, with passengers buying tickets amid fresh fish stalls (at their busiest in the evenings). Fares are also 10% cheaper than at Piraeus, although the bus fare into Athens erodes most of this saving. Connections with Athens are good, with hourly buses departing from the port slip road (extra buses gather on the quay and meet ferries) to both the city centre and the airport. The catch to all this is that the number of ferries is smaller, and travellers can face a longer wait for a boat (usually on the scruffy, but popular, beach just south of the port). Rafina departure times are listed on separate EOT information sheets from Piraeus departures. Athenian papers also carry them.

⊨
Most tourists are in transit so there are no rooms. There are a few hotels, but to be honest none are worth considering unless you are very desperate. The *Korali* (☎ 22477) is the best of a bad lot. More pokey is the *Akti* (☎ 24776), while the large *Avra* (☎ 22781/3) is bordering on the derelict.

Λ
A well-signed beach site 2 km north of the port (though the walk seems longer). Excellent facilities, but usually empty: the Balkan war has depleted the numbers motoring from central Europe.

Salamina / Salamis

ΣΑΛΑΜΙΝΑ; 93.5 km²; pop. 23,000.

CODE ☎ 24670

Cowering behind the shipyards and rows of rusting ships anchored west of Piraeus lies the famous, but lamentably ugly, island of Salamis (known these days as Salamina). Its great claim to fame comes via the battle between the Greek and Persian trireme fleets in 480 BC which took place in the narrow straits between the north-east side of the island and the mainland. This encounter, one of the great naval battles in history, prevented the Persian conquest of Greece and in so doing altered the destiny of European civilization. Unfortunately, Salamis has been in decline from this high point ever since, and after 2,500 years this means that things are pretty bad. The close proximity of Athens has resulted in it becoming little more than a smoggy suburb of the capital. Not the cleanest water to swim in either (this is one of the few places in the Aegean where bathing is a health hazard), so unless you are clocking up islands / ferry hops, or are a student of military history, then sadly, it is worth giving a miss. None of the settlements has much to offer; the capital, Salamina, is dusty and lacking even a modicum of town planning, while Selinia (the nearest thing Salamis has on offer to a 'resort') is rather scruffy. Nicer, in a very quiet way, are the villages of Eantio and Peristeria.

Bus services are good along the limited routes run, but the south of the island (easily the nicest part with even the odd patch of forest cover on the hillsides) is not served. The main ferry link runs from the mainland suburb of **Perama** to **Paloukia** on the east coast, while a second operates from **Steno** to **Nea Peramos**. In addition, commuter boats run frequently to Piraeus Great Harbour.

⊨

There are no rooms on Salamis, but there are budget hotels at Selinia and Eantio.

2
CYCLADES CENTRAL

ANTIPAROS · IOS · NAXOS · PAROS · SANTORINI / THIRA

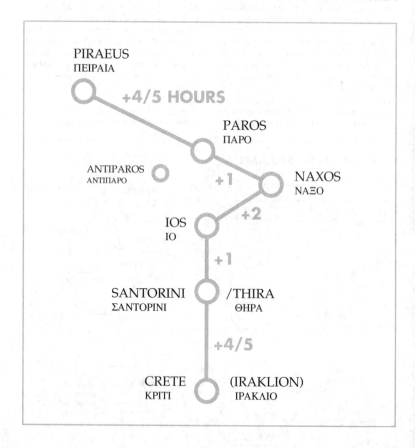

General Features

The Cyclades derive their name from being said to 'circle' the island of Delos — birthplace of the god Apollo. In practice, they lie in a semicircle south of a line running from the north-west to the south-east drawn just north of Delos.

Within the Cyclades the islands fall neatly into four subgroups, with Paros and the Central Cyclades line islands now forming the true centre of the group. The Central Cyclades consist of a number of islands that are known by name to most visitors to Greece. Among these, the photogenic volcanic island of Santorini is deservedly

popular, being identified with the legend of Atlantis; disco-laden Ios is known by repute to every student under the sun; Paros has a happy mix of almost everything; and Naxos has an excellent blend of atmosphere and golden beaches.

However, unspoilt islands these are not. Given that most new island hoppers make for an island that they've at least heard of, it is inevitable that this group should have become the main artery in the ferry system, seeing more visitors than the rest of the Cyclades put together. Out of High Season they are fine, but in summer these islands can seem very crowded.

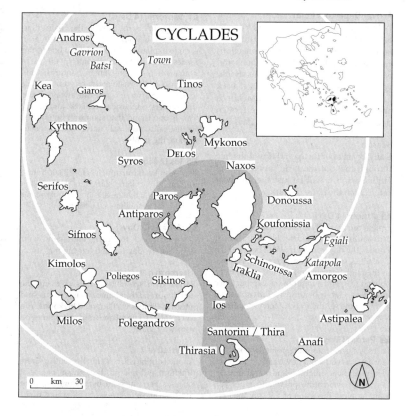

Example Itinerary [2 Weeks]

This justifiably popular group of islands forms the backbone of the Greek ferry system. High Season connections are so good that they make for extremely relaxed island hopping. With ferries almost as frequent as red buses down Oxford Street, even the most timid of travellers can wander without fear. The main islands can be done in any order since there are boats all times of the day. You won't be short on company either. Even so, with a little effort, you can escape the worst of the crowds almost whenever you choose.

Arrival/Departure Point

With good ferry links to Athens/Piraeus, Santorini, Mykonos and Crete (Iraklion) — all ports with charter flight connections — you are spoilt for choice. Athens and Santorini remain the safest options should you find yourself in a rush to get back for your return flight. Crete and Mykonos are a little less easy, since you are often dependent on a single boat each day.

Season

Daily boats operate up and down the line through most of the year, though out of High Season it will be just the one boat rather than the daily dozen.

1 Athens [1 Day]

Unless you are really unlucky with your flight arrival time, you should be able to ship out of Piraeus the day you fly in. With boats to the Cyclades Central line mornings and evenings in the High Season, you are not going to be obliged to spend a night in the capital. Once in Athens grab a handful of Euros, a meal and, of course, the NTOG ferry departure sheets and go.

2 Paros [3 Days]

Paros is a genial stopping point for your first few days, as you wind down and acclimatise. Plenty of beaches, nightlife and that all-important Greek island atmosphere, and, when you want to avoid the worst of the sun, the cave on Antiparos makes an interesting excursion easily to hand.

3 Naxos [2 Days]

More relaxing than Paros, Naxos is the next stop down the line. If you don't want to stay you can always visit on a day trip from Paros; a morning boat will set you down in time for lunch and you can then pick up a Paros-bound evening Santorini—Piraeus boat.

If you visit on one of the days that the small *Express Skopelitis* (p. 266) heads to Amorgos you can take her as far as Paros (Piso Livadi) several days a week (these vary according to the season) and then a bus over the island back to Paros Town.

4 Santorini [4 Days]

Although Ios is the next in the chain, time spent there is unlikely to leave you in a fit state to explore Santorini. Pick up one of the ferries running down the line in the early hours when heading on to Santorini (this way you don't waste a day of your holiday looking for a room). You can always make up lost sleep on the nearest black sand beach. This is one island that shouldn't be missed. Realistically, you will need three days to explore the sights.

5 Ios [2 Nights]

Ios doesn't wake up much before 23.00 hours. The mixture of sun, 'slammers' and sand is so over the top that most island hoppers can't stand it for more than a day or two.

1 Athens [2 Days]

Get a boat back to Athens and spend your flight 'safety' day in hand touring the city.

Alternative 1

Rather than spend two days enjoying the delights of Naxos, advance your schedule and return to Piraeus via Paros and **Mykonos**. You can glean the latest Paros departure times on your way south.

Alternative 2

Another option is to head further south to **Crete (Iraklion)** and take in the Minoan palace at Knossos. Ferry links are more tenuous this far south, so allow 3 days to do the round trip.

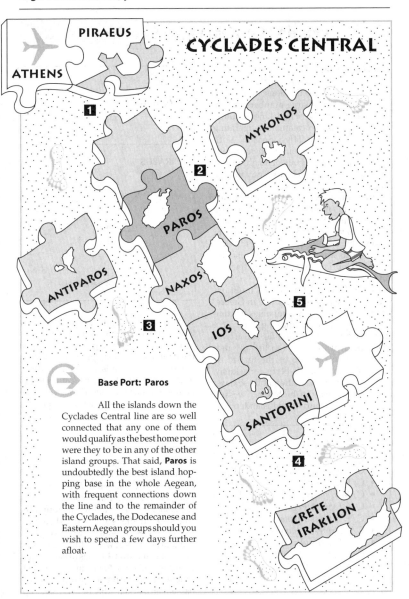

PIRAEUS

ATHENS

CYCLADES CENTRAL

1

MYKONOS

2

PAROS

ANTIPAROS

NAXOS

5

3

IOS

Base Port: Paros

SANTORINI

4

All the islands down the Cyclades Central line are so well connected that any one of them would qualify as the best home port were they to be in any of the other island groups. That said, **Paros** is undoubtedly the best island hopping base in the whole Aegean, with frequent connections down the line and to the remainder of the Cyclades, the Dodecanese and Eastern Aegean groups should you wish to spend a few days further afloat.

CRETE IRAKLION

Cyclades Central Ferry Services

Main Car Ferries

Because all the islands on this line are popular tourist destinations, ferries are geared to moving large numbers of passengers — fast. The rich pickings result in a dozen ferries and catamarans operating down the line in High Season, with departures from Piraeus both mornings and evenings. Even out of High Season there are usually two boats a day in each direction. Complementing the Cyclades Central Line ferries are tourist boats and a large number of regular ferries heading on to Samos, Crete, Rhodes and the Dodecanese, which pick up extra income by making stops along this line (these boats are described in the chapter most appropriate to their overall itinerary and are listed below).

The Cyclades Central line has traditionally been the most competitive in Greece, with the leading ferry companies fighting for pole position, deploying their best and newest boats. A decade ago it was not unknown for ferries to literally race each other to Paros to be the first to tie up at the then single-berth ferry quay, but things are rather different these days; the large increase in high speed vessels has made both tourists and islanders less

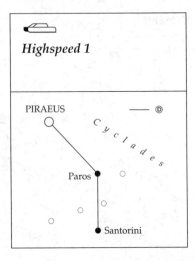

Highspeed 1

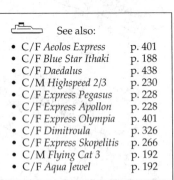
willing to contemplate long ferry journey times (Piraeus to Santorini takes 10 hours by regular ferries calling at all the ports on the line). The result is a growing tendency to target a few islands and then sail direct to them. The much better facilities found on the new custom-built ferries and catamarans, coupled with their high speed, is even pulling traffic away from domestic airlines.

C/M *Highspeed 1*
Hellas Flying Dolphins; 1998.

A venerable six years old, this boat is the old lady of the HFD *Highspeed* fleet. Compared to her three younger sisters she is looking just a tad worn around the edges — but she is still better than most regular ferries by a long way. Offering very fast journey times, with a top speed of 38 knots, she runs from Piraeus to Paros in just under three hours, Santorini in five. This enables her to cream off the top end of the passenger market. Able to carry over 600

Milopotas –
the most popular beach
on Ios

Every Sunday morning and
evening a hapless youth is
sent up into the highest
campanile in Ios Town to
ring the bells …

IOS

Chora Hilltop Views of the Campanile
& Evening Ferries calling at Ios Port
(with Sikinos on the horizon)

Cyclades Central

Ios Town: the Chora Hill

ANTIPAROS
Main Street & Kastro

PAROS
Morning Ferries Arrive
at Paros (viewed from
Parikia Beach)

Sightseeing on
Parikia Beach

How to make mad,
passionate, erotic
love on the back
of a Great Striped
Man–Seating
Whale …

PAROS
Parikia Town

Temple Site Kastro Church

MINISTRY OF CULTURE
21th INFORMATE OF PREHISTORIC
& CLASSICAL ANTIQUITIES

TEMPLE OF ATHENA

Paros Ferry Quay (with Passenger
Sheds & Windmill)

NAXOS
Town/Chora

Naxian Ferry Ticket Agency

A small inter-island ferry arrives at Naxos

Cyclades Central

The Doorway of Ariadne's Palace often prompts speculation over the size of her lover — the god Dionysos …

Temple of Apollo / Ariadne's Arch
NAXOS

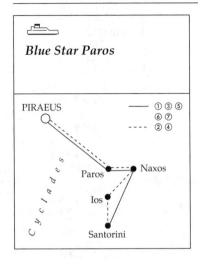

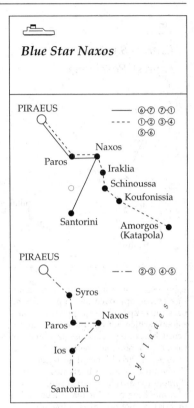

passengers (in rows of aircraft-type seating) and 150 cars, she is very popular and is usually full on journeys out of Piraeus in High Season (for this reason it is always advisable to book ahead with this vessel). She is particularly popular with locals. Tourists also seem to prefer her — though these cats have windows that do nothing to help the majority enjoy the scenery go by and no sun-deck, so travel is relegated from being part of the 'holiday experience' to a chore. As on all the *Highspeed* vessels you are expected to sit in the numbered seat indicated on your ticket.

C/F *Blue Star Paros*
Blue Star/Strintzis; 2002; 16500 GRT.
Since their arrival in 2002 two new Korean-built ferries on the Cyclades Central Line, the *Blue Star Paros* and *Blue Star Naxos*, have quickly established themselves as the premier regular ferries on the route. The two boats, identical in design and layout, now run a morning and evening departure from both ends of the line. Major changes in 2004 are unlikely. If they do occur they are most likely to involve Ios: on the 3rd of July 2003 the mayor of the island and some

forty islanders (armed with black rubbish-bin liners on sticks) held a half-hour protest on the ramp of the *Blue Star Paros* over Blue Star's failure to provide a daily high-speed service from Athens (the trigger for this action — filmed by a conveniently passing TV news crew — was the decision to have the *Blue Star Paros* only call at Ios on return runs to Piraeus). The company's response, if any, is likely to arrive in 2004.

C/F *Blue Star Naxos*
Blue Star/Strintzis; 2002; 16500 GRT.
Sister-ship to the *Blue Star Paros* (above), this boat's facilities are equally first rate, with

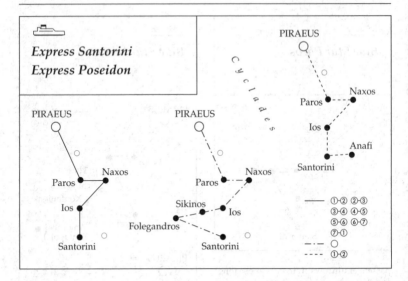

Express Santorini
Express Poseidon

shiny escalators (only on the right-hand side as you approach the ship) whisking passengers up to well-equipped deck-class saloons which are complete with an on-board burger-bar franchise (a branch of *Goody's* — a popular Greek chain).

Fares are 20% higher than regular ferries because these new boats are 20% faster (Piraeus to Paros in 4 hours instead of 5+). The only negative thing that can be said of them is the amount of free seating: sun-deck space is very limited, and the arrangement of chairs inside seems to encourage 'empty seat hogging' by other passengers.

Hellas Ferries Boats

The company operating the greatest number of regular ferries down the Cyclades Central Line is Hellas Ferries. Ferries in their fleet are interchanged regularly, so sailing times tend to be more important than the name of the boat. As for the ferries themselves, they share several depressing characteristics: all are very old and near the end of their working lives (as the painted-over rust indentations — up to 2 cm deep — on their outside decks testify), all tend to keep to time less well than their modern counterparts, and the attitude of the crews to backpackers is more reminiscent of keepers in a zoo's monkey house than anything to do with customers. The only plus is that these boats are cheaper than any others!

C/F *Express Santorini*
Hellas Ferries / HFD; 1974; 4590 GRT.
Introduced in 1994, the *Express Santorini* (formerly the French *Chartres*) has over the years gained a well-merited reputation for anti-backpacker discrimination. Join the ship at either Piraeus or Santorini and a pair of waistcoated goons will be at the (recently refurbished) deck-class saloon door stopping non-Greeks from entering. Fortunately these idiots aren't very 'with it' and they can easily be avoided by waiting until the first rush of boarders is over (after which they often disappear). Those that get into the deck-class saloon will find a reasonable sandwich bar franchise and seats full of Greeks.

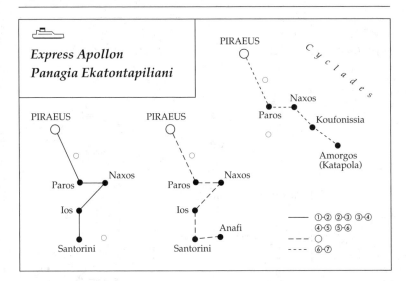

C/F *Express Poseidon*
Hellas Ferries / HFD; 1973; 5284 GRT.
The *Express Poseidon* has moved on and off this route several times, covering for other ferries. She tends to be used as the overnight boat from Piraeus because — originally built for the France—North Africa routes she is well endowed with cabins, while her public rooms are small and awkwardly placed. Sadly, while the other boats in the Hellas Ferries fleet had an internal make-over a couple of years ago, this ferry missed out: she is looking very shabby and in need of a refit.

C/F *Panagia Ekatontapiliani*
Hellas Ferries / HFD; 1972; 5590 GRT.
Formerly the *Apollo Express 2*, this ferry has managed to achieve the notable feat of having four names in as many years. Renamed the *Panagia Ekatontapiliani* (after the 'church of one hundred doors' on Paros), she was again renamed *Express Artemis* when HFD bought her. Her popularity took a nose-dive the day after the *Express Samina* disaster in 2000 when she suffered

a power failure just as she was entering Naxos — forcing other ferries to divert and take on her passengers.

Conveniently, the church leaders on Paros complained about her name change, and HFD responded accordingly. No company is likely to object to having a ferry named after a church with 100 doors. If you are worried about safety what could possibly be more reassuring? Sadly, this elderly ferry hasn't half as many doors and has to settle for merely having an unpronounceable name (most agents just call her '*Panagia*').

Identical to the *Express Apollon*, she started out life as the cross-Channel *Hengist*. She is due to retire sooner rather than later as she is approaching the domestic ferry age-limit in Greece.

C/F *Express Apollon*
Hellas Ferries / HFD; 1973; 5101 GRT.
Now on the Cyclades West line, this ferry (see p. 228) could be moved back to the Cyclades Central to cover for the three HFD boats here (particularly out of High Season).

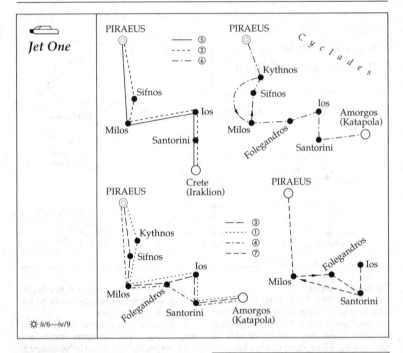

Jet One

☼ ii/6—iv/9

C/M *Jet One*

AegeanJet; 1995; 499 GRT.

Formerly the Strintzis/Blue Star *SeaJet 1*, this medium-sized catamaran ran successfully as a solo boat in 2002 on a wide-ranging itinerary. At the start of the 2003 High Season she was involved in a major incident south of Santorini when one of her hulls took on water (other ferries evacuated the passengers at sea). She was replaced by a hydrofoil. It is unclear if she will reappear in 2004.

The main characteristic of her schedules is a morning start from either Crete or Amorgos, calling at islands on the southern ends of the Cyclades Central and Cyclades West Lines, and a late afternoon departure from Piraeus back down the route. The result is an invaluable series of links if you want to cross between lines.

Flying Cat 4

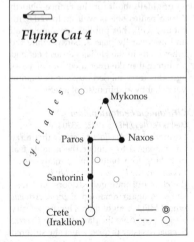

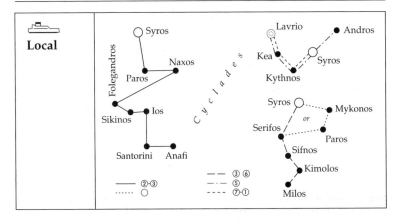

Local

Syros
Folegandros
Naxos
Paros
Ios
Sikinos
Santorini   Anafi

Lavrio
Kea
Kythnos
Andros
Syros
Syros
Serifos
Sifnos
Kimolos
Mykonos
or
Paros
Milos

Cyclades

②-③   ○
③ ⑥
⑤
⑦-①

C/M *Flying Cat 4*
Hellas Flying Dolphins

This small, but attractive, catamaran moved from the Northern Sporades route in 2002 to provide a very useful connecting service from Crete to the Cyclades Central and Cyclades North lines (schedules changed little in 2003). A nice boat, but apt to be disrupted once the summer *meltemi* winds start to blow: don't rely on this vessel if she is on the route again in 2004 and you are returning to Crete to collect a flight home.

Local Syros-based Ferry

One of the relatively few concessions to the summer tourist influx made by ferry operators is the regular appearance of a — very old — ferry running out of Syros to the Cycladian islands, providing hoppers with a series of useful connections (when running). Sadly, the timetables are often more tantalizing than tangible: in 2002 a tub called C/F *Santorini Sky* (operated by Golden Ferries) stayed in port most of the time, while in 2003 an ancient AK Ventouris boat — the C/F *Panagia Tinou* — ran the service for a few weeks before disappearing (this was probably due to a lack of customers, as she made a point of sailing at completely different times to her published timetable).

Paros—Antiparos Taxi-Boats

Three small boats roll between Paros and Antiparos, providing an hourly 40-minute 'tourist' link. Don't be surprised if you have to take the Punta ferries (see overleaf) back, because of over-choppy afternoon seas. The three boats tried a failed attempt to combine forces in 2000, enabling one to buy open-dated return tickets. However, it is now back to throat-cutting normal and you now buy single tickets (€2) on the vessel you travel on (no computer ticketing with these boats). One — usually the *Antiparos Express* — also runs a Paros—Sifnos (Faros) service three times a week.

Antiparos Express
Kasos Express
Panagia Parou

Paros
(Parikia)
Antiparos

⑩

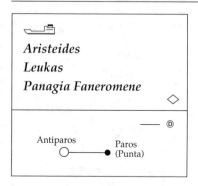

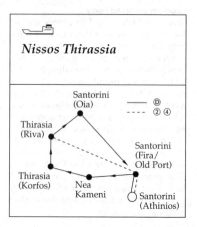

Antiparos—Punta Ferries

Several small ferries provide a vehicle link across the straits between Antiparos Town and the quay at Paros (Punta). Their only redeeming feature is the fare: at €0.50 it is much cheaper than the Paros town boats, even allowing for the Punta—Parikia bus fare (€1).

C/F *Nissos Thirassia*

One landing-craft ferry operates a 'life-line' ferry service to Thirasia disguised as a Santorini caldera tour. Actually, stopping off at the hot springs to allow tourists a quick bathe is quite an enterprising way of subsidizing a ferry link! In High Season the *Nissos Thirassia* runs a twice-weekly day-return service (usually departing around 07.45 from Fira Old Port) that offers a much cheaper way (€4.50 Rtn.) of spending five hours on uncrowded Thirasia than taking a caldera tour.

Tour Boats

The large number of ferries conspires against the existence of large numbers of Cyclades tourist boats. These only exist where ferry links are weak. There are a number of vessels of note; the largest run daily day trips from various ports on Crete to Santorini. The biggest of these are the *Minoan Prince*, the *Artemis*, the *Vergina Sky*, and the unattractive *Maria PA*. All these boats rely on package tourists, who

are willing to pay their extortionate fares (usually around €70).

Lightweight tourist boats also operate in the Central Cyclades. Not for sea-sickies, and expensive, they offer extra hopping options: in 2003 these included Paros to Delos (€30), Paros to Serifos (€28), and Ios to Sikinos (€25). These boats really come into their own if you want to have a quick look at the Little Cyclades, as they run good-value day trips that enable you to get a look at Iraklia and Koufonissia (€30). The only problem with these boats is that they are totally tourist dependent: if not enough tickets are sold then they don't run.

Cyclades Central Islands & Ports

ANTIPAROS

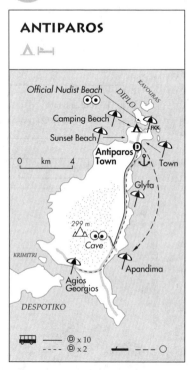

Official Nudist Beach

Camping Beach

Sunset Beach

Antiparos Town

Town

Glyfa

0   km   4

299 m

Cave

KRIMITRI

Apandima

Agios Georgios

DESPOTIKO

Ⓓ x 10

Ⓓ x 2

Antiparos

ΑΝΤΙΠΑΡΟΣ; 55 km²; pop. 820.

CODE ☎ 22840
POLICE ☎ 61202
FIRST AID ☎ 61219

One of those less well-known islands that have more going for them than their larger and more popular neighbours, Antiparos is a gem. If your idea of the perfect island includes excellent sand beaches, a spot of nudism, a cosy atmosphere, a picturesque port filled with prune-faced fishermen mending their nets, and plenty of discreet

nightlife then Antiparos is it. As a result the island attracts many day-trippers from Paros who head either for a beach or the other attraction, the famous cave.

In many ways Antiparos is a strange place, having been severed from Paros as the result of an earthquake around 550 BC. The straits between it and Paros are very shallow (which is why all ferries are obliged to sail around the top of Paros when heading for Santorini) and narrow, with the fields on the western side of the island rolling into the sea. The only settlement, **Antiparos Town** — straddling the flat northern tip of the island and with a fortress at its centre — forms the focus of island life. Enough of the old town survives to give plenty of atmosphere, though the environs are dominated by establishments offering accommodation.

Apart from the tavernas and boutiques lining the winding main street, the town's great attraction lies in its beaches. Within easy walking distance there is one guaranteed to suit most tastes. Families head for the shallow and sheltered beach to the north of the port, while the good sand beach opposite **Diplo** island (reached via the track to the campsite and then a 100 m path to the right) is the preserve of windsurfers (boards can be hired) and nudists (this is one of only three official nudist beaches in Greece). More hardy types in search of solitude head for Sunset Beach; windswept and with an abandoned air, it is the place for contemplating the meaning of life (and what one is doing with it) and for quietly drowning oneself if one isn't happy with the conclusions.

Drowning one's sorrows back in town is even easier as bars aplenty cluster around the fortress and trickle down the main street. The town also has several discos (notably establishments in the inland town windmill and near the *Galini* hotel).

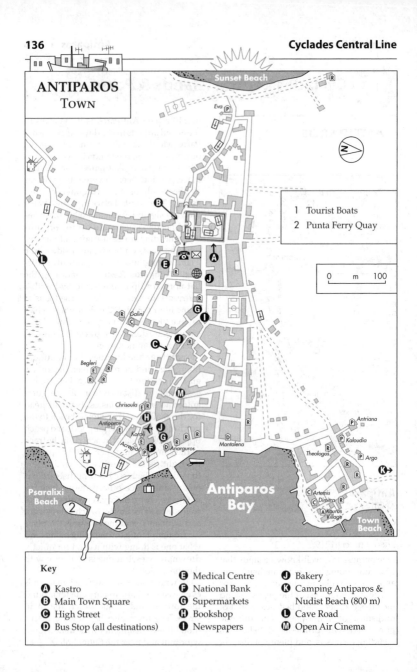

ANTIPAROS
TOWN

1 Tourist Boats
2 Punta Ferry Quay

0   m   100

Sunset Beach

Eva

Galini

Begleri

Chrisoula

Antiparos

Koroli

Acrogiali

Anarguros

Mantalena

Antriana

Kaloudia

Theologos

Argo

Artemis

Dimitra

Kouros
Village

Psaralixi
Beach

**Antiparos
Bay**

Town
Beach

Key

A Kastro
B Main Town Square
C High Street
D Bus Stop (all destinations)
E Medical Centre
F National Bank
G Supermarkets
H Bookshop
I Newspapers
J Bakery
K Camping Antiparos &
Nudist Beach (800 m)
L Cave Road
M Open Air Cinema

The rest of the island is relatively unde-veloped; a decent road has only recently been completed, allowing buses to run south to the cave, and occasionally to Agios Georgios on the south-west coast. There is a comfortable scatter of holiday homes along the coast road, as well as taverna-backed sand beaches at **Glyfa** and at **Apandima** (the mooring point for boats bringing visitors to the cave).

The beach at **Agios Georgios** is remote, but worth the effort of getting to. The hills behind are nothing to look at, but were once home to a major early Cycladic settlement. The first to have ever been sys-tematically explored, the site yielded up a large number of Cycladic figures that now form the nucleus of the British Museum's impressive collection.

This site (along with a number of others on Antiparos and Paros) was excavated by another of those 19 c. young gentlemen travellers, an Englishman by the name of **James Theodore Bent**. With his Irish wife, Mabel, he toured the Cyclades in 1883–84. This was a time when the islands were completely off the beaten track (so much so that only Syros had proper roads). Bent not only introduced the world to the art of the early Bronze Age Cycladic culture, but also penned one of the most famous — and readable — of 19 c. travel books describing his tour.

In ancient times Antiparos was known as 'Oliaros'. It has always been too small to be a significant historical force in its own right, being dependent to a greater or lesser extent on Paros. Like Paros it was a subject of Athens, fol-lowing Parian support for the losing Persians at Salamis (480 BC). In the middle ages it was in the hands of the Dukes of Naxos. Turkish rule between 1537–1821 was briefly broken by the 1770–74 Russian occupation.

⊫

There is plenty of accommodation in Town, though it is pricey. Top of the range is the A-class *Kouros Village* (☎ 61084) and the C-class *Artemis* (☎ 61460), both with good views over the harbour. Equally good, but less

THE CYCLADES
OR
LIFE AMONG THE INSULAR GREEKS
JAMES THEODORE BENT - 1885

15. PAROS

ON landing at Paroikia, the chief town of Paros, you immediately come in contact with the speciality of the place: the little jetty on which you land is made of marble, marble pillars for mooring boats to are jotted here and there, and you realise before long that Paros is nothing but one huge block of marble covered with a thin coating of soil. In ages long gone by these central *idu*...

16. ANTIPAROS

A more wretched fever-stricken lot than the six hundred inhabitants of the one village of Antiparos I never saw; it is just one of the usual fortified Kastros of the islands, with the backs of the houses fitting close together, so as to form a circular wall. It has gates which are now never closed, and its streets, are filthily dirty; and, as it lies low, in summer time it is a hotbed of fever. The priest, whom I afterwards learnt did not bear an excellent character, and who had narrowly escaped being unfrocked for his naughty ways, is the ruling spirit of the place..... People believe that these old wizards *... make a mistake* once the old man *... in front*

ANTIPAROS CAVE

It is not the pleasantest of all sensations to be dangling in the air over an abyss, the depth of which you cannot measure by the uncertain light of your torch, and to be solely dependent on your ability in holding a rope which is tied to a stalactite for your safety. Down, down we went, descending three difficult places by ropes and two by ladders until we were safely landed in a perfect sea of stalactites and stalagmites of dazzling beauty. We had brought with us a large quantity of dried brushwood with which to kindle a light, and by this means we were able to penetrate with our eyes the labyrinth of sparkling chambers...

Bent's Full Text is now online
@
greekislandhopping.com
Complete with
ITINERARY MAPS
BACKGROUND INFO
Island Hopping in the Footsteps of James Theodore Bent ...

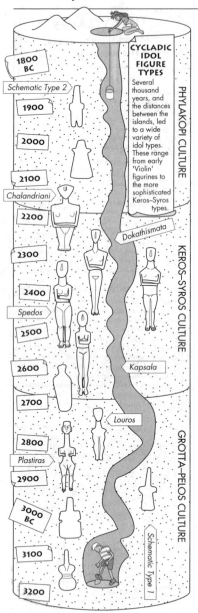

CYCLADIC IDOL FIGURE TYPES

Several thousand years, and the distances between the islands, led to a wide variety of idol types. These range from early 'Violin' figurines to the more sophisticated Keros-Syros types.

PHYLAKOPI CULTURE

1800 BC

Schematic Type 2

1900

2000

2100

Chalandriani

2200

Dokathismata

KEROS-SYROS CULTURE

2300

2400

Spedos

2500

2600

Kapsala

2700

Louros

2800

Plastiras

2900

GROTTA-PELOS CULTURE

3000 BC

3100

3200

Schematic Type 1

well-placed, is the inland *Galini* (☎ 61420). The remainder of the hotel accommodation is cheaper. This includes the waterfront D-class *Mantalena* (☎ 61206), and several E-class establishments in the streets behind the waterfront buildings — the *Korali* (☎ 61236), *Antiparos* (☎ 61358), *Chrisoula* (☎ 61224) and the popular *Argo* (☎ 61419/61186). Budget travellers should note that the E-class *Begleri* (☎ 61378) is more expensive than the C-class establishments! Room availability is good, but many bookings are on a long-stay basis, so arrive early in High Season.

Λ

Camping Antiparos (☎ 61221): 1 km along a dirt track north of the town. Some complaints about passport recovery problems, so visit with caution. Tents are pitched in bamboo compounds. Mini-bus meets boats.

∞

Nudist beach aside (which in High Season sadly attracts more timid than enlightened fans), Antiparos has two sights of note. The first is a small medieval **Kastro** (c. 1440) at the heart of Antiparos town: though until one is inside it one is hard put to recognize it at all. Sited at the end of the high street, it is a rectangular structure that in its heyday looked akin to a three-storeyed Alamo-like stockade, with houses lining the inside walls. In the years since it has been painted white, the top storey has gone, and windows and doors have been let into the outside wall. As a result, from the outside, the walls now look like any typical white cubist Cycladic row of buildings. On the south side, however, you will find a small unpainted Gothic archway — the original single doorway in the walls. Even today it is the only way you can gain access to the courtyard of the stockade-cum-castle without going through one of the houses. This ensures that something of the original enclosed atmosphere remains (though better examples of this type of fortification exist on Kimolos and Folegandros). Stairs directly facing the archway run up to a central 'hump' with good views over the building.

The best sight on the island is the **Antiparos Cave**. A couple of centuries ago this cave was one of the most famous in the world; so much so that it inspired many by its reputation alone. Not least among these was Johann Wyss (the author of *Swiss Family Robinson*) who — picking up on the juxtaposition of an island and a cave — appears to have derived the idea for the Rock House from reading of the Antiparos cave, acknowledging the debt by having the narrator say:

'I had … read the description of the famous grotto of Antiparos.'

After this build-up the cave itself inevitably suffers in comparison with both the myth and some other caverns accessible today. However, even allowing that discriminating troglodytes are likely to be disappointed, for most the cave is a gentle and rewarding introduction to the underworld. Certainly there are enough buses hell-bent on getting you there (and making an equally big hole in your pocket). For this reason you should exercise caution; if you are not careful the cave is not the only pitfall that you could encounter. You should be aware of the following:

(1). In the summer of 2003 the round tour bus-trip to the cave was €3.50. One-way tickets cost €1.75. Several agency buses and the regular island bus (a mere €1) run to the cave but tickets are not interchangeable; it pays to buy single tickets so that you can return on the first available bus back.

(2). Tours and bus tickets do not include the cave ticket price of €3.

(3). Buses decant passengers on a bend of a road half-way up a mountainside. Here you will be met by mules with touting owners. Those taking up the offer to be taken for a ride are apt to feel bigger asses than their mounts when they find that the cave entrance is only 150 m up the path.

(4). Low Season sees buses reduced to a trickle; so expect delays when both departing and returning. In addition, the cave is often locked, prompting further delays.

Once inside Mt. Agios Gianni you will find yourself in a cave that has been on the tourist map almost as long as the Parthenon, and unfortunately it is as badly damaged. Many of the stalagmites and stalactites (sexist mnemonic: tights come down) are broken. In times past the cave's fame ensured that stalagmites were carried off by the Russian navy to the Kremlin. More recent damage was inflicted during the last war when German soldiers used the stalactites for rifle practice. The walls are also covered with graffiti dating back 300 years, the more notable vandals including King Otho of Greece (in 1840) and Lord Byron. Tales persist of a stalactite inscribed by some failed assassins of Alexander the Great hiding in the cave. Graffiti is less of a problem

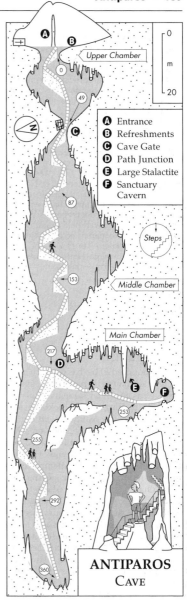

- **A** Entrance
- **B** Refreshments
- **C** Cave Gate
- **D** Path Junction
- **E** Large Stalactite
- **F** Sanctuary Cavern

Upper Chamber

Steps

Middle Chamber

Main Chamber

ANTIPAROS
CAVE

today as movement in the cave is restricted to a narrow stairway barely wide enough for two people to pass (in High Season rotund visitors have been known to commit mass murder simply trying to pass by on the other side). Low handrails are provided for midgets, but at several points the stairs are built onto stalagmites and taller vertigo suffers could be in for a heady time. The cave is floodlit, but it might be worthwhile bringing a torch as power cuts are not unknown in this part of the world.

Pottery has been found in the cave indicating occupation back to archaic times, though the nearest it has ever come to fame was in 1673 when a potty Frenchman (one M. de Nointel) organised a Christmas Day mass (complete with fireworks) in the main chamber — the congregation being 500 of the bemused population of Paros (who were paid to indulge this exhibition of antiquarian eccentricity). Just over a century later — in 1774 — the locals built the chapel at the cave entrance to prevent anything like this happening again.

Ios

ΙΟΣ; 108 km²; pop. 1,650.

CODE ☎ 22860
PORT POLICE ☎ 91264
POLICE ☎ 91222
HOSPITAL ☎ 91227

Ios (pronounced *EE*os) has gained a reputation and a half as *the* party island since it emerged as a popular student destination in the 60s, offering a heady cocktail of sun, sand and sex. The reality is a little more complicated, for a lot depends on when you go and which part of the island you visit. From mid-July to the end of August the crowds pour in, and Ios attempts to live up to its reputation — those looking for a traditional, unspoilt Greek island would do better to avoid it, but for the rest of the year, even if partying isn't your thing, it is worth paying a call for Ios has a lot going for it. In many ways Ios is an ideal holiday island; it has two of the best beaches to be found anywhere in Greece, a picturesque old chora, good connections for day trips to other islands, and — most importantly of all — a buzz about it that you just don't

find anywhere else. It is difficult not to get caught up in the atmosphere, and, as you don't have to join the all-night party, it is possible to turn a blind eye to the excesses of those that do and simply embrace those aspects of the island that appeal to you. In some respects the island's reputation is rather overblown, for although the days of the youthful hanger-out are not exactly over, a growth in the number of families visiting (thanks to the thirty-somethings returning to the haunts of their giddy youth) is beginning to restore the balance a bit. The telling fact that Paros and Fira Town on Santorini both now have more nightspots is also rarely acknowledged, in part because the nightspots on Ios are heavily concentrated in the centre of town and not obscured among a plethora of competing attractions.

Not all is sweetness and light, however, and Ios does have a less appealing side that the island's more passionate fans are loath to accept. The height of the season sees it ludicrously overcrowded, with the attendant problems of noise, poor sanitation, alcohol abuse and theft — all of which are more evident than on other islands. The locals have got in on the act as well, with some of the bars adding god-knows-what to spirits and cocktails, invariably with dire consequences for the drinker a few hours later. Violence is also a problem: the rumour mill regularly churns out rape figures running at over a dozen each summer (occasional victims being male). How much truth there is in such sobering bar talk is hard to establish, as the police are not keen on highlighting this aspect of island life.

Describing the geography of Ios is easy enough, for there are only three main points of reference, with a bare 4 km between them: the Port, the Chora set up on the hill behind (known as the Village), and the Beach (Milopotas) on the other side of the chora hill. At first sight the island seems innocuous enough, for the port of **Gialos** is quite sleepy — give or take a dozen bars.

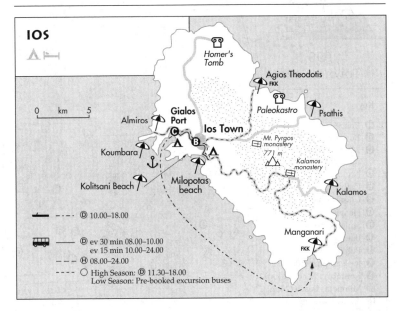

IOS

Homer's Tomb

Agios Theodotis
FKK

0   km   5

Almiros

Gialos Port
Ios Town

Paleokastro
Psathis

Koumbara

Mt. Pyrgos monastery
771 m

Kalamos monastery

Kolitsani Beach

Milopotas beach

Kalamos

Manganari
FKK

ⓓ 10.00–18.00

ⓓ ev 30 min 08.00–10.00
ev 15 min 10.00–24.00
ⓗ 08.00–24.00

○ High Season: ⓓ 11.30–18.00
Low Season: Pre-booked excursion buses

Indeed, it is positively quiet compared to its counterparts on Paros and Santorini, besides being far more attractive than either of them. For this reason it attracts those who want to be able to escape the worst excesses of the island's nightlife, and has a good supply of hotels, along with an excellent bakery and several restaurants. It is only when you step inside the supermarket and discover that the check-out racks are filled with condoms that you first get a hint that something, somewhere, could be up.

Behind the port climbs the old mule **stairway** up to the Chora. This offers an appealing alternative to the new road, but thanks to slippery, sloping steps that are awkward enough when one is sober (never mind when one is totally sozzled and in the dark), it accounts for the fact that there is always someone hopping around with a leg in plaster, and the widely advertised doctors' practices in the town. Most visitors prefer to use the two island buses instead. These are more crowded than buses else-

where — and this is really saying something. Until you have tried travelling on an Ios bus in one of the 'rush hours', you haven't fully enjoyed the Greek island experience. The sardine-tin times are between 11.00–14.00 when heading for the beach, 15.00–18.00 returning from the beach, and after 21.00 heading for the village. The buses do nothing else except run from the Port to the Chora and then down to Milopotas and Koumbara.

Ios Town (alias the Village) at the top of the muleway-cum-stairs is a real contradiction, the islanders having made a far better job of combining a pretty chora village with a heavy bar and disco scene than their counterparts on the other popular islands. During daylight hours it retains much of its former small village atmosphere, and at first sight you would be hard put to know that it was anything more. Come dusk, the windows and doors of the lower town buildings open to reveal a profusion of bars and boutiques.

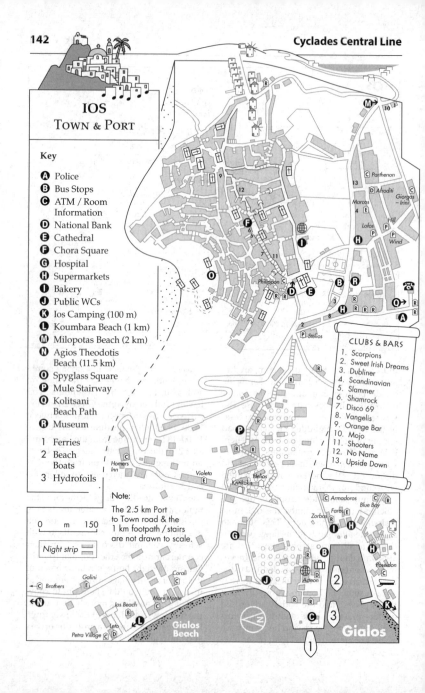

IOS
Town & Port

Key

- **A** Police
- **B** Bus Stops
- **C** ATM / Room Information
- **D** National Bank
- **E** Cathedral
- **F** Chora Square
- **G** Hospital
- **H** Supermarkets
- **I** Bakery
- **J** Public WCs
- **K** Ios Camping (100 m)
- **L** Koumbara Beach (1 km)
- **M** Milopotas Beach (2 km)
- **N** Agios Theodotis Beach (11.5 km)
- **O** Spyglass Square
- **P** Mule Stairway
- **Q** Kolitsani Beach Path
- **R** Museum

1 Ferries
2 Beach Boats
3 Hydrofoils

CLUBS & BARS

1. Scorpions
2. Sweet Irish Dreams
3. Dubliner
4. Scandinavian
5. Slammer
6. Shamrock
7. Disco 69
8. Vangelis
9. Orange Bar
10. Mojo
11. Shooters
12. No Name
13. Upside Down

Note:
The 2.5 km Port to Town road & the 1 km footpath / stairs are not drawn to scale.

0   m   150

Night strip

Gialos Beach

Gialos

After bars, beaches are the great attraction of Ios. **Milopotas Beach** is one of the best in the Aegean; a long stretch of golden sand, it is large enough to accommodate even the High Season crowds and is backed by a scatter of bars and tavernas. However, in summer it is wind-blasted by the *meltemi*. Visitors to Ios of a decade ago will mourn the arrival of a road running the length of the beach that has destroyed the nudism at the far end.

The rest of the island — being arid and very hilly — is quiet, though regular buses (starting at the port) now run to the main beaches. The best of these is the superb stretch of sand taking in several bays at **Manganari** on the south coast. Reasonably quiet to date, this beach is set to become much busier as the dirt road used to access it is now being upgraded and metalled (beach boats also visit). **Agios Theodotis**, on the east coast, is almost as good, with the skimpy ruins of a Venetian kastro in lieu of the former's disco/taverna and windsurfing school. Both have a nude end, unlike the official nude beaches at oily **Koumbara** (which is now very restrained thanks to the arrival of hotels and a regular bus service) and at **Kolitsani**. This latter beach is in a small cove (favoured by yachts as a quiet mooring point) that is best reached via the path that runs east from the town post office road.

😝

Ios, formerly known as 'Io' or 'Nio', was a much prized island in history thanks to its harbour (the Turks called it 'Little Malta'). The island was allied to Athens and shared her political fortunes through the Classical and Hellenistic periods. It was captured by the Romans in the 1 C. BC and became a place of exile. In the Byzantine period Ios was repeatedly visited by pirates. Between 1207–96 the island was part of the Duchy of Naxos; thereafter the Venetians ruled. Turkish pirates arrived in 1558 in 14 galleys, laying waste to the buildings and taking the population into

slavery. Ios was uninhabited for 21 years before it was resettled by Albanians and the few survivors from the pirate raid. Like the rest of the Cyclades the island was briefly under Russian rule from 1770–74, before finally breaking away from Turkish rule in 1821.

🛏

Rooms are plentiful on Ios, though the usual caveat about arriving early in the day applies here as well. Start at the accommodation office on the ferry quay. If you are staying more than a fortnight (it is not unknown for people to get off a ferry and then ask in the nearest ticket agency for a three-month room!) then negotiate a reduced rate. If you are staying for several weeks you will be expected to pay your bill on a weekly basis.

The **Port** is well equipped with several good mid-range hotels (though ferry noise can be a problem). These include the C-class *Armadoros* (☎ 91201), *Blue Bay* (☎ 91533) and the *Poseidon* (☎ 91091). There is also the somewhat noisy D-class *Acteon* (☎ 91207) over the ticket agency, and the E-class *Faros* (☎ 91569). Nearby **Gialos Beach** offers some of the most relaxed rooms on Ios. These include the beach-side C-class *Corali* (☎ 91272) and *Mare Monte* (☎ 91564), the expensive *Petra Village* (☎ 91409) and B-class *Ios Beach*, and the D-class *Leto* (☎ 91279).

The **Chora** has a plentiful supply of rooms — mostly in the new part of town — and a number of reasonable hotels. Best among these are the D-class *Afroditi* (☎ 91546) and the C-class *Parthenon* (☎ 91275). The C-class *Giorgos Irini* (☎ 91527) is also popular, as is the *Philippou* (☎ 91290) near the Cathedral, and the E-class *Marcos* (☎ 91060).

The road to and behind **Milopotas Beach** also has a large number of pensions and hotels perched along it. These include the C-class *Far Out* (☎ 91446), *Delfini* (☎ 91340), and *Nissos Ios* (☎ 91306), and the E-class *Aegeon* (☎ 91392). Milopotas is also home to the expensive B-class *Ios Palace* (☎ 91269). Finally, if you are really seeking the quiet life on Ios, there are also some rooms at **Agios Theodotis Beach**.

Å

Thanks to the high student numbers, Ios is equipped with three campsites, but even this is not enough at the height of the season when you will find tents pitched peg to peg by the early evening. The rest of the year there is space aplenty. Regardless of when you visit, you should take extra pains to secure all valuables as petty theft is depressingly common.

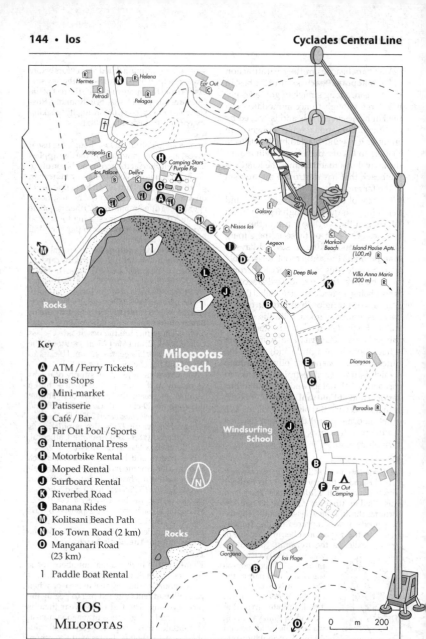

Key

Ⓐ ATM / Ferry Tickets
Ⓑ Bus Stops
Ⓒ Mini-market
Ⓓ Patisserie
Ⓔ Café / Bar
Ⓕ Far Out Pool / Sports
Ⓖ International Press
Ⓗ Motorbike Rental
Ⓘ Moped Rental
Ⓙ Surfboard Rental
Ⓚ Riverbed Road
Ⓛ Banana Rides
Ⓜ Kolitsani Beach Path
Ⓝ Ios Town Road (2 km)
Ⓞ Manganari Road
    (23 km)

1 Paddle Boat Rental

IOS
MILOPOTAS

Milopotas
Beach

Windsurfing
School

Rocks

Rocks

Hermes
Petradi
Pelagos
Helena
Far Out
Acropolis
Ios Palace
Delfini
Camping Stars / Purple Pig
Galaxy
Nissos Ios
Aegeon
Markos Beach
Island House Apts. (100 m)
Villa Anna Maria (200 m)
Deep Blue
Dionysos
Paradise
Far Out Camping
Gorgona
Ios Plage

0 m 200

Thanks to the number of long-stay (i.e. a couple of months or more) visitors — many of whom are strapped to find the funds to party *and* pay their camping bills — it is all but impossible to stay a week without hearing of someone losing cash from their tent. As for the sites:

Ios Camping (☎ 91329), a good site complete with a swimming pool, lies opposite the ferry quay. Its convenient location is not the money-spinner that it should be, as most campers prefer to be near the beach and head for the sites behind Milopotas beach.

Camping Stars (☎ 91302), nearest the village road, is a well-established if small site, showing its age. It has plenty of tree cover, and tries to compete at the port for the party types by calling itself 'The Purple Pig'. Note: the only things partyish or purple on-site are the painted gates and lamp-posts.

Far Out Camping (☎ 91468) at the end of Milopotas. Its 'far out' location and amenities combine to make it a venue in its own right (don't come here if you enjoy your beauty sleep). Facilities include a pool complete with rock music, DJ and a bungee-jump crane. There is a pool-side ear-piercing service if the loudspeakers haven't already done the job for you.

≋✿

All the large clubs (which need more space) now lie along the road and strip of building-free ground (thanks to ownership disputes) that divide the old and new halves of the town. Things don't really get going much before 23.00 (it is a truism of Ios that the sun sets as a new day dawns), after which life gets wilder by the hour. Shutting — or rather falling — down time is 03.00–04.00. If you are young, and male, and have come to Greece looking for the girl of your dreams, you will probably find Ios disappointing; most nightspots seem to find males outnumbering females by two to one (though this improves considerably outside High Season). Nightspots catering for those with minority sexual orientations are also all but non-existent. Bars can change name and in popularity regularly, so recommendations are difficult. Getting feedback from revellers is equally hard: most end up joining the masses doing an extended bar and club crawl. The exact itinerary has never been recorded because no one who has done it has ever been in a fit state to remember anything about it the next day.

Of the bigger dance clubs (and none have particularly large dance areas), *Scorpions* seems to have had the edge of late, but the *Dubliner* and *Sweet Irish Dreams* also draw crowds. Finally, there are a good collection of quieter bars in the port; these do a reasonable trade until the late boat to Piraeus departs, whereupon the action moves into the town.

👓

The official and oft-quoted sight is **Homer's Tomb** — or rather the alleged stones from which it was made (now topped with a modern headstone bearing the poet's name). Lying near the north coast of Ios, it is merely one of several prehistoric graves excavated by a Dutch traveller in 1770. Paasch van Krienen claimed to have found a stone in it inscribed 'Homer' (the stone next to this one — now marked 'Simpson' — is just someone repeating the joke 230 years later). These graves are all but impossible to get to and, frankly, not worth the effort of the difficult journey. As a result, most visitors justifiably prefer to get stoned in the bars and discos of Ios Town instead.

The one Ios sight not to be missed is the view from the top of the **Chora Hill**. Finding your way up through the warren of streets is, admittedly, half the fun of it (a couple of stairways that disintegrate into steep tracks on the western side of the Chora will eventually get you there), but there is usually a steady trail of sunset-watchers heading in the same direction to help you. The top, adorned with several chapels and a scree slope of pebbles, offers fantastic views of the port framed with the island of Sikinos behind in one direction, and the Chora and distant Santorini in another. The best time to visit is at sunset, when the port is bathed in a golden glow, and the wine-dark harbour sea is furrowed by a procession of ferries running up from Santorini en route to Piraeus; the combination offers one of the best panoramic views in the Greek islands.

Naxos
ΝΑΞΟΣ; 448 km²; pop. 18,000.

CODE ☎ 22850
PORT POLICE ☎ 22300
POLICE ☎ 22100
FIRST AID ☎ 23333

Naxos can lay claim to being one of the most popular Greek islands — at least with island hoppers. Not only are the numbers visiting higher than for any other island,

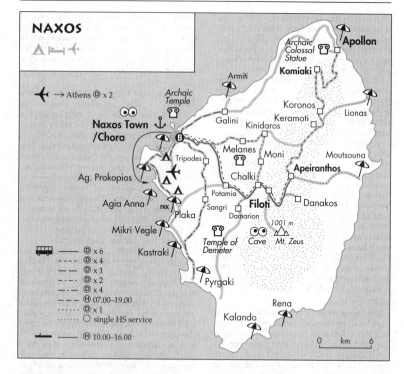

NAXOS

→ Athens ⊕ x 2

Naxos Town /Chora

Armiti

Archaic Temple

Galini

Kinidaros

Komiaki

Koronos

Keramoti

Lionas

Archaic Colossal Statue

Apollon

Melanes

Moni

Moutsouna

Tripodes

Ag. Prokopios

Chalki

Apeiranthos

Potamia

Agia Anna

FKK

Plaka

Sangri

Damarion

Filoti

Danakos

Mikri Vegle

Kastraki

Temple of Demeter

Cave

1001 m

Mt. Zeus

Pyrgaki

Rena

Kalando

⊕ x 6
⊕ x 4
⊕ x 1
⊕ x 2
⊕ x 4
⊕ 07.00–19.00
⊕ x 1
○ single HS service

⊕ 10.00–16.00

0   km   6

but the average length of stay is also greater than that for other popular islands. This isn't surprising given that Naxos offers an alluring mix of an attractive port town, a succession of wonderful, easily accessible sand beaches (complete with proper sand-dunes), an interior landscape of lush valleys and ruin-topped skylines, and good links with other islands. Writers — ancient and modern — have regularly labelled Naxos as the most beautiful of the Cyclades. Not only is it the largest island in the group, but it is a popular day-trip destination, and the primary jumping-off point for Amorgos and the Little Cyclades. Thanks to a prosperous agricultural base Naxos has long been able to ignore the tourist market, but this is now changing. The last decade has seen the

opening of an airport, and a large increase in the number of tourists. Fortunately, their impact has been relatively benign, as the tourist strip is confined to Naxos Town and its environs. At the moment Naxos thus enjoys just enough tourism to make the 'typical' tourist feel comfortable, but not so much that the island's character is irredeemably damaged.

Naxos Town is the arrival point for all but air visitors. Hardly representative of the island as a whole, it is a mass of contradictions, offering a mix of a brash, touristy waterfront, a warren of lovely little backstreets winding up to a Venetian Kastro, and one of the most dramatic harbours in the Aegean — thanks to the romantic skyline arch of a ruined temple on the causeway-linked islet at the edge of the town (Naxos is one island where it is difficult not to know that you have arrived at the right place). The temple-topped rock provides a beguiling promise to arriving ferry passengers of things to come.

Surprisingly, as far as most tourists are concerned, Naxos is still something of a one-town island; most are content to divide their time between Naxos Town (or Chora) and the miles of fine sandy beaches that run down the coast to the south, where campsites and nudity abound. First impressions of the town can be rather mixed, as the enchantment of the temple is somewhat offset by an increasingly glitzy waterfront; the cute old hardware shops of just a few years ago have now given way to tourist shops and cash dispensing machines. Most of the town's amenities are to be found here, including a good bookshop and a bus station complete with timetables. The municipal authorities have also woken up to the tourists' occasionally more pressing needs and have installed a WC and shower house on the main street behind the promenade. Step into the streets behind the main street and wander into the chora, and you will discover the older and more attractive face of the town. The collection of castle, Greek chora and Venetian houses combine to make for shady, and interesting wandering, and near the castle walls you will find several good restaurants to augment the collection running the length of the promenade.

The coastline south of Naxos Town is a **beach strip** without equal in the islands. Running for kilometres between headland and cove are a succession of excellent sand beaches. The nearest lies on the edge of town at **Agios Georgios**. This is a good family beach, even if the large numbers visiting mean that it isn't the cleanest. A small headland to the south divides it from the low 'dam' that was built (at great cost to the wildlife) to prevent the salt flats behind — that are now home to the island airport — from flooding. A very windy beach has grown up along the north side of the

dam, which is popular with windsurfers and ignored by everyone else (note: there is an excellent windsurfing school here, offering a good opportunity to try repeatedly falling off a surfboard in shallow, sandy-bottomed waters). **Stelida** beach to the west is more popular with bathers and has a taverna.

South of the Stelida headland lie the bigger beaches (now sadly being marred by unsympathetic hotel and holiday home development). **Agios Prokopios** is the first of these. Home to a motley collection of establishments offering beds and bars (the more unscrupulous come complete with bouncers), the only paved street in town is the main road. Be sure to take a look at the small salt lakes behind the beach to the north of this beach 'resort'; dry in summer, the beds are caked with a layer of salt. Travelling in the opposite direction the coast road runs as far as **Agia Anna** beach. Thereafter a dusty track leads you to the quieter **Golden** and **Plaka** beaches. Beach boats also run from Agia Anna and Naxos Town to the isolated beaches of **Kalando** and **Rena** on the south coast.

In spite of its attractive main town, Naxos's fame has always rested on its verdant but hilly hinterland where an attractive rural Greek atmosphere pervades. Farming is still an important feature of the local economy (the island is noted for its wines and cheeses), and indeed, has been so profitable that it is only now that Naxos is really jumping on the tourism bandwagon. Sadly, roads have yet to catch up with this trend and are in a positively lethal condition in parts (this is one island where it is better to stick to buses rather than resort to mopeds). Most tourists tend to compromise and see the interior via a daily tour bus that heads along the meandering mountain roads (that run through pretty **Komiaki** — the highest village on the island) to the small developing northern 'resort' of **Apollon**. With an indifferent beach and little nightlife, few people stay here, however, and the fishing village subsists on the tour parties taking in the local sight — the giant Kouros (see p. 152) — and lunch before returning to civilization.

Two settlements en route also attract attention. The first is the attractive hillside village of **Filoti**, which, in addition to lying at the centre of the fertile Tragaia Valley and offering a view of an appealing unspoilt Greek island community, is also the starting point for the 2-hour trek to the summit of **Mt. Zeus** (the highest peak in the Cyclades). Serious hikers will find that it is worth attempting the ascent (despite the poorly marked paths) to marvel at the view of the archipelago, and the cave halfway up, where the god was supposed to have been born, and then nurtured by an eagle. The second village of note is **Apeiranthos**. Arguably the most attractive on the island, it has several Venetian towers and streets paved with the island's famous marble. The village is also home to a small Archaeological Museum housing some Early Cycladic figures. The village school also houses a small Geological Museum which charts the area's 17–19 c. emery mining industry. This was responsible for the road to the former port of **Moutsouna** — now a quiet beach backed by holiday homes. The remainder of the east coast of Naxos is quiet in the extreme, with tourists something of a rarity. This is in part due to the open cast mining south of Lionas, which reduces its tourist appeal for obvious reasons.

According to Herodotus, the inhabitants of Naxos were Ionians of Athenian origin. The island was sacked by a Persian expedition in 490 BC. The islanders responded by sending four ships to fight at Salamis, thereafter joining the Delian League and the control of Athens. In the Hellenistic and Byzantine periods the island drifted in quiet obscurity. The change came in 1207 when the island was captured by Marco Sanudi who founded the Venetian Duchy of Naxos. His family and its successor the Crispis ruled over most of the Cyclades until the Turkish conquest in 1566. In 1770–74 the island was briefly held by the Russians, gaining its freedom from the Turks in 1821.

The various ticket and travel agencies on the waterfront road are a good starting point when bed hunting (assuming you escape the room owners besieging the ferries). **Naxos Town** is home to the bulk of the island accommodation, with an easily located batch of hotels in the northern town. Nearest the ferry quay is the D-class *Oceanis* (☎ 22436), with the E-class *Anna* (☎ 22475) and *Savvas* (☎ 22213) down the street behind. There is also a nice hotel in the C-class *Grotta* (☎ 22215) beyond the *Apollon* (☎ 22468). In addition to several places offering rooms, the promenade has a cluster of C-class hotels at its southern end, including the *Hermes* (☎ 22220) and the *Coronis* (☎ 22626). The warren of streets around the castle is also home to a number of hotels, while the maze of streets to the north contains the *Panorama* (☎ 22330) and the pricey *Chateau Zevgoli* (☎ 22993), along with the D-class *Anixis* (☎ 22112) and a youth hostel/pension, the *Dionysos* (☎ 22331). These are better bets if you don't want to have to stagger far from the town's largest disco back to your bed.

The **Agios Georgios Beach** area is also well endowed with hotels and pensions, including the E-class *Soula* (☎ 23637) and *St. George* (☎ 23162). On the town road to the beach stands the C-class *Helmos* (☎ 22455) and the E-class *Folia* (☎ 22210) to the south. Two other hotels of note are the E-class *Korali* (☎ 23092) behind the beach supermarket, and, three blocks behind, the C-class *Zeus* (☎ 22912).

The beach strip is gradually being developed; at **Agios Prokopios** there are a scatter of pensions and the E-class *Agia Prokopios*. **Agia Anna** is more up-market with three C-class hotels near the beach: the *Iria Beach* (☎ 24178), the *Agia Anna*, and the *Artemis* (☎ 24880).

Λ

There is very fierce competition between the three sites that lie on the beach road running south of Naxos Town, so much so that it is not unusual to be approached on ferries by students (working off their camping bills) handing out promotional flyers in High Season. The sites have very different attractions, so it is worthwhile deciding what your priorities are before choosing between them:

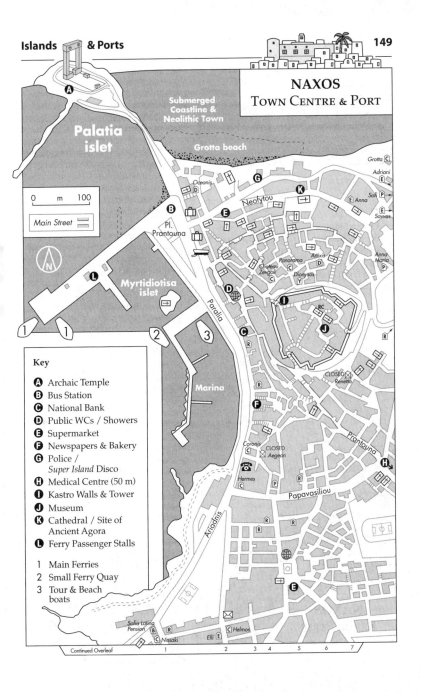

NAXOS
TOWN CENTRE & PORT

Palatia islet

Submerged Coastline & Neolithic Town

Grotta beach

Oceanis

Neofytou

Grotta C

Adriani E

Sofi P

Anna E

Savvas E

0 m 100

Main Street

Pl. Prantouna

Chateau Zevgoli

Panorama

Anixis D

Dionysos Y

Anna Maria P

Myrtidiotisa islet

Paralia

RC

Marina

CLOSED Renetta

Prantouna

Coronis C

CLOSED Aegean

Hermes

Papavasiliou

Ariadnis

Sofia Latina Pension

Nissaki C

Elli E

Helmos C

Continued Overleaf

1 2 3 4 5 6 7

Key

A Archaic Temple
B Bus Station
C National Bank
D Public WCs / Showers
E Supermarket
F Newspapers & Bakery
G Police / *Super Island* Disco
H Medical Centre (50 m)
I Kastro Walls & Tower
J Museum
K Cathedral / Site of Ancient Agora
L Ferry Passenger Stalls

1 Main Ferries
2 Small Ferry Quay
3 Tour & Beach boats

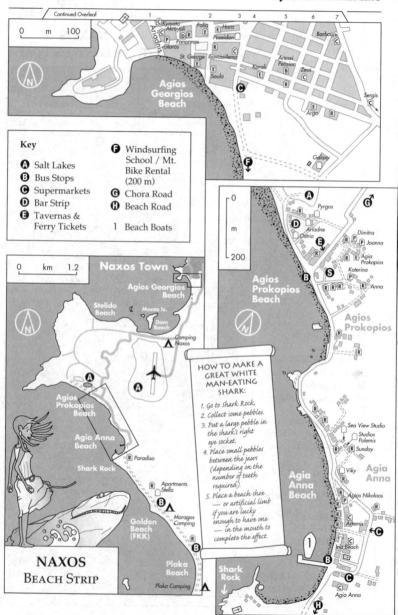

Key

A Salt Lakes
B Bus Stops
C Supermarkets
D Bar Strip
E Tavernas & Ferry Tickets
F Windsurfing School / Mt. Bike Rental (200 m)
G Chora Road
H Beach Road
1 Beach Boats

Continued Overleaf

0 m 100

Agios Georgios Beach

Kymata
Akroyali
Folia
Panormos
Glaros
Hara
Poseidon
St. George
Iliovassilema
Soula
Korali
Ariessi Pensiona
Zeus
Barbouni
Sergis
Argo
Galaxy

0 km 1.2

Naxos Town

Agios Georgios Beach

Stelida Beach
Manto Is.
Dam Beach

Agios Prokopios Beach

Agia Anna Beach

Shark Rock

Paradiso

Apartments Stella

Golden Beach (FKK)

Maragas Camping

Plaka Beach

Plaka Camping

NAXOS
BEACH STRIP

Camping Naxos

HOW TO MAKE A GREAT WHITE MAN-EATING SHARK:

1. Go to Shark Rock.
2. Collect some pebbles.
3. Put a large pebble in the shark's right eye socket.
4. Place small pebbles between the jaws (depending on the number of teeth required).
5. Place a beach shoe — or artificial limb if you are lucky enough to have one — in the mouth to complete the effect.

0 m 200

Pyrgos
Ariadne
Ostria
Dimitra
Joanna
Agia Prokopios
Katerina
Anna

Agios Prokopios Beach

Agios Prokopios

Sea View Studio
Studios Polemis
Sunday
Viky

Agia Anna

Agios Nikolaos

Agia Anna Beach

Artemis
Inia Beach

Shark Rock

Agia Anna

Naxos Camping (☎ 23501) is the nearest site to Naxos Town (2 km). This makes it the most convenient for nightlife addicts. The downside is that, knowing that they will get the town fans, they don't bother to provide much else. Even so, the site is large, with plenty of shade, clean (if aging) facilities and a roadside pool. Agios Georgios beach is a 1 km walk up the road. Tends to be popular with (and employ) Brits.

Maragas Camping (☎ 24552), is 7 km from the town. It is a typical (if large) beach site. The absence of anywhere else to go ensures that the beach-fronting bar is well patronized. The site is ever-popular with the younger beach-loving crowd. Echoes of hippydom pervade.

Plaka Camping (☎ 42700) is the newest site on Naxos (opening in 1997). If your idea of perfect camping is a good beach and immaculate facilities then it is a good bet; however, its isolated position means that if you want anything more you are dependent on hourly buses or your own wheels. Beware the site brochure: adorned with a faked photo depicting the reception block on the beach, it ignores the sand dunes and the dirt road separating it from the sea.

≥✿

Naxos Town and its beach strip to the south play host to most of the island's nightlife. This is surprisingly tame given the popularity of Naxos, which has thrived regardless on a diet of good beaches peopled by holidaying couples wallowing in dreamy romance. The brasher singles scene is only now emerging (though so far its impact on the town is minimal), with more bars and clubs arriving each year. Recent arrivals include the *Ocean Club Disco* behind the National Bank and the nearby *Musique Café*, the *Caesar's Club* and the *Super Island*,

all on the promenade. Two other nearby bars can get very lively — *Mike's Bar* and *The Jam* (tucked away behind the OTE). A popular collection of nightspots lies along the main port—Grotta road just off the ferry quay, the best being the *Empire, Seven* and the *Loft Bar* near the police station on the Port—Grotta road. Turning south, the promenade is home to the imaginatively named *Greek Bar*. Agios Georgios beach also has a number of discos attached to the hotels and other bars in the nearby streets.

👓

Naxos Town offers the best sightseeing options. First of these is the **Archaic Temple** (6 C. BC) and its remarkably well-preserved cella doorway on Palatia islet. Reached by braving a surf-kissed causeway (that was home to half a dozen windmills in medieval times), it is now expected of most visitors that they will come away with at least one photograph of themselves standing astride the base stones inside the arch (this isn't quite as famous a shot as being snapped holding up the leaning tower of Pisa, but it runs it pretty close). Little remains of the rest of the temple apart from the floor and assorted stones. Originally having 12 Ionic columns on each side and 6 at each end, the building was converted into a church, and until the late Middle Ages was surrounded by houses.

The temple is something of an enigma, as no surviving literature from antiquity mentions it. With no inscriptions from the site recovered either, debate rages as to to whom it was dedicated; the main candidates are Dionysos or Apollo. Sentiment favours the former, but its age and the particular affinity that the Archaic Naxians enjoyed with Delos and its Apollo sanctuary suggest the latter. What is known is that it is a contemporary of similar massive temples built during this period at Athens and Samos. The fragments that survive also testify to the fact that this impressive temple was never finished: the stone 'knobs' adorning some of the stones on the archway were left by the builders on otherwise finished blocks to help hoist them into position. Their removal was one of the last acts in a temple's completion: it never happened here.

The temple arch was initially believed by antiquarians to be the doorway of Ariadne's palace, for tradition has it that Naxos was the home of the god Dionysos. It was on Palatia

HOW TO MAKE MAD, PASSIONATE, EROTIC LOVE (IN THE DARK) ON THE BACK OF A GREAT WHITE MAN-EATING SHARK:

SEE p. 673–692

that he is supposed to have ravished Ariadne, the beautiful maiden abandoned here by the Athenian hero Theseus after their escape from Knossos on Crete. Quite why Theseus dumped the girl who — with her ball of thread — gave him the means of escape from the Labyrinth after killing the Minotaur isn't known. Three millennia on, attempts to unravel the threads of this relationship are dangerous; however it is a fair bet that Ariadne was both very highly strung and apt to whine. Dionysos, the god of wine and pleasure, loved both a good vintage and Ariadne: he built her a palace, only to find that she (being a mere mortal) inconsiderately went and died on him; whereupon he got the hump, threw her bridal crown of seven stars into the night sky (these now form the constellation Corona Borealis) and went off and invented orgies.

The **Old Town** (largely a product of the period of Venetian rule between 1207–1566 when members of the Sonudi family set up shop as the Dukes of Naxos) runs around the 13 c. castle walls and is filled with geraniums and a lovely warren of little streets to get lost in. The **Kastro**, built on the site of the ancient acropolis, contains a Roman Catholic cathedral and a **Museum** (one of the few where you can see some of the Early Cycladic marble figurines so sought after by art thieves). The Kastro is well preserved (and graced with the escutcheons of various Venetian noble families), though

its heart has a somewhat antiseptic feel to it: this is in part because the ruling Venetian community that lived here constructed it as their own non-Greek part of town, and the islanders have not managed to shake off their ambivalent feelings towards it since.

The windswept northern shoreline of the town, known as **Grotta**, is also of interest, thanks to a couple of caves and the submerged remains of an Early Cycladic town (presumably complete with drowned figurines) just off the beach. Remains of the Classical and Roman town are harder to spot. Some excavation is going on in the Grotta area, but major buildings — such as the theatre — have yet to be located. The site of the agora is known; it stood, north of the Kastro, on the site of the current cathedral square.

Around Naxos are a number of archaeological sites of varying merit. The most visited of these are the ancient marble quarries at **Melanes** and **Apollon**, where there are the partially carved remains of large male statues known as **Kouroi**. These are stylized figures which were abandoned half-completed due to faults in the stone. The colossal **Apollon Kouros** (7 c. BC) is easily the best of the three; 10.5 m tall (making the figure five times life-size), it is a giant rough sketch in stone of a god — probably Dionysos.

The two **Melanes Kouroi**, despite being abandoned in something nearer their intended final form, are much smaller (being only just over life-size) and of a much cruder design than the Apollon figure. Most visitors to Melanes only see the better preserved kouros: the second figure is hidden away down an overgrown track some 300 m to the south. The remains of a finished Naxian colossal figure of similar size to the Apollon Kouros can be seen on the nearby island of Delos (see p. 202). Naxos was a major exporter of sculpture during the Archaic period (the famous lions on Delos were also carved from Naxian marble), but as with Paros, export — rather than local construction — was the order

Corona Borealis

THE APOLLON KOUROS
OVERHEAD VIEW

SCALE

of the day, so Naxos itself has comparatively little Archaic material on show.

Remains of ancient structures are to be found in remoter areas. The most noteworthy of these is a **Temple of Demeter** that lies halfway down the road from Naxos Town to the beach hamlet at Pyrgaki. Dating from the 6 C. BC, it was unusual in having a square floor plan with 5 Ionic columns on its pedimental side, and a roof made up of marble beams and thin marble tiles that allowed a diffused light into the interior. The cella is also noteworthy as all the inside wall stones were left uncut, with the result that the temple's holy of holies would have resembled a cave or grotto, illuminated by the translucent marble roof. The building survived until the 9 C. AD, when it was destroyed and the site abandoned. Now recognized as important because of the uniqueness of its architecture, the temple has been partially reconstructed, and now has a small museum attached.

Naxos is also noted for its **Towers** (over 30 in number, they are known as 'Pyrgi' and are the remains of fortified manor houses), **Castles**, and even the odd fortified monastery for good measure. These litter the interior; most date from medieval times. The closest one to the tourist strip is well-preserved **Paleopirgos Castle**, one hour's walk inland via a track running from Plaka beach. Most of the Pyrgi require hard walking if you want to visit them, but they do offer a good starting point for those who enjoy walking holidays, and Naxos is a popular island among walkers. Anyone taking time to explore the island by foot should step first in the direction of the bookshop on the promenade and buy a copy of Christian Ucke's excellent *Walking the Greek Islands: Naxos and the Small Cyclades* (€11.70); this offers 26 suggested routes and a lot of background detail.

The final great sight on Naxos is the **Mount Zeus** and **Cave of Zeus** combination. Not a trek for the faint-hearted, the walk (described in detail in the guide above) from the hill village of Filoti to the summit takes in the cave where, tradition has it, Zeus was raised. Truth to tell, the cave isn't on a par with the larger cave on Antiparos. Relatively shallow, it is more of a sloping cavern 150 m deep and is home to a substantial colony of bats and a curious species of large yellow spider. Few visitors venture much beyond the entrance (where there are the remains of a rough altar) if only because most don't appreciate the need to bring a torch until they get into it.

Paros
ΠΑΡΟΣ; 194 km²; pop. 7,900.

CODE ☎ 22840
PORT POLICE ☎ 21240
POLICE ☎ 21221
FIRST AID ☎ 22500

A large and well-placed island, Paros has become the de facto hub of the Greek ferry system in recent years, and it is now difficult for Cycladic island hoppers to avoid calling at some point during their holiday. As a result, Paros is apt to get horribly overcrowded at the peak of the High Season. In part this is due to the charms of the island itself, for it is ringed with good sandy beaches, is fertile inland (in a dusty sort of way), and now has plenty of nightlife into the bargain.

Paros's main port and tourist centre is at **Parikia** (though you find that except on the island itself all ticket agents and schedules simply refer to it as 'Paros'). Occupying a sheltered bay on the west coast, it has been the main island centre since the Bronze Age, when an early Cycladic village existed on the site. It briefly lost its role as the island capital during the Ottoman period, when inland Lefkes took over (being far less vulnerable to pirate attack). Today the port town has re-emerged as the undisputed centre on the island, ribboning ever further along the shore. At its heart lies a typical Cycladic chora, complete with the odd wall of a Venetian kastro built on the site of the ancient acropolis in 1207. Neither is the best examples of its type (though the chora manages to retain a surprising amount of charm even when it is swarming with tourists), but they are suitable symbols, in their way, of Paros as a whole.

Very much tied to the shoreline, Parikia does not extend inland to any great extent, and is neatly divided by the road running south from the recently extended ferry quay (Prombona St.). To the west lies the old part of town, to the east the modern hotel and beach strip. Between the two lies the church of Ekatontapiliani, discreetly tucked

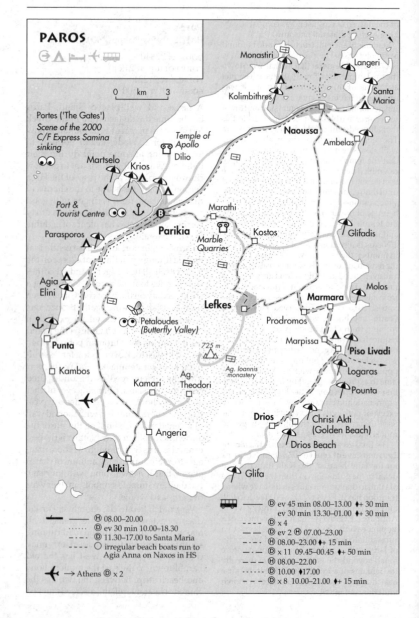

PAROS

Portes ('The Gates')
*Scene of the 2000
C/F Express Samina
sinking*

Martselo

Krios

Temple of
Apollo
Dilio

Monastiri

Kolimbithres

Langeri

Santa
Maria

Naoussa

Ambelas

Port &
Tourist Centre

Parosporos

Agia
Elini

Punta

Kambos

Petaloudes
(Butterfly Valley)

Kamari

Ag.
Theodori

Angeria

Aliki

Glifa

Parikia

Marathi

*Marble
Quarries*

Kostos

Lefkes

725 m

Ag. Ioannis
monastery

Glifadis

Molos

Marmara

Prodromos

Marpissa

Piso Livadi

Logaras

Pounta

Drios

Chrisi Akti
(Golden Beach)

Drios Beach

0   km   3

──── ⊞ 08.00–20.00
······ Ⓓ ev 30 min 10.00–18.30
─·─· Ⓓ 11.30–17.00 to Santa Maria
──── ◯ irregular beach boats run to
Agia Anna on Naxos in HS

✈ → Athens Ⓓ x 2

──── Ⓓ ev 45 min 08.00–13.00 ♦+ 30 min
         ev 30 min 13.30–01.00 ♦+ 30 min
──── Ⓓ x 4
──── Ⓓ ev 2 ⊞ 07.00–23.00
─·─· ⊞ 08.00–23.00 ♦+ 15 min
─·─· Ⓓ x 11   09.45–00.45 ♦+ 50 min
──── ⊞ 08.00–22.00
······ Ⓓ 10.00 ♦17.00
──── Ⓓ x 8   10.00–21.00 ♦+ 15 min

out of sight behind a park-cum-wood of pine trees. All the essential facilities are to be found within easy distance of the quay 'square' and its distinctive windmill. The building block opposite the quay is devoted en masse to ticket agents (it also has the best luggage deposit in Parikia: a 24-hour affair — stairs lead up to it from two sides of the block).

Behind the waterfront buildings lies the town's main square; decorated with shrubs and trees of a sort, it has more the feel of a crossroads between the various quarters of the town and the ferry quay. This reflects the fact that the waterfront is the real centre of activity in the town. Apart from the section composed of the whitewashed kastro walls, it is lined with restaurants, bars, shops and hotels, though it has to be said that it isn't the most photogenic in the Aegean by a long way. The best thing it has going for it is its orientation — it is ideally positioned for sitting back and admiring the sunset over a drink or two. At night it is very lively, and in High Season is packed with crowds and mosquitoes drinking up the atmosphere along the promenade. This ends in a small headland decked with a windmill (with a couple more hidden amid the hotels on the hill behind). The waterfront east of the ferry quay is quieter (though this is relative) and home to some of the better restaurants in town. Up one of the backstreets behind lies an open air cinema, with current release films in English, served up with popcorn and all the trimmings, in someone's back yard. A second cinema — the *Rex* — lies on the ring road at the back of the town.

Parikia also has a number of beaches within easy reach. The best and most popular is the main town beach, opposite the tourist hotel and restaurant strip east of the ferry quay (during the small hours it plays host to drunken bathers kitted out in their underclothes). There is another — albeit more skimpy — beach on the east side of the bay that is also crowded, and a less attractive strand on the west end of the town promenade. All are adequate for

the odd day of sunbathing, but are pretty inferior compared to some of the other beaches on Paros. One of these, a collection of coves a boat ride across the bay at Krios, is easily accessible from Parikia, and has many fans thanks to the opportunity it offers to remove more beach-wear than is acceptable nearer the town (i.e. everything). Buses from Parikia are usually very crowded, and geared to moving tourists to beaches further afield. Both the bus station (in the form of a dinky little kiosk) and the beach boats operate from points just to the east of the ferry quay.

The fenced-off ferry quay is one of the largest in the Cyclades and in High Season sees ferries queuing up to berth during the midday and midnight busy periods. Waiting ferry passengers are corralled in three quayside passenger stalls. At the ferry end of each is a gate that is unlocked when the ferry calls; it therefore pays to be in the correct stall (the port police chalk up the names of the next three boats due in on blackboards on the town side of each). When arriving at Paros you should also note that the quay exit gate is on the west/old town side of the passenger stall block (this is kept locked until the first arrivals reach it, to prevent stall-jumping by departing passengers). On Paros the sheer number of tourists also dictates that it is advisable to buy your tickets well in advance if you are planning to take one of the smaller ferries in High Season. Apart from the crowds, the only problem you are likely to encounter is the delightfully large choice of connections available. During the Low Season Paros remains the best-served Aegean island, though daily departures rarely reach double figures.

Around Paros there are a number of tourist resorts and beaches that are easily accessible thanks to the good (but invariably very crowded) bus service. The picturesque chora town of **Naoussa**, set in a bay on the northern coast and dominated by a tall Orthodox church, has rapidly expanded to become the island's second major tourist centre. Smaller and prettier

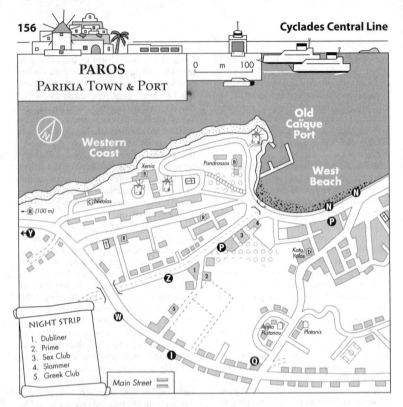

PAROS
PARIKIA TOWN & PORT

0   m   100

Western Coast

Old Caïque Port

Xenia

Pandrossos B

West Beach

Nicolas C

R (100 m)

Kato Yalos D

Anna Platanou   Platanis

NIGHT STRIP
1. Dubliner
2. Prime
3. Sex Club
4. Slammer
5. Greek Club

Main Street

than Parikia, it shares one thing in common, in as much as it is also bursting at the seams with tourists during the summer months. At the height of the season numbers get quite oppressive as its capacity to absorb them is not nearly so great. At the centre of the town is a whitewashed chora. Laid out in an almost grid-like pattern, it is more boutique-filled than its Parikia counterpart. In spite of this, it is the taverna-lined waterfront that is the great draw, with a charming caïque harbour backed by pretty Venetian houses (now doubling as dreamy tavernas) and protected on the seaward harbour wall side by the remains of a kastro-cum-tower — now reduced to a surf-kissed breakwater. Running through, and dominating, the centre of town is a dry (in summer) river bed that is home to the town bus stop.

The chora lies to the east, gradually ascending the hillside to the dominating church and a handful of derelict windmills to the north. West of the river bed the town is reduced to a ribbon of houses running a mere two or three blocks deep along the coast. This coast road is home to the OTE and police station as well as the best Naoussa can offer by way of a beach; be warned, this isn't a lot. As a result, boats run from the waterfront to beaches around the bay, and round the headland to the beach at Santa Maria (also reached via a daily bus from Parikia or a local bus from Naoussa).

The number three resort destination, **Piso Livadi**, is a quaint little village gathered around a cute little harbour on the east side of the island, with a thrice-weekly High Season

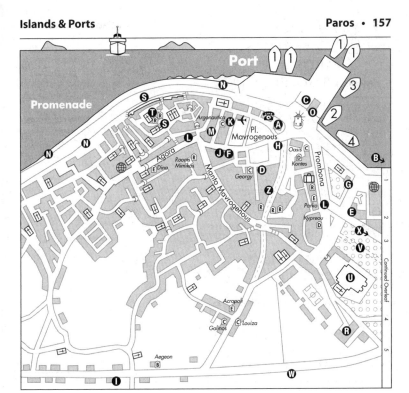

Key

A Tourist Information Office
B Bus Station (15 m)
C Hotel Information Kiosk
D Police / Tourist Police
E Hospital / Clinic
F National Bank of Greece
G Public WCs
H Taxi Rank
I Supermarket
J Bakery
K Pharmacy
L International Press
M Paros Craft Shop
N Tavernas

O Ferry Passenger Stalls
P Night Strip
Q Cinema Rex
R Archaeological Museum
S Frankish Kastro Walls
T Foundations of the
  Temple of Aphrodite
U Ekatontapiliani
  Cathedral &
  Baptistry
V Pine Wood Park
W Ring Road
X Naoussa Road
Y Punta Road
Z Street / River Bed

1 Ferries
2 Antiparos Town
  & Cave Tour
  Boats
3 Hydrofoils
4 Krios Beach &
  Camping
  Taxi Boats

*Panagia
Ekatontapiliani —
The Cathedral Church*

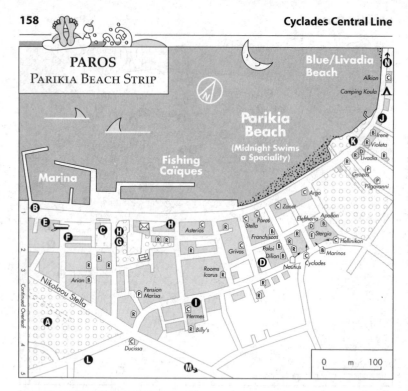

PAROS
PARIKIA BEACH STRIP

Blue/Livadia Beach

Parikia Beach
(Midnight Swims a Speciality)

Fishing Caïques

Marina

Key

- **Ⓐ** Pine Wood Park
- **Ⓑ** Bus Station (all destinations)
- **Ⓒ** Excavated Classical & Hellenistic Cemetery
- **Ⓓ** Open Air Cinema
- **Ⓔ** Books & International Press
- **Ⓕ** Large Supermarket
- **Ⓖ** Mountain Bike Rental
- **Ⓗ** Moped Rental
- **Ⓘ** Supermarket
- **Ⓙ** Pizzeria
- **Ⓚ** Bar Strip
- **Ⓛ** Parikia Town Ring Road
- **Ⓜ** Naoussa Road
- **Ⓝ** Krios & Dilio Roads

link to Naxos and Amorgos, besides being a nice place to stay if you are seeking to escape the worst of the crowds. This said, a resort is rapidly developing behind a couple of good beaches immediately to the south of the village at Logaras and Pounta, and is attracting a fair number of the younger crowd.

At the top of the isolated cone-shaped hill that climbs up behind Piso Livadi is a medieval fortress, complete with a disused monastery and the church of Agios Antonios. Access is via a small road that starts in the backstreets behind the windmill at nearby Marpissa (which backs right onto Piso Livadi).

Piso Livadi is also conveniently close to the island's best beach (all the best beaches on Paros are to be found along this stretch of coast) at **Chrisi Akti** (Golden Beach). As the name suggests, this is an excellent stretch of sandy coast and is popular with windsurfers (despite the pretensions of less attractive Santa Maria beach to the north). Nearby lies the village of **Drios**; now rapidly being spoilt by ugly uncontrolled hotel development, it is the destination of Parikia buses.

The fourth centre of note is at **Aliki** on the south coast. Little more than a quiet beach village, it offers a peaceful and more relaxing alternative to the main resorts. In High Season it also has an irregular taxi-boat service to Antiparos (sometimes continuing east to a beach on the islet of **Despotiko**). Other destinations have less going for them.

The inland chora village of **Lefkes** developed as the island capital during the days when pirates ruled the seas, forcing the abandonment of the traditional centre at Parikia. Built in the shape of a vague amphitheatre in the hills, it is well worth a look and is an appealing hangover from the days before Paros was irredeemably changed by tourism. Access is easy via the frequent Parikia—Piso Livadi buses, though it is better to avoid them when the masses are either travelling to or from the east coast beaches.

Parikia buses also run hourly to the middle of nowhere. This is the lonely small quay at **Punta**, landing place for the regular Antiparos car ferries (times are posted up at Punta on the chapel wall near the ferry quay).

The combination of size, fertility and marble has ensured that Paros has always been an important island. As early as the 7 C. BC it was sufficiently powerful to send a colony to Thassos (the standard procedure employed by Greek city states and islands for dealing with population overspills). In 490 BC Paros sided with the Persians at the Battle of Salamis (via one trireme), and thereafter found itself under the control of Athens. Like the other Cycladian islands, Paros drifted out of the scene in the Hellenistic and Byzantine periods, enjoying increasing pirate activity and diminishing prosperity.

In the medieval period Paros was an important component of the Duchy of Naxos until 1389. Conquered by the Turks in 1537, Paros saw the Russian fleet use it as a winter base in 1770–71, and the island remained in Russian hands until 1774 when the Turks regained control. Independence was achieved in 1821.

Paros had (until 2000) a good Accommodation Office on the ferry quay with staff that would phone around for you. Hopefully it will be back in business this year. Meantime, plentiful offers of rooms greet boats arriving before 18.00 (many by room owners from nearby Antiparos), but prices rise in High Season when the morning ferries from Piraeus start arriving after midday. From then on you will have to be prepared to pay up or look further afield. Naoussa is the best bet, as the town is plastered with 'Rooms' signs. Piso Livadi also has a reasonable supply.

Well-endowed **Parikia** is home to the greatest number of the island's hotels. These are divided between the old part of town (mostly smaller, budget establishments) and the new, tourist-dominated suburb to the east (which is home to the bulk of the package tour hotels). Other hotels lie around the town environs — including the expensive *Xenia* (☎ 21394), located 100 m west of the town's west beach behind a couple of windmills.

Mid-range hotels mostly cater for package tourists, but they are quick to snap up island hoppers to fill any empty beds. Some even have signs outside indicating vacancies. The waterfront east of the ferry quay includes the C-class *Asterias* (☎ 21797), *Stella* (☎ 21502) and the *Argo* (☎ 21367). Quieter hotels lie in the streets behind, including the *Cyclades* (☎ 22048) and the new *Hotel John* (☎ 22797). If you want to splash out at the middle end of the range, the C-class *Argonautica* (☎ 21440) is conveniently placed behind the main town square with attractive, if pricey, rooms. Near the ferry quay are a couple of reasonable D-class establishments that are easy to find: the *Kontes* (☎ 21096) and the *Kypreou* (☎ 21383). The latter is the cheaper of the two.

Another popular group of hotels lie along the river bed cum road: the C-class *Galinos* (☎ 21480), *Louiza* (☎ 22122) and E-class *Acropoli* (☎ 21521). Other E-class hotels in town include the *Dina* (☎ 21325) and the *Parko* (☎ 22213). At the budget end of the market are a number of establishments offering rooms (these are effectively backpackers' pensions), notably *Rooms Icarus* (☎ 21695) in the new strip and the better *Rooms Mimikos* (☎ 21437) in the chora part of town.

Other towns also have hotels on offer. **Naoussa** is the best equipped, with the B-class *Naoussa* (☎ 51207), overlooking the waterfront, standing out from the rest. **Piso Livadi** has fewer rooms, but they are much quieter. One of the best is the C-class *San Antonio* overlooking the village.

▲

On Paros there are a large number of sites: *Camping Koula* (☎ 22081): nice olive-grove site and the nearest to the port. The site cashes in on its convenient location, though sleepers sometimes experience more disruption than most from 03.00 ferry arrivals and disco returnees. There is a strictly enforced 23.00–07.00 noise ban (lovers have to moan quietly) and free WC-rolls are issued to all.

Camping Krios (☎ 21705) is one of the newer sites on the beach opposite the port. Sadly let down in the past by a lack of regular cleaning, it seems to be better these days. The taxi-boat link to Parikia (last at 19.30) is also not conducive to nightlife or catching an early morning ferry (though there is a fair mini-bus service).

Parasporos Camping (☎ 21394) is a better site 3 km south of the town, with mini-buses that also provide campers with a free service to and from town. Good on-site facilities include a pool. Past years have seen free tents provided to campers out of High Season.

Camping Naoussa (☎ 51398) is one of the better sites on Paros if a frenetic nightlife isn't a priority; again, mini-buses meet boats.

Camping Surfing Beach (☎ 51013), nestling in the scrub behind Santa Maria beach, is the newest site on Paros, and popular with windsurfers. Facilities are good, with a free shuttle service to and from Parikia.

Camping Agia Elini is an indifferent site on one of the best island beaches.

Captain Kafkis Camping (☎ 41392), 1 km outside Piso Livadi, is for those who like a quiet life with fair facilities. The site now has a mini-bus advertising it as 'The Green Site'.

≋☆

Nightlife in **Parikia** is dominated by the large *Dubliner* / *Paros Rock* / *Comma* complex. Built on two levels, this is the real hot spot in town, with two dance floors and a few quiet corners where you can find out the name of the person you are trying to get off with (something that

you usually have to leave until morning on Ios). The other clubs have less going for them: *Prime* club is a disco that is haunted by older revellers, while the *Sex Club* is so noisy that it doesn't appeal to anybody and is usually thinly filled. The *Greek Club* relies on holidaying locals.

A visit to one of the open-air cinemas also just qualifies as nightlife (it makes a good starter to an evening of bar crawling). However, don't be surprised to find the locals diving for the entrance if the national anthem is played. The Greek anthem, with its 158 verses, is the longest in the world (in most places the locals just sing the first two and then whistle the rest, but it's never wise to chance it).

👓

Considering that Paros was famed in antiquity for the quality of its marble (Parian marble is more translucent than other types in Greece — that is to say, light penetrates further through it, giving it a sparkling white, light-absorbent appearance) it is sad that the island boasts no Classical archaeological site of importance (though there are the scanty remains of a temple at Dilio). The famous **Marble Quarries** do survive outside Marathi, though few visitors venture beyond the cave-like entrance.

The **Venetian Kastro** (1260 AD) at **Parikia** was largely constructed from the remains of archaic **Temples of Demeter & Apollo**, remnants of which can be seen in the form of the circular column drums now embedded in the surviving kastro walls and the black foundations of the temple base. The town does, however, have one notable architectural monument: the 6 c. AD cathedral church of **Ekatontapiliani**. This rather odd name (thought to be a corruption of 'in the lower town') now means 'Our Lady of the 100 doors' — for the building was supposed to have had as many. Truth to tell you would be hard put to know it today, though a number of architecture students have managed to trace a dozen on their first attempt and 99 after a few ouzos. The 100th is believed to have been carried off by the Turks (a delightful notion as it suggests in a subtle way that the old enemy is completely unhinged along with it). Tradition also claims that the church was designed by Isidore of Miletus, with the

Santorini Taxi Boat

Caldera View from
Oia/Ia

**SANTORINI
/THIRA**

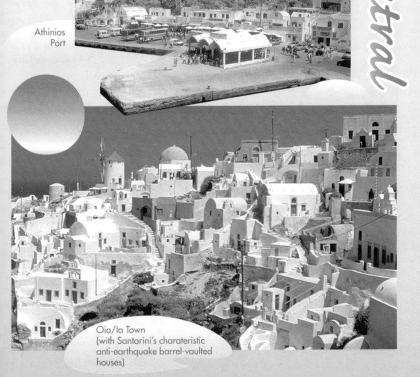
Athinios
Port

Oia/Ia Town
(with Santorini's charateristic
anti-earthquake barrel-vaulted
houses)

SANTORINI
Akrotiri Excavation

Boxing Children Fresco

Building Delta (East Side)

West House & Triangular Square

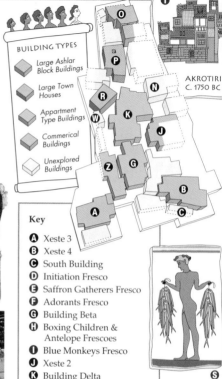

BUILDING TYPES

Large Ashlar Block Buildings

Large Town Houses

Appartment Type Buildings

Commerical Buildings

Unexplored Buildings

AKROTIRI C. 1750 BC

Key

- **A** Xeste 3
- **B** Xeste 4
- **C** South Building
- **D** Initiation Fresco
- **E** Saffron Gatherers Fresco
- **F** Adorants Fresco
- **G** Building Beta
- **H** Boxing Children & Antelope Frescoes
- **I** Blue Monkeys Fresco
- **J** Xeste 2
- **K** Building Delta
- **L** Stone Sacral Horns
- **M** Lilies or Spring Fresco
- **N** Xeste 5
- **O** Sector Alpha
- **P** House of the Ladies
- **Q** Fresco of the Ladies
- **R** West House
- **S** Fisherboys Fresco
- **T** Miniature Fresco
- **U** Bathroom
- **V** Triangular Square
- **W** House of the Anchor
- **X** Propylon
- **Y** Telchines Road
- **Z** Building Gamma

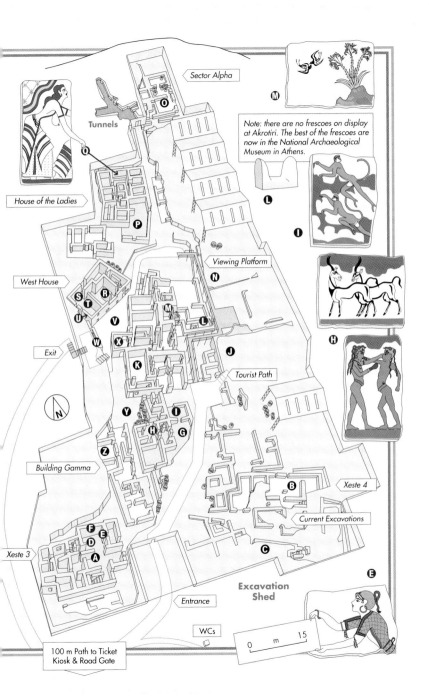

Sector Alpha

M

Note: there are no frescoes on display
at Akrotiri. The best of the frescoes are
now in the National Archaeological
Museum in Athens.

Tunnels

Q

L

I

House of the Ladies

P

Viewing Platform

N

West House

S T R

M

U

V

L

H

Exit

W X

J

K

Tourist Path

Y

I

Z

H G

Building Gamma

B

Xeste 4

Current Excavations

F E

D

Xeste 3

A

C

E

Excavation
Shed

N

Entrance

WCs

0   m   15

100 m Path to Ticket
Kiosk & Road Gate

SANTORINI/THIRA
Views of the Volcano
(Kameni Islands)

SYROS
Ermoupolis

Cyclades

THIRASIA
Busy Main Street in August

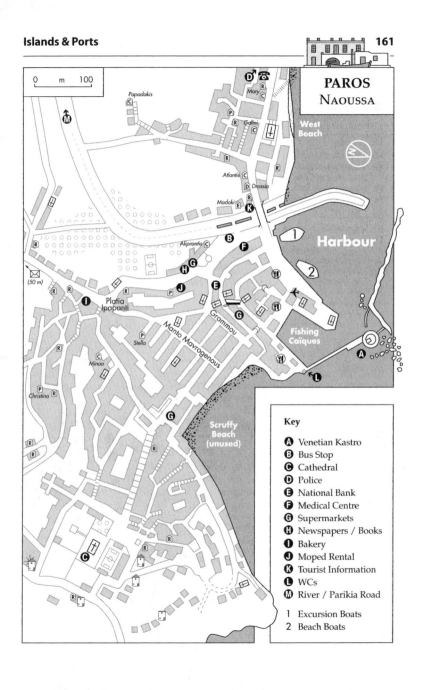

PAROS
NAOUSSA

0 m 100

Papadakis C

West Beach

Harbour

Mary C
Galini C
Atlantis C
Drossia D
Madaki E
K

Aliprantis C
B
F
H G
E
J
Grammou
G

1
2

Platia
Ipapanti

Manto Mavrogenous
Stella P
Minoa C
Christina P

Fishing
Caïques

A

L

G

Scruffy
Beach
(unused)

C

Key

A Venetian Kastro
B Bus Stop
C Cathedral
D Police
E National Bank
F Medical Centre
G Supermarkets
H Newspapers / Books
I Bakery
J Moped Rental
K Tourist Information
L WCs
M River / Parikia Road

1 Excursion Boats
2 Beach Boats

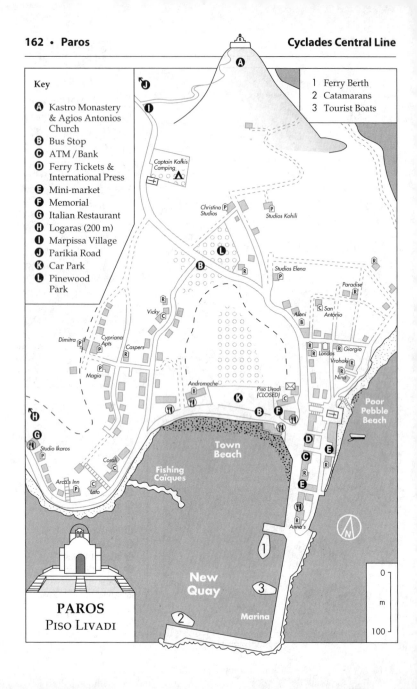

Key

Ⓐ Kastro Monastery & Agios Antonios Church
Ⓑ Bus Stop
Ⓒ ATM / Bank
Ⓓ Ferry Tickets & International Press
Ⓔ Mini-market
Ⓕ Memorial
Ⓖ Italian Restaurant
Ⓗ Logaras (200 m)
Ⓘ Marpissa Village
Ⓙ Parikia Road
Ⓚ Car Park
Ⓛ Pinewood Park

1 Ferry Berth
2 Catamarans
3 Tourist Boats

Captain Kofkis Camping

Christina Studios
Studios Kohili
Studios Elena
Paradise
San Antonio
Aleni
Vicky
Dimitra
Cypriana Apts
Caspers
Londos
Giorgio
Vrohaki
Nina
Magia
Andromache
Piso Livadi (CLOSED)
Poor Pebble Beach
Town Beach
Studio Ikaros
Coroli
Fishing Caiques
Arca's Inn
Lefo
Anna's

PAROS
Piso Livadi

New Quay

Marina

0
m
100

construction carried out by his pupil Ignatius. When it was completed, Isidore is said to have been so jealous of the church's beauty that he attacked his pupil on the roof with the result that both fell to their deaths. Given that Isidore was one of the architects responsible for the infinitely more wondrous Agia Sofia in İstanbul/Constantinople one suspects this is hyperbole. The oldest part of the building is Roman anyway. The **Archaeological Museum** behind the church has part of the Roman pavement uncovered in the church on display amongst other island exhibits.

South of Parikia, the old town of **Lefkes** is the main destination for tour buses thanks to its old chora atmosphere. The main sights in town are the churches — notably the white marble church of the Holy Trinity.

The final destination of note is the **Valley of the Butterflies** (alias tiger moths) at **Petaloudes** (from May to July). These gather before dying to mate in this quiet spot. Unfortunately, the poor creatures are now subjected to clapping and shouting exhibitions by tourists — thus alarming them into flight: the clouds of butterflies are, after all, what they have come to see. This is very debilitating for animals nearing the end of their lives and trying to conserve energy, and is producing dire consequences; as every jump means they have the energy for one less hump, their numbers are declining rapidly.

Santorini / Thira
ΣΑΝΤΟΡΙΝΙ / ΘΗΡΑ; 73 km²; pop. 7,100.

CODE ☎ 22860
TOURIST POLICE ☎ 22649
PORT POLICE ☎ 22239
HOSPITAL ☎ 22237

The most spectacular (and one of the most expensive) of all the Greek islands, Santorini is subject to ever-increasing waves of tourists drawn by the landscape, the archaeological discoveries at Akrotiri, and the legend of Atlantis. The island is commonly known by two names: the Venetian 'Santorini' (after the 3 c. AD St. Irene who died in exile hereabouts) or its Classical name of 'Thira' (now reinstated as its official name). 'Santorini' is more popular with tourists. Ferry operators usually prefer 'Thira' (also transcribed as

'Fira'), in the interests of brevity on ship destination boards.

The island is the largest fragment of a volcanic archipelago made up of the broken remnants of the largest caldera on earth. It is now thought by many to be the origin of the Atlantis legend, the inpouring of the sea into the caldera during a massive eruption c. 1640 BC giving early sailors the impression that the greater part of the island had sunk, taking the Minoan settlements on the island with it. Within the caldera, subsequent volcanic eruptions (the last in 1925–26) have spawned new islets of ominous, black, razor-sharp lava. The volcano is now quietly simmering with sulphur emissions and hot springs. If this wasn't enough by way of icing the tourist cake, the caldera rim is frosted with scenic white cubist towns that take a tumble every time an earthquake hits. The island also has a reputation as a home for vampires. All this ensures that Santorini is on the itinerary of every cruise ship, day-tripper and casual tourist within range, and usually full to overflowing, regardless of the time of year (a major problem in itself, as the island has no fresh water springs; supplies are tankered in daily from the mainland).

The centre of activity on Santorini is **Fira Town** (also transcribed as 'Thira' and 'Phira'). This large island capital is perched precariously on the edge of the caldera rim, with a switchback staircase (carpeted with donkey droppings) down the crater wall, and a cable-car for those who don't care for the donkey rides or the 587 awkward steps. These run to the old port of Skala Fira — and its mooring buoys for cruise ships — below the town. Now unashamedly a tourist centre, Fira has preserved enough of its charm to make a visit enjoyable. This might not seem to be the case if you arrive in the early hours when the main town square is thronged with tourists enjoying what amounts to an open air party, but once the surprisingly efficient town street cleaners have done their dawn stuff and revealed once again the black lava stone

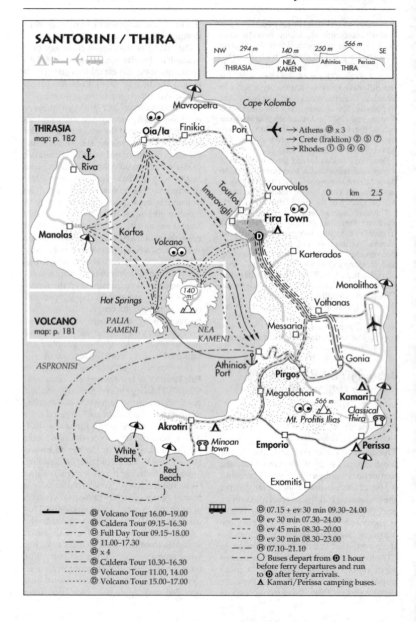

SANTORINI / THIRA

NW 294 m   140 m   250 m 566 m   SE
                    NEA   Athinios Perissa
        THIRASIA   KAMENI   THIRA

Mavropetra   Cape Kolombo

THIRASIA
map: p. 182

Riva

Oia/Ia   Finikia   Pori

→ Athens ⒹD x 3
→ Crete (Iraklion) ② ⑤ ⑦
→ Rhodes ① ③ ④ ⑥

Tourlos
Imerovigli

Vourvoulos

0   km   2.5

Manolas   Korfos

Fira Town

Volcano

Karterados

140
m

Monolithos

Hot Springs

Vothonas

VOLCANO
map: p. 181

PALIA
KAMENI

NEA
KAMENI

Messaria

ASPRONISI

Athinios
Port

Gonia

Pirgos

Megalochori

566 m

Kamari

Classical
Thira

Mt. Profitis Ilias

Akrotiri

Minoan
town

Emporio

Perissa

White
Beach

Red
Beach

Exomitis

— Ⓓ Volcano Tour 16.00–19.00
- - - Ⓓ Caldera Tour 09.15–16.30
-·-·- Ⓓ Full Day Tour 09.15–18.00
—— Ⓓ 11.00–17.30
-··- Ⓓ x 4
- - - Ⓓ Caldera Tour 10.30–16.30
········· Ⓓ Volcano Tour 11.00, 14.00
········ Ⓓ Volcano Tour 15.00–17.00

— Ⓓ 07.15 + ev 30 min 09.30–24.00
- - - Ⓓ ev 30 min 07.30–24.00
- - - Ⓓ ev 45 min 08.30–20.00
-··- Ⓓ ev 30 min 08.30–23.00
-·-·- Ⓗ 07.10–21.10
- - - ○ Buses depart from Ⓓ 1 hour
before ferry departures and run
to Ⓓ after ferry arrivals.
▲ Kamari/Perissa camping buses.

used to cobble the streets, a vague semblance of the Greek island idyll is restored, and even enhanced by the weird nature of the place. For Fira Town rolls dramatically with the landscape, falling fast from the caldera rim to the coastal plain, with its views of neighbouring Anafi. The rim itself is by no means level, and has the buildings rolling up and down every photogenic step of the way.

The great attraction in town is the view over the caldera and the volcano (principally from Ipapantis St.). Bars clutter up the best viewing places, fronting the warren of boutique-filled backstreets behind. Hidden away in these are several museums. Along the rim you will find occasional fragments of buildings that fell into the caldera on the 9th of July 1956, during an earthquake that all but levelled the town — killing 53 people and destroying 2,400 homes (one is apt to wonder if the restaurants perched precariously on the rim are really such a good idea). If losing many of its old buildings wasn't bad enough, Fira has suffered further disfigurement thanks to the large disused pumice quarry at the southern edge of the town, a gaping hole in the caldera wall that has been excavated to the pre-eruption level, revealing the stumps of petrified trees.

To get the most out of Fira you have to pick your moment. Early mornings are the best time to explore — it is cooler, the rising sun gives the buildings a lovely warming glow, ferries glide silently across the caldera over a cobalt-blue sea, and the streets are free from the camera-clutching hordes and the moped packs that cruise round looking for someone to mow down. As the sun sets the town comes into its own again as the vibrant nightlife scene takes over.

The island ferry terminus is at **Athinios**, 4 km south of Fira. Little more than a long quay — complete with a passenger shed (and in 2002 a loose pony wandering around) — at the bottom of the caldera cliff face, it is backed with ticket agencies, tavernas (to be avoided as they charge their captive market exorbitant prices) and a WC at the far end. It exists here solely because it was at this point that it was possible to cut a switch-back road down the cliff-side. In spite of this, access is still very limited; in High Season the number of vehicles attempting to reach the quay can result in major traffic jams, and it is not unknown for bus passengers to have to walk down the cliff to join their boats. These often hang around for a few hours: Santorini's popularity is reflected in the ferry schedules — some 9 hours' sailing from Piraeus, the island is an obvious terminus for boats doing a daily round trip.

The caldera rim also has other settlements clinging to it. The most important of these is the pretty small northern town of **Oia** (otherwise transcribed as 'Ia' and pronounced as 'EEa'). Also badly damaged by the 1956 earthquake, the town has been rebuilt after a fashion. Promoted as the 'Paris of the Aegean' for no apparent reason other than its photogenic nature (the best picture-postcard caldera rim views are invariably of Oia), it has fewer crowds and a nicer small-town atmosphere than Fira; this along with a reconstructed windmill and superb sunset views brings in the tour parties by the coach load. Sunsets aside, Oia is best explored during the day. Relatively cheap buses run from Thira (though the road is a disappointment as it runs too far inland for travellers to enjoy sweeping caldera views), leaving you to explore at your own pace. When you are tired of walking you always have the option of descending one of the two cliff-side stairways to the tiny port below the town. This has seen ferries decant passengers into taxi boats in past years, but now relies on fish-dish tavernas for its income. There is also a cliffside path running back into the caldera basin and ending at swimming rocks with a small — chapel-topped — lava stack 20 m offshore.

Following the rim around there are several other villages that are increasingly filled with expensive tourist accommodation, but

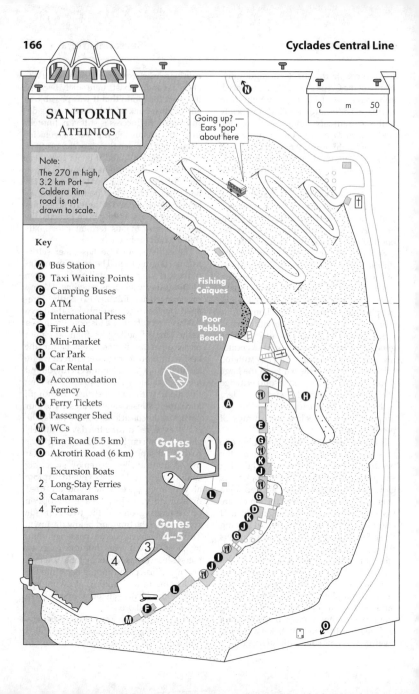

SANTORINI
ATHINIOS

Note:
The 270 m high,
3.2 km Port —
Caldera Rim
road is not
drawn to scale.

Going up? —
Ears 'pop'
about here

0   m   50

Key

Ⓐ Bus Station
Ⓑ Taxi Waiting Points
Ⓒ Camping Buses
Ⓓ ATM
Ⓔ International Press
Ⓕ First Aid
Ⓖ Mini-market
Ⓗ Car Park
Ⓘ Car Rental
Ⓙ Accommodation
   Agency
Ⓚ Ferry Tickets
Ⓛ Passenger Shed
Ⓜ WCs
Ⓝ Fira Road (5.5 km)
Ⓞ Akrotiri Road (6 km)

1 Excursion Boats
2 Long-Stay Ferries
3 Catamarans
4 Ferries

Fishing
Caïques

Poor
Pebble
Beach

Gates
1–3

Gates
4–5

which are still noticeably less spoilt than the main towns. The biggest of these are **Finikia**, just outside Oia, and **Tourlos** and **Imerovigli**. These last two run into the residential northern section of Fira Town (not shown on the map overleaf).

Turning inland from the caldera rim, the bulk of the island slopes steeply away and looks rather scruffy, being dry and treeless; the land is given over to producing tomatoes and ground-crawling vines that provide the wine for which Santorini is famous. The most accessible vineyards — with imaginative names like 'Volcano' — are to be found near Kamari, and they thrive on a procession of tour coaches that bring the masses to get their tongues around labels like 'Lava'. The reds certainly live up to the billing, giving the tastebuds a big bang that rapidly dwindles to an ashy nothing.

Dotted around the grey volcanic landscape between the vines are a number of whitewashed villages, which these days serve to mop up the tourists who can't find beds elsewhere. The largest of these — such as impressive hilltop **Pirgos**, and less dramatic **Emporio** and **Gonia** — have become minor centres in their own right. The best, however, is the dusty village of **Akrotiri** on the southern wing of the caldera rim. Only now opening up to tourism, it still retains much of its traditional character, thanks to the odd windmill, though the nearby Minoan town excavation is helping to change this. The town also offers good views of the volcano set against the backdrop of the towns of Fira and Oia on the caldera rim (telescopes are provided on the headland to the west of the town). The downside to Akrotiri is the lack of a convenient nearby beach.

Volcanic islands are not generally noted for having brilliant beaches, and Santorini is no exception. Beaches there are in profusion, but most are strewn with black pebbles or pumice. However, on the south-east coast the beaches consist of wide stretches of black sand which, although it lacks

sparkle and gets painfully hot (leaving sun worshippers looking like so many rows of pink sausages in a Teflon frying pan), has prompted the emergence of two large and successful beach resorts at Perissa and Kamari. Both are unashamedly tourist centres and nothing more, but they cater for very different markets.

Perissa is very much the haven of the independent and down-market budget traveller, with a host of pensions, rooms and bars along a main road running inland from the beach (as of 2000 it has even aquired its own waterpark for good measure). **Kamari** is better established and more up-market, with a lot of package tour hotels and a much more sophisticated waterfront. It is also conveniently placed for the island's airport. The two resorts are separated by an iron curtain of a headland which is topped by the ruined Classical and Roman capital of the island. Access on the Perissa side is via a well-trodden, but poor, path that requires a good hour's hard walking. On the Kamari side there is a longer switchback road (built for the coach tours) that is serviced by mini-buses. Both road and path arrive at a roundabout of sorts, usually complete with a van selling refreshments.

Other beaches on Santorini are to be found near the Minoan excavation at Akrotiri. The site — and its regular bus link to Fira — is only a short walk from the southern shore and caïques to two more of the island's beaches, Red Beach and White Beach. Both are named after the colour of their cinders-cum-sand. Oia also has an indifferent beach nearby, at Mavropetra.

Santorini has been occupied since at least 2000 BC. It first made an impact in the post-prehistorical period when it joined Milos in fighting against Athens in the Peloponnesian War. However, it fell to Athenian control regardless. During the Hellenistic period it was used by the Ptolemies as a naval base. From 1207 until the Turkish conquest in 1537 it was ruled by Venetian families and the Duchy of Naxos, finally gaining its freedom in 1821.

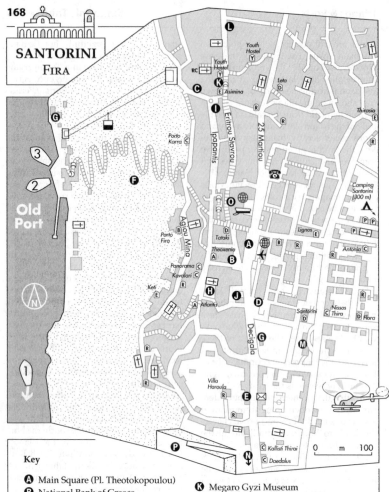

SANTORINI
FIRA

Old Port

3

2

1

Porto Karra

Porto Fira

Panorama

Kavalari

Keti

Atlantis

Villa Haroula

Ipapantis

Eritrou Stavrou

25 Martiou

Agiou Mina

Decigala

Camping Santorini (300 m)

Lignos

Antonia

Nissos Thira

Santorini

Flora

Youth Hostel

Youth Hostel

Asimina

Leta

Thirasia

Theoxenia

Tataki

Kallisti Thirai

Daedalus

RC

0   m   100

Key

Ⓐ Main Square (Pl. Theotokopoulou)
Ⓑ National Bank of Greece
Ⓒ Cable Car Ticket Office
Ⓓ Bus Station (all destinations)
Ⓔ Police
Ⓕ Stairway / Mule Track to Old Port
Ⓖ Public WCs
Ⓗ Cathedral
Ⓘ Archaeological Museum
Ⓙ Museum of Prehistoric Thira

Ⓚ Megaro Gyzi Museum
Ⓛ Old Style (unwhitewashed) Street
Ⓜ Medical Centre
Ⓝ Road to Port (4 km) & Heliport (2 km)
Ⓞ Nightclub Strip
Ⓟ Pumice Quarry (disused)

1   Athinios Port / Ferry Terminus (4 km)
2   Old Port Tour Boats & Thirasia Ferry
3   Cruise Ship Taxi-Boat Arrival Point

⊨

The supply of beds dries up early in High Season on Santorini. Even if you arrive on the first of the Piraeus morning boats (berthing around 15.00), you could have to settle for a night in a campsite or hostel before finding something more to your taste. The more expensive hotels tend to lie on the caldera rim (if you choose to stay in one, it pays to forget both your bank balance and the fact that when the last earthquake struck most of the rim-side buildings ended up a lot nearer sea level than they were before). Top of the range, and a landmark in its own right, is the chunky A-class *Atlantis* (☎ 22232) near the cathedral. Nearby lies the B-class *Porto Fira* (☎ 22849). To the north of this is the C-class *Porto Karra* (☎22 979), while two more C-class hotels lie up the slope: the *Panorama* (☎ 22481) and *Kavalari* (☎ 22455).

The east side of Fira Town offers the best prospect of finding a bed in High Season, with a number of 'cheaper' hotels. These include the C-class *Nissos Thira* (☎ 23252) and *Antonia* (☎ 22879), the D-class *Santorini* (☎ 22593) and *Flora* (☎ 81524), and the E-class *Lignos* (☎ 23 101) and *Thirasia* (☎ 22546). The road to the campsite is also worth trying, as it is lined with pensions. Other hotels lie to the south of the town, including the C-class *Kallisti Thirai* (☎ 22317) and the *Daedalus* (☎ 22834). More hotels are being built to the south, overlooking the ugly old pumice quarry — pretty desperate stuff. The cable-car area of town also has a number of cheaper establishments. These include three youth hostels — the *Youth Hostel* (☎ 22722) on Eritrou Stavrou being easiest to find — and the E-class *Asimina* (☎ 22034). Inland the D-class *Leta* (☎ 22540) stands near the main road. A final option is to head for the village of **Karterados**, which mops up the tourist overspill at the cost of a thirty-minute walk into town.

Perissa is also popular, with two large hostels on the outskirts of town. There are also plenty of pensions and small hotels offering

relatively cheap beds. These include the E-class *Meltemi* (☎ 81325), *Boubis* (☎ 81202), and *Marousiana* (☎ 81124) on the main road. Rather more up-market is the D-class *Marianna* (☎81286), complete with pool.

Kamari has fewer non-pre-booked beds on offer, and outlets offering rooms are decidedly thin on the ground. The better bets here are the C-class *Akis* (☎ 31670) and *Adonis* (☎ 31956), the D-class *Blue Sea* (☎ 31481) and *Andreas* (☎31692), and the E-class *Dionysos* (☎ 31310). Other towns with hotels and rooms include **Oia** — complete with a good youth hostel: *Youth Hostel Oia* (☎ 71465) — and **Pirgos** on the road to the port.

▲

There are four campsites on Santorini; most have mini-buses meeting ferries:

Camping Santorini (☎ 22944) lies down the hill from Fira Town, and is easily the most convenient if you want to be close to the island's transportation hub and nightlife. The site has a small swimming pool, a small but good mini-market — that even sells international newspapers — and reasonable tree cover. Prices are typical for Santorini (i.e. €1.50 more expensive than sites on Paros but still cheaper than Mykonos).

Perissa Beach Camping (☎ 81343) is an equally expensive and crowded beach site right in the centre of Perissa. The camping entrance also seems to act as a general information centre. With a fair amount of tree cover, the site is great if you want to stagger straight from bar to sea via a tent. The downside is the noise level and the salt-water showers.

Caldera View Camping (☎82010), outside the village of Akrotiri, is the newest site on Santorini. The site has a swimming pool and new facilities; it also has a large number of bungalows that provide the bulk of the site's income. On the wrong side of the road to actually have a 'view' of the caldera and too far from the island's beaches or nightlife, this site is really struggling to attract campers.

Kamari Camping (☎ 31453) is a municipal site (which means poorer facilities and fewer campers). Located on the main road out of Kamari, it suffers from being 1.7 km from its namesake beach and looking half-abandoned. Only open from June to September, it does have plenty of shade. No mini-bus service.

≋✿

Radiating out from Fira's main square are a profusion of bars and clubs that have one characteristic in common — they are all expensive. As Santorini will make a huge hole in your pocket you could do worse than dance in one; the *Tithora Club*, near the top of the port stairway, offers a dance floor in an old pumice

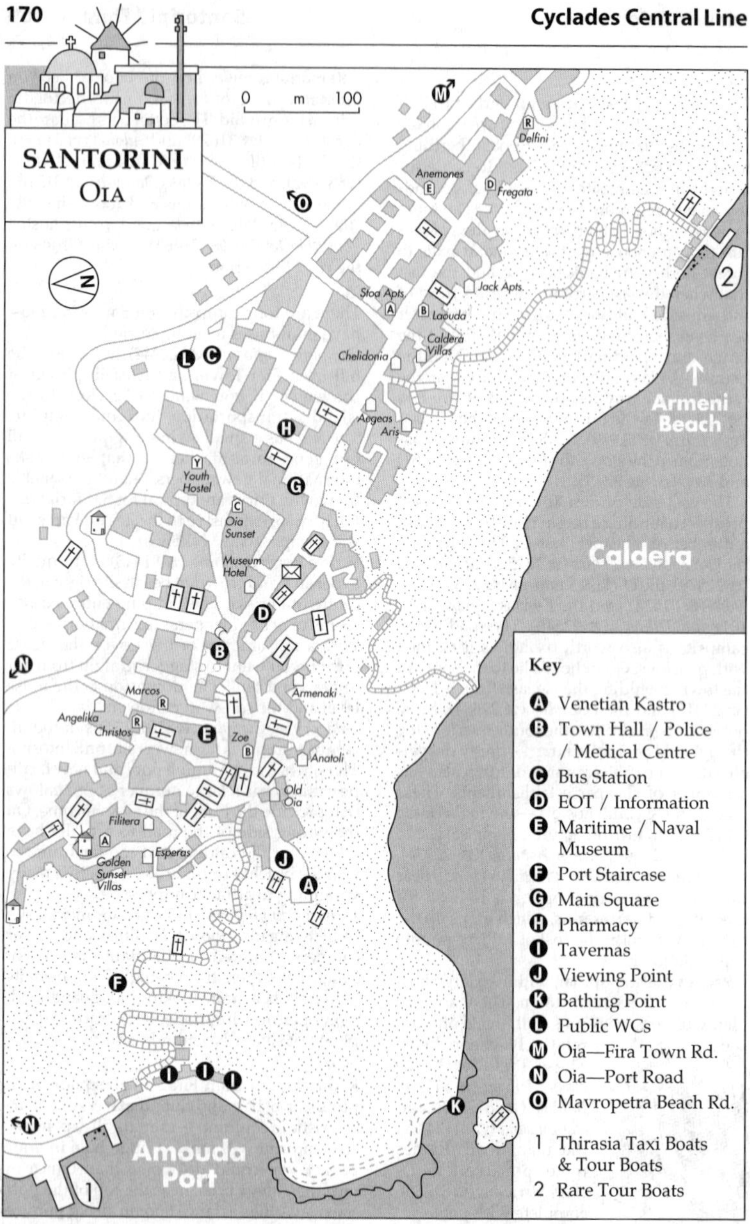

SANTORINI
OIA

0   m   100

Delfini

Anemones E

D *Fregata*

Stoa Apts. A

B *Laouda*

Jack Apts.

Chelidonia

Caldera Villas

L C

H

Aegeas Aris

Y *Youth Hostel*

G

C *Oia Sunset*

Museum Hotel

D

B

Marcos R

Angelika

Christos R E *Zoe* B

Armenaki

Anatoli

Old Oia

Filitera

A

Esperas

Golden Sunset Villas

J

A

F

N

I I I

N

Amouda Port

1

M

R

N

O

↑
Armeni Beach

Caldera

2

K

2

Key

A Venetian Kastro

B Town Hall / Police / Medical Centre

C Bus Station

D EOT / Information

E Maritime / Naval Museum

F Port Staircase

G Main Square

H Pharmacy

I Tavernas

J Viewing Point

K Bathing Point

L Public WCs

M Oia—Fira Town Rd.

N Oia—Port Road

O Mavropetra Beach Rd.

1 Thirasia Taxi Boats & Tour Boats

2 Rare Tour Boats

cave and troglodyte male dancers. There are also three other large discos / clubs in town: the *Dionysos*, the *Enigma* and the *Koo Club* — all are located in the nightstrip area just to the north-west of the main town square. Popular bars in Fira include the *Blue Note* (a bar turned disco also near the main square) and the very expensive *Tropical* (on the caldera rim).

◎◎

The whole 'Thira' archipelago is one vast tourist attraction, and there is sufficient sightseeing to fill a good four days, though tour buses — all taking in the inevitable winery — manage to cram a lot into a few hours. The highlights (not necessarily in their pecking order) are:

1. Ancient Thira.
The remains of the Hellenistic capital (known as Ancient Thira) on the headland between Perissa and Kamari.

2. Museum of Prehistoric Thira (p. 174).
One of the most important museums in the Greek islands, and a good introduction to the archaeological discoveries on Santorini.

3. The Akrotiri Excavation (p. 174).
One of the most important archaeological sites in the world.

4. The Volcano / Kameni Islands (p. 180).
The most visually impressive sight in the Greek islands.

In addition to the above, there are a number of 'lesser' sights that would still merit star status were they to be located on any other Greek island. **Fira** is home to several of these. First and foremost is the **Thera Foundation Exhibition** in the Petros M. Nomikos Center (the main caldera-view street north of the cable-car has a number of signs pointing the way). Housed in a series of galleries cut into the pumice, the Foundation has an excellent exhibition of three-dimensional life-size reproductions of **'The Wall-paintings of Thera'** (€3). At first sight a display of a bunch of fresco copies wouldn't seem to be much of a draw, but the quality of the computer-derived reproduction is fantastic. Even with the opening of the Museum of Prehistoric Thira, the Foundation display remains the best place to appreciate these art works, and the only place where you can see an ensemble of all the frescoes unveiled to date in one location.

Fira also has two more museums: the old **Archaeological Museum** (filled largely with post-Minoan artifacts), and a privately run town museum — known as the **Megaro Gyzi** — which is a repository for odds and ends. Its most interesting exhibits are unlabelled photos of the pre-1956 earthquake town. The northern town of **Oia** also has a good, if small, **Nautical Museum** (open ②–⑦ 12.30–16.00, 17.00–20.30), complete with a number of 19 c. ships' figure-heads.

Ancient Thira
Santorini has such a wealth of volcanic and prehistoric material to look at that anything dating from the historical period is apt to be treated rather casually. In fact, the island has some of the best-preserved Archaic to Roman era remains in the Aegean.

A few centuries after the eruption that destroyed the Minoan settlement on Santorini, the fertile volcanic soils brought colonizing Doric Greeks to the island. The new centre emerged on the east coast, on the easily defendable high headland north of Perissa (see map on p. 173), and the remains of the town (dating from the Archaic to the Roman era) can be explored. The site has yet to be fully excavated; the exposed remains mainly consist of nondescript foundations and a poorly preserved theatre. The site is more of scenic than archaeological merit. Its main attractions are a number of very faint carvings of an erotic (well, okay, 'porno') nature on some of the buildings, and, on the headland, an early Archaic temple of Apollo that has a ground plan more in common with a house. There is also an agora, a stoa and the remains of several large Hellenistic houses.

Open ⑥ ex ① 09.00–15.00 (last admissions at 14.30); entrance is free. One word of warning: although the site closes at 15.00 it is advisable to depart a good fifteen minutes before this, as the caretaker takes care of stray tourists by unleashing a couple of large Rottweilers. Being chased across a hilltop peninsula through the remains of a Hellenistic town by a ferocious dog is certainly a holiday experience you won't forget in a hurry, although you will certainly leave the site in one.

Expensive mini-buses run to Ancient Thira from Kamari and cost €3 one-way, €4.50 return. Given this, it isn't very surprising that the site is a popular destination for island walkers, along with nearby Mt. Profitis Ilias, which is topped by a radar station and monastery.

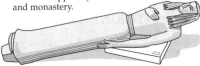

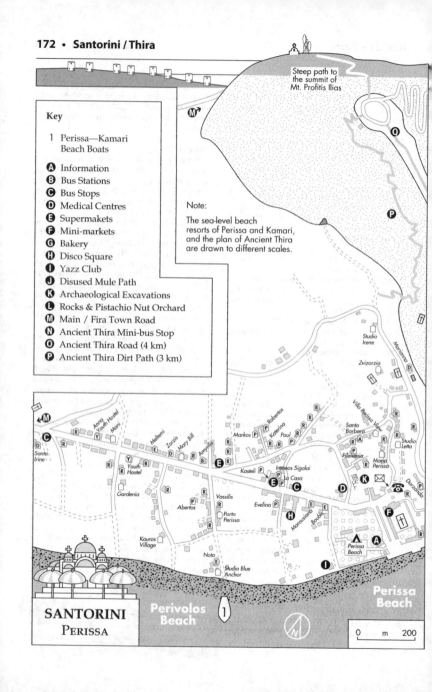

Key

1   Perissa—Kamari Beach Boats

Ⓐ Information
Ⓑ Bus Stations
Ⓒ Bus Stops
Ⓓ Medical Centres
Ⓔ Supermakets
Ⓕ Mini-markets
Ⓖ Bakery
Ⓗ Disco Square
Ⓘ Yazz Club
Ⓙ Disused Mule Path
Ⓚ Archaeological Excavations
Ⓛ Rocks & Pistachio Nut Orchard
Ⓜ Main / Fira Town Road
Ⓝ Ancient Thira Mini-bus Stop
Ⓞ Ancient Thira Road (4 km)
Ⓟ Ancient Thira Dirt Path (3 km)

Steep path to
the summit of
Mt. Profitis Ilias

Note:

The sea-level beach
resorts of Perissa and Kamari,
and the plan of Ancient Thira
are drawn to different scales.

SANTORINI

PERISSA

Perivolos Beach

Perissa Beach

0   m   200

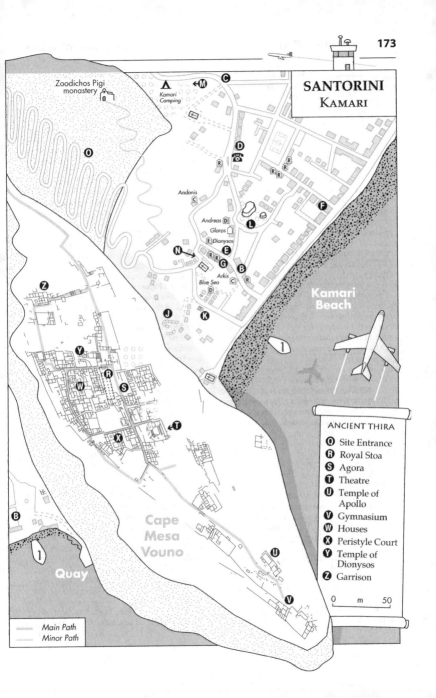

SANTORINI
KAMARI

Zoodichos Pigi monastery

Kamari Camping

Andonis C
Andreas D
Glaros
Dionysos E
Arkis C
Blue Sea

Kamari Beach

Cape Mesa Vouno

Quay

Main Path
Minor Path

ANCIENT THIRA

O Site Entrance
R Royal Stoa
S Agora
T Theatre
U Temple of Apollo
V Gymnasium
W Houses
X Peristyle Court
Y Temple of Dionysos
Z Garrison

0   m   50

Museum of Prehistoric Thira

Standing by Fira Town bus station, and built to house the finds from the Akrotiri excavation, this new museum joined the tourist map in 2000. Open ②–⑦ 08.30–15.00 (entrance fee is €3: tickets from the separate building inside the mueum grounds, include entry to Fira's regular Archaeological Museum), it is set to become one of the most important museums in Greece. Although it is not particularly large, the quality of the exhibits and the detailed explanatory texts is very high, and it is easy for even the uninitiated to spend the best part of an hour taking in the displays: the museum offers a superb introduction to the Akrotiri site and the pre-eruption island.

One of the few gripes one can make about the museum is its confusing entrance. Visitors are expected to turn left on entering (from a door on the caldera rim side of the building) to read the explanatory text on the discovery of Akrotiri and then, ignoring the alluring glimpse of frescoes and gold further on, turn back and go around the galleries in an anti-clockwise direction. The first exhibits pre-date the city of Akrotiri and therefore aren't, at first sight, particularly interesting. However, there are important gems to be found here. Not least of these are the **Cycladic Idols**. The examples here are unusual in (a) being carved out of local pumice rather than marble, and (b) possessing 'male' attributes: until recently only female idols had been recovered from excavated sites. Male figures of unknown provenance had appeared via the black market, but given the large number of fake idols in circulation, it was unclear if any were genuine.

Having dispensed with pre-Minoan era culture in a few cases, the museum soon gets down to the serious business of displaying the Akrotiri artifacts. To set the scene it starts with a large **Model of the Excavations**. This leads on into a number of gallery sections devoted to various aspects of life in the town. The first of these deals with day-to-day household items. Highlights of these first display cases are the **Plaster Cast of a Three-Legged Table** (as at Pompeii wooden artifacts from Akrotiri are 'recovered' by pouring plaster into holes that appear in the volcanic ash — the origi-

nal wood having long since disintegrated), and a small **Clay Oven** (both illustrated top right opposite). Nearby is a large **Bathtub** that is much more 'pot'-like than its Knossos counterpart (compare the illustration on this page with that on p. 306). This gallery leads into exhibits on writing and painting (including some of the famous **Pithoi Jars**). This in turn naturally leads into the frescoes. Unfortunately, only a few are on display: the best come from two rooms in the **House of the Ladies**, and include the famous **Ladies Fresco** and the less interesting **Lilies Fresco**. Further fresco fragments (including one showing an African figure) are scattered through the rest of the museum, which hereafter focuses on pottery. Because Akrotiri was abandoned by its inhabitants prior to the eruption, smaller or valuable items (pottery excepted) are rare. A notable exception is a 10 cm long snub-nosed **Gold Ibex Figurine**: recovered from the site in December 1999, it takes pride of place as the climax to the museum display.

The Akrotiri Excavation

Nestling in an undistinguished ravine that runs down to the sea beyond Akrotiri village lies the Pompeiian-like Minoan town (map between pages 160–161) that has elevated Santorini to the top of the archaeological world map. A complete town buried by the ash and pumice from the massive eruption that blew the pre-Santorini island apart, Akrotiri is a sightseeing 'must' — even though the accessible area is quite small (you will be hard put to make a visit to the excavation last half an hour). Buses run direct to the site from Fira Town. Open ②–⑦ 08.30–15.00; the entrance fee is €5. If you really want to appreciate what is on view you can't do much better than read *Art and Religion in Thera* (€7) beforehand; this is an excellent guide (complete with reconstructions of the fresco rooms) and is on sale in tourist shops in Fira Town.

Note: over the next year or so the Akrotiri site is likely to experience severe disruption while the old protective shed over the site is replaced by a futuristic glass and steel 'bio-climatic shelter'. All movable exhibits have already been removed, and the archaeologists have stopped work. It is even possible that the site will be closed for a period as the existing iron-framed shed has a roof with a very high asbestos content (which could cause contamination problems when it is removed).

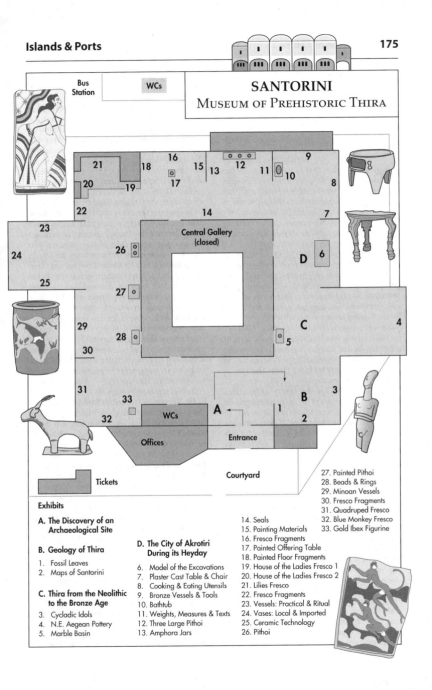

Bus Station

WCs

SANTORINI
MUSEUM OF PREHISTORIC THIRA

Central Gallery
(closed)

D

C

B

A ←

1

2

3

4

5

6

7

8

9

10

11

12

13

14

15

16

17

18

19

20

21

22

23

24

25

26

27

28

29

30

31

32

33

WCs

Offices

Entrance

Tickets

Courtyard

Exhibits

A. The Discovery of an Archaeological Site

B. Geology of Thira
1. Fossil Leaves
2. Maps of Santorini

C. Thira from the Neolithic to the Bronze Age
3. Cycladic Idols
4. N.E. Aegean Pottery
5. Marble Basin

D. The City of Akrotiri During its Heyday
6. Model of the Excavations
7. Plaster Cast Table & Chair
8. Cooking & Eating Utensils
9. Bronze Vessels & Tools
10. Bathtub
11. Weights, Measures & Texts
12. Three Large Pithoi
13. Amphora Jars

14. Seals
15. Painting Materials
16. Fresco Fragments
17. Painted Offering Table
18. Painted Floor Fragments
19. House of the Ladies Fresco 1
20. House of the Ladies Fresco 2
21. Lilies Fresco
22. Fresco Fragments
23. Vessels: Practical & Ritual
24. Vases: Local & Imported
25. Ceramic Technology
26. Pithoi

27. Painted Pithoi
28. Beads & Rings
29. Minoan Vessels
30. Fresco Fragments
31. Quadruped Fresco
32. Blue Monkey Fresco
33. Gold Ibex Figurine

Part of the pleasure of visiting Akrotiri is that the 35-century-old site is still under excavation. Archaeologists are slowly unearthing an incredible Minoan town, with all the attributes of high civilization that have come to be the hallmark of this remarkable pre-Greek people. These range from the humble street drains (that didn't appear elsewhere in the Mediterranean for a millennium) and inside WCs (that weren't a feature in European homes until a century ago) to the surprisingly modernist appearance of their houses (equipped with large windows and central light wells). Most amazing of all are the large number of wall frescoes — most reduced to fragments that have to be painstakingly reassembled — that exhibit a spontaneity and freshness that seem wholly contemporary (an illusion greatly enhanced by the boxing boys fresco, which depicts two pubescent naked youths sporting Michael Jackson look-a-like hairstyles). Sadly, almost all of the better known frescoes on view are in the National Archaeological Museum in Athens, but even without them the site is still impressive enough.

Because Akrotiri is still under excavation, tourists are confined to a predetermined route that runs though a couple of streets of the town. Some 10,000 m² of the site has now been excavated. Estimates as to the town's size range from 30,000 to 200,000 m². Neither the harbour (thought to lie in a now pumice-filled inlet west of the current excavation) nor any overtly public buildings (if they exist) have been unearthed.

Discovered in 1967, the site was the reward for years of searching. Following the discovery of the Minoan civilization (with the excavation of the palaces on Crete) archaeologists were increasingly wont to ask why they were finding palaces and villas but nothing resembling towns or commercial centres. Their absence implied that they must have existed elsewhere in the Aegean and attention turned to possible sites, notably to Santorini where, in 1867, a fresco-filled house had been uncovered and subsequently lost. Akrotiri came to light thanks to its location in a ravine; the stream that formed it eroded the layers of pumice to reveal evidence of buildings beneath. Once a

prospering 16 C. BC town that — if the street plan revealed to date is typical — looked similar to Greek island choras today, it was abandoned (probably thanks to early earthquakes that were the harbinger of the main eruption) by its inhabitants a couple of decades prior to the explosion that ripped the heart out of the island. Covered by layers of volcanic ash, the quake-damaged buildings, some several storeys high, have been preserved. Frescoes aside, the houses have limited contents, as the townsfolk had time to hurriedly collect valuables when they abandoned their homes.

On entering the excavation shed, you arrive in an open area from which a path runs north along the line of the former stream that exposed the site. On either side of the entrance you can see the remains of two major buildings — **❶ Xeste 3** and **❷ Xeste 4** — that are often ignored by tourists heading for the ticket check. In fact, both are examples of the most important building type uncovered to date. They are large mansions with ashlar block façades, and notable for possessing removable interior wooden panel walls in the major front rooms along with 'lustral basins', which appear to have had some religious use. **Xeste 4** has only been partially excavated (work stopped in 1974, when Professor Marinatos — Akrotiri's discoverer — died in a wall collapse, has now resumed). A further house at **❸**, known as the **South Building**, has also yet to be explored. All these buildings appear to have major frescoes within them. Indeed, **Xeste 3** (the only one excavated to date) has provided the richest haul of frescoes recovered from one building. These include the **Monkey Musician Fresco** (depicting blue monkeys — a sacred animal in Minoan art — playing lyres and pipes), **❹ The Initiation Fresco** (portraying youths preparing for a coming of age ritual), **❺ The Saffron Gatherers Fresco** (showing young girls picking blooms) and **❻ The Adorants Fresco** (which depicts a number of young women and a 'Demeter-like' mother-earth goddess).

Once you pass the ticket check visitors arrive at **❼ Building Beta**. Badly damaged by the stream, it is an example of the second type of building uncovered, being a large structure filled with small rooms. The layout and the lack of kitchen facilities (there is usually only one per block) suggest that the inhabitants lived in a communal, rather than family, unit. These houses appear to represent the lowest housing rank. They did, however, have frescoed rooms like the other buildings, and Building Beta has provided us with several of the best known Akrotiri frescoes: the **Boxing Children and Antelope Frescoes**, and the **Blue Monkeys Fresco**. At the end of this structure the path arrives at a small square and **Xeste 2**, a third (unexplored) ashlar block mansion.

From this point, tourists have to walk along a viewing platform that runs past the central area of the excavation. This is dominated by the block at known as **Building Delta**. Easily identified by the **Stone Sacral Horns** now sitting on the wall beside the walkway (they are believed to have once adorned the top of the building), this is another of the communal-living-type buildings. Within it archaeologists discovered the almost complete **Lilies** (or **Spring**) **Fresco**, depicting a landscape of lilies and swallows. The swallows provide a poignant insight into the changed conditions on the island, for Santorini is now one of the few Aegean islands not to see swallows nesting in the summer (the dry volcanic ash isn't adhesive enough for them to build their mud nests), though they do still wistfully fly around looking for suitable sites. To the east of Building Delta are the tops of the walls of the unexplored building **Xeste 5** at .

At the end of the viewing platform the path turns west, taking you past the northern section of the site. Currently roped off, it is inaccessible to tourists beyond tiptoe views. Following the line of the former torrent bed, this open area leads to , the most northerly part of the excavation. Known as **Sector Alpha**, it is the site of a **Pithoi Jar Storehouse** several storeys high, and apparently some kind of communal food warehouse or shop. It marks the spot where digging commenced at Akrotiri in 1967, and where the first fresco fragments were found. These include a fragment showing a North African man and a palm tree, and a swallow fragment (illustrated below). Just visible at stands the **House of the Ladies**. An important town house (it is the only building so far discovered with a light well), it has yielded up the **Fresco of the Ladies** (depicting some well-endowed women robing a lost figure), and the **Papyrus Fresco** (deftly painted with yellows, blues and reds, as the painters of the Akrotiri frescoes had no green pigments at their disposal). This fresco suggests trade links with Egypt, as this plant is not native to Greece. Unfortunately, the House of the Ladies

looks a bit of a mess because, in the eruption, the ground storey collapsed, the upper floor falling on top of it.

After running past the northern façade of Building Delta (notable for having a stairwell filled with 'karate-chopped' stairs), the tourist path turns south-west, following the path of one of the ancient town's streets now known as the **Telchines Road**. On the opposite side of the path to the Building Delta stairs is a small pithoi jar display against the wall of the **West House**. Along with the House of the Ladies, this is an example of the third type of building on the site, being a large independent town house for the middle rank of Akrotiri society (though again interpretations differ as — judging by the contents — the large upstairs window belonged to a 'weaving room'; this suggests some commercial activity was taking place in the building). Smaller than the ashlar-block mansion type, this house was nonetheless well adorned with frescoes, yielding up , the famous **Fisherboys**, and the tapestry-like river and nautical festival scenes on the **Miniature Fresco**. This narrow strip fresco is of particular importance as it appears to be a pictorial narrative of a voyage between four towns (ending at Akrotiri itself). Its information on the ships and houses of the period is invaluable and unique. Another unique feature of the West House — though it is not possible to see this wonder — is the upstairs bathroom at (complete with a latrine connected to a pipe running down inside the external wall). This led to a mains drain under the **Triangular Square**. This is the most impressive part of the site, thanks to the height of the buildings.

The tourist path formerly ended at the Triangular Square (the exit stairs ran up over the unexcavated **House of the Anchor**), but while the roof rebuilding is going on tourists get to see more of the site as they now have to follow the path through the **Propylon**, or entrance hall, of Building Delta, and then down , the Telchines Road to the so-called **Mill-House Square** (this is another of the tiny open areas that appear to have played an important part in the ancient town's life). From this square, the street narrows, running between Building Beta and a similar type of building at : **Building Gamma**. Still only partly excavated (only the street-side area has been explored), this structure has also yielded up its first fresco fragments.

the story of
Atlantis and
Listen, then, Santorini
Socrates
to a tale, which,
though strange, is
certainly true...

The Atlantis Legend

You can't travel far around Santorini without coming across claims that the island is the site of Atlantis. The problem is, almost any lost civilization—and certainly sunken city—has the same claims made for it too, with the more ardent Atlantis theorists embracing everyone from Hawaii to visiting aliens from bizarre worlds similar to their own. The trouble with the Atlantis mystery is that it is too attractive to clear up. The problem for the alien lovers is that serious scholars are increasingly inclined to stamp this particular X-file 'Solved'.

The Atlantis story is briefly this: There once was a mighty maritime civilization that ruled the waves and many islands as far as Egypt and Italy. Over the generations they became extremely wealthy, building the great island city of Metropolis, and hunting bulls in its temple precincts. But greed and a lust for power overtook their rulers, angering the gods, who undertook retribution by sinking both the people and city into the sea which 'disappeared in one terrible day and night'.

In fact, the Atlantis tale, although it sounds like the stuff of Greek myth, isn't Greek at all — but is an old Egyptian story. Who the old Egyptian was who told it isn't known, but the philosopher Plato says that the tale was spun to the Athenian leader Solon on a visit c. 590 BC, while he was being ribbed about the Greeks being a new people, lacking a long written historical tradition and ignorant of their ancestry. On his return from Egypt, Solon is said to have repeated the tale to Plato's great grandfather, and it was passed down thereafter as a family story. Plato used it in two of his written educational dialogues. There is a brief account in *Timaeus* (c. 350 BC) and an implausibly detailed fragment in the uncompleted *Critias* (c. 340 BC).

Plato's Contribution

Although Plato preserved the story, he also added a number of red herrings. Not least of these is that he was using the tale to make philosophical points, probably distorting details to that end. Certainly the Egyptian names have been replaced with appropriate Greek ones ('Atlantis' and 'Metropolis' cannot have been part of the original tale).

Plato's better geographical and poorer historical knowledge than the original Egyptian storytellers also appear to have created further misconceptions. Atlantis was said to lie in the 'far west'. Plato naturally placed it in the Atlantic (the western limit of his world), but the term is relative to where one is and the world one knows (hence later attempts to locate Atlantis in the Americas and beyond). It is clear from other evidence that the limit of the known world for the inward-looking and desert-locked Egyptians 900 years before Plato's day extended no further west than Sicily at best (they knew of the Minoans, and called them the people of 'Keftiu').

Plato's weaker historical knowledge also prevented him from connecting the story with the local pre-Greek Minoan civilization. Thanks to the Dark Ages — the 350-year period in Greek history when the art of writing was forgotten — the Classical Greeks had no knowledge of the earlier Minoans beyond the garbled oral myth of King Minos and the Minotaur.

Finally Plato's use of scale and numbers is seriously awry. He describes Atlantis as 'larger than Africa and Asia' (though these terms only applied to the Mediterranean coastlines of each continent), dates the events as taking place 9,000 years before his day, and gives detailed measurements for Metropolis. Interestingly, the Santorini eruption was 900 years earlier, and similarly knocking zeros off his Metropolis figures produces an area similar to that occupied by the Santorini volcano.

The Case for Minoan Santorini

Separating fact from fiction isn't easy with a tale like this: it is always dangerous to select favourable details to one's case while ignoring others that contradict it. However, within the whole there is enough corroborating detail to suggest that the Minoan civilization and its subsequent demise, following the Santorini eruption, is the basis of the Atlantis myth:

1. Even allowing for 900 years' worth of exaggeration, the latest geological models of the pre-c. 1640 BC island are uncannily close to Plato's description of Metropolis. The 'island within an island' concept is unique to both this one story and this one location.

2. The existence of a city-topped island in the pre-c. 1640 BC eruption caldera is supported

by the Miniature/Flotilla Fresco discovered at Akrotiri. This appears to show a substantial settlement covering an island lying within a cliff and hill-backed lagoon.

3. Both Minoans and Atlantians were noted for having a highly advanced civilization characterized by opulent buildings with running water and baths, wide-ranging trade, a powerful fleet and a highly unusual bull cult that involved ritual activity with loose bulls in building precincts.

4. Both Minoan and Atlantian civilizations suffered catastrophic and rapid collapse following a natural disaster that involved an island disappearing into the sea.

5. Finally, Plato says that the concentric island rings of Metropolis had walls plated respectively with tin and bronze. The tin walls of the inner island were blown sky high in the eruption, but look across the Santorini caldera at sunset today, and romantics point out that it is surely clear to all but the meanest doubter that the walls of plated bronze are still standing, broken in parts, but taller than ever.

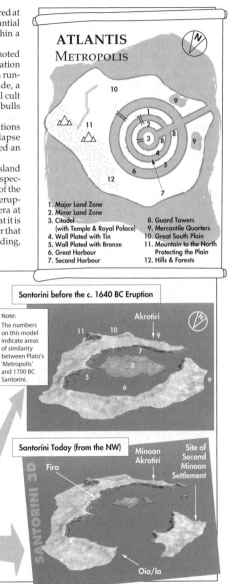

ATLANTIS
METROPOLIS

1. Major Land Zone
2. Minor Land Zone
3. Citadel
   (with Temple & Royal Palace)
4. Wall Plated with Tin
5. Wall Plated with Bronze
6. Great Harbour
7. Second Harbour
8. Guard Towers
9. Mercantile Quarters
10. Great South Plain
11. Mountain to the North
    Protecting the Plain
12. Hills & Forests

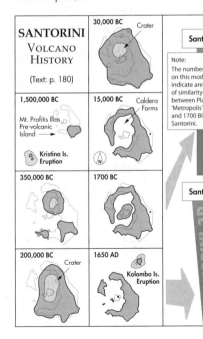

SANTORINI
VOLCANO HISTORY

(Text: p. 180)

30,000 BC — Crater

1,500,000 BC

Mt. Profitis Ilias
Pre-volcanic
Island →

Kristina Is.
Eruption

15,000 BC — Caldera Forms

350,000 BC

1700 BC

200,000 BC — Crater

1650 AD

Kolombo Is.
Eruption

Note:
The numbers on this model indicate areas of similarity between Plato's 'Metropolis' and 1700 BC Santorini.

Santorini before the c. 1640 BC Eruption

Akrotiri

11   10   9
7
3
5
6

Santorini Today (from the NW)

Minoan Akrotiri

Site of Second Minoan Settlement

Fira

Oia/Ia

SANTORINI 3D

The Volcano: 1. History

Santorini is one of the most intensely studied volcanos in the world. Quite apart from having the largest caldera on earth (with the exception of the few so-called 'super volcanos'), it is also one of the most explosive — sea water rushing into a crater of molten magma is always apt to cause a massive bang (these occur roughly every 20,000 years).

Volcanic activity in the Santorini region isn't confined to the visible eruptive matter: as the Eurasian plate buckles (see: inside back cover) the earth's crust in this area is slowly cracking in a north-easterly direction. The eruptions began with the formation of the Kristina islets 20 km to the south-west of Santorini. At that early time Santorini was a small non-volcanic island (this original island now forms Mt. Profitis Ilias). In 1650 there was an eruption 7 km to the north-east of Santorini, with the brief appearance of Kolombo (Columbus) islet. Kolombo sank when the eruption ended (it is now an underwater cone, with its summit some 17 m below sea level), but it is likely to one day reappear to form a permanent island between Ios and Santorini.

One important development to emerge from recent studies of the Santorini system is a reassessment of the volcano's appearance prior to the c. 1640 BC eruption which did so much damage to the Minoans. Until recently it had been assumed that it would have looked similar to the high mountain cone of Krakatoa — another island volcano (albeit three times smaller) — which blew itself apart in 1883 with an explosion that was heard half way around the globe. However, examination of the caldera wall has shown that in many places it has a thin pre-eruption soil covered with pumice — indicating it had already formed when the c. 1640 BC eruption took place, and that the 'high mountain cone' phase of Santorini's life belonged to an earlier epoch.

The Volcano: 2. Kameni Islands

Since the c. 1640 BC eruption emptied the caldera bay, new islands (the 'Burnt Islands') have again risen out of the sea in subsequent eruptions. The largest, the volcano islet of **Nea Kameni** (New Kameni), is a popular sight on the itineraries of all boat tours, though the sun-baked 20-minute walk along a cinder track can be a bit of a strain. Most tours don't give you time to wander off: the guides lead you direct to the main crater, walking at a pace which

suggests that they know the time of the next eruption and don't want to hang around.

The objective of this route march is the **Georgios Crater**. It does nothing more than give off a bad smell from a number of steaming fumeroles, and is not the idyll that it seems from Santorini (where fake postcards are on sale depicting it as a glowing inferno). This said, excursions are good value for they offer a unique opportunity to walk over the cinder-black lava of a sleeping volcano. Visitors find a daunting, frying-pan-hot landscape lacking refreshment facilities (bring water) and vegetation (the only tree is on Palia Kameni).

Tour boats also call at the hot springs for a popular swim session in a narrow cove off the small and older island of **Palia Kameni**. The hot springs (for 'hot' read 'warm') offer those prepared to swim ashore the chance to wallow in a salty mud-bath. Those left on board get to view the spectacle of several hundred people splashing in a scene that looks like a rehearsal for a shot at the end of the *Titanic* movie.

Palia Kameni was the first island to emerge, in an eruption in 196 BC. A second briefly put in an appearance in 46 AD, before Mikri Kameni emerged in 1573. Nea Kameni appeared in 1711, was enlarged in the eruption of 1866–68 when the Georgios crater appeared, and was joined with Mikri Kameni in the 1925–26 eruption. As Santorini must be due for another one soon, you should note that before the last two, the waters around the islands turned a milky colour due to underwater sulphur emissions. If this phenomenon recurs, catching the next ferry to anywhere is a very good idea.

All **tour boat itineraries** visit Nea Kameni and the hot springs. There are three basic packages on offer: the Full Day Tour (09.15–18.20) costs €17 and takes in the works, including a sail round to Cape Akrotiri. The Caldera Round Trip (09.15–16.30) excludes this run and is better value at €12, while the two half-day burnt islands (alias 'Volcano') trips — the first also taking in the hot springs (15.20–19.30); the second, the town of Oia (10.30–16.30) — are a more rushed €9. Students receive a 20% discount. Also note that tour tickets can be up to €3 cheaper at the port.

In 2003 a Submarine Tour of the caldera was launched. This hour-long trip costs €61, with a connecting taxi-boat service from Fira Old Port. Forget the 'follow the traces of Lost Atlantis' blurb — they were all blown somewhere east of Cyprus during the Minoan eruption.

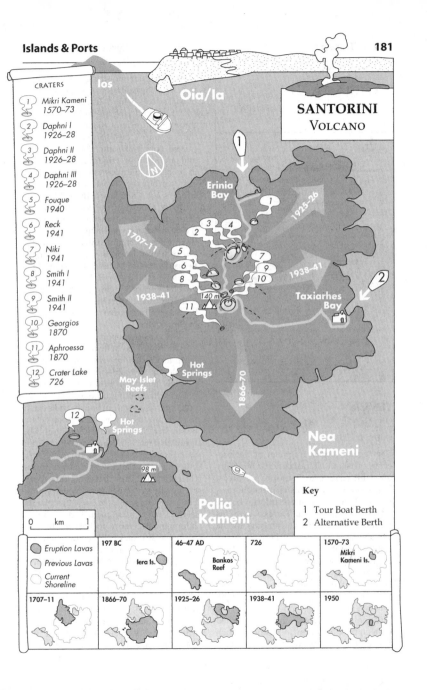

SANTORINI
VOLCANO

CRATERS

1 Mikri Kameni 1570–73
2 Daphni I 1926–28
3 Daphni II 1926–28
4 Daphni III 1926–28
5 Fouque 1940
6 Reck 1941
7 Niki 1941
8 Smith I 1941
9 Smith II 1941
10 Georgios 1870
11 Aphroessa 1870
12 Crater Lake 726

Ios

Oia/Ia

Erinia Bay

1925–26

1707–11

1938–41

1938–41

Taxiarhes Bay

1866–70

140 m

Hot Springs

May Islet Reefs

Hot Springs

Nea Kameni

98 m

Palia Kameni

0 km 1

Key

1 Tour Boat Berth
2 Alternative Berth

Eruption Lavas
Previous Lavas
Current Shoreline

197 BC — Iera Is.
46–47 AD — Bankos Reef
726
1570–73 — Mikri Kameni Is.
1707–11
1866–70
1925–26
1938–41
1950

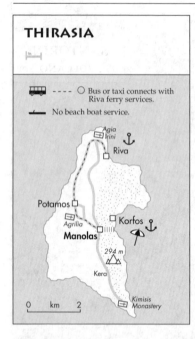

THIRASIA

Bus or taxi connects with Riva ferry services.

No beach boat service.

Agia Irini

Riva

Potamos

Agrilia

Korfos

Manolas

294 m

Kera

Kimisis Monastery

0   km   2

Thirasia

ΘΗΡΑΣΙΑ; 9 km²; pop. 260.

CODE ☎ 22860

The second largest fragment of the pre-eruption island, Thirasia offers a blissfully quiet alternative to Santorini's crowds. The island — and particularly the chora — is a miniature version of Santorini before tourism swamped all. Thirasia owes its tranquillity to an earlier swamping, for the island was joined to northern Santorini until an eruption in 236 BC collapsed the land bridge between them. Without it, and lacking the good beaches that would encourage the development of the island as a tourist destination in its own right, Thirasia remains very quiet.

The only settlement of any size is perched high on the caldera rim at **Manolas**. Much smaller than Fira (of which it has views),

it is an irregular and stringy affair, ribboning along the caldera rim without a maze of backstreets behind. Its appeal lies in its size; for wandering around is to journey through an unspoilt island village rather than a tourist destination. Odd houses carved hobbit-like into the pumice cliffs and a couple of windmills simply add to its charm (Fira lost all its mills in the 1956 earthquake). Most visitors are day-trippers who arrive via the caldera rim staircase (boasting the usual awkward steps and donkey transport), but beyond the existence of several tavernas in the town their impact is confined to the old port of **Korfos** tucked inside the northern wing of the caldera below Manolas. Little more than indifferent shingle beach backed by half-a-dozen tavernas and the odd shop, it is the usual destination for the small caldera tour boats as well as regular taxi-boats from Oia on Santorini.

Thirasia's second port is located in an isolated northern bay at **Riva**. This is the usual berth for the landing-craft ferry (that also doubles up as a caldera tour boat). Unfortunately, it isn't the most prepossessing of places with nothing on offer beyond the odd taverna, a string of houses and a dusty road; its only feature of note is a long pebble beach that is rendered all but unusable by the oil that mars it. The exposed quay is the usual home of the island bus that does little other than serve caldera tour parties during their brief sojourn on the island. Other boats are met by two 'truck-taxis' which shuttle between Riva and Manolas (€2) along the island's only paved road. Those who are hopping with empty pockets will find the walkable dirt track between the chora and the port a better option.

The rest of the island feels like the back of beyond and is scarred in places thanks to years of pumice quarrying. In fact much of Thirasia is now lining the banks of the Suez Canal, as it was a principal source of both materials and manpower. This activity also exposed some of the first 'Minoan' remains to be discovered in the archipelago (in 1869), alerting archaeologists to Santorini's potential. Unfortunately, the site has long since been lost. Tours try to make up for this by stopping at the diminutive hamlet of **Potamos** (home to an ugly multicoloured campaniled church) and at even smaller **Agrilia**.

The only hotel on Thirasia is the excellent, purpose-built *Cavo Mare* (☎ 23349); complete with pool, it stands on the crest of the island with stunning views of the caldera in one direction and the wild surf-kissed outer shores of the island on the other. In the High Season town tavernas also offer rooms.

Unless you stay on Thirasia you won't have time to take in more than the port and town. Those that do stay shouldn't miss the walk along the caldera rim to the southern tip and its 1851-built Kimisis monastery. Running from Manolas, the path passes through the abandoned pumice-cliff house village of **Kera**. Riva also has a 'sight': to the west of the bay is the church of **Agia Irini** — a structure of no great distinction, it is notable for giving neighbouring Santorini (literally 'Saint Irene') its Venetian name.

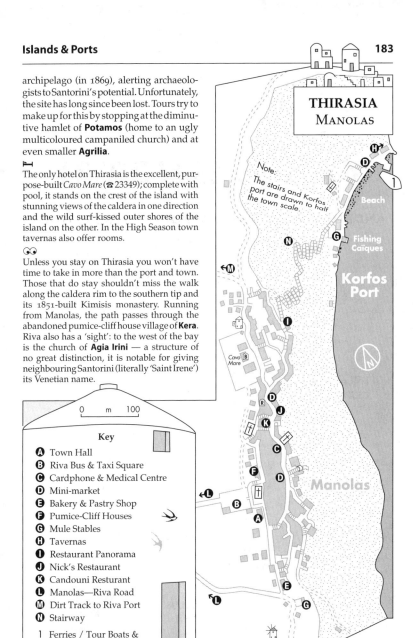

THIRASIA
MANOLAS

Note:
The stairs and Korfos port are drawn to half the town scale.

Korfos Port

Manolas

0 m 100

Key

Ⓐ Town Hall
Ⓑ Riva Bus & Taxi Square
Ⓒ Cardphone & Medical Centre
Ⓓ Mini-market
Ⓔ Bakery & Pastry Shop
Ⓕ Pumice-Cliff Houses
Ⓖ Mule Stables
Ⓗ Tavernas
Ⓘ Restaurant Panorama
Ⓙ Nick's Restaurant
Ⓚ Candouni Resturant
Ⓛ Manolas—Riva Road
Ⓜ Dirt Track to Riva Port
Ⓝ Stairway

1 Ferries / Tour Boats &
   Oia Taxi Boats

3
CYCLADES NORTH

ANDROS · DELOS · EVIA · MYKONOS · SYROS · TINOS

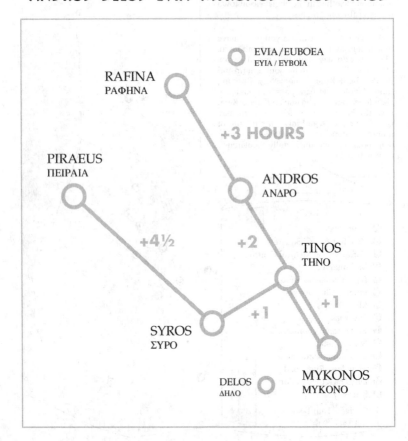

EVIA/EUBOEA
ΕΥΙΑ / ΕΥΒΟΙΑ

RAFINA
ΡΑΦΗΝΑ

+3 HOURS

PIRAEUS
ΠΕΙΡΑΙΑ

ANDROS
ΑΝΔΡΟ

+4½   **+2**

TINOS
ΤΗΝΟ

+1   **+1**

SYROS
ΣΥΡΟ

MYKONOS
ΜΥΚΟΝΟ

DELOS
ΔΗΛΟ

General Features

The Northern Cyclades Line covers those Cycladic islands to the east of Piraeus and the 'Athenian' port of Rafina, and is served by daily boats from both. The islands lying along this line include the former Mecca of the Greek World — the sacred island of Delos (birthplace of the God Apollo) — and its modern equivalent, the island of Tinos (home to the most important shrine of the Orthodox church in Greece). Delos lies, in theory if not in fact, at the centre of the Cyclades. While all the islands vary greatly in their characteristics, the one feature common to all is a tendency to be extremely windy. The *meltemi* 'hits' these Greek islands the hardest and they form something of a buffer for the rest of the Cyclades.

Cosmopolitan Mykonos and its satellite Delos remain the best-known islands on this line, the former being numbered among the most popular of all the Greek islands. Syros is often mentioned in older guidebooks as being the hub of the Cycladic ferry network, as its 19 c. commercial port of Ermoupolis is the formal capital of the group; however, the island has faded into relative obscurity and can now only boast half the number of ferry sailings of its southern neighbour Paros.

The remaining islands are very much orientated to Greek rather than international tourism. Andros and Evia (now little more than an extension of the Greek mainland) remain well off the beaten track. Tinos is less so, thanks to the constant stream of locals enjoying a spot of religious pilgrimage, and has hordes of little old ladies descending upon it to join the — mainly package — tourists at the height of the season for the feast of the Assumption of the Virgin Mary. As for Giaros, long famed as a place of exile, it has just been abandoned by the Greek military, and there are plans to open it to tourists at some point in the future.

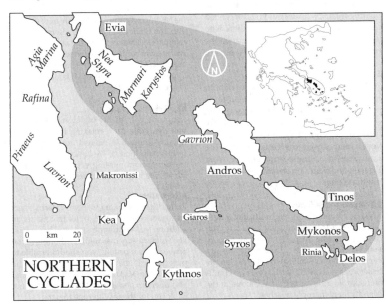

Example Itinerary
[2 Weeks]

The two ferry routes running out of Piraeus and Rafina that meet at Mykonos combine to provide a nice island hopping circuit that is both easy and for the inexperienced reasonably safe. Boats are sufficiently frequent down both lines for you to be sure of a daily boat up and down at least one of the lines even out of High Season.

Arrival/Departure Point

There are two easy alternatives when visiting islands on this line: Athens and Mykonos. Athens is invariably the cheaper of the two, and with far more frequent flights into the bargain. You can do the loop easily from either base. Mykonos is chosen here as it offers a more relaxed start and end to a holiday and a pleasant alternative to arriving at and rushing back to Athens.

The other ports en route are well worth visiting for a few hours but you don't need to stay overnight to see such as there is to see; the loop to Athens can effectively be undertaken as a long weekend excursion.

Season

As Mykonos is served by boats out of both Piraeus and Rafina, ferry links tend to be better either end of the High Season than elsewhere. The result is that from early June to the end of October coverage is very good down the line. During the Low Season a single ferry service from Piraeus and Rafina normally operates on alternate days.

1 Mykonos [4 Days]

Mykonos offers the opportunity for a very relaxed start to a Greek island holiday. You can happily idle away the first few days of your stay with day trips to Delos and Paros and even Tinos if you want to cut corners later on. In between you can tilt at Mykonos windmills and start an all-over body tan on one of the island's many naturist beaches.

2 3 Tinos/Andros [1 Day]

If you take the daily 08.00 Mykonos—Rafina ferry to Tinos you'll arrive in time for a late breakfast. An interesting day stop, you can either stay overnight or have the option of picking up the afternoon boat to Andros (note: accommodation is thin on the ground there) or on to Rafina, where you can take an evening bus into Athens.

4 5 Rafina/Athens [4 Days]

If you are not tied to budget accommodation it will be to your advantage to pre-book your Athens hotel accommodation while on Mykonos via one of the ticket agents. It will be hard not to arrive in the capital at any other time than the evenings (hardly an ideal time to start hunting for your bed). Thereafter you will be free to explore at your own pace and adjust the length of your stay as your fancy takes you.

6 Syros [1 Day]

On the schedule of Piraeus—Mykonos ferries, Syros offers an interesting day out. The difficulty comes in getting off the island since the Mykonos link is usually only once daily. If you don't fancy staying here you might have to repair to Tinos or Paros for the night. After Athens you could find Syros something of an anticlimax; but the island does ensure that you appreciate how much nicer Mykonos is during the rest of your stay.

1 Mykonos [4 Days]

Returning with plenty of days to spare gives you the scope for a relaxing finish to your holiday (though in August 'relaxing' isn't a useful definition of Mykonos!). Not having to worry about missing your return flight is something not to be underestimated.

Alternative

Rather than returning via Syros, **Paros** offers an attractive alternative (or for that matter an addition to your itinerary). A stop here could necessitate a stay overnight — though, if you arrive in the morning, you should be able to pick up a catamaran or ferry on an evening run back to Mykonos. A Paros stop would also open up possible calls to Naxos, Ios and Santorini for those with time to hand.

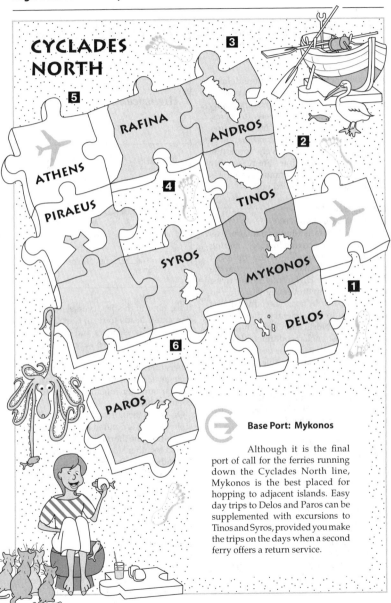

CYCLADES NORTH

Base Port: Mykonos

Although it is the final port of call for the ferries running down the Cyclades North line, Mykonos is the best placed for hopping to adjacent islands. Easy day trips to Delos and Paros can be supplemented with excursions to Tinos and Syros, provided you make the trips on the days when a second ferry offers a return service.

Cyclades North Ferry Services

Main Car Ferries

Although the Cyclades East Line is defined within this section as a single line, in practice it is not a complete through route. Daily ferries run both from Piraeus (to Syros, Tinos and Mykonos) and Rafina (to Andros, Tinos and Mykonos); the combination of the two sub-lines effectively forms the 'line'. Regular ferry times are reasonably well established; more annual variation is found with the high speed vessels.

C/M Highspeed 4

Hellas Flying Dolphins; 2000.
This large Australian-built catamaran was one of the new arrivals in 2000. Offering very fast journey times — with a top speed of 40 knots — she has taken over from the *Highspeed 3*. The *Highspeed 4* runs a twice daily round trip (reversing direction in the afternoon). In 2002 she added Paros and Naxos to the itinerary, thus linking the Cyclades North and Central lines. She ran an almost unchanged timetable in the summer of 2003, using the port of Tourlos on her calls at Mykonos. Able to carry 600 passengers and 70 cars, she is having a major impact as many locals seem happy to pay the premium fares that come with her. A popular boat in High Season, it is advisable to book ahead.

C/F Aeolos Express II

NEL Lines; 2001; 6000 GRT.
Looking something akin to a floating version of Concorde (thanks to her aero-dynamic pointed bow), this is one of

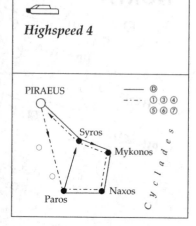

Highspeed 4

PIRAEUS

three new high-speed vessels (36 knots) that cause heads to turn. Capable of carrying 1000 passengers and 200 vehicles, they are proving to be very popular with locals and tourists alike: one dividend of this is that there was thus little reason to change her 2002 timetable in 2003, so a regular summer itinerary seems to have been established.

On-board facilities are good; the aircraft style seating is divided by a central partition — imagine the cabins of two jumbo jets bolted together side by side with a drinks bar at the back. On the downside there are no sun decks, luggage is never allowed in the seating area, and the light construction of these boat makes for a rock-and-roller of a ride in rough seas. In 2003 she was docking at the Old Port when visiting Mykonos.

C/F Blue Star Ithaki

Blue Star/Strintzis; 2000; 16500 GRT.
One of the first of a new generation of boats built specifically for the Greek domestic market, this ferry has been one of the

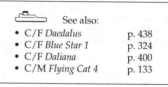

See also:
- C/F *Daedalus*   p. 438
- C/F *Blue Star 1*   p. 324
- C/F *Daliana*   p. 400
- C/M *Flying Cat 4*   p. 133

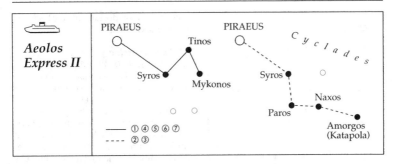

most sought-after boats since her arrival in 2001. On-board facilities are first rate, with shiny escalators whisking passengers up to a well-equipped deck-class saloon, which boasts comfortable seating and a burger-bar franchise (a branch of *Goody's* — a popular local chain). Add to this the fact that the crew treat people like customers instead of unwelcome monkeys, and you have a large, smooth-sailing vessel that is one of the best domestic boats in Greece.

As with the other Blue Star boats, tickets cost 20% more than other (slower) regular ferries. In 2003 she was using the Old Port when visiting Mykonos.

C/F *Express Aphrodite*

Hellas Ferries / HFD; 1977; 11500 GRT.
Formerly the UK-built *Stena Hibernia*, this large ferry appeared on the Cyclades North line in 1997, taking the morning slot out of Piraeus and quickly establishing herself as the regular cheap ferry on the Piraeus branch of the line. She has run a daily service ever since — docking at the Old Port when visiting Mykonos.

Times are unlikely to change in 2004, though she is now the least attractive option on this route: her interior layout seems curiously dated (more redolent of a grubby 1960s ferry rather than something designed in the later 1970s). Sadly, it looks as if she could be around for a while yet as she is comparatively young for an old boat, and has a higher than average passenger carrying capacity.

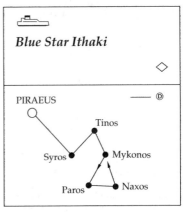

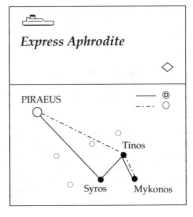

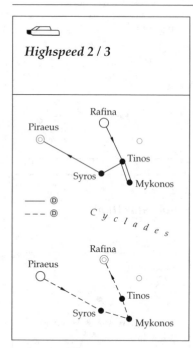

Highspeed 2 / 3

As is usual with older Hellas Ferries boats there are anti-backpacker goons on station when passengers board to prevent access to the large deck-class saloon. The only consolation is that the upper outside decks are higher up than most ferries — so you get bird's-eye views of the island harbours.

C/M *Highspeed 2* – C/M *Highspeed 3*
Hellas Flying Dolphins (HFD); 2001.
In 2003 two large car-carrying catamarans — the *Highspeed 2* and *Highspeed 3* — combined forces to work together down the Cyclades North and Cyclades West lines (see p. 230), one of them stopping overnight at Rafina. As with other catamaran services, these boats are very popular and you should book tickets as soon as practicable in High Season — these are currently the best boats running out of Rafina. In 2003

these boats were docking at Tourlos when visiting Mykonos.

C/F *Express Athina*
Hellas Ferries / HFD; 1973; 5171 GRT.
Formerly the *Panagia Tinou 2*, this ferry appeared in Greece at the end of the 1998 season. Now in Hellas Ferries colours, her major fault is a propensity to bob around like a cork in even calm conditions: this is one Greek ferry on which you could end up feeling seasick the moment she leaves harbour. In poor conditions mass throw-ups are not unknown: this is probably why she visits the very windy seas off Mykonos. In 2003 she docked at the Old Port when visiting Mykonos.

C/F *Express Penelope*
Hellas Ferries / HFD; 1972; 5109 GRT.
Formerly the flagship of a one-boat Rafina company, this ferry has operated the route since 1992. Now owned by the ubiquitous Hellas Ferries, she is now just another boat in the large HFD fleet. Formerly the cross-Channel *Horsa*, she is sister of the *Express Apollon* and *Panagia Ekatontapiliani* and looks identical. On-board facilities, however, are a touch above her former stable mates (though this isn't saying much these days). In 2003 she docked at the Old Port when visiting Mykonos.

C/F *Superferry II*
Blue Ferries / Strintzis; 1974; 5052 GRT.
The third 'regular' ferry operating out of Rafina down the Cyclades North line is the *Superferry II*. In the past this boat has been an escalator and a patisserie ahead of any of her rivals, but with the arrival of the high-speed catamarans she is suddenly looking her age. Even so, her open-deck plan is far in advance of much of the competition, and she feels ten years newer than boats such as the *Express Penelope*, although she is barely two.

A good boat, thanks to her large open-plan interior (the Rafina—Mykonos route is usually far too windy for comfortable sun-deck

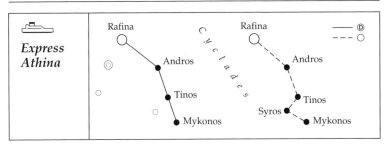

Express Athina

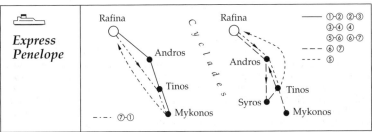

Express Penelope

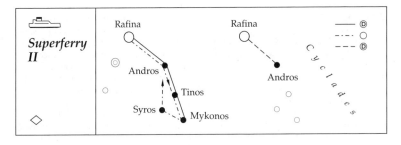

Superferry II

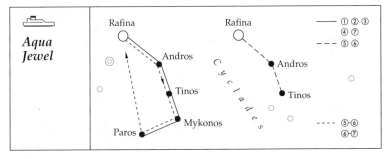

Aqua Jewel

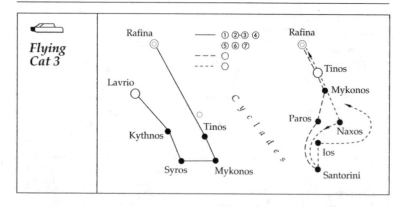

travel in High Season), her sole drawback is that backpackers are 'encouraged' to leave packs in the tiny luggage room at the top of the escalator. The *Superferry II*'s schedule is unlikely to change much in 2004. In 2003 she docked at the Old Port when visiting Mykonos.

C/F *Aqua Jewel*
Alpha Ferries

The new arrival on the line in 2003 was something of a surprise as it took the form of a tarted up older boat, painted a rather noisy turquoise blue. Run by the little-known Alpha Ferries, the slightly under-sized (compared to the competition) *Aqua Jewel* looked to be struggling to pick up customers last year, despite running the first service of the day out of Rafina, and having reasonably attractive interior seating. This could just be a lack of advertising, but it is likely to induce timetable changes this summer. In 2003 she docked at the Old Port when visiting Mykonos.

C/M *Flying Cat 3*
Hellas Flying Dolphins

Originally named *Athina 2004* in honour of the awarding of the 2004 Olympic Games to Athens, this passenger-only catamaran arrived in 1998. Within a year she was renamed *Super Cat Athina*, only to

be renamed again when she was bought by Hellas Flying Dolphins. Her appearance and specification is very similar to the two *Flying Cats* operating down the Saronic Gulf line, with the usual pricier hydrofoil-range fares.

Described as a 'turbo cat' and with an advertised speed of 50 knots, she has struggled to find a regular slot (in past years she has even undertaken a longer mid-week run to Amorgos). Her big drawback is her small size: on windier days (of which there are many) in July and August her activities are curtailed as she can't cope with the sea conditions, so don't be too surprised to find your sailing has been cancelled.

In 2003 she abandoned Tinos as her home port — adopting Lavrio instead, and running daily to Rafina and back via Kythnos and the Cyclades North islands. This doesn't look to be the most lucrative itinerary in Greece: expect further changes in 2004.

C/M *SeaJet 2*
Blue Star / Strintzis; 1995; 499 GRT.

The *SeaJet 2* arrived in 1999, and until 2002 ran in tandem with a sister vessel down the Cyclades North line. She was all set to run solo through the summer when she crashed into the harbour breakwater at the old port on Tinos. This left her engine room flooded,

MYKONOS
Town Waterfront

Mosaic & Plaster 'Pebble'
from a Delos Beach

Paraportiani Church
& Little Venice House

DELOS
Delian Lioness

Rubble Field & Mt. Kynthos

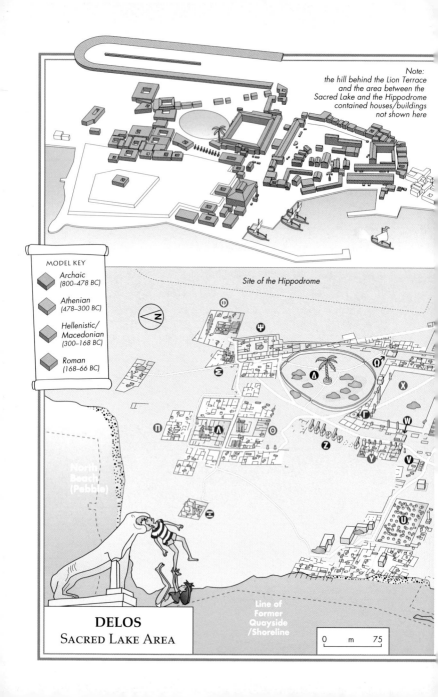

Note:
the hill behind the Lion Terrace
and the area between the
Sacred Lake and the Hippodrome
contained houses/buildings
not shown here

MODEL KEY

Archaic
(800–478 BC)

Athenian
(478–300 BC)

Hellenistic/
Macedonian
(300–168 BC)

Roman
(168–66 BC)

Site of the Hippodrome

N

North
Beach
(Pebble)

Line of
Former
Quayside
/Shoreline

DELOS
SACRED LAKE AREA

0   m   75

Key

A Agora of the Competialists
B Stoa of Philip V
C South Stoa
D Propylaea
E Oikos of the Naxians
F Base of the Colossal Statue of the Naxians
G Stoa of the Naxians
H Great Temple of Apollo /Temple of the Delians
I Temple of the Athenians
J Porinos Naos of Apollo
K Treasuries
L Neorion/Monument of the Bulls
M Altar of Zeus Soter & Polieus
N Agora of the Delians
O Sanctuary of Dionysos
P Stoa of Antigonos
Q Minoa Fountain
R Artemision & Colossal Statue of the Naxians
S Thesmophorion
T Agora of Theophrastos
U Hypostyle Hall
V Dodekatheon Temple
W Letoon/Temple of Leto
X Agora of the Italians
Y Granite Monument
Z Terrace of the Lions
T Sacred Palm Tree
A Sacred Lake
◎ Koinon of the Poseidoniasts of Beirut
A House of the Diadumenos
B Hillside House
U House of the Comedians
E House of the Lake
O Palaestra of Granite
W Palaestra of the Lake
O Temple of Anios

Path to Stadium

Museum

Refreshments

Main Path
Minor Path

Path to Mount Kynthos

The Colossal Statue of the Naxians c. 1673

Basilica of Agios Kyrikos

LORENA BOBBITT WOS HERE

SANCTUARY AREA

Path to Theatre

Mt. Kynthos. See Map 2

Sacred Harbour

Site Entrance

Tickets

Ancient Commercial Harbour

New Mole

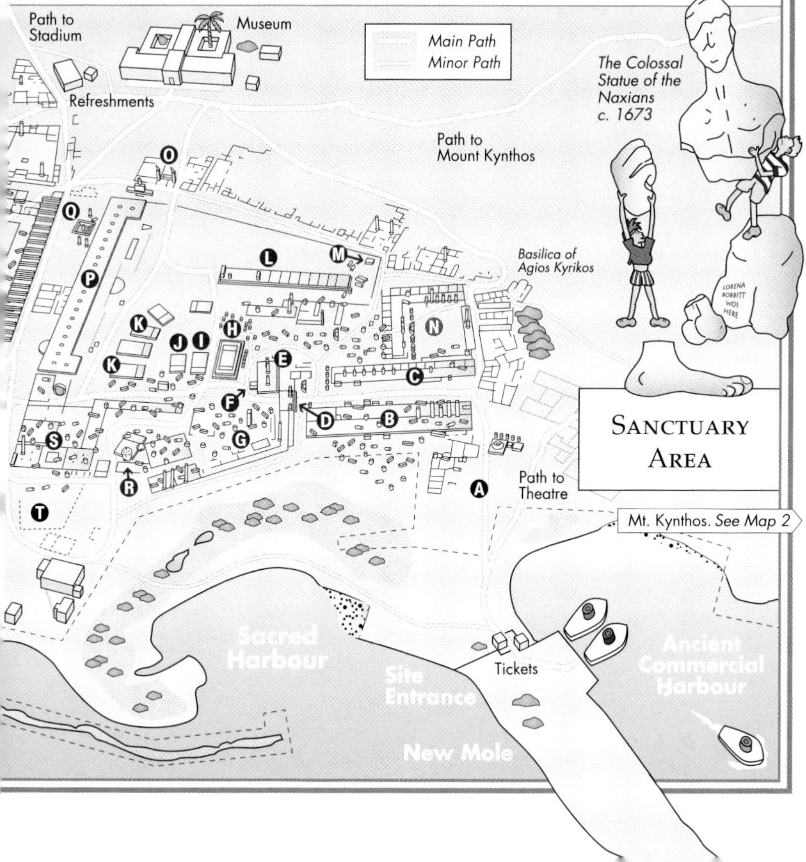

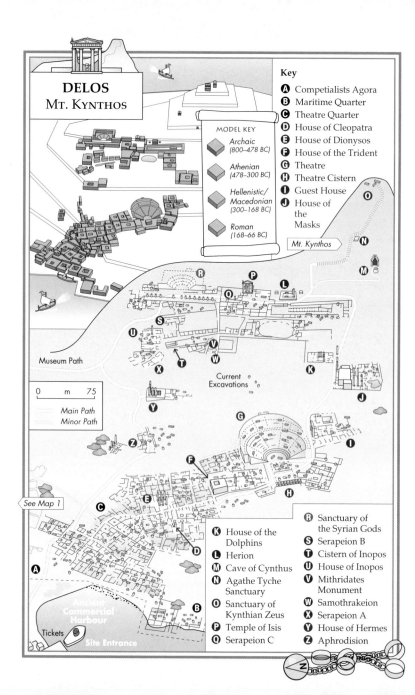

DELOS
Mt. Kynthos

MODEL KEY
- Archaic *(800–478 BC)*
- Athenian *(478–300 BC)*
- Hellenistic/ Macedonian *(300–168 BC)*
- Roman *(168–66 BC)*

Mt. Kynthos

Museum Path

0   m   75

Main Path
Minor Path

Current Excavations

See Map 1

Ancient Commercial Harbour

Tickets

Site Entrance

Key
- **A** Competialists Agora
- **B** Maritime Quarter
- **C** Theatre Quarter
- **D** House of Cleopatra
- **E** House of Dionysos
- **F** House of the Trident
- **G** Theatre
- **H** Theatre Cistern
- **I** Guest House
- **J** House of the Masks
- **K** House of the Dolphins
- **L** Herion
- **M** Cave of Cynthus
- **N** Agathe Tyche Sanctuary
- **O** Sanctuary of Kynthian Zeus
- **P** Temple of Isis
- **Q** Serapeion C
- **R** Sanctuary of the Syrian Gods
- **S** Serapeion B
- **T** Cistern of Inopos
- **U** House of Inopos
- **V** Mithridates Monument
- **W** Samothrakeion
- **X** Serapeion A
- **Y** House of Hermes
- **Z** Aphrodision

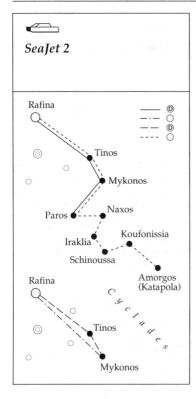

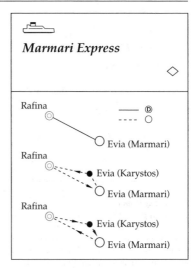

enough. Her destination isn't a popular one for island hoppers, so most are content to view her from a distance.

C/F *Evia Star*
Local

A new arrival in 2001, this gaudily painted orange-hulled boat is rarely used by tourists. She used to call at the Evian port of Karystos, but in 2002 was — like the *Marmari Express* above — only visiting Marmari.

but after a few months out of action she was back running in 2003. Occasional floods of sea water aside, on-board conditions are generally good — provided you can live with the regular diet of TV movies (guaranteed to end 15 minutes after you reach your destination). If she isn't around in 2004 the probability is that a *Flying Cat* will be deputizing.

C/F *Marmari Express*
DD Ferries

A small but useful ferry that appeared in 2000 on the Evia (Marmari) route. Clearly a recently rebuilt and refurbished vessel, she is not in the first division, but is adequate

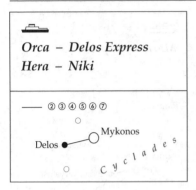

Delos Tour Boats

The island of Delos is only accessible via small tourist boats. Note: these often don't run in heavy seas, so it pays to be flexible about plans to visit Delos. Aim to go when you can, rather than allocating a specific day (and don't forget that there is no service on Mondays when the site is closed). The best of these boats run direct from Mykonos several times a day in High Season (you can pick up your boat on any of its return runs, so you can spend up to 5 hours on Delos). Return tickets (you can't buy single tickets) cost the same (€5) for all three boats, but are not interchangeable.

Boat tickets do not include the entrance fee for the archaeological site.

Tour boats from Tinos, Naxos and Paros also visit Delos, but all include a stop at Mykonos, restricting your time sightseeing on Delos to around 1½ hours. The fares are also much higher (Naxos—Delos trips cost around €25 because you are buying a day trip to several islands). The Naxos-based *Ariadne of Naxos* is the best of these boats, the *Naxos Star* being on the small side: their timetables change frequently. The Tinos-based *Tinos Sky* offers a minor advantage as her sailing times to Delos are significantly shorter.

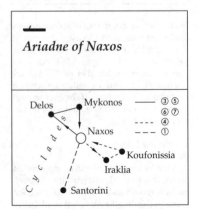

Cyclades North Islands & Ports

Andros
ΑΝΔΡΟΣ; 380 km²; pop. 9,020.

CODE ☎ 22820
GAVRION POLICE ☎ 71220
ANDROS TOWN POLICE ☎ 22300
HOSPITAL ☎ 22222

Despite being the second largest and most northerly of the Cyclades, Andros is only slowly edging its way onto the tourist map. A combination of rich vegetation and mountains has failed to bring the crowds. The only obvious reason for such a paradox is the lack of any notable population centre, for Andros really has a lot going for it if a downbeat, understated beach holiday is your kind of thing. The locals of course have long been in the know, and like Kea, Andros has been the preserve of Greek, rather than foreign, tourists, with many of the better-off Athenians having villas on this appealing island.

Despite the fact that Andros is on a major ferry route, independent island hoppers don't visit in large numbers; the great majority of visitors are package tourists who spend their time on the south coast, split between the port of Gavrion and the tourist resort village of Batsi to the east. Relatively few venture across the island to the capital at Chora, a symptom of the limited bus service; Andros is another of those islands that are best explored with your own transport.

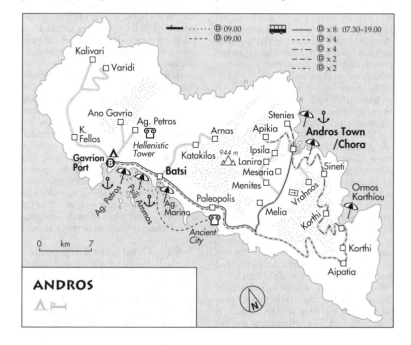

Most visitors arrive by ferry and thus find themselves deposited at the port of **Gavrion**. Set in a deep inlet, it consists of an intimidatingly large (and very dusty) ferry quay, backed by a little port village strung along the waterfront behind. All the usual facilities (including an information office housed in an old dovecot) lie along the shore: Gavrion is one of those 'what you can't see isn't there' sort of places, besides being very windy. Island buses (centred on Andros Town; Gavrion times are posted up in shops and ticket agents) turn around by the ferry quay before running back along the coast to the capital. More often than not they take any arriving tourists with them, as Gavrion offers little incentive to linger (writing in 1884 J. T. Bent said that 'of all places in the world Gavrion is one of the most desolate'). Things have improved somewhat today, but the port beach is a sadly indifferent affair (most people who stay in town migrate to the excellent sand beaches that run down the coast towards Batsi), and the commanding hilltop church of Agios Nikolaos that dominates the town reveals itself to be too new to be interesting when you get close up to it.

The main tourist resort on Andros is at **Batsi** (in Greek 'ΜΠΑΤΣΙ', and also transcribed as 'Vatsi') some 8 km east of Gavrion. Unashamedly a tourist town, it has developed from a tiny hamlet since the last war to become the island's premier resort. Given that it is so new and lacking an atmospheric centre, the town has managed to acquire a surprising amount of character with an attractive and lively waterfront (it is easy to see why some tourists choose to return regularly). Thereafter it is divided into two halves by a tree-filled valley, with the east (and older) side of the town clambering rapidly up a staircase-cluttered hillside, while the western 'hotel strip' end lies along the plain behind the beach.

However, there is little to see beyond the sea and the usual collection of tourist tavernas and bars. Serious nightlife is harder to find — a reflection of the fact that Batsi is very much a 'family holiday' orientated resort — and you don't have to wander around for long to come across bored-looking teenagers (dreaming wistfully of Ios Town, Faliraki on Rhodes, and Malia on Crete) who are just not quite old enough to be allowed on parent-free vacations. The limited nightspots are located on the outskirts of town.

Batsi's importance to tourists has grown of late, and it is now the base for the island's beach boats, with daily departures to a number of good sand beaches in the coves and bays either side of the town (these include a nudist beach at Delavogias on the south-east side). Most are accessible from the well-made main road, and moped or car hire fans will find themselves enjoying a major advantage over other tourists, as they can thus guarantee a stretch of sand beach all for their very own.

The island capital, **Andros Town** (also known as **Chora**), is a very different affair from the island's other port towns. Unusually for a capital, it is sited on the more exposed northern coast, and is home to a number of a wealthy Greek families. This, combined with the lack of accommodation and nightlife, and poor ferry and bus links, means that many island hoppers are happy to place Andros Town on their 'island capitals we can afford to miss' list. The accommodation situation is so bad that Andros Town usually has to be explored as a day trip excursion. Sightseeing fans will find more of interest as the town is home to a couple of excellent museums. As an added bonus, the bus ride (just over an hour from Gavrion — it is one of the cheapest island tours around) across the island passes through some very attractive countryside.

Sited on a wind-buffeted, finger-narrow peninsula, the majority of the buildings in the town are typical neo-classical 19 c. red-tile roofed piles. The main street dominates the town, running its length and dotted with shops and up-market boutiques. It ends in a small square adorned with an ugly bronze

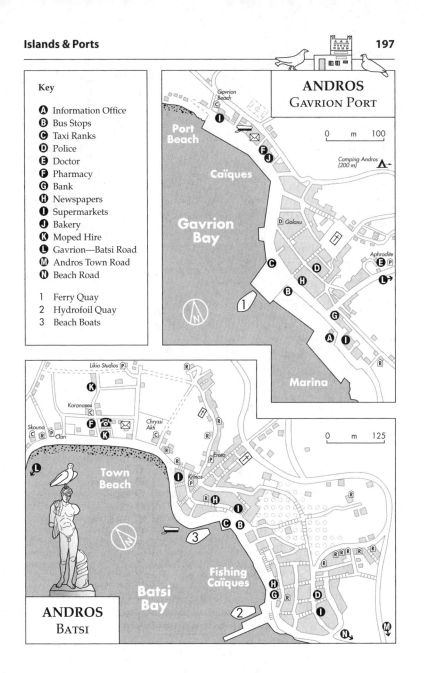

Key

- **A** Information Office
- **B** Bus Stops
- **C** Taxi Ranks
- **D** Police
- **E** Doctor
- **F** Pharmacy
- **G** Bank
- **H** Newspapers
- **I** Supermarkets
- **J** Bakery
- **K** Moped Hire
- **L** Gavrion—Batsi Road
- **M** Andros Town Road
- **N** Beach Road

1 Ferry Quay
2 Hydrofoil Quay
3 Beach Boats

ANDROS
GAVRION PORT

0 m 100

Camping Andros
(200 m)

Gavrion
Beach

Port
Beach

Caïques

Gavrion
Bay

Galaxu

Aphrodite

Marina

Likio Studios

Karanasos

Skouna
Clari

Chryssi
Akti

Erato

Krinos

Town
Beach

Fishing
Caïques

Batsi
Bay

0 m 125

ANDROS
BATSI

ANDROS
CHORA / TOWN

Key

- **A** Venetian Kastro
- **B** Police
- **C** Bus Station
- **D** Taxi Station
- **E** Archaeological Museum
- **F** Modern Art Museum
- **G** Maritime Museum & Unknown Soldier Statue

- **H** National Bank of Greece
- **I** Banks
- **J** Pharmacy
- **K** Bakery
- **L** Tavernas
- **M** Public WCs
- **N** Cinema
- **O** Disco (400 m)
- **P** School
- **Q** Agia Thalassini Church
- **R** Kairis Square
- **S** Chora—Gavrion Road

1 Ferry Berth
2 Rare Hydrofoils

Kastrou Bay

Plakoura / Old Port

North Beach

Paraporti Beach

Xenia

Aegli

0   m   150

(entitled 'The Unknown Sailor') waving out to sea, and a Maritime Museum that is usually closed. The sailor's view of the horizon is blocked by a islet topped by the remains of a long abandoned Venetian kastro. Known as the Mesa Kastro, it was built between 1207–33, and is reached via a narrow, arched bridge. The whitewashed buildings and the backstreets behind this square are the most appealing part of town, and are all that remains of the medieval capital of Kato Kastro. At the landward end of the old part of town are a notable Archaeological Museum and a Museum of Modern Art. Both have enjoyed the patronage of the wealthy Goulandri family — Andros is another of those islands that has among its sons a family of benevolent shipping millionaires.

The rest of the island remains virtually tourist free, thanks to the lack of a decent bus service and obvious sightseeing destinations: Andros is a good island to visit if unspoilt hill villages filled with dovecots (a legacy of the period of Venetian rule) appeals. The most visited inland settlement is **Mesaria** on the Andros Town road. This village retains a number of medieval buildings, including several ruined tower houses. Mesaria also has a 10 c. Byzantine church. Just up the road is the picturesque village of **Menites**, a settlement with an even greater ancestry: the main church stands on the site of a temple of Dionysos. In the mountains south of Andros Town stands the Monastery of Panachrantou. Founded in 961, it is home to St. Panteleimon's skull. Armed with healing powers, this relic packs quite a bit of pilgrim-pulling power. The monastery is just one of many possible destinations for walkers on Andros; other suggested island walks can be found in a local guide — *A Practical Guide to Andros* — which is on sale locally.

😰

Andros has always enjoyed a quiet existence on the fringes of history. Its location so close to Athens ensured that it was under the control of whichever power controlled that city. This changed in 200 BC when the Romans took con-

trol and handed over to Pergamon. Devastated in the Byzantine period by pirates, Andros fell under Venetian control from 1207, until the Turks took the island in 1556.

🛏

Accommodation is thinly spread around the island. In **Gavrion** the waterfront *Galexu* (☎ 71228) offers rooms for the desperate along with the better *Gavrion Beach* (☎ 71312). **Batsi** is host to the bulk of the island's accommodation, with the *Chryssi Akti* (☎ 41236), *Skouna* (☎ 41240) and *Karanasos* (☎ 41480) — complete with restaurant — being augmented by several pensions and plenty of hillside rooms. In **Andros Town** the best bet is the C-class *Aegli* (☎ 22303). There is also an expensive *Xenia* (☎ 22270) overlooking the beach and port on the north side of the town.

A

Camping Andros (☎ 71444): a reasonable site just behind Gavrion, it tries to make up for its odd location by providing all the facilities; these include a swimming pool, restaurant and pool table.

👓

Sightseeing is limited as the major archaeological sites have yet to be seriously explored. The most accessible object of interest is a 20 m high **Hellenistic Tower**: a 3 km hour-long hike inland from Gavrion. Known as the 'Tower of Agios Petros', conjecture varies wildly as to its purpose and age, with Mycenaean to Byzantine dates being suggested.

The remains of the ancient city of **Paleopolis** offer an attractive boat excursion from Batsi. Largely unexcavated, the old capital (from 600 BC to 500 AD) is sited down a steep path off the town road and also under the sea (the site has one beach, where visitors are not encouraged to carry a bucket and spade). Tourists visit to enjoy the pretty valley walk between the beach and the modern village. Of ruins there are few signs; the most notable discovery is a 2 c. BC marble copy of a bronze statue of Hermes by Praxiteles. Unusually, the island has managed to retain this major piece of sculpture and it is the prize exhibit in the Andros Town **Archaeological Museum**. The **Museum of Modern Art** is also worth exploring (despite having several works by the sculptor of the Unknown Sailor), if only for the strange 'sound' exhibits that follow you around.

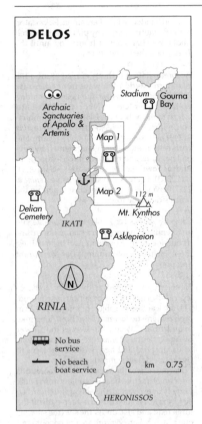

DELOS

Stadium Gourna Bay

Archaic
Sanctuaries
of Apollo &
Artemis

Map 1

Map 2   112 m

Delian
Cemetery   Mt. Kynthos
        IKATI

        Asklepieion

N

RINIA

No bus
service

No beach
boat service   0   km   0.75

HERONISSOS

Delos
ΔΗΛΟΣ; 3.6 km²; pop. 20.

Easily the smallest populated island in the
Cyclades (though technically Delos isn't
part of the group as it can't 'circle' itself),
Delos is also one of the most famous. Home
to one of the most important sanctuaries
in ancient Greece, the island is now one of
the great classical archaeological sites of
the Mediterranean, not least because it was
all but abandoned during the Roman era
and thus remains unspoilt by the gradual
accretion of later buildings.

Tradition had it that in an effort to escape the
amorous attentions of the god Zeus, a wench
named Asteria ignored the maxim that no
woman is an island and contrived to meta-
morphose into one, thereafter drifting where
tide and current would take her, sometimes
above the surface, other times submerged.
Not unnaturally, this did nothing for ancient
ferry schedules, and Poseidon finally inter-
vened and anchored the island of 'Asteria'
to the sea floor. As a result it was thereafter
known as 'Delos' or 'visible'. Years passed only
for another of Zeus's escaping lovers — Leto
— to land on the island, disguised as a swan,
and give birth to the twin deities Apollo (the
most popular of all the Greek gods) and his
sister, Artemis.

This set Delos up nicely: with a background
of divine sex and religion it not unnaturally
became a leading spiritual centre in ancient
Greece. This role was bolstered by a quadren-
nial games festival on a par with the Olympics,
and the island's emergence as the trade centre
of the Aegean. In its later years, during the
Hellenistic period, its trade markets came to
overshadow the sanctuary, and the excavated
complex of temples and markets is an impressive testament to this double life. That said,
the extant structures are confined to jumbled
foundations, thanks to a history of systematic
demolition.

A major Mycenaean site, Delos took off as a
sanctuary with the construction of a Temple
of Apollo in the early 7 c. BC (largely under
Naxian patronage). As the sanctuary grew in
importance, it underwent various stages of
ritual purification. This started in 540 BC with
the removal of all graves to neighbouring
Rinia island. This was followed in 426 BC
with an edict making it illegal to give birth or
die on Delos (this policy is maintained today
via a ban on overnight stays, and if that was
not discouragement enough, the only hotel
has been in ruins for 1600 years). The 426
BC edict prompted the growth of a town on
Rinia (otherwise known as 'Larger Delos')
— where one could be born or die and not
get blamed for it. On the political front, such
moves helped Delos emerge as a non-partisan
sanctuary — a sort of mini-Switzerland amid
the warring Greek city states, under the
control of none.

With the rise of the 4 c. BC Persian threat
Delos was chosen as the nominal centre of the

anti-Persian alliance of Greek city states, and it was to Delos that each sent contributions to a common war chest. However, the Delian League (as the alliance was known) was soon dominated by Athens, and this led to political control of the island passing to Athens, and the neutering of Delian influence. Thereafter, under Athenian patronage, the commercial aspect of Delos became ascendant.

After 250 BC Delos came under the control of the kings of Macedonia, and gradually emerged as the largest slave market in the Mediterranean. The geographer Strabo (64 BC – 19 AD) estimated that on a typical day 10,000 slaves would change masters. The wealth that came with this trade brought about the island's downfall. After coming under Roman control in 168 BC, it was sacked in 88 BC by Mithridates Eupator, king of Pontos, in his war with Rome. Having lost 20,000 of its population in the attack, Delos was sacked again in 69 BC by the pirates of Athenodoros, an ally of Mithridates. Delos never recovered. Abandoned by her rich patrons, and her trade functions re-centred elsewhere, she settled into a period of long decline that culminated with the arrival of Christianity — an event that destroyed her tarnished remaining religious role. From the 6 C. AD Delos appears to have been abandoned. In 1566 the Turks occupied the island, the tiny population doing a brisk trade selling much of the masonry, and burning the fine marble to make lime, before being driven away by the establishment of a pirate base on the island that survived into the early 19 C.

༽༼

Visitors to Delos should bring a sunhat, good shoes and beverages (refreshments are scandalously expensive on Delos; e.g. a can of cola costing €0.60 in a supermarket will set you back €5 here). Local visitors from Mykonos also wear stout shoes for fear of deadly snakes, but this is just paranoia; there aren't any deadly snakes in Greece. All tour boats arrive at a mole (complete with barrier and ticket kiosk on

the island side) built out of the debris from the excavations. In poor sea conditions boats berth on the other side of the island in Gourna Bay.

There is a site entrance fee of €5 (this is included in the price of *some* agency tours — it is advisable to check when buying) which also includes the museum. Establish carefully boat return times. You will need 2–3 hours in order to visit all the major features on the site — all are marked with stones inscribed in Greek and French. Unfortunately, there isn't a set route to follow when exploring Delos. Tourists peel off in all directions as soon as they pass the ticket kiosk. Given the summer heat, an anti-clockwise circuit is best as you can attempt the summit of Mt. Kynthos while still fresh; this means starting with Map 2, and then taking in the sites on Map 1 and the museum as you find them.

The rather ugly concrete-clad site museum is the most imposing building on the island. Fortunately, once you gain admission (you will have to show your entrance ticket) you will find that inside it is among the better archaeological museums in Greece. The eight galleries are home to a good collection of sculpture, mosaics, plaster wall paintings, household utensils and jewellery.

The Sanctuary Area
The heart of ancient Delos was made up of the central Sanctuary and Sacred Lake areas (see the double-page colour map between p. 192–193). On arriving at the site most tourists head for the enormous rubble field that once was the Sanctuary Area. In its prime it was the heart of Delos, containing the shrines to Apollo and holy sites dating back to Mycenaean times.

All arrivals to Delos start from ❶ the Hellenistic **Agora of the**

DELOS
SLAVE MARKET
SPECIALS!

ORGY GIRL —
10,000 TALENTS!
WITH FREE
PET HUNK
ATTACHED!

Competialists. This was a market dividing the religious and commercial areas of Delos; it is adorned with the bases of monuments erected by guildsmen. The main path from this crossroads ran north. This was the **Sacred Way** (or **Dromos**), the processional road to the sanctuary, and bounded by **B** the **Stoa of Philip V** (C.150 BC), named after a king of Macedon, and **G** the **South Stoa** (3 C. BC). Both were filled with shops.

The religious part of the site began with **D** the **Propylaea** (2 C. BC). This was the ceremonial gateway to the main sanctuary precinct (the **Hieron of Apollo**). It boasted three doors and four pillars (the bases of which survive, along with a statue base on the west side that has the footprints left by some long-lost bronze hero). Just inside stood one of the oldest buildings on Delos: **E** the **Oikos of the Naxians** (7 C. BC), an odd shrine with open ends and a roof supported by a row of internal pillars. Along its north wall stands **F** the **Base of the Colossal Statue of the Naxians**.

This famous sculpture (see **R**) was a 6 C. BC **Kouros** of Apollo that stood over 10 m high — i.e. more than twice the height of the Heraion Kouros now on display in the Archaeological Museum in Vathi, Samos (see p. 426). The broken base is inscribed 'I am of the same marble, both statue and base' on its east side and 'The Naxians to Apollo' on its west. The statue looked out to sea, over the monuments within **G** the L-shaped **Stoa of the Naxians** (6 C. BC). First among these was the **Bronze Palm Tree of Nicias** (417 BC) which was lost when the Apollo fell on it during a storm; only its base survives.

North of the Oikos lie the foundations of three Apollo temples. Delos is unusual in that later temples were built alongside (rather than replacing) earlier buildings. This had the side effect of leaving the site with a series of small temples, rather than acquiring one great temple, as other major shrines did. The focus provided by the sacred harbour also prompted another change in tradition, as all the temples have their main entrances on their west sides, instead of the usual east (it was normal building practice for the main door, opening on the statue within, to face the rising sun). The largest and newest of these temples was **H** the **Great Temple of Apollo (Temple of the Delians)**. Built on the founding of the Delian League in 478 BC, this was the only temple on Delos to have columns on all four sides.

North of it lies **I** the **Temple of the Athenians** (425–417 BC). Built out of Pentelic marble by Athenian workmen, it was highly decorated with sculptures. **J** the **Porinos Naos of Apollo** (6 C. BC) was the oldest temple, with columns only across its west front.

Running in an arc north and east of the three Apollo temples are the foundations of **K** the **5 Treasuries**. All date from the 6 or 5 C. BC, and lead round to several more important sanctuary precinct buildings. First among these is **L** the 3 C. BC **Neorion** (otherwise known as the **Monument of the Bulls** because of its decorative reliefs). This is one of the most unusual buildings known from ancient Greece. A stoa with a two-storey north end, it housed a trireme in its lower southern half. This glorified warship shed was built by Antigonos Gonatas to commemorate a naval victory over the Ptolemies. To the east lie the remains of several buildings housing minor cults, the **Bouleuterion** (6 C. BC) and the **Prytaneion**. To the west lies **M** the **Altar of Zeus Soter & Polieus** (3 C. BC).

South of the precinct boundary lies **N** the **Agora of the Delians**. This was lined with 2 C. BC stoas on its north and east sides and a 3 C. BC stoa on its south. Behind this complex stood a late Christian **Basilica of Agios Kyrikos**, along with a series of houses, including the **House of Kerdon** (marked by a couple of columns). The precinct boundary street runs north from here to **O** the **Sanctuary of Dionysos**, a popular tourist venue (thanks to the two broken giant phalli on pillars), and the nearby **Monument of Gaius Billienus** (1 C. BC), the marble torso of a Roman general. This backs onto **P** the foundations of the massive **Stoa of Antigonos** (3 C. BC), a ceremonial building surrounded by monuments. These include **Q** the water-and-frog-filled **Minoa Fountain** (6 C. BC) on its north side and, on the south, the semicircular **Graphe** or **Oikos**, the Mycenaean tomb of Arge and Opis (the maidens who supposedly attended Leto at Apollo's birth).

Artemis was worshipped in the north-west corner of the sanctuary; **R** the **Artemision** (c. 175 BC) was built on the site of an Archaic temple which was built over a Mycenaean shrine. It is easily located as it is now the home of the divided white marble torso of the **Colossal Statue of the Naxians** (this was cut in two and its head lost in pre-18 C. AD attempts to remove it — one of the statue's hands is in the site museum, and a foot is in the British Museum).

South of the Artemision lie the confused remains of several rather obscure and oddly named buildings: the **Keraton** (4 C. BC), a building that was used in a bizarre crane-dance ritual first stepped by Theseus, the **Oikos of the Andrians & Heiropoion** (otherwise known as the **Monuments of the Hexagons**), and the **Thesmophorion**, a 4 C. BC shrine complex that included a **Temple of Demeter**.

The Sacred Lake Area

Lying north of the Apollo temples precinct and the Stoa of Antigonos is the Sacred Lake Area. The Sacred Lake (so called because it was on its banks that Apollo and Artemis were born) marked the boundary of the Archaic sanctuary. With the rise of Delos as a trading centre, the area later became an up-market mansion district.

The main street leading to the Sacred Lake runs from ❼ the **Agora of Theophrastos** (126 BC) on the north side of the Sacred Harbour. When commercial forces were in the ascendant even the Sacred Harbour was put to commercial use with the building of ⓤ the **Hypostyle Hall** or **Stoa of Poseidon** (3 C. BC), a many-pillared merchants' exchange that was open on the harbour side. Now reduced to a field of capitals and bases, it was graced by 44 Doric and Ionic pillars (their absence is a clear sign of deliberate demolition). To the east stood ⓥ the **Temple of the Dodekatheon** (4 C. BC); dedicated to the 12 gods (see p. 72), it replaced an earlier Archaic structure.

Around the corner lies ⓦ the **Letoon** (or **Temple of Leto**). Built in the 6 C. BC, it honoured the mother of Apollo and Artemis, and — unusually — faced south, in order to face their temples. The surviving base of the building is easy to miss, thanks to the more impressive remains that stand either side, namely ⓧ the **Agora of the Italians** (2 C. BC), a large two-storey peristyle building named after its excavators, and ⓨ the **Granite Monument** (2 C. BC), a large building constructed out of granite blocks that is thought to have been a religious meeting house.

The high point of any tour of Delos is undoubtedly ❷ the **Terrace of the Lions** (7 C. BC). Powerful, deftly carved, archaic figures, now reduced to a weathered minimalist

perfection, they stood guard, looking over the Sacred Palm from which Leto hung to give birth to Apollo and Artemis. Thought to have once been up to 16 strong, only 5 lions survive *in situ*.

The body of a 6th was removed in the early 18 C. to guard the Arsenal in Venice. Unfortunately, the locals touched it up, replacing the original head with something more in keeping with the traditional Venetian Lion (complete with mane). The result is best summed up by the poor creature's expression of pained surprise; a case of being not so much maned as maimed. The Greek government has requested the torso's return and it is difficult not to sympathize given the poor beast's obvious distress (see below).

The site ❼ of the **Sacred Palm Tree** is probably the circular trunk-sized hole amid the foundations next to ⓐ the **Sacred Lake**. Dry since 1925 (when it was drained for fear of malarial mosquitos), it was originally perfectly circular and graced with swans. However, during the Hellenistic period, when the mansion district was built, the secular merchants (no doubt still being broken on a wheel in Hades) had the street to the harbour widened, prompting the narrowing of the lake and leaving it with the current oval shape. When it was drained the existing wall was erected to mark its perimeters, and a commemorative palm tree planted in the centre.

North of the Sacred Lake are the remains of several 3 C. and 2 C. BC mansions. Two have yielded up statues: ⓞ the **Koinon of the Poseidoniasts of Beirut** was built by Syrian merchants (a statue of Aphrodite whopping a cupid with a slipper — now in the National Archaeological Museum in Athens — was found here); ⓝ the **House of the Diadumenos** was   named after

a 2 C. BC copy of Polykleitos' Apollo. Other houses have more to see: ⊖ the **Hillside House** has been excavated out of the hill and gives an overhead view of the typical internal layout, while ⓪ the **House of the Comedians** has a good example of a central cistern (complete with water and Kermit-green frogs) with part of its roof-cum-floor intact. Some way north stands the **House at Scardana**. Turning east brings you to ⊖ the **House of the Lake**, which has a pretty little peristyle court, while ⓪ the large **Palaestra of Granite** (2 C. BC) behind it is dominated by a large water-filled cistern divided into quarters. ⓪ the **Palaestra of the Lake** (3 C. BC) is more nondescript, but also has a cistern.

Behind it lies the line of the **Wall of Triarius** (66 BC), built by a Roman legate to protect against pirates. The wall ran over demolished ancient buildings past ⓪ the **Temple of Anios** (7 C. BC), a small temple dedicated to a mythical king of Delos. From here a path runs north-east, past the site of the vanished U-shaped **Hippodrome**. Built c. 200 BC, it was later demolished to build defensive walls. Its predecessors, the **Gymnasium** (3 C. BC) and **Stadium** (C. 274 BC), survive in part on the east side of Delos, but see few tourists. Beyond them are the remains of a number of houses and a large 2 C. BC **Synagogue**.

Mount Kynthos

The Mount Kynthos area (see the colour map facing p. 193) contains a diverse mix of buildings. The theatre and residential buildings are the main attractions; some of the latter are among the best preserved 3 and 2 C. BC houses in Greece. Most retain walls up to chest height (these are not shown on the map for fear of rendering it unusable) and many adorned with mosaics have undergone some rebuilding. The mosaics — many quite famous — are something of a disappointment as they need watering to bring out their colours.

Along with visitors heading for the central sanctuary district, ❹ the **Agora of the Competialists** is the starting point for exploration of the Mount Kynthos district. Running down to the south is ❺ the **Maritime Quarter**. Little visited today, this area is made up of warehouse buildings. Most are only partly excavated, but enough has been discovered to show that this was where the slave market flourished. The tourist path, however, moves in the direction

of ❻ the **Theatre Quarter** (the residential area near the theatre), where all the buildings have been explored.

A walk up the ancient main street will bring you to a marked side-street leading off to ❼ the **House of Cleopatra & Dioscurides** (137 BC); named after the statues of two wealthy Athenians to be seen within (this Cleopatra is not the queen of Egypt with the famously lovely nose: in fact, this lady hasn't even got a head), it has the remains of a typical peristyle pillared central courtyard. The statues on site are reproductions: the originals are now standing in the site museum.

Further up the main street lies ❽ the **House of Dionysos**. The first of the 'mosaic' houses, it is named after the impressive mosaic of Dionysos riding nose-saddle on a panther. Similarly, ❾ the rebuilt **House of the Trident** has a trident mosaic. Both houses can be locked and are only open if sufficient site staff have turned up for guard duty.

The main residential street finally emerges at ❿ the **Theatre** (4 C. BC). Now badly preserved in detail (its seating proved too tempting to masonry thieves) it is still impressive. Climbing to the level of the higher tiers, it is easy enough to imagine it filled with a 5,500 capacity crowd. It is unique among ancient theatres in having a stage building constructed on its circular orchestra or stage: the **Skene**. Possibly three floors high (to allow the 'gods' to appear from above) it had colonnaded lower storeys. Only foundations remain, with rubble running back to ⓿ the **Theatre Cistern**. This stored rainwater running off the theatre. Some 22.5 m long and 6 m wide, it is filled with water; its roof is missing, though the supporting arches remain.

The tourist path ascends the hill south of the theatre past a marble-lined doorway that marks ⓿ the **Guest House**. Thought to have been an inn, it is notable for having the deepest cistern of any house on Delos. It is 8.3 m deep and guarded with protective rails. Those that don't fall in will find the path continuing up to ⓿ the **House of the Masks** (named after a mosaic illustrating a series of actor's masks). A large building, it had shops along its street side. Nearby stands ⓿ the **House of the Dolphins**, a smaller, richer structure with mosaics depicting cupids riding dolphins.

Once past the House of the Dolphins the tourist path emerges at an upper sanctuary level. This area contains a number of small temples, as well as shrines devoted to eastern deities (a reflection of the island's days as an international trading centre). The first recognisable building is ❶ the **Herion** (c. 500 BC). A small temple dedicated to Hera, its columns survive. This temple also marks the point where the main path divides. One branch steps up to the summit of **Mt. Kynthos** (don't miss the tiny path running to the mysterious **Cave of Cynthus** or **Grotto of Hercules** at ⓜ. Dating from the 3 C. BC, it contained a statue of the hero under its roof of pitched granite slabs, and has a circular marble altar outside the door). The main path runs up past the foundations of ❶ the **Sanctuary of Agathe Tyche** (of which little survives) before reaching the summit. Here stood ❶ the **Sanctuary of Kynthian Zeus & Athena** (7 C. BC). Once similar in size to the Herion, the only surviving remains are a few slippery foundation stones from which you get blown into next week trying to take in the superb panoramic views.

Returning to the Herion, the path moves on to a relatively isolated area of Delos (reflecting the comparatively late date of the majority of its religious buildings). The first building of note is ❶ the heavily restored **Temple of Isis** (3 C. BC), complete with a headless statue of Isis standing within its walls. Nearby is ❶ **Serapeion C**, a small stoa-lined court. Further along this terrace is ❶ the **Sanctuary of the Syrian Gods** (c. 100 BC) which included a religious amphitheatre for witnessing ceremonies. Below this terrace is the site of a second stoa-lined court: ❺ **Serapeion B** (2 C. BC), and below that ❶ the **Cistern of Inopos** (3 C. BC). Still filled with green water, it was built to collect the fountainhead waters of the Inopos, the sacred river of Delos. Legend had it that its source was the Nile. Nearby is ❶ the **House of Inopos**. South of the cistern lie the remains of ❶ the **Monument of Mithridates Eupator** (c. 100 BC), a king of Pontos. This stood in front of ❶ the **Samothrakeion** (4 C. BC), a temple to the Great Gods of Samothrace.

East of the cistern, in the largely unexcavated area, lie other buildings of interest, notably ❽ **Serapeion A** (3 C. BC), a third stoa-lined court, and — accessed via a narrow path branching off the museum path — ❶ the **House of Hermes** (4 C. BC). This two-storey house is the best-preserved peristyle court mansion on Delos. Further along this path lies ❷ the **Aphrodision** (4 C. BC), a tiny temple of Aphrodite. From here the path rejoins the main sanctuary area.

Evia / Euboea
EYIA / EYBOIA; 3580 km²; pop. 165,000.

CHALCIS: CODE ☎ 22210
POLICE ☎ 22100
KIMI: CODE ☎ 22220
POLICE ☎ 22555
FIRST AID ☎ 22322

The second-largest island in Greece, mountainous Evia (or Euboea) is not a member of the Cyclades; it is included in this chapter thanks to its links with the North Cycladic islands via hydrofoils running to both and ferries running out of Rafina. In fact, Evia isn't popular with island hoppers and remains stubbornly well off the tourist map, lacking the beaches or sights that would bring the crowds. The island's position on the north-east coast of Attica does little to help, as linked by a bridge and motorway to Athens it is often seen as merely an adjunct to the mainland it hugs so closely. Even the main town can't seem to make up its mind and clings to both island and mainland. Ferry connections are poor, being confined to a number of minor crossing points to the mainland at intervals along the coast (this tells you all you need to know about the island's roads) and the main Skyros—'mainland' link. These are all local services and times vary little during the year.

The island capital is at **Chalcis**, located halfway up the west coast at the narrowest point of the Evian Strait (known as the Euripus Channel). The town was an important centre in ancient Greece, thanks to its strategic position on the straits, but is now an ugly commercial centre with only a distinctive Turkish quarter, and a popular, up-market waterfront to redeem it. The old-fashioned swing bridge that straddles the 30 m strait marks the boundary between the chic northern and southern commercial quarters; the straits are too narrow to admit cargo vessels north of the bridge. Not unnaturally the town is also the hub of the island bus services. These are wide ranging, but infrequent, and on difficult roads. This, and the distances involved, means that Evia is not really a moped island either. If getting around is not very easy, getting overland to Evia is: bus and rail links with Athens are very good.

Around Evia are a number of towns or villages with little in common. **Eretria** is the most notable of them, and is now emerging as a poor tourist resort. Like Chalcis, it was a major ancient city in the 6 C. BC, before Athens dominated the region and it fell into decline. Indeed, by the beginning of the 19 C. the population was so small that the town was used to rehouse those inhabitants of Psara that managed to escape the 1824 Turkish devastation of that island. As a result Eretria is also known as **Nea Psara**. Set on a dry dusty plain, it is a garden of Eden short of beautiful thanks to the half-empty grid layout of the incomplete new town, but the plentiful archaeological remains of the ancient city are some compensation, as is the good beach east of the harbour.

Other centres have less going for them. **Loutra Edipsos** is Greece's premier spa, emerging as a popular holiday destination in the late 19 C. However, it has yet to emerge as a modern tourist resort and is marred by the rather dismal air of a faded watering hole. More cheerful spots are to be found elsewhere. **Limni** is a coastal village turned resort, as is **Pefki** on the northern coast, but even so, there is little disguising the fact that neither are worth flying all the way to Greece for. The latter does, however, receive occasional visits from Sporades' hydrofoils.

The southern half of Evia is dominated by two port villages, **Karystos** and **Marmari**. Both have direct ferry links with Rafina and tend to clog up with escaping Athenians during the weekends. Karystos is the nicer of the two, set in a wide bay with a Venetian-built harbour. Marmari has less charm but does offer regular boat trips to the small wooded Petali Islands (**Megalo Petali** & **Xero**) 1 km to the south.

Kimi port (as distinct from Kimi Town, a hillside village 4 km inland) is the principal jumping off point for Skyros and its links with the other Northern Aegean destinations. It is tucked beneath the mountain range that makes up the backbone of Evia, and is a very pretty little place with an excellent beach just below the harbour. Unfortunately, beds are thin on the ground.

Thanks to Evia's motorway link with Athens, Kimi is a de facto mainland port with regular buses, and most visitors pass straight through. The link with Skyros is the mainstay of ferry activity. Other departures (usually twice weekly to the Sporades in High Season) are poorly advertised, and remain easier to arrive than depart on.

⊨

Considering its size, Evia is poorly equipped with hotels, and rooms are a rarity. **Chalcis** offers the greatest choice of beds thanks to its hotel-littered waterfront. Unfortunately, the majority are pricey, top end of the market establishments. Top of the range is the A-class *Lucy* (☎ 23831). Budget hotels lie nearer the bridge. These include the *Kentrikon* (☎ 71525) and the very noisy (and primitive) *Kymata* (☎ 21317) and *Iris* (☎ 22246). Meantime, on the mainland side you will find the quieter *Hara* (☎ 25541) is very reasonable.

Eretria has several mid-range hotels including the good C-class *Xenia* (☎ 61202). As it stands alone on a causeway-linked islet on the east side of the town (recently renamed **Dream Island**) noise is not a problem. **Kimi Port** has rooms and two hotels, the best being the C-class *Beis* (☎ 22604).

Å

There is camping on Evia — 19 sites in all — but they are poorly placed and totally geared up to serving motor-campers rather than backpackers. Island hoppers are likely to find that the reasonable site near **Pefki**: *Camping Pefki* (☎ 22960 41121) is of most use. There is also a fair site near **Eretria**: *Camping Milos* (☎ 22290 60420).

∞

If you discount the attractive pine-clad mountain scenery, the **Euripus Channel** in **Chalcis** is Evia's most noteworthy sight, and boasts a 2500 year pedigree as a tourist attraction thanks to the odd combination of land and currents which make the tide change eight times a day. Since the building of the first bridge

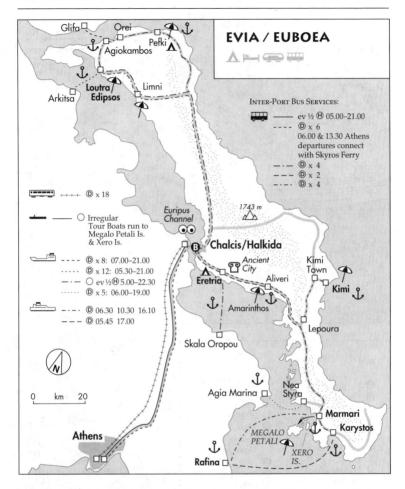

EVIA / EUBOEA

Glifa
Orei
Pefki
Agiokambos
Loutra / Edipsos
Arkitsa
Limni

INTER-PORT BUS SERVICES:

— ev ½ Ⓗ 05.00–21.00
---- Ⓓ x 6
       06.00 & 13.30 Athens
       departures connect
       with Skyros Ferry
—·— Ⓓ x 4
—··— Ⓓ x 2
—···— Ⓓ x 4

Ⓓ x 18

○ Irregular
   Tour Boats run to
   Megalo Petali Is.
   & Xero Is.

---- Ⓓ x 8: 07.00–21.00
····· Ⓓ x 12: 05.30–21.00
—·— ○ ev ½ Ⓗ 5.00–22.30
····· Ⓓ x 5: 06.00–19.00

---- Ⓓ 06.30 10.30 16.10
—— Ⓓ 05.45 17.00

Euripus
Channel

1743 m

Chalcis/Halkida

Ancient
City

Eretria

Kimi
Town

Kimi

Aliveri

Amarinthos

Lepoura

0   km   20

Skala Oropou

Agia Marina

Nea
Styra

Marmari

Karystos

MEGALO
PETALI

XERO
IS.

Athens

Rafina

over the 30 m-wide narrows in the 5 C. BC, the locals have wondered over the phenomenon. Aristotle is reputed to have drowned when he threw himself into the sea in exasperation at his inability to explain it. His successors still haven't come up with the answer but, given the murky state of the water, have generally opted for cleaner forms of suicide.

Signs of the ancient city are as well hidden as the seabed, and archaeology fans will do best to head for the **Archaeological Museum**, which houses finds from all over the island. The remains of ancient **Eretria** offer better sightseeing; the great rival of Chalcis (the two cities fought a succession of wars for control over the plain that separates them) has a notable theatre (largely denuded of stone), several important houses and a section of city wall, complete with the best-preserved Archaic period gate in Greece.

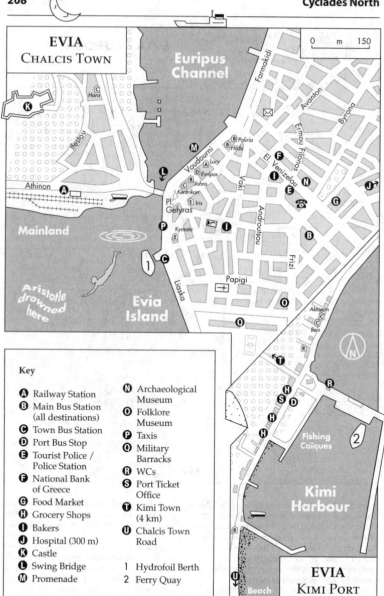

EVIA
CHALCIS TOWN

Euripus Channel

Mainland

Evia Island

Aristotle drowned here

Key

- **A** Railway Station
- **B** Main Bus Station (all destinations)
- **C** Town Bus Station
- **D** Port Bus Stop
- **E** Tourist Police / Police Station
- **F** National Bank of Greece
- **G** Food Market
- **H** Grocery Shops
- **I** Bakers
- **J** Hospital (300 m)
- **K** Castle
- **L** Swing Bridge
- **M** Promenade

- **N** Archaeological Museum
- **O** Folklore Museum
- **P** Taxis
- **Q** Military Barracks
- **R** WCs
- **S** Port Ticket Office
- **T** Kimi Town (4 km)
- **U** Chalcis Town Road

- **1** Hydrofoil Berth
- **2** Ferry Quay

Kimi Harbour

Fishing Caiques

EVIA
KIMI PORT

Beach

GIAROS

No bus service

No beach boat service

Prison

489 m

Sea Cliffs

GLARONISI

0   km   5

Giaros
ΓΙΑΡΟΣ; 19 km²; pop. 0.

Travel on a ferry out of Piraeus to Paros and the first substantial island you steam past is Giaros (also transcribed 'Yiaros'). This is somewhat ironic, because this is the only Cycladic island which has never been accessible to the hordes that swarm across the Aegean each summer. Long without a resident population, Giaros has been under military control since WW2. Little more than a barren hilltop with a very crinkly coastline, it was turned into a military prison camp for political dissidents between 1967–74 when the Colonels seized power (the task of the first innmates was to construct their own prision!), and since the restoration of democracy it has been used as a naval base — complete with a gunboat firing range.

However, things are now set to change. In January 2002 Giaros was declared by a presidential decree to be a 'national monument' and released from military control. There are now plans to restore the prison buildings, build a new pier and turn the island into a tourist attraction. Since

the announcement was made, silence has reigned, but it is just possible that tours will start up — probably from Syros — in 2004. If you get the chance to go, take it, as Giaros promises to offer a Greek island experience like no other — though given the recent use of the island as naval firing range, it might not be wise to wander away from designated tourist areas, or go beachcombing in search of interesting shells.

Giaros can claim one notable footnote in history: in 37 AD it was suggested that two leading Romans — Silanus and Marsus Vibius, who attracted the wrath of the dying Emperor Tiberius — be exiled to the island after facing charges of treason and adultery. In the event the Roman Senate decided that this punishment would be inhuman and the two ended up suffering the 'torments' of banishment to Amorgos instead.

As Rome's power waned, Giaros took on a new identity as a base for pirates (known hereabouts as 'corsairs') — a role that continued well into the Middle Ages. This history of operating as prison before pirates move in seems to be being repeated today: in February 2001, as the military moved out, modern day pirates — in the form of refugee smugglers — moved in, marooning 35 illegal immigrants (mainly Kurds and Iraqis) on the island, after they were intercepted by the Greek Coast Guard en route to Kythnos.

Mykonos
ΜΥΚΟΝΟΣ; 88 km²; pop. 5,700.

CODE ☎ 22890
PORT POLICE ☎ 22218
POLICE ☎ 22482
FIRST AID ☎ 23994

Now among the most heavily touristed (and expensive) of all the Greek islands and the location for the get-away-from-it-all film *Shirley Valentine*, Mykonos is one of those islands that are really superb at the quieter times of the year, but which descend into the realms of the truly awful at the peak of the High Season (with over 750,000 visitors a year some of the residents

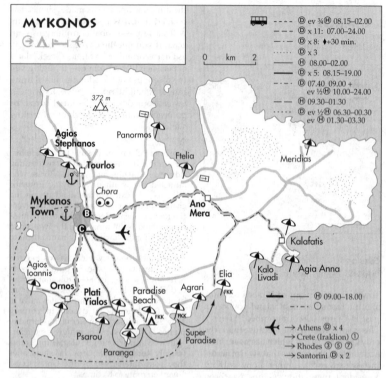

even go island hopping to get away from the chaos — especially in mid-July to mid-August). The island has been near the top of the Greek island tourist map since the mid-1960s, courtesy of one of the most scenic harbours in the Mediterranean, a profusion of good sand beaches tolerating nudism, and the nearby premier sightseeing island of Delos. Sadly, the prolonged exposure to heavy tourism is reflected in the terrible damage wrought on the landscape — thanks to the excessive amount of hotel and holiday-home building — and on the local tourist industry (the attitude on Mykonos to tourists is increasingly reminiscent of Athens: i.e. forget the old-fashioned Greek ideal that 'visitors are guests' and

screw them for every penny you can get out of them instead). Sadly, on Mykonos you need to check your change carefully — even on buses — and keep an eye out for double-charging in supermarkets.

Formerly a preserve of the world's jet-setters, Mykonos always has exhibited wildly inflated prices, thanks to a scene dominated by expensive boutiques and nightclubs where French and the male gay scene thrive. A procession of cruise ships calling provides little incentive to keep prices down (you should reckon on paying a 25% premium for the pleasure of a stay on Mykonos). Notwithstanding the cost of living, backpackers also swarm over the island each summer in increasing numbers, their great redeeming function being to make the island much safer for the single male who, in years past, was apt to find out what the fairer sex have to put up with. Unfortunately, Mykonos also attracts a goodly number of rowdy urban Greeks, seemingly attracted by the island's reputation for loose living. At their best they clog the roads with mass moped displays; at their worst they have, in past years, included a rapist with a rather nasty knife, and a mass convention of graffiti artists. All this sounds pretty dire, but if you are careful when here, and come at the right time, Mykonos is still a very rewarding place to visit.

The only large settlement on a small island, **Mykonos Town** is the overburdened hub of all this activity. Centred on the famous crescent-shaped harbour bay with its headland topped with windmills, it is an attractive maze of whitewashed cubic houses riddled with alleyways deliberately contrived to distract both would-be pirates (to say nothing of tourists) and the *meltemi* wind that attacks Mykonos very hard each summer. The largest of its kind in the Cyclades, the chora street maze is so intricate that it happily baffles seasoned visitors. Sooner or later you will be obliged to head for either the hills and the roads that surround the town, or the chaos that is the bus square at Plati Yialos, or the harbour itself, in order to re-establish your bearings.

The harbour, naturally the focal point of the town, is stunningly attractive when viewed from the hill behind the quay. However, the heavy waterfront mix of tavernas, souvenir and (expensive) gold and silver shops, backed by bars, nightclubs and restaurants, quickly dispels any pretence that this is an unspoilt island town. This is not to say that Mykonos Town doesn't exude Greek island charm, for it does — almost to excess. But it is difficult to escape the impression that it is contrived and done purely for the tourists' benefit. This can be seen in the spate of windmill rebuilding on the hills around the town. Further

building work is going on, in an effort to relieve the pressure. A ring road around the town opened in 1999, and a new port opened 2.5 km up the coast at Tourlos (see overleaf).

Fortunately, amidst the tourists and building, echoes of the old Mykonos can still be found; the locals who aren't in the tourist industry somehow manage to carry on with their daily routine, seemingly oblivious to the mayhem around them, and still walk down to the waterfront each morning to buy produce and freshly caught fish. Tourists also get in on the act by relieving the fishermen of any part of their catch that they can't sell, so that they can throw fish to the very photogenic pelican that is allowed to flap the streets at will.

Actually, the history of the Mykonos pelican (the island's famous mascot, and a beast that is snapped in virtually every photo-orientated Greek island guidebook) is worth a brief mention as it provides a good insight of how the island has gone ever down. The original pelican landed on Mykonos in 1956 during a storm, and rapidly emerged as a premier attraction. The locals persuaded it to stay by clipping its wings and naming it Petros. In the event this was a slight misnomer as it was pe*trol* that did for it: the poor thing was run over in 1985 — a victim of the island's traffic injury boom. Fortunately, its killer — a passing taxi driver — also fancied himself as a taxidermist and attempted to recover the situation by stuffing his victim. This was not an unqualified success, as the deception was noticed; the islanders thereafter

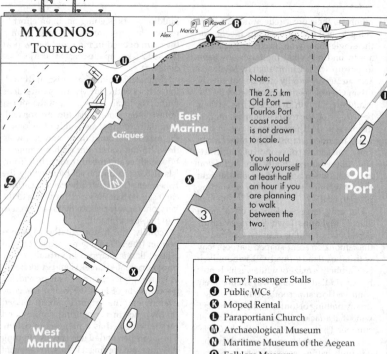

MYKONOS

TOURLOS

Caïques

East Marina

West Marina

New Port

Old Port

Note:

The 2.5 km Old Port — Tourlos Port coast road is not drawn to scale.

You should allow yourself at least half an hour if you are planning to walk between the two.

Key

- **A** Buses to New Port (Tourlos) / Accommodation Office / Tourist Police / Camping Bus pick-up point
- **B** Bus Station (N. & Central Mykonos)
- **C** Bus Station (Pl. Plati Yialos)
- **D** Police
- **E** Tourist Police
- **F** National Bank of Greece
- **G** Supermarket
- **H** Newspapers / Bookshop
- **I** Ferry Passenger Stalls
- **J** Public WCs
- **K** Moped Rental
- **L** Paraportiani Church
- **M** Archaeological Museum
- **N** Maritime Museum of the Aegean
- **O** Folklore Museum
- **P** Windmill Museum
- **Q** Little Venice
- **R** Town Ring Road
- **S** Cathedral
- **T** School of Fine Arts
- **U** Taverna
- **V** Motorbike Rental
- **W** Coast Road
- **X** Bus Drop-off / Pick-up Points
- **Y** Main Bus Stops on the Coast Road
- **Z** Agios Stephanos Road (1 km)
- 1 Old Port Ferry Quay
- 2 Smaller Ferries
- 3 Ferry & Large Catamaran Berth
- 4 Delos Tour Boats
- 5 Excursion Boat Berth
- 6 Cruise Ships Only

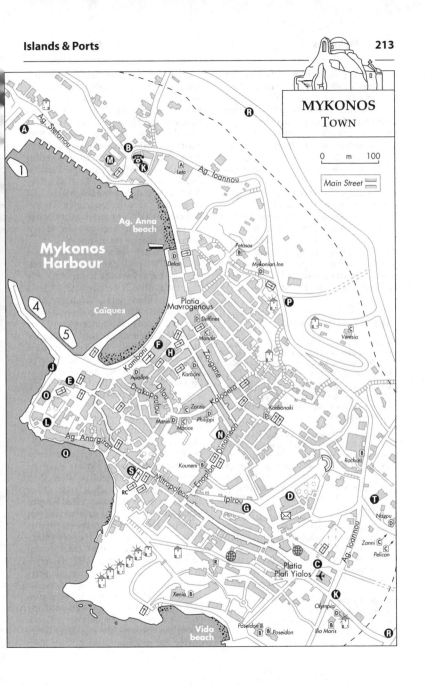

MYKONOS
TOWN

0   m   100

Main Street

Mykonos
Harbour

Caïques

Ag. Stefanou

Ag. Anna
beach

Ag. Ioannou

Leto

Petasos

Delos

Mykonian Inn

Platia
Mavrogenous

Delfines

Mando

Ventsia

Kambani

Apollon

Dilou

Karboni

Zougane

Kalogera

Drakopoulou

Zorzis

Mania

Philippi

Manos

Karbonaki

Dinameon

Ag. Anargiron

Kouneni

Enoplon

Rochari

Mitropoleos

RC

Ipirou

Xenia

Platia
Plati Yialos

Nazou

Zanni

Pelican

Olympia

Poseidon II

Poseidon

Ilio Maris

Vida
beach

decided to install Petros in the Craft and Folklore Museum and get in a couple of replacements (now usually to be found near the waterfront, looking vainly for a refuge from the camera-snapping crowds), hoping that no one would notice the difference.

If the pelicans have got any sense, they keep their feathers well down at night, for Mykonos Town after dark is something else; in High Season the place literally throbs. Unfortunately, some hereabouts throb too much, particularly when confronted by an unattached female, and Mykonos has had more than its share of problems (those who find all this difficult to square with the fact this is the *Shirley Valentine* island should note that the film was produced well out of season when the pretence of a dreamy, idyllic Greek island could be maintained).

Mykonos — Which Port?

• When you buy at ferry ticket on Mykonos check carefully which of the island's two ports (**Old Port** or **Tourlos**) your boat or catamaran is departing from.

• If you buy a ticket for a boat departing from Mykonos on another island, be sure to check on its departure point with a local ticket agent when you get to Mykonos.

The new port at **Tourlos**, looking like a large offshore runway (linked by a bridge to the island), was built primarily to cater for cruise ships too large to enter the **Old Port**. Some larger ferries and catamarans are now using it too. This is regularly causing serious confusion for island hoppers, and almost every day sees passengers caught at the wrong port when their boat turns up.

Unfortunately the distance between the two ports makes it difficult to rectify the problem once a boat has docked — though those caught do try: in 2003 the world was even treated to the sight of a desperate running island hopper pushing her wheelchair-bound partner along the coast road in the dark, in a breathless attempt to catch a night boat.

Mykonos Town—Agios Stephanos buses call at both ports during daylight hours, but there is no transport at Tourlos at night. There are no ticket or refreshment facilities at Tourlos.

After Mykonos Town and its nightlife, the island's beaches are the other big draw — particularly those on the south coast, which offers an appealing mix of windy headlands and bays decorated with long strands of fine sand. These start at **Plati Yialos**, a crowded, hotel-backed beach with a small quay from which caïques shuttle along the coast to Paradise, Super Paradise and Elia beaches. All bar Plati Yialos have their nudist end. **Paradise Beach** is the most famous (and crowded), though it is somewhat overrated. The beach bar attached to the campsite really goes to town when it comes to charging rip-off prices.

Nudism is confined to a few brave women and a clutch of posing gay men on the western end. **Super Paradise** has traditionally been the gay beach, but these days it has a pretty even mix of sexes, and more nudity than Paradise. **Elia Beach** is the best of the four and is predominately nude. All four are linked by a rough path. Taking the overspill from these crowded strands are the windy north-coast beaches. However, most are only good for sunbathing fans, as offshore currents can be dangerous. The best of these beaches are to be found at **Panormos** and **Ftelia**.

The interior of Mykonos is hilly and barren with surprisingly few villages. However, farms and the massive numbers of new holiday homes now under construction and ruining every skyline leave the landscape cluttered with whitewashed cubic architecture in abundance. Other centres are small; the most visited is **Agios Stephanos**, which has a substandard (for Mykonos) beach that is nonetheless popular because it is easy to get to. The only village of any size inland is at **Ano Mera**. Home to a museum and a 6 c. church, it is the centre of one of the few remaining unspoilt parts of the island.

Buses run frequently around Mykonos, particularly between the town and all the popular beaches. Unusually for a Greek island they operate into the small hours during the summer months. Ferry links are also good. Sailings to Rafina (usually labelled 'Athens') are widely advertised without mention of the stops at Tinos and Andros.

Lying so close to Delos, ancient Mykonos found itself eclipsed by its more famous neighbour. Lacking notable cities or sanctuaries, it was best known — thanks largely to the writer Strabo — for being the home of an excessively large number of bald men (some things don't change). When Athens took control of Delos via the Delian League, rule over Mykonos inevitably came as part of the package, and thereafter the island's fate was tied to that city. This only changed with the collapse of the Byzantine empire. Mykonos then found herself first under the rule of the Dukes of Naxos and, once that brief dynasty foundered, under Venetian control (via Tinos). Mykonos briefly played an important part in the War of Independence against the Turks when, in 1822, it repulsed an attack after joining the embryonic Greet state.

Mykonos has a hotel and room information office on the ferry quay; this makes life easy, but not that easy as beds fill up early in High Season. Perhaps more than with any other island it pays to arrive before noon.

The town has a number of C and D 'standard' (one hesitates to say 'priced') hotels, including the waterfront *Apollon* (☎ 22223) and a varied collection on Kaloaera St., including the C-class *Zorzis* (☎ 22167) and *Marios* (☎ 22704) and the D-class *Maria* (☎ 24212) and *Philippi* (☎ 22294). The hills behind the town are another fertile hunting ground, and include the noisy *Olympia* (☎ 22964), the better-placed *Nazou* (☎ 22626) and C-class *Zanni* (☎ 22486) and *Pelican* (☎ 23454). *Paradise Beach Camping* also offers popular chalets. At the top end of the market is the A-class *Leto* (☎ 22207), which earlier in the last century played host to the King of Greece, and those similarly well-off ever since. A second bet if you want everything from satellite TV to saunas and jacuzzis are the three *Petasos Hotels* on Mykonos: one in the town (☎ 22608), and two at Plati Yialos (☎ 23437).

Mykonos has two sites five minutes' walk from each other (via the coast path). Competition between them ensures a frantic grab for campers off the boats. Both charge the same rates and are among the most expensive in the Aegean (reckon on paying at least €1.50 more per day than elsewhere).

Camping Mykonos (☎ 24578) is a newish site on a headland beside Paranga beach. Now the best on the island (though this is relative and, compared to sites on other islands, isn't saying a lot), its facilities include a reception internet link. The site is served by hourly buses running to Mykonos Town. Let down by a pricey mini-market and very basic washing facilities.

Paradise Beach Camping (☎ 22852): forget the 'Paradise' bit — this is the site that threatens to give Hell a good name. The site's proud boast that it has been around since 1969 is fully borne out by its awful, often filthy, washing facilities. Add to this some very unenthusiastic staff and a mini-market that charges double the rates found in supermarkets, and one is left wondering why anyone chooses to stay here. The answer is the non-stop beach disco (latterly with fireworks three nights a week): dancing on bar tops from mid-day on.

Nightlife is scattered around the town. The hottest venues change with each year, though there are regular favourites. These include the big *Hard Rock Café* complex on the Ano Mera road (reached via free mini-buses from the town) and a cluster of bars near the Paraportiani church. These include the *Windmill Disco*, the *Irish Disco* and the *Scandinavian Bar*. More up-market venues are to be found behind the waterfront at Little Venice and the yacht marina near the ferry quay.

Mykonos lacks archaeological or historical sites (the proximity of neighbouring Delos did little to encourage building during the Classical period), but **Mykonos Town** offers plenty by way of compensation. Although the Venetian kastro that once adorned the western promontory of the town is long gone, a row of wooden galleried houses known as **'Little Venice'** remain from the period, the multicoloured balconies hanging over the sea providing one of the town's picture-postcard views. On the site of the kastro now stands the

Paraportiani, a group of picturesque chapels plastered together in 'melting ice cream' fashion. The rest of the town also lends itself to exploration, though most only dates from the 18 — 19 c. There are also a clutch of museums worth visiting:

A working **Windmill Museum** is open to tourists on the hillside east of the harbour; admission is free and you should take a look (this is the only working example you can visit in the islands).

The **Archaeological Museum** (open ②–⑦ 08.30–15.00; entrance fee €1.50) contains finds from Delian graves on the nearby island of Rinia (when Delos was sanctified, all burials were re-interred on Rinia). Commanding pride of place among the exhibits is a 7 c. BC red terracotta pithoi vase decorated with a relief that is the earliest known depiction of the wooden horse of Troy.

Hidden away in an old town house is the **Maritime Museum of the Aegean** (open ⓪ 10.30–13.00, 18.30–21.00; entrance fee €3). Although not quite up to the standard of its Santorini (Oia) counterpart, the museum still offers a rewarding hour's browsing. The exhibits consist of a pretty varied collection of nautical odds and ends spread over three rooms, and a lawned back garden (the latter being home to assorted gravestones and the top 20 feet of a late 19 c. lighthouse). Maps and models on an Aegean theme make up the bulk of the collection (including the *Endeavour*, the ship made famous by the explorer Captain Cook, who apparently discovered the Aegean by way of Australia).

Finally, the **Craft and Folklore Museum** (open ⓪ 17.30–20.30) takes the form of a restored 17 c. sea captain's house. Replete with contemporary artifacts, it offers a glimpse of pre-tourist island life.

Syros

ΣΥΡΟΣ; 86 km²; pop. 21,000.

CODE ☎ 22810
PORT POLICE ☎ 22690
TOURIST POLICE ☎ 22620
POLICE ☎ 23555

Imagine a relatively small, arid island with a large mainland-sized town built on the east coast, and you have some idea what Syros is like. An oddity among Greek islands, Syros

was able to avoid the chaos and destruction encountered by most islands at the hands of pirates from the 17 c. on, thanks to the existence of a strong Roman Catholic community that sought and got the patronage and protection of the King of France. Thanks to this connection, the island was able to retain its coastal settlements rather than retreat from them to inland centres, and even during the War of Independence was able to maintain a precarious neutrality, making it a haven for refugees. The influx of refugees (notably from Chios) fleeing Turkish suppression also served to give the town economy a massive boost.

Building on this background, the main town of **Ermoupolis** ('The city of Hermes') developed rapidly in the 19 c. (thanks to its role as *the* mid-Aegean coaling port) to become the largest in the Cyclades and the capital of the group. The town is divided into three quarters. This might sound Greek but is perfectly logical given the geography; for the waterfront and its environs are backed by two building-clad hills — each topped with a church, one Roman Catholic, the other Orthodox. Add to this a superb natural harbour, and they combine to produce one of the most impressive approaches when viewed from a ferry.

Closer inspection reveals a rather more chequered picture, for the rapid commercial rise of the town is reflected in its buildings, which are more in keeping with the dowdy capitals of Chios and Sami rather than the white cubist buildings that are such a feature of the Cyclades. Fortunately the islanders have made a conspicuous — and largely successful — effort to improve things in recent years and the all-new polished-up Ermoupolis is now beginning to exude something of a buzz in High Season. Dead on Sundays and out of shopping hours, the town explodes into life once night falls. Quiet streets filled with down-at-heel shops suddenly fill with tables and tavernas, with various entertainments on offer in the main square. The miscellany of faded neo-classical charm gives Syros

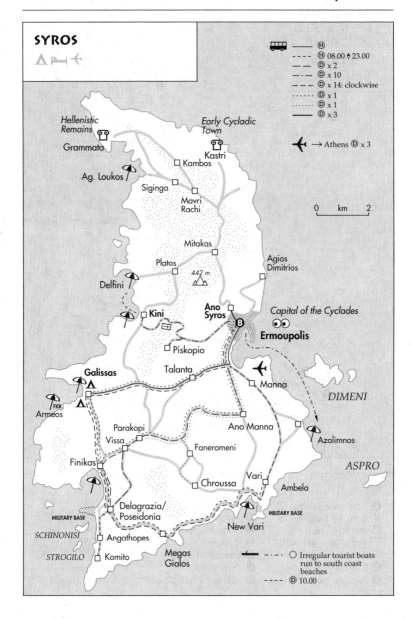

SYROS

Hellenistic
Remains
Grammata

Early Cycladic
Town
Kastri

Kambos

Ag. Loukos

Siginga

Mavri
Rachi

Mitakas

Platos

442 m

Delfini

Kini

Ano
Syros

B

Capital of the Cyclades

Ermoupolis

Agios
Dimitrios

Piskopio

Talanta

Galissas

Armeos

FKK

Parakopi

Vissa

Finikas

Delagrazia/
Poseidonia

MILITARY BASE

SCHINONISI

STROGILO

Angathopes

Komito

Megas
Gialos

Manna

DIMENI

Ano Manna

Faneromeni

Azolimnos

ASPRO

Chroussa

Vari

Ambela

New Vari

MILITARY BASE

0   km   2

⊕ 08.00 ⧫ 23.00
Ⓓ x 2
Ⓓ x 10
Ⓓ x 14: clockwise
Ⓓ x 1
Ⓓ x 1
Ⓓ x 3

→ Athens Ⓓ x 3

○ Irregular tourist boats
run to south coast
beaches
Ⓓ 10.00

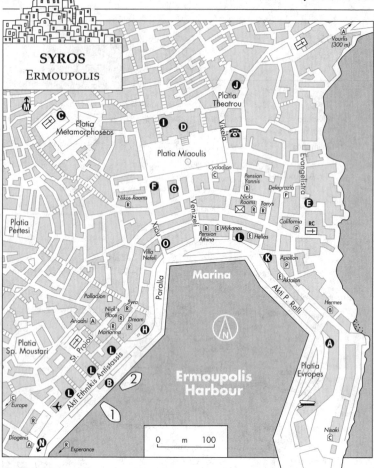

SYROS
ERMOUPOLIS

Key

- **A** EOT Tourist Office & WCs / Showers
- **B** Bus Station & Ferry Passenger Stalls
- **C** Cathedral
- **D** City Hall
- **E** National Bank of Greece
- **F** Police
- **G** Tourist Police
- **H** Accommodation Kiosk
- **I** Archaeological Museum
- **J** Theatre
- **K** International Press
- **L** Ferry Tickets
- **M** Ano Syros Path (2 km)
- **N** Industrial Museum
- **O** Street Market
- **1** Ferry Quay
- **2** Hydrofoil Berths

something neighbouring islands cannot match: it is worth a visit just to capture the contrast with the cute Cycladic-village look that dominates elsewhere.

The two town hills also contrast greatly with each other and the lower town. Catholic **Ano Syros** is easily the more interesting as the buildings on its upper slopes form the nucleus of the original island chora. On your left-hand side as you enter the harbour, it has a meandering staircase running down to the lower town. Attempting this climb is the most popular sightseeing trip in town, and you can take in the British Cemetery halfway up the hill (where the victims of a WW1 troopship sinking are interred). The Orthodox hill town on **Vrontado** only dates from the 19 c. and, bar the domed church that marks it out from the more kastro-like church topping Ano Syros, it has little of interest.

The recent tourist influx has yet to make much impact on the rest of the island. North of Ermoupolis, tourists will find they have become the main local attraction, though ever-increasing numbers of hill-walkers head for the area. The main resort (courtesy of the best island beach — though this isn't saying a lot) is at scruffy **Galissas** on the west coast. Once a widely spread out agricultural community, it has seen considerable in-filling with tourist accommodation that does nothing to create an attractive sense of community. The town is a disappointing spot, with no real centre (its most notable feature being a derelict concrete pitch-and-putt course on the main 'street').

Weekends find the tree and reed-bed backed beach packed with islanders, so if you like solitude you will do better going elsewhere. One possible option — provided your body is up to it — is to take the stairway and path over the southern headland to the island's recognized nudist beach at Armeos (voyeurs shouldn't get their hopes up as there are usually as few nudists as clothes on view: Syros isn't a noted naturist destination).

South of Galissas is a second resort strip running from **Finikas** down to **Delagrazia** (alias **Poseidonia**). However, the beaches are even more scruffy (though less crowded), and one has to search pretty hard to justify stopping here with so many other good beach islands close to hand. The remaining southern half of Syros is, if truth be told, best seen from a bus: merely a collection of small villages scattered over low-lying countryside and lacking tourist appeal.

Ferry links with Syros are adequate but no more: long gone are the days when Ermoupolis was the hub of the Cycladic ferry system. In fact Syros is somewhat out on a limb these days, seeing a greater number of odd-ball calls than most islands. The Port Police have a complete list of the day's sailings chalked up in the doorway of their barrack-like building. Ferries and hydrofoils berth by the passenger stalls on the other side of the harbour. The taxi and bus stations are also here. Frequency of buses to the main centres is good, but dominated by one-way services.

In prehistoric times Syros was an important centre (though most remains lie in the less accessible far north of the island). In the Classical and Hellenistic period the main city, Syria (which until recently was still used as an alternative name for the island), stood on the site of Ermoupolis, but almost nothing survives. It was abandoned during the pirate-infested Middle Ages in favour of Ano Syros. Syros wasn't an active player in the 19 c. War of Independence, but the island was irrevocably changed by it thanks to the influx of refugees from scorched Chios and Psara. Thereafter it grew to become Greece's largest 19 c. coal bunkering port.

There are beds aplenty in **Ermoupolis**; most are at the budget end of the market, and are advertised by a forest of signs. Given the comparatively small numbers of tourists visiting Syros, finding a bed is rarely a problem and there is now a quayside kiosk to help you. The relocation of the ferry berth to the west side of the harbour is prompting a rash of new hotel and room conversions. These include the plush A-class *Ariadni* and the quayside *Dream Rooms*. At the bottom end of the market are *Tony's*, buried in the warren of streets behind the waterfront, the better located *Apollon* (☎ 22158) and *Athina* (☎ 23600). More up-market hotels are not so centrally placed. Nearest is the B-class *Hermes* (☎ 28011) with its own tiny private beach. On the west side of the port is the C-class *Europe* (☎ 28771), and to the north-east stands the A-class *Vourlis* (☎ 28440). Elsewhere on Syros beds are few except at **Galissas**, which has a supply of rooms.

Å

Two sites exist on Syros at **Galissas**. Set in a pistachio nut-tree grove, *Two Hearts Camping* (☎ 42052) is the best. Don't be put off by the romantic pitch to their advertising — broken single hearts are also admitted. Mini-buses meet all boats. *Camping Yianna* (☎ 42418) is rather run down and might not be open.

ᴥ

Ermoupolis offers the main sightseeing on Syros, and unusually for a Greek island town is well endowed with street names (the west European influence coming to the fore again). Several blocks up from the waterfront is the impressive **Miaoulis Square**. Adorned with a statue of the Greek hero of the War of Independence after which it is named, and a bandstand, it is lined with bars along all but the north side. To the west side of the town hall dominating the square is a small **Museum** housing exhibits from other Cycladic islands too small to possess one (the exhibits include a few Cycladic figures from Keros and Amorgos). Just north-east of the square you will also find a miniature version of La Scala **Opera House**: built in 1862, it has been closed almost ever since. In the industrial area south of the port is a good **Industrial Museum** — the main building (one of three) being a converted lead-shot factory.

The hills north of **Kastri** offer possibly the most intriguing and (unless you like hard hill-walking) inaccessible sites on the island. Ringing the top of one are the walls of one of the largest of the **Early Cycladic** culture villages discovered. It clearly was defensive in function (the odd horseshoe-shaped bastion aside, the surviving 'ramparts' look just like typical hill farm walls), and was accompanied by a large cemetery that has yielded up a number of important Cycladic figurines.

Tinos

ΤΗΝΟΣ; 193 km²; pop. 7,730.

CODE ☎ 22830
PORT POLICE ☎ 22348
POLICE ☎ 22100
FIRST AID ☎ 22210

The spiritual centre of modern Greece, mountainous Tinos even outshines Patmos for raw pilgrim-pulling power. Billed as the Lourdes of the Aegean, Sundays and the Virgin Mary-related festivals on the 25th March (Annunciation), and particularly the 15th of August (Feast of the Assumption), see the main centre of Tinos Town jam-packed with the faithful. If you plan to stay, then you should try to avoid arriving on Tinos on Saturdays and in the week preceding these festivals. The focus of all this activity is an icon housed in the church that dominates the town: the Panagia Evangelistra (or Megalochari, meaning 'Great Joy'). As a result of this, Tinos has thrived happily on Greek rather than foreign tourism (something all too evident in the all-Greek timetables outside ticket agencies), and it is only now starting to emerge as a foreign tourist destination.

Coated with a sprinkling of small villages and over 1200 picturesque dovecots (the island speciality), Tinos is very attractive. However, it remains very much of a 'one town' island and is best explored via excursions from the port and centre of **Tinos Town**. A largely modern affair, it owes its existence solely to the church and icon; and this shows, for as you approach by ferry, the seemingly thin scatter of buildings looks to have a rather tenuous hold on the foreshore. Once within the confines of the harbour mole the town reveals itself to be a substantial, but largely modern, settlement — no old-world chora charm here. Its most conspicuous feature is the main street that runs up the hillside from the waterfront to the impressive walls and ornate plaster façade of the church at the back of the town. In fact, Tinos Town is dominated by three streets: the waterfront (replete with ticket agencies, restaurant, and a good super-market south of the Port Police office), the pedestrianized Evangelistrais (lined with a number of particularly tacky souvenir shops that sell plastic bonsai trees among other things) and Leoforos Megalocharis, the main processional road to the church: on feast days devout pilgrims process up it on their knees, stopping off only to buy candles — some up to 2 m high — from shops along the way. This all sounds serious stuff, yet the town feels a very relaxed, laid-back sort of place, and is a nice base for exploration.

Tinos Town also has a couple of beaches reasonably close to hand. The closest — Ag. Fotias beach — is a walk away, 500 m past the town's campsite. However, the best is at **Kionia** (now the island package tourist centre). Buses run frequently from Tinos Town, or if you are feeling energetic you can walk along the coast past the scanty remains of a temple to Poseidon and Amphitrite and a small stoa. Poseidon was the island's

favourite deity after he relieved Tinos from a plague of snakes by sending along a flock of hungry storks ('Tinos' is derived from the Phoenician word for snake: *tenok*). These days finding a snake is very difficult and on a par with working out where your ferry is going to dock. Depending on conditions, ferries can dock at one of three quays; you'll have to ask where your boat will berth.

Tinos Town aside, the island is very quiet (apart from the incessant cooing of doves). The former capital lay on the upper slopes of **Mt. Exombourgo**. If you care to attempt the steep walk, you will find the remains of the Venetian fortress behind a monastery and part of the Archaic city wall. The summit was an important landmark in ancient times, when sailors navigated by always keeping in sight of land. Local tradition had it that, when it was obscured by cloud, it was a sure sign that unsettled weather was on the way, but you should take this with a pinch of salt as even in High Season the island peak is often hidden from view.

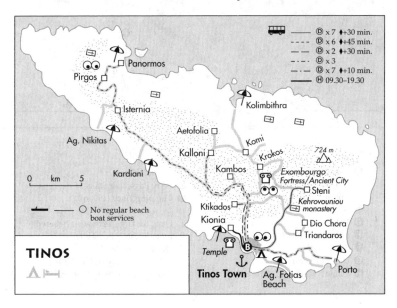

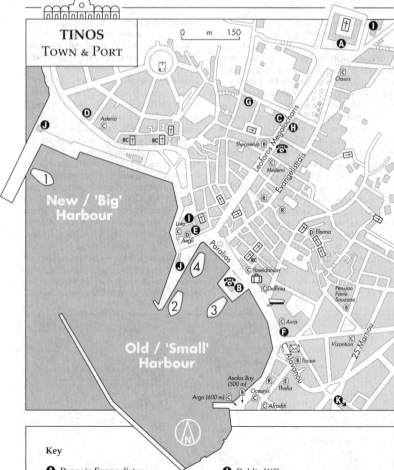

TINOS
Town & Port

0   m   150

New / 'Big' Harbour

Old / 'Small' Harbour

Asteria
Oassis
Theoxenia
Meltemi
Leto
Aegli
Paralias
Poseidonion
Delfinia
Eleana
Pension Favie Souzane
Avra
Vizantion
Tinian
Aeolos Bay (500 m)
Oceanis
Thalia
Argo (600 m)
Afroditi
Leoforos Megalochari
Evangelistrais
Alavanou
25 Martiou

1
2
3
4

Key

Ⓐ Panagia Evangelistra
   Church (Megalochari)
Ⓑ Bus Station (all destinations)
Ⓒ Archaeological Museum
Ⓓ Police Station
Ⓔ National Bank of Greece
Ⓕ Supermarket
Ⓖ Cultural Centre
Ⓗ Clinic / Medical Centre

Ⓘ Public WCs
Ⓙ Ferry Passenger Stalls
Ⓚ Camping Tinos (150 m)

1 Quay for large ferries (unsheltered)
2 Inner Ferry Quay (sheltered)
3 Quay for smaller ferries /
  Catamaran / Hydrofoil Berth
4 Tourist boat departure point

The villages of Tinos are, in the main, pretty mountainside affairs little visited by tourists, with the notable exception of the attractive northern centre of the island, the hill village of **Pirgos**. Now home to a substantial sculpting community — which thrives in these parts thanks to several quarries producing high-quality marble — it is a very attractive place in its own right. Most of the local marble is exported via the nearby small port village of **Panormos**, which is redeemed by a passable beach and a few rooms. Buses run to both daily (other villages have irregular bus calls), though Sunday services are not good. Buses also provide good links to the 12 c. village-like monastery at **Kehrovouniou**, another popular excursion destination. If you are easily irritated by other people's personal habits then avoid sitting next to priests or little old ladies on the island buses. These delightful souls indulge in the practice of crossing themselves every time they pass a chapel or roadside shrine. There are said to be 643 chapels on Tinos.

In ancient times the island was known as 'Ophiousa', which like 'Tinos' is snake related. It was forced to provide ships for the invading Perisans in 480 BC, but one of its triremes deserted, and gave the Athenian fleet the information it needed to come up with a winning strategy at the Battle of Salamis. The island's role as a focus of Greek nationalism was further advanced by its being the last of the Aegean strongholds to succumb to Turkish rule (in 1715) after 500 years as a bastion of Venetian control. Tinos was also the scene of a pivotal event in WW2, when the torpedoing of the visiting Greek warship *Elli* outside the town harbour, on Assumption Day 1940 by an Italian submarine (before Greece had formally joined the war on the side of the allies), served to encourage Greek resistance to the notion of capitulating to Italian demands for surrender without a fight.

Tinos Town has plenty of hotels and some rooms. Prices are slightly higher than average, but on pilgrimless nights you can usually haggle advantageously. Arrive at festival time, however, and well … you may have heard of the 'feeding of the five thousand', but the streets of Tinos Town sees an annual re-enactment of the less talked about 'sleeping of the five thousand' that came after that memorable nosh-up. Budget beds are limited to a scatter of rooms and two D-class hotels; the quayside *Aegli* (☎ 22240) and the backstreet *Eleana* (☎ 22561). The majority of hotels are C-class, the more appealing being those along the waterfront. These include the *Oceanis* (☎ 22452), the *Avra* (☎ 22242), the *Delfinia* (☎ 22289) and the B-class *Tinion* (☎ 22261).

Tinos Camping (☎ 22344): a reasonable site. Blown clean daily, it has plenty of tree cover, and a dovecot — complete with peacocks — in lieu of a mini-market (there is a good supermarket 200 m opposite the site entrance).

The stucco-plastered church of **Panagia Evangelistra** (complete with the icon causing all the fuss) is the main sightseeing destination on Tinos, though the icon is so encased in gold and glass that it is difficult to get anything other than a brief impression. The **icon** is reputedly the work of St. Luke (the time involved in pursuing a second career as a painter no doubt explains why the author of the third gospel copied roughly 60% of Mark's gospel into his own), and if true shows a remarkable anticipation of later Byzantine art. Reputedly from a church destroyed by pirates in the 10 c., it is widely believed to be endowed with healing powers. It came to light in 1822 after a passing nun saw a hunky bronzed workman digging in a field and had a vision (of what, history hasn't recorded). Given instructions where to dig he unearthed the icon, miraculously unharmed. The church was built on the discovery site. The icon's appearance during the birth throes of the Greek state has further enhanced its symbolic importance to the Greek people. Take care to observe the church dress code; it is very strictly enforced here.

Tinos Town is also host to the island's **Archaeological Museum**; the exhibits include a late Hellenistic sundial and odd fragments recovered from the temple of Poseidon and the Mt. Exombourgo Kastro. **Pirgos** also has a couple of museums — one devoted to the current crop of local artists, the other to the town's most famous son: the leading Greek sculptor of the 19 c., Ianoulis Chalepa.

4
CYCLADES WEST

**FOLEGANDROS · KEA · KIMOLOS · KYTHNOS
MILOS · SERIFOS · SIFNOS · SIKINOS**

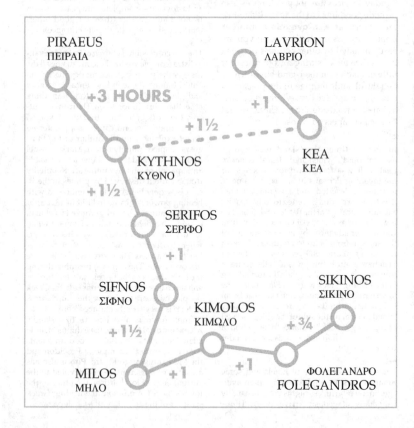

PIRAEUS
ΠΕΙΡΑΙΑ

LAVRION
ΛΑΒΡΙΟ

+3 HOURS

+1

+1½

KYTHNOS
ΚΥΘΝΟ

KEA
KEA

+1½

SERIFOS
ΣΕΡΙΦΟ

+1

SIFNOS
ΣΙΦΝΟ

SIKINOS
ΣΙΚΙΝΟ

KIMOLOS
ΚΙΜΩΛΟ

+¾

+1½

+1

+1

ΦΟΛΕΓΑΝΔΡΟ
FOLEGANDROS

MILOS
ΜΗΛΟ

General Features

The Western Cyclades Line runs in an irregular 'L'-shaped chain around the rim of the group. A paucity of camping sites and budget accommodation produces the odd combination of fewer backpackers and greater numbers of Greek holidaymakers than elsewhere, thus helping to keep the islands free from the worst trappings of mass tourism. In fact out of the High Season July/August peak foreign tourists are thin on the ground.

The chain is peculiar in that the nearer the island is to Athens, the fewer foreign tourists it tends to see. Northerly Kea — served by the mainland port of Lavrio — is very much of an Athenian's get-away-from-it-all weekend island, but very quiet in mid-week. Kythnos and Serifos are quite

off the beaten track despite the frequency of Piraeus ferries. Sifnos, on the other hand, is the only island in the group that comes close to being labelled 'touristy' and even this is mild by Central Cyclades standards. Milos — famous as the island where the Venus de Milo was discovered — attracts tourists by virtue of name recognition and is slowly emerging as a resort island in its own right.

Neighbouring Kimolos makes an interesting day excursion but is very much of a minor island, as are the two at the tail end of the line, Sikinos and Folegandros. Bridging the Central and Western lines, they do not fit comfortably into either, being serviced by boats steaming down both, but as they are more characteristic of the Western Cyclades they are covered here.

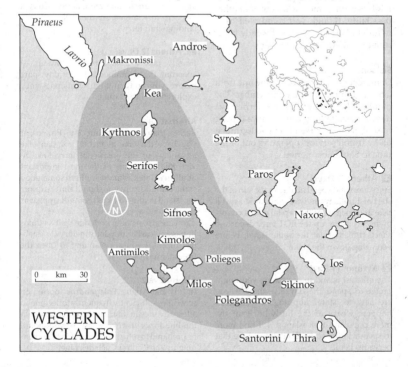

Piraeus

Lavrio

Makronissi

Andros

Kea

Kythnos

Syros

Serifos

Paros

Sifnos

Naxos

Kimolos

Antimilos

Poliegos

Ios

0   km   30

Milos

Sikinos

Folegandros

WESTERN
CYCLADES

Santorini / Thira

Example Itinerary [2 Weeks]

Those looking for a fortnight's holiday that combines the sights of Athens with some relaxed island hopping without huge crowds could do worse than the Western Cyclades. An atmosphere of sleepy indifference rules. The islands are close to the capital and fairly quiet (unless you travel at the weekends), yet with enough going on so that you don't end up feeling as if you had been washed up at the back of beyond.

Arrival/Departure Point
None of the islands boast an international airport, and connections with other island groups are so poor that Athens is the only viable starting point. During the High Season Santorini becomes another possibility; though you could well have to hop to Paros for one of the daily boats running into the line from there.

Season
Daily services operate down the line from late June through to late September. The month either side of this sees ferries five days a week falling to three days during the rest of the year. Don't depend too much on hydrofoil services operating out of the June to September period.

1 Athens [2 Days]
Since you can't spend all day in the sun at the start of a holiday anyway, you might as well take in the sights of the capital over a couple of days (picking up the EOT ferry departure sheets/timetable at the same time), before venturing down the chain.

2 Kythnos [1 Day]
The quietest island in the group; you might prefer to spend the day elsewhere if you are new to island hopping. Experienced hoppers weary of the hurly-burly of the more popular Greek islands will find more to savour in the somnolent atmosphere that pervades here.

3 Serifos [2 Days]
A day is all that is needed to take in the port and dramatic Chora hanging on the hill behind. After this you can retire to the beach and wait — if needs be for an extra day — for a *morning* ferry to Sifnos; enabling you to take your pick of the accommodation on arrival there.

4 Sifnos [4 Days]
As this is the best beach island in the group (and by this stage you should be better conditioned to enjoy spending more extended time in the sun), Sifnos offers the opportunity to enjoy a few days of complete relaxation.

5 6 Milos/Kimolos [3 Days]
Milos provides the best sightseeing in the Western Cyclades. Three days can be happily spent between the catacombs, beach and, if you are feeling more adventurous, a day trip to Kimolos via the Pollonia-based landing-craft ferry.

1 Athens [2 Days]
Finally, take a boat direct to Piraeus — spending the recommended clear day spare before your return flight finishing your exploration of the capital.

Alternative 1
Rather than returning direct to Piraeus, if you have the time available, you can take advantage of the occasional ferry links to visit **Kea**. Once one of the most important of all the Greek islands, it offers some good sightseeing. Ideally, you should aim to explore the island in mid-week as rooms disappear as the weekend approaches.

You are also recommended to visit Kythnos in passing earlier in your itinerary (to establish times) if you are planning to catch the irregular ferries.

Alternative 2
In July and August **Folegandros** appears on schedules sufficiently frequently to become an alternative destination. However, ferries down this line do not visit every day, and you should be prepared to return to Piraeus via boats running up the Central Cyclades Line.

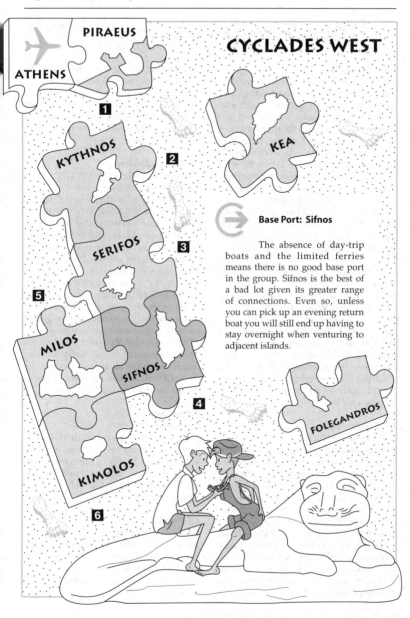

CYCLADES WEST

PIRAEUS

ATHENS

1

KYTHNOS **2**

KEA

Base Port: Sifnos

The absence of day-trip boats and the limited ferries means there is no good base port in the group. Sifnos is the best of a bad lot given its greater range of connections. Even so, unless you can pick up an evening return boat you will still end up having to stay overnight when venturing to adjacent islands.

SERIFOS **3**

5

MILOS

SIFNOS

4

FOLEGANDROS

KIMOLOS

6

Cyclades West Ferry Services

Main Car Ferries

The Cyclades West line is the most self-contained of all the Cycladic routes, thanks to a combination of fewer tourists, a shorter sailing time to Piraeus, and the fact that the islands lie too far to the west for ferries heading for other chains to feel inclined to call in. As a result, the Cyclades West islands rely on a smaller pool of boats than the other Cycladic lines, with services dominated by just a couple of boats and a catamaran that gets booked solid at weekends.

A further odd characteristic of the line is that there isn't anything akin to a 'standard' itinerary; almost every possible combination of ports is attempted, though the pattern of services sees only minor changes each summer (mostly, one suspects, to relieve the monotony). This state of affairs is largely due to the relative unpopularity of the northern islands, which leads ferries to either ignore them or only call on their outward runs. Links with other lines remain poor, as does the amount of tourist-boat activity. This is, however, slowly changing: the pressure of tourism in the rest of the Cyclades is encouraging increasing numbers of visitors — and occasional Cyclades Central Line ferries — onto this line.

C/F Express Pegasus
Hellas Ferries / HFD; 1977; 4810 GRT.
On the route since 1996 this ferry has undergone regular name changes (she originally sailed as the *Pegasus*, then between 2000–01 as the *Express Dionyssos*). Although quite a small vessel, she is popular with locals. Her limited capacity is, however, something of a liability in High Season: and unfortunately, this is one of those boats whose crew attempts to prevent non-Greek backpackers from entering the deck-class saloons on boarding. Those able to argue their way inside will find the usual TVs and aircraft-seating, along with locked WCs

and air-conditioning that often leaves the interior feeling like a floating freezer.

The *Express Pegasus* runs in tandem with the *Express Apollon* below — the boats are fully interchangeable, and share a set of itineraries between them, swapping runs from time to time.

C/F Express Apollon
Hellas Ferries / HFD; 1973; 5101 GRT.
Formerly the *Apollo Express*, the *Express Apollon* has been on the Central Cyclades Line since the 1980s only to be forced onto the secondary Cyclades West line in 2003 by more modern competition. She was still able to visit a couple of her old haunts by taking on all the extended runs beyond Milos to Ios and Santorini.

Originally the cross-Channel *Senlac* (she was named after the hill on which the Battle of Hastings was fought), her new Greek owners re-christened her after the god of archery. This is surely one in the eye for all those who maintain that ferry owners have no sense of humour. Sadly, humour doesn't extend as far as her crew who are amongst the worst offenders when it comes to anti-backpacker discrimination.

C/F Daliana
G.A. Ferries; 1970; 5528 GRT.
A token piece of competition to the Hellas Ferries hegemony on this route was provided in 2003 by the *Daliana* (see p. 400) and her weekly sojourn down the line via Syros and Paros. She is likely to be replaced in 2004.

C/F Romilda
G.A. Ferries; 1974; 5169 GRT.
A second G.A. Ferries boat also made the run at one stage last summer (excluding Paros from her itinerary). There is a better chance of the *Romilda* remaining on the route in 2004.

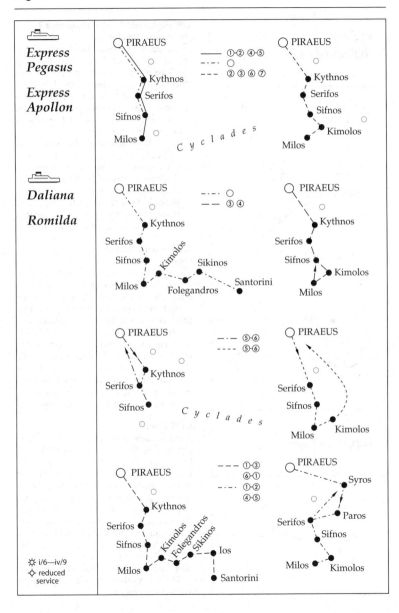

Express Pegasus

Express Apollon

Daliana

Romilda

☼ i/6—iv/9
◇ reduced service

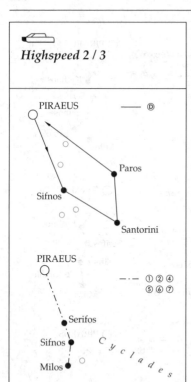

C/M *Highspeed 2* – C/M *Highspeed 3*
Hellas Flying Dolphins; 2001.

High speed catamarans have been operating on the Cyclades West route since 2001. The level of service and the itineraries have fluctuated wildly during the last three years. In 2003 all links with Kythnos were dropped, and the return leg of the Santorini run was via Paros (instead of the previous year's return call at Sifnos).

Hopefully things won't change much in 2004: but if things run true to form they will. The chances are that the excellent Australian-built *Highspeed 3* will remain on the route, though she shared it in 2003 with the *Highspeed 2*. Regardless of which *Highspeed* is running the service you can be sure that they will be fast and running to time.

C/F *Antiparos Express*
Local

The last two summers have seen a thrice-weekly link between Paros and Sifnos via one of the Antiparos island ferries. The only thing they don't tell you on Paros is that this boat docks at the southern Sifnos fishing village of Faros rather than the island's main port. This is useful if you want a day trip to the nearby Chrisiopigi monastery, but otherwise is more inconvenient than not. Note: this boat is slow (just under two hours one way), and small, and she rolls a lot in anything other than calm seas.

LANE Lines

A useful adjunct to regular Cyclades West ferries is by the two Crete-bound LANE Lines boats. The *Vitsentzos Kornaros* and the *Ierapetra L* (see p. 292) both regularly stop at Milos on their outward and return runs to Crete (so much so, that their midnight appearance has come to mark the end of the evening promenade time at Adamas). Apart from their inconvenient calling times, there is little that can be said against the *Vitsentzos Kornaros* and the *Ierapetra L*. Both boats vary itineraries at the Cretan end, but as Milos is visited regardless, this never matters very much.

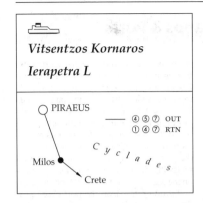

Vitsentzos Kornaros
Ierapetra L

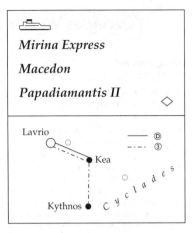

Mirina Express
Macedon
Papadiamantis II

C/F *Nissos Kimolos*
Karametsos Ferry Lines

This small landing-craft ferry runs between Kimolos and Milos anything up to five times daily in High Season (depending on day-tripper coach excursions to Kimolos from Milos). If these aren't running then three round trips daily is more usual. Changes are unlikely in 2004.

C/F *Mirina Express*
Goutos Lines; 1975; 1168 GRT.

This vessel has become the mainstay of the Lavrio—Kea route. Greek-built, she has the traditional, but now rare, external staircases for passengers at her stern. Internally she is rather characterless, though a reasonable deck-class saloon means that there is no need to buy a higher-class ticket to travel in reasonable comfort on this boat. Her only

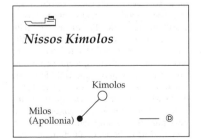

Nissos Kimolos

weakness comes with the weekend rush, when Athenian commuters fill her to bursting: at such times it is best to buy tickets in advance. In July 2000 she had to make an unscheduled late trip to Kea after a fully loaded ferry — the now defunct *Karystos Express* — was stormed and boarded by irate passengers without tickets, who were desperate to travel on the last boat to the mainland. You have been warned!

C/F *Macedon*
Local; 1972; 1974 GRT.

Now the main companion to the *Mirina Express*, the *Macedon* is a chunky-looking ex-Japanese boat. Solid and reliable, though a bit long in the tooth, she covers the Lavrio—Kea run, leaving Kythnos to her partner.

C/F *Papadiamantis II*
Local; 1973; 1060 GRT.

Extra back-up is put on the Lavrio—Kea route during the High Season (doubling the total number of sailings). For the last two summers this has been the ugly and pokey *Papadiamantis II*. Formerly on the North Sporades line, she is named after the Skiathos playwright and poet, though this boat is anything but poetry in motion.

Cyclades West Islands & Ports

Folegandros
ΦΟΛΕΓΑΝΔΡΟΣ; 32 km²; pop. 650.

CODE ☎ 22860
PORT POLICE / POLICE ☎ 41249
FIRST AID ☎ 41222

A 'romantic' island boasting one road and no large shops, Folegandros has long been known as a get-away-from-it-all sort of place. In the last few years it has attracted a select clientele of up-market island lovers drawn by the quiet laid-back atmosphere. The islanders, eager to get the economic benefits of tourism but not over-keen on the more tacky aspects of the trade, have happily promoted this image, with the result that Folegandros has managed to retain its traditional lifestyle yet also take advantage of a relatively small number of visitors with money to spend.

If your object in island hopping is to find a port of respite from the modern world then you could do far worse than be washed up here — provided, of course, that your budget can stand it. This is not to say that those with limited funds — and you should note that the island is one of the few without a bank — should be put off visiting (those that are miss a lot); you just have to work on the assumption that this is one place where you might have to splash out a bit for a day or two if you visit in High Season, when the available accommodation is hard put to keep up with demand. Much will depend on the time of year that you visit.

Out of High Season Folegandros could never be described as crowded, but during July and August the island often seems to be so, simply because the port and town are very small and have difficulty coping with those that do call. In fact, compared to any of the 'popular' islands the numbers visiting are surprisingly low.

At first sight Folegandros appears to live up to its historical role as a place of exile, courtesy of its arid and rocky landscape, but as is so often the case with Greek islands, first impressions can be misleading. The dusty little port in Karavostasis bay doesn't do the island justice. Relatively new, it is little more than a motley collection of tourist-generated buildings trailed around a rather poor beach. Now used as the island caïque harbour, the fishermen weighing their catches and mending nets on the quay inadvertently add some colour, and with each season the port becomes a little more lively. The locals have tried to tart it up as best they can (latterly by adding an elaborate staircase down to a second, very poor, beach over the quayside headland), but it remains more of a place to pass through rather than stay in. Two roads run out of the port. The first skirts the port beach and then round the bay and over a headland before running down to Livadi beach (an indifferent strand of sand) with the campsite on the hillside behind. The second is the main island road, running up to the Chora and the settlements behind. Buses run regularly between the two (times are posted up at the 'bus station' on the ferry quay).

Chora is the only large centre and lies 4 km from the port. One of the most attractive of the traditional whitewashed cubist Cycladic villages, it is a mini Mykonos Town without the crowds, and feels like the sort of place where everybody obviously knows everybody else and everybody else's grandmother besides. Part of the secret of its appeal is its location. Set atop a 200 m cliff on the northern coast it shares that 'living on the edge of the world' feeling common to the caldera towns on Santorini. However, unlike the latter, Chora doesn't look the dizzy views in the eye (though there are several good vantage points), but for the most part turns in on itself. The result is a cosy huddle of houses and churches cen-

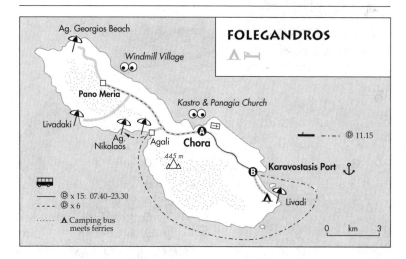

tred on a couple of leafy squares (thanks to a number of large plane trees) decked with pots of red geraniums and check-cloth taverna tables that leave one feeling that one is tucked away in the heart of a provincial French hill village.

Chora is a great place for romantic evening meals (to say nothing of futile cliff-edge gestures if all you end up with is a spot of unrequited love or the taverna bill). Joking aside, Folegandros has figured in press reports of late thanks to several tourists disappearing off cliff paths without even the consolation of a broken heart to justify their fall. Visitors who manage to stay topsides will find that the old Kastro quarter is the best part of town. This neatly hides the cliff-edge from view, besides offering the most attractive example of the medieval house-stockade forts built to defend Cycladic islands from pirate attacks. Its interior is a real delight, the flower-filled aisles of whitewashed houses being adorned with brightly painted balconies and ranks of external staircases (each with its own resident cat). New development in the town (largely up-market hotels and apartment blocks) is confined to strips along the access roads,

the liveliest being along the Pano Meria road which has several bars and a disco en route to the Fani Vevis pension.

After passing by Chora the main road runs west along the spine of the island. Although there is a regular bus service along it, it is also a ready-made excursion if you are up to the walk; the best strategy is to take the bus to **Pano Meria** and then return to Chora. The walk isn't too stressful, and winds through a delightfully unspoilt rural island landscape, with a mix of farms, derelict windmills and churches. Pano Meria isn't much of a place, but is a useful starting point. Little more than a loose scatter of houses and farmsteads along the island spine road, it only becomes apparent that you are here when the bus goes no further.

Beach fans have to walk from the spine road down unmade tracks to the shoreline: the first beach of note is the excellent sand strand at **Agali** (also known as Vathi) complete with several tavernas and outlets offering rooms. From here a coastal path winds its way to a second good beach at **Ag. Nikolaos**. Both can be reached by a daily High Season beach caïque.

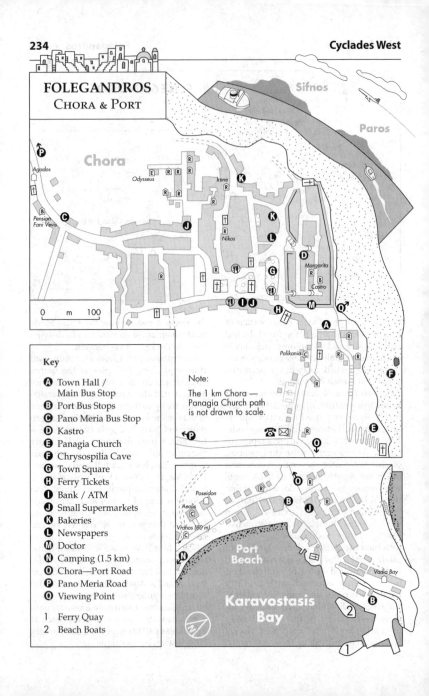

FOLEGANDROS
Chora & Port

Chora

Sifnos

Paros

Agados

Odysseus
Irene
Pension
Fani Vevis

Nikos

Margarita

Castro

0   m   100

Polikania

Key

Ⓐ Town Hall /
    Main Bus Stop
Ⓑ Port Bus Stops
Ⓒ Pano Meria Bus Stop
Ⓓ Kastro
Ⓔ Panagia Church
Ⓕ Chrysospilia Cave
Ⓖ Town Square
Ⓗ Ferry Tickets
Ⓘ Bank / ATM
Ⓙ Small Supermarkets
Ⓚ Bakeries
Ⓛ Newspapers
Ⓜ Doctor
Ⓝ Camping (1.5 km)
Ⓞ Chora—Port Road
Ⓟ Pano Meria Road
Ⓠ Viewing Point

1   Ferry Quay
2   Beach Boats

Note:

The 1 km Chora —
Panagia Church path
is not drawn to scale.

Poseidon

Aeolis

Vrahos (80 m)

Port Beach

Vadia Bay

Karavostasis Bay

Folegandros has enjoyed a very chequered history, with periods of quiet prosperity alternating with devastation. In the 4 C. BC the island was a member of the Delian League, but by the Macedonian era it had been abandoned. Later a pirate haunt, it came under Venetian rule and the Kastro was built. However, the island had been abandoned again by 1416, and was later repopulated by inhabitants from Sifnos. The Turks took Folegandros in 1617, but Turkish and Pirate raids in 1715, 1774 and 1794 left the island abandoned. Again repopulated, Folegandros joined the Greek state in 1828.

Rooms are available to rent in the port, but most tourists take the bus that meets all boats to **Chora**, which is both prettier and has more options. The most appealing of these are in the old kastro: the small B-class *Castro* (☎ 41230) and the *Margarita Rooms* (☎ 41321). Rooms are scattered around the town with hotels confined to the outskirts, notably the new C-class *Polikania* (☎ 41322) on the port road. The Chora—Panagia Church path also has some plush furnished apartments along it. More down-market rooms lie on the west side of town, along with the E-class *Odysseus* (☎ 4139). The Chora—Pano Meria road has a couple of pensions, including the deceptively dour-fronted B-class *Fani Vevis* (☎ 41237). **Karavostasis Port** also has several hotels including the C-class *Aeolis* (☎ 41205).

A

Camping Livadi (☎ 41204); 2 km west of the port along the coast path. Lack of competition (and water) is all too evident with the very poor washing facilities — hence the freelance camping on the adjacent beach. Bring foodstuffs with you as the campsite restaurant takes advantage of the longish walk to the port (a mini-bus meets ferries). Tents are available for hire, but view before you pay: some of the 'two person' jobs are *very* small.

The only major island sights regularly visited are the **Chora** and its **Kastro** (built in 1212 AD). The attractive whitewashed **Panagia Church** lies on the cliff-hill on the north-east side of the Chora, and stands on the foundations of the ancient city wall that stood on the site. Although it is quite a climb to the church the wonderful views over the town and island are more than worth it.

Walking is a popular activity on Folegandros (thanks in part to a good map showing all the major paths). Even the less ambitious have been known to head along the road to **Pano Meria**. Although the village is little more than a string of houses (and the odd windmill) strung along the spine of the island, the scenery is worth the effort. Pano Meria is also home to the only museum on Folegandros: the **Folk Museum** has the usual collection of rural island exhibits. A second excellent source of information on sale on the island is a picture-filled guidebook called *Folegandros — The place, the people, the history.*

Kea

KEA; 131 km²; pop. 1,700.

CODE ☎ 22880
PORT POLICE ☎ 21344
POLICE ☎ 21100
FIRST AID ☎ 22200

Despite being only three hours from Athens, Kea (also transcribed as 'Tzia') is one of the hidden pearls of the Aegean, retaining much of its rural charm and now popular with those who like walking holidays. This is something of an unfamiliar role for an island that was home to an important Minoan outpost and was one of the cradles of Greek civilization.

Kea has always been, and remains, an island set apart from the rest. Not only did it manage to support four city states where most islands could barely manage one, but it was also a pioneer of social change by introducing a compulsory celebratory cup of hemlock when its citizens reached retirement age at 70. These days the locals buy holiday homes instead. As a result, the island tends to fill up quickly on weekends with Athenians escaping the city smog: Kea is comparatively fertile for a Cycladic island and is graced with countryside that is noticably greener than neighbouring Kythnos. If you intend to stay during High Season then plan for a mid-week arrival. Foreign tourists are comparatively thin on the ground, and nightlife is sparse and scattered.

All ferries and hydrofoils dock at the small port of **Korissia**, a tapering port-village that is now emerging as the island's main 'resort', sited on the west side of Agios Nikolaos bay. On the south is a long sand beach and the largest collection of accommodation on the island. However, apart from these attractions there is little incentive to linger. In truth, the waterfront lacks interest thanks in part to the bland topography of this part of the bay. The port beach also isn't the world's greatest, being quite awful at the quayside end (it improves noticeably as you progress around the bay). Korissia is also more substantial than it looks from the sea, with more building in the valley floor behind the waterfront. This part of town is dominated by the red brick chimney of a

derelict Victorian enamel and metallurgy factory. This sounds rather dour, but it doesn't impact on the touristy areas. Further evidence of late 19 c. activity lies on the north side of Korissia bay: an excellent natural harbour, the bay was an important coaling station in the years leading up to WW1, and the roofless coal stores still stand at Kokka near the village of **Vourkari** — laid out like a miniature version of Korissia and now a growing up-market resort thanks to a large yachting marina located here.

Buses run from the port to Vourkari and, more frequently, to the red-tile roofed main town of **Ioulis** or **Chora**. Visible from the port, it sits in a natural amphitheatre in the hills, overlooked by a handful of ruined windmills that are all that remain of the 26

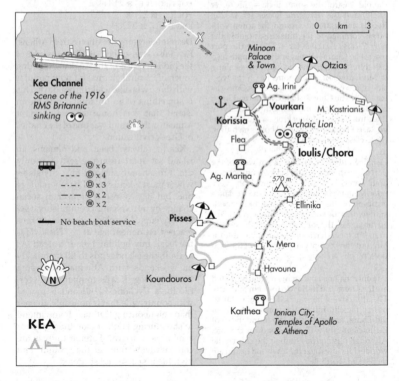

Kea Channel
Scene of the 1916 RMS Britannic sinking ◉◉

Minoan Palace & Town

⚓ Otzias

Ag. Irini

⚓ **Vourkari**   M. Kastrianis

Korissia

Archaic Lion

Flea

◉◉ **Ioulis/Chora**

0   km   3

Ⓓ x 6
Ⓓ x 4
Ⓓ x 3
Ⓓ x 2
Ⓦ x 2

No beach boat service

Ag. Marina   570 m

Ellinika

Pisses Λ

K. Mera

Koundouros   Havouna

Karthea   *Ionian City: Temples of Apollo & Athena*

KEA
Λ ⌂

N

that once topped the so-called Mountain of Mills. The town is built around nine springs (now decorated with mule troughs) and clings to a couple of hillsides; the old Kastro dominates one, and the Chora the other. The streets are too narrow to admit vehicles, and this remains a very attractive working town packed with tiny houses, though most visitors simply pass through in search of the famous Kea Lion. Ioulis is also the best base for exploring the rest of island.

The rest of Kea is an odd mix of unspoilt countryside and holiday-villa-filled villages. Best of these is the delightfully named **Pisses**. In the normal course of things one would assume that this name was just an unhappy accident, but the existence of another hamlet bearing the equally appealing name of 'Flea' suggests that the islanders have really got this place-naming thing down to a fine art. With a good sand beach backed by a prosperous market-garden valley, Pisses is served by a very inadequate once-daily bus service. The northern hamlet of **Otzias** is better served, but, filled with holiday villas, is of little interest, as is the south-west coast 'resort' of **Koundouros**; now tarted up with pseudo-windmill homes near the tiny quay, it sees hydrofoils en route to Korissia. Walkers, meantime, will find bus-free **Flea** has more buzz as a destination than most thanks to its location in a ravine with 13 cute watermills.

Known in antiquity as Keos, Kea's history began with the Minoan settlement at Ag. Irini. In the 6 c. BC the four cities were established. Kea fought with the Athenians at Salamis, and later joined the Delian League in 478 BC. During the Hellenistic period pirate attacks disrupted the local enconomy and by the 2 c. BC the city of Poiessa was abandoned. Others followed and by the 4 c. AD only Ioulis was still inhabited. Kea suffered more pirate raids, followed by capture by the Venetians in 1207. The Turks held the island between 1537–1821.

Rooms are on offer in Korissia and the Chora. Hotel and pension options are thin

on the ground, though this shouldn't mean difficulty in finding a bed in mid-week. **Ioulis** has one superbly placed B-class pension (on top of the old kastro site), the *Ioulis* (☎ 22177) — complete with a terrace restaurant — and a small E-class hotel charmingly placed on one of the main town alleys, the *Filoxenia* (☎ 22057). **Korissia** has the C-class hotel *Karthea* (☎ 21204) on the waterfront and a B-class 'motel', the *Tzia Mas* (☎ 21305), at the better end of the beach. However, the best hotel in town lies down a dusty track behind the beach: the newish B-class *Korissia* (☎ 21484, 21355). **Koundouros** also has one hotel: the pricey B-class *Kea Beach* (☎ 31230).

A

Camping Kea (☎ 31335): a nice site on the best island beach at Pisses 16 km from the port, it suffers from its isolated location.

∞

The oldest and most accessible of the Kea sites is on the promontory north of the port: the foundations of a **Minoan Palace** at Agia Irini. There is little here but a jumble of thick-walled foundations: the remains of half-a-dozen elaborate houses (with cellars complete with drains), streets with public benches, and defensive walls. The site takes its name from the red-tiled church on the promontory.

The most impressive sight on Kea — the grey granite 6 c. BC **Lion of Kea** — lies on an olive-groved hillside on the far side of Ioulis; 6 m long, it is carved sphinx-like from an outcrop of rock and looks back across the valley towards the town wearing an enigmatic smile. This often seems to wear a little thin when the inevitable parties of tourists queue up to be photographed bestriding his head.

One objectless site of interest is the steamy, mirror-smooth **Kea Channel**. Although there is nothing to see except 'sea, sea, sea', the strait is the last resting place of the *Britannic* (sister-ship of the *Titanic*). Originally laid down as the *Gigantic*, she was renamed after the *Titanic* disaster. Launched in 1914, she struck a mine off Kea on the 21st of November 1916 — while serving as a hospital ship during the WW1 Dardanelles campaign. Fortunately she was sailing to collect casualties, so was half empty at the time. She sank in a mere 55 minutes

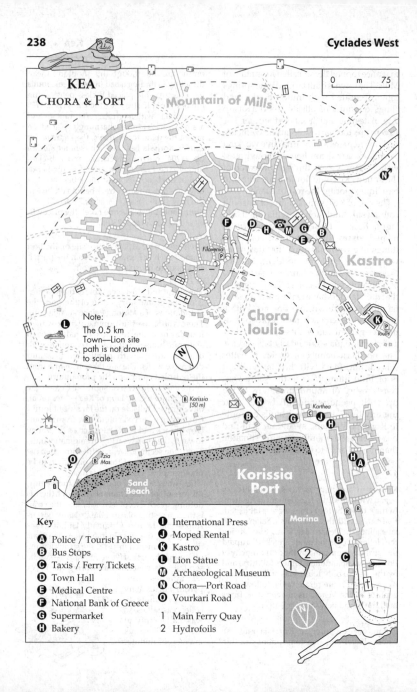

KEA
CHORA & PORT

Mountain of Mills

Filoxenia

Kastro

Chora / Ioulis

Ioulis

Note:
The 0.5 km
Town—Lion site
path is not drawn
to scale.

Korissia
[50 m]

Karthea

Tzia Mas

Sand Beach

Korissia Port

Marina

Key

Ⓐ Police / Tourist Police
Ⓑ Bus Stops
Ⓒ Taxis / Ferry Tickets
Ⓓ Town Hall
Ⓔ Medical Centre
Ⓕ National Bank of Greece
Ⓖ Supermarket
Ⓗ Bakery

Ⓘ International Press
Ⓙ Moped Rental
Ⓚ Kastro
Ⓛ Lion Statue
Ⓜ Archaeological Museum
Ⓝ Chora—Port Road
Ⓞ Vourkari Road

1 Main Ferry Quay
2 Hydrofoils

with the loss of only 30 lives (after two of her lifeboats were sucked into her rotating propellers, as her captain vainly headed for Korissia in a last-gasp attempt to beach her). Like her sister, she was the largest vessel semi-afloat at the time of her sinking, and still holds the record as the largest liner on the sea bed. Lying on her starboard side in 110 m of water, she is now attracting ever more attention. This started in 1995 when Dr R. Ballard — the discoverer of the *Titanic* — explored the ship and found her excellently preserved, with even her smokestacks extant (albeit separated from her hull). The ship is pictured in *Lost Liners* (Hodder & Stoughton/Madison Press). Dr Ballard has a long-term ambition to use the *Britannic* to establish 'the world's first undersea museum', with internet tourists. Meantime, the wreck is now dived on each summer, due to its condition and shallow location: turned end up, over half the vessel would stand out of the water. One result is a number of web sites with photos of the wreck (see the Kea 'Links' page on greekislandhopping.com for the best of them). An indifferent TV movie of the sinking also appeared in 2000.

Of the four classical cities surprisingly little remains except at remote **Karthea** (for which you will need your own transport), where there are the dramatic cliff-side remains of a late Archaic temple of the Pythios Apollo. **Ioulis** (home of the 5 c. BC Simonides) has the remains of a **Venetian Kastro** built out of the ruins of a second temple to Apollo. There is also an **Archaeological Museum** housing island finds in the town. The third city (Korissia) produced a famous Kouros statue (now in Athens) but otherwise (like the fourth of Kea's cities Poiessa — near Pisses) there is little extant on the ground today. Elsewhere on Kea you will find the substantial remains of a **Hellenistic Watchtower** at **Ag. Marina** and a monastery at M. Kastrianis.

Kimolos

ΚΙΜΩΛΟΣ; 38 km²; pop. 800.

CODE ☎ 22870
PORT POLICE ☎ 22100
POLICE ☎ 51205
FIRST AID ☎ 51222

A good island to escape the crowds and the more commercial trappings of tourism, Kimolos is named after the 'kimolia'

or chalk that was mined here before fuller's earth (used in the manufacture of porcelain) took over as the dusty mainstay of the local economy: ferries running along the northeast side of the islands pass hillsides badly scarred with opencast mines. This sounds singularly uninviting, yet the sea view creates a very false impression, for the southern half of Kimolos has a nice sleepy backwater atmosphere with a number of fine sand beaches (notably at Aliki). In addition, the islanders are among the declining number that treat visitors as honorary members of their large extended family.

Those looking for a tranquil holiday in traditional surroundings will find Kimolos to be a minor gem. More cautious island hoppers will find that in High Season Kimolos can also be visited as a day-trip destination; weekly tour boats run from Milos, and ticket agents on Sifnos have recently taken to advertising ferry day trips (taking advantage of those boats running down the line to the Central Cyclades and then returning, such services typically

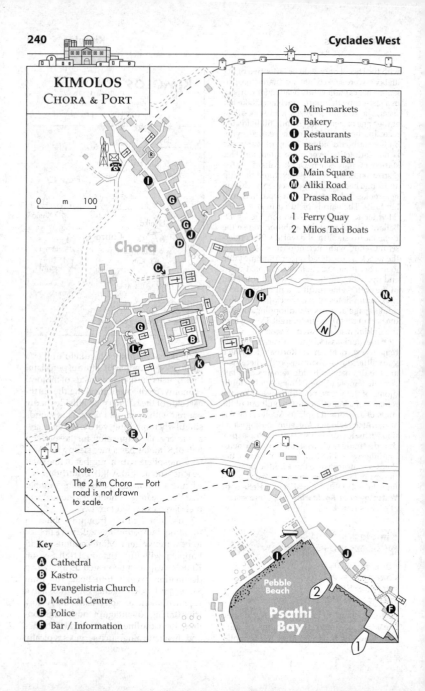

KIMOLOS
CHORA & PORT

0   m   100

Chora

Ⓖ Mini-markets
Ⓗ Bakery
Ⓘ Restaurants
Ⓙ Bars
Ⓚ Souvlaki Bar
Ⓛ Main Square
Ⓜ Aliki Road
Ⓝ Prassa Road

1   Ferry Quay
2   Milos Taxi Boats

Note:
The 2 km Chora — Port
road is not drawn
to scale.

Pebble
Beach

**Psathi
Bay**

Key
Ⓐ Cathedral
Ⓑ Kastro
Ⓒ Evangelistria Church
Ⓓ Medical Centre
Ⓔ Police
Ⓕ Bar / Information

give day hoppers just over five hours on Kimolos).

All regular ferries (and the landing-craft ferry that makes the 15-minute run to and from Pollonia on the north coast of Milos) dock at the small port of **Psathi** on the south-east coast. Little more than a quiet bar-backed quay beside a beach lined with odd trees and fishermen's houses, it looks suitably like the back of beyond; though this is somewhat deceptive as it is often quite lively, thanks to a couple of tavernas, a bar and a very popular beach restaurant. The air of abandon is greatly enhanced by the crescent of hills behind the port, most topped with derelict windmills. This is relieved by the attractive hilltop chora that trickles down the hillside toward the port. The chora and port are linked by an easily walked 1.5 km road — islanders will often offer visitors a ride on the back of a truck in the absence of any public transport (Kimolos is this sort of a place).

Chora itself is a pretty, unspoilt, working island village complete with a dominating 'cathedral' (a disappointing 20 C. building). Deftly hidden away in the ramshackle streets in its centre is another of those stockade-type kastros built to protect the inhabitants from the marauding pirates of four centuries ago. The town has grown up around this, and latterly along the valley floor road to the north. Consisting mainly of housing, there is no obvious centre of town (most of the important services have been added on at the edges). There are small squares where the inhabitants gather (the one on the west side of the kastro being the most 'cosy'). Shops are spread equally thinly all over town (and choice of goods tends to be limited as tourism has yet to reach a point where retailers stock up with outsiders in mind).

The rest of the island is quiet, though somewhat noisier than in past years thanks to another of those large EU road-building grants. This has seen Kimolos acquire the less than idyllic Tarmac roads that have scarred many of the smaller Greek islands,

spoiling the place for some visitors. In this case the upgraded roads run from Chora to the ugly mining hamlet of **Prassa** on the north-east corner of the island, and the much more appealing beach hamlet of **Aliki** on the south coast.

Kimolos's history is closely tied to neighbouring Milos. The island was formerly known as Echinousa (after a sea-urchin). Mining for fuller's earth started by the 4 C. BC. Thereafter little is known of the island's history. It later became a pirate's lair, before the Venetians took control, renaming it 'Argentiera' (silver) after the mines here. After the Turks took the island in 1566 Kimolos returned to its piratical past, joining Greece in 1821.

The lack of hotels reflects the small number of overnight visitors to Kimolos. Fortunately, accommodation isn't as thin on the ground as it looks from the map opposite (rooms are not advertised; locals either meet boats or rely on tavernas to refer customers on).

Most rooms are in **Chora** (or in the case of the *Meltemi Bar Rooms*, on the far side of it). The nearest the island has to a hotel is the large purpose-built rooms outlet on the port—Chora road. Tavernas backing on to **Aliki** beach also offer beds, notably *Taverna Aliki* (☎ 51340). Freelance camping is tolerated on the remoter beaches.

Kimolos has, from its earliest history, been dominated by its large neighbour Milos. This limited development on the island, and with it possible sights. These do exist, but most are located in the remoter parts of the island and take some effort to visit. **Chora** is the exception; it has some notable buildings (not least the Cycladic stockade-type kastro), and — if you are up to the climb — superb panoramic views of the chora, port and nearby islands (including large Poliegos opposite the port, which is used for grazing goats) from the top of the windmill-lined hill behind the town.

Sharing similar features with the stockade kastros on Antiparos and Folegandros, the Kimolos **Kastro** is in many ways the best of the three, as it hasn't been modified by later openings in its walls, or painted to a picture-postcard perfection. The interior houses are much as they originally were (in a run-down sort of way), lining the inner walls and with characteristic rows of external staircases. All are inhabited, and look on to the central block of buildings that make up the core of the kastro. The core buildings (the churches aside) are ruinous. From the ground the kastro appears to share a similar symmetrical shape as its Antiparos counterpart. However, from the air its north wall can be seen to bulge out to meet the summit of the chora hill (the kastro is built against the summit rather than atop it). Access is via two original gateways, the one on the east side offset from the centre and bearing the date 1556. Some of the internal features come from a 13 C. fortification.

The **Chora Churches** are also worth a look. The best of these is the lovely old **Evangelistria** (1608) just outside the north walls of the kastro; bare of plaster, it stands in warm contrast to the surrounding whitewashed buildings.

The chora aside, the main points of interest are a sulphur spring at the northern hamlet of **Prassa**, a surviving **Tower** of the ubiquitous ruined Venetian kastro (built on the slopes of the island's highest mountain, Paliokastro), and the site of the island's **Ancient Capital** on the west coast; it is now submerged between Kimolos and Agios Andreas islet (otherwise known as Daskaleio) near Ellinika beach. Finally, near Kambana beach are the remains of a number of **Mycenaean Tombs**.

Kythnos

ΚΥΘΝΟΣ; 86 km²; pop. 1,500.

CODE ☎ 22810
PORT POLICE ☎ 32290
POLICE / TOURIST POLICE ☎ 31201
FIRST AID ☎ 31202

A friendly, rocky little place three hours' sailing south of Athens with few tourist facilities, Kythnos (also often transcribed as 'Kithnos') is not the sort of island where the casual island hopper will be tempted to linger. The main attraction of the place is its very lack of attractions: a feature more likely to appeal to the jaded palette of the experienced island hopper than a novice. None of the island centres (primarily the port, the chora and Driopida) can offer excessive amounts of tourist appeal beyond the undeniable attraction of being 'unspoilt'

communities, while the rest of the island is spectacularly undramatic.

The port of **Merihas** is untidily strung around three sides of a small bay on the west coast and is very slowly emerging as a resort village in lieu of better alternatives elsewhere. Truth to tell, things haven't got very far; it has a pebbly-sand beach of sorts backing onto a tree- and taverna-lined waterfront that is also home to a number of rather down-at-heel looking small stores and not a lot else, beyond growing clusters of holiday homes and rooms on the hillsides and valley behind. Things aren't helped by one over-large hotel — the *Possidonion* — totally out of character and scale with the other buildings, now being reduced to a derelict hulk and the preserve of the occasional squatter. This is hardly the stuff of romantic quayside evening strolls — unless you are a new town architect from a former communist bloc country. However, Merihas isn't all bad; almost all the island accommodation worth knowing about is here and there are better beaches concealed beyond the two headlands to the north of the ferry quay, the best being a long tree-backed strip of sand two headlands along the Port—Chora road.

An erratic bus service links the port with the main towns (times are posted in the front windscreens). Inland there are two settlements of note: the capital at Chora, and the village of Driopida. In ancient times Kythnos was divided between them, and even today they manage to all but ignore each other (an attitude made easier by the need to take different roads from the port to each of them).

Set amid a gently undulating plain of brown stubble fields and low hills topped with windmills, **Chora** (also known as **Kythnos**), for all its lack of 'sights', offers an attractive destination, with friendly inhabitants and plenty of whitewashed charm. It more than makes up for Merihas. The island's comparative lack of popularity has ensured that it has remained surprisingly unspoilt, with no tourist accommodation and only two or three small souvenir shops marring the main street that runs the length of the town. The side streets are also appealing, with a donkey lingering around every other corner. Fortunately, in this part of the world they earn their keep in the traditional way instead of lugging well-heeled tourists around. Chora also does its bit for Greek island church architecture; churches here add to the variety by having their bells hung on the outside walls (usually near the door). At various points in the town you will find signs to the wind park that sits on the hills rising behind the far end of town. A destination worth attempting as it requires you to explore the length of the town, don't go expecting Disneyland: there is nought there but several modern power-generating windmills poignantly positioned alongside derelict traditional mills.

Other towns on Kythnos have less going for them. First among these (at least with the elderly Greeks who make up the bulk of the island's visitors) is the 19 c. spa resort and fishing port at **Loutra** on the north coast. Unfortunately, a thimbleful of the thermal waters has more fizz than all the tourists here put together, and if you want to be spared a depressing experience then avoid the town. **Driopida** is more uplifting; located in a fertile hill valley, its houses are topped with red-tile roofs reminiscent of town houses on Kea. Sadly, accommodation is non-existent.

The rest of Kythnos is very low-key, consisting mainly of arid treeless hills, highly terraced, and speckled with the thyme from which the rich island honey derives its distinctive flavour. Given that Kythnos barely recognizes the existence of tourists (because it sees so few), it is almost superfluous to add that the best island beach — on the east coast at **Ag. Stefanou** — is not served by buses, and thus is inaccessible, unless you fancy the dusty walk down the hillside from Driopida. A better option is to walk up the western coast from Merihas to **Fikiado**, a golden causeway of sand that links Kythnos with the islet of Agios Loukas.

KYTHNOS

Formerly known as 'Themia', Kythnos was a minor player in antiquity. The island provided two triremes to fight at Salamis, later joining the Delian League. Thereafter it was ruled from Athens. Its subsequent history mirrored that of nearby Kea, with pirate raids followed by capture by the Venetians in 1207. The Turks held Kythnos between 1537–1821.

Even in High Season you can't walk far from the ferry quay without islanders calling out 'Room?' The comparative lack of tourists all but guarantees a cheap bed on demand. Most rooms are to be found at **Merihas**, though it is worthwhile ascertaining where your bed is

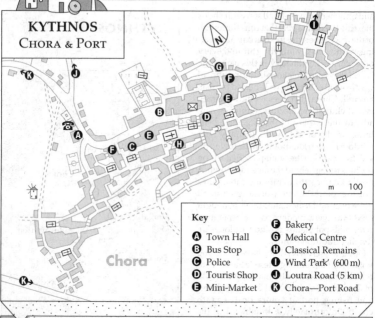

KYTHNOS
CHORA & PORT

Chora

0   m   100

Key

A Town Hall
B Bus Stop
C Police
D Tourist Shop
E Mini-Market
F Bakery
G Medical Centre
H Classical Remains
I Wind 'Park' (600 m)
J Loutra Road (5 km)
K Chora—Port Road

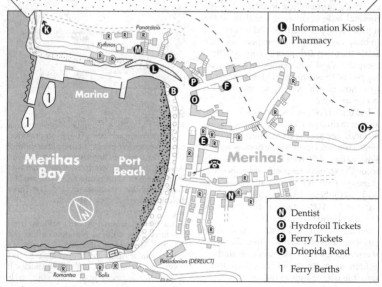

Panorama

Kythnos

Marina

Merihas Bay

Port Beach

Merihas

Possidonion (DERELICT)

Romantsa   *Solis*

L Information Kiosk
M Pharmacy

N Dentist
O Hydrofoil Tickets
P Ferry Tickets
Q Driopida Road

1 Ferry Berths

before accepting an offer: some are at the top of taxing hillside staircases that one wouldn't want to tackle more than once a day. If you want to phone ahead, try the rooms near the dentist — complete with early morning calls (well, screams) from 08.00 (☎ 32284, 32104) — or the second establishment offering rooms past the small chapel on the south side of the bay (☎ 32105). Hotel accommodation is much thinner on the ground, being confined to the mid-range *Kythnos* (☎ 32092). The island also has three C-class establishments all in the wrong place — i.e. the spa 'resort' of **Loutra**. At the bottom end of the range is the relatively inexpensive *Xenia Anagenissis* (☎ 31217). This is followed by the pricier *Kythnos Bay* (☎ 31218) and the *Meltemi* (☎ 31271).

◐◐

Visitors don't come to Kythnos for the sightseeing, and it is pretty limited. **Chora** has some unidentifiable small fragments from ancient buildings tucked away in a small 'garden' just off the main street, and Driopida lays claim to the notable **Katafiki Cave** at the head of its valley. The cave extends for over a kilometre and has several lakes. Sadly, it is currently closed due to the lack of funds needed to employ guides (one of the tourist shops at Merihas has a cave guidebook on sale). Hill walkers will (hopefully) find a **Venetian Kastro** on the northern tip of the island that is notoriously difficult to get to. A more practical walk runs between Chora and Driopida. Finally, there are many **churches** littering the hillsides, but an increasing number are locked following a series of icon thefts.

Milos

ΜΗΛΟΣ; 161 km²; pop. 4,500.

CODE ☎ 22870
PORT POLICE ☎ 22100
TOURIST OFFICE ☎ 22445
POLICE ☎ 21378

Like its more scenic neighbour Santorini, Milos is volcanic in origin, offering a vivid contrast with the islands higher up its respective ferry line. However, similarities are apt to end there for Milos is a very different sort of place, and it is worth taking some pains to pay a visit just to experience the contrasts. One of the most obvious of these is the level of tourism, for Milos has come very late onto the sightseeing scene, having traditionally relied on mining as the mainstay of the local economy. This is now changing fast and the locals have made strenuous efforts in the last five years to develop their tourist facilities (which, to be honest, were a bit on the basic side before). With these in place now is the ideal time to pay the island a visit — before the island's charms bring in too many new visitors.

First impressions of Milos are apt to be somewhat contradictory, for the island hides many of its finer points amid a rather bizarre hilly landscape — the result of repeated ancient eruptions, mining activity and the workings of archaeologists looking vainly for the arms of the Venus de Milo (the Hellenistic statue of an over-plump Aphrodite that has ensured that most people are at least familiar with the island's name).

With the exception of the north and west, Milos is very sparsely populated. Few tourists venture beyond the triangle of settlements made up of Adamas, Plaka — and its associated villages — and Pollonia (so much so, that the bus service doesn't even extend to the eastern half of the island).

The port of **Adamas** is now the biggest of the three and the best base for exploring the island. It now boasts a recently redeveloped waterfront and promenade, and arguably the finest ferry passenger shed in the islands. Built upon a weathered plug of magma, Adamas enjoys the views across the central bay (which looks more like a lake as the entrance is hidden from view). Although it might look similar in shape to Santorini on a map, this bay isn't a caldera, but just the chance result of a large number of small eruptions building the island in this shape. Either side of the town are small sandy beaches. There are also several discos in town that are the sum total of the island's nightlife. Adamas is also well endowed with tavernas (the best lie on the coast road to the east of the area shown on the map overleaf).

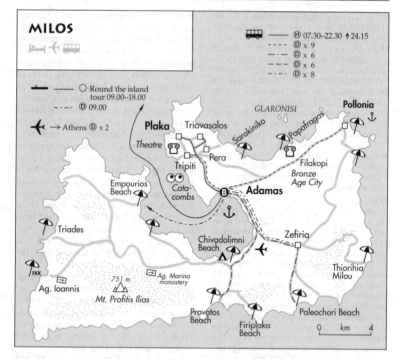

MILOS

⊞—⊁—🚌

🚌 ——— Ⓗ 07.30–22.30 ⚓24.15
- - - - Ⓓ x 9
— - — Ⓓ x 6
— — — Ⓓ x 6
- - - · Ⓓ x 8

⊁—— ○ Round the island
tour 09.00–18.00
- - - · Ⓓ 09.00

⊁ → Athens Ⓓ x 2

GLARONISI

Pollonia ⚓

Plaka   Triovasalos
Theatre 🏛️🏛️
Σαρακίνικο
Ⓗ🏛️ Παπαφράγας

Tripiti 🏛️🏛️   Pera
Filakopi
_Bronze
Age City_

Empourios
Beach ⚓   Cata-
combs   **Ⓑ** **Adamas**
⚓

Triades ⚓

Chivadolimni
Beach   Zefiria

Thiorihia
Milou

FKK ⚓   ⊞ _Ag. Marina
monastery_
Ag. Ioannis   751 m
Mt. Profitis Ilias

Provatos
Beach
Firiplaka
Beach
Paleochori Beach

0   km   4

North of Adamas lies the classical centre of Milos. This part of the island is dominated by a cluster of four villages, the prettiest of which, **Plaka**, is the island capital. Easily the most photogenic part of Milos, it is an unspoilt whitewashed chora with the usual warren of streets to get hopelessly lost in, and with superb views and a couple of museums worth visiting. Dominating the town is another volcanic mound topped with a number of chapels, all that remain of the old Venetian castro-cum-town. The other villages in the quartet are close enough to walk to: the best is **Tripiti**, running down from a windmill-topped hill to the remains of the ancient island capital and the lovely string of waterfront fishermen's houses that make up the tiny old port of **Klima**.

The second major tourist centre of note lies on the north-east coast at **Pollonia** (also known as Apollonia). Fringing a sheltered bay, it started life as a small fishing village, but has now developed into low-key pension and holiday home style resort (though this latter term is a bit misleading — the atmosphere of Pollonia is more akin to Greek village on holiday). Even in spite of the inevitable abandoned opencast mine eating away an overlooking hillside, it is one of the more scenic parts of the island, with a very attractive windswept northern headland. The ferry to neighbouring Kimolos also helps bring visitors to Pollonia (along with some nice tavernas and rooms): the overall result is that most visitors to Milos pay a call at some point during their stay.

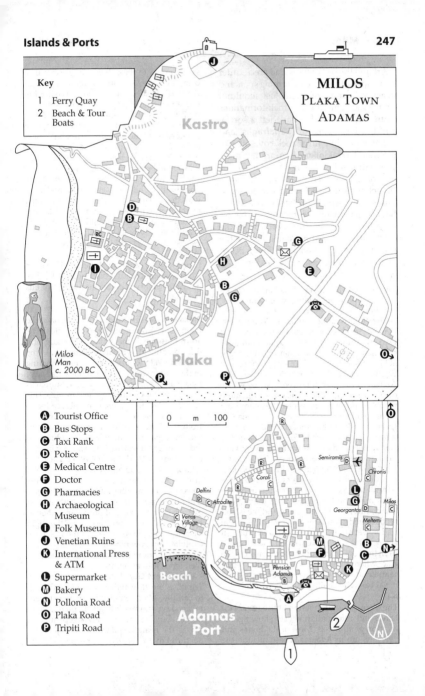

Key

1. Ferry Quay
2. Beach & Tour Boats

MILOS
PLAKA TOWN
ADAMAS

Kastro

RC

Milos Man c. 2000 BC

Plaka

Ⓐ Tourist Office
Ⓑ Bus Stops
Ⓒ Taxi Rank
Ⓓ Police
Ⓔ Medical Centre
Ⓕ Doctor
Ⓖ Pharmacies
Ⓗ Archaeological Museum
Ⓘ Folk Museum
Ⓙ Venetian Ruins
Ⓚ International Press & ATM
Ⓛ Supermarket
Ⓜ Bakery
Ⓝ Pollonia Road
Ⓞ Plaka Road
Ⓟ Tripiti Road

0   m   100

Semiramis
Chironis
Delfini
Corali
Afrodite
Georgantas
Milos
Venus Village
Meltemi
Pension Adamas

Beach

Adamas Port

Around the rest of the island are a scatter of wonderfully scenic swimming spots and beaches — some of which just shouldn't be missed. The unusual rock-formations of the Milan coastline have left a sort of cliff-lined sea canal at **Papafragas**, and weathered white lunar rock coves at **Firiplaka** and **Sarakiniko**. There are also more conventional beaches in abundance. The best of these served by the bus system is the pebble beach at **Paleochori**, with several buses running daily in High Season. If you have your own transport you can do better: a set of wheels can transport you to the monastery and goat-inhabited west of the island where it is possible to find a beach all to yourself, even in High Season.

Thanks to its large, sheltered harbour Milos was an important island in ancient times, rivalling Naxos as a centre of pre-Hellenic civilization, with an important Minoan settlement developing on the northern coast at Filakopi. Prior to this Milos appears to have been a major trading post thanks to the availability of obsidian, a volcanic glass that could be cut to make sharp tools. Mycenaean and Archaic settlement followed apace, and by the Classical era Milos was one of the more notable of the minor players in the internecine struggles of the Greek city states. The island's great moment in history occurred in 416 BC when Milos refused to join Athens in her war with Sparta and Corinth (an event later immortalised by the historian Thucydides via the 'Melian Dialogue' in his *History of the Peloponnesian War*). By way of a reprisal the Athenians voted for the execution of all the adult males on the island. With the women and children sold into slavery and the island repopulated with Athenians, Milos — even under Venetian (1207–1566) and Turkish (1566–1821) rule — kept a very low profile from then on, apart from a short period in the 17 c. when it emerged as a notorious pirate centre, and WW1 when it was used as an Allied naval base and coaling station.

☍

The ferry quay Information Office (☎ 22445) hands out information sheets showing the location of all hotels. Most of the hotels and pensions are in **Adamas**. These include the

spiffy, pricey C-class *Venus Village* (☎ 22030) complex, complete with swimming pool and the port's best beach. Also ideally placed to take advantage of this are the C-class *Afrodite* (☎ 22020) and the D-class *Delfini* (☎ 22001). More hotels are to be found on the east side of the port. Near the waterfront are the C-class *Meltemi* (☎ 22284) and *Milos* (☎ 22087) along with the D-class *Georgantas* (☎ 21955). On the Plaka road behind are the C-class *Chronis* (☎ 22226) and the D-class *Semiramis* (☎ 22117). The Adamas 'hill' has less accommodation, with the C-class *Corali* (☎ 22204) augmented by the B-class pension *Adamas* (☎ 22322) and a number of rooms. Around the rest of the island the only hotel of note is the friendly D-class *Panorama* (☎ 21623) at **Klima**.

Λ

Camping Milos (☎ 31410), located 6.5 km from Adamas on the coast directly opposite the ferry quay, is a clean, well-equipped site. A mini-bus meets all ferries.

☁☁

Plaka and the surrounding villages have the main concentration of sights on Milos. The **Town Museum** is inevitably something of a disappointment as the main attraction — the **Venus de Milo** (C. 320 BC) — is now residing in the Louvre in Paris (it is represented here by a plaster replica). This famous statue was discovered by a farmer in a field in 1820. This was reported to the French ambassador to Constantinople, who arranged for its purchase from the Turks and had it shipped to Paris. Rumours persist that when this plumpish lady was first unearthed she was not brachially disadvantaged (the first two Frenchmen who saw the statue reported the existence of arms). Quite what happened to them is the subject of any number of tall tales, the best embracing ransom demands, with almost every islander having, if not an arm, then at least a hand in the business. Like the Elgin Marbles, this piece of sculpture has been exploited by government ministers seeking a popularist profile, with regular requests to the French for her return.

The **Ancient City**, down the road at nearby Tripiti, is worth wandering around, though to call the extant remains a city casts a very misleading impression given their scanty nature. Built on a relatively steep hillside, it was the island capital from around 1000 BC through to the Byzantine period. The

Key

A Tripiti Village Bus Stop
B Main Path to Archaeological Site
C Entrance to the Catacombs
D Circular Bastion
E Internal Defensive Wall
F Stadium
G Discovery site of the Venus de Milo / Gymnasium
H Foundations of Baptistry & Early Christian Font

I Roman Theatre
J Site of Main City Temple?
K Roman Baths
L Private Houses
M 'Hall of the Mystai' Mosaic
N Sections of City Wall
O Road to Triovasalos Village (1 km)
P Road to Plaka Village (1 km)
Q Road to Adamas Port (4 km)
R Current hiding-place of the Venus de Milo's arms

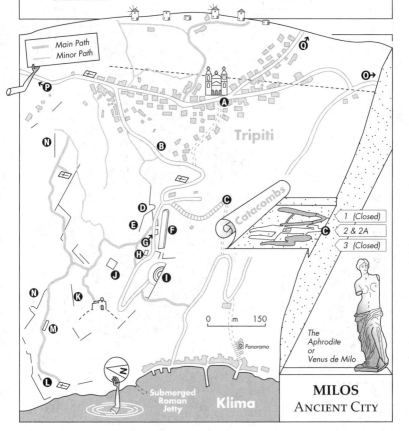

Main Path
Minor Path

Q →
O →
P
A
Tripiti
N
B
Catacombs
C
D
E
F
G
H
J
I
N
K
M
L

1 (Closed)
2 & 2A
3 (Closed)

0   m   150

Panorama

The Aphrodite or Venus de Milo

Submerged Roman Jetty
Klima

MILOS
ANCIENT CITY

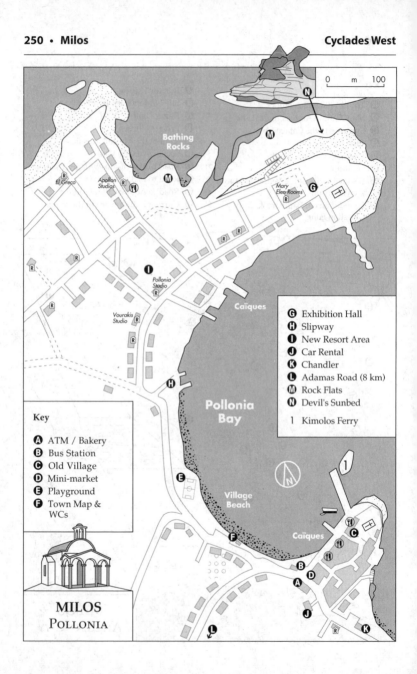

0 m 100

Bathing Rocks

El Greco

Apollon Studios

Mary Elen Rooms

G Exhibition Hall
H Slipway
I New Resort Area
J Car Rental
K Chandler
L Adamas Road (8 km)
M Rock Flats
N Devil's Sunbed
1 Kimolos Ferry

Pollonia Studio

Vourakis Studio

Caïques

Pollonia Bay

Key

A ATM / Bakery
B Bus Station
C Old Village
D Mini-market
E Playground
F Town Map & WCs

Village Beach

Caïques

MILOS
POLLONIA

best preserved remains are parts of the **City Walls** along with a **Roman Theatre**. A plaque also stands on the site where *the* statue was discovered (there are plans to erect a copy of the Venus on the site): it is thought to have graced a niche in a gymnasium that stood near the stadium. The lower part of the city stood behind an ancient harbour and was dominated by a small temple-topped hill (a small church now stands on the site).

Easily the most impressive remains of the ancient city are the **Catacombs**, the earliest known Christian site in Greece (they are thought to date from the 1 c. AD when St. Paul was shipwrecked on Milos, an arrival that appears to have prompted the locals to dig a series of tunnels capable of hiding away the entire population). The site of burials and worship for close on 400 years, they lie just outside the East Gate of the city wall. Dug into the easily worked volcanic rock, they originally took the form of three unconnected tunnels (the longest being some 184 m) with secondary chambers leading off them. Since their discovery in 1840, connecting corridors have been dug between them and two of the three entrances closed off. Only the central catacomb is open to the public (the Adamas information office has current opening times). Once inside you will find yourself in a long, floodlit chamber with burial niches in the walls and floor, along with cavities for oil lamps. Estimates as to the numbers interred range from 2000—8000, but as 'dem bones' appear to have risen up and legged it during repeated pillaging in the island's piratical years, it is impossible to arrive at an accurate figure.

The catacombs also feature in one of the more original day excursions in the Greek islands: Milos has a **Mining and Geology Tour** that starts with the above and ends at a working mine. **Adamas** is also home to a new **Mining Museum** (open ◎ 09.15–13.45, 18.45–21.15). Sited on the waterfront 500 m east of the port, it is easily spotted by the rusting mine wagons adorning the entrance.

The other major site on Milos is the **Bronze Age Town** at **Filakopi**. The site offers plenty for archaeologists to ponder on, but little for the layman. The jumble of walls (extending under the sea) are not readily intelligible, but are important as one of the largest Minoan towns outside Crete and Santorini. Later a Mycenaean centre, it remained the island

capital until its decline c. 1100 BC. Finds are in the Plaka museum, but the best — including the 'flying fish fresco' — are in the National Archaeological Museum in Athens.

Boat trips around Milos (€14.50) also make an interesting excursion, passing the volcanic **Glaronisi** islets en route to the uninhabited (rare chamois goats excepted) island of **Antimilos** to the north-west, and Kimolos.

Serifos
ΣΕΡΙΦΟΣ; 70 km²; pop. 1,100.

CODE ☎ 22810
PORT POLICE ☎ 51470
POLICE ☎ 51300
HOSPITAL ☎ 51202

Serifos is one of those islands that always seems to end up near the top of the list of 'one of those places the ferry calls at on the way to the island you are heading for'. This is a pity, because in many respects the island has more going for it than its more popular neighbour Sifnos. Equally distressing, a goodly number of the citizens of Athens are in the know about this and descend like a plague of locusts for weekends and summer holidays: be warned, ferries departing Serifos for Athens on Sundays are almost certain to be booked solid before you get a chance to buy a ticket.

Athenians aside, sun-baked Serifos is blessed with a laid-back, relaxed ambience. During Low Season weekdays, at least, the island offers a tantalizing glimpse of what Ios might have been like if it hadn't been discovered by the partying masses; the set-up is not dissimilar, with a small port overlooked by an appealing chora, coupled by a good beach a headland away. Serifos is as barren and with as poor a road system as Ios, too; as a result few visitors venture beyond the closely connected port—chora—beach combination.

The only means of arrival and escape is the cosy beach and pine-fringed harbour of **Livadi**. Set in a deep-cut bay on the south coast, it is home to most of the island's facilities, from the bank, supermarket and nightlife (don't expect too much on this

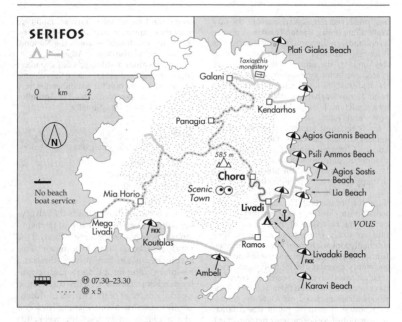

SERIFOS

Plati Gialos Beach

Taxiarchis monastery

Galani

0 km 2

Kendarhos

Panagia

Agios Giannis Beach

585 m

Psili Ammos Beach

Chora

Agios Sostis Beach

No beach boat service

Mia Horio

Scenic Town

Lia Beach

Livadi

VOUS

Mega Livadi

FKK

Koutalas

Ramos

Livadaki Beach
FKK

Ambeli

07.30–23.30

x 5

Karavi Beach

score) to almost all the accommodation options. However, for all this, the port is very small and charmingly primitive. The one feature of note is the over-large ferry quay built onto the headland that protects the harbour bay.

The bay itself is lined by hotels and houses offering rooms. These look onto a passable sand beach (though the dust thrown up by cars negotiating the port's one-way traffic system means that it pays to walk to the east of the hotel strip). A better beach lies to the west of the ferry quay at **Livadaki**. This is supposedly designated as one of the island's two nude beaches, but the crowds turn this into an all-family affair during the summer months. Those looking for the chance to reveal more to fewer people should consider taking the short path that runs from the end of Livadaki beach over the headland to **Karavi** beach. The more energetic might also consider taking the track that runs from the far end

of the harbour beach to the succession of charming beaches on the east coast. These start with **Lia** and run up to **Agios Giannis** — passing en route the island's best beach, a long stretch of sand backed by a couple of tavernas at **Psili Ammos**.

New arrivals to Serifos are now confronted with a sign on the quay welcoming you 'to the island with Europe's most beautiful beach — *Sunday Times 25/5/2003*'. This is a bit disingenuous (to put it mildly) as the newspaper in question had twenty of its writers nominate their top European beach: Psili Ammos was merely one of those listed. Moreover, the recommendation doesn't call the beach beautiful, but instead dwells more on the merits of two tavernas behind it which 'make a good beach a great one' (the liquid refreshment on sale here is pretty potent stuff). About an hour's walk from the port bay, the beach can also be reached via a track running down from Chora. Beyond Psili Ammos is a longer beach at **Agios Giannis**; usually very quiet, it tends to be the sole preserve of the occasional nude hiker.

A second walking option (provided you are prepared to keep your clothes on) is the old mule path running from the road behind the port up a steep hillside to the island's only town. The path and modern road repeatedly meet and turn away all the way up the hillside — like a pair of virgin lovers' furtive glances, with mule water troughs taking the part of occasional tears along the way. Unless you attempt it during the heat of the middle of the day it is an easy and pleasant walk, though at some points where path and road meet you have to look quite hard to pick up where the path continues.

Just over 2 km long, the path finally wanders into the lower slopes of the island capital at **Chora**. Straddling the slopes of a finger of rock pointing skyward (complete with a whimsical small chapel placed deftly on the tip) Chora is not to be missed. It deserves a visit for it is one of the most photogenic choras around: a mini-Astipalea Town, complete with a ridge of windmills, and a hill topped with whitewashed chapels and the scanty remains of a kastro. The views over Chora and the port bay from the top are suitably breathtaking, and worth the effort of finding your way through the narrow warren of streets (many in a poor state of repair).

The main hill aside, Chora neatly divides into two quarters. The older section runs in an arc north along the hill spine until it reaches the windmills (most of the houses run down the east slope before farming terraces take over). The 'new' town cascades down the south slope of the Chora hill, and there is limited access between the two. Still very much a residential town with few concessions to tourism, Chora lacks landmarks (thereby guaranteeing you will get lost in it for a street or two). Fortunately, it is not so big that this is much of a problem and some relief is to be gained by the provision of working water taps at

strategic points on the edge of the chora and the old road.

The rest of Serifos is not visited by the great majority of tourists. Consisting of arid, stone-littered hills ('Serifos' means 'stoney') that are relieved only by odd patches of vegetation (like equally dry Santorini, the island's principal crops are tomatoes and ground-creeping vines) and a scatter of isolated farms, it doesn't exactly invite exploration, though ambitious walkers will find plenty to please them. The dull red-brown landscape isn't really enhanced by the litter of rusting remains from the island's — now defunct — iron mining industry. This thrived a century ago but declined between the world wars: its only lasting impact was in the field of Greek industrial relations — a 1916 miners' strike saw the deaths of several strikers before workers' rule was established. More appealing are the small villages connected by poor roads. These lead variously to the island's other official nudist beach at Koutalas, and to the **Taxiarchis** monastery on the north coast.

An earlier island attraction is presumably still lying around somewhere and, if discovered, is probably better left where you find it; for Serifos was the childhood home of Perseus, the Greek hero who cut off the head of the Gorgon Medusa (a personified shriek who, if looked at directly in the eye, would turn the viewer into stone). Armed with this little trinket, Perseus went around the island flashing it at anyone who didn't take his fancy; this included the king and most of the population. This seems to have left the modern inhabitants in a quandary: on the one hand this mythological hero provides the only event in the history of Serifos worth talking about, yet he presumably did to death their ancestors. As a result Perseus, although a hero, is all but ignored here.

Elsewhere Perseus was a popular figure. Not to be confused with the god Hermes, he was armed with a mirror shield (provided by his patron Athena), a pair of winged boots, a head-satchel and cap of invisibility, and a sickle. His foe Medusa was one of the horror figures of Greek mythology. Noted for having a head of snakes instead of hair, she was made to appear infinitely more terrible by Classical artists who represented her as a beautiful maiden. Her beheading and Perseus's subsequent pursuit by her two sisters (Sthenno 'the Strong' and Euryale 'the wide-leaping') was a popular theme in Ancient Greek art.

Serifos was one of the early democracies, with the first experiments coming as early as the 7 C. BC. During the Persian Wars the island first sided with the Persians, but deserted to the Greek cause during the Battle of Salamis. It later came under Athenian control via the Delian League, and was subsequently ruled by the Macedonians, the Ptolemies and Romans. During the later Roman years it was used as a place of exile. In obscurity during the Byzantine era, Serifos was captured by the Venetians in 1207, before falling to the Turks in 1617. Briefly under Russian control between 1770–74, Serifos joined Greece in 1821.

⊨

Most of the accommodation on Serifos is to be found in and around the port of **Livadi**. This includes the B-class pension *Naias* (☎ 51585) and the more expensive B-class hotel *Areti* (☎ 51479) overlooking the beach. At the far end of the port beach stands the equally pricey *Asteri* (☎ 51191). In addition there are four C-class hotels: the *Naias* (☎ 51585), the *Eliza* (☎ 51763), the *Maistrali* (☎ 51381) — topped with flags and charging rates above most B-class hotels — and the *Serifos Beach* (☎ 51209), complete with restaurant and tucked down a side alley. At the budget end of the range is the D-class *Albatros* (☎ 51148) along with the E-class *Cyclades* (☎ 51315). A scatter of rooms — notably the faded *Captain George Rooms* (☎ 51274) near the main square — are complemented by new establishments behind the port beach and along the campsite, Chora and Ramos roads.

Λ

Coralli Camping (☎ 51500), 400 m west of the port (mini-buses go 2 km around the port one-way system to get there), is one of the best and cleanest sites in Greece, on the beach with shady shrubs and a pool. Bungalows are also rented out. The only weak point is lack of choice as to where you can pitch your tent.

The Myth of Perseus & the Gorgons

Once upon a time Acrisius, the king of Argos, was warned by an oracle that his daughter Danaë would produce a son who would kill him. Whereupon he imprisoned her in a bronze chamber (an ancient variation on the chastity belt). Needless to say the god Zeus — disguised as a golden shower (of what it is probably politic not to ask) — visited her and nine months later Perseus appeared. Loath to kill his grandson, Acrisius promptly put him into a chest with his mother and cast it out to sea. It drifted to Serifos, where mother and son were received cordially by the local king Polydectes, who fell violently in love with Danaë, allowing both mother and son to live in his palace. Danaë, however, successfully rejected the king's advances until Perseus was fully grown. Polydectes then sought to get him off the scene while he pursued his mother by sending him off on a seemingly impossible task — to fetch the head of the Gorgon Medusa. This Perseus did with a little help from his friends, notably the goddess Athena, the god Hermes, and some Gorgon-hating sea nymphs.

On returning to Serifos, Perseus turned Polydectes and his courtiers into stone by producing the head of Medusa after he discovered that the king had attempted to force his mother into marriage. After returning the gifts of Hermes and his patron Athena (who thereafter wore the Aegis cape, adorned with the Gorgon's head and fringed with snakes), Perseus and his mother decided to return to the mainland, where en route to his home he mis-threw a discus while competing in some funeral games, accidentally killing a member of the crowd — his grandfather.

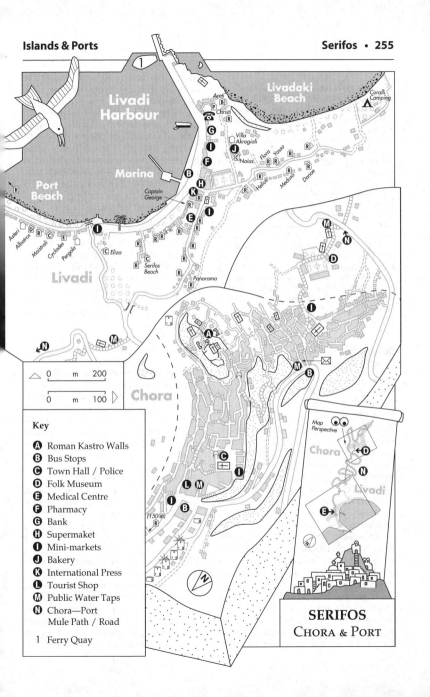

Livadi Harbour

Livadaki Beach

Coralli Camping

Areti
Christi
Villa Akrogiali

Marina

Naias
Flora
Yasso
Helios
Meduso
Danae

Port Beach

Captain George

Livadi

Adeni
Albatros
Maistrali
Cyclades
Pergola

Eliza

Serifos Beach

Panorama

Chora

△ 0   m   200

0   m   100 ▷

(150 m)

Key

- Ⓐ Roman Kastro Walls
- Ⓑ Bus Stops
- Ⓒ Town Hall / Police
- Ⓓ Folk Museum
- Ⓔ Medical Centre
- Ⓕ Pharmacy
- Ⓖ Bank
- Ⓗ Supermaket
- Ⓘ Mini-markets
- Ⓙ Bakery
- Ⓚ International Press
- Ⓛ Tourist Shop
- Ⓜ Public Water Taps
- Ⓝ Chora—Port
  Mule Path / Road

- 1 Ferry Quay

Map Perspective

Chora

Livadi

SERIFOS
Chora & Port

👓

The main sight on Serifos should have been the **Roman Kastro** on the Chora hill. Sadly, it was reduced to walls by pirates in 1210. Even less is to be seen of the temple of Athena that preceded it (most of its stones are now in the walls of two nearby churches). Near the other end of history's spectrum is the Town Hall. Built in 1909, it stands resplendent in the main square, glorying in the contrast it offers with the whitewashed houses that surround it.

The **Ancient Capital** which was at Mia Horio has left few traces, and in lieu of anything else, the castle-like **Taxiarchis Monastery**, built c. 1600 AD, is the main sightseeing destination, though access isn't easy; the surest way of getting there is to pack a few bottles of water and walk it: the round-trip from the town takes a little over four hours. Despite being attacked and looted on a number of occasions by pirates, it is still home to a notable collection of artifacts. Finally **Panagia** has the island's oldest church. Built c. 950 BC, it is adorned with 14 C. wall paintings.

Sifnos
ΣΙΦΝΟΣ; 89 km²; pop. 2,200.

CODE ☎ 22840
PORT POLICE ☎ 31617
TOURIST OFFICES ☎ 31977, 32190
FIRST AID ☎ 31315

The most touristed island in the Cyclades West group, Sifnos is still fairly quiet by Central Cyclades Line standards. Much of the island's popularity can be attributed to its hilly landscape, sprinkled with typical white Cycladic villages and several good beaches; sightseeing usually gives way to general exploring, given the limited number of sights of interest.

During the Archaic period Sifnos was very prosperous, thanks to the discovery of gold deposits. By way of a thanks offering for this good luck the islanders were in the habit of making an annual gift of a golden egg to the god Apollo's shrine at Delphi (this wasn't as odd as it sounds, for the oracle stone at Delphi, the *Omphalos* marking the centre of the world, was egg-shaped; it was the point where two eagles — flying from the opposite ends of the earth — met). The story has it that one year they sent a gilt egg instead and, surprise, surprise, their mines (which by now had extended out under the sea) were mysteriously flooded. This had a catastrophic effect on the island's fortunes, and by the Classical period Sifnos had ceased to be a major player and relied on pottery production for its livelihood — the islanders presumably working on the practical notion that if you can't dig up pots of gold you can at least make the pots.

These days Sifnos is one of those leading the pack in the second eleven of Greek islands. Despite its popularity, it suffers from a shortage of accommodation. This is one of the few islands where there is a real possibility of not being able to find a High Season bed (and those that are available tend to be expensive); it pays to arrive on a morning boat if you haven't phoned ahead.

All ferries dock on the 'wrong' side of the island (relative to the main settlements) where a narrow gorge provides a natural harbour at **Kamares**. Considering how small the port is, it is a surprisingly lively place thanks to its de facto role as the tourist centre, defying the stark hills that climb high above it, seeming to almost bundle it into the sea. Clinging to the shoreline you will find waterside tavernas by the score, a growing number of bars which are acquiring quite a reputation of oversharp dealing, several travel agents and a sand-and-pebble beach of some length and dubious quality. Accommodation is spread thinly, but evenly, around the back of the settlement, and is for the most part hidden behind clumps of trees and the half-hearted attempt to turn the road behind the beach into a promenade. Near the ferry quay there is also a helpful tourist information office. Frequent buses run from a turn-around point near the quay into the interior, making escape very easy — though most journeys seem to require you to change at Apollonia. All buses run east and south as the northern third of the

Cyclades West

Chora Square Taverna
Menu & Chair

SERIFOS
Chora Houses

How to keep cool in Greece:
Example 21

MILOS
Apollonia Beach

KEA
Archaic Lion
& Tourist Circus

Cliff-top Chora Views on
Folegandros

Cyclades West

Kastro Houses & Main Square Church
FOLEGANDROS

ANAFI
Chora Square

IRAKLIA
Quay & Village

Waiting for ferries —
Koufonissia style

KOUFONISSIA
Port Village Beach & Fishing
Caïques

Lifeboat
from the
original

C/F Skopelitis

Cyclades East

AMORGOS
Chora

Chora Bus Station
Square

Waterfront at
Katapola

Amorgos:
Conch-blowing
fishermen sell
their catch in
the streets of
Chora

ASTIPALEA
Chora Windmills
& Kastro

Cyclades East

island is all but unpopulated, the gold mines now being inaccessible even to the archaeologically minded. The bus ride itself is something of a revelation as the road runs up a valley filled with olive and fig trees; for Sifnos is not the barren island that the sea views suggest, and agriculture still plays an important role in its economy.

The modern 'capital' of **Apollonia** lies 5 km inland. As island capitals go it is a regular odd-ball, being merely one of four closely placed hill villages that has grown (by virtue of its role as the island's crossroads) to become the de facto nucleus. Lacking a historical heart of note, the settlement has grown along the roads to the neighbouring villages rather than in a traditional manner, creating an unusual village-cum-suburb web of buildings. Tourist

activity is centred on the bland square in the heart of this jumble; little more than a road junction fringed with houses it doesn't do the town justice, though all essential services are conveniently to hand. In fact, the tourist-shop-cluttered street behind the square is supposed to be the true centre of the universe hereabouts. For Apollonia to have any appeal you have to enjoy walking; if you do so, you can be rewarded with an interesting day clambering up and down the whitewashed streets. The best views are to be found on the windmill-topped hill above **Pano Petali** — the mills themselves being rather fun thanks to their fish-shaped weathervanes (a more interesting piece of religious symbolism than the more usual cross). The farmyard-backed backstreets behind **Exambela** are also quaint in a

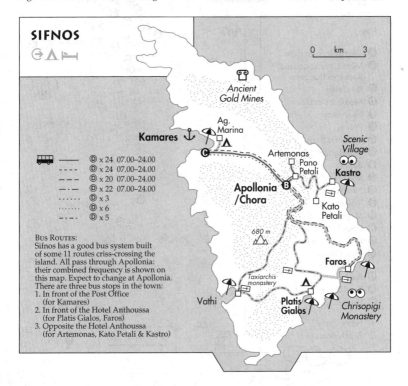

SIFNOS

0   km   3

Ancient
Gold Mines

Ag.
Marina

Kamares

Scenic
Village

Artemonas

Pano
Petali

Kastro

**Apollonia
/Chora**

Kato
Petali

680 m

Faros

Taxiarchis
monastery

Vathi

**Platis
Gialos**

Chrisopigi
Monastery

Ⓓ x 24   07.00–24.00
Ⓓ x 24   07.00–24.00
Ⓓ x 20   07.00–24.00
Ⓓ x 22   07.00–24.00
Ⓓ x 3
Ⓓ x 6
Ⓓ x 5

BUS ROUTES:
Sifnos has a good bus system built of some 11 routes criss-crossing the island. All pass through Apollonia: their combined frequency is shown on this map. Expect to change at Apollonia. There are three bus stops in the town:
1. In front of the Post Office
   (for Kamares)
2. In front of the Hotel Anthoussa
   (for Platis Gialos, Faros)
3. Opposite the Hotel Anthoussa
   (for Artemonas, Kato Petali & Kastro)

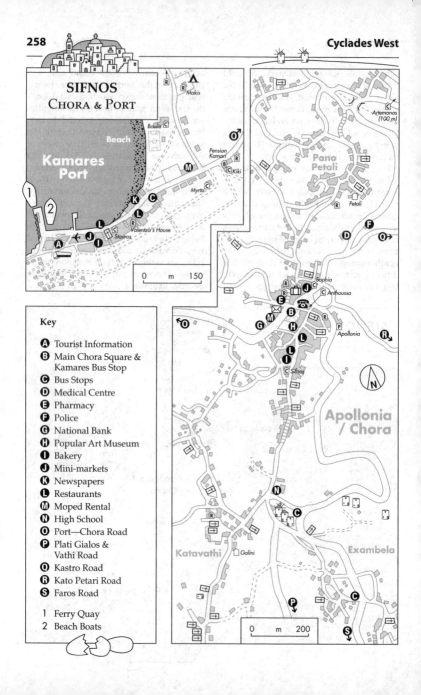

SIFNOS
CHORA & PORT

Makis

Boulis

Beach

Kamares Port

Pension Kamari

Kiki

Myrto

M

K C

L

Valentza's House

Stavros

A J I

1
2

Artemonas (100 m)

Pano Petali

Petali

F

D Q

Sophia

Anthoussa

E

G M B H

L

I

Apollonia

P

R

N

Apollonia / Chora

Katavathi

Galini

C Sifnos

N

C

Exambela

P

C

S

0   m   150

0   m   200

Key

A Tourist Information
B Main Chora Square & Kamares Bus Stop
C Bus Stops
D Medical Centre
E Pharmacy
F Police
G National Bank
H Popular Art Museum
I Bakery
J Mini-markets
K Newspapers
L Restaurants
M Moped Rental
N High School
O Port—Chora Road
P Plati Gialos & Vathi Road
Q Kastro Road
R Kato Petari Road
S Faros Road

1 Ferry Quay
2 Beach Boats

downbeat sort of way. Both offer excellent views of the comparatively isolated east coast former capital of Kastro, which is just within walking distance if you are not tempted by the bus.

The string of beaches along the south coast are the island's other great attraction. Of these, the best is at taverna-backed **Vathi** and is now visited by a new road and buses. A dirt track also runs from Vathi to the south-coast beach resort at **Platis Gialos**. A line of tavernas, rooms and the odd hotel strung along the foreshore, it is the main beach and resort on Sifnos. Its main weak point is the lack of serious shopping facilities and services. Further east lies the less popular small village of **Faros**, complete with three small beaches.

😲

According to Herodotus the population of Sifnos were the wealthiest in the Greek islands in the pre-Classical period, thanks to the gold and silver mines. The islanders fought alongside Athens at Salamis, continuing in reasonable prosperity until the Byzantine era when pirate attacks took their toll. Sifnos was incorporated into the Duchy of Naxos in the 13 c., later coming under control of the despotic Da Coronia in 1307. Pirate attacks continued until the island's capture by the Turk Barbarossa. Briefly under Russian control between 1770–74, Sifnos joined Greece in 1821.

🛏

Good tourist offices on the port waterfront and Apollonia main square are of major help finding accommodation. There are four hotels in **Apollonia**, and all are C-class. Nearest the town square is the *Anthoussa* (☎ 31431), with the *Sophia* (☎ 31238) tucked away in a nearby street. Quieter than both is the *Sifnos* (☎ 31624) away to the south. The *Artemonas* (☎ 31303), 1 km to the north-east, is nice, but inconveniently placed. There is also a pension in town — the *Apollonia* (☎ 31490).

Kamares has accommodation in the form of the C-class *Stavros* (☎ 31641), the *Myrto* (☎ 32055), *Kiki* (☎ 32329), *Boulis* (☎ 321 22), and the B-class pension *Kamari* (☎ 31710). There are also rooms — including half-a-dozen establishments on the north side of the bay (not shown on the map opposite): these will

appeal to worshippers of Aphrodite as they will have to undertake romantic moonlit walks along the length of the beach when their partner needs feeding and watering.

Other settlements also have a scatter of hotels: **Faros** has the D-class *Sifneiko Archontiko* (☎ 31822) along with the expensive B-class *Blue Horizon* (☎ 31442), and **Platis Gialos** the B-class *Platys Gialos* (☎ 31324) and the D-class *Filoxenia* (☎ 322212).

A

Kamares has a friendly site — *Camping Makis* (☎ 32366): very small, but with new washing facilities. Late arrivals in July/August are sometimes turned away. *Camping Plati Gialos* (☎ 31786) is a remote — and usually empty — site tucked 1 km behind the resort.

👀

The most popular sight is the small **Chrisopigi Monastery** sited on a small islet (linked to Sifnos by a causeway) lying west of Faros. Equally photogenic is the former capital at **Kastro**. Largely built between the 14–19 c., it is now an impeccably kept little village that has retained most of its medieval character and shouldn't be missed. Not least among its sights are the old whitewashed houses complete with brightly painted wooden huts on their balconies: a Greek variation of the outside privy. Best of all is the unspoilt atmosphere, though tourists are arriving in some numbers. Of the other villages around Apollonia, Venetian-built **Artemonas** is the most attractive, with the Kohi church built on the foundations of a Temple of Artemis.

Sikinos

ΣΙΚΙΝΟΣ; 41 km²; pop. 330.

CODE ☎ 22860
POLICE ☎ 51222
FIRST AID ☎ 51211

If you want to experience an 'unspoilt' Greek island you can't pick much better than Sikinos. A hilly gem close to Ios, it is only in recent years that a ferry quay, roads and a hotel have appeared, changing the scruffy beach port bay but otherwise unaltering the working island atmosphere. After Anafi, Sikinos is the least touristed large island in the Cyclades, and offers a unique insight as to what Ios and other popular islands

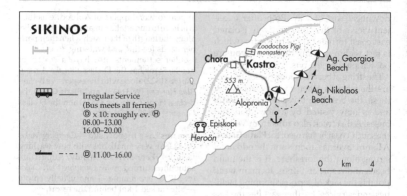

SIKINOS

Zoodochos Pigi monastery
Chora □ **Kastro**
Ag. Georgios Beach
553 m.
Ag. Nikolaos Beach
Alopronia (A)
ⴲⴲ Episkopi
Heroön

—— Irregular Service
(Bus meets all ferries)
Ⓓ x 10: roughly ev. Ⓗ
08.00–13.00
16.00–20.00

— - - - Ⓓ 11.00–16.00

0   km   4

were like in pre-tourist days. Apart from a restaurant in both village and port, there are few concessions to tourism, and much of the island's attractiveness stems from the fact that the donkeys constantly processing through the only town are carrying water rather than tourists. Another plus is the hospitality of the islanders, who have the unusual distinction of being of Cretan stock (their ancestors repopulated the island in the 16 c.).

Sikinos is visited via Cyclades East and occasional Cyclades Central ferries which call at the tiny bay port of Alopronia, home to summer caïques (running to several good south coast beaches) and buses to Kastro/Chora, a settlement consisting of two closely sited villages. Climbing up the spines of opposing hillsides, they are delightful, picturesque examples of their kind. **Kastro** is the larger and its lower quarter is now the de facto 'town' centre. Shrunken **Chora** is a suburb, with a trail of ruined houses and mills running up the hillside behind.

Sikinos was once called 'Oinoe' (wine) thanks to the vines that grew here. Like its neighbours it joined the Delian League in the 4 c. BC. Never really large enough to maintain its own security, Sikinos suffered from repeated pirate attacks until it came into the hands of the Spanish Da Coronia family in 1307. In 1467

control of Sikinos passed to the Gozadinis, an Italian Frankish family, who renamed the island 'Syrandros'. The Turks captured the island in 1617, it was briefly held by the Russians between 1771–74, and it finally joined Greece in 1829.

⊨

A reasonable supply of rooms scattered around the port is augmented by a small number in Kastro/Chora. Few in the latter have signs: owners meet boats instead. The only hotel, *Porto Sikinos* (☎ 51220), is newish and pricey: rooms start at €45.

൦൦

Kastro/Chora aside, the only sights on Sikinos are two unusual defunct (and locked up) monasteries. The closest is **Zoodochos Pigi**, overlooking the main town. Once fortified, it gives Kastro its name. Those negotiating the steep path up to it are rewarded with superb views.

More ambitious sightseers have the option of making the scenic and windswept walk across the island (via the new road) to **Episkopi**, a delightfully adapted Roman templet now masquerading as a monastery. Originally thought to be a Hellenistic temple to Hera (hence Heroön), it is now deemed more likely to have been a 3 c. AD mausoleum. It is the only surviving remnant of the ancient centre of the island which was here rather than at Kastro. Virtually intact, it was converted into a monastery in 1673, after being damaged in an earthquake. There are said to be the remains of a second ancient sanctuary on the north-east tip of the island.

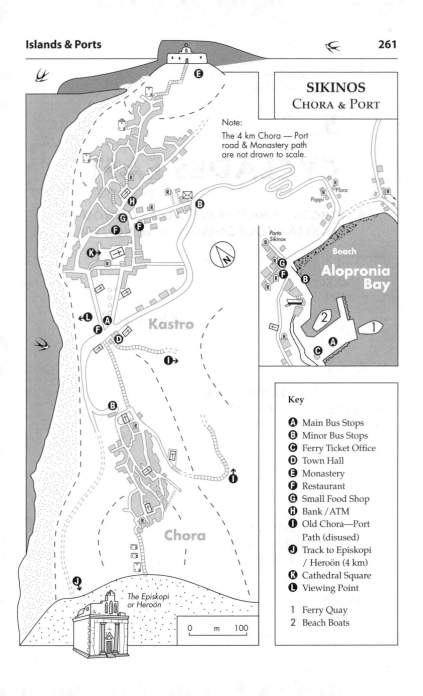

SIKINOS
CHORA & PORT

Note:

The 4 km Chora — Port road & Monastery path are not drawn to scale.

Flora

Poppi

Porto Sikinos

Beach

Alopronia Bay

Kastro

N

Chora

The Episkopi or Heroön

0   m   100

Key

Ⓐ Main Bus Stops
Ⓑ Minor Bus Stops
Ⓒ Ferry Ticket Office
Ⓓ Town Hall
Ⓔ Monastery
Ⓕ Restaurant
Ⓖ Small Food Shop
Ⓗ Bank / ATM
Ⓘ Old Chora—Port Path (disused)
Ⓙ Track to Episkopi / Heroön (4 km)
Ⓚ Cathedral Square
Ⓛ Viewing Point

1 Ferry Quay
2 Beach Boats

5
CYCLADES EAST

AMORGOS · ANAFI · ASTIPALEA · DONOUSSA
IRAKLIA · KOUFONISSIA · SCHINOUSSA

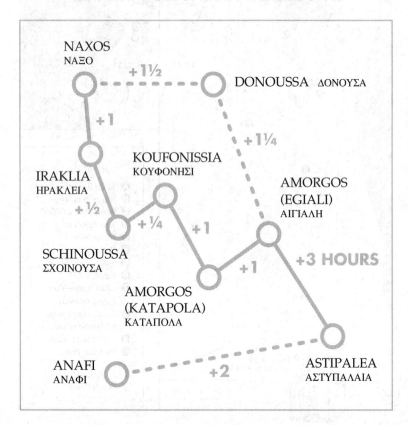

NAXOS
ΝΑΞΟ

+1½

DONOUSSA ΔΟΝΟΥΣΑ

+1

+1¼

KOUFONISSIA
ΚΟΥΦΟΝΗΣΙ

IRAKLIA
ΗΡΑΚΛΕΙΑ

AMORGOS
(EGIALI)
ΑΙΓΙΑΛΗ

+½

+¼

+1

SCHINOUSSA
ΣΧΟΙΝΟΥΣΑ

+1

+3 HOURS

AMORGOS
(KATAPOLA)
ΚΑΤΑΠΟΛΑ

ANAFI
ΑΝΑΦΙ

+2

ASTIPALEA
ΑΣΤΥΠΑΛΑΙΑ

General Features

In the centre of the Aegean lie a number of islands that do not fall easily into chapters organised by ferry routes. Rather than distort the reader's perception of those routes by describing them elsewhere, these islands are gathered together here. All are relatively untouristed (though this is slowly changing): the last redoubt of the pre-tourist era, and all the better for it. The fact that they are untainted by mass tourism is their great charm: in many ways these are the *real* Greek islands!

The best known (and most accessible) is scenic Amorgos. It lies at the end of the line for most ferries that call — as does quiet Anafi to the south. To the east lies Astipalea, administratively one of the Dodecanese,

but more characteristic in appearance of the Cyclades and usually served by ferries visiting the other islands in this chapter (hence its inclusion here).

The minor Cycladic islands running south-east of Naxos to Amorgos make up the balance of this chapter. Variously known as the 'little', 'lesser', 'minor', or 'small' Cyclades, they are all little gems. Only four are inhabited (Iraklia, Koufonissia, Schinoussa and relatively isolated Donoussa), and all are small enough to make you feel as if you really are on an island, since it is almost impossible not to lose sight of the sea. These islands are a true delight — if you can live without banks and discos. All have small, friendly populations that subsist on fishing.

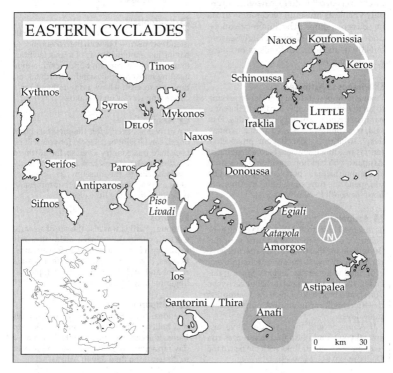

EASTERN CYCLADES

Example Itinerary [2/3 Weeks]

This chapter covers two islands — Amorgos and Astipalea — widely hailed as amongst the most attractive and unspoilt in the Aegean. Lying off the main ferry routes, they are passed over as impracticable by most island hoppers restricted to a fortnight's travelling. Yet, in fact they can easily be incorporated into a tight timetable. The trick is to tackle them as primary objectives. By visiting them first you can build them into a wider-ranging island-hopping holiday, and as Amorgos was a major centre of the Early Cycladic culture, the itinerary below takes in other islands similarly blessed. However, don't expect to find idols standing on every hilltop; they rarely exceeded 30–40 cm in height and are only visible as museum pieces and copies in souvenir shops. The itinerary can be undertaken in two weeks in High Season; outside it, abandon Koufonissia or take a leisurely three.

1 Piraeus to Astipalea

Piraeus is the best starting point when seeking to get to Astipalea simply because of the comparative frequency of ferry connections. That said, you could still be faced with a two-day delay awaiting a boat. If your prospective ferry is heading elsewhere before arriving at Astipalea you can hop ahead and pick it up at the intermediate port. Alternatively, you can spend the time sightseeing in Athens or hopping south to nearby Aegina.

2 Astipalea

Your length of stay on Astipalea is going to be delimited by the paucity of a means of escape. Beyond saying that the overall pattern of ferry connections remains the same each summer it is difficult to generalize as ferry times at this end-of-the-line island tend to change each year. You should be able to plan on the assumption that a ferry will be running to Amorgos within three days.

If Amorgos and the Cyclades have less appeal you should also find that ferries run to Kalimnos (with its links with the rest of the Dodecanese) twice a week.

3 Amorgos (Egiali)

The great majority of visitors to Amorgos head for Katapola, but if you didn't encounter a long delay at Athens, those who like quiet island ports should find themselves with plenty of time to stop off at Egiali first. When you are ready to move on you can take either a bus or ferry on to Katapola.

4 Amorgos (Katapola)

Once at Katapola you are effectively plugged back into the ferry mainstream. With daily boats to Naxos you are within easy striking distance of the Cyclades Central Line. Katapola is also the best jumping off point for the Little Cyclades and Koufonissia, but if the *Express Skopelitis* isn't running daily, you should allow for the possibility of being stranded on the beach a day longer than intended, either here or on Koufonissia.

5 Koufonissia

Koufonissia offers a fair degree of small island escapism — but with the reassurance of having just enough by way of tourist facilities to hand. Even if you can't find a caïque-tour heading for Keros, the island is worth taking time out to visit. Allow a day in hand for a connecting service on to Naxos.

6 Naxos

An arrival at Naxos after the previous ports of call can be a bit of a shock, for you will be back in tourist country. Even so, the northern coast of the town was host to a major Early Cycladic village, the museum has a clutch of idols, and a souvenir shop near the promenade is devoted to selling little else.

7 Paros

Although Parikia was also the site of an early Cycladic village the main reason to call now is to pick up a ferry or tour boat on to Antiparos. Besides, if you have found the other islands restful and idyllic you won't be tempted to linger for long here anyway.

8 Antiparos

The ideal place to while away the last days of a holiday, Antiparos is quiet, yet close to Paros. It is easy to lounge on the beach for a day, nip across to Parikia and take a night boat to Piraeus for a final day in Athens.

EASTERN CYCLADES

Base Port: Naxos

Not the best collection of islands for springboard island hopping. **Naxos** offers the greatest number of possibilities with easy hops to Paros and Antiparos as well as tour boats to the Little Cyclades and Koufonissia. Links with Amorgos (Katapola) are daily in High Season and thrice weekly for most of the remainder of the year.

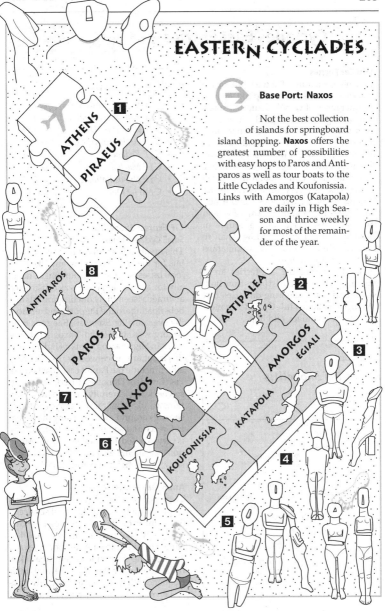

Cyclades East Ferries

Main Car Ferries

The isolated nature of the islands in the Eastern Cyclades has conspired against the emergence of vessels dedicated solely to providing services to this chain. Instead, boats that normally run elsewhere take time out to make an extended run that includes various islands in the group. This means that services and boats change quite a lot each year, though the overall pattern changes very little, with ferries running from the Cyclades Central and North lines running on to Amorgos (and sometimes Astipalea), and a couple of Cyclades Central boats adding Anafi to their schedules. Occasional catamarans also venture to Amorgos.

Complementing the car ferries are a growing number of tourist boats from both Naxos and Paros. Offering day trips that take in two or more Little Cyclades islands, they can be useful for odd hops.

See also:
- C/F *Express Santorini*   p. 130
- C/F *Panagia Ekatonta*.   p. 131
- C/F *Blue Star Naxos*   p. 129
- C/F *Aeolos Express II*   p. 188
- C/F *Rodanthi*   p. 326
- C/F *Marina*   p. 326
- C/F *Nissos Kalimnos*   p. 327
- C/M *Jet One*   p. 132

C/F *Express Skopelitis*
Small Cyclades Lines; 1998.

This invaluable small car ferry is the local bus for the Little Cyclades, and like most local buses is apt to fill to bursting. Unusually for a Greek ferry she was constructed at Piraeus (seemingly out of spare bits and bobs floating around the port), and replaced the even smaller *Skopelitis*. She runs from Amorgos (Katapola) to Naxos six days a week in High Season. Out of High Season, this is cut to a twice-weekly run. Her runs either include the Parian east-coast port of Piso Livadi or Donoussa (the days do vary, so check this carefully). On-board conditions are okay, but this isn't saying a lot, as she rolls around more than any other boat in Greece and some of her outside seating is very exposed. If Katapola is your destination you should also note that this boat is slow, rarely arriving before 22.00.

Anafi Mail Boats

Two caïques — the *Alkyon* and *Ag. Nikolaos* — provide a twice-weekly mail service to Santorini on the days that ferries don't call. They only take passengers from Anafi to Santorini (times from Anafi port's Jeyzed Travel). The downside is the time taken (two hours to a ferry's one) and their frequency (they don't run on windy days — i.e. most days in July and August).

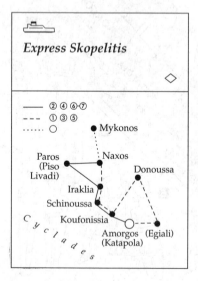

Cyclades East Islands & Ports

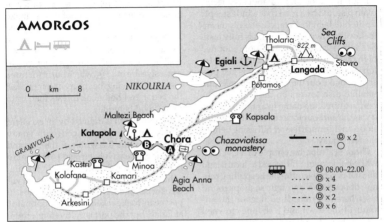

Amorgos
ΑΜΟΡΓΟΣ; 117 km²; pop. 1,720.

CODE ☎ 22850
PORT POLICE ☎ 71259
POLICE ☎ 71210
FIRST AID ☎ 71208

The most easterly of the Cyclades, Amorgos has been one of the least touristed of the large Aegean islands. This is rapidly changing as its reputation grows, for Amorgos *should* be on the itinerary of any Cycladic island hopper. It is rugged, mountainous, often battered by choppy seas, and at first sight more intimidating than many other islands. But once ashore, it turns out to be very friendly and charmingly unspoilt.

The 'Amorgos' experience is dominated by the island's mountainous terrain. One consequence of this is that the road system has been very poor, the two main settlements at each end of the island only recently being connected by a good road and regular bus. As a result, ferries call at both centres (ticket agents habitually use the port names in lieu of 'Amorgos' on

timetables), and even the islanders tend to think of their end as a separate entity to the other half.

Katapola, the principal port, lies on the more populous western half of Amorgos. Tucked into a suitably scenic and well protected bay on the north coast, it is rapidly acquiring all the trappings of a mini resort (including one of the best pizzerias in the Cyclades and a patisserie). It also offers the best facilities on the island, though this isn't saying a great deal in some respects: shopping — as elsewhere on Amorgos — is rather limited. The port beach, backed by a narrow raised promenade, is more for show than lying on (such surf as there is looks curiously soapy), and a regular taxi boat chugs across the bay to a much better beach behind the eastern headland.

Katapola is sufficiently spread out to have three centres of activity. The largest is on the ferry quay side, which contains the nucleus of tourist facilities and a waterfront lined with tavernas; the second is the hill behind the bay beach, which is dominated by a large church, with islanders' housing clustered around it; while the far side of the bay is home to a growing number of tourist apartments.

Fanning out behind Katapola is a fertile plain bisected by a road that winds steeply up the hills behind. Katapola literally means 'below the town', a name that is fully justified as the island's capital at Chora is located high on the cloud-clad hillside behind (as ferries steam toward the bay it is just possible to make out the Chora windmills and satellite dish towers on the skyline). The port acquired the name in antiquity when it was the harbour for ancient Minoa which stood on the much nearer hill rising behind the ferry quay.

Chora is a superb example of a Cycladic white-cubic town. Still geared to local island life, it has yet to acquire the bespoiling retinue of boutiques and tourist shops found elsewhere. The ruined buildings on the outskirts of the town and a skyline crowned with derelict windmills (for some unclear reason each extended family on Amorgos had to have its own mill) add greatly to the unspoilt character of the place. This is enhanced further by delightful small tree-filled squares and melting ice-cream-style churches that in turn generate a cosmopolitan touch via the odd artist sketching in dreamland.

The main street (inaccessible to vehicles) winds up the floor of the shallow valley in which the town lies, arriving at the windy top of the southern cliffs of the island. Here there is a viewing point (under one of the town's two satellite dish towers) and the top of the staircase that winds down to both the main tourist attractions on Amorgos: the monastery of Chozoviotissa and the road to the island's most popular beach — at **Agia Anna** — a tiny pebble affair known for nudism (both can also be reached by bus). To the north looms Mt. Profitis Ilias which, even in summer, is usually accompanied by a playful cloud chasing its tail around the upper slopes. This intimidating spectacle sets the tone for the wild mountain hinterland that is little frequented by tourists thanks to the paucity of bus services.

Egiali, the island's second port, is significantly smaller than Katapola, and feels much newer, with more of a quiet beach resort atmosphere. In fact the scatter of holiday apartments and hotels that make up much of the settlement running up the hill behind the ferry quay are built on the remains of an ancient city. Sadly, nothing is visible, and all later buildings went west in a massive fire in 1835, which burnt for three weeks, destroying the entire settlement and the cedar and holly-oak forests that, until then, stood behind it.

Modern Egiali is defined by an excellent family sand beach (fringed with shady trees) that runs the width of the bay and the wide, intensively farmed plain behind it. Embracing both port and plain is a ring of hills topped with attractive, unspoilt villages at **Langada**, **Tholaria** and **Potamos**. In past years backpackers have predominated at Egiali, but the port is cultivating a more up-market image with the first package-tour operators starting to move in, and an increasing number of beach-bound day trippers from Chora and Katapola using the island bus service (the first and last buses running the length of the island are thus rather crowded in High Season).

Amorgos was a sufficiently important island in antiquity that it could boast three cities (all sited along the northern coast) at Minoa, Egiali and Arkesini (at Kastri). None, however, really made much of an impact on the course of history, and Amorgos was best known by the Roman era as one of the 'gentler' islands of exile. Amorgos was pillaged extensively from the 7 c. on by pirates, with the centres of population moving away from the coast to places such as Chora. During the 9 c. Byzantine control was re-established, and held sway until 1207 when the Venetian Ghizi family took the island, maintaining a perilous hold on power until 1446 when the ruling house on Astipalea — the Quirini family — gained control. Amorgos fell to the Turk Khayr-ad-Din Barbarossa in 1537, becoming an unstable pirate-ridden island thereafter. It broke away from Turkish rule in 1822 and joined the new Greek state shortly after.

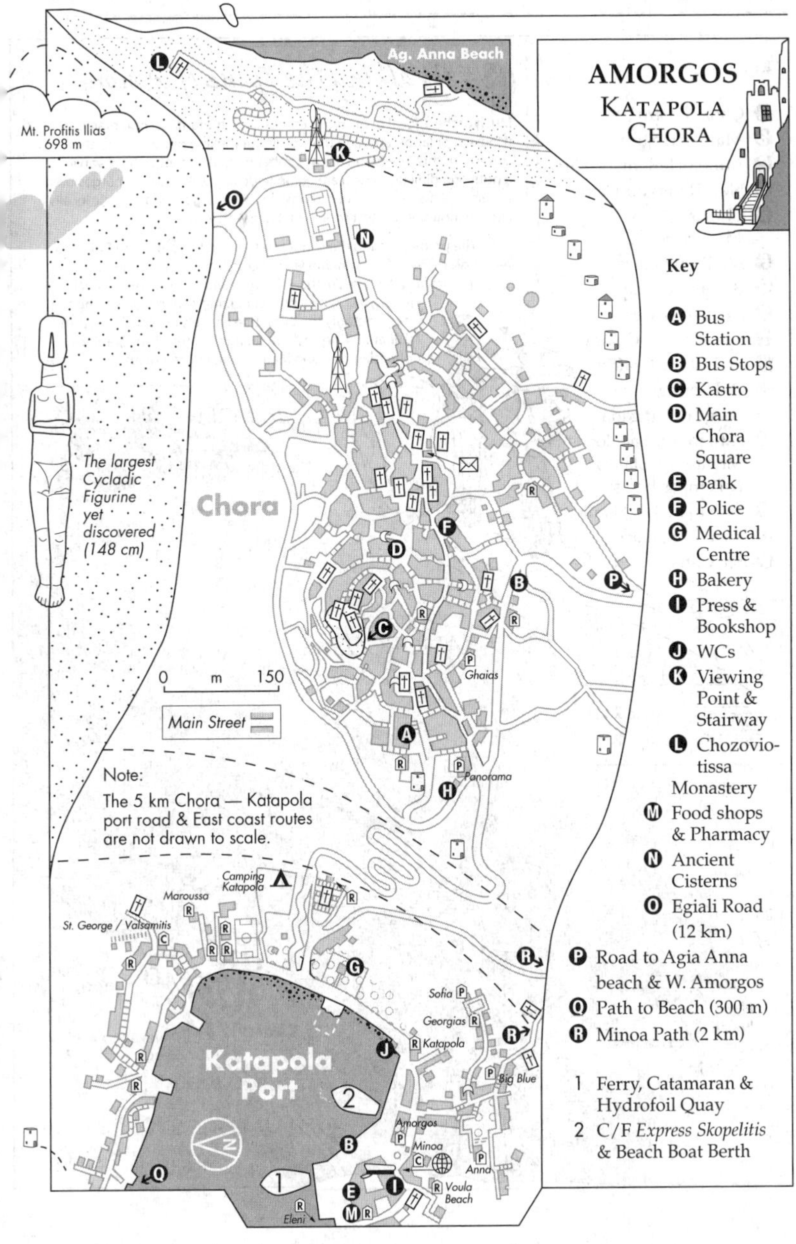

AMORGOS
KATAPOLA
CHORA

Mt. Profitis Ilias
698 m

The largest Cycladic Figurine yet discovered (148 cm)

Chora

0   m   150

Main Street

Note:
The 5 km Chora — Katapola port road & East coast routes are not drawn to scale.

Ag. Anna Beach

Ghaias

Panorama

Camping Katapola

Maroussa

St. George / Valsamitis

Katapola Port

Sofia

Georgias

Katapola

Big Blue

Amorgos

Minoa

Anna

Voula Beach

Eleni

Key

Ⓐ Bus Station
Ⓑ Bus Stops
Ⓒ Kastro
Ⓓ Main Chora Square
Ⓔ Bank
Ⓕ Police
Ⓖ Medical Centre
Ⓗ Bakery
Ⓘ Press & Bookshop
Ⓙ WCs
Ⓚ Viewing Point & Stairway
Ⓛ Chozovio-tissa Monastery
Ⓜ Food shops & Pharmacy
Ⓝ Ancient Cisterns
Ⓞ Egiali Road (12 km)
Ⓟ Road to Agia Anna beach & W. Amorgos
Ⓠ Path to Beach (300 m)
Ⓡ Minoa Path (2 km)

1 Ferry, Catamaran & Hydrofoil Quay
2 C/F *Express Skopelitis* & Beach Boat Berth

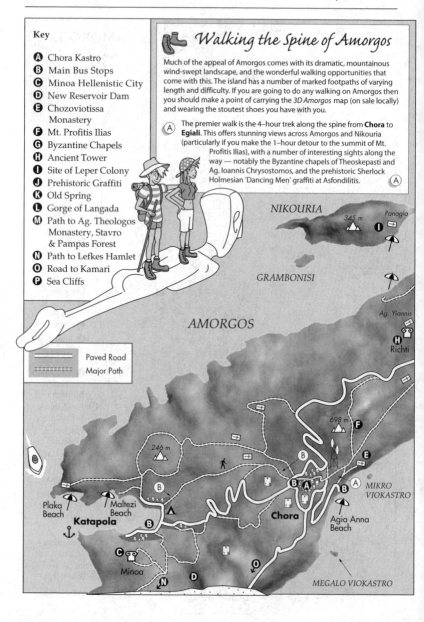

Key

Ⓐ Chora Kastro
Ⓑ Main Bus Stops
Ⓒ Minoa Hellenistic City
Ⓓ New Reservoir Dam
Ⓔ Chozoviotissa Monastery
Ⓕ Mt. Profitis Ilias
Ⓖ Byzantine Chapels
Ⓗ Ancient Tower
Ⓘ Site of Leper Colony
Ⓙ Prehistoric Graffiti
Ⓚ Old Spring
Ⓛ Gorge of Langada
Ⓜ Path to Ag. Theologos Monastery, Stavro & Pampas Forest
Ⓝ Path to Lefkes Hamlet
Ⓞ Road to Kamari
Ⓟ Sea Cliffs

Walking the Spine of Amorgos

Much of the appeal of Amorgos comes with its dramatic, mountainous wind-swept landscape, and the wonderful walking opportunities that come with this. The island has a number of marked footpaths of varying length and difficulty. If you are going to do any walking on Amorgos then you should make a point of carrying the *3D Amorgos* map (on sale locally) and wearing the stoutest shoes you have with you.

Ⓐ The premier walk is the 4–hour trek along the spine from **Chora** to **Egiali**. This offers stunning views across Amorgos and Nikouria (particularly if you make the 1–hour detour to the summit of Mt. Profitis Ilias), with a number of interesting sights along the way — notably the Byzantine chapels of Theoskepasti and Ag. Ioannis Chrysostomos, and the prehistoric Sherlock Holmesian 'Dancing Men' graffiti at Asfondilitis. Ⓐ

NIKOURIA
Panagia
345 m
Ⓘ

GRAMBONISI

Ag. Yiannis

AMORGOS

Paved Road
Major Path

Ⓗ
Richti

698 m Ⓕ

Ⓔ

246 m

Ⓐ
MIKRO
VIOKASTRO

Plaka Beach
Maltezi Beach

Katapola

Chora
Agia Anna Beach

Ⓒ
Minoa

Ⓝ   Ⓓ

MEGALO VIOKASTRO

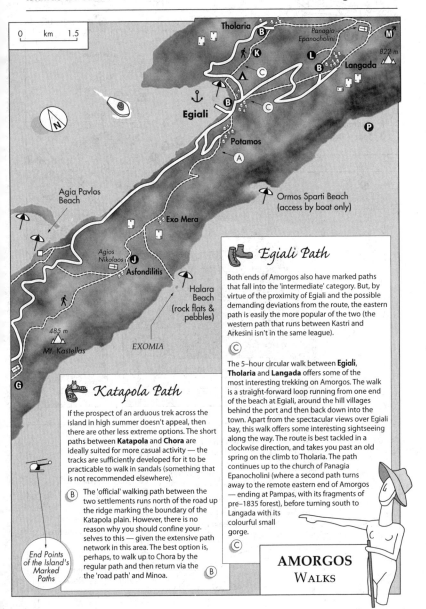

0   km   1.5

Tholaria

Panagia
Epanocholini

822 m

Langada

Egiali

Potamos

Ormos Sparti Beach
(access by boat only)

Agia Pavlos
Beach

Exo Mera

Agios
Nikolaos
Asfondilitis

Halara
Beach
(rock flats &
pebbles)

485 m
Mt. Kastellas

EXOMIA

End Points
of the Island's
Marked
Paths

👢 Egiali Path

Both ends of Amorgos also have marked paths
that fall into the 'intermediate' category. But, by
virtue of the proximity of Egiali and the possible
demanding deviations from the route, the eastern
path is easily the more popular of the two (the
western path that runs between Kastri and
Arkesini isn't in the same league).

Ⓒ

The 5-hour circular walk between **Egiali**,
Tholaria and **Langada** offers some of the
most interesting trekking on Amorgos. The walk
is a straight-forward loop running from one end
of the beach at Egiali, around the hill villages
behind the port and then back down into the
town. Apart from the spectacular views over Egiali
bay, this walk offers some interesting sightseeing
along the way. The route is best tackled in a
clockwise direction, and takes you past an old
spring on the climb to Tholaria. The path
continues up to the church of Panagia
Epanocholini (where a second path turns
away to the remote eastern end of Amorgos
— ending at Pampas, with its fragments of
pre-1835 forest), before turning south to
Langada with its
colourful small
gorge.

Ⓒ

🐢 Katapola Path

If the prospect of an arduous trek across the
island in high summer doesn't appeal, then
there are other less extreme options. The short
paths between **Katapola** and **Chora** are
ideally suited for more casual activity — the
tracks are sufficiently developed for it to be
practicable to walk in sandals (something that
is not recommended elsewhere).

Ⓑ The 'official' walking path between the
two settlements runs north of the road up
the ridge marking the boundary of the
Katapola plain. However, there is no
reason why you should confine your-
selves to this — given the extensive path
network in this area. The best option is,
perhaps, to walk up to Chora by the
regular path and then return via the
the 'road path' and Minoa.   Ⓑ

AMORGOS
WALKS

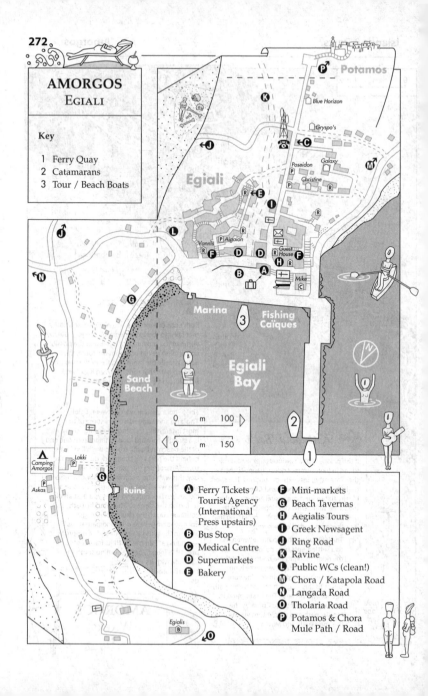

AMORGOS
EGIALI

Key

1 Ferry Quay
2 Catamarans
3 Tour / Beach Boats

Potamos

Blue Horizon

Gryspo's

Galaxy

Poseidon

Christine

Egiali

Guest House

Mike

Vannis Aigaion

Marina

Fishing Caiques

Egiali Bay

Sand Beach

| 0 | m | 100 |
| 0 | m | 150 |

Camping Amorgos

Lakki

Askas

Ruins

Egialis

A Ferry Tickets / Tourist Agency (International Press upstairs)
B Bus Stop
C Medical Centre
D Supermarkets
E Bakery
F Mini-markets
G Beach Tavernas
H Aegialis Tours
I Greek Newsagent
J Ring Road
K Ravine
L Public WCs (clean!)
M Chora / Katapola Road
N Langada Road
O Tholaria Road
P Potamos & Chora Mule Path / Road

⊨

Hotels and rooms fill fast in High Season, though the island doesn't have a reputation for being short of beds: new building is keeping up with demand. **Chora** has a limited number of establishments (often without signs) offering rooms and a couple of pensions, the *Panorama* and the larger *Ghaias* (☎ 71277), but building restrictions aimed at preserving the town have limited the options here. The vast majority of visitors stay at one of the two ports instead.

Katapola has the greater number of beds. The pensions include the *Amorgos* (☎ 71214) and the *Sophia*. In addition, the port has two notable C-class hotels: *St. George/Valsamitis* (☎ 71228), on the far side of the port bay, and the excellent C-class *Minoa* (☎ 71480), which also houses the island's internet cafe.

Egiali has a wider mix of accommodation that includes the B-class hotel *Egialis* (☎ 73393), with its panoramic views, and C-class *Mike* (☎ 73208). The village is overlooked by the good, but pricey *Poseidon Rooms* (☎ 73452).

Λ

Both ports have sites offering plenty of shade. At **Katapola** is *Camping Katapola* (☎ 71257): inexpensive, and reasonable out of High Season, it gets crowded in August. Popular with French school groups, it can sometimes feel like a playground during a fire drill. Washing facilities are a bit on the primitive side and would benefit from more frequent cleaning.

Egiali has *Camping Amorgos* (☎ 73333): a cheaper and much quieter site complete with a mini-bus that meets ferries arriving at Katapola (this is one way to get a free bus ride the length of the island).

👀

The island sight is the spectacularly impressive **Chozoviotissa Monastery** (1088 AD), complete with a miraculous icon of the Virgin (open ⊗ 08.00–13.00). Plastered into the side of a cliff 300 m above sea level, it is eight storeys high with rooms only 5 m wide at best, and largely carved out of the cliff-face. It justifies adding Amorgos to any itinerary. As is usual with religious sites, 'formal' clothing must be worn by all visitors (no shorts or bikinis). If you suffer from claustrophobia you might find the labyrinth of small rooms and narrow staircases less than appealing.

Chora itself is more scenic than sight-filled. The best it has to offer is the finger of rock poking up from the whitewashed buildings:

this is home to an unimpressive wall of a tiny 13 c. Venetian **Kastro**. Sadly, there is no museum, so major finds — such as the largest **Cycladic Idol** yet discovered (it is almost life size and was unearthed at **Kapsala**) — are now in the National Archaeological Museum in Athens.

Minoa, the ancient city overlooking Katapola port, offers another worthy excursion. The site is predominantly on the landward side of the 290 m high hill, and is reached via an old mule path, then unmade road running up from the back of Katapola. The city took its name from a rock hole near the summit which local tradition said was the tomb of King Minos. The remains have only been partially excavated, so there isn't a vast amount to see beyond jumbled foundations. However, don't let this put you off: the site is free and has good explanatory notices at the entrance, detailing the layout (both ascertained and — in the case of the theatre — conjectured). Best of all are the stunning views of Katapola and Chora: if you don't attempt any other walks on Amorgos, it is worthwhile making this short one.

Beach boat excursions are another attraction: regular boats leave for neighbouring islets, notably the good beach on the ex-leper colony islet of **Nikouria** (Egiali boats visit) and the beach islet of **Gramvousa** (occasional Katapola boats visit).

Anafi
ΑΝΑΦΙ; 38 km²; pop. 340.

CODE ☎ 22860
POLICE ☎ 61216
TOURIST OFFICE ☎ 61253
MEDICAL CENTRE ☎ 61215

Only one hour's sailing east of Santorini, at first sight it seems something of a paradox that Anafi is one of the least accessible islands in the Aegean: so much so, that 'Anafi' is the Greek equivilent of 'Timbuktu'. Myth has it that the island sprang up out of the sea by order of Apollo when the legendary Argonauts, sailing north from Crete, were overwhelmed by a 'pall of darkness' and found themselves in desperate need of a sanctuary. Their plight must have been pretty desperate as Anafi lacks most of the basics; apparently the Argonauts didn't need water as the island isn't furnished with a spring. Covered by a 25 m thick blanket

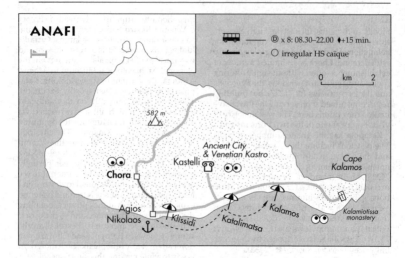

ANAFI

🚌 —— Ⓓ x 8: 08.30–22.00 ⬥+15 min.
⚓ - - - - ⭕ irregular HS caïque

0   km   2

582 m
△△

Ancient City
& Venetian Kastro
Kastelli 👁👁   Cape
Chora □   Kalamos

Agios
Nikolaos ⚓   Klissidi   Katalimatsa   Kalamos 👁👁   Kalamiotissa
                                                      monastery

of pumice from the c. 1470 BC eruption of Santorini (it has been suggested that this incident in the *Argonautica* reflects a vague folk memory of it), Anafi has never been a prosperous place.

Those who are washed up on Anafi's mountainous shores will find a barren island that — approached from the south — looks like a double-humped mountain top sticking out of the sea (NB. the 'Enter' page on this book's web site is decorated with a basic 3D model of it), but for all its stark barrenness the 'living on the edge of the world' atmosphere is superb. So much so, that Anafi is attracting increasing numbers of visitors drawn to the laid-back isolation and a succession of sandy, crowd-free beaches.

This is one island that really is worth a visit, but like many of the smaller islands medical facilities are very limited. Any serious problems require an air ambulance lift to either Rhodes or the mainland. This resulted in the death of a patient in June 2002 when the air ambulance helicopter crashed at night into one of the island's steep hillsides shortly after taking off, killing all on board.

The only settlement on Anafi is a photogenic hilltop chora overlooking a diminutive cliff-backed port. Anafi's **Chora** can lay claim to be one of the last truly unspoilt Cycladic choras, and is a pretty place in a downbeat sort of way, with Santorini-style anti-earthquake barrel-roofed houses and exterior baking ovens. The government has recently slapped a building restriction order on the village to protect it from growing tourist development pressures, for as word has spread about the delights of Anafi, so have the number of new buildings dedicated to tourist accommodation around the chora's fringes.

This is quite important, for the chora is almost all fringes: although its setting is little short of majestic, it lacks an obvious centre of focus; the hilltop at its heart is missing its all-important kastro (now long since lost) — though it offers superb views over the town. Instead, the main centres are the bus squares at each end of the chora: the eastern sees more activity, while the western is a quiet picture-postcard affair.

To date there is no bank (though this must surely be rectified sooner rather than later), but there are a couple of tiny food-cum-

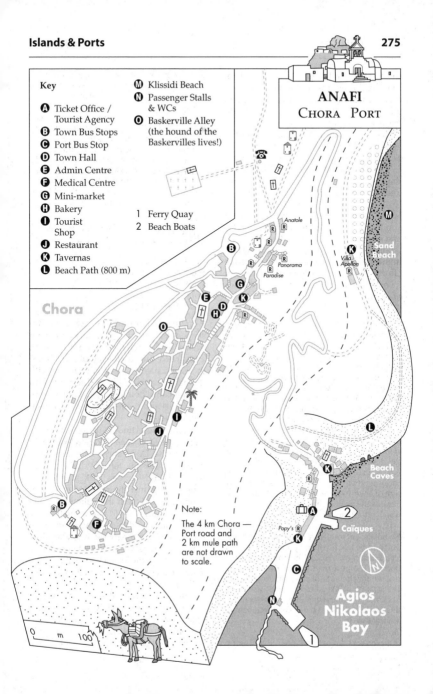

ANAFI
CHORA PORT

Key

- **A** Ticket Office / Tourist Agency
- **B** Town Bus Stops
- **C** Port Bus Stop
- **D** Town Hall
- **E** Admin Centre
- **F** Medical Centre
- **G** Mini-market
- **H** Bakery
- **I** Tourist Shop
- **J** Restaurant
- **K** Tavernas
- **L** Beach Path (800 m)
- **M** Klissidi Beach
- **N** Passenger Stalls & WCs
- **O** Baskerville Alley (the hound of the Baskervilles lives!)

1 Ferry Quay
2 Beach Boats

Chora

Anatole

Panorama

Paradise

Villa Apollon

Sand Beach

Beach Caves

Caïques

Popy's

Note:

The 4 km Chora — Port road and 2 km mule path are not drawn to scale.

Agios Nikolaos Bay

0   m   100

tourist shops and a restaurant. A new 4 km road has brought with it a pint-sized bus that scuttles frequently between the chora and port (the old 1.5 km mule track still exists for energetic traditionalists).

The port of **Agios Nikolaos** is — rather surprisingly given its size — the real hub of Anafi life (such as it is). Everyone seems to pass through at some point during the day and as a result it has several tavernas and a travel agency that acts as a money exchange. A short cliffside-path walk away is attractive tree-backed **Klissidi** beach: in summer it is now quite crowded (the far end seeing the odd nudist). Less crowded strands lie further along the coast at **Katalimatsa** and **Kalamos**. Both are well worth the effort envolved in getting to them, though if you opt to walk the coast path good shoes are a must.

Too impoverished and lacking in resources to ever be a major centre, little is known of Anafi's early history, beyond that deduced from ancient remains at Katalimatsa and Kastro (which suggest a small but well-established community has always managed to live here). Little excavation has been done, and most of the visible remains of note were removed to St. Petersburg by the Russians during their period of control between 1770–74.

Beyond the *Argonautica* Anafi's only other moment of fame came with the movie *Raider's of the Lost Ark* — when the island appears as the destination on the route map where the Ark is finally opened with dramatic results. Sadly, neither mountain cavern, ark, nor any sign of enemy storm-troopers are to be found here, as the nearest the film crew got to Anafi was North Africa.

ᕁ

No hotels, but rooms are on offer at the Chora, port and beach. If you are phoning ahead try *Jeyzed Travel* (☎ 61253) who are based at the port. At the port road end of the **Chora** are two establishments of note offering rooms: *Ta Plagia* (☎ 61308), and *Panorama Rooms* (☎ 61292). If you fancy something more secluded then try *Villa Apollon* (☎ 61237) tucked behind **Klissidi Beach**.

Λ

In past years August has seen anything up to 60+ tents lining the back fringes of Klissidi beach. However, freelance camping has recently been banned on the island.

👓

If you are seeking a genuine unspoilt Greek island Anafi is it. If nightlife is more your thing then the best sight on offer is the ferry arriving to pick you up. The more adventurous will find a ruined **Venetian Kastro** at Kastelli, and a deserted **Kalamiotissa Monastery** (built on the foundations of a **Temple of Apollo** supposedly set up by the Argonauts) atop the hill that dominates the eastern end of the island.

Astipalea

ΑΣΤΥΠΑΛΕΑ; 95 km²; pop. 1,150.

CODE ☎ 22430
PORT POLICE ☎ 61208
TOURIST OFFICE ☎ 61217
POLICE ☎ 61207
FIRST AID ☎ 61222

Administered from Kalimnos, butterfly-shaped Astipalea is technically a member of the Dodecanese group. Yet, in both appearance and frequency of ferry links, the island has far more in common with the neighbouring Eastern Cyclades, with a white-cubist house chora (complete with windmills and castle) and typical barren, arid hillsides.

Even the locals find Astipalea's membership of the Dodecanese somewhat anachronistic (the 'Dodecanese' only came into being in 1908: the term is derived from the '12 islands' under Turkish rule that protested against the removal of special privileges held from the Sultan since the 16 C.). The story is told that when the new Greek state's borders were agreed in 1830 the map used to draw the boundary line was so bad that Astipalea was mistakenly positioned on the Turkish side of the line, losing its status as member of the Cyclades in the process.

Now well on the Greek side of the line — if not back in the Cyclades — Astipalea's relative remoteness, lack of nightlife (there are only three discos!) and reasonable — but not spectacular — beaches have

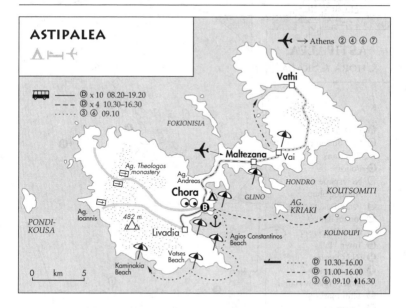

ASTIPALEA

→ Athens ② ④ ⑥ ⑦

Vathi

Ⓓ x 10 08.20–19.20
Ⓓ x 4 10.30–16.30
③ ⑥ 09.10

FOKIONISIA

Maltezana

Vai

Ag. Theologos
monastery

Ag.
Andreas

HONDRO

KOUTSOMITI

Chora

GLINO

AG.
KRIAKI

Ag.
Ioannis

482 m.

Livadia

Agios Constantinos
Beach

KOUNOUPI

PONDI-
KOUSA

Vatses
Beach

0   km   5

Kaminakia
Beach

Ⓓ 10.30–16.00
Ⓓ 11.00–16.00
③ ⑥ 09.10 ♦16.30

all conspired to keep the masses and tour operators requiring reliable and frequent ferry links at bay. All this is now slowly changing; one only has to sail between the folds of Astipalea's wings and see the castle-topped chora for a certain fascination to take hold. The end-of-the-world sense of introspection that pervades is enhanced by the combination of the island's beach-comber scruffiness (there are insufficient tourists to fund municipal cleanups here) and the picturesque litter of islets around the coastline.

Astipalea is a perfect spot to quietly unwind and soak up some Greek island atmosphere, free from crowds, yet in tangibly exotic surroundings. Folks come here to clamber up the hillsides behind the town and drink in the views. Buffeted by the wind (Astipalea is very exposed; so the *meltemi* 'wind tunnel' effect is particularly noticeable here), this is an island which encourages you to feel exhilaratingly alive. Rich, blue sea-filled vistas drenched in a

dreamy bright sunlight worthy of an Alpine ski-slope and all that sort of stuff.

Coming back down to earth, the only settlement of any significance is the main **Chora** and port complex, an odd mix of staircases and new buildings running up to one of Greece's nicer old towns. Finding your way around is not particularly difficult: just keep climbing and sooner or later you arrive at the castle entrance. It offers a shady (and wind-free) retreat in the form of a passage that burrows quaintly under one of the two surviving whitewashed interior churches to the forecourt, and spectacular views of the coastline and beach islets to the south.

Most tourist facilities are to be found fringing the **Port** (an area made up of buildings constructed since WW2), in the saddle-top windmill square above, and strung along the stairways and roads between the two. The popular port beach is lined with tavernas and mini-markets and is the nearest thing you will find to the

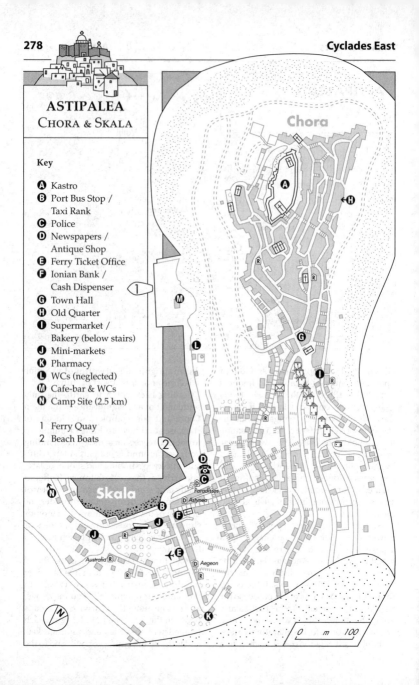

ASTIPALEA
Chora & Skala

Key

- **A** Kastro
- **B** Port Bus Stop / Taxi Rank
- **C** Police
- **D** Newspapers / Antique Shop
- **E** Ferry Ticket Office
- **F** Ionian Bank / Cash Dispenser
- **G** Town Hall
- **H** Old Quarter
- **I** Supermarket / Bakery (below stairs)
- **J** Mini-markets
- **K** Pharmacy
- **L** WCs (neglected)
- **M** Cafe-bar & WCs
- **N** Camp Site (2.5 km)

1   Ferry Quay
2   Beach Boats

centre of town: the chora square is usually too windy for those left standing to want to linger in it for long. Astipalea has a single bank—a waterfront branch of the Commercial (complete with an ATM). The National Bank of Greece has a 'representative' next to the *Aegeon* hotel.

Reliable buses run from both the port and chora squares. The prime destinations are **Livadia** to the west of the port, site of the island's best beach and backed by a fertile valley that gave the island renown in Classical times as a source of market garden produce, and to the east **Maltezana** (also known as **Analipsis**), a former pirate lair noted as the spot where a French commander — Captain Bissiou — died in 1827 by firing his corvette to avoid capture; the closest Astipalea has to a resort beach, the nearest thing you'll see to skulls and cross-bones are paraded by elderly nudists.

The rest of the island lacks decent roads; buses crawl to Astipalea's second port at **Vathi** only twice a week. Blessed with a good beach and set in a deep fjord-like cove, this is a scenic village with a good cave, but it really only comes into its own during the winter months when heavy seas occasionally force ferries to berth here. Hill paths lead to several hilltop monasteries on the island and to a number of narrow tree-filled valleys.

😊

Surprisingly, given its rather remote location, Astipalea was an island of some note in antiquity. It never acquired the status of the major islands such as Kos or Rhodes, but it was a noted centre for agriculture and fishing. Its most famous son was a boxer by the name of Kleomedes. Disqualified for killing his opponent (one Ikkos of Epidavros) at the 71st Olympic games, he returned to Astipalea in disgrace and did a Samson, pulling down the pillars of the island school and killing all the children along with himself (his late opponent obviously got in at least one good head blow).

Astipalea briefly came to prominence as a base for a Roman fleet engaged in anti-piracy operations, before falling into obscurity during

the Byzantine period. Its isolation served it well between 1207 and 1522 when it was ruled by the Venetian Quirini family. Thereafter it was under Turkish rule until 1919, and then Italian until joining the Greek state in 1947.

Room supply is good, with owners meeting the boats and three inexpensive, but reasonable, hotels (all D-class) in the lower part of the town. The best of these — notably the clean but spartan *Paradissos* (☎ 61224) — and the *Astynea* (☎ 61209) are on the waterfront. The *Aegeon* (☎ 61236) lies on the chora road. Rooms are also available in the houses on the north side of the port bay (these have great views of the floodlit Kastro at night) and also in Livadia and Maltezana.

A

Camping Astipalea (☎ 61238): a pleasant and shaded (if isolated) pebble-beach site 2.5 km east of the port. Mini-bus meets ferries.

👀

Astipalea's great attraction is its imposing **Kastro**. Built on the site of the ancient acropolis, it is a 9 c. Byzantine fortification, later rebuilt after a fashion by the Venetians. Never a traditional castle, it thereafter evolved into a medieval apartment-block of sorts during the centuries of piracy that followed.

In its prime it was home to some 4,000 people, its walls containing a labyrinth of staircases and four-storey buildings (if contemporary accounts of it are anything to go by then the island has lost an amazing tourist attraction). This was extant until the 1920s, when the development of the port shifted the axis of settlement away from the chora, prompting partial demolition. An earthquake in 1956 destroyed most of the remaining buildings, leaving the interior little more than a shell, with only the churches and the fragmentary remains of the houses that nestled against the window-choked walls (now a storey lower than in times past) surviving.

Little of pre-medieval Astipalea survives. Odd fragments of buildings are to be found in the Kastro walls and the island has yielded up a number of important inscriptions. The most unusual remains are found at Maltezana (or to be more accurate — on the fringes of a reed bed, a couple of fields past the small Analipsis quay), where well-preserved **Zodiac Mosaics** from the 5 c. AD **Talaras Bathhouse** are on view.

Donoussa

ΔΟΝΟΥΣΣΑ; 13 km²; pop. 100.

CODE ☎ 22850

Rising steeply out of the sea east of Naxos, isolated Donoussa is the second largest and least visited of the Little Cyclades. Tucked behind the untouristed east coast of Naxos, it lies too far north to be a convenient stop for ferries serving the other islands in the group, though the island is served well enough in High Season.

Once ashore, you will find that Donoussa is a tranquil, friendly place that has a growing reputation among those looking to 'enjoy' a tranquil week or two in a largely unspoilt Greek island community. For good measure the island has several good sandy beaches on the south coast and three hamlets on the girdling coastal road. The largest settlement lies in a bay on the south-east coast at **Agios Stavros**. Although it is a rather scruffy place, it

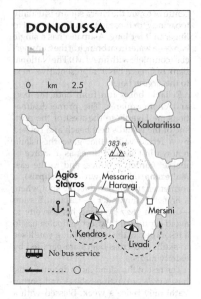

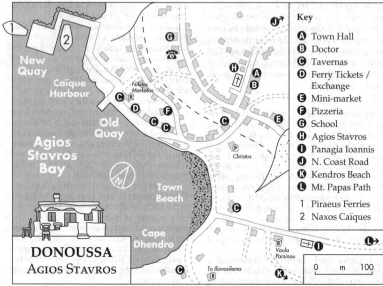

Key

ⓐ Town Hall
ⓑ Doctor
ⓒ Tavernas
ⓓ Ferry Tickets / Exchange
ⓔ Mini-market
ⓕ Pizzeria
ⓖ School
ⓗ Agios Stavros
ⓘ Panagia Ioannis
ⓙ N. Coast Road
ⓚ Kendros Beach
ⓛ Mt. Papas Path

1 Piraeus Ferries
2 Naxos Caïques

DONOUSSA
AGIOS STAVROS

is home to most of the available tourist accommodation. However, outside the half-dozen tavernas, little English is spoken, and there is only one general store. A souvenir shop/ticket agency on the waterfront also offers exchange facilities with rates so bad that it is more advantageous to head back to Naxos for a couple of days and visit a bank there instead.

The rest of Donoussa offers rewarding walks and several excellent empty beaches at **Kendros** and **Livadi**. Both tend to suffer at the height of the summer from the miscellany of campers living free-style (this can include nudity) behind the sand — sans toilets! The island's hamlets are studies in unspoilt rural communities, **Mersini** being the most prosperous thanks to the existence of a spring which is the island's main water supply.

Isolated **Kalotaritissa** has appeal as a walking destination. In past years the coastal walk was the main activity Donoussa had to offer. Unfortunately, the coastal dirt road has now been metalled (enabling the island's two vehicles to have grand prix races), so the 16 km circumambulation isn't quite as appealing as it once was.

⊨

All the accommodation is at **Agios Stavros**. Rooms are not over-abundant (take up offers made when ferries arrive). The pension *Christos* (☎ 51555) is complemented by several establishments offering rooms. These include the waterfront *Nikitas Markolas* (☎ 51566) and the *Voula Parsinou* (☎ 61455).

Iraklia
HPAKΛEIA; 17.5 km²; pop. 110.

CODE ☎ 22850

A hilltop sticking out of the sea that tapers away into low hills to the north, Iraklia (usually pronounced 'Heraklia', and not to be confused with Heraklion / Iraklion, the capital of Crete) is marginally the most accessible of the Little Cyclades, thanks to occasional tour-boat trips from Naxos Town. Like Donoussa, the island has a growing reputation for 'get-away-

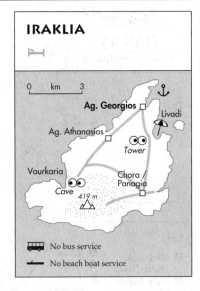

IRAKLIA

from-it-all' fans but, unlike the other Little Cyclades, it hasn't yet resorted to building extra facilities to meet growing High Season demand.

All ferries call at the north-coast port of **Agios Georgios**. Set in a deep inlet, it is a rather scruffy, ramshackle affair, with two main streets of sorts, bisected by a small ravine that winds up the most fertile valley on the island. The village boasts all the usual lack of amenities with a scattering of tavernas and a single food shop (that sells bread and milk imported from Naxos and ferry tickets for all but two lines). Additional pluses are a sandy harbour beach backed by shady trees, and friendly locals who treat those staying more than a day or two as honorary villagers (though most rooms are carefully sited on the outskirts of town). This is not without advantages as most visitors find themselves nicely placed to walk to Iraklia's best sand beach at **Livadi**. This is a wide, taverna-backed strand with views across the narrow strait to Schinoussa (10 minutes' sailing time away).

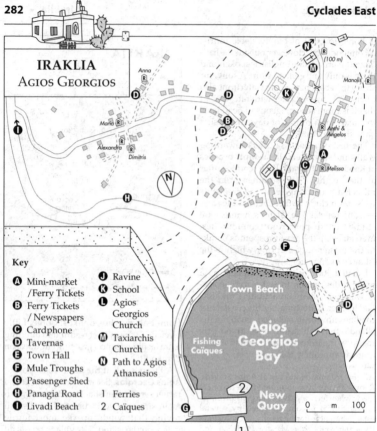

IRAKLIA
AGIOS GEORGIOS

Key

A Mini-market
    /Ferry Tickets
B Ferry Tickets
    / Newspapers
C Cardphone
D Tavernas
E Town Hall
F Mule Troughs
G Passenger Shed
H Panagia Road
I Livadi Beach
J Ravine
K School
L Agios
    Georgios
    Church
M Taxiarchis
    Church
N Path to Agios
    Athanasios
1 Ferries
2 Caïques

Town Beach

Agios
Georgios
Bay

Fishing
Caïques

New
Quay

0   m   100

    The rest of the island offers an ideal retreat for leisurely walks, though past visitors will be disappointed to find that the Port—Panagia mule path has been replaced with an EU-sponsored road wide enough to pass for a runway. Little used beyond Livadi, it runs past a hill overlooking the beach on which stands the impressive remains of a tower — dating from the days when these islands were notorious pirates' nests — to the old hillside chora at **Panagia** (now home to a mere half-a-dozen houses and a church).

    A surviving mule path runs from the back of Agios Georgios up the west coast and

on to a cave (complete with stalactites) near Vourkaria Bay.

Room supply is okay out of peak season but in July and August there are days when late arrivals can't find a bed — it pays to either phone ahead or arrive early. Prices are high regardless of season (€3 more than on Naxos). All the beds on Iraklia are in Agios Georgios — the largest group include the *Maria* (☎ 71485), the *Alexandra* (☎ 71482), and the nearby *Anna* (☎ 71145). Rooms in the village itself include the *Anthi & Angelos* (☎ 71486), the *Melissa* (☎ 71539) and the *Manolis* (☎ 71569). There is also some freelance camping at the far end of Livadi beach.

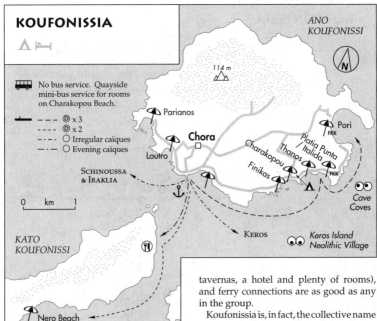

KOUFONISSIA

No bus service. Quayside mini-bus service for rooms on Charakopou Beach.

ⓓ x 3
ⓓ x 2
○ Irregular caïques
○ Evening caïques

SCHINOUSSA & IRAKLIA

0   km   1

KATO KOUFONISSI

Nero Beach

ANO KOUFONISSI

N

114 m

Parianos

Chora

Loutro

Charakopou

Thanos

Platia Punta / Italida

Pori
FKK

Finikas

FKK

Cave Coves

KEROS

Keros Island Neolithic Village

Koufonissia

ΚΟΥΦΟΝΗΣΙ; 3.8 km²; pop. 280.

CODE ☎ 22850

This being Greece, it is not surprising that the smallest inhabited island in the Little Cyclades is the most heavily populated, and indeed, touristed. Koufonissia is becoming quite a trendy place to visit, for although it can offer only the usual mix of beaches and mule tracks, the former are of a high quality and the generally cosy beach island atmosphere gives it an edge over its companions. If you have time to visit only one of the Little Cyclades, or are a little wary of venturing too far from the tourist trail, then Koufonissia is probably the island to go for. Truth to tell, part of its attraction is that it does have at least a modicum of facilities (i.e. a post office,

tavernas, a hotel and plenty of rooms), and ferry connections are as good as any in the group.

Koufonissia is, in fact, the collective name for two islands: Ano (upper) Koufonissi and Kato (lower) Koufonissi — though these days the name is generally taken to mean the former. Ano Koufonissi is the main island (its low-lying companion being little more than a reef rising a few metres above sea level and used for grazing goats), and is home to the only settlement and the ferry quay. Hemmed in by Kato Koufonissi and Glaronissi, with mighty Naxos dominating the northern horizon and the much taller island of Keros close to the south, Koufonissia has a wonderful little-kid-in-the-playground feel about it.

The island is easily identified thanks to the white-roofed windmill to the left of the quay as you view it from the ferry. In addition, it is low and flat, tapering gently down to the sea on the south side. Moreover, you will invariably find a picturesque flotilla of fishing caïques

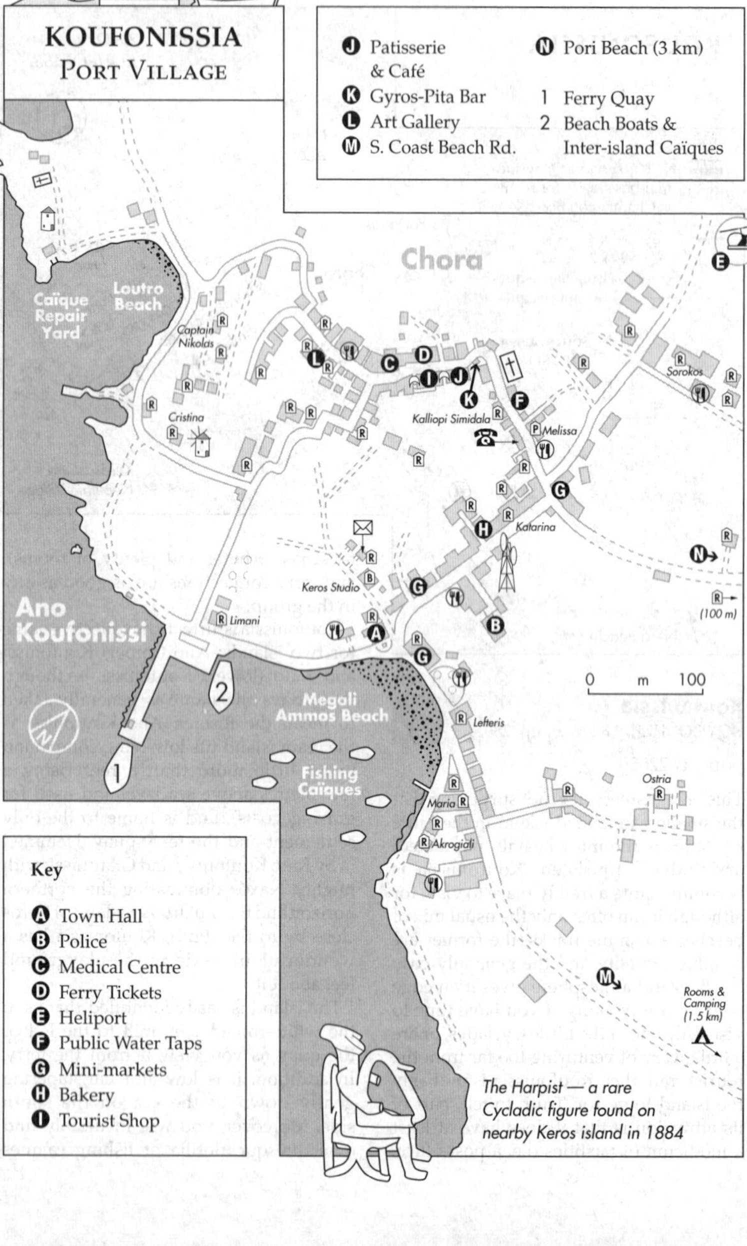

KOUFONISSIA
PORT VILLAGE

J Patisserie
  & Café
K Gyros-Pita Bar
L Art Gallery
M S. Coast Beach Rd.

N Pori Beach (3 km)

1 Ferry Quay
2 Beach Boats &
  Inter-island Caïques

Chora

Caïque
Repair
Yard

Loutro
Beach

Captain
Nikolas

Cristina

Ano
Koufonissi

Kalliopi Simidala

Melissa

Sorokos

Katarina

Keros Studio

Limani

N→

(100 m)

0   m   100

Megali
Ammos Beach

Fishing
Caïques

Lefteris

Ostria

Maria

Akrogiali

M↘

Rooms &
Camping
(1.5 km)

*The Harpist — a rare
Cycladic figure found on
nearby Keros island in 1884*

Key

A Town Hall
B Police
C Medical Centre
D Ferry Tickets
E Heliport
F Public Water Taps
G Mini-markets
H Bakery
I Tourist Shop

moored in the sandy bay to the east of the ferry quay.

Standing on the gentle hill behind the quay is the **Port Village**. This has all the essential facilities (with the exception of a bank and a good supermarket: the food stores on Koufonissia are very poorly stocked compared to most) and is pretty enough in a ragged sort of way, but in truth it is a rather tame affair compared to most island choras. The old-style main street aside, most of the newer buildings are holiday homes or tavernas.

Fortunately, no one comes to Koufonissia for much other than the beaches. Most of these are gentle crescents of golden sand gracing a series of wide coves running south from Parianos on the west coast to Pori on the east. All are accessed via dirt tracks. The beaches get progressively better the further east you go. Charakopou and Thanos are the busiest, thanks to the rooms, taverna and campsite. The very limited tree-cover on Koufonissia is also at its poor best here.

Nudism is supposedly banned on the island, but the islanders seem very laid-back about this, and **Platia Punta** and **Pori** are de facto nudist affairs thanks to their comparative isolation. Both are reached by a dirt path that meanders along the edge of the low-cliffed coastline. This has been badly eroded by the sea, producing a succession of coves each with a tiny cave under the cliff path. In August each is usually home to a latter-day troglodyte couple, whose presence can be deduced by the scent of evaporating suntan oil wafting up to the cliff path.

Pori is the best beach and worth the effort of getting to it, but be warned: the coastal path walk is much longer than it looks thanks to the indented coastline. There is an inland mule path to Pori, but this is less picturesque thanks to the lack of turquoise seas, caves, coves and nudists.

Beach boats run from the port to Pori and also to neighbouring **Kato Koufonissi**, where there is a quiet sand beach at Nero. The island's other great attraction is a taverna with such a high reputation that it struggles to keep up with the demand in High Season.

⊨

The port village is increasingly devoted to providing rooms for summer visitors. If you are phoning ahead there is plenty of choice. Harbour views are offered by the *Maria* (☎ 71436), the *Akrogiali* (☎ 71685) and the *Keros Studio* (☎ 71600).

In the centre of town is the pension *Melissa* (☎ 71454), the *Katarina* (☎ 71455) and the *Kalliopi Simidala* (☎ 71462). Those looking for something more tucked away should try either the *Sorokos* (☎ 71453) or the *Ostria* (☎ 71671). In addition to rooms in the port village, a number of rooms are also available behind Charakopou beach.

Λ

Camping Charakopou (☎ 71683): a pleasant — if windswept — site behind a taverna between Charakopou and Thanos beaches. With limited washing facilities and a lack of tree cover, the site has a very camping-in-the-sand-dunes feel about it. The site was closed for most of 2002 owing to alleged certification problems, forcing would-be campers to freelance on the beaches. In view of this, it would be wise to arrive in 2004 assuming that official camping isn't likely to be a viable option.

ᐁᐁ

Caïques regularly make trips to neighbouring islands (including Volaka on Naxos). Occasional boats go to the Neolithic village site on neighbouring **Keros**. This large hilltop poking out of the water is far more impressive a sight than Koufonissia, looking as if it ought to be the most important of the Little Cyclades. However, apart from the obligatory mad monk, it is uninhabited, and used for grazing. This is all something of a comedown from its days as a major centre of the Early Cycladic culture (c. 3000–2000 BC).

Excavations on the west coast at the end of the 19 c. produced over 100 Cycladic figures — the largest group found to date, including the famous harpist and flautist (both are now in the National Archaeological Museum in Athens). This reflects the island's role as an idol manufacturing centre. If you charter a caïque (expect to pay at least €50 for a day round-trip) to take you across, take care you don't end up instead at the remains of a medieval village on the north coast.

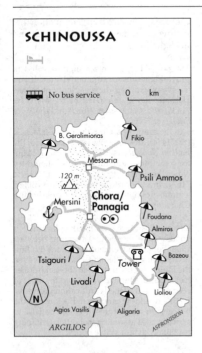

SCHINOUSSA

No bus service

0   km   1

B. Gerolimionas

Fikio

Messaria

120 m

Psili Ammos

Mersini

**Chora/
Panagia**

Foudana

Almiros

Tsigouri

Bazeou

Tower

Livadi

Lioliou

Agios Vasilis

Aligaria

ARGILIOS

ASPRONISSI

Schinoussa

ΣΧΙΝΟΥΣΣΑ; 8.5 km²; pop. 100.

CODE ☎ 22850

Once in a while a Greek island appears on the horizon that is so nice that it is almost a shame to tell people about it: dreamy and diminutive Schinoussa (pronounced 'Skinoussa') is one of these. A collection of lumpy, low, windmill-topped hills, it isn't an obvious example of an island paradise, but in a very downbeat way it is. The rather barren and uninviting aspect that Schinoussa presents from the deck of a ferry is revealed, on landing, to be made up of a quaint mix of hills, the odd olive grove and scattered areas of pasture.

Unfortunately, the island needs hordes of guidebook readers dropping in every year like a hole in its ferry quay; its charm comes from nothing more than being so delightfully unspoilt. How long it will remain this way is another matter. To date it has been well served by its poor harbour, which for many years discouraged visitors by forcing ferries to dump passengers into taxi boats, and, even now a proper quay has been built, it still discourages casual island hoppers by looking so intimidatingly quiet (the inlet has only three buildings to its name).

The only settlement of any size is known variously as '**Chora**' or '**Panagia**'. Skilfully sited on a low ridge between the island's low hills, it commands good views without being too obvious itself — a hangover from the pirate days which saw Schinoussa depopulated several times (the current inhabitants are descendants of Amorgos stock who repopulated the island in the early 1800s). For the most part, Chora is a less than photogenic single-street affair, but despite having few older buildings, it has a very appealing small-town atmosphere — largely thanks to the few concessions to tourism.

This is not to say that it is totally absent. The main street is home to the usual litter of tavernas (most offering rooms) and occasional small shops, and finally peters out into a couple of tracks that wander down to the popular beach at Livadi and to the east coast beaches. In fact, Schinoussa is well endowed with beaches: there are up to a dozen around the coast. However, although adequate, they are made of grey, coarse sand and are not on a par with the golden strands to be found on neighbouring islands — a fact that partly explains Schinoussa's relative unpopularity.

The rest of the island can best be described as looking like a group of interconnected low rock dunes. Schinoussa is made up of some nine hillocks (the northern two topped with derelict windmills, with another on the hill between Tsigouri beach and the chora). With the notable exception of the port—Chora road, all the roads on the island are dirt-track affairs and the

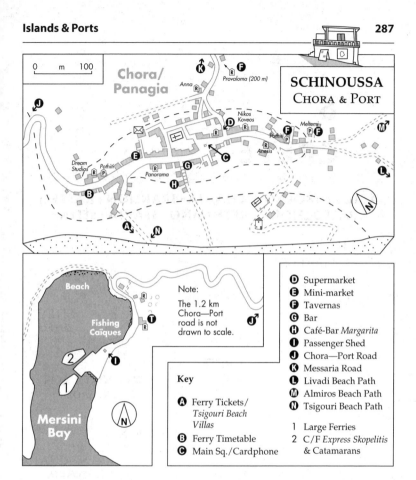

0 m 100

Chora/ Panagia

SCHINOUSSA
CHORA & PORT

Note:

The 1.2 km Chora—Port road is not drawn to scale.

Beach

Fishing Caïques

Mersini Bay

Key

Ⓐ Ferry Tickets/ *Tsigouri Beach Villas*
Ⓑ Ferry Timetable
Ⓒ Main Sq./Cardphone
Ⓓ Supermarket
Ⓔ Mini-market
Ⓕ Tavernas
Ⓖ Bar
Ⓗ Café-Bar *Margarita*
Ⓘ Passenger Shed
Ⓙ Chora—Port Road
Ⓚ Messaria Road
Ⓛ Livadi Beach Path
Ⓜ Almiros Beach Path
Ⓝ Tsigouri Beach Path

1 Large Ferries
2 C/F *Express Skopelitis* & Catamarans

preserve of the island's mule population, which seems to outnumber the human inhabitants.

The only other settlement is the hamlet of **Messaria**, north of Chora, which is home to some 20 people. Ironically, given the comparative lack of inhabitants and visitors, Schinoussa has the best water supply of any island in the Little Cyclades, thanks to the existence of three springs. In the absence of tourists, they water the wild chewing-gum bushes (mastica) that cover the hillsides instead.

Given its size, Chora has a surprising number of rooms on offer. As with Iraklia, expect to pay €3 above other island rates. Accommodation in Chora starts with the *Pension Pothiti* (☎ 71184) and the *Dream Studios* (☎ 71175). At the other end of town are the *Meltemi* and the *Anesis* (☎ 71180). Other options lie on the Messaria road with the *Anna* (☎ 71161), the *Agnadema* (☎ 71987) and the solitary *Provaloma* (☎ 71185). If you want both ferry tickets and a nearby beach then *Tsigouri Beach Villas* (☎ 71930) is for you. There is also some freelance camping behind Livadi beach.

6
CRETE

AGIOS NIKOLAOS · CHANIA · IRAKLION · KASTELI
PALEOCHORA · RETHIMNO · SFAKIA · SITIA

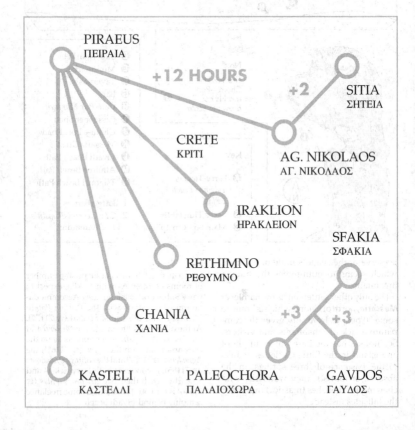

Crete

IRAKLION
Venetian Harbour &
Kastro Runway

Minoan Palace:
North Entrance Bastion
& Racing Bull Relief

KNOSSOS

Venetian Kastro/
Rocco al Mare:
Capless Minaret

Minoan Palace:
Sacred Horns

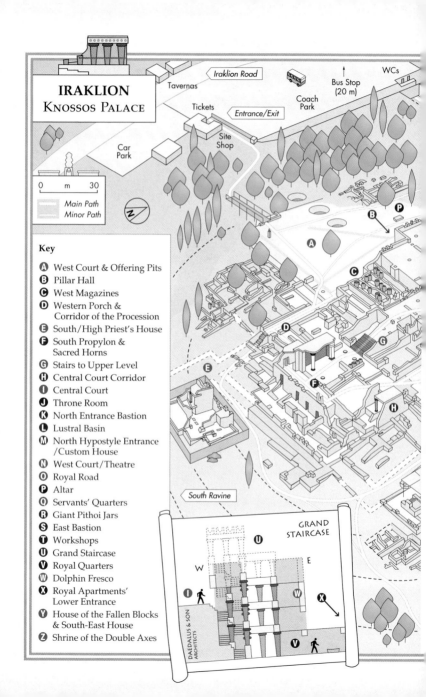

IRAKLION
KNOSSOS PALACE

Iraklion Road

Tavernas

Tickets

Entrance/Exit

Site Shop

Car Park

Coach Park

Bus Stop (20 m)

WCs

| 0 | m | 30 |

Main Path
Minor Path

Key

- **A** West Court & Offering Pits
- **B** Pillar Hall
- **C** West Magazines
- **D** Western Porch & Corridor of the Procession
- **E** South/High Priest's House
- **F** South Propylon & Sacred Horns
- **G** Stairs to Upper Level
- **H** Central Court Corridor
- **I** Central Court
- **J** Throne Room
- **K** North Entrance Bastion
- **L** Lustral Basin
- **M** North Hypostyle Entrance /Custom House
- **N** West Court/Theatre
- **O** Royal Road
- **P** Altar
- **Q** Servants' Quarters
- **R** Giant Pithoi Jars
- **S** East Bastion
- **T** Workshops
- **U** Grand Staircase
- **V** Royal Quarters
- **W** Dolphin Fresco
- **X** Royal Apartments' Lower Entrance
- **Y** House of the Fallen Blocks & South-East House
- **Z** Shrine of the Double Axes

South Ravine

GRAND STAIRCASE

DAEDALUS & SON ARCHITECTS

W   E

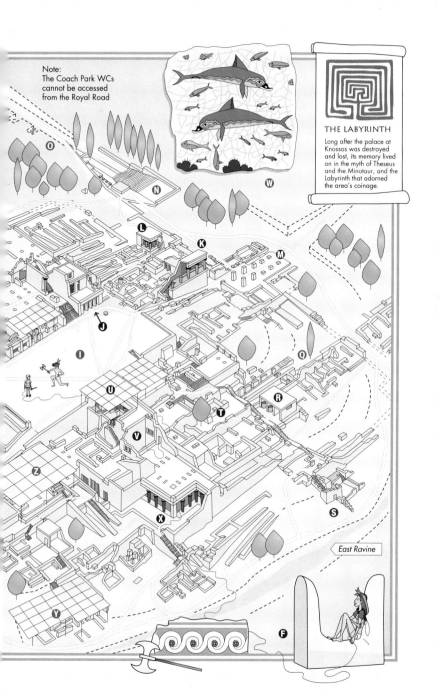

Note:
The Coach Park WCs
cannot be accessed
from the Royal Road

THE LABYRINTH

Long after the palace at
Knossos was destroyed
and lost, its memory lived
on in the myth of Theseus
and the Minotaur, and the
Labyrinth that adorned
the area's coinage.

East Ravine

C/M
Express Haroulla
(in Goutos Colours) &
C/F Superferry II
at Mykonos Town

C/F Rodanthi
Departs from Santorini

C/F Aeolos
Express
C/F Express
Santorini

A typical High Season ferry embarkation scene
on one of the smaller islands
(in this case Koufonissia)

General Features

Crete is such a large island that it justifies a separate volume in several popular guide series. A goodly number of island hoppers also sample the island in passing: for the most part restricting their visits to the string of port cities along the northern coast. These are worthy destinations in their own right and play such an important role in Cretan life that it is almost better to think of Crete as half-a-dozen 'city-states' sharing the same island. The modern capital of Iraklion (Venetian 'Candia') is the most visited thanks to its good ferry and air links, though it doesn't have half the atmosphere of the former capital of Chania or nearby Rethimno.

The remaining cities of Agios Nikolaos, Sitia and Kasteli have less going for them, but they do have important ferry links for wide-ranging island hoppers. In addition to the north coast ports, the south-west coast has a miniature ferry system of its own that invites exploration — as does the odd collection of associated islets scattered around the Cretan coast.

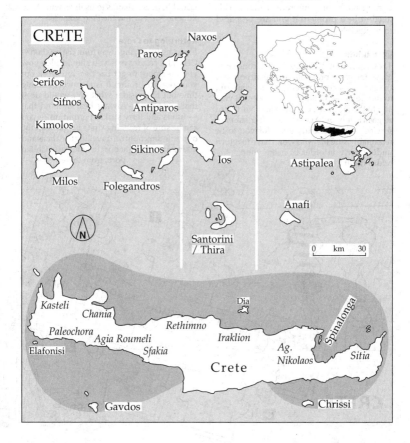

CRETE

Naxos
Paros
Serifos
Sifnos
Antiparos
Kimolos
Sikinos
Ios
Astipalea
Milos
Folegandros
Anafi
Santorini / Thira
0   km   30

Kasteli
Chania
Dia
Spinalonga
Paleochora
Rethimno
Agia Roumeli
Iraklion
Elafonisi
Sfakia
Ag. Nikolaos
Sitia
Crete
Gavdos
Chrissi

Crete-based Itineraries

Many regular island hoppers choose to avoid annual visits to Athens by flying to and from Crete. This is an attractive option (by any standards Crete is a much more appealing destination), but you do have to be careful given the limited nature of the ferry links between Crete and the islands. Not only is there the very real possibility that you will have to wait a day or two before being able to jump across, but you also have the problem of getting back for your return flight. This needn't be a problem if you are prepared to be flexible.

1 Iraklion

The Cretan capital is the obvious starting point given the close proximity of the airport and the good ferry connections. Regular boats run to the Central Cyclades and Rhodes all year and to the Northern Cyclades and North-ern Aegean in July and August. Moreover, summer services are sufficiently good for you to be reasonably sure that you won't have to return unduly early in order to make your return flight.

2 Agios Nikolaos & Sitia

The two east Crete towns of Agios Nikolaos and, to a lesser extent, Sitia are also worth considering as starting points, having regular links with the Cyclades West island of Milos and the south Dodecanese islands to Rhodes. However, they are not particularly frequent: if you are flying into Iraklion visit the EOT / NTOG office and get their current timetable before heading for these towns.

3 Kasteli

The small port of Kasteli on the west side of Crete also has options for really ambitious island hoppers, thanks to its links with Anti-kithera, Kithera and the Peloponnese.

Returning to Crete

If you are venturing away from the Iraklion—Central Cyclades axis you should plan how you are going to get back as you work out your outward route. It is also worth taking time out to consider what you would do if that went down. Always bear in mind that — funds and ferry strikes permitting — you can be sure of reaching Crete by going in the opposite direction: i.e. travelling to Athens and taking an overnight boat to a choice of Cretan ports from there.

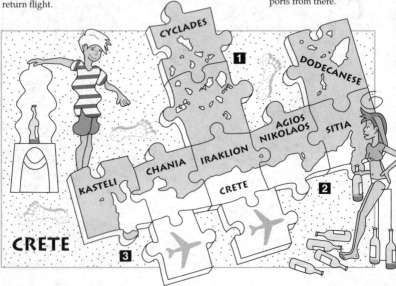

Cretan Ferries

Main Car Ferries

Crete is the sole destination for a number of dedicated boats, as well as being used as a springboard by long-haul ferries heading to other destinations. The former are reliable and can be timed to the minute. However, indirect ferries can be up to four hours late; Crete is often at the end of scheduled routes and thus delays (thanks to the distance from Piraeus) tend to be longer than elsewhere in the system. Such ferries either steam down from the Central Cyclades or ricochet off Crete en route to Rhodes.

In High Season Cretan links are significantly enhanced by boats running a thrice-weekly service between Thessalonika and Iraklion, via the Sporades and Cyclades island chains. In 2003 *Daedalus* ran solo on the route (see p. 438). As they provide a unique service into the Northern Aegean, they are described and mapped in that chapter.

C/F *Festos Palace* – C/F *Knossos Palace*
C/F *Olympia Palace*
C/F *Europa Palace*
Minoan Lines

Festos Palace; 2000; 30000 GRT.
Knossos Palace; 2000; 30000 GRT.
Olympia Palace; 2001; 30000 GRT.
Europa Palace; 2002; 30000 GRT.

After years of little change to direct services between Piraeus and the capital of Crete, Iraklion saw a major shake-up in 2001 thanks to the arrival of new high-speed ferries (*Festos Palace* and *Knossos Palace*) that cut the travel time from 11 to 6 hours. At a stroke Minoan have managed to outclass all the competition with these boats. They are very popular, and it pays to book several days ahead — otherwise you could well be disappointed. Facilities on board are first rate: these are arguably the best domestic boats in Greece. Two further high-speed boats, the *Olympia Palace* and *Europa Palace*, could also move onto the route if competition intensifies further.

C/F *Kriti I* – C/F *Kriti II*
C/F *Aptera* – C/F *El. Venizelos*
ANEK Lines

Kriti I; 1979; 14385 GRT.
Kriti II; 1979; 14375 GRT.
Aptera; 1973; 7058 GRT.
El. Venizelos; 1992; 23000 GRT.

ANEK, after running two boats on the Piraeus—Iraklion service for many years in a gentle state of competition with Minoan, really suffered in 2001 with the arrival of the new high speed ferries above. As a short-term measure they moved three of their large Adriatic boats, the impressive *El. Venizelos*, *Kriti II* and the *Kriti II* onto the route, but they can't compete on speed or facilities. The hopelessly small *Aptera* will surely have to be moved in 2004. ANEK will struggle again this year unless they bring in new ferries of their own.

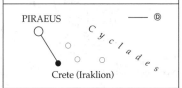

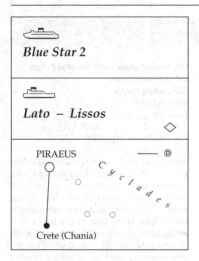

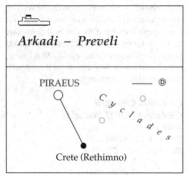

C/F *Blue Star 2*
Blue Star Ferries; 2000; 20000 GRT.

The new arrival in 2003, this fast boat moved from the Adriatic to much protest from other ferry operators serving Crete. Able to make the Piraeus—Chania run in just under 6 hours, and offering excellent facilities, the competition are justified in being worried. Even a remote berth on the outer fringes of Piraeus Harbour hasn't put passengers off. If you are travelling via Chania then this is the boat!

C/F *Lato* – C/F *Lissos*
ANEK Lines
Lato; 1975; 15504 GRT.
Lissos; 1972; 9893 GRT.

For many years ANEK have found a profitable niche offering a daily service to the north-western town of Chania (via its port at Souda). The boats on the route are well established, both are okay — though no match for the *Blue Star 2*. They are now attempting to compete by going down the 'hey, we may be older and slower, but our tickets are also cheaper' route. Expect changes in the next year or two — if only because the Lissos is nudging the compulsory ferry retirement age barrier.

C/F *Arkadi* – C/F *Preveli*
ANEK Lines
Arkadi; 1983; 4097 GRT.
Preveli; 1980; 5653 GRT.

If Iraklion isn't your objective, the two boats offering a daily link with Rethimno

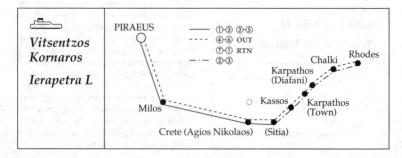

offer a second alternative travel option. Although smaller than their rivals on other routes, these ANEK boats have the advantages of being significantly newer and less crowded vessels. Both are well maintained. The *Arkadi* has been on the route for eight years and was rejoined in 2001 by the larger *Preveli*. Schedules don't change much, though there are odd variations every other year. In the past these have included a stop at Sifnos and an extended run to Rhodes.

C/F *Vitsentzos Kornaros*
LANE Lines; 1976; 9735 GRT.

In past years Crete has seen several ferry companies attempting to make a go of a thrice-weekly link from Piraeus to Agios Nikolaos and Sitia via Milos. Unfortunately, neither Cretan port offers lucrative pickings and all have failed to make the route pay (the bulk of the traffic consists of lorries running between these ports and Athens). The latest company to have a go is the LANE Lines operation (now a subsidiary of ANEK Lines). Armed with a comparatively clapped-out vessel — the *Vitsentzos Kornaros* (the ex-cross-Channel *Pride of Winchester*) — they have kept a thrice-weekly service going for several years, providing in addition a life-line service for the unpopular Dodecanese islands that lie between Crete and Rhodes. On occasions operating a Rhodes—Crete return run in between trips to and from Piraeus.

C/F *Ierapetra L*
LANE Lines; 1975 (rebuilt 1995); 6135 GRT.

Formerly the ANEK's *Talos*, this ferry was a new arrival on the Greek domestic scene in 1999. Operating in tandem with the *Vitsentzos Kornaros* she runs three times a week down to Crete (sometimes excluding Milos on her return runs). Unfortunately the day this happens varies from year to year. On-board conditions are significantly better than on her larger running-mate. This is in part because the route is relatively unpopular, so they are less crowded.

Southern Crete Services
A. N. E. ND. Y. K. Ferries

Five small ferries, operated by one of the most awkwardly named ferry lines in Greece, run along the south-west coast of Crete from the ports of Paleochora and Sfakia/Chora Sfakion. Their primary role is ferrying tourists disgorged from the mouth of the Samarian Gorge to adjacent coastline towns, but they also offer an irregular service to the remote island of Gavdos to the south (the bulk of the weekday services have lately been from Paleochora, while weekend runs have been out of Sfakia).

Timetables are available from the EOT branch in Iraklion. Although these boats are supposed to service the mountain-locked fishing hamlets, they remain very tourist-dependent, and only a limited service — April to October — operates out of the July/August peak. A weekly Sfakia—Gavdos service operates all year round (formerly this ran from Paleochora).

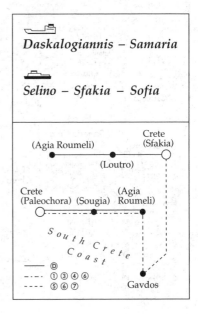

Daskalogiannis – Samaria

Selino – Sfakia – Sofia

Cretan Ports

Crete
KPITI; 8259 km²; pop. 460,000.

The fifth largest island in the Mediterranean and the largest in Greece, Crete is larger than some independent island states and has plenty to occupy the visitor. Geography and history have combined to mark the island out as one of the most diverse in Greece. Long and mountainous, it marks the southern boundary of the Aegean Sea, supping up the contents of any rain-clouds that might have otherwise attempted to venture further north as well as acting as a giant breakwater for the southern Aegean as a whole. Crete is also an island of great strategic importance, for without control of it no power was able to fully command the rest of the Aegean. As a result, the island is littered with the remains of all the great powers from the region, and indeed, appears to have been the power-base of the earliest of them all — the Bronze Age Minoan civilization. Their palaces are among the top sight-seeing destinations, though later Greek and Roman temples, Byzantine churches, Venetian fortresses, Ottoman mosques, and WW2 German battlefields also lie thick on the ground.

If this was not enough, Crete is also very fertile and, following in the tradition of its role as an important grain producing island in the ancient world, now is the major supplier of market garden produce to Greece. The self-sufficiency gained by

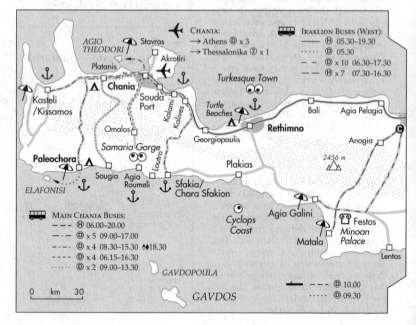

this has given the Cretans a reputation for hot-headed independence and radical politics. Tourism, although not vital to the economy, is now rampant thanks to good beaches, impressive sightseeing and a climate befitting an island lying further south than the northern coast of Tunisia. All major settlements now lie on the north coast which has developed into an English-speaking tourist strip that looks increasingly closer to Benidorm rather than the bucolic, unspoilt Greek island idyll.

Fortunately, the south coast (the resort town of Ierapetra aside) and greater part of the hinterland — rugged and mountainous, covered in pine forests and wildly beautiful — remain remarkably untainted and invite exploration, though comparatively few visitors to Crete venture beyond the spectacular walk down the longest gorge in Europe at Samaria. This winds down to the nicest part of the island — the collection of small port villages and dreamy shoreline of the south-west coast from Matala (with its history of 1970s hippy troglodytes) to the dusty town of Paleochora and its caïques to the exquisite islet of Elafonisi with its sandy beaches and turquoise seas.

The size of Crete has resulted in ferry links with the mainland developing to six ports on the northern coast. All significant towns in their own right, they provide good bases for exploring the adjacent coastlines and hinterland. They are linked by the island's main road (which runs the length of the northern coast, with feeder roads running south from the main towns to the mountain villages and the south coast) and are served by frequent buses. The island bus service is excellent, making travel on Crete both easy and cheap, besides providing a valuable link between ferry routes. The only minor problem of note are the distances; these are very long by Greek island standards.

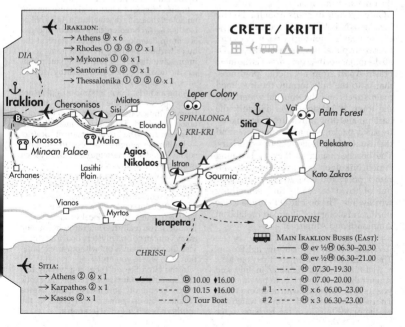

Agios Nikolaos
ΑΓΙΟΣ ΝΙΚΟΛΑΟΣ; pop. 19,000.

CODE ☎ 28410
TOURIST POLICE ☎ 22321
POLICE ☎ 22338
TOURIST INFORMATION ☎ 22357

The premier port of eastern Crete (though given the paucity of ferry connections this isn't saying a lot), Agios Nikolaos is an attractive — though all too obviously tourist — town perched on a tiny headland deep within the Mirambelou Gulf. Named after the patron saint of sailors, the town's name is a common one, and not to be confused with other ports in the Gulf of Corinth or on Anafi. In fact, for most of its life it was known as Lato, but the Venetians chose to rename it and the modern authorities have simply opted for a Hellenised version of the name (though you will still find local bus drivers referring the town as San Nikolaos).

Only a couple of hours from Iraklion by bus, Agios Nikolaos marks the eastern edge of the heavily built-up Cretan package-tourist strip that lies between the two. Of all the major north-coast ports it is the most brash. Apart from a general 'prettiness' thanks to the hilly terrain, the tree-lined main streets and the unusual waterfront, the town lacks sights. As a result, the harbour and downtown area is dominated by sickly package-tourist eating spots and the usual mix of holiday shops and bars. The beaches (such as they are) around Agios Nikolaos are overcrowded and rather poor: you have to go quite a way out of town to really find something worthwhile. The best lie at Elounda to the north, and along the Sitia road (notably at Ammoudi and Almyros).

🛏️

Accommodation fills up early in High Season. This is also one town where it pays to have a well-filled wallet: certainly in July and August this is not the place to prevaricate if your boat or bus is met with offers of a room. The easiest hotels to find lie on the waterfront on the opposite side of the harbour to the ferry quay. These include the C-class *Alcestis* (☎ 22454) and (250 m north-west) the B-class *Coral* (☎ 28363) and the B-class pension *Lida* (☎ 22130). Finally, the C-class *Mandraki* (☎ 28880) lies east of the bus station, and further up the hill is an establishment (easily identified via the green 'Rooms' sign) offering very cheap rooms at a price — the price being the minimalist facilities.

Δ

The nearest site to the town, *Gournia Moon Camping* (☎ 28420 93243), is well a way from the centre at Gournia, near a Minoan palace.

👓

The town itself has no buildings of particular merit, thanks to the Turks who demolished the Genoese fortress. Instead the heart of the town is dominated by a **lagoon**-like sea-lake inner harbour of reputedly measureless depth. The reality doesn't live up to the mystique: the 'lake' (which is some 55 m deep) was only connected to the sea in 1907 when the existing channel was dug. It is lined by expensive tavernas whose prices are only matched by the rip-off bar on the main ferry quay.

In the absence of a historical centre the one notable sightseeing destination in Agios Nikolaos is the **Archaeological Museum** (located 500 m up Paleologou St., which starts at the inner harbour bridge), which is home to an impressive display of artifacts (giant pithoi jars included) recovered from nearby Minoan sites — including Malia.

Being a tourist town, a number of pleasure boats operate from the port, though most of them are ludicrously expensive, given the distances involved. The most popular of these excursions is to the Cretan version of Alcatraz — the former Knights' fortress turned leper colony island of **Spinalonga** (see p. 319), which is invaded most days a week.

Taxi-boat services also operate to the resort of **Elounda** and the quiet village of **Plaka**. There are also excursions to the remains of the Roman city of **Olous** up the coast, as well as Bird and Kri-Kri (named after the local species of goat) islands. If you really feel like throwing money away you can go on a mystery boat tour (these visit the same islands but without an explanation as to where you are).

In the High Season there is a weekly bus and boat trip to **Chrissi** (see p. 317), the exotic beach island off south-east Crete. Agios Nikolaos buses connect with boats at the southern beach resort of **Ierapetra**.

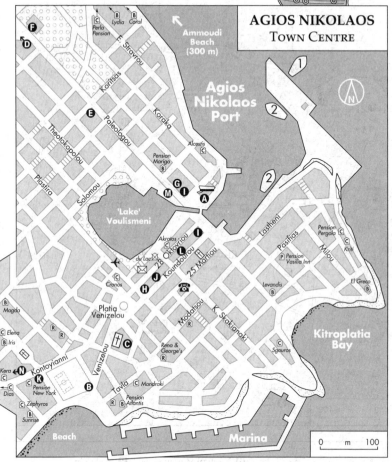

AGIOS NIKOLAOS
TOWN CENTRE

Perla Pension · B Lydia · B Coral

Ammoudi Beach (300 m)

Agios Nikolaos Port

E. Stavrou

Koritsas

Theotokopoulou

Pateologou

Plastira

Solomou

Koraka

Alcestis C

Pension Marigo

1

2

2

G I

M I

A

'Lake' Voulismeni

Lastheni

Akratos C I
Oktoviou C
du Lac 28 L Koundourou
C Cronos H J
25 Martiou

Pension Pergola C
C Kriti

Pasifias

P Pension Vasilia Inn

Milou

Levandis B

El Greco B

Platia Venizelou

Modatsou
K. Skakianaki

Kitroplatia Bay

B Magda

C Elena
B Iris

R

R

Kera N
C Kontoyianni
C Dias
K Pension New York
B

Venizelou

Tavla

C Mandraki

Pension Atlantis

R B

C Zephyros
B Sunrise

Rena & George's R

C Sgouros

Beach

Marina

0 m 100

Key

- **A** Municipal Tourist Office
- **B** Bus Station
- **C** Cathedral
- **D** Hospital (150 m)
- **E** Tourist Police Office
- **F** Archaeological Museum
- **G** Folk Museum
- **H** National Bank of Greece
- **I** Bank
- **J** English Bookshop
- **K** Moped Rental
- **L** Ferry Tickets
- **M** Taxi Rank
- **N** Sitia Road
- **1** Ferry Quay
- **2** Tour Boats

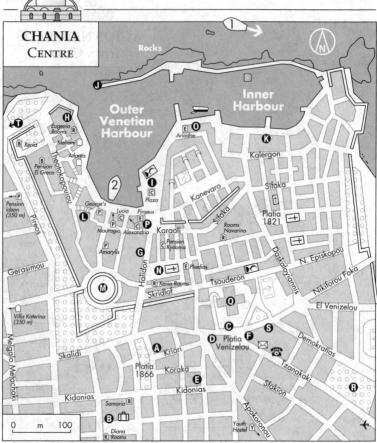

CHANIA CENTRE

Rocks

Outer Venetian Harbour

Inner Harbour

Eugenia Rooms

Xenia

Meltemi

Atlantis

Pension El Greco

Pension Ideon (350 m)

Theotokopoulou

Pireos

George's

Lucia

Piraeus

Mouragio

Alexandria

Amarylis

Karaoli

Pension Kydonia

Rooms Navarino

Ariadne

Kalergon

Sifaka

Platia 1821

Kanevaro

Sifaka

Plaza

Gerasimou

Halidon

Xenia Rooms

Phedias

Tsouderon

Skridlof

Dastalogyannis

N. Episkopou

Nikiforou Foka

El Venizelou

Villa Katerina (350 m)

Megalo Marachaki

Skalidi

Platia 1866

Kriari

Koraka

Kidonias

Kidonias

Platia Venizelou

Demokratias

Tzanakaki

Stakion

Apokoronou

Kidonias

Samaria

Diana Rooms

Youth Hostel

0　　m　　100

Key

Ⓐ NTOG / EOT Office
Ⓑ Main Bus Station
Ⓒ Souda Bus Stop
Ⓓ Youth Hostel Bus Stop
Ⓔ Tourist Police Office
Ⓕ National Bank of Greece
Ⓖ Archaeological Museum
Ⓗ Nautical Museum
Ⓘ Mosque of the Janissaries (Old EOT)
Ⓙ Venetian Lighthouse
Ⓚ Venetian Arsenal
Ⓛ Renieri Gate
Ⓜ Shiavo Bastion
Ⓝ Cathedral
Ⓞ Police
Ⓟ Bookshop
Ⓠ Turkish Market
Ⓡ Gardens
Ⓢ ANEK Ticket Office
Ⓣ Beach & Pool (200 m)

1　Ferry Terminal (6 km East at Souda)
2　Beach & Tour Boats

Chania

XANIA; pop. 50,000.

CODE ☎ 28210
TOURIST POLICE ☎ 24477
NTOG ☎ 26426
EMERGENCY ☎ 22222

The capital of Crete until 1971, Chania (pronounced Han*y*a) is now the number two city on the island. As such, it is the beneficiary of the second daily direct service between Crete and Piraeus. Chania boasts one of the most attractive town centres on Crete, retaining much of its Venetian/ Turkish heart and offering an attractive caïque-filled harbour lined with tavernas (complete with expensive package tourist orientated menus). Unfortunately, some of the outer suburbs are pretty ropy, and the town's modern port (thanks to the inability of the old harbour to handle large vessels) is located an inconvenient 6 km to the east of the town centre — across the Akrotiri headland at Souda.

In addition to the heavy package tourist trade, local prices are pushed up by the military personnel from the nearby Akrotiri NATO air and naval base. The military presence is strong in the area (i.e. 'photography banned' notices abound, and there are always plenty of unattached males in the local discos), but in the main it doesn't detract from the town.

Inevitably, the harbour is the main centre of activity. Used as the set for the film *Zorba the Greek*, it is easily the most attractive on Crete — even with the crowds. Taxi boats run from here (ferry fans shouldn't miss the free raft across the harbour to the Fortella restaurant) to local beaches and the small islet of **Agio Theodori**. The winding streets behind the waterfront are inevitably very boutique-laden, but also contain a fair number of easily found pensions.

All the main services are to be found in the centre — apart from the bus station, which lies outside the old city walls, some five blocks in from the waterfront. Chania is the main junction for the Eastern Crete

bus system with good links to Paleochora and the ports on the south Cretan coast, as well as the villages in the White Mountains that rise behind the town.

🛏️

Rooms are in limited supply, but pricier beds are less hard to come by. The NTOG / EOT office can help you find a bed. The B-class *Samaria* (☎ 51551) is right next to the bus station and easily located; so too is the E-class *Piraeus* (☎ 54154) on the Old Port waterfront. Like all the hotels and pensions in this area it is rather noisy. Tucked behind the Nautical Museum are the much more expensive B-class *El Greco* (☎ 90432) and A-class *Palazzo* (☎ 43255). The Old Harbour and the main street (Halidon St.) between the Old Harbour and the bus station have a number of pensions in the side-streets behind them. There is also a *Youth Hostel* (☎ 53565) at 33 Drakonianou Street, south of the town centre.

▲

Camping Chania (☎ 31138). A reasonably good site 3 km beyond Chania on the road to Kasteli (take the Kasteli bus and ask for the camping).

👓

Known as the 'Venice of Greece' the town itself is the main sightseeing attraction. Needless to say, this being Greece, it is without a single canal, the city acquiring the label by virtue of its largely Venetian-built centre. Although heavily bombed during WW2, the heart of Chania is graced with a remarkable collection of Venetian buildings (now protected by government decree). First among these are the **City Walls**; built c. 1590 after the Barbary pirate Barbarossa sacked nearby Rethimno. The city fathers' fear was such that they added a 15 m deep moat to the outer side for good measure. The harbour was also fortified (the ruins of the **Arsenal** can be seen on the waterfront), and a **Nautical Museum** is now housed in the old walls.

Within the old town there are a number of 16 c. **Venetian Churches**: the one on the main street now houses the city **Archaeological Museum**, which contains material from the town's early Minoan settlement through to the classical period.

Two centuries of Turkish rule have also left their mark, most notably in the form of the lovely multi-domed waterfront **Mosque of the Janissaries** — built to mark the Ottoman conquest of the city in 1645.

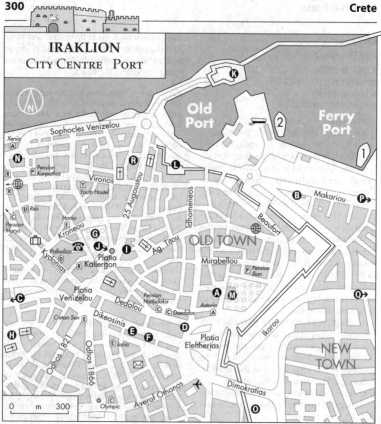

IRAKLION
CITY CENTRE PORT

Old Port

Ferry Port

OLD TOWN

NEW TOWN

Xenia
Sophocles Venizelou
Pension Karpathos
Vironos
Youth Hostel
Rea
Hania
Kroneou
Pension Marys
Palladion
Lydonias
Platia Kallergon
Ag. Titou
Idhomeneos
Makariou
Beaufort
Mirabellou
Pension Ilion
Platia Venizelou
Dedalou
Perision Hadjidakis
Daedalos
Astoria
Ikarou
Cretan Sun
Dikeosinis
Ionia
Odhos 1821
Odhos 1866
Averof Othonos
Dimokratias
Olympic
Platia Eleftherias

0   m   300

Key

- **A** NTOG / EOT Office
- **B** Main Bus Station / WCs
- **C** SW Bus Station (Festos / Ag. Galini)
- **D** Bus Stop (Hotels & Camping)
- **E** Tourist Police Office
- **F** Police
- **G** El Greco Park
- **H** Cathedral
- **I** Loggia / National Bank of Greece
- **J** Turkish Fountain

- **K** Venetian Fortress
- **L** Venetian Arsenal
- **M** Archaeological Museum
- **N** Historical Museum
- **O** Venetian City Wall
- **P** Port (Vehicle Entrance 300 m)
- **Q** Airport (4 km) / McDonald's (30 m)
- **R** Travel Agent / *Bureau de Change*

- **1** Ferry Quay (Ferry Terminal Building 200 m East)
- **2** Hydrofoil / Catamaran Berth

Iraklion
ΗΡΑΚΛΕΙΟ; pop. 102,000.

CODE ☎ 2810
PORT POLICE ☎ 282002
TOURIST POLICE ☎ 283190
EOT / NTOG OFFICE ☎ 228203
EMERGENCY (FOR MOST OF CRETE) ☎ 100

The main port and modern capital of Crete, Iraklion (alias Heraklion) does its best to equal Athenian grime at its worst, but doesn't quite make it. Instead, the city has to settle for looking as if it is suffering the effects of a catastrophic explosion at a local cement factory. However, it is not all dust and grime: the mollifying existence of the well-preserved Venetian city walls, waterfront fortress and arsenal do something to redeem the ambiance, and the Archaeological Museum (home to the largest display of Minoan artifacts in the world) is enough to justify adding the city to any itinerary.

Iraklion is a very popular starting point for Greek island hopping holidays, thanks to the international airport on the city limits. In fact many regular island hoppers prefer to start from here, just to avoid the horrors of Athens airport (Iraklion airport is one of the leading charter flight destinations in Greece). The city is also the hub of the island bus system and an important ferry junction. Ferry links are adequate, if not brilliant. In addition to the daily service to Piraeus, in High Season you can also be fairly sure of at least one boat every other day to Santorini and the Cyclades, and a ferry every third day to Rhodes. Ferry arrivals will find themselves on a long commercial quay, the east end being reserved for international boats. On the west side of the fence that separates this international section, you will find a ferry passenger terminal with ticket offices (most are only open for a few hours each day). Boats arriving in the early hours berth here regardless of line.

Behind the commercial quay stands the New Town, an ugly expanse of concrete that is best ignored. A short walk west, however, will bring you to the main city bus station and the old town.

The old town was the old Venetian capital of Crete (the later Turks preferring Chania) and is easily identified by the massive city walls that surround it. Built during the 16th and 17th centuries, they are so substantial that they enabled the inhabitants of Candia (the city only acquired the ugly name of Iraklion with Cretan independence) to withstand a Turkish siege for over two decades before the city capitulated in 1699. Better still, they have even managed to defy the combination of WW2 bombing and later property developers who have done much to destroy the heart of the old town.

Today the old centre is dominated by 25 Augoustou Street (home to many ferry ticket agencies and not much else) which runs up from the old port to the main square — Platia Kallergon; this is the hub of the old town (though, if truth be told, the attractive and shady El Greco park to the east is a more pleasant spot), and home to a number of tavernas popular with the locals. Once night falls, the square ceases to be a frenetic road junction and marks instead the boundary of the pedestrian zone, opening onto the side streets south of Dikeosinis Street which are home to the best of the tourist-orientated restaurants and shops.

Apart from sightseeing and ferry links, Iraklion has little to offer, and although a large number of tourists pass through, they rarely stay long: Iraklion remains very much a city for its inhabitants and day-trippers. Nightlife is poor (for foreign tourists at any rate) and as a beach destination it doesn't score highly either. If you are looking to wash off the dust, the hotel strip (starting 4 km west of the centre) bus takes you to a sandy strip of sorts. To the east, there is a fair sand beach at Amnissos (take the #1 bus), 8 km from Iraklion centre: plane spotters will love it as it is directly under the airport flight path. Like all beaches near Iraklion it is very windy.

⊨

There are few rooms on offer in Iraklion but plenty of hotel accommodation. Top of the range are the A-class *Xenia* (☎ 284000) on the waterfront and the *Astoria* (☎ 229002) overlooking leafy Eleftherias Square. C-class hotels lie pretty thick on the ground. These include the *Olympic* (☎ 288861) and the *Daedalos* (☎ 224391); both offer good value rooms if your budget isn't too tight. Being old and dusty, the old town also has plenty of D-class establishments close to the centre. There are two worth trying: the *Palladion* (☎ 282563) and the *Rea* (☎ 223638). E-class hotels are more dubious but will do for a night in a pinch. The *Cretan Sun* (☎ 243794) is too noisy for comfort, though the rooms are pleasant enough. Finally, in addition to a number of pensions, there is a good *Youth Hostel* (☎ 286281) at 5 Vironos/Cyronos St. complete with fairly priced rooms, a café/bar, and baggage storage facilities.

Δ

The size of Cretan towns ensures that sites are inconvenient distances from centres. Iraklion is no exception, the nearest being an excellent beach site: *Camping Creta* (☎ 28970 41400), lying 30 minutes east via a #18 bus, then a 20-minute walk.

👀

Iraklion boasts two attractions that draw the crowds. The **Minoan Palace** at **Knossos** (see opposite) is the big pull: 5 km from the town centre, it is an easy bus ride (#2 bus runs every 20 minutes from the bus station: tickets from the kiosk by the bus stop) and is the most important Minoan site on the island. The **Archaeological Museum** (open ① 12.30–19.00, ②–⑦ 08.00–19.00; entrance fee €4.40) in Iraklion is rich in associated finds, and offers a shady, fresco-filled retreat from the midday heat of the city streets. Star exhibits include the Knossos frescoes, a large wooden model reconstruction of the palace, and finds from the smaller Minoan palace complexes at Festos and Malia.

Iraklion also has a second museum: the less frequented **Historical Museum**. This houses exhibits ranging from Byzantine icons of saints to memorabilia of the heroes of the independence struggle (Crete only joined Greece in 1913) to photos of the German occupation in WW2. The museum is also home to the only painting now in Greece of the country's most famous painter — El Greco (alias Domenikos Theotocopoulos) — who was born in Iraklion in 1541.

Hunting around the town, you will find a few architectural lights amid the grey modern buildings. First and foremost is the **Rocca al Mare** — the wonderfully well-preserved Venetian 16 c. kastro that stands at the entrance to the old harbour; its front portal is still adorned with a Venetian winged lion. It is open ⑩ 08.00–15.00; entrance fee €2. Inside you will find assorted dank halls filled with cannon, a mule stairway to the upper levels and a delightful capless miniature minaret added by the Turks (tourists can ascend for views over the fortress). Near the Rocco al Mare are the remains of the **Venetian Arsenal**, now reduced to a few heavily restored arches (often used by local fishermen for storing nets) that herald the seaward end of 25 Augoustou Street, which runs up to the main square (Platia Kallergon). This is dominated by the ornate **Morosini Fountain** (1625), a charming lion-inspired work commissioned by the nephew of the vandal who blew up the Parthenon in Athens. To the east of the fountain is a reconstructed contemporary **Venetian Loggia**, which was damaged by bombing in the last war.

Thanks to its position as the central Crete bus hub, Iraklion is also a good jumping-off point from which to visit the Minoan palace sites on **Malia** and **Festos** (also transcribed as 'Phestos'). Regular buses run past Malia and some five a day venture to Festos. Both sites are open ⑩ 08.00–19.00; entrance fee €5. Unlike Knossos, neither site has undergone 'reconstruction' and both are as excavated. For this reason alone, a visit to one is worthwhile as you will get a good insight into what newly excavated Knossos looked like. Malia is the better preserved and is unusual in its coastal plain location. The palace at Festos is more dramatically sited on a hilltop above the Messara plain, and has a more sophisticated theatre-cum-dancing floor than the famous example at Knossos.

Iraklion buses also run across the island to the southern coast town of **Matala**. Famous in the 1960s as a hairy hippy haven (who took to getting as high as possible while living in the local beach-cliffs — these are honeycombed with caves that have been inhabited by men and Cyclops since Neolithic times), the town is now a much tamer family resort.

Knossos

The Palace of Knossos (see colour map between pages 288–289) was the centre of Minoan civilization between 3000–1400 BC. Its fame was such that faint memories of it, and its name ('Knossos' is not Greek and is thought to be close to the site's earlier Minoan name), lingered on in Greek myth long after the site of the palace and the Minoan civilization were forgotten. By the Classical period, a thousand years after its destruction, beyond the myths and a horribly pessimistic belief that a Golden age had long since given way to a more prosaic age of Iron, no local recollection of the pre-Greek Minoan culture survived. Elsewhere the Minoans were remembered — not least in Egypt where the story of their fall possibly came to be immortalized in the Atlantis legend (see p. 178).

Incredibly, beyond the odd painted pot and some clay tablets bearing a strange script that turned up in Mycenaean palace excavations in the 19 C., the Minoans remained completely unrecognised until Sir Arthur Evans began excavating at Knossos in 1900. The site had long been recognised as one of potential importance, but even so, his unearthing of a massive, elaborate, surprisingly modern-looking palace adorned with frescoed walls, pillared light wells and drains (a feature not found in other European civilizations for a millennium), yet lacking defensive walls (suggesting an awesome military command of the region), was equal to any other 20 C. archaeological discovery.

Evans continued to excavate at Knossos until the 1930s, and also undertook considerable rebuilding, replacing the lost wooden pillars and beams with concrete substitutes. Had his sponsors not balked at providing additional funds for concrete he would probably have rebuilt the whole complex. The result gives you plenty to see (even if this sort of 'reconstruction' is nowadays regarded as over enthusiastic) and offers a nice compromise between the impression given of the former palace as it was and the warren of foundations that recall the palace of Greek legend, the famous Labyrinth where the Athenian hero Theseus fought the dreaded Minotaur before running off with the King's daughter, Ariadne. Worth recalling, it ran something like this:

The Myth of Theseus & the Minotaur

Far away and long ago there lived a king called Minos. He presided over a powerful maritime empire. Unfortunately for Minos, his wife, Queen Pasiphae, took a fancy for the idea of a night in bed with a large white bull that the king had refused to sacrifice to Poseidon (a strange desire which rather suggests that King Minos was King Minus-an-inch-or-two when it came to the tackle department). Pasiphae sought out the chief craftsman — Daedalus — and ordered him to devise some kind of heifer-shaped sex aid that would allow her to... Well, anyway, one hell of a night and nine months later she gave birth to the Minotaur, the monstrous creature with the body of a man and the head of a bull. King Minos then ordered Daedalus to construct the labyrinth in which the Minotaur was hidden away. Here it lived on an annual diet of 14 Athenian youths and maidens who were pushed into the entrance and never seen again. Daedalus, meantime, was imprisoned to prevent him from divulging the secret of the labyrinth (to say nothing of indulging the queen's fancies) whereupon, with his son Icarus, he made some wings out of feathers and wax and flew to Sicily by way of Ikaria (where Icarus died after flying too near the sun). Meantime, back at the labyrinth, Theseus, the son of the king of Athens, disguised as one of the annual sacrificial youths, killed the Minotaur with the help of Ariadne, who gave him a ball of thread that enabled him to escape from the labyrinth. The couple then fled to Naxos where the highly strung Theseus unceremoniously dumped his love, returning to Athens alone.

The palace uncovered by Sir Arthur Evans is multi-layered and complex, the structure being built around the four sides of a flattened hilltop. Originally built in the Middle Minoan period c. 1950 BC, the palace was destroyed (along with all the other early Minoan palaces) c. 1700 BC, probably as the result of a massive earthquake. Rebuilt in the opulent style reproduced by Evans, the succeeding structure boasted the staircases, light wells and plaster-coated walls that make it so distinctive, although to call it a 'palace' is rather misleading, for the building complex at Knossos appears to have not only been the focus of political and religious life, but was also the centre of judicial, administrative, commercial and industrial activity. The hectares around the site contain the remains of a number of associated Minoan villas and houses, and a small town.

The massive eruption of Santorini c. 1640 BC triggered the collapse of the Minoan civilization, with all the Cretan palaces being destroyed — Knossos among them (seemingly by fire). Partially rebuilt by alien Mycenaean Greeks, it was the only Minoan palace site that wasn't abandoned. However, it didn't survive for long, being finally destroyed — possibly as the result of a raid by invaders — c. 1400 BC. Thereafter, the palace hill (still known as 'Knossos') was home to a small undistinguished Archaic settlement that survived into the Roman era.

Visitors to the palace today no longer need a ball of string to find their way around. From the moment they arrive at Knossos, life becomes very easy: you just follow the crowds. These start at the main road (lined with tavernas and tourist shops) which runs between the palace site and the small modern village of Knossos (where a limited number of rooms are available). Iraklion buses stop near the large coach park (complete with WCs) at the site entrance.

Open ® 08.00–19.00, the ticket fee is €5 (students: €3. In past years ISIC-holding students have been admitted free). Now surrounded by large pine trees, the site is accessed from the west. Most visitors explore the features of Knossos in the sequence given below, but you are free to wander (though rumour has it that plans are in hand to confine access to parts of the site, as heavy tourism is wearing down the floors).

On entering the site, visitors pass along a tree-lined avenue which ends with a bust of Sir Arthur Evans. This stands on the edge of the palace **West Court** that is dominated by **Ⓐ** three tree-filled circular **Offering Pits** used in Minoan worship. Into these were thrown ceremonial pottery vessels (an odd habit curiously replicated by the later Greeks with their passion for smashing platters after meals).

Behind the West Court stands the reconstructed west façade of the palace. Although roped off, doorways enable you to peer into **Ⓑ** the **Pillar Hall**, the first of the palace's estimated thousand rooms. Next door are **Ⓒ** the **West Magazines**. These are long storage pits containing the large pithoi jars used to store oil and wine (the palace had a secondary role as a communal warehouse for the region). Originally they were unlit rooms deep in the bowels of the building. The path brings you to the **Western Propylon** (porch) and **Ⓓ** the **Corridor of the Procession** (which takes its name from the fresco depicting gift-bearers and a goddess figure).

From the Western Porch the path divides: one branch runs off to the roped-off **Ⓔ South /High Priest's House**, outside the palace walls. This is closed while it awaits restoration, but it is possible to see the rebuilt red-tapered Minoan pillars that adorn the building. Meanwhile the tourist route turns back, past **Ⓕ** the **South Propylon** or gatehouse (complete with a fake white tapered column). To the east of this structure stands a pair of large **Sacred Horns** (now a popular seat for tourist photos): part of the Minoan bull-cult, they were replicated many times over in a smaller form as a decorative device along the tops of the palace walls. From the back of the South Propylon run **Ⓖ** the **Stairs** that led into the religious wing of the palace (follow them up today and you are able to get a better view of the pithoi in the West Magazine).

A path from the South Propylon runs east to **Ⓗ** the **Central Court Corridor**, which now contains a reproduction of the famous **Prince of the Lilies Fresco**. One of the most famous frescoes found at Knossos (and adopted as the symbol of Minoan Lines), it shows a kilted youth wearing a crown of lilies and peacock feathers. However, the figure is made up from fragments that could belong to three different individuals, and is a good example of the high degree of 'reconstruction' undertaken by Evans.

The corridor leads to ❶ the **Central Court** — a feature common to all Minoan palaces but implemented at its best at Knossos. This formed the centre of palace life, with the various quarters of the palace opening out onto it. The court is also thought to be the place where the famous bull-leaping contests, or rites, were performed. Artwork found on the site and elsewhere suggests that young men would grab the lowered horns of a charging bull, then, as the animal attempted to free itself by rearing its head, would use the momentum of that movement to somersault over the horns, landing on their feet on the animal's back before jumping clear. This was clearly a far more sophisticated exercise than modern bull-fighting, and was probably an integral part of Minoan religious ritual.

The **West Side Buildings** adjacent to the Central Court appear to have contained the religious centre of the palace. The most famous of the remains is ❷ the **Throne Room**. Arguably the most interesting room on the site, it is viewed via a basin-filled anteroom (complete with a second dummy throne placed so tourists can photograph each other sitting on it). The throne you can't sit on was originally thought to be that of the ruler at Knossos (hence its title: 'the throne of Minos'), but is now believed to have seated a High Priest. Made of gypsum, it has gypsum benches on either side, above which are frescoes of griffins and lilies (the design dates from the Mycenaean occupation). The throne's shape is also of interest as it mimics a wooden ceremonial chair design. The Throne Room is also a good example of the degree of reconstruction undertaken by Evans: photographs of the excavation show that the throne's back stood several feet above the height of

the surrounding walls, with only the griffin's feet surviving from the frescoes. All of this room (and the storey above) from seat height is, therefore, 'fake'. The frescoes, along with most of the others found, have been reconstructed from fragments. Applauded at the time, they have come in for criticism since, following the discovery of the better-preserved Akrotiri frescoes on Santorini. By comparison, the Knossos reconstructions (produced by a Swiss father-and-son artist combination with the name of Gillieron) look curiously lifeless, and in some instances the fragments were completely misinterpreted (in the most notorious 'reconstruction', the remains of a blue monkey ended up being rebuilt as the figure of a youth).

Directly to the south of the Throne Room are the remains of the **Central Staircase** that served the west wing of the palace. Today it ascends to the rebuilt floor level at the top of the South Propylon stairs, and then further on up to nowhere (though the views are good). Ascending to the first level, then weaving your way around the back of the staircase, you come to the small reconstructed chamber over the Throne Room. This contains the light well that descends into the room and a number of fresco fragments on its walls. The covered-over ruins to the south of the Central Staircase yielded up the famous statuettes of the topless snake-waving ladies.

Returning to the Central Court and then heading north, the path leads down past the most photographed architectural feature on the site: the rebuilt tapered columns of ❸ the **North Entrance Bastion**. The most impressive of the entrances to the palace complex (thanks in part to the steepness of the hillside corridor at this point), it is home to the reconstructed **Racing Bull Relief**. Although the notion is a bit fanciful, it has been suggested that this wall remained visible among the ruins of the palace into the Archaic period, helping to give rise to the legend of the Labyrinth and the Minotaur. Behind it are yet more rooms and storage chambers, and ❹ the **Lustral Basin**: a small reconstructed sanctuary complete with tapering pillars.

Following the path down past the North Entrance Bastion brings you into the square-pillared chamber now known as ❿ the **North Hypostyle Entrance** or **Custom House**. It is believed that this room was an accounting point where goods (brought up

BULL LEAPING

from the harbour 5 km away) and personnel were checked into the palace. Turning west from the Custom House, the path runs on to a feature of greater fame:  the **West Court** or **Theatre**. Truth to tell, it doesn't conform much to modern ideas as to what a theatre should look like, being merely an earthquake-damaged paved area with a flight of steps and no seating. It has been identified as a 'theatre' for want of any other feature at Knossos that could serve as the 'dancing floor which Daedalus made for Ariadne in broad Knossos' described by Homer. In reality it is more of a terminus for the **Royal Road** that runs west from it. Described as the oldest paved road in Europe, the road dates from the earliest palace period. Originally, it was lined with houses and led to the **Little Palace** (a large Minoan villa that stood nearby) and the town that is thought to have built up outside the palace complex. Today, the deeply excavated path runs into the supporting wall of the site coach park, and has partially excavated buildings on its south side. Nearer the palace, excavation has opened up a path that runs back to the entrance court past the **Altars**. A second excavated Minoan road runs north of the Custom House to an inaccessible building known as the North Pillar Hall.

East of the Custom House, the site path drops away sharply (all the east-side rooms of the palace were built on the slope of the hill). The north-east corner of the palace was home to the **Servants' Quarters**: now little more than a jumble of meaningless foundations, their function has been determined by the contents when excavated. The singular exception to these incomprehensible ruins is the re-roofed room on the edge of this quarter containing the **Giant Pithoi Jars**. These stand over 2 m high, and are the largest found at Knossos. The 'room' they are in was once part of the complex of eastern storage rooms in the palace. The best means of seeing these is to take the staircase running from the central court to the **East Bastion**. The stairs divide the servants' quarters and storerooms from the **Workshops**, where the palace craftsmen did their stuff. Individual rooms (directly opposite the Giant Pithoi Jars) have been identified as potters' and stonecutters' workshops. The craftsmen in the latter carved stone utensils out of blocks of basalt imported from the Peloponnese.

The south-east sector of the palace containing the royal quarters was the most luxurious part of the complex. Unfortunately, the reconstructed buildings are closed on and off while they undergo periodic restoration, so they might not be open during 2004 (the 1900s concrete used to replace the lost wooden pillars and beams has flaked and cracked, and proved no durable substitute for the missing originals).

When this building is closed visitors have to make do with standing at the Central Court entrance and peering down into the reconstructed **Grand Staircase**, that in its prime stood five storeys high (only the bottom two of the three rebuilt storeys contain a significant amount of original material). Built around a light well adorned with the usual colonnades of tapering pillars (originally upturned trees) and spacious verandas adorned with frescoes, the Grand Staircase is the single most impressive architectural feature of the palace, besides marking Knossos out as a royal residence above the rest (other palaces on Crete had nothing to match it). It formed a royal approach to the **Royal Quarters**, with bathrooms on each floor (off the south-west corners) and doorways leading off into shrines and private rooms. The rebuilt staircase has been used to display reconstructions of a number of frescoes found in nearby rooms, notably the Mycenaean-period figure-of-eight shields and the lovely **Dolphin Fresco**. Fortunately the original fragments of these frescoes are on display in the Iraklion Archaeological Museum, so not all is lost if the Grand Staircase is still closed when you visit.

Sadly, if the staircase is closed you will miss out on the Royal Quarters, which are closed along with it. The nearest you will get to seeing them is to glimpse into the **Royal Apartments Lower Entrance** (this is reached via the

GRAND STAIRCASE
& QUEEN'S
APARTMENTS

CLOSED
for
renovation

path that runs around the site or — from the Central Court — via the East Bastion steps). From here you can just make out the **Hall of the Double Axes** (now thought to be the King's Audience room as the remains of a throne — complete with a four-pillared canopy — were discovered here) and the **King's Megaron**. This private royal room had a private balcony and was the original home of the figure-of-eight shield frescoes. Evans believed the room contained another throne.

Another room leading off the Hall of the Double Axes leads to the **Queen's Megaron**. Smaller than the King's Megaron, it was also adorned with frescoes — the most famous being the Dolphin Fresco. From this room runs a gallery complete with a triple window that opens out onto a light well. On this gallery stands the **Queen's Bathroom** (complete with a small painted hip-bath) and the **Queen's Toilet Room** which served as a dressing room. It, too, had a window and door into the light well (the door provided access to another small room off the light well that served as her most private of throne rooms).

The floor of the light well is also known as the **Court of the Distaffs**, after a symbol carved on the walls. From it runs a second corridor that leads to the **Treasury Room**. In this room Sir Arthur Evans discovered a number of fragments from gold and ivory objects. These are believed to have fallen from a room immediately above. The private royal living quarters are also lost; they are thought to have been located on the upper floors of the royal quarter of the palace.

The eastern edge of the palace now sits at the base of a small pine-shaded valley formed by the excavation of the lower hill rooms. From the Royal Quarters, the path runs on to the covered-over remains of the south-east corner of the palace. These include a number of 'private' apartments now named after their excavated remains: ❶ the **House of the Fallen Blocks** (no guesses as to what you will find here), the **House of the Channel Screen**, the **House of the Sacrificed Oxen**, the **House of the Monolithic Pillars**, the **South-East House**, and west of that ❷ the **Shrine of the Double Axes**. The double-headed axe was another popular Minoan motif; known as a 'Lavrys' it is thought by some to be the origin of the word 'Labyrinth' — meaning 'palace where the Lavrys is worshipped' (though others claim this is a load of bull).

Kasteli

ΚΑΣΤΕΛΛΙ; pop. 2,800.

CODE ☎ 28220
PORT POLICE ☎ 22024

A small, rather drab town on the western edge of Crete offering all the essential facilities but no more, Kasteli is often called, by ticket agents and maps alike, by its older name of **Kissamos**. The only ferry connections are the services to Kithera, Piraeus and the southern Peloponnese, a fact reflected in the location of the ferry quay, over 2 km west of the town centre on a particularly quiet stretch of coastline.

The solitude of the surrounding countryside — particularly the Gramvoussa Peninsula to the west — is the only real attraction, given that the town (complete with an uninspiring centre and a comparatively poor beach) itself lacks zip at all times of the day. Despite being the local transportation hub, the absence of frequent buses means you will need to hire a moped or car to explore the wilds.

►━┥

A plentiful supply of rooms are on offer in the town square and waterfront, even at the height of the season. There are also a number of reasonable hotels, including the C-class *Kissamos* (☎ 22086), *Castle* (☎ 22140) and the *Peli* (☎ 22343). There is also one B-class hotel/pension, the *Astrikas*, and one D-class outlet with expensive apartments, the *Mandy* (☎ 22825).

Λ

Camping Mythimna (☎ 31444): very quiet, 5 km east of the town centre on an excellent beach (take a Chania-bound bus and ask to be dropped at the campsite). There is also a semi-official site closer to hand — *Camping Kissamos* (☎ 23444). Complete with pool, it lies 200 m west of the town centre.

👓

Sightseeing is thin on the ground if you don't have your own wheels. The best thing on offer is the 7 km trek (buses are rare) inland to the village of **Polirinia** which has the substantial remains of an **Ancient City** (complete with an aqueduct commissioned by Hadrian) on the hillside above the current centre.

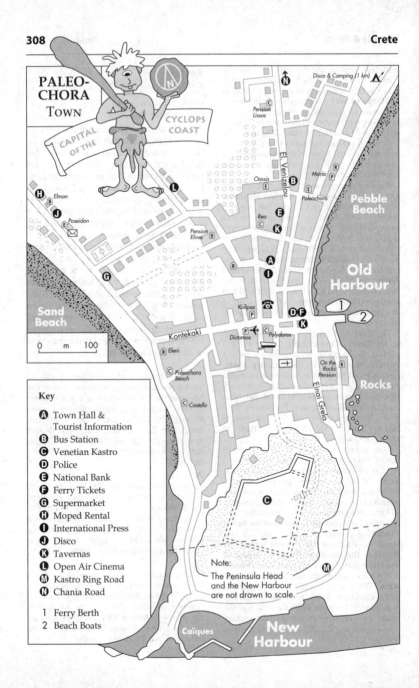

PALEO-CHORA TOWN

CAPITAL OF THE
CYCLOPS COAST

Disco & Camping (1 km)

Pension Lissos

El. Venizelou

Oassis

Maria

Paleochora

Pebble Beach

Rea

Elman

Poseidon

Pension Eliros

Sand Beach

0   m   100

Kontekaki

Kalipso

Dictamos

Polydoros

Eleni

Paleochora Beach

Castello

On the Rocks Pension

Einai Greia

Old Harbour

Rocks

Key

- **Ⓐ** Town Hall & Tourist Information
- **Ⓑ** Bus Station
- **Ⓒ** Venetian Kastro
- **Ⓓ** Police
- **Ⓔ** National Bank
- **Ⓕ** Ferry Tickets
- **Ⓖ** Supermarket
- **Ⓗ** Moped Rental
- **Ⓘ** International Press
- **Ⓙ** Disco
- **Ⓚ** Tavernas
- **Ⓛ** Open Air Cinema
- **Ⓜ** Kastro Ring Road
- **Ⓝ** Chania Road

1 Ferry Berth
2 Beach Boats

Note:
The Peninsula Head and the New Harbour are not drawn to scale.

Caïques

New Harbour

Paleochora

ΠΑΛΑΙΟΧΩΡΑ; pop. 3,000.

CODE ☎ 28230
PORT POLICE ☎ 41214
POLICE ☎ 41111
FIRST AID ☎ 41211

The south-west coast of Crete is charac-
terised by cliffs, ravines and a number of
small, isolated settlements. The region is
also famed as Cyclops country, though there
is little sign of these one-eyed giants today.
The main town on the coast is **Paleochora**. A
dusty peninsular town that is increasingly
under the sway of up-market package tour
operators, it lies caught between the sea on
two sides and the remains of a Venetian
Kastro (constructed in 1279 and destroyed
by the pirate Barbarossa), which offers some
exceptional views of the neighbouring
coastline, and an attractive base for a few
days while one explores the region.

The town's shoreline is graced with
a popular sand beach on the west side
and a pebble affair on the east (its comparative lack of appeal making it popular
with nudists). In addition, Paleochora is
host to a usually full-to-bursting daily boat
which heads for the idyllic brush-covered
beach islet of **Elafonisi** to the south-west.
Paleochora itself isn't the most attractive
town on Crete, but it is pleasant enough,
with the main streets closed to traffic during
the summer evenings.

Paleochora also has a regular small ferry
that runs east along the coast to a number
of secondary settlements. **Sfakia** (also
known as **Chora Sfakion**) is the next largest in size and lies at the other end of the
line. Its main attraction is the bus service
with Chania which ferries large numbers
of tourists home after their walk down the
Samaria Gorge.

During WW2 all the traffic was the other
way, as the village was a major Allied evacu-
ation point in the latter stages of the Battle
of Crete. **Agia Roumeli**, at the mouth of the
Samaria Gorge, is a tourist trap of little
merit. Now living off the large number of

tourists walking the gorge, it has a passable beach but little else to recommend it.
In between these three 'major' ports are
two tiny fishing hamlets also served by
the south coast ferry service. **Lutro** is the
least developed — thanks to the lack of a
beach — but can be reached via a coastal
path from Sfakia. **Sougia** has a beach and
growing numbers of tourists. It also lies at
the mouth of a second gorge — the **Agia Irini
Gorge**. Local ticket agencies offer organized
tours from Paleochora.

The coastline east of Sfakia is riven with
further gorges. These start with the **Kavi
Ravine** 1 km to the east, the 8 km **Imbros
Gorge** — accessible from the inland hill village of Imbros (which in turn is reached via
a Chania bus) — and the more inaccessible
Kallikrates Ravine and the **Aradena Gorge**,
which remain the preserve of heavy-duty
trekkers.

This area of coastline effectively termi-
nates with the 'resort' at **Matala** (accessed
by bus from Iraklion), home to a good beach
backed by cliffs pock-marked with caves
that look to have once been home to a colony
of Cyclops. During the 1960s these hapless
giants failed to keep a spare eye out for
squatters and the hippy brigade moved
in, changing all the boulders on the caves,
and generally making a nuisance of themselves. Most are now company executives
so things have calmed down a bit. Even
so, this part of Crete is still an odd mixture
of local conservatism and discreet foreign
liberalism.

⊨

Rooms are available in all ferry ports, but
supplies are necessarily limited. Most are
to be found in Paleochora. At the budget
end of the range are the E-class *Paleochora*
(☎ 41023) and *Oasis* (☎ 41328), the C-class
Polydoros (☎ 41068) and *Rea* (☎ 41307), and
some pensions including the dangerously
named *On the Rocks* (☎ 41713).

A

Camping Paleochora (☎ 41120) lies 2 km east
of the town in an olive grove behind a pebble
beach. A beach disco keeps campers awake
several nights a week in summer.

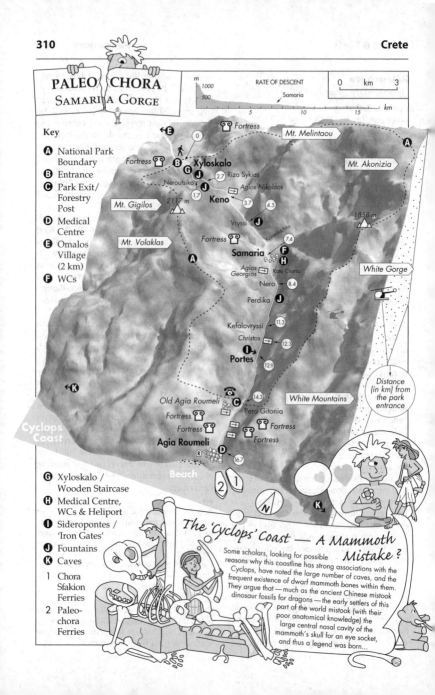

PALEO CHORA
SAMARIA GORGE

RATE OF DESCENT

m — 1000
— 500

Samaria

0 ___ km ___ 3

5   10   15   km

Key

A National Park Boundary

B Entrance

C Park Exit/ Forestry Post

D Medical Centre

E Omalos Village (2 km)

F WCs

Fortress

←**E**

(0)

Fortress

B **G** Xyloskalo

J

Neroutsiko

Riza Sykias

(2.7)

J

(1.7)

Agios Nikolaos

Keno

Mt. Melintaou

Mt. Akonizia

Mt. Gigilos   2117 m

(3.7)   (4.5)

Vryssi

J

Kolardáchtis

(7.4)

1858 m

Mt. Volaklas

Fortress

A

Samaria   **F**
H

Agios Georgios   Kato Chorio

Nero   (8.4)

Perdika   **J**

Kefalovryssi   (11.3)

Christos   (12.3)

Portes

(12.9)

White Gorge

White Mountains

Distance (in km) from the park entrance

Old Agia Roumeli   **C**
(14.3)

Fortress

Fortress

Pera Gitonia

Fortress

Fortress

Agia Roumeli

D

B   (16.7)

Beach

(2)   (1)

K

N

←**K**

Cyclops Coast

G Xyloskalo / Wooden Staircase

H Medical Centre, WCs & Heliport

I Sideropontes / 'Iron Gates'

J Fountains

K Caves

1 Chora Sfakion Ferries

2 Paleo-chora Ferries

The 'Cyclops' Coast — A Mammoth Mistake?

Some scholars, looking for possible reasons why this coastline has strong associations with the Cyclops, have noted the large number of caves, and the frequent existence of dwarf mammoth bones within them. They argue that — much as the ancient Chinese mistook dinosaur fossils for dragons — the early settlers of this part of the world mistook (with their poor anatomical knowledge) the large central nasal cavity of the mammoth's skull for an eye socket, and thus a legend was born...

∞
Chania is the best jumping-off point for the
Samaria Gorge. 18 km long and ranging
from 3.5 km down to 3 m wide, the gorge
is Crete's Lilliputian Grand Canyon (and
the longest canyon in Europe). It has been a
national park since the 1960s. Local ecologists
are becoming increasingly concerned by the
numbers visiting the gorge (an average of
2,000 a day now do the walk in the summer
months). Paths are being eroded, and the rare
horned Cretan ibex (the kri-kri) and the golden
eagles that once thrived here are departing for
the less noisy hillsides of the adjacent gorges
along this coast.

Walking the Gorge
The gorge is open from the 1st of May to the 31st
of October (at other times of the year the rivers
are high and the danger from falling rocks is
too great). It is patrolled by National Forest
Service staff who ensure that visitors don't
come to grief, attempt to stay overnight, or
enter outside the permitted hours (08.00–15.00:
from 15.00 to sunset visitors are allowed to visit
only the first 2 km of each end. All visitors are
checked in and out).

  Buses run daily to the village of **Omalos** at the
northern entrance to the gorge from Iraklion
(05.30: 3–4 hours), and four times daily from
Chania (1 hour). The trek down the gorge
takes some six hours with good shoes, and
is very pretty — particularly in the spring.
High Season travellers will find the walk less
attractive, the numbers of trekkers turning a
communion with nature into a noisy hobbit's
walking party. It is best to do the walk early
in the day to be sure of picking up a Sfakia
ferry from **Agia Roumeli** in time for the last
bus (usually 18.30).

1. Xyloskalo—Neroutsiko
[1.7 km, 45 minutes]. The gorge officially begins
at Xyloskalo, at an altitude of 1200 m. The
name means 'wooden staircase' after the early
stairway that was built down the steep wall of
the gorge. These days it has been replaced with
a proper stone and pine-tree-lined path that
descends steeply to the Neroutsiko spring.

2. Neroutsiko—Riza Sykias
[1 km, 20 minutes]. From Neroutsiko the path
follows the bed of a small spring, descending
much more gently to Riza Sykias.

3. Riza Sykias—Agios Nikolaos
[1 km, 20 minutes]. Riza Sykias is a second

spring which joins the path at this point, with
the gorge widening out as it approaches Agios
Nikolaos.

4. Agios Nikolaos—Vryssi
[0.8 km, 15 minutes]. Agios Nikolaos is a
small whitewashed chapel nestling under
some large cypress trees. Site of a spring, it
has had a religious function since Minoan
times. The path continues under the trees to
the Vryssi fountain.

5. Vryssi—Samaria
[2.9 km, 1 hour]. Crossing the river bed,
the path runs past hilltops decorated with
Turkish fortresses and on to the bridge that
leads to Samaria, the abandoned village at the
heart of the gorge. The inhabitants were forced
to leave when the National Park was created.
Only the churches survive intact.

6. Samaria—Perdika
[1.6 km, 20 minutes]. From Samaria the
gorge passes a second abandoned village
and becomes much deeper: the path runs
parallel to the river bed, before arriving at
the Perdika spring.

7. Perdika—Kefalovryssi
[2.3 km, 45 minutes]. From Perdika the
walls of the gorge rise steeply, and for
much of the time the path and river bed are
indistinguishable.

8. Kefalovryssi—Christos
[1 km, 20 minutes]. At Kefalovryssi the gorge
briefly opens out to reveal a spring shaded
by plane trees. A little further, and the path
comes to the small Church of Christ.

9. Christos—Portes
[0.6 km, 15 minutes]. The highlight of the gorge
is at **Portes / Sideropontes** ('the iron gates'),
where its width narrows to 3 m, while the walls
rise over 300 m. Rockfalls are common in the
early mornings and at nightfall — thanks to
the activities of Cretan ibex and changes in
rock surface temperatures.

10. Portes—Park South Entrance
[1.4 km, 30 minutes]. After the gates, the gorge
quickly widens again, slowly descending to
the National Park guard post.

11. Park South Entrance—Agia Roumeli
[2.4 km, 45 minutes]. From the south entrance
the path runs along the right bank of the river,
through a wide valley to Agia Roumeli.

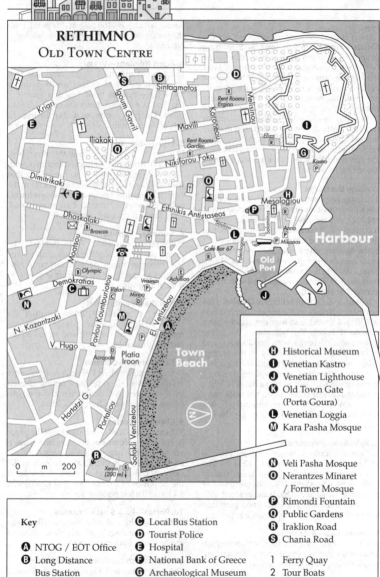

RETHIMNO
OLD TOWN CENTRE

Harbour

Old Port

Town Beach

0   m   200

Key

A NTOG / EOT Office
B Long Distance Bus Station
C Local Bus Station
D Tourist Police
E Hospital
F National Bank of Greece
G Archaeological Museum
H Historical Museum
I Venetian Kastro
J Venetian Lighthouse
K Old Town Gate (Porta Goura)
L Venetian Loggia
M Kara Pasha Mosque
N Veli Pasha Mosque
O Nerantzes Minaret / Former Mosque
P Rimondi Fountain
Q Public Gardens
R Iraklion Road
S Chania Road
1 Ferry Quay
2 Tour Boats

Rethimno
ΡΕΘΥΜΝΟ; pop. 20,000.

CODE ☎ 28310
TOURIST POLICE ☎ 28156
POLICE ☎ 25247
NTOG OFFICE ☎ 29148

Of the major port towns along Crete's north coast, Rethimno is the jewel in the crown; for not only can it claim to have the best preserved historical centre — German bombing in WW2 left it comparatively unscathed — packed with an interesting mix of Venetian and Ottoman buildings (the particularly rich Turkish overlay add-ing much to the exotic atmosphere of the town), but it is unique in having a very good town beach into the bargain.

With its very attractive harbour (complete with a very helpful NTOG / EOT office on the waterfront), and the largest Venetian castle in Greece, it is not surprising that Rethimno is developing as a popular package tourist resort destination. Hotels are mushrooming up all over the place — particularly along the coast east of the town — and doing little to enhance the ugly suburbs (one of the few negative points) around the old town.

If it wasn't for the tourists the old town would offer the chance to walk back a few centuries thanks to the narrow streets lined with unspoilt buildings (some of the Turk-ish houses have even retained their origi-nal wooden balconies), to say nothing of a couple of minarets attached to buildings that started life as Venetian churches.

In spite of its being laid out in a regular fashion it is easy to get lost in the maze of the old town (it is worth allowing for this before you start exploring); fortunately you don't have to go far in any direction before coming upon a recognisable landmark. The taverna-lined Venetian harbour in particu-lar is a visual delight, but also the town's bane. Too small to accommodate large boats, and prone to silting up, it accounts for the town's relative obscurity in the last couple of centuries.

Ferry connections reflect this state of affairs and are scanty — consisting of boats running direct to Piraeus augmented with occasional more expensive tourist boats to Santorini.

🛏

The popularity of Rethimno leads to higher prices, so you may have to ask around, though there are rooms and pensions aplenty — most within a block of the town beach or waterfront. There is also a Youth Hostel (☎ 22848) at 41 Tombasi St. With some forty hotels in the town or its environs finding a bed isn't difficult. Finding a cheap bed is a bit more tricky. The best bets are the D-class *Minoa* (☎ 22508), *Kastro* (☎ 24973), *Acropole* (☎ 27470) and the E-class *Achillion* (☎ 22581). Higher up the range is the C-class *Valari* (☎ 22236) near the National Bank and the B-class *Olympic* (☎ 24761) by the bus station.

Å

Camping Elisabeth (☎ 28694): a reasonable site 4 km east of the town. There is also a second site further out: *Camping Agia Galini* (☎ 91386).

👓

The **Venetian Kastro** is the obvious attraction in the town. Known as the **Fortezza** it was built in 1574 after repeated Barbary pirate raids. One of the best preserved Venetian castles in Greece, in its prime its walls almost held a town in themselves, but most of the interior buildings have gone now (apart from the former church that was later converted into a mosque) and you have to make do with the lovely views over the town.

Somewhat surprisingly (considering how much of the old centre has survived) the Ve-netian town walls have all but disappeared, the only remnant being one gate known as the **Porta Goura** (1572). Within the alleyways stands a Venetian **Loggia**. Built c. 1600, it served as a meeting place for the town's officials. Nearby flows the 17 c. **Rimondi Fountain**, a late Venetian addition to the town. The later Turkish presence offers another sightseeing option: the climb to the top of the minaret of the 18 c. **Nerandzes Mosque**, with its views over the castle and town.

Rethimno also has **Archaeological** and **Historical Museums** housing a variety of (indif-ferent) finds, from its Minoan origins to its later role as a haven for scholars fleeing the Turkish conquest of Constantinople.

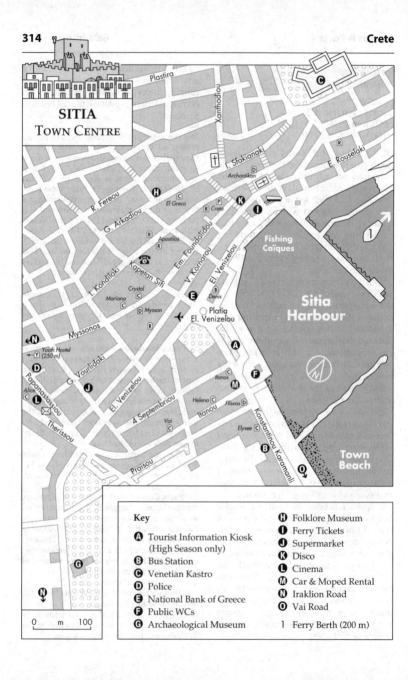

SITIA
TOWN CENTRE

Plastira

Xanthoudiou

I. Sfakianaki

E. Rouselaki

Archontikon

R. Fereou

H

C
El Greco

R **P**
R Creta

K

I

G. Arkadiou

Em. Foundalidou

V. Kornarou

El. Venizelou

Apostilos
R
R

Kapetan Sifi

I. Kondilaki

Fishing
Caïques

Crystal
C
Mariana
C

D Mysson

R

E

B
Denis

Platia
El. Venizelou

**Sitia
Harbour**

Myssonos

N

Youth Hostel
Y (250 m)

D

G. Vourlidaki

Papanastassiou

Alice
C
L

J

El. Venizelou

4 Septembriou

A

C
Itanos

M

F

Helena **C**
Flisvos **D**

Itanou

Vai
C

Elysee **C**

B

O

Konstantinou Karamanli

**Town
Beach**

Praisou

Therissou

N

0   m   100

G

Key

A Tourist Information Kiosk
   (High Season only)
B Bus Station
C Venetian Kastro
D Police
E National Bank of Greece
F Public WCs
G Archaeological Museum

H Folklore Museum
I Ferry Tickets
J Supermarket
K Disco
L Cinema
M Car & Moped Rental
N Iraklion Road
O Vai Road

1 Ferry Berth (200 m)

Sitia
ΣΗΤΕΙΑ; pop. 8,000.

CODE ☎ 28430
PORT POLICE ☎ 22310
TOURIST POLICE ☎ 24200
POLICE ☎ 22266
FIRST AID ☎ 24311

The most easterly port on Crete, scenic Sitia is very much the poor relation compared to the other towns along the northern coast when it comes to ferry connections. However, it beats the pants off Agios Nikolaos as an attractive destination. Set in a wide bay, the Venetian-built town (that nonetheless manages to feel more like a regular island chora, being all white houses and stair-cases) attracts its share of tourists in High Season, thanks in part to its lovely fishing port atmosphere and a three-day annual August wine festival (grapes and raisins are the region's principal exports).

The town, which is built like an irregular amphitheatre around the port, is also blessed with a reasonable sand beach that extends east for over a kilometre, and has a couple of days of sightseeing for those who want it. The municipal tourist information kiosk that opens every summer in the main square offers information on the sights and accommodation options.

⊨

In **Sitia** rooms are plentiful (except for the end of August Sultana Festival), with over a dozen hotels in the centre. For a reasonable bed try the B-class pension *Denis* (☎ 28356) on the waterfront. At the budget end of the range is the D-class *Archontiko* (☎ 22993), and the *Pension Artemis* (☎ 22564). There is also a *Youth Hostel* (☎ 22693) 500 m from the town centre (towards Iraklion) at 4 Therissou St.

◑◑

Thanks to a good **Archaeological Museum** (housing finds from the Minoan palace at Zakros), and a passable **Folklore Museum** in the town, there is enough to keep you occupied if you have to wait for a boat. The only building of note is the restored **Kastro** on the hill behind the town. Really a glorified fort rather than a full-blown castle, it was built in 1204 and later enlarged by the Venetians,

repelling a Barbary pirate raid in 1538 before falling to the Turks in 1651. In the absence of any significant Turkish remains (the town lay in ruins for the two centuries following its capture), popular tourist-buses also head east to the good sand beach (graced with islets offshore) at **Vai**: the beach, however, isn't the reason the tourists come, for behind the sand is the only natural **Palm Forest** in Europe. Looking like a piece of transplanted North Africa, it is now a national park.

Sitia is the north coast port for the finger of land that makes up the eastern extremity of Crete. The windmill-cluttered hinterland known as the Lasithi plain is very quiet, with poor roads: you usually have to double back to Agios Nikolaos to get to the other population centres on the south coast. Fringing the Libyan Sea, they escape the attentions of the *meltemi* wind that slams into Crete's northern coast and thus enjoy calmer seas during the summer. The only large town is at **Ierapetra**, which can be reached by regular buses from Sitia.

Ierapetra
ΙΕΡΑΠΕΤΡΑ; pop. 10,750.

CODE ☎ 28420

Built on the site of an important Minoan and later Roman town, Ierapetra (pronounced 'EErapetra') was very late in embracing tourism. Today the town has a small, but noisy and vibrant, tourist industry (centred heavily on the waterfront), but the main focus of economic activity still centres on market-garden agriculture. With a large fertile plain behind the town and something approaching a mild North African climate, Ierapetra is well placed and takes every advantage of its location. So much so, that a good number of the visitors are seeking casual work in the industry. The same climatic conditions make it a poor choice of destination in July and August as it can get insufferably hot.

Sadly, the town itself doesn't live up to its history. The problem is finding any, for apart from a very small old town that dates from the years of Ottoman rule, the rest of the place is post-1960 concrete. The pluses are a good (grey) sand town beach and — for

IERAPETRA
CENTRE

Key

ⓐ Venetian Kastro
ⓑ Archaeological
   Museum
ⓒ Napoleon's House
ⓓ Turkish Fountain
ⓔ Clock Tower
ⓕ Town Hall

Popy   Four
       Seasons
Nikos ⓡ
ⓗ
ⓙ
Cretan
Villa Ⓓ
**Platia
El Venizelou**
ⓞ
Katerina
El Greco
Iris Ⓓ ⒸⒸ
Lashenou
Nikiphorou Foka
☏
Kaminos
Ⓒ
Leon ⓟ
**Platia
Eleftherias**
Ersi
Ⓒ
ⓘ
Zakros
Ⓒ
ⓘ
Adrianou   ⓕ
ⓑ ⓖ
←ⓡ
Opt. Vasamidi
Kiprou
ⓝ
Pl.
Emmanuel
Kothri
ⓚ
Promenade
Houta
✉
Agiou Georgiou
Vitzenizos Kornaros
ⓛ
ⓟ
**Town
Beach**
Coral Ⓓ
ⓟ
Gorgona Ⓟ ⓜ
Idomeneos
Zafiri
Ⓓ
ⓓ
Erotokritos ⓡ
ⓒ
ⓟ
**Old
Town**
ⓛ
ⓔ †
ⓐ
Beach
**Fishing
Caïques**
Marina
Ⓝ
Harbour

0   m   150

ⓖ Information Centre
ⓗ Bus Station
ⓘ Bank / ATM
ⓙ Hospital (200 m)
ⓚ Pharmacy
ⓛ Taverna
ⓜ International Press
ⓝ Covered Market
ⓞ Stadium (50 m)
ⓟ Boat Tickets
ⓠ Agios Nikolaos &
   Sitia Road
ⓡ Myrtos Road

1 Excursion Boats to
   Chrissi Is. &
   Koufonisi Is.

island hoppers — regular caïques that run to **Chrissi** island during the summer months (see below).

Ierapetra has a good amount of budget accommodation: notably, the D-class *Cretan Villa* (☎ 28522) near the bus station, the beach front D-class *Iris* (☎ 23136) and C-class *El Greco* (☎ 28471). In the centre of town are the noisier D-class *Coral* (☎ 22848) and the pensions *Gorgona* (☎ 23935) and *Diagoras* (☎ 23898).

There is nothing to be seen of the Minoan and Roman towns (the last remaining major building, a bathhouse, was lost two hundred years ago). The few surviving fragments are housed in a one-room **Archaeological Museum**. The other sightseeing attractions include a small **Venetian Kastro**, rebuilt in 1626 after an earthquake. The Old Town also boasts a Venetian town house where **Napoleon** stayed while returning to France from Egypt following the Battle of the Nile.

Crete: Minor Islands

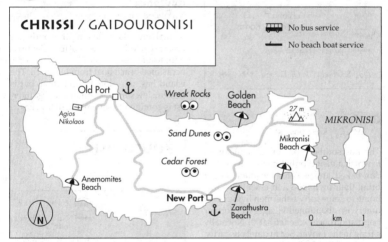

Chrissi
ΧΡΥΣΗ; 6 km²; pop. 0.

Formerly known as Gaidouronisi ('donkey island'), the small island of Chrissi is a nature reserve (now without donkeys) and beach island sitting in the Libyan sea 10 km to the south of the Cretan town of Ierapetra. Daily excursion boats (€5) run from the town in High Season.

Blessed with an intriguing mix of good clean sandy beaches, backed by sand dunes

and a small forest of cedar trees, Chrissi is the nearest thing in Greece to a plausible desert island. Usually uninhabited, it has a couple of tavernas (located at the new harbour) that open during the tourist season and freelance camping has been tolerated in the past. Chrissi is traversed via a dirt track that links the new harbour with its predecessor (complete with a nearby chapel and lighthouse) to the north-west and the best of the beaches — Golden Beach — to the north-east.

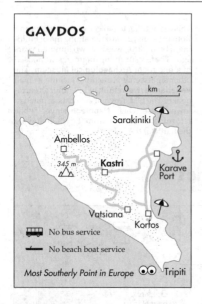

GAVDOS

0   km   2

Sarakiniki

Ambellos

345 m   **Kastri**

Karave Port

Vatsiana

Korfos

No bus service

No beach boat service

Most Southerly Point in Europe   Tripiti

Gavdos
ΓΑΥΔΟΣ; 34 km²; pop. 50.

The most southerly part of Europe, Gavdos is worth a visit if only for curiosity value. Sun-baked and isolated (visitors should bring their own food and essentials), it is home to some forty fishermen living on in otherwise abandoned villages (the former population once exceeded 8,000). Normally sitting in the Libyan Sea in quiet obscurity, the island hit the headlines in June 1996 when Turkey—in the wake of the argument over the sovereignty of Imia (see p. 337) —claimed Gavdos was 'disputed territory', a delicious piece of nonsense as Turkey is hundreds of kilometres away.

Despite its tiny population Gavdos has a post office/OTE, a doctor and— bizarrely — a policeman, all housed in the capital of Kastri. The island has quiet beaches at Korfos (at the mouth of a small fertile valley) and Sarakiniki: the only other bathers are likely to be the doctor and the policeman.

A few rooms are available in both Karave and Kastri (pre-booking is possible via travel agents in Paleochora). Freelance camping is also tolerated in season.

The nearest Greece has to a ghost-town island, Gavdos lacks sights beyond an air of wild abandon. However, it does offer some interesting walks. Those trekking to the end of Europe at Tripiti will, however, be able to enjoy the incongruous sight of oil tankers passing by like spook ships from another age. Occasional caïques also venture to uninhabited **Gavdopoula** to the north-east.

Koufonisi
ΚΟΥΦΟΝΗΣΙ; 11 km²; pop. 0.

A small low island close off the south-east coast of Crete, Koufonisi (not to be confused with Koufonissia in the Cyclades) sees the occasional beach boat from Ierapetra. The island has no resident population, but is host to a few summer farmers. Tourist interest is confined to several small beaches.

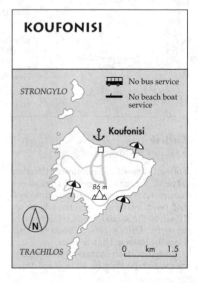

KOUFONISI

STRONGYLO

No bus service

No beach boat service

Koufonisi

86 m

N

TRACHILOS

0   km   1.5

Spinalonga
ΣΠΙΝΑΛΟΝΓΑ; 1 km²; pop. 0.

Spinalonga is a small islet on the north-east coast of Crete. The island is dominated by a well-preserved Venetian fortress that skirts the entire coastline. It is now billed by excursion boat operators at Agios Nikolaos as the 'island of the living dead' thanks to its history as a leper colony between 1903–55.

It is this role that takes centre stage today. For although Spinalonga was supposedly a hospital, in reality it was a dumping ground, with lepers of all ages (including children) deliberately marooned here, living in the former Turkish village built within the fortress's massive curtain walls. Guided tours (usually included in the tour boat price of €18) are standard, as all the buildings are now derelict and most in a ruinous state of repair. Tours take in the circuit path that runs inside the enceinte, visiting all the major landmarks — these include the leper's cemetery and the battlements.

As an excursion destination Spinalonga offers good value and an interesting experience, but there is no escaping the fact that the island is a melancholy place: this isn't a day-trip for those who want to party.

The Venetian fortress is so substantial that it has obliterated any evidence of earlier constructions. Built in 1579, it achieved fame across Europe as a bastion of heroic resistance for holding out against Turkish attack for thirty years after the rest of Crete had succumbed to Ottoman rule (it finally fell in 1715). Thereafter it housed a Turkish garrison and their families. By 1898, when Crete effectively joined modern Greece, the Turkish population was over 3,000. Most left, but a good number refused to leave their homes. In 1903 the Greek government decided to turn Spinalonga into a leper colony, and for some reason the remaining Turkish inhabitants opted to leave — very quickly.

The new inhabitants didn't get the same opportunities. Attempts at escape by lepers were discouraged by removing all the baths from the island (after several were used as makeshift boats), while in WW2 four escaping lepers were shot by German troops.

Although many of the lepers did their best to make the most of life on the island, their existence was very hard. All food and water had to be brought in, and supplies were very irregular. Medical necessities were also often lacking (hence the stories of limb amputations without anaesthetics).

The worst horror story concerns an 18-year-old girl who was dumped on the island after being diagnosed with leprosy of the throat. Shortly after arriving she choked on an apple. The following day her body was interred in the leper cemetery. As is usual in Greece, the grave was opened four years later (by which time all soft matter has rotted away) so that the bones could be moved and the grave reused. To the horror of those who removed the stone slab covering the grave, the girl's bones were not in their laid-out position, and it was clear from their location that she must have awoken from a comatose state only to find herself entombed alive. The last lonely hours of this girl's terrible life don't bear thinking about, but do sum up the tragedy of Spinalonga.

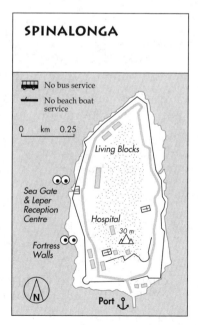

SPINALONGA

No bus service

No beach boat service

0   km   0.25

Living Blocks

Sea Gate & Leper Reception Centre

Hospital

30 m

Fortress Walls

N

Port

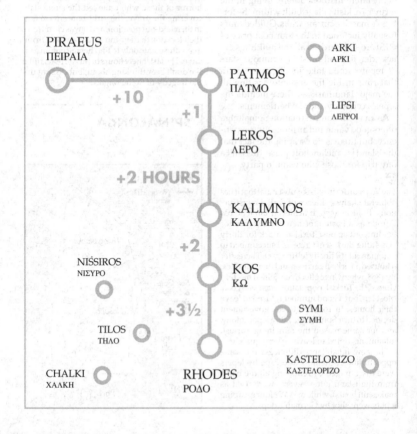

7

DODECANESE LINES

CHALKI · KALIMNOS · KARPATHOS · KOS · LEROS
LIPSI · NISSIROS · PATMOS · RHODES · SYMI · TILOS

PIRAEUS
ΠΕΙΡΑΙΑ

ARKI
ΑΡΚΙ

PATMOS
ΠΑΤΜΟ

+10

+1

LIPSI
ΛΕΙΨΟΙ

LEROS
ΛΕΡΟ

+2 HOURS

KALIMNOS
ΚΑΛΥΜΝΟ

NISSIROS
ΝΙΣΥΡΟ

+2

KOS
ΚΩ

+3½

SYMI
ΣΥΜΗ

TILOS
ΤΗΛΟ

KASTELORIZO
ΚΑΣΤΕΛΟΡΙΖΟ

CHALKI
ΧΑΛΚΗ

RHODES
ΡΟΔΟ

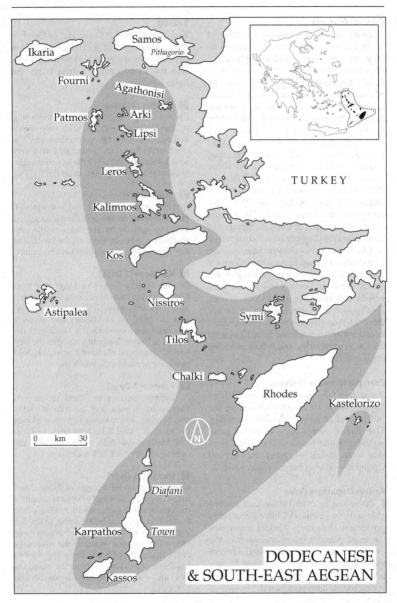

Ikaria

Samos
Pithagorio

Fourni

Agathonisi

Patmos   Arki

Lipsi

Leros

TURKEY

Kalimnos

Kos

Astipalea   Nissiros

Symi

Tilos

Chalki

Rhodes

Kastelorizo

0   km   30

Diafani

Karpathos   *Town*

Kassos

**DODECANESE
& SOUTH-EAST AEGEAN**

General Features

Running down the Aegean coastline of Turkey, the Dodecanese chain derives its name from the Greek 'dodeka' or 'twelve', after the major islands in the group which revolted against Turkish rule in 1908. The islands possess a unique character thanks to a combination of the strong architectural heritage inherited from the Knights of St. John (who left at least one castle on every island), the Italian occupation between 1913 and 1943 (when a deliberate attempt was made to Italianize the islands), the allure of day trips to the Turkish mainland (visible from most islands), and the duty-free status that has accompanied their late entry into the Greek state. The tourist influx has resulted in the development of a considerable pleasure boat industry that augments the ferry infrastructure, making island hopping easy. Ferry connections are mostly confined to the group (though occasional ferries do venture beyond the geographical boundaries of the Dodecanese). Finally, isolated Astipalea, though part of this post-1908 group, has more in common in history, appearance and ferry links with the Eastern Cyclades, and is thus included in Chapter 5.

Example Itinerary [2 Weeks]

If you aren't the most adventurous island hopper the Dodecanese chain offers the prospect of an easy and relaxed holiday. The islands offer a popular mix of good sightseeing and beaches. The only downside is an Italian — rather than typical Cycladic — atmosphere in many towns.

Arrival/Departure Point

Rhodes, Kos or even Piraeus are reasonable starting points. All have good entry points into the group. Rhodes is perhaps the most popular (so it is chosen in the example here); though lying at the end of the chain with poorly connected islands immediately north of it, it is an indifferent springboard/base port island.

Season

Early June through to the end of October sees a high level of services. Out of this period ferries only run 3—4 days per week and the all-important tourist boats are far less evident.

1 Rhodes [2 Days]

Rhodes is a good starting point if venturing up the Dodecanese chain, with easy flights and plenty to see while you acclimatize. The city tourist office also distributes current ferry schedules and with these in hand you can start to fill in the details of your itinerary.

2 Kos [4 Days]

Arriving on Kos you will find yourself well placed to take advantage of the island's good hopping options by staying a while and alternating between days on the beach and day hops to Nissiros and Turkey (Bodrum).

3 Kalimnos [2 Days]

Can be happily 'done' as a day trip from Kos if you don't want to change your accommodation. Otherwise, it is an easy hop and you can head on to Mirities and spend a couple of days between the beach and the islet of Telendos. Kalimnos also has the best beach boats to the island of Pserimos should you want to try out the beach there.

4 Patmos [3 Days]

A suitably spectacular island to aim for, Patmos has a nice lazy mixture of sights and beaches. You can also add other islands to your tally and take boat trips to Lipsi and Marathonisi/Arki before catching the overnight ferry back to Rhodes.

1 Rhodes [3 Days]

One of the great advantages of flying direct to the Dodecanese is that your final couple of days are spent in far nicer surroundings than those offered by Athens. Returning to Rhodes with plenty of time to spare before your return flight means you can take advantage of the many tourist boats down the coast to Lindos, as well as day trips to the islands of Symi and — with a little more circumspection — Chalki.

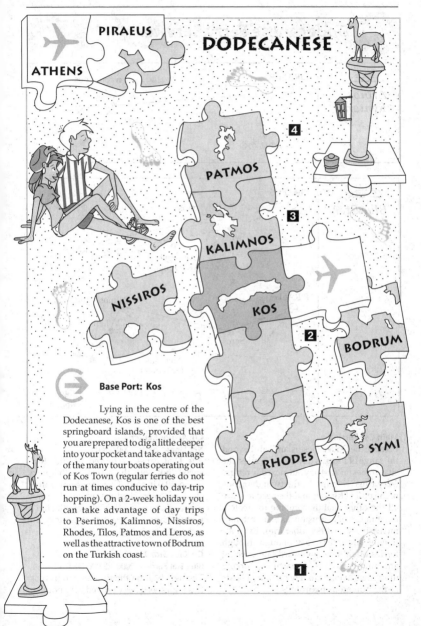

PIRAEUS

DODECANESE

ATHENS

4

PATMOS

3

KALIMNOS

NISSIROS

KOS

2

BODRUM

Base Port: Kos

Lying in the centre of the Dodecanese, Kos is one of the best springboard islands, provided that you are prepared to dig a little deeper into your pocket and take advantage of the many tour boats operating out of Kos Town (regular ferries do not run at times conducive to day-trip hopping). On a 2-week holiday you can take advantage of day trips to Pserimos, Kalimnos, Nissiros, Rhodes, Tilos, Patmos and Leros, as well as the attractive town of Bodrum on the Turkish coast.

RHODES

SYMI

1

Dodecanese Ferry Services

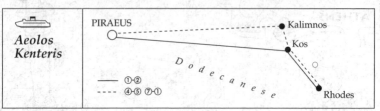

Aeolos Kenteris

PIRAEUS ○ ○ Kalimnos
Kos
D o d e c a n e s e
—— ①-②
- - - ④-⑤ ⑦-①
Rhodes

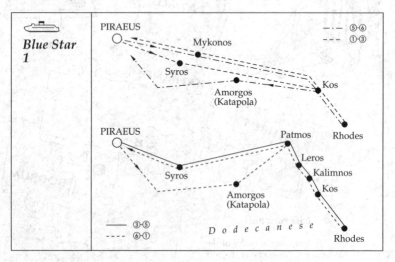

Blue Star 1

PIRAEUS ○
Mykonos
Syros
Amorgos (Katapola)
Kos
Rhodes
—·— ⑤-⑥
- - - ①-③

PIRAEUS ○
Patmos
Leros
Syros
Kalimnos
Kos
Amorgos (Katapola)
—— ③-⑤
- - - ⑥-①
D o d e c a n e s e
Rhodes

Main Car Ferries

Because the Dodecanese islands are beyond the range of Piraeus day-return ferries, the chain relies on 'first day out, next day return' ferry runs. Unhappily, the twin demands of the pull of Rhodes and the need to serve all the other islands combine to create a fair amount of confusion, as boats attempt increasingly diverse itineraries. Even so, moving around is easy enough, though ferries often have awkward late evening and night arrivals/departures, forcing morning travellers to rely on tourist boats or the numerous hydrofoils.

C/F *Aeolos Kenteris*

NEL Lines; 2001; 6000 GRT.

The Dodecanese acquired its first high speed link with the arrival of this ferry (see p. 402) in 2002. There were only minor changes to her schedules in 2003. The only downside to using this boat are the fares: with distances as great as these they are rather steep.

C/F *Blue Star 1*

Blue Star Ferries; 2000; 20000 GRT.

The new boat on the Rhodes run in 2003, this high speed ferry proved very popular,

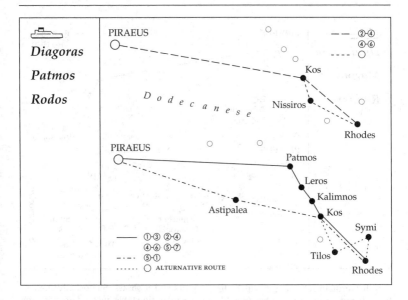

running to the Dodecanese four times a week, with some useful cross-line stops in the Cyclades en route. An impressive ferry with a double escalator up to the main passenger saloon, she offers the best facilities of any boat on the line. She is also the only boat to offer high speed links to Patmos and Leros (though only two calls a week in each direction). Highly recommended — even if the tickets come at a price.

C/F Diagoras
D.A.N.E. Sea Lines.
Financially troubled D.A.N.E Sea Lines run three ferries to the Dodecanese. Formerly the premier company on the line, they are now the 'best of the rest'. The C/F *Diagoras* falls neatly into this category: an attractive enough boat, but no competition for the new high speed craft. In addition to a couple of sorties into the Dodecanese, she also made a couple of runs between Piraeus and Crete (Iraklion) in 2003. She combines with the *Patmos* and *Rodos* on a rolling 8-day timetable, so with all these

D.A.N.E. Sea Lines boats the route is far more important than the ferry name (which is apt to change each week).

C/F Patmos
D.A.N.E. Sea Lines; 1972; 7480 GRT.
A regular in the Dodecanese since 1992, the *Patmos* is a medium-sized, if rather boring, ferry. Her one great selling-point is the fact that she offers good deck-class facilities. In the past she has run an irregular schedule. High Season sees her taking on an extended run from Rhodes to Thessalonika. Otherwise she runs in tandem with the *Rodos* offering a daily afternoon departure each way — though the calls at intermediate islands tend to vary. Like most of the large Dodecanese boats she is among the older Greek ferries, though she doesn't seem it.

C/F Rodos
D.A.N.E. Sea Lines; 1973; 6475 GRT.
The *Rodos* formerly ran a direct 12-hour service between Piraeus and Rhodes, but now visits the other Dodecanese islands

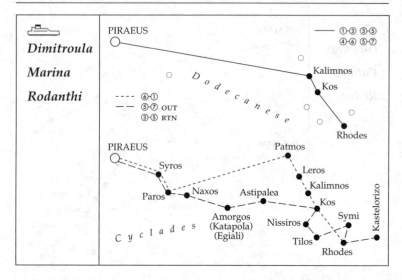

Dimitroula

Marina

Rodanthi

as well. Normally reliable, and with better than average on-board facilities (notably a good deck-class saloon), she suffered a major engine fire in 1991, forcing passengers to be transferred in mid-Aegean to a rescue boat. Since then she has had a helicopter pad on her sun deck in lieu of passenger seating. Attitudes to backpackers are reasonably relaxed. Overall, this is one of the better boats on the route.

C/F *Dimitroula*
G. A. Ferries; 1978; 7222 GRT.
A reasonably large vessel (see p. 439) the *Dimitroula* returned to this line in 2003 (after a summer deputizing for another ferry on another line). Given her history of route changes, it will be a miracle if she stays in place this year.

C/F *Marina*
G.A. Ferries; 1971; 5941 GRT.
The G.A. Ferries' fleet is looking shabby these days (part owned by Hellas Flying Dolphins it hasn't received much investment of late). The *Marina* has been on the Piraeus—Rhodes route for the last seven

years and it shows. She usually runs an irregular timetable in tandem with the *Rodanthi* (timetables simply say '*Marina* or *Rodanthi*'). The main thing that can be said in her favour is that she is better than her partner. In past years she possessed that rarest of rarities, a swimming pool full of sea water — to say nothing of a sun deck adorned with palm sun-umbrellas (now looking as if a hurricane has struck).

C/F *Rodanthi*
G.A. Ferries; 1974; 8273 GRT.
This big ferry moved onto this line from the Cyclades in 1997. Formerly a comfortable boat, she was looking very down-at-heel in 2003, with both her interior deck-class facilities and sun-deck seating looking shabby in the extreme. Her inflatable life-rafts also looked to be in an ancient condition (to go by the flaps of rough plastic glued over their release mechanisms). If you are still inclined to travel on her after reading the above, then there is one very minor plus: this is one boat that hasn't discriminated against backpackers trying to gain entry to the interior deck-class facilities.

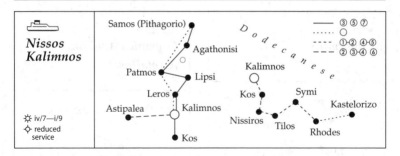

C/F *Nissos Kalimnos*
A. N. E. Kalimnos Sea Lines; 1988; 754 GRT.

The only small car ferry sailing solely within the Dodecanese, this Greek-built vessel operates out of Kalimnos and provides an invaluable service to adjacent islands. Run by a one-boat company, her itinerary has barely changed over the last eight years (though the days routes are run have sometimes varied). For the most part reliable — if occasionally very late — this ferry broke down in July 1992, leaving her passengers with nought to do but admire the view while listening to the soporific 'lip-lip' of the sea kissing the ship's sides. The *Nissos Kalimnos* was also laid up in the early part of 2001 (when a succession of other vessels were put on her route — this ferry acts as the local mail boat for some of the smaller islands). Unfortunately, she boasts a shabby interior, seriously awful WCs, and a lack of air-conditioning.

C/M *Dodekanesos Express*
Dodekanisos Speedways

The first of several new catamarans to appear in the Dodecanese in the last couple of years, this orange-hulled, medium-sized passenger-only craft appeared out of the blue in late June 2000. Running daily out of Rhodes up the line, she is poorly advertised in the islands and hasn't made much impact to date (finding a current timetable can be a problem on many of the islands). This is a great pity, for this craft is easily the most civilized way of travelling up and down the Dodecanese. She is as fast as the competing hydrofoils but offers a far superior ride for a similar fare. The lack of advertising means that she isn't too full, and she boasts a powerful air-conditioning system and a number of TVs. Like the hydrofoils, she uses the port of Agia Marina when calling at Leros. In 2003 she offered a much-need day-trip option to Kastelorizo.

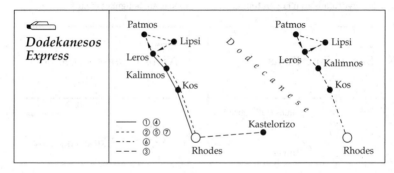

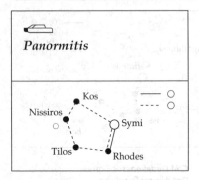

C/M *Panormitis*

Arriving in mid-2002, this vessel has yet to settle down into an established routine. Operated by ANE Symi, she confined her wanderings last year to making daily round trips between Symi and Rhodes alongside the existing cats and hydrofoils. Prior to her arrival in Greece, her operators were advertising a much wider range of destinations, so look out for timetable changes.

Samos Tour Boats

The large number of package tourists now based on the south coast of Samos has spawned a minor excursion-boat boom (though hydrofoils remain the primary beneficiaries of this custom). As a result, it is possible to island hop at least four days a week using these vessels. They are particularly useful during the Low Season when hydrofoils aren't operating.

C/F *Olympios Apollon* – C/F *Atromitos*

Landing-craft ferries operate out of Kalimnos to the resort of Mastihari on Kos. Running three times daily, they exist in part to serve charter holiday-makers running to and from the airport on Kos. At the same time, these rather uninspiring boats also provide a useful evening standby for any day-trippers who have missed their tour boat and are marooned on Kalimnos or Kos. The *Atromitos* wasn't operating in 2003.

T/B *Nikos Express* – T/B *Chalki*

Two caïques turned tour boats provide Chalki with its main link with the wider world, running daily to Rhodes (where they connect with the daily bus service to and from Rhodes Town). The *Nikos Express* is the better of the two, though both are apt to roll for the full 90-minute crossing. Tickets are bought on board.

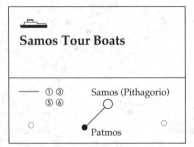

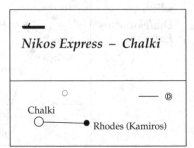

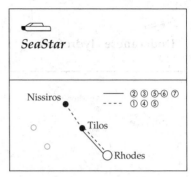

Dodecanese Tour / Island Boats

The inconvenient departure times of many ferries in the Dodecanese mean that most island hoppers resort to at least one of the tourist craft shown on this page. Although they cost a bit more, the convenience value makes them worth it, and they partly exist to provide one-way journeys for those not enamoured with day-tripping.

Kos is the main base for tour boats, with two large and comfortable vessels — the *Stefamar* and the *Nissos Kos* — augmented by smaller boats. They swap destinations several times a week, but in practice combine to run a daily service to Nissiros, Kalimnos and Pserimos; a quick wander around the town's travel agents or along the waterfront will enable you to find out which one you want. Tickets are sold on the quayside prior to departure as well as at travel agents. You can also pick these

vessels up on their return runs, if they have spare capacity (when tickets are sold on board). The same is true of the smaller boats operating out of Patmos to Lipsi, and the larger Rhodes—Symi boats.

One of the most useful in the past has been the *Symi II*. Worth looking out for as she runs an early morning Symi—Rhodes service, she returns to Symi filled with tourists. The new catamaran *Symi III* runs alongside, and augments the new C/M *Panormitis*. As a means of getting to Symi in time to find accommodation she has been invaluable, but in 2003 the operators weren't keen on one-way backpackers using her.

Tilos is also now in on the 'get tourists to visit our island by having our own daily boat link to Rhodes' act, having recently stumped up the cash to buy its own catamaran — the *SeaStar* — which now operates out of Rhodes to the island.

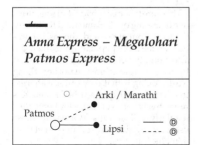

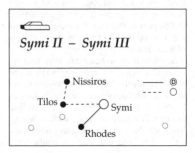

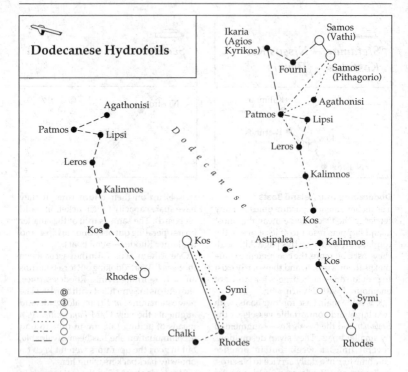

Hydrofoils

Local hydrofoils provide an invaluable addition to ferries in the Dodecanese, if only because they don't require night travel (a depressing feature of many ferry departure times). The downside is that most of these boats are quite old, but rust and mould don't seem to be denting their popularity in this part of the world, even if the years are now taking their toll on the numbers of these boats still operating.

Given that these boats are very tourist-orientated, it is not surprising that there are considerable fluctuations in levels of activity, with little happening outside the June to September period. If you are not travelling in High Season it is very much a case of looking to see what is running when you arrive. The links that you can confidently

expect to find are daily Kos—Rhodes and Rhodes—Kos runs. These boats thrive on day-trippers as they leave early morning and return in the evenings (note: they often fill up in High Season, so it is best to buy tickets at least 24 hours before you want to travel).

There are two major hydrofoil operators, one operating out of Samos and Kalimnos, the second out of Kos and Rhodes. In addition, on the more popular routes, there are also a number of smaller one-or-two-boat hydrofoil operations. Another thing worth noting is that they can use alternative harbours or quays (Rhodes and Kos respectively) or even ports (at Leros they regularly call at Agia Marina) to those used by regular ferries, and timetables don't indicate this.

Dodecanese Islands & Ports

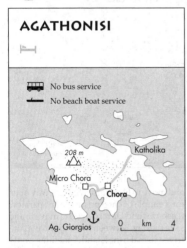

AGATHONISI

No bus service

No beach boat service

208 m

Katholika

Micro Chora

Chora

Ag. Giorgios

0   km   4

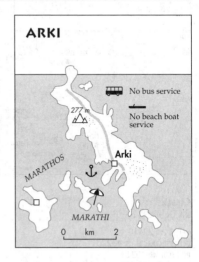

ARKI

No bus service

277 m

No beach boat service

MARATHOS

Arki

MARATHI

0   km   2

Agathonisi

ΑΓΑΘΟΝΗΣΙ; 13 km²; pop. 110.

CODE ☎ 22470
PORT / REGULAR POLICE ☎ 23770

Poorly connected Agathonisi is home to a small fishing community, six islets (all uninhabited), and a large ferry quay. An uninspiring hilly island covered with thorn bushes, it remains the preserve of the odd northern European grimly determined to get away from it *all*. The best reason to visit is the sense of elation that comes on leaving it; you can guarantee that you will return from your holiday feeling you have really achieved something. Unfortunately, the sum of the parts is considerably less than the whole. The two hamlets aren't worth spending three days on the island for and the only activity on offer is walking the donkey path to an abandoned village at Katholika.

Two port pensions offer a total of 12 beds.

Arki

ΑΡΚΟΙ; 7 km²; pop. 50.

CODE ☎ 22470

Consisting of scrub-covered dune-hills unrelieved by anything of interest, one dour fishing village and a dozen-odd islets, Arki is not on the tourist map. The island also has no ferry quay, so boats steam aimlessly around on the off-chance of meeting a passenger-filled caïque. More important, there is no regular caïque to the nearby uninhabited islet of **Marathi** (complete with a delightful beach backed by a couple of seasonal tavernas) — the destination for most 'Arki' advertised Patmos boats (check your exact destination if taking one of these). Marathi excepted, visitors should bring their own food, shelter, spade and nut-bucket.

Accommodation is limited to two tavernas offering rooms in Arki. One of the tavernas on Marathi also offers summer rooms.

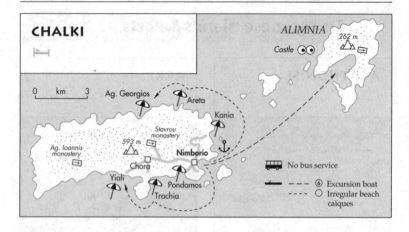

Chalki
ΧΑΛΚΗ; 28 km²; pop. 300.

CODE ☎ 22410
PORT POLICE ☎ 45220
POLICE ☎ 45213
FIRST AID ☎ 45206

If you are seeking out that elusive Greek island that just isn't like any other Greek island then Chalki (pronounced 'Hal-key', and often transcribed as Khalki, or Halki) should be pretty high up your hit list. A small, barren, undistinguished island located just west of Rhodes, Chalki is little more than a bone-dry rock (the island takes its name from the bronze that was once mined here). Indeed, Chalki has no fresh water supply, and as a result, all produce and fresh water is tankered in from Rhodes twice a week. To help conserve stocks, tap water is heavily adulterated with sea water: drink from a tap on Chalki and you'll end up thirstier than before you started.

On top of this, a touch of early 1900s sponge-blight and a failed 1980s attempt to turn the island into a summer UNESCO youth conference centre, and circumstances were dire enough to ensure that most of the islanders (who formerly eked out a living via sponge fishing) opted to cut their losses

and move to Florida, leaving the way open for a couple of enterprising tour operators (*Laskarina* and *Direct Greece*) to move in and save the day. Between them they have contrived to make the island something pretty special: for the truth is that Chalki is really an up-market tourist resort in the middle of nowhere masquerading as an unspoilt Greek island.

At first sight everything seems pretty normal, for the island has only one settlement of note in the form of a typically picturesque, semi-dilapidated port town backed by neglected hinterland, but when you look closer it is clear that the port of **Nimborio** is by no means a typical Greek island town despite initial appearances. A trail of red tiled Venetian (or if you prefer Symi or neo-classical) style mansion houses set around a horseshoe-shaped bay, and with a skyline topped by three ruined windmills, it is quite attractive, but when you start walking the streets it quickly becomes clear that many of the properties have been converted into holiday villas.

Add to the above the diminishing number of houses still in ruins and it is doubtful if more than a third of the houses are actually occupied by islanders. This is not to say that Chalki is all about tourism, for there is a

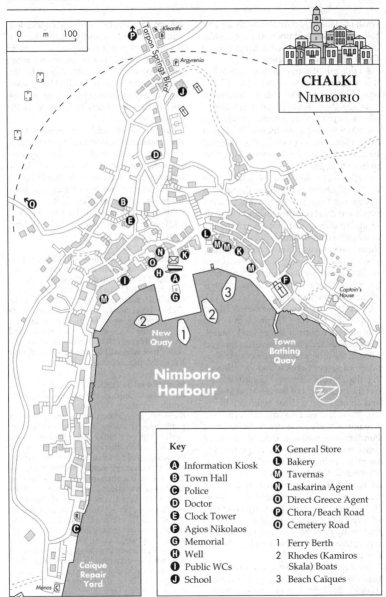

CHALKI
NIMBORIO

0   m   100

Kleanthi

Tarpon Springs Blvd.

Argyrenia

Nimborio Harbour

New Quay

Town Bathing Quay

Captain's House

Caïque Repair Yard

Manos

Key

- **A** Information Kiosk
- **B** Town Hall
- **C** Police
- **D** Doctor
- **E** Clock Tower
- **F** Agios Nikolaos
- **G** Memorial
- **H** Well
- **I** Public WCs
- **J** School
- **K** General Store
- **L** Bakery
- **M** Tavernas
- **N** Laskarina Agent
- **O** Direct Greece Agent
- **P** Chora/Beach Road
- **Q** Cemetery Road

1 Ferry Berth
2 Rhodes (Kamiros Skala) Boats
3 Beach Caïques

small nucleus of genuine town life adding colour to the several hundred upper-middle class Brits playing at being make-believe Greek villagers for a fortnight.

All this might sound unduly critical but it is not meant to be so: to be fair, Chalki would be in serious trouble without these tour operators, as the island is just too far off the popular ferry routes to rank high on the island hopper's hit list, and hasn't really enough going for it by way of either beaches or sightseeing to have more appeal in its own right.

Furthermore, there is a lot to be said in favour of Chalki as a holiday destination if you don't want to do anything except unwind with a book for a fortnight (there is no nightlife, no tourist shops, and no bank), or are blessed with children able to entertain themselves and want a quiet holiday where you can let them roam the streets at will without worrying about their safety (there are no watersports, and no cars or mopeds as there is nowhere to go).

Of course, as any experienced island hopper can tell you, the problem is that this just isn't normal for a Greek island. The Greek islands never were like this and none of the others are: Chalki is a glorious fake — a sort of Greek island variation on Agatha Christie's *Bertram's Hotel* (but without the excitement of having Miss Marple and an organizing crime syndicate living in). Even the island's main beach — a 15-minute walk away from the town at **Pondamos** — is now artificial (courtesy of some imported sand); the original being swept away in a bad winter storm in 1995. Worse still, the absence of a 'normal' mix of tourists contributes to a rather odd atmosphere: painted in tour brochures as the ultimate unspoilt island, in an odd sort of way Chalki ends up feeling more spoilt than many more heavily touristed islands. It is a place you will either love or hate, and this can be bad news.

The flip side to escapist islands is that they can be difficult to escape from. Most islands offer a choice of alternatives within easy reach if you find your own is less than you had hoped for: sadly, Chalki doesn't. If you don't like it then you could be in real trouble: it is not unknown for more disenchanted holidaymakers to take the daily boat and bus to Rhodes City (a two-hour trip each way) several times a week simply to enjoy a few hours back in the normal world.

Of course it is possible to escape on Chalki itself: walkers not afraid of rougher terrain will find the island offers something and the waterfront is enlivened by half-a-dozen tavernas that hum into the small hours. This is in part because of a lack of beds for independent travellers (many end up beating a hasty retreat) and the awkward 05.30 departure time of the daily 'lifeline' boat to Rhodes.

⇥

Unless you are travelling well out of season then you should phone ahead and book a room. The options are limited to the small *Captain's House* (☎ 45201), the B-class pension *Kleanthi* (☎ 45334), the *Argyrenia* (☎ 45205), and the C-class hotel *Manos* (☎ 45295). None have distinguishing signs on display. Villas run by *Laskarina* or *Direct Greece* are pre-booked well in advance but both have agents on the waterfront who will be able to advise if they have any spare rooms.

👁👁

Nimborio (alias Emborio) can claim to have one notable sight in the form of the tallest campanile in the Dodecanese: it dominates the town in addition to adding plenty of photogenic character. The only 'sightseeing' destination on Chalki is the former **Chora**, topped with a chapel-filled castle built by the Knights of St. John and complete with a derelict monastery nearby. Set safely inland, it is now all but abandoned, and sees almost as few tourists as it did pirates: faced with the choice between a very steep walk from the port (the road rises 300 m in 2 km) and caïques heading for tiny scraps of beaches around the island, most opt for the latter.

The main sightseeing excursion is also a caïque-ride away on the adjacent island of **Alimnia**. Blessed with some excellent beaches, an abandoned village, and a castle straddling a ridge on the south-eastern side, the island has more going for it than Chalki.

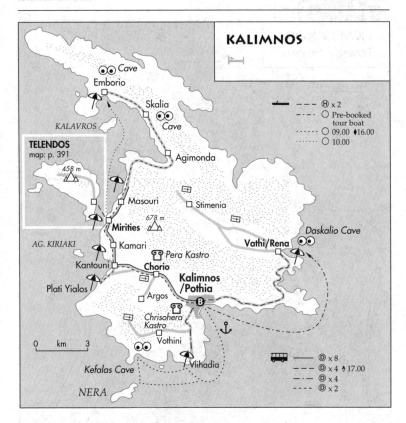

KALIMNOS

Cave
Emborio
Skalia
Cave
KALAVROS
⊕ x 2
○ Pre-booked tour boat
○ 09.00 ◆16.00
○ 10.00
TELENDOS
map: p. 391
Agimonda
458 m
Masouri
Stimenia
Mirities
678 m
Daskalio Cave
AG. KIRIAKI
Kamari
Vathi/Rena
Pera Kastro
Kantouni
Chorio
Kalimnos /Pothia
Plati Yialos
Argos
Chrisohera Kastro
0   km   3
Vothini
⊕ x 8
⊕ x 4 ◆ 17.00
⊕ x 4
⊕ x 2
Kefalas Cave
Vlihadia
NERA

Kalimnos

ΚΑΛΥΜΝΟΣ; 111 km²; pop. 14,500.

CODE ☎ 22430
PORT POLICE ☎ 24444
POLICE ☎ 22100
HOSPITAL ☎ 28851

A number of Dodecanese islands have laid claim to being the sponge-fishing centre of the Aegean — Symi not least among them — but relatively quiet Kalimnos has a better claim than most. Yet to embrace mass tourism, Kalimnos is a medium-sized island north of Kos that hides its attractions behind superficially forbidding mountains and one of the largest and most dour of island towns (population 11,000) in the Aegean. First impressions are, however, misleading, for between the mountains lie dark pockets of verdant vegetation, and there is certainly enough on the island to see if you don't mind poking around in dark holes to find it. In fact, holes are something of an island speciality. Not only are they abundant in the island's sponges, but Kalimnos has three caves visited by irregular excursions, and a whole lot more scattered around the island in which you can risk getting irrecoverably lost.

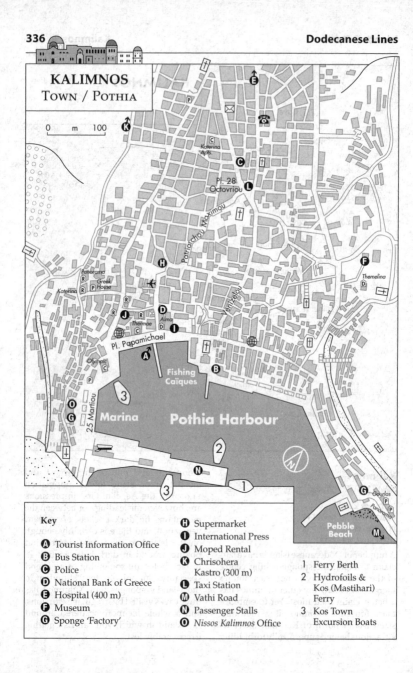

KALIMNOS
Town / Pothia

0   m   100

Pothia Harbour

Marina

Fishing Caïques

Pebble Beach

Pl. Papamichael

Pl. 28 Octovriou

Patriarchou Maximou

Venizelou

25 Martiou

Panorama

Katerina

Greek House

Thermae

Olympic

Alma

Themelina

Katerina Apts.

Gourlas

Panorama

Key

- **A** Tourist Information Office
- **B** Bus Station
- **C** Police
- **D** National Bank of Greece
- **E** Hospital (400 m)
- **F** Museum
- **G** Sponge 'Factory'
- **H** Supermarket
- **I** International Press
- **J** Moped Rental
- **K** Chrisohera Kastro (300 m)
- **L** Taxi Station
- **M** Vathi Road
- **N** Passenger Stalls
- **O** *Nissos Kalimnos* Office

1 Ferry Berth
2 Hydrofoils & Kos (Mastihari) Ferry
3 Kos Town Excursion Boats

Kalimnos hit the headlines in 1996 thanks to a dispute with Turkey over the neighbouring islet of Imia. Used by Kalimnot farmers to graze goats, Imia saw groups of Greek and Turkish marines landing on the island in order to tear down each other's flags and raise their own. Add to this a couple of gunboats, and the incident threatened to become a very nasty affair until mediating US diplomats negotiated a joint stand-off. Fortunately this dispute has gone off the boil in the years since.

Gunboats notwithstanding, ferries call at the capital, **Pothia** (also known as **Kalimnos Town**), which fills the floor of a sheltered bay on the mountainous south coast. Also the object of daily excursion boats from Kos Town, the Italianesque waterfront is arguably one of the best of its type in the Dodecanese. Lined with trees and tavernas, it manages to offset the unappealing size of the town that sprawls behind it surprisingly well, offering an attractive spot in which to watch the world go by. The townsfolk have made a conspicuous effort in the last few years to enliven the waterfront area and there is now a good scatter of street cafes and tavernas, backed by the inevitable sponge shops. Sadly, the rest of the town has too much of the world going by for comfort: the locals treat the narrow streets as if they were a motorbike rally course, and this makes exploration uncomfortable to say the least. The only consolation is that the lack of sights means that Pothia offers little temptation to linger.

Day trippers from Kos aside, most tourists seem to spend a day in the capital and then rapidly head on over the hills to the expanding resort/beach strip running along the north-west coast, opposite the island of Telendos (the big draw hereabouts). At the centre of the strip is the village of **Mirities**, which has little to offer besides an indifferent white-pebble beach and regular caïque services to Leros and Telendos (there are better beaches along the coast to the south). In truth the village is more of a hilly, tree-lined road along which has grown a fringe

of hotels, tavernas and tourist shops. In many ways the setting is quite attractive: it is certainly a vast improvement on Pothia; the problem again is the motorbike traffic — the shady pine-tree idyll is compromised too often for comfort.

From Mirities the hotel strip dribbles along the coast to become the resort of **Masouri**. There isn't a clear point at which one ends and the other begins, but if you are travelling by bus it is worth noting that the route used takes the hill road to Masouri and then doubles back along the coast to Mirities. The small beach village of **Kantouni**, with its large incomplete hotel (only the top two of five floors have been finished), is also visited by the Mirities bus.

Buses on Kalimnos are a law unto themselves: they tend to be the shortened variety in order to cope with Pothia's narrow streets. Summer timetables are posted up regularly, but most of the drivers seem happy to keep to the winter one: they are not too keen on taking your money either — this is one island where you buy tickets from shops adjacent to bus stops.

Bus links as far north as Masouri are adequate, but very limited along the road that takes you to the northern finger of Kalimnos which is very quiet. Despite this, it is worth visiting thanks to an interesting cave just outside the village of **Skalia** and the blissful isolation of the pebble beach village of **Emborio**, which is attracting a growing number of those in the know.

The rest of Kalimnos tends to be little explored. The best and most popular alternative destination is the deep inlet of **Vathi** on the east coast. Set in a citrus-filled market-garden valley, the harbour of **Rena** offers a hotel, a few rooms and a notable sea cave (visited by tour boats from Pothia). If you fancy spending four hours getting to Vathi the hard way you can always attempt the walk from Pothia over the top of the island (the old dirt track runs up from behind the museum) in the happy knowledge that there is a bus that will get you back.

Sponge Fishing and Kalimnos

Kalimnos is the sponge capital of the Mediterranean, and formerly of the world. The
island grew very rich on the fruits of sponge
fishing, but this came at a terrible price for
the inhabitants. Today the industry still exists (Kalimnos is home to the only surviving
sponge fishing fleet in Greece), but it is a
shadow of its former self and, in reality,
is little more than a convenient branding
label to draw in the tourists. Once you get
to Kalimnos there is surprisingly little of this
industry on show. Visitors will find the inevitable sponge sellers and a couple of small
sponge 'factories' in waterfront buildings
— where you can see the bleaching process
under way. But that is it.

The Sponge

Long considered to be part of the plant
kingdom, sponges have only comparatively
recently been reclassified as animals (for
over two thousand years the locals had
been wondering why the little vegetables
squeaked when they hit them). In fact
sponges are the fibrous excreta of colonies
of micro-organisms. They feed by drawing
nutrients from sea water passed through
the pores in their bodies. Under the sea,
sponges are an inconspicuous black or dull
grey colour: the beguiling golden yellow of
the objects you see on sale is only achieved
by a lot of painful labour.

The traditional processing of a sponge
is briefly thus: after being cut from rocks
on the seabed, it arrives on board a fishing
boat exuding a nasty smell and possessing
a tough surface layer. The first stage of the
processing involves stamping on the poor
smelly little critter to squash all the 'milk'
out of it. It is then left under a sheet in the
sun to warm up and kill off any organisms
still alive inside. Once cooked, the sponge is
strung on a line and then repeatedly washed
in the sea and beaten with sticks
(to break down the hard outer
surface). Finally, irregular
areas are trimmed off.
The second stage
takes place
on shore in
the sponge
factories:
the sponge
is quickly

dunked for a few seconds in a mix of potas-
sium permanganate and sulphuric acid, to
bleach it to the golden or light yellow colour
we are so familiar with (the length of the
dunking determines its shade of yellow),
and then washed in fresh water.

Sponge Fishermen

If anyone is tempted to think that the sponges have had a raw deal from the sponge fishing industry, give a thought to the sponge
fishermen: if anything, they had it worse.

Kalimnos has long been at the forefront of
the sponge industry (other islands with notable fleets included Hydra, Poros, Spetses
and Symi). At its prime the island had the
largest fleet in the Aegean, with over 350
boats setting out during the summer fishing season (the waters — even in this part
of the world — were too cold during the rest
of the year). In the second half of the 19th
century Kalimnos sponges were well known
though out Europe, but over-fishing and
injury brought about a rapid decline in the
industry's fortunes. By 1920 only Kalimnos,
Hydra and Symi still possessed fleets, and
by 1950 Kalimnos was on her own.

The Kalimnot fleet enjoyed two distinct
periods of prosperity. The first was achieved
by sheer numbers of boats. Each of the 350-
odd vessels in the fleet carried up to a dozen
divers who would make several dives a day.
Without oxygen, they would free-fall naked
to the seabed holding onto a large stone,
hack off sponges with an axe and return
to the surface (all within the space of 2–4
minutes). Despite the obvious limitations
of this method of fishing, enough sponges
were recovered during a season to make it
worthwhile. The limitations, however, were
obvious. Divers couldn't go deeper than 30
m and stocks of sponges so near the surface
were soon fished out — forcing the fleet to
venture ever further afield.

The second, and more deadly, period of
prosperity came with the introduction of
helmeted diving suits (locally known as
the 'skafandro') from 1865. These enabled
the divers to go down to depths of 70 m
— thanks to the use of compressed air
pumped down from the surface. This greatly
increased production as the fleet was able
to exploit the large stocks of previously untouched sponges at these greater depths. But
this did not come without cost to the divers.

Many suffered from the 'bends' after second or third dives, returning to boats without any decompression facilities.

At the time the causes of the 'bends' (when small bubbles of excess nitrogen enter the bloodstream and block blood flow to limbs and organs if a diver attempts to surface too quickly) weren't clearly understood. Nor were the dangers of making several dives a day appreciated — at least at first. The heaviness of the diving suit itself also contributed to the problem: it was so difficult to walk around in that divers took deeper breaths and so absorbed more compressed air.

The divers were only hired hands. They couldn't dictate working conditions and suffered accordingly. Between 1886 and 1910 an estimated 10,000 Aegean sponge divers died, and a further 20,000 ended up crippled with varying degrees of paralysis. The population of Kalimnos was particularly hard hit. At one point the island's boats were returning with only half the divers they set out with, and the womenfolk took to meeting them wearing black shawls. The Kalimnots even developed a macabre sponge-divers' dance (called the 'mihanikos') in which a dancing youth suddenly falls to the ground and then drags himself around on shaking legs with the aid of a stick.

There was an attempt at a revolt against using the suits: in 1882 they were banned on Kalimnos, but the economic damage inflicted by going back to the old diving technique was such that the suits were back within a couple of years (and continued in use until the aqua-lung arrived in the 1960s).

From the 1920s on improved safety measures and equipment cut down the toll of death and injury in the Kalimnos fishing fleet, but a long term decline had set in. The new diving suits resulted in massive overfishing of sponge beds. Further decline came with the arrival of cheap synthetic sponges in the 1950s, and just to top things off in 1986 the Aegean sponge population was devastated by mystery disease — though it is now reviving.

Buying Sponges

These days a surprising number of tourists seem to be turned off by the idea of rubbing themselves down using the body of an animal that has been stamped on, cooked alive in the sun, beaten repeatedly with sticks, and then dunked in a vat of acid for good measure. But if you are tempted to buy one for your bath, here are some pointers to look out for:

1. Avoid them if they are either black, squeak when you squeeze them, or are still moving.

2. Look at the pattern of holes in the sponge (small, densely-packed holed sponges are to be preferred and cost more).

3. Check the consistency of the texture over the whole sponge.

4. Size — avoid small cut-off remnants: don't end up buying a leg for the price of a whole body.

5. Shape: different shapes attract different prices. There are a number of sponge species with oddball names such as 'elephant's ear', 'Turkey cup' in addition to the more predictable 'Honeycomb' (Kapadiko) varieties.

6. Enquire about the nationality of your sponge: the majority of the sponges now on sale on Kalimnos — and in Greece for that matter — are imported from as far afield as the Caribbean and the Red Sea, rather than animals caught locally.

⊢

Surprisingly for such a large island Kalimnos lacks a campsite. There are, however, plenty of beds available, most in Pothia and Mirities, and in the former you can easily seek help via the helpful tourist office housed in a waterfront beach hut on the opposite side of the harbour to the ferry quay.

Pothia has a pretty mixed collection, starting with the waterfront C-class *Olympic* (☎ 28801) and *Thermae* (☎ 29425), along with the D-class *Alma* (☎ 28969). A quieter D-class hotel, the largely package tour *Villa Themelina* (☎ 22682), stands near the museum. A clutch of establishments lie up in the backstreets rising behind the harbour. These include the C-class *Panorama* (☎ 23138) and *Katerina Rooms* (☎ 22532) — not to be confused with the package tourist-dominated *Katerina Apartments* near the back of the town — along with the excellent pension *Greek House* (☎ 22559).

Mirities also has over a dozen hotels including the D-class *Myrties* (☎ 47512) and E-class *Paradise*. Finally, **Rena** has the C-class *Galini* (☎ 31241) and the pension *Manolis* (☎ 22641), and **Emborio** also has a few rooms.

⊙⊙

Pothia was built on the back of the sponge-fishing industry and has little by way of sights. The most visible things on show are a number of bronze waterfront **Statues**. These are staggeringly ugly, modern affairs: the worst is a figure of Poseidon who looks as if he has been caught sitting on a very private sort of throne. Another offering (on the far side of the harbour) is a look-a-like of Copenhagen's Little Mermaid who doesn't, thanks to lumps.

Strangely, the perverse fates have since sent Kalimnos relief from this assault on artistic taste. The island is now an archaeological hot spot, with major ancient statues now turning up every other year. The first appeared on Christmas Eve 1995 when a local fisherman netted one of the best **Hellenistic bronzes** ever discovered. Now known as the **Peplophoros Daughter of Kalimnos** the 2 m high figure of a veiled woman dates from the late 4 C. BC, and is thought to possibly be the work of the sculptor Praxiteles. It has been described as the only example of its kind to survive from the period. A grateful government gave the fisherman a million drachmas by way of a reward for not trying to sell it on the black market. Unfortunately, it also rapidly took

the figure to Athens for conservation. Given the statue's importance, the betting is that it is unlikely to see Kalimnos again.

Some consolation came in February 1997 when a fisherman pulled from the waters north of Telendos a **Macedonian Head** (see p. 338). Made of copper, the male figure sports a moustache and a broad-rimmed hat. Unusually, the glazed enamel eyes (usually missing on recovered bronzes) are intact. One of the figure's legs was also fished up.

If this wasn't statuary enough, the world went mad in March 2001 when an islander digging a well came across a statue burial site. Subsequent excavations revealed **35 Marble Statues**. All over 1.2 m tall and dating from the 2 C. BC, the figures were mutilated prior to burial (fortunately the damaged parts were all buried together so repair should be possible). They are thought to be victims of the Emperor Theodosius (378–395 AD), a fanatical Christian, who persecuted ancient Greek religion. The statutes are believed to have decorated the cella halls of the Temple of Delius Apollo just outside Mirities (the stones of which now make up the ruinous 5 C. AD **Church of Jerusalem** that now occupies the site). In time they will no doubt be housed in Pothia's — currently small — **Archaeological Museum**. At the moment they are on Rhodes.

Pothia is also the starting point for tour boats that run to the main sea cave: **Kefalas Cave**. Famous for its stalagmites and stalactites, this cavern is said to be that in which the god Zeus hid from his immortal father before killing him (gods can do *anything*). These boats also often stop off at the islet of **Nera** to the south-west, where there is a monastery. Other tour boats irregularly visit the **Daskalio Cave** at Vathi. If you fancy venturing further afield, Pothia has also lately seen the arrival of regular day-trips to **Kos** and **Bodrum**.

Elsewhere on Kalimnos you will find two reasonable castles: the **Castle of the Knights of St. John** (alias **Chrisohera Kastro**), complete with its own monastery, outside Pothia, is the better preserved, but a better excursion is to be had visiting the second, the abandoned fortress-village (complete with nine preserved whitewashed chapels) of **Pera Kastro**, just outside the old capital of Chorio, thanks to its impressive views. The beach hamlet at **Vlihadia** is host to a small family-run **Sea World Museum**. Interesting exhibits include a large number of encrusted amphoras.

Karpathos

ΚΑΡΠΑΘΟΣ; 301 km²; pop. 5,400.

CODE ☎ 22450
PORT POLICE ☎ 22227
TOURIST POLICE ☎ 22218
POLICE ☎ 22222
HOSPITAL ☎ 22228

Along with Kassos to the south and Saria to the north, the island of Karpathos forms a small archipelago midway between Rhodes and eastern Crete. An appealing destination if you are looking for a quiet, relatively unspoilt Greek island, it remains a tricky spot to get to: the great majority of visitors are package tourists flying in direct from Europe. Given the low level of ferry links (the 'two boats in each direction' pattern of weekly services has been running for a good many years now), you should allow a couple of days in hand, if you visit, to make your escape.

Like Amorgos, Karpathos enjoys a history of division with the two sides of the island effectively separated by inhospitable terrain, with the result that ferries call at two island ports. The similarities end there, however, because Karpathos has higher mountains, has much more tree cover (though this has been sadly diminished by recent forest fires), is graced with some excellent beaches and — thanks to the large expatriate community (many now in the US) who send back funds — is now among the most affluent islands in the Aegean. In spite of the appearance of regular charter flights, tourism has yet to take off (and there is not much sign of it doing so), with the somewhat paradoxical effect of creating a High Season surplus of demand for what limited facilities do exist.

Buses run to the most popular island beach at Ammopi, but the service is otherwise generally very poor. Other transport options are pretty dire, the taxis being too expensive except for the shortest journeys, and car and moped hire limited by the poor quality of the road network and the lack of fuel stops outside the capital.

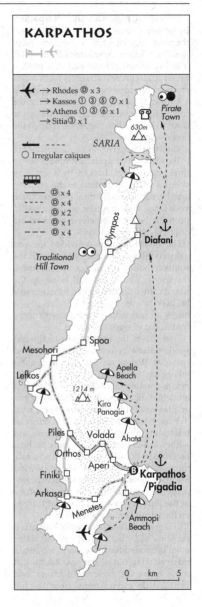

KARPATHOS

→ Rhodes ⑩ x 3
→ Kassos ① ③ ⑤ ⑦ x 1
→ Athens ① ③ ⑥ x 1
→ Sitia ③ x 1

○ Irregular caïques

━━━ ⑩ x 4
--- ⑩ x 4
-·-· ⑩ x 2
-·- ⑩ x 1
--- ⑩ x 4

Pirate Town

SARIA

630m

Olympos

Diafani

Traditional Hill Town

Spoa

Mesohori

Apella Beach

Lefkos

1214 m

Kira Panagia

Piles   Volada   Ahata

Orthos

Aperi

Finiki   **Ⓑ Karpathos /Pigadia**

Arkasa

Menetes

Ammopi Beach

0   km   5

The capital, **Pigathia** (called '**Karpathos**' by locals and timetable writers alike), lies at the more populous, flatter southern end of the island. Surprisingly for an island capital, it lacks a historical heart and is, in truth, a rather drab concrete affair. Its main assets are a picturesque harbour setting and a 4 km sandy beach that runs north of the town. High Season caïques also run up the coast to several beaches, ending up at the best — Apella.

The main tourist resort on Karpathos lies to the south of the capital at **Ammopi** where three sandy bays, backed by a growing taverna village, play host to the growing number of tourists. If Ammopi doesn't take your fancy, then irregular caïques also run from the beach to quieter coves backing onto the drab airport road.

The rest of Karpathos is divided between a dozen villages (most of which lie in the southern half). First among these is **Aperi**, the former chora and still home to the island cathedral: dominated by expensive holiday homes built by US émigrés, it offers an interesting contrast with more traditional villages elsewhere.

From Aperi the road climbs to the less spoilt **Volada** before topping the island spine at **Orthos**, at 510 m the highest village on the island (bring a pullover) before running down to one of the most attractive hill villages on Karpathos at **Piles**, and the resort of **Lefkos**. However, a rival to Piles exists at **Menetes**, which offers an interesting mix of old mansion-style and whitewashed houses (depending on how posh a part of town you are in) and a folk museum. Beyond Menetes lies the growing resort village of **Arkasa**. Straddling a narrow gorge, it is home to the scanty remains of one of the four Mycenaean cities that thrived on the island, and a good beach.

Villages in the northern half of Karpathos are few and far between; the island at this point becomes little more than a mountain ridge sticking out of the sea. Rough dirt roads (more the preserve of hikers than vehicles) do extend north from the hill villages of Mesohori and Spoa, but caïques running between Pigadia and the small northern port of **Diafani** remain the principal means of travelling between the two halves of the island.

In fact, quiet Diafani largely owes its survival to the package tourists en route to explore the famous hill village of **Olympos**. Easily the most photogenic village on the island, lofty Olympos — complete with restored windmills galore — straddles a steep ridge, and is notable for retaining a traditional village lifestyle (with the women conspicuously decked out in 19 c. dress). Sadly, this is increasingly a show for the tourists' benefit. This is not to say that the local girls all dive for the nearest pair of jeans the moment the tourist bus heads down the hill, but the town now does have more suspiciously non-traditional souvenir shops than most.

⊨

There is no camping on Karpathos bar an unofficial site 30 minutes' walk north of **Diafani**. Fortunately, beds are plentiful, even in High Season. Most budget accommodation is in **Karpathos Town**. At the bottom end of the range are a couple of pensions offering rooms: *Harry's Rooms* (☎ 22188), north of the bus station, and *Carlos Rooms* (☎ 22477), along with two E-class hotels: the *Zephyros*, and the *Avra* (☎ 22388), a block inland. Moving up the price range, the D-class *Coral* and *Anessis* (☎ 22100) are topped by the C-class *Karpathos* (☎ 22347) and *Atlantis* (☎ 22777).

In **Diafani** you will also find offers of rooms, pensions and several hotels, including the quayside E-class *Chryssi Akti* (☎ 51215).

∞

Sightseeing is very limited, the best thing on offer being the High Season taxi boats — the *Karpathos II* and *Chrisovalandou* — that run up the coast to **Diafani** (buy cheap tickets on board). The latter boat also visits the uninhabited island of **Saria** beyond, complete with a deserted 'pirate' town noted for having the remains of some oddly shaped houses (i.e. cone-like roofs). This can also be reached via caïque from Diafani, which has a bus link to Olympos: a tour bus in all but name, its Karpathos town counterparts offer the best way of seeing the southern villages.

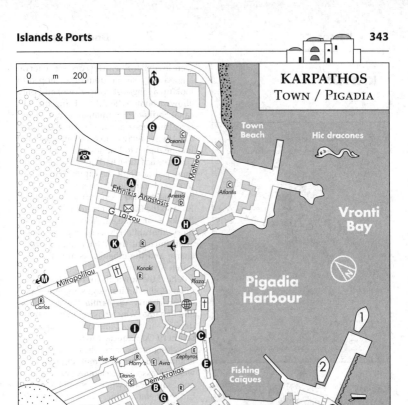

KARPATHOS
Town / Pigadia

Key

Ⓐ Tourist & Regular Police
Ⓑ Bus Station
Ⓒ National Bank of Greece
Ⓓ Hospital
Ⓔ Waterfront Clock Tower
Ⓕ Town Hall
Ⓖ Supermarket
Ⓗ Pharmacy
Ⓘ Bakery
Ⓙ Newspapers
Ⓚ Moped & Car Hire
Ⓛ WCs
Ⓜ Airport & Menetes Road
Ⓝ Aperi, Spoa & Diafani 'Road'
Ⓞ Ammopi Beach Road

1 Ferry Quay
2 Beach & Excursion Boats

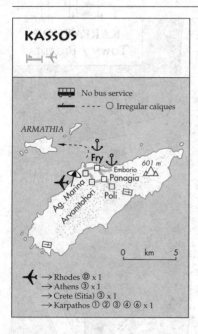

KASSOS

🚌 No bus service

⚓ ---- ○ Irregular caïques

ARMATHIA

Fry

Emborio   601 m

Panagia

Ag. Marina

Arvanitohori

Poli

0   km   5

✈ → Rhodes ⓓ x 1
✈ → Athens ③ x 1
✈ → Crete (Sitia) ③ x 1
✈ → Karpathos ① ② ③ ④ ⑥ x 1

Kassos
ΚΑΣΟΣ; 66 km²; pop. 1,184.

CODE ☎ 22450
PORT POLICE ☎ 41288
POLICE ☎ 41222
HOSPITAL ☎ 41333

An arid, mountainous island with more cliffs than beaches, Kassos is definitely not on the tourist map and has seen ferry services dwindle over the last decade, and its population over the last two centuries. It has an odd history, having been subjected to an attack by a band of marauding Egyptians who carried off most of the women and children in 1824 with the thanks of their Ottoman overlords (Kassos was another of those small islands with a large fleet that enthusiastically joined the 1824 bid for Greek independence, only to see savage retribution). The few male members of the population who were not killed or enslaved

were invited to Suez a few decades later on a goodwill visit (no doubt they hoped to look up a long-lost wife or two) and only allowed home when they'd dug the odd canal. Sadly, the Egyptians have not offered ferry links since, and it is best to allow three days to get away or take advantage of the lifeline flights to Rhodes and Crete.

Kassos has three harbours: the new ferry quay just north of the capital **Fry**, the old ferry port at the small taverna-backed harbour of **Emborio** 1 km round the bay from Fri, and the tiny caïque harbour known as Bouka — at Fri itself. Also transcribed as 'Phry', the capital is a peculiarly ramshackle affair, but for all that, it has a certain scruffy charm and the inhabitants are all smiles (often American).

Behind the 'town' lie four closely located villages, all exhibiting signs of gentle decay — particularly **Ag. Marina**, the old capital, and **Panagia**, which has yet more of those derelict early 19 c. mansions so typical of southern Dodecanese towns.

Lacking roads or beaches the rest of the island is little visited. **Armathia**, an islet just west of Kassos, sees caïques heading for a good sand beach when sufficient numbers can be generated; otherwise the main tourist activity is hill walking.

⮌

So few tourists call that facilities are very poor. Harbour tavernas offering rooms and two C-class hotels combine to cater for the few that do call (they can more than handle the number of visitors, even in High Season). Best is the *Anagennisis* (☎ 41323), with the poor *Anessis* (☎ 41201) limping in behind.

👀

Kassos is not noted for its sightseeing. That said, there are sights of a sort. Most notable is the **Sellai Cave** near the airfield, complete with all the usual subterranean accoutrements.

The village of **Poli** is also of some interest, being located (as its name suggests) on the site of the **Ancient City** (complete with the scanty remains of the old Acropolis). A Byzantine church now adorns the site. A second church of note stands at nearby **Arvanitohori**, which is partly carved out of the bedrock of the hillside.

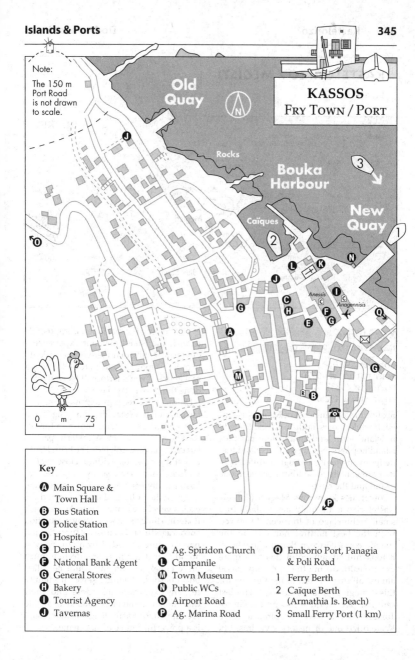

Note:

The 150 m Port Road is not drawn to scale.

Old Quay

KASSOS
Fry Town / Port

Rocks

Bouka Harbour

3

Caïques

New Quay

2

1

Anessis

Anagennisis

Key

- **Ⓐ** Main Square & Town Hall
- **Ⓑ** Bus Station
- **Ⓒ** Police Station
- **Ⓓ** Hospital
- **Ⓔ** Dentist
- **Ⓕ** National Bank Agent
- **Ⓖ** General Stores
- **Ⓗ** Bakery
- **Ⓘ** Tourist Agency
- **Ⓙ** Tavernas
- **Ⓚ** Ag. Spiridon Church
- **Ⓛ** Campanile
- **Ⓜ** Town Museum
- **Ⓝ** Public WCs
- **Ⓞ** Airport Road
- **Ⓟ** Ag. Marina Road
- **Ⓠ** Emborio Port, Panagia & Poli Road
- **1** Ferry Berth
- **2** Caïque Berth (Armathia Is. Beach)
- **3** Small Ferry Port (1 km)

0 m 75

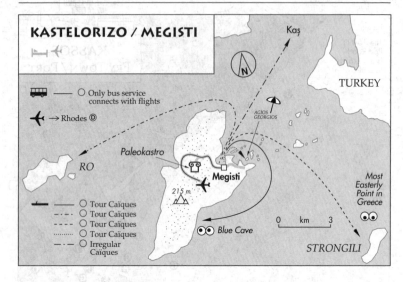

KASTELORIZO / MEGISTI

Kaş

TURKEY

🚌 —— ○ Only bus service
connects with flights

✈ → Rhodes ⓓ

AGIOS
GEORGIOS

Paleokastro

RO

Megisti

215 m.

Most
Easterly
Point in
Greece

—— ○ Tour Caïques
–·–· ○ Tour Caïques
–––– ○ Tour Caïques
········· ○ Tour Caïques
–·— ○ Irregular
       Caïques

👀 Blue Cave

0   km   3

STRONGILI

Kastelorizo

ΚΑΣΤΕΛΟΡΙΖΟ; 9 km²; pop. 210.

CODE ☎ 22410
PORT POLICE ☎ 49270
POLICE ☎ 49333
FIRST AID ☎ 49267

Six hours steaming east of Rhodes, isolated Kastelorizo is both a Greek tragedy in island form, and an absolute must for island hoppers looking for that island that defies even the usual range of differences that are usually to be found between one island and the next.

Sometimes known as Megisti ('large'), Kastelorizo is the only large island in a small archipelago of fourteen. Endowed with the best natural harbour on the Asiatic coast between Beirut and Makri, it took full advantage of this to acquire great wealth during the 19 c. only to see almost all turn to ruin in the fighting for this strategic prize in the first half of the last century. Two world wars and the Greco-Turkish conflict have conspired to leave Kastelorizo one of history's victims, but even allowing the fact that it is impossible to visit the island and not experience a powerful feeling of tragedy, there is plenty to quietly enjoy — in truth Kastelorizo is a real gem — even if it doesn't feel quite the done thing to 'party' here.

Union with Greece in 1947 has brought a measure of quiet stability, but lying 90 km east of Rhodes and under 3 km from Turkey, Kastelorizo — the most easterly part of Greece — is very isolated. The brutal truth is that it isn't viable without close contact with the Anatolian coast, yet to date, that hasn't really been a practical proposition — given the politics of the region and the exclusively Greek inhabitants. As a result, it floats in a limbo sea, with a tiny population encouraged to stay by a mix of subsidies and new housing provided by a government afraid that if the numbers decline much more Greek sovereignty could be called into question. A strong sense of identity felt by expatriate islanders and their descendants (who book solid all available accommodation at the height of the season) is a powerful source of sustenance.

The government is doing its best to turn things around, and 2003 saw a couple of very positive developments. First, part of an inter-governmental conference was held on the island during Greece's 6-month presidency of the EU. This brought the foreign ministers of Europe to the island (with a day trip to Turkey — to open up links in this direction). The second notable change was the arrival of a catamaran service from Rhodes that allowed day trips to the island for the first time.

😨

First the tragedy. For most of its history Kastelorizo has been a relatively insignificant island, controlled by whichever power was master of Rhodes; its significance being primarily military, courtesy of the castle that gave it its name (Kastelorizo means 'Red Castle'). However, as the Ottoman Empire opened up to European traders in the first half of the 19 c. the island economy developed quickly — thanks to its harbour and its location on the east–west trade route.

By 1850 Kastelorizo was very wealthy, with many of its population of 17,000 owning property on the island and in the adjacent mainland town of Kaş (ironically pronounced 'Cash'). Tragedy was heralded with a change in governing policy by the ruling Turks in 1908, which resulted in a local revolution in 1913 followed by an unstable period of self rule that saw the island cut off from the Anatolian mainland and economic decline setting in. Worse was to follow with the arrival of WW1. The French occupied the island in 1915, turning it into a naval base. This prompted Turkish forces to blockade the island and shell the harbour and town in 1917.

In 1921 the French handed over Kastelorizo to the Italians under the Treaty of Sèvres that gave the Dodecanese islands to Italy, thereby condemning the island's economy to a prolonged period of decline: the lack of any contact (never mind trade) with the mainland and changes in shipping routes proved to be a fatal double blow. The Italians attempted to turn Kastelorizo into a passenger seaplane base (serving Rome—Beirut flights) but this wasn't successful. Their integration policy, which sought the Italianization of the Dodecanese islands by banning the speaking of Greek in schools and public places, proved an even greater disaster, being fiercely resisted by the islanders. This left the Italians ill-disposed to help rebuild the town after it was badly damaged by an earthquake in 1926. As a result of all this, the town's population fell from 9,000 in 1910 to 1,400 in 1940.

In 1941 WW2 came to Kastelorizo when the British briefly captured the island only to see the Italians rapidly retake it. With the Italian surrender in 1943 the British regained control, and the heart of the old town was then subjected to dive-bomb attacks by German planes. This resulted in massive damage and the decision to evacuate the remaining island population to Cyprus. Following their departure, in 1944 a fire completed the devastation of the town, the burnt-out buildings being bulldozed by the British for safety reasons. Some islanders asserted it was to cover up looting by the garrison, a hard claim to substantiate given the years of decline that preceded the war and the bomb damage to the town during it.

The final tragedy was yet to come: in 1946 the elderly British ship *Empire Patrol* — overloaded with 500 returning islanders — sank after a fire broke out on board: 33 of them died.

Megisti or **Kastelorizo Town** has less than a third of its former buildings still standing. Old postcards and guidebooks on sale from waterfront shops reveal the pre-WW2 town to have looked very like a second Symi, with similar tiers of mansion-style buildings crowding around the magnificent, wide, U-shaped harbour bay. Only the houses behind the back of the harbour survive in any numbers, the castle hill that once formed the centre of town now being reduced to bulldozed rubble.

The waterfront — shorn of many of its buildings by German bombing — is on the verge of being rebuilt. One new house (presumably a copy of its predecessor on the site) has appeared in the 'gap' backing onto the new ferry quay, and concrete footings for several more houses have been marked out (this is a way of registering plots by expatriate islanders). The attractive pastel

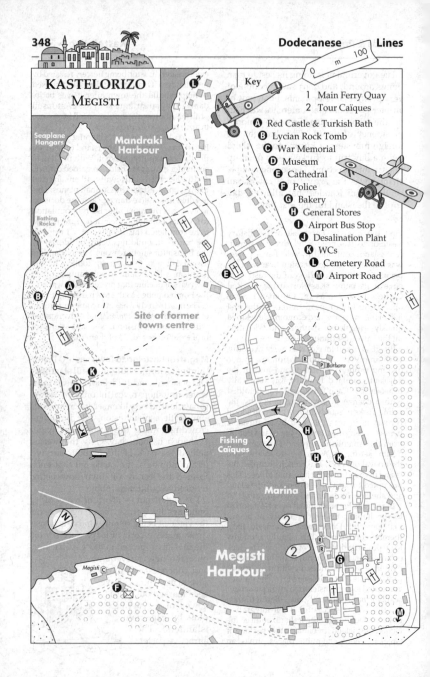

KASTELORIZO
MEGISTI

Seaplane
Hangars

**Mandraki
Harbour**

Bathing
Rocks

J

Key

1   Main Ferry Quay
2   Tour Caïques
A Red Castle & Turkish Bath
B Lycian Rock Tomb
C War Memorial
D Museum
E Cathedral
F Police
G Bakery
H General Stores
I   Airport Bus Stop
J Desalination Plant
K WCs
L Cemetery Road
M Airport Road

L

E

A

B

Site of former
town centre

K

D

C

I

C

H

H

K

R Barbara
P

Fishing
Caïques

2

1

Marina

2

2

N

**Megisti
Harbour**

G

Megisti **C**

F

M

painted waterfront buildings that have survived are home to the new 'centre' of town and here you will find the bulk of the town's shops and tavernas (which happily sprawl to the edge of the harbour as the quayside street is too narrow to admit vehicles).

The backstreets are more sobering: for the most part rows of semi-derelict houses and blocked off alleyways, they have a distinct ghost-town feel to them. The only one of any length runs up the periphery of the castle hill; once a backstreet, it is now the main town artery between the waterfront and the partially rebuilt main square (now home to the cathedral, several churches, odd houses and a barracks).

Paths also lead across the hill to the former main stairway (now reduced to an impressive flight of steps ascending into demolished oblivion) and to the castle. The castle is the only significant survival from the old town centre (bar a small redundant Turkish bath and a ruined windmill), and is really little more than a glorified tower (albeit a pretty impressive one). Access is via a steep metal staircase that runs up against one of the side turrets. Walking on, the path passes a new museum and then runs down to the pitiful collection of houses around the locked mosque. On the other side of the hill is the small harbour of **Mandraki**: semi-derelict and home to a desalination plant, it is backed by hills now being developed with government-built homes. A road of sorts also leads to a headland that is home to the town cemetery.

Kastelorizo not only enjoys very high summer temperatures (without the cooling influence of the *meltemi* these are regularly over 40 °C) but also has a high military presence. The main garrison lies on the airport road and does much to add to the frontier-town feel of the place. When tensions with Turkey are running very high, armed patrols parade along the waterfront and helicopters occasionally pass low overhead, in serious anticipation that Kastelorizo — an isolated Greek thorn in

the soft underbelly of the Turkish Mediterranean coast — will be the first victim of a Turkish attack on Greece.

All this sounds pretty grim, but Kastelorizo is actually a very cheerful place in High Season. This is largely thanks to the many Australian expatriate visitors who do much to add to the vitality of the town: 80% of those able to claim Kastelorizian ancestry are now settled in Australia (in this part of Greece a man doesn't bring a phrase book; he just brings his Sheila). The only downside is that with so many expats around, others can end up feeling a bit like outsiders.

The **rest of the island** is difficult to visit unless you like hiking. Walkers will enjoy Kastelorizo thanks to an excellent walking guide, *Capture Kastelorizo* (€10), by Marina Pistisonis (who describes herself as 'A Greek Aussie but always a Kassie at heart'). Available in a waterfront shop, it is also a good introduction and guide to the island as a whole. The main destination is the ancient acropolis at **Paleokastro**.

🛏

Accommodation in August is in very short supply: if you haven't booked you are cooked. In a worst-case scenario, try the police station and ask for a spare cell! Out of High Season you can always find a bed and will be met with offers when ferries dock. The only hotel is the expensive B-class *Megisti* (☎ 49221). This is augmented by several pensions. Most easily found is the *Barbara* (☎ 29295); others are signless and include the *Kristallo* (☎ 41209) behind the main square and the *Paradisos* (☎ 49074) near the west end of the port. There are also Rooms (☎ 29074) opposite the *Barbara*.

There isn't a campsite, and freelance camping isn't an option given the high military presence. Roughing it in the small patches of woodland on the outskirts of town isn't viable as their floors are littered with pine needles and spent cartridges: both are deadly, though the former are surprisingly toxic and will leave those who make an impromptu bed out of them looking like a walking example of some strange boil-producing disease a day or two later.

The 1380-built **Castle** is the main sight in town, followed by the free **Museum**. It contains an odd assortment of finds from the ancient acropolis at Paleocastro, earthenware from a medieval wreck off the south-west coast, and a collection of local house artifacts and costumes. Cut out of the rock beneath the castle is the only **Lycian Tomb** to be found in Greece (though there are plenty on the coast opposite). If you feel minded to attempt the short clamber up the steep cliff-side steps you will find a tomb with a view with room for six. Finally, although the **Cathedral** only dates from the 19 c. it is also of interest as the columns in the nave were taken from the temple of Apollo at Patara in Lycia (back in mainland contact days).

Thanks to a roadless and hilly interior, sightseeing is limited to Paleocastro and boat excursions to the **Blue Cave / Fokiali Cavern** — the best sea-cave in Greece if not the Med. Tour boats run from the harbour, making irregular runs to Turkey and to the outlying islands of **Strongili** and **Ro** (which has passed into Greek nationalist folklore thanks to its last inhabitant — a little old lady — who heroically ran up the Greek flag each day until her death in 1986. Her grave is one of the first things you see on landing on the island).

As is the case with many Greek islands, some of the more interesting 'sights' are no longer there to see. Kastelorizo has its sightseeing ghost in the form of the aircraft carrier *Ben My Chree* (Manx for 'girl of my heart'). One of the first half-dozen carriers in the Royal Navy, she was launched in 1908, starting out as a passenger steamer running between Liverpool and Douglas. On the outbreak of WW1 she was rebuilt as a carrier, with the addition of a flight deck and a prominent stern hangar (that housed 4 Sopwith camels and 2 Short seaplanes). Between 1915–16 she served in the Dardanelles during the Gallipoli campaign, and in January 1917 she sailed to Kastelorizo to replenish the supplies of the French garrison. Forced to use the main harbour because of her size (she was 375 feet long), she was shelled by the Turkish mainland artillery batteries. Her hangar received a direct hit on the 9th of January 1917, setting it on fire. Within half an hour the ship had been abandoned and continued to blaze until she sank on the morning of the 11th. In 1919 the hulk was refloated, towed to Piraeus, and sold to a German scrap merchant.

Kos

ΚΩΣ; 290 km²; pop. 21,500.

CODE ☎ 22420
PORT POLICE ☎ 26594
TOURIST POLICE ☎ 28227
POLICE ☎ 22222
HOSPITAL ☎ 22330

Thanks to an attractive mixture of sand and sights, Kos (often transcribed as 'Cos') is a justifiably popular package tourist destination. Large for a Greek island (45 km from east to west), Kos is long and tapering, with a high spine of mountains running along its southern side. The second largest island in the Dodecanese, it lies midway down the chain, and is the de facto hub of much of the group's ferry and hydrofoil activity, with virtually every boat putting in an appearance. Kos also has an unsurpassed number of tourist craft operating to neighbouring islands and the Turkish coast, a mere 5 km away, which dominates the eastern horizon.

Kos was an important centre in the ancient world, its capital being one of the major commercial ports in the Aegean. Unlike Rhodes, Kos was never large enough to be a major force in its own right, leaving it more prone than most of the larger islands to the vicissitudes of history: it variously relied on the patronage of Egypt (under the Ptolemies), Rome (from 130 BC) and Rhodes (from the 1 C. AD) for its protection. Its shaky geology has also played a major role: it was devastated by massive earthquakes on several occasions, notably in the 6 C. AD. (which totally flattened the ancient city, founded in 336 BC) and again as recently as 1933. As a result, much of its fame was derived from an odd mix of figures and famous associations rather than economic or military prowess. First among the historical figures were Hippocrates (460–357 BC) — the so-called 'Father of Medicine' — who was born and had his school here, and a famous painter contemporary of Alexander the Great named Apelles. Kos was also a noted producer of fine wine, and scandalously, in the Roman era, see-through silk garments beloved by senators' wives and the transvestite Emperor Caligula.

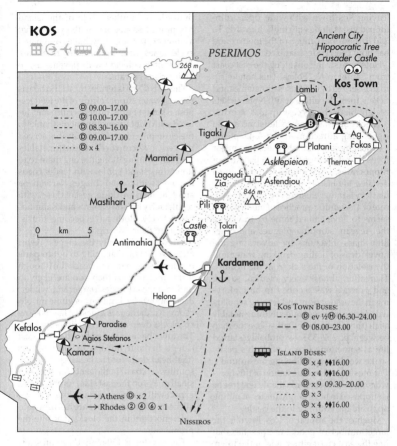

Kos Town, the main port and capital of the island, lies on the sandy east coast with views across to Turkey. It is a gentle, wide-avenued centre of flowers and trees that would be very restful if it wasn't for a spot of mass tourism. For the most part the more scenic parts of town have stood up to this remarkably well, but the streets north of the castle-dominated old harbour (and indeed, the coastline north and south) are dominated by a heavy concentration of hotels, discos and tee-shirt shops that will

either be your idea of holiday heaven or a variation of hell: this is the secret of the town's success for there is something here to appeal to all tastes — unless you like solitude. The centre is very Italianesque in feel, having been largely rebuilt during the interwar occupation years (courtesy of the massive 1933 earthquake). Some consolation for the loss of any tangible 'Greek' atmosphere is to be found in the Italian disinclination to rebuild over any archaeological remains that came to light, leaving Kos Town with wide, open, ruin-topped vistas along with the boulevards. To add to the appeal, much of the town centre has now been pedestrianized.

Hotels are strung out along the east coast from Lambi to Ag. Fokas. This hotel-strip road is served by city buses (timetables and tickets from the office at ❽). Note: tickets bought on the buses cost up to 20% extra.

The city buses also run to the island's main sightseeing attraction — the Asklepieion — a healing sanctuary that became a major focus for pilgrimage thanks to the fame of **Hippocrates**. Local guides will give you a detailed life history of this figure, though his story is rather elusive. The earliest advocate of a 'scientific' practice of medicine, he seems to have gained fame by travelling the Aegean, stopping plagues and other little mass infections by advocating the novel ideas of boiling drinking water and the isolation of the sick from the healthy. Thereafter, almost every medical saying and practice was ascribed to him, glorying in the association, and leaving scholars wondering if he ever said anything notable at all (the Hippocratic Oath — see the map between p. 352–353 — probably started life as something like: 'I wish this pesky snake would stop following me around'). The most recent manifestation of this hero-worship by association is the ancient tree he is supposed to have taught under, standing opposite the entrance to the castle.

Much of the appeal of Kos Town is the large number of good sand beaches that line the east coast either side of the town. The beach and hotel strip to the north of the centre is now very developed, and one is often hard put to see the sand for sun umbrellas and tourists. The beach strip to the south of the castle is the more appealing (though it is slowly deteriorating), with emptier strands, and lined with palm and eucalyptus trees and a cycleway running alongside the main road.

Bicycle hire is deservedly very popular in Kos Town as the wide streets and flat layout are well suited to this mode of transport

(indeed, the northern side of the island has proved so popular with cyclists that a number of roads now have designated cycle lanes running parallel to them). These often coincide with pavements, so pedestrians beware.

The rest of Kos is fertile (the island boasts the best water supply of any of the Dodecanese islands) but is rather scruffy and littered with military encampments thanks to the close proximity of Turkey. It is served by very overcrowded buses (timetables from ❽) running along the one main road down the island spine, with feeder roads linking it with coastal villages. Kardamena and Mastihari are the largest of these, with regular ferry links to Nissiros and Kalimnos respectively. Both have become tourist resorts in their own right.

Kardamena is easily the biggest resort after Kos Town, managing to outdo parts of it for discos, bars and beach life (though if this mix appeals then you are likely to find Faliraki on Rhodes a larger and 'wilder' destination). Lacking any significant old centre, Kardamena is a mass of hotels some six blocks deep and over a kilometre long. The town has a crowded beach on its west side, a harbour filled with tourist boats (that head daily for the beaches along the south-west coast) in the centre and several small quays on the east side. As one would expect with a major package tourist town, all the important facilities are readily available: most are in the blocks that line the promenade.

The bus stop is 150 m up the main street running up behind the ferry quay. Sad to say it, but this is in many ways the biggest attraction in town, for there is very little of Greece to be found here: one could just as easily be in any other down-market package tour resort filled with beer-and-chips type Brits and Germans (the former often propping up bars showing videos of ancient UK

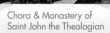

Chora & Monastery of
Saint John the Theologian

PATMOS

View of Chora
& the Ferry Quay

Greece is a great
place for girls who
break up with their
boyfriends — there
are bronzed hunks
to be had on every
island waterfront …

SYMI
The C/F *Nissos Kalimnos*
Docks at Gialos Port

Sponge Diver
Bronze

Asklepieion:
View from the
Upper Terrace

Statue Niches in the
Middle Terrace Wall

Kos Town:
Main Square Mosque

KOS Old Harbour
Waterfront

Dodecanese

Key

Ⓐ Entrance Stairs & Small Roman Bath
Ⓑ Entry Propylon
Ⓒ Galleries
Ⓓ Statue Niches & Middle Terrace Wall
Ⓔ Statue Torsos
Ⓕ Fountains
Ⓖ Roman Latrines (not in use)
Ⓗ Second Staircase
Ⓘ Great Altar of Asklepios
Ⓙ Early Temple of Asklepios
Ⓚ Priests' Quarters
Ⓛ Exedra/Public Platform
Ⓜ Temple of Apollo
Ⓝ Lesche (Conference Hall)
Ⓞ Upper Andria/Terrace Wall
Ⓟ Monumental Staircase
Ⓠ Large Temple of Asklepios
Ⓡ Galleries
Ⓢ Patients' Rooms
Ⓣ Sacred Wood & Small Temple
Ⓤ Large Roman Baths

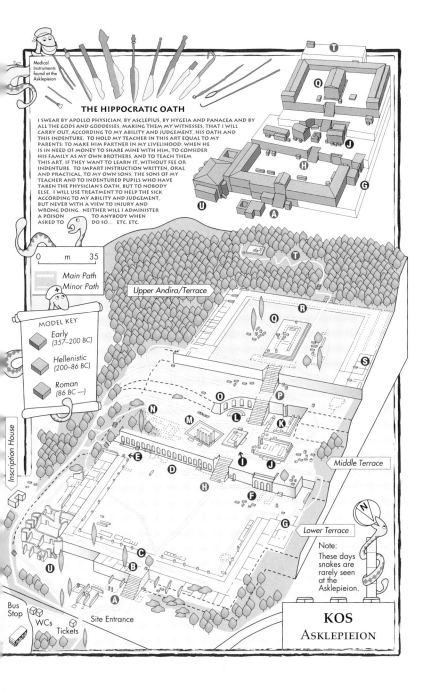

Medical Instruments found at the Asklepieion

THE HIPPOCRATIC OATH

I SWEAR BY APOLLO PHYSICIAN, BY ASCLEPIUS, BY HYGEIA AND PANACEA AND BY ALL THE GODS AND GODDESSES, MAKING THEM MY WITNESSES, THAT I WILL CARRY OUT, ACCORDING TO MY ABILITY AND JUDGEMENT, HIS OATH AND THIS INDENTURE. TO HOLD MY TEACHER IN THIS ART EQUAL TO MY PARENTS: TO MAKE HIM PARTNER IN MY LIVELIHOOD; WHEN HE IS IN NEED OF MONEY TO SHARE MINE WITH HIM, TO CONSIDER HIS FAMILY AS MY OWN BROTHERS, AND TO TEACH THEM THIS ART, IF THEY WANT TO LEARN IT, WITHOUT FEE OR INDENTURE. TO IMPART INSTRUCTION WRITTEN, ORAL AND PRACTICAL, TO MY OWN SONS, THE SONS OF MY TEACHER AND TO INDENTURED PUPILS WHO HAVE TAKEN THE PHYSICIAN'S OATH, BUT TO NOBODY ELSE. I WILL USE TREATMENT TO HELP THE SICK ACCORDING TO MY ABILITY AND JUDGEMENT, BUT NEVER WITH A VIEW TO INJURY AND WRONG DOING. NEITHER WILL I ADMINISTER A POISON   TO ANYBODY WHEN ASKED TO   DO SO... ETC. ETC.

0   m   35

Main Path
Minor Path

MODEL KEY

Early
(357–200 BC)

Hellenistic
(200–86 BC)

Roman
(86 BC —)

Inscription House

Upper Andira/Terrace

Middle Terrace

Lower Terrace

Note:
These days
snakes are
rarely seen
at the
Asklepieion.

N

Bus Stop

WCs   Tickets

Site Entrance

KOS
ASKLEPIEION

RHODES
Lindos Acropolis &
Faliraki Shop Sign

EXCHANGE
RENT   HERE
FANS WHEEL CHAIRS
WALKING   STICKS
CRUTCHES

KASTELORIZO
Megisti at Dawn
(with mainland Turkey in the
background)

LEROS
Windmill at
Agia Marina

EVENING ARGOS

WELL-WISHERS
FLOOD
AEGEAN

TOURISTS BLAMED
FOR LOSS OF KEY
GREEK ISLANDS !

DELPHI ORACLE
— LATEST —
"Glub, glub, glub,
glub..."

NISSIROS
Town Well

Dodecanese

TV comedy shows or enjoying the wet bikini and tee-shirt contests). On the plus side are the tour-boat links with nearby Nissiros.

Mastihari, the largest settlement on the north coast, also has a sand beach but is much quieter than Kardamena and offers a better mix of tourism and regular town. Built on a wide, flat promontory, it has a small harbour (rather smelly), a ferry link to Kalimnos, and a single major street running directly inland. It also has a bus stop at the town end of the ferry quay — the only problem being lack of services after 18.00. If you arrive on the evening ferry from Kalimnos en route to Kos Town you will need to take a taxi (€20).

The best beach in town lines the wide bay to the west of the centre (which has recently seen its waterfront given a major make-over), while the eastern half of town is dominated by several large hotel complexes. In this respect it mirrors the north coast village of **Tigaki**. This small settlement offers a popular alternative to the Kos Town beaches, via its impressively large expanse of sand that is popular with windsurfers. Like adjoining Mastihari, it consists of a promenade (complete with a disco) and a main street that runs directly inland to the main island road.

Inevitably, the more attractive destinations are harder to get to. The best beaches are tucked away under the western 'fin' of the island beneath the hilltop windmilled village of **Kefalos** (site of the pre-Kos Town ancient capital of the island) 45 km from Kos Town. This is easily the best part of Kos, quieter and more fertile than the rest of the island. This area has some notable pine woods south-west of Antimahia, known as Plaka. These are now an attractive picnic spot for island coach tours and those with their own transport. Although hotel development has also encroached onto the landscape, the area is still relatively unspoilt.

The largest beach centre is at **Kamari**. This is a resort village with a lovely sandy strand,

the remains of an ancient agora, a couple of discos and a large *Club Med* complex behind Agios Stefanos beach (named after a ruined early basilica on the small headland that separates the beach from the village). Just offshore is the attractive chapel-topped islet of Agios Nikolaos.

To the east are a series of superb beaches reached via boats or bus stops along the main road. These include the imaginatively named Paradise, Sunny and Magic beaches. The inland towns have less going for them. The majority of visitors to Kos end up passing through **Antimahia**. Distinguished by having the only working windmill on Kos, the town is better known for being the jumping-off point for the charter-flight airport. To the north-east is the unspoilt village of **Pili**: built alongside its beautiful, ruined medieval counterpart, it is more worthy of a look.

🛏

High Season sees a rush for the available hotel space and rooms, and understandably so, for Kos, an island overloaded with upper and mid-range package tour hotels, is poorly supplied with budget accommodation, given the number of visitors it sees. It thus pays to arrive on a morning boat (i.e. Rhodes hydrofoil rather than afternoon ferry). The limited budget rooms available in **Kos Town** are divided between seven establishments. To the south of the ferry quay the D-class *Hara* (☎ 22500) lies one block behind the beach road that is home to package tour hotels for a kilometre each side of the town (if funds aren't too much of a problem then finding a bed in one of them is never very difficult). Alternatively, you can try the C-class *Maritina* (☎ 23241) near the OTE.

Although it is on a busy street, it is not as noisy as the clutch of hotels overlooking the Old Harbour. These consist of the E-class *Kalymnos* (☎ 22336), the reasonable but popular D-class *Helena* (☎ 22986) near the internet café, and *Dodecanessus* (☎ 28460). There is also one good pension in the centre of town — the *Acropoli* (☎ 22244). To the north lies a second, the *Alexis* (☎ 28798). Although rooms are not so plentiful as on the Cycladic islands there are a reasonable number scattered around the town: the owners, however, are in the habit of only meeting the major boats.

KOS
TOWN CENTRE

Key

- **A** Tourist Information Office
- **B** Island Bus Station
- **C** Taxi Station
- **D** City Hall, Customs & City Bus Stop / Tickets
- **E** Police & Tourist Police
- **F** National Bank of Greece
- **G** Hospital
- **H** Museum
- **I** Castle
- **J** Castle Entrance / Plane Tree of Hippocrates
- **K** Harbour Area Excavations
- **L** Site of Ancient Acropolis

- **M** Odeon (restored)
- **N** Western Area Excavations
- **O** Casa Romana
- **P** Knights' City Wall & *McDonald's*
- **Q** Cathedral
- **R** Supermakets
- **S** International Press
- **T** Pharmacies
- **U** Produce Market
- **V** Bar Strips
- **W** Cinema Orfeus
- **X** Ferry Terminal / WCs
- **Y** Ferry Passenger Stalls
- **Z** Public WCs

1. Car Ferries
2. Island Excursion Boats
3. Bodrum Day Boats
4. Tour Boats
5. Hydrofoil Quay
6. Hydrofoil Berth
7. Turkish Day Boats

- **F** Asklepieion (4 km) & Western Kos
- **A** Lambi Rd. (2 km)
- **Ψ** Psalidhi & Agios Fokas Coast Road

ANCIENT CITY
10. Temple of Pandimos Aphrodite
11. Temple of Heracles
12. Small Temples
13. Roman Agora
14. Stoas (4 c. BC)
15. City Wall
16. Site of East Wall Gate
17. Harbour Baths
18. North Baths
19. Roman House

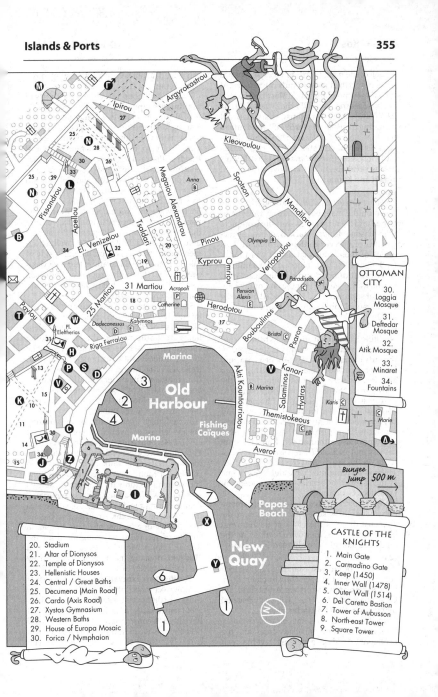

Argyrokastrou

Ipirou

Kleovoulou

Spoison

Mandilara

Megaiou Alexandrou

Anna

Pissandrou

Apellou

Tsaldari

El. Venizelou

Pinou

Olympia

Kyprou

Omirou

Veriopoulou

Paradissos

25 Martiou

31 Martiou

Acropoli

Herodotou

Pension Alexis

Catherine

Pavlou

Dadecanessus

Kalymnos

Pl. Eleftherias

Riga Ferraiou

Bouboulinas

Psaron

Bristol

Marina

Akti Kountouriotou

Kanari

Old Harbour

Marina

Salaminos

Hydras

Fishing Caïques

Themistokeous

Karis

Marina

Averof

Marie

Papas Beach

New Quay

Bungee Jump | *500 m*

OTTOMAN CITY

30. Loggia Mosque
31. Deftedar Mosque
32. Atik Mosque
33. Minaret
34. Fountains

CASTLE OF THE KNIGHTS

1. Main Gate
2. Carmadino Gate
3. Keep (1450)
4. Inner Wall (1478)
5. Outer Wall (1514)
6. Del Caretto Bastion
7. Tower of Aubusson
8. North-east Tower
9. Square Tower

20. Stadium
21. Altar of Dionysos
22. Temple of Dionysos
23. Hellenistic Houses
24. Central / Great Baths
25. Decumena (Main Road)
26. Cardo (Axis Road)
27. Xystos Gymnasium
28. Western Baths
29. House of Europa Mosaic
30. Forica / Nymphaion

Each of the main tourist villages on Kos has more hotels than most islands can muster. At the budget end of the range **Mastihari** has the D-class *Faenareti* (☎ 51395), the E-class *Zevas* (☎ 22577) and some good rooms on the waterfront including the *Panorama* (☎ 59145). **Kardamena** has the D-class *Paralia* (☎ 51205) and the E-class *Olympia*, and **Kefalos**, the D-class *Sidney* and E-class *Eleni* and *Maria* (☎ 71308). Rooms are also available at all the above as well as at **Tigaki** and **Kamari**.

Λ

Camping Kos (☎ 23275): 3½ km south of Kos Town on the main beach road. A well-maintained and friendly family-run site (complete with reasonable mini-market) set in an attractive mix of a flower garden and orchard. This is one of those sites that tempt you to stay far longer than you intended. No mini-bus service, but campers can take the coast-road bus or walk. The site is at the end of the long straight section of road — bounded by tourist facilities (including a couple of supermarkets) and by a cycleway.

≈☆

Nightlife in **Kos Town** often looks to be in a not dissimilar condition to Hippocrates' tree: by the early hours the town is festooned with limp limbs propped up by bars. The main nightclub area lies on the north-east boundary of the Harbour Excavation, though the northern part of town along Kanari St., home to the *Playboy Club* (famed for disco light shows) and the *Beach Boys* bar (arguably home to the best music), is also replete with bars. Other discos in town are also in the northern Kanari/Lambi district and include *Disco Heaven*, the *Kalua* (both on the beach) and the *Disco Rock Club*. There is also the inevitable outdoor cinema — in this case the *Orpheus* — on the waterfront (Vassileos Georgiou).

Nightspots aren't hard to find in **Kardamena** either. The most visible establishments are the *Tropicana* disco in the block at the east end of the promenade, and *Disco Starlight* on the landward side of the main road into town.

◎◎

Kos is one of the best islands going when it comes to sightseeing. First and foremost there is the **Asklepieion**, one of the greatest shrines in Greece (described overleaf, it is easily reached by bus from the Old Harbour).

Kos Town itself is the other big crowd-puller. By mixing exploration, shady trees, and the occasional drink at a passing taverna, you can spend a relaxed and interesting day's sightseeing.

The most obvious attraction is the **Castle of the Knights** (open ②–⑦ 08.30–15.00; tickets €3). Begun in 1450, it initially consisted of just the keep and the inner enceinte (curtain wall). Following the unsuccessful Turkish assault of 1480, in 1495 the Grand Master of Rhodes, Pierre d'Aubusson, had the outer enceinte constructed, the task being completed by his successor Fabrizio Del Carretto in 1514; their coats-of-arms (see the Rhodes City map between pages 384–385) are carved on the walls at various points. Most of the masonry used in the castle was pillaged from the ancient city and Asklepieion. It was also used to construct the **Knights' City Wall**, a fragment of which survives on the north side of the Harbour Area Excavation, and includes a gateway and the south-west tower. The castle also had a moat, which now houses the road that runs under the bridge.

Standing opposite the castle bridge is the impressive 14 m girthed (and now hollow) **Plane Tree of Hippocrates** — its not so plain limbs artistically supported with scaffolding and cut-up tractor tyres. Supposedly the one he taught under, it is at best about 500 years old. It shades a Turkish fountain (dry) constructed from fragments of ancient buildings, and the best of Kos Town's several mosques: **Gazi Hassan Pasha Mosque** (1786). Sadly, none of them are open to the public.

Immediately to the south of the mosque lies the largest excavated area of the ancient city, the **Harbour Area Excavation** (entry free). This roughly corresponds with the site of the medieval city. The bulk of the excavation consists of foundations and the inner stone cores of temples (only the long-gone exteriors were faced with marble); it is the preserve of lizards during the day and couples serenading the moon at night. Amid the rubble are the remains of a temple of Aphrodite and a couple of reconstructed columns from the Roman Forum. More interesting is the town **Museum**, housing the finds not shipped by the Italians to Rhodes.

The **Western Excavation** area to the east of the town centre is (thanks to Italian restorers) the best of the ancient sites. A number of pillars that formed the gymnasium's peristyle court have been 'reconstructed', and the streets still bear the ruts worn into the stones by ancient carts. The site also has walls complete with

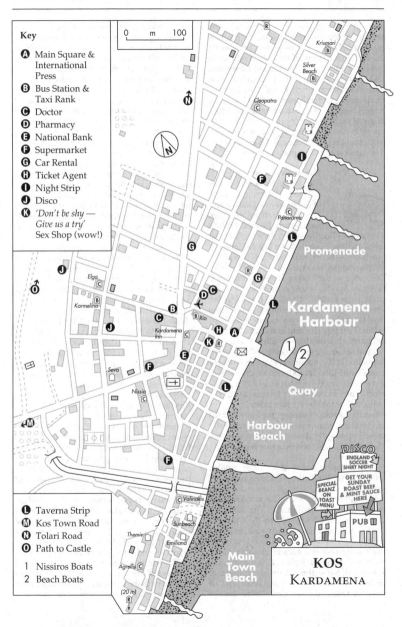

Key

- **A** Main Square & International Press
- **B** Bus Station & Taxi Rank
- **C** Doctor
- **D** Pharmacy
- **E** National Bank
- **F** Supermarket
- **G** Car Rental
- **H** Ticket Agent
- **I** Night Strip
- **J** Disco
- **K** 'Don't be shy — Give us a try' Sex Shop (wow!)

- **L** Taverna Strip
- **M** Kos Town Road
- **N** Tolari Road
- **O** Path to Castle

1 Nissiros Boats
2 Beach Boats

0   m   100

Krismari

Silver Beach

Cleopatra

Panorama

Promenade

Kardamena Harbour

Quay

Harbour Beach

Elga

Karmelina

Kardamena Inn

Rio

Seva

Nissia

Valinakis

Sunbeach

Themis

Emiliana

Agrellis

Main Town Beach

DISCO
ENGLAND SOCCER SHIRT NIGHT

SPECIAL BEANZ ON TOAST MENU

GET YOUR SUNDAY ROAST BEEF & MINT SAUCE HERE

PUB

KOS
KARDAMENA

(20 m)

original painted plasterwork, though the ancient Acropolis isn't visible, its position marked only by the mosqueless minaret on the hill. To the south of these excavations lie two other attractions: the restored **Odeon** and also a rebuilt example of a Roman Villa (the Italians not surprisingly opted to reconstruct this building rather than one of the Hellenistic houses nearby), the **Casa Romana**, a mixture of pools and mosaics. Worth a look: don't be put off by the singularly ugly cement exterior of the building — Roman houses always were decorated with pretty plain exteriors.

The Asklepieion

(See map between pages 352–353.) The remains of one of the most imaginative and effective creations of Greek architecture lie on a hillside 4 km west of Kos Town. Overlooking both the town and the Turkish strait, the Asklepieion (open ②–⑦ 08.30–15.00; tickets €3) was the leading medical sanctuary in the Greek world. Dedicated to the God of Healing, Asklepios (a son of Apollo, whose symbol was a snake curling up a staff), it was — thanks to the revenue that accompanied the pilgrims that flocked there — an architectural and cultural centre. The sanctuary was founded a century after the death of Hippocrates (357 BC) and because of his associations developed thereafter. Built on four terraces carved out of a gentle hillside adorned with a sacred wood, it was considered a masterpiece of Hellenistic architecture in its day, and boasted a series of famous paintings by Apelles to heal the spirit when they couldn't manage the body. Offices to the latter were undertaken by a priestly order supposedly descended from the god. The sanctuary also offered a much-used right of asylum.

Despite losing some of its most notable art works to Rome, the Asklepieion thrived until the 6 C. AD, when it was reduced to rubble either by the Anatolian attack on Kos in 554 AD or an earthquake. The ruins lay undisturbed until 1450, when the Castle of the Knights was constructed in Kos Town, the need for building blocks being sated by the readily available ancient masonry in the town and at the Asklepieion. As a result, the site was all but stripped bare of architectural members and its location passed out of memory. One of the lost great shrines known

only through literary sources, the search for the Asklepieion began in earnest in 1896. The probable site was eventually pinpointed by an English archaeologist, W. R. Paton, in 1902 — though it was left to a local antiquarian, G. E. Zaraphtis, and his German archaeologist sponsor, Rudolf Herzog, to crudely excavate the remains in a classic early archaeological 'grub-and-grab' dig — that enabled him to walk off with the glory and his sponsor with the more attractive finds. From 1904 on Zaraphtis began a much better and more systematic excavation that continued until his death in the 1933 earthquake. Thereafter Italian archaeologists did as much building as excavating, rebuilding the impressive terrace walls (with rough tuffstone blocks in lieu of smooth marble) and staircases, and adding a pillar or two for good measure. The visible remains are therefore as much of a 'fake' as the Minoan palace at Knossos on Crete, but, as in that case, the reconstruction is really inspired and of great value to those seeking an appreciation of the site's former grandeur.

Today the Asklepieion is approached via a pleasant suburb road that emerges through an avenue of cypress trees at a large coach and bus park. A short path takes you past a drinking-water tap to the ticket kiosk at the entrance to the site. At this point you have to choose between taking the path up the south side of the site and then walking down the terraces from the upper terrace or taking the ancient route (i.e. walking up the staircases). The description below assumes the latter, if only because it is easier to climb, rather than descend, stairways without hand rails.

Directly inside the site entrance are the foundations of a small Roman bathhouse (with hypocaust floor in the hot room and a beautifully preserved plunge pool complete with steps), where pilgrims would cleanse themselves before entering the sanctuary proper. The modern path runs past this to ❶ the **Entrance Stairs**. Consisting of 24 steps they climb to the **Lower Terrace** and the site of the formal gateway to the sanctuary, ❷ the **Entry Propylon**, now marked only by a pillar base under a shady tree. The vision — on passing through it — of the wedding-cake terrace layers ascending to the main temple is now only to be dimly gleaned. So too is the enclosed 'courtyard' atmosphere of the Lower Terrace created by ❸ the **Galleries** — pillared, stoa-like buildings which once ran from either side of the gate to the middle terrace wall. Even so, the Lower Terrace retains the wide, open aspect that graced it in antiquity, and it was probably on this terrace that athletic contests associated with festivals honouring the god were held. Unfortunately, the votive statues that were such a feature of this terrace have long gone. All that remains are **D** the rebuilt **Statue Niches**. In one of these niches stood a very famous statue of antiquity now lost — the Aphrodite by the even more famous sculptor Praxiteles. The only figures remaining are the **Torsos** at **E**, propped against the **Middle Terrace Wall**. On the stoa side of the path at **E** you will also find one of the few remaining statue bases (complete with the ghostly footprints of its owner) that adorned this terrace.

Walking along to the north side of the terrace wall you arrive at **F** the **Fountains**. Fed by both sulphurous and iron-rich springs, these were revered for the supposed healing properties of the water. The later Romans debased the atmosphere by building **G** the **Latrines** nearby (no doubt the steady tinkle of water dribbling into the sacred pool prompted too many to go in search of a sacred tree or two).

Returning back along the terrace you come to **H** the **Second Staircase**. Running up to the Middle Terrace via 30 steps, it brings you onto the real heart of the sanctuary, for directly in front of you is **I** the **Great Altar of Asklepios** (4 C. BC), the oldest building of the Asklepieion. Now reduced to its foundations, it was similar (albeit on a smaller scale) to the Great Altar at Pergamon, with a central stairway running up to the winged base. The base was also roofed, and one of the ornate roof coffers lies on the edge of the foundations.

To the north lies the oldest temple in the sanctuary: **J** the **Asklepios Early/Small Temple.** Dating from the 4 C. BC, it was built in the Ionic style (two of the columns have been restored) and functioned as the sanctuary treasury after it was replaced as the main shrine on the site. In this capacity it housed a series of wooden panel paintings by Apelles. One — the Aphrodite Anadyomene — was regarded as a masterpiece of ancient art. It was carried off to Rome by the Emperor Augustus. On the Lower Terrace side are the bases for lost votive statues, while tucked away on the Upper Terrace side is a Roman building on Greek foundations **K**, believed to have been the **Priests' Quarters**.

Opposite the Priests' Quarters are the semi-circular foundations of **L** the **Exedra / Public Platform**. An odd building, with no clear function, suggestions as to its purpose have ranged from a public bench to an assembly point for priests or doctors. The terrace wall behind it has several more statue niches. To the east, the Romans in-filled the terrace by building **M** an irregularly orientated **Temple of Apollo**, now the most visible of all the buildings on the site thanks to the seven fake columns erected by the Italians to give you something to look at. Two of them contain fluted fragments of the original drums.

To the south, now little visible and partly overgrown with trees, are the foundations of **N**, usually known as the **Lesche** or **Conference Hall** — though the precise function of the building remains unclear. Given the snake cult associated with the god Asklepios, it is somewhat surprising that the Asklepieion does not appear to have possessed a snake house (its counterpart at Epidavros had a magnificent Tholos built for this purpose), so perhaps this was it. Snake rooms were common at medical shrines, for these lovely little critters were deemed to have healing powers — given the numbers of lame men who suddenly acquired the ability to run very fast when faced with one (to say nothing of the numerous compulsive stammerers suddenly able to say 'Asklepieion' three times in as many seconds at the first time of asking).

Behind the buildings on the Middle Terrace is **O**, the first stage of the double **Upper Terrace Wall**. In fact, the Middle Terrace can be divided into two (hence the four terraces), but as the upper part of the Terrace is too small to contain buildings, it is viewed as merely a halfway point up **P** the **Monumental Staircase**. This consists of two closely positioned flights that rise 60 steps to the **Upper Terrace** and its superb views over both the site and Kos Town.

Dominating the centre of the Upper Terrace is **Q** the **Large Temple of Asklepios**. Built in the 2 C. BC, this was the main temple on the site to the god. Doric in style, it was an irregularly shaped 6 x 11 columned building, notable in its day for having the lowest of its three steps made of black marble (though you would be hard-pressed to know it now). Today only the foundations and part of the interior floor survive.

Around the side and back perimeter of the terrace ran ❽ the **Galleries**, forming a peristyle backdrop to the temple, and closing in the rear of the site. At some later date, additions — in the form of cell-like cubicles — were made to the back of the side galleries: now little more than unintelligible foundations, these are thought to have been ❾ **Patients' Rooms**.

From the back of the terrace a path winds into ❼ the **Sacred Wood** — a delightful, shady canopy of pine trees that surrounds the site — emerging a hundred metres later in a small grove adorned with the remains of a **Small Temple** of unknown attribution (only the foundations of the base remain). Returning to the main terrace, another path runs to the southern end and joins the main path running down the south side of the site. This takes you past a disused museum (still adorned outside with blocks containing inscriptions found on the site) and the back of the **Large Roman Baths**. Dating from the 1 C. AD, this is a late but major structure, again boasting hypocaust floor pillars. The now high walls have been extensively repaired by the Italians (this is Roman after all!). However, one of the front rooms — at ❿ — retains some original painted plaster (though there is little visible detail). From here the path returns past the small bathhouse to the site entrance.

The Rest of the Island

Additional minor sites are scattered around Kos. The most impressive of these is the **Antimahia Castle**. Sited atop a hill north of the airport and Kardamena, it can be reached either via a 3 km path from the airport—Kos Town road—or a 10 km track that starts 700 m east of Kardamena. Built by the Knights of St. John in the first half of the 16 c., it is triangular in shape, with corner turrets. Within the ruined walls are the remains of a number of houses and a couple of churches. A second site worth taking in lies at **Therma** — a 4 km walk from **Ag. Fokas** — where hot springs run down to the sea.

Finally, Kos has boat excursions aplenty, with craft running across the 5 km straits to **Bodrum** in Turkey and to all the adjacent islands, including the beach islet of **Pserimos**. This is a crowded beach island reserved for day-trippers seeking (in vain) to escape the crowds. Boats berth at a small quay serving the small settlement on the west coast.

Leros

ΛΕΡΟΣ; 53 km²; pop. 8,200.

CODE ☎ 22470
PORT POLICE ☎ 23256
POLICE ☎ 22222
HOSPITAL ☎ 23251

Leros is a real oddity among the Greek islands. Conveniently placed between the popular islands of Patmos and Kos, it is sufficiently attractive to deserve its fair share of the crowds — even despite its lack of obvious sights — and yet, although it is well served by ferries, the island remains stubbornly off the tourist trail. There is, of course, a reason, and that is its very unsavoury reputation. This is so bad that leaflets issued to tourists by the Municipality of Leros are, unusually, forced to acknowledge the problem thus:

'In 1958 the Community of Psychopaths was established at Leros, which is still here today, under the name of 'State Therapeutical Hospital of Leros'. Stemming from that, by mistake or sometimes in purpose, an infamous picture of Leros has been promoted, which in no way can identify with the island and its people. Since 1989 various press reports in Greek and foreign press presented in excess the negative sides of such an establishment'.

In short, a past Greek government came up with the idea of conveniently placing all lunatics and severely mentally handicapped adults in one location — Leros. The media reports in question were humiliating accounts, widely publicized across Europe, that patients in the hospital were being kept in concentration-camp-like conditions.

Happily, thanks to international pressure, a £9.3 million EU grant, and the surreptitious dumping of a number of patients to institutions just as bad on other islands (such as Lesbos — see p. 418) things have now improved, though the legacy of this nasty episode lives on in the lack of visitors. Greek tourists tend to avoid the island in droves (its name has become a byword hereabouts carrying much the same resonances that 'Bedlam' has acquired in English). In many ways this is unfortunate, because Leros has a fair bit going for it in a downbeat sort of way, and you are likely to find that the islanders are both welcoming and almost pathetically grateful that you are mad enough to have paid them a visit (note: given the circumstances, it is probably wise not to look *too* mad).

Its reputation notwithstanding, Leros is not by any means a typical Greek island. Superficially, it is not dissimilar to Patmos, being small and hilly, with a deeply indented coastline offering a number of sheltered bays complete with — predominantly pebble — beaches. However, the years of Italian rule between the world wars have left a greater mark than on other islands in the chain, and it is fair to say that Leros still retains the atmosphere of an Italian island. This is largely because the crumbling plastered 1930s buildings, the harbour and military roads (lined with plane trees) are Italian built, with the tiny nucleus of the Greek chora failing to make an impact.

Most visitors to the island arrive at the port of **Lakki**, set in a deep inlet on the south-west coast. Thanks to the shelter offered by this bay, Leros was a major naval base and was occupied by the Allies at the start of the last war. The island was successfully attacked by German forces in 1943, with 5,000 casualties (war cemeteries are scattered around the island — the largest British cemetery being near Alinda). The memory of this does little to relieve the atmosphere that is set by the airfield-like lights of a mental hospital complex on the southern shore. Used to detain political prisoners by the Colonels between 1967–1974, it makes the perfect asylum as any sane person within its precincts would soon be driven mad by the sight of the means of escape constantly steaming in and out of the harbour.

The port town is a very artificial affair, revealing its Italian-planned origins. The roads were laid out, impressive waterfront buildings were erected and then, well, not

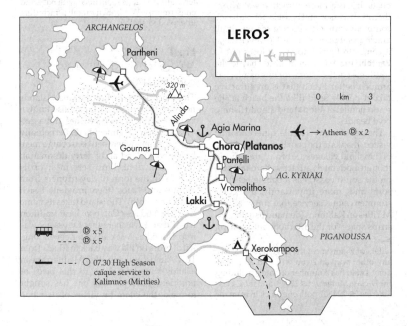

LEROS

ARCHANGELOS

Partheni

320 m

Alinda

Agia Marina

Chora/Platanos

Gournas

Pantelli

Vromolithos

AG. KYRIAKI

Lakki

0   km   3

→ Athens Ⓓ x 2

PIGANOUSSA

Xerokampos

Ⓓ x 5
Ⓓ x 5

○ 07.30 High Season
caïque service to
Kalimnos (Mirties)

a lot really, as the local economy has never grown enough to allow a town to fully develop in the space provided. The result is a mix of odd buildings and clumps of trees that is a bit ghost-townish. On the plus side, accommodation is easily found (even if the views are not very appealing), along with all services, and in summer the promenade has been known to play host to a circus, complete with little top.

The bus service on Leros is so poor that taxis thrive along the walkable 3 km road to the chora at **Platanos**. Slightly more Greek in appearance, it lies under the protecting walls of the imposing Kastro, but is somewhat spoilt by indifferent buildings, a rather dingy atmosphere and the busy road running through the centre. All the main services lie on the street which runs down to the little port of Agia Marina.

The 19 C. main port, **Agia Marina** is now rather neglected, though it is still used by hydrofoils, catamarans (in certain weather conditions) and the island's excursion boats. It has a more attractive waterfront than its successor, and boasts a pebble beach complete with a distinctive sea windmill gracing a submerged mole. However, when it comes to tourist appeal, it loses out to **Pantelli**, tucked away in a little bay to the south-east of the Chora, for this hamlet has a much better beach that is an attractive mix of pebbly sand (like the beach at the resort hamlet of **Alinda**) and the odd fishing boat besides.

The rest of Leros is fertile, quiet and little visited, thanks to the poor bus service. None of the island villages are of any great merit, though moderately attractive **Xerokampos**, on the south coast, has a pebble beach of sorts and, more importantly, a regular summer caïque service that runs daily to Mirities on Kalimnos (demand usually outstrips space for the afternoon return trip).

🛏

Offers of rooms meet the large ferries; arrive any other way and you will find an empty quay. **Lakki** has a number of hotels including the D-class *Miramare* (☎ 22043) and the E-class *Katerina* (☎ 22460), both one block in from the

waterfront. Up-market hotels lie inland, with the attractive C-class *Artemis* (☎ 22416) supported by the B-class *Agelou Xenon* (☎ 22514). **Chora** also has a couple of pensions: most conspicuously the *Platanos* (☎ 22608) housed in an incongruously tall modern building overlooking the main square, and the nicer *Elefteria* (☎ 23550) on the Lakki road. **Agia Marina** has a few apartments on the beach road but no other advertised accommodation. **Pantelli** (off the map) also has a scatter of pensions and taverna rooms, as does the package resort village at **Alinda**.

▲

Camping Leros (☎ 23372): at Xerocampos. Olive-grove site with more trees than tents.

👓

The 12 C. **Castle** built by the Knights of St. John on the site of a Byzantine fortress is the one and only attraction. It contains a church and offers panoramic views of the island and the large number of islets nearby. Tourists can visit (the stairway to the castle starts to the right of a small florist's just off the Chora main square). The nearest thing Leros has to a museum is contained in the tourist office block on the ferry quay: a single room filled with odds and ends (mostly WW2 memorabilia, including unexploded shells).

Lipsi
ΛΕΙΨΟΙ; 16 km²; pop. 650.

CODE ☎ 22470

The most developed of the small islands north of Patmos, quiet Lipsi (also known as Lipsos) offers good beaches and a get-away-from-it-all atmosphere. Perpetually hovering somewhere between being a mere beach-boat island and a ferry destination in its own right, Lipsi sees most of its visitors in the form of day-trippers from Patmos and Leros (there are daily beach boats from both). The island takes its name from the goddess Calypso: local tradition has it that it was here that Odysseus was imprisoned as a sex slave for seven long, hard, years on his way back to Ithaca from Troy. Almost as many other Mediterranean islands have laid claim to this piece of notoriety, but only this one has sought to make the claim by virtue of its name

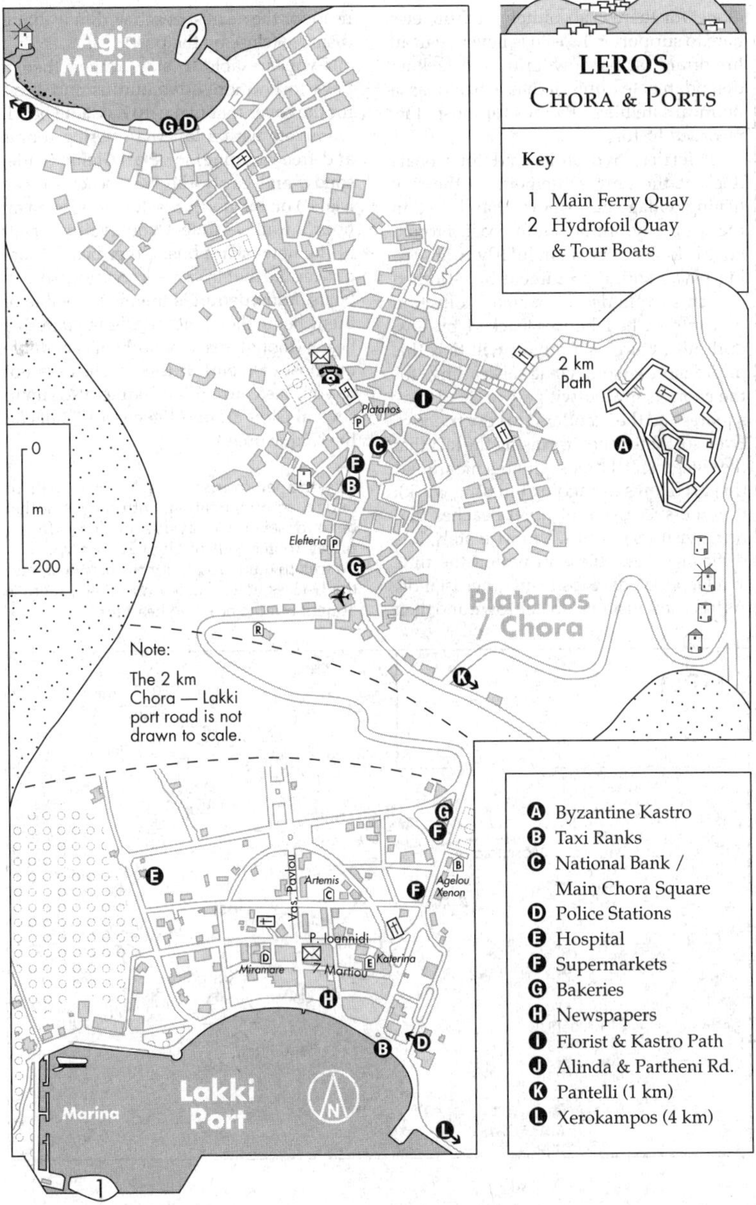

Agia Marina

2

J

G D

LEROS
CHORA & PORTS

Key

1 Main Ferry Quay

2 Hydrofoil Quay
& Tour Boats

2 km
Path

I

Platanos
P

C

0

m

200

F

B

A

Elefteria
P

G

Platanos / Chora

R

K

Note:

The 2 km
Chora — Lakki
port road is not
drawn to scale.

G
F

E

B
Agelou
Xenon

Artemis
C

F

Vas. Pavlou

P. Ioannidi

D
Miramare

Kalerina

7 Martiou

H

B

D

Marina

Lakki Port

N

L

Ⓐ Byzantine Kastro

Ⓑ Taxi Ranks

Ⓒ National Bank /
Main Chora Square

Ⓓ Police Stations

Ⓔ Hospital

Ⓕ Supermarkets

Ⓖ Bakeries

Ⓗ Newspapers

Ⓘ Florist & Kastro Path

Ⓙ Alinda & Partheni Rd.

Ⓚ Pantelli (1 km)

Ⓛ Xerokampos (4 km)

alone; for there is absolutely nothing else here to support it. Lipsi has never been an important island; low, arid, and lacking defendable features it has existed as a political satellite of Patmos for most of its recorded history.

All ferries, hydrofoils and tour boats dock at the only settlement — the tiny fishing village-cum-chora that is set in the deep bay on the south coast. From a boat it looks to be a singularly uninspiring place, with a prominent blue-domed church surrounded by a small collection of whitewashed houses backed by low, arid hills. Once ashore you will find this impression is somewhat misleading, for the chora is graced with a couple of cosy squares and the islanders are very friendly. Even so, there is no disguising the fact that the village isn't the most photogenic around (in part thanks to ongoing building work): it is the succession of quiet beaches that bring visitors to Lipsi. Unfortunately, it is difficult to take these in within the time available on day-trips from other islands. As it is, most visitors 'do' the town and then head for the nearest beach within walking distance (close by the port).

If you are able to stay longer, then it pays to be more adventurous and head for the coves that make up **Katsadia** beach (complete with a taverna offering rooms and free camping), or **Plati Gialos** (wide, sandy, and easily the best beach on the island) on the north coast. It is close on an hour's walk — unless you avail yourself of the new island bus. Other beaches are quieter and the objective of occasional beach boats. **Monodendri** is the most notable of them, being the island's designated nudist beach (though discreet nudism is possible on most of them). If the beaches are not to your taste, irregular caïques also run to several islets around the coast (details on the caïque quay).

⊢⊣

Day-tripper tourism has left a dearth of budget accommodation, with the result that beyond several quayside outfits offering pricey rooms (out of High Season you will do well to hunt around for the best deal) and the D-class hotel *Calypso* (☎ 41242), there is nought but the beach to head for.

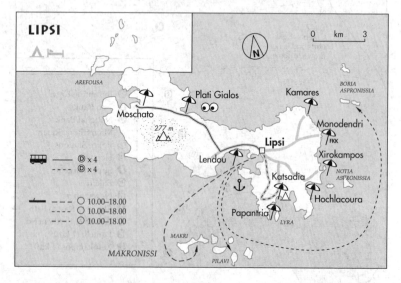

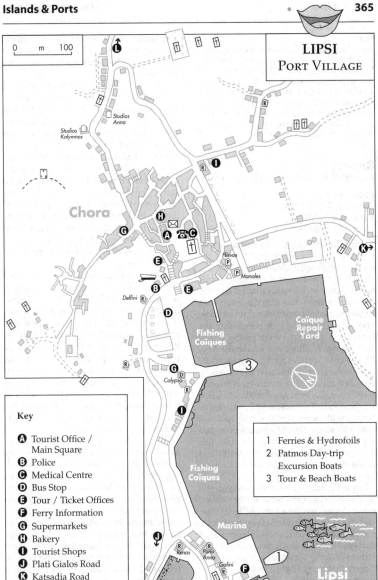

0   m   100

LIPSI
PORT VILLAGE

L

Studios Anna

Studios Kalymnos

Chora

H

G

A

C

E

Flisvos P

P Manoles

B

Delfini R

E

D

Fishing Caïques

Caïque Repair Yard

G

D

Calypso R

3

I

Fishing Caïques

Marina

J

Renas R

Pano Anna R

Galini R

F

1

2

Beach

Lipsi Port

Key

- **A** Tourist Office / Main Square
- **B** Police
- **C** Medical Centre
- **D** Bus Stop
- **E** Tour / Ticket Offices
- **F** Ferry Information
- **G** Supermarkets
- **H** Bakery
- **I** Tourist Shops
- **J** Plati Gialos Road
- **K** Katsadia Road
- **L** Monodendri Road

1 Ferries & Hydrofoils
2 Patmos Day-trip Excursion Boats
3 Tour & Beach Boats

K→

👓

Lipsi lacks sights (unless you include thirty-odd churches or chapels built in the last three hundred years), but in spite of this the village has an information office in the main square — complete with a **Museum** of sorts that is short of notable contents. Prize exhibits are an assortment of plastic bottles full of 'Holy' water (allegedly) and the remains of a passing American's pet rock collection.

Nissiros

ΝΙΣΥΡΟΣ; 41 km²; pop. 1,100.

CODE ☎ 22420
PORT POLICE ☎ 31222
POLICE ☎ 31201
FIRST AID ☎ 31217

A small island just to the south of Kos, Nissiros is to be numbered among the more picturesque Dodecanese islands, attracting considerable day-tripper traffic and worthily so. It is easily the best day-trip destination from Kos (Rhodes excepted), thanks to a lovely small island atmosphere and a real Jekyll and Hyde personality. For Nissiros is a volcano cone jutting out of the Aegean. In shape not unlike the Aeolian islands north of Sicily, it looks oddly out of character in this part of the world. Another feature that contrasts markedly with other southern Aegean islands is that it is (thanks to the volcanic soil) remarkably fertile, with outer slopes thickly planted with vineyards, fig and almond trees, and wild flowers. These combine to make this a gorgeous island to visit in the spring and an excellent shady walking destination any time of the year.

Climb the hillside, however, and you will see the other face of Nissiros, for the verdant outer slopes conceal a very different interior: this takes the form of a deep and barren crater caked with a yellow sulphurous mud that smells as bad as it looks. Tradition has it that when the Olympian gods arrived in Greece they had to fight a race of giants for control of the earth. Nissiros was formed as the result of a battle between Poseidon and the giant Porphyris; the god speared

a lump of Kos and dumped it on the giant, burying him alive — hence the volcano's rumblings as he periodically tries in vain to break free.

Nissiros has one town of note — the port of **Mandraki** — and a number of minor villages, including two (Emborio and Nikia) on the crater rim. Mandraki is an attractive centre that to date has managed to cater to the tourist hordes without losing its whitewashed narrow street charm. Not very large, the port side of town is just a main street ribboning along the northern shore. The promenade, however, is not the centre of Mandraki life: the town almost has its back to it, preferring instead to huddle in the valley between the volcano and the headland that plays host to the small Venetian castle that stands guard over the town.

Just about large enough for the casual visitor to get lost in for a hundred metres or so, Mandraki invites relaxed exploration. In addition to the castle and shoreline, the town has some lovely unspoilt streets and small squares (the main square — Ilikiomeni — lying on the inland edge of town). The atmosphere reflects the gentle, unhurried island village life, and even if the islanders no longer draw water from the picturesque town well that stands in Pilaoulli square, Mandraki offers a blissful contrast with the brash commercial bustle of Kos and Rhodes.

This is not to say that Nissiros is slow to sell itself. Thanks to the volcano, the quayside is lined with tour agents selling trips to the crater and there is even an island-cum-volcano model for good measure. Tour buses run from the quay to the crater floor and the crater rim villages. Island buses also start from here, but go no further than the crater rim, as well as to other inhabited hot spots around the island (there are hot water springs to be found outside **Nikia** and also at **Loutra**, now the home of a rather run-down spa).

Both the crater rim villages of **Nikia** and **Emborio** have viewing points along with steps/paths down into it. Nikia is the better of the two, both as a viewing station and in the degree of inhabitation. Thanks to the building of a number of holiday homes it is quietly thriving, while Emborio is now half abandoned (the population having retreated to the small beach village of Pali).

Like Santorini, Nissiros has black or red sand beaches, but in the main these are poor affairs (people generally come to Nissiros to have a day off from burning on a beach), the best being **White beach** near **Pali** (the only white sand beach of any size on the island), followed by **Lies** beach (made up of tiny grey pebbles). The nearest beach to Mandraki (**Koklaki**) lies below the cliffs on the west side of town, and is reached by a hazardous (beware of falling rocks) path that runs around the shoreline under the kastro. The beach is made up of large blue volcanic 'pebbles' and is more scenic than comfortable. On the ferry front, connections are comparatively poor, but daily boats from Kos (Town and Kefalos) and Rhodes hydrofoils make Nissiros easily accessible.

🛏

There are plenty of rooms in **Mandraki**, with some in Pali and Nikia. Hotel accommodation is adequate, even if there isn't much at the top of the range. The nearest Nissiros comes to luxury is the C-class *Porfyris* (☎ 31376). Hotels just to the left as you leave the ferry quay include the *Three Brothers* (☎ 31344) and the *Romantzo* (☎ 31340); these are on a par with the B-class pension *Haritos* (☎ 31322) on the Loutra road.

More down-market is the pension *Drossia* (☎ 31328) in the town. Out of Mandraki the only hotel of note is the C-class *White Beach* (☎ 31497/8) on the hill just before you get to Pali.

👀

Even without the volcano **Mandraki** would attract tourists to Nissiros, being a scenic whitewashed chora with 2 castles. Above the town stands the Venetian Knights of St. John **Castle** (1315) which contains a multi-iconed monastery within its walls, while 1 km inland stands the older **Kastro**: complete

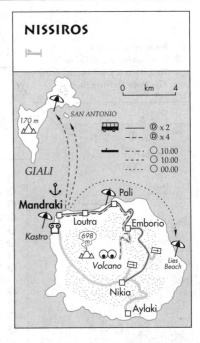

with a Cyclopian wall and gateway built out of imposing lava blocks, it marks the site of the ancient acropolis (though there is little to see within the enclosure). It can be reached via the road south of Mandraki or via a cliff-top track. Occasional boat excursions are also available to **Giali** — a small double-hilled island which has a pleasant beach surprisingly unmarred by the pumice quarrying in the hillside behind it — and to a beach on the islet of **San Antonio**.

The **Volcano**, however, is the great attraction, and better done first thing if you are on a day trip. Tour buses run to the crater floor, returning 2–3 hours later. The more ambitious (armed with plenty of water and half a day) might also consider walking the path that runs from Mandraki, over the rim, past Mt. Profitis Ilias and down into the crater. As with other Greek volcanos, Nissiros is not all fountains of magma and pillars of steam, but more a lunar landscapey hole — in this case with 5 shallow craters set in the main crater floor.

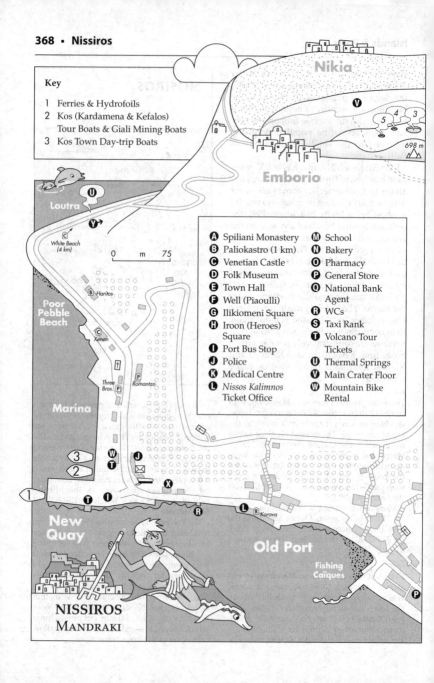

Nikia

Emborio

Key

1 Ferries & Hydrofoils
2 Kos (Kardamena & Kefalos)
  Tour Boats & Giali Mining Boats
3 Kos Town Day-trip Boats

Loutra

White Beach
(4 km)

0   m   75

Poor
Pebble
Beach

Haritos

Xenon

Three
Bros.

Romantzo

Marina

698 m

Ⓐ Spiliani Monastery
Ⓑ Paliokastro (1 km)
Ⓒ Venetian Castle
Ⓓ Folk Museum
Ⓔ Town Hall
Ⓕ Well (Piaoulli)
Ⓖ Ilikiomeni Square
Ⓗ Iroon (Heroes)
  Square
Ⓘ Port Bus Stop
Ⓙ Police
Ⓚ Medical Centre
Ⓛ *Nissos Kalimnos*
  Ticket Office

Ⓜ School
Ⓝ Bakery
Ⓞ Pharmacy
Ⓟ General Store
Ⓠ National Bank
  Agent
Ⓡ WCs
Ⓢ Taxi Rank
Ⓣ Volcano Tour
  Tickets
Ⓤ Thermal Springs
Ⓥ Main Crater Floor
Ⓦ Mountain Bike
  Rental

Karava

New
Quay

Old Port

Fishing
Caïques

NISSIROS
MANDRAKI

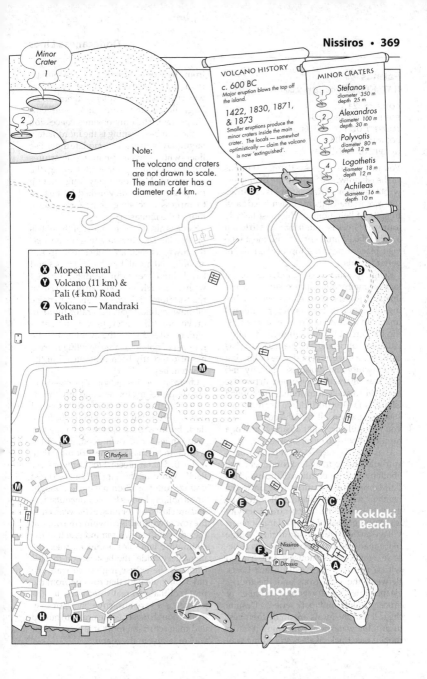

Minor Crater
1

2

VOLCANO HISTORY

c. 600 BC
Major eruption blows the top off the island.

1422, 1830, 1871, & 1873
Smaller eruptions produce the minor craters inside the main crater. The locals — somewhat optimistically — claim the volcano is now 'extinguished'.

MINOR CRATERS

1 *Stefanos*
diameter 350 m
depth 25 m

2 *Alexandros*
diameter 100 m
depth 30 m

3 *Polyvotis*
diameter 80 m
depth 12 m

4 *Logothetis*
diameter 18 m
depth 12 m

5 *Achileas*
diameter 16 m
depth 10 m

Note:

The volcano and craters are not drawn to scale. The main crater has a diameter of 4 km.

Ⓧ Moped Rental
Ⓨ Volcano (11 km) & Pali (4 km) Road
Ⓩ Volcano — Mandraki Path

C *Porfyris*

M

K

O **G**
P

E **D** **C**

F

Nissiros
P
P *Drossia*

A

Q **S**

Koklaki Beach

H **N**

Chora

Patmos

ΠΑΤΜΟΣ; 34 km²; pop. 2,600.

CODE ☎ 22470
PORT POLICE ☎ 31231
TOURIST OFFICE ☎ 31666
POLICE ☎ 31303
HOSPITAL ☎ 31577

Volcanic in origin, cosy Patmos (famous as the island where St. John the Evangelist wrote the Book of Revelation) is an attractive mix of small hills and beach-lined bays. In spite of being one of the most heavily touristed Greek islands it manages to retain a very relaxed atmosphere, and most who visit place it near the top of their list of better islands.

Religious tourism is the mainstay of the local economy and a procession of cruise liners release a flood of tourists, overwhelming attempts to maintain a reverential image. In a recent effort to stem the tide, the Patriarch of Constantinople declared Patmos a holy island, and extra backing has come via a government decree outlawing 'promiscuity and looseness'. Nudity and discos are theoretically banned. In practice however, this delightful monastery-topped island is far less forbidding than all this sounds, and on all but the town beach you will still encounter a happy ratio of a hundred boobs to every brother.

The island's success in mixing things spiritual and tourists temporal has come about by a tacit separation of the two. This deft compromise confines religion to the heights, while the island's playgrounds grace the shoreline. The centre of activity is the port of **Skala**. Now the largest resort village on the island, it is an attractive little place made up of tavernas and Cycladic-style whitewashed houses, and fringed with a marina replete with beach boats. Between the waterfront and the tourist establishments are a goodly number of grocery stores and patisseries. Despite the fact that the locals are doing their best to ruin the waterfront by turning it into a moped race track, Skala is still a long way

from the worst excesses of mass tourism found on other islands. Though there are waterfront tavernas aplenty, there are no large hotels and Tinos-tacky souvenir shops here. The only obvious concession to the numbers visiting is the inordinately large quay built to accommodate the cruise liners whose tears-and-bunting departures enliven evening promenades along the waterfront. Most only stay long enough for passengers to be whisked by bus up to impressive-looking Chora for a quickie tour of the monastery.

Skala is also home for most of the hotels on the island. Fortunately, these do not mar the town, as they are judiciously spread around, and are all low-lying. The second bay behind the north headland (graced with a church and an early Christian roadside tomb) is home to the island's noisy oil-powered electricity generator, the town graveyard (disconcertingly illuminated with candles during the evenings) and a number of hotels. A large yachting marina has also recently been constructed in the adjacent bay.

Chora is a very insipid sort of place—lacking shops, rooms for rent and any 'lived-in' sense at all. A maze of whitewashed mansion-style buildings skirting the high, dark, buttressed walls of the monastery, it is too quiet for its own good, and, filled with churches, has become little more than a glorified outer precinct to the monastery itself. Many of the larger houses (most dating from the 18 c.) have been bought up as holiday homes by wealthy outsiders and are closed up for most of the year. Only the row of windmills crowning the ridge at the edge of the town remind one that the chora once had a less sanitized role. The monastery aside, the best reason to visit Chora is the excuse it gives to walk the old 3 km mule path that runs up from the port (not that you really need one, for the journey is a very attractive one). An easy walk (though most people prefer to bus up and then return on foot), it is an excellent way of taking in the island.

The rest of the island has much more going for it, being a lovely mix of bays and beaches tucked away within the folds of an intricate coastline. Beach caïques run from Skala to the best of these — **Psiliamos** to the south and the multicoloured pebble **Lampi** on the north coast, as well as to the adjacent beach islands of Lipsi and Arki (most 'Arki' taxi boats in fact go to a beach and taverna on the adjacent islet of Marathi).

The only other settlements of any size at all are at **Kambos** — which is a pleasantly unspoilt hill village complete with an attractive pebble beach — and **Grikos**, billed as a 'resort' village (though it has fewer hotels than Skala).

In addition to the beach boats, Patmos has a good bus service running between the main centres. Photocopied timetables for these and all regular ferries are available from the information office located in the quayside post office building.

🛏

Plenty of rooms are available, thanks to the island's pilgrim status. Offering hordes meet all boats. The tourist office in the block behind the ferry quay also has lists of hotels. The majority are to be found in Skala, which is also the name of the premier hostelry — the B-class hotel *Skala* (☎ 31343). At the north end of the port, it is close by other up-market establishments, including the *Patmion* (☎ 31313). Best of the mid-range hotels are the C-class *Chris* (☎ 31001) and *Hellinis* (☎ 31275). Cheaper hotels are also plentiful. Just off the quay is the D-class *Rex* (☎ 31242), and behind the town are the *Kastro* (☎ 31554), the *Plaza* (☎ 31217), and cheaper *Rodon* (☎ 31371).

⛺

Camping Stefanos alias *Patmos Flowers Camping* (☎ 31821) lies 2 km away, around the harbour and over the hill at Melloi. A bambooed site, it is one of the best in Greece, but suffers from the island's water shortages in High Season. The new mini-bus only ventures to the port in High Season and usually has to make two

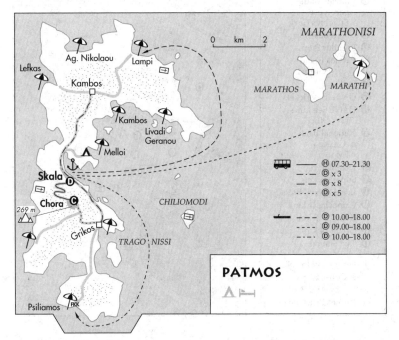

PATMOS

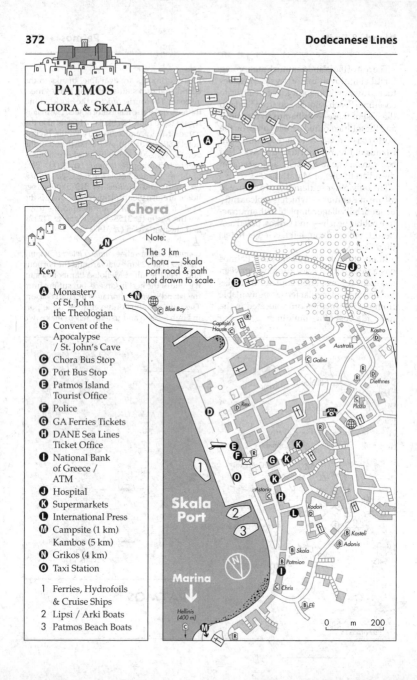

PATMOS
CHORA & SKALA

Note:

The 3 km
Chora — Skala
port road & path
not drawn to scale.

Key

Ⓐ Monastery
of St. John
the Theologian

Ⓑ Convent of the
Apocalypse
/ St. John's Cave

Ⓒ Chora Bus Stop

Ⓓ Port Bus Stop

Ⓔ Patmos Island
Tourist Office

Ⓕ Police

Ⓖ GA Ferries Tickets

Ⓗ DANE Sea Lines
Ticket Office

Ⓘ National Bank
of Greece /
ATM

Ⓙ Hospital

Ⓚ Supermarkets

Ⓛ International Press

Ⓜ Campsite (1 km)
Kambos (5 km)

Ⓝ Grikos (4 km)

Ⓞ Taxi Station

1 Ferries, Hydrofoils
& Cruise Ships

2 Lipsi / Arki Boats

3 Patmos Beach Boats

Chora

Blue Bay

Captain's
House

Kastro

Australis

Galini

Diethnes

Rex

Plaza

Skala
Port

Astoria

Rodon

Kasteli

Adonis

Skala

Patmion

Chris

Marina

Hellinis
(400 m)

Efi

0   m   200

journeys to the site when large ferries come in. A pick-up truck also collects campers.

∞

The main attraction is impossible to miss: the castle-like **Monastery of St. John the Theologian** standing majestically atop Mt. Kastelli. Founded in 1088, it started out as merely a hilltop monastery, but repeated pirate raids prompted its fortification. This process continued when the island fell under the rule of the Dukes of Naxos (from the 13 c. to the 16 c.) who allowed it an unusual degree of autonomy, so that when the Turks finally took control of the Aegean, Patmos — like Mt. Athos — was able to retain semi-independent status.

The present castle layout is relatively recent: a damaging earthquake in 1956 that brought down a tower and several walls prompted its partial rebuilding. Open daily: precise times vary, but it is always open ①–⑥ 08.30–13.00, ⑦ 10.00–12.00. Entry is free, though you must take care to be modestly dressed (no shorts or bikini tops). Surly monks do wonders for the atmosphere — successfully repelling all boarders since the monastery's foundation. As a result it is a treasure house containing over 890 early Christian manuscripts (notably an early 6 c. version of St. Mark's Gospel), a large collection of icons, and the most important display of monastic artifacts in Greece. Built on the site of the ancient acropolis, fragments of a temple of Artemis also litter the building.

Halfway up the Skala—Chora road and mule-track you will come to the second major monastery on Patmos: the **Convent of the Apocalypse** (opening times as above), built over the cave where St. John saw and dictated (to his disciple Prochoros) all. Banished to the island in 95 AD by the Emperor Dominian for winding up the population of Ephesus, he spent 15 years in a cave writing the Book of Revelation. Quite why he was disposed to conjure up such happy notions as 'And I looked, and behold a pale horse: and his name that sat on him was Death, and Hell followed with him' remains a mystery; modern Patmos encourages far happier thoughts, and the island in St. John's day (complete with a picturesque temple in place of the forbidding monastery) had even more going for it.

Finally, when you have had enough of Patmos, boat trips offer a taste of freedom. Daily tour boats head for Lipsi, hydrofoils for Samos.

Rhodes

ΡΟΔΟΣ; 1398 km²; pop. 68,000.

CODES: (TOWN) ☎ 22410
(REST OF THE ISLAND) ☎ 22440
PORT POLICE ☎ 28888
NTOG / EOT OFFICE ☎ 23255
TOURIST POLICE ☎ 27423
POLICE ☎ 7423
HOSPITAL ☎ 22222

The largest island in the Dodecanese, Rhodes (known locally as 'Rodos'), is one of the most touristed islands in Greece thanks to an attractive mix of good beaches, plenty of sightseeing, an unspoilt interior, and a sound reputation for being the sunniest island in the Aegean (it sees over 300 days of sunshine a year). This is probably just as well, for myth has it that when Zeus divided up the world he forgot to allocate a portion to the sun god, Helios, who promptly took for his own the fertile island of Rhodes that was just then emerging from the sea.

Even allowing for repeated earthquakes and invasions, Rhodes has been pretty much sunny-side up ever since, for the island has something for just about everyone. The main tourist strip runs down the east coast: a necklace of sand beaches hung between the two sightseeing jewels of Rhodes City and the acropolis-topped town of Lindos.

Inevitably there is a significant downside to this: with package tourists descending all year round, the island now has a reputation as a home for the worst of the binge-drinking brigade. Rhodes also comes more expensive than many other islands, and clearly doesn't feel the need to cater for independent travellers in great numbers. On the plus side, the heavy tourist presence has encouraged a proliferation of pleasure boats augmenting the ferries that call — thanks to the island's role as a terminus on the domestic ferry network and point of call for international services to Cyprus, Israel and Egypt. The combination makes Rhodes an attractive point from which to start an island hopping holiday.

Sightseeing fans will find rich pickings on Rhodes thanks to the island's colourful history. For most of the classical period Rhodes was — like most others — a bit player in the wider struggle between Greek and Persian and Athens and Sparta, swapping sides whenever it was deemed politic to do so. She first left her fingermarks on the pages of history following the death of Alexander the Great when she sided with Ptolemy in the wars between his successors, prompting one of his rivals, Demetrius Poliokretes, to lay siege to Rhodes City in 305 BC. The siege failed in spectacular fashion (the townsfolk selling the abandoned siege engines and using the money to build the mighty Colossus). Inspired by the victory and growing success as a trading centre, Rhodes came into its own as a Hellenistic power centre, boasting an artistic school that produced works of the calibre of the famous Winged Victory of Samothrace and gave — according to Strabo — Rhodes City over 2000 statues, and a navy that controlled the Eastern Aegean.

However, Rhodes was eclipsed by the rise of Roman power, paying the price for supporting Julius Caesar (by way of retribution she was captured in 44 BC by Cassius and stripped of her art works), and finally becoming part of the Empire in 70 AD. Further damage followed with regular earthquakes and invasions of Goths (269 AD), Persians (620), Saracens (653), and Fourth Crusaders (1204).

Stability of a sort came with the arrival of the crusading Knights of St. John in 1309, who fortified Rhodes City, establishing it as the home of the Knights Hospitallers, and the European front line against the Ottoman Turks. Besieged in 1444 and 1480, Rhodes City finally fell in 1522. Treated badly by the Turks (who stigmatized islands that had resisted them), Rhodes was occupied by the Italians between the world wars, finally joining Greece in 1947.

Rhodes City

The story of Rhodes City is really the story of three cities (Ancient, Medieval and Modern). It was founded as a unifying capital in 408 BC by three ancient cities that previously had ruled the island. Lying on the northern tip of Rhodes and now home to over 60% of the population, it is a bustling centre packed with history and tourists. No matter how you arrive,

the chances are you will end up here. The main bus terminus lies on the boundary between the Modern City and the walled Medieval City. Arrive by ferry and you will be decanted onto the large quay abutting the Old City walls; hydrofoils and tourist boats usually dock at Mandraki Harbour, but sometimes use the main ferry quay.

Ancient City

Unfortunately, the fact that Rhodes has been continually occupied since its foundation in 408 BC has led to the obscuring of most traces of the ancient city. In its time it was deemed beautiful and notable. Built on a green field site, it was the product of the famous town planner Hippodamos of Miletus, and was laid out in a grid form with distinct commercial, residential, administrative and religious quarters. Fragments of the city walls reveal that it ran east to west across the neck of the peninsula between the Great Harbour and the Upper Acropolis (which stood outside the city walls). At its centre was the Lower Acropolis, which was home to the Great Temple of Helios (now the site of the Palace of the Grand Masters).

The most notable surviving remains visible today are the foundations from a 3 c. BC **Temple of Aphrodite** just inside the Old City walls (which also contain other assorted fragments that include foundations from the city walls). The Upper Acropolis is also hidden away. Lying to the west of the current Old City, it is also known as Mt. Smith (after an English admiral who used it as a spyglass hill) and is now a park (it is open all day, all week, and entry is free). The site offers a shady view of the best-preserved **Stadium** in the Greek islands and small **Theatre**, as well as several standing columns of a **Temple of Apollo** (over-heavily restored by its Italian excavators). The **Archaeological Museum** (open ②–⑦ 08.30–15.00; entrance fee: €3) contains most of the surviving movable Ancient City remains. These include a notable head of Helios (see p. 380), and a famous 1 c. BC marble statuette of a bathing, nude Aphrodite drying her hair, known as the 'Aphrodite of Rhodes'.

APHRODITE
OF
RHODES

1 C. BC

GLUE

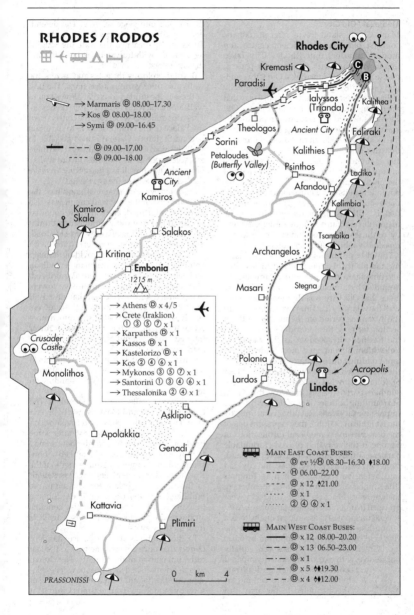

RHODES / RODOS

→ Marmaris Ⓓ 08.00–17.30
→ Kos Ⓓ 08.00–18.00
→ Symi Ⓓ 09.00–16.45

---- Ⓓ 09.00–17.00
---- Ⓓ 09.00–18.00

Rhodes City

Kremasti

Paradisi

Ialyssos
(Trianda)

Kalithea

Theologos

Ancient City

Faliraki

Sorini

Kalithies

Petaloudes
(Butterfly Valley)

Psinthos

Ladiko

*Ancient
City*

Kamiros

Afandou

Kolimbia

Kamiros
Skala

Salakos

Tsambika

Kritina

Archangelos

Embonia
1215 m

Masari

Stegna

→ Athens Ⓓ x 4/5
→ Crete (Iraklion)
  ① ③ ⑤ ⑦ x 1
→ Karpathos Ⓓ x 1
→ Kassos Ⓓ x 1
→ Kastelorizo Ⓓ x 1
→ Kos ② ④ ⑥ x 1
→ Mykonos ③ ⑤ ⑦ x 1
→ Santorini ① ③ ④ ⑥ x 1
→ Thessalonika ② ④ x 1

*Crusader
Castle*

Polonia

Acropolis

Monolithos

Lardos

Lindos

Asklipio

Apolakkia

Genadi

MAIN EAST COAST BUSES:
——— Ⓓ ev ½Ⓗ 08.30–16.30 ♦18.00
– – – Ⓗ 06.00–22.00
– – – Ⓓ x 12 ♦21.00
······ Ⓓ x 1
······ ② ④ ⑥ x 1

Kattavia

Plimiri

MAIN WEST COAST BUSES:
——— Ⓓ x 12 08.00–20.20
– – – Ⓓ x 13 06.50–23.00
–·–·– Ⓓ x 1
— — Ⓓ x 5 ♦♦19.30
– – – Ⓓ x 4 ♦♦12.00

PRASSONISSI

0   km   4

Medieval / Old City

Many Greek island towns offer a dramatic contrast between the ancient centre and modern quarters, but Rhodes City takes this to extremes with the character-packed, moated and walled medieval Old City seemingly standing apart from a quintessentially Italianesque New Town. This is not to say that the Italians didn't leave their mark on the Old City, for they did in a large way, repairing the walls and medieval buildings, and allowing the locals to tear down the forest of minarets that the Turks had added to the Byzantine city churches that had been converted into mosques. Occupying the eastern half of the ancient city, the Old City also contains reminders of its more illustrious past, including a hint of the former grid street layout that is still visible in the position of the main thoroughfares — now rather distorted by centuries of encroachment by buildings repeatedly rebuilt after earthquakes.

The Old City offers several days of sightseeing and plenty of opportunity to get lost time and time again in the warren of narrow streets. Bounded by a moated wall breached by 11 gates, the Old City was divided by an inner wall (now largely lost) into two sections, from the Byzantine period on, the smaller northern section forming the inner defensive core of the fortified city. Known as the **Kastro** or **Collachium**, it contained most of the important buildings during the 14 and 15 c., when the city housed the West European Knights of St. John; the lowly Greeks lived in the larger southern part of the city, known as the Chora. Surrounding both sections of the town are the impressive **City Walls**. Rebuilt several times by the Knights of St. John, they represent one of the best-preserved medieval fortifications in Europe. In their day they proved a formidable barrier to Turkish ambitions to take the island, protected by a deep, dry moat, and divided into defensive sections known as **Tongues** (the Knights of St. John recruited members to their order right across Europe, and they were grouped in units according to language). After several unsuccessful assaults, it finally took a 6-month siege by 200,000 Turks to capture the city, held by 290 Knights supported by 6,000 local Greek soldiers. The losses were equally impressive, with 50,000 Turks killed compared to 2,000 defenders. The high death rate among the Ottomans can in part be attributed to the arrival of the cannon into siege warfare. The defenders' casualties were so low because, once the Turks finally breached the wall, the Knights negotiated a withdrawal in return for leaving the city intact.

Beyond exploring the gates and towers, the walls also offer various attractions. The best of these is the guided tour that allows you to walk along the walls (②, ⑦ 14.15; tickets: €3). This runs anticlockwise from the courtyard of the Palace of the Grand Masters to the stairs beyond St. John's Gate. It is also possible to walk the moat — which was always dry (there are access points at intervals in the walls). Below the north wall is a daily *Son-et-lumière* that tells the story of the 1522 siege.

Protected by the moat against land attack, the seaward side of the city wall circuit was also formidably fortified. The walls here bounded the **Great Harbour** (now significantly diminished by the building of a seaward-side road, a new mole and the enlarged ferry quay), with the impressive **Marine Gate** providing the main entrance to the city. The ancient moles built on both sides of the harbour were also utilized, with the construction of impressive towers that guarded a massive chain that closed off the entrance. Today only one of these towers survives (the **Tower of the Mills**); its much more romantic-looking partner, the lost **Nailac Tower** (named after a Grand Master and adorning many early drawings of the city), collapsed in an earthquake in 1863. The Italians did plan to rebuild it, but WW2 put paid to that ambition, so tourists have to make do with standing on its base instead.

Within the walls, the biggest pull is **The Palace of the Grand Masters**. Sadly, it is a fake. The original — converted into a prison by the Turks — blew up in 1856 after some bright spark (no doubt a warder determined to prove that cigarettes do kill) ignited a thousand tonnes of forgotten gunpowder that the Knights had left in one of the dungeons. Rebuilt in the 1930s as a palace for Mussolini, the building (open ②–⑦ 08.30–15.00; €6) is home to many Kos Town mosaics. It also contains an interesting museum that houses artifacts from all three cities.

To the south-east of the Palace stands a **Loggia** that once covered the way to the lost cathedral church of the Knights. The church was also demolished in the gunpowder explosion, and the Italians built a reconstruction of sorts by modelling Evangelismos Church (at

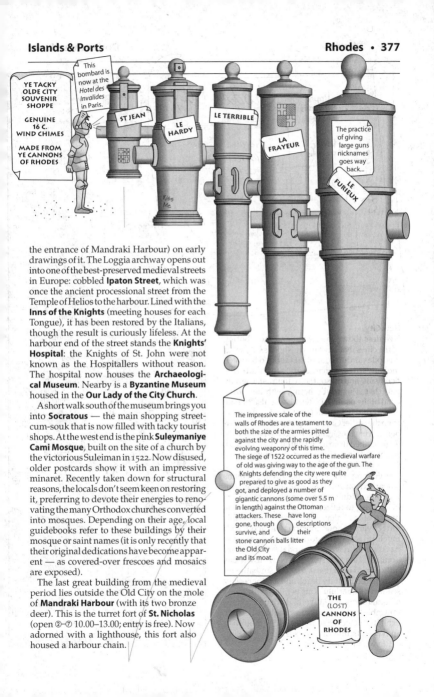

YE TACKY OLDE CITY SOUVENIR SHOPPE

GENUINE 16 C. WIND CHIMES

MADE FROM YE CANNONS OF RHODES

This bombard is now at the *Hotel des Invalides* in Paris.

ST JEAN

LE HARDY

LE TERRIBLE

LA FRAYEUR

The practice of giving large guns nicknames goes way back...

LE FURIEUX

Kiss Me

The impressive scale of the walls of Rhodes are a testament to both the size of the armies pitted against the city and the rapidly evolving weaponry of this time. The siege of 1522 occurred as the medieval warfare of old was giving way to the age of the gun. The Knights defending the city were quite prepared to give as good as they got, and deployed a number of gigantic cannons (some over 5.5 m in length) against the Ottoman attackers. These ☐ have long gone, though ☐ descriptions survive, and ☐ their stone cannon balls litter the Old City and its moat.

THE (LOST) CANNONS OF RHODES

the entrance of Mandraki Harbour) on early drawings of it. The Loggia archway opens out into one of the best-preserved medieval streets in Europe: cobbled **Ipaton Street**, which was once the ancient processional street from the Temple of Helios to the harbour. Lined with the **Inns of the Knights** (meeting houses for each Tongue), it has been restored by the Italians, though the result is curiously lifeless. At the harbour end of the street stands the **Knights' Hospital**: the Knights of St. John were not known as the Hospitallers without reason. The hospital now houses the **Archaeological Museum**. Nearby is a **Byzantine Museum** housed in the **Our Lady of the City Church**.

A short walk south of the museum brings you into **Socrates** — the main shopping street-cum-souk that is now filled with tacky tourist shops. At the west end is the pink **Suleymaniye Cami Mosque**, built on the site of a church by the victorious Suleiman in 1522. Now disused, older postcards show it with an impressive minaret. Recently taken down for structural reasons, the locals don't seem keen on restoring it, preferring to devote their energies to renovating the many Orthodox churches converted into mosques. Depending on their age, local guidebooks refer to these buildings by their mosque or saint names (it is only recently that their original dedications have become apparent — as covered-over frescoes and mosaics are exposed).

The last great building from the medieval period lies outside the Old City on the mole of **Mandraki Harbour** (with its two bronze deer). This is the turret fort of **St. Nicholas** (open ②–⑦ 10.00–13.00; entry is free). Now adorned with a lighthouse, this fort also housed a harbour chain.

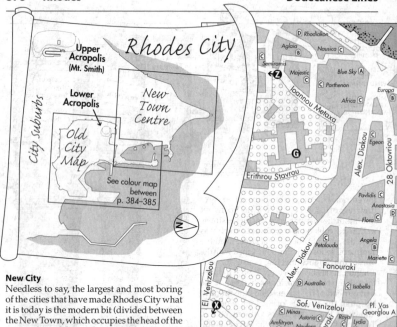

New City

Needless to say, the largest and most boring of the cities that have made Rhodes City what it is today is the modern bit (divided between the New Town, which occupies the head of the peninsula, and the southern suburbs). The only part that is worth bothering with lies at the head of the peninsula (which was also the site of part of the Ancient City). It takes its name from the earlier Greek settlement that emerged here during the Ottoman period (when Greeks were banned from living within the Old City). Sadly, nothing of this survives beyond five windmills behind the western beach.

Following WW1, the occupying Italians embarked on an extensive rebuilding pro-gramme, adding many grandiose buildings in an effort to reflect the town's status as the capital of the Italian Dodecanese. Add to this thirty years of hotel construction, and it isn't much of a surprise to find that these days package-tourist accommodation and bars dominate. As a result, the New Town has little else to offer, bar a bracing sunbathe on aptly named Windy Beach and a rather seedy sea-level **Aquarium**. This is filled with a mix of local marine life (alive, and not on a restaurant table for once), and rarer or almost extinct exhibits (including some intriguing moon fish and several stuffed monk seals fighting a losing battle with moths).

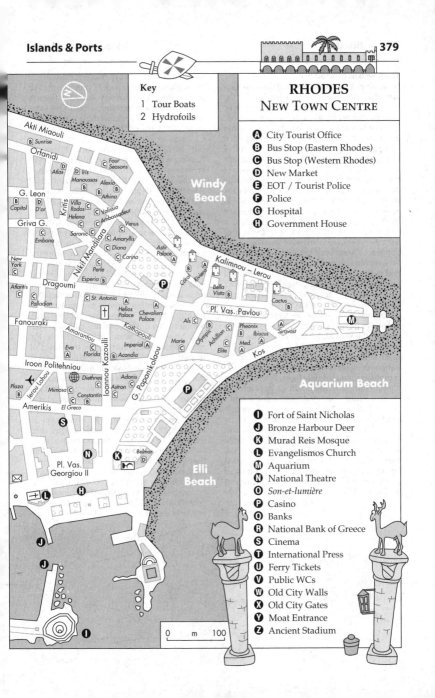

Key

1 Tour Boats
2 Hydrofoils

RHODES
NEW TOWN CENTRE

Ⓐ City Tourist Office
Ⓑ Bus Stop (Eastern Rhodes)
Ⓒ Bus Stop (Western Rhodes)
Ⓓ New Market
Ⓔ EOT / Tourist Police
Ⓕ Police
Ⓖ Hospital
Ⓗ Government House

Ⓘ Fort of Saint Nicholas
Ⓙ Bronze Harbour Deer
Ⓚ Murad Reis Mosque
Ⓛ Evangelismos Church
Ⓜ Aquarium
Ⓝ National Theatre
Ⓞ Son-et-lumière
Ⓟ Casino
Ⓠ Banks
Ⓡ National Bank of Greece
Ⓢ Cinema
Ⓣ International Press
Ⓤ Ferry Tickets
Ⓥ Public WCs
Ⓦ Old City Walls
Ⓧ Old City Gates
Ⓨ Moat Entrance
Ⓩ Ancient Stadium

Akti Miaouli
Orfanidi
G. Leon
Griva G.
Dragoumi
Fanouraki
Iroon Politehniou
Amerikis

Windy Beach
Aquarium Beach
Elli Beach

Kalimnou – Lerou
Pl. Vas. Pavlou

Pl. Vas. Georgiou II

0   m   100

The Colossus of Rhodes

Best summed up as the original Statue of Liberty, the Colossus of Rhodes was one of the Seven Wonders of the World. Built c. 290 BC with the money obtained by selling the siege engines left after the unsuccessful attempt by Demetrios to take the city in 305/4 BC, it was designed by Chares of Lindos, a pupil of the famous Lysippos (Alexander the Great's favoured sculptor). The figure took 12 years to complete and was the largest colossal statue ever made in ancient Greece and one of the most renowned in the ancient world. Made of bronze (probably on an iron and stone frame), it only stood for 63 years before it collapsed — along with most of the rest of the city — during a massive earthquake in 227/6 BC. Thereafter it lay as a wondrous ruin for over nine centuries, until it was broken up and removed in 653 AD, after the island fell under Arab rule, exaggerating legend having it that it took nine hundred camels to transport the bronze from Aleppo to Syria.

No trace of the statue has been found, nor did ancient writers describe its pose. This has opened the way for a flood of theories as to where it stood and what it looked like. The most famous of these was dreamed up by Italian renaissance artists, who opted for the compelling image of giant figure bestriding the harbour entrance, and holding a light into the bargain. Sadly, all the evidence is against such a notion. First, the figure just wasn't tall enough to have been capable of such a feat even if its feet had been capable of sustaining it upright in such an unstable posture. Secondly, the statue fell onto land (if it had been straddling the harbour entrance it would surely have toppled into the sea). Thirdly, ancient writers comment on the figure's beauty and height (pacing out the length of the fallen Colossus was obviously a popular pastime) but make no mention of

its posture. It is always dangerous to argue from silence, but the lack of remarks on this score means one can say that the figure's pose was literally 'unremarkable'. This same argument also tells against the notion that the figure acted as a lighthouse. So, what did the Colossus look like?

If Chares kept to the Lysippian tradition (and he is known primarily as a pupil of Lysippos) it is reasonable to assume that the Colossus had much in common with the Lysippian statues of Alexander that rapidly became the model for statues of many other heroes and gods (Apollo not least among them). This 'Alexander' pose was a derivative of the kouros form with the left foot traditionally placed slightly forward but with a much more relaxed gait and a reduction in the ratio of head to body size from the traditional 7:1 to the Lysippian 10:1 (giving the figure a hunky torso look). Using fragments of various Lysippian figures, it is possible to come up with a plausible reconstruction of the fallen Colossus as it might have looked on the day of the annual Vestal Virgin Brass-Rubbing Club outing in any of the centuries that followed. This bit of fun is made easier thanks to the head of Helios (identifiable by the crown of holes that would have held the gold sun-rays) in the Rhodes Archaeological Museum. Dating from a hundred years of the construction of the Colossus (it could even be a copy of it), it is a variant of the Lysippian head of Alexander. A second great aid to reconstruction is the fact that the statue's height is known: it was 31 metres high (making it a metre shorter than the Statue of Liberty, measured from head to toe). A further check on its size comes from the comment of Pliny, who wrote — no doubt from personal experience — that it was only with difficulty that a man could put his arms round the figure's thumb (he is curiously reticent about what Mrs Pliny could just about get her arms around).

Where the Colossus stood is also the cause of much debate among scholars today thanks to the almost total absence of evidence, combined with the fragmentary understanding of the layout of the Ancient City. Colossal statues traditionally stood either near the temple of the god to whom they were dedicated (e.g. the statue of Apollo on Delos) or at port entrances, usually on the end of man-made moles. On Rhodes, the Temple of Helios is thought to have stood on the site now occupied by the Masters' Palace.

During the 1930s, the Italians extensively excavated before rebuilding the palace, and found nothing to suggest that the Colossus stood in this area. The port alternatives also present problems as there were five ancient harbours, and all Rhodian moles are man-made. In order to be sure of visiting the site of the Colossus, you therefore need to take in the Tower of the Mills, the base of the lost Nailac Tower, the landward entrance of Mandraki harbour and the Fort of St. Nicholas on the Mandraki harbour mole. This last location is arguably the most likely site for the Colossus. The site's champions point to a number of curved marble blocks built into the walls of the circular central tower of the fort that appear to come from a Hellenistic structure with the same 17 m diameter; the suggestion being that the tower is built directly onto the remains of the lost base of the Colossus.

Helios: The Sun God

The deity that inspired the Colossus of Rhodes has left his mark in more tangible ways beyond the memory of his statue. Widely respected in the Eastern Mediterranean (Apollo occupied his role as the god of light in the rest of the Greek world) from the Archaic period on, Helios was particularly associated with beginnings, rebirth and light coming up out of darkness. The ancients believed that he rode a chariot of fire across the sky each day before spending the night sailing around the dark side of the world in a giant cup. From the Hellenistic period on, his cult developed from basic superstitions (it was considered dangerous to turn one's back on the rising sun) to a point from the mid-2 C. AD when it became the religion of the Roman world. Even the Emperor Constantine — who made Christianity the state religion of the Empire — combined worship of the 'Unconquered Sun my companion' with his Christianity, for the first decade of his rule.

As a result, the church ended up inadvertently adopting holy days that had no biblical significance, merely because they had already become established as holy days in the Empire thanks to the brief flirtation with Helios. Not least of these was the use of Sunday as the day of worship rather than the Jewish Sabbath. Sunday — as the first day of the week — was literally 'Sun'-day: the day of the sun god. (Note: this guide adopts the European timetable convention of numbering Monday — the first working day — as ①). Helios's birthday was also absorbed into Christianity. The 25th of December (the first day that could be shown to be getting longer after the winter equinox) was a popular feast day in the Eastern Mediterranean from the 5 C. BC on. Not content with nabbing the sun god's birthday and day of worship, the early church made off with his symbol too. All ancient gods had an identifying symbol (see p. 72–73); Helios's was a sunburst — represented as an orb, or points of light around the head — the original halo: all of which leads one to wonder how many clergymen have looked forlornly across ranks of empty pews of a Sunday morning and mourned the fact that Helios wasn't also the god of orgies.

SOUVENIRS

UP

THE COLOSSUS OF RHODES
RECONSTRUCTED FROM THE LYSIPPIAN-STYLE HEAD OF HELIOS IN RHODES, THE TORSO OF A LYSIPPIAN BRONZE OF ALEXANDER, AND THE FEET AND GOOLIES OF A LYSIPPIAN APOLLO.

Car Hire on Rhodes

Take great care if you are planning to hire a car on Rhodes. In 2003 a UK TV programme (*Package Holiday Undercover*) tested cars from nine car-hire outlets on the island; only two of the vehicles examined by an AA mechanic met the MOT road-worthiness standard required for UK cars.

If you do opt for car hire ignore the spotless paint-work and look closely at tyres and lights (take a second person with you to check on rear brake lights), and if possible test drive it for a block to give brakes and gearbox a trial.

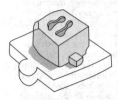

Lindos

After Rhodes City the next great centre and sightseeing attraction is the picturesque, acropolis-topped village of Lindos. Although it isn't the island capital, Lindos has a pedigree that puts most Greek island capitals to shame. Of the three early Doric Greek cities of Rhodes, it was the only one that had sufficient going for it to survive the collective decision to found a new capital at Rhodes City. This was, in large part, due to its having a major shrine that remained the premier shrine on the island even after Rhodes City was built. Indeed, the famous Temple of Athena Lindia that stood atop the dramatic coastal acropolis was famed throughout the Greek world. Gradually fortified during the Roman and Byzantine eras, the acropolis ensured that the ancient city beneath its walls remained occupied, developing in the last few centuries into a scenic whitewashed village complete with narrow cobbled streets (now protected from further development by a government decree).

Even without the acropolis, the village would be a sightseeing destination of note, and it is not surprising that Lindos has emerged as a premier day-trip destination, with a procession of tour buses and boats running down from Rhodes City and arriving at the small leafy town square or the pitifully small harbour quay. Even with the crowds lining up to take donkey rides or being ripped off by the local refreshment prices (expect to pay at least 20% more than you would elsewhere), Lindos defiantly manages to retain a fair measure of charm. In short, it is well worth taking time out to visit.

In addition to the acropolis and the foundations of a 4 C. BC theatre, the village also has a number of notable 17 C. mansion houses with ornately carved doorways, and a Byzantine church decorated with frescoes. Most visitors, however, seem to find the tourist shops and the sandy beaches either side of the village more interesting (this is partly because the mansions are not easily identifiable from their exteriors).

Lindos village lies in a hollow, sand-wiched between the seaward acropolis and the hills that surround the village. Either side of the acropolis are beach-lined bays. The northern bay — usually known as the **Grand Harbour** — is home to the town beach, and the small quay where the day-tripper boats from Rhodes City berth. The southern bay is reputedly the point where St. Paul arrived on the island in 43 AD and is now known as St. Paul's, or the **Small Harbour**. Legend has it that the bay was formed when the rocks opened up to protect St. Paul, as his ship battled against seas that threatened to shipwreck him. This was no doubt a wonderful event for the saint, but it must have left the owners of the land pretty browned off.

Lindos also has problems beyond passing saints knocking holes in the coastline, and the crowds. In 1994 the village received considerable publicity for flying an EU Blue Flag (awarded to particularly clean beaches), while scientific tests revealed that Lindos Bay was heavily contaminated with human sewage-feeding bacteria. Lindos later replaced its sewage system. However, part of the problem was deemed to be yachts emptying their septic tanks into Lindos Bay, and the new sewage system doesn't clean up this contamination.

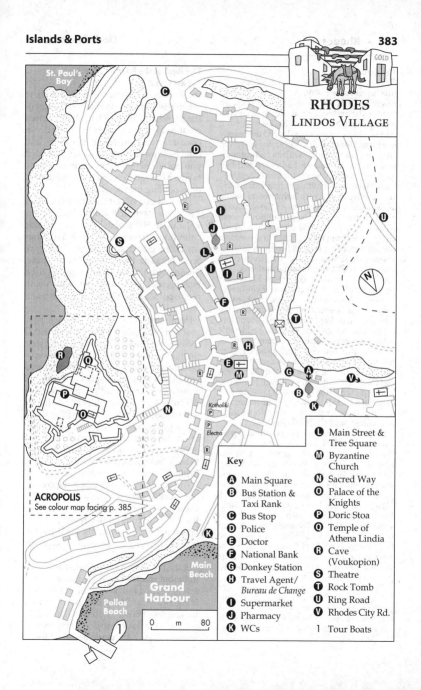

RHODES
LINDOS VILLAGE

St. Paul's Bay

ACROPOLIS
See colour map facing p. 385

Katholiki

Electra

Grand Harbour

Main Beach

Pellas Beach

Key

- **A** Main Square
- **B** Bus Station & Taxi Rank
- **C** Bus Stop
- **D** Police
- **E** Doctor
- **F** National Bank
- **G** Donkey Station
- **H** Travel Agent/ *Bureau de Change*
- **I** Supermarket
- **J** Pharmacy
- **K** WCs
- **L** Main Street & Tree Square
- **M** Byzantine Church
- **N** Sacred Way
- **O** Palace of the Knights
- **P** Doric Stoa
- **Q** Temple of Athena Lindia
- **R** Cave (Voukopion)
- **S** Theatre
- **T** Rock Tomb
- **U** Ring Road
- **V** Rhodes City Rd.
- **1** Tour Boats

0 m 80

The Acropolis

Open ②–⑦ 08.30–15.00 and ① 12.30–15.00 (the entrance fee is €6), the acropolis (see the colour map opposite p. 385) is one of the most spectacular archaeological sites in Greece; so much so, that the 116 m rock has been drawing tourists since antiquity, thanks to ❹ the **Temple of Athena Lindia**. Built in 348 BC, the surviving structure is a tiny affair with its end columns and side walls (it never had columns down its sides) partially reconstructed. It replaced earlier temples (including its immediate Classical predecessor, which burnt down) dating as far back as the 10 C. BC. As the sanctuary grew in importance other buildings were added, the most notable being ❺ the formal gateway or **Propylaea** (407 BC) to the temple precinct, and ❻ a large, 42-column, double-winged **Doric Stoa** (208 BC) that formed the entrance to ❼ a **Monumental Stairway**. The construction of this majestic Stoa heralded a phase of Hellenistic sanctuary embellishment on the grand scale, and was a precursor to the major development along similar lines of the Asklepieion on Kos. As with the Asklepieion, the Italian excavators attempted a considerable amount of reconstruction (rescuing many of the stones that were reused in later buildings on the site). Unfortunately, like that at the Rhodes City acropolis, the touch is not quite so deft, and the overall impression, although positive, is one of excess (the amount of tasteless new material is apt to leave the unfortunate impression that these remains are more akin to those of bombed-out WW2 buildings).

During the Byzantine period, the acropolis was fully fortified, a process completed with the construction work carried out by the Knights of St. John. Within the walls they also rebuilt ❺ a medieval castle on a grand scale, turning it into a fortified **Palace** (complete with the now ruined Byzantine church of Agios Ioannis). This final phase of fortification saw the best survival on the site brought within the walls: the **Trireme Relief**. Measuring 4.6 m long and 5.5 m high, it was carved by Pythocretes on the cliff wall and shows the stern and rudder of an ancient Greek warship. The relief served as the base for a statue of a priest named Hagesandros.

Finally, outside the acropolis walls on the seaward side, there is a large cave (only partly accessible). Lying directly underneath the main temple, it seems to have added to the religious significance of the site during the Dark Ages.

The Rest of the Island

1. East Coast

While Rhodes City and Lindos dominate the tourist industry on Rhodes, the rest of the island also has much to offer. The east coast sees regular boats running down each morning, stopping at resorts and sand beaches en route to Lindos. Provided you can afford them, they are preferable to taking a bus (and cooler), as the coast road does not hug the shoreline.

The first port of call is usually the faded 1920s spa town of **Kalithea**: built by the Italians, it offers a delightfully quixotic collection of pseudo-Moorish buildings set in an odd landscape of small park areas between the rocks of the seashore. These days, the world has moved on (in every sense) down the coast to the youth nightspot Mecca of Greece — the disco and bar resort of Faliraki.

Home to wild — 'girls, don't tell your mothers'—nightlife, **Faliraki** was branded 'possibly the most dangerous holiday destination in the world' by one UK newspaper in 2003, after a series of incidents that included several drink-related deaths, and a number of arrests for public indecency. Add to this a very unhealthy reputation for sex attacks, and it is not surprising that a major police clampdown is now the order of the day. In 2004 it is planned that some 30 British police officers will be in the resort to help the local force control the — mostly British — drunken revellers.

The next major beach down the coast is rocky **Ladiko**. The place where much of *The Guns of Navarone* was filmed, it has been known as 'Antony Quinn' beach (after the late film star who played the lead), but this is now changing as too many visitors are simply asking 'Who?'.

South of Ladiko come the resort beaches of **Kolimbia** and **Tsambika** (which has a monastery-topped hill behind the beach, offering good views along the coast), and the far less spoilt beach at **Stegna**. This is best reached via a track that runs down from the inland village of **Archangelos**. After Lindos,

Harbour Windmills

19 c. Clock Tower
(Offers good views
over the Old City)

Marine Gate

ΜΕΛΑΣ
CHARCOAL GRILL GREEK TRADITIONAL TAVERN

Choosing Lunch
at an Old City Taverna

OLD CITY
Ippokratous Square Fountain
& Socratous Street

Rhodes

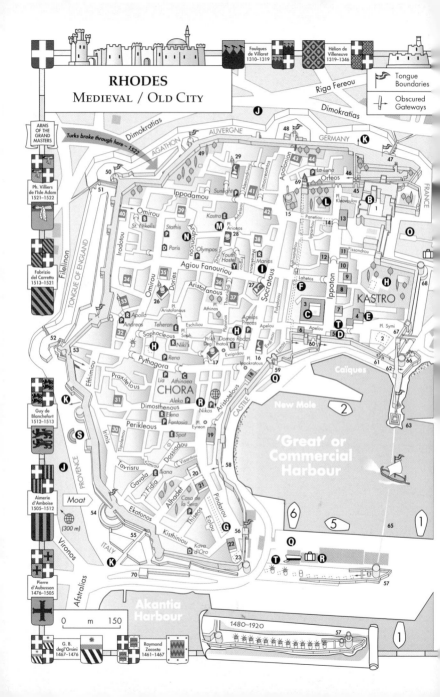

RHODES
MEDIEVAL / OLD CITY

Foulques de Villaret 1310–1319

Hélion de Villeneuve 1319–1346

Tongue Boundaries

Obscured Gateways

Riga Fereou

Dimokratias

J

Dimokratias

AUVERGNE

GERMANY

K

48

ARMS OF THE GRAND MASTERS

Turks broke through here – 1522

AGATHON

43

44

46

47

Ph. Villiers de l'Isle Adam 1521–1522

50

51

Ippodamou

49

29

Apollonia

La Luna Orfeos

69

45

B

1

O

Fabrizio del Carretto 1513–1521

40

Omirou

St Nikolis

39

Stathis

Andronicou

Kastro

Pl. Arionos

28

15

Panetiou

14

13

L

Pl. Kleovoulou

Pissandrou

11

FRANCE

Paris

Olympos

38

Marips

Socratous

M

Youth Hostel

12

10

9

H

Guy de Blanchefort 1512–1513

34

35

36

Dories

Aristotanous

27

F

Lahetos

8

C

E

KASTRO

K

33

26

Pl. Athinos

37

Pl. Thoudidi

Agelos Precas

P

3

7

T

D

Pl. Symi

2

67

Apollo

Andreas

32

Sophocleous

Teheran

Eschiliou

Pl. Soph.

Domos Rodas

Apelou

6

Apelou

S

5

66

Aimerie d'Amboise 1505–1512

K

H

Niki's

Rena

17

Evipidou

Ippokratous

16

Pl.

60

61

62

Q

Pythagora

Praxitelous

Lia

Athinaea

C

Rhodes

Aristotelous

59

Caïques

63

J

31

CHORA

Aleka

P

R

CASTILE

New Mole

2

Dimosthenous

Nikas

Perikleous

Elena

Fantasia

30

Spot

19

Eyreon

58

'Great' or Commercial Harbour

Pierre d'Aubusson 1476–1505

Tavrisru

Simiou

Dossiadou

Iliana

Vizantiou

20

Gavala

Fidia

Alhadef

21

Casa de la Sera

Pindarou

G

56

5

65

1

Moat

54

Ekatonos

Kisthiniou

Thiseos

Eolou

55

Kava d'Oro

22

Q

23

K

70

T

R

57

0   m   150

Vironos

Afstralias

Akantia Harbour

1480–1920

57

1

G. B. degl'Orsini 1467–1476

Raymond Zacosta 1461–1467

BYZANTINE CHURCHES

30. Agia Ekaterini
31. Agia Triada
32. Aghii Theodori
33. Agia Kyriaki
34. Archangelos Michaii
35. Agios Fanourios
36. Agios Spiridon
37. Archangelos Michaii
38. Agios Konstantinos
39. Agios Nikolaos
40. Agios Athanasios
41. Agia Paraskevi
42. Aghii Apostoli
43. Agios Georgios
44. Agios Marcos

OLD CITY GATES & TOWERS

45. Artillery Gate
46. St. Anthony Gate
47. Amboise Gate
48. St. George Tower
49. Tower of Spain
50. St. Mary / Virgin Tower
51. St. Athanase Gate
52. Koskinou / St. John's Gate
53. Koskinou / St. John's Tower
54. Tower of Italy / Carretto
55. Italy Gate (1924)
56. St. Catherine's / Mill Gate
57. Tower of the Mills / France

58. Port Gate (1924)
59. Marine Gate
60. Arnardo Gate
61. Arsenal Gate
62. St. Paul's Gate
63. Nailac Tower Base
64. Lost Nailac Tower
65. Harbour Chain Line
66. St. Paul's Tower
67. Liberty Gate (1924)
68. St. Peter's Tower
69. Clock Tower
70. Akantia Bastion

Key

- **Ⓐ** City Tourist Office
- **Ⓑ** Grand Masters Palace Museum
- **Ⓒ** Archaeological Mus.
- **Ⓓ** Byzantine Museum
- **Ⓔ** Folk Art Museum
- **Ⓕ** Kastro Inner Wall
- **Ⓖ** Ancient City Wall
- **Ⓗ** Classical Excavations
- **Ⓘ** Drinking Fountain
- **Ⓙ** Moatside Park
- **Ⓚ** Moat Access Points
- **Ⓛ** Turkish Library
- **Ⓜ** Turkish Baths
- **Ⓝ** Folk Dancing Theatre
- **Ⓞ** *Son-et-lumière*
- **Ⓟ** Italian Cathedral
- **Ⓠ** Taxi Stations
- **Ⓡ** Public WCs
- **Ⓢ** Moat Theatre
- **Ⓣ** ATM / Bank

1. Ferries
2. Catamarans
3. Tour Boats
4. Hydrofoils
5. Cruise-ships
6. Turkish Day Boats

Makariou

Plessa

Platia Vas. Georgiou II

(100 m)

Pl. Eleftherias

24

Mandraki Harbour

Marina

Akti Boumbouli

3

4

25

64

CITY LANDMARKS

1. Palace of the Grand Masters / Temple of Helios Site
2. Temple of Aphrodite
3. Hospital of the Knights
4. Inn of Auvergne
5. 'Our Lady of the Chateau' Church
6. Inn of England
7. Inn of Italy
8. Inn of France
9. 'Palace of Zizim'
10. Chapel of France
11. Inn of Provence
12. Inn of Agathon / Spain
13. Loggia
14. 'St. John of the Collachium' Site
15. Suleymaniye Cami Mosque
16. Chadrevan Mosque
17. Ibrahim Pacha Cami Mosque
18. Castellinia
19. Admiralty / Bishop's Palace
20. 'Our Lady of the City' Church
21. Hospice of St. Catherine
22. St. Pantaleon

23. 'Our Lady of Victory'
24. Site of Ancient & Medieval Dockyards
25. St. Nicholas Fortress / Site of the Colossus ?
26. Redjeb Pasha Mosque
27. Agha Mosque
28. Mastapha Mosque
29. Hamza Bey Mosque

4

1

25

The Colossus of Rhodes (attempting the pose favoured by 15 c. illustrators)

 Dieudonné de Gozon 1346–1353

 Pierre de Corneillan 1354–1355

 Roger de Pins 1355–1365

 Raymond Béranger 1365–1374

 Robert de Juilly 1374–1377

 Ferdinand d'Hérédia 1377–1396

 Philibert de Naillac 1396–1421

 Antoine Fluvian 1421–1437

 Jean de Lastic 1437–1454

 Jacques de Milly 1454–1461

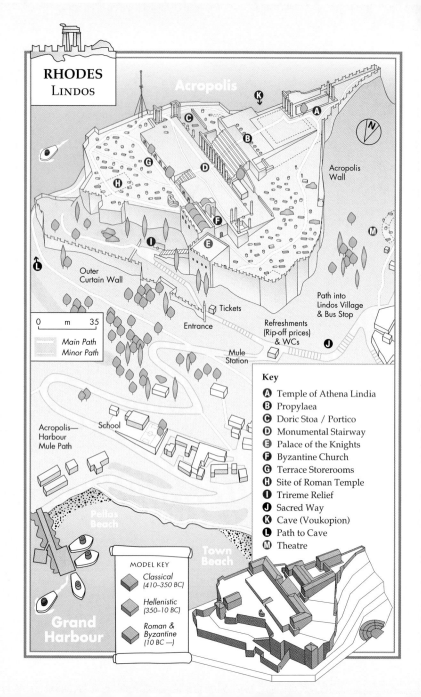

RHODES
LINDOS

Acropolis

Ⓚ

Ⓐ

Ⓒ

Ⓑ

Acropolis Wall

Ⓖ

Ⓓ

Ⓗ

N

Ⓕ

Ⓘ

Ⓔ

Ⓜ

Ⓛ

Outer Curtain Wall

Tickets

Entrance

Path into Lindos Village & Bus Stop

Refreshments (Rip-off prices) & WCs

Ⓙ

Mule Station

| 0 | m | 35 |

Main Path
Minor Path

Acropolis—Harbour Mule Path

School

Pallas Beach

Town Beach

Grand Harbour

Key

Ⓐ Temple of Athena Lindia
Ⓑ Propylaea
Ⓒ Doric Stoa / Portico
Ⓓ Monumental Stairway
Ⓔ Palace of the Knights
Ⓕ Byzantine Church
Ⓖ Terrace Storerooms
Ⓗ Site of Roman Temple
Ⓘ Trireme Relief
Ⓙ Sacred Way
Ⓚ Cave (Voukopion)
Ⓛ Path to Cave
Ⓜ Theatre

MODEL KEY

Classical (410–350 BC)
Hellenistic (350–10 BC)
Roman & Byzantine (10 BC —)

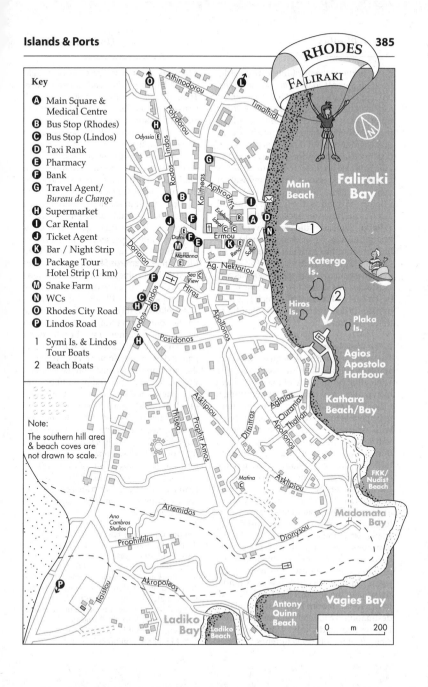

Key

- **A** Main Square & Medical Centre
- **B** Bus Stop (Rhodes)
- **C** Bus Stop (Lindos)
- **D** Taxi Rank
- **E** Pharmacy
- **F** Bank
- **G** Travel Agent/ *Bureau de Change*
- **H** Supermarket
- **I** Car Rental
- **J** Ticket Agent
- **K** Bar / Night Strip
- **L** Package Tour Hotel Strip (1 km)
- **M** Snake Farm
- **N** WCs
- **O** Rhodes City Road
- **P** Lindos Road

1 Symi Is. & Lindos Tour Boats
2 Beach Boats

Note:

The southern hill area & beach coves are not drawn to scale.

RHODES

FALIRAKI

Athinodorou

Polydorou

Lindos

Rodos

Odyssia

Kallitheas

Aphroditis

Timalhidi

Main Beach

Faliraki Bay

Edelweiss

Ermou

Doration

Dafni

Marianna

Ag. Nektariou

Sea View

Hiras

Rena

Sofia

Posidonos

Apollonos

Rodos

Lindos

Katergo Is.

Hiras Is.

Plaka Is.

Agios Apostolo Harbour

Asklipiou

Thisea

Prophit Amos

Dimitras

Apollonos

Aglaias

Ouranias

Thalian

Kathara Beach/Bay

Matina

Ariemidos

Asklipiou

Dionysou

FKK/ Nudist Beach

Madomata Bay

Ano Cambros Studios

Prophitililia

Akropoleos

Ifaisiou

Ladiko Bay

Ladiko Beach

Antony Quinn Beach

Vagies Bay

0   m   200

this is perhaps the most interesting settlement on the east coast (it is also the largest 'village' on the island). Set in a valley noted for its orange groves, Archangelos is made up of typical white-cubist houses, but has the added bonus of a very impressive Castle of the Knights (built in 1467) and a fresco-decorated late Byzantine church (1377). The village is also on the tour-bus circuit as it is a leading hand-woven carpet and leather boot manufacturing centre.

South of Lindos the only significant resort is the pine-tree backed beach village at **Pefki**. Thereafter the coast is very quiet (though the beaches are good enough), with buses reduced to a trickle: **Kattavia** sees a service only three times weekly. However, if you have your own transport, then this part of Rhodes is a delight — particularly the beach islet of **Prassonissi**, which is linked by a sandy beach causeway to the southern tip of the island.

2. The West Coast

The west coast of Rhodes is greener, quieter and less popular than the east coast. The winds that hit this side of the island have blown away any chance of it becoming a major package tourist strip. Beaches tend to be pebble rather than sand, and littered with driftwood; escapist beachcombers will love them. Tourist development on this side of Rhodes is largely confined to the coast between Rhodes City and the airport at **Paradisi**. This is as developed as the top half of the west coast. Thereafter, you are into country dominated by farms and vineyards. In spite of this, many visitors to Rhodes venture down this coast during island excursions, for the coast road is the jumping-off point for a number of sightseeing destinations. Regular — but infrequent — buses also run down this coast to the sights. The best served of these is **Trianda**, the stop for the ancient city of Ialyssos and, to the south, **Mount Filerimos**. This latter destination is a low hill picturesquely clad in pine trees and a mix of Byzantine and Knights of St. John era churches.

Beyond the airport, the wes-coast high-way is joined by the road to **Petaloudes**. This is the inland butterfly valley where millions of tiger moths are scared into flight by almost as many tourists between late June and early September. Like the similar site on Paros, the numbers of moths are declining each year, thanks to the tourists.

The next notable destination after Petaloudes is **Kamiros**. This is the second abandoned west coast ancient city and the third most popular sightseeing destination on the island. Thereafter the road continues along an ever quieter coast: a single daily Rhodes City bus gathers passengers at the rather sad hamlet of Kamiros Skala en route to Monolithos. **Kamiros Skala** (not to be confused with the ruined city) has a daily caïque link to Chalki (times on the ferry timetable sheet issued free in Rhodes City).

Monolithos is the most important village on the southern half of the west coast. In truth it is a rather poor beach resort redeemed by a Castle of the Knights perched on an overlooking hill. Arguably the most impressive castle on the island, it was built in the 15 c. Today it offers stunning views across the sea to the island of Chalki, and some dangerously crumbling walls on its sea-cliff side. Beyond Monolithos, the island is very sparsely populated. Like much of the mountainous interior of Rhodes, it remains surprisingly untouristed. Those wishing to visit these unspoilt parts of the island will need a good road map and their own transport; car hire comes into its own when exploring an island the size of Rhodes.

Rhodes City is the best place to stay if you don't have your own wheels, as it is at the hub of the transportation network. The city has a good supply of rooms (the tourist office also offers a room-finding service). The New Town is dominated by block-booked package tourist hotels (though they often have empty rooms). Most of the independent travellers' accommodation is to be found in the best part of town, in the Old City, but rates are at least 10% higher than on other islands.

At the bottom end of the range you will find pensions aplenty, among the best being the *Nikos* (☎ 23423) and the *Aleka* (☎ 33701) — both within easy distance of the port (look for 'CHORA' on the Old City map). A street to the north-east is home to the good *Rena* (☎ 26217), and tucked quietly away on the south side of town are two more good-value establishments: the *Andreas* (☎ 34156) and the *Apollo Rooms* (☎ 35064). Thanks to the competition, E-class hotels are all pretty reasonable. These include the *Spot* (☎ 34737), the *Domos Rodos* (☎ 25965) and the *Teheran* (☎ 27594). The cheap *Kastro* (☎ 20446) near the Turkish baths has noisy rooms overlooking a square. D-class hotels include the excellent, if out of the way, *Kava d'Oro* (☎ 36980) and *Paris* (☎ 26356).

Outside of Rhodes City there are plenty of options (though camping is not one of them — the island's only site at Faliraki closed in 2001). If you are looking for nightlife then **Faliraki** has several inexpensive, if noisy, hotels on its bar-fronted main street, including the C-class *Ideal* (☎ 85518) and *Edelweiss* (☎ 85442, 85305), and the E-class *Dafni* (☎ 85544).

Lindos has few accommodation options of note beyond a couple of expensive pensions, the *Katholiki* (☎ 31445) and the *Electra* (☎ 31266). Both need to be booked ahead by phone regardless of the season.

👓👓

Most island hoppers, if they are island hopping, will have their work cut out just taking in the sights in Rhodes and Lindos without having time to venture further afield, though Rhodes has sufficient sightseeing to fill a 2–week holiday.

Top of the list are the other two pre-408 BC cities (both accessible by bus from Rhodes City). **Kamiros** is, in fact, the best preserved of the three former centres of power. Abandoned after Rhodes City was built, much of the city plan is still visible, but sightseeing suffers considerably thanks to the lack of notable major buildings.

The remains at **Ialyssos** are far more fragmentary and consist of the foundations of a 3 C. BC **Temple of Athena Polias and Zeus Polios** on the site of the ancient acropolis. Unlike Kamiros, a settlement of sorts survived at Ialyssos until comparatively recently. Its close proximity to Rhodes City ensured that it was a centre of operations for besiegers of the city: both the Knights of St. John and Suleiman used it as a base prior to their conquests of the island.

Symi

ΣΥΜΗ; 58 km²; pop. 2,500.

CODE ☎ 22410
PORT POLICE ☎ 71205
TOURIST OFFICE ☎ 71215
POLICE ☎ 71111
FIRST AID ☎ 71290

A small island half tucked within the folds of the indented Turkish coast, hilly Symi (inappropriately pronounced 'Seamy') is both a popular day-tripper destination from Rhodes, and the prized objective for an exclusive few able to find overnight accommodation. There are two stories as to how the island got its name. The first is that Symi is named after a little-known goddess daughter of Ialyssos who was carried away from Rhodes by a passing boat-builder, who thereafter upset her by doing nothing but ignore her while he built boats. This story is as boring as he was and not worth going into further. The alternative tale has it that the island was originally called 'Simia' or 'monkey island'. Besides being far more appealing, this explanation is also much more plausible given the hilly nature of the terrain (you almost need to be a monkey to get around here). Of course, day-trippers from Rhodes aside, there isn't a monkey in sight: the simian bit comes from Prometheus (the man who stole fire from Zeus) who — myth would have it — was subsequently imprisoned and died here after the wrathful god zapped 1.6% of his DNA, thereby turning him into a monkey.

Symi was once one of the most prosperous islands in the Aegean, thanks to the combined industries of shipbuilding and sponge fishing. Its pre-WW2 history is not unlike nearby Kastelorizo; for Symi likewise enjoyed considerable prosperity coupled with political autonomy during the period of Ottoman rule, only to see its fortunes dramatically wane with the rise of the steamship and the island's isolation from the Anatolian mainland, following the Italian takeover of the Dodecanese after WW1.

Having cut down its trees to furnish wood for its shipbuilding industry, barren Symi depended thereafter on timber from mainland Turkey to maintain its output of over 500 caïques a year. Once this was lost, and the sponge fishing declined, the island fell into comparative poverty. Not even the re-growth of a good part of its forest cover was able to reverse the island's decline. Salvation of a sort came with the Turkish invasion of Cyprus in 1974, when Symi emerged as a popular Rhodes day-tripper excursion (in lieu of Turkish Marmaris, which was

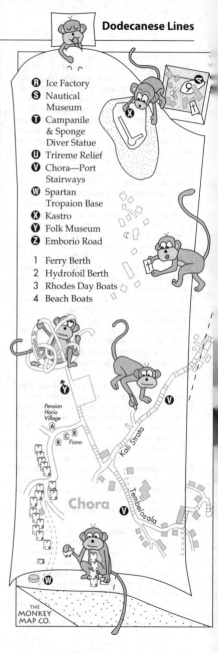

R Ice Factory
S Nautical Museum
T Campanile & Sponge Diver Statue
U Trireme Relief
V Chora—Port Stairways
W Spartan Tropaion Base
X Kastro
Y Folk Museum
Z Emborio Road

1 Ferry Berth
2 Hydrofoil Berth
3 Rhodes Day Boats
4 Beach Boats

Pension Horio Village
A
R C R Fiona

Kali Strata

Chora

Tembelosala

THE MONKEY MAP CO.

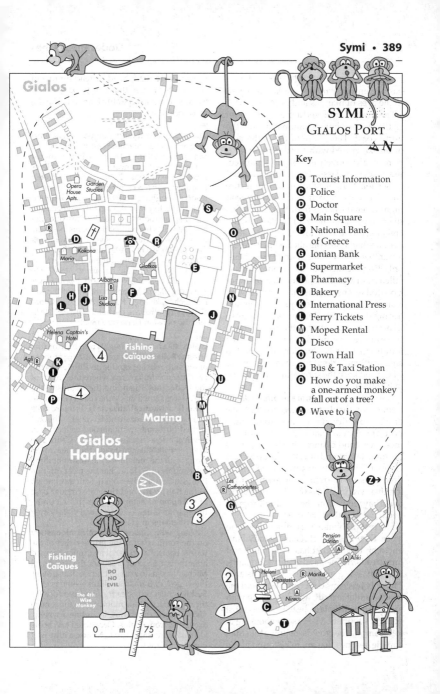

Gialos

SYMI

GIALOS PORT

△N

Key

- **B** Tourist Information
- **C** Police
- **D** Doctor
- **E** Main Square
- **F** National Bank of Greece
- **G** Ionian Bank
- **H** Supermarket
- **I** Pharmacy
- **J** Bakery
- **K** International Press
- **L** Ferry Tickets
- **M** Moped Rental
- **N** Disco
- **O** Town Hall
- **P** Bus & Taxi Station
- **Q** How do you make a one-armed monkey fall out of a tree?
- **A** Wave to it

Opera House Apts.

Garden Studios

Kokona

Maria

Glafkos

Albatros

Lisa Studios

Helena Captain's Hotel

Agli

Fishing Caïques

Gialos Harbour

Marina

Fishing Caïques

DO NO EVIL

The 4th Wise Monkey

0   m   75

Les Catherinettes

Pension Dorian

Aliki

Heleni

Anastasia

Marika

Nireus

Z→

necessarily out of bounds). Since then it has become ever more popular, overly so in the eyes of many island hoppers.

The only large settlement on Symi is the port—chora combination on the north coast. The centre of life is the port of **Gialos**, graced with a waterfront that is pure magic: a lovely mix of pastel painted, red-tiled, neo-classical mansions arranged in serried tiers around an amphitheatre bay. The scene is particularly attractive at night when the banks of dull orange lights seem to roll into the sea like the glowing embered lip of a lava flow. Daylight reveals a somewhat more complicated picture, for a number of the houses are mere shells, reflecting the fact that the population has fallen from 30,000 in the late 19 c. to under 3,000 today. The waterfront (complete with a campanile near the ferry quay) is crowded during the daytime, but quickly reverts to its normal sleepy self once the tour boats go; these arrive after midday and then depart four hours later, having done their best to enhance Symi's reputation as an expensive island and keep the sponge and herb shops in business.

The upper town of **Chora** retains an air of tranquillity, thanks to the need to climb one of the two stairways running up from the port. This is more than enough to dissuade most. A second disincentive is the state of the town (at the end of WW2 the departing Germans chose to blow up a couple of hundred houses). The remaining town is large, if rather scrappy, but is worth a visit thanks to the bay views from the windmill-topped headland and the Kastro hill.

The rest of Symi is very quiet, thanks to a coastline of steep cliffs and sandy bays and a hinterland that has nought but odd farmsteads, hamlets and goat-tracks galore; this makes it a good hill walking island. The only bus runs between Gialos and the beach hamlet at **Pedi**, which — along with sandy **Agios Nikolaos** beach — sees most of Symi's tourists. Visitors not choosing to loiter among the crowds, or brave the small shingle beaches that are to be found along

the **Emborio** road, head instead for one of the beach caïques that run to bays down Symi's east coast (pebbly **Nanou** being the most popular).

The lack of accommodation puts great pressure on capacity in High Season. Usually you can find something (at a price), but in August you can expect to encounter huge problems if you haven't booked ahead or arrived on a morning boat: it is common for late arrivals to resort to roughing it on the mosquito-haunted waterfront to await the next day when they can snap up rooms vacated by those moving on. **Gialos** has the bulk of the rooms. Near the ferry berth are the expensive A-class *Aliki* (☎ 71665), *Nireus* (☎ 72400) and the *Dorian* (☎ 71181). Best bets behind the harbour are the *Albatros* (☎ 71707), the *Kokona* (☎ 71549), the tiny *Glafkos* (☎ 71358) and the *Opera House Apts* (☎ 72034). On the Chora side of the bay is the cheapish *Agli Rooms* (☎ 71665). **Chora** also has a few rooms, the hotel *Fiona* (☎ 72088) and the pension *Horio* (☎ 71800).

👓

Gialos has a number of sights ranging from the **Trireme Relief** on the waterfront (a 1945 replica of the ship relief at Lindos on Rhodes) to the *Les Catherinettes* taverna where the Treaty of the Dodecanese (handing the islands to the Allies) was signed that same year. There is also a two-floor **Nautical Museum** (€3); the exhibits consist of half-a-dozen model caïques, the odd stuffed bird and an unlabelled collection of nautical bric-a-brac (mostly brac). **Chora** also has a fair **Folk Museum** (follow the blue arrows) along with the remains of the **Kastro** built by the Knights of St. John, but the most original things in town are the majestic stairway known as the **Kali Strata**, and the large circular base of a **Tropaion** (victory monument) set up by the Spartans after a nearby naval victory over the Athenians in 411 BC.

Along with Gialos, **Panormitis Monastery** on the south coast is the prime target of the tourist boats. This palatial institution (named after the patron saint of sailors, the Archangel Michael) seems to exist for tourists. It also owns the largest of Symi's satellites — the islet of **Seskli**, which provides fruit and produce for the monastery's lone monk. Some tours have visits in their itineraries, including a weekly excursion from Gialos. Occasional taxi boats also make the short trip to **Nimos**, a hilly islet north of Gialos.

Telendos
ΤΕΛΕΝΔΟΣ; 5 km²; pop. 90.

CODE ☎ 22430

Hidden away behind Kalimnos, Telendos is a substantial hilltop, sitting like a giant boulder 700 metres offshore. The island is supposed to resemble the head of a petrified princess caught at the moment she was looking out to sea for her long lost lover. This tradition baffles most as the resemblance doesn't exactly hit you in the eye.

The nearest most visitors to the Dodecanese get to Telendos is the ferry view of the island's forbidding west side. Those in the know are more than happy to keep this arrangement, for although the mountain isn't exactly cosy, the fishing village that nestles along the coastline opposite the Kalimnos resort of Mirities is. Even the three caïques (complete with carpeted decks) that run every half hour across the straits add to the feeling, giving an escapist edge to the place: when you are on Telendos you really do feel as if you have pulled up a drawbridge linking you to the rest of the world (which is still on view in a comfortably visible way).

The only village, backed by slopes covered with a light confetti of pine trees, is so small that the waterfront is the main street in all but name. The only facilities are a tiny mini-market and half a dozen tavernas. Telendos really does give you the chance to experience life in a working Greek island fishing village. When you want tourist facilities and shopping then a quick caïque ride to Mirities is an easy way of fulfilling the need.

One reason why Telendos hasn't come to the fore are its beaches. The most accessible — white pebble **Hohlaka** (alias 'Chochlaka') lies at the bottom of a low cliff behind the village. It is apt to be quite windy. The islanders have attempted to improve its appeal by adding sun-beds — as they have at the other main beach at Paradise (pebbles and dark sand) to the north of the village.

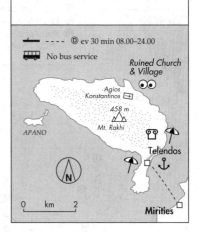

TELENDOS

⊶ ---- ⒹD ev 30 min 08.00–24.00

🚌 No bus service

Ruined Church & Village

Agios Konstantinos 🏕

458 m

Mt. Rakhi

APANO

Telendos

Ⓝ

0   km   2

Mirities

🛏
No hotels, but a surprising number of beds are available. Waterfront establishments offering rooms include *Studio Rita* (☎ 47914), *Rooms Fotini* (☎ 47401), *On the Rocks* (☎ 48260) and *Villa Erminia* (☎ 47446).

😋
Originally joined to Kalimnos, Telendos was merely a hill that overlooked the ancient Kalimnos capital of 'Pothia' that had been built on low land between the two. A massive earthquake in 554 AD changed all that: the ancient capital did a 'Port Royal' and sank under the modern straits, and the newly created Telendos island became a sleepy backwater.

👓
Sightseeing on Telendos is surprisingly plentiful — though most of it consists of **ruined churches**. The easiest of these to find is 6 C. AD **Agia Triada** behind the town. The remains of another three lie at the abandoned village on the north coast if you care to attempt the walk to **Agios Konstantinos**. The southern spur of the island has fragments of a **Roman bath** — the only ancient remains still extant. Of the lost city of Pothia under the sea, nothing is visible, though 'tis said that you can sometimes hear church bells tolling under the waves'.

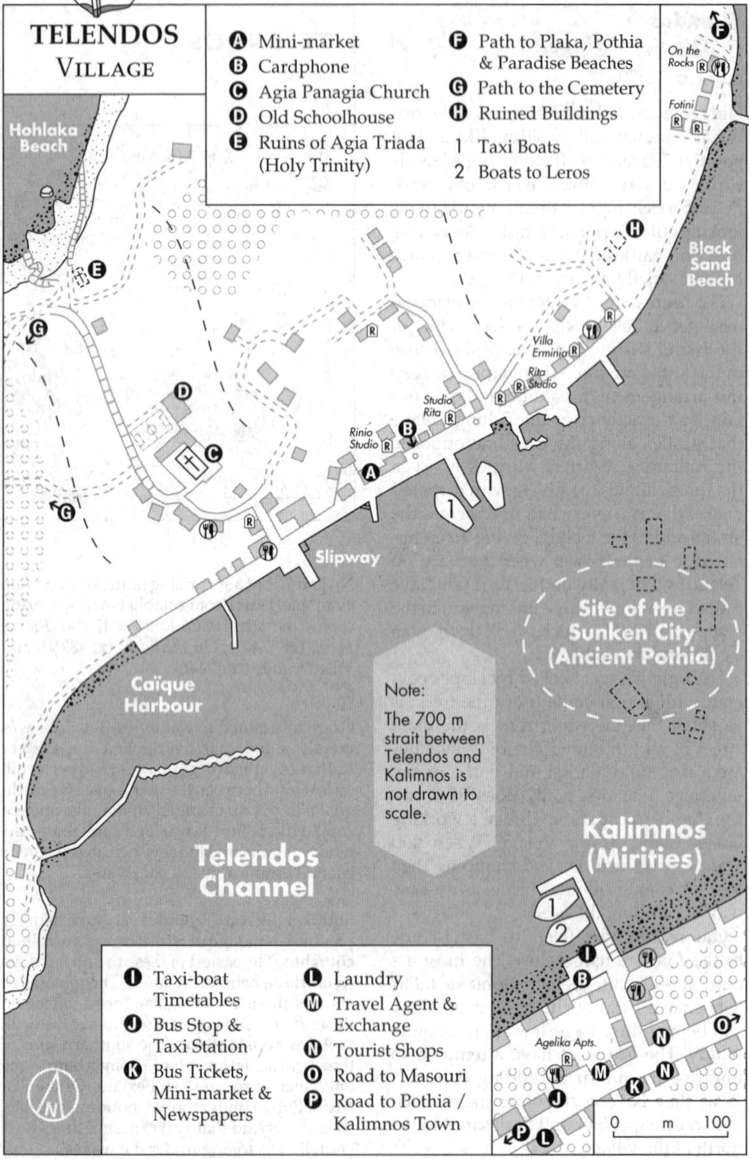

TELENDOS
VILLAGE

A Mini-market
B Cardphone
C Agia Panagia Church
D Old Schoolhouse
E Ruins of Agia Triada
(Holy Trinity)

F Path to Plaka, Pothia
& Paradise Beaches
G Path to the Cemetery
H Ruined Buildings

1 Taxi Boats
2 Boats to Leros

Hohlaka Beach

E
G

H

Black Sand Beach

On the Rocks

Fotini

Villa Erminia

Rita Studio

Studio Rita

Rinio Studio

D
C

B
A

G

1
1

Slipway

Site of the Sunken City (Ancient Pothia)

Caïque Harbour

Note:

The 700 m strait between Telendos and Kalimnos is not drawn to scale.

Telendos Channel

Kalimnos (Mirities)

1
2

I

B

Agelika Apts.

N

O

N

M

K

J

P
L

I Taxi-boat
Timetables
J Bus Stop &
Taxi Station
K Bus Tickets,
Mini-market &
Newspapers

L Laundry
M Travel Agent &
Exchange
N Tourist Shops
O Road to Masouri
P Road to Pothia /
Kalimnos Town

0   m   100

N

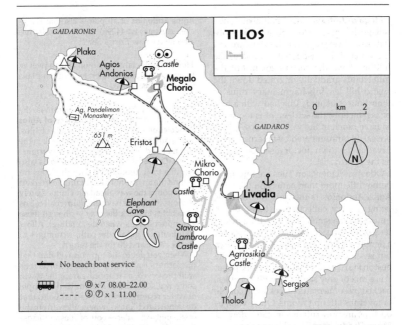

Tilos

ΤΗΛΟΣ; 63 km²; pop. 320.

CODE ☎ 22410
PORT POLICE ☎ 44350
POLICE ☎ 44222
FIRST AID ☎ 44210

A sleepy island even in High Season, tiny Tilos is an attractive and cosy place, made up of hills topped with castles, quiet orchard valleys and empty beaches. For years it has been all but ignored by tourists, perhaps because at first sight it looks rather dull compared to almost every other island in the Dodecanese. Other factors also come into play, with rumours of internecine feuds between the islanders (resulting in few tourist facilities emerging) whispering up and down the Dodecanese, reflecting past antagonism between the two communities on the island. Happily today there is nothing on Tilos to support them: the islanders are generally very friendly and welcoming.

Even better, unlike many small islands in the region, you can be reasonably sure of finding a room of some sort no matter when you visit.

Having abandoned several tiny hill villages, the island population is now divided between the port of Livadia and the tiny capital of Megalo Chorio, the two being linked by a recently paved road. **Livadia** is the more vibrant of the two centres with a plethora of new hotel and apartment building going on behind the old waterfront. Although tourism is the only economic god now worshipped in town, Livadia has managed to retain much of its former homely small island appeal, with a leafy central square, sleepy tavernas (that only come to life once darkness falls) and a handful of friendly shops. The port quay also gives way to a long clean beach that unfortunately is little used, as it is made up of large pebbles that are just a bit too big for comfort.

Megalo Chorio is a small, half-abandoned village that sits on a foothill at the back of a flat plain. In ages past it clustered around the walls of the castle that dominates the hilltop above the current town, but the inhabitants gradually migrated down the kastro hill leaving fragmentary ruins of their houses behind. Touched with a hint of melancholy, the settlement is too small to have much in the way of shops, which are easily outnumbered by tavernas. As at Livadia, the town doctor also doubles up as the pharmacist.

Other settlements on Tilos are tiny, most being little more than names on the map. **Agios Andonios** is the only one of note, being a sorry collection of half-a-dozen houses near a small jetty huddling near a long scruffy 'beach' backed by the turret of a derelict windmill. **Eristos** is even smaller, but is set to grow thanks to its beach. The best on the island and at times over-popular, it is a mix of grey sand and white pebbles, backed by some mature trees and a couple of tavernas offering rooms. Other villages on Tilos are now ruinous, notably derelict **Micro Chorio**, abandoned in the 1950s.

The main roads on Tilos have recently been made up with concrete, and keep to the valley floors. These are surprisingly fertile, with lovely shady, mature oak trees, fields of silage and collections of hives (the island is known for its honey). With the improved road system has also come a new blue bus (a cut-down regular bus type). Bus times are hard to find (they are only listed on the information kiosk on the quay at Livadia), but in summer services are frequent enough.

⊨

Livadia has the bulk of the accommodation including two hotels: the C-class *Irini* (☎ 44293) (hidden away in a jungle of a garden) and the E-class *Livadia* (☎ 44266). There are also a number of apartments charging hotel rates — including the good C-class *George Apartments* — and pensions. Most island rooms are also at Livadia. **Megalo Chorio** also has establishments offering rooms, including the *Milou* (☎ 44204) and *Elecantakia* (☎ 44213).

Agios Andonios of all places also has the B-class *Australia* (☎ 44296), and **Eristos** also has a hotel: the new *Eristos Beach*.

Δ

There is no official campsite on Tilos: however, freelance camping is tolerated at both Plaka and Eristos beaches.

👓

The main sightseeing destination is the 1470-built fortified hill **Monastery of Agios Pandeleimon** on the north-west side of Tilos. The island bus runs there twice a week in summer and waits an hour before returning.

The **Castle** above **Megalo Chorio** is also worth a visit, though the path that runs up behind the town isn't for the faint-hearted. At some points the way ahead isn't immediately obvious (the locals have piled up small cairns of pebbles to mark the way — though these are more obvious when descending). Allow 45 minutes to get up the path, 15 minutes to do the castle and 30 for the return.

When you get to the top you will find that the fortress isn't nearly as large, nor is it as well preserved, as it appears from the town: some walls are all but missing and a couple of water cisterns have unguarded holes that descend to god-knows-where. Views from the castle are spectacular — both of Tilos and across the straits to Nissiros, which from this vantage point really looks like a volcano.

A few years back, a small island near Siberia received considerable publicity after the discovery that it was home to a species of **Dwarf Mammoth** a couple of hundred thousand years earlier. What is less well known is the fact that they came to Tilos for their summer holidays (the fossilized bones of those killed in moped accidents litter caves on the island). The town hall at Megalo Chorio is home to a small bones **Museum**.

Finally, hill walkers and hikers will love Tilos. Armed with a good island map (two are on sale in Livadia: go for the good blue rather than the poor white one), it is possible to wander at will, exploring the series of castles that run down the spine of the island, including one at **Mikro Chorio** which is worth the walk anyway. A walk to the Agios Pandelimon monastery on the north-west coast also enables you to take in **Agios Andonios Beach**. This has a sobering reminder of the dangers of over exposure thanks to the petrified remains of three sailors who were caught napping by an eruption of Nissiros c. 600 BC.

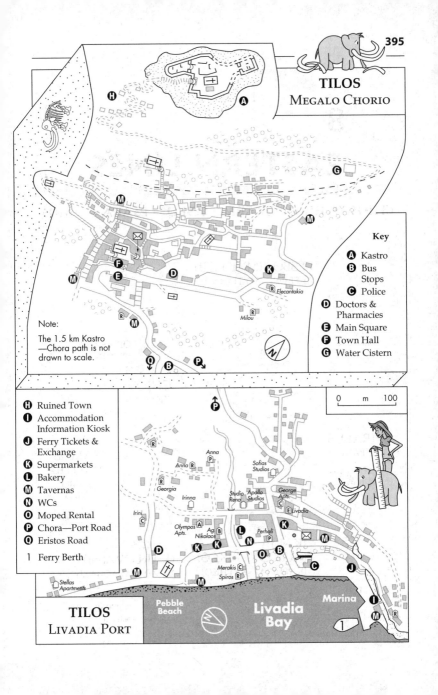

TILOS
MEGALO CHORIO

Key

- **A** Kastro
- **B** Bus Stops
- **C** Police
- **D** Doctors & Pharmacies
- **E** Main Square
- **F** Town Hall
- **G** Water Cistern

Note:

The 1.5 km Kastro—Chora path is not drawn to scale.

Elecantakia

Milou

H Ruined Town
I Accommodation Information Kiosk
J Ferry Tickets & Exchange
K Supermarkets
L Bakery
M Tavernas
N WCs
O Moped Rental
P Chora—Port Road
Q Eristos Road
1 Ferry Berth

0   m   100

Anna
Anna
Sofias Studios
Georgia
Studio Rena
Apollo Studios
George Apts.
Livadia
Irinna
Irini
Olympos Apts.
Ag. Nikolaos
Perhall
Stellas Apartments
Merakis
Spiros

TILOS
LIVADIA PORT

Pebble Beach

Livadia Bay

Marina

8
EASTERN LINES

CHIOS · FOURNI · IKARIA · LESBOS · PSARA · SAMOS

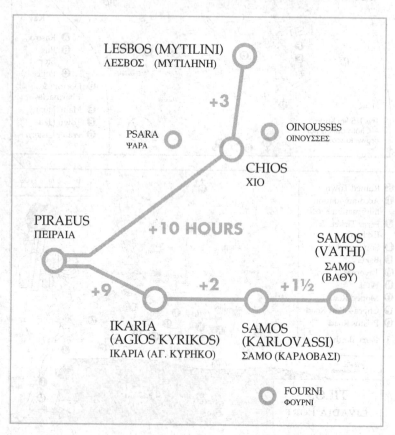

LESBOS (MYTILINI)
ΛΕΣΒΟΣ (ΜΥΤΙΛΗΝΗ)

+3

PSARA
ΨΑΡΑ

OINOUSSES
ΟΙΝΟΥΣΣΕΣ

CHIOS
ΧΙΟ

PIRAEUS
ΠΕΙΡΑΙΑ

+10 HOURS

SAMOS
(VATHI)
ΣΑΜΟ
(ΒΑΘΥ)

+9

+2

+1½

IKARIA
(AGIOS KYRIKOS)
ΙΚΑΡΙΑ (ΑΓ. ΚΥΡΗΚΟ)

SAMOS
(KARLOVASSI)
ΣΑΜΟ (ΚΑΡΛΟΒΑΣΙ)

FOURNI
ΦΟΥΡΝΙ

General Features

The Eastern Aegean Line is made up of two separate routes running from Piraeus east across the Aegean to those Greek islands adjacent to the Turkish coast north of the Dodecanese. All the ferries operating Eastern Line services follow the natural geographical division of the islands into the two sub-groups, either running Piraeus—Ikaria—Samos, or Piraeus—Chios—Lesbos (Mytilini).

The more southerly route takes in the large and increasingly popular island of Samos as well as the less well known Ikaria. Each boasts two regular ports at which ferries can call, giving scope for alternations in schedules. The more northerly route runs across to Chios and then up the Turkish seaboard to Lesbos (Mytilini); both are large islands which have remained economically independent of the tourist hordes but which are increasingly attracting Grecophiles jaded by the over-tourism encountered elsewhere.

Northern route sailings are almost exclusively confined to the major ports of Chios Town and Lesbos (Mytilini), but a number of ferries then continue on into the northern Aegean to varying ports of call. Both groups also include minor islands little visited by tourists: Fourni and Samiopoula off Samos, Oinousses and Psara accessible from Chios.

Links between the two lines remain poor, but are slowly improving with a connecting Chios—Samos service three days a week. Equally indifferent are connections with the Dodecanese which are so thin on the water that locals utilize Patmos-bound tourist boats.

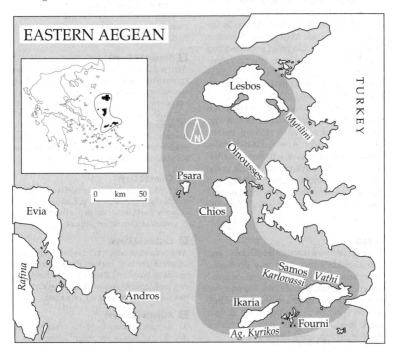

Example Itinerary [2 Weeks]

An itinerary based on the Eastern Lines is for those who prefer a scattering of trees rather than High Season crowds with their Greek islands, and are happy to settle for quiet taverna eating and making their own entertainment. It is unlikely to appeal to those who like to boogie between boats. The islands en route are comparatively quiet thanks to a mix of fewer ferry connections and the need to get a bus to the nearest reasonable beach (on the popular Cycladic islands you only have to fall overboard near to port to find yourself on one). The crowds are missing more than they realise.

Arrival/Departure Point

On a fortnight's holiday there are two easy flight options: Athens and Samos (more poorly served Lesbos (Mytilini) is a third possible option). Athens is the easiest to get back to in a rush. Samos is an equally accessible point provided you travel in an anticlockwise direction (thus ensuring you can pick up one of the daily Piraeus—Samos links in the latter part of the trip if needs be).

If you have three weeks at your disposal then Mykonos, Santorini or Kos can also be considered as viable starting points. However, unlike Athens and Samos, neither will give you advance information on the 2–3 days per week link in the itinerary: the Samos—Chios crossing, and this is a disadvantage given that you will have to structure your plans around the days it runs.

Season

Travel in late June through late October and you shouldn't encounter any problems. Low Season sees difficulties in crossing between the Samos and Chios lines; ferries along both decline from the daily High Season services to the usual 3–4 days a week level, with links to the Northern Aegean disappearing altogether.

1 Athens [2 Days]

Quite apart from the city sights, Athens offers agents in Piraeus who will show you the Miniotis Ferries timetable (if they are operating) when you ask about links between Chios and Samos. With this info you can then work out how many days you have either side of this weak link and allocate nights and stops accordingly.

2 Paros [2 Days]

As there are not usually morning and evening boats out of Piraeus along the Samos line it is often more convenient to make for better connected Paros and then jump from there onto a Samos boat. It also breaks up an otherwise 12-hour voyage and offers a quick dash down to Naxos and the Cyclades Central Line if you have a third week to hand.

3 Ikaria [1 Day]

An optional island (it is a good idea to build in extra flexibility by having one in any itinerary) you can fit (time willing) into a tight schedule.

4 Samos [3 Days]

Arriving at Vathi the number one priority is to confirm the Monday and Friday boat to Chios is running (in the unlikely event of this service not operating — and it has for the last few years — you always have the option of heading south by picking up a tourist boat from Pithagorio down to Patmos and the Dodecanese). This established, you can fill the available time on excursions to Pithagorio and Turkey.

5 Chios [2 Days]

Once on Chios you have optional hops to neighbouring Oinousses, to Turkey, and even adjacent Psara if the notion of a couple of days of untouristed isolation appeals.

6 Lesbos [2 Days]

A nice island on which to relax before catching an overnight boat back to Piraeus. Irregular ferries to Volos and Rafina (via the Northern Aegean) are also options if you don't mind a bus ride into Athens at the other end.

1 Athens [2 Days]

Arrive back in Athens with the precautionary day in hand before your flight home.

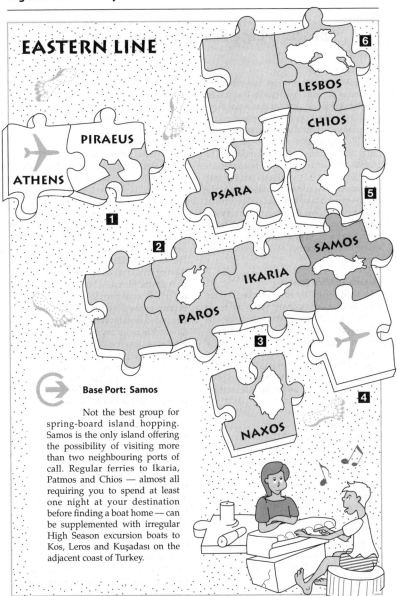

EASTERN LINE

ATHENS
PIRAEUS
PSARA
LESBOS
CHIOS
SAMOS
IKARIA
PAROS
NAXOS

1 **2** **3** **4** **5** **6**

Base Port: Samos

Not the best group for spring-board island hopping. Samos is the only island offering the possibility of visiting more than two neighbouring ports of call. Regular ferries to Ikaria, Patmos and Chios — almost all requiring you to spend at least one night at your destination before finding a boat home — can be supplemented with irregular High Season excursion boats to Kos, Leros and Kuşadası on the adjacent coast of Turkey.

Eastern Line Ferry Services

Main Car Ferries

The level of ferry services has remained consistent over the last decade. Traffic is far less dependent on tourism than some other parts of the Greek system, with regular daily connections in both directions, as the ferries provide important services to what are all fairly large islands by Greek standards. The islands of Fourni and Psara, however, are irregularly served by Piraeus ferries, with calls often only added to schedules at the last moment. These links should be treated with caution. Low Season can see services fall to a low of a four-days-a-week level, with Northern Aegean links all but non-existent, and services to Turkey severely curtailed.

Piraeus—Samos Ferries

The southern Piraeus—Ikaria—Samos route is now seeing change after a decade of little change. In part this is because this is the route run by the infamous *Golden Vergina,* which as the *Express Samina* sank so tragically at the end of September 2000, while running her regular evening itinerary to Samos via Paros. Bar the few high speed ferries, all the boats on the line are starting to look seriously dated.

C/F *Aeolos Express*

NEL Lines; 2000; 6000 GRT.

The first of the trio of high speed boats (with the very distinctive pointed bows), the *Aeolos Express* expanded her 2001 Cyclades Central Line service to cover Ikaria and Samos in 2002. In spite of her significantly higher ticket prices (e.g. Ikaria to Naxos: €28), she appeared to have no great difficulty attracting custom.

Leg room in the airline-style seating is a bit tight, but otherwise it is difficult to fault this very well maintained vessel. All luggage is stowed in racks either on the car deck or at the far ends of the passenger deck. If you are venturing to Ikaria, check carefully which port this boat is calling at: she is prone to ring the changes and sometimes ticket agents on other islands aren't sure themselves.

C/F *Express Olympia*

Hellas Ferries / HFD; 1973; 4657 GRT.

This elderly ferry moved to this route in 2000, with a reputation for poorly maintained facilities and anti-backpacker activities. Now refurbished, if not re-crewed, it is difficult to rate her as she can either offer a pleasant ride (when half empty) or — when packed to bursting — claim the laurels for being the least attractive ferry in Greece. In late August 2003 she broke down soon after leaving Piraeus and had to be towed back to port. On the plus side, her saloon (if you can get into it) conspires to add a touch of the bizarre to the island hopping experience: decorated with murals of the white cliffs of Dover, it is an incongruous hangover from her days as the cross-Channel *Earl Granville*. Her schedules vary considerably with the season: at peak periods she tends to run a direct service to Ikaria and Samos five times a week, while calls at smaller islands are reserved for the rest of the year.

C/F *Daliana*

G.A. Ferries; 1970; 5528 GRT.

An ex-Japanese boat, the elderly *Daliana* replaced her identical sister, the *Milena,* on the Samos line in 1999. Both ferries have small smoke-stacks astern, comfortable interior deck-class facilities, and sun-deck bench seats for sleeping-bag fans. Given her age and generally run-down state, it is to be hoped that *Daliana* will have been retired by the summer of 2004 — though it is just possible that her operators will squeeze one more year's use out of her. If she is replaced then expect another equally knackered G.A. Ferries fleet vessel to replace her.

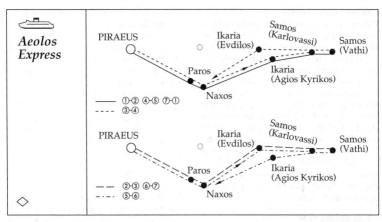

Aeolos Express

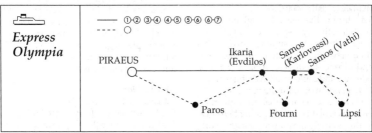

Express Olympia

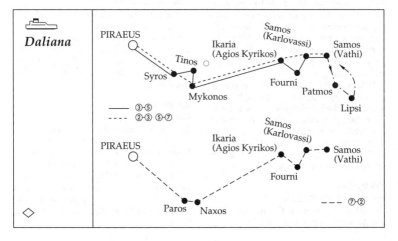

Daliana

Piraeus—Chios Ferries

Piraeus to Lesbos and Chios services have been dominated by one company — the Maritime Co. of Lesbos (NEL Lines) — for many years. The lack of heavy tourist traffic in the northern Aegean hasn't encouraged other operators to move in (though each summer sees someone try their luck on the route). Meantime, despite their near monopoly, NEL achieve a commendable standard, both in terms of the quality of their fleet and the level of service. The company is, however, something of a timetable-compiler's bane, as it tends to pool its boats. For these reasons the services opposite are mapped together rather than by individual boat.

C/F *Aeolos Kenteris*
NEL Lines; 2001; 6000 GRT.

The third of the new NEL high-speed ferries (all with very distinctive pointed bows) has for the last two summers divided her time between the Piraeus—Lesbos route and trips to Rhodes (see p. 324). This is an odd mix, and could result in changes in 2004 if demand on either route increases.

There is also a chance that political considerations will dictate her routing in August as this is surely the only ferry in the world to be named after an athlete competing in the Athens Olympics (a national hero, Costas Kenteris won the 200 Metres title in Sydney, and is planning to defend his title this year. Outside Greece he is little known thanks to his habit of only attending major meetings).

Tickets on the *Aeolos Kenteris* tend to be pricey because of this boat's high speed status and the long hops she makes. However, she is easily the best boat on the route, and well worth splashing out on. (Those without the spare Euros are still catered for by NEL as the *Aeolos Kenteris* tends to run in tandem with regular ferries.)

C/F *Mytilene*
NEL Lines; 1973; 6702 GRT.

The *Mytilene* is now the number two regular ferry in the NEL fleet. Her design is something of a problem: the search for the sun deck or the WCs is apt to be hard on the feet, and her turnaround times are not good thanks to the limited entry/exit facilities given the numbers she can carry: if you are particularly safety-conscious you might want to avoid her.

If you are picking her up at the start of her route it is also worth joining her at least an hour before her departure: although the deck-class passenger lounge is large, demand for seats always exceeds supply in High Season.

C/F *Taxiarchis*
NEL Lines; 1976; 10750 GRT.

A new arrival in 1999, this ferry took over much of the itinerary of one of the smaller NEL boats, including the traditional High Season weekend Mytilini—Volos run. Formerly the trans-Adriatic *Agia Methodia*, this vessel is hardly the most inspiring recent arrival in the Aegean, but a reasonable mid-range boat, even though she is obviously a converted container ferry.

C/F *Theofilos*
NEL Lines; 1975; 19212 GRT.

The largest regular ferry in the NEL fleet, this boat arrived in the Aegean in 1995 after running as the Australian *Abel Tasman* (followed by a brief spell as the trans-Adriatic *Pollux*). She has taken on all the 'heavy' peak-demand passenger runs. As with the *Mytilene*, life on board isn't exactly cosy: she is just too big for comfort. That said, she is an excellent overnight ferry with good-value cabins.

C/F *Milena*
G.A. Ferries; 1970; 5491 GRT.

The only competition to NEL on the Piraeus—Chios—Lesbos route in 2003 came from the tired old *Milena* (see p. 436). In truth the service was half-hearted at best, with only one round trip a week. This boat is unlikely to be repeating the service in 2004 thanks to ferry age limitations, but the chances are that another token competing ferry will appear.

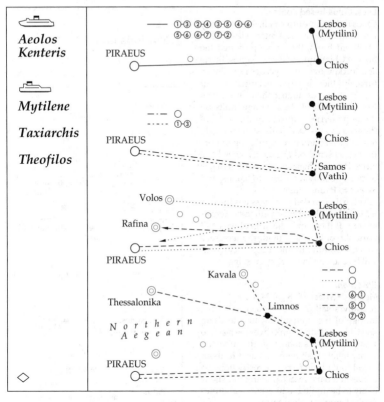

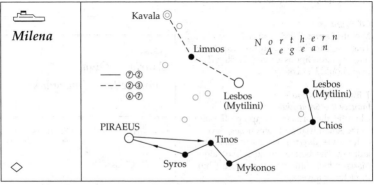

Local Chios-based Boats

Chios is the home of a small, regional ferry line: Miniotis Ferries. Armed with several small old boats, they have provided the bulk of Chios links to Psara, Samos, Ikaria and Turkey over the last decade. Unfortunately, they have been largely out of action of late as almost their entire fleet has fallen foul of the new age-limits on domestic ferries imposed in the wake of the 2000 *Express Samina* disaster, with only one boat remaining in regular operation. In their absence other larger ferries have moved to cover their most important routes — most notably the Chios to Samos, and Samos to Patmos runs.

At the time of going to press it is unclear if Miniotis will reappear with 'new' ferries in 2004. If they don't the larger boats will no doubt continue to provide the necessary cover. Meantime, the older boats below can still be used on the Turkey crossing.

C/F *Chioni*

Miniotis Ferries; 1968; 572 GRT.
A really small ferry that has carried the burden of the company's Chios to Psara and Chios to Patmos links over the last two years, the *Chioni* is about to go the same way of her fellow fleet members as it is about to fall foul of the ferry age restrictions on domestic boats. In 2004, therefore, she is likely to be limited to international duties on the Chios—Turkey service.

C/F *Psara*

Miniotis Ferries; 1963; 250 GRT.
This rusty 'tour boat' is only used to provide day trips to Oinousses and Turkey. This boat should be avoided.

T/B's *Maria – Olga – Inousse II – Smargdaki*

Chios is the primary jumping-off point to the small island of Oinousses. Several older style day-tripper boats make the journey. The best of these is the caïque *Maria*, which runs day trips from Chios three times a week.

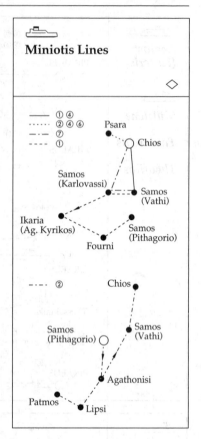

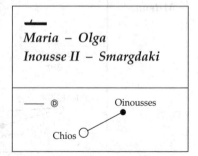

Eastern Line Islands & Ports

Chios
ΧΙΟΣ; 852 km²; pop. 54,000.

CODE ☎ 22710
TOURIST OFFICE ☎ 24217
TOURIST POLICE ☎ 26555
PORT POLICE ☎ 44433
FIRST AID ☎ 23151

Relatively untouristed (thanks to an ugly main port with no good beaches close by) nor offering much in the way of photogenic sightseeing, the large island of Chios remains quiet with its low-key attractions hidden away. To do the island justice you need to take time to explore away from the capital, for Chios has a merited reputation for having some of the most fertile and attractive terrain to be found in the Aegean. Indeed, in many ways the landscape is the best thing about Chios, as well as being the source of its quiet affluence, thanks to the growing of mastica (the sticky stuff used to make paint adhere to walls and chewing-gum to everything else). This resin, which oozes out of the trunk of a low bush, gave the island its wealth: during the Middle Ages it was the only source of mastic production in the world.

Most of Chios is mountainous, with the mastica bush crop covering much of the south, while the north is forested — though major fires in 1981 and 1987 inflicted considerable damage to this region. A more recent and lucrative contribution to the local economy has come via the sea, for almost every Greek shipping tycoon in sight seems to hail from here or the neighbouring satellite of Oinousses.

A bastion of quiet prosperity, Chios has enjoyed a very low-key history for much of its existence. Most of its population appear to have been too busy making a mint through growing and chewing gum to have had time for philosophical speculation or political struggle. This only changed in the 19 c. and the devastating impact of the island's brief sojourn into the limelight haunts Chios still. Like many islands located close to the Turkish coast Chios suffered in the struggle for Greek independence. Having joined the rebellion by a number of islands against Turkish rule in 1822, Chios was singled out (along with neighbouring Psara) — largely for convenient geographical reasons — for the most severe retribution. On the orders of the Sultan the entire island was sacked, with its buildings burnt. Over 30,000 islanders were massacred in the process and a further 70,000 (mainly women and children) were enslaved and deported. A devastating earthquake arrived in 1881, just in time to nicely set back the island's recovery. This is now complete, though the scars of the last two centuries are still very evident.

The capital, **Chios Town**, has retained its late 19 c. industrial port waterfront and this has little to recommend it. Demolished by the 1881 earthquake, subsequent rebuilding has left the town an inadequate harbinger to the attractiveness of the rest of the island. As one might expect on Greece's premier chewing-gum growing island, Chios Town is home to a large expatriate North American community that returns to the island each summer. The back streets behind the waterfront offer an incongruous mix of crumbling mansions, pool bars and New Yorker run pizza bars. The quayside is more reminiscent of a mini version of Piraeus than any other harbour in Greece.

The centre of activity lies near the north-western corner: this is where all the large ferries dock, with the most scenic part of the town behind (complete with a closed mosque and a large tree-filled square/park). In an attempt to humanize the waterfront, the western side is now pedestrianized during the evening, the local mosquitos taking full advantage of

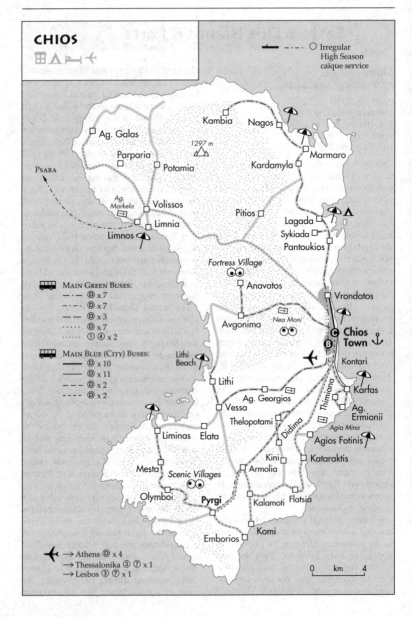

CHIOS

—— ---- ○ Irregular High Season caïque service

PSARA

1297 m

Kambia

Nagos

Ag. Galas

Parparia

Potamia

Marmaro

Kardamyla

Ag. Markela

Volissos

Pitios

Limnia

Lagada

Sykiada

Pantoukios

Limnos

Fortress Village

Anavatos

Vrondatos

MAIN GREEN BUSES:
— · — ⑩ x 7
— · · — ⑩ x 7
— — ⑩ x 3
· · · · · ⑩ x 7
· · · · · ① ④ x 2

MAIN BLUE (CITY) BUSES:
——— ⑩ x 10
——— ⑩ x 11
— — — ⑩ x 2
— - — - ⑩ x 2

Avgonima

Nea Moni

Chios Town ⚓

B

Lithi Beach

Kontari

Lithi

Karfas

Ag. Georgios

Vessa

Thelopotami

Ag. Ermionii

Agia Mina

Liminas

Elata

Agios Fotinis

Kini

Kataraktis

Mesta

Scenic Villages

Armolia

Olymboi

Pyrgi

Kalamoti

Flatsia

Komi

Emborios

✈ → Athens ⑩ x 4
→ Thessalonika ③ ⑦ x 1
→ Lesbos ③ ⑦ x 1

0   km   4

the humans taking in the night air (this is one harbour where it can be quite potent). Commendable though this effort is, the waterfront just doesn't lend itself to romantic evening strolls (it is too smelly for one thing), and once the crowds have departed taxis and motor-bikes use it as a race track into the small hours, when they give way in turn to packs of stray dogs which chase each other along its length instead. All this is rather a pity because the town does have enough in it to justify a short visit once you get behind the grubby, down-at-heel feel of the place, thanks to a castle, a warren-streeted old quarter and several small museums.

Getting away is easy as most of the major villages on Chios are linked by the island bus services. Blue city buses — in their eagerness to escape the capital — run well beyond Chios town environs to cover the whole central portion of the island, while less consistent Green long distance buses (both start from their own terminals near the town park) serve the rest. Timetables for both services (and ferries) are provided by an official NTOG / EOT office on Kanari St. (a sidestreet off the north-east corner of the harbour).

Southern Chios has most to offer the tourist thanks to a series of scenic medieval fortress villages in the mastica-growing region. These settlements, known as the **'mastic villages'** (mastichoria), should be a must on the itinerary of anyone spending more than a day on Chios. Their numbers vary according to which local guidebook you happen to pick up, but the total is in the high teens. They share a number of common characteristics, with a line of houses built around their perimeter that doubled to form a defensive wall (the populations of the mastic villages were the only ones to escape alive in the 1822 destruction of Chios).

Protective watchtowers stand on any exposed corners along the wall, and the streets within adopt the Cycladic warren pattern, deliberately designed to confuse any enemy that managed to get in. In the centre of most of the villages is a well-protected church or tower that provided a final point of refuge. **Pyrgi** is the biggest and prettiest of these villages, and is noted for the whitewashed houses that adorn its streets and a main square that is over-painted with a wide variety of geometric blue patterns that extend even to the underside of the balconies. Nearby lies the smallest of the mastichoria, **Armolia** — a noted pottery production centre.

Mesta is also worth exploration, for although not as pretty as some, it retains more of its medieval buildings (including the largest church on the island) and with it, its old-world atmosphere. **Olymboi**, on the road between Pyrgi and Mesta, is in many ways the best preserved, with little building beyond its almost rectangular walls and a well-preserved central tower. It also has a port at **Liminas** that until a few years ago saw the odd ferry. Nowadays only the occasional tourist boat disturbs the waves.

To the west of Chios Town is one of the most northerly of the mastic villages at **Vessa**. Built on the side of a hill, it offers an easy half-day's excursion. While just to the south are a couple of other popular destinations: **Karfas** with its reasonable beach — now rapidly developing as the island's premier tourist resort — and the monastery of Agia Mina, site of another massacre by the Turks.

North of the town, buses run frequently to **Vrondatos** and the Daskalopetra or 'teaching rock', which tradition associates with Homer (Chios — an island without many ancient notables of its own — is yet another of those islands that claim him as a son). North of this resort the island is a quiet, tourist-free zone. The largest village is at **Kardamyla**, though it isn't much bigger than its equally rustic and undisturbed neighbours. Whitewashed Volissos on the west coast has more to offer, with remnants of a fortress and a pretty little harbour at **Limnos** with caïques to Psara.

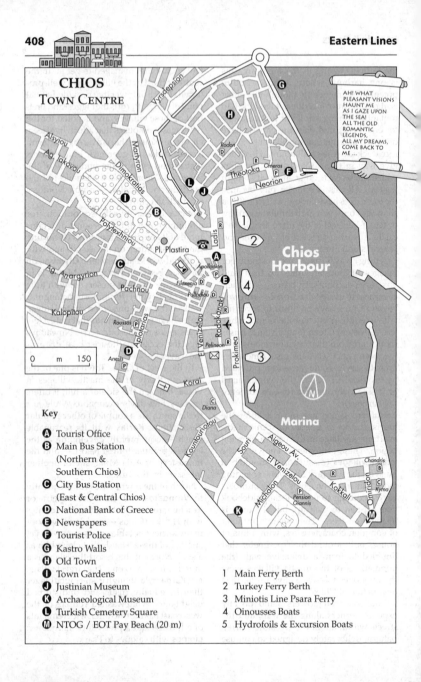

CHIOS
TOWN CENTRE

AH! WHAT
PLEASANT VISIONS
HAUNT ME
AS I GAZE UPON
THE SEA!
ALL THE OLD
ROMANTIC
LEGENDS,
ALL MY DREAMS,
COME BACK TO
ME ...

Chios
Harbour

Marina

0   m   150

Key

A Tourist Office
B Main Bus Station
    (Northern &
    Southern Chios)
C City Bus Station
    (East & Central Chios)
D National Bank of Greece
E Newspapers
F Tourist Police
G Kastro Walls
H Old Town
I Town Gardens
J Justinian Museum
K Archaeological Museum
L Turkish Cemetery Square
M NTOG / EOT Pay Beach (20 m)

1 Main Ferry Berth
2 Turkey Ferry Berth
3 Miniotis Line Psara Ferry
4 Oinousses Boats
5 Hydrofoils & Excursion Boats

◄

The lack of tourists means that accommodation options are adequate but not vast. Chios Town has the most beds, but in High Season finding an empty one come the evening can be a problem; ticket agencies will phone around for you. Best (and most expensive) hotel in town is the *Chandris* (☎ 25761), hiding in the street below the harbour. Nearby is the popular mansion *Kyma* (☎ 44500). The *Radon* (☎ 24335) in the old town also offers a quiet atmosphere and reasonable prices. Noisier, but clean, are the *Diana* (☎ 24656) and cheaper *Filoxenia* (☎ 22813). Rooms along the waterfront are popular and generally good value, though the best lie in the old town. Most of the towns also have hotels (Karfas being the best served, with five) along with a scatter of rooms in Pyrgi and Mesta.

A

Completely off the backpacker trail, Chios isn't well endowed with camping facilities. The only site is *Chios Camping* (☎ 74111) and this isn't up to much. An exposed, isolated beach site 14 km north of Chios Town, it is too remote to send a bus to meet ferries.

👓

Lacking any notable sites from the Classical, Hellenistic or Roman periods, the main attraction on Chios is an 11 c. **Byzantine Monastery** at **Nea Mona**, 15 km west of Chios Town. Carefully tucked away in the foothills, it is founded on the spot where shadowy myth says three passing hermits discovered an icon. Quite what three hermits were doing in each other's company in the first place isn't clear, nor is the picture of how they happened upon the icon any clearer. This remains an event more weird than wonderful. Be this as it may, the monastery thrived and is now home to some of the finest Byzantine frescoes and mosaics known. Many date from the monastery's foundation in 1042, though a fair number were lost in a damaging earthquake in 1881.

The monastery's charnel house is also home to a ghoulish display of skulls, tastefully arranged in glass-fronted bookcases. Victims of the 1822 massacre of the island's population by the Turks (who axed to death those members of the population who had sought refuge in the church, along with 600 monks), they stare at visitors in serried rows like a hungry crowd of evangelicals looking for converts. Another relic of Greek nationalism housed in

the monastery is a grandfatherish clock that was carried away by the Greek inhabitants of Smyrna (modern İzmir) when they fled the city in 1923. Note: the dial is melodramatically set to Constantinople time; so it doesn't do to check your wristwatches by it.

East of the monastery lies another popular sight: the abandoned cliff village of **Anavatos** whose inhabitants did a collective jump as the Turks approached (sightseeing on Chios is not for the squeamish).

Chios Town has a few sights worth hunting out, including the remains of the Genoese **Kastro** (1433) housing the **Turkish Quarter** to the north of the harbour. The only part of the town to survive the 1881 earthquake, it was badly damaged, but still boasts some impressive fortification walls and an impressive moat. Less inspiring are the **Archaeological Museum** and Cathedral. The town is also home to the **Justinian Museum** (devoted to church art). Those with more cash in hand can also splash out on a day-trip to Turkish **Çeşme** on the coast opposite.

Fourni

ΦOYPNOI; 37 km²; pop. 970.

CODE ☎ 22710
PORT POLICE ☎ 44433
POLICE ☎ 44427
FIRST AID ☎ 112

Fourni is the largest island in a small rocky archipelago lying between Ikaria, Samos and Patmos. If you are looking for something close to an unspoilt island, then look no further: for Fourni is one of the few genuine articles left in Greece. Formerly the home of Byzantine pirates, the island is quiet even in High Season, only recently emerging as a regular ferry destination and still lacking proper roads. Unfortunately, as word gets around, this is starting to change and Fourni now sees regular day boats from Ikaria dropping in to augment the tourists that seek it out.

The bulk of the population lives in the chora settlement of **Fourni**. Home to a large fishing fleet, Fourni is very much a working town: its waterfront is usually covered with mounds of yellow nets, and the well sup-

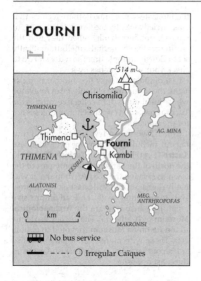

FOURNI

Chrisomilia

THIMENAKI

Thimena

Fourni

THIMENA

Kambi

AG. MINA

KESIRIA

ALATONISI

MEG.
ANTRHROPOFAS

0   km   4

MAKRONISI

🚌 No bus service

⚓ ----- ○ Irregular Caïques

plied fish tavernas behind stand cheek by jowl with a tiny ice factory (the production lines run from late afternoon). At the end of the harbour is a usable beach (the two combining to form the centre of town life). Littered with caïques all year round, the beach becomes a playground for the local kids in summer — offering an appealing change to the usual monotonous rows of tanning tourists encountered elsewhere.

The town itself is unusual without having tangible sights on offer (beyond the inevitable derelict windmills topping the hills ringing the port). The narrow, over-straight, mulberry tree-lined main street is an odd mix of quaint provincial Greece combined with a rare — for the islands at any rate — grid layout (this pattern gives way to the usual chaotic street arrangement once the land rises behind the main square). Most of the few facilities in town (bar the anonymous medical centre which is marked only by the presence of an ambulance parked outside) are located on either the main street or the rather bland square that lies at its end.

Thanks to a combination of inbreeding and eating excessive amounts of fish the — very friendly — locals are apt to be a bit eccentric at times. The Fourni versions of those notorious little old ladies in black have been known to jump fully clothed into the sea (black hat and all) in order to play with bathing kids (looking like something out of Roald Dahl's *The Witches* in the process).

It is also not uncommon to find parents feeding toddlers with bowls of runny white yuk while they walk along the town beach of an evening. If you like fish/shellfish then don't be put off by such exhibitions of madness, for fish lovers will find that Fourni is the next thing to paradise. Prices, however, are surprisingly high; with the island fleet sending most of its catch to Athens, the locals have come to accept city prices as normal. Even so, it is difficult to resist giving one's wallet a nip when confronted with a waterfront taverna bathed in the glow of the setting sun, its tables heaving with red lobsters (this, and the heaving toddlers on the beach, add up to a really colourful spectacle).

Emptier beaches lie to the north and south of the village if you are prepared to negotiate the rough tracks that run to them. The locals aren't terribly keen on island walking and prefer to take taxi caïques to the other villages on Fourni at Chrisomilia and Kambi. The second inhabited islet in the archipelago — **Thimena** (complete with one untouristed hillside hamlet) — is also visited by caïques, but strangers are not made over-welcome.

🚤

Fourni village is home to all the available accommodation. There are no hotels, but even in August you can be sure of being greeted with offers of rooms.

👓

Fourni has little sightseeing, bar the lidless **Hellenistic Sarcophagus** that stands in the town square acting as a litter bin, and a few blocks south of the town, at **Marmari** cove: a relic from the days when Fourni was used as a marble quarry for the city of Ephesus on the adjacent Turkish coast.

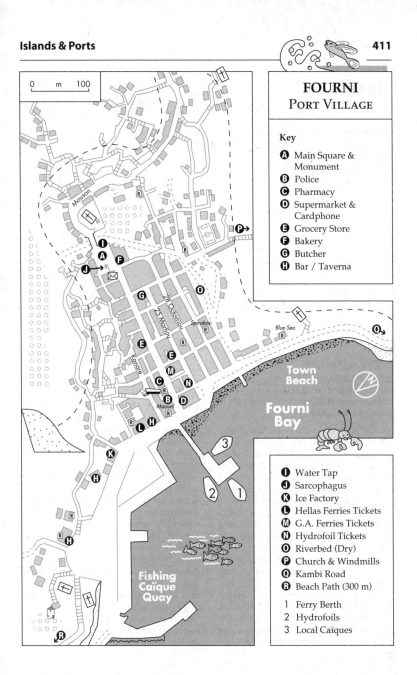

FOURNI
Port Village

Key

A Main Square & Monument
B Police
C Pharmacy
D Supermarket & Cardphone
E Grocery Store
F Bakery
G Butcher
H Bar / Taverna

O Water Tap
J Sarcophagus
K Ice Factory
L Hellas Ferries Tickets
M G.A. Ferries Tickets
N Hydrofoil Tickets
O Riverbed (Dry)
P Church & Windmills
Q Kambi Road
R Beach Path (300 m)

1 Ferry Berth
2 Hydrofoils
3 Local Caïques

0 m 100

Mouson

28 Oktovriou

25 Martiou

Kanare

Spirakos

Blue Sea

Maouni

Town Beach

Fourni Bay

Fishing Caïque Quay

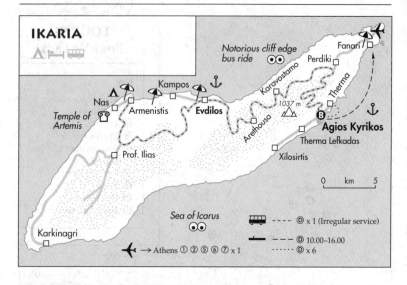

IKARIA

Notorious cliff edge bus ride ◉◉

Fanari

Perdiki

Kampos

Karavostamo

Therma

Nas

Armenistis

Evdilos

1037 m

Temple of Artemis

Arethousa

Agios Kyrikos

Therma Lefkadas

Prof. Ilias

Xilosirtis

0   km   5

Sea of Icarus ◉◉

🚌 ---- Ⓓ x 1 (Irregular service)

Karkinagri

—— --- Ⓓ 10.00–16.00

✈ → Athens ① ② ⑤ ⑥ ⑦ x 1

······ Ⓓ x 6

Ikaria

IKAPIA; 260 km²; pop. 9,500.

CODE ☎ 22750
TOURIST OFFICE ☎ 22222
PORT POLICE ☎ 22207
HOSPITAL ☎ 22330

Named after the unfortunate Icarus who fell and drowned (in the sea of the same name), after the wax holding the feathers to his man-made wings melted on flying too near the sun, wing-shaped Ikaria is a mountainous island with a thin covering of trees standing on the slopes like so many pins in a cushion. In fact, those who like the usual trappings of tourism will find that the view from the ferry is almost the most comfortable thing about the island.

Often used as a place of exile, Ikaria seems to lack a coherent sense of identity. With five changes of name in the last two thousand years, a three-month existence as an independent state in 1912 before union with Greece, a failed 19 c. spa resort (boasting thermal springs so radioactive that they had to be closed down), and more recently,

a freelance hippy colony on the northern coast monopolizing the best beaches, this is perhaps not too surprising. But it does leave the island with a decidedly faded air: the locals haven't got much and don't seem to expect much either. The few tourists who call are often left feeling much the same; though if you are prepared to grub around, with a bit of effort Ikaria offers an interesting and highly rewarding variation of the Greek island theme.

The main town of **Agios Kyrikos** lies on the south-east coast and the scanty remains of an ancient city. Most of the current buildings date from the 19 c. when the port expanded to serve the nearby spa resort at Therma. As a result, it hasn't developed much beyond a street or two behind the waterfront, and is filled with the cheaper and uglier type of old-style Aegean mansion house. The only quarter with any atmosphere lies north of the *Hotel Adam*: a warren of narrow streets filled with shoe shops.

On the plus side, the backstreets clambering up the hillside behind the boulder-strewn waterfront exude an air of quiet,

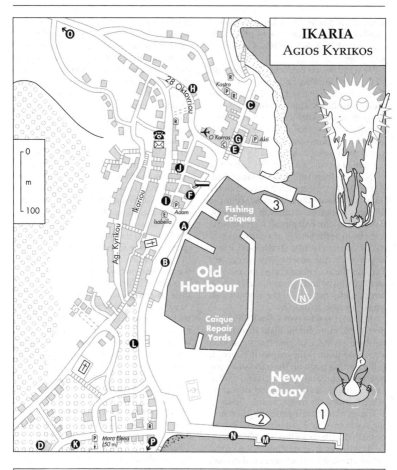

IKARIA
AGIOS KYRIKOS

Key

A Main Square
B Bus Stop
C Police Station
D Hospital
E Bank
F Newspapers

G Pharmacy
H Supermarket
I Bakery
J Pizzeria
K Rex Cinema
L Moped Rental
M Sculpture of Icarus

N Passenger Stalls
O Evdilos Road
P Xilosirtis Road

1 Ferry Berth
2 Hydrofoil Berth
3 Therma/Fourni Caïques

small town domesticity (Agios Kyrikos is another of those Greek towns filled with cats), and the whole town is well endowed with trees.

The waterfront is the focus of all life, with all the usual facilities and several tavernas doing their best to inject a (very) little bon-homie into things. This isn't due to any lack of spirit of the inhabitants, who are very friendly, it is just that Agios Kyrikos isn't geared up to any sort of tourism. Unless you have a fancy to visit nearby Therma (crammed around a narrow bay to the east of the town) there isn't much to see or do in Agios Kyrikos, except stroll along the ferry quay and admire the modernist sculpture of Icarus that greets all arrivals. Quite why the failed aviator is depicted caught in what appears to be the beak of an enormous bird isn't immediately clear. (Truth to tell, it isn't any clearer if you come back ten years later.) Perhaps the sculptor decided to spice the story up a bit by adding a mythical Halcyon bird, quietly nesting on the waves when Icarus decided to drop by.

Most tourists who visit Agios Kyrikos are doing little more, for the main attraction of the town is its role as the local transportation hub. In addition to the caïques to Fourni, it is the starting point for the only island bus link: a service that is very unreliable—often terminating at Evdilos — and departing when full rather than on schedule. Buses on Ikaria are a law unto themselves (the morning bus from Agios Kyrikos to Evdilos starts out at Evdilos because the driver lives there: he thus drives an empty bus to the capital before starting his working day; it doesn't seem to have occurred to anyone that he could carry the odd paying passenger as well). When you can get aboard, the bus provides excellent value for money thanks to a cliff-edge ride that will leave you with a vivid insight as to what Icarus saw and felt as he fell to sea.

At the end of the mountain road lies the more appealing north side of the island (home to pine forests, vineyards, and the island's best beaches). **Evdilos**, the bus's final destination, is Ikaria's second port. It offers an interesting example of the way tourism is changing the face of the islands. Until recently it was a pretty sad sort of place, being a village in decline and offering few facilities or temptations to linger. Today just enough tourists are passing through to encourage development without ruining the unspoilt cosy atmosphere, and it is now arguably the more attractive of Ikaria's ports.

Huddled around a small hilly bay, Evdilos offers a picturesque waterfront (albeit in a charmingly shabby sort of way) backed by a confetti of loosely scattered houses and churches on the green hills behind (most cling to the hill road that runs parallel to the harbour). The village has two centres: the first is on the headland near the ferry quay and is reached by an impressive, if rather steep, staircase; the second is around the old harbour where the waterfront is dominated by leafy tavernas that come into their charming own after dark.

Provided you aren't trying to exist on a backpacker's budget, then Evdilos could be a very attractive option. The two up-market hotels seem to thrive on the sort of holiday maker who would be comfortable on an island like Chalki, but who prefers to be surrounded by local islanders rather than fellow vacationers. In short, Evdilos is ideal for spooning lovers who want dreamy evenings in tavernas with lots of local colour. Those looking for nightlife and cheap accommodation will be disappointed.

Ferry links are surprisingly good for a second island port, and the quay is invariably lined with a fleet of taxis whenever a boat comes in. Most disembarking here are those in the know — heading for the wide sand beach at **Armenistis**, 15 km along the coast. The village on the headland beyond is now witness to the first signs of Ios-like disco and taverna development (though this is a bit misleading as the scale of the scene here is much smaller). Some 2 km further west lies the pretty hamlet of **Pappas** and the nearby archaeological site at

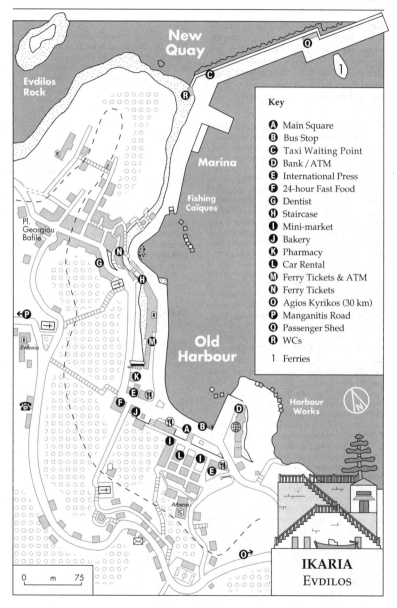

New
Quay

Evdilos
Rock

Marina

Fishing
Caïques

Pl.
Georgiou
Bafile

Old
Harbour

Harbour
Works

Key

- **A** Main Square
- **B** Bus Stop
- **C** Taxi Waiting Point
- **D** Bank / ATM
- **E** International Press
- **F** 24-hour Fast Food
- **G** Dentist
- **H** Staircase
- **I** Mini-market
- **J** Bakery
- **K** Pharmacy
- **L** Car Rental
- **M** Ferry Tickets & ATM
- **N** Ferry Tickets
- **O** Agios Kyrikos (30 km)
- **P** Manganitis Road
- **Q** Passenger Shed
- **R** WCs

1 Ferries

Evdoxia

Atheras

IKARIA
EVDILOS

0   m   75

Nas, after which roads degenerate into dirt tracks. From this point Ikaria is the preserve of walkers, and thus little visited. In past years rare ferries have made a taxi-boat rendezvous off the hill village of **Karkinagri**, providing a link with the outside world in lieu of a terrestrial means of access.

In antiquity Ikaria had something of an identity crisis, being variously known as Makris, Dolichi, and Doligi (all names derived from its oblong shape), and Ichthyoessa (derived from the plentiful fishing to be found hereabouts). The island was home to three major towns. The most important was at **Kampos** and called Oinoi. It lasted until the late Byzantine period. The second city of note was just east of Therma and also grew up around hot springs. It was swept into the sea by a landslide in the 1 C. BC. Both cities sided with Athens and then Macedon in the wider power struggles in Greece, before coming under the control of the kings of Pergamum. Decline followed and by the late Byzantine period Ikaria was used as a place of banishment for members of the imperial family. During the late Middle Ages the Genoese Arangi family ruled before the Turks took Ikaria in 1521. The island rebelled from Turkish rule in 1912, declaring the 'Free State of Ikaria', joining Greece later that year.

On the south coast gloomy **Therma** has a monopoly on faded up-market waterfront hotels, while **Agios Kyrikos** has a motley collection of cheaper establishments, including the B-class pension *Adam* (☎ 22418), the C-class *O Karras* (☎ 22494) and E-class hotel *Isabella* (☎ 22839) — all on the waterfront. More attractive is the pension *Kastro* (☎ 22474), which offers rooms overlooking the town.

Evdilos currently has two pricey hotels which are either B-class or expensive C-class according to which source you consult. The newer and better of the two is the *Atheras* (☎ 31434), which offers attractive singles starting at €45. The more expensive *Evdoxia* (☎ 31502) has lovely views over the port, but a horrible staircase every time you want to get to it. Rooms are generally scarce elsewhere on the island — though a few exist at Evdilos (arrive early), and there are a goodly number at **Armenistis**. There is also unofficial freelance camping at Armenistis and at Nas.

The only great archaeological site of interest on Ikaria is a **Temple of Artemis** at Nas, foundations of which survive along with remnants of the harbour. In the 19 C. a marble statue of the goddess Artemis was unearthed at the site but an enlightened priest put paid to the island's chances of making it as a major sightseeing destination by burning it in a lime kiln on the grounds that it was a pagan idol. The other archaeological site of note is a 3 C. BC **Hellenistic Tower** at Faros.

Agios Kyrikos sees frequent water taxis running to the ugly spa and hotel hamlet of Therma, 4 km from the town, a fair beach at **Fanari**, and more interesting daily High Season caïques to the Fourni archipelago. Waterfront signs pointing out the town museum (150 m south of the hospital) take you on a town walk to a long abandoned building.

On the west side of Agios Kyrikos lies a second, less popular spa village, at **Therma Lefkadas**, with the hamlet of **Xilosirtis** further down the road. After that the southern coast is little more than a steep mountainside falling into the sea.

Lesbos

ΛΕΣΒΟΣ; 1630 km²; pop. 104,600.

MYTILINI CODE ☎ 22510
NTOG TOURIST OFFICE ☎ 22776
PORT POLICE ☎ 28888
HOSPITAL ☎ 28457

The third largest Greek island, Lesbos (pronounced Les*vos*) is more popular with locals rather than with foreign holidaymakers (this latter category largely confined to those individuals who go everywhere, and sundry loving couples — usually female — searching out their feminist roots). Thanks to good olive oil and ouzo (the aniseedy national drink) brewing industries, the island is economically self-sufficient, with little need to develop tourism.

This is an island that will appeal most to those who don't want to be surrounded by other tourists and 'tourist' culture. Having your own wheels is also a help, given the limited nature of local bus services. These are inconveniently centred on the east coast capital of Mytilini, and infrequent into the

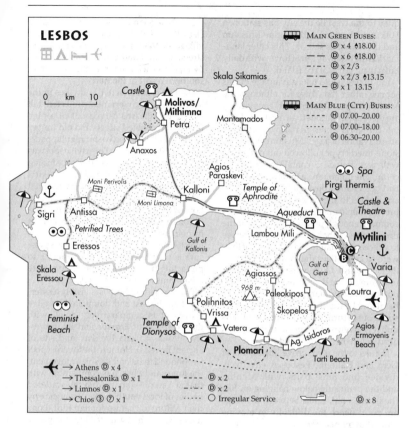

LESBOS

Main Green Buses:
— Ⓓ x 4 ♦18.00
— — Ⓓ x 6 ♦18.00
— · · — Ⓓ x 2/3
— · · — Ⓓ x 2/3 ♦13.15
— — — Ⓓ x 1 13.15

Main Blue (City) Buses:
— — — — Ⓗ 07.00–20.00
· · · · · Ⓗ 07.00–18.00
· · · · · · Ⓗ 06.30–20.00

0   km   10

Skala Sikamias

Castle
Molivos/
Mithimna
Petra
Mantamados
Anaxos

Moni Perivolis
Agios
Paraskevi
Kalloni
Temple of
Aphrodite

Sigri   Antissa
Moni Limona
Aqueduct

Petrified Trees   Lambou Mili
Eressos
Gulf of
Kallonis

Spa
Pirgi Thermis

Castle &
Theatre

Mytilini

Skala
Eressou
Gulf of
Gera
Varia

Agiassos
968 m
Paleokipos
Loutra

Feminist
Beach
Polihnitos
Vrissa
Skopelos

Temple of
Dionysos   Vatera
Ag. Isidoros
Agios
Ermoyenis
Beach

Plomari
Tarti Beach

✈ → Athens Ⓓ x 4
→ Thessalonika Ⓓ x 1
→ Limnos Ⓓ x 1
→ Chios ③ ⑦ x 1

— · — Ⓓ x 2
— · — Ⓓ x 2
· · · · · ○ Irregular Service
Ⓓ x 8

bargain, making quick movement around the island difficult without your own transport. Given that sights are spread inconveniently around Lesbos and that much of the stark landscape reflects the island's volcanic origins, it is perhaps not surprising that most short-stay island hoppers confine themselves to Mytilini and the lovely northern resort town of Mithimna/ Molivos. This is a pity because the west side of the island is much the best.

Mytilini, the island capital, is the destination for all ferries and is one of those ports which operators prefer to refer to

direct in preference to the island's name. At first sight very appealing, straddling a promontory adorned with an impressive castle and a busy harbour crowned with a prominent pineapple-domed church, this large town has a lot in common with other large Greek towns and cities in that it is dead to the world on Wednesday and Saturday afternoons and all of Sunday. The rest of the time it is very stimulating: a Greek island town full of friendly locals and no tourists.

All the facilities are within a Euro's throw of the inner harbour waterfront. Along the quay to the west lie the city bus station, a Folk Art Museum, a Byzantine Museum and the main bus station. This latter landmark is the best way out of town, with daily links to all parts of the island.

You may wish to take advantage of this sooner rather than later for although the Mytilini townsfolk are friendly enough they are more superstitious than most, and leapt into the world's press in 1994 when, during an excavation of a 19 c. Muslim cemetery, a stone-lined crypt hollowed out of the city wall was found to contain a vampire's coffin. The inhabitant, a middle-aged man, had been nailed through his neck, pelvis, and ankles to the casket base in order to prevent him from rising again. This was a common enough practice in Greece at the time (as was the habit of nailing horseshoes to a deceased's hands and feet so that if they were to go walkies the locals would hear them coming). Quite what this particular unfortunate had done to deserve his fate is not known. Rumour, probably malicious, has it that he was a misogynist who rashly spoke out of turn in a lesbian bar; but this is unlikely given that he appears to have been dead before he was nailed down.

Thanks to the olive-grove lined Gulfs of Gera and Kallonis, Lesbos is effectively divided into three parts, with Mytilini and the peninsula below hanging on like the island's tail. Links between the three are poor: hence the difficulty in moving around by public transport.

To date, the northern part of the island has been the focus of the tourist industry, thanks to the attractive castle-topped northern coast town of **Molivos** (officially known by its older name of **Mithimna**), 62 km from Mytilini. Once Mytilini's great rival for control of the island it has benefited immeasurably from losing out and not ending up the home of innumerable grimy 19 c. mansions. Instead, cobbled streets, a pebble beach and photogenic houses are the order of the day. The village of **Petra** 5 km to the south is also emerging as a resort thanks to its better beach.

The best island beaches, however, lie elsewhere. The surprisingly quiet resort village of **Vatera** has an amazing 7 km stretch of sand and can be reached direct by bus or beach boat from the indifferent southern resort of **Plomari**.

The bus route is better as it takes in the lovely old (and government protected) hill village of **Agiassos** carved out of a pine forest with cobbled streets and old timber houses, and the objective for regular package-tourist excursions. This idyllic spot was revealed in press reports in 1999 to be hiding a terrible secret, for on the village outskirts is an Orthodox church-run mental hospital where a number of patients (some formerly housed at Leros) are kept in appalling conditions (i.e. being tied to their beds and left in their own excrement, in filthy, cockroach-infested buildings). Fortunately, press pressure is now forcing the government into protecting the village's more unfortunate inhabitants as well as its buildings.

The west side of Lesbos is visibly less fertile than the east and dominated by olive groves. It is comparatively quiet, with the exception of **Eressos** and its impressive beach at Skala Eressou (and site of ancient Eressos). Home to the feminist poet Sappho and the island's lesbian movement, the long sandy beach is comparable with that at Vatera — apart from the scattered bodies of local youths driven to suicide by their failure to chat up foreign fluff. Lone males will do better to head for the pretty west-coast fishing village of **Sigri** — an ideal spot for quiet romance away from the crowds, and an infinitely more attractive place than the capital, and home to the occasional summer ferry service.

Both size and location have conspired to give Lesbos an important place in Aegean history. The island has always been a significant player in the region. Oligarchy was the preferred method of rule in antiquity, with Pittacus (one of the seven sages) numbered among its rulers. The island's proximity to Asia meant that it fell to the Persians in 527 BC, and was only freed in 479 BC, joining the Delian League.

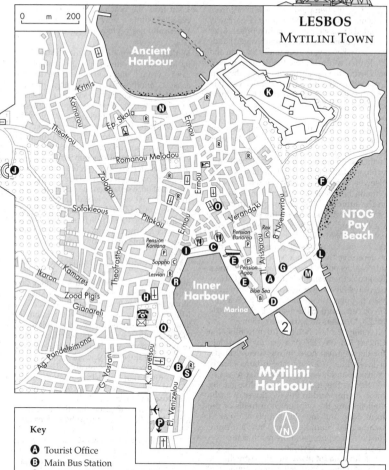

LESBOS
MYTILINI TOWN

0　m　200

Ancient Harbour

Krinis

Komarou

Theatrou

Ep. Skala

Romanou Melodou

Zalogou

Sofokleous

Pitakou

Ermou

Ermou

Theofrastou

Kamares

Ikaron

Zood Pigis

Gianareli

Ag. Pandeleimona

G. Yatani

Aq. Pandeleimona

K. Kavetsou

El. Venizelou

Verandaki

Pension Pariorea

Pension Kontana

Sappho

Lesvion

Rek

T. Aristarou

Noemvriou

Pension Agea

Blue Sea

Inner Harbour

Marina

Mytilini Harbour

NTOG Pay Beach

Castle

Statue of Liberty

Flea Market

Ferry Quay

Turkey Ferry

N

Key

Ⓐ Tourist Office
Ⓑ Main Bus Station
Ⓒ City Bus Station
Ⓓ Port Building / ATM
Ⓔ Ticket Agencies
Ⓕ Wooded Picnic Area
Ⓖ Old Archaeological Museum
Ⓗ Byzantine Museum / St. Theodore's Church

Ⓘ Art and Craft Museum
Ⓙ Ancient Theatre
Ⓚ Castle
Ⓛ Statue of Liberty
Ⓜ Swimming Pool
Ⓝ Flea Market
Ⓞ Cathedral

Ⓟ Hospital (500 m)
Ⓠ Taxi Station
Ⓡ International Press
Ⓢ Supermarket / ATM

1　Ferry Quay
2　Turkey Ferry

In 428 BC it attempted to break away from Athenian control; an act that only narrowly avoided a massacre by way of a reprisal. After the Peloponnesian War Lesbos changed hands regularly, being variously under Spartan and Ptolemian control before the Romans moved in. During the Byzantine era Lesbos became a place of exile, and was later under Venetian and then Genoese control. It fell to the Turks in 1462 and joined Greece in 1912.

⊨

A Tourist Police office lies just off the ferry quay offering accommodation details. Most of it is well away from **Mytilini Town**. In town (which is where you often need to be thanks to ferry departure times that prohibit sleeping elsewhere) options are more limited. Rooms offer the best value for money, but fill quickly in the summer. Most are on or near Ermou St., though the best lie on the south side of the harbour. The hotels are a pretty diverse collection. The B-class *Blue Sea* (☎ 23994) offers the prospect of an easy, if pricey, bed, but this is deceptive thanks to a 'strictly no riff-raff' admissions policy (note: if you are wearing a backpack then *you* are 'riff-raff'). The C-class *Sappho* (☎ 28888) is more accommodating, but very popular (phone ahead in High Season). If you can afford it, the nearby B-class *Lesvion* (☎ 22038) offers an attractive option.

Usually the last hotel in town to fill is the C-class *Rex* (☎ 28523): a leading candidate for the weirdest hotel in the Greek islands, it looks like a down-beat Addams Family mansion, and boasts hollowed mattresses so old that getting into bed is not unlike getting into a coffin. Add to this the cloves of garlic embellishing the wrought iron trellis of the front door, and the photograph of a naked two-headed Siamese infant boy adorning the hotel reception, and the result is the cheapest hotel in Mytilini.

In **Mithimna / Molivos** there is so much accommodation on offer that one is spoilt for choice. The tourist office near the bus stop can help find a bed, but it pays to check how far from the waterfront any bed is before you accept it. The town has B-class hotels in abundance and little else; these include the *Poseidon* (☎ 22530 71570) by the bus stop, and the *Sea Horse* (☎ 22530 71320).

A

Camping Mithimna (☎ 22610 71169): a reasonable site 2 km east of Mithimna,

1 km from the beach. *Camping Dionysos* (☎ 22520 61340) is a new site just inland from Vatera and has yet to really get going.

👓

Mytilini is dominated by the **Castle**, built in 1373 on the site of the old acropolis; it can be visited, but, overlooking the Turkish coast, is another of those photographically sensitive sites. Impressive views of the castle can, however, be gleaned from the hillside that is home to the bowl (sans seats) of the 3 C. BC **Hellenistic Theatre** that marked the edge of the ancient town. Mosaics found in excavations nearby are now residing in the good **Archaeological Museum** 50 m north-east of Mytilini's ferry quay. Other undoubted town sights are no longer extant. These include the canal that once separated the castle peninsula from the rest of the island (Ermou Street follows much of its former course) and the wacky looking tower (see illustration below) that once adorned the end of the — just visible — eastern mole of the now defunct northern harbour.

Elsewhere on the island the hamlet of Moria, 4 km outside Mytilini, has the impressive remains of a 3 C. AD **Roman Aqueduct** that watered Mytilini. Odd fragments survive along its 20 km length, notably at Lambou Mili. Some way beyond are the remains of Temples of Aphrodite and Dionysos. **Mithimna / Molivos** offers some of the best sightseeing on Lesbos courtesy of the 14 C. Genoese **Kastro** built on the site of the ancient acropolis, and the almost too picturesque cobbled and stone-house town that lies below. Finds from the ancient town (including sarcophagi) are in the **Museum** in the town hall.

The west side of Lesbos has the remains of a building alleged to be **Sappho's Home** and, on the road to Antissa, the curious remains of a **Petrified Forest** dated as being from one to twenty million years old. Several of the excavated old tar-coloured tree stumps have been set up like pillars from some very early Greek temple, and there is also a useful museum attached to the site. Finally, **Sigri** on the west coast has a very atmospheric 18 C. cannon-filled **Turkish Fortress**. Similar in design to the castle at Kos Town (see p. 355), it also stands on a promontory with a picturesque town on its landward side, and a quay on the seaward.

Oinousses

ΟΙΝΟΥΣΣΕΣ; 16 km²; pop. 420.

CODE ☎ 22720
POLICE ☎ 55222

Oinousses (also transcribed as 'Inousses')
is the collective name for a group of nine
tiny islands that lie off the north-east coast
of Chios. The only inhabited island — the
largest in the group — goes under the
same name and is ignored by all regular
ferry services.

Blessed with several good beaches, attractively clear seas and one large town that
feels more like a city suburb on the slide than
an island capital, Oinousses has the distinction of being the birthplace of several of
Greece's richest shipping owners. Summers
therefore see luxury yachts in the harbour,
their owners visiting luxury villas tucked
discreetly away in an otherwise attractive,
but declining, town. The strong seafaring
tradition hereabouts sees many of the men-
folk working away: the result is a curious
mix of affluence combined with boarded-
up summer holiday homes. For this reason
tourism is all but ignored as the remaining
islanders (many of whom work in fishing-
related industries) have enough coming in
to be able to resist the temptations to turn
their home into a resort island.

The most obvious consequence of all
this is that tourist facilities are scarce to
the point of being non-existent (beyond
the normal bank-cum-post office), and the
usual welcoming attitude typical of most
Greek islanders is thin on the ground if you
try to sleep on it (you will as likely as not
be rounded up by cadets from the island's
nautical school). Those that resort to the
only hotel fare somewhat better.

The town harbour likewise reflects the
absent nature of tourism: it is a bit bleak
with only one taverna — though it has a
lot of potential, with a veritable concertina
of small quays and a harbour protected by
three islets (one topped with a monastery
and another with a church). Given the lack
of accommodation, beaches and sights,

OINOUSSES

0   km   4

PASAS

Oinousses

MANDRAKI

🚌 No bus service

⛵ No beach boat service

the island is best visited on a day-tripper
boat basis (frequency varies according to
the time of year). In addition to visiting
Oinousses proper, these boats often also
stop at the privately owned harbour-mouth
church islet of **Mandraki**, 300 m from the
town quay.

⊨

No rooms, but a nice, if pricey, C-class hotel
in the town — the *Thalassoporos* (☎ 55475) —
usually has rooms available.

👓

Oinousses is relatively bereft of things to see
or do other than lie on the beach (the best are
in quiet coves to the west of the town).

The only attraction in town is a well-stocked
Maritime Museum filled with mementos
donated by local shipping millionaires. This
means that most visitors are reduced to doing
the coastal walk to the **Evangelismou Convent**
on the western tip of the island. Home to the
mummified corpse of a shipping billionaire's
daughter who snuffed it shortly after becoming
a nun, the monastery was rebuilt as a shrine
to her memory by her father (who has now
joined her in her mausoleum). The fact that her
body hadn't decomposed after its traditional
three-year stint underground (in Greece graves
are reused, so once the flesh has rotted the
bones of the deceased are usually interred
elsewhere) was taken as a (fortuitous — for
the monastery's finances at any rate) sign of
sainthood.

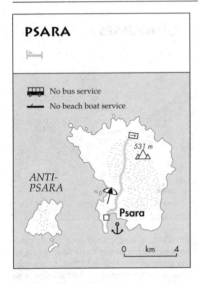

PSARA

🛏

🚌 No bus service

⚓ No beach boat service

531 m
🏔

*ANTI-
PSARA*

☂ **Psara**

⚓

0   km   4

Psara
ΨΑΡΑ; 45 km²; pop. 460.

CODE ☎ 22740

Barren and dusty Psara rarely figures on tourist itineraries and, ignored by most ferry operators, wallows quietly in the shadows of its own grim history. An obscure island in ancient times, it came to prominence (along with the Saronic islands of Hydra and Spetses) in the early 19 c., thanks to an indigenous fleet of merchant adventurers. Psara was thus well placed to play a prominent part in the early liberation struggle of the independent Greek state, but — lying just off the Turkish mainland — very badly placed when it came to avoiding the wrath of the Turks that came after. By way of setting an example to would-be rebellious islands the Turks laid waste to the island in 1824, killing the bulk of the population (inflated by refugees from other islands) of 20,000 (3,000 escaping by boat to found a town on Evia: Nea Psara). Psara has never really recovered from the event the Greeks call the 'holocaust'. Some survivors drifted back; the island has never prospered. Almost all live in the only town of **Psara**. Traversing a headland on the south coast, it is hardly the typical island town. Photographs suggest that it is quite developed, but the reality is rather different. With few made-up roads and not much in the way of shops, the town feels like an undeveloped version of Lipsi. Town buildings — which for the most part are gloriously undistinguished — are pretty scattered, as there is no pressure on space. Most of the town life — such as it is; for the settlement feels like one large suburb — centres on the waterfront square which is home to one bar, a couple of shady trees and a memorial adorned with miniature cannon. A gun-manned bastion of sorts has also been built on the northern headland of the caïque harbour which is also home to a couple of tavernas. On the plus side the typical 'family' small island atmosphere pervades, and there are a reasonable number of American-English speakers in the streets thanks to expatriates returning 'home' each summer.

The rest of the island is barren and has little to offer apart from walks to distant windmills or empty beaches (sadly, most are poor quality: the best lie along the road to the north-east of the town) and an 18 c. monastery on the north side of the island.

🛏

The thin supply of beds on the island are dominated by a prison converted to a hotel by the EOT, the B-class *Miramare* on the north side of town, and the *Xenonas Pension* (☎ 612 93). There are also a few rooms.

👓

Sightseeing on Psara is thin on the ground. The Turks took a lot of trouble to ensure that there was nothing left to look at, totally demolishing the castle that stood on the headland still known as **Paleokastro**. Now topped by a couple of chapels it offers sun-baked views across to Antipsara but little more. A few ruinous pre-holocaust buildings survive, and there is a small museum on the outskirts of town that is usually closed.

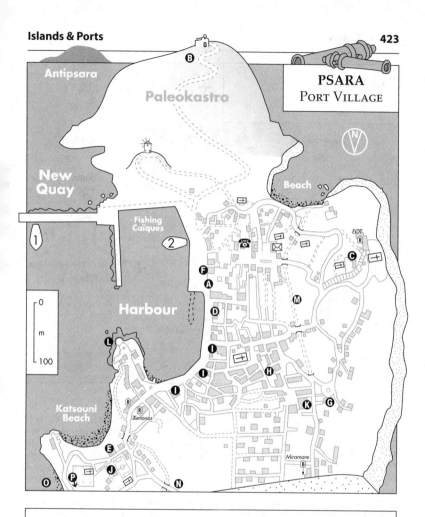

PSARA
PORT VILLAGE

Antipsara

Paleokastro

New
Quay

Beach

EOT

Fishing
Caïques

Harbour

Katsouni
Beach

Xerionas

Miramare

Key

- **A** Town Square
- **B** Site of Venetian Kastro
- **C** Police
- **D** National Bank of Greece
- **E** Museum
- **F** Main Square Bar &
  Ferry Tickets
- **G** Supermarket
- **H** Bakery
- **I** Tavernas
- **J** School
- **K** Old Water Wells
- **L** Cannon Memorial
- **M** Ravine (dry in summer)
- **N** Village Ring Road
- **O** Lazoreta Beach
- **P** Dirt Track to
  Lakka Beach &
  Limnos Beach

1 Ferry Berth
2 Berth for (rare)
  Excursion Caïques

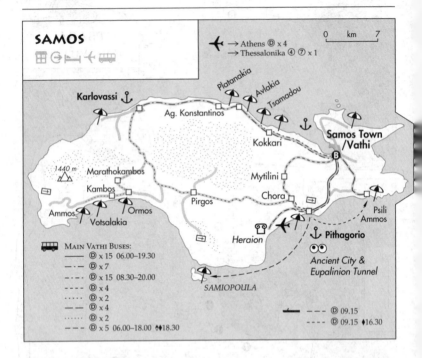

Samos
ΣΑΜΟΣ; 472 km²; pop. 41,500.

CODE ☎ 22730
TOURIST OFFICE ☎ 28530
PORT POLICE ☎ 27318
HOSPITAL ☎ 27407

A large island just to the north of the Dodecanese, mountainous Samos (the name is thought to derive from the Phoenician word for 'high') is known for its tree-clad slopes (though a series of devastating fires in July 2000 destroyed 50% of its tree cover), a scattering of reasonable beaches, and top end of the package tourist market. Island hoppers are not noted for visiting in large numbers.

Thanks to its large size, Samos boasts three modern centres with ferry connections. The most important of these is **Samos Town** (or

Vathi as it appears on all timetables). The modern island capital, it is easily the biggest town on Samos (bus timetables simply refer to it as 'Samos'). It consists of a wide ribbon of houses, four or five blocks deep, that winds around a horseshoe-shaped bay, with steep, wooded hills climbing quickly up behind. Like all large towns in this part of the Aegean, the waterfront is adorned with commercial, 19 c. buildings in the neo-classical style, many topped with red-tile roofs. If you venture here by way of Pithagorio the hillside views over the town are superb, with the vivid mix of blue seas, red roofs and green hills.

This all adds up to a pretty and attractive picture, but Vathi somehow lacks charm once you descend to street level: it is too big, and once you delve beyond the waterfront the backstreets prove to be rather drab and dingy affairs. The overall feel of Vathi is much more akin to that of a mainland town, and one without much tourist activity at that. This feeling is reinforced by the fact that the whole place shuts down on Sundays and Wednesday afternoons (tourist towns on most other islands all but ignore mainland conventions such as this).

This is not to say that Vathi is a place to be avoided. The pluses certainly are there when you look for them: Vathi has a small but excellent Archaeological Museum, a diminutive shady park, and a number of good tavernas in the street one block behind the ferry side of the harbour (avoid the poor affairs on the waterfront itself). The most attractive part of Vathi climbs up the windmill-topped hill to the south of the harbour; called Old Vathi, it is the pre-19 c. heart of the town.

Vathi isn't noted for its beaches, but a number of fine pebble strands lie an easy bus ride away along the coast. The most developed of these is at **Kokkari**, which has evolved into the largest north-coast tourist resort. Further west are quieter, but attractive, options at **Tsamadou**, **Avlakia** and **Platanakia**; all are pebble, but are fringed with pine woods and the coast road. Though the latter feel remote, they are easily visited via the hourly Vathi—Karlovassi buses which stop at all of them.

Thanks to its role as the hub of the bus system, Vathi is the best base if you want to explore the island by public transport. It also dominates ferry activity and as a result ends up on the itineraries of most island hoppers who venture into the Eastern Aegean. It is the terminus for all Piraeus—Ikaria—Samos ferries, with invaluable linking services on to Chios, Turkey, and the well-preserved ancient Greek city of Ephesus, is also a popular hop away from here.

As usual in this part of the world political tensions are evident: the Port Police are very sensitive when Turkish boats are in, and are quick to shepherd interested spectators away from them. Sleeping on the ferry quay is also a non-starter thanks to the attentions of mice and men (or in Vathi's case rats and policemen).

The second of the island's ports is commercial **Karlovassi**. Only 50 minutes from Vathi by bus, it is sited on the north-west coast, an hour's steaming closer to Piraeus. This port had its heyday during the late 19 c. when boats were slower and it formed the nearest convenient link with the mainland. Even today most Vathi-bound ferries call en route. It might thus sound an attractive option if you don't want to spend more time than you can help on a ferry, but you are best advised to give Karlovassi a miss: this place is best summed up as 'positively dire'. At first sight it looks pleasant enough: the ferry harbour (tucked neatly behind a wooded hillock 1 km west of the town) is actually quite cosy, with a couple of tavernas and several reasonable hotels, but Karlovassi proper is awful. The waterfront is all but derelict, with run-down 19 c. neo-classical warehouses giving way to a drab concrete-built town beyond. The all-important bus stop is 2 km from the port in the tiny old chora part of town.

One of Karlovassi's few plus points is that it is the jumping-off point for the south-west coast (though Vathi and Pithagorio are equally good if you don't mind longer journey times). This is in many ways the most attractive part of Samos, being an appealing mix of taverna-lined beaches and fishing villages that form a relaxed and unexploited backwater. **Votsalakia** and **Ammos** beaches are easily the best and usually quiet, even in High Season.

The third Samian port of **Pithagorio** on the south coast offers a complete contrast to the northern ports. Now the centre of the island's tourist industry, it has a very attractive atmosphere and the bulk of the island sights, but bar a few tourist boats and a daily summer hydrofoil (most heading for Patmos) it is poorly connected with the ferry network, with only a couple of regular departures each week. The modern town lies directly over the ancient capital of

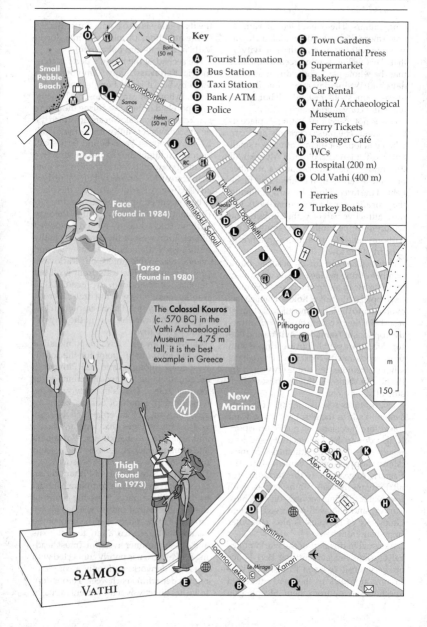

Key

- **A** Tourist Infomation
- **B** Bus Station
- **C** Taxi Station
- **D** Bank / ATM
- **E** Police
- **F** Town Gardens
- **G** International Press
- **H** Supermarket
- **I** Bakery
- **J** Car Rental
- **K** Vathi / Archaeological Museum
- **L** Ferry Tickets
- **M** Passenger Café
- **N** WCs
- **O** Hospital (200 m)
- **P** Old Vathi (400 m)
- **1** Ferries
- **2** Turkey Boats

Small Pebble Beach

Koundourioti

Boni (50 m)

Samos

Helen (50 m)

Port

1

2

Face (found in 1984)

Torso (found in 1980)

Themistokli Sofouli

Likourgou Logotheti

Avli

Aeolis

The **Colossal Kouros** (c. 570 BC) in the Vathi Archaeological Museum — 4.75 m tall, it is the best example in Greece

Thigh (found in 1973)

New Marina

N

Pl. Pithagora

0

m

150

Alex. Pashali

Smirnis

Ioannou Lekati

Le Mirage

Kanari

SAMOS
VATHI

the island. Known at the time as 'Samos', it is not to be confused with the modern capital with that name on the north coast. In fact, Pithagorio has changed names several times, and the current name only dates back to 1953 when the town was re-christened in honour of the island's most famous son: the mathematician Pythagoras (from the Middle Ages until 1953 the town was called Tigani).

Despite the numbers of package tourists in town (hotel development along this coast has been extensive thanks to the large number of good sand beaches), Pithagorio manages to retain a surprisingly dreamy air, with a snug taverna- and tree-lined small harbour backed by red-roofed town behind. Unfortunately, all this means that the town is expensive — a reflection of the top-island-resort status it enjoys. This is set to get worse now that a huge new yachting marina has been built in the bay just east of the town. Tourism has at least ensured the existence of regular taxi boats to Psili Ammos beach as well as to **Samiopoula** islet (visiting a north-side beach and taverna).

Samos was one of the most important islands in ancient Greece, and particularly noted as a centre of learning. This reputation was derived from her most famous sons, notably Aesop (of fable fame), Pythagoras, Epicurus, Aristarchus (the astronomer who worked out that the earth revolved around the sun), and the navigator Kolaios — the Columbus of the ancient world — who dared to sail a ship through the Pillars of Hercules in 650 BC. Politically the island was rather unstable, with the ruling aristocracy producing a series of tyrants, the most famous being Polykrates, who came to power in 540 BC. Following his capture and execution by the mainland-ruling Persians the island lost effective independence. Samos fought on the Persian side at the Battle of Salamis, but changed sides soon after.

The island was later part of the Delian League and stayed loyal to Athens during the Peloponnesian War. It did, however, change hands several times, and had its entire population replaced by Athenian colonists in 365 BC (the original inhabitants returned in 321 BC). Samos was later ruled by the Ptolemies of Egypt, before coming under Roman control in 129 BC. Thereafter decline set in; the island was subject to repeated pillaging from 82 BC

Exhibits

1. Early Statue Torsos
2. Later Statue Torsos
3. Geneleos Family Group
4. Kouroi Fragments
5. Colossal Kouros
6. Fragments of second Colossal Kouros
7. Hellenistic Statues
8. Pottery Room (no labels!)
9. Heraion Small Finds Room
10. Wooden Exhibits
11. Gold Coins and Pot
12. Bronze Room
13. Ivory & Painted Vases

NEW BUILDING

Ticket Check

Upper Floor

Lower Floor

Offices

Tickets

Entrance

OLD BUILDING

SAMOS
VATHI MUSEUM

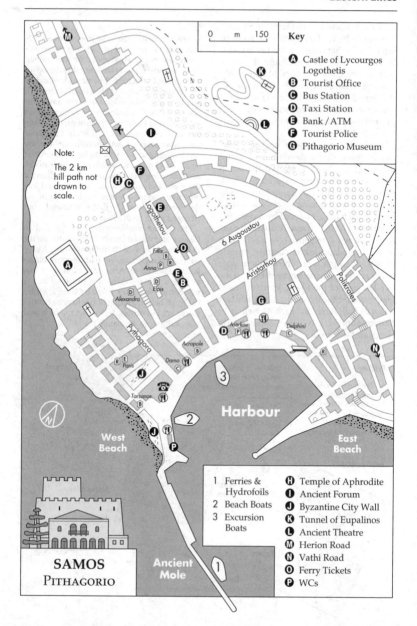

Key

- **A** Castle of Lycourgos Logothetis
- **B** Tourist Office
- **C** Bus Station
- **D** Taxi Station
- **E** Bank / ATM
- **F** Tourist Police
- **G** Pithagorio Museum

Note:

The 2 km hill path not drawn to scale.

1 Ferries & Hydrofoils
2 Beach Boats
3 Excursion Boats

- **H** Temple of Aphrodite
- **I** Ancient Forum
- **J** Byzantine City Wall
- **K** Tunnel of Eupalinos
- **L** Ancient Theatre
- **M** Herion Road
- **N** Vathi Road
- **O** Ferry Tickets
- **P** WCs

SAMOS
PITHAGORIO

Harbour

West Beach

East Beach

Ancient Mole

on (the raiders even included Anthony and Cleopatra who stopped off in 39 BC and made off with everything of value that could be moved). During the Byzantine period Samos was in steady decline. After the island was conquered by the Turks in 1473 it was forcibly depopulated, and remained so for some two hundred years. The recolonized island finally achieved union with Greece in 1912.

ᴴ

Budget accommodation is thin on the ground in the popular towns, and there is no camping. As a result Samos can be a tricky island on which to find a reasonably priced bed in August: at this time of the year it pays to phone ahead. Ticket agencies have lists of accommodation, as do the Tourist Police.

Vathi has a reasonable supply of accommodation. The waterfront has a number of hotels including the well-placed *Aeolis* (☎ 28904), and the very well maintained C-class *Samos* (☎ 28377), which has pricey but good value rooms (prices are advertised on a board outside). Nearer the budget end of the range is the pension *Avli* (☎ 22939) in a former convent school when 'nun' but the cheapest will do.

Pithagorio has a tourist office/booth just off the main street with accommodation information. The quayside has a number of pricey but justifiably popular hotels hidden behind the tavernas, including the B-class hotel/pensions *Tarsanas* (☎ 61162) just off the ferry quay, and the *Acropole* (☎ 61261), along with the almost as pricey C-class *Damo* (☎ 61303) and *Delphini* (☎ 61205). The streets behind offer the prospect of better hunting. On the main street is the B-class *Fillis* (☎ 61296) and behind, the budget D-class *Alexandra* (☎ 61429) and E-class *Paris* (☎ 61513). These are augmented by several minor pensions and a limited number of rooms.

Karlovassi is such an ugly place finding a bed is rarely a problem. Cheapest option is a Youth Hostel behind the large Panagia Church, but there are hotels in town. At the bottom end are the D-class *Morpheus* (☎ 32672), the *Astir* (☎ 33150) and, outside the town, the *Aktaeon* (☎ 32356) on the port road.

ᴼᴼ

Given that Samos was one of the better-endowed islands with monuments in ancient times, the extant remains are something of a disappointment: much has gone and the remainder can comfortably be taken in during the course of an extended day trip to the island.

The only sightseeing of note at Vathi is the town's **Archaeological Museum** (plan on p. 427; open ® ex ① 08.30–15.00; tickets are €3). This isn't the largest museum in the islands by any means, but it is one of the most interesting as it houses all the finds from the on going excavations at the Heraion (see overleaf). It has had an extension built to house the more recent discoveries. Not least among these is the **Colossal Kouros**, which was one of a pair that stood on the sacred way. Originally painted in gaudy colours, it is now admired for the rippling veins in its marble. Other star exhibits include the **Geneleos Family** statues, a collection of bronze griffin heads, and very rare fragments of wooden Hellenistic furniture preserved by the Heraion site's marshy soil.

Pithagorio is the sightseeing town on Samos, though at first sight this might seem rather surprising as there doesn't initially appear to be much to see beyond the exhibits in its **Archaeological Museum**. In fact during the 6 c. BC the tyrant Polykrates left a series of monumental works here. No doubt it was a considerable source of satisfaction to him when, crucified (by the Persians in 522 BC) on the Turkish coast opposite the town, he hung around and surveyed the wondrous constructions he had commissioned. All survive — in various states of repair — today. These include the **Temple of Hera** (usually known as the **Heraion** and described overleaf) and the best preserved of the Polykratic monuments, the **harbour mole** (now the ferry quay); most tourists walk its length without knowing it to be any different from quays the islands over. The quay reflects the fact that Pithagorio hides all but scant remains of the ancient city. Beyond odd collections of stones and the foundations of some Hellenistic houses behind the **Castle of Legothetis** (built in 1824 by a hero of the independence movement) only the ruinous **Theatre** and **City Walls** skirting the tops of the hills behind give a hint as to what was here before.

The oddest of the Polykratic monuments is well hidden (though signposts around the town give the game away today): the 1034 m **Tunnel of Eupalinos** (named after its architect and completed in 524 BC), hewn through the mountain, was designed to guarantee water supplies to the city as well as offering a means of escape. The first claustrophobic 70 m is open to the public ® ex ① 9.00–14.00; the entrance fee is €1.50.

The Heraion

Lying 9 km west of the ancient capital of Samos at Pithagorio is the massive **Temple of Hera** — more usually known as the **Heraion**. Open ②–⑥ 08.30–15.00; the entrance fee is €3. Although it is the main sightseeing attraction on Samos, the Heraion is more likely to appeal to archaeology fans than casual visitors, the remains consisting of foundations and a single incomplete column that is now the island's totem. All of the major finds are in the Vathi Museum as there isn't one on site.

One of the most unusual things about the Heraion is the site itself: for at first sight this major shrine is bizarrely set in an anonymous field that has nothing of the grandeur of an Acropolis to enhance it (a characteristic also shared by the site of the Great Temple of Artemis on the nearby Turkish coast). This apparent whimsy on the part of the ancients becomes clear when one appreciates that temples were usually surrounded by groves of trees and gardens (a fact now lost on most modern visitors to what are usually dry, dusty, treeless excavation sites), and these factors came to the fore in the siting of the Heraion.

Placed on the banks of the Imbrasos stream in a meadow of lygos trees (a variety of willow) that was believed to be the birthplace of the queen goddess Hera, its location so far out of town makes more sense once one remembers that ancient temples were not the equivalent of the modern church or mosque but were more akin to glorious hotels, built as a private residence for the god or goddess when they happened to be in the neighbourhood (the theory being that the better the temple, the better the chance that the patron deity would be tempted to visit and then stay). Worship generally took place at nearby altars.

Easily the most impressive feature on the site is the surviving column of ❹ the **Heraion** or **Temple of Hera**. A famous building, it had the odd role of being the eighth of the seven wonders of the world (getting into later lists that excluded Babylon). The structure extant today was the fourth temple on the site. Four times the size of the Parthenon in Athens, it had 3 x 8 30 m columns at its east end, 3 x 9 along the west and 24 x 2 down each side; it was begun in the 6 c. BC, but never finished, though the Romans added steps along the east front. The massive temple was really like a roofed bed of nails: a mass of columns reflecting the

concreteless Archaic Greeks' inability to solve the problem of bridging large internal spaces. The three temples that preceded it stood more to the east, the first recently surrendering the claim to be the oldest known temple built with columns at each end and down its sides. Like the later second temple it was small: the third temple built in the 6 c. BC by Rhoikos was the first Great Temple on the site. Destroyed by fire c. 525 BC after standing for only 25 years, its extant successor was built by Polykrates.

Alongside the Heraion other buildings were erected, notably ❸ the **Temple of Aphrodite** or **Hermes**, and ❻ the now invisible **South Stoa**, now vaguely marked by ❼ the base of the **Ciceros Monument** (2 C. AD), home to statues of the Roman orator Cicero and his brother Quintus. To the east stands an enigmatic group of stones that are thought to be the **Kolaios Ship Base** ❺ on which stood the first ship to sail on the Atlantic (it was viewed by the ancients with all the awe of an Apollo space capsule).

The area in front of the Heraion was the religious hot spot on the site. Originally the area was a paved square bounded by ❻ the **Rhoikos Altar** (6 c. BC) which was built on the site of an ancient **Lygos Tree Shrine**. The later Romans in-filled, adding ❻ a **Temple** (on the site of the earlier Heraion temples), ❿ the **Monopteros Altar / Temple**, ❶ a second **Temple** (2 C. AD) along with ❷ a tiny **Bathhouse**. In the early Christian era a **Basilica** ⓚ was also constructed.

The area to the north of the Heraion has revealed traces of several structures including ❶ a **Mycenaean Tholos Tomb** and ⓜ the **North Stoa**. This is the site of the earliest known example of this uniquely Greek form of architecture. Originally a wooden structure, it was replaced in stone in the Hellenistic period. A small town grew up to the east of it and several ⓝ **Hellenistic Houses** have been excavated. Temples, however, lined the sanctuary precinct: the foundations of two, ⓞ **Temple A** and ❷ a **Temple of Aphrodite**, are still extant. Nearby lie the foundations of an Archaic shrine with ⓠ the base of the **Genelos Statue Group**. Copies of several of the statues have been erected on the base. The originals are the only survivals from the 2000 statues that graced ⓡ the **Sacred Way**, the paved road running from the Heraion to Pithagorio, and now irreparably damaged by the island airport runway which bisects it.

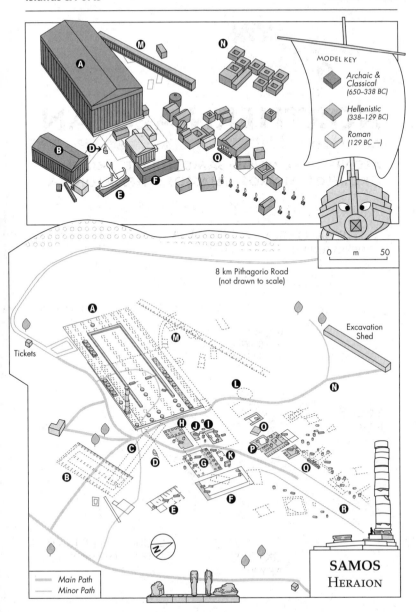

MODEL KEY

Archaic &
Classical
(650–338 BC)

Hellenistic
(338–129 BC)

Roman
(129 BC —)

0   m   50

8 km Pithagorio Road
(not drawn to scale)

Tickets

Excavation
Shed

SAMOS
HERAION

Main Path
Minor Path

9

NORTHERN AEGEAN

**ALONISSOS · LIMNOS · SAMOTHRACE · SKIATHOS
SKOPELOS · SKYROS · THASSOS · THESSALONIKA**

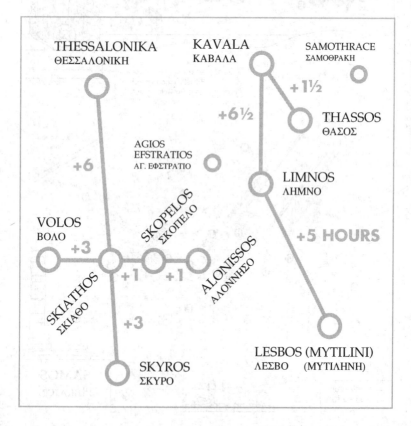

THESSALONIKA
ΘΕΣΣΑΛΟΝΙΚΗ

KAVALA
ΚΑΒΑΛΑ

SAMOTHRACE
ΣΑΜΟΘΡΑΚΗ

+1½

+6½

THASSOS
ΘΑΣΟΣ

AGIOS
EFSTRATIOS
ΑΓ. ΕΦΣΤΡΑΤΙΟ

+6

LIMNOS
ΛΗΜΝΟ

VOLOS
ΒΟΛΟ

SKOPELOS
ΣΚΟΠΕΛΟ

+5 HOURS

+3

+1   +1

ALONISSOS
ΑΛΟΝΝΗΣΟ

SKIATHOS
ΣΚΙΑΘΟ

+3

SKYROS
ΣΚΥΡΟ

LESBOS (MYTILINI)
ΛΕΣΒΟ   (ΜΥΤΙΛΗΝΗ)

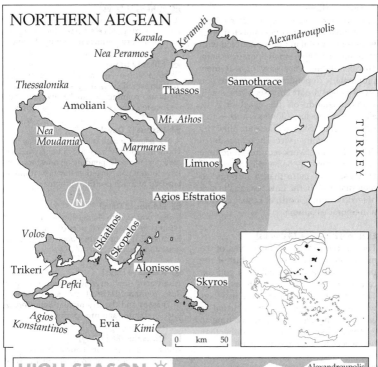

NORTHERN AEGEAN

Kavala · *Keramoti* · *Alexandroupolis*

Nea Peramos

Thessalonika

Thassos · Samothrace

Amoliani · *Mt. Athos*

Nea Moudania · *Marmaras*

Limnos

Agios Efstratios

Volos · Skiathos · Skopelos

Trikeri · Alonissos

Pefki · Skyros

Agios Konstantinos · Evia · Kimi

TURKEY

0   km   50

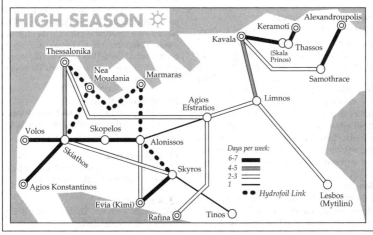

HIGH SEASON ☀

Alexandroupolis

Keramoti

Kavala · Thassos

(Skala Prinos)

Samothrace

Thessalonika

Nea Moudania · Marmaras

Agios Efstratios · Limnos

Volos · Skopelos

Skiathos · Alonissos

Agios Konstantinos

Skyros

Days per week:
6-7
4-5
2-3
1
●●● *Hydrofoil Link*

Evia (Kimi)

Rafina · Tinos

Lesbos (Mytilini)

General Features

The Northern Aegean is characterized by a combination of poorly connected large islands and mainland ports, coupled with an easily accessible small Sporades chain. Travel is either very easy or extremely problematic depending upon where you are. The 'easy' part consists of the small, wooded islands off the coast of Evia: Skiathos, Skopelos, Alonissos and — to a lesser extent — Skyros. These are linked by a good hydrofoil service. The remainder of the northern network requires more time and really can only be happily negotiated by those with more than a fortnight at their disposal. In the Low Season the lack of ferries running north of Lesbos curtails non-Sporades options.

Example Itinerary [3 Weeks]

The Northern Aegean offers some of the nicest Greek island hopping, but at the price of a loss of flexibility as you are constrained by the few boats available. This itinerary has been achieved in 8 days with a lot of luck. It is more usual to encounter delays, and allowing time to explore, you should allow three rather than two weeks to complete the circuit.

Arrival/Departure Point

There are charter flight airports at three points on the circuit: Athens, Kavala and Thessalonika and you can happily operate from any of them. Athens is the best should you need to get back in a rush, with daily bus or boat connections. Similarly, as you are visiting poorly connected ports it is better to travel anti-clockwise as the latter destinations all have easy ferry links to the mainland and bus links to the capital, reducing any danger of finding yourself caught out and missing a flight home.

Season

July and August only: the months either side see reduced services sinking away to all but nothing in the Low Season.

1 Athens [3 Days]
An easy starting point with access to NTOG ferry departure sheets from which you can deduce departure times further up the line.

2 Chios [2 Days]
Worth a stop-over, Chios has a lot to offer. You can establish in Athens when subsequent boats are running down the line and thus deduce the times of Chios—Lesbos ferries.

3 Lesbos [2 Days]
A nice island, which is just as well given that you will probably have to wait a day or two for a boat north. Depending on how long you have to wait you can either stay in Mytilini or head up to much prettier Mithyma.

4 Limnos [2 Days]
Unless you have to change here you can treat Limnos as an optional port of call that can be missed if your Lesbos boat north leaves you running late.

5 Kavala [4 Days]
An attractive town in which to rest up for a few days. You should take advantage of the ferries to **Thassos** and the less regular **Samothrace** boat — stamina and time permitting.

6 Thessalonika [1 Day]
Athens buses run every hour from Kavala so you can run across at your leisure and pick up either hydrofoil or ferry to Skiathos. This is one of the weak connections in the chain as weekend services out of Thessalonika can be booked solid. Should this happen you can take a train to Volos and then a Skiathos-bound hydrofoil or ferry from there.

7 Skiathos [3 Days]
Another nice resting point with good Athens links if the need arises via Volos. Even so, try to find time to continue on to Skyros.

8 Skyros [2 Days]
The final island in the loop with ferry links with Kimi and the waiting bus to Athens.

1 Athens [2 Days]
Arrive back with two days to spare if you have a flight pre-booked.

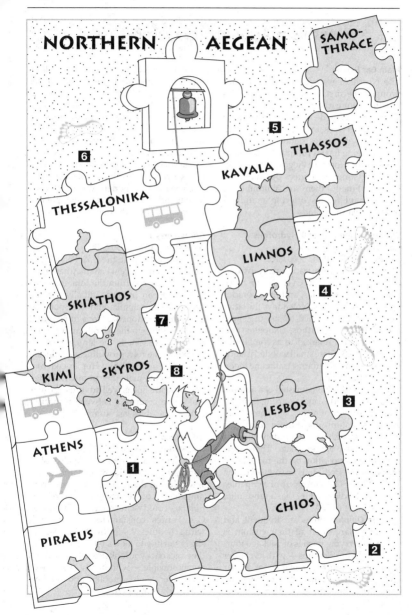

Northern Aegean Ferry Services

Main Car Ferries

The North Aegean ferries fall into four groups. The first is composed of ferries bustling along the small Sporades line. The second is made up of ferries running summer services from Thessalonika to Crete via the Cyclades islands. The third are wide-ranging ferries running to mainland ports in the Northern Aegean (the majority being summer services operating via Lesbos). Finally, there are a number of shorter-haul ferries offering mainland links to adjacent islands.

Sporades Line Ferries & Hydrofoils
Hellas Ferries / HFD;
Express Haroulla; 1994; 5000 GRT.

The Greek islands are traditionally divided into two groups: the Cyclades or those islands 'circling' Delos, and the Sporades or 'scattered' islands. Nowadays the latter term is usually applied to just the small archipelago of Skiathos, Skopelos and Alonissos (also referred to as the Northern Sporades). These small wooded islands attract considerable tourist traffic and therefore ferry activity.

In the past this has consisted of a number of small car-ferries, most starting from the mainland town of Volos, but some from Agios Konstantinos. But in 2003 this changed as services were consolidated between three larger boats. There now is no true competition on the route as all the boats and hydrofoils are owned by the Hellas Flying Dolphin group of companies or their subsidiaries (HFD has a substantial shareholding in G.A. Ferries).

Flying Dolphin times are frequent and regular (a large part of their custom is obtained ferrying parties of package tourists to and from Skiathos — with its charter flight airport), but the timetable sees regular changes, and with the lack of competition some streamlining of services is now taking place. The overall package always ends up much the same. Itineraries A and B (see opposite) are the most widely run. Occasional calls at isolated ports — notably Evia (Pefki) — have occurred in past years.

The only HFD boat on the route is now the *Express Haroulla*: the largest catamaran operating in Greece and one of the best boats for deck-class passengers into the bargain, she is a vehicle-carrying, passenger ferry-sized boat, with a modern, open deck-class lounge and a sun deck. In 2003 she operated twice daily down the line from Volos.

C/F *JetFerry 1*
G.A. Ferries; 1995; 3950 GRT.
The only fast boat in the G.A. Ferries fleet (in fact the only decent boat they have), the *JetFerry 1* moved from the Ionian islands to the Aegean in 2002. Initially she ran between Thessalonika and the Sporades. This was abandoned in 2003 in favour of a daily service to the islands out of Agios Konstantinos. She is the largest boat yet to take on the role, providing a significant upgrade to this link. Her speed and appointments make her popular, though her times are not as well advertised (there was some confusion between respective island timetables last summer).

C/F *Milena*
G.A. Ferries; 1970; 5491 GRT.
The elderly *Milena* (see p. 402) made a token appearance in the Sporades three days a week during the summer of 2003 — running the rest of the time out of Lesbos. The itinerary could well change in 2004 — given G.A. Ferries' constant habit of tinkering with schedules. As for the *Milena* herself, she is starting to look a bit ragged around the edges once you look closely, but facilities are reasonable — with plenty of sun-deck space. Her age is a problem and her days are clearly numbered.

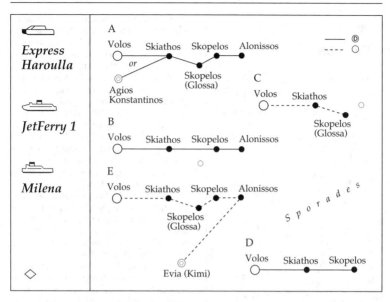

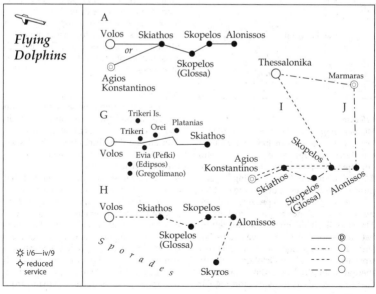

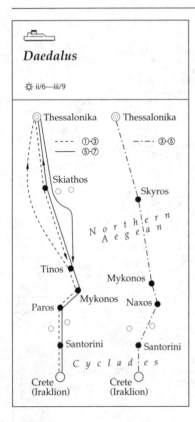

Daedalus

☼ ii/6—iii/9

Thessalonika   Thessalonika

- - - - ①-③   —·—· ③-⑤
—— ⑤-⑦

Skiathos

Skyros

Northern Aegean

Tinos

Mykonos

Mykonos   Naxos

Paros

Santorini   Santorini

Cyclades

Crete   Crete
(Iraklion)   (Iraklion)

C/F *Daedalus*

Minoan Lines; 1973; 7323 GRT.

Since 1989 the Aegean has seen at least one ferry running an extremely useful summer thrice-weekly service between Thessalonika and Crete, linking several groups of islands en route. In the past the service existed solely to provide the large numbers of islanders now working in Thessalonika with a quick means of getting back home for their summer vacations, but since 2001 this period has been extended from May through to October — clearly there are enough islanders now working in Greece's second city to justify more regular

ferry links. All this results in some extreme variations in the numbers travelling. The boats are bursting when heading south in the early part of the High Season (pre-booking is essential), and empty when running north: in mid-to-late August they are empty heading south and full running north. Out of the High Season things tend to be pretty quiet and calls at Skiathos (and in the past Skyros as well) are dropped.

The *Daedalus* first appeared on this route in 2002 and is the largest boat making the run. Despite her years, she is a well-fitted-out boat, having been switched from the competitive trans-Adriatic service. This was reflected in her superior facilities (though a couple of years on this route are apt to take quite a toll). Even so, if you are a deck passenger looking to overnight on the cheap in a saloon or corridor seating she remains an attractive option.

The Minoan High Season timetable has seen only minor changes since 1997, so hopefully the *Daedalus* will run a near identical service in 2004. Changes in 2003 were confined to the dropping of a call at Syros in preference for a stop at Skyros (an island that seems to drop in and out of the itinerary every other year). Out of High Season days of the week and the number of sailings change.

G.A. Ferries

Serious competition for Minoan Lines on the Thessalonika to Crete route arrived in 1997 with the arrival of a G.A. Ferries boat. Running a similar three round-trips a week service, G.A. Ferries maintained the service until 2002 when the number of trips was cut to one, before stopping at the end of that summer. There was no G.A. Ferries service in 2003. It is, however, possible that some sort of link will re-emerge in 2004 as this company — with its elderly fleet of boats — is increasingly struggling to compete elsewhere. Even though there were always running a smaller boat to Minoan (which changed with depressing regularity), there did appear to be sufficient demand from

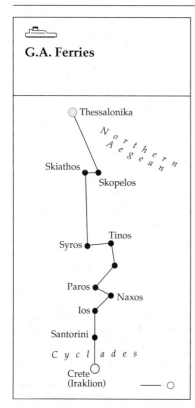

G.A. Ferries

Thessalonika

Northern Aegean

Skiathos
Skopelos

Syros
Tinos

Paros
Naxos

Ios

Santorini

Cyclades

Crete
(Iraklion) —— ○

the large population of Thessalonika to justify having a second boat running to the Cyclades and Crete.

C/F *Dimitroula*
G.A. Ferries; 1978; 7222 GRT.
The Northern Aegean also plays host to a third 'north coast to southern island' summer service, but unlike the other links this is very much a High Season six-week peak-period-only service, and involves one ferry running down the Greek islands along the Turkish seaboard to Rhodes. In past years a number of ferry companies have taken a turn providing the

Dimitroula

☼ ii/7—iii/8

Alexandroupolis

Northern Aegean

Limnos

Lesbos (Mytilini)
Chios

Samos (Vathi)

Dodecanese

Kos

Rhodes

—·—· ⑦-②

service — so expect changes both to the boat and the days the route is run — these consistently change every year though the route remains. The *Dimitroula* (see p. 326) had the job in 2003.

C/F *Nissos Limnos*
Local; 1969; 4797 GRT.
This elegant old boat (originally the cross-Channel *Vortigern*) sailed down the Cyclades West line for many years as the *Milos Express*, and later *Express Milos*. She was sold by Hellas Ferries last year as she is approaching compulsory retirement age. By rights she won't be running in 2004 (it looks as if she was just thrown into the Northern Aegean last year as a stop-gap measure). If she is operating again then think twice about using her; this isn't a boat one willingly travels on overnight these days. Deck-class facilities are just about adequate (with a large saloon near her stern), but her external seating is utilitarian, and her decks and lifeboats have had too many coats of paint over the years for comfort.

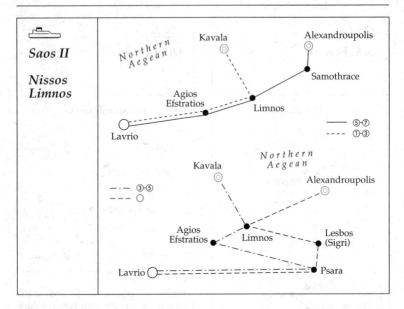

C/F *Saos II*
A.N.E.S.

After complaints from islanders on Limnos and Agios Efstratios about the low level of ferry services in the spring of 2002 this boat appeared out of nowhere, operating out of the mainland port of Lavrio. A relatively small vessel, this ferry is just about up to the job — though she is sure to be booked solid at the height of the season. She started her life on the route by offering an odd-ball link in the form of a call at Samothrace (thus enabling this remote island to join the mainstream ferry network), and has maintained it ever since. Expect changes in 2004, though the overall pattern of services isn't likely to change that much: the islands are too far apart to encourage much variation in itineraries.

C/F *Lykomides*
Skyros Line; 1973; 1169 GRT.
A small car-ferry operated by a one-boat company, the small *Lykomides* runs solely between the ports of Evia (Kimi) and Linaria on Skyros. A little-changing daily 'lifeline' service runs throughout the year, with a second and an occasional third trip in High Season; she has been buried away in this quiet corner of the world for the best part of twenty years. However, her days are numbered as she is reaching retirement age: a new ferry should be on the route within a couple of years. Reliability is good and facilities are reasonable. Athens buses link up with Kimi sailings (see p. 78).

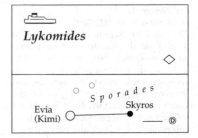

Thassos—Mainland Ferries

A service provided by nine landing-craft car ferries. Most are run by the local A.N.E.T. Line and are named along the lines of *Thassos I, Thassos II* etc. Tickets are bought from kiosks on the quayside or on board. The main service is the 70-minute crossing between Kavala and the Thassos port of Skala Prinos. A 30-minute crossing between Thassos Town and Keramoti attracts more vehicles. Reliability and frequency (every 2 hours) of these boats is good. Skala Prinos ferries also provide a four times daily (mainly commercial vehicle) service to the roadside hamlet of Nea Peramos, 20 km west of Kavala.

C/F *Arsinoe*

Arsinoe Lines; 1980; 800 GRT.
Named after a temple on Samothrace, this boat retains one of those — now rare — traditional Greek chapels on her sun deck. Surprisingly, it is not locked, but open to the passengers and their prayers. Finally, the WC sinks are regularly polished, proving that even the most wistful of prayers can occasionally be answered in one. She has been joined by another ferry (the C/F *Caviros*) and two hydrofoils: the *Niki* (also operated by Arsinoe Lines), which runs to Samothrace and occasionally to Kavala and Limnos, and the *Thraki III* (a Thracian Lines vessel).

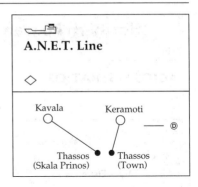

H/Fs *Marina II – Thission Dolphin*

Kavala is the home of a couple of hydrofoils that combine to provide a six times daily service to Thassos Town. Popular with tourists and locals alike, they are faster than taking a ferry to Skala Prinos and then a bus on to Thassos Town. The *Thission Dolphin* is operated by A.N.E.T. Line, while the *Marina II* is owned by NEL Lines. During the summer season at least one of them will make additional morning and evening day-tripper runs to ports down the west coast of Thassos. Operated in much the same way as a bus service, tickets for both boats are usually bought on the quayside or on board.

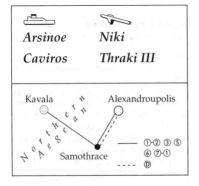

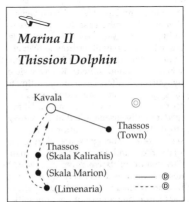

⚓ Northern Aegean Islands & Ports

AGIOS EFSTRATIOS

Alonitisi Beach

Agios Efstratios

303 m

0   km   3

🚌 No bus service

⛴ No beach boat service

Agios Efstratios
ΑΓΙΟΣ ΕΥΣΤΡΑΤΙΟΣ; 43 km²; pop. 300.

A remote, sun-baked island with vegetation (mostly scrub and scattered oak trees) hidden away in the folds of the rocky hills, Agios Efstratios sits like a drowned camel's hump to the south-west of Limnos (from where it is administered). Rarely visited by tourists, it offers close on the ultimate in 'get-away-from-it-all' experiences (the locals routinely assume all arrivals have inadvertently disembarked at the wrong stop). Used as an isolation camp for some 5,000 political prisoners during the 1930s, the island has never been popular. Any chance of its emerging as a tourist destination was effectively demolished in 1968, when an earthquake put paid to the picturesque houses of the only settle-

ment on the west coast. This in itself was unlucky enough, but unfortunately the military junta ruling Greece at the time decided to help out and sent the army to the rescue. Helpfully demolishing the damaged town, they rebuilt it with ugly concrete prefabricated buildings laid out in military formation. They also bulldozed the town beach beyond repair in the process. The islanders have been in mourning ever since.

Given the limited attractions of the town, which now depends on a mix of fishing and a dust-generating cement factory (donated by a past Greek government in an attempt to bolster the island economy), most visitors take to walking, as the island is criss-crossed with goat tracks that wander into hidden folds in the hills and down to deserted beaches. The best is a long strand of volcanic sand on the north coast, a three-hour walk from the chora. One further word of warning: Agios Efstratios is one of the few places where few of the locals speak English — some Greek or a phrase book is a necessity.

🛏
A tiny pension (housed in one of the few pre-earthquake buildings still standing) and some tavernas offering rooms are the sum of the island's facilities.

Agios Konstantinos
ΑΓΙΟΣ ΚΩΝΣΤΑΝΤΙΝΟΣ

Figuring larger on schedules than in real life, this port is something of a nonentity as a destination in its own right. Little more than a stopping point on the main intercity highway from Athens to the north of the country, there is scant reason to stay. The 'town' backs onto the mountains of Attica and is only four blocks deep. The main road runs along the waterfront, with the ferry quay an apologetic extension to the promenade, and adjacent to a leafy central

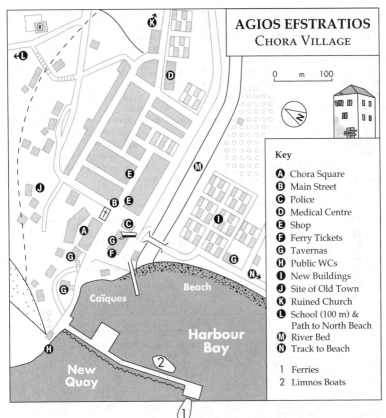

AGIOS EFSTRATIOS
CHORA VILLAGE

0   m   100

Key

Ⓐ Chora Square
Ⓑ Main Street
Ⓒ Police
Ⓓ Medical Centre
Ⓔ Shop
Ⓕ Ferry Tickets
Ⓖ Tavernas
Ⓗ Public WCs
Ⓘ New Buildings
Ⓙ Site of Old Town
Ⓚ Ruined Church
Ⓛ School (100 m) &
   Path to North Beach
Ⓜ River Bed
Ⓝ Track to Beach

1   Ferries
2   Limnos Boats

Caïques

Beach

Harbour Bay

New Quay

square. Most visitors are only staying until the next ferry or Athens bus leaves, and the facilities reflect this: on the plus side there are a number of reasonable tavernas, along with the inevitable ticket agencies. There is a bus station (with hourly services to Athens) several blocks from the ferry quay. If you are travelling via a Hellas Flying Dolphins hydrofoil, you can take advantage of the pricey company buses that are laid on to meet the hydrofoils (buy your bus ticket along with the hydrofoil ticket: Athens-bound buses terminate near the ancient stadium).

Alexandroupolis
ΑΛΕΞΑΝΔΡΟΥΠΟΛΗ; pop. 34,600.

CODE ☎ 25510
TOURIST OFFICE ☎ 24998
POLICE/TOURIST POLICE ☎ 26418

A rather drab modern town on the northern Aegean coast redeemed only by a lively promenade decked with a lighthouse, Alexandroupolis is named after an obscure 19 C. king of Greece rather than Alexander the Great (who renamed half the cities of Asia after himself during his campaigns). This fact eloquently sums the place up, and not even the annual July to August wine festival can dispel the 'okay, but not a great place' impression. In truth for all its attempts to appear to be a significant city, there is a distinct frontier-town feel to Alexandroupolis. The city's location near the Turkish border makes it both difficult to get to (it's the de facto end of the line for both ferries and the coastal bus service) and a useful stepping stone for journeys into Turkey (thanks to the daily buses to İstanbul).

Sadly, there is no reason to come to the city itself and most visitors only stay long enough to catch a ferry or hydrofoil to Samothrace, or one of the seven buses a day to Kavala, or the Athens railway link.

The waterfront is naturally the centre of activity, and is dominated by a high esplanade topped with an elderly, but fully functional, lighthouse that is increasingly surrounded with (empty) taverna seating that isn't up to the grandiose scale of its surroundings. A steep descent from the waterfront street brings you to the extensive — but under-utilized — port and an area of scruffy, reclaimed land that is variously used as a car park or as a fairground area whenever a small travelling circus hits town.

Key

Ⓐ Main Square & Lighthouse (1880)
Ⓑ Bus Station
Ⓒ Railway Station
Ⓓ Police / Tourist Police
Ⓔ National Bank of Greece
Ⓕ Pharmacy
Ⓖ Cathedral / Ecclesiastic Art Museum
Ⓗ WCs
Ⓘ Ferry & Hydrofoil Tickets
Ⓙ Road to Komotini & Kavala
Ⓚ Road to Kipi & Turkey

1 Ferry Berth
2 Hydrofoil Berths

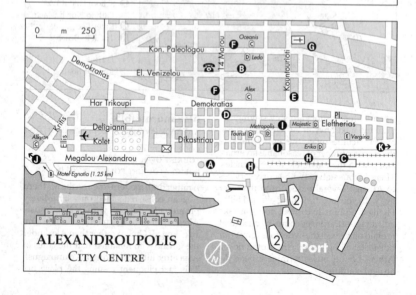

ALEXANDROUPOLIS
CITY CENTRE

The city-centre streets behind the waterfront do nothing to enhance the impression of the place: for the most part they are typical of modern Greek towns, and have no noteworthy sightseeing to relieve the concrete and glass monotony. The nearest that come to 'character' are those abutting the port and railway station area.

◪

The wine festival produces considerable pressure on the limited accommodation available in High Season. The Tourist Office has lists of rooms in the town, but if you arrive after midday the only option likely to be open to you is an expensive waterfront B-class *Motel Egnatia* (☎ 37630), 2 km west of the ferry quay.

There are, however, a number of hotels in town worth a try first, the best bets being away from the waterfront. These include the D-class *Ledo* (☎ 28808) and *Majestic* (☎ 26444) and the C-class *Alex* (☎ 26302) and *Alkyon* (☎ 23593/5).

Alonissos

ΑΛΟΝΗΣΟΣ; 64 km²; pop. 1,500.

CODE ☎ 24240
PORT POLICE ☎ 65595
POLICE ☎ 65205
MEDICAL CENTRE ☎ 65208

The least populated of the larger Sporades, Alonissos is a very popular destination for daily day-tripper boats from Skiathos and Skopelos, thanks to an attractive port lined with low cliffs garnished with pine trees, a pretty hilltop chora and a nearby marine nature reserve that is one of the few remaining homes for the threatened Mediterranean monk seal. The island is also rapidly developing as a rather chic holiday destination in its own right. The fact that it is less touristed than its neighbours makes it appealing to increasing numbers of visitors attracted by the quiet beaches (accessible only via a flotilla of caïques, thanks to the dirt track roads), the friendly islanders and the overwhelmingly cosy ambiance of the place — if you want to unwind on a quiet Greek island then Alonissos can't be beaten. Given this, it is best to allow for extended

stays here when planning your holiday: seductive Alonissos is one of those places where one can't help but linger.

The largest settlement on Alonissos is now the port of **Patitiri**. Nestling in a delightfully piratesque cliff and taverna-decked cove, it has managed to acquire considerable charm despite the fact that it is modern village from roof to cellar, thanks to a disastrous earthquake in 1965 which left it in ruins and the hilltop capital of Chora badly damaged. Coming after extensive depopulation that followed after the island's vineyards were wiped out in 1950 by disease, the earthquake prompted the junta then ruling Greece to dictate that the remaining islanders be rehoused in the rebuilt port. Thanks to tourism, prosperity has returned and Alonissos is now quite busy when the tour boats are in. Fortunately, they don't stay more than a few hours so the dreamy nature of the place isn't interrupted for too long.

Other settlements remain tiny in comparison. Thanks to the island's growing popularity **Chora** is now seeing houses renovated thanks to the large number of people wanting holiday homes, but the lack of a significant year-round population means that it isn't reverting to its previous significant status. Fortunately those that do live there seem content with it continuing as no more than the major sightseeing destination hereabouts. The only other significant settlement of note is the hamlet of **Steni Vala**. Tucked neatly away in a creek halfway up the east coast it is served by the daily taxi-boats than run out of Patitiri. Here you will find tavernas, a shop, and the HQ of the Hellenic Society for the Protection of the Monk Seal.

◪

Alonissos has 14 hotels divided between **Patitiri** port and the suburb of **Votsi** some 20 minutes' walk to the north. Most are B and C category establishments with prices at the top end of the range. Among the most expensive is the B-class *Alkyon* (☎ 65450) on the waterfront, but the east cliff-top hotels offer better views for less, notably the E-class *Liadromia*

ALONISSOS

Beaches: 1. Marpounta 2. Megalo Mortia
3. Vithisma 4. Chrisi Milia
5. Kokkinokastero 6. Kalamaki
7. Ag. Dimitrios

(☎ 65521), and the pricier B-class pension *Cavos* (☎ 65216).

Å

Alonissos has two small, unofficial sites. *Camping Rocks* lies 1.5 km from the port. An idyllic, mature pine-forest site (albeit with rudimentary facilities), has been empty/closed for last two summers (though signs are still up). Come 22.00 the reason why becomes clear thanks to the nearby *Rocks Disco*; the largest and loudest on the island, its great attraction is that, when you and your partner are too beat to bounce around the dance floor, you can retire to a tent and then bounce to the beat on the forest floor without suffering any loss in music volume. The second site, *Camping Ikaros* (☎ 65258), is at isolated Steni Vala, but can fill up with one or two campers in August (it is usually closed most of the rest of the year).

∞

Tours on Alonissos centre on the **Marine Park**. Boats leave daily from Patitiri to north coast sea caves and then on to a monastery on **Kira Panagia** island and a beach on **Gioura** island (which also has yet another of those 1000 stalagmite caves with Cyclops legends attached). However, don't go expecting to see any seals: the islands are home to an estimated 20 pairs out of a world population of 800. Pessimists predict the species will be extinct within a decade. **Peristera**, lying across a narrow strait off the east coast of Alonissos, is also a beach-boat destination. There is also a small fishing village straddling the neck of the island.

Sightseeing on Alonissos itself is more limited — an inevitable consequence of the island's history as a minor satellite of Skopelos. In 2000 a privately operated **Historical and Folklore Museum** appeared in Patitiri. Open ⊙ 09.00–21.00 (€3), it houses a large collection of traditional artifacts reflecting the island's rural and agrarian heritage. Unfortunately the labelling is poor to non-existent, but in most cases the displays are reasonably self-explanatory, ranging from the contents of a typical house to the various tools of various professions from cobbler to saddle-maker. An upper floor has a collection of maps of the island, and some shells and a mine (all of the military variety).

Finally, walkers should note that Alonissos is a pine-clad heaven, with a number of gentle wooded walks to beaches. You can buy locally an excellent walking and swimming guide called *Alonissos On Foot* (€9).

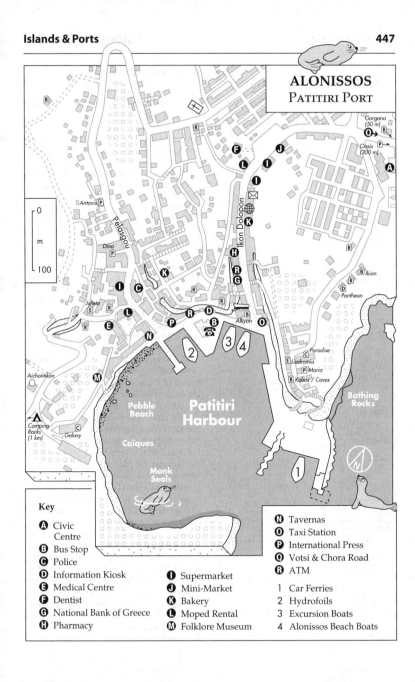

ALONISSOS
PATITIRI PORT

Gorgona
(50 m)

Oasis
(300 m)

Pelasgou

Antonis

Dina

Julieta

Ikon Dolopon

Ikion

Pantheon

Paradise

Lipdromia

Maria

Kabos / Cavos

Aichonirikon

Camping
Rocks
(1 km)

Galaxy

Alkyon

Pebble
Beach

**Patitiri
Harbour**

Caïques

**Monk
Seals**

**Bathing
Rocks**

Key

A Civic Centre
B Bus Stop
C Police
D Information Kiosk
E Medical Centre
F Dentist
G National Bank of Greece
H Pharmacy
I Supermarket
J Mini-Market
K Bakery
L Moped Rental
M Folklore Museum

N Tavernas
O Taxi Station
P International Press
Q Votsi & Chora Road
R ATM

1 Car Ferries
2 Hydrofoils
3 Excursion Boats
4 Alonissos Beach Boats

AMOLIANI & MT. ATHOS

KIROPOTAMINA

Tripiti

Amoliani

Ftelies

Tsarki
Bay

Ⓓ x 2

DHRENIA

0   km   3

Ouranopolis

Ierissos

Xerxes
Canal

Nea Rodha

AMOLIANI   Tripiti

N

Ouránopolis

Metoni
Hourmitsis

Esfigmenou

22

Ouranopoli—
Thessalonika
Ⓓ 07.15, 17.30

Vatopediou

2
3
4

21

Pantoratoros

Ⓓ 09.30 ♦18.30   5   20
                                            19   18
◯ Irregular   6
Tour Boats   17   Iviro

Other Monasteries: Dafni   16
1. Zografou, 2. Kastamonitou,
3. Dohiariou, 4. Xenofontas,   15
5. Skiti Evan. Theotokou,   7
6. Ag. Pandelimonos,
7. Simonos Petras,
8. Ossiou Grigoriou,   8
9. Ag. Dionisiou, 10. Ag. Paviou,
11. Theotokou, 12. Ag. Annis,   9
13. Ag. Triados,
14. Magistis Lavras,   10   Mt. Athos
15. Karakallou, 16. Filotheou,   2033 m
17. Timiou Prod. Iviron,   11
18. Ag. Pandelimonos,
19. Koutioumousiou,   12
20. Profitis Iliou,   Megistis
21. Ag. Dimitriou,   13   Lavras
22. Hiliandariou,   14

0   km   6

Amoliani & Mt. Athos

Accessible from Thessalonika, the island of Amoliani and the neighbouring Mt. Athos peninsula are well off the ferry lanes and tend to be the preserve of the mainland tourist rather than the island hopper. Amoliani is about as far removed as you can get from the rest of the Greek ferry system, and really only features on the hit lists of island hoppers who are determined to do every Greek island.

Amoliani is an unassuming little place. It is home to one hamlet which offers a few rooms as well as dirt roads to good beaches at Ftelies and Tsarki (also known as Alikes) bays. Passenger boats run from Tripiti, a quay on the Ouranopolis road. **Ouranopolis** is the last settlement before the 'border' that closes off the Mt. Athos peninsula from the rest of the world. The town is a bit of a tourist trap, but does offer boat trips to the Dhrenia islets offshore as well as along the coast of Mt. Athos.

Mt. Athos, a politically autonomous and closed collection of medieval monasteries, is one of those curiously Greek sightseeing attractions which you can see from the sea but can't visit. As a result, tour boats simply cruise off-shore without landing, but each morning one does a 'provision' run, stopping at various monasteries en route to Dafni where the few males with the almost impossibly hard-to-obtain permits to visit disembark. Females (both human and animal) are banned, but this hasn't stopped the peninsula emerging as an important wildlife sanctuary (the monks obviously go in for some pretty odd habits). Tourist boats also run down the east coast from **Ierissos**. Near Ierissos are the scanty remains of the trans-peninsula canal dug in 480 BC for the invading Persian fleet (en route to the Battle of Salamis) of King Xerxes. His abortive invasion of 491 BC having come to grief when his fleet was wrecked off the tip of Mt. Athos, he opted for the drastic solution of digging his way west on his return visit.

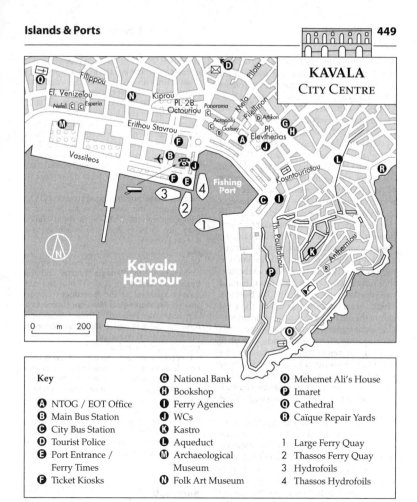

KAVALA
CITY CENTRE

0   m   200

Key

🅐 NTOG / EOT Office
🅑 Main Bus Station
🅒 City Bus Station
🅓 Tourist Police
🅔 Port Entrance /
    Ferry Times
🅕 Ticket Kiosks

🅖 National Bank
🅗 Bookshop
🅘 Ferry Agencies
🅙 WCs
🅚 Kastro
🅛 Aqueduct
🅜 Archaeological
    Museum
🅝 Folk Art Museum

🅞 Mehemet Ali's House
🅟 Imaret
🅠 Cathedral
🅡 Caïque Repair Yards

1 Large Ferry Quay
2 Thassos Ferry Quay
3 Hydrofoils
4 Thassos Hydrofoils

Kavala

ΚΑΒΑΛΑ; pop. 57,500.

CODE ☎ 2510
NTOG/EOT OFFICE ☎ 222425
POLICE ☎ 222905
HOSPITAL ☎ 228517

If you exclude hydrofoils from the equation, Kavala (ancient Neapolis) is easily the premier port of the Northern Aegean, with good links to the otherwise unconnected islands of Thassos and Samothrace, and also — in High Season — the Athenian port of Rafina, the Dodecanese and Rhodes. If this wasn't reason enough to venture in this direction, the city itself is one of the nicest in Greece; set against a backdrop of rolling hills, it nestles snugly between their lower folds and the shoreline, with a picturesque Turkish quarter topped with an imposing castle, an aqueduct and traditional caïque-building thrown in for good measure. Sadly the strong tourist presence is evident in local prices.

The city centre is surprisingly compact, dividing into two quarters. To the east lies the old town dominated by the castle set upon the building-clad promontory ringed by the old city wall (known as the Panagia Quarter). Outside the walls, the old town continues to the north under the arches of the delightful aqueduct that once took water to the castle. The inlet to the east is littered with boat-builder's yards. To the west lies the old fishing harbour, still home to a fair number of working caïques. They sit somewhat incongruously against a backdrop of 'modern' buildings (and the ugly main city square — Pl. Elevtherias) that now make up the new town behind the very busy road that divides the two. Things are a bit more relaxed on the west side of the old harbour, with several reasonable restaurants with views over the castle backing onto a long promenade, complete with sun-bleached lawns and the odd tree for good measure. The rest of the new town isn't up to much, but has the merit of a reasonable scatter of shops (though supermarkets are thin on the ground) and a busy bus station.

The absence of many competing ferry companies means that ticket agents are confined to three outlets on the quayside serving the large boats and ticket kiosks for the Thassos boats on the quay. Buy in advance if you can, but if you find the kiosks closed then tickets are bought on board after the ferry has departed. The quay has ferry times up at the entrance gate kiosk (in Greek) and a procession of large landing-craft type car ferries and a hydrofoil heading for Thassos. The Samothrace ferry berths on the east side of the harbour under the castle walls.

🛏
A good NTOG/EOT office on the edge of Pl. Eleftherias. has free city maps and will help you find where the one empty bed is to be located. Hotel accommodation is rather limited, and at the bottom end of the scale very poor; this is one city where it pays to look up-market a bit. Within an easy walk of the waterfront there are a number of C-class establishments: the *Acropolis* (☎ 22 3643) and *Panorama* (☎ 22 4205) — both near the old harbour, and the *Esperia* (☎ 22 9621) and *Nefeli* (☎ 22 7441) near the museum. Best of the down-market options is the D-class *Attikon* (☎ 22 2257) a couple of blocks behind the EOT office. If you can afford to splash out then the waterfront B-class *Galaxy* (☎ 22 4521) is the best hotel in the centre.

▲
Nearest to the port is a poor, treeless NTOG site 3 km to the west. 5 km to the east is *Irini Camping* (☎ 22 9776): a good trailer park site. A better bet is to hop over to a site on Thassos.

👓
Main sights in Kavala are the maze of streets that make up the **Panagia Quarter** and the **Byzantine Kastro** (⊙ 10.00–17.00), the old quarter spanned by the **Aqueduct** (c. 1550) and an **Archaeological Museum** (home to a disparate collection culled from sites around Kavala). There is also a **Municipal Museum** full of the usual round of bric-a-brac dating from the early 19 c. on.

If you have more than a day in Kavala then you should consider venturing 15 km north-east of the city to the remains of the ancient city of **Philippi**: the site of the battle in which Octavian (later the Emperor Augustus) defeated the murderers of Julius Caesar, Cassius and Brutus, in 42 BC. Straddling the main road, the remains are substantial and include a well-preserved latrine (this is more than modern Kavala can boast). Kavala buses run every ½ hour.

Keramoti
ΚΕΡΑΜΩΤΗ

An isolated port turned growing resort, Keramoti owes its existence to the fact that it is the nearest point on the mainland to Thassos. A reasonable sand beach has enabled it to grow into a minor destination in its own right, with a reasonable number of rooms and a campsite. Package tourists often pass through via the ferries serving Thassos Town en route for Keramoti airport, some 20 km to the north-west.

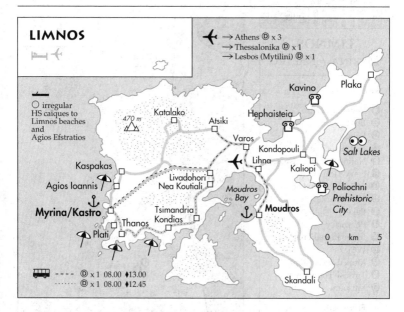

Limnos

ΛΗΜΝΟΣ; 477 km²; pop. 16,000.

CODE ☎ 22540
PORT POLICE ☎ 22225
TOURIST OFFICE ☎ 22315
POLICE ☎ 22200
HOSPITAL ☎ 22203

The home of Hephaistos, the divine smith, Limnos (also commonly transcribed as 'Lemnos') is a fertile, volcanic island opposite the entrance to the Dardanelles — a strategic location that attracts a strong military presence. An accompanying lack of tourists (who are missing a lovely island) has ensured a continuation of the traditional island culture now sadly absent elsewhere. This, coupled with good beaches, very friendly islanders and an attractive (in a weird volcanic molehill, lumpy, sort of way) main port of Myrina, are all the more reason to visit. Somewhat less appealing is the reputation of the curative properties of the local soil; indeed, Limnosian mud

pills were viewed as a sort of Viagra-like wonder drug by much of the ancient world. These days the locals seem less adept at weaving money-spinning yarns to ensnare gullible visitors.

Myrina (also known as Kastro, thanks to the floodlit castle built on the ancient acropolis) is very much the centre of island life. It is a prosperous little working town with an interesting warren of backstreets leading off from the main street that snakes its way from the cute little square backing onto a small caïque harbour near the constantly enlarging ferry quay, under the castle walls and then east into the suburbs. Lined with an odd mix of hardware shops, discos and men's clothing outlets (it is difficult to forget that Limnos has a large army garrison), it is very much the focus of town life. Either side of the castle are the town's sandy beaches; the one to the north is decidedly more up-market.

Limnos is a good destination if you have your own transport, and very frustrating

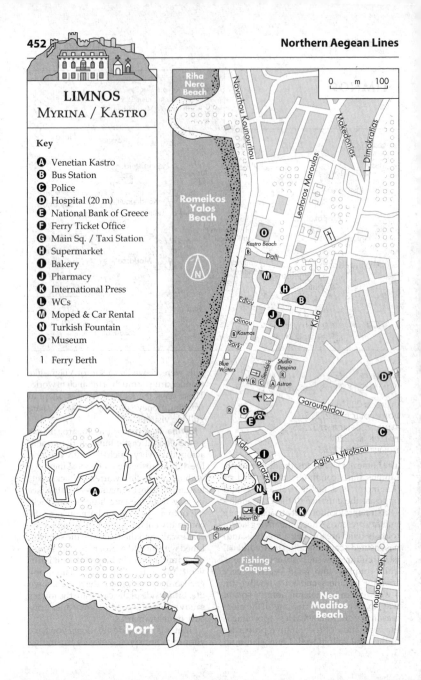

LIMNOS
MYRINA / KASTRO

Key

Ⓐ Venetian Kastro
Ⓑ Bus Station
Ⓒ Police
Ⓓ Hospital (20 m)
Ⓔ National Bank of Greece
Ⓕ Ferry Ticket Office
Ⓖ Main Sq. / Taxi Station
Ⓗ Supermarket
Ⓘ Bakery
Ⓙ Pharmacy
Ⓚ International Press
Ⓛ WCs
Ⓜ Moped & Car Rental
Ⓝ Turkish Fountain
Ⓞ Museum

1 Ferry Berth

—given the almost non-existent bus service — if you haven't. The two halves of the island contrast greatly. The east side is flat and fertile, with two lakes adding to the oddly un-Greek landscape of cornfields and grazing cattle, while the west has a starker rocky volcanic terrain and the bulk of the best beaches. Apart from Myrina the only large settlement is at **Moudros** (the forward Allied military base during the ill-fated Gallipoli campaign; thanks to the sheltered bay, it also safely housed the Allied generals).

Buses link the town with the capital, but unfortunately the service is geared to moving islanders into Myrina for work in the mornings and returning them at night. With only two services offering a same-day return to Myrina, buses are all but useless for tourism purposes. Short of hiring a moped, the best way to see the remote sites of interest on Limnos is to take the once-a-week bus excursion (unfortunately, the day varies).

⊨

In High Season a Tourist Police office is open in Myrina's town hall which will help you find a bed. This usually means directing you to one of the **Myrina** hotels (of which there is a reasonable selection). On the waterfront the D-class *Aktaion* (☎ 22258) and the C-class *Lemnos* (☎ 22153) are easily found and reasonable. Harder to find is the C-class *Sevdalis* (☎ 22691), which lies in a side street one block beyond the OTE square on the town's main street. More up-market establishments tend to lie near the beaches. These include the B-class *Paris* (☎ 23266) and the expensive *Kastro Beach* (☎ 22148), which lies at the east end of the town's north beach.

⌖

Limnos was an important island during the Archaic period, and the primary archaeological site — the city of **Poliochni** even predates Troy on the adjacent Turkish coast. Tours visit the rather confused archaeological remains along with those of the classical city at **Hephaisteia**. This was built on the spot where the god Hephaistos landed and lamed himself after Hera threw him from the summit of Mt. Olympus in a fit of 'peak'. The tangible remains include fragments of a temple to the god and an odeon.

Marmaras
ΜΑΡΜΑΡΑΣ

A resort on the middle fork (known as Sithonia) of the Halkidiki peninsula, Marmaras (alias Nea Marmaras) is on hydrofoil itineraries. A pricey resort with a reasonable beach, bus links to Thessalonika, and a campsite, the main incentive to visit is the boat tour along the coast offering a glimpse of the monasteries of Mt. Athos. Marmaras is the easiest departure point for island hoppers wanting a look; the daily excursion costs €28.

Nea Moudania
ΝΕΑ ΜΟΥΔΑΝΙΑ

An over-touristed small town on the Northern Aegean's west coast just north of the left-hand fork (alias Cassandra) of the Halkidiki peninsula, Nea Moudania is the weekend getaway resort for Thessalonika, and now sees a number of hydrofoils calling en route to the Sporades.

Beyond the crowded beach, some over-expensive hotels and a crowded campsite, it has very little to recommend it — unless you are in a hurry to continue on to Cassandra. Hourly buses to Thessalonika offer frequent means of escape.

Nea Peramos
ΝΕΑ ΠΕΡΑΜΟΣ

Unless you have a vehicle, this mainland port 15 km west of Kavala is not really a practical proposition given the 'inter-city' nature of local buses. However, host to several daily landing-craft ferries running to Thassos, it offers a short cut to motorists arriving from or departing to the west. Set in a cosy, open-mouthed bay, this hamlet (complete with beach, kastro and campsite) is an infinitely more relaxing jumping-off point to Thassos than Kavala. If you are prepared to stop overnight, Nea Peramos is worth considering as a quiet overnight excursion for Thassos trippers.

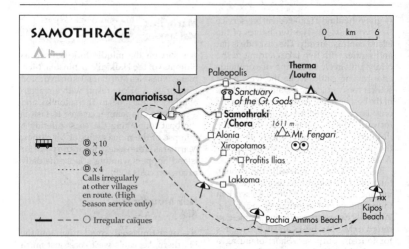

Samothrace
ΣΑΜΟΘΡΑΚΗ; 178 km²; pop. 2,800.

CODE ☎ 25510
PORT POLICE ☎ 41305
POLICE ☎ 41203
FIRST AID ☎ 41217

A dramatic, heavily wooded mountain peak rising from the sea, Samothrace was an island of spiritual pilgrimage in the ancient world; partly, one suspects, because it was as difficult to get to then as it is now. First impressions of a comparatively bleak and mountainous island are enhanced by the almost apologetic way the main island town and port of **Kamariotissa** clings to the foreshore against a backdrop of undulating hills devoid of vegetation bar the odd wind-broken tree and stubbly cornfields. A couple of horribly modern electricity-generating windmills on the long western spur do nothing to relieve the almost forbidding sense of isolation. This tends to do Samothrace something of a disservice for once ashore it is quite a friendly place.

All the nightlife and essentials are to be found in the port along with most of the accommodation. For once on a Greek island,

English is little spoken as most visitors are German or Scandinavian.

Almost all tourist activity is confined to the northern coast thanks to the impressive archaeological remains of the Sanctuary of the Great Gods at Paleopolis and the spa village at Therma. Other island villages see few tourists. Buses run regularly to the whitewashed island capital at **Chora**; a jumble of whitewashed houses tucked comfortably out of sight in a fold in the foothills, it is devoid of hotels and all the other trappings of modern tourism and topped with the remains of a lovely castle. Equally attractive is the pretty hill village of **Profitis Ilias** (buses also head for here calling irregularly at other villages en route).

Buses also run direct to the campsites via **Therma** (also known as Loutra). As the name implies, this is a spa resort of sorts and now the main tourist centre on the island, though trees outnumber tourists for the greater part of the year.

Not really a beach island, Samothrace does have two excellent examples along its south coast that are sadly only accessible by dirt track or irregular caïque on the south coast at Pachia Ammos and delightfully remote Kipos.

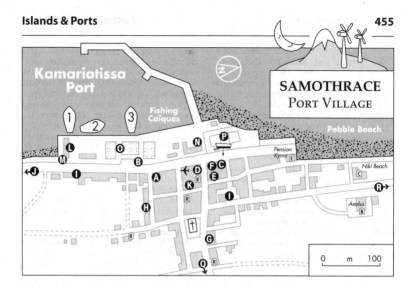

Kamariotissa Port

SAMOTHRACE
PORT VILLAGE

Pebble Beach

Pension Kyma

Niki Beach

Aeolus

Fishing Caïques

0   m   100

Key

A Information / Bus Office
B Bus Stop
C Police
D National Bank of Greece
E Pharmacy
F Supermarket
G Grocery Store

H Bakery
I Moped Rental
J Disco & Promontory
K Bar / Ferry Tickets
L Passenger Stalls
M WCs
N Old Lighthouse
O Waterfront Park

P Beach Square
Q Chora Road
R Therma Road

1 Ferry Berth
2 Hydrofoil Berth
3 Irregular Beach
   Caïques

⊢

Rooms and hotels are scattered thinly between the port, Paleopolis, Therma and Chora. Low numbers of visitors means low prices. At the **Port** you will find, at the northern end of the waterfront, the C-class *Niki Beach* (☎ 41561), with the pricey B-class *Aeolus* (☎ 41595) close by, along with a pension, the *Kyma* (☎ 412 68). **Paleopolis** has the B-class *Xenia* (☎ 41230) and the C-class *Kastro* (☎ 41850) close to hand. **Therma** is also blessed with a couple of establishments: the B-class *Kaviros* (☎41577) and the C-class *Mariva* (☎ 41759).

▲

There are two north-coast High Season only sites: poor *Camping Loutra* (☎ 41784), is 3 km east of Therma. *Multilary Camping* (☎ 41759) is a much better site 2 km further on.

👁

Samothrace offers two great attractions, the most obvious being **Mt. Fengari** (the 'Mountain of the Moon'). Used by Poseidon as a seat while he observed the Trojan war, mortals seeking serious hill walking (via Therma) find that when they get to the summit after a day's climb that the ground is still warm.

The **Sanctuary of the Great Gods** at Paleopolis sees far more visitors. The remains of one of Greece's premier places of pilgrimage (the first historian, Herodotus, was initiated into the rites, and Alexander the Great's parents met and fell in love here), it is sadly diminished, but is located in a marvellous woody ravine setting that more than makes up for the limited remains. The sanctuary was pre-Greek in origin, being originally dedicated to the Great

Mother Earth goddess Axieros and a fertility god, Kadmilos. The Greeks quickly conflated these figures with their own Demeter and Hermes and so kept local traditions going for the best part of a millennium. What those traditions were is still something of a mystery. Ancient writers were loath to mention them thanks to the belief in shadowy demon figures (known as the Kabeiroi) who were thought to harbour implacable wrath towards any that divulged the sanctuary's secrets. However, it is known that anyone could be initiated into the sanctuary's mysteries and that the torch-lit night-time ceremony had two stages (the first involving purification, the second, initiation into the rites). Despite earthquakes and pirate attacks, the sanctuary (politically independent throughout its life) was only abandoned with the adoption of Christianity by the Roman Empire, and most of the important buildings were rebuilt several times during the course of their lives.

Access to the site today is via a footpath running inland from the main coast road. Walking past the hotel and the museum along the path running parallel with the central ravine stream, on your right you will see the remains of **❹** the **Milesian Building** (so called because of an inscription associated with it), and behind it **❺** a **Byzantine Fort** built from stones from the sanctuary.

The most important buildings were all located on the 'island' of land bounded by the (usually dry) streams running down the ravines. Crossing the stream brings you to **❻**; the rotund **Arsinoeion**, also an important structure though of much later date. Built c. 285 BC, it was the largest circular building ever constructed by the ancient Greeks. Commissioned by Queen Arsinoe of Thrace, it was used for public sacrifice. To the north is **❼** the **Anaktoron** (also known as the 'Hall of the Lords'); it was one of the oldest buildings on the site, being in continuous use from the 6 C. BC to the 4 C. AD. It was used for the first stage of the initiation rites. In the Roman period a robing room, **❽** the **Sacristy**, was added to the building, when it was substantially rebuilt.

Turn south of the Arsinoeion and you come to **❾** the **Temenos** (an open air precinct with a ceremonial entrance on the north-east side), and **❿** the **Hieron**. Now the most prominent building on the site, thanks to its columns, the

temple was the location for the second stage of the initiation. The remains of spectator seating line the interior walls. On its west side lie the scanty foundations of **⓫** the **Hall of Votive Gifts** (c. 540 BC), little evident now, but important in that it survived for close on a thousand years without rebuilding. Next door is the **Altar Court** at **⓬**, dedicated by a half-brother of Alexander the Great. The path now crosses a culvert that ran under the theatre stage. **⓭**, the site of the **Theatre** is now a tree-covered depression and barely recognisable, as almost all the seats were removed for the construction of later fortifications.

Once you have passed the theatre, the paths divide. The eastern path wanders over the stream and a hill (that was home to **⓮** the **South Necropolis**) before coming to the substantial foundations of **⓯** the **Propylon of Ptolemy II**, a formal gateway constructed for the use of the local townspeople (the ancient capital — Paleopolis proper — stood to the east of the sanctuary). When originally built it had the stream channelled to emerge through it. On the west side of that stream are two rather obscure buildings: **⓰** a **Circular Building** and **⓱** a **Doric Structure** dedicated by Phillip III and Alexander IV.

The western path turns west up the hillside behind the theatre, bringing you to the foundations of **⓲** the **Nike Niche**: a small building cut into the hillside that was built specifically to house **⓳** the famous **Winged Nike (Victory) of Samothrace**. Made of Parian marble, this sculpture is the site's greatest archaeological find, and (bar the missing head) is now in the Louvre. It takes the form of an 'angel' standing on the prow of a ship. The Nike niche was in fact a fountain house, and the prow stood in a double-level floor basin filled with water.

The path continues up the hill to the higher level behind the theatre and **⓴** a **Stoa**. Plenty of fragments lie scattered around but nobody has yet found the time to reassemble them. Between the stoa and the ravine stream at **㉑** lie scanty remains of **Hellenistic Buildings** (purpose unknown).

Finally, returning to the main path you come back to the site's **Archaeological Museum**: it is well laid out and worth a visit, though — as with many 19 C. excavated sites — all the important sculptures found on the site have long since found their way into French and Austrian museums.

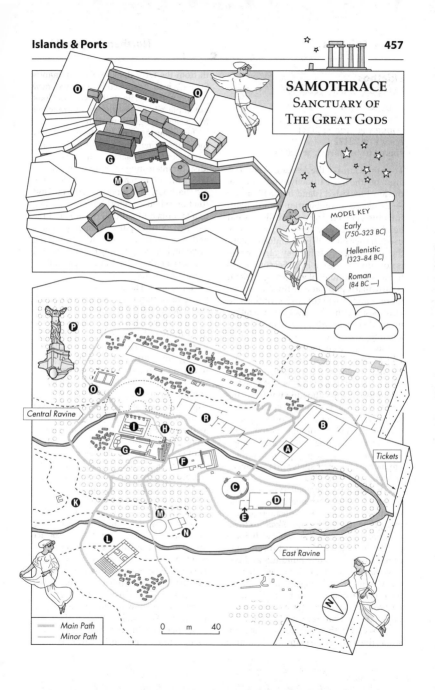

SAMOTHRACE
SANCTUARY OF
THE GREAT GODS

MODEL KEY

Early
(750–323 BC)

Hellenistic
(323–84 BC)

Roman
(84 BC —)

Central Ravine

Tickets

East Ravine

Main Path
Minor Path

0   m   40

Skiathos

ΣΚΙΑΘΟΣ; 61 km²; pop. 4,900.

CODE ☎ 24270
PORT POLICE ☎ 22017
TOURIST POLICE ☎ 21111
POLICE ☎ 23172
FIRST AID/HOSPITAL ☎ 22040

The mini-Corfu of the Aegean, Skiathos is arguably the most attractive and certainly the most touristed island in the Sporades — thanks to a combination of a delightful pine-clad landscape, excellent sand beaches, good ferry links and a heavily used charter flight airport. Unfortunately, the cosy 'ideal family holiday' atmosphere is now under siege in High Season thanks to the sheer number of visitors. The island is particularly popular with British package tourists and Italians of all descriptions. In years past Skiathos has always been a rather up-market package tour destination, but of late things seem to be sliding downwards — the only exception being local prices, which are apt to be on the expensive side compared to most other islands.

The net result of all this is that those in the know mark Skiathos down as one of the best Greek islands going for spring/early summer visits and a spot to be avoided during the height of the season. That said, even when the crowds are in town it remains a very friendly place, and there are plenty of quieter spots you can escape to if you are so minded.

As with many of the smaller Greek islands Skiathos has one substantial settlement and no other major centres. Considering how many tourists pass through, **Skiathos Town** weathers the storm remarkably well. Set in an islet-littered bay, it is a picturesque mix of red-tile roofs, white buildings and bell towers, set against the rich green hills.

The crowds that throng the narrow streets have had a major impact. For the most part this has taken the form of boutiques, patisseries and bars rather than neon lights and discos, but there are blots on the landscape; the worst is the main street running

in from the ferry dock — Papadiamantis St. — which has recently acquired new paving, naff street lights that wouldn't look out of place in *Disneyland*, and a branch of *McDonald's* for good measure.

The restaurant-lined waterfront is far more appealing, and adds greatly to the cosmopolitan ambiance of the town. It is ideal for interesting evening promenades, taking in the beach boats tied up in the old harbour, the wooded **Bourtzi islet** (that once housed a fort but now is home to a taverna and cultural centre), and the assorted portrait painters, sponge sellers and street entertainers — to say nothing of campaigners protecting the endangered monk seals that breed in this part of the world — that appear out of nowhere once darkness falls. The town is also endowed with a yacht marina, and several flotilla sailing holiday companies are based here.

The **south coast road** (the only one made up on the island) is home to the great majority of the island's large package tour hotels. Strung irregularly, like so many octopi out to dry, along the sheltered southern coast they hug the high ground, and the larger complexes usually have a coast road supermarket nearby (there are well over a dozen along the coast road). This isn't as depressing as it sounds as the mix of wooded headlands and small bays — most with golden sand beaches — works very well, and the hotels are almost lost amidst this attractive jumble — there are no high-rise buildings damaging the views.

The road is very busy, particularly at rush periods, but at least it is almost impossible to get lost, and there are frequent taxis and bus stops along its length. The **bus service** is one of the more 'interesting' features of Skiathos. The bus stops carry no name but have a number instead: this saves tourists from having to remember the name of their cove, bay or hotel. Fares are €0.90 or €1.10, depending on how far down the line you want to go. This might not be very far as the buses here would give those on Ios a run for their money in a tourist sardine contest.

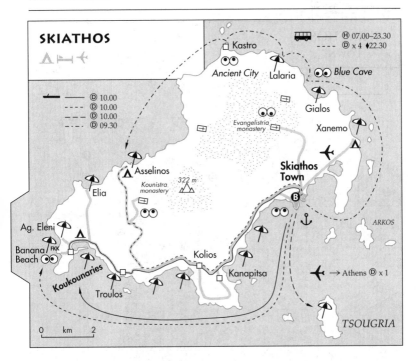

SKIATHOS

- Kastro
- Ancient City   Lalaria
- Blue Cave
- ⊞ 07.00–23.30
- ⊙ x 4 ♦22.30
- ⊙ 10.00
- ⊙ 10.00
- ⊙ 10.00
- ⊙ 09.30
- Evangelistria monastery
- Gialos
- Xanemo
- Asselinos
- Kounistra monastery
- 322 m
- Elia
- Skiathos Town
- B
- ARKOS
- Ag. Eleni
- Banana/ FKK Beach
- Kolios
- Kanapitsa
- → Athens ⊙ x 1
- Koukounaries
- Troulos
- 0   km   2
- TSOUGRIA

The trouble is that although the buses run every 15 minutes, they simply can't cater for the massive demand. The battle to get on and off also pushes up journey times to a sometimes intolerable extent.

The primary destinations lie at each end of the road; in the evenings everyone is heading for Skiathos Town, while in the mornings the big draw is **Koukounaries** beach, a long crescent-shaped stretch of sand filled with bodies of various hues, and sporting a sea-water lagoon, complete with wildlife sustaining reed-bed backed by yet more umbrella pines. A short walk away is quieter **Banana Beach**, reputedly the best naturist beach in the Mediterranean — most of the bananas on display tend to be middle-aged and Italian.

The north coast is very quiet, without hotels or settlements of note, thanks to a lack of roads and the strong winds that turn the beaches into a beachcomber's paradise. In fact, the only easily accessible point is at **Asselinos** (reached via a dusty woodland track that runs past the odd stud farm), which is a blissfully quiet and verdant little valley only let down by a rather tatty beach. Equally underdeveloped is the wooded interior of the island which is popular with hikers.

The east coast is similarly the preserve of those looking for a quiet life; the one blot on their happiness being the noisy airport (see p. 461). There is a poor beach at **Xanemo**, and you will have to resort to beach boats if you want to do better. **Lalaria** on the north-east corner is the best bet; a very picturesque tapering pebble beach at the base of a cliff, it is more Beachy Foot than Head and is well worth the cost of a visit.

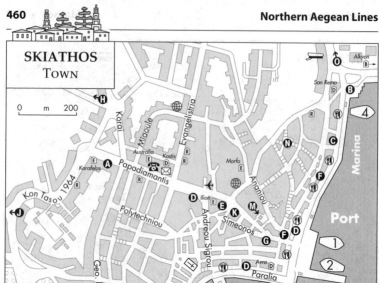

SKIATHOS TOWN

0   m   200

Alkyon

San Remo

Marina

Port

Koraï

Mïaoule

Evangelistria

Australia

Kostis

Karafelas

Papadiamantis

Kon Tasou 1964

Polytechniou

Morfo

Ananiou

Ilion

Simeonos

Andreou Sigrou

Geo. Maraitou

Avra

Paralia

Old Harbour

Bourtzi islet

Key

- **A** Police Station
- **B** Bus Station
- **C** Car Rental & Taxi Rank
- **D** Bookshop & International Press
- **E** National Bank of Greece
- **F** Travel Agent / Ferry Tickets
- **G** *McDonald's*
- **H** Car Rental (50 m) & Cinema (200 m)
- **I** Site of Old Kastro (replaced with school: now a theatre)

- **J** Junction with Ring Road (20 m)
- **K** Pharmacy
- **L** Hospital / Medical Centre
- **M** Papadiamantis House Museum
- **N** Spyglass Church with Campanile
- **O** Town Ring Road to all destinations
- **P** War Memorial

1   Ferry Quay
2   Hydrofoil Berth
3   Tourist & Beach Boat Quay
4   East Coast Beach Boat Quay

⊢

Rooms can be hard to come by in High Season, though of late large ferries are met by a few townsfolk offering beds. A quayside kiosk just north of the ferry quay provides useful accommodation advice. Hotels there are aplenty on Skiathos. Most are block-booked by package tour operators. Seeking out untaken-up rooms is an option, though you will find almost all the A to C class hotels are well out of town, bar the B-class *Alkyon* (☎ 22981) on the airport road.

Within Skiathos Town there are a number of budget establishments: the poor D-class *Avra* just off the waterfront, the *San Remo* (☎ 22078) at the other end of the harbour and the *Kostis* (☎ 22909) behind the post office. E-class hotels are to be found near Papadiamantis St. These include the *Ilion* (☎ 21193), the *Morfo* (☎ 21737), the basic *Australia* (☎ 22488) and the *Karafelas* (☎ 21236). All adequately offer the basics at a reasonable price.

A

There are three sites on Skiathos: nearest to the port is a municipal campsite at Xanemo. Under the airport flight path, it does a roaring trade but attracts few campers.

The newest site is *Koukounaries Camping* (☎ 49290) and is easily the best for the beach of the same name and buses to Skiathos Town, though it is expensive. Summer prices are maintained throughout the year, but on the plus side the grass, flower and willow-tree filled site is very well maintained too. There is also a good supermarket 40 m west of the site entrance at Bus Stop 23.

If solo camping in a grassy field is more to your taste, then laid-back *Asselinos Camping* (☎ 49312) is to be recommended (though it no longer seems to have a bus — so you will have to walk the 2 km from the south coast road).

◯◯

Skiathos Town is the island's main attraction: though it lacks tangible sights (substantial rebuilding following bombing damage in WW2 hasn't helped). The only 'sight' as such is the well-preserved late 19th century home of the writer **Alexandros Papadiamantis** (1851–1911). One of Greece's most notable literary figures, he grew up on Skiathos and returned to die. A journalist turned author, he penned over 100 novels and short stories (most based on island life) — the most famous being *The Man Who Went to Another Country*, *The Gypsy*, and *The Murderess*. Translations of several are on sale in the town's bookshop. Perhaps they are losing something in translation, but his work can be a bit heavy going.

As for his house, it is a simple homestead. Unfortunately, Papadiamantis had as few possessions as his fellow islanders and the building reflects this wonderfully. Minimalists and creaky floorboard fans will love it: most others seem to leave with the impression that the removal men have already been in.

The southern waterfront is home to a second memorial to long departed island sons. In this case it is a cannon and flag decorated **War Memorial**. Placed in honour on a quay of its own, it commemorates the men who were summarily rounded up and executed in 1943 by the German troops — as a reprisal for local resistance to occupation. Sadly its inscription is only in Greek, so its significance isn't appreciated by most tourists. However, the event itself still colours many islanders' attitude to visitors — as when visiting Crete; it helps if you are a national of one of the Allied powers.

Most tourists visit Skiathos Town at least once a day if only to pick up the daily tour boats heading on to Skopelos and Alonissos, the beach boats (most heading for Koukounaries, Banana and a beach on the adjacent islet of **Tsougria**), or the anticlockwise island boat tour. The island boat tour also stops briefly at the **Blue Cave**, a sea cave on the east coast, and at **Kastro**, site of the medieval centre of the island until it was abandoned in the 19 C. after piracy was no longer a threat to the islanders' security. Set on an all but impregnable headland, it is now a picturesque ruin of houses, streets and churches.

Excursions also run to two monasteries: **Kounistra** to the west (for the view) and **Evangelistria** (a popular donkey-ride destination north of Skiathos Town, famed in Greece as the place where the Greek flag was first raised in 1807 by a group of conspiring independents).

Finally, if you want some really inspired sightseeing try the beach road running past the end of the airport runway. Supposedly closed every time a flight leaves, it made headlines in 1996 after three tourists unwittingly stood behind the engines of a departing jet. When it took off they did as well, one landing on a nearby beach, a second waist-deep in the sea and the third ending up on a mainland-bound hydrofoil with a broken jaw.

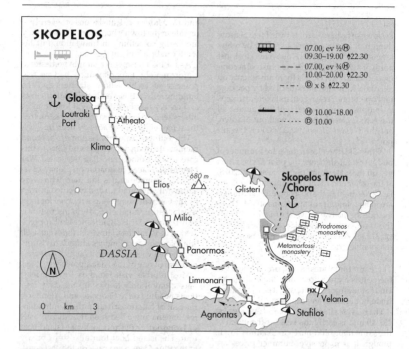

Skopelos

ΣΚΟΠΕΛΟΣ; 96 km²; pop. 4,700.

CODE ☎ 24240
PORT POLICE ☎ 22180
POLICE ☎ 22235
FIRST AID/HOSPITAL ☎ 22220

The largest island in the Sporades group, Skopelos has less sparkle than neighbouring Skiathos. The beaches are not as good (most are pebble), there is less sightseeing, and the main town has far less going on. Even so, it is an attractive island — covered in pine forests and (thanks to flatter terrain) more agriculture as well. With the easy links to the airport on Skiathos, Skopelos has seen a dramatic rise in tourism as package tour operators have moved in, promoting the island as an ideal quiet family-holiday destination. Independent travellers are far less visible, but their numbers are on

the increase as the appeal of over-touristed Skiathos wanes, and many are apt to rank it ahead of Skiathos thanks to its more relaxed, laid-back atmosphere.

The main settlement is **Skopelos Town**, tucked beneath a ring of sheltering hills in a deep bay on the northern coast. This is something of a disadvantage as, lying on the exposed side of the island, ferry and hydrofoil services are subject to regular disruption. On windy days these, and other tourist boats, are often diverted to a small wooded inlet at **Agnontas** on the sheltered south side, where confused passengers are unceremoniously decanted onto an empty quay seemingly in the middle of nowhere (the three village tavernas aren't immediately obvious). When this happens free buses into town are laid on.

Skopelos Town has retained much of its whitewashed traditional appearance,

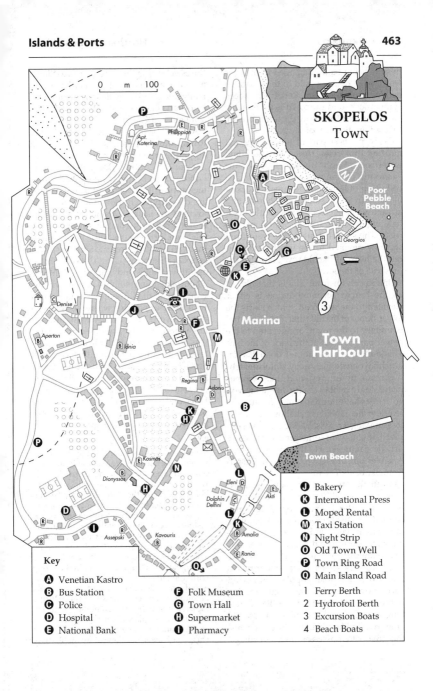

SKOPELOS
TOWN

Poor Pebble Beach

Georgios

Denise

Aperton

Ignia

Regina

Adonis

Marina

Town Harbour

Kosmos

Dionyssos

Eleni

Akti

Dolphin / Delfini

Town Beach

Kavouris

Amalia

Assepski

Rania

Key

Ⓐ Venetian Kastro
Ⓑ Bus Station
Ⓒ Police
Ⓓ Hospital
Ⓔ National Bank

Ⓕ Folk Museum
Ⓖ Town Hall
Ⓗ Supermarket
Ⓘ Pharmacy

Ⓙ Bakery
Ⓚ International Press
Ⓛ Moped Rental
Ⓜ Taxi Station
Ⓝ Night Strip
Ⓞ Old Town Well
Ⓟ Town Ring Road
Ⓠ Main Island Road

1 Ferry Berth
2 Hydrofoil Berth
3 Excursion Boats
4 Beach Boats

despite being badly damaged in the 1965 earthquake that put paid to the Chora on neighbouring Alonissos. Repairs have been sympathetic, and the town is undeniably attractive, but somehow the total adds up to less than the sum of the parts.

Easily the best part of town is the old quarter that rises from the tree-lined waterfront steeply up the slopes of the kastro hill on the west side of the bay: a collection of labyrinthine streets chock-a-block with steep staircases, chapels and attractive houses — many with over-hanging wooden balconies and red-tile roofs. The streets abutting the waterfront are now devoted to the tourist industry, but the heart of the old town remains the preserve of the locals.

One knock-on from this is that almost all the tourist accommodation is either elevated to the ring road, which skirts the lower slopes of the hills that make a natural boundary to the town, or relegated to the newer part of town at the back of the bay. This latter area is also home to a small town beach beyond the ferry quay. Unfortunately, it is made up of grey sand that becomes increasingly pebbly the further along you go. It does have one redeeming feature: the sea floor hereabouts is shallow and rock-free, making it a passable kiddie beach in a pinch. If you want something a little more private, caïques run to the otherwise inaccessible, but attractive, beach at **Glisteri** from Skopelos Town.

Given that there is only one metalled road and a good bus service, visiting the rest of the island is very straightforward. Most of the bus stops are at beach hamlets. **Stafilos** can lay claim to being the over-crowded main island beach: it owes this role thanks largely to being a walkable 4 km from Skopelos Town. **Panormos** is the next beach, and popular with wind surfers (there is also unofficial camping in the coves on either side). **Milia** offers a long strand of pebbly sand and is usually quiet, while **Elios** is home to the nearest thing Skopelos possesses to a resort village.

Buses venturing this far then run to **Klima**, a semi-abandoned village that has never really recovered from the 1965 earthquake, before arriving at the island's second major settlement of Glossa.

A small picturesque and unspoilt hill town, **Glossa** perches majestically in amphitheatre fashion on a hillside above the port of Loutraki. Despite its narrow winding streets and whitewashed buildings appeal, it attracts few visitors — most are day-trippers from Skopelos Town on tours of the island. Despite this, three or four hydrofoils call daily at the port below the town. Ferries also called in past years (note: all timetables refer to Skopelos Town simply as 'Skopelos'; Glossa is usually listed as if it were an island in its own right).

Loutraki, lying some 4 km down the winding hill road (there is a donkey path with more appeal for walkers), is now a diminutive fishing hamlet with an over-large harbour. In ancient times, however, it was home to a significant Roman town (it takes its name from the baths that were built here). The waterfront is lined with attractive tavernas, and the few original buildings are now surrounded by a growing number of hotels and purpose-built tourist rooms. The port also boasts a large windswept pebble beach to the north of the quay.

Skopelos shares a similar quiet history to her neighbours. Lacking size and arable land, the Northern Sporades were never particularly wealthy. Lying close to the mainland, they became part of the Athenian empire and were later sacked by Philip V of Macedon in 220 BC. The only really notable event in their history came just before the battle of Salamis in 480 BC when a preliminary skirmish took place off Skiathos between three Greek triremes and a Sidonian squadron of the Perisan fleet.

Skopelos was the only island in the group with a significant city. In ancient times the island was called Peparethos by the Greeks, becoming Skopelos in the Roman era. During the Byzantine period it was another unfancied island used as a place of exile. With the arrival of the Franks it came under the rule of the Duchy of Naxos, until a visit by the Barbary

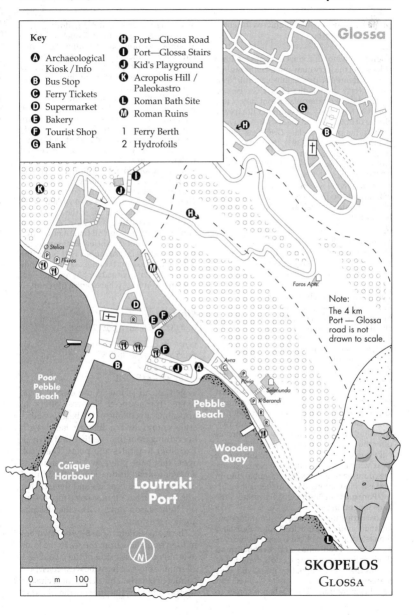

Key

Ⓐ Archaeological Kiosk / Info
Ⓑ Bus Stop
Ⓒ Ferry Tickets
Ⓓ Supermarket
Ⓔ Bakery
Ⓕ Tourist Shop
Ⓖ Bank

Ⓗ Port—Glossa Road
Ⓘ Port—Glossa Stairs
Ⓙ Kid's Playground
Ⓚ Acropolis Hill / Paleokastro
Ⓛ Roman Bath Site
Ⓜ Roman Ruins

1 Ferry Berth
2 Hydrofoils

Glossa

Stelios
Flisvos
Faros Apts.

Note:
The 4 km Port — Glossa road is not drawn to scale.

Avra
Pavia
Selenunda
K Berandi

Poor Pebble Beach
Pebble Beach
Wooden Quay
Caïque Harbour
Loutraki Port

0   m   100

SKOPELOS
GLOSSA

pirate Barbarossa who slaughtered the entire population in 1538.

⊨

There are plenty of rooms in **Skopelos Town** (a kiosk on the ferry quay offers information). Hotel beds are also reasonably plentiful. Nearest the ferry quay is the E-class *Georgios* (☎ 22308), but like other waterfront hotels it is apt to be a bit noisy. For a quieter life try the cluster of hotels behind the town beach. These include the pricey C-class *Delfini* (☎ 23015), the D-class *Eleni* (☎ 22393), the E-class *Stella* (☎ 22081) and *Rania* (☎ 22486). At the upper end of the market are the B-class *Amalia* (☎ 22688), the *Dionyssos* (☎ 23210) and, nearer the centre of town, *Ionia* (☎ 22568). Glossa's port of **Loutraki** also has several pensions with sea views on offer, as well as the largish C-class hotel *Avra* (☎ 33550).

Λ

There are no official sites, but freelance camping has been tolerated at Velonio (the unofficial nudist beach), and at Panormos beach — though it has been discouraged of late.

👓

The town and beaches are the main attractions; sightseeing on Skopelos tends to come in a poor third. **Skopelos Town** provides just about enough to justify a day-trip from a neighbouring island, but lacks specific sights. The **Kastro** is a serious disappointment, now being reduced to little more than a couple of walls that hardly grab the eye, though the town is interesting enough.

The only museum in town is the tiny **Folk Art Museum** hidden away in the backstreets, and largely passed by. Once you start wandering (well okay, given the number of staircases, climbing) around backstreets the churches offer the main landmarks. The town is reputedly home to some 120 of them, but it isn't clear which clubs and bars the person doing the counting frequented before embarking on his task. First among the churches is the cliff-top **Panagia ston Pirgho** which overlooks the harbour entrance.

Coach trips around the island are quite popular, and usually take in at least one of the island monasteries. Three of these open their doors to visitors, **Prodromos** and **Evangelismou** (both dating from the 18 c.: now denuded of monks they are occupied by nuns) and 16 c. **Metamorfossi** (now uninhabited, so you can be a bit more uninhibited when it comes to

observing the dress code). In addition, tour boats operate daily out of Skopelos Town to Skiathos and Alonissos (including the Marine Park). If you fancy city sightseeing in the heat of the day, ticket agencies also offer day trips to Athens (via early morning hydrofoil and coach) — at a price.

With plenty of shade and scenery Skopelos is an excellent island for **walking**, even in high summer. Walkers should buy the snappily titled *Sotos Walking Guide to Local Beauty Spots & Places of Historical Interest* by Heather Parsons (€6), which is on sale in several waterfront shops.

Finally, **Loutraki** also has limited sightseeing thanks to the fragmentary remains of the ancient city of **Selinous** which once stood here. The only obvious remains are 4 whitewashed column fragments in front of the Avra hotel, but once you visit the Archaeological information kiosk nearby you will find photos of the overgrown site of the ancient **Bathhouse**, the largely inaccessible **Acropolis** Hill. Sadly, the port has no museum: the more significant finds — notably a torso of a statue of Aphrodite — are now in the Volos Archaeological Museum.

Skyros
ΣΚΥΡΟΣ; 208 km²; pop. 2,900.

CODE ☎ 22220
PORT POLICE ☎ 96475
POLICE ☎ 91274
FIRST AID ☎ 92222

A gem of an island to the east of Evia, Skyros (pronounced Sk*ee*-ros) offers an appealing mix of one of the best Cycladic-style choras and a history laced with everything from transvestism and a Greek Excalibur to pirates and poets. The weak spots that have prevented it emerging as a major tourist destination are the limited number of good beaches and the fact that it is too far from regular ferry routes (out of High Season links with other islands are non-existent).

The main settlement of **Skyros Town** lies hidden from view near the sea in the folds of a hill on the east side of the island — a 20-minute bus ride from the west-coast port hamlet of **Linaria**. This desire for seclusion was prompted by the piracy of the 16 and 17

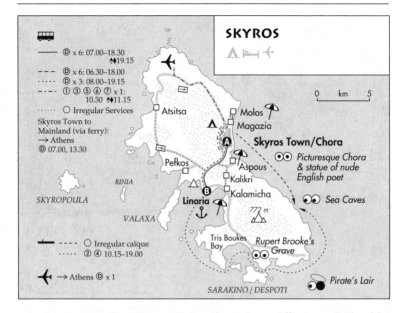

SKYROS

⊕ x 6: 07.00–18.30
　　　◆◆19.15
⊕ x 6: 06.30–18.00
⊕ x 3: 08.00–19.15
① ③ ⑤ ⑥ ⑦ x 1:
　　10.30 ◆◆11.15
○ Irregular Services

Skyros Town to
Mainland (via ferry):
→ Athens
⊕ 07.00, 13.30

0   km   5

Atsitsa

Molos
Magazia
Skyros Town/Chora
⊚⊚ *Picturesque Chora
& statue of nude
English poet*

Pefkos
Aspous
Kalikri
Kalamicha
RINIA

Linaria

⊚⊚ *Sea Caves*

SKYROPOULA

VALAXA

772 m

○ Irregular caïque
② ④ 10.15–19.00

Tris Boukes
Bay

*Rupert Brooke's
Grave* ⊚⊚

→ Athens ⊕ x 1

Pirate's Lair ⊚⊚

SARAKINO / DESPOTI

c., but did not prevent 'Three Entrance Bay'
at the southern end of the island becoming
a notorious Pirate Lair. During the Heroic
Age the warrior Achilles had much the
same hideaway idea with equally little
success, for foreseeing his death at Troy,
he hid on Skyros disguised as a girl only
to let his frock slip when Odysseus (offering a particularly heroic sword for sale)
discovered him and dragged him by the
heel to its date with destiny (see p. 551).
Surprisingly, there is nothing commemorating this event in the town. Instead, you will
find a bronze of another poetic warrior who
died with a sore point — Rupert Brooke,
the First World War poet, who came off
worse in a fight with a mosquito, dying
unheroically here of his wound in 1915, en
route to Gallipoli. If he sauntered around
the island wearing as little as his statue it
is not surprising that he was smitten and,
all things considered, he was lucky not to
share the fate of the third notable to come a
cropper here — the hero Theseus who was

thrown over a cliff onto a nudist beach by
the then king of Skyros, Lykomides. These
days the townsfolk are more friendly, in part
because the Chora has managed to retain
much of its unspoilt charm thanks to the
bulk of the island accommodation being
located a bus-ride away on the beach. The
car-free Chora is dominated by the castle
and the main street which winds up the hill
towards it, and is particularly appealing in
the evenings when the streets are thronged
with gossiping locals. It is, however, often
quite windy.

Rupert Brooke's grave aside, the rest of
the island is little visited by tourists: most
visitors to Skyros confine themselves to the
chora and the relatively close resort villages
of **Magazia** and **Molos** which are linked by a
good sand beach (the island bus service isn't
geared to getting tourists anywhere else).
Those hiring their own transport to explore
further will find the expense well worth
it. The southern half of Skyros is mountainous, the north flatter and more fertile,

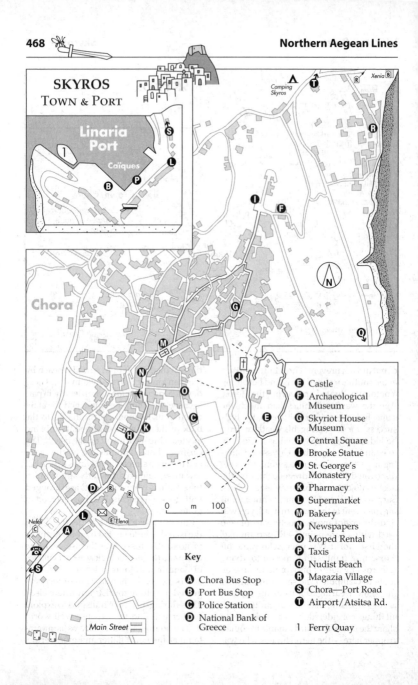

SKYROS
Town & Port

Linaria Port

Caïques

Camping Skyros

Xenia

Chora

N

Key

Ⓐ Chora Bus Stop
Ⓑ Port Bus Stop
Ⓒ Police Station
Ⓓ National Bank of Greece

Ⓔ Castle
Ⓕ Archaeological Museum
Ⓖ Skyriot House Museum
Ⓗ Central Square
Ⓘ Brooke Statue
Ⓙ St. George's Monastery
Ⓚ Pharmacy
Ⓛ Supermarket
Ⓜ Bakery
Ⓝ Newspapers
Ⓞ Moped Rental
Ⓟ Taxis
Ⓠ Nudist Beach
Ⓡ Magazia Village
Ⓢ Chora—Port Road
Ⓣ Airport/Atsitsa Rd.

1 Ferry Quay

0   m   100

Main Street

Nefeli

Ⓔ Elena

and the whole delightfully unspoiled and well wooded with pine trees (making this magnificent hill walking country, even at the height of summer). The only downside is the sometimes heavy military presence — though there is no obvious reason that would account for the numbers of soldiers stationed here — beyond the charm of the island.

Skyros has also attracted media attention thanks to a 'holistic holiday community' established at remote **Atsitsa** on the north-west coast (with a centre in Chora). Offering mind/body/spirit courses for those asking questions like 'What is stopping me from being who I really am?', the community has been accused of encouraging marital breakdown thanks to the allegedly high number of subsequent divorces by holiday-makers. This is unfair, because anyone who chooses to spend a holiday alone 'painting the soulscape' is obviously in a marriage that is in pretty serious trouble anyway. To do the community justice, most who go on these courses return swearing by them and the impact on Skyros is far less obtrusive than most tourist-related activities.

However, this doesn't stop some of the locals asking 'Why us?' First someone erects a bronze nude of a poet they have never heard of in the middle of town (at a time when most chaste village maidens wouldn't have known what a poet's lyric metre was, still less seen one), and now they have ranks of skinny-dipping middle-management types asking 'Where am I going?' On Skyros this question at least is easy to answer, as ferry connections are confined to the link with Kimi, the odd boat to Thessalonika and the Cyclades, and the — now very rare — hydrofoils to the Sporades.

⊨

There is a reasonable supply of rooms on Skyros spread between the town and the beach villages of Magazia and Molos. Hotels are thin on the ground and rather pricey, though the island is worth it. The best establishments are also in the beach villages to the north. **Molos** has the new A-class *Skyros Palace* (☎ 91994) on the beach (a large apartment complex on the beach with its own pool), the B-class *Angela*

(☎ 91764), and the new C-class *Paradissos* (☎ 91220). Closer to the town lies the B-class *Xenia* (☎ 91209), a lovely hotel on the beach under the kastro at **Magazia**. Hotel options in Chora are limited, your best bets being the C-class *Nefeli* (☎ 91964) on the road just before you enter the town and the E-class *Elena* (☎ 91738) behind the Post Office. Chora also has a good supply of rooms — though these tend to be offered by owners on the ferry quay rather than bearing identifying signs in town.

Å

Although backpackers are not thick on the ground there are two sites on Skyros. *Skyros Camping* (☎ 92458) is near the chora. A field site located between the beach and the chora hill, it isn't popular due to the poor facilities on offer. A second — and more attractive option — is provided by an unofficial site operated by a taverna on the beach in the bay just to the north of Linaria port.

👓

Chora, with its traditional Skyriot houses and blue and white 'Delftware' pottery (a noted Skyriot product) is the main attraction on the island. The streets are so narrow vehicles are confined to the outskirts, and like all good choras it just invites you to get lost and then lost again. The town climbs to an impressive **Venetian Kastro** of Byzantine origin, with fantastic views over the town and island as well as housing a small **Archaeological Museum** which sadly lacks any outstanding exhibits. Below the castle walls is the **Monastery of St. George**. All three suffered minor damage in an earthquake that rocked the island on the 26th July 2001, but almost everything is now back to normal.

The chora also has a folk museum in the form of a traditional house (known as the **Faltaits Museum**) decked out with examples of the island wares (though most of the town houses retain the fittings and platters that give the museum its atmosphere).

The grave of **Rupert** ('If I should die, think only this of me: That there's some corner of a foreign field that is forever England') **Brooke** is set under a small grove of olive trees in the **Pirate Bay** on the south of Skyros, and is the premier destination of tourist caïques (which occasionally also visit the pirate base — one of the largest in the Aegean — of **Despot's Island**) and bus tours (the most accessible way of seeing Skyros). The east coast cave was also a **Pirate Grotto** in its day.

Thassos

ΘΑΣΟΣ; 398 km²; pop. 16,000.

CODE ☎ 25930
PORT POLICE ☎ 22106
POLICE / TOURIST POLICE ☎ 22500
FIRST AID ☎ 22190

A large, beautiful island tucked against the northern Aegean seaboard, Thassos is the most northerly inhabited island in Greece. Mountainous and green, with over half of its surface covered with cedar, oak and pine forests (now criss-crossed with bulldozed fire gaps to keep any forest fires under control) and fringed with good sand beaches, the island has emerged as a popular (if somewhat pricey) north European package-holiday destination, as well as attracting caravaners willing to motor through the Balkans. Fortunately, hotel development, although evident, is by no means over-conspicuous thanks to reasonable spacing around the attractive 95 km coastline, and the island is further improved by being out of the reach of the backpacking hordes that so damage the dreamy Greek island idyll elsewhere.

The main settlement at **Limenas** (also popularly known as **Thassos Town**) lies in a large bay on the north coast — offering the shortest crossing point to the mainland (12 km). A very pleasant mix of modern town and ancient city ruins, it reflects the island's history as a quietly prosperous state during the ancient period (its wealth generated by gold and silver mines and marble quarrying). With a scatter of later Turkish houses, in-filled with modern (invariably tourist-related) buildings, the town is probably akin to what Kos Town would have looked like today if both Crusaders and Italians had not come a-building. Even the presence of tourist outlets and discos accompanying the holidaymakers fails to diminish the appealing relaxed atmosphere.

Activity naturally centres on the waterfront, which is surprisingly diverse with three distinct zones: the ferry quay (home to most of the services and shops), the ancient harbour (base for tour and beach boats, starting point for town tours, and offering leafy night-time waterfront promenades), and the popular town beach (backed by restaurants and tavernas). The tree-filled streets behind are thinly lined with buildings that are rarely more than one deep.

Movement around Thassos is dominated by the coast road that runs in a rough circuit around the island. Most buses travel in an anticlockwise direction to connect with the main port of **Skala Prinos** perched on an east coast spit: a tourist-dominated hamlet, but with more going for it than many Greek ports with a number of tavernas and holidaymaker-orientated shops, a goodly number of trees dividing the outlets offering accommodation and a working caïque repair yard.

South of Skala Prinos the west coast is fairly quiet with the bulk of the island's low-key agriculture and scattered beach villages until it reaches **Limenaria** on the south coast. The island's main resort (courtesy of a long, narrow sand beach) and the only other large town, it is largely a product of the mining industry in the early years of the last century, though this fact is somewhat misleading as the only dark holes these days are provided by the local discos. These exist in numbers, as if trying to compensate for the damaged landscape around the town: this southern part of the coast is the most spoilt part of Thassos thanks to extensive forest fire damage in recent years.

Those in search of scenery will do better to head on to neighbouring resort villages of **Pefkari** and **Potos** which have quieter beaches. Potos is also a convenient place to pick up buses heading inland to the island's medieval capital at **Theologos**. Now reduced to a quiet, whitewashed hill village, Theologos has only benefited from its isolation.

The attractive beach at **Makriammos** aside, the east coast of Thassos is the best on offer. More scenic (the road deviates from the coast to take in the attractive mountain villages of **Panayia** and **Potamia**; the latter is

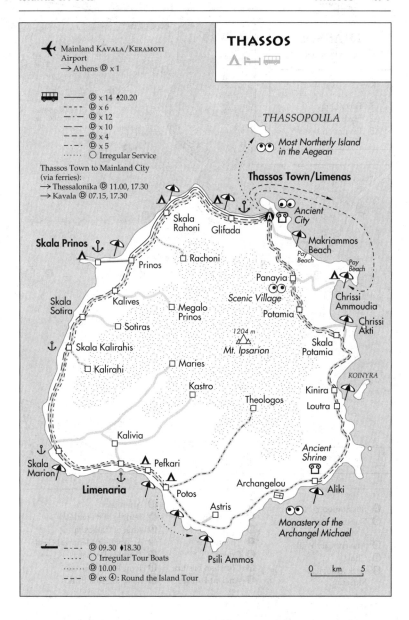

Mainland KAVALA/KERAMOTI
Airport
→ Athens Ⓓ x 1

──── Ⓓ x 14 ♦20.20
---- Ⓓ x 6
-·-· Ⓓ x 12
── Ⓓ x 10
--- Ⓓ x 4
-··- Ⓓ x 5
······ ○ Irregular Service

Thassos Town to Mainland City
(via ferries):
→ Thessalonika Ⓓ 11.00, 17.30
→ Kavala Ⓓ 07.15, 17.30

THASSOPOULA

Most Northerly Island
in the Aegean

Thassos Town/Limenas

Skala
Rahoni   Glifada

Ancient
City

Makriammos
Beach

*Pay
Beach*

Skala Prinos

Prinos

Rachoni

Panayia

*Pay
Beach*

Chrissi
Ammoudia

Scenic Village

Skala
Sotira

Kalives

Megalo
Prinos

Potamia

Chrissi
Akti

Sotiras

1204 m

Skala
Potamia

Skala Kalirahis

Mt. Ipsarion

KOINYRA

Kalirahi

Maries

Kinira

Kastro

Theologos

Loutra

Kalivia

*Ancient
Shrine*

**Skala
Marion**

Pefkari

Archangelou

Aliki

Limenaria

Potos

Astris

Monastery of the
Archangel Michael

Psili Ammos

──-·- Ⓓ 09.30 ♦18.30
····· ○ Irregular Tour Boats
······· Ⓓ 10.00
--- Ⓓ ex ④: Round the Island Tour

0   km   5

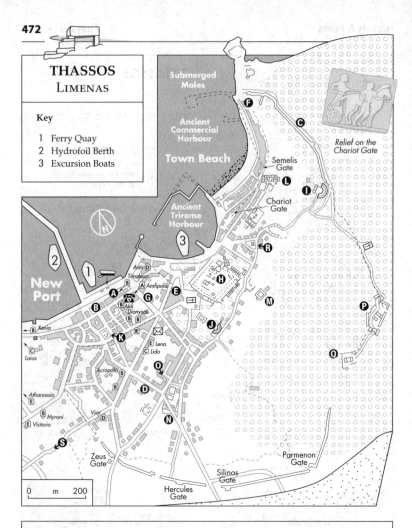

THASSOS
LIMENAS

Key

1 Ferry Quay
2 Hydrofoil Berth
3 Excursion Boats

Submerged
Moles

Ancient
Commercial
Harbour

Town Beach

Relief on the
Chariot Gate

Semelis
Gate

Chariot
Gate

Ancient
Trireme
Harbour

New
Port

Astri
Timoleon
Amfipolis
Akti
Dionysos
Xenia
Laios
Lena
Lido
Acropolis
Athanassia
Myroni
Victoria
Vioy

Zeus
Gate

Parmenon
Gate

Silinos
Gate

Hercules
Gate

0   m   200

- **A** Bus Station / Police
- **B** National Bank of Greece / Main Square
- **C** Ancient City Walls
- **D** Clinic
- **E** Archaeological Museum
- **F** WCs
- **G** Newspapers
- **H** Agora
- **I** Theatre
- **J** Odeon
- **K** Christian Basilica
- **L** Ancient Houses
- **M** Artemision
- **N** Temple of Hercules
- **O** Arch of Caracalla
- **P** Acropolis / Medieval Castle
- **Q** Temple of Athena
- **R** Temple of Dionysos
- **S** Road to Skala Prinos

a popular tour destination in consequence), it runs down to the picture-postcard village of **Aliki** and, arguably the most attractive part of the island, the long, golden sand pine-backed beach running from **Kinira** to **Psili Ammos**.

![icon]

Thassos Town is the best place to stay on the island. A few rooms are around. The wide range of hotels in Thassos Town have prices that are higher than average, and the balance of accommodation is towards the upper end of the range. At the top is the A-class *Amfipolis* (☎ 23101). B-class hotels include *Xenia* (☎ 71270) and the pensions *Acropolis* (☎ 22488), *Myroni* (☎ 23256), *Akti* (☎ 22326) and *Dionysos* (☎ 22198). C-class hotels are confined to the *Lido* (☎ 22929) and *Laios* (☎ 22309). At the bottom end of the range are the D-class *Astir* (☎ 22160), and E-class *Victoria* (☎ 22556), *Lena* (☎ 22793) and *Athanassia* (☎ 22545).

Λ

There are several sites at Skala Prinos including a pleasant NTOG / EOT site: *Camping Prinos* (☎ 71171), 700 m west of the ferry quay. Complete with its own pebble beach, it is easy to get to without your own transport, but like other sites it is geared to the trailer/camper market and full of young families in High Season.

Other sites are more isolated and invariably have a full range of facilities (including reasonable mini-markets). *Camping Ioannidis* (☎ 71477) and *Camping Perseus* (☎ 81352) at Skala Rahoni are well placed and worth considering. Even better — if you can live with the isolation — are south coast *Pefkari Camping* (☎ 51595) and east coast *Chryssi Ammoudia Camping* (☎ 61207).

👓

Thassos Town offers an easy day's sightseeing, along with a readily accessible beach. Ancient remains are scattered liberally around the town, though in almost every case nothing but foundations survive. Most obvious of these is the **Agora**, which backs onto the ancient harbour and houses the remains of a couple of Roman stoas, a tholos (a small circular temple) and several monumental altars. Nearby is a small **Archaeological Museum** (it has a notable 3 m high Archaic kouros, various pieces of sculpture, labels in French and no entry fee).

To the south lies a small **Odeon** fronted by a tiny remnant (50 m) of a paved **Hellenistic Street**. This led to the triumphal **Arch of Caracalla**, now reduced to some impressively large foundations. Other survivals consist of temples to assorted gods along with a well-preserved **Theatre**. Hidden away in the forest, this theatre is one of the most appealing in the Greek islands. However, the number of pine trees enthusiastically growing amid the tiers of bench seats does suggest that the occasional performances put on here for the tourists' benefit are a bit on the wooden side.

Perhaps the most impressive feature of the ancient town is the well-preserved 4 C. BC **City Wall** that skirts the hills around the modern town and includes the old Acropolis. The wall fragments are in varying states of repair, along with the gates that each take their name from the Archaic reliefs carved on them. A wooded path (complete with street lamps) runs from the theatre up to the **Acropolis** — its ancient remains now incorporated into the walls of a ruined **Medieval Castle** (built in 1259). From the Acropolis the path runs on to a **Temple of Athena**. Little remains of the building, but the views over Thassos Town are worth the walk.

The buses that run around the coast road are also popular with visitors. Mornings and late afternoons they make a circuit of the island — thus offering tourists the opportunity to make 'day trips' to the destination of their choice. Most either make for the east-coast villages of **Panayia** and **Aliki** (the latter offering the remains of a small Doric shrine and ancient marble quarries), or head for the **Monastery of the Archangel Michael**, which has a gift shop staffed by some very friendly nuns and a hut full of fancy dress 'cover-ups' for the underdressed (a catagory which tends to include most holidaying visitors).

Thessalonika
ΘΕΣΣΑΛΟΝΙΚΗ; pop. 406,500.

CODE ☎ 2310
PORT POLICE ☎ 531504
NTOG OFFICE ☎ 263112
TOURIST POLICE ☎ 544162
POLICE ☎ 522589

The 1997 European City of Culture and the second city of Greece, Thessalonika (often abbreviated to plain 'Salonika') commands attention as an important bus and rail junction, but the city has to work hard to keep the many tourists passing through. With a population approaching half a million, along with all the smog, crowds and concrete of the capital Athens — but without the mitigating grace of an Acropolis complex — Thessalonika has limited appeal unless you are prepared to venture well away from the waterfront.

Founded in 316 BC by the Macedonian commander Cassander (husband of Alexander the Great's half-sister), the city, unlike most other important centres in Greece, was never a major city state in its own right (hence the lack of Classical antiquities); instead, ideally placed on the trade route between the Levant and the Balkans, it has thrived as a major staging post from the Roman era (when it became the capital of the province of Macedonia) to the present day. Its history, therefore, is one of repeated changes in ruler as the warring powers in the region through the centuries have fought to secure its strategic position, leaving a legacy of impressive Byzantine churches and an even more spectacular city wall. Poets and philosophers are conspicuous by their absence: Thessalonika just wasn't their sort of town. Trade has always been the order of the day and with it came waves of immigrants (notably 1492, when 20,000 Spanish Jews settled in the city, and 1923, when Greeks emigrating from Turkey arrived in numbers).

The last hundred years have not been particularly kind to the city. Victim of a devastating fire in 1917 (which resulted in the waterfront and commercial centre being totally destroyed and then reconstructed on a grid system, with only the odd rebuilt church or ancient monument poking incongruously amid the new buildings giving a reminder of the city of old), Thessalonika saw its commercial stuffing all but knocked out during WW2 when the occupying German forces deported the large Jewish population to the death camps. This was followed by a major earthquake in 1978 that inflicted considerable damage on the rich legacy of Byzantine churches (many only

recently rebuilt after the fire). These three events have combined to take much of the zip out of the city's step, and the pervading downtown atmosphere is one of a utilitarian, if cosmopolitan, commercialism; this is all rather a pity given that this city is often the first port of call for visitors to Greece — courtesy of its position on the main railway line to Europe. Even so, while this isn't Greece at its best, there is certainly enough sight-seeing to fill a couple of leisurely days. If you are looking for something more, then you would be better advised to move on, for although the city has an active nightlife, swimming is a non-starter: tucked up in the Thermaic Gulf, the seas hereabouts are not as clean as they might be.

No matter how you arrive, the easiest way of getting your bearings is to head for **the waterfront** (which would be attractive enough were it not for the harbour seemingly doubling up as the city's primary sewage disposal system). Those that brave the brown waves and murderous traffic that bedevil the promenade will find a helpful NTOG/EOT office located midway along it offering free city maps (though finding your way around the centre is easy enough provided you stick to the main streets).

Most of the sights are to be found in the north and eastern sections of the city. The former (just to the north of the area on the map opposite) includes the well-preserved city walls and the only part of the pre-1917 town to survive the flames. Now known as the Kastra district, it is an atmospheric maze of tiny streets more reminiscent of a Turkish town and offers a considerable contrast with the bland wide boulevards (albeit fairly leafy ones) running between the large squares of the rebuilt centre.

As befits a major city, bus links are good all year, though the bus stations are poorly marked, hard to find and best reached via taxi. However, Thessalonika is not well served by ferries, though island hoppers can justify a visit by virtue of those boats (often booked solid by locals at the start of the local holiday season) that do run.

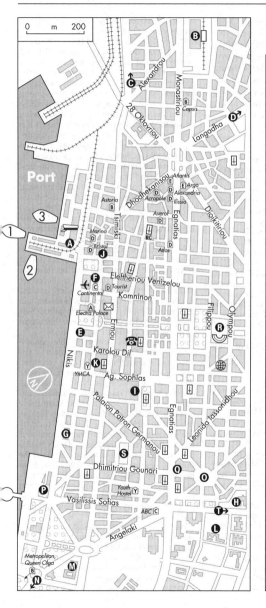

THESSALONIKA
CITY CENTRE

Key

Ⓐ Port Entrance /
   Customs Building
Ⓑ Railway Station
   (all destinations)
Ⓒ Main Bus Station:
   Athens & West
   (700 m)
Ⓓ Bus Station:
   Kavala & East
   (1 km)
Ⓔ NTOG / EOT Office
Ⓕ British Consulate
Ⓖ US Consulate
Ⓗ Hospital
Ⓘ Tourist Police
Ⓙ Banks
Ⓚ Cathedral
Ⓛ University
Ⓜ Archaeological
   Museum
Ⓝ Folk Museum
   (800 m)
Ⓞ Rotunda
   (Ag. Georgios)
Ⓟ White Tower
Ⓠ Arch of Galerius
Ⓡ Roman Agora
Ⓢ Palace of Galerius
Ⓣ Acropolis & City
   Walls (500 m)

1 Domestic Ferries
2 International Ferries
3 Hydrofoil Berth

Thessalonika is a little-known jumping-off point for the islands, and a preferable alternative to an uncomfortable night train-bound to Athens. Those prepared to pay will find regular ferries heading south (though not as many as in years past). Another service missing in 2003 were the daily hydrofoils running to the Sporades islands in High Season.

⊨

As the nearest camping is 25 km away at Agia Triada (via a #72 or #73 bus), most budget travellers head for the hotels near the railway station. These usually fill up early in High Season. Phone ahead if you can; best bets lie in the centre of town and include the D-class *Alexandria* (☎ 536185), *Ilissia* (☎ 528492) and *Atlas* (☎ 537046), and the E-class *Argo* (☎ 519 770) and *Atlantis* (☎ 540131).

Near the port both the D-class *Marina* (☎ 538917) and the C-class *Continental* (☎ 277563) offer reasonable rooms. To the east lies the expensive A-class *Electra Palace* (☎ 23 2221). There is also a *Youth Hostel* (☎ 225946) at 44 Alex. Svolou St. If things get really desperate you can always try the port area D-class *Bristol* (☎ 530351). A remarkable survival of both fire and earthquake, this dilapidated dump offers corridors reminiscent of a 19 C. hospital and rooms filled with crumbling plaster glued together with squashed mosquitoes. For some unknown reason they usually have spare beds even in High Season.

๛

If you only have a short time in Thessalonika then you should abandon all other sightseeing for the **Archaeological Museum**. Housing the contents of Phillip II of Macedon's (Alexander the Great's father) tomb at Vergina (closed to tourists), it contains a collection of art and goldware not to be missed, including the gold casket decorated with the star of Macedon in which Phillip's partially cremated bones were interred. They are now laid out near the casket.

The museum has gained, in both prominence and the number of visitors, from the dispute over the use of the name Macedonia by the former Yugoslav republic to the north. Philip II's remains are seen as irrefutable proof that 'Macedonia is Greek'; in this respect the Greeks do have a point, as the population of ancient Macedon were Greek-speakers (albeit regarded by the sophisticates of Athens and

mainstream Greece as quaintly accented provincial cousins) and not Slavs.

The city's main sights all lie to the southeast of the port/railway station area and can be divided into ancient and Byzantine / medieval categories. Most impressive in the former category is the excellently preserved **Rotunda**: an intact Roman building dating back to 306 AD. Having served as everything from a museum to a mosque (the surviving abandoned minaret is very conspicuous), it is now the university church of Agios Georgios, but is usually closed to tourists. Other ancient remains are fragmentary but more accessible. The **Arch of Galerius** (303 AD) is the best preserved, and was erected to celebrate the Roman Emperor's victory of the Persians at Armenia and Mesopotamia. It is decorated with reliefs depicting the battles. Galerius also built a **Palace** but only foundations of this, the Roman **Agora** and **Hippodrome**, are extant and there is little on public display.

The great architectural jewels in Thessalonika's crown are the Byzantine churches dotted around the city and the Medieval fortifications. Most famous of the churches is the rather plain-looking **St. Demetrius** standing near the Agora (it lies over the remains of the Roman city baths). Noted for its fine mosaics, it was badly damaged in the 1917 fire, and the current building is a copy in all but name.

More substantive (and venerable) are the largely intact **City Walls** to the north of the downtown area. Originally they extended east as far as the **White Tower**. Otherwise known as 'Lefkos Pirgos', this is a medieval construction built on older foundations, and now the nearest the city has to an identifiable emblem. Used for executions during Turkish rule, it was christened the 'Bloody Tower' by the locals after the sultan imprisoned and massacred his rebelling personal bodyguards here in 1826. The sultan took umbrage at the burgers' new name for his little home from home and painted the tower white by way of a response. It is now open to tourists, and contains a **Byzantine Museum** that is put to shame by the city views available from the top of the tower.

With your passport to hand you can also get into the home of the founder of modern Turkey, **Kemal Attaturk**, who was born in the city in 1881. Maintained by the Turkish government, and closed whenever Greco-Turkish tensions run high, the house lies east of the Kastra district, on Apostolou St.

Volos

ΒΟΛΟΣ; pop. 71,400.

CODE ☎ 24210
PORT POLICE ☎ 38888
NTOG OFFICE ☎ 23500

The number four city of Greece, Volos (or Bolos) is set deep in a bay north of Evia, and is the mainland jumping-off point for the Northern Sporades island chain. Long an important port, the modern town lies atop the ancient city of Iolkos, home of Jason the Argonaut, from whence he set out in search of, and returned with, the mythical Golden Fleece.

Sadly, there is little to show of this pastoral ancestry these days — except the ugly appearance of a city that looks as if it ought to be the sort of place which manufactures sheep dip. As a result, most visitors just pass through, being either day-trippers from the islands or Athens-based groups

'doing a Greek island' or using the town as a jumping-off point for the very attractive oak-wooded Mount Pelion peninsula rising up behind. This popular tourist attraction (hence the helpful NTOG tourist office in Volos town centre) was home to the half-man, half-horse Centaurs that have long since hoofed it from the city-clad foothills to quieter parts, despite the existence of a good Archaeological Museum on Volos's bustling waterfront.

The means of getting away are very good, with a dozen buses a day to Athens as well as a rail link to Larissa. Ferry connections with the Sporades are good all year, though other sea connections (including the uninspiring fishing hamlet-clad islet of **Trikeri** to the south) are less consistent.

⊢

Both the D-class *Iasson* (☎ 26075) and E-class *Europa* (☎ 23624), just off the ferry quay, provide indifferent rooms that serve in a pinch. Private room availability is very poor.

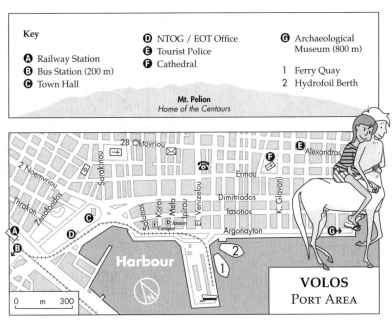

Key

Ⓐ Railway Station
Ⓑ Bus Station (200 m)
Ⓒ Town Hall
Ⓓ NTOG / EOT Office
Ⓔ Tourist Police
Ⓕ Cathedral
Ⓖ Archaeological Museum (800 m)

1 Ferry Quay
2 Hydrofoil Berth

Mt. Pelion
Home of the Centaurs

28 Oktovriou
2 Noemvriou
Sarakinou
Thrakon
Zenofondos
Solonos
Korai
Meta
Spirou
El. Venizelou
Ermou
Dimitriados
Iasonos
Argonayton
K. Giovani
Alexandras
Ⓔ *Europa*
Ⓓ *Iasson*

Harbour

0   m   300

VOLOS
PORT AREA

10
ARGO-SARONIC LINES

**AEGINA · ANGISTRI · ANTIKITHERA · GYTHIO · HYDRA
KITHERA · MONEMVASSIA · NEAPOLI · POROS · SPETSES**

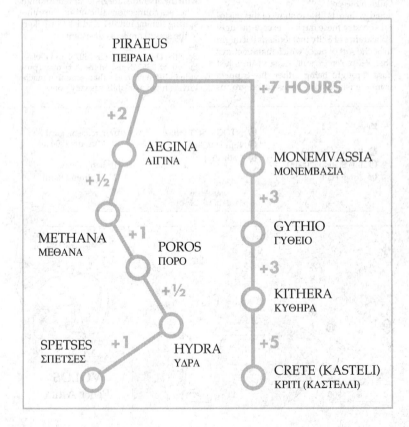

PIRAEUS
ΠΕΙΡΑΙΑ

+7 HOURS

+2

AEGINA
ΑΙΓΙΝΑ

MONEMVASSIA
ΜΟΝΕΜΒΑΣΙΑ

+½

+3

METHANA
ΜΕΘΑΝΑ

+1

POROS
ΠΟΡΟ

GYTHIO
ΓΥΘΕΙΟ

+3

+½

KITHERA
ΚΥΘΗΡΑ

SPETSES
ΣΠΕΤΣΕΣ

+1

HYDRA
ΥΔΡΑ

+5

CRETE (KASTELI)
ΚΡΙΤΙ (ΚΑΣΤΕΛΛΙ)

General Features

This 'Argo-Saronic' chapter encompasses ferry services to islands within the Saronic Gulf proper, as well as those running down the so-called 'Argoid' or East Peloponnesian coast to Kithera and Crete. Ferries confine their runs within one of the two branches, the all important linking services being provided by hydrofoils. The islands and ports also reflect this divide and range from among the most heavily touristed in Greece (within the Saronic Gulf, where the short distance to the capital provides a ready tourist and commuter market), to coastal hamlets further south that have all but fallen out of the ferry network and only see occasional hydrofoils. Connections reach their nadir on Antikithera, the small island most poorly served by regular ferry in the Aegean. There is thus little middle ground between the two groups. Ports are either over-touristed with a veritable procession of landing-craft type ferries and hydrofoils running around (Aegina, Poros, Hydra, and Spetses all qualify for this category thanks to their popularity as day-tripper and European package tour islands), or they can be almost too quiet for comfort (the Peloponnese and island of Kithera) relying on a couple of infrequent ferries and an occasional long-range High Season hydrofoil. Aristotle and his golden mean clearly never found much favour in these parts.

If you like the idea of island hopping against a background of such extremes, then this route offers a happy mix of days when you can visit up to eight ports in 24 hours (if you feel mad enough to try it), and others when you have to wait as long for a ferry. One set of boats definitely to be avoided are those doing the 'three-island' day cruise trips widely advertised in Athens and taking in Aegina, Poros and Hydra. You can do these yourself over the course of a day for half the price (using hydrofoils and catamarans), and save even more using the local ferries.

1 Angistri
2 Methana
3 Souvala

4 Ag. Marina
5 Kosta
6 Porto Helio
7 Galatas

SARONIC GULF & EAST PELOPONNESE

Example Itinerary [2 Weeks]
The mix of over-touristed and relatively inaccessible ports of call offers an interesting holiday for those who like variety. Even so you will have to be prepared to compromise and adjust your schedule (particularly the latter part). Arrive on a favourable day and it is quite possible to get down the group (returning either via Crete and a direct boat back to Piraeus or by bus back up the Peloponnese). Otherwise you will have to skip a port.

Arrival/Departure Point
Athens is easily the best airport on offer. If you are offered a cheap flight to either airports on the Peloponnese or Crete ignore the temptation; they are just too difficult to get back to in an emergency.

Season
If you are prepared to give it an extra week then this itinerary could be followed all year round or you could return via the Central Cyclades Line. Otherwise the usual High Season advantages in terms of frequency of service apply.

1 Athens [2 Days]
An easy starting point and an easy first hop: all the boats start from the same quay at Piraeus and offer frequent starts for Aegina so you won't have to hang around for long.

2 Aegina [1 Day]
An interesting first port of call with enough to fill a day with sightseeing. But the inescapable evidence of mass tourism does little to nurture a get-away-from-it-all Greek island atmosphere. Accommodation can also be a problem so if you are having real difficulty you could take an evening boat on down the line or alternatively, pick up an evening ferry to the neighbouring small beach island of Angistri.

3 Poros [1 Day]
The town itself can be done in a couple of hours but this does make a good base of operations if you prefer to 'do' the adjacent islands as outings from one base. Mainland excursions to Mycenae and the famous theatre at Epidavros are possible from here too.

4 Spetses [2 Days]
The best beach island in the group and thus the best place to rest up for a couple of days while you wait for a hydrofoil or ferry south. The mainland village of Kosta is also easily accessible, with buses to nearby tourist sites.

5 Monemvassia [2 Days]
After being pampered by the profusion of services thus far the jump to Monemvassia can come as something of a shock. It seems like the end of the world but in fact it is quite a civilized little place. If a hydrofoil or the ferry is not offering your required hop on south you can always take a bus to Napoli and pick up the ferry from there.

6 Kithera [2 Days]
This quiet island offers a complete contrast with its northern Saronic sisters and is a worthy destination to aim for in its own right. That said, the first priority on arrival must be establishing when you can get off. If the wait for a boat on to Crete is too long you always have a boat to Gythio or Napoli on the Peloponnese (both offering bus links with Athens) as a safety option to fall back on. Alternatively, if you have tarried too long in the Saronic Gulf you can give the island a miss and head directly on to Crete.

7 Crete [2 Days]
Dumped on the eastern end of Crete you will have to get a bus from Kasteli to Chania and then another on to Iraklion. Here you can take time out to visit Knossos and the Archaeological Museum before taking the overnight boat back to Piraeus.

1 Athens [2 Days]
If you are planning to venture as far down this line as Crete you could do worse than skip a day in the capital at the beginning of your holiday to give you an extra day's safety at the end of your trip. Either way, as usual give yourself at least one clear day back in Athens before your return flight.

AEGINA
Temple of Aphaia

The C/F *Aias* arrives at Aegina
(with the Hidden Harbour in the
foreground and Angistri Is. on
the horizon)

HYDRA
Main Street &
Cannon

ANGISTRI
Main Ferry Quay & Church
at Skala Port Village

POROS
Northern Suburbs
of Poros Town

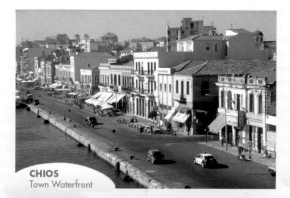

CHIOS
Town Waterfront

The P/S *Fourni Express*
Departs from Fourni
Village Beach

SAMOS
The Roman Catholic
Church on Vathi
Waterfront

Northern Coast east of
Karlovassi

Eastern Lines

FOURNI
Village Beach

SKOPELOS
Panagia ston Pirgho
at Skopelos Town

The C/F *Macedon*
Moored at Skopelos Town

ALONISSOS
Alonissos' Beach Boats
in Patitiri Bay

A *Minoan Flying Dolphin*
hydrofoil — a common
visitor to the Sporades &
Argo–Saronic islands

THASSOS
View of Thassos Town
from the Acropolis

Northern Aegean

Ionian

KEFALONIA
Sami Beach & Tide Mill
Wheel

CORFU/KERKYRA
Old Town & Palace Wall
Staircase

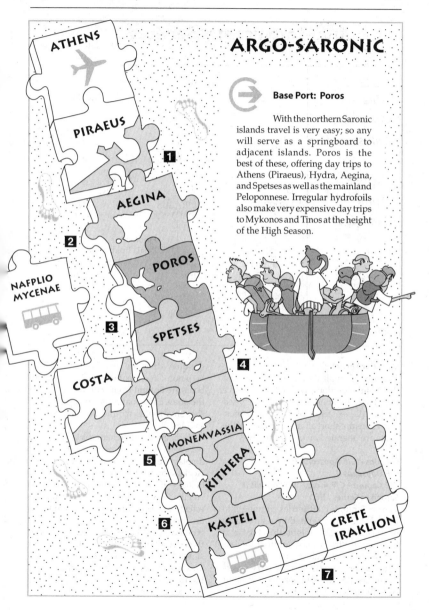

ATHENS

PIRAEUS

1

AEGINA

2

NAFPLIO
MYCENAE

POROS

3

SPETSES

COSTA

4

MONEMVASSIA

5

KITHERA

6

KASTELI

CRETE
IRAKLION

7

ARGO-SARONIC

Base Port: Poros

With the northern Saronic islands travel is very easy; so any will serve as a springboard to adjacent islands. Poros is the best of these, offering day trips to Athens (Piraeus), Hydra, Aegina, and Spetses as well as the mainland Peloponnese. Irregular hydrofoils also make very expensive day trips to Mykonos and Tinos at the height of the High Season.

Argo-Saronic Ferry Services

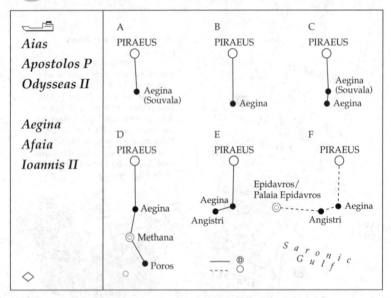

Aias
Apostolos P
Odysseas II

Aegina
Afaia
Ioannis II

A
PIRAEUS
Aegina
(Souvala)

B
PIRAEUS
Aegina

C
PIRAEUS
Aegina
(Souvala)
Aegina

D
PIRAEUS
Aegina
Methana
Poros

E
PIRAEUS
Aegina
Angistri

F
PIRAEUS
Epidavros/
Palaia Epidavros
Aegina
Angistri

S a r o n i c
G u l f

Main Car Ferries

The mix of small islands tucked against the mainland, along with either massive popularity or none at all, has conspired against the existence of large car ferries. Ferry runs are short affairs, and most of the boats are operated by one company.

C/F *Aias* – C/F *Apostolos P*
C/F *Odysseas II*
C/F *Aegina* – C/F *Afaia* – C/F *Ioannis II*
Saronikos Ferries / HFD

The six landing-craft ferries running into the Saronic Gulf operated by a subsidiary of *Hellas Flying Dolphins* berth in the Great Harbour at Piraeus, just south of the bus station/ferry terminal building. Departure times do not appear on EOT ferry sheets but are posted up in Greek (for a 48-hour period) on a small Port Police kiosk on the quay (they are usually very ready to help non-Greek-readers). Tickets for these boats are bought from stalls at the back of the quay. Each boat runs one or several of the above routes, with additional weekend sailings.

The boats are interchangeable, with little between them in terms of facilities. Most display destination boards and nursery clocks showing their departure time. Most boats — if not offering a direct service to Aegina Town — include it on extended schedules. Departures for Aegina (Souvala) are primarily for commercial vehicles. None of these boats heads further south than Poros but they offer the cheapest (and slowest) travel down the line. All services are duplicated by smaller passenger craft, but these landing-craft car ferries offer the cheaper tickets.

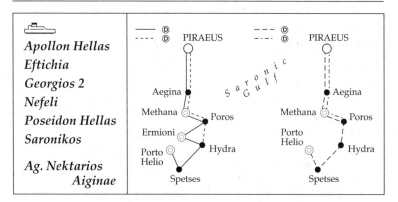

| Apollon Hellas |
| Eftichia |
| Georgios 2 |
| Nefeli |
| Poseidon Hellas |
| Saronikos |
| Ag. Nektarios |
| Aiginae |

In addition to landing-craft ferries, the Saronic Gulf is served by a number of small regular boats. Faster than the landing-craft types, they venture further down the line, but primarily exist to ensure that a service can be maintained during the winter when poor sea conditions confine small boats to port. Until 2000 they competed against each other, but most belong to one fleet and are frequently switched around.

C/F Apollon Hellas
Saronikos Ferries / HFD; 1990; 1820 GRT.
One of the newer, larger and better boats in this small fleet, this vessel was a new arrival in 2000.

C/F Eftichia
Saronikos Ferries / HFD; 1974; 869 GRT.
The sharp-nosed *Eftichia* — a passenger boat converted to a full car ferry — is the smallest fully fledged ferry on the line. Usually overcrowded to bursting as a result, she can offer a less relaxing journey than her companions.

C/F Georgios 2
Saronikos Ferries / HFD; 1990; 3438 GRT.
The largest of the small ferries on this route, the *Georgios 2* appeared in 1997. She was tied up and out of action in 2000, but has been running around successfully since. She is a pleasant enough craft and popular too.

C/F Nefeli
Saronikos Ferries / HFD; 1990; 2847 GRT.
The second 'new' boat of 2000 (though she is anything but), this vessel was often deployed on the twice-daily Poros run.

C/F Poseidon Hellas
Saronikos Ferries / HFD; 1999; 2100 GRT.
A new arrival in 1999, this ferry runs twice daily to Poros, swapping around with the equally new *Apollon Hellas*.

C/F Saronikos
Saronikos Ferries / HFD; 1974; 1126 GRT.
A roofed-over landing-craft ferry, the *Saronikos* runs in tandem with the *Eftichia*; the vessels make alternate runs, with one boat going on to Poros while the other starts later and turns back at Aegina.

C/F Ag. Nektarios Aiginae
Local; 1999; 1500 GRT.
Formerly the *Panagia Skiathou* this new boat is a refugee from the Northern Sporades line where it failed to compete successfully with the 100% monopoly operated by the Hellas Flying Dolphin sub-line. Now hoping for better luck breaking their monopoly on the Saronic Gulf service to Spetses, this boat started operating in 2002. The newest boat on the line, she should be popular, but her design ('nautical gothic') is a tad old-fashioned and this could put some off.

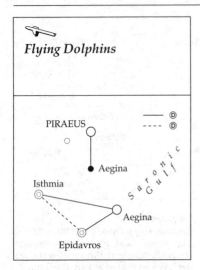

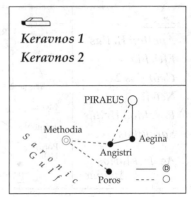

H/F *Flying Dolphin 1—30*
Hellas Flying Dolphins

For reasons that aren't clear, hydrofoils heading direct to Aegina never seem to venture beyond this destination. The probable reason is that the boats tend to be very popular in the rush hours and at weekends (so it pays to book your return if it is going to coincide with these times). The island of Aegina is also developing as a jumping-off point for additional hydrofoils to Epidavros. In years past an additional link ran to the entrance of the Corinth Canal, at Isthmia, ferrying tour parties to nearby ancient Corinth.

C/Ms *Keravnos 1 – Keravnos 2*

For the last few years a small catamaran — the *Keravnos 1* — has run around the upper reaches of the Saronic Gulf, running out of Piraeus a number of times a day, her primary destinations being Aegina and Angistri. In 2000 she was joined by a second equally small cat called the *Keravnos 2*. Both boats are a bit on the old side, but have been extensively refurbished: the decision by *Hellas Flying Dolphins* to make-over

all their competing hydrofoils in 2000 has obviously prompted a major refit.

H/F *Dolphins I—IV*
Saronic Dolphins

A local hydrofoil service has now existed for seven years, running an hourly service to the resort of Agia Marina on Aegina. The limited popularity of the route has forced changes since the addition of Souvala, and latterly Paros and Hydra, to occasional itineraries. More variations could occur in 2004 as these boats don't look to be particularly successful. In 2003 one of these craft was moved to the Cyclades to cover for the missing *Jet One* catamaran. It is unclear if this service will resume in 2004.

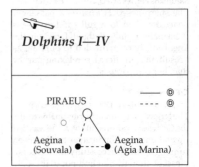

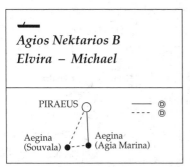

Small Passenger Boats

In addition to the regular ferries, hydrofoils and catamarans, a number of smaller passenger craft operate to the islands of Aegina and Angistri. For the most part small vessels incapable of journeying far, they rely on commuters for their custom; each boat runs several times daily to its own set destination. Departures for the following 48 hours are posted up on the Saronic Gulf quay Port Police kiosk (they are listed separately at the end of the regular ferry departure times). Tickets for these boats are either bought on board or from ticket 'desks' on the quayside. With the growth in the number of hydrofoils their popularity is on the wane, so some could well be missing in 2004.

Most likely to be of use are flashy **Elvira**, and **P/S Michael**: both provide a link with

the resort of Agia Marina on Aegina. Note: these boats take at least double the hydrofoil journey time. Also of interest is the **P/S Kitsolakis Express** which heads direct to the 'beach' island of Angistri. A more popular and enjoyable means of access is via a large caïque — the **T/B Angistri Express** — that runs four times daily in High Season from Aegina Town to the main Angistrian port at Skala and then smaller Megalochorio (alias Milos) along the coast.

Finally, there is the **P/S Manaras Express**; she also ventures to Angistri (via Aegina) but is less prepossessing, being a tiny tub of a boat that looks to have been cobbled together out of old banana boxes. She runs for the benefit of those who like to live dangerously and is usually filled with locals visiting Athens on shopping expeditions.

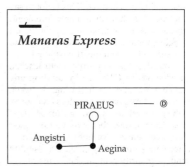

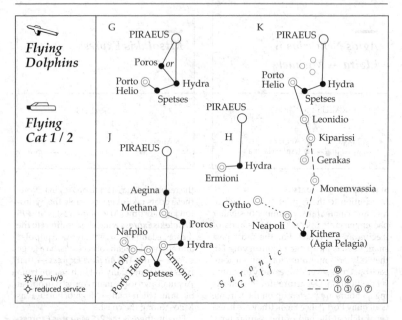

Flying Dolphins

Flying Cat 1 / 2

☼ i/6—iv/9
◇ reduced service

H/F *Flying Dolphin 1—30*
Hellas Flying Dolphins

Hydrofoils are both the most versatile and quickest way of hopping around the Saronic Gulf, so much so that some islands (e.g. Hydra) largely depend on them. They are popular, easy to use, and usually keep good time (the protected Saronic Gulf waters ensure that most of these services run reasonably to schedule). This is not to say that they don't have their share of problems. In the summer of 2000 one caught fire off Aegina, forcing all on board to jump into the sea and swim to nearby fishing boats. Despite this, it can pay to buy a return ticket: particularly for (1) last hydrofoils from any given port, and (2) hydrofoils between Poros and Aegina, and Spetses and Poros, which are relatively few in number. Last year saw all these boats move from their former base at Zea Marina to Piraeus Great Harbour — increasing their accessibility and popularity still further. Itinerary G

is the most consistent of the routes run; most take in ports along J. During the High Season there is a service (K) down to Kithera four days a week.

C/Ms *Flying Cat 1 – Flying Cat 2*
Hellas Flying Dolphins

Operating alongside the hydrofoils are two very swish and popular catamarans, usually running itinerary G. Times are included in the hydrofoil timetable, and ticket prices are the same. This being so, take these boats if you can, as the ride is faster, smoother and quieter (though the *Flying Cat 2* is noisier than most cats) into the bargain.

C/Ms *Hydra Cat – Spetses Cat*
Saronic Catamarans

In 2002 these two boats were advertised, a kiosk was erected at Piraeus (manned by a friendly lady without timetables) and then — nothing. The boats didn't appear. Hopefully they will finally be around in 2004.

C/F *Mirtidiotissa*
ANEN Lines; 1976; 2889 GRT.

One of the few subsidized ferry routes left in Greece runs down the Peloponnese coast and on to Crete. Until 1997 the itinerary had changed little in years, though days of operation and ferries regularly did, with the boat detailed to run the route calling at all the small ports on the Peloponnese coast before visiting Kithera and Crete. However, since then the Peloponnese has been dropped from schedules, and Piraeus departures have fallen to one or two a week. The vessel providing the link since 2000 is the *Mirtidiotissa* (the ex-*Anemos*, now operated as a one-ferry company). Unfortunately this boat has a recent history of failing safety checks, so it is very difficult to recommend using her.

C/F *Nissos Kithera*
This is a small ferry bought by the islanders of Kithera to maintain a daily link with the mainland. In addition to performing this useful function, she ventures further afield, providing extra links to Gythio and Crete (Kasteli). Although small, she is easily the best boat hereabouts.

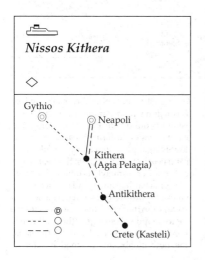

Argo-Saronic Islands & Ports

AEGINA

Bus routes:
- —— ○ ev ¾ ⊕ 06.15–20.30
- ---- ⑩ x 13: 06.15–20.30
- —·—· ⑩ x 11: 06.15–20.30
- ······ ⑩ x 5

Souvala

Vagia

Agii

Mesagros

Kipseli

Palaiochora

Temple of Apollo
Kolona

Kontos

Temple of Aphaia

Aegina Town

Alones

Ag. Marina

Faros

Marathon

Portes

Mt Oros/
Temple of Zeus
532 m

—— ⑩ x 12

MONI

Perdika

Sfentouri

0   km   2

Aegina

ΑΙΓΙΝΑ; 84 km²; pop. 10,000.

CODE ☎ 22970
TOURIST POLICE ☎ 23243
FIRST AID ☎ 22222

Lying a mere 20 km south of Piraeus, Aegina (pronounced '*Ee–genah*') is among the most touristed of the Greek islands. Its close proximity to Athens makes it a popular package-tourist destination (and incidentally, an ideal spot in which to fill a day in hand before a flight home), but despite this, out of August it is not noticeably overcrowded. If you don't mind commuting each day, the island is quite a nice base for 'doing' the capital, besides offering pleasant wooded, low-lying mountain scenery and plenty of sand beach coves for (given the cleanliness of the water) somewhat dubious bathing.

Aegina has had an up and down history: emerging during the 5 C. BC as a serious rival to Athens, it lost the inevitable regional power struggle that followed. Forcibly repopulated by the Athenians, the new inhabitants deemed it safer to grow pistachio nuts rather than dream of power: Aegina is now the nut capital of Greece (you'll find free hand-outs all along the waterfront along with plenty of highly priced bags). In 1829 Aegina briefly again came to the fore when it became the first capital of the Greek state (before losing out to Athens for a second time).

Aegina Town, complete with its neo-classical frontage from its days as the capital, is the main centre and by far the best of the possible ferry destinations. The waterfront is lined with tavernas and tourist shops (pistachio nuts figuring prominently in the displays of wares) near the ferry quay, but once you move along the waterfront or inland a street or two, the town reveals itself to be a surprisingly unspoilt small island town surrounded by nut orchards and offering a day of gentle tourism. The town is very much centred around the ferry quay, the tourist presence all too evident by the existence of horses and carriages standing along the promenade awaiting a fare. But either side of this the waterfront is attractive despite a busy road.

To the south, in the ancient commercial harbour, you will find full-to-overflowing caïques selling fruit and veg, with a fresh fish market housed in a quayside alley opposite. To the north lie the remains of the ancient trireme harbour. This was famous in the ancient world, though its name — it was known as the 'hidden harbour' — has caused more than one scholar to scratch his head because it isn't, well, exactly 'hidden', even after two and a half thousand years. Behind it rises the lightly wooded former acropolis at Kolona (with good views over the Saronic Gulf and the town and the fine beach to the north).

Along the beach road lie the bus ticket kiosk and several budget hotels and restaurants. Ticket agencies are surprisingly thin on the ground; the quayside Port Police kiosk has ferry departure times posted up daily (in Greek), with ticket kiosks (often only staffed half an hour before the ferry is due to depart) either side. Note: if you are planning to return to Athens via late

afternoon/evening hydrofoil you should buy your ticket on arrival as they tend to get booked up.

Aegina's bus service is limited but good, running frequently along the northern coast to the island's second town of **Agia Marina**. Linked by small passenger ferry to Piraeus, it is an unabashed package tour resort with all the trimmings. Even so, so far as disco-cities on the sand go it is better than most.

If night-life is a priority then Agia Marina will appeal; otherwise the walk up the pine-forested hill to the Temple of Aphaia is likely to be of greater interest (the 2 km path looks to have been made by a runaway bulldozer). If you are visiting Aegina for a day it is worth considering taking the ferry to Agia Marina, walking up to the temple then taking a bus to Aegina Town and a ferry back to Athens from there.

Other coastal villages are less developed, but gradually falling to the tourist hordes, or failing this, have become villa-filled suburbs for the more affluent Athenians. The small fishing port of **Perdika** on the south-west coast is the most attractive, and surprisingly unspoilt, with some rooms on offer besides boats to the delightfully quiet pine-clad islet of **Moni**.

The third of Aegina's ports, **Souvala**, is a resort village with a reasonable beach and a large quay (adorned with landing-craft ferries that are used by lorries unwilling to negotiate the streets of Aegina town).

▱

Most of Aegina's hotels are pre-booked by tour operators or inconveniently placed. In town there are plenty of mid price range options. The best of these are: the *Brown* (☎ 22271) at the south end of the town, along with the hotels north of the port; the *Marmarinos* (☎ 23510) just has the edge, though there is little between the *Plaza* (☎ 25600), *Avra* (☎ 22303), *Artemis* (☎ 25195) and the budget *Togias* (☎ 24242). Those looking for something a little different should try the *Pension Pavlou* (☎ 22795), which offers pricey, but atmospheric, rooms in an old town house. Being so close to Athens, Aegina sees regular rooms fill up very quickly in High Season; so arrive early.

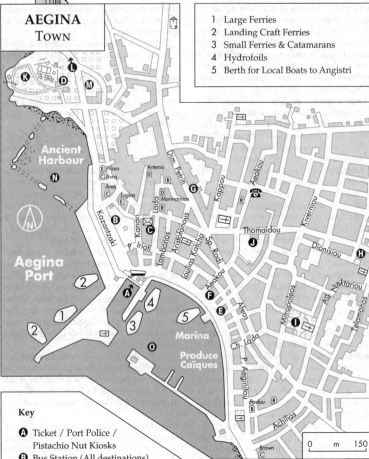

AEGINA
Town

1 Large Ferries
2 Landing Craft Ferries
3 Small Ferries & Catamarans
4 Hydrofoils
5 Berth for Local Boats to Angistri

Ancient Harbour

Aegina Port

Marina

Produce Caïques

Key

Ⓐ Ticket / Port Police / Pistachio Nut Kiosks
Ⓑ Bus Station (All destinations)
Ⓒ Regular & Tourist Police
Ⓓ Archaeological Museum / Site of Ancient Theatre
Ⓔ National Bank of Greece
Ⓕ Newspapers
Ⓖ Medical Centre
Ⓗ Hospital
Ⓘ Cathedral / Former Museum
Ⓙ Markello's Tower
Ⓚ Acropolis & Temple of Apollo
Ⓛ Road to Beach (50 m) & Aphaia (10 km)
Ⓜ Site of the Ancient Stadium
Ⓝ Remains of the 'Hidden Harbour'
Ⓞ Ancient Commercial Harbour

0   m   150

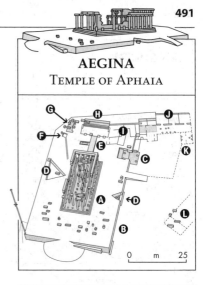

AEGINA
TEMPLE OF APHAIA

👓

A crumbling lone column of a **Temple of Apollo** stands as a marker indicating the site of Aegina's ancient acropolis on the northern edge of the town. The walls were demolished by the Athenians, so little but jumbled foundations remain. The temple once resembled the temple of Aphaia but you would be hard pressed to know it now. This site (known as Kolona or 'column') is also home to Aegina's reasonable **Archaeological Museum** (08.30–15.00 ex ①), which houses a display of coins (Aegina was the first island to mint its own currency — its symbol was the turtle) and the 6 c. BC 'Aegina Sphinx'.

The rest of Aegina Town is stronger in atmosphere than sightseeing detail, the one exception being the oddly turreted **Markello's Tower**. Built in 1802, this curiously cute structure was the office-cum-home of Greece's first governor, and the tiny ground floor is now a home for local art exhibitions.

The island's major draw is the small 5 c. BC **Temple of Aphaia** (Ⓓ 08.00–15.00/17.00). Named after a minor daughter goddess of Zeus, it is set atop a pine-tree-clad hill 10 km from Aegina Town, and is one of the best preserved in Greece, with a unique 2-storey inner colonnade (it is one of the few temples to retain its interior columns). The pedimental sculptures, however, now reside in Munich. Similarities with the Athenian acropolis extend beyond 'lost' sculptures: it is advisable to visit early to avoid the crowds. On the plus side, the temple is very appealing, being a more approachable size than the later temples in Athens. Built around 490 BC, it reflects the transition between the Late Archaic and Classical traditions. The terrace setting with its views and lightning mast (one set of gable sculptures in classical times and the western end seem to have been demolished by lightning strikes — the last in 1969) also helps to give the building a character all its own. Note: only limited refreshments (i.e. beer and orange juice) are available from a taverna at the site.

Aegina also had another major temple of interest — the **Temple of Zeus** on the peak of Mt. Oros. Only the foundations survive, with few tourists venturing up the mountain path to view the remains. The final site of note is the monastery of **St. Catherine** on the road east of Aegina Town. It lies west of the abandoned former hill capital of **Palaiochora** on the site of a Temple of Aphrodite.

Key

Ⓐ Temple of Aphaia
Ⓑ Rebuilt Sanctuary Precinct Wall
Ⓒ Classical Propylon (gateway)
Ⓓ Foundations of 6 c. BC Precinct
Ⓔ Ceremonial Ramp & Altar
Ⓕ Cistern & Base of Sphinx Column
Ⓖ Remains of Archaic Altar
Ⓗ Classical Altar
Ⓘ Archaic Priest's Quarters & Baths
Ⓙ Classical Priest's Quarters
Ⓚ Outer Propylon
Ⓛ Anti-peribolus (precinct) Building

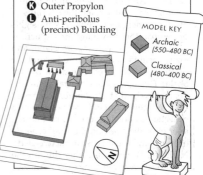

MODEL KEY

Archaic
[550–480 BC]

Classical
[480–400 BC]

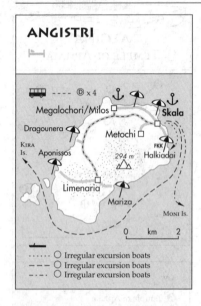

ANGISTRI

Megalochori/Milos
Skala
Dragounera
Metochi
KIRA Is.
Aponissos
294 m
FKK
Halkiadai
Limenaria
Mariza
MONI Is.
0   km   2

····· ○ Irregular excursion boats
- - - ○ Irregular excursion boats
-·-· ○ Irregular excursion boats

Angistri

ΑΓΚΙΣΤΡΙ; 17 km²; pop. 530.

CODE ☎ 22970

A small, low satellite of Aegina, pine-clad Angistri is a popular day-excursion destination for beach-loving Athenians too afraid of the pollution in the Saronic Gulf to venture to beaches closer to home. In addition, Angistri is increasingly finding a summer role absorbing the overflow of her larger neighbour, but, lacking sights or centres, the prevailing atmosphere is very much of a beach resort island, and many visitors fail to venture beyond the prettyish beaches near the main port at **Skala**. This spread-out coastal plain settlement is the de facto centre: dominated by a tall new church, it is made up of a collection of hotels and tavernas and not a lot else (the coast on the southern side of the quay is the most attractive part). Nightlife, however, is rather thin on the ground (there is only one disco): Angistri

is for the thirty- or forty-somethings rather than the younger crowd.

The daily Aegina boat stops at Skala, and also runs along the north coast to Angistri's second port at **Megalochori** (often also known — in the interests of brevity if nothing else — as '**Milos**'). Home to a narrow street chora of sorts, the island's diminutive bus calls here en route from Skala to the comparatively quiet 'capital' at **Limenaria**. This is an untouristed village: the only attraction is the escape from the coastal crowds.

Angistri is somewhat unusual for a Greek island in having shingle rather than sand beaches. These are scattered pretty evenly around the coastline, and all are within an easy shady pine-tree walk of the hotel areas. **Dragounera** beach, sited in a small cove, is among the best and only a short walk from the bus stop. **Halkiadai** beach has become a de facto nudist beach in recent years, though how much you see is very dependent on when you go.

👀

There is little to see on Angistri, but caïques undertake sunset cruises around the island, and travel agents offer more excursions to nearby destinations than you will find on most Greek islands. In fact, Angistri is an excellent base for a number of day-tripping sorties. **Athens** and **Aegina** are within easy reach thanks to regular catamarans and tour boats, and there are expensive (€16.50) day trips on offer to Hydra and Poros for those too scared to brave the ferry system. More appealing — and unique — are excursions to **Ancient Corinth** and the **Corinth Canal** (€22), and to the famous **Ancient Theatre** at **Epidavros**, where (in July and August only) you can see an evening performance of a classical play as part of the excursion (tickets for Epidavros are also sold in Athens). Note: on excursions from Angistri, archaeological site admission and theatre performance tickets are NOT included in the excursion ticket price.

🛏

Reasonable supply of rooms and some 22 D- and E-class hotels, but these are apt to fill with Athenian 'weekenders' from Friday on. There is no camping: this is very much a day-tripper and package-tour dominated island.

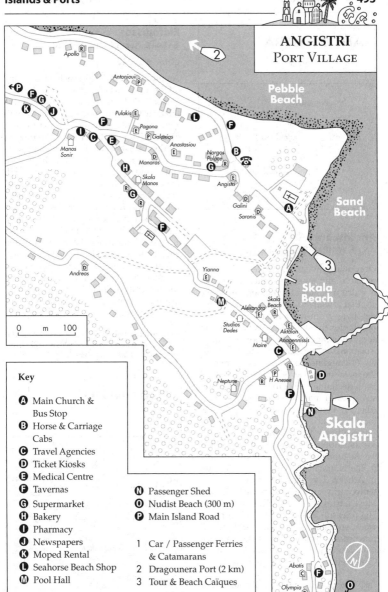

ANGISTRI
PORT VILLAGE

Pebble Beach

Sand Beach

Skala Beach

Skala Angistri

Apollo

Antonioui

Pulakis

Pagona

Galaxias

Anastasiou

Manaras

Nargos Palace

Manos Sonir

Skala Manos

Angistri

Galini

Saronis

Andreas

Yianna

Alexandro

Skala Beach

Studios Dedes

Aktaion

Maire

Anagennissis

Neptune

H Anesee

Abatis

Olympia

Key

- **A** Main Church & Bus Stop
- **B** Horse & Carriage Cabs
- **C** Travel Agencies
- **D** Ticket Kiosks
- **E** Medical Centre
- **F** Tavernas
- **G** Supermarket
- **H** Bakery
- **I** Pharmacy
- **J** Newspapers
- **K** Moped Rental
- **L** Seahorse Beach Shop
- **M** Pool Hall

- **N** Passenger Shed
- **O** Nudist Beach (300 m)
- **P** Main Island Road

- **1** Car / Passenger Ferries & Catamarans
- **2** Dragounera Port (2 km)
- **3** Tour & Beach Caïques

ANTIKITHERA

Potamos

0 km 4

Galaniana

No bus service

No beach boat service

Antikithera
ΑΝΤΙΚΥΘΗΡΑ; 29 km²; pop. 115.

Occupying the straits between the Peloponnese and western Crete, this island is a dry mountain top poking out of the sea that is likely to appeal only to extreme get-away-from-it-all fanatics. The tiny population lives in two dusty hamlets and sees few strangers. The oppressive air of isolation is encouraging the younger islanders to emigrate, so those that do remain see fewer friends as well. The only school has a declining role of four, and the island struggles to maintain the bare essentials (the vet hereabouts doubles up as the local doctor).

These days Antikithera is best known for its shipwrecks, one of which yielded up the bronze Ephebe of Antikithera now in the National Archaeological Museum in Athens. The Elgin Marbles were also temporarily sunk here en route to Britain. Most ferries steer well clear, and out of High Season links are reduced to one a week, so the island is inaccessible for all practicable purposes. If you want a quick look you can visit via a ferry en route to Crete, returning north 6 hours later.

Take a room here and you will double your host's annual income!

Elafonissos
ΕΛΑΦΟΝΗΣΙ; 19 km²; pop. 270.

CODE ☎ 27340

An attractive, isolated beach island lying off the southern Peloponnese coast town of Neapoli, Elafonissos ('deer's island') was linked to the mainland by a causeway until 1677. The only settlement lies at the site of this divide: a church now standing in glorious isolation (along with Elafonissos's only tree) from the other buildings on a spit of land tapering towards the mainland. Elafonissos town is a pretty fishing village that offers an ideal base if your notion of getting away from it all includes an absence of banks and other tourists. In addition, the island is blessed with clean seas and a superb sand beach 4 km south of the village (accessible via an irregular boat). Caïques augment ferry links, running to Neapoli (30 minutes east). There is also a landing-craft mainland service operating to a track running off the Neapoli—Peloponnese road.

Some rooms and 2 B-class pensions in the village: the *Asteri Tis Elafonissou* (☎ 61271) and the cheaper *Elafonissos* (☎ 61268).

ELAFONISSOS

⊙ x 2

0 km 4

Elafonissos

276 m

Sarakiniko

Levki Bay

No bus service

⊙ 10.00–16.00

Epidavros
ΕΠΙΔΑΥΡΟΣ

The name 'Epidavros' is applied to three closely related places. On ferry timetables it refers to the small Peloponnesian port of **Palea Epidavros** — host to three campsites, a dozen hotels, a reasonable beach and the scanty remains of an ancient city. Some 6 km up the coast is **Nea Epidavros** — an attractive hamlet backed by orange groves. Finally, there is **Ancient Epidavros** — the famous sanctuary to the god of healing, Asklepios, and now one of Greece's premier archaeological sites thanks to its notable theatre, easily the finest ancient theatre ever built, and by marvellous good fortune also the best preserved. Buses run to the site daily from Athens and from Palea Epidavros, 15 km away (taxis also run

EPIDAVROS
ANCIENT SANCTUARY

Key

- **A** Theatre
- **B** Gymnasium
- **C** Temple of Asklepios
- **D** Tholos
- **E** Stadium
- **F** Katagogion (160-room hotel)
- **G** Portico of Kotys / Palaestra
- **H** Abaton (dormitory for the sick)
- **I** Temple of Artemis
- **J** Temple of Themis
- **K** Sanctuary of the Egyptian Gods
- **L** Greek Baths
- **M** Roman Baths
- **N** Roman Houses
- **O** Roman Odeon
- **P** North Hall
- **Q** Fountain House
- **R** Path to the Propylaea (gateway)

Main Path
Minor Path

Museum

Tickets

Coach Park

Road to Palaia Epidavros

ARISTOPHANES
THE BIRDS

ACT 3

ENTER
PEISTHETAIROS ...

Modern productions of ancient plays at Epidavros are popular. However, don't come here expecting to see an accurate recreation. In Classical times the all-male cast donned terracotta masks, and in comedies such as *The Birds*, players wore tights with heavily padded buttocks and an over-long leather phallus that could be waved around to great comic effect. The bordering-on-crude nature of Old Attic Comedy accounts for the ambivalent attitude of the more conservative modern Greeks. As fine literature they laud the plays, but an excess of reality is rarely encouraged.

5 c. BC Comic Actor in costume

0   m   75

direct). Neighbouring Nafplio also has a bus service to the site, and regular tours — some including performances at the theatre—are available from nearby islands such as Angistri, Aegina and Poros.

ᏉᏉ

Set among the attractive rolling wooded slopes of Mt. Kynortion, Ancient Epidavros (open ②–⑦ 08.30–15.00; tickets €3) as an important sanctuary to the healing god Asklepios (of staff and serpent fame). Although it didn't rank as highly as its counterpart on Kos, easier accessibility ensured that it became very affluent — a fact reflected in the quality of its buildings. The site was home to what was popularly considered the greatest **Theatre** in the Greek world (thanks to its unrivalled symmetry, beauty and perfect acoustics), and, if this wasn't enough, Epidavros was also the home of a **Tholos** (a circular pillared hall) that was deemed by many of its contemporaries to be simply the most beautiful Greek building — full stop. Both these circular structures were built by the famed architect Polykleitos, c. 350 BC. The perfectly preserved theatre, with seating for 14,000, is a sightseeing must. In July and August is home to the Epidavros festival, hosting performances of classical plays — *The Birds* of Aristophanes being a favourite.

Contrasting vividly with the extant theatre are the other buildings on the site — which consist only of foundations. Only fragments (now housed in the site **Museum**) survive of the famous, highly decorated, colonnaded Tholos, but these (coupled with the description by Pausanias, who recorded that it was decorated with paintings by Pausias) are sufficient to give us a good idea of its form. Other foundations of note are those of the **Stadium** (the sanctuary hosted its own games), a small **Temple of Asklepios** and an impressively large 4-quad **Katagogion** (a hotel that had 160 sleeping cells).

Ermioni
EPMIONI

A suburb commuter town on the Peloponnese coast. Tourists with any sense avoid disembarking here as there is nothing to see or do: the town lacks even a serviceable beach. The majority of vessels calling are hydrofoils.

Gerakas
ΓΕΡΑΚΑΣ

Located in a mini-loch half-way down the eastern Peloponnese, this small and uninspiring hamlet (without buses or a beach) has little but a road into the interior. In past years regular hydrofoils and rare ferries have called at the port (none of the latter were operating in 2000).

Gythio
ΓΥΘΕΙΟ; pop. 4,950.

CODE ☎ 27330
PORT POLICE ☎ 22262
TOURIST POLICE ☎ 27310 28701
POLICE ☎ 22271

The most important town strung along the south coast of the Peloponnese, Gythio offers an attractive Venetian house-fronted promenade, decked out with a number of reasonable fish restaurants and set close against the green foothills of Mount Laryssion. A good base for exploring the region, it is a pretty — if somewhat over-touristed — port with quite a history. Sparta's naval base during the Peloponnesian war, it was attacked and sacked by the Athenian navy in 455 BC (relations are now on a friendlier footing, with 4 buses running daily between the two — via Sparta). During the Roman era the town became an important production centre for murex — the imperial purple dye — extracted from sea molluscs by a method now lost. Most of ancient Gythio is now equally invisible: the only survival of note is a small theatre 400 m north of the current town. Ferry links are also rather poor as Gythio lies tucked 2–3 hours' steaming up the Gulf of Lakonia. Along with the odd tourist boat, they combine to provide an almost daily service to Kithera and its links with the outside world.

⊨

There are a dozen or more hotels in Gythio, but they tend to be comparatively expensive: this is up-market package tour country. The cheapest are the waterfront D-class *Akaion* (☎ 22294) and *Kranae* (☎ 22249). Fortunately rooms are on offer and well signposted around the harbour area of the town.

A
Several olive-grove sites lie just off a good beach 5 km south of the town. Buses run hourly past the camping strip, though the sites rely on trailer-campers rather than backpackers.

◌◌
The main sight lies just to the south of the promenade: the small causeway-linked islet of **Marathonisi** (ancient Kranai). Famed in antiquity as the spot where Paris spent his first night with Helen (whose face launched the first thousand Greek ferries) while carrying her off to Troy, the islet attracted the curious from the first, prompting the erection of a Hellenistic temple of Aphrodite and a number of other shrines. As late as 1770, garbled tales of the Jolly Roger prompted the islet's Turkish masters in faraway Istanbul to sanction the building of a fortress tower (newly restored) to keep non-existent local brigands in hand. Apart from this construction, a couple of chapels, and a suitably phallic modern lighthouse, Marathonisi has no other buildings but is disappointingly covered in shrubby trees and hosts an annual summer pan-Hellenic mosquito convention so large that one wonders if any mortal has ever managed an untroubled night's sleep here.

Hydra
ΥΔΡΑ; 52 km²; pop. 3,000.

CODE ☎ 22980
PORT POLICE ☎ 52279
TOURIST POLICE ☎ 52205

A hilltop sticking out of the Aegean lacking roads or beaches, Hydra (pronounced *'EE-dra'*) has overcome the disadvantages of a generally dour appearance to become one of the most touristed spots in Greece. This is due to a combination of a very attractive fortified harbour town and the close proximity of Athens (making it a perfect day-tripper island). Sadly, the numbers calling have turned the place into a tourist trap and the island is now arguably one of the least idyllic in the whole Aegean, with a constant procession of hydrofoils and tour-boats bringing in the crowds and encouraging the most expensive island prices in Greece.

Apart from the town, with its harbour walls adorned with cannon, Hydra has little to offer. Decked with steep hill paths and a scattering of monasteries, and with a car and motorbike ban, it is often touted as a

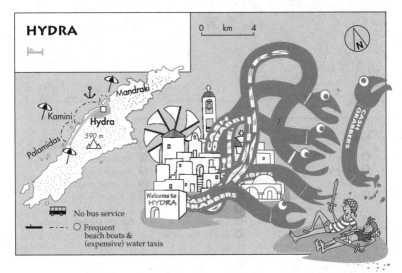

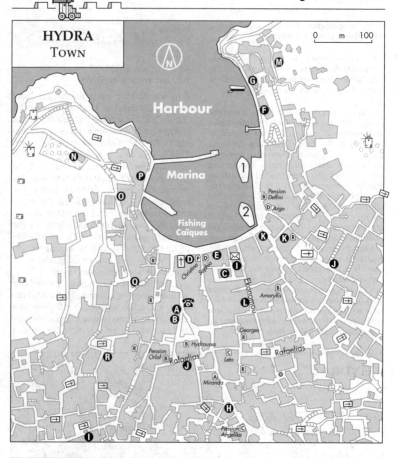

HYDRA TOWN

0   m   100

Harbour

Marina

Fishing Caïques

1
2

B Pension Delfini
D Argo

K   K R

B Amaryllis

Ekonomou

Christina
Sahia

B Hydroussa

Georges

C Leto

Rafaelias   Rafaelias

A Miranda

Pension Orlof B

Pension C
Angelika

Key

A Tourist Police
B Hospital
C Market
D Panagia Monastery / Clock Tower
E National Bank of Greece
F Museum

G Old Arsenal / Port Police
H Doctor
I Supermarket
J Pharmacy
K Bakery
L Cinema
M Kriezis Mansion

N Koundouriotis Mansion
O Tombasis Mansion
P Voulgaris Mansion
Q G. Voulgaris Mansion
R L. Koundouriotis Mansion

1 Ferry / Hydrofoil Berth
2 Taxi Boats

hill-walking destination given the absence of anything else to do. Bathing areas are confined to three poor northerly beaches served by expensive taxi boats, and from rocks beneath the cannon-topped ramparts on the south promontory of the town.

Pricey hotels and rooms. Book ahead if at all possible. The A-class *Miranda* (☎ 52230) and B-class *Hydroussa* (☎ 52217) are the premier hotels in town and with prices to match. Those on a tight budget will fare better at the C-class *Leto* (☎ 53385), the pension *Angelika* (☎ 53202) or the D-class *Argo* (☎ 52452). Also on the waterfront is the rather run-down D-class *Sophia* (☎ 52313). Right under the monastery belfry, certain disadvantages become all too apparent on the hour, every hour.

Poor and insignificant in ancient times, Hydra's transformation into a gold and jewellery boutique has its origins in the 17th and 18th centuries, when, lying on the periphery of both Turkish and Venetian spheres of influence, the island bred a succession of autonomous buccaneer flash Harrys who successfully exploited the growth of Euro-Levantine trade. The town thrived and grew to support a population of 28,000 before post-independence decline reduced the numbers to around 3,000, eking out an existence by sponge fishing until tourism took off. Since then they have reverted to their piratical habits, practising on the hapless victims decanted by the tour boats.

For most tourists **Hydra Town** is Hydra. Very photogenic, it is snugly tucked into a fold in the barren hills and consists of neo-classical mansions, built during the years of prosperity, fanning up the hillsides behind the port. The bursting waterfront is distinguished by the 18 c. **Panagia Monastery**, built from the stones of the famous Temple of Poseidon on Poros.

The largely undamaged **harbour fortifications** are also impressive and do wonders for the feel of the town. Carefully restored (boutiques aside), it is worth stopping off for a look, before catching a hydrofoil to the next port of call when you feel a comparatively inexpensive drink coming on. On the hillsides climbing up either side of the harbour are the 19 c. mansions built by the leading pirate families of the day.

Despite sharing the same name as a mythical monster called the Hydra, the island has no connection with this wee beastie (in fact the monstrous, multi-headed water snake — that grew two new heads each time one was cut off — lived in the Lernaean marshes in Argolis). This is not to say that monsters are unknown here: some even rent accommodation on Hydra. Not least of these is the indicted war criminal Slobodan Miloševič and his family. Formerly an annual visitor (and very popular with the locals), 'Slobber' is unlikely to be around in 2004, but if you are very unlucky you might bump into his — to quote *The Sunday Times* — 'gun-toting, car-mad, bleach-haired priapic' playboy son, Marko (who hid out the Kosovo crisis hereabouts).

Kalamata
ΚΑΛΑΜΑΤΑ; pop. 41,910.

CODE ☎ 27210
PORT POLICE ☎ 22218
TOURIST POLICE ☎ 23187

The second city of the Peloponnese (after Patras), Kalamata is a sprawling concrete conurbation well off the regular ferry trail. Tucked away in the deepest recess of the Messiniakos Gulf, it has a rail link with the rest of Greece and buses to Athens (8 daily) and Patras (2 daily). The bad news is that the bus station is 3 km from the port. To be honest, from any perspective Kalamata is a very ugly city. Badly damaged by a massive earthquake in 1986, it has never really recovered from the event. A minor quake also struck in August 2000, bringing down a few ceilings.

Limited number of budget hotels on or near the waterfront, including the *Plaza* (☎ 82590), the *Nevada* (☎ 82429) and the *Pension Avra* (☎ 82759). Offers of rooms are very rare.

A

Camping Patista (☎ 29525), 2 km east of the ferry quay, is an okayish beach site.

With most of the Venetian and Turkish era buildings flattened by the earthquake, the only site of note that the city has left is a **Frankish Kastro** on a low acropolis just north of the bus station.

Kiparissi

ΚΥΠΑΡΙΣΣΙ

An idyllic hamlet on the Peloponnesian coast offering a pleasant mixture of red-tiled houses, trees and a good shingle beach that attracts the occasional day-tripper hydrofoil. In past years Kiparissi also saw ferry visits, but with the upgrading of the mountain roads these have disappeared.

Kithera

ΚΥΘΗΡΑ; 278 km²; pop. 2,600.

CODE ☎ 27350
PORT POLICE (AGIA PELAGIA) ☎ 33280
PORT POLICE (KAPSALI) ☎ 31222
POLICE ☎ 31206
FIRST AID ☎ 31243

Arguably deserving of the title of the last unspoilt large Greek island, Kithera (also transcribed as 'Kythera') lies in glorious isolation from other island chains like a lump of rare meat falling off the Peloponnese fork. Unfortunately, there are few eaters; the remoteness of the place means that ferry connections are very limited, and most visitors are not island hoppers but travellers to the Peloponnese. The lack of an island chain to call its own has always left Kithera at something of a loose end.

Historically Kithera was administered as part of the Ionian group, but although sharing a similar history (of Venetian rather than Turkish rule), its appearance is more in common with the Cycladic islands. These days local schizophrenia is further enhanced by the additional complications of the island now being administered direct from Athens, and a largely migrant population. Like Kastelorizo in the Dodecanese, this is another Greek island where everyone seems to own an Australian passport. This results in Kithera being either appealingly full or uncomfortably empty as the number of town houses converted into holiday homes grows. However, bucking this trend, an increasing number of expatriates are choosing to retire on the island. While welcoming, they are not keen to see their dream island degenerate into yet another tourist resort.

A more serious handicap to enjoying the island is the limited nature of the public services (this is, in part, a consequence of the lack of tourists). Public transport is very poor: the school bus runs down the road bisecting the island twice daily in the summer, with frequent, but expensive, taxis making the most of this. If you want to make the most of Kithera then you need to bring or hire your own transport.

Most visitors arrive via the northern hamlet of **Agia Pelagia** (though of late ferries have been arriving at various ports). A dreamy — if rather unprepossessing — sort of place, Agia Pelagia has emerged over the last decade as the island's primary port and now sees the bulk of the ferry traffic as well as any calling hydrofoils.

On the back of the ferry traffic have come a growing number of tavernas and outlets offering rooms, but these are so spread out that they do little to encourage a cosy atmosphere. In this respect, the over-long quay hardly helps either. On the plus side, there are small coves either side of the port with quiet, sandy beaches. This is just as well as Agia Pelagia isn't really the best base from which to explore Kithera. If this is what you have come to do, then moving south opens up more options.

Tourists bent on sightseeing usually head straight for the scenic hilltop capital of **Chora** (home to a lovely, quiet, white-washed village with a notable number of oddly shaped chimneys) that meanders up the spine of a hill to an impressive but ruinous castle, or the resort port of **Kapsali** that lies below. Kapsali now sees few ferries — except when conditions prevent boats docking at Agia Pelagia or the increasingly popular dock at **Diakofti**. It has to rely on two pebble beaches in a bay divided by a small chapel-topped headland, plus its bar life, for its appeal.

Other beaches are equally remote. The island's best sand beach lies beyond

Kapsali on the south-east coast at Fryiammos, though without a moped it is a long dirt-track walk away.

The rest of Kithera is home to empty villages on rolling low hills with little vegetation; the best of these lies along the main island road at **Potamos**. Now slowly emerging as a convenient halfway-house between the settlements at each end of the island (though it lies well to the north), Potamos is home to the island's regular Sunday market and larger shops.

🛏

Hotels are scattered thinly around the island, but the majority of beds are now to be found at **Agia Pelagia**. The D-class *Kytheria* (☎ 33321) and the B-class *Filoxenia* (☎ 33610), both close to the ferry quay, mop up evening arrivals, but you will find plenty of other offers of beds. Potamos also has some rooms and the *Pension Porfyra* (☎ 33329).

Chora meantime has the pricey, but lovely, B-class *Margarita* (☎ 31694) and a couple of cheaper pensions — notably *Pension Keti* (☎ 31318) — and some unsigned rooms.

Kapsali has the luxury B-class pension *Raikos* (☎ 31629), both rather pricey. Budget accommodation — notably the D-class *Aphrodite* (☎ 31328) and rare rooms along the beach — is usually snapped up in season.

▲

Camping Kapsali (☎ 31580): a struggling pinewood site on the outskirts of Kapsali, only open late June through to early September.

👓

The **Chora**, straddling a narrow 500 m ridge, and the Venetian **Kastro** (built in 1503) are the most accessible attractions that Kithera has to offer. The latter looks impressive from a distance but the remains are rather 'bitty'. The best reason to visit is the panoramic views of Kapsali and the coast. In Chora there is also a small town **Museum**. The most popular excursion is to the pretty village of **Milopotamos** with its fine **Cave of Agia Sophia**, and nearby, a Venetian castle.

Between Chora and Milopotamos lies the village of **Livadi**, complete with a bridge dating from the period of British rule (1814–1864). Looking incongruously out of place on a Greek island, it would happily pass as a railway viaduct anywhere in southern England. Kithera was noted in antiquity as the place where the

KITHERA

0   km   7

✈ → Athens Ⓓ x 4

Agia Pelagia ⚓

Potamos

Paleochora

✈ Diakofti

Cave

Milopotamos

Paleopolis

506 m

City & Temple of Aphrodite

Karvounades

Livadi

Kalamos

Chora

Cycladic Style

Kapsali

Fryiammos

Chora & Venetian Kastro

Resort Village

🚌 ····· Ⓓ x 2: Ag. Pel: 09.00, 14.30
Kapsali: 11.00, 17.00

No beach boat service

goddess Aphrodite was born (or drawn) out of the sea (a claim also made by Cyprus). Kithera's claim was not disputed in antiquity and the centre (at **Paleopolis**) was home to a notable **Temple of Aphrodite** that the Roman-era travel writer Pausanias deemed to be the oldest, most beautiful, and most venerated in the world. A church constructed partly from the remaining temple stones now stands on the site.

The final site of note is the medieval town of **Paleochora** — abandoned after the island's entire population was sold into slavery by the pirate Kemal Reis in 1537.

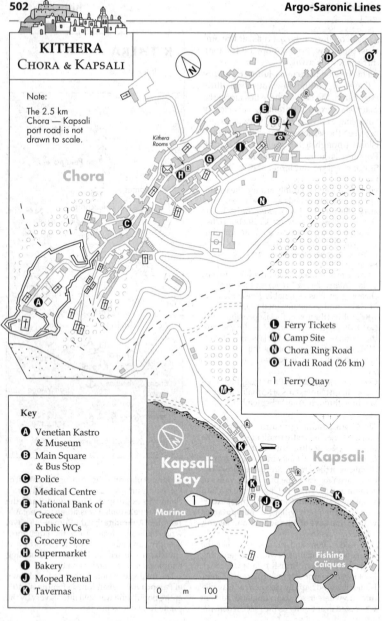

KITHERA
CHORA & KAPSALI

Note:

The 2.5 km
Chora — Kapsali
port road is not
drawn to scale.

Kithera Rooms

Chora

Kapsali Bay

Marina

Kapsali

Fishing Caïques

Ⓛ Ferry Tickets
Ⓜ Camp Site
Ⓝ Chora Ring Road
Ⓞ Livadi Road (26 km)

1   Ferry Quay

Key

Ⓐ Venetian Kastro
    & Museum
Ⓑ Main Square
    & Bus Stop
Ⓒ Police
Ⓓ Medical Centre
Ⓔ National Bank of
    Greece
Ⓕ Public WCs
Ⓖ Grocery Store
Ⓗ Supermarket
Ⓘ Bakery
Ⓙ Moped Rental
Ⓚ Tavernas

0   m   100

Leonidio
ΛΕΩΝΙΔΙΟ

A small coastal town served by hydrofoils in the summer months. Commuters and the odd tourist escaping the crowds are the only beneficiaries of the service: there isn't any reason to stop off here.

Methana
ΜΕΘΑΝΑ; pop. 998.

Another small port — this time on a peninsula jutting north from the Peloponnese into the Saronic Gulf. Ferries as well as hydrofoils call but most of the traffic is local rather than tourist. Like Leonidio most visitors ship out on the same boat they arrive on.

Monemvassia
ΜΟΝΕΜΒΑΣΙΑ

CODE ☎ 27320
PORT POLICE ☎ 61266
POLICE ☎ 61210

A distinctive small town at the southern end of the Peloponnese, Monemvassia (or rather its adjacent mainland town of Gefira) lives off the tourism generated by the mini Gibraltar-cum-boulder offshore. From the ferry both look a bit austere but this is deceptive: there are souvenir shops and tavernas aplenty on the mainland, while the boulder town lies on the southern flank out of view. They are linked by a causeway that also provides a convenient quay for both the single ferry that calls and High Season hydrofoils.

⤐

Plenty of rooms are available as well as hotels. These include the E-class *Akroyali* (☎ 61306) and D-class *Aktaeon* (☎ 61234); both are near the causeway along with the C-class *Minoa* (☎ 61209). The A-class pension *Kastro* (☎ 61413) provides a more pricey alternative.

▲

Camping Paradise (☎ 61680): a lovely and quiet site 3½ km south of the town.

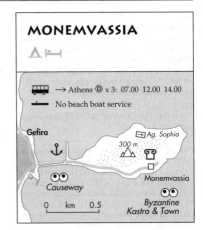

MONEMVASSIA

🚌 → Athens ⒟ x 3: 07.00 12.00 14.00
⛴ No beach boat service

Gefira
⚓
Causeway
0   km   0.5

Ag. Sophia
300 m
Monemvassia
Byzantine
Kastro & Town

👀
The 350 m '**Rock**' looks barren from the north, but once the ferry steams past the eastern side the remains of a fortress (dating back to Homeric times) and a medieval village dominate the rock. The main Byzantine centre on the Peloponnese, its (largely abandoned) upper and lower towns offer an interesting day's exploration, besides being the site of an important event in the struggle for Greek independence: an unjustifiable massacre of every man in the Turkish garrison in 1821.

Nafplio
ΝΑΥΠΛΙΟ; pop. 10,700.

CODE ☎ 27520
PORT POLICE ☎ 22974
POLICE ☎ 28131

Tucked into the Peloponnese coastline, stately Nafplio — also transcribed as 'Nauplion' — was briefly capital of the embryonic Greek state (1827–34) between Aegina and Athens and is visited by occasional hydrofoils. The tourist presence is high, thanks to the combination of a building programme which stalled when 'capital' status was lost, leaving the best preserved Venetian town in Greece, along with the daily influx from the nearby resort of **Tolo** (linked by bus and hydrofoil).

⊢

Rooms aren't thick on the ground, but there are plenty of budget hotels. The side streets near the ferry quay hide a number of them, including the musty D-class *Acropole* (☎ 27796). Best of the mid-range hotels is the *Agamemnon* (☎ 28021). Right at the top of the range, there is an A-class *Xenia* (☎ 28981) in the town.

A

Nearest is *Tolo Camping* (☎ 59133), a crowded site 8 km to the east.

಄

The old town is worth a day's exploration, the highlights being three impressive castles (the most impressive is the islet of **Bourtzi** — a mini Alcatraz opposite the town waterfront; daily taxi boats make the 20-minute crossing 09.00–13.00, 16.00–19.00) and a small **Archaeological Museum** with an interesting display of Mycenaean artifacts.

Neapoli
ΝΕΑΠΟΛΗ

CODE ☎ 27340
PORT POLICE ☎ 22228
TOURIST POLICE ☎ 27310 28701

The most southerly port on the Peloponnese, Neapoli is tucked in the lip of the Gulf of Lakonia. Not that there is much to be laconic about, for there is nought here but a poorly connected and dusty town. The austere, 'end of the known world' feeling that pervades (that led to the ancients believing that the entrance to Hades — the underworld — lay at the southern tip of the Peloponnese) will do little for the tourist who likes his nightlife, though this is a resort town of sorts thanks to the long narrow beach bisected by the ferry quay. Most holidaymakers seem to be Greeks escaping the crowds elsewhere. If you are looking to get away from it all then Neapoli might have appeal — and nearby Elafonissos offers some attractive consolation.

⊢

Limited rooms, and three B-class pensions: the *Alivali* (☎ 22287), the *Arsenakos* (☎ 22991) and the *Limira Mare* (☎ 22208).

Peloponnese
ΠΕΛΟΠΟΝΝΗΣΟΣ

The Peloponnese is an important region of mainland Greece. As such it falls outside the remit of most Greek island guides, but is included here because many island hoppers visit — usually passing rapidly through en route from Patras to Athens, or, less commonly, because they take island-based excursions to sightseeing destinations within the region, or visit ports on the Peloponnesian coast (these are singled out as separate destinations within this chapter). The rest of the Peloponnese — an area with an impressively diverse landscape, so rich in history and sights that it would justify a guidebook in its own right — is also worth a brief mention.

In both an etymological and a literal sense the Peloponnese can claim honorary island status. The name literally means 'island of Pelops', and reflects the fact that even the ancients recognized that, but for the narrow Corinth isthmus which joins it to the rest of the Greek mainland, it was an island. On several occasions they attempted to turn this into reality by digging a canal (the Emperor Nero even set to with a solid gold shovel: a case of one clod getting to grips with another). For want of resources it remained stubbornly attached to the mainland until the 19 c., when the Corinth Canal turned the 'nissos' (island) in Peloponnissos into reality. Today rail and road bridges cross the canal — now a tourist destination in its own right. Sadly, it is so narrow that if you cross via the new Patras—Athens highway bridge you are unlikely to be aware that it exists at all.

The majority of visitors to the Peloponnese come via tour bus — though there is a reasonable coastal bus system and rail network. Unfortunately, like most transport in Greece, they are geared to moving people to and from Athens. This can make life difficult if you are trying to explore the region — as all roads and rails seem to lead to the Corinth Canal. This said, the bus system is robust enough to

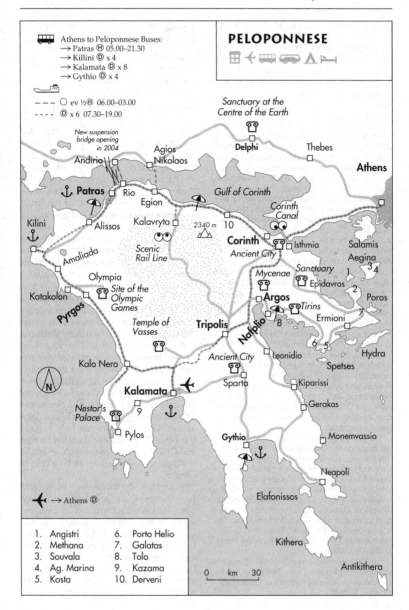

Athens to Peloponnese Buses:
→ Patras Ⓗ 05.00–21.30
→ Killini Ⓓ x 4
→ Kalamata Ⓓ x 8
→ Gythio Ⓓ x 4

– – – ○ ev ½Ⓗ 06.00–03.00
- - - - Ⓓ x 6 07.30–19.00

New suspension
bridge opening
in 2004

PELOPONNESE

Sanctuary at the
Centre of the Earth

Delphi

Thebes

Athens

Agios
Nikolaos

Andirio

⚓ **Patras**

Rio

Egion

Gulf of Corinth

Kilini
⚓

Alissos

Kalavryta

2340 m
△ 10

*Corinth
Canal*

Isthmia

Salamis

Aegina

Amaliada

*Scenic
Rail Line*

Corinth
Ancient City

Sanctuary

1

3 4

Olympia

*Site of the
Olympic
Games*

Mycenae

Epidavros

2

Poros

Katakolon

Argos

Tirins

Ermioni

Pyrgos

*Temple of
Vasses*

Tripolis

Nafplio

8

7

6 5

Hydra

Kalo Nero

Ancient City

Leonidio

Spetses

Ⓝ

Kalamata

9

Sparta

Kiparissi

Gerakas

Nestor's
Palace

Pylos

Gythio
⚓

Monemvassia

→ Athens Ⓓ

Neapoli

Elafonissos

1. Angistri
2. Methana
3. Souvala
4. Ag. Marina
5. Kosta

6. Porto Helio
7. Galatas
8. Tolo
9. Kazama
10. Derveni

Kithera

Antikithera

0   km   30

get you most places, provided you are not in a hurry. Those wishing to make a rapid journey from, say, Gythio to Patras have to catch the Athens bus to the Corinth Canal (most buses set down and pick up on the north side), and then pick up a Patras-bound bus from there.

∞

It is the sightseeing, rather than beaches or the considerable beauty of the landscape, that tends to pull tourists into the area. Although it never scaled quite the same cultural and artistic heights as Athens, the Peloponnese was just as important a powerhouse of Greek culture. It came to the fore during the Mycenaean era, when the cities of Mycenae, Tirins and Pylos dominated the Greek world. The hilltop citadel of **Mycenae** is the best known, thanks to Schliemann's discovery of the Mask of Agamemnon (now in the National Archaeological Museum in Athens). **Tirins** also has a less visited citadel, while remote **Pylos** has the remains of **Nestor's Palace**, nestling under protective roofing.

Once the classical world emerged, so too did their successor powers in the cities of Argos, Corinth and Sparta. The latter two successfully overcame Athens at the height of her power to win the 30-year contest dubbed by the Athenian historian Thucydides as 'The Peloponnesian War'. **Ancient Corinth** (not to be confused with the very modern city nearby) is a major sightseeing draw, with the remains of a stumpy-pillared Archaic Temple of Apollo set amid a confused jumble of later Greek and Roman architectural remains. **Sparta**, on the other hand, didn't go in for culture in a big way, and this is reflected in a lack of remains that leaves the modern town without income-generating sights.

The Peloponnese was also host to the greatest games in the Greek world at **Olympia**. The site is not in island hopper's territory (though rare and very expensive excursions have been made from Ionian islands in the past), but the remains of the sanctuary are well worth the trouble of a visit. Leading remains are the Temple of Zeus, the Stadium where the games took place and the well-stocked museum. The scenery, with the nearby Alpheios river (which later covered the site with preserving mud), is also delightful.

Finally, to the south-east lies one of Greece's greatest temples, the 420 BC **Temple of Apollo** tucked away in the mountains at **Vasses** (alias 'Basses/Bassae').

Poros

ΠΟΡΟΣ; 28 km²; pop. 4,500.

CODE ☎ 22980
PORT POLICE ☎ 22274
TOURIST POLICE ☎ 22462
HEALTH CENTRE ☎ 22222

Poros marks the limit for the landing-craft ferries running out of Piraeus. It is actually made up of two islands (**Sphalria** and **Kalaureia**) separated by a narrow canal and connected by a bridge, and takes its modern name from the narrow strait that separates it from the mainland: 'Poros' meaning 'passage'. In fact Poros is an extremely odd island; for the straits — rather than the island itself — are the focus of activity, with settlement running along the shores on either side and the bulk of the island relegated to hinterland. The 'island' sensation is strangely thin, with an atmosphere more reminiscent of a large coastal town ribboned around a narrow bay. Perhaps because of this and a lack of good beaches, Poros attracts less tourism than her neighbours. However, the island is a nice base for visiting nearby mainland sights and adjacent islands.

Poros Town is the only settlement of any significance, occupying most of Sphalria Island. It consists of whitewashed and red-tile houses banked between the long quay and a stubby hill topped with a campanile. On first arriving, the waterfront can come as a bit of a shock; for not only is it the third smelliest in the Aegean (after Piraeus and Chios) but is adorned with several of the tackiest tourist shops to be found in Greece.

Fortunately, the further you walk south from the ferry quay the better it gets; developing into an attractive mix of tavernas and yachts, with a myriad of taxi-boats and small car ferries scuttling across the straits to the mainland village of Galatas (the path ends at some rocks where the town children bathe). The backstreets are also reasonably attractive in a downbeat sort of way: but it is difficult to imagine anyone coming to Poros for the architecture. One suspects the main reason some tourists come back year after year is the low-key 'niceness' of the island, though if truth be told you don't have to go far to find better. Perhaps this is why cycle hire is so popular here — as it offers easy access to better mainland beaches.

Settlement on the wooded main island is largely confined to tourist developments along the straits (served by frequent buses). The coast south of the town is the busiest, with the bulk of the island's poor beaches (all pebble) and the now unused but pretty monastery of **Kalavrias** (alias Zoodochos Pigi). At the other end of the strait lies Russian Bay, home to an 1828 nautical conference in which Britain, France and Russia discussed the future of the independent Greek state. En route you will pass the beach at Neorio, arguably the best of the island's poor collection. Walk inland, and Poros improves considerably, the abundance of trees being some compensation for the demolition of the WCs

on the waterfront of Poros Town.

Galatas is much more dowdy than Poros Town, though some efforts have been made to tart up the waterfront. Unless you are heading for the campsite there is no great reason to venture here.

🛏

Poros Town offers the best chance of finding a room south of Aegina. There are also a number of easily located hotels along the waterfront. Closest to the ferry quay are the B-class *Latsi* (☎ 22392), the *Saron* (☎ 22279), and the C-class *Aktaion* (☎ 22281). More expensive hotels tend to be out of town on Kalavrias, the largest being the B-class *Poros* (☎ 22216).

There are also several waterfront hotels in **Galatas** if you draw a blank in Poros Town. These include the D-class *Saronis* (☎ 22356) and the C-class *Galatia* (☎ 22227) and *Papasotiriou* (☎ 22841).

A

Camping Kirangelo (☎ 24520): small mainland site 1 km inland on the road north of Galatas. Avoid the tent village on the coast north of Galatas: this is a hospital resort run by the local health service for the elderly insane.

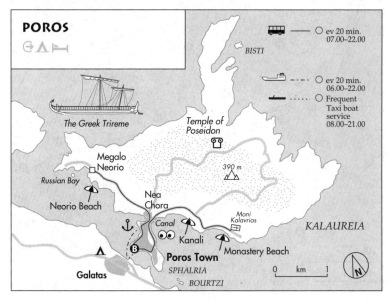

POROS

BISTI

○ ev 20 min.
07.00–22.00

○ ev 20 min.
06.00–22.00

○ Frequent
Taxi boat
service
08.00–21.00

The Greek Trireme

Temple of
Poseidon

Megalo
Neorio

390 m

Russian Bay

Nea
Chora

Neorio Beach

Moni
Kalavrias

KALAUREIA

Canal

Kanali

Poros Town

Monastery Beach

Galatas

SPHALRIA

BOURTZI

0   km   1

N

POROS
POROS TOWN

Key

Ⓐ Campanile
Ⓑ Bus Stop
Ⓒ Police / Supermarket
Ⓓ National Bank
Ⓔ Doctor
Ⓕ Pharmacies
Ⓖ Taxi Rank

Ⓗ Grocery Stores
Ⓘ Bakery
Ⓙ Newspapers
Ⓚ Restaurants
Ⓛ Camping (700 m)
Ⓜ Museum
Ⓝ Nautical School

1 Large Ferries
2 Hydrofoils
3 Landing Craft Berths
4 Taxi Boat Berths

Trireme Berth

Poros Island

Marina

Papadopoulou

Demosthenous

25 Martiou

Georgiou Michail

Latsi

Galatas (Mainland)

Fishing Caïques

25 Martiou

Vasiliadou

Galatia

Papasotiriou

Saronis

Monessi

Saron

Aktnion

7 Brothers

Mitropoleos

Note:
the 360 m wide
strait is not
drawn to scale

0   m   100

GG

Poros Town has little of sightseeing interest beyond the waterfront itself and a small **Archaeological Museum** south-east of the ferry quay (the Venetians preferring to fortify one of the Bourtzi islets rather than build in the town). On the north side of Sphalria lies Greece's **Naval Cadet School** in the former home of the 19 c. Arsenal. As a result, when she isn't on good will voyages, it is occasionally possible to see the replica **Greek Trireme** (so named because such vessels were powered by three banks of oars) tied up at the end of the ferry dock (a night watchman is kept permanently aboard to stop tourists doing untold damage). Now officially part of the Hellenic Navy, the cadets have the dubious pleasure of rowing her each summer along with parties of invited foreign oarsmen.

Once out of the town, you will find Poros is all pine trees and hills, with an inland road around Kalaureia. This circuit offers a day's gentle strolling, taking in the views from the hills as well as the remains of the ancient city of Kalaureia. This settlement was home to one of ancient Greece's premier religious centres in the form of the 6 c. BC **Temple of Poseidon** (later demolished to furnish the masonry for Hydra Town's quayside monastery); here the great orator Demosthenes committed suicide in 322 BC (by nibbling on his poisoned pen while writing a farewell epistle — the original poison pen letter — to his family when his creditors seized him from the temple where he had sought sanctuary).

Porto Helio
ΠΟΡΤΟ ΧΕΛΙ

CODE ☎ 27540
PORT POLICE ☎ 51408

An extremely large tourist town that is better avoided. This resort has become the natural terminus for ferries and hydrofoils running down the islands in the gulf — so most depart northwards (up to ten daily). Irregular smaller craft do put in occasionally, but the local market is insufficient to generate much traffic.

ம

Pre-booked hotels predominate, but some pricey rooms are available.

Spetses
ΣΠΕΤΣΕΣ; 22.5 km²; pop. 3,500.

CODE ☎ 22980
PORT POLICE ☎ 72245
TOURIST POLICE ☎ 73100
FIRST AID ☎ 72472

Sufficiently far from the capital to escape the worst of the day-trippers, yet still close enough to be served by daily Piraeus ferries (just), Spetses is a gentle, small, pine-forested island particularly popular with English tourists (suburbia rather than the fish-and-chips brigade). This is in part due to the island's being the setting for John Fowles' novel *The Magus*, a popular tome that has ensured that many holidaymakers come to Spetses disposed to admire the place. The horses and traps that run along the waterfront of Spetses Town don't hurt either, though the paucity of good beaches results in a daily mass migration around the island that is not conducive to relaxed holiday-making.

Mansioned **Spetses Town** is apt to disappoint on first acquaintance: considering that it is the only settlement of any size on the island, the centre area is poorly laid out without the natural charm of most of the Cycladic island choras. It is also comparatively expensive. The tourist area is firmly focused around the streets near the new port. This is rather sad, as the too shallow old port is now reduced to a little-visited yacht marina. In fact, it is much the more attractive of the two, with the headland to the south graced with three windmills for good measure.

An island-wide ban on cars has served to increase the suburbs of Spetses Town while restricting the growth of other tourist centres. Movement around the island is thus greatly restricted. As a result, crowded buses run along the northern coast hotel strip as well as to the most popular beach on Spetses — at Ag. Anargiri. Better reached by beach boat (you don't have to fight for a place like you do on the afternoon buses heading back to Spetses Town), it offers the

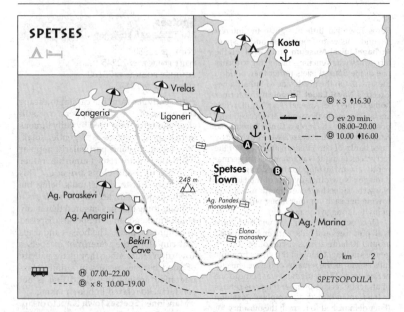

best sand beach on the island. Beach boats also run across the straits from Spetses Town to the adjacent beach near the quiet village of **Kosta**, supplementing the landing-craft ferry running to the village itself several times a day.

Tourist boats also make the crossing to Kosta and Porto Helio. Be very wary of some of these boats: they divide up into 'normal' multi-passenger beach boats and so-called sea 'taxis', individually hired and charging ludicrous 'tourist' fares.

⊨

Arrive early: block bookings by package tour operators mean that beds are scarce. Tourist agencies east of the ferry dock have lists, and one, *Takis Travel* (☎ 72888) — sited near the ferry quay — acts as an agent for most of the island hoteliers, the residue being covered by *Pine Island Tours* (☎ 72464). Close by the ferry quay are a number of hotels worth a try. These include the budget E-class *Alexandri* (☎73073), the D-class *Saronicos* (☎73741) and the C-class *Faros* (☎ 72613). Near the town beach are the D-class *Klimis* (☎73777) and *Stelios* (☎72364),

the latter complete with restaurant. Those with money to spend should try the A-class Edwardian *Posidonion* (☎ 72308).

Δ

Camping Kosta (☎ 51571). Quiet mainland site 1 km west of Kosta village. A member of the *Harmonie* camping club scheme.

∽

Spetses, like Aegina and Hydra, played an important part in the struggle for Greek independence, furnishing the rebels with a cross between a Greek Boudicca and Lord Nelson in the form of a female admiral, Laskarina Bouboulina. Spetses Town has a **Museum** in one of the 18 c. mansions housing her bones and other independence material. The 8th of September also sees the commemoration of an 1822 naval victory when a Greek fireship forced an attacking Turkish fleet to withdraw from Spetses. This is re-enacted with the burning of a cast-adrift taxi-boat each year.

Apart from the attractive **Bekiri Sea Cave** at **Ag. Anargiri** beach, Spetses lacks sights: agencies make a killing selling highly priced tours to worthy attractions on the Peloponnese such as Epidavros and Corinth.

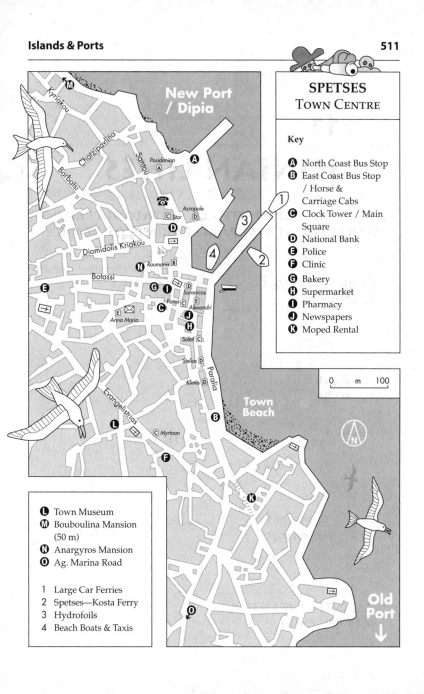

New Port / Dipia

Kyriakou

Chatzipavlina

Barbatsi

Samou

Posidonion Ⓐ

A

Diomidolis Kriakou

C Star

Acropole
Ⓓ

D

N Roumanis Ⓑ

Botassi

E

G **I**

C Faros

Saronicos
Ⓓ
C Ⓔ Alexandri

J

H

Soleil Ⓒ

Stelios Ⓓ

Klimis Ⓓ

Paralia

B

Evangelistrias

L

C Myrtoon

F

K

O

E Anna Maria

Town Beach

Old Port

SPETSES
TOWN CENTRE

Key

Ⓐ North Coast Bus Stop
Ⓑ East Coast Bus Stop / Horse & Carriage Cabs
Ⓒ Clock Tower / Main Square
Ⓓ National Bank
Ⓔ Police
Ⓕ Clinic
Ⓖ Bakery
Ⓗ Supermarket
Ⓘ Pharmacy
Ⓙ Newspapers
Ⓚ Moped Rental

0   m   100

Ⓛ Town Museum
Ⓜ Bouboulina Mansion (50 m)
Ⓝ Anargyros Mansion
Ⓞ Ag. Marina Road

1 Large Car Ferries
2 Spetses—Kosta Ferry
3 Hydrofoils
4 Beach Boats & Taxis

11

IONIAN LINES

ANTIPAXI · CORFU · ITHACA · KEFALONIA · KILINI
LEFKADA · PATRAS · PAXI · ZAKINTHOS / ZANTE

CORFU/KERKYRA
ΚΕΡΚΥΡΑ

IGOUMENITSA
ΗΓΟΥΜΕΝΙΤΣΑ

+2

+9 HOURS

+2

PAXI
ΠΑΞΟΙ

LEFKADA
ΛΕΥΚΑΔΑ

ANTIPAXI
ΑΝΤΙΠΑΞΟΙ

ITHACA
ΙΘΑΚΗ

+2

+1

KEFALONIA
ΚΕΦΑΛΟΝΙΑ

PATRAS
ΠΑΤΡΑ

+3

+3

ZAKINTHOS/ZANTE
ΖΑΚΥΝΘΟ / ΖΑΝΤΗ

KILINI
ΚΥΛΛΗΝΗ

+1½

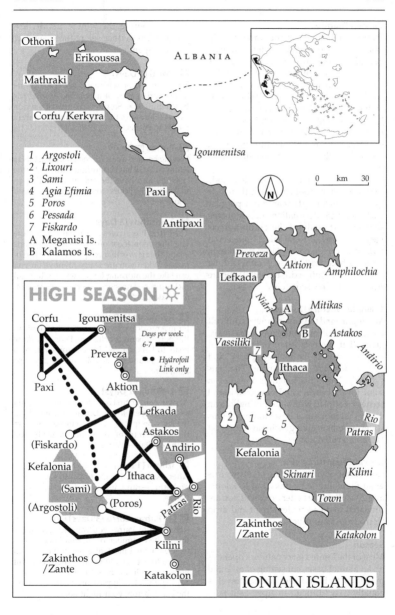

Othoni
Erikoussa
Mathraki
Corfu/Kerkyra

ALBANIA

Igoumenitsa

1 Argostoli
2 Lixouri
3 Sami
4 Agia Efimia
5 Poros
6 Pessada
7 Fiskardo
A Meganisi Is.
B Kalamos Is.

Paxi

Antipaxi

0   km   30

N

Preveza   Aktion   Amphilochia
Lefkada
Nidri   A   Mitikas
                B   Astakos
Vassiliki   Andirio
           7
           Ithaca
        4
      2   3   Rio
         1   5   Patras
          6
      Kefalonia   Kilini
           Skinari
                    Town
Zakinthos
/Zante   Katakolon

IONIAN ISLANDS

HIGH SEASON ☼

Corfu   Igoumenitsa
              Days per week:
              6-7 ▬▬▬
         Preveza
                    ●● Hydrofoil
         Aktion   Link only
Paxi

              Lefkada
         Astakos
(Fiskardo)   Andirio

Kefalonia
         Ithaca
(Sami)

(Argostoli)   (Poros)
                    Patras   Rio
                    Kilini
Zakinthos
/Zante   Katakolon

General Features

The Ionian Islands lie uncomfortably adrift from the rest of the Greek ferry system, guarding the entrance to the Adriatic Sea. By Greek standards most are on the large side, but as they have comparatively small population ratios and lie close to the mainland, a fully integrated ferry structure has never emerged. Poor ferry links are not helped by the profusion of airports, with Corfu, Zakinthos, Kefalonia and mainland Preveza/Aktion near Lefkada all offering viable arrival points.

With the exception of Corfu, the islands see fewer independent travellers than their Aegean counterparts. Zante is a popular package tourist destination but being at the southern extremity of the group attracts very few ferries. Kefalonia is quiet and lacking a conveniently placed population centre. Ithaca (of Odysseus fame), along with Paxi and Antipaxi, is too small to figure strongly on ferry schedules.

Example Itinerary [2 Weeks]

Moving around the Ionian group is difficult but practicable on a one-hop-a-day basis, given that there is often only one boat between poorly connected ports, and bus services are equally poor. The plus side to going to the Ionian Islands lies in some lovely beaches and pine-clad island scenery, coupled with shimmeringly clean water that looks as if Poseidon has set his waternymphs to giving each wavelet a good lick and a rub daily.

Arrival/Departure Point

Corfu is the obvious starting point given its good flight and ferry links, but Kefalonia and Zakinthos are better options if you are prepared to do a smaller circuit and drop Corfu from your itinerary.

Season

Most of the limited ferry network operates on an annual basis, consisting of essential mainland to island services. So travel is equally easy/difficult in April as it is in August. During the winter months less popular links either see reduced services or are suspended.

① Corfu [2 Days]

This is one group where it is better to explore in the earlier part of a holiday, leaving the beach until later. So, after a couple of days on Corfu, take one of the international overnight ferries to Patras.

② Patras [1 Day]

Having booked a seat on the afternoon bus to Kilini you will have a few hours to explore the city. You also have the option of heading on to Athens (3½ hours) for a couple of nights if you want to visit the capital.

③ Zakinthos [3 Days]

The Patras bus arrives at Kilini in time for the late afternoon ferry on to Zakinthos — one island that is worth a couple of days' exploration. When you are ready to move on you can take the morning ferry back to Kilini and pick up the connecting afternoon service on to Kefalonia (Argostoli).

④ Kefalonia [2 Days]

From Argostoli take a bus across Kefalonia to the port of Sami for the best beds and daily boats to Lefkada and Ithaca. You could also stay longer and do these islands as day trips from here.

⑤ Lefkada [2 Days]

Arriving on the first boat you can use Vassiliki as a base for exploring Lefkada before taking the ferry on to Ithaca. This will leave you on the northern tip of the island. Take a bus on to the capital — Vathi.

⑥ Ithaca [1 Day]

After exploring Ithaca, finish in the capital of Vathi — and its daily ferry link with Patras.

② ① Patras/Corfu [3 Days]

Returning to Patras you can pick up one of the limited number of international ferries (e.g. Minoan Lines) offering travel within Greece to get back to Corfu, where you will have a couple of days to take in Paxi and Antipaxi via Corfu pleasure boats, or lie on the beach before your flight home.

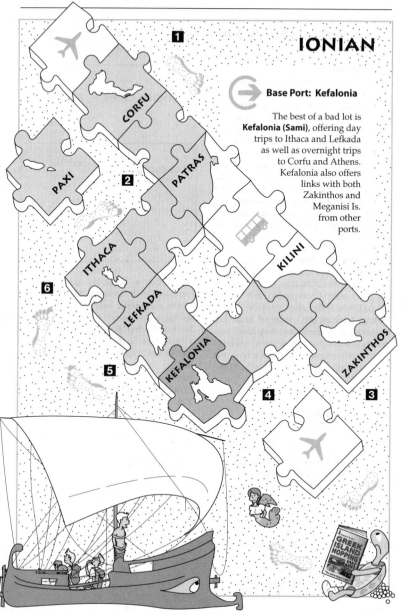

IONIAN

Base Port: Kefalonia

The best of a bad lot is **Kefalonia (Sami)**, offering day trips to Ithaca and Lefkada as well as overnight trips to Corfu and Athens. Kefalonia also offers links with both Zakinthos and Meganisi Is. from other ports.

Ionian Ferry Services

Main Car Ferries

Given the lack of any obvious pattern of progression between islands, and the over-long sailing time between the north and south Ionian Islands, it is not surprising that many ferry services are small ferries operating out of a mainland port to an adjacent island, rather than running up or down the chain. Moving between islands, therefore, often involves bouncing off the mainland by changing ferries at a mainland port. Moreover, useful inter-connecting ferries often run solo on routes, and you are pretty vulnerable should they not be operating.

Hellas Flying Dolphins

The jokers in the Ionian Island pack are hydrofoil and catamaran services. Over the years several companies have started up and then failed after a season. Hellas Flying Dolphins are supposed to be the next ones to try their luck; they have been granted a licence to run a service from Patras up to Igoumenitsa, though they have yet to convert this into a service, and as time goes by it looks increasingly unlikely that they will.

Minoan Lines & ANEK Lines

At the time of going to press the only ferry link between the north and south Ionian Islands was provided by the international ferries of the Greek-owned Minoan and ANEK Lines (landlubbers not in the know travel the complicated bus route from Igoumenitsa to Preveza/Lefkada, and then continue island hopping from there). This situation was caused by Greek cabotage laws which prevented foreign ferry operators from providing domestic ferry services. However, the market has now been opened up to foreign competition so, in theory at any rate, any trans-Adriatic operator can now provide domestic tickets. In fact, it is

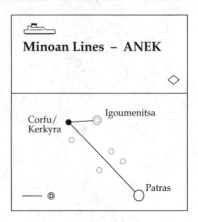

easy to buy a 'domestic' ticket between Patras or Kefalonia and Corfu.

With a domestic ticket you are waved through passport control. The only downside is that 'deck' tickets do mean the outside deck on these boats — you've no entitlement to an inside seat on these boats and the crews aren't over-keen on seeing their lounges turned into backpackers' dormitories. Cabins or cheap aircraft-type seats can, however, be booked for overnight trips.

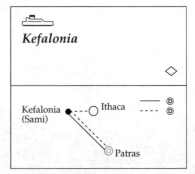

C/F *Kefalonia*
Blue Ferries / Strintzis; 1975; 3472 GRT.
Formerly the premier boat on the line, the *Kefalonia* appeared in the Ionian Sea in 1995. Despite the arrival of the better *JetFerry 1*, this boat continued to operate a morning service from the islands to Patras, her big selling-point being her unique calls at Ithaca. Now the *JetFerry 1* has moved to the Aegean and the *Kefalonia* reigns supreme again. In past years she has occasionally operated to Argostoli via Kilini. Overall, she is an attractive boat, and if she isn't in the same class as the newest arrivals in Greece facilities are the best of any regular boat in the group, with escalators and an open-plan passenger saloon.

Kilini—Argostoli Link
Local
This is the one ferry route in the Ionian islands that has consistently found it difficult to attract a ferry for more than one season or so. The service between Kilini and the capital of Kefalonia ought to be

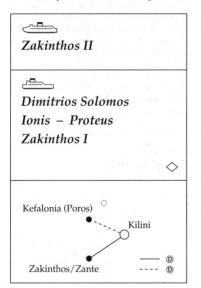

Zakinthos II

Dimitrios Solomos
Ionis – Proteus
Zakinthos I

Kefalonia (Poros)
Kilini
Zakinthos/Zante

Dimitrios Solomos
Ionis – Proteus
Zakinthos I

Kefalonia (Argostoli)
(Lixouri)
Kilini

viable (particularly given the poor nature of public transport on the island), but a succession of ferries have tried it for a season and then moved on. In 2003 the service was maintained by the collection of ferries that normally service the Kilini—Zakinthos link. If this is repeated in 2004 (as seems likely) then be prepared for any of the boats below to be operating the service.

C/F *Zakinthos II* – C/F *Dimitrios Solomos*
C/F *Ionis* – C/F *Proteus* – C/F *Zakinthos I*
Zakinthos II; 2002.
Ionis; 1977; 2963 GRT.
Proteus; 1973; 1160 GRT.
Zakinthos I; 1973; 2157 GRT.
Five ferries provide the link between the mainland and Zakinthos, with a new high speed boat—the *Zakinthos II*—due in 2003, but yet to appear (this should happen in 2004). The service runs eight times daily in the summer, four times daily in the Low Season. In 2002 they took on the Kefalonia (Poros) link as well.

All independently operated, the boats run by rota, and you buy a ticket for a crossing rather than a specific boat (this is likely to change once the *Zakinthos II* arrives). Of the regular ferries, the *Ionis* is arguably the best boat (though none of them are up to much) followed by the *Zakinthos I*. The grubby *Proteus* is the boat to avoid.

C/F *Agia Marina*

For over a decade a useful small landing-craft type car ferry has provided a morning and evening link between the port of Sami on Kefalonia and the otherwise unused quay of Pisaetos on Ithaca. In past years this service was run by the *Aphrodite L*, as part of a twice-daily run up to Vassiliki on Lefkada via Fiskardo. Since 1997, however, the boat on this line has been obliged to cover on the Kefalonia—Astakos mainland route (the previous ferry ran into the 'not more than 35 years old' ferry law). This makes life difficult for travellers as the Fiskardo—Lefkada link is otherwise very awkward. Sadly, it would appear that this is unlikely to change in 2004: you might have to take a bus from Astakos to Lefkada.

C/F *Captan Aristidis* – C/F *Meganisi*

These two landing-craft ferries combine to run a daily service from Lefkada to northern Kefalonia and Ithaca, as well as providing the small island of Meganisi with its main link with the outside world. The *Captan Aristidis* is easily the better of the pair and usually takes the Ithaca run, while the pitifully small *Meganisi* is usually confined to the Meganisi run. In 1996 she had to combine both as the *Captan Aristidis* was deputizing elsewhere. In the summer both boats are swamped by Italian

motorists: car owners should arrive on the quayside early to secure a passage, then you can sit back and enjoy the sight of massed ranks of arguing tourists desperate to get a passage home.

C/F *Ionion Pelagos*

Each summer sees this stumpy, diminutive landing-craft ferry operate the shortest crossing between Kefalonia and Zakinthos (Skinari, alias Agios Nikolaos). Services have remained unchanged in years, with the link only existing between mid-May and early October. However, unless you have your own transport, this is a poor link even when it is in operation — given the absence of bus services (out of the July—August High Season peak) to both ports of call.

C/F *Theologos* – H/F *Santa II / III*

Landing-craft type ferries have provided the daily Corfu—Paxi island service for the last few years. For a long time threatened by the arrival of stiff competition from a catamaran and an advertised ferry that never appeared, they remain in service (though the name of the boat running the service does change from year to year). The only competition comes via a small tourist boat — the P/S *Pegassus* — which runs daily to Corfu town from Paxi.

Corfu—Mainland Links

An island the size of Corfu naturally attracts a number of popular ferry links with the mainland. Most services run to the port of Igoumenitsa, but there are others worth looking out for. For most of the 1990s a daily link existed between Corfu and the mainland port of Amphilochia (a route that cuts the Athens bus journey time by almost half): sadly, it has not operated since 2001 — unlike the boats below.

Large Corfu—Igoumenitsa Services

The Corfu—Igoumenitsa run is attracting a growing number of larger car ferries — vital during the winter months when the landing-craft ferries often can't operate.

C/F *Agios Spiridon*

Kerkira Lines; 1972; 2574 GRT.
Formerly the *Hellas Express*, this ferry did time in the Cyclades for many years. Docking at Corfu's international port she now runs frequently to Igoumenitsa.

C/F *Ekaterini P*

Fast Ferries
An unmissable orange-hulled boat, seemingly trying to cash in on the success of Superfast by adopting a similar name.

C/F *Pantokrator*

Feax Express Lines; 1989; 4926 GRT.
A new arrival on this route, this blue-hulled boat is reasonably large, but seems much older than her real age.

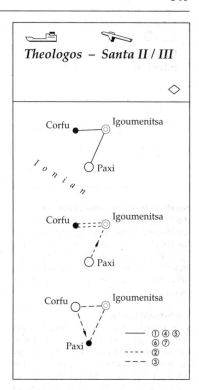

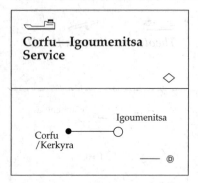

Corfu—Igoumenitsa Service

Small Corfu—Igoumenitsa Services
The 90-minute Corfu—Igoumenitsa crossing has some dozen landing-craft operating an hourly service on a rota basis from a quay 400 m north of Corfu Town's International ferry terminal building. Unchanging schedules are posted up on the quayside ticket office.

Corfu Local Ferries
Corfu also has a number of minor services with limited tourist appeal. The most useful of the mainland links is the 5 x ⑩ service between the island's second port of Lefkimi and Igoumenitsa. Lefkimi also has had an inconsistent link with Paxi, though this has diminished in recent years. Tourist boats (the P/S's *Rena S/II*, *Petrakis*, *Sotirakis* and *Sotirakis II*) also offer extra Paxi, Antipaxi and Plataria connections, as well as an Albania service.

P/S *Alexandros K II*
Corfu Town also has a limited service to the three minor islands to the north of Corfu. The *Alexandros K II* — a small passenger boat that can also manage a couple of cars — departs soon after dawn several days a week from Corfu's Old Port. Times don't change much, but (Othoni aside) these islets are more frequently visited via tourist boats from the north Corfu resort town of Sidari.

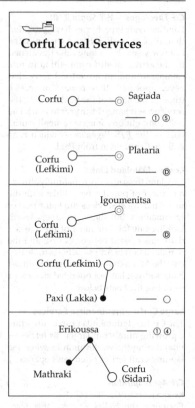

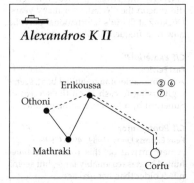

Ionian Islands & Ports

Astakos
ΑΣΤΑΚΟΣ

CODE ☎ 26460

A small village on the mainland west coast, Astakos was formerly the home port of a single ferry running daily to Ithaca and Kefalonia. It is still the departure point for the produce caïques that keep the small fishing community that struggles along on the isolated island of Kalamos (which lies to the north-west) supplied with essentials. However, erratic ferry connections aside, Astakos has little going for it. In truth, the beach aside, the most interesting thing in town is the bus stop.

ᖨ

Astakos has three hotels that cater for the few that get caught here. Top of the range is the B-class *Stratos* (☎ 41096). There are also two budget hotels in town: the D-class *Beach* (☎ 41135) and the *Byron* (☎ 41516).

Corfu / Kerkyra
ΚΕΡΚΥΡΑ; 592 km²; pop. 89,600.

TOWN CODE ☎ 26610
NTOG/TOURIST POLICE ☎ 30265
EMERGENCY ☎ 100
PORT POLICE ☎ 34036
HOSPITAL ☎ 25400

Long considered one of the most beautiful of the Greek islands thanks to the abundant rainfall and vegetation, Corfu (or Kerkyra as it is known locally) is now among the most package-touristy parts of Greece. This being so, you have to venture quite far to escape the crowds, but on the plus side the island doesn't attract millions each year without good reason: it is beautiful, people and all. Ruled by the British between 1815 and 1864, the island retains a colonial feel — thanks in part to it being wetter than other islands out of High Season, and the large number of holiday homes scattered around. On the

downside, Corfu has made the news thanks to attacks by Albanian pirates (a tourist was killed in 1996). Overlooking the Albanian coast, Corfu proved tempting; even the *Club Med* resort has come under fire. The Greek authorities provided a 50-strong task-force to prevent further incidents. This now seems to be working and the island has enjoyed several untroubled years.

As with the other large Ionian islands, the main settlement — **Corfu Town** — lies on the east coast along with most of the tourist development (patronized largely by Brits). On Corfu this is particularly heavy, with a hotel strip running from **Pirgi** down to **Benitses** (the booze and snooze resort of Greece) that contrives to place Corfu close to the top of the 'expensive island' rankings. Luckily, both island and capital are sufficiently attractive to overcome this handicap, with even the worst resorts having the kernel of a former fishing village at their heart.

Unless nightlife is a priority, the over-crowding to be found in Corfu Town and the east coast villages will soon tempt you into venturing further afield. The north and west sides of the island have most to offer. Along the north coast Kassiopi (the centre of Corfu in Roman times) is an attractive fishing village resort overlooked by the remains of a 12 c. castle built on the site of a Temple of Zeus. **Sidari**, backed by rich farmland, is a less picturesque but equally lively village offering excursion boats to the islets north of Corfu as well as several reasonable beaches. However, the west coast has the best of Corfu's beaches, including Agios Georgios (both north and south), Glifada, Agios Gordis, Pelekas and **Mirtiotissa** (arguably the best beach: its isolation ensures it gets the thumbs — among other things — up from nudists). The cliffs at **Paliokastritsa** are also a great draw — particularly at sunset.

The southern limb of Corfu is quieter, with the exception of the large resort at **Messoighi** and the youth-dominated **Kavos**, a beach and disco village where one goes to get drunk and then laid (or, more often, laid by a drunk). Nearby **Lefkimi** sees a limited number of ferry services, though the bulk of these operate to Corfu Town. Most ferries that call are international, and the island sees an irritating stacking of services, with most ferries departing in the same direction within a couple of hours of each other and then nothing for the rest of the day.

⊨

The EOT (☎ 37520) and Tourist Police in Corfu Town offer free town as well as hotel and room information. Hotel beds are adequate for most of the year, but there is pressure on bed space in High Season. Near the New Port are a few rooms and the elderly but just bearable *Ionian* (☎ 39915), while the Old Port has the over-popular budget *Constantinoupolis* (☎ 39826) and *Acropolis* (☎ 39569).

Nearer the top end of the market is the delightfully placed (and pricey) *Arcadion* (☎ 37670) overlooking the cricket pitch. Out of town there is a poor *IYHF Hostel* (☎ 91292) at Kontokali, but best of all is the increasingly notorious *Pink Palace* (☎ 53103/4) complex on the west coast at Agios Gordis. It offers €20 rooms, built-in nightlife (so good that rumour has it that they always try to get you drunk the night before you leave in order to stop you going) and a free mini-bus service to and from Corfu Town. Agents meet boats.

⚑

The nearest camping to Corfu Town is *Camping Kontokali* (☎ 91170), 5 km to the north: a basic site, it scores on convenience rather than facilities on offer. There are better sites: mini-buses lay siege to the ferry terminal when the morning ferries come in and are thereafter conspicuous by their absence. The best sites lie away from the tourist strip, and as usual in the Ionian islands are geared up to motor caravans: *Vatos Camping* (☎ 94393) and *Paliokastritsa Camping* (☎ 2663 41204) on the west coast are attractive, along with the clutch of sites abutting the northern beaches. Nightlife lovers usually stick to the sites on the tourist strip north of Corfu Town. These include Dassia's *Kada Beach Camping* (☎ 93595) and *Corfu Camping* (☎ 93246) at Ipsos.

◌◌

Corfu Town is the premier tourist attraction thanks to a delightful mix of Venetian, French and British Georgian buildings straddled by a couple of fortresses partially demolished by the British when they left the islands in the 1860s. The focus of the town is park-like **Spinada** Square or Esplanade, the site of the famous cricket pitch now used early Saturday mornings as a practice marching ground by the local High School band. The square is bounded on the western side by the **Liston**, a row of tall arcaded houses-cum-cafés built during the brief period of French rule (1807–14), and on the east side by the moated **Old Fortress** — built on the Corfu ('two hills') promontory, and once the site of a Temple of Hera.

North of the cricket pitch lies the **Royal Palace**, looking like a Georgian English country house. It was built in 1819 to house a series of British High Commissioners who considered themselves sufficiently high to require a throne room of the regal rather than the convenience variety. These days the recently refurbished building is home to a display of Chinese and Japanese porcelain and bronzes (the collection of a former Greek ambassador in the Far East).

Some 50 m south of the square lies Corfu's **Archaeological Museum**: home to the famous pedimental sculptures (dominated by a primitive figure of a Gorgon — considered to be among the greatest Archaic-period sculptures) from the Temple of Artemis (580 BC) in the ancient town. The museum is also home to an assorted collection of Classical and Roman sculpture recovered from various sites on the island. The best of these lies just south of Corfu Town: the ancient city of Kerkyra (now little more than foundations — including the Temple of Artemis). Beyond the ruins lies Kanoni, jumping-off point for a couple of monastery-topped islets. The first — **Vlakerani** — is linked to Corfu by a picture-postcard causeway, while **Pontikonissi** (or Mouse Island) is reached by regular caïque and is said to be the boat of Odysseus turned into stone by the wrathful Poseidon.

Further afield, Corfu has a disparate collection of other sights. Nearest to Corfu Town is the 1891-built **Royal Palace** (now a casino) at Achillion; the summer home of Kaiser Wilhelm II from 1908–14, it was the birthplace of Prince Phillip. Far prettier is the cliff and beauty

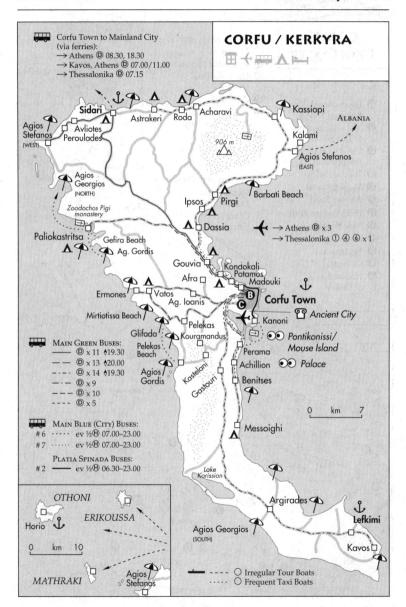

CORFU / KERKYRA

Corfu Town to Mainland City
(via ferries):
→ Athens Ⓓ 08.30, 18.30
→ Kavos, Athens Ⓓ 07.00/11.00
→ Thessalonika Ⓓ 07.15

Sidari
Agios Stefanos (WEST)
Avliotes
Peroulades
Astrakeri
Roda
Acharavi
Kassiopi
ALBANIA
Kalami
906 m
Agios Stefanos (EAST)
Agios Georgios (NORTH)
Zoodochos Pigi monastery
Ipsos
Pirgi
Barbati Beach
Paliokastritsa
Gefira Beach
Ag. Gordis
Dassia
→ Athens Ⓓ x 3
→ Thessalonika ① ④ ⑥ x 1
Gouvia
Kondokali
Potamos
Madouki
Ermones
Vatos
Afra
Ag. Ioanis
B
C
Corfu Town
Ancient City
Mirtiotissa Beach
Kanoni
Pelekas
Glifada
Pelekas Beach
Kouramandus
Agios Gordis
Perama
Kastelani
Achillion
Gastouri
Benitses
Pontikonissi/ Mouse Island
Palace

MAIN GREEN BUSES:
—— Ⓓ x 11 ⏰19.30
— — Ⓓ x 13 ⏰20.00
-·- Ⓓ x 14 ⏰19.30
-··- Ⓓ x 9
– – Ⓓ x 10
---- Ⓓ x 5

MAIN BLUE (CITY) BUSES:
6 ···· ev ½⊕ 07.00–23.00
7 ···· ev ½⊕ 07.00–23.00

PLATIA SPINADA BUSES:
2 —— ev ½⊕ 06.30–23.00

Messoighi

0   km   7

OTHONI
ERIKOUSSA
Horio
Lake Korission
Argirades
Lefkimi
0   km   10
Agios Georgios (SOUTH)
Kavos
MATHRAKI
Agios Stefanos

—— ---- ○ Irregular Tour Boats
···· ○ Frequent Taxi Boats

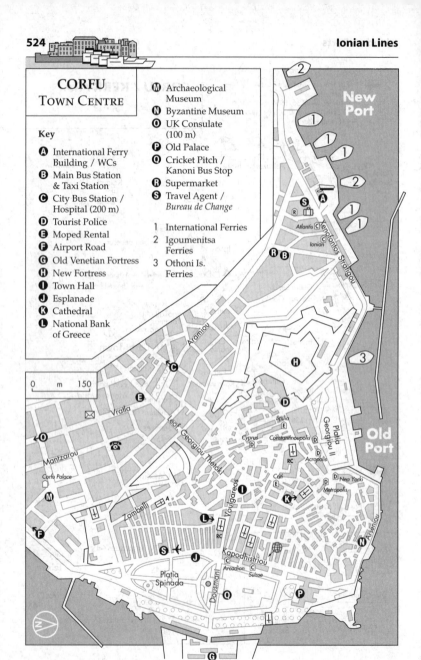

CORFU
TOWN CENTRE

Key

- **A** International Ferry Building / WCs
- **B** Main Bus Station & Taxi Station
- **C** City Bus Station / Hospital (200 m)
- **D** Tourist Police
- **E** Moped Rental
- **F** Airport Road
- **G** Old Venetian Fortress
- **H** New Fortress
- **I** Town Hall
- **J** Esplanade
- **K** Cathedral
- **L** National Bank of Greece
- **M** Archaeological Museum
- **N** Byzantine Museum
- **O** UK Consulate (100 m)
- **P** Old Palace
- **Q** Cricket Pitch / Kanoni Bus Stop
- **R** Supermarket
- **S** Travel Agent / *Bureau de Change*

1   International Ferries
2   Igoumenitsa Ferries
3   Othoni Is. Ferries

New Port

Old Port

0   m   150

spot of **Paliokastritsa**, home to a castle (c. 1200 AD) and monastery (1228) replete with icons (icon fans should also check out the **Byzantine Museum** in Corfu Town).

To the north-east of Corfu lie three islets also open to island hoppers. They see few tourists, but those that call usually end up raving about them. Regular ferries leave from Corfu Town, but given that each can be 'done' in a couple of hours it is better to visit by excursion boat from Sidari. Arid and hilly **Othoni** is the largest, and the only one with a resident summer tourist population. Even so, it is very quiet with nothing to do except lounge on the beach and make the dusty walk to the inland chora. **Erikoussa** is the main objective for the Sidari excursion boats thanks to a good sand beach at the port village. **Mathraki**, the smallest, sees few tourists and her beaches are home to nesting loggerhead turtles each summer. Rooms are available on all three islets. Erikoussa also has a hotel.

Gulf of Corinth Ports

Running north of the Peloponnese from the Corinth Canal to the entrance to the Ionian Sea lies the Gulf of Corinth. Two landing-craft ferry links cross it, though both will disappear when a new suspension bridge over the Gulf is completed some time in 2004. The easterly link runs from **Agios Nikolaos** on the north coast to **Egion** on the Peloponnese. The much busier western link — at the new bridge site — links **Andirio** to **Rio** (10 km north-east of Patras), running frequently day and night, and used by the Corfu—Athens bus. There is also a ferry link between the mainland ports of **Aktion**, north of Lefkada, and **Preveza** (home to the remains of a notable Roman city and a good number of waterfront hotels), a town on the headland to the north (see p. 535). Finally, the small town of **Amphilochia** — deep inside the Preveza Gulf — had a Corfu catamaran link in previous years offering a quick connection with Athens buses. Sadly, this route seems to be totally moribund, so it is a link to look for, but not a connection to build into pre-planning.

Igoumenitsa
ΗΓΟΥΜΕΝΙΤΣΑ; pop. 6,500.

CODE ☎ 26650
WATERFRONT GNTO/EOT ☎ 22227
TOURIST POLICE ☎ 22222
POLICE ☎ 22100

Set within the inner recesses of a deep and steamy calm bay, this is one of those places which always prompt the question 'Where are we?' from puzzled ferry passengers. In fact, Igoumenitsa — despite being a surprisingly small place — is Greece's major western port north of the Gulf of Corinth and thus on the itineraries of many ferries (though in practice few foot passengers choose to set down here). The long waterfront is fairly pleasant — given its commercial role — with a park of sorts (filled with bushes used for highly dubious purposes — given the absence of a public WC) and a frontier town air, but walk a street inland and you will find a dusty collection of drab Greek streets of the kind that bedevils many an otherwise pretty place. If you are stuck in town for the day then you would do well to head 5 km north to the beach at **Drepanos** which is a much nicer part of the world. Igoumenitsa, meantime, offers nothing to do except catch the ferry to Corfu or Italy, or a bus to another Greek destination.

Buses run (from the bus station a block in from the waterfront) direct to Athens (⊕ 08.30, 11.00, 13.30, 19.45), Thessalonika (⊕ 11.45) and also to Preveza (⊕ 11.45, 15.30) — with its short ferry hop to Aktion and the link to Lefkada (last bus 16.10).

⊨
Most folks head for Corfu Town rather than stay in the dozen-odd hotels in Igoumenitsa. However, there are advantages in staying here, not least because there is far less pressure on beds. In a pinch try the D-class *Egnatias* (☎ 23648) and *Lux* (☎ 22223) or the C-class *Epirus* (☎ 22504), all on or near the waterfront. Ticket agents also offer some rooms.

A
Kalami Beach Camping (☎ 71245), awkwardly placed, 4 km south of the town.

Ithaca
ΙΘΑΚΗ; 96 km²; pop. 4,000.

CODE ☎ 26740
PORT POLICE ☎ 32209
POLICE ☎ 32205
HOSPITAL ☎ 32282

A small and very hilly island, Ithaca is literally two barely connected mountain peaks poking out of the sea. Ithaca lies steeped in the romance of myth rather than offering much in reality beyond a quiet tranquillity. The legendary home of Odysseus (alias Ulysses), hero of the *Odyssey* — and

the siege of Troy, too, in a way (he was the devious hero who came up with the idea of the wooden horse) — there is little to do here except walk the hills, indulge in a little quiet romance and wonder why he spent ten years trying to get back. Indeed, there is little to show that he was ever here at all: no dead dogs on the beaches, no remains of a palace (home to his wife Penelope), and no sign of the suitors and attendant orgy girls — Ithaca has yielded little significant archaeological evidence to suggest it was a centre of power at the time.

The modern centre, such as it is, consists of the red-tiled house village of **Vathi** tucked deep into a bay in the middle of the island. Devastated in the 1953 earthquake that rocked all the southern Ionian Islands, it has been rebuilt sympathetically, and offers a taste of rural island life, spiced with the more tourist-orientated waterfront looking onto the prison islet of **Lanzareto** that graces the mouth of the bay.

Ferry links are good, considering the insignificance of Ithaca as a tourist island (thanks largely to poor pebble beaches and few obvious sights), with boats running to three island ports. The majority of large ferries head for Vathi, with daily High Season landing-craft ferries serving both the small northern port of **Frikes** (from Lefkada) and **Pisaetos** (from Kefalonia). Pisaetos also sees occasional international boats that can't find the time to steam round to Vathi. This 'port' is no more than an isolated quay below a steep hillside decorated with a switchback dirt track road, which defies the island bus and sees as few taxis.

Ithaca has a solitary bus that teeters along the precipitous hill roads to uninspiring **Stavros** (complete with several places offering rooms) and the hamlet villages on the northern half of the island, as well as to **Perahori**, the former centre in pirate-troubled days. High Season also sees taxi boats running from Vathi to the attractive pebble-beach villages of **Kioni** and Frikes. Formerly quiet fishing villages, they offer a gentle spot in which to spend a day or two.

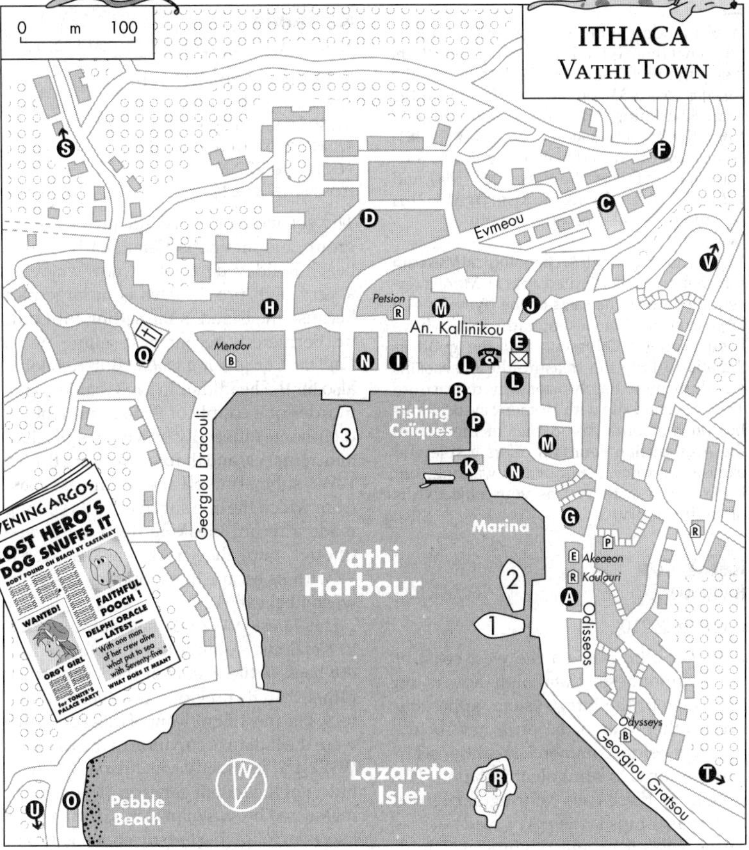

ITHACA
VATHI TOWN

0   m   100

Evmeou

Petsion

An. Kallinikou

Mendor

Georgiou Dracouli

Fishing
Caïques

3

**Vathi
Harbour**

Marina

Akeaeon

Kaulouri

2

1

Odisseos

Odysseys

Georgiou Gratsou

**Lazareto
Islet**

**Pebble
Beach**

EVENING ARGOS

LOST HERO'S
DOG SNUFFS IT

BODY FOUND ON BEACH BY CASTAWAY

FAITHFUL
POOCH !

WANTED!

DELPHI ORACLE
— LATEST —

With one more
shot got to see
what crew alive
with humanity.
WHAT DOES IT MEAN?

ORGY GIRL

Key

A	Tourist Information
B	Bus Stop & Taxi Rank
C	Police
D	Tourist Police
E	National Bank of Greece
F	Hospital
G	Town Hall
H	Archaeological Museum
I	Pharmacy
J	Bakery
K	Public WCs
L	Ticket Agent
M	Moped Rental
N	Tavernas
O	Circe Club
P	Pl. Elastathiou Dracouli
Q	Cathedral
R	Former Prison
S	Sarakiniko Bay Road
T	North Ithaca Road
U	Loutsa / Skinos Bay Road
V	Perahori Road
1	Ferry Berth
2	Irregular Hydrofoils
3	Beach Boats

⊢

Accommodation on Ithaca is pretty limited, and what there is tends to be expensive. **Vathi** has some rooms and two B-class hotels: the *Mendor* (☎ 32433), on the waterfront near the caïque harbour, and at the western edge of town the hotel/pension *Odysseus* (☎ 32381) — also on the waterfront. There is also a C-class hotel in **Frikes**, the *Nostos* (☎ 31644), and a B-class hotel in Kioni: the *Kioni* (☎ 31362). A few rooms are also on offer at both.

∽

Vathi is host to a small **Archaeological Museum** which in truth has limited appeal. More interesting by far is the **Cave of the Nymphs** — a large cavern 1 km west of Vathi, said to have been used by Odysseus and the goddess Athena to hide the treasure the Phaeacians gave him immediately prior to his return from Troy. A second site with Homeric associations lies on the south-east corner of the island: the **Arethousian Fountain** offers a splendid excuse for some pleasant hill walking, but bring liquid with you as your objective is often drunk dry.

Katakolon
ΚΑΤΑΚΟΛΟ

CODE ☎ 26210

A sleepy little port on the west coast of the Peloponnese, Katakolon hovers on the fringe of the ferry system, appearing every other year or so on a new boat's itinerary before commercial realities set in and it returns to somnolent isolation. The reason for these calls by irregular ferries and cruise ships is the port's ready access to the site of ancient Olympia (27 km), home to the most important Temple of Zeus and the Olympic games. Actually, the port is quite attractive itself, with an impressively long beach, several tavernas and hotels. Buses connect with the town of Pirgos (12 km away) and its links with Olympia (where you will find three campsites and a youth hostel).

⊢

Accommodation options in town are confined to three establishments: the A-class pension *Zefyros* (☎ 41170), the C-class hotel *Ionio* (☎ 41494), and the D-class *Delfini* (☎ 41214).

Kefalonia
ΚΕΦΑΛΛΩΝΙΑ; 781 km²; pop. 31,800.

ARGOSTOLI CODE ☎ 26710
SAMI CODE ☎ 26740
ARGOSTOLI NTOG OFFICE ☎ 22248
SAMI PORT POLICE ☎ 22031
POLICE ☎ 22200
HOSPITAL ☎ 22434

The second largest island in the Ionian group, mountainous Kefalonia is a quiet beach-holiday destination now enjoying a very high profile. This is in large part because the island is the setting for Louis de Bernières's recent best-selling novel *Captain Corelli's Mandolin*. But Kefalonia also hit the headlines in 1998 thanks to the murder of a couple of British residents in their home (allegedly by a couple of Albanian refugees) and the discovery of a British WW2 submarine off the south-east coast from which the one survivor of its sinking made a record-breaking deep-sea escape (though until the wreck was discovered — with its escape hatch open — his story wasn't believed).

This latest WW2 tale has simply added to Kefalonia's ability to promote itself on the back of the events of the last century rather than its previous 3,000 years of history. The most significant of these episodes were the Italian occupation of the island in WW2 and its bloody conclusion (when all but 33 of the Italian garrison of 9,000 were massacred by German forces during their take over following the surrender of Italy in 1943), and the devastating earthquake that rocked the Ionian Islands in 1956, during which almost all the buildings on Kefalonia collapsed. These events provide the setting for (and are excellently described in) *Captain Corelli's Mandolin*.

Kefalonia is very much an island of visual contradictions. On the one hand it boasts some spectacular mountain scenery with a coastline of green pine-clad hills and sandy beach-lined coves, all bathed in a timeless light that makes one feel as if one is walking around in a polarized photograph; on

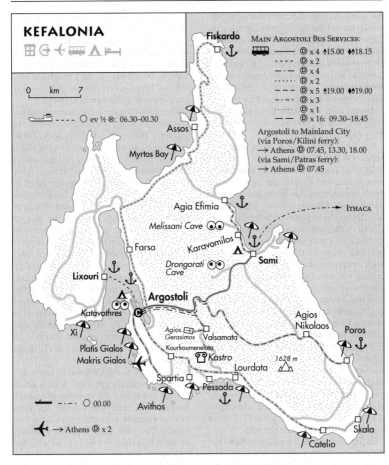

KEFALONIA

0   km   7

⌂ --- ○ ev ½ ⊗: 06.30–00.30

Fiskardo

Assos

Myrtos Bay

Agia Efimia

Melissani Cave ⊙⊙

Farsa

Drongorati ⊙⊙
Cave

Karavomilos

Sami

Lixouri

Katavothres ⊙⊙

Argostoli

Xi

Platis Gialos

Makris Gialos

Agios
Gerasimos   Valsamata

Kourkoumenelata

Kastro

Spartia

Pessada

Avithos

Agios
Nikolaos   Poros

1628 m

Lourdata

Skala

Catelio

— --- ○ 00.00

✈ → Athens ⓓ x 2

MAIN ARGOSTOLI BUS SERVICES:

——— ⓓ x 4 ◆15.00 ◆◆18.15
---- ⓓ x 2
—·— ⓓ x 4
······ ⓓ x 2
——— ⓓ x 5 ◆19.00 ◆◆19.00
—··— ⓓ x 3
······ ⓓ x 1
—— ⓓ x 16: 09.30–18.45

Argostoli to Mainland City
(via Poros/Kilini ferry):
→ Athens ⓓ 07.45, 13.30, 18.00
(via Sami/Patras ferry):
→ Athens ⓓ 07.45

→ ITHACA

the other hand the island has been shorn of almost every attractive building that it once possessed. Unfortunately, the hurried rebuilding after the 1956 earthquake was more practical than poetic, leaving a result best summed up by Captain Corelli: 'Everything here used to be so pretty, and now everything is concrete.' Don't, however, be put off by this lament: even without its old architecture Kefalonia is a very attractive

place, though you will encounter considerable difficulties in exploring the island if you are without your own transport. Kefalonia's fans tend to divide their time between a small hotel, a quiet beach, and a good book (an estimated one in five visitors now come armed with *the* novel).

Size disparities are Kefalonia's great problem: the island is too big while the population centres are widely scattered and too small. As a result of both this — and the misfortune of the capital growing up on the far west side when all ferry links are either with the mainland or islands on the other three sides of the compass — an amazing seven island ports have emerged offering ferry services. This wouldn't be a problem if there was an adequate bus service running between them but sadly there is not, and from midday on, you have to resort to the very expensive taxis.

Kefalonia's ports are a pretty disparate collection. **Argostoli**, the capital, is majestically sited in a picturesque bay beneath the mountains, and despite the lack of good ferry connections has managed to retain some sense of centre but very little else; it abjectly fails to do justice to its setting. From the air or the overlooking hillsides it looks fantastic, but once you arrive in town you will find yourself surrounded by drab concrete structures: its buildings (many deliberately left with half-built top floors — so that the owners don't have to pay the local roof tax) would put Kefalonia very high in any 'Greek island with the ugliest capital' contest. Even the waterfront, complete with yachting marina, lacks sparkle. There is an EOT office just south of the ferry port, but otherwise there is nowhere to visit. Even the locals prefer to live on the western side of the bay at **Lixouri**, a port town almost as large as the capital, made up of nought but suburbs tarted up with the odd statue. A small landing-craft ferry (the C/F *Agios Gerasimus*) runs between the two.

Of the other ports: the village of **Sami** has become the 'international' berth and the nearest thing Kefalonia has to a main ferry port and tourist resort. It was also used as the main location during the shooting of the film of *Captain Corelli's Mandolin* (if you visit Kefalonia and then view the film afterwards, it becomes an exercise in 'spot the location'). With a pleasant, taverna-lined waterfront that is atmospheric enough at night (though a bit too bland for comfort during the day), and a fine pebble beach to the north of the port, it is the easiest

place to stay if you are island hopping, though again there isn't a great deal here beyond the hotels, promenade, and several supermarkets battling with each other for the limited custom. Nightlife, such as it is (and to be honest, 'it' isn't much), is also centred here, but reflects the fact that few people come to Kefalonia to party.

The remaining ports/settlements on the island are poorly connected, but make pleasant places in which to stay; **Poros** is the most accessible thanks to the Kilini ferry. It consists of a large village with a long waterfront, which is more scruffy beach than promenade. It is connected to Argostoli by the same road that branches south to the small tourist resort village of **Skala**, with beaches (some of the best on the island) to the east a second home to the loggerhead turtle (see p. 544).

Fiskardo, perched on the northern finger, is the only village to retain most of its attractive, pre-earthquake Venetian buildings. These are clustered around a petite tree-lined bay, easily making it the most photogenic of the ports; the downside is that it is host to day-trippers from the rest of the island (it is so isolated that it is an attractive day-trip destination) and Lefkada in consequence.

The village of **Agia Efimia**, 10 km north of Sami, is quietly attractive with a small pebble beach and the remains of a small Roman villa crumbling nearby. The final port, at **Pessada**, is another very attractive village, but it has ferry schedules written by local taxi drivers and is to be avoided unless you have your own transport.

Kefalonia is primarily a beach island and has them in abundance. Finding one isn't difficult. Among the best known are those at **Makris Gialos** and **Platis Gialos**. These end at the small islet of **Tourkopodaro** (connected to Kefalonia by a beach).

Taverna-backed **Avithos** is also justifiably popular thanks to its fine red sand. Lixouri also has a notable red sand beach at **Xi**. The beach at **Spartia** is more isolated and is backed by picturesque steep white cliffs.

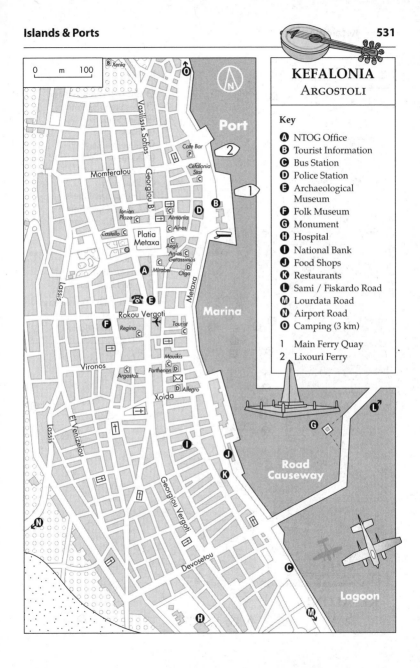

0   m   100

KEFALONIA
ARGOSTOLI

Key

A NTOG Office
B Tourist Information
C Bus Station
D Police Station
E Archaeological Museum
F Folk Museum
G Monument
H Hospital
I National Bank
J Food Shops
K Restaurants
L Sami / Fiskardo Road
M Lourdata Road
N Airport Road
O Camping (3 km)

1   Main Ferry Quay
2   Lixouri Ferry

Port

Marina

Road Causeway

Lagoon

Vasilissis Sofias
Momferatou
Georgiou B'
Ionian Plaza
Castello
Platia Metaxa
Mirabel
Xenia
Cafe Bar
Cefalonia Star
Armonia
Ainos
Aegli
Agias Gerassimos
Olga
Metaxa
Rokou Vergoti
Regina
Tourist
Mouikis
Parthenon
Allegro
Vironos
Argostoli
Xoida
El Venizelou
Lassis
Georgiou Vergoti
Devosetou

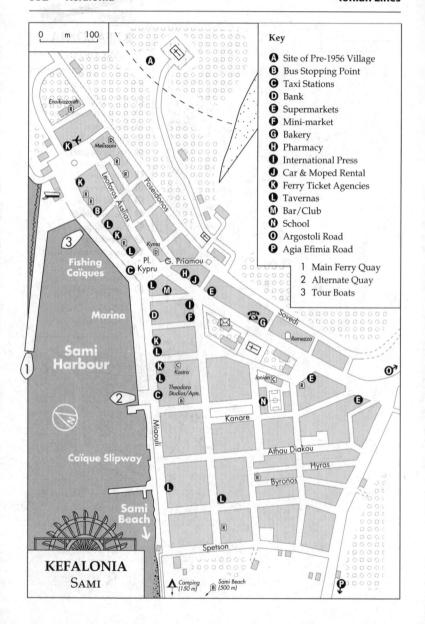

Key

- **A** Site of Pre-1956 Village
- **B** Bus Stopping Point
- **C** Taxi Stations
- **D** Bank
- **E** Supermarkets
- **F** Mini-market
- **G** Bakery
- **H** Pharmacy
- **I** International Press
- **J** Car & Moped Rental
- **K** Ferry Ticket Agencies
- **L** Tavernas
- **M** Bar/Club
- **N** School
- **O** Argostoli Road
- **P** Agia Efimia Road

1 Main Ferry Quay
2 Alternate Quay
3 Tour Boats

KEFALONIA
SAMI

⊨

Bed supply is good on Kefalonia, despite
the island being well off the backpacker trail
and popular with Italian motorists hopping
across the Adriatic (the tragic fate of the Italian
WW2 garrison has left the islanders with a soft
spot for the citizens of this occupying nation).
However, beds on Kefalonia are pricey. The
EOT office in Argostoli offers help in tracking
spare beds down, along with free maps, bus
timetables, and ferry information.

Sami has several convenient hotels. Two,
the C-class *Ionion* (☎ 22035) and D-class
Kyma (☎ 22064), are both one block behind
the promenade (the latter off the town square).
Several blocks further back, with good bay
views across to Ithaca, is the D-class *Melissani*
(☎ 22464). There are also several houses offering rooms in the backstreets. **Poros** also has a
good number of rooms advertised.

Argostoli has hotels aplenty; for a good
budget hotel try the D-class *Allegro* (☎ 22268)
or *Parthenon* (☎ 22246). More up-market are
the C-class *Tourist* (☎ 22510), *Agios Gerasimos*
(☎ 28697) and the *Mouikis* (☎ 23032). If you
want to splash out, then there is a B-class *Xenia*
(☎ 22233) at the north end of town.

A

There are two reasonable sites on the island:
most convenient is *Caravomilos Beach* (☎
26740 22480) at **Sami**. A nice, mature tree-
filled 'family' site behind a pebble beach, but
(thanks to the large number of Italian motorists) very expensive. *Argostoli Beach* (☎ 26710
23487) — a member of the *Sunshine Camping
Club* scheme — is 2 km north of **Agostoli** and
offers marginally better value.

ᏮᏮ

Apart from a poor **Archaeological Museum**,
the only 'sight' Argostoli has on offer is a small
monument on the causeway across the neck
of the bay south of the town — built to commemorate the glory of the British Empire (the
British built most of the island's roads during
50 years of rule in the 19th century); it is now
inscription-less but otherwise intact. During
1992, the mayor of Sami (a part-time archaeologist) discovered a major 14 c. BC Mycenaean
beehive-shaped tomb on the outskirts of town,
reopening speculation as to whether Kefalonia
was the true 'Ithaca' of Odysseus — given
the absence of finds there and the better
topographical 'fit' of Kefalonia to the island
described by Homer. This discovery will presumably be open to the public at some point.

Meantime, **island bus tours** out of Argostoli
are very popular. These take in the **Venetian
Kastro** of St. George, 9 km south of Argostoli,
and the **Monastery of Agios Gerasimos** (home
to the body of a monk who is now the island's
little-known patron saint).

Fans of *Captain Corelli's Mandolin* are also
visiting the island in increasing numbers with
the express purpose of finding the Kefalonia
described in the book. Needless to say the
earthquake hasn't left much. The old village
of **Farsa** is now a deserted ruin on a hillside
above the Argostoli—Lixouri road, while
Argostoli has lost the attractive tavernas that
once lined Metaxa Square. As a result of this
dearth of sites, many fans have to make do
with visiting the beach beyond the village of
Spartia from where Captain Corelli (and his
mandolin strings) made his bid for freedom,
and imbibing the odd beverage at the *Café
Tselenti* (supposedly the model for Drosoula's
taverna) in **Fiskardo**.

The most impressive sightseeing Kefalonia
has to offer — beyond the island's lush
mountain and coastal scenery — are its caves.
These include the red-walled **Drongorati Cave**
(entrance fee €5) 4 km south-west of Sami
(which has such good acoustics that concerts
are occasionally held in it), and the 100 m
long **Melissani Cave** (entrance fee €5) on the
Sami—Agia Efimia road (complete with a
subterranean lake and tour boats).

En route you will find a **Tide-Mill Wheel**
at **Karavomilos** — one of a number scattered around the Kefalonian coastline. The
best known is at **Katavothres**, just north of
Argostoli. For many years this (now over-
touristed) site attracted interest thanks to
the odd phenomenon of the sea seemingly
flowing into the apparently inexhaustible
sink hole found here. Frequent attempts to
track where the water went, with everything
from dyes to petrol and saw-dust, proved
fruitless until 1963, when a party of Austrian
geologists put 140 kg of a water soluble green
dye down the sink hole. Fourteen days later
faint traces of the dye appeared 20 km away
on the other side of the island at Karavomilos
and Melissani cave.

Tour buses also combine with ferries to
provide excursions to (1) **Zakinthos** (via
Pessada), (2) the ruins of **Olympia** — home
to the original Olympic Games and the famous
Temple of Zeus (via Poros and Kilini) — and,
(3) day trips to **Ithaca** and **Lefkada**.

Kilini
ΚΥΛΛΗΝΗ

CODE ☎ 26230

The major jumping-off point to the island of Zante, Kilini is a dusty little port with a beach on the west coast of the Peloponnese some 30 km south of Patras. Overland connections are poor; simply getting to this port is apt to be a pain. Two buses a day leave Patras during the week (08.00, 14.55), with only the first running during the weekends. At Kilini they stop at the ticket office block behind the ferry quay, usually only skidding into town at breakneck speed a few minutes before ferries are due to depart. There is also a rail link between the ports — but no passenger trains.

╾

The Tourist Police office (☎ 92211) on the quay will point you in the direction of the limited (but rarely full) port rooms. The nearest hotels are 5 km to the south at **Kastro**.

Lefkada / Lefkas
ΛΕΥΚΑΔΑ; 303 km²; pop. 23,000.

CODE ☎ 26450
POLICE / TOURIST OFFICE ☎ 22346
HOSPITAL ☎ 22336

An island sufficiently close to the mainland to have a road link (via a bridge to the capital of Lefkada Town), Lefkada is barren and austere but spectacular thanks to its mountains and islet-littered coast. Tourist development has largely confined itself to the east and southern coasts, but is comparatively restrained, offering an appealing mix of taverna and tradition. Unusually for a Greek island, the capital — Lefkada Town — is not a ferry port. With the lagoon to the north now home to a yachting marina, and salt flats between it and the mainland, it doesn't feel like a coastal town. Tradition has it that Lefkada was joined to the mainland until a canal was dug in the 5 c. BC separating the town from the mainland. Earthquake damage is also

all too evident here, but fortunately most of the Venetian churches that make the town have survived, and the ad hoc rebuilding of houses (now limited to a maximum of two storeys high) has produced a charming tin-roof and plaster touch. This is one town that has actually been enhanced by earthquake 'repairs'. Unfortunately, accommodation is limited in the town and it is best visited as a day trip from one of Lefkada's ports.

Buses run frequently between the capital and main island towns, most passing through the resort port of **Nidri**, the starting point for boat tours circumnavigating a number of islets, including **Skorpios** — owned by the Onassis family. A number of boats advertise swims *on* the island. Even if this was physically possible, in practice you are not allowed to venture beyond the beach if you are allowed to land, and usually swims are from the boat just offshore. Despite this, these excursions offer value for money thanks to the visit to the sea cave on Meganisi. One boat even goes to Lefkada's best sand beach at **Porto Katsiki** — also visited by caïques from the port of **Vassiliki**. Home to the best windsurfing in Europe, off a poor pebble beach, this village gets very crowded, but is worth a look in the late afternoon when up to 100 windsurfers are skimming effortlessly up and down the bay. The best beaches on Lefkada are all on the remoter west side. In addition to Porto Katsiki there is an excellent sand beach behind the headland at **Ag. Nikitas**.

╾

High package tourist presence (courtesy of the airport at Aktion: sometimes advertised as Lefkada airport) has driven up prices and reduced the available accommodation. **Lefkada** is the most likely town to have beds on offer. The E-class *Patrae* (☎ 22359) near the Agricultural Bank in the central square has a good reputation, as does the C-class *Santa Mavra* (☎ 22342) and the nearby E-class *Vyzantion* (☎ 22629). More up-market are the promenade B-class *Niricos* (☎ 24132) and *Lefkas* (☎ 23916). **Vassiliki** also has some budget hotels: the C-class *Lefkatas* (☎ 31229) and E-class *Paradissos* (☎ 31256), and a supply of B-class hotels full of package tourists.

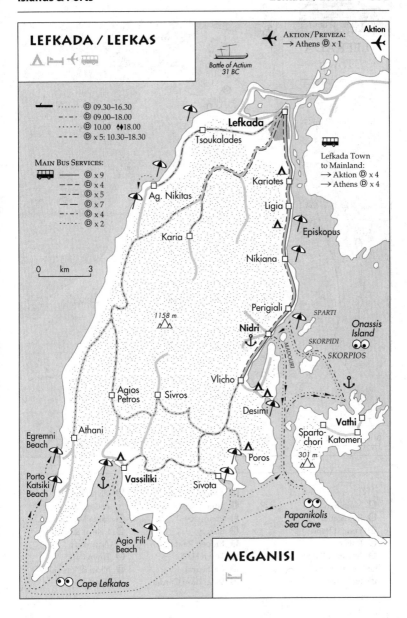

LEFKADA / LEFKAS

AKTION/PREVEZA:
→ Athens Ⓓ x 1

Aktion

Battle of Actium
31 BC

⊙ 09.30–16.30
⊙ 09.00–18.00
⊙ 10.00 ⚓18.00
⊙ x 5: 10.30–18.30

MAIN BUS SERVICES:
Ⓓ x 9
Ⓓ x 4
Ⓓ x 5
Ⓓ x 7
Ⓓ x 4
Ⓓ x 2

0   km   3

Lefkada

Tsoukalades

Lefkada Town
to Mainland:
→ Aktion Ⓓ x 4
→ Athens Ⓓ x 4

Kariotes

Ag. Nikitas

Ligia

Episkopus

Karia

Nikiana

1158 m

Perigiali

SPARTI

Nidri

**Onassis
Island**

SKORPIDI

SKORPIOS

Vlicho

Agios
Petros

Sivros

Desimi

Sparto-
chori

Vathi

Katomeri

Egremni
Beach

Athani

Poros

301 m

Porto
Katsiki
Beach

Vassiliki

Sivota

Agio Fili
Beach

*Papanikolis
Sea Cave*

MEGANISI

Cape Lefkatas

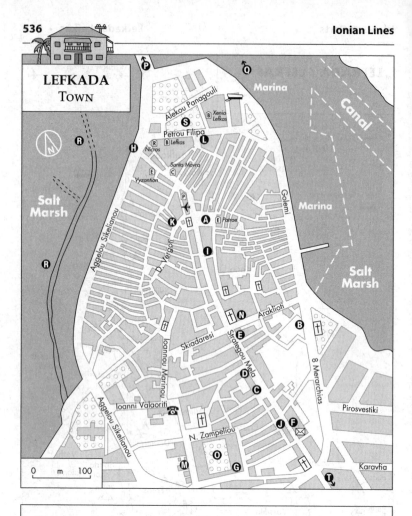

LEFKADA
Town

Key

- **A** Main Square
- **B** Bus Station
- **C** Tourist Police
- **D** Police
- **E** National Bank of Greece
- **F** Ionian Bank
- **G** Hospital
- **H** Taxi Station
- **I** Supermarket
- **J** Pharmacy
- **K** Bakery
- **L** Moped Rental
- **M** Town Hall
- **N** Cathedral
- **O** Valaoritou Garden
- **P** Chain Bridge & Causeway
- **Q** Santa Maura Fort
- **R** Line of Roman Aqueduct
- **S** Town Park
- **T** Nidri & Vassiliki Road

Λ

There are six sites on the island: *Camping Vassiliki Beach* (☎ 31308), full-to-bursting with windsurfers, is the most convenient; *Camping Desimi Beach* (☎ 95225), 3 km south of Nidri, is less so but offers more space. *Camping Kariotes Beach* (☎ 71103) is the nearest to Lefkada Town. The other sites — *Episkopos Beach* (☎ 92410), *Santa Mavra Camping* (☎ 95493) and *Poros Beach* (☎ 95452), running down the east coast — are geared to motorists.

⊙⊙

Lefkada's sights are more made up of places where things happened rather than things to see; over the years the island has become a veritable shrine to the sticky side of romance. Story has it that Aristotle, when a very old man, was asked if he regretted that his manly 'powers' had waned. He is said to have observed that it was the best thing that had ever happened to him, as it was 'like being unchained from a lunatic'.

Lefkada is, from top to tail, a testament to the acuteness of this observation. **Cape Lefkatas** became the Beachy Head of the ancient world after Sappho (the famous lesbian poet of antiquity) jumped off after experiencing a touch of unrequited love — for a middle-aged man. The tip of this peninsula housed a **Temple of Apollo** (fragmentary remains extant) whose priests thought this action a terribly good idea and took to chucking sacrificial victims — with symbolic lover's dove wings tied to their limbs — over the edge in years thereafter (they were collected by boat after they hit the water).

Given the close proximity of this lover's leap, it is surprising that Anthony and Cleopatra didn't take advantage of it in 31 BC after the disastrous naval **Battle of Actium** against Octavian, which took place just to the north of Lefkada just offshore from the airport of Preveza / Aktion. Instead, they winged it to Egypt and jumped into the next world from there.

Romance struck again in the 19 c. when the German archaeologist Wilhelm Dörpfeld hit upon the idea that Lefkada was Homer's Ithaca and then spent futile years trying to prove it. Dying of old age before the total discrediting of his theory could prompt him to test the merits of Sappho's leap, he left some **Bronze Age Tomb** excavations south of Nidri — now little visited — and a bronze bust of himself on the town waterfront.

Meganisi

ΜΕΓΑΝΗΣΙ; 23 km²; pop. 250.

CODE ☎ 26450

A small island off the south-east coast of Lefkada, Meganisi is linked by a daily ferry from Nidri as well as several tour boats. If you are not planning to stay overnight then the latter are a better way of quickly seeing this gentle island. Most boats also call at the fishing village of **Vathi**, the largest settlement on the north coast, and occasionally at its tidier neighbour — **Spartochori** — as well.

⋈

A reasonable supply of rooms exist in all three villages. There is also a pricey A-class hotel in Katomeri: the *Meganissi* (☎ 51639).

⊙⊙

Nidri tourist boats run daily to the **Papanikolis Cave** on the west coast, said to be the second largest sea cave in Greece. The locals claim that they successfully hid a Greek submarine in it for much of the last war, but, appealing as this idea is, the more cynical will perceive that it must have been a very small submarine.

Patras

ΠΑΤΡΑ; pop. 141,530.

CODE ☎ 2610
TOURIST OFFICE ☎ 22 0902
NTOG OFFICE ☎ 65 3368
FIRST AID ☎ 150

The busiest international port in Greece after Piraeus, Patras is a popular destination for ferries running down the length of the Adriatic or south from Italy. However, the presence of thousands of holidaymakers passing through daily brings out the worst rip-off merchants in Greece, the practical upshot being that if you want either a top-class meal or bed you have to look pretty hard to find it. The city is also suffering from an influx of illegal immigrants, who, having broken into the EU via Greece, are now looking to cross over to richer Italy.

The third largest city in Greece, Patras's fate was sealed with the decision to rebuild

PATRAS
CITY CENTRE

Key

- **A** International Ferry Terminal / NTOG
- **B** Main Bus Station
- **C** Railway Station
- **D** Public WCs
- **E** Tourist Police / National Bank
- **F** Local Bus Station
- **G** Bakery
- **H** Newspapers
- **I** Roman Odeon
- **J** Acropolis
- **K** Cathedral
- **L** Hospital
- **M** Museum
- **N** Ticket Kiosks

1 Domestic Ferries
2 Hydrofoils (if any)

International Ferries
(typical locations):
3 Ventouris Ferries
4 Minoan Lines
5 ANEK Lines
6 H.M.L. Ferries
7 Blue Star
8 Superfast

9 Vergina Ferries
10 Adriatica
11 Marlines
12 Agoudimos Lines
13 Poseidon Lines
14 A. K. Ventouris

the centre (following its destruction during the War of Independence) using an uninteresting grid pattern. The grime-laden buildings, relieved only by attractive park-like squares, offer little incentive to hang around, and few tourists do.

Fortunately, all facilities and means of escape are on or near the waterfront. The downside of this is that, alongside the ferry terminus and the railway and bus stations, the quayside road is loaded with the worst 'restaurants' in Greece (offering warmed-up greasy — rather than Grecian — cuisine) and the usual collection of ticket agents. Given this, the best advice has to be to feed before you arrive in the port area of town; that way you can still enjoy your holiday without being ripped off.

Most ticket agencies are only interested in selling international tickets, and all will accept credit cards — unless you are buying a ticket for a purely domestic boat. The latter are still sold on a cash basis. You will also find tickets for most domestic ferries and hydrofoils (if any) on sale from kiosks at **◐**.

A relatively recent change at Patras has been the introduction of signpost 'Gates' along the waterfront. Your ticket agent should be able to indicate from which your boat will depart, but all international travellers still have to clear passport control in the International Ferry Terminal (**◓**) to get their boarding pass and have it stamped (this is checked on boarding). Domestic ticket holders just show their tickets.

Patras is naturally a major destination for both trains and buses. The former depart from a quayside station every couple of hours and then crawl to Athens or the Peloponnese; the latter are based at a waterfront bus station (complete with a pricey, but popular, snack and drink shop) and offer a far wider variety of destinations. The most important of these are to: Athens (℗ 05.00–21.00), Thessalonika (℗ 08.30, 15.00) and Kilini (℗ 08.00, 14.45). Finally, the big Adriatic ferry lines run ultrasmooth air-conditioned buses to and from

the centre of Athens. Seats can be booked along with your ticket.

➤

The friendly NTOG office (☎ 42 3866) located in the ferry terminal can point you in the direction of a room. The port area of town has the greatest concentration, with the waterfront D-class *Splendid* (☎ 27 6521) along with the C-class *Acropole* (☎ 27 9809) offering tolerable rooms at better than most prices. Near the bus station you will find the noisy C-class *Adonis* (☎ 22 4213) and the *Mediterranee* (☎ 27 9602) — located on Ag. Nikolaou, the main shopping street. The up-market *Rannia* (☎ 220114) lies on the next block east. Patras also has a couple of good pensions at the southern end of the port, the *Marie* (☎ 33 1302) and the *Nicos* (☎ 27 6183). There is also an IYHF *Youth Hostel* (☎ 42 7278) 2 km north at 68 Iroon Polytechniou.

Λ

There are several sites beyond the outer suburbs of Patras. The best is *Camping Rion* (☎ 99 1585): on the beach 7 km north.

◉◉

Patras has just enough sights to keep you occupied while you await your ferry. Greeks head for **St. Andrew's Cathedral**, a major shrine thanks to its role as the repository of the saint's head.

Others make for the **Venetian Castle** on the site of the ancient **Acropolis**. Classical remains are confined to a restored **Odeon**. Patras also has a small **Archaeological Museum** (② to ⑦ 08.30–15.00).

Paxi / Paxos
ΠΑΞΟΙ; 25 km²; pop. 3,000.

CODE ☎ 26620
POLICE ☎ 31222
PORT POLICE ☎ 31259
FIRST AID ☎ 31466

Lying just south of Corfu, tiny Paxi (also known as 'Paxos') is largely the domain of up-market English and Italian tourists; its tranquil atmosphere is severely tested by daily invasions of day-trippers from both Corfu Town and the mainland resort of Parga. These two tourist groups combine to make Paxi a comparatively expensive destination. Backpackers are a rarity thanks

PAXI / PAXOS

---- ⊕ 09.00–20.00
--·-- ⓓ 10.00 Seven Sea Cave boat tour
······ ⊕ 10.00–18.00

Lakka

Ipapanti
(Sea
Cave)

(Porto)
Longos

Fountana

Magazia　　Bogdanatika

Stachai
(Sea
Caves)

Gaios
Town　　New
　　　　Port
Old Port　　AG. NIKOLAOS

PANAGIA

Ortholithos
Stack

Porto
Sputzo

MOGONISI

KALTSIO-
NISSI

🚌 ——— ⓓ x 4
- - - ⓓ x 6
No ⑦ Bus Service

Vrikes
Beach

Voutoumi
Beach

ANTIPAXI

Ormos
Agrapidias

0　　km　　2

to the island's pricey reputation, and a lack of budget accommodation. The residents won't thank this book for saying it, but in High Season day-tripping is the best way for island hoppers to get a taste of the main town. The rest of the year (and once day-trippers have gone) it is a much more tranquil spot, reverting to a Patmos-like cosiness.

The main centre is at **Gaios Town**. Protected by two pine-clad islets (one topped with the remains of a Venetian fortress) nestling within the port bay, it has more charm than many island capitals, despite the inevitable 1953 earthquake damage. Fortunately, most of the lovely red-tiled houses that line the horseshoe waterfront survived unscathed, and contrast attractively with the sea-canal and islets. Because of the narrowness of the channel the town now has an 'Old Port' harbouring caïques and tour boats, while ferries now dock at the 'New Port', a quay 600 m along the coast road. The waterfront aside, the town is little more than the main square with a couple of major streets behind, adding greatly to the village feel of the place. The town's only major weakness is the beach; a tiny pebble affair, it does little more than encourage visitors to opt for the caïques that head for two south-coast beaches.

The rest of Paxi (along with Antipaxi to the south) is characterized by low hills on the east side and dramatic cliffs and views on the west. Add to this the carpet of ancient olive groves — containing 200,000 trees — and Paxi's homely size, and the result is a near-perfect walking island.

Buses run regularly from a dusty square at the back of Gaios Town across the island to the small hamlet ports of Lakka and Longos (both of which have seen local ferry links with Corfu in the past). **Longos** is the more attractive settlement of the two, with a couple of tavernas overlooking a small caïque harbour. **Lakka** (also a popular destination for Corfu tour boats) is larger, but relies more on its narrow pine-lined bay for its not inconsiderable scenic appeal.

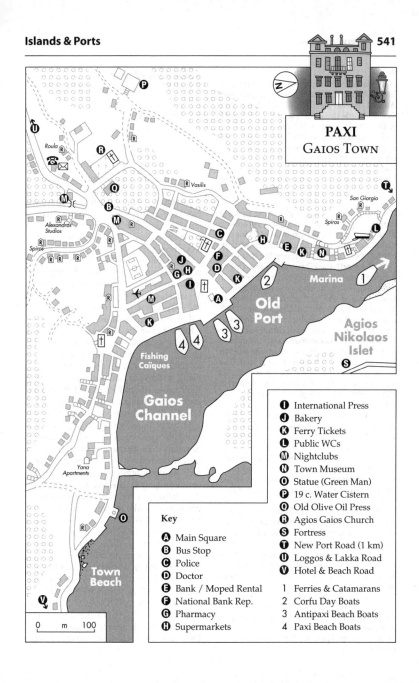

PAXI
GAIOS TOWN

Roula

Vasilis

San Giorgio

Spiros

Alexandros
Studios

Spiros

Marina

Old
Port

Agios
Nikolaos
Islet

Fishing
Caïques

Gaios
Channel

Yana
Apartments

Town
Beach

0 m 100

Key

 A Main Square
 B Bus Stop
 C Police
 D Doctor
 E Bank / Moped Rental
 F National Bank Rep.
 G Pharmacy
 H Supermarkets

 I International Press
 J Bakery
 K Ferry Tickets
 L Public WCs
 M Nightclubs
 N Town Museum
 O Statue (Green Man)
 P 19 c. Water Cistern
 Q Old Olive Oil Press
 R Agios Gaios Church
 S Fortress
 T New Port Road (1 km)
 U Loggos & Lakka Road
 V Hotel & Beach Road

 1 Ferries & Catamarans
 2 Corfu Day Boats
 3 Antipaxi Beach Boats
 4 Paxi Beach Boats

🛏

Hotels are few and pre-booked. If you can, phone ahead to reserve a room in July and August. **Gaios** has the bulk of the rooms. These include the *Vasilis* (☎ 32404), complete with a leafy garden, the *Spiros* (☎ 31172) and *Alexandros Studios* (☎ 32133) on the hill opposite the bus stop square, and the *Spiros* (☎ 32434) and *San Giorgio* (☎ 32223) on the Port Police headland. Elsewhere on the island **Lakka** has the D-class *Erida* hotel and a couple of tavernas offering rooms.

👁👁

Gaios has just enough sightseeing to keep the day-trippers fully occupied. First among these is the town **Museum** housed in the old British Residency building. Although it is only a three-room affair, it is among the best of its kind and worth the €3 entrance fee. Exhibits include a rusty pistol that in its prime could shoot six bullets at once, a pair of equally rusty forceps and a five million drachma banknote. The museum also sells a town-walk map with notes on notables from churches to chimneys. Other sites worth hunting out are the statue of the **Green Man** on the waterfront (commemorating a Paxiot sailor who tried to set fire to a Turkish fleet in 1821 and was captured and burnt alive for his pains) and the intriguing 19 c. cistern — complete with a country-house-style grand staircase — on the hill behind the town.

From Gaios there are also excursions to the mainland village of **Parga**, a lovely white-washed town tucked under a hillside decked with trees and with a Crusader fortress on a headland above the town. Caïques also visit the west coast of Paxi, which has three major **Sea Caves** and a limestone stack called **Ortholithos** poking out of the waters like a monstrous finger of stone.

Tourist boats also leave hourly from Gaios for the large satellite of **Antipaxi** to the south, thanks to a proliferation of sandy strands running down the east side of the island. Most boats call at the two large beaches north of the hamlet of **Ormos Agrapidias**, leaving you to walk to others should you covet greater seclusion.

The best and most popular beach is **Voutoumi** — a lovely stretch of golden sand that justifies the walk from the first (and most visited beach) at **Vrikes** — home to some unofficial camping given the absence of any other accommodation on the island.

Zakinthos / Zante

ZAKYNΘOΣ; 402 km²; pop. 30,200.

CODE ☎ 26950
PORT POLICE ☎ 22417
POLICE ☎ 22550
HOSPITAL ☎ 22514

One of the most popular Greek islands, Zakinthos (known to the Venetians as 'Zante') was once described as 'the flower of the Orient'. Regrettably, what was once an undeniably attractive island has been badly scarred by the unhappy combination of a major earthquake (in 1953) and insensitive package tourist development that leads some visitors wishing for another one. The island does not see vast numbers of island hoppers as it is inconveniently placed at the foot of the Ionian chain, with poor ferry connections: the only link of note runs from mainland Kilini to Zakinthos Town.

Rebuilt after the earthquake, **Zakinthos Town** is a considerable improvement on similar reconstruction on Kefalonia, with all the churches and important buildings being restored to something approaching their pre-earthquake state. That said, all look somewhat artificial and the town could never be described as cosy. This is in part due to the exceptionally large harbour that runs the length of the town. Ferries normally dock on the northern quay, but if the berths are full it is not unknown for new arrivals to disgorge their passengers on the southern quay (at the end of which stands Ag. Dionissiou church and its distinctive campanile — like its more famous model adorning St. Mark's Square in Venice, it is a reconstruction of a collapsed original).

All the main facilities are to be found along the waterfront, with the exception of the bus station which lies a block behind. The main focus of town life, however, lies to the north of the port, which is bordered by a reasonable NTOG / EOT pay beach. Hills rise quite steeply behind the town, limiting development to the coastal strip. On a crest above the town are the remains

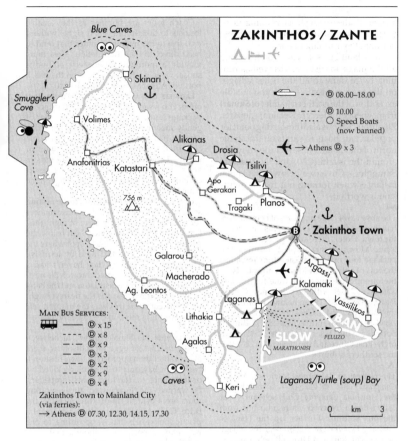

ZAKINTHOS / ZANTE

Blue Caves

Smuggler's Cove

Skinari

Volimes

Anafonitrias   Katastari

Alikanas
Drosia
Tsilivi
Apo Gerakari
Tragaki
Planos

756 m

Zakinthos Town

Galarou

Macherado

Ag. Leontos

Argassi
Kalamaki
Vassilikos

Laganas

Lithakia

Agalas

BAN
SLOW   PELUZO
MARATHONISI

Caves
Keri

Laganas/Turtle (soup) Bay

08.00–18.00
10.00
Speed Boats (now banned)
→ Athens ⓓ x 3

MAIN BUS SERVICES:
⟶ ⓓ x 15
---- ⓓ x 8
-·- ⓓ x 9
— ⓓ x 3
--- ⓓ x 2
-··- ⓓ x 9
······ ⓓ x 4
Zakinthos Town to Mainland City (via ferries):
→ Athens ⓓ 07.30, 12.30, 14.15, 17.30

0   km   3

of a Venetian kastro. Severely damaged by the earthquake, it is no longer a major attraction, though the views over the town are impressive.

Zakinthos offers an enjoyable combination of a fertile plain running the length of the island's east side, and a mountainous western half, made more accessible via regular coach excursions. Tourist activity is spread along the southern bay and the east coast (popular with cyclists) either side of Zakinthos Town itself. To the north it is centred on the resortified villages of **Planos**

/**Tsilivi** and more attractive **Alikanas**, to the south at **Argassi**. Argassi aside, the southern peninsula is arguably the prettiest part of the island — offering a succession of cove beaches backed by a wooded interior that climbs to the summit of Mt. Skopos, which rises up between **Kalamaki** and Argassi. The low peak is adorned with the scant remains of a temple of Artemis.

Marring all this, on the south coast lies the truly awful disco and beach resort of **Laganas**. Now the second largest settlement after Zakinthos Town, its main arteries resemble a giant 'T', the upper stroke running along the beach, with an over-long hotel and restaurant alley running inland.

The island bus service is good, serving all the major tourist areas as well as running twice daily to all the other villages on the map overleaf — with the notable exception of the northern hamlet of **Skinari** from whence the ferry to Kefalonia departs. Zakinthos Town is also the starting point for popular tour boats to sights on the scenic north of the island. These include a day trip around the island (€30) and the beach at Smuggler's Cove (see below): this is one instance when forking out for an excursion is worth it.

⊨

The absence of large numbers of backpackers has limited the number of rooms on offer in the town. Hotels there are in profusion on the island. Most, however, are pre-booked solid by package tour operators. **Zakinthos Town** has the bulk of hotels likely to have empty beds. At the top end of the range is the waterfront B-class *Xenia* (☎ 22232), with the pricey new C-class *Palatino* (☎ 27780) 100 m behind. Nearby lies the *Diana* (☎ 28547). Cheaper options are the *Apollon* (☎ 22838) and *Aegli* (☎ 28317). Budget options are the D-class *Ionian* (☎ 22511) north of the Post Office and the *Omonia* (☎ 22113) in the southern suburbs.

Λ

The nearest to Zakinthos Town is the good *Camping Zante* (☎ 24754) — a member of the *Sunshine Camping Club* scheme — at Tsilivi Beach (reached via regular bus from the bus station). Further up the coast is *Camping Paradise* (☎ 61888), near the village of Mesogerakari and Drosia Beach. Laganas Bay is also home to a couple of sites: *Camping Laganas* (☎ 51585) in an olive grove 1 km west of the end of the town beach is one of the worst sites in Greece. Further west lies the better *Tartarouga Camping* (☎ 51417), down the road from the village of Lithakia.

∞

All over Greece you will find postcards of a rusty wreck of a cargo ship set in a crescent beach of golden sand backed by towering cliffs: a beach boat runs daily to **Smuggler's Cove** (€28) as well as to the **Blue Caves** on the northern tip of the island — generally reckoned to be among the best sea caves in Greece.

Coach tours are popular as they enable tourists to take in the island sights without recourse to the main bus routes that tend to head direct to their destination. Most tours include a mountain monastery, cliff-edge sunset views and the salt-pans on the beach north of Alikanas (alias Alikes beach).

Laganas Bay (also known as **Turtle Bay**) offers you a sight of the unacceptable face of package tourism. Blessed with a number of gently shelving beaches of a particularly fine sand, it has been the nesting area for some 80% of the Mediterranean's population of the shy **Loggerhead Turtle** for thousands of years, only to find a disco-city tourist resort of the tackiest kind (**Laganas**) develop on the main beach.

Unfortunately the tourist and turtle nesting seasons are the same, with dire consequences for the turtles. Coming ashore at night they lay eggs in the sand a mere 50 cm below the surface (when they can find a spot where the sand hasn't been packed hard by tourists). These hatch (assuming they haven't had a sun-umbrella pole rammed through the nest) at night, some eight weeks later, and the baby turtles then crawl towards the nearest bright light (in years past this was the moonlit sea: these days it is more likely to be the nearest disco).

Meantime the female turtles, in between laying batches of eggs (or jettisoning them at sea rather than approach a neon-lit shore), bask in the bay, only to be regularly killed by, or lose limbs to, the tour boats' propellers. Be warned: the 'guaranteed' turtle-spotting tours are a cynical rip-off (this includes the price, €35). At best you will be looking at a plastic look-a-like that — according to one newspaper report — is so life-like that 'even aficionados have been fooled'; at worst you will be disturbing a very shy reptile at a very vulnerable time.

The situation is so bad that the World Wildlife Fund and Greenpeace have called for the entire bay to be declared a marine national park. Some locals disagree: the stringent zoning laws aimed at protecting the beaches are regularly flouted, while boat operators engage in sporadic punch-ups with outraged conservationists. All in all you will do better to avoid Laganas; there are plenty of good beaches on the east coast and less environmentally destructive nightlife elsewhere.

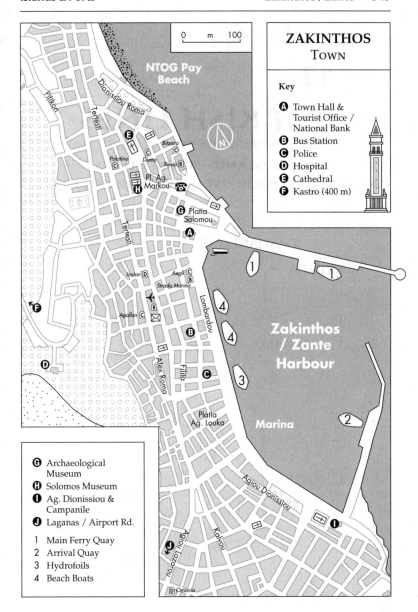

ZAKINTHOS
TOWN

NTOG Pay Beach

Key

Ⓐ Town Hall &
   Tourist Office /
   National Bank
Ⓑ Bus Station
Ⓒ Police
Ⓓ Hospital
Ⓔ Cathedral
Ⓕ Kastro (400 m)

Zakinthos
/ Zante
Harbour

Marina

Ⓖ Archaeological
   Museum
Ⓗ Solomos Museum
Ⓘ Ag. Dionissiou &
   Campanile
Ⓙ Laganas / Airport Rd.

1 Main Ferry Quay
2 Arrival Quay
3 Hydrofoils
4 Beach Boats

12
TURKISH LINES

GREEK ISLAND — TURKEY LINKS
DARDANELLES · İSMİR · İSTANBUL · TURKISH ISLANDS

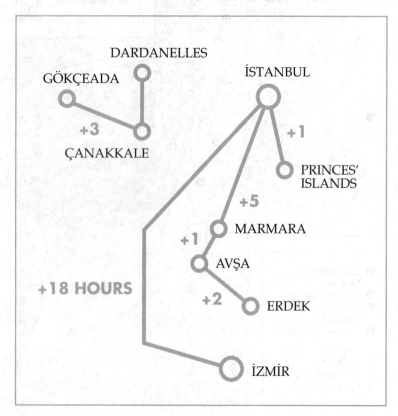

General Features

Given its size, Turkey is endowed with a remarkably poor ferry system. This is a historical accident born out of modern Turkey's failure to retain any of the large Aegean islands (apart from those guarding the entrance to the Dardanelles) once controlled by the Ottoman empire. As a result, ferries on the Turkish Aegean seaboard are — with the odd exception — confined to small international boats providing day-trip excursions to adjacent Greek islands: the ongoing political tension between Greece and Turkey prevents the emergence of more substantial links. Such islands where Turkey has sovereignty are tiny affairs that serve only to encourage local taxi boats bringing day-trippers from nearby resorts, rather than acting as the necessary catalyst for the emergence of a ferry system. South of the Dardanelles, Turkey is the land of the local bus rather than the ferry. This absence of anything that could remotely be called an Aegean ferry system means that hopping in Turkish waters is, for most tourists, usually a day-trip option while following a Greek domestic route.

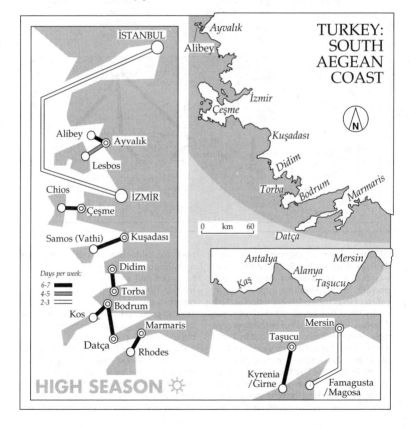

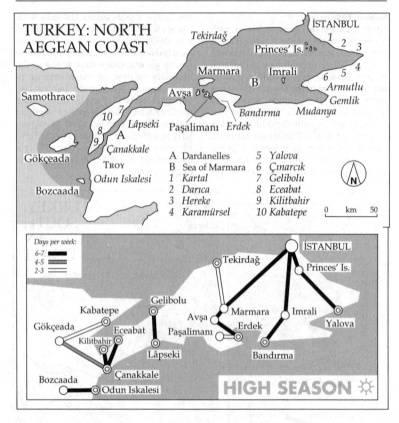

TURKEY: NORTH AEGEAN COAST

A   Dardanelles
B   Sea of Marmara
1   Kartal
2   Darıca
3   Hereke
4   Karamürsel
5   Yalova
6   Çınarcık
7   Gelibolu
8   Eceabat
9   Kilitbahir
10 Kabatepe

0   km   50

Days per week:
6-7
4-5
2-3

HIGH SEASON ☼

From the Aegean entrance of the Dardanelles through the Sea of Marmara to İstanbul, a very different state of affairs prevails, with something approaching a coherent ferry network in existence (backed up by short bus hops), courtesy of some dozen ex-'Greek' islands. For the most part these are served by boats provided by Turkish Maritime Lines (Turkey's national flag line). This excellent company is responsible for the bulk of the Dardanelles and Sea of Marmara services as well as the commuter boats operating along the Bosphorus. However, effective ferry competition does not really exist since the only other companies operating out of Turkish ports are confined to routes and ships too insignificant to interest Turkish Maritime. Moreover, this company often has a controlling interest in Turkish ports and charges a steep levy for use which discourages competition on all but the most popular routes.

The islands are little visited (except by holidaying Turks), and are very much a product of the messy aftermath of the border drawn up following the Greco-Turkish war of 1920–23. Home to almost exclusively ethnic Greek populations, the inhabitants found themselves on the 'wrong' side of the border, and though largely exempted from the forced population exchanges that occurred between the World Wars, most have subsequently left for Greece (thanks in part to cultural intimidation — something ethnic Turks 'stranded' in Greece also encountered). Home to new Turkish populations, they all have something of a 'someone's-sleeping-in-my-bed' air, with churches either abandoned or converted into mosques and the old Greek place names replaced with suitably Turkish successors.

From the Greek perspective these are very much the 'unlucky Greek islands' — all 13 of them — and reflect the fact that the modern border between Greece and Turkey is historically and archaeologically a very artificial one, something akin to a cultural Berlin Wall enhanced by enforced population exchanges. For most of history the power that reigned supreme on one side of the Aegean also held sway on the other. The Turkish Aegean seaboard is thus littered with cities that to the ancients were as 'Greek' as Athens or Corinth are today.

Ironically, the archaeological remains tend to be better preserved than their Western Aegean counterparts, for deforestation of the mountains of Asia Minor caused extensive silting up of harbours on the Eastern Aegean seaboard leading to these cities being abandoned by the end of Roman rule, while prominent Greek cities elsewhere remained inhabited and grew into the built-over population centres of today. Hopping across to Turkey for a day for a spot of ancient 'Greek' city sightseeing combined with a Turkish coffee, and — it has to be said — a good whiff of the Orient besides, has thus become a popular feature of Greek island hopping holidays.

In the past the omnipresent threat of hostilities between Turkey and Greece — that reached its peak with the 1974 Turkish invasion of Cyprus after a military Cypriot regime sought union with Greece — has severely limited, and for a time curtailed,

ferry links. This uncomfortable situation has eased in recent years, but a number of reciprocal measures enforced after the Cyprus invasion have had an impact on Greek island—Turkey services.

Decrees that passengers could only travel to the other country on the ship of the country they were departing from (producing two fleets at every crossing point) are no longer enforced (though the competing fleets remain). A second charter-flight ticket-issuing requirement that tourists who have entered Greece cannot spend a night in Turkey without losing their right to use the return half of their ticket is more serious and *remains in force*.

Fares

Turkey offers very good value for money, with the general cost of living about 25% cheaper than Greece. Ferry and catamaran ticket prices are similarly lower, though the number of useful sea travel options are also well down — given the limited nature of the Turkish ferry system. International travellers should also not forget that even small boats running between Greek islands and Turkey attract international port taxes.

Language

Modern Turkish is not the easiest of tongues to grapple with. Along the coast tourists can happily get by with a mix of English and German, but place names are often a bit of a mouthful. If you are planning to do more than a day trip or hop to İstanbul you should bring a language guide with you. Otherwise you can just about get by pronouncing:

Turkish	English
C	J
Ç	Ch
I	U
İ	E
J	S
Ö	Eu
Ş	Sh

Example Itineraries

Turkey has justly become a popular Greek-island-hopping day-excursion destination. If you find yourself on one of those islands offering excursions you should hop across; the contrast in culture and atmosphere is an experience well worth the cost of tickets. If you are on something longer than a two-week charter-flight return ticket, then Turkey offers some interesting island hopping possibilities too.

Arrival/Departure Point

The lack of anything other than local boats making the crossing to Turkey means that the islands of the Dodecanese and Eastern Aegean are the best starting points. Rhodes, Kos and Samos all have frequent charter flights.

A: Day Trips to Turkey

Day trips operate from Rhodes to Marmaris, Kos to Bodrum, Samos to Kuşadası, Chios to Çeşme and Lesbos to Ayvalık. Fares tend to be broadly similar regardless of which crossing you use, and reflect the fact that most of the 'ferries' are expensive day-tripper boats. You are usually left to your own devices in Turkey, but you can travel from Samos as part of a tour if so minded. Greek craft from Kos and Rhodes tend to be excursion boats, while their Turkish counterparts are closer to ferries. This distinction can become quite important, for if you travel by ferry you will be deemed an independent traveller and your passport will be stamped on entering and leaving the country. Travellers on excursion boats, because they have a return ticket, are issued with a landing pass while passports (unstamped) are held by passport control. Ferries also have well-advertised return times. Excursion boats don't — so be careful to establish when excursion boats depart for home; they do NOT wait for late passengers. Miss the boat and you'll have to stay overnight, thereby jeopardising your right to your charter flight home. Finally, it is all but impossible to change Turkish Lira

in Greek banks (best bet is to try branches of the National Bank of Greece). Turkish banks, after years of refusing to change Drachmas are now happy to accept Euro notes. Travellers cheques are no problem. If you do return from a day trip armed with wads of Turkish banknotes the best way of changing them is to offer them to day-trippers boarding the next day's boat.

B: Turkish Excursion [10 Days]

Those with time to hand will find that a trip to Troy and Constantinople (both dear to Greek hearts) is easily achieved:

■ Lesbos

The closest crossing point to Troy, Lesbos offers regular ferries to Ayvalık. Crossing points further south are also practicable options if you don't mind changing buses up the Turkish coast.

■ Ayvalık [1 Day]

Worth a day's exploration, with nearby Alibey to visit. Thereafter you can get a bus on to Çanakkale.

■ Çanakkale [3 Days]

Easily the best base for exploring the region, with plenty of accommodation and easy access to Troy and the battlefields of Gallipoli. Each offers a day of leisurely tourism, before heading on to Bandırma by bus.

■ ■ Bandırma / Princes' Is. [1 Day]

From Bandırma you have several options. You can either take a regular ferry to İstanbul or break the journey with a visit to the Princes' Islands or travel via Erdek and Avşa.

■ İstanbul [3 Days]

Three days gives you time to do the sights and hop up the Bosphorus. Thereafter you can consider returning to Greece.

Return [2 Days]

Most direct route out of High Season is the weekly ferry from İstanbul to Piraeus. Otherwise the fastest return is via ferry to İzmir (though you can always return via ferry to Bandırma and then an İzmir train) and then bus to Çeşme and ferry to Chios.

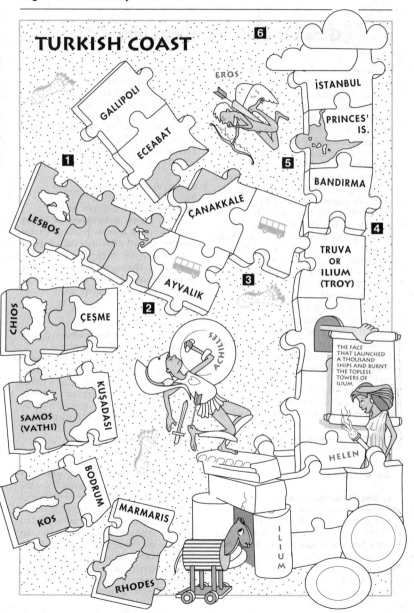

Greek Island — Turkey Links

Crossing between Greece and Turkey you must use a designated crossing point. Five Greek islands adjacent to the Turkish Aegean coast have ferry connections. However, the level of service varies greatly. Most are only advertised on a local basis, and exist courtesy of tourist day trippers. Services are curtailed out of High Season (most operate from May to October).

This tourist-driven regime is also reflected in the type of craft, and how much you pay: the greater the demand the more competitive the fare. This makes the popular islands of Kos and Rhodes the busiest crossing points (both have large Turkish resorts opposite them to push up the demand). The ferries are little more than pleasure boats that can often take one or two cars driven aboard — with the aid of a couple of planks of wood as a makeshift ramp. There are also a growing number of hydrofoils and catamarans.

It is standard practice at all ports to buy your ticket a day in advance. In practice, foot passengers can usually get on an afternoon boat (there are usually morning and late afternoon departures from both Greek and Turkish sides of a crossing), provided they get tickets first thing in the morning on the day of travel. Port taxes of €5 for one-way crossings, €12 for open return tickets, should be added to the 2003 prices listed here.

Crossing points:

Lesbos (Mytilini)—Ayvalık
Journey time: 80 minutes.
Fare: €60 one way, €80 open return.
The most northerly and utilitarian crossing point. Fewer tourists than elsewhere. Small passenger ferries (that carry the odd car) supposedly run daily in High Season, otherwise on alternate days. It is best to plan on the assumption of a 24-hour wait here.

Chios—Çeşme
Journey time: 90 minutes.
Fare: €37 one way, €48 open return.
Best crossing point for vehicles. Miniotis Ferries' car ferry service is well advertised (though you can't be sure which of their boats will be on the run), and tickets can be bought as far afield as Piraeus. Like Lesbos, a do-it-yourself crossing point.

Samos (Vathi)—Kuşadası
Journey time: 90 minutes.
Fare: €40 one way, €75 open return.
Traffic is mainly from Greece to Turkey in the form of tourists heading for the remains of nearby Ephesus. Also popular with longer-stay backpackers heading into Turkey. Occasional tourist-boats also make the crossing, often calling at Samos (Pithagorio) and even Leros en route.

Kos—Bodrum
Journey time: 50 minutes.
Fare: €20 one way, €34 open return (hydrofoils: €57 one way, €75 open return).
Tourist boats make the 1-hour crossing in equal numbers from both directions, as both centres are popular tourist resorts. Greek boats tend to be small cruisers, Turkish, larger affairs. Cars and motorcycles can be taken across here on the Turkish boats.

Rhodes—Marmaris
Journey time: 110 minutes.
Fare: €58 one way, €80 open return.
The most southerly crossing point. As Greek boats find day excursions down the Rhodian coast to Lindos or to the island of Symi more profitable, daily hydrofoils dominate Greece-to-Turkey traffic, and all travel must be booked in advance (turning up at the last moment doesn't work here). Turkish boats coming to Greece for the day are equally full of package tourists. Weekday services are consistent, but weekend travel is erratic.

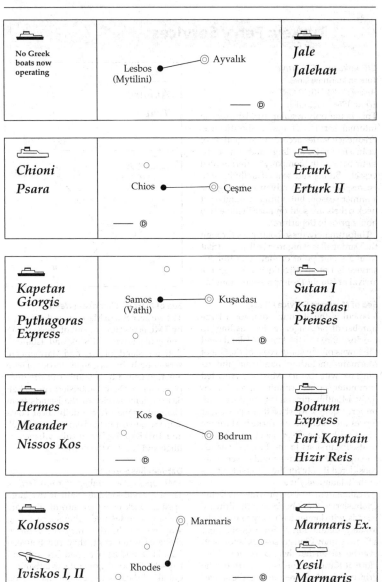

No Greek boats now operating

Lesbos (Mytilini) ● —— ◎ Ayvalık

Jale
Jalehan

—— Ⓓ

Chioni
Psara

○
Chios ● —— ◎ Çeşme

—— Ⓓ

Erturk
Erturk II

Kapetan Giorgis
Pythagoras Express

○
Samos (Vathi) ● —— ◎ Kuşadası
○

Sutan I
Kuşadası Prenses

—— Ⓓ

Hermes
Meander
Nissos Kos

○
Kos ●
○
◎ Bodrum

—— Ⓓ

Bodrum Express
Fari Kaptain
Hizir Reis

Kolossos

Iviskos I, II

◎ Marmaris
○
Rhodes ●
○

—— Ⓓ

Marmaris Ex.

Yesil Marmaris

Turkey: Ferry Services

C/F *Ankara* —C/F *Truva*
Turkish Maritime Lines
Ankara; 1983; 10552 GRT.
Truva; 1966; 3422 GRT.

This is the only regular Turkish Aegean internal service of major significance. Frequency varies according to the time of year. The ferries are large and run on the same basis as the company's international vessels. Bunks and seats usually have to be reserved well in advance during the summer season, but a limited number of deck tickets are sold on board (some two hours prior to departure).

Unfortunately, these boats pass through the Dardanelles at night on both legs so that from a scenic point of view this 18-hour service is not all it could be, though the arrival at İstanbul is impressive enough.

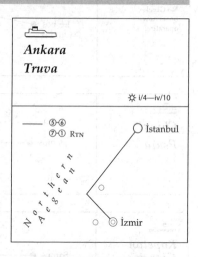

Sea of Marmara Services (East)
İstanbul is the starting point for a large number of passenger ferries heading up the Bosphorus, to the Princes' Islands and the towns on the south coast of the Sea of Marmara (including Bandırma and its rail link with İzmir). Most are crowded commuter services running several times daily. Monthly timetables are posted up on ferry quays. Most of these passenger ferries are operated by Turkish Maritime Lines, with a large fleet of well-maintained boats. Excursions to the Princes' Islands and up the Bosphorus should be seriously considered if only for the waterside views of the İstanbul skyline.

A catamaran service is provided by Deniz Otobüsleri to the suburbs and the Princes' Islands, with longer-haul daily connections to Bandırma and Yalova. Services start from a floating quay (you get seasick before you even board) on the other side of the Golden Horn at Karaköy. This is the berth for the Princes' Islands express ferries; the slower ferries start at Eminönü.

Sea of Marmara Services (West)
The western Sea of Marmara is dominated by TML boats running out of the Kapıdağ peninsula town of Erdek and İstanbul. Both the islands of Avşa and Marmara are served daily by passenger ferries. These are augmented by a number of irregular private craft: Deniz Otobüsleri run a High Season daily service to the islands from İstanbul, while private daily local boats ship the odd car to the islands from Erdek and the Kapıdağ peninsula villages of Ilhan and Narli to the north.

Dardanelles Services
TML operate a number of ro-ro ferries. These are odd-looking affairs with a large open car deck, over the centre of which are the ship's bridge and cabin space sitting atop an overhead gantry. Very much sheltered-water craft, they run between Çanakkale and Eceabat, and Gelibolu and Lâpseki. The locally operated Kilitbahir—Çanakkale boat is not as large and runs on demand rather than hourly.

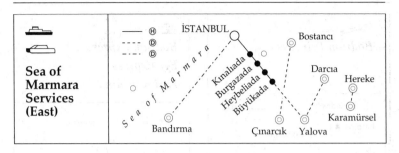

Sea of Marmara Services (East)

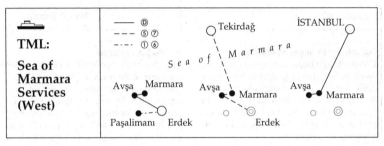

TML: Sea of Marmara Services (West)

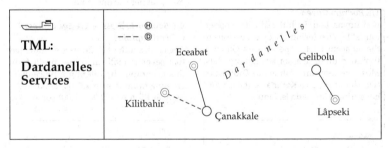

TML: Dardanelles Services

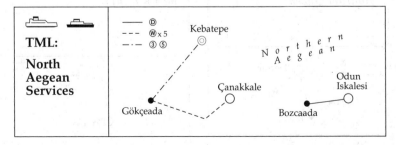

TML: North Aegean Services

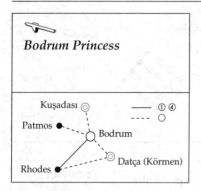

Turkish North Aegean Services
Gökçeada and Bozcaada are served exclusively by TML boats. Bozcaada has a twice daily service, while Gökçeada is served five days a week from Çanakkale, the remaining days from the small Gelibolu port of Kabatepe. Current timetables are available at Çanakkale.

T/B Bodrum Queen
Bodrum harbour is cluttered with wooden tourist boats offering pricey excursions to the adjacent islets. The *Bodrum Queen* is typical, running to assorted offshore islets. Most common are sailings to **Otok Is.** or two-island trips to **Korada Is.** (beach and hot springs) and **Ada Is.** (aquarium).

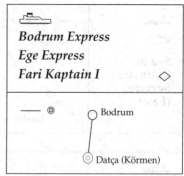

H/F Bodrum Princess
This frequently repainted Turkish hydrofoil runs out of Bodrum in the High Season, providing a direct service to Rhodes two days a week. During the remainder of her life she makes irregular excursions along the Turkish coast and day trips to Patmos and Kos. Note: you can't pick up this boat except at her starting point.

**C/F Bodrum Express — C/F Ege Express
C/F Fari Kaptain I**
The coast south of Bodrum is so indented that several small car ferries profit from this geography by offering a twice-daily crossing from Bodrum (09.00, 17.00) to the quay at **Körmen** (09.00, 17.00) some 7 km

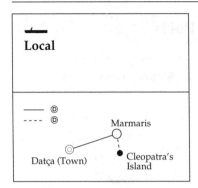

north of Datça (bus service into town included in the price of the ferry ticket). A second summer service operates twice daily (09.00, 17.00) between Torba (again, ferry-ticket buses depart from Bodrum) to Didim (alias Didyma) to the north, home to a major temple of Apollo.

Marmaris Taxi Boats

Daily taxi boats run from Marmaris along the coast of the Datça peninsula to the town of Datça (some even continuing on to the ancient city of Knidos). In doing so they open up the possibility of doing a loop running Rhodes—Marmaris—Datça—Bodrum—Kos—Rhodes.

Turkey—North Cyprus Services:
Mersin—Famagusta

Occupied northern Cyprus is served by boats out of two Turkish south-coast ports. From the Turkish perspective these are full-blown international services. However, as Turkey is the only country which recognizes the legitimacy of the so-called Turkish Republic of Northern Cyprus, these ferry links are de facto internal Turkish services.

Mersin (ancient Tarsus) — a large noisy seaport with nothing to recommend it beyond the ferry link — is the best of the Turkish ports, with the thrice-weekly Turkish Maritime Lines' elderly C/F *Yeşilada* operating to the war-ruined derelict resort of Famagusta (now Turkish **Magosa**). Weekend sailing continues on to Syria (Lattakia).

Taşucu—Kyrenia

Slightly closer to the Aegean is the resort town of Silifke and its port Taşucu. Again there is nothing of any interest in the place except the means of leaving it. Small ferries (*Liberty* and *Ertürk*) and hydrofoils make the 7- and 3½-hour crossings respectively to the once attractive port of Kyrenia (now **Girne**) daily in High Season, three times weekly during the rest of the year (though days and times are never very consistent).

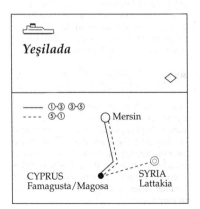

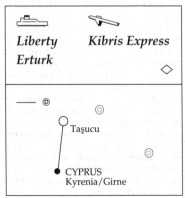

Turkish Islands & Ports

ALIBEY / CUNDA / MOSCHONISSI

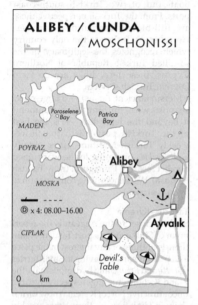

AVŞA / OPHIOUSSA

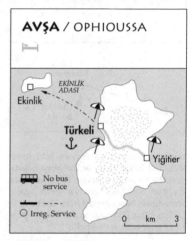

Alibey / Cunda
ΜΟΣΧΟΝΙΣΣΙ

A small island north of Ayvalık, Alibey is linked by causeway to the mainland. This had a major impact on the former Greek population, who, unusually, were forced out and replaced by displaced Cretans of Turkish stock between the wars. This at least ensures that the island retains a Greek atmosphere, with a typical resortified town (linked by both ferry and hourly bus to Ayvalık), and several reasonable beaches (the best lying on the west coast). Northern Alibey is quiet and contains the nearest thing to the island 'sight' in Poroselene bay: famous in antiquity as the home of a dolphin who saved a drowning boy and did other party tricks for passing writers — notably Pausanias.

Avşa
ΟΦΙΟΥΣΣΑ

The most popular central Sea of Marmara island, Avşa has emerged in recent years as the getaway destination for the better off in İstanbul and its environs. The only town is a mass of hotels and not much else (the nearby beaches and vineyard landscape being the great attraction). In addition to frequent ferry links, occasional taxi boats head out to nearby Ekinlik.

Ayvalık

A new earthquake-damaged town, more ramshackle than scenic, Ayvalık owes its present importance to the nearby attractions of Troy and the Çanakkale—İzmir road running through the town. Alibey aside, the only ferry link is the 'daily' Lesbos service. A good base for exploring the region with regular buses to Bergama (and the ruins of Pergamum).

Bandırma

The main city on the Sea of Marmara south coast, Bandırma is a major transportation hub, with regular buses to all the major Aegean and Marmarian towns, an important rail link to İzmir, and regular ferries to İstanbul. Home to both cement and sulphuric acid factories, the city is not likely to be in many visitors' lists of Turkish trip highlights, but is normally tolerable enough if you are just passing through. Unfortunately, times in these parts aren't normal. Since early 1999 all shops and cafés in the town have been closed as part of the security clampdown over the captured Kurdish separatist leader Abdullah Ocalan (housed on nearby Imrali — see p. 565). Visitors to Bandırma are likely to find things very unpleasant in 2004. Avoid the town if at all possible.

Bodrum
ΑΛΙΚΑΡΝΑΣΣΟΣ

If you are planning to take a day trip from the Dodecanese to Turkey you will find that Bodrum is easily the most attractive of the ports on the Turkish seaboard that are accessible from the Greek islands. Now a major resort town, Bodrum can nonetheless boast a very attractive centre offering plenty of sightseeing.

The mosque- and bazaar-filled town is one of the prettiest in the Aegean (the quayside girl selling drinks from inside a large plastic orange aside) and worth a day's visit in its own right. Those readers not constrained by the overnight limitations imposed on charter flight tickets who choose to stay in Bodrum should find the experience even more rewarding: the town is an attractive base from which to explore a coastline famed for beaches and beauty.

Only a very short ferry-ride from adjacent Kos Town, Bodrum is in many ways her Greek counterpart's twin sister. Both are modern package-tour resort towns with their centres built within the remains of notable ancient cities; both have a relaxed street plan, a scatter of minarets and palms gracing their skylines, and harbours dominated by impressive castles built by the same order of the Knights of St. John. However, Bodrum has two singular advantages that make it the more impressive of the two: the first is the Castle of St. Peter (which is much more substantial than the 'all curtain walls and no keep' affair on Kos); the second is the fact that the town is home to the remains of one of the Seven Wonders of the World: the Mausoleum — the famous tomb of the Hellenistic king of the city, Mausolus.

Modern Bodrum stands atop ancient Halicarnassos. Founded c. 1200 BC, this Greek city rapidly prospered thanks to its good harbour and ideal position on the trade routes of the time. In Classical times it was also famed as the birthplace of the so-called 'Father of History' — the first recognized historian, Herodotus (c. 484–c. 429 BC), though these days his work is regarded as part faction, part travelogue, mostly good fun: filled with good tales, scandalous gossip and a large measure of historical detail about the war between Persia and the Greek states, his 'History' (literally 'enquiry' in the Greek) is one of the most readable of ancient books.

When the Persians advanced to the Aegean in 540 BC, Halicarnassos, which was in no position to resist, came under the overlordship of a succession of Carian kings, aiding the Persians at the Battle of Salamis (480 BC). The most famous of these rulers was Mausolus (377–353 BC), thanks to the tomb commissioned by his wife Artemisia II. The city was regained by the Greeks when Alexander the Great moved east in 334 BC, and came under Roman control in 129 BC. It was successfully attacked by pirates in 62 BC, after which it regained its prosperity under such figures as Cicero. In 1402 AD it was captured by the Knights of St. John, who surrendered it in 1523 without a fight (as part of the terms of withdrawal from the region following the surrender of Rhodes).

Although there are plenty of beds in town, rooms are hard to find in High Season: it is

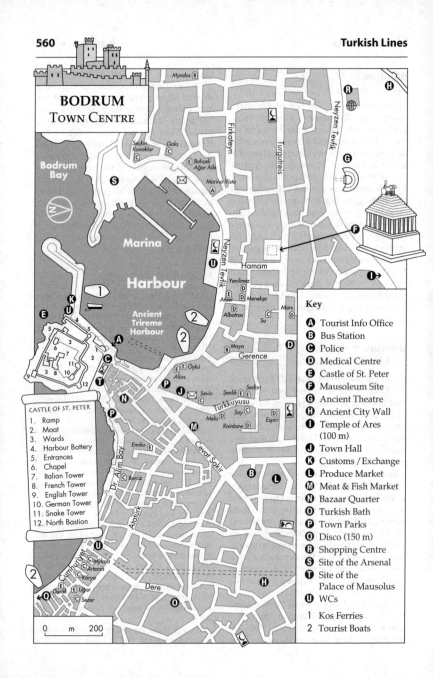

BODRUM
Town Centre

Bodrum Bay

Marina

Harbour

Bodrum Bay

Ancient Trireme Harbour

Myndos **B**

Seçkin Konaklar **C**

Gala **C**

Bahçeli Ağar Aile **E**

Marina Vista **A**

Firkateyn

Turgutreis

Neyzen Tevfik

Hamam

F

I →

Yenilmez **D**

Ataer **E**   Menekşe **D**

Albatros **D**

Mars **D**

Su **C**

Maya **E**

Gerence

D

Öykü **E**

Alias **E**

Sevin **C**

Şenlik **E E**

Sedan **E**

Turkkuyusu

Melis **D**   Say **C**

Rainbow **D**

Espiri **D**

Emiko **E**

Cevat Şakir

Baraz **C**

Dr. Alim Bey

Atatürk

Mylasa **C**

Artemis **C**

Karya **C**

Durak **E**   Uğar **E**

Sezer **C**

Cumhuriyet

Dere

2 ← **Q** ←

0   m   200

CASTLE OF ST. PETER
1. Ramp
2. Moat
3. Wards
4. Harbour Battery
5. Entrances
6. Chapel
7. Italian Tower
8. French Tower
9. English Tower
10. German Tower
11. Snake Tower
12. North Bastion

Key

A Tourist Info Office
B Bus Station
C Police
D Medical Centre
E Castle of St. Peter
F Mausoleum Site
G Ancient Theatre
H Ancient City Wall
I Temple of Ares (100 m)
J Town Hall
K Customs / Exchange
L Produce Market
M Meat & Fish Market
N Bazaar Quarter
O Turkish Bath
P Town Parks
Q Disco (150 m)
R Shopping Centre
S Site of the Arsenal
T Site of the Palace of Mausolus
U WCs

1 Kos Ferries
2 Tourist Boats

essential to arrive on a morning boat. Best bets in the town centre are the good *Sedan* (☎ 252-316 0355), the *Su* (☎ 252-316 6906) and *Rainbow* (☎ 252-316 5170). Have money? — try *Marina Vista* (☎ 252-316 0356).

A

The town has a couple of horrible sites. Best is *Uçar Camping* at Dere Sok, but it is only worth considering if you can't find a room.

≋☆

Bodrum has a well-merited reputation as a disco and bar hot-spot. This is in part due to the famous waterfront *Halikarnas Disco* with its deafening loudspeaker system. Other discos are to be found on the waterfront to the east of the castle and at the resort of Gümbet (which lies 5 km west of the old town).

∞

Sadly, the most famous structure in Bodrum — the **Mausoleum** (351 BC) — is all but invisible. After surviving intact until the 12 C. AD, it suffered earthquake damage, and was finally demolished by the Knights of St. John in 1522, when the stones were used to strengthen the castle against the cannons newly acquired by the Turks. Other fragments are now in the British Museum. The site is now home to a deep pit sporting a few blocks and foundations, along with a model of the monument in all its glory. The **Castle of St. Peter** is now the principal sight. Built between 1402–37 on the islet of Zephyrion, it is in very good condition. It is home to a good **Underwater Archaeology Exhibition** (based on ancient wrecks excavated during the 1970s) and a very sad monkey on a string.

Bozcaada
ΤΕΝΕΔΟΣ

A small Aegean island a few kilometres south-west of Troy, Bozcaada was known for over two millennia by the name recorded by Homer: Tenedos. Closed to tourists until the late 80s for military reasons (check with the tourist office in Çanakkale for the latest information regarding the need for possible visitor's permits), the island is one of the least spoilt and most attractive around. The only town lies on the north-east corner and is dominated by a well-preserved Genoese castle the equal of any in the Aegean. It lies

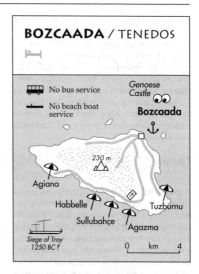

BOZCAADA / TENEDOS

🚌 No bus service

▬ No beach boat service

Genoese Castle ∞

Bozcaada ⚓

230 m

Agiana

Habbelle

Sullubahçe

Tuzburnu

Agazma

Siege of Troy 1250 BC?

0   km   4

on the site of Justinian's warehouses, for the island was used as a granary storage base in the Byzantine era.

South of the town the shoreline is fringed by a succession of empty sand beaches, the best on the south coast proper, and it was to here that the Greek fleet retreated out of sight when they left the wooden horse outside the gates of Troy. The island economy continues to depend almost entirely on viticulture; mass tourism has yet to discover the delights of the — still very Greek — cobbled town, with its restaurant-fronted waterfront and dusty hotels in the streets behind.

Çanakkale

The largest port and best stopping-point on the Dardanelles (known to the Greeks as the Hellespont), Çanakkale is a pretty town offering plenty to do thanks to the combination of a well-preserved castle (home to a naval museum), a well-stocked archaeological museum, the Dardanelles ferry link, and the half-hourly buses from the town centre to Truva (the modern name for ancient Troy). The centre of town boasts a conspicuous clock tower, and in close proximity to this landmark you will find all the essentials — including the city tourist office. Nearby tour operators offer day packages to both Troy and the Gallipoli battlefields across the Dardanelles (tours to this latter destination are the best way to visit given the absence of a good peninsula bus service).

Çeşme

A quaint little town with a pretty castle and interesting waterfront. Out on a limb at the end of the İzmir peninsula, it has become the main port for large international ferries along with the regular Chios boats — the pull of İzmir (a 90-minute bus ride away) being great. An appealing place to spend one's time with plenty of accommodation and camping to hand.

Datça

Deftly placed on one of the most attractive stretches of the Turkish coast, this quiet town, surrounding green pine forest and turquoise bay-lined Datça peninsula, is the real reason to hop from Rhodes to Marmaris. Taxi boats (and hourly buses) go to Datça from there. The town has plenty of rooms, a campsite, and is the jumping-off point (via tour boat or taxi) for Knidos, 34 km away on the tip of the peninsula. A major city in Classical times, it was home to the masterpiece of the sculptor Praxiteles — a (lost) statue of Aphrodite.

Eceabat

Main destination for Çanakkale ferries crossing to the Gelibolu peninsula. There isn't much here beyond the ferry terminal itself, Kilitbahir being the traditional landing point adjacent to Çanakkale.

Erdek

An attractive (courtesy of a lack of modern building) town on the Kapıdağ peninsula, Erdek is the main jumping-off point for the Sea of Marmara islands. The town has all the necessary tourist facilities (behind the tree- and restaurant-lined waterfront). Dolmuş taxis run frequently to nearby Bandırma, with its bus links to Çanakkale and other major centres.

Gelibolu

Known to most by its former name of Gallipoli, Gelibolu is the major port on the European side of the Dardanelles, giving its name to the whole peninsula (and of course, the disastrous WW1 Gallipoli campaign in which the Allies fought the Turks). Ferries dock on the outer quay, behind which lie two inner harbours bisected by a bridge. Pretty enough in a quiet sort of way, the town is home to a castle and also boasts a quayside statue of its most famous son, Piri Reis, a 16 c. cartographer and navigator. Hourly buses to İstanbul make Gelibolu more accessible than ferry links would suggest.

Gökçeada
ΙΜΒΡΟΣ; 597 km².

The only large Aegean island in Turkish hands, Gökçeada is still widely known by its former Greek name of Imbros (or Imroz). Heavily fortified thanks to its strategic position at the entrance of the Dardanelles, tourist access was prohibited until the late 80s when visitors with permits were admitted (information regarding any current requirements can be obtained from the tourist office in Çanakkale). Red tape has relaxed further since, but the number of tourists remains very small.

Visits to Gökçeada remain the preserve of the dedicated island hopper, intent on 'doing' every Greek or Aegean island,

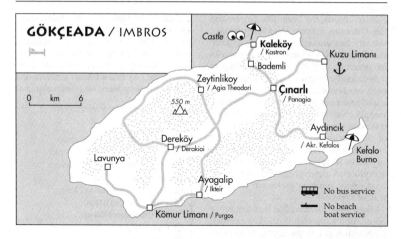

GÖKÇEADA / IMBROS

Castle
Kaleköy / Kastron
Bademli
Kuzu Limanı
Zeytinlikoy / Agia Theodori
Çınarlı / Panagia
0   km   6
550 m
Aydıncık
Dereköy / Derakioi
/ Akr. Kefalos
Kefalo Burno
Lavunya
Ayagalip / Ikteir
No bus service
No beach boat service
Kömur Limanı / Purgos

rather than the casual tourist. Green and very hilly, there is little disguising that of all the Turkish islands, this one more than any other feels — thanks to the heavy military presence — like an occupied zone. Although exempted from the 1920s population exchanges, the exclusively Greek inhabitants have been driven out over the last 30 years — unsung casualties of the Cyprus conflict. In the absence of a bus service, tourism is confined to the former chora (now Çınarli), and the town of Kaleköy — home to the island's best beach and an impressive castle. Both are linked by dolmuş taxi to the port at Kuzu Limanı.

Imrali
ΚΑΛΟΛΙΜΝΟ

The former Greek island of Kalolimno, Imrali is very much the unlucky 13th of the inhabited Turkish islands and definitely not on the tourist trail: if you end up landing here then something has gone very seriously wrong. At first sight it looks to be just another small barren island covered with a scattering of trees, and with a small port town, but in fact Imrali is Turkey's very own Alcatraz. Home to a high security prison

(from where the 'hero' of the film *Midnight Express* swam to freedom), the island has received considerable press attention of late as it is currently the home of the captured Kurdish separatist leader Abdullah Ocalan (now serving a life-sentence). In February 1999 the Turkish authorities removed the 250 prisoners normally housed here in order to hold a prisoner deemed so dangerous that naval boats constantly circle the island, while the neighbouring coastal towns of Bandırma and Mudanya have had all their shops and cafés closed.

Further captures of Kurdish separatists, and the huge devastation wrought by the massive 1999 earthquake (which left over 14,000 in the region dead), have ensured that Imrali and the whole south and east coastline of the Sea of Marmara are likely to remain an unattractive area for tourists through 2004.

İstanbul
ΚΩΝΣΤΑΝΤΙΝΟΥΠΟΛΗ / ΒΥΖΑΝΤΙΟ

One of the great cities of the world, İstanbul is well worth almost any amount of effort involved in getting to it. Formerly known as Constantinople and then Byzantium, it was in turn the capital of the Eastern

Roman Empire, the Byzantine Empire and the Ottoman Empire. Not surprisingly, the city has enough sightseeing to keep the dedicated explorer busy for weeks (so much so, that it is worth investing in a dedicated city guide). Ferry links, however, are few and far between (though a goodly number of cruise ships call), but if you are on an extended tour of the Aegean it is worth considering taking advantage of the weekly service running between İstanbul and İzmir to pay a visit. The city owes so much to the sea and boasts a skyline so atmospheric that arrival by boat easily remains the most attractive way of approach.

Like Athens, İstanbul has seen a massive population explosion in the last century. Although it is not the capital of modern Turkey it is easily the most populous city, with a population now well in excess of 3 million. Similarities with the Greek capital do not end there, as the city has a good supply of cheap accommodation (some of it earthquake-proof) close to a historic centre surrounded by a sea of modern concrete. The same problems of pollution and traffic congestion that bedevil Athens are also to be found here.

İstanbul's principal port is located at Eminönü, adjacent to the Galata bridge over the Golden Horn. All large ferries depart from here (a convenient quay as it backs onto the old part of the city that is home to all the major sights and the bulk of the budget accommodation). However, the İzmir ferry often lands its passengers at a quay 2 km to the north, on the far side of the Golden Horn.

Eminönü is also the departure point for cruises up the Bosphorus. These are just regular passenger ferries calling at all the European and Asian ports up to the entrance of the Black Sea (if you've ever fancied hopping a dozen or more times between Europe and Asia before dinner then this is your chance). Boats normally stop at the final Black Sea entrance port of **Anadolukavağı** for a couple of hours, so that

passengers can get off on the Asian shore and buy overpriced kebabs and seafood dishes. Other ferries cross the Bosphorus — either to the port directly on the other side or visiting several ports on both. Normally you buy brass tokens emblazoned with the *Turkish Maritime Lines* insignia at

---

Key

- **A** Tourist Office (Agia Sophia)
- **B** Tourist Office (National Bank)
- **C** Main Post Office / Telephones
- **D** Sikeci Railway Station
- **E** Topkapı Bus Station (2 km)
- **F** US Consulate (100 m)
   UK Consulate (400 m)
- **G** Galata Bridge
- **H** Atatürk Bridge
- **I** TML Ticket Office
- **J** Youth Hostel
- **K** Budget Hotel Area
- **L** Galata Tower
- **M** Agia Sophia Museum
- **N** Blue Mosque
- **O** Hippodrome
- **P** Topkapı Palace
- **Q** Agia Irine
- **R** Beyaut Mosque
- **S** Süleymaniye Mosque
- **T** Yeni Cami Mosque
- **U** University
- **V** Egyptian Bazaar
- **W** Grand Bazaar
- **X** Atatürk Statue
- **Y** Gülhane Park
- **Z** Topkapı Palace Walls

- 1   International Ferry Port
- 2   Alternative Ferry Port (Arrivals)
- 3   Ferries to Princes' Islands & Boats running the length of the Bosphorus
- 4   Ferries to Kadiköy
- 5   Trans-Bosphorus Ferries
- 6   Karaköy Ferry Quay
- 7   Golden Horn Ferries

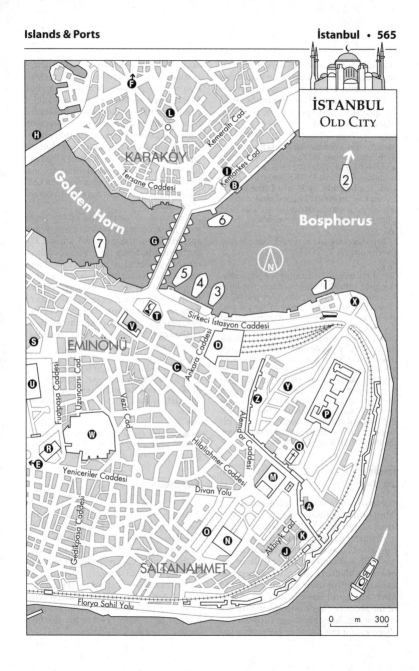

İSTANBUL
OLD CITY

Golden Horn

Bosphorus

KARAKÖY

Kemeraltı Cad.

Kemankeş Cad.

Tersane Caddesi

EMİNÖNÜ

Sirkeci İstasyon Caddesi

Ankara Caddesi

Fuatpaşa Caddesi

Uzunçarşı Cad.

Vezir Cad.

Alemdar Caddesi

Hilaliahmer Caddesi

Yeniceriler Caddesi

Divan Yolu

Gedikpaşa Caddesi

Ahırkapı Cad.

SALTANAHMET

Florya Sahil Yolu

0   m   300

the quay or from street traders. The crossing will set you back no more than a few pence/cents. Ferries are numerous on the southern crossings. Timetables can be found on quaysides (European ports shown in black; Asian in red).

ᕼ

Most budget accommodation is in the Old City in the small streets backing onto Agia Sophia and the Blue Mosque. The total of five youth hostels includes one IYHF hostel at 6 Caferige Cad. The helpful City Tourist Office is at 31 Divan Yolo on the old Hippodrome, and can advise on accommodation as well as offer plenty of blurb on the major sights.

Λ

Noisy short-stay site at *Londra Mocamp* near the city airport.

ᏀᏀ

Top of any touring hit list must be **Agia Sophia**, the great cathedral church of the Byzantine Empire, built in 532–37 AD. After the fall of Constantinople to the Turks in 1453 it was converted into a mosque. Atatürk turned the building into a museum as part of a secularization drive in 1935. Nearby stands the beautiful **Blue Mosque**. Built in 1609–16, it is a (failed?) Ottoman attempt to construct a building that surpassed Agia Sophia. The **Topkapı Palace** (home of the Sultans, their harems, and one of the greatest displays of crown jewels) is the other truly great show in town — if one discounts the unmissable bustle of the **Grand Bazaar**. Remnants of the ancient city also survive: the most evident of these are the **Hippodrome** and **City Walls**.

İzmir
ΣMYPNA

The largest city on the Turkish Aegean coast, İzmir (formerly the Greek Smyrna) is now a major metropolis. Sadly, little architecture of character remains in what is now one of the ugliest cities (not many Aegean towns are lumbered with a 'Park of Culture') in one of the Mediterranean's most attractive bays: the Gulf of İzmir. The bulk of the old town was burnt down with the collapse of the abortive Greek attempt to take the coast of Asia Minor between 1919–22. The sheer size of the rather uninteresting (an ancient Agora and Fortress aside) wide-boulevarded modern city does at least ensure a regular ferry link with İstanbul. Most foreign visitors are taking advantage of either ferries or the railway (this is the only Turkish city on the Aegean coast with such a link), or are en route to the ruins of the ancient city of Pergamum (reached via frequent buses to the new town of Bergama). İstanbul ferries leave from the international ferry berth (complete with a dusty locked-up duty-free centre) at the eastern corner of the gulf.

The centre of the city lies on the south side. The accompanying suburban sprawl spreads far to the west and around the northern side, hence the existence of three trans-bay commuter services: 1. From **Konak** quay (west of city centre) to **Urla** (south side of the gulf midway between İzmir and Çeşme). 2. From Konak quay to **Karşıyaka** (on the north of the gulf). 3. From **Pasaport** quay (centre of the city seafront) to **Alsancak** (200 m west of the International Ferry dock).

ᕼ

Finding a bed for the night in İzmir is rarely a problem. Cheap pensions and hotels are densest around the railway station. The city bus station also houses a helpful tourist office.

Λ

Nearest sites are at Çeşme. The village has several sites: notably *Fener Mocamp* on the promontory north of the harbour.

Kabatepe

A small town on the west side of the Gelibolu peninsula, Kabatape has an infrequent ferry link with Gökçeada, an excellent beach and a museum dedicated to the 1915–16 Gallipoli campaign. Local taxis run to nearby ANZAC cove and the many cemeteries that house the 200,000 dead. Local public transport is relatively poor over the whole peninsula: buses or dolmuş taxis from Eceabat are the best means of getting to the town.

Kilitbahir

The narrowest crossing point on the Dardanelles runs between Kilitbahir and Çanakkale (1300 m) — hence the minor ferry link. Worth a visit thanks to the castle, built by Mehmet the Conqueror in 1452, that gives substance to the town's name, which means 'Key to the sea'.

Kuşadası

A rapidly growing tourist resort midway down Turkey's Aegean coast, Kuşadası is named 'Pigeon Island' — after a fortified islet linked to the town via a causeway. It draws the hordes thanks to its role as the jumping-off point to the nearby ruins of Ephesus, the best preserved of ancient Greek cities. A stream of cruise ships call, upping prices to Greek levels. The port used to figure more prominently on ferry schedules until the late 1990s.

⊨

Good supply of rooms via ticket agencies.

⚓

Camping Önder: 2 km north of the town, this site has reasonable facilities.

Lâpseki

A small port that owes its existence to adjacent Gelibolu on the opposite side of the Dardanelles, Lâpseki is very much of an overspill town, relying on the ferry link between the two.

Marmara

The largest island in the Sea of Marmara, and from which it takes its medieval name, Marmara is a mountainous and rather inhospitable-looking place. The island was famous in the ancient world as one of the best sources of white marble: the whole northern half is composed of little else, leaving a windswept landscape with little vegetation and well scarred with three thousand years of quarrying. Southern Marmara has more going for it, with a fringe of pine trees and the best of the small population centres. Ferries stop at assorted points around the coast. Boats to Marmara town (home to two budget hotels and the island bank) often stop at Gundoğdu en route, and the former capital at Saraylar sees boats running north.

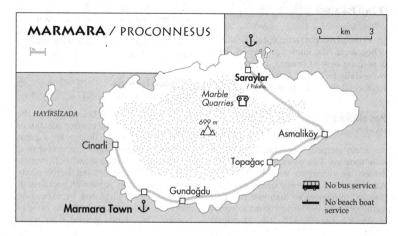

MARMARA / PROCONNESUS

⚓

0   km   3

Saraylar
/ Palatia

Marble Quarries

HAYİRSİZADA

699 m

Asmaliköy □

Cinarli □

Topağaç □

Gundoğdu

Marmara Town ⚓

🚌 No bus service

⚓ No beach boat service

Marmaris

The most southerly Turkey—Greece crossing point, Marmaris has grown from a small fishing village to one of Turkey's leading tourist resorts. The town ribbons along the coast at the head of an islet-littered bay, against an attractive backdrop of mountains and pine trees, but lacking anything approaching a major 'sight', seeing is reduced to 'souking' up tourism with a Turkish flavour. There is enough going on to keep you happily occupied for a day but this is arguably the least interesting of Turkey's day-tripper ports. The ferries and hydrofoils to Rhodes are now the only regular services, though previous years have seen long-haul international ferries calling. Taxi boats run along the coast to Datça and to nearby **Cleopatra's Island** (sand imported from Egypt courtesy of one Marcus Antonius). Now sadly overrated and overcrowded.

Ⓗ
Tourist Office opposite the ferry quay offers maps and a room-finding service.

Ⓐ
Best site is *Camping Berch* west of the port.

Odun Iskalesi

Small mainland port adjacent to the island of Bozcaada. Also known as Yukyeri, there is nothing here of interest, excepting the twice-daily ferry link. Dolmuş taxis meet ferries and run to Çanakkale.

Paşalimanı
ΗΑΛΟΝΙ

An oddly shaped, low-lying island with little tourism. The economy is primarily driven by viticulture and shell-fishing. All settlements are very small and even 'hamlet' implies more than you will find on the ground. Most ferries run to the largest cluster of houses (and the island mosque)

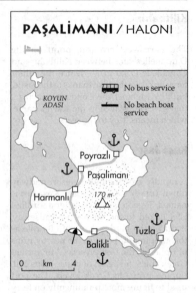

PAŞALİMANI / HALONI

KOYUN ADASI

🚌 No bus service

🚤 No beach boat service

⚓ Poyrazlı

⚓ Paşalimanı

Harmanlı

170 m

Tuzla

Balıklı

0　　km　　4　⚓

at Paşalimanı, but you should be aware that boats (especially those operating out of the small village ports north of Erdek on the Kapıdağ peninsula often prefer to dock at other points—notably the wooded settlement of Balikli. Facilities ashore are all but non-existent, so bring provisions with you. Best way to visit is via a day trip, crossing by private boat on one of the days that a scheduled ferry offers a means of return.

Princes' Islands
10 km²; pop. 15,000.

A group 20 km to the south of the Bosphorus, these nine car-free islets (four accessible by ferry — though the express boats usually only call at the largest two) are a popular destination with both tourists and locals alike, performing the role of city parks. The largely Armenian populations are now being displaced by increasing numbers of jet-setters building holiday homes. The islands gained their name as places of exile for Byzantine nobles and then members of the Sultan's family. Sadly, these days harems are few on the ground — though one island was briefly used as a rabbit farm. **Büyük** is the largest of the islands, and its Greek title (Prinkipo) gave the name to the group. Today it has a plethora of restaurants, hotels, horses and carriages, and gardens. **Heybeli** is a quieter version of the same, with a naval college and a Greek Orthodox school of theology. The interiors of both are wooded, as is smaller **Burgaz**, the only other island to boast a reasonably sized settlement.

Northern **Kınalı** is home to one tiny hamlet, and, along with **Sedef**, exists as a beach destination. The remaining islands are little more than rocks with only **Kaşik** readily accessible (via Heybeli beach boats). **Yassi** is now a prison and thus closed to tourists, while **Sivri** has an odd history as dumping ground for stray dogs rounded up from the streets of İstanbul, and **Tavsan** is uninhabited.

Tekirdağ

The only port of note on the northern Sea of Marmara coast, Tekirdağ is poorly connected with the rest of the Turkish ferry system, but offers good bus links with İstanbul. A growing resort town, outlying beaches are the main attraction.

Yalova

The destination of a number of İstanbul—Princes' Islands ferries, Yalova is a commuter town on the southern Sea of Marmara coast. Yalova also has daily links with **Darıca** and **Kartal** on the adjacent coast, as does **Çınarcık**, which also sees occasional Princes' Islands boats. These are the best of the local services (the service between the towns of **Hereke** and **Karamürsel** being the other link) between equally uninspiring towns off the tourist map.

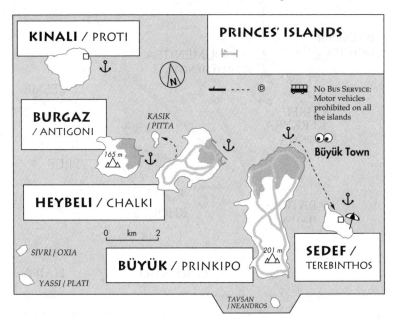

13

INTERNATIONAL LINES

CYPRUS · EGYPT · GREECE · ISRAEL · ITALY (ANCONA BARI · BRINDISI · VENICE) · LEBANON · TURKEY

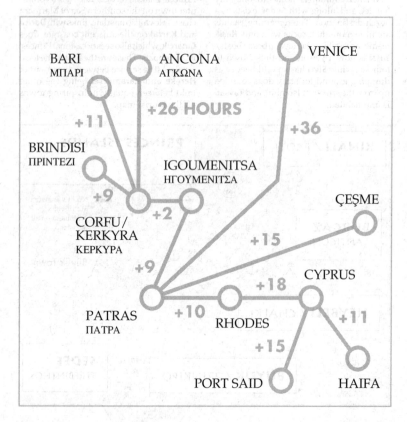

EASTERN
MEDITERRANEAN

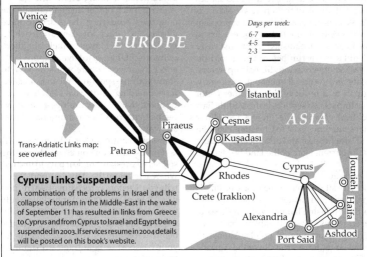

Days per week:
6-7
4-5
2-3
1

Trans-Adriatic Links map:
see overleaf

Cyprus Links Suspended

A combination of the problems in Israel and the collapse of tourism in the Middle-East in the wake of September 11 has resulted in links from Greece to Cyprus and from Cyprus to Israel and Egypt being suspended in 2003. If services resume in 2004 details will be posted on this book's website.

General Features

The Eastern Mediterranean is rather lop-sided in the distribution of ferry services. Beyond the extensive Greek and Croatian domestic systems there is little traffic other than international lines, and the bulk of these are confined to the Adriatic. Long-haul services across the Mediterranean are more constricted (when operating), with most services running along an Italy—Israel/Egypt axis. Operators largely ignore Albania, Syria, Lebanon, and Libya.

1. Eastern Mediterranean

The number of 'true' long-haul ferries is very small — for, given the journey times and the subsequent level of fares, few routes can compete with the relative cheapness of air travel. Some of the ferries, thanks to six to eight hour stop-overs in each port, are advertised as cruise ship operations. They are cheaper in all respects than true cruise liners but have the saving grace of allowing you more flexibility in planning your itinerary.

The lack of trans-Adriatic style competition on these longer routes also makes itself felt: many of the ferries are older ex-Greek domestic boats (this can be a problem considering the amount of time one has to spend aboard), banished to one last rusty Mediterranean run before being sold off to less safety-conscious SE Asia operators. Boats and routes also change frequently, in part as a result of this. Another factor that impacts on services is the Middle East political situation: the 'lifeline' ferry links that sometimes exist to Christian Lebanon and Israel appear and disappear according to the current state of the land borders.

2. Adriatic

The Adriatic is very much part of Italy's back yard and treated as something akin to the English Channel, with the coastal resort towns of her rather bland east coast serving as jumping-off points. Almost all of the larger ferries run down the Adriatic to Greece, encouraged by the tourist hordes

who pass through each summer as well as the freight trade generated by Greece's membership of the EU (now greatly enlarged thanks to the closure of the land route through the war-torn countries of former Yugoslavia).

This is a potent combination that produces the most competitive international ferry services in the Mediterranean: even deck-class passengers are treated with a modicum of respect. Ferries are much larger than those on other routes (with bigger or faster boats appearing every year), but you do have to be wary of maverick companies; the profits in this part of the world are such that the temptation to chuck on a clapped-out ferry to make a few easy Euros is often irresistible. Every year you will see at least one boat Nero would happily send his mother to sea in. Fortunately, they are easy enough to spot; a company producing a brochure without pictures of their boats is almost an admission that they are too clapped-out to survive a camera's critical eye.

Embarkation & Immigration Controls

As with much of Continental Europe the countries bordering the Adriatic have adopted a rather low-key approach to border controls. However, their 'abolition' within the EU has yet to have an appreciable effect in Greece (where you still have to show your passport and get an associated ferry boarding card). This said, it should be noted that all EU countries greet arriving passengers with the minimum of fuss anyway.

Passport control (when it happens at all) is now usually done on board ship in the self-service restaurant, so it pays to find out where it is before the arrival-at-port queue tells you. Customs procedures (where they exist) take place ashore. Embarking tends to be more complex; you are usually required to report for boarding 2–3 hours before departure so you have time to get your passport or boarding card stamped by immigration.

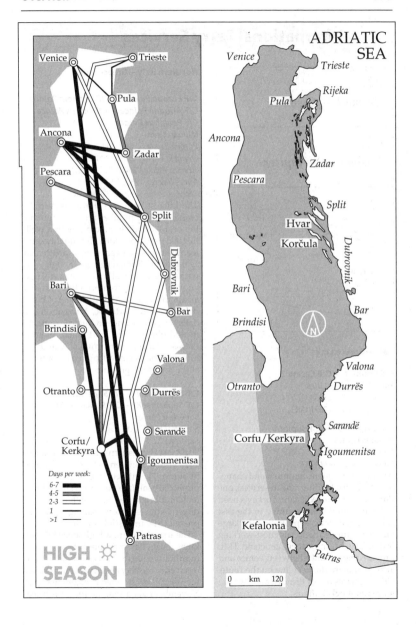

International Ferry Services

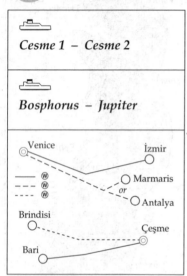

Italy—Greece Links

C/F Cesme 1 – C/F Cesme 2
Turkish Maritime Lines
Cesme 1; 1973; 18858 GRT.
Cesme 2; 1972; 17691 GRT.

C/F Bosphorus – C/F Jupiter
Anatolia Ferries
Bosphorus; 1962; 4727 GRT.
Jupiter; 1964; 3984 GRT.
Among the frequent chopping and changing of Eastern Mediterranean services one thing does remain constant: Turkey's need to have several boats running to the east side of the Adriatic — providing the large number of Turkish nationals guest-working in the EU with a link to their homeland. TML provide regular links between Venice and Turkey and are the best line on the route. Other services out of Brindisi and Bari are more rust-bucket affairs.

Northern Italy—Greece Links

C/F Europa Palace – C/F Olympia Palace
C/F Ariadne Palace – C/F Ikarus Palace
C/F Pasiphae Palace
Minoan Lines
Europa Palace; 2002; 30000 GRT.
Olympia Palace; 2001; 30000 GRT.
Ariadne Palace; 2002; 30000 GRT.
Ikarus Palace; 1997; 31000 GRT.
Pesiphae Palace; 1998; 31000 GRT.
The biggest name on the trans-Adriatic crossing, Minoan Lines are also arguably the best Adriatic line going, with a well-merited reputation for a high-quality service. Even deck-class passengers are treated as if they are human beings (though — as with all international boats — you will find your journey more comfortable if you book an aircraft-type seat). With a fleet of boats running up the Adriatic, Minoan offer a daily 23-hour service to Venice (route C) in addition to their traditional 19-hour Patras—Ancona run (routes A and B). Minoan Lines seem well placed to continue at the top of the pile in 2004.

C/F Superfast V – C/F Superfast VI
C/F Superfast XI – C/F Superfast XII
Superfast Ferries
Superfast V, VI; 2000.
Superfast XI, XII; 2002.
Superfast Ferries arrived in the Adriatic in 1995 with two new ferries that took the route by storm. The attraction of large and well-promoted boats (thanks to their streamlined look and bright red hulls) offering a fast direct Patras—Ancona sailing (route B) proved to be irresistible to many.

The arrival of the new high speed Minoan Lines' boats has prevented the company from building on this success. Superfast also received some very negative publicity after the *Superfast III* suffered a major mishap in November 1999; an engine-room fire broke out in mid-Adriatic, forcing the ship to be abandoned (with Greek TV providing a running commentary by broadcasting the mobile-phone calls of panic-stricken passengers as they were herded into lifeboats). Ten Kurdish stowaways died. The fact that a fire could take hold so quickly, and burn out the stern of the ship, does raise questions about modern ferry design. In spite of this, the boats deserve to be recommended.

C/F *Blue Sky* – C/F *Blue Horizon*
Blue Ferries / Strintzis
Blue Sky / Blue Horizon.
Once a great power in the Adriatic, Strintzis (now re-badged as 'Blue Star Ferries') has built new boats, but is focusing on the Aegean. The company has a loose link-up with Superfast Ferries, so does not compete against them in the Adriatic — running just two boats to Venice. The *Blue Sky* and *Blue Horizon* are looking distinctly small, dated and poor competition to rival Minoan's fast alternatives. This lack of competitive edge is reflected in the fact that they sail as 'Blue Ferries' rather than 'Blue Star Ferries'.

C/F *Olympic Champion*
C/F *Hellenic Spirit* – C/F *Kriti V*
C/F *Lefka Ori* – C/F *Sophocles V*
ANEK Lines
Olympic Champion; 2001; 30000 GRT.
Hellenic Spirit; 2002; 30000 GRT.
Kriti V; 2000; 30000 GRT.
Lefka Ori; 1991; 29420 GRT.
Sophocles V; 1990; 13384 GRT.
The main rival of Minoan Lines on the Piraeus—Crete routes, financially troubled ANEK also provide a competing Adriatic service, though they have lost much of their competitive edge lately. The company is now addressing this by introducing large, new, custom-built vessels, but it seems to be a case of too little, too late. ANEK hardly better their position by operating boats to out-of-the-way Trieste (route D), instead of the popular Venice favoured by their rivals. This aside, ANEK boats are clean, reliable and have an enviable safety record.

Europa Palace
Olympia Palace
Ariadne Palace
Ikarus Palace
Pasiphae Palace

Superfast V—VI, XI—XII

Blue Sky
Blue Horizon

Olympic Champion
Hellenic Spirit – *Kriti V*
Lefka Ori – *Sophocles V*

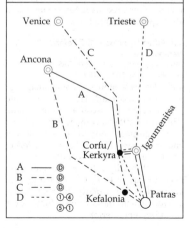

Bari—Greece Links

C/F *Ariadne Palace 1* – C/F *Prometheus*
Minoan Lines
Ariadne Palace 1; 2001; 28000 GRT.
Prometheus; 2001; 28000 GRT.
So many new boats are now on the Patras to Ancona and Venice runs that ferry operators are turning their attention to the Bari link by moving excess capacity here. Minoan are the latest to join in the act with the *Prometheus* and *Ariadne Palace 1* (formerly the *Oceanus*) arriving in 2003. Now the best boats on this route, their apperance is also another salvo in the on-going war with Superfast. Recommended.

C/F *Superfast I* – C/F *Superfast II*
Superfast Ferries
Superfast I, II; 1995; 23663 GRT.
These two high-powered Superfast ferries have been on the Bari run for a couple of years. Their arrival caused a contraction in the number of operators on the route as no one else was in a position to compete. They deserved to clean up and all but did so — until Minoan arrived. Despite being less than ten years old, both these vessels are losing their competitive edge, though facilities are still way above most Greek domestic boats. It is possible that they could be replaced with newer siblings in the Superfast fleet in 2004.

C/F *Athens Express* – C/F *Polaris*
Ventouris Ferries
Athens Express; 1969; 6416 GRT.
Polaris; 1975; 20326 GRT.
In past years Ventouris Ferries managed to carve out a nice market by packing a route with its boats to discourage competition. This strategy failed with the arrival of fast, better equipped vessels and they are now minor players. They subsist by offering the budget option for commercial vehicles, with hardly a tourist in sight. Any that do buy tickets run when they see the boats — particularly the poor *Athens Express*, which boasts a weedy funnel over an indifferent interior.

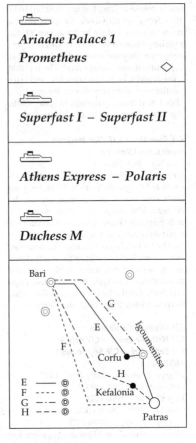

Ariadne Palace 1
Prometheus   ◇

Superfast I – *Superfast II*

Athens Express – *Polaris*

Duchess M

C/F *Duchess M*
Marlines; 1970; 2786 GRT.
In years past Marlines were quite a big player on the trans-Adriatic ferry scene, but their policy of buying older ferries and then rebuilding them proved a disaster when the likes of Superfast and Minoan introduced purpose-built high speed boats. Marlines are now reduced to running this one ferry in the area. Sadly, the *Duchess M* is far too small and way too old for anyone to take seriously. A boat to be avoided.

Blue Bridge

Kapetan Alexandros A
Penelope A

Afrodite II
Maria G

Erotokritos
King Minos

Ouranos

Egnatia III
Poseidonia

◇

Brindisi ⊚
K
I
L
J
M
Igoumenitsa
Corfu /
Kerkyra
I —— ⒟
J - - - ⒟
K -·-·- ⒟
L ---- ⒟
M -··-·· ○
Kefalonia
(Sami)
Patras

Brindisi—Greece Links

C/F *Blue Bridge*
Blue Ferries / Strintzis
Blue Bridge; 1976; 12067 GRT.
The Brindisi—Greece route is the short
and cheap Adriatic crossing. As a result it
attracts a succession of smaller and older
boats unable to make a go of it elsewhere.
The comparatively low cost of the tickets
has made the Brindisi run an unattractive
option for the companies operating new
high speed ferries — to date!
  Blue Ferries offer the best of a bad lot with
the *Blue Bridge*. This boat is easily the biggest
(and best) ferry running to Brindisi, with
a reasonable interior. Her main weakness
is that she runs solo: so the company isn't
offering a daily service in both directions.
Recommended — until something better
comes along.

C/F *Kapetan Alexandros A*
C/F *Penelope A*
Agoudimos Lines
Kapetan Alexandros A; 1962; 3250 GRT.
Penelope A.
Formerly the Rafina-based *Alekos*, the tiny
and heavily rebuilt ferry *Kapetan Alexandros
A* moved into this Adriatic route in 1992.
She has continued on it ever since — being
joined in 2000 by the *Penelope A*. During the
High Season they usually run a daily one-
way Igoumenitsa—Corfu—Brindisi service
(itinerary L). Expect the latter boat to be
running this year, but how long her partner
will remain viable is open to question.

C/F *Afrodite II* – C/F *Maria G*
Med Link Lines / NEL Lines
Afrodite II; 1967; 4190 GRT.
Maria G; 1976; 7020 GRT.
Med Link Lines (recently bought up by NEL
Lines) run a couple of elderly but reasonable
boats on the Brindisi route (running itiner-
ary J), in past years occasionally pulling
them off to take on a summer long-haul
Turkey service. Since 1996 this company's
ferries have made additional stops at
Kefalonia during the High Season.

C/F *Erotokritos* – C/F *King Minos*
Minos Lines
Erotokritos; 1974; 12888 GRT.
King Minos; 1972; 9652 GRT.
Another of the companies operating older ferries on the route, this outfit bought up a couple of Minoan's older boats. Barely repainted, and looking the worse for wear, these ferries might be okay for island hoppers and ferry fans on a nostalgia trip, but can be happily avoided by everyone else.

C/F *Ouranos*
Fragline; 1967; 11600 GRT.
After the best part of a decade running in tandem with a feebly small companion, the *Ouranos* has run solo on route L since 1995. A reasonable enough boat if you are not too demanding, she isn't sufficiently high-powered to make a go of it on any of the other Adriatic routes, and is looking extremely dated. Best avoided.

C/F *Egnatia III*
C/F *Poseidonia*
Hellenic Mediterranean Lines
Egnatia III / Poseidonia.
HML Ferries, once one of the mainstays of the Brindisi—Patras route with four boats, have now all but disappeared from the scene. They are still here, but their profile has sunk considerably. This is a great pity as their innovative itineraries take in islands otherwise inaccessible except by domestic ferries (notably Kefalonia, Paxos and Zakinthos). Much of this enterprising activity is due to the fact that HML rely on dated small ferries and need to have some means of competing with other lines. Worth looking out for, they are in need of some streamlined timetabling — their range of schedules is so great that it is impossible to say where their boats will be on any given day — without much head-scratching over their near incomprehensible timetable.

C/M *Ventouris High Speed I*
C/M *Ventouris High Speed II*
Since 1996 catamarans have operated an up-market Italy—Greece service on this route. The Brindisi—Corfu—Igoumenitsa link has been dominated by two Ventouris cats for the last two years (this is little help in predicting what will run in 2004, however, as these boats change with depressing regularity). Very expensive, and catering for affluent Italians, scheduling for all these boats tends to be 'elastic', to say the least.

P/S *Petrakis* – P/S *Sotirakis*
Prior to the Kosovo crisis, tour boats ran from Corfu to Albanian Sarandë, doing the 90-minute run several days a week (these are apt to change each year). Formerly ex-Royal Navy wooden-hulled minesweepers, these boats, if operating, will require you to buy your ticket at least one day in advance (see p. 583 for details).

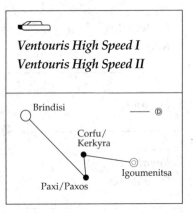

Ventouris High Speed I
Ventouris High Speed II

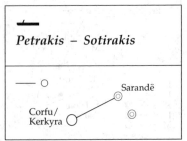

Petrakis – Sotirakis

Trans-Adriatic Ports (Non-Greek)

Alexandria
Egypt is too far removed from the rest of the ferry network to figure widely on schedules. Services that do exist are rather irregular with most operating via the Cypriot port of Limassol. Alexandria is an attractive neo-colonial city with good bus and rail links to the capital Cairo, some three hours' drive to the south. The port area is very extensive, though ferry traffic has declined with the reopening of the Suez Canal and Port Said.

Ancona
The number two destination for north-bound Patras ferries, Ancona is a substantial — but thanks to its commercial activities not particularly attractive — city on the upper Italian Adriatic coast. It sees considerable ferry traffic thanks to good road connections north (and hence is a natural departure point for holidaying Italians from the northern cities) and trans-European rail links (daily departures for Frankfurt and Munich). Nearby Rimini also has a daily overnight express train to Milan, Frankfurt and Amsterdam.

⊨⊣

Those mad enough to want to stay will find several cheap hotels opposite the railway station, which is home to a tourist information kiosk that issues free city maps along with accommodation information.

Ashdod
Very much Israel's second port, lying just north of the Gaza Strip, Ashdod very occasionally appears on cruise/ferry schedules. Links are very erratic indeed. Given the troubled state of the Gaza Strip an increase in ferry activity is unlikely.

Bari
An attractive — if unspectacular — city, Bari is too far south down the Italian boot to be an appealing port of call for travellers heading on to Northern Europe, nor is it sufficiently north to appeal to holidaying Italians either. As a result, it is very much the number three west-Adriatic ferry port. On the same rail line as Brindisi, but a longer journey by ferry, your

chances of finding a train seat in summer are likely to be limited.

Brindisi
This pleasant city is the destination for the majority of the Patras—Italy ferries. This is due to the easy turn-around time (22 hours), thus allowing two ferries to combine and offer a daily service in each direction. This is the best arrival point if Rome or southern Italy is your next port of call. However, if you are passing through Italy you will still be faced with a long drive or rail journey north.

⊨⊣

Accommodation can be a problem thanks to occasional waves of boat people from Albania (most of whom are temporarily housed in local hotels before being returned).

Cyprus
Offering an interesting mix of sun, sand and antiquities — to say nothing of Greek and British military cultural lifestyles co-existing side by side — Cyprus offers a worthy stopover should you be hopping between Greece and Israel or Egypt. Since the 1974 Turkish invasion the Cypriot Republic has been confined to the southern 60% of the island. Despite this the south has prospered while the isolated Turkish-occupied north (set up as an unrecognized Turkish Cypriot republic) remains stagnant. The UN-monitored Green Line between the two sides of the island cannot be crossed at any point. A peace process of sorts has been crawling along for years, but was all but wrecked with the fatal shooting of two Cypriot protesters in August 1996. It would be unrealistic to expect the situation to improve in the foreseeable future.

Given that northern Cyprus can only be accessed via Turkish ports, those services are covered in Chapter 12. You should also note the potential pitfall of having a Turkish-Cypriot stamp in your passport. This can (though not always) cause severe difficulties when entering Greece, since you can be deemed to have inevitably been in receipt of 'stolen property' (e.g. by staying in a hotel owned by a displaced Greek Cypriot). Your

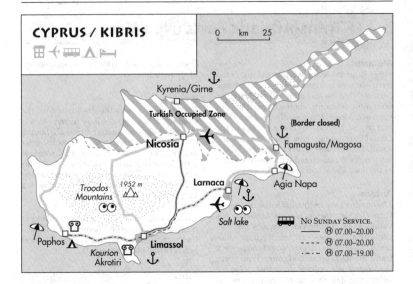

CYPRUS / KIBRIS

0   km   25

Kyrenia/Girne

Turkish Occupied Zone

(Border closed)

Nicosia

Famagusta/Magosa

Larnaca   Agia Napa

Troodos   1952 m
Mountains

Salt lake

No Sunday Service.
——— ⊕ 07.00–20.00
- - - ⊕ 07.00–20.00
-·-·- ⊕ 07.00–19.00

Paphos

Kourion
Akrotiri

Limassol

new 'criminal' status will go down even less well if attempting to enter Greek Cyprus: you could well be denied entry.

With the division of the island has come a shift in the focus of Cypriot life, from the divided capital of Nicosia, to the south coast ports. **Limassol** (an unplanned concrete town) has became the de facto centre of Greek Cyprus as well as the ferry hub of the Eastern Mediterranean beyond Greece. The centre is quite pleasant in a garrison town way, the British forces base at Akrotiri dominating the local economy. Helpful tourist offices at both ferry terminus building (linked to the centre by bus #1) and waterfront have free maps showing all hotels and guest houses.

The island's second port is at **Larnaca**, a prosperous resort that has grown up since the invasion thanks to the new international airport and the need to replace lost Famagusta. The Costa del Sol atmosphere of the seafront (complete with a poor beach) contrasts greatly with the ghost town ferry terminus (Larnaca is one of the quietest international ferry ports in the Med.) 2 km east of the centre.

Λ

Geroskipou Camping: the only island site, on the beach 3 km to the east of Paphos.

Tourist offices carry information on all the easily accessible sights from Limassol. These are the ruined cities at Kourion and Paphos and the Troodos mountains: a cool retreat from the heat of the coast.

Durrës

The principal port of Albania and its nearby capital of Tirana, ugly Durrës is not a leading candidate for an increase in ferry activity in the near future. Until the recent wave of liberalization the thrice-monthly ferry link to Trieste was one of the principal means of entering the country.

Haifa

Haifa is a large (and not particularly attractive) port on the northern edge of Israel's Mediterranean seaboard. Conflict with her neighbours means that the country has no land route to Europe, and this is reflected in the relatively high level of ferry traffic linking Haifa with Limassol, Rhodes and Piraeus. This link operates three days a week in High Season and is maintained at twice-weekly level throughout the rest of the year. Since the peace treaty with Egypt irregular services to

Alexandria and Port Said are also on offer, but most are tourist/cruise ship vessels with prices to match. Most casual non-vehicle traffic on both these routes is gleaned from the ranks of the backpacker and kibbutz brigade. Security problems within the country are reflected on ferries that include Israel in their itineraries. This is tighter than on other boats and even if your destination is not Israel you can expect rigorous questioning on boarding.

Jounieh

A small port set safely in the Christian enclave of the Lebanon in a wide bay 20 km north of Beirut. A ferry link was established on the outbreak of the civil war that left Beirut port in ruins. For the bulk of the last 30 years operated a 'rat' run to Larnaca on Cyprus. Services were suspended in 1994.

Otranto

Cornered on the heel of Italy, Otranto is too remote to attract ferry traffic bar the odd maverick boat, and even then only because it offers the shortest (a beguiling advertising point) Adriatic crossing from Corfu and Igoumenitsa. Poor road and rail connections with the rest of Italy.

Port Said

Lying on the north-eastern entrance to the Suez Canal, Port Said has regained its role among Egypt's premier commercial ports following the reopening of the waterway. Good bus links with Cairo, which is just as well since — canal excepted — there is little of interest here. Fortunately the Cairo road follows the bank of the canal (free sightseeing) so that arrival here has some advantages. That said, if you are arriving as an independent traveller outside a cruise/tour visit, you should allow 3–4 hours to negotiate the tortuous local immigration and customs processing operation.

Sarandë

This shop- and restaurant-free town on Albania's southern coastline is visited by Corfu tour boats four days a week. Services resumed in 2002 after several years' suspension thanks to the Kosovo conflict. Passengers pre-book four days in advance to enable visas to be prepared. When booking you are asked to provide your surname, forenames, father's name, place of birth, date of birth, nationality, and occupation. Fares are quite high: €35 one way, €50 return (plus a US$30 visa). Given the shortages in Albania, it is necessary to take absolutely everything you are likely to need — bar drinking water — with you.

Trieste

Argued over by Yugoslavia and Italy after the last war, Trieste voted to join the latter in a UN plebiscite. Despite this, it retains strong connections with the Slovenian Istrian peninsula and is awkwardly linked with the rest of Italy (though it is the terminus for several trans-Europe trains — notably to Budapest and Geneva). The northern gateway to Slovenia and Croatia, the city remains a ferry backwater — with only ANEK Lines regularly calling. Tucked away at the head of the Adriatic, the city is unlikely to see an increase in traffic.

Valona

Albania's third and most northerly port, it saw its first regular ferry service in 1993. A town with few facilities, it is unlikely to develop in the future. Conditions of passage as for Sarandë above.

Venice

Considering how great an impact Venice has had over the history and culture of the Mediterranean it is surprising how little it figures on ferry schedules (being confined to one or two daily boats to Greece in High Season, with irregular boats to Turkey some years). This is due to the same geographical difficulty that affects Trieste: being at the head of the Adriatic the city does not figure prominently on trans-European road or rail routes.

Since motoring in Venice is handicapped by the canal system, and the former Yugoslavia (a couple of hours away by road) is only very slowly returning to the fringes of the tourist map, it is inevitable that the *Stazione marittima* is under utilised. This is a pity, as arriving in Venice by boat is one of the best landfalls going, with ferries passing the Grand Canal and St Mark's Square. It is almost worth waiting for a Venice-bound ferry simply to enjoy this experience. In practice, however, Venice remains the preserve of long-distance travellers. This could change as new fast ferries (Igoumenitsa in 16 hours) come into service.

PORT TABLES

& REFERENCE:
FERRY COMPANIES · INTERNET · USEFUL GREEK · INDEX

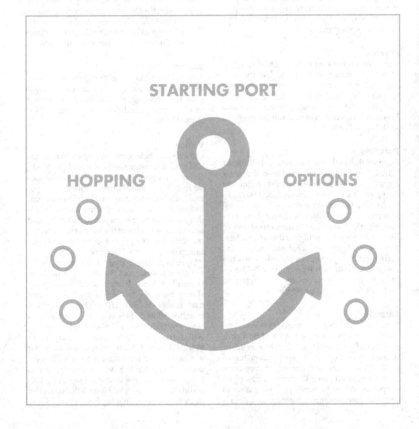

STARTING PORT

HOPPING

OPTIONS

Note:

The following Port Tables show *typical* High Season ferry times. Islands and ports are listed alphabetically. Those islands that are known by two common names (eg. Santorini / Thira) are listed

under the first (e.g. Santorini). Island ports are not listed separately by name but appear under their respective island's name. Minor ferry services already shown on island maps are not listed again here.

Aegina

Argo-Saronic p. 488

○ Typical daily departures:

06.10	Saronikos Ferries	Piraeus.
07.30	*Nefeli*	Piraeus.
07.40	*Keravnos 1/2*	Piraeus.
08.40	*Poseidon Hellas*	Methana. Poros.
08.45	Saronikos Ferries	Piraeus.
08.55	*Apollon Hellas*	Methana. Poros. Hydra. Spetses. Porto Helio.
09.00	Saronikos Ferries	Methana. Poros.
09.10	*Eftichia*	Poros. Hydra. Ermioni. Spetses.
09.10	*Georgios 2*	Methana. Poros. Spetses. Porto Helio.
09.30	*Angistri Express*	Angistri.
10.00	*Keravnos 1/2*	Angistri.
10.00	Saronikos Ferries	Piraeus.
11.40	*Poseidon Hellas*	Piraeus.
11.45	*Keravnos 1/2*	Piraeus.
12.15	*Angistri Express*	Angistri.
12.20	*Apollon Hellas*	Piraeus.
12.30	Saronikos Ferries	Piraeus.
14.00	*Angistri Express*	Angistri.
15.15	*Keravnos 1/2*	Angistri.
15.45	Saronikos Ferries	Piraeus.
15.50	*Angistri Express*	Angistri.
17.00	Saronikos Ferries	Piraeus.
17.20	*Apollon Hellas*	Methana. Poros.
17.55	*Eftichia*	Piraeus.
18.30	*Georgios 2*	Piraeus.
18.30	*Poseidon Hellas*	Piraeus.
19.00	*Angistri Express*	Angistri.
20.30	*Apollon Hellas*	Piraeus.

Ⓢ Ⓖ Ⓓ

14.15	Saronikos Ferries	Piraeus.
16.30	Saronikos Ferries	Piraeus.
18.00	Saronikos Ferries	Piraeus.
19.15	Saronikos Ferries	Piraeus.

Ⓖ Ⓓ

10.45	Saronikos Ferries	Angistri.
16.00	Saronikos Ferries	Epidavros.

≈ *Flying Dolphins* include:

Ⓗ 08.00–19.00 Piraeus (Great Harbour).

Ⓓ 09.45 17.15 Poros. Hydra. Spetses.

Aegina (Agia Marina)

Ⓓ

06.30	*Elvira*	Piraeus.
09.30	*Michael*	Piraeus.
13.00	*Agios Nektarios B*	Piraeus.
17.00	*Michael*	Piraeus.
18.45	*Agios Nektarios B*	Piraeus.

≈ *Saronic Dolphins* include:

Ⓓ	07.30	09.15	12.30	15.15
	17.15	19.15	21.00	Piraeus.

Aegina (Souvala)

Ⓓ

08.15	Saronikos Ferries	Piraeus.
12.00	Saronikos Ferries	Piraeus.

Ⓓ ex Ⓖ

17.30	Saronikos Ferries	Piraeus.
19.30	Saronikos Ferries	Piraeus.

Ⓖ

16.30	Saronikos Ferries	Piraeus.

≈ *Saronic Dolphins* include:

Ⓓ	06.40	08.00	09.45	12.45
	14.15	16.15	18.15	21.15	Piraeus.

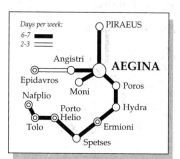

Days per week:
6-7 ▬
2-3 ═

PIRAEUS

Angistri

AEGINA

Epidavros

Nafplio Moni

Poros

Porto Helio

Hydra

Tolo Ermioni

Spetses

Agathonisi

Dodecanese p. 331

②
08.30 Miniotis Ferries Arki. Lipsi. Patmos.
15.00 Miniotis Ferries Samos (Pithagorio).

③ ⑦
13.15 *Nissos Kalimnos* Samos (Pithagorio).
16.00 *Nissos Kalimnos* Arki. Patmos. Lipsi.
Leros. Kalimnos.

⑤
13.15 *Nissos Kalimnos* Samos (Pithagorio).
16.00 *Nissos Kalimnos* Arki. Patmos. Lipsi. Leros.
Kalimnos.

⑥
08.35 Hydrofoil Patmos. Lipsi.
Leros (Agia Marina).
Kalimnos. Kos.
17.25 Hydrofoil Samos (Pithagorio).
Samos (Vathi).

Agios Efstratios

Northern Aegean p. 442

②
04.30 *Saos II* Limnos. Kavala.

③ ⑦
05.20 *Saos II* Lavrio.

④
10.00 *Saos II* Limnos. Kavala.

⑤
05.30 *Saos II* Psara. Lavrio.

⑥
04.30 *Saos II* Limnos. Samothrace.
Alexandroupolis.

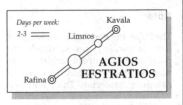

Agios Konstantinos

Northern Aegean p. 442

Ⓓ
10.00 MFD Hydrofoil Skiathos. Skopelos (Glossa).
Skopelos. Alonissos.
14.00 MFD Hydrofoil Skiathos. Skopelos.
19.15 MFD Hydrofoil Skiathos. Skopelos (Glossa).
Skopelos. Alonissos.

①
12.00 *JetFerry 1* Skiathos. Skopelos.
Alonissos.

②
12.00 *JetFerry 1* Skiathos. Skopelos.
Alonissos.

③
12.00 *JetFerry 1* Skiathos. Skopelos.
Alonissos.

④
12.00 *JetFerry 1* Skiathos. Skopelos.
Alonissos.

⑤
09.00 *Milena* Skiathos. Skopelos.
15.00 *JetFerry 1* Skiathos. Skopelos.
Alonissos.

⑥
12.00 *JetFerry 1* Skiathos. Skopelos.
Alonissos.

⑦
12.00 *JetFerry 1* Skiathos. Skopelos.
Alonissos.

Alexandria

Egypt p. 579

○
00.00   *Princesa Amorosa*   Cyprus (Limassol). Haifa.

Alexandroupolis

Northern Aegean p. 443

Ⓓ
08.00   *Arsinoe/Caviros*   Samothrace.
15.30   *Arsinoe/Caviros*   Samothrace.

①
08.30   *Niki H/F*   Samothrace.
12.00   *Dimitroula*   Limnos.
                      Lesbos (Mytilini).
                      Chios.
                      Samos (Vathi).
                      Kos.
                      Rhodes.
15.30   *Niki H/F*   Samothrace. Thassos.

②
08.00   *Arsinoe*   Samothrace.
12.30   *Niki H/F*   Samothrace.
15.15   *Niki H/F*   Samothrace.
16.00   *Arsinoe*   Samothrace.

③
09.30   *Niki H/F*   Samothrace.
14.00   *Niki H/F*   Samothrace.
18.00   *Niki H/F*   Samothrace.

④ ⑦
09.30   *Niki H/F*   Samothrace.
14.00   *Niki H/F*   Samothrace.
18.00   *Niki H/F*   Samothrace.

⑤
09.30   *Niki H/F*   Samothrace.
15.30   *Niki H/F*   Samothrace.

⑥
09.30   *Niki H/F*   Samothrace.
14.00   *Niki H/F*   Samothrace.
14.30   *Saos II*   Samothrace. Limnos.
                      Agios Efstratios.
                      Lavrio.
18.00   *Niki H/F*   Samothrace.

Alonissos

Northern Aegean
p. 445

Ⓓ
06.30   MFD Hydrofoil   Skopelos. Skopelos
                        (Glossa). Skiathos. Volos.
06.45   MFD Hydrofoil   Skopelos. Skopelos
                        (Glossa). Skiathos.
                        Agios Konstantinos.
11.45   MFD Hydrofoil   Skopelos. Skiathos. Volos.
14.00   MFD Hydrofoil   Skopelos. Skopelos
                        (Glossa). Skiathos. Volos.
16.00   MFD Hydrofoil   Skopelos. Skopelos
                        (Glossa). Skiathos.
                        Agios Konstantinos.

①
12.30   *Express Haroulla*   Skiathos. Volos.
16.30   *JetFerry 1*   Skopelos. Skiathos.
                             Amorgos (Katapola).

② ③
12.30   *Express Haroulla*   Skiathos. Volos.
16.30   *JetFerry 1*   Skopelos. Skiathos.
                             Amorgos (Katapola).

④
12.30   *Express Haroulla*   Skiathos. Volos.
16.30   *JetFerry 1*   Skopelos. Skiathos.
                             Amorgos (Katapola).

⑤
12.30   *Express Haroulla*   Skiathos. Volos.
20.30   *JetFerry 1*   Skopelos. Skiathos.
                             Agios Konstantinos.

⑥
12.30   *Express Haroulla*   Skiathos. Volos.
16.00   *JetFerry 1*   Skopelos. Skiathos.
                             Amorgos (Katapola).

⑦
12.30   *Express Haroulla*   Skiathos. Volos.
16.00   *JetFerry 1*   Skopelos. Skiathos.
                             Amorgos (Katapola).

ALEXANDROUPOLIS

Kavala ◎

Samothrace

Days per week:
6-7 ▬▬▬
2-3 ══

ALONISSOS

Volos ◎

Skiathos

Agios
Konstantinos

(Glossa) Skopelos
(Town)

Days per week:
6-7 ▬▬▬
4-5 ▬▬▬

Amorgos (Egiali)

Cyclades East
p. 268

Amorgos (Katapola)

Cyclades East
p. 267

① |
07.15 | *Express Skopelitis* | Donoussa. Koufonissia. Schinoussa. Iraklia. Naxos.
19.45 | *Express Skopelitis* | Amorgos (Katapola).

③ |
07.15 | *Express Skopelitis* | Donoussa. Koufonissia. Schinoussa. Iraklia. Naxos.
12.00 | *Dimitroula* | Amorgos (Katapola). Donoussa. Naxos. Paros. Syros. Piraeus.
19.45 | *Express Skopelitis* | Amorgos (Katapola).

⑤ |
01.20 | *Dimitroula* | Astipalea.
07.15 | *Express Skopelitis* | Donoussa. Koufonissia. Schinoussa. Iraklia. Naxos.
08.20 | *Dimitroula* | Amorgos (Katapola). Donoussa. Naxos. Paros. Piraeus.
19.45 | *Express Skopelitis* | Amorgos (Katapola).

⑥ |
10.30 | *Dimitroula* | Astipalea. Kos. Nissiros. Tilos. Symi. Rhodes. Kastelorizo.

⑦ |
11.20 | *Romilda* | Donoussa. Naxos. Paros. Piraeus.

① |
06.00 | *Express Skopelitis* | Amorgos (Egiali). Donoussa. Koufonissia. Schinoussa. Iraklia. Naxos.
06.00 | *Express Skopelitis* | Amorgos (Egiali). Donoussa. Koufonissia. Schinoussa. Iraklia. Naxos.
07.10 | *Jet One* | Santorini. Ios. Milos. Kythnos. Piraeus.

② |
06.00 | *Express Skopelitis* | Koufonissia. Schinoussa. Iraklia. Paros (Piso Livadi). Naxos.
06.30 | *Blue Star Naxos* | Koufonissia. Schinoussa. Iraklia. Naxos. Paros. Piraeus.
13.30 | *Aeolos Express II* | Mykonos. Tinos. Syros. Piraeus.
23.00 | *Marina/Rodanthi* | Astipalea. Kalimnos. Kos. Rhodes.

③ |
04.00 | *Patmos/Rodos* | Piraeus.
06.00 | *Express Skopelitis* | Amorgos (Egiali). Donoussa. Koufonissia. Schinoussa. Iraklia. Naxos.
07.10 | *Jet One* | Santorini. Ios. Folegandros. Milos. Sifnos. Piraeus.
12.45 | *Dimitroula* | Donoussa. Naxos. Paros. Syros. Piraeus.
13.30 | *Aeolos Express II* | Mykonos. Tinos. Syros. Piraeus.
22.50 | *Patmos/Rodos* | Astipalea. Kalimnos. Nissiros. Rhodes.

④ |
01.45 | *Marina/Rodanthi* | Piraeus.
06.00 | *Express Skopelitis* | Koufonissia. Schinoussa. Iraklia. Paros (Piso Livadi). Naxos.

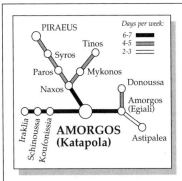

| 06.30 | *Blue Star Naxos* | Koufonissia. Schinoussa. Iraklia. Naxos. Paros. Piraeus. |
| 07.10 | *Jet One* | Santorini. Folegandros. Milos. Piraeus. |

⑤
00.35	*Dimitroula*	Amorgos (Egiali). Astipalea.
06.00	*Express Skopelitis*	Amorgos (Egiali). Donoussa. Koufonissia. Schinoussa. Iraklia. Naxos.
09.00	*Dimitroula*	Donoussa. Naxos. Paros. Piraeus.

⑥
06.00	*Express Skopelitis*	Koufonissia. Schinoussa. Iraklia. Paros (Piso Livadi). Naxos.
06.30	*Blue Star Naxos*	Koufonissia. Naxos. Paros. Piraeus.
07.10	*Jet One*	Santorini. Ios. Milos. Sifnos. Kythnos. Piraeus.
09.45	*Dimitroula*	Amorgos (Egiali). Astipalea. Kos. Nissiros. Tilos. Symi. Rhodes. Kastelorizo.
16.20	*Blue Star 1*	Piraeus.

⑦
04.45	*Blue Star 1*	Patmos. Leros. Kos. Rhodes.
10.30	*Romilda*	Amorgos (Egiali). Donoussa. Naxos. Paros. Piraeus.
12.30	*Panagia Ekatontapiliani*	Koufonissia. Naxos. Paros. Piraeus.

Anafi

Cyclades Central
p. 273

②
| 04.15 | *Express Santorini* | Santorini. Ios. Naxos. Paros. Piraeus. |

④
| 07.00 | *Romilda* | Santorini. Folegandros. Sikinos. Ios. Naxos. Paros. Piraeus. |

⑥
| 07.00 | *Romilda* | Santorini. Folegandros. Sikinos. Ios. Naxos. Paros. Piraeus. |

○
| 00.00 | *Panagia Tinou* | Santorini. |

○
| 00.00 | *Mail Boat* | Santorini. |

Ancona

Italy p. 579

Ⓓ
13.30	Superfast Ferries	Igoumenitsa. Patras.
16.30	ANEK Lines	Igoumenitsa. Patras.
17.00	Minoan Lines	Igoumenitsa. Patras.
19.00	Superfast Ferries	Patras.

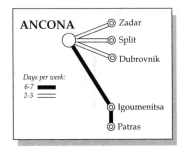

Andros

Cyclades North
p. 195

①		
09.30	*Aqua Jewel*	Tinos. Mykonos. Paros.
10.00	*Express Athina*	Tinos. Mykonos.
10.00	*Superferry II*	Tinos. Mykonos.
11.00	*Express Penelope*	Rafina.
15.30	*Express Athina*	Rafina.
16.15	*Superferry II*	Rafina.
17.30	*Aqua Jewel*	Rafina.
19.45	*Express Penelope*	Tinos. Mykonos.
21.10	*Superferry II*	Rafina.

②		
09.30	*Aqua Jewel*	Tinos. Mykonos. Paros.
10.00	*Express Athina*	Tinos. Mykonos.
10.00	*Superferry II*	Tinos. Mykonos.
11.00	*Express Penelope*	Rafina.
15.30	*Express Athina*	Rafina.
16.15	*Superferry II*	Rafina.
17.30	*Aqua Jewel*	Rafina.
19.45	*Express Penelope*	Tinos. Mykonos.
21.10	*Superferry II*	Rafina.

③		
09.30	*Aqua Jewel*	Tinos. Mykonos. Paros.
10.00	*Express Athina*	Tinos. Mykonos.
10.00	*Superferry II*	Tinos. Mykonos.
11.00	*Express Penelope*	Rafina.
15.30	*Express Athina*	Rafina.
16.15	*Superferry II*	Rafina.

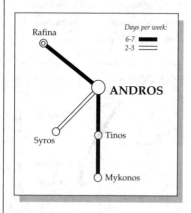

Rafina

ANDROS

Syros

Tinos

Mykonos

Days per week:
6-7 ▬▬▬
2-3 ═══

17.30	*Aqua Jewel*	Rafina.
21.10	*Superferry II*	Rafina.

④		
09.30	*Aqua Jewel*	Tinos. Mykonos. Paros.
10.00	*Express Penelope*	Tinos. Mykonos.
10.00	*Superferry II*	Tinos. Mykonos.
11.00	*Express Penelope*	Rafina.
16.15	*Superferry II*	Rafina.
17.00	*Express Penelope*	Rafina.
17.30	*Aqua Jewel*	Rafina.
19.40	*Express Athina*	Tinos. Mykonos.
21.10	*Superferry II*	Rafina.

⑤		
01.00	*Express Athina*	Rafina.
09.30	*Aqua Jewel*	Tinos.
09.45	*Express Penelope*	Tinos.
10.00	*Express Athina*	Tinos. Mykonos.
10.00	*Superferry II*	Tinos. Mykonos.
13.00	*Aqua Jewel*	Rafina.
13.15	*Express Penelope*	Rafina.
15.30	*Express Athina*	Rafina.
16.15	*Superferry II*	Rafina.
19.00	*Aqua Jewel*	Tinos. Mykonos. Paros. Rafina.
19.45	*Express Penelope*	Tinos. Mykonos.
20.40	*Express Athina*	Tinos. Mykonos.
21.10	*Superferry II*	Rafina.

⑥		
01.30	*Express Athina*	Rafina.
09.30	*Aqua Jewel*	Tinos.
10.00	*Express Athina*	Tinos. Mykonos.
10.00	*Superferry II*	Tinos. Mykonos.
11.00	*Express Penelope*	Rafina.
13.00	*Aqua Jewel*	Rafina.
15.30	*Express Athina*	Rafina.
16.15	*Superferry II*	Rafina.
18.30	*Aqua Jewel*	Tinos. Mykonos. Paros. Rafina.
19.45	*Express Penelope*	Tinos. Mykonos.
21.10	*Superferry II*	Rafina.

⑦		
09.30	*Aqua Jewel*	Tinos. Mykonos. Paros.
10.00	*Express Athina*	Tinos. Mykonos.
10.00	*Superferry II*	Tinos. Mykonos.
11.00	*Express Penelope*	Rafina.
15.30	*Express Athina*	Rafina.
16.15	*Superferry II*	Rafina.
17.30	*Aqua Jewel*	Rafina.
19.45	*Express Penelope*	Tinos. Mykonos.
21.00	*Express Athina*	Rafina.
21.30	*Superferry II*	Rafina.
22.15	*Express Penelope*	Syros. Tinos. Mykonos.

Angistri

Argo-Saronic
p. 492

Ⓓ
07.00	*Angistri Express*	Aegina.
07.15	*Keravnos 1/2*	Aegina. Piraeus.
10.00	*Angistri Express*	Aegina.
11.20	*Keravnos 1/2*	Aegina. Piraeus.
13.00	*Angistri Express*	Aegina.
15.00	*Angistri Express*	Aegina.
18.00	*Angistri Express*	Aegina.

①
05.55	*Manaras Express*	Piraeus.
07.10	*Kitsolakis Express*	Piraeus.
09.45	*Manaras Express*	Piraeus.
14.30	Saronikos Ferries	Aegina.
16.10	*Manaras Express*	Piraeus.
17.15	Saronikos Ferries	Aegina. Piraeus.

②
07.10	*Kitsolakis Express*	Piraeus.

② ③ ④
06.10	*Manaras Express*	Piraeus.
16.40	*Manaras Express*	Piraeus.

③
07.10	*Kitsolakis Express*	Piraeus.
14.30	Saronikos Ferries	Aegina.
17.15	Saronikos Ferries	Aegina. Piraeus.

④
07.10	*Kitsolakis Express*	Piraeus.

⑤
09.45	*Manaras Express*	Piraeus.
12.40	*Kitsolakis Express*	Piraeus.
14.30	Saronikos Ferries	Aegina.
15.30	*Manaras Express*	Piraeus.
17.15	Saronikos Ferries	Aegina. Piraeus.
20.15	*Manaras Express*	Piraeus.

⑥
06.15	*Kitsolakis Express*	Piraeus.
09.00	*Manaras Express*	Piraeus.
11.45	Saronikos Ferries	Aegina.
12.10	*Kitsolakis Express*	Piraeus.
15.45	Saronikos Ferries	Aegina. Piraeus.
17.00	*Manaras Express*	Piraeus.

⑦
12.00	Saronikos Ferries	Aegina.
15.00	*Manaras Express*	Piraeus.
16.00	*Kitsolakis Express*	Piraeus.
19.10	*Manaras Express*	Piraeus.
19.45	Saronikos Ferries	Aegina. Piraeus.

○
12.00	Saronikos Ferries	Epidavros.
14.30	Saronikos Ferries	Epidavros.

Antikithera

Argo-Saronic
p. 494

⑤
00.30	*Mirtidiotissa*	Kithera. Piraeus.
12.15	*Nissos Kithera*	Kithera (Agia Pelagia). Neapoli.

⑥
03.15	*Mirtidiotissa*	Crete (Kasteli).

⑦
12.15	*Nissos Kithera*	Kithera (Agia Pelagia). Neapoli.
16.45	*Mirtidiotissa*	Kithera (Agia Pelagia). Gythio.

Antiparos

Cyclades Central
p. 135

Ⓓ Ⓗ
07.00–24.00;		
ev. 30 min		
10.30–20.30	*Agioi Anargiri*	Paros (Punta).

Ⓓ
x 10	*Antiparos Express/ Kasos Express/ Panagia Parou*	Paros.

Days per week:
6-7 ▬▬
2-3 ══

○ PIRAEUS

Aegina

Epidavros

ANGISTRI

Paros (Town)

Days per week:
6-7 ▬▬

Paros (Punta)

ANTIPAROS

Arki

Dodecanese p. 331

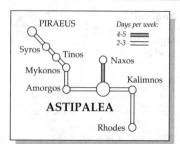

②
| 10.00 | Miniotis Lines | Lipsi. Patmos. |
| 13.30 | Miniotis Lines | Agathonisi. Samos (Pithagorio). |

③ ⑤ ⑦
| 12.05 | *Nissos Kalimnos* | Agathonisi. Samos (Pithagorio). |
| 17.00 | *Nissos Kalimnos* | Patmos. Lipsi. Leros. Kalimnos. |

Ashdod

Israel p. 579

○
| 18.00 | *Princesa Amorosa* | Limassol. Port Said. |

Astakos

Ionian Line p. 521

Ⓓ
| 13.00 | *Agia Marina* | Kefalonia (Sami). |

Astipalea

Cyclades East p. 276

②
| 06.45 | *Nissos Kalimnos* | Kalimnos. |

③
01.00	*Marina/Rodanthi*	Kalimnos. Kos. Rhodes.
01.45	*Patmos/Rodos*	Amorgos (Katapola). Piraeus.
09.40	*Dimitroula*	Amorgos (Egiali). Amorgos (Katapola). Donoussa. Naxos. Paros. Syros. Piraeus.
23.45	*Marina/Rodanthi*	Amorgos (Katapola). Piraeus.

④
| 01.00 | *Patmos/Rodos* | Kalimnos. Nissiros. Rhodes. |
| 01.15 | *Nissos Kalimnos* | Kalimnos. |

⑤
| 06.00 | *Dimitroula* | Amorgos (Egiali). Amorgos (Katapola). Donoussa. Naxos. Paros. Piraeus. |

⑥
10.15	*Nissos Kalimnos*	Kalimnos.
13.00	*Dimitroula*	Kos. Nissiros. Tilos. Symi. Rhodes. Kastelorizo.
15.00	Hydrofoil	Kalimnos. Kos. Symi. Rhodes.

Avşa

Turkey p. 558

Ⓓ
| 00.00 | TML | Marmara. İstanbul. |

Ⓓ ex ⑦
| 00.00 | TML | Marmara. |
| 00.00 | TML | Erdek. |

Ⓓ x ④
| 00.00 | Deniz Otobusleri | Marmara. İstanbul. |

⑤ ⑦
| 00.00 | TML | Marmara. Tekirdağ. |

Ayvalık

Turkey p. 558

Ⓓ
| 08.00 | *Jale/Jalehan* | Lesbos (Mytilini). |
| 17.00 | *Jale/Jalehan* | Lesbos (Mytilini). |

Bandırma

Turkey p. 559

Ⓓ
| 01.15 | TML | İstanbul. |
| 14.30 | TML | İstanbul. |

Bari

Italy p. 579

ⓓ		
20.00	Superfast Ferries	Igoumenitsa. Patras.
20.00	Ventouris Ferries	Corfu. Igoumenitsa.

① ③		
16.00	Minoan Lines	Igoumenitsa. Patras.
19.00	AK Ventouris	Patras.

② ⑤		
16.00	Minoan Lines	Igoumenitsa. Patras.

④ ⑦		
16.00	Minoan Lines	Corfu. Igoumenitsa. Patras.

⑥		
16.00	Minoan Lines	Corfu. Igoumenitsa. Patras.
19.00	AK Ventouris	Patras.

○		
20.00	*Dame M/Duchess M*	Igoumenitsa.

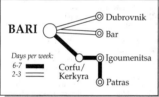

BARI

Days per week:
6-7 ▬▬▬
2-3 ═══

Dubrovnik
Bar
Corfu/ Kerkyra
Igoumenitsa
Patras

Bodrum

Turkey p. 559

ⓓ		
09.00	*Bodrum Princess*	Kos.
09.00	*Fari Kaptain I*	Kos.
09.30	*Bodrum Express*	Datca (Körmen).
11.00	Bodrum T/Bs	Orak Is.
11.00	Bodrum T/Bs	Korada Is. Ada Is.
16.00	*Hermes*	Kos.
17.00	*Bodrum Express*	Datca (Körmen).

Bozcaada

Turkey p. 561

ⓓ x 2	TML	Odun Iskalesi.

Brindisi

Italy p. 579

ⓓ		
00.00	*Ventouris High Speed I/II*	Paxi. Corfu. Igoumenitsa.
09.00	HML Ferries	Igoumenitsa. Corfu.
10.30	*Blue Bridge*	Corfu. Igoumenitsa.
14.00	*Santa Eleonora*	Corfu. Paxi.
19.00	*Brindisi/Valentino*	Igoumenitsa. Patras.
20.00	Med Link Lines	Patras.
20.45	*Ouranos*	Igoumenitsa. Corfu.
22.00	*Kapetan Alexandros*	Igoumenitsa.

Ⓐ		
18.00	Poseidon Lines	Igoumenitsa. Patras.
20.00	HML Ferries	Corfu. Paxi. Kefalonia (Sami). Patras.
20.00	HML Ferries	Corfu. Igoumenitsa. Kefalonia (Sami). Patras.
20.00	Med Link Lines	Kefalonia (Sami). Patras.
22.00	HML Ferries	Corfu. Igoumenitsa. Patras.

②		
20.00	*Maria G*	Çeşme.

③		
20.00	*Poseidon*	Çeşme.

⑥		
16.00	*Maria G*	Çeşme.
20.00	*Poseidon*	Çeşme.

ⓦ		
00.00	*Cesme 1/2*	Çeşme.

○		
20.00	HML Ferries	Zakinthos. Patras.
20.00	Med Link Lines	Igoumenitsa.

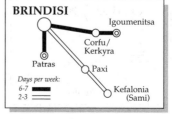

BRINDISI

Igoumenitsa
Corfu/ Kerkyra
Patras
Paxi
Kefalonia (Sami)

Days per week:
6-7 ▬▬▬
2-3 ═══

Çeşme

Turkey p. 562

Ⓓ

| 08.00 | Erturk I | Chios. |
| 18.00 | Capetan Stamatis | Chios. |

○

| 20.00 | Poseidon/Maria G | Brindisi. |

Chalki

Dodecanese p. 332

Ⓓ ex ⑦

| 05.30 | Chalki/ Nikos Express | Rhodes (Kamiros Skala). |

① ⑤

| 17.00 | Vitsentzos Kornaros | Rhodes. |

②

| 01.15 | Vitsentzos Kornaros | Karpathos (Diafani). Karpathos (Town). Kassos. Crete (Sitia). |
| 17.40 | Vitsentzos Kornaros | Rhodes. |

③

| 06.45 | Vitsentzos Kornaros | Karpathos (Diafani). Karpathos (Town). Kassos. Crete (Sitia). Crete (Agios Nikolaos). Milos. Piraeus. |
| 16.00 | Hydrofoil | Rhodes. Tilos. Nissiros. Kos. |

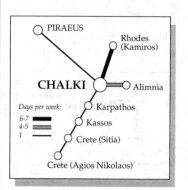

```
          ○ PIRAEUS
                         ○ Rhodes
                           (Kamiros)

  CHALKI  ○━━━━━○ Alimnia

Days per week:    ○ Karpathos
  6-7 ▰▰▰
  4-5 ▰▰▰        ○ Kassos
  1   ━━━
               ○ Crete (Sitia)

      ○ Crete (Agios Nikolaos)
```

⑥

| 06.45 | Vitsentzos Kornaros | Karpathos (Diafani). Karpathos (Town). Kassos. Crete (Sitia). Crete (Agios Nikolaos). Milos. Piraeus. |
| 17.00 | Ierapetra L | Rhodes. |

⑦

| 06.45 | Ierapetra L | Karpathos (Diafani). Karpathos (Town). Kassos. Crete (Sitia). Crete (Agios Nikolaos). Milos. Piraeus. |
| 09.00 | Chalki/ Nikos Express | Rhodes (Kamiros). |

Chios

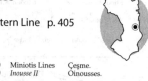

Eastern Line p. 405

Ⓓ

| 08.00 | Miniotis Lines | Çeşme. |
| 14.00 | Inousse II | Oinousses. |

①

06.00	Mytilene	Lesbos (Mytilini).
10.30	Daliana	Samos (Vathi). Samos (Karlovassi). Fourni. Ikaria (Agios Kyrikos). Piraeus.
15.00	Taxiarchis	Piraeus.
22.00	Mytilene	Piraeus.

②

00.40	Dimitroula	Samos (Vathi). Kos. Rhodes. Kastelorizo.
03.20	Milena	Lesbos (Mytilini).
04.30	Theofilos	Lesbos (Mytilini).
12.00	Taxiarchis	Lesbos (Mytilini).
21.00	Taxiarchis	Samos (Vathi). Piraeus.
22.00	Aeolos Kenteris	Lesbos (Mytilini). Limnos. Thessalonika.
22.00	Theofilos	Piraeus.

③

04.00	Mytilene	Lesbos (Mytilini).
19.45	Aeolos Kenteris	Piraeus.
22.00	Mytilene	Piraeus.

④

04.30	Theofilos	Lesbos (Mytilini).
08.00	Taxiarchis	Piraeus
22.00	Theofilos	Piraeus.

⑤

04.00	Mytilene	Lesbos (Mytilini).
22.00	Aeolos Kenteris	Lesbos (Mytilini).
22.00	Mytilene	Piraeus.

⑥
04.30	*Theofilos*	Lesbos (Mytilini). Limnos. Thessalonika.
07.30	*Taxiarchis*	Lesbos (Mytilini).
10.30	*Aeolos Kenteris*	Piraeus.
22.00	*Aeolos Kenteris*	Lesbos (Mytilini).

⑦
10.30	*Aeolos Kenteris*	Piraeus.
14.00	*Milena*	Mykonos. Tinos. Syros. Piraeus.
18.00	Miniotis Ferries	Samos (Karlovassi). Samos (Vathi).
21.15	*Dimitroula*	Lesbos (Mytilini). Limnos. Alexandroupolis.
22.00	*Theofilos*	Piraeus.

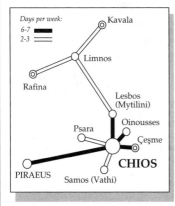

Days per week:
6-7
2-3

Kavala
Limnos
Rafina
Lesbos (Mytilini)
Oinousses
Psara
Çeşme
CHIOS
PIRAEUS
Samos (Vathi)

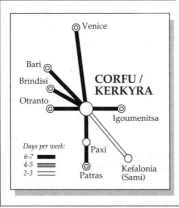

Venice
Bari
Brindisi
CORFU / KERKYRA
Otranto
Igoumenitsa
Days per week:
6-7
4-5
2-3
Paxi
Kefalonia (Sami)
Patras

Corfu / Kerkyra

Ionian Line   p. 521

Ⓓ
01.00	*Blue Bridge*	Brindisi.
07.00	Ventouris Ferries	Igoumenitsa.
08.30	*Ouranos*	Brindisi.
09.00	*Santa Eleonora*	Brindisi.
18.30	*Blue Bridge*	Igoumenitsa.
18.30	*Santa Eleonora*	Paxi.
23.00	Ventouris Ferries	Bari.

Ⓐ
00.00	HML Ferries	Brindisi.
00.00	HML Ferries	Paxi. Kefalonia (Sami). Patras.
00.00	HML Ferries	Igoumenitsa. Kefalonia (Sami). Patras.

①
07.00	*Blue Horizon/Blue Sky*	Igoumenitsa. Venice
07.00	Minoan Lines	Igoumenitsa. Venice.
10.30	ANEK Lines	Trieste.
13.00	*Blue Horizon/Blue Sky*	Igoumenitsa. Patras.
14.30	Minoan Lines	Patras.

②
| 07.00 | *Blue Horizon/Blue Sky* | Igoumenitsa. Venice |
| 14.30 | Minoan Lines | Patras. |

③
07.00	Minoan Lines	Igoumenitsa. Venice.
14.30	Minoan Lines	Patras.
22.30	*Blue Horizon/Blue Sky*	Patras.

④
07.00	Minoan Lines	Igoumenitsa. Venice.
10.30	ANEK Lines	Trieste.
12.00	ANEK Lines	Igoumenitsa. Patras.
22.30	*Blue Horizon/Blue Sky*	Patras.
23.30	Minoan Lines	Igoumenitsa. Patras.
24.00	Minoan Lines	Bari.

⑤
06.00	*Blue Horizon/Blue Sky*	Igoumenitsa. Venice.
07.00	Minoan Lines	Igoumenitsa. Venice.
14.30	Minoan Lines	Patras.

⑥
06.00	*Blue Horizon/Blue Sky*	Igoumenitsa. Venice.
07.00	Minoan Lines	Igoumenitsa. Venice.
09.00	*Petrakis/Sotirakis*	Sarandë.
14.30	Minoan Lines	Patras.
23.30	Minoan Lines	Igoumenitsa. Patras.
24.00	Minoan Lines	Bari.

⑦
07.00	Minoan Lines	Igoumenitsa. Venice.
12.00	ANEK Lines	Igoumenitsa. Patras.
13.00	*Blue Horizon/Blue Sky*	Igoumenitsa. Patras.
14.30	Minoan Lines	Patras.
23.30	Minoan Lines	Igoumenitsa. Patras.
24.00	Minoan Lines	Bari.

Domestic Services:

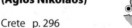

Ⓗ
06.00–22.00
| | Local C/F | Igoumenitsa. |

Ⓓ
09.30	*Agios Spyridon*	Igoumenitsa.
14.00	*Agios Spyridon*	Igoumenitsa.
14.00	*Pegasus* T/B	Paxi (Old Port).
19.30	*Agios Spyridon*	Igoumenitsa.

①
| 12.45 | Local C/F | Igoumenitsa. Paxi. |

②
| 12.45 | Local C/F | Igoumenitsa. Paxi. |

② ⑥
06.30	Local P/S	Erikoussa.
		Mathraki.
		Othoni.

③
| 07.30 | Local C/F | Igoumenitsa. Paxi. |
| 17.00 | Local C/F | Paxi. |

④ ⑤ ⑥
| 12.45 | Local C/F | Igoumenitsa. Paxi. |

⑦
| 12.45 | Local C/F | Igoumenitsa. Paxi. |

○
| 00.00 | | Paxi. Preveza. |
| | | Amphilochia. |

Corfu (Lefkimi)

Ⓓ
06.00 09.00 12.00
16.00 18.00
| | Local C/F | Igoumenitsa. |

Corfu (Sidari)

① ④
| 11.00 | Othoni Line | Erikoussa. |
| | | Mathraki. Othoni. |

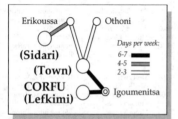

Crete
(Agia Roumeli)

Crete p. 309

Ⓓ
09.30 14.00 15.45 17.00
	South Crete Line	Lutro. Sfakia.
18.00	South Crete Line	Sfakia.
16.30	South Crete Line	Sougia. Paleochora.

Crete
(Agios Nikolaos)

Crete p. 296

Ⓓ
| 10.00 | Tour Boats | Spinalonga. |

①
07.30	*Vitsentzos Kornaros*	Crete (Sitia). Kassos.
		Karpathos (Town).
		Karpathos (Diafani).
		Chalki. Rhodes.

②
| 07.30 | *Ierapetra L* | Crete (Sitia). |
| 19.00 | *Ierapetra L* | Piraeus. |

③
| 18.00 | *Vitsentzos Kornaros* | Milos. Piraeus. |

④
| 07.30 | *Ierapetra L* | Crete (Sitia). |
| 19.00 | *Ierapetra L* | Piraeus. |

⑤
07.30	*Vitsentzos Kornaros*	Crete (Sitia). Kassos.
		Karpathos (Town).
		Karpathos (Diafani).
		Chalki. Rhodes.

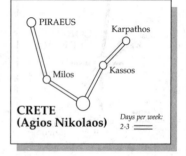

⑥		
07.30	*Ierapetra L*	Crete (Sitia). Kassos. Karpathos (Town). Karpathos (Diafani). Chalki. Rhodes.
18.30	*Vitsentzos Kornaros*	Milos. Piraeus.
⑦		
18.00	*Ierapetra L*	Milos. Piraeus.

Crete (Chania)

Crete
p. 298

ⓓ		
21.00	*Lato/Lissos*	Piraeus.
23.30	*Blue Star 2*	Piraeus.

Crete (Iraklion)

Crete
p. 300

ⓓ		
07.15	*Maria PA/ Vergina Sky*	Santorini.
09.15	*Flying Cat 4*	Santorini. Ios. Paros. Naxos. Mykonos.
21.00	*Kriti I/Kriti II*	Piraeus.
22.00	*Festos Palace/ Knossos Palace*	Piraeus.
①		
13.00	*Daedalus*	Santorini. Paros. Mykonos. Tinos. Thessalonika.
②		
07.00	*Jet One*	Santorini. Ios. Milos. Sifnos. Piraeus.
③		
18.00	*Daedalus*	Santorini. Naxos. Mykonos. Skyros. Thessalonika.
⑤		
07.00	*Jet One*	Santorini. Ios. Milos. Piraeus.

The following diagram shows shipping routes with days per week indicators:

Days per week:
6-7 ▬▬
4-5 ▬
2-3 ═
1 —

Thessalonika, Skiathos, Tinos, Mykonos, Ancona, PIRAEUS, Paros, Karpathos, Rhodes, Santorini, Limassol, **CRETE (Iraklion)**, Haifa

21.00	*Daedalus*	Santorini. Paros. Mykonos. Tinos. Skiathos. Thessalonika.
⑥		
12.30	*Festos Palace/ Knossos Palace*	Piraeus.
⑦		
12.30	*Festos Palace/ Knossos Palace*	Piraeus.

Crete (Kasteli)

Crete
p. 307

① ③ ⑥		
08.00	*Mirtidiotissa*	Antikithera. Kithera (Agia Pelagia). Gythio *or* Kalamata.
② ⑦		
08.00	*Mirtidiotissa*	Kithera (Agia Pelagia).
④		
14.00	*Mirtidiotissa*	Kithera (Agia Pelagia). Gythio *or* Kalamata.
⑦		
08.00	*Mirtidiotissa*	Gythio.

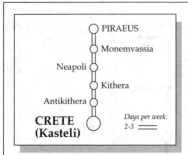

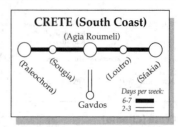

① ④ ⑥ ⑦
09.00   South Crete Line   Gavdos.

Crete (Paleochora)

Crete p. 308

ⓓ
08.15   South Crete Line   Sougia.
                             Agia Roumeli.
10.00   South Crete Line   Elafonisi.
②
08.30   South Crete Line   Gavdos.

Crete (Rethimno)

Crete
p. 312

ⓓ
19.30   *Arkadi/Preveli*   Piraeus.
②
06.45   *Vergina Sky*   Santorini.

```
PIRAEUS          Days per week:
 |                6-7  ▬▬
 |      CRETE
 |      (Rethimno)
```

Crete (Sfakia)

Crete p. 309

ⓓ
10.30 11.45 13.45 15.45
        South Crete Line   Lutro. Agia Roumeli.

Crete (Sitia)

Crete p. 314

①
09.30   *Vitsentzos Kornaros*   Kassos.
                                 Karpathos (Town).
                                 Karpathos (Diafani).
                                 Chalki. Rhodes.
②
10.00   *Vitsentzos Kornaros*   Kassos.
                                 Karpathos (Town).
                                 Karpathos (Diafani).
                                 Chalki. Rhodes.
16.00   *Ierapetra L*   Crete (Agios Nikolaos).
                                 Piraeus.
③
15.30   *Vitsentzos Kornaros*   Crete (Agios Nikolaos).
                                 Milos. Piraeus.
④
16.00   *Ierapetra L*   Crete (Agios Nikolaos).
                                 Piraeus.

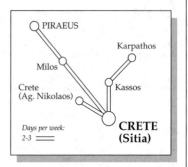

⑤
09.30   *Vitsentzos Kornaros*   Kassos.
                                Karpathos (Town).
                                Karpathos (Diafani).
                                Chalki. Rhodes.

⑥
09.30   *Ierapetra L*   Kassos.
                                Karpathos (Town).
                                Karpathos (Diafani).
                                Chalki. Rhodes.
15.30   *Vitsentzos Kornaros*   Crete (Agios Nikolaos).
                                Milos. Piraeus.

⑦
15.30   *Ierapetra L*   Crete (Agios Nikolaos).
                                Milos. Piraeus.

Cyprus (Limassol)

Cyprus p. 580

○
15.00   *Princesa Marissa*   Port Said.
16.00   *Nissos Kypros*   Rhodes. Tinos.
                              Piraeus.

○
15.00   *Princesa Amorosa*   Port Said.
18.00   *Salamis Star*   Port Said. Haifa.
19.30   *Princesa Marissa*   Haifa. Port Said.
20.00   *Sea Harmony*   Haifa.

○
14.00   *Salamis Star*   Rhodes. Santorini.
                              Piraeus.
15.00   *Princesa Cypria*   Rhodes.
                              Lesbos (Mytilini).
                              Tinos. Piraeus.
19.30   *Princesa Marissa*   Haifa.
20.00   *Nissos Kypros*   Haifa.

○
17.00   *Princesa Amorosa*   Port Said.
                              Ashdod.

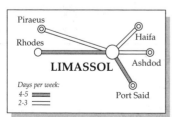

Piraeus
Rhodes
Haifa
LIMASSOL   Ashdod

Days per week:
4-5 ▬▬▬
2-3 ═══
Port Said

Turkish Occupied Ports:

Famagusta / Magosa

② ④ ⑦
22.00   *Yeşilada*   Mersin.

Kyrenia / Girne

Ⓓ
13.00   Hydrofoil   Taşucu.

② ③ ④
13.00   *Liberty / Ertürk*   Taşucu.

Datça (Körmen)

Turkey p. 562

Ⓓ
09.00   *Bodrum Express*   Bodrum.
17.00   *Bodrum Express*   Bodrum.

Delos

Cyclades North p. 200

Ⓓ ex ①
11.45   *Delos Express*   Mykonos.
12.20   *Hera/Orca*   Mykonos.
12.30   *Delos Express*   Mykonos.
12.30   *Niki*   Mykonos.
13.45   *Hera/Orca*   Mykonos.
14.15   *Delos Express*   Mykonos.
14.15   *Niki*   Mykonos.
15.00   *Delos Express*   Mykonos.
15.00   *Hera/Orca*   Mykonos.

Donoussa

Cyclades East
p. 280

①
08.30   *Express Skopelitis* Koufonissia. Schinoussa.
                              Iraklia. Naxos.
18.30   *Express Skopelitis* Amorgos (Egiali).
                              Amorgos (Katapola).

③
08.30   *Express Skopelitis* Koufonissia. Schinoussa.
                              Iraklia. Naxos.
13.45   *Dimitroula*   Naxos. Paros. Syros.
                              Piraeus.
18.30   *Express Skopelitis* Amorgos (Egiali).
                              Amorgos (Katapola).

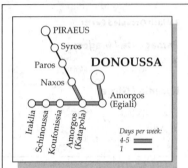

④
23.35 *Dimitroula* Amorgos (Katapola).
Amorgos (Egiali).
Astipalea.

⑤
08.30 *Express Skopelitis* Koufonissia. Schinoussa.
Iraklia. Naxos.
10.00 *Dimitroula* Naxos. Paros. Piraeus.
18.30 *Express Skopelitis* Amorgos (Egiali).
Amorgos (Katapola).

⑥
08.45 *Dimitroula* Amorgos (Katapola).
Amorgos (Egiali).
Astipalea. Kos. Nissiros.
Tilos. Symi. Rhodes.
Kastelorizo.

⑦
12.20 *Romilda* Naxos. Paros. Piraeus.

Durrës

Albania p. 580

② ④
12.00 Adriatica Bari.
③ ⑥
19.00 Adriatica Trieste.
⑦
12.00 Adriatica Ancona.

Eceabat

Turkey p. 562

Ⓓ ev 2Ⓗ 08.00–03.00 Çanakkale.

Egion

Ionian p. 525

Ⓓ x 10 including:
07.30 10.30 13.30 17.00 19.00
Panagia T. II Agios Nikolaos.

Elafonissos

Argo-Saronic p. 494

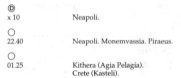

Ⓓ
x 10 Neapoli.

◯
22.40 Neapoli. Monemvassia. Piraeus.

◯
01.25 Kithera (Agia Pelagia).
Crete (Kasteli).

Epidavros

Argo-Saronic p. 495

①
09.50 *Flying Dolphin* Aegina.
16.00 Saronikos Ferries Angistri.
Aegina.
Piraeus.
19.55 *Flying Dolphin* Aegina.

③
17.15 Saronikos Ferries Angistri. Aegina.
Piraeus.

⑤
16.00 Saronikos Ferries Angistri. Aegina.
Piraeus.

⑥
14.00 Saronikos Ferries Angistri. Aegina.
Piraeus.

⑦
14.00 Saronikos Ferries Aegina.
Piraeus.
18.30 Saronikos Ferries Angistri.
Aegina.
Piraeus.

Erdek

Turkey p. 562

Ⓓ ex ⑦
00.00 TML Avşa. Marmara.

① ⑥
00.00   TML   Paşalimanı.

⑤ ⑦
00.00   TML   Avşa. Marmara. Tekirdağ.

Ermioni

Argo-Saronic p. 496

Ⓓ
12.30   Saronikos   Spetses.
14.30   Saronikos   Hydra. Poros.
                      Methana.
                      Aegina. Piraeus.

③ ⑥
12.40   Georgios 2   Spetses. Porto Helio.
15.30   Georgios 2   Poros. Methana. Aegina.
                      Piraeus.

 Flying Dolphins include:
Ⓓ
x 6   Hydra. Piraeus.
x 4   Poros.

Evia (Kimi)

Northern Aegean
p. 206

Ⓓ ex ⑦
11.00   Lykomides   Skyros.
17.00   Lykomides   Skyros.

⑦
13.00   Lykomides   Skyros.
19.00   Lykomides   Skyros.

○
22.15   Skopelos.
                      Alonissos.

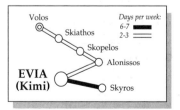

Volos   Days per week:
    Skiathos   6-7 ▬▬▬
        Skopelos   2-3 ═══
            Alonissos
EVIA
(Kimi)   Skyros

Evia (Marmari)

Cyclades North
p. 206

Ⓓ
06.00   Marmari Express   Rafina.

① ② ③ ④
10.30   Evia Star   Rafina.
13.45   Marmari Express   Rafina.
17.17   Evia Star   Rafina.
18.30   Marmari Express   Rafina.

⑤
10.30   Marmari Express   Rafina.
13.30   Evia Star   Rafina.
15.30   Marmari Express   Rafina.
18.30   Evia Star   Rafina.

⑥
09.30   Marmari Express   Rafina.
10.30   Evia Star   Rafina.
13.45   Marmari Express   Rafina.
17.17   Evia Star   Rafina.

⑦
09.30   Marmari Express   Rafina
14.00   Marmari Express   Rafina.
17.17   Marmari Express   Rafina.
20.45   Evia Star   Rafina.

Folegandros

Cyclades West
p. 232

①
16.55   Express Apollon   Sikinos. Ios. Santorini.

②
12.45   Express Apollon   Kimolos. Milos. Sifnos.
                            Serifos. Kythnos.
                            Piraeus.

③
11.15   Jet One   Milos. Sifnos. Piraeus.
20.50   Jet One   Ios. Santorini.
                           Amorgos (Katapola).

④
00.30   Romilda   Santorini. Anafi.
09.45   Jet One   Milos. Piraeus.
12.00   Romilda   Sikinos. Ios. Naxos.
                           Paros. Piraeus.
20.15   Jet One   Santorini.
                           Amorgos (Katapola).

⑥
00.30   Romilda   Santorini. Anafi.
12.00   Romilda   Sikinos. Ios. Naxos.
                           Paros. Piraeus.

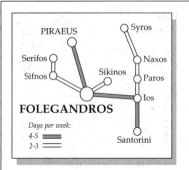

PIRAEUS ○ Syros

Serifos ○

Naxos

Sifnos ○ Sikinos

Paros

Ios

FOLEGANDROS

Days per week:
4-5 ▬▬
2-3 ══ Santorini

⑦		
01.10	*Express Apollon*	Sikinos. Ios. Santorini.
17.55	*Jet One*	Santorini. Ios.
19.10	*Express Apollon*	Kimolos. Milos. Sifnos. Serifos. Kythnos. Piraeus.

Fourni

Eastern Line p. 409

Ⓓ		
07.00	*Maria Express*	Ikaria (Agios Kyrikos).
①		
03.40	*Daliana*	Samos (Karlovassi). Samos (Vathi). Chios.
08.00	Miniotis Ferries	Ikaria (Agios Kyrikos). Samos (Karlovassi). Samos (Vathi).
10.50	Hydrofoil	Ikaria (Agios Kyrikos). Samos (Pithagorio).
16.05	Hydrofoil	Patmos. Leros (Agia Marina). Kalimnos. Kos.

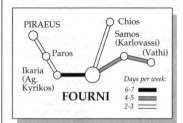

PIRAEUS ○ Chios

Samos
(Karlovassi)
Paros (Vathi)

Ikaria
(Ag.
Kyrikos) *Days per week:*

FOURNI 6-7 ▬▬
4-5 ▬▬
2-3 ══

18.40	*Daliana*	Ikaria (Agios Kyrikos). Piraeus.
20.30	Miniotis Ferries	Samos (Pithagorio).
③		
02.50	*Daliana*	Samos (Karlovassi). Samos (Vathi). Patmos. Lipsi.
08.55	Hydrofoil	Ikaria (Agios Kyrikos). Patmos. Lipsi. Leros (Agia Marina). Kalimnos. Kos.
18.30	Hydrofoil	Samos (Pithagorio). Samos (Vathi).
18.40	*Daliana*	Ikaria (Agios Kyrikos). Mykonos. Syros. Piraeus.
⑤		
08.55	Hydrofoil	Ikaria (Agios Kyrikos). Patmos. Lipsi. Leros (Agia Marina). Kalimnos. Kos.
13.00	Hydrofoil	Ikaria (Agios Kyrikos).
14.35	Hydrofoil	Patmos. Kos. Rhodes.
18.30	Hydrofoil	Samos (Pithagorio). Samos (Vathi).
⑥		
02.50	*Daliana*	Samos (Karlovassi). Samos (Vathi). Patmos. Lipsi.
18.40	*Daliana*	Ikaria (Agios Kyrikos). Mykonos. Syros. Piraeus.
⑦		
08.55	Hydrofoil	Ikaria (Agios Kyrikos). Patmos. Lipsi. Leros (Agia Marina). Kalimnos. Kos.
18.30	Hydrofoil	Samos (Pithagorio). Samos (Vathi).

Gavdos

Crete p. 318

②		
15.30	South Crete Line	Sougia.
②		
15.30	South Crete Line	Paleochora.
⑥ ⑦		
16.00	South Crete Line	Sfakia.
⑥ ⑦		
00.00	South Crete Line	Paleochora.

Gelibolu

Turkey p. 562

Ⓓ x 7	06.00–23.00	Lâpseki.

Gökçeada

Turkey p. 562

Ⓦ x 5   TML   Çanakkale.

Gythio

Argo-Saronic p. 496

① ③
12.30	Nissos Kithera	Kithera (Agia Pelagia). Neapoli.
○		
17.00	Mirtidiotissa	Kithera (Agia Pelagia).
○		
07.00	Mirtidiotissa	Kalamata.

Haifa

Israel p. 580

○		
19.00	Princesa Marissa	Port Said. Limassol.
20.00	Sea Harmony	Limassol. Rhodes. Santorini. Tinos. Piraeus.
○		
20.00	Princesa Cypria	Limassol. Rhodes. Lesbos (Mytilini). Tinos. Piraeus.
20.00	Salamis Star	Limassol. Rhodes. Santorini. Piraeus.
○		
20.00	Nissos Kypros	Limassol. Rhodes. Tinos. Piraeus.
20.00	Princesa Marissa	Limassol. Port Said.

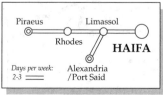

Hydra

Argo-Saronic p. 497

Ⓓ
12.00	Eftichia	Ermioni. Spetses.
12.00	Apollon Hellas	Spetses. Porto Helio.
15.00	Apollon Hellas	Poros. Methana. Aegina. Piraeus.
15.15	Eftichia	Poros. Methana. Aegina. Piraeus.
17.50	Georgios 2	Spetses. Porto Helio.
20.00	Georgios 2	Piraeus.

🐟 Flying Dolphins include:
Ⓓ x 10   Piraeus.
    x 7   Poros. / Spetses. Porto Helio.

Igoumenitsa

Ionian Line p. 525

International Services:

Ⓓ
05.30	Superfast Ferries	Patras.
07.00	Ouranos	Corfu. Brindisi.
08.00	Brindisi/ Valentino	Patras.
08.00	Minoan Lines	Patras.
08.30	ANEK Lines	Patras.
11.00	Kapetan Alexandros	Brindisi.
20.00	Superfast Ferries	Ancona.
20.30	HML Ferries	Corfu. Brindisi.
21.30	Ventouris Ferries	Corfu. Bari.
23.00	ANEK Lines	Ancona.
23.30	Blue Bridge	Corfu. Brindisi.

Ⓐ
00.30	HML Ferries	Corfu. Brindisi.
02.30	Poseidon Lines	Patras.
02.30	Poseidon Lines	Brindisi.
06.15	HML Ferries	Kefalonia (Sami). Patras.
07.00	Adriatica	Corfu. Brindisi.
09.00	Adriatica	Patras.

①
01.00	Minoan Lines	Patras.
08.30	Blue Horizon/ Blue Sky	Venice
09.00	ANEK Lines	Corfu. Trieste.
10.00	Minoan Lines	Venice.
12.30	ANEK Lines	Patras.
12.30	Minoan Lines	Corfu. Patras.
14.00	Blue Horizon/ Blue Sky	Patras.
22.00	Minoan Lines	Bari.

②		
01.00	Minoan Lines	Patras.
08.30	*Blue Horizon/Blue Sky*	Venice
10.00	ANEK Lines	Trieste.
12.30	Minoan Lines	Corfu.
		Patras.
22.00	Minoan Lines	Bari.

③		
01.00	Minoan Lines	Patras.
10.00	Minoan Lines	Venice.
12.30	ANEK Lines	Patras.
12.30	Minoan Lines	Corfu.
		Patras.
20.30	*Blue Horizon/Blue Sky*	Corfu. Patras.
22.00	Minoan Lines	Bari.

④		
01.00	Minoan Lines	Patras.
09.00	ANEK Lines	Corfu.
		Trieste.
10.00	Minoan Lines	Venice.
13.30	ANEK Lines	Patras.
20.30	*Blue Horizon/Blue Sky*	Corfu. Patras.
22.00	Minoan Lines	Corfu. Bari.

⑤		
01.00	Minoan Lines	Patras.
07.30	*Blue Horizon/Blue Sky*	Venice.
10.00	ANEK Lines	Trieste.
10.00	Minoan Lines	Venice.
12.30	Minoan Lines	Corfu. Patras.
22.00	Minoan Lines	Bari.

⑥		
01.00	Minoan Lines	Patras.
07.30	*Blue Horizon/Blue Sky*	Venice.
10.00	Minoan Lines	Venice.
12.30	ANEK Lines	Patras.
12.30	Minoan Lines	Corfu. Patras.
14.30	ANEK Lines	Trieste.
22.00	Minoan Lines	Corfu. Bari.

⑦		
01.00	Minoan Lines	Patras.
10.00	Minoan Lines	Venice.
12.30	Minoan Lines	Corfu. Patras.
13.30	ANEK Lines	Patras.
14.00	*Blue Horizon/Blue Sky*	Patras.
22.00	Minoan Lines	Corfu. Bari.

Domestic Services:

Ⓓ Ⓗ 05.00–22.00 | Corfu.

Ⓓ		
07.30	11.00	14.00
16.00	19.30		Corfu (Lefkimi).
05.45	11.30	16.15	
	Agios Spyridon	Corfu.

○		
09.30	Local C/F	Corfu.
15.00	Local C/F	Paxi.

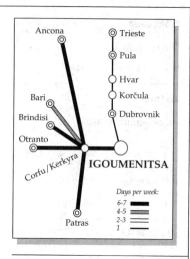

Days per week:
6-7
4-5
2-3
1

Ikaria
(Agios Kyrikos)

Eastern Line   p. 412

Ⓓ		
13.00	*Maria Express*	Fourni.

①		
02.50	*Daliana*	Fourni. Samos (Karlovassi).
		Samos (Vathi). Chios.
09.00	*Aeolos Express*	Naxos. Paros. Piraeus.
09.00	Miniotis Ferries	Samos (Karlovassi).
		Samos (Vathi).

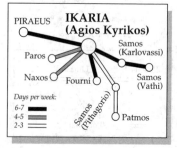

Days per week:
6-7
4-5
2-3

15.30	Hydrofoil	Fourni. Patmos.
		Leros (Agia Marina).
		Kalimnos. Kos.
19.20	*Daliana*	Piraeus.
19.30	Miniotis Ferries	Fourni.
		Samos (Pithagorio).
22.45	*Aeolos Express*	Samos (Vathi).

②
| 09.00 | *Aeolos Express* | Naxos. Paros. Piraeus. |

③
02.00	*Daliana*	Fourni. Samos (Karlovassi).
		Samos (Vathi). Patmos.
		Lipsi.
09.25	Hydrofoil	Patmos. Lipsi.
		Leros (Agia Marina).
		Kalimnos. Kos.
19.40	*Daliana*	Mykonos. Syros. Piraeus.
22.45	*Aeolos Express*	Samos (Vathi).

④
| 22.45 | *Aeolos Express* | Samos (Vathi). |

⑤
09.00	*Aeolos Express*	Naxos. Paros. Piraeus.
09.25	Hydrofoil	Patmos. Lipsi.
		Leros (Agia Marina).
		Kalimnos. Kos.
14.00	Hydrofoil	Fourni. Patmos. Kos.
		Rhodes.
17.25	Hydrofoil	Fourni. Samos (Pithagorio).
		Samos (Vathi).

⑥
02.00	*Daliana*	Fourni. Samos (Karlovassi).
		Samos (Vathi).
		Patmos. Lipsi.
09.00	*Aeolos Express*	Naxos. Paros. Piraeus.
19.40	*Daliana*	Mykonos. Syros. Piraeus.

⑦
09.25	Hydrofoil	Patmos. Lipsi.
		Leros (Agia Marina).
		Kalimnos. Kos.
11.10	Hydrofoil	Samos (Pithagorio).
14.30	Hydrofoil	Patmos.
		Leros (Agia Marina).
		Kos. Kalimnos.
17.25	Hydrofoil	Fourni. Samos (Pithagorio).
		Samos (Vathi).
22.45	*Aeolos Express*	Samos (Vathi).

Ikaria (Evdilos)

Eastern Line p. 414

②
| 03.10 | *Express Olympia* | Samos (Karlovassi). |
| | | Samos (Vathi). |

IKARIA
(Evdilos)

PIRAEUS

Days per week:
6-7 ▬

Samos
(Vathi)

Samos
(Karlovassi)

| 09.30 | *Express Olympia* | Piraeus. |
| 22.45 | *Aeolos Express* | Samos (Vathi). |

③
| 09.00 | *Aeolos Express* | Naxos. Paros. |
| | | Piraeus. |

④
03.10	*Express Olympia*	Samos (Karlovassi).
		Samos (Vathi).
09.00	*Aeolos Express*	Naxos. Paros.
		Piraeus.
09.30	*Express Olympia*	Piraeus.

⑤
03.10	*Express Olympia*	Samos (Karlovassi).
		Samos (Vathi).
09.30	*Express Olympia*	Piraeus.
22.45	*Aeolos Express*	Samos (Vathi).

⑥
03.10	*Express Olympia*	Samos (Karlovassi).
		Samos (Vathi).
09.30	*Express Olympia*	Piraeus.
22.45	*Aeolos Express*	Samos (Vathi).

⑦
03.10	*Express Olympia*	Samos (Karlovassi).
		Samos (Vathi).
09.00	*Aeolos Express*	Naxos. Paros.
		Piraeus.
09.30	*Express Olympia*	Piraeus.

Ios

Cyclades Central p. 140

①
06.10	*Express Poseidon*	Santorini.
09.30	*Jet One*	Milos. Kythnos. Piraeus.
11.30	*Express Poseidon*	Naxos. Paros. Piraeus.
11.50	*Flying Cat 4*	Paros. Naxos. Mykonos.
16.05	*Panagia*	
	Ekatontapiliani	Santorini.
16.50	*Flying Cat 4*	Santorini.
		Crete (Iraklion).
18.15	*Express Apollon*	Santorini.

20.55	*Jet One*	Santorini.
		Amorgos (Katapola).
21.20	*Panagia*	
	Ekatontapiliani	Naxos. Paros. Piraeus.
②		
00.40	*Express Santorini*	Santorini. Anafi.
06.10	*Express Poseidon*	Santorini.
09.20	*Express Santorini*	Naxos. Paros.
		Piraeus.
09.30	*Jet One*	Milos. Sifnos.
		Piraeus.
11.25	*Express Apollon*	Sikinos. Folegandros.
		Kimolos. Milos. Sifnos.
		Serifos. Kythnos.
		Piraeus.
11.30	*Express Poseidon*	Naxos. Paros. Piraeus.
11.50	*Flying Cat 4*	Paros. Naxos. Mykonos.
16.05	*Panagia*	
	Ekatontapiliani	Santorini.
16.25	*Blue Star Paros*	Naxos. Paros. Piraeus.
16.50	*Flying Cat 4*	Santorini.
		Crete (Iraklion).
20.00	*Jet One*	Santorini.
		Crete (Iraklion).
21.20	*Panagia*	
	Ekatontapiliani	Naxos. Paros. Piraeus.
③		
00.55	*Blue Star Naxos*	Santorini.
06.10	*Express Santorini*	Santorini.
10.30	*Jet One*	Folegandros. Milos.
		Sifnos. Piraeus.
11.30	*Express Santorini*	Naxos. Paros. Piraeus.
11.50	*Flying Cat 4*	Paros. Naxos. Mykonos.
16.05	*Panagia*	
	Ekatontapiliani	Santorini.
16.50	*Flying Cat 4*	Santorini.
		Crete (Iraklion).
21.10	*Jet One*	Santorini.
		Amorgos (Katapola).
21.20	*Panagia*	
	Ekatontapiliani	Naxos. Paros. Piraeus.
23.00	*Romilda*	Sikinos. Folegandros.
		Santorini. Anafi.
④		
00.40	*Express Poseidon*	Santorini.
06.10	*Express Santorini*	Santorini.
09.20	*Express Poseidon*	Naxos. Paros. Piraeus.
11.30	*Express Santorini*	Naxos. Paros. Piraeus.
11.50	*Flying Cat 4*	Paros. Naxos. Mykonos.
13.20	*Romilda*	Naxos. Paros. Piraeus.
16.05	*Panagia*	
	Ekatontapiliani	Santorini.
16.25	*Blue Star Paros*	Naxos. Paros. Piraeus.
16.50	*Flying Cat 4*	Santorini.
		Crete (Iraklion).
21.20	*Panagia*	
	Ekatontapiliani	Naxos. Paros. Piraeus.
⑤		
00.55	*Blue Star Naxos*	Santorini.
06.10	*Express Poseidon*	Santorini.
09.30	*Jet One*	Milos. Piraeus.
11.30	*Express Poseidon*	Naxos. Paros. Piraeus.

PIRAEUS
Syros
Mykonos
Serifos
Naxos
Sifnos
Paros
Folegandros
IOS
Sikinos

Days per week:
6-7
4-5
2-3

Santorini

11.50	*Flying Cat 4*	Paros. Naxos. Mykonos.
16.05	*Express Santorini*	Santorini.
16.50	*Flying Cat 4*	Santorini.
		Crete (Iraklion).
20.30	*Jet One*	Santorini.
		Crete (Iraklion).
21.20	*Express Santorini*	Naxos. Paros. Piraeus.
23.00	*Romilda*	Sikinos. Folegandros.
		Santorini. Anafi.
⑥		
00.40	*Panagia*	
	Ekatontapiliani	Santorini.
06.10	*Express Poseidon*	Santorini.
08.50	*Panagia*	
	Ekatontapiliani	Naxos. Paros. Piraeus.
10.30	*Jet One*	Milos. Sifnos. Kythnos.
		Piraeus.
11.30	*Express Poseidon*	Naxos. Paros. Piraeus.
11.50	*Flying Cat 4*	Paros. Naxos. Mykonos.
13.20	*Romilda*	Naxos. Paros. Piraeus.
16.05	*Express Santorini*	Santorini.
16.50	*Flying Cat 4*	Santorini.
		Crete (Iraklion).
20.10	*Jet One*	Santorini.
		Amorgos (Katapola).
21.20	*Express Santorini*	Naxos. Paros. Piraeus.
⑦		
02.30	*Express Apollon*	Santorini.
06.10	*Express Poseidon*	Santorini.
11.30	*Express Poseidon*	Naxos. Paros. Piraeus.
11.50	*Flying Cat 4*	Paros. Naxos. Mykonos.
16.05	*Express Santorini*	Santorini.
16.50	*Flying Cat 4*	Santorini.
		Crete (Iraklion).
17.50	*Express Apollon*	Sikinos. Folegandros.
		Kimolos. Milos. Sifnos.
		Serifos. Kythnos.
		Piraeus.
21.20	*Express Santorini*	Naxos. Paros. Piraeus.

Iraklia

Cyclades East   p. 281

Ⓓ
Ferries and Catamarans as **Schinoussa**
Times for boats to:

Naxos & Piraeus:
Schinoussa departure time +30 minutes.

Amorgos:
Schinoussa departure time –30 minutes.

İstanbul

Turkey   p. 563

Ⓓ Ⓗ
06.45–21.00		Princes' Islands.
		[x 5 steaming on to
		Yalova or Çinarcik.]

Ⓓ
09.30	20.00	Bandırma.
10.30	13.30	Bosphorus 'Tour'.
08.00		Armutlu. Mudanya.
08.00		Marmara. Avşa.

| x 4 | Deniz Otobusleri | Marmara. Avşa. |

⑤
| 17.30 | TML | İzmir. [③ August only] |

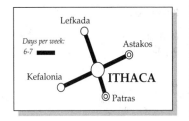

Ithaca (Frikes)

Ionian Line
p. 526

Ⓓ
11.00	*Meganisi*	Kefalonia (Fiskardo).
		Lefkada (Nidri).
13.00	*Nidri*	Lefkada (Nidri).

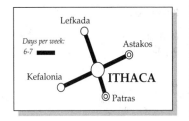

| 17.45 | *Nidri* | Kefalonia (Fiskardo). |
| | | Lefkada (Nidri). |

Ithaca (Pisaetos)

Ionian Line   p. 526

Ⓓ
07.40	*Agia Marina*	Kefalonia (Sami).
09.35	*Agia Marina*	Astakos.
17.00	*Agia Marina*	Kefalonia (Sami).

Ⓞ
| 21.00 | HML Ferries | Brindisi. |

Ithaca (Vathi)

Ionian Line   p. 526

Ⓓ
| 07.00 | *Kefalonia* | Kefalonia (Sami). Patras. |
| 16.30 | *Kefalonia* | Kefalonia (Sami). Patras. |

İzmir

Turkey   p. 566

② ⑦
| 14.00 | TML | İstanbul. |
③
| 16.00 | *Ankara* | Venice. |

Kabatepe

Turkey   p. 566

③ ⑦
| 13.00 | TML | Gökçeada. |

Kalimnos

Dodecanese
p. 335

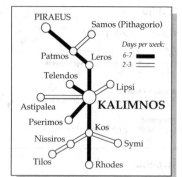

PIRAEUS

Samos (Pithagorio)

Days per week:

Patmos   Leros   6-7

2-3

Telendos

Lipsi

Astipalea   **KALIMNOS**

Pserimos

Kos

Nissiros

Symi

Tilos

Rhodes

Ⓓ
07.00	15.50	19.30		
			Olympios Apollon/ Atromitos	Kos (Mastihari).

①
02.30	*Patmos/Rodos*	Kos. Rhodes.
04.15	*Marina/Rodanthi*	Kos. Rhodes.
07.00	Hydrofoil	Kos. Leros (Agia Marina). Patmos.
07.00	*Nissos Kalimnos*	Kos. Nissiros. Tilos. Symi. Rhodes.
11.40	*Dodekanesos Express*	Leros (Agia Marina).
14.45	Hydrofoil	Leros (Agia Marina). Patmos. Samos (Pithagorio).
15.30	*Dodekanesos Express*	Kos. Rhodes.
18.45	Hydrofoil	Kos.
20.30	*Patmos/Rodos*	Leros. Patmos. Piraeus.

②
01.45	*Marina/Rodanthi*	Kos. Rhodes.
02.30	*Patmos/Rodos*	Kos. Tilos. Symi. Rhodes.
03.30	*Nissos Kalimnos*	Astipalea.
07.00	Hydrofoil	Kos. Leros (Agia Marina). Lipsi. Patmos. Samos (Pithagorio).
10.50	Hydrofoil	Kos.
11.40	*Dodekanesos Express*	Leros (Agia Marina). Patmos. Lipsi.
14.45	Hydrofoil	Lipsi. Patmos. Samos (Pithagorio).
15.30	*Dodekanesos Express*	Kos. Rhodes.
17.55	Hydrofoil	Kos.
20.30	*Patmos/Rodos*	Leros. Patmos. Piraeus.
22.45	*Marina/Rodanthi*	Piraeus.
23.45	*Patmos/Rodos*	Astipalea. Amorgos (Katapola). Piraeus.

③
02.30	*Patmos/Rodos*	Kos. Rhodes.
03.00	*Marina/Rodanthi*	Kos. Rhodes.
07.00	*Dimitroula*	Astipalea. Amorgos (Egiali). Amorgos (Katapola). Donoussa. Naxos. Paros. Syros. Piraeus.
07.00	Hydrofoil	Kos. Nissiros. Tilos. Rhodes.
07.00	*Nissos Kalimnos*	Leros. Lipsi. Patmos. Arki. Agathonisi. Samos (Pithagorio).

14.45	Hydrofoil	Leros (Agia Marina). Lipsi. Patmos. Samos (Pithagorio).
17.25	Hydrofoil	Kos.
19.45	*Marina/Rodanthi*	Astipalea. Amorgos (Katapola). Piraeus.
20.30	*Patmos/Rodos*	Leros. Patmos. Piraeus.
22.00	*Nissos Kalimnos*	Astipalea.

④
01.45	*Marina/Rodanthi*	Kos. Rhodes.
03.00	*Patmos/Rodos*	Nissiros. Rhodes.
07.00	Hydrofoil	Kos. Rhodes.
07.00	*Nissos Kalimnos*	Kos. Nissiros. Tilos. Symi. Rhodes.
08.15	Hydrofoil	Leros (Agia Marina). Lipsi. Patmos. Samos (Pithagorio).
11.40	*Dodekanesos Express*	Leros (Agia Marina). Patmos. Samos (Pithagorio).
14.45	Hydrofoil	
15.30	*Dodekanesos Express*	Kos. Rhodes.
17.55	Hydrofoil	Kos.
21.45	*Aeolos Kenteris*	Kos. Rhodes.
22.45	*Marina/Rodanthi*	Piraeus.

⑤
01.45	*Marina/Rodanthi*	Kos. Rhodes. Kastelorizo.
02.30	*Patmos/Rodos*	Kos. Rhodes.
07.00	*Nissos Kalimnos*	Leros. Lipsi. Patmos. Arki. Agathonisi. Samos (Pithagorio).
08.15	Hydrofoil	Leros (Agia Marina). Lipsi. Patmos. Agathonisi. Samos (Pithagorio).
11.40	*Dodekanesos Express*	Leros (Agia Marina). Patmos. Lipsi.
12.20	Hydrofoil	Kos.
15.30	*Dodekanesos Express*	Kos. Rhodes.
17.45	Hydrofoil	Kos.

20.30	*Patmos/Rodos*	Leros. Patmos. Piraeus.
23.15	*Marina/Rodanthi*	Piraeus.

⑥

01.45	*Marina/Rodanthi*	Kos. Rhodes.
07.00	*Nissos Kalimnos*	Astipalea.
08.20	Hydrofoil	Leros (Agia Marina). Lipsi. Patmos. Samos (Pithagorio).
11.15	Hydrofoil	Kos.
11.40	*Dodekanesos Express*	Leros (Agia Marina). Lipsi. Patmos.
14.45	Hydrofoil	Leros (Agia Marina). Lipsi. Patmos. Agathonisi. Samos (Pithagorio).
15.30	*Dodekanesos Express*	Kos. Rhodes.
16.55	Hydrofoil	Kos.
17.00	Hydrofoil	Kos. Symi. Rhodes.
22.45	*Marina/Rodanthi*	Piraeus.

⑦

02.30	*Patmos/Rodos*	Kos. Rhodes.
03.00	*Diagoras*	Kos. Rhodes.
03.45	*Marina/Rodanthi*	Kos. Rhodes.
07.00	*Nissos Kalimnos*	Leros. Lipsi. Patmos. Arki. Agathonisi. Samos (Pithagorio).
11.40	*Dodekanesos Express*	Leros (Agia Marina). Patmos. Lipsi.
12.20	Hydrofoil	Kos.
14.45	Hydrofoil	Leros (Agia Marina). Lipsi. Patmos. Samos (Pithagorio).
15.30	*Dodekanesos Express*	Kos. Rhodes.
17.55	Hydrofoil	Kos.
20.30	*Patmos/Rodos*	Leros. Patmos. Piraeus.
21.45	*Aeolos Kenteris*	Kos. Rhodes.
22.45	*Marina/Rodanthi*	Leros. Patmos. Piraeus.

⑥

10.15	*Vitsentzos Kornaros*	Kassos. Crete (Sitia). Crete (Agios Nikolaos). Milos. Piraeus.
14.00	*Ierapetra L*	Karpathos (Diafani). Chalki. Rhodes.

⑦

10.15	*Ierapetra L*	Kassos. Crete (Sitia). Crete (Agios Nikolaos). Milos. Piraeus.

Karpathos (Diafani)

Dodecanese p. 342

① ⑤

15.00	*Vitsentzos Kornaros*	Chalki. Rhodes.

②

03.20	*Vitsentzos Kornaros*	Karpathos (Town). Kassos. Crete (Sitia).
15.30	*Vitsentzos Kornaros*	Chalki. Rhodes.

③

08.45	*Vitsentzos Kornaros*	Karpathos (Town). Kassos. Crete (Sitia). Crete (Agios Nikolaos). Milos. Piraeus.

⑥

08.45	*Vitsentzos Kornaros*	Karpathos (Town). Kassos. Crete (Sitia). Crete (Agios Nikolaos). Milos. Piraeus.
15.00	*Ierapetra L*	Chalki. Rhodes.

⑦

08.45	*Ierapetra L*	Karpathos (Town). Kassos. Crete (Sitia). Crete (Agios Nikolaos). Milos. Piraeus.

Karpathos

Dodecanese p. 342

① ⑤

14.00	*Vitsentzos Kornaros*	Karpathos (Diafani). Chalki. Rhodes.

②

04.30	*Vitsentzos Kornaros*	Kassos. Crete (Sitia).
14.30	*Vitsentzos Kornaros*	Karpathos (Diafani). Chalki. Rhodes.

③

10.15	*Vitsentzos Kornaros*	Kassos. Crete (Sitia). Crete (Agios Nikolaos). Milos. Piraeus.

Days per week:
2-3 =====

PIRAEUS

Rhodes

KARPATHOS (Town)

Kassos

Santorini

Crete (Sitia)

Crete (Agios Nikolaos/Iraklion)

Kassos

Dodecanese   p. 344

① ⑤
12.15	*Vitsentzos Kornaros*	Karpathos (Town). Karpathos (Diafani). Chalki. Rhodes.

②
06.10	*Vitsentzos Kornaros*	Crete (Sitia).
12.45	*Vitsentzos Kornaros*	Karpathos (Town). Karpathos (Diafani). Chalki. Rhodes.

③
12.00	*Vitsentzos Kornaros*	Crete (Sitia). Crete (Agios Nikolaos). Milos. Piraeus.

⑥
12.00	*Vitsentzos Kornaros*	Crete (Sitia). Crete (Agios Nikolaos). Milos. Piraeus.
12.15	*Ierapetra L*	Karpathos (Town). Karpathos (Diafani). Chalki. Rhodes.

⑦
12.00	*Ierapetra L*	Crete (Sitia). Crete (Agios Nikolaos). Milos. Piraeus.

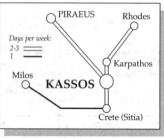

Kastelorizo/ Megisti

Dodecanese   p. 346

②
18.00	*Dimitroula*	Rhodes. Symi. Tilos. Nissiros. Kos. Kalimnos. Astipalea. Amorgos (Egiali). Amorgos (Katapola). Donoussa. Naxos. Paros. Syros. Piraeus.

③
16.00	*Dodekanesos Ex.*	Rhodes.

⑤
12.15	*Marina/Rodanthi*	Rhodes. Kos. Kalimnos. Piraeus.

⑦
03.45	*Dimitroula*	Rhodes. Kos. Samos (Vathi). Chios. Lesbos (Mytilini). Limnos. Alexandroupolis.

Kavala

Northern Aegean   p. 449

Ⓓ
07.50 09.30 12.00 14.00 16.00 18.00 19.30	ANET Line	Thassos (Skala Prinos).
07.00 12.30 14.00 18.30	Hydrofoil	Thassos (Town).
08.30 15.30	Hydrofoil	Thassos (Limenaria).

②
20.30	*Milena*	Limnos. Lesbos (Mytilini).
20.30	*Saos II*	Limnos. Agios Efstratios. Lavrio.

④
14.00	*Arsinoe*	Samothrace.
20.30	*Saos II*	Limnos. Agios Efstratios. Psara. Lavrio.

⑥
15.30	*Arsinoe*	Samothrace.
22.00	*Milena*	Limnos. Lesbos (Mytilini).

⑦
14.30	*Arsinoe*	Samothrace.
21.00	*Taxiarchis*	Limnos. Lesbos (Mytilini). Chios. Piraeus.

◯
00.00	*Nissos Limnos*	Limnos. Agios Efstratios. Psara. Rafina.

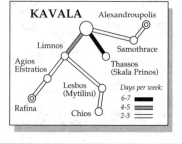

Kea

Cyclades West　p. 235

①
12.00	Mirina Express	Lavrio.
13.30	Macedon	Lavrio.
18.30	Mirina Express	Lavrio.

②
07.00	Macedon	Lavrio.
10.30	Mirina Express	Kythnos.
14.30	Mirina Express	Lavrio.
16.30	Macedon	Lavrio.
18.30	Mirina Express	Lavrio.

③
| 07.00 | Macedon | Lavrio. |
| 13.30 | Macedon | Lavrio. |

④
07.00	Macedon	Lavrio.
07.00	Mirina Express	Lavrio.
12.00	Mirina Express	Lavrio.
13.30	Macedon	Lavrio.

⑤
07.00	Macedon	Lavrio.
09.00	Mirina Express	Lavrio.
12.00	Mirina Express	Lavrio.
15.00	Macedon	Lavrio.
15.30	Mirina Express	Lavrio.
18.30	Macedon	Lavrio.
19.00	Mirina Express	Lavrio.

⑥
06.00	Mirina Express	Lavrio.
07.00	Macedon	Lavrio.
10.20	Mirina Express	Lavrio.
10.30	Macedon	Lavrio.
16.00	Mirina Express	Lavrio.
17.00	Macedon	Lavrio.
19.30	Mirina Express	Lavrio.

⑦
07.00	Macedon	Lavrio.
13.30	Macedon	Lavrio.
15.15	Mirina Express	Lavrio.
15.30	Mirina Express	Lavrio.
18.30	Macedon	Lavrio.
19.00	Mirina Express	Lavrio.
21.30	Macedon	Lavrio.
22.30	Mirina Express	Lavrio.

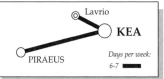

Kefalonia (Argostoli)

Ionian Line　p. 530

Ⓗ	Local	Kefalonia (Lixouri).
Ⓓ		
08.00		Kilini.
15.00		Kilini.

Kefalonia (Fiskardo)

Ionian Line　p. 530

Ⓓ		
10.30	Meganisi	Lefkada (Nidri).
12.00	Nidri	Ithaca (Frikes).
		Lefkada (Nidri).
17.00	Meganisi	Lefkada (Vathi).
19.00	Nidri	Lefkada (Nidri).

Kefalonia (Lixouri)

Ionian Line　p. 530

Ⓗ	Local	Kefalonia (Argostoli).
Ⓓ		
08.15		Kilini.
15.15		Kilini.

Kefalonia (Pessada)

Ionian Line　p. 530

Ⓓ		
07.45	Ionion Pelagos	Zakinthos (Skinaria).
17.30	Ionion Pelagos	Zakinthos (Skinaria).

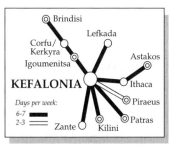

Kefalonia (Poros)

Ionian Line p. 530

Ⓓ
05.00 15.30 20.30
    Dimitiros Miras/Ionis/
    Proteus/Zakinthos I   Kilini.

Kefalonia (Sami)

Ionian Line
p. 530

International Services:

Ⓐ
11.30   HML Ferries   Patras.
12.00   HML Ferries   Patras.
19.30   HML Ferries   Igoumenitsa.
                        Corfu.
                        Brindisi.
21.00   Med Link Lines Brindisi.
23.45   HML Ferries   Paxi. Igoumenitsa.
                        Corfu. Brindisi.

Domestic Services:

Ⓓ
06.45   *Agia Marina*   Ithaca (Pisaetos).
08.35   *Kefalonia*   Patras.
08.45   *Agia Marina*   Ithaca (Pisaetos).
                          Astakos.
15.50   *Agia Marina*   Ithaca (Pisaetos).
17.50   *Kefalonia*   Patras.
23.30   *Kefalonia*   Ithaca.

Keramoti

Northern Aegean p. 450

Ⓓ
07.15 09.15 11.15 13.15 15.15 16.45
17.45 18.45 19.45 20.45 21.45 22.30
        ANET Line   Thassos (Town).

KERAMOTI

Days per week:
6-7 ▰

Thasssos (Town)

Kilini

Ionian Line p. 534

Ⓓ
10.15   *Dimitiros Miras/Ionis/*
         Proteus/Zakinthos I   Zakinthos.
11.00   *Proteus/Zakinthos I*   Kefalonia (Lixouri).
                                  Kefalonia (Argostoli).
14.30   *Dimitiros Miras/Ionis/*
         Proteus/Zakinthos I   Zakinthos.
17.30   *Dimitiros Miras/Ionis/*
         Proteus/Zakinthos I   Zakinthos.
18.30   *Dimitiros Miras/Ionis/*
         Proteus/Zakinthos I   Kefalonia (Poros).
20.15   *Dimitiros Miras/Ionis/*
         Proteus/Zakinthos I   Zakinthos.
22.30   *Dimitiros Miras/Ionis/*
         Proteus/Zakinthos I   Kefalonia (Poros).

Kefalonia (Poros)   *Days per week:*
(Argostoli)   6-7 ▰

Zakinthos
/Zante   **KILINI**

Kilitbahir

Turkey p. 567

Ⓓ x 6
00.00   TML   Çanakkale.

Kimolos

Cyclades West p. 239

Ⓓ
08.00 13.15 17.30
        Nissos Kimolos   Milos (Pollonia).

①
12.15   *Romilda*   Milos.
14.45   *Romilda*   Sifnos. Serifos. Paros.
                            Syros.
15.35   *Express Apollon* Folegandros. Sikinos. Ios.
                            Santorini.

②
14.05   *Express Apollon* Milos. Sifnos. Serifos.
                            Kythnos. Piraeus.
17.15   *Romilda*   Milos.
19.50   *Romilda*   Sifnos. Serifos. Paros.
                            Syros. Piraeus.

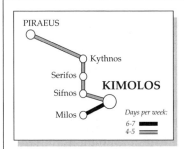

PIRAEUS

Kythnos

Serifos

Sifnos

KIMOLOS

Milos

Days per week:
6-7
4-5

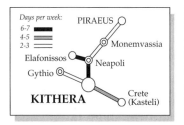

Days per week:
6-7
4-5
2-3

PIRAEUS

Monemvassia

Elafonissos

Neapoli

Gythio

KITHERA

Crete
(Kasteli)

22.15	*Express Pegasus*	Milos. Sifnos. Serifos. Piraeus.
③		
14.05	*Express Apollon*	Milos. Sifnos. Serifos. Kythnos. Piraeus.
④		
14.05	*Express Apollon*	Milos. Sifnos. Serifos. Kythnos. Piraeus.
23.15	*Daliana*	Milos. Sifnos. Serifos. Paros. Syros. Piraeus.
⑥		
00.30	*Express Apollon*	Piraeus.
14.00	*Express Pegasus*	Milos.
23.50	*Express Apollon*	Folegandros. Sikinos. Ios. Santorini.
⑦		
14.00	*Express Pegasus*	Milos.
20.35	*Express Apollon*	Milos. Sifnos. Serifos. Kythnos. Piraeus.

Kiparissi

Argo-Saronic p. 500

○		
00.00		Kithera (Agia Pelagia). Antikithera. Crete (Kasteli).

🌊 *Flying Dolphins* include:
ⒹⓍ1   Piraeus.

Kithera (Agia Pelagia)

Argo-Saronic
p. 500

⑥		
19.45	*Mirtidiotissa*	Antikithera. Crete (Kasteli).
23.30	*Mirtidiotissa*	Gythio.

① ③		
09.30	*Nissos Kithera*	Gythio.
① ② ④ ⑦		
19.45	*Mirtidiotissa*	Crete (Kasteli)
⑦		
03.45	*Mirtidiotissa*	Crete (Kasteli).
○		
01.30	*Mirtidiotissa*	Piraeus.
14.30	Hydrofoil	Monemvassia. Gerakas. Kiparissi. Spetses. Hydra. Piraeus.

Kos

Dodecanese
p. 350

Ⓓ		
08.00	Hydrofoil	Rhodes.
10.00	Tour Boat	Kalimnos.
10.00	Tour Boat	Pserimos.
10.00	Tour Boat	Nissiros.
16.00	*Bodrum Princess*	Bodrum.
18.00	Hydrofoil	Rhodes.
19.15	Hydrofoil	Kalimnos.
①		
04.30	*Patmos/Rodos*	Rhodes.
05.30	*Marina/Rodanthi*	Rhodes.
08.15	Hydrofoil	Leros (Agia Marina). Lipsi. Patmos.
08.30	*Nissos Kalimnos*	Nissiros. Tilos. Symi. Rhodes.
10.00	*Aeolos Kenteris*	Piraeus.
10.15	Hydrofoil	Leros (Agia Marina). Patmos. Samos (Pithagorio).
10.50	*Dodekanesos Ex.*	Kalimnos. Leros (Agia Marina).
16.20	*Dodekanesos Ex.*	Rhodes.
18.00	Hydrofoil	Rhodes.
18.45	*Patmos/Rodos*	Kalimnos. Leros. Patmos. Piraeus.
19.15	Hydrofoil	Kalimnos.
22.00	*Aeolos Kenteris*	Rhodes.

②

02.15	*Nissos Kalimnos*	Kalimnos.
03.30	*Marina/Rodanthi*	Rhodes.
04.10	*Blue Star 1*	Rhodes.
04.30	*Patmos/Rodos*	Tilos. Symi. Rhodes.
07.30	Hydrofoil	Kalimnos. Leros (Agia Marina). Lipsi. Patmos. Samos (Pithagorio).
08.00	Hydrofoil	Rhodes.
08.15	*Dimitroula*	Rhodes. Kastelorizo.
10.50	*Dodekanesos Ex.*	Kalimnos. Leros (Agia Marina). Patmos. Lipsi.
16.20	*Dodekanesos Ex.*	Rhodes.
18.00	Hydrofoil	Rhodes.
18.45	*Patmos/Rodos*	Kalimnos. Leros. Patmos. Piraeus.
19.15	Hydrofoil	Kalimnos.
21.30	*Marina/Rodanthi*	Kalimnos. Piraeus.
22.55	*Blue Star 1*	Mykonos. Piraeus.

③

04.15	*Marina/Rodanthi*	Rhodes.
04.30	*Diagoras*	Rhodes.
04.30	*Patmos/Rodos*	Rhodes.
05.45	*Dimitroula*	Kalimnos. Astipalea. Amorgos (Egiali). Amorgos (Katapola). Donoussa. Naxos. Paros. Syros. Piraeus.
08.00	Hydrofoil	Rhodes.
10.15	Hydrofoil	Leros (Agia Marina). Patmos. Samos (Pithagorio).
18.00	Hydrofoil	Rhodes.
18.30	*Marina/Rodanthi*	Kalimnos. Astipalea. Amorgos (Katapola). Piraeus.
18.45	*Patmos/Rodos*	Kalimnos. Leros. Patmos. Piraeus.
21.50	*Diagoras*	Piraeus.

④

03.30	*Marina/Rodanthi*	Rhodes.
05.40	*Blue Star 1*	Rhodes.
07.30	Hydrofoil	Kalimnos. Leros (Agia Marina). Lipsi. Patmos. Samos (Pithagorio).
08.00	Hydrofoil	Rhodes.
08.15	Hydrofoil	Leros (Agia Marina). Patmos. Agathonisi. Samos (Pithagorio).
08.30	*Nissos Kalimnos*	Nissiros. Tilos. Symi. Rhodes.
10.50	*Dodekanesos Ex.*	Kalimnos. Leros (Agia Marina).
14.40	*Patmos/Rodos*	Samos (Vathi). Thessalonika.
16.20	*Dodekanesos Ex.*	Rhodes.
18.00	Hydrofoil	Rhodes.
19.15	Hydrofoil	Kalimnos.
21.30	*Marina/Rodanthi*	Kalimnos. Piraeus.
22.30	*Aeolos Kenteris*	Rhodes.
22.55	*Blue Star 1*	Leros. Patmos. Syros. Piraeus.

⑤

02.15	*Nissos Kalimnos*	Kalimnos.
03.30	*Marina/Rodanthi*	Rhodes. Kastelorizo.
04.30	*Diagoras*	Nissiros. Rhodes.
04.30	*Patmos/Rodos*	Rhodes.
07.30	Hydrofoil	Kalimnos. Leros (Agia Marina). Lipsi. Patmos. Agathonisi. Samos (Pithagorio).
08.00	Hydrofoil	Rhodes. Symi.
10.50	*Dodekanesos Ex.*	Kalimnos. Leros (Agia Marina). Patmos. Lipsi.
16.20	*Dodekanesos Ex.*	Rhodes.
18.00	Hydrofoil	Rhodes.
18.45	*Patmos/Rodos*	Kalimnos. Leros. Patmos. Piraeus.
19.15	Hydrofoil	Kalimnos.
20.00	*Diagoras*	Piraeus.
22.00	*Marina/Rodanthi*	Kalimnos. Piraeus.

⑥

03.30	*Marina/Rodanthi*	Rhodes.
04.20	*Blue Star 1*	Rhodes.
07.30	Hydrofoil	Kalimnos. Leros (Agia Marina). Lipsi. Patmos. Samos (Pithagorio).
08.00	Hydrofoil	Rhodes. Symi.
10.30	*Patmos/Rodos*	Rhodes.
10.50	*Dodekanesos Ex.*	Kalimnos. Leros (Agia Marina). Lipsi. Patmos.
12.50	*Blue Star 1*	Amorgos (Katapola). Piraeus.
15.30	*Dimitroula*	Nissiros. Tilos. Symi. Rhodes. Kastelorizo.
16.30	*Dodekanesos Ex.*	Rhodes.
18.00	Hydrofoil	Symi. Rhodes.
19.15	Hydrofoil	Kalimnos.
21.30	*Marina/Rodanthi*	Kalimnos. Piraeus.

PIRAEUS

Days per week:
6-7
4-5
2-3

Patmos
Lipsi
Leros
Kalimnos
Pserimos
KOS
Bodrum
Symi
Nissiros
Tilos
Rhodes
Kastelorizo

⑦
04.30	*Diagoras*	Rhodes.
04.30	*Patmos/Rodos*	Rhodes.
05.00	*Marina/Rodanthi*	Rhodes.
07.30	Hydrofoil	Kalimnos. Leros (Agia Marina). Lipsi. Patmos. Samos (Pithagorio).
08.00	Hydrofoil	Rhodes.
08.15	Hydrofoil	Leros (Agia Marina). Patmos. Samos (Pithagorio).
09.50	*Blue Star 1*	Rhodes.
10.15	Hydrofoil	Nissiros.
10.50	*Dodekanesos Ex.*	Kalimnos. Leros (Agia Marina). Patmos. Lipsi.
13.30	*Dimitroula*	Samos (Vathi). Chios. Lesbos (Mytilini). Limnos. Alexandroupolis.
16.20	*Dodekanesos Ex.*	Rhodes.
18.00	Hydrofoil	Rhodes.
18.45	*Patmos/Rodos*	Kalimnos. Leros. Patmos. Piraeus.
19.15	Hydrofoil	Kalimnos.
21.25	*Blue Star 1*	Leros. Patmos. Syros. Piraeus.
21.30	*Marina/Rodanthi*	Kalimnos. Leros. Patmos. Piraeus.
21.50	*Diagoras*	Piraeus.
22.30	*Aeolos Kenteris*	Rhodes.

Kos (Kardamena)

Dodecanese
p. 352

ⓓ
| 09.00 | *Nissiros Express* | Nissiros. |

Kos (Mastihari)

Dodecanese
p. 354

ⓓ
09.00   16.30   22.00
| | *Olympios Apollon/Atromitos* | Kalimnos. |

Kosta

Argo-Saronic   p. 510

ⓓ
| 10.30   13.30   17.00 | *Alexandros M* | Spetses. |

① ② ③ ④ ⑤
| 06.50   08.00   18.30 | *Alexandros M* | Spetses. |

Koufonissia

Cyclades East
p. 283

①
| 09.30 | *Express Skopelitis* | Schinoussa. Iraklia. Naxos. |
| 17.30 | *Express Skopelitis* | Donoussa. Amorgos (Egiali). Amorgos (Katapola). |

②
00.40	*Blue Star Naxos*	Amorgos (Katapola).
07.00	*Express Skopelitis*	Schinoussa. Iraklia. Paros (Piso Livadi). Naxos.
07.15	*Blue Star Naxos*	Schinoussa. Iraklia. Naxos. Paros. Piraeus.
17.45	*Express Skopelitis*	Amorgos (Katapola).

③
| 09.30 | *Express Skopelitis* | Schinoussa. Iraklia. Naxos. |
| 17.30 | *Express Skopelitis* | Donoussa. Amorgos (Egiali). Amorgos (Katapola). |

④
00.40	*Blue Star Naxos*	Amorgos (Katapola).
07.00	*Express Skopelitis*	Schinoussa. Iraklia. Paros (Piso Livadi). Naxos.
07.15	*Blue Star Naxos*	Schinoussa. Iraklia. Naxos. Paros. Piraeus.
17.45	*Express Skopelitis*	Amorgos (Katapola).

⑤
| 09.30 | *Express Skopelitis* | Schinoussa. Iraklia. Naxos. |
| 17.30 | *Express Skopelitis* | Donoussa. Amorgos (Egiali). Amorgos (Katapola). |

⑥
00.20	*Blue Star Naxos*	Amorgos (Katapola).
07.00	*Express Skopelitis*	Schinoussa. Iraklia. Paros (Piso Livadi). Naxos.
07.15	*Blue Star Naxos*	Naxos. Paros. Piraeus.
15.20	*Express Skopelitis*	Amorgos (Katapola).

⑦
00.45	*Panagia Ekatontapiliani*	Amorgos (Katapola).
09.30	*Romilda*	Amorgos (Katapola). Amorgos (Egiali). Donoussa.
13.30	*Panagia Ekatontapiliani*	Naxos. Paros. Piraeus.

Kuşadası

Turkey p. 567

Ⓓ
| 08.00 | *Fari Kaptain/Sultan I* | Samos (Vathi). |
| 17.00 | *Kapetan Giorgis* | Samos (Vathi). |

Kythnos

Cyclades West p. 242

①
01.45	*Express Apollon*	Piraeus.
10.45	*Express Apollon*	Serifos. Sifnos. Milos. Kimolos. Folegandros. Sikinos. Ios. Santorini.
12.05	*Flying Cat 3*	Syros. Mykonos. Tinos. Rafina.
19.05	*Express Pegasus*	Serifos. Sifnos. Milos.
20.30	*Flying Cat 3*	Lavrio.

②
12.05	*Flying Cat 3*	Syros. Mykonos. Tinos. Rafina.
12.15	*Mirina Express*	Kea. Lavrio.
19.05	*Express Pegasus*	Serifos. Sifnos. Kimolos. Milos.
19.15	*Express Apollon*	Piraeus.

③
10.45	*Express Apollon*	Serifos. Sifnos. Kimolos. Milos.
19.15	*Express Apollon*	Piraeus.
20.30	*Flying Cat 3*	Lavrio.

④
10.45	*Express Apollon*	Serifos. Sifnos. Kimolos. Milos.
12.05	*Flying Cat 3*	Syros. Mykonos. Tinos. Rafina.
19.05	*Express Pegasus*	Serifos. Sifnos. Milos.
19.15	*Express Apollon*	Piraeus.
20.30	*Flying Cat 3*	Lavrio.

⑤
| 12.05 | *Flying Cat 3* | Syros. Mykonos. Tinos. Rafina. |
| 20.30 | *Flying Cat 3* | Lavrio. |

⑥
10.50	*Express Pegasus*	Serifos. Sifnos. Kimolos. Milos.
12.05	*Flying Cat 3*	Syros. Mykonos. Tinos. Rafina.
19.00	*Express Apollon*	Serifos. Sifnos. Milos. Kimolos. Folegandros. Sikinos. Ios. Santorini.
19.00	*Express Pegasus*	Piraeus.
20.00	*Express Pegasus*	Serifos. Sifnos.
20.30	*Flying Cat 3*	Lavrio.
23.30	*Express Pegasus*	Piraeus.

⑦
10.50	*Express Pegasus*	Serifos. Sifnos. Kimolos. Milos.
12.05	*Flying Cat 3*	Syros. Mykonos. Tinos. Rafina.
13.00	*Mirina Express*	Kea. Lavrio.
19.00	*Express Pegasus*	Piraeus.
20.30	*Flying Cat 3*	Lavrio.

Lavrio

Athens & Piraeus p. 120

Ⓓ
| 09.00 | *Macedon/ Mirina Express* | Kea. |
| 19.00 | *Macedon/ Mirina Express* | Kea. |

①
11.15	*Flying Cat 3*	Kythnos. Syros. Mykonos. Tinos. Rafina.
15.30	*Mirina Express*	Kea.
20.00	*Saos II*	Agios Efstratios. Limnos. Kavala.

②
09.00	*Mirina Express*	Kea. Kythnos.
11.15	*Flying Cat 3*	Kythnos. Syros. Mykonos. Tinos. Rafina.
16.30	*Mirina Express*	Kea.

③
| 19.30 | *Mirina Express* | Kea. |
| 20.00 | *Saos II* | Psara. Agios Efstratios. Limnos. Kavala. |

④
| 10.00 | *Mirina Express* | Kea. |
| 11.15 | *Flying Cat 3* | Kythnos. Syros. Mykonos. Tinos. Rafina. |

⑤
10.00	*Mirina Express*	Kea.
11.15	*Flying Cat 3*	Kythnos. Syros. Mykonos. Tinos. Rafina.
14.00	*Mirina Express*	Kea.

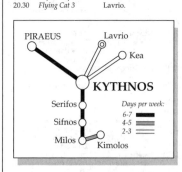

| 20.00 | *Saos II* | Agios Efstratios. Limnos. Samothrace. Alexandroupolis. |
| 21.30 | *Mirina Express* | Kea. |

⑥
11.15	*Flying Cat 3*	Kythnos. Syros. Mykonos. Tinos. Rafina.
12.00	*Macedon*	Kea.
18.00	*Mirina Express*	Kea.

⑦
09.00	*Mirina Express*	Kythnos. Kea.
11.15	*Flying Cat 3*	Kythnos. Syros. Mykonos. Tinos. Rafina.
20.30	*Mirina Express*	Kea.

Lefkada (Nidri)

Ionian Line   p. 534

Ⓓ
x 6: 07.20 11.45 13.15
17.00 18.30 20.00
	Meganisi	Meganisi (Vathi). Meganisi (Spartohori).
08.30	*Meganisi*	Kefalonia (Fiskardo).
10.00	*Nidri*	Kefalonia (Fiskardo). Ithaca (Frikes).
15.30	*Meganisi*	Kefalonia (Fiskardo).
16.30	*Nidri*	Ithaca (Frikes). Kefalonia (Fiskardo).

Lefkada (Vassiliki)

Ionian Line   p. 534

○
01.00	HML Ferries	Brindisi.
11.10	*Agia Marina*	Kefalonia (Fiskardo). Ithaca (Pisaetos). Kefalonia (Sami).
12.45	HML Ferries	Corfu.
17.00	*Agia Marina*	Kefalonia (Fiskardo). Ithaca (Pisaetos). Kefalonia (Sami).

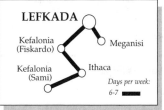

LEFKADA
Kefalonia (Fiskardo)
Meganisi
Kefalonia (Sami)
Ithaca
Days per week:
6-7

Leros

Dodecanese p. 360

①
00.50	*Patmos/Rodos*	Kalimnos. Kos. Rhodes.
03.00	*Marina/Rodanthi*	Kalimnos. Kos. Rhodes.
21.30	*Patmos/Rodos*	Patmos. Piraeus.

②
| 00.50 | *Patmos/Rodos* | Kalimnos. Kos. Tilos. Symi. Rhodes. |
| 21.30 | *Patmos/Rodos* | Patmos. Piraeus. |

③
00.50	*Patmos/Rodos*	Kalimnos. Kos. Rhodes.
08.45	*Nissos Kalimnos*	Lipsi. Patmos. Arki. Agathonisi. Samos (Pithagorio).
20.30	*Nissos Kalimnos*	Kalimnos.
21.30	*Patmos/Rodos*	Patmos. Piraeus.

④
| 04.00 | *Blue Star 1* | Kos. Rhodes. |

⑤
00.35	*Blue Star 1*	Patmos. Syros. Piraeus.
00.50	*Patmos/Rodos*	Kalimnos. Kos. Rhodes.
08.45	*Nissos Kalimnos*	Lipsi. Patmos. Arki. Agathonisi. Samos (Pithagorio).
20.30	*Nissos Kalimnos*	Kalimnos.
21.30	*Patmos/Rodos*	Patmos. Piraeus.

⑦
00.50	*Patmos/Rodos*	Kalimnos. Kos. Rhodes.
02.00	*Diagoras*	Kalimnos. Kos. Rhodes.
02.45	*Marina/Rodanthi*	Kalimnos. Kos. Rhodes.
08.10	*Blue Star 1*	Kos. Rhodes.
08.45	*Nissos Kalimnos*	Lipsi. Patmos. Arki. Agathonisi. Samos (Pithagorio).
20.30	*Nissos Kalimnos*	Kalimnos.
21.30	*Patmos/Rodos*	Patmos. Piraeus.
23.05	*Blue Star 1*	Patmos. Syros. Piraeus.
23.45	*Marina/Rodanthi*	Patmos. Piraeus.

Leros (Agia Marina)

Dodecanese p. 362

① ④
09.10	Hydrofoil	Patmos. Fourni. Ikaria (Agios Kyrikos). Samos (Pithagorio).
09.30	Hydrofoil	Lipsi. Patmos.
09.45	Hydrofoil	Kalimnos. Kos.
11.25	Hydrofoil	Patmos. Samos (Pithagorio).
14.30	*Dodekanesos Ex.*	Kalimnos. Kos. Rhodes.

| 15.40 | Hydrofoil | Patmos. Samos (Pithagorio). Samos (Vathi). |
| 16.30 | Hydrofoil | Kos. Kalimnos. |

② ⑤ ⑦

09.10	Hydrofoil	Lipsi. Patmos. Samos (Pithagorio).
09.25	Hydrofoil	Lipsi. Patmos. Samos (Pithagorio).
09.55	Hydrofoil	Kalimnos. Kos.
12.40	*Dodekanesos Express*	Patmos. Lipsi.
14.30	*Dodekanesos Express*	Kalimnos. Kos. Rhodes.
15.40	Hydrofoil	Lipsi. Patmos. Samos (Pithagorio). Samos (Vathi).
16.30	Hydrofoil	Kos. Kalimnos.
17.00	Hydrofoil	Kalimnos. Kos.

③

09.10	Hydrofoil	Lipsi. Patmos. Samos (Pithagorio).
11.25	Hydrofoil	Patmos. Samos (Pithagorio).
11.25	Hydrofoil	Kalimnos. Kos.
15.40	Hydrofoil	Lipsi. Patmos. Ikaria (Agios Kyrikos). Fourni. Samos (Pithagorio). Samos (Vathi).
16.30	Hydrofoil	Kalimnos. Kos.
16.50	Hydrofoil	Kos. Rhodes.

⑥

09.20	Hydrofoil	Lipsi. Patmos. Samos (Pithagorio).
09.25	Hydrofoil	Lipsi. Patmos. Samos (Pithagorio).
10.20	Hydrofoil	Kalimnos. Kos.
12.40	*Dodekanesos Express*	Lipsi. Patmos.

14.30	*Dodekanesos Express*	Kalimnos. Kos. Rhodes.
15.40	Hydrofoil	Lipsi. Patmos. Agathonisi. Samos (Pithagorio). Samos (Vathi).
16.00	Hydrofoil	Kalimnos. Kos.
16.30	Hydrofoil	Kos. Kalimnos.

Lesbos (Mytilini)

Eastern Line
p. 416

Ⓓ

| 08.00 | *Jale/Jalehan* | Ayvalık. |

①

01.00	*Dimitroula*	Limnos. Alexandroupolis.
12.00	*Taxiarchis*	Chios. Piraeus.
18.00	*Mytilene*	Chios. Piraeus.
21.30	*Dimitroula*	Chios. Samos (Vathi). Kos. Rhodes. Kastelorizo.

②

09.00	*Milena*	Limnos. Kavala.
17.00	*Taxiarchis*	Chios. Samos (Vathi). Piraeus.
18.00	*Theofilos*	Chios. Piraeus.

③

00.45	*Aeolos Kenteris*	Limnos. Thessalonika.
08.00	*Milena*	Limnos. Skopelos. Skiathos. Volos.
17.00	*Aeolos Kenteris*	Chios. Piraeus.
18.00	*Mytilene*	Chios. Piraeus.

④

| 18.00 | *Theofilos* | Chios. Piraeus. |

⑤

| 08.00 | *Taxiarchis* | Piraeus. |
| 18.00 | *Mytilene* | Chios. Piraeus. |

⑥

08.30	*Aeolos Kenteris*	Chios. Piraeus.
10.00	*Theofilos*	Limnos. Thessalonika.
12.00	*Milena*	Limnos. Kavala.

⑦

07.30	*Taxiarchis*	Limnos. Kavala.
08.30	*Aeolos Kenteris*	Chios. Piraeus.
09.00	*Mytilene*	Piraeus.
10.00	*Milena*	Chios. Mykonos. Tinos. Syros. Piraeus.
18.00	*Theofilos*	Chios. Piraeus.

Lesbos (Sigri)

○

| 09.00 | | Limnos. Agios Efstratios. |
| 21.00 | | Psara. Rafina. |

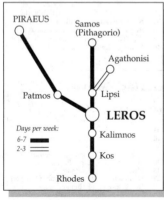

PIRAEUS

Samos (Pithagorio)

Agathonisi

Patmos

Lipsi

LEROS

Kalimnos

Kos

Rhodes

Days per week:
6-7
2-3

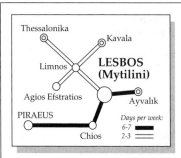

Thessalonika
Kavala
Limnos
LESBOS (Mytilini)
Agios Efstratios
Ayvalık
PIRAEUS
Chios
Days per week:
6-7
2-3

Limnos

Northern Aegean
p. 451

①
06.00	*Dimitroula*	Alexandroupolis.
06.00	*Taxiarchis*	Lesbos (Mytilini). Chios. Piraeus.
16.00	*Dimitroula*	Lesbos (Mytilini). Chios. Samos (Vathi). Kos. Rhodes. Kastelorizo.

②
06.00	*Saos II*	Kavala.
14.45	*Milena*	Kavala.

③
01.00	*Milena*	Limnos. Lesbos (Mytilini).
03.00	*Saos II*	Agios Efstratios. Lavrio.
03.30	*Aeolos Kenteris*	Thessalonika.
13.15	*Aeolos Kenteris*	Lesbos (Mytilini). Chios. Piraeus.
13.45	*Milena*	Skopelos. Skiathos. Volos.

④
12.30	*Saos II*	Kavala.

⑤
03.00	*Saos II*	Agios Efstratios. Psara. Lavrio.

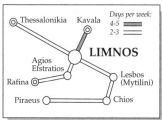

Thessalonikia
Kavala
Days per week:
4-5
2-3
LIMNOS
Agios Efstratios
Rafina
Lesbos (Mytilini)
Piraeus
Chios

⑥
03.35	*Milena*	Lesbos (Mytilini).
06.00	*Saos II*	Samothrace. Alexandroupolis.
15.30	*Theofilos*	Thessalonika.
16.30	*Milena*	Kavala.

⑦
02.15	*Milena*	Lesbos (Mytilini).
05.00	*Saos II*	Agios Efstratios. Lavrio.
10.00	*Theofilos*	Lesbos (Mytilini). Chios. Piraeus.
15.00	*Taxiarchis*	Kavala.

Lipsi

Dodecanese   p. 362

ⓓ
08.00	*Captain Makis*	Leros.
16.00	*Megalo./Pat. Ex.*	Patmos.

①
10.00	Hydrofoil	Patmos. Samos (Pithagorio).
16.00	Hydrofoil	Leros (Agia Marina). Kos. Kalimnos.

②
09.25	Hydrofoil	Leros (Agia Marina). Kalimnos. Kos.
09.40	Hydrofoil	Patmos. Samos (Pithagorio).
10.30	Miniotis Ferries	Patmos.
13.00	Miniotis Ferries	Arki. Agathonisi. Samos (Pithagorio).
14.00	*Dodekanesos Ex.*	Leros (Agia Marina). Kalimnos. Kos. Rhodes.
16.00	Hydrofoil	Leros (Agia Marina). Kos. Kalimnos.
16.05	Hydrofoil	Patmos. Samos (Pithagorio). Samos (Vathi).
16.30	Hydrofoil	Leros (Agia Marina). Kalimnos. Kos.

③
09.40	Hydrofoil	Patmos. Samos (Pithagorio).
10.00	*Nissos Kalimnos*	Patmos. Arki. Agathonisi. Samos (Pithagorio).
10.50	*Daliana*	Samos (Vathi). Samos (Karlovassi). Fourni. Ikaria (Agios Kyrikos). Mykonos. Syros. Piraeus.
10.55	Hydrofoil	Leros (Agia Marina). Kalimnos. Kos.
16.05	Hydrofoil	Patmos. Ikaria (Agios Kyrikos). Fourni. Samos (Pithagorio).
19.30	*Nissos Kalimnos*	Leros. Kalimnos.

④
09.25	Hydrofoil	Leros (Agia Marina). Kalimnos. Kos.

09.40	Hydrofoil	Patmos. Samos (Pithagorio).
16.05	Hydrofoil	Patmos. Samos (Pithagorio).
		Samos (Vathi).
16.30	Hydrofoil	Leros (Agia Marina).
		Kalimnos. Kos.

⑤
10.00	Hydrofoil	Patmos. Samos (Pithagorio).
10.00	*Nissos Kalimnos*	Patmos. Arki. Agathonisi.
		Samos (Pithagorio).
10.55	Hydrofoil	Leros (Agia Marina).
		Kalimnos. Kos.
14.00	*Dodekanesos Ex.*	Leros (Agia Marina).
		Kalimnos. Kos. Rhodes.
16.00	Hydrofoil	Leros (Agia Marina). Kos.
		Kalimnos.
19.30	*Nissos Kalimnos*	Leros. Kalimnos.

⑥
09.50	Hydrofoil	Patmos. Samos (Pithagorio).
09.55	Hydrofoil	Leros (Agia Marina).
		Kalimnos. Kos.
10.00	Hydrofoil	Patmos. Samos (Pithagorio).
10.50	*Daliana*	Samos (Vathi).
		Samos (Karlovassi). Fourni.
		Ikaria (Agios Kyrikos).
		Mykonos. Syros. Piraeus.
13.10	*Dodekanesos Ex.*	Patmos. Leros (Agia Marina).
		Kalimnos. Kos. Rhodes.
16.00	Hydrofoil	Leros (Agia Marina). Kos.
		Kalimnos.

⑦
09.50	Hydrofoil	Patmos. Samos (Pithagorio).
10.00	*Nissos Kalimnos*	Patmos. Arki. Agathonisi.
		Samos (Pithagorio).
10.55	Hydrofoil	Leros (Agia Marina).
		Kalimnos. Kos.
14.00	*Dodekanesos Ex.*	Leros (Agia Marina).
		Kalimnos. Kos. Rhodes.
16.30	Hydrofoil	Leros (Agia Marina).
		Kalimnos. Kos.
19.30	*Nissos Kalimnos*	Leros. Kalimnos.

Marmara

Turkey p. 567

Ⓓ x 4
| 00.00 | Deniz Otobusleri | Avşa. |
| 00.00 | Deniz Otobusleri | İstanbul. |

⑤ ⑦
| 00.00 | TML | Avşa. Erdek. |
| 00.00 | TML | Tekirdağ. |

Marmaris

Turkey p. 568

Ⓓ
| 09.00 | 16.00 | *Yesil Marmaris* | Rhodes. |

Meganisi (Spartochori)

Ionian Line
p. 537

Ⓓ
| 08.00 | 14.00 | *Meganisi* | Lefkada (Nidri). |

Meganisi (Vathi)

Ionian Line p. 537

Ⓓ
07.45	*Meganisi*	Meganisi (Spartochori).
		Lefkada (Nidri).
13.45	*Meganisi*	Meganisi (Spartochori).
		Lefkada (Nidri).
17.00	*Meganisi*	Lefkada (Vathi).

Mersin

Turkey p. 557

① ③ ⑤
| 22.00 | *Yeşilada* | Famagusta. |

Methana

Argo-Saronic p. 503

Ⓓ
06.30	Saronikos Ferries	Aegina. Piraeus.
09.40	*Eftichia*	Poros.
09.55	*Apollon Hellas*	Poros. Hydra. Spetses.
		Porto Helio.
10.00	*Saronikos*	Poros. Hydra. Ermioni.
		Spetses.
10.25	*Georgios 2*	Poros. Spetses.
		Porto Helio.
11.20	*Eftichia*	Aegina. Piraeus.
11.20	Saronikos Ferries	Aegina. Piraeus.
14.00	Saronikos Ferries	Aegina. Piraeus.
16.45	*Apollon Hellas*	Aegina. Piraeus.
17.10	*Saronikos*	Aegina. Piraeus.
17.25	*Georgios 2*	Aegina. Piraeus.
18.20	*Eftichia*	Poros.
19.30	*Eftichia*	Aegina. Piraeus.

⑤
| 18.55 | Saronikos Ferries | Aegina. Piraeus. |

⑦
| 18.00 | Saronikos Ferries | Aegina. Piraeus. |

Milos

Cyclades West p. 245

①
01.15	*Ierapetra L*	Piraeus.
11.15	*Jet One*	Kythnos. Piraeus.
11.30	*Highspeed 2/3*	Sifnos. Serifos. Piraeus.
13.30	*Romilda*	Kimolos. Sifnos. Serifos. Paros. Syros.
14.30	*Express Apollon*	Kimolos. Folegandros. Sikinos. Ios. Santorini.
19.20	*Jet One*	Ios. Santorini. Amorgos (Katapola).
23.00	*Express Pegasus*	Sifnos. Serifos. Piraeus.
24.00	*Ierapetra L*	Crete (Agios Nikolaos). Crete (Sitia).

②
10.00	*Jet One*	Sifnos. Piraeus.
11.30	*Highspeed 2/3*	Sifnos. Serifos. Piraeus.
15.30	*Express Apollon*	Sifnos. Serifos. Kythnos. Piraeus.
18.40	*Romilda*	Kimolos. Sifnos. Serifos. Paros. Syros. Piraeus.
19.35	*Jet One*	Ios. Santorini. Crete (Iraklion).
23.30	*Express Pegasus*	Sifnos. Serifos. Piraeus.

③
15.30	*Express Apollon*	Sifnos. Serifos. Kythnos. Piraeus.
19.35	*Jet One*	Folegandros. Ios. Santorini. Amorgos (Katapola).
24.00	*Ierapetra L*	Crete (Agios Nikolaos). Crete (Sitia).

④
01.15	*Vitsentzos Kornaros*	Piraeus.
11.05	*Jet One*	Piraeus.
11.30	*Highspeed 2/3*	Sifnos. Serifos. Piraeus.
15.30	*Express Apollon*	Sifnos. Serifos. Kythnos. Piraeus.
23.00	*Express Pegasus*	Sifnos. Serifos. Piraeus.
24.00	*Vitsentzos Kornaros*	Crete (Agios Nikolaos). Crete (Sitia). Kassos. Karpathos (Town). Karpathos (Diafani). Chalki. Rhodes.

⑤
00.30	*Daliana*	Sifnos. Serifos. Paros. Syros. Piraeus.
11.15	*Jet One*	Piraeus.
11.30	*Highspeed 2/3*	Sifnos. Serifos. Piraeus.
19.00	*Jet One*	Ios. Santorini. Crete (Iraklion).
23.30	*Express Apollon*	Kimolos. Piraeus.
24.00	*Ierapetra L*	Crete (Agios Nikolaos). Crete (Sitia). Kassos. Karpathos (Town). Karpathos (Diafani). Chalki. Rhodes.

PIRAEUS

Kythnos

Serifos

Sifnos

Kimolos Folegandros

Sikinos

MILOS

Santorini

Rhodes

Days per week:
6-7
2-3
1

Karpathos

Kassos

Crete (Ag. Nikolaos)   Crete (Sitia)

⑥
11.30	*Highspeed 2/3*	Sifnos. Serifos. Piraeus.
12.00	*Jet One*	Sifnos. Kythnos. Piraeus.
15.30	*Express Pegasus*	Sifnos. Serifos. Kythnos. Piraeus.
22.45	*Express Apollon*	Kimolos. Folegandros. Sikinos. Ios. Santorini.

⑦
01.15	*Vitsentzos Kornaros*	Piraeus.
11.30	*Highspeed 2/3*	Sifnos. Serifos. Piraeus.
15.30	*Express Pegasus*	Sifnos. Serifos. Kythnos. Piraeus.
16.45	*Jet One*	Folegandros. Santorini. Ios.
21.35	*Jet One*	Piraeus.
22.00	*Express Apollon*	Sifnos. Serifos. Kythnos. Piraeus.
24.00	*Vitsentzos Kornaros*	Crete (Agios Nikolaos). Crete (Sitia). Karpathos (Town). Karpathos (Diafani). Chalki. Rhodes.

Milos (Pollonia)

Ⓓ
| 09.00 | 14.15 | 18.30 |
| | *Nissos Kimolos* | Kimolos. |

Monemvassia

Argo-Saronic p. 503

② ③ ④ ⑤

06.00	*Flying Dolphin*	Spetses. Piraeus.

① ⑤ ⑦

13.15	*Flying Dolphin*	Spetses. Piraeus.
16.05	*Flying Dolphin*	Spetses. Piraeus.

① ⑥ ⑦

10.40	*Flying Dolphin*	Neapoli. Kithera.

⑤

23.00	*Myrtidiotissa*	Kithera (Agia Pelagia). Antikithera. Crete (Kasteli).

Mykonos

Cyclades North p. 209

Ⓓ ex ①

08.30	*Delos Express*	Delos.
09.00	*Orca / Hera*	Delos.
09.30	*Delos Express*	Delos.
09.30	*Niki*	Delos.
09.55	*Delos Express*	Delos.
10.15	*Orca / Hera*	Delos.
10.45	*Niki*	Delos.
11.00	*Delos Express*	Delos.
11.40	*Orca / Hera*	Delos.

Ⓓ

12.45	*Blue Star Ithaki*	Paros. Naxos.
16.45	*Blue Star Ithaki*	Tinos. Syros. Piraeus.
20.30	*Highspeed 2/3*	Tinos. Rafina.

①

08.30	*Express Penelope*	Tinos. Andros. Rafina.
09.50	*Sea Jet 2*	Paros.
10.30	*Highspeed 2/3*	Tinos. Syros. Piraeus.
11.00	*Highspeed 4*	Naxos. Paros. Piraeus.
11.50	*Sea Jet 2*	Tinos. Rafina.
12.00	*Aeolos Express II*	Tinos. Syros. Piraeus.
12.00	*Aqua Jewel*	Paros.
13.00	*Express Athina*	Tinos. Andros. Rafina.
13.30	*Superferry II*	Tinos. Andros. Rafina. Crete (Iraklion).
14.00	*Flying Cat 3*	Tinos. Rafina.
14.30	*Express Aphrodite*	Tinos. Syros. Piraeus.
14.30	*Flying Cat 4*	Naxos. Paros. Ios. Santorini.
15.00	*Aqua Jewel*	Tinos. Andros. Rafina.
18.30	*Sea Jet 2*	Tinos. Rafina.
18.45	*Flying Cat 3*	Syros. Kythnos. Lavrio.
20.30	*Aeolos Express II*	Tinos. Syros. Piraeus.
21.45	*Highspeed 4*	Syros. Piraeus.

22.35	*Daedalus*	Tinos. Thessalonika.
22.50	*Milena*	Chios. Lesbos (Mytilini).

②

08.30	*Express Penelope*	Tinos. Andros. Rafina.
09.50	*Sea Jet 2*	Paros.
10.30	*Highspeed 2/3*	Tinos. Syros. Piraeus.
11.00	*Highspeed 4*	Naxos. Paros. Piraeus.
11.30	*Aeolos Express II*	Amorgos (Katapola).
11.50	*Sea Jet 2*	Tinos. Rafina.
12.00	*Aqua Jewel*	Paros.
13.00	*Express Athina*	Tinos. Andros. Rafina.
13.30	*Superferry II*	Tinos. Andros. Rafina. Crete (Iraklion).
14.00	*Flying Cat 3*	Tinos. Rafina.
14.30	*Express Aphrodite*	Tinos. Syros. Piraeus.
14.30	*Flying Cat 4*	Naxos. Paros. Ios. Santorini.
15.00	*Aqua Jewel*	Tinos. Andros. Rafina.
15.45	*Aeolos Express II*	Tinos. Syros. Piraeus.
18.30	*Sea Jet 2*	Tinos. Rafina.
22.15	*Daliana*	Ikaria (Agios Kyrikos). Fourni. Samos (Karlovassi). Samos (Vathi). Patmos. Lipsi.

③

03.20	*Blue Star 1*	Piraeus.
05.30	*Daedalus*	Paros. Santorini. Crete (Iraklion).
08.30	*Express Penelope*	Tinos. Andros. Rafina.
09.50	*Sea Jet 2*	Paros.
10.30	*Highspeed 2/3*	Tinos. Syros. Piraeus.
11.00	*Highspeed 4*	Naxos. Paros. Piraeus.
11.30	*Aeolos Express II*	Amorgos (Katapola).
11.50	*Sea Jet 2*	Tinos. Rafina.
12.00	*Aqua Jewel*	Paros.
13.00	*Express Athina*	Tinos. Andros. Rafina.
13.30	*Superferry II*	Tinos. Andros. Rafina. Crete (Iraklion).
14.30	*Express Aphrodite*	Tinos. Syros. Piraeus.
14.30	*Flying Cat 4*	Naxos. Paros. Ios. Santorini.
15.00	*Aqua Jewel*	Tinos. Andros. Rafina.
15.45	*Aeolos Express II*	Tinos. Syros. Piraeus.
18.30	*Sea Jet 2*	Tinos. Rafina.
18.45	*Flying Cat 3*	Syros. Kythnos. Lavrio.
21.45	*Highspeed 4*	Syros. Piraeus.
23.10	*Daliana*	Syros. Piraeus.

④

03.00	*Daedalus*	Skyros. Thessalonika.
08.30	*Express Penelope*	Tinos. Andros. Rafina.
09.50	*Sea Jet 2*	Paros.
10.30	*Highspeed 2/3*	Tinos. Syros. Piraeus.
11.00	*Highspeed 4*	Naxos. Paros. Piraeus.
11.50	*Sea Jet 2*	Tinos. Rafina.
12.00	*Aqua Jewel*	Paros.
12.45	*Aeolos Express II*	Tinos. Syros. Piraeus.
13.30	*Superferry II*	Tinos. Andros. Rafina. Crete (Iraklion).
14.00	*Flying Cat 3*	Tinos. Rafina.
14.30	*Express Penelope*	Tinos. Andros. Rafina.
14.30	*Express Aphrodite*	Tinos. Syros. Piraeus.
14.30	*Flying Cat 4*	Naxos. Paros. Ios. Santorini.

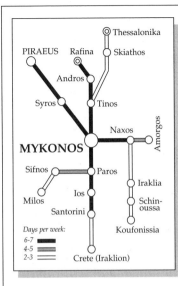

PIRAEUS Rafina
Thessalonika
Skiathos
Andros
Syros Tinos
Naxos
Amorgos
MYKONOS
Sifnos Paros
Iraklia
Milos Ios
Schin-
oussa
Santorini
Koufonissia
Crete (Iraklion)

Days per week:
6-7
4-5
2-3

15.00	*Aqua Jewel*	Tinos. Andros. Rafina.
18.30	*Sea Jet 2*	Tinos. Rafina.
18.45	*Flying Cat 3*	Syros. Kythnos. Lavrio.
21.45	*Highspeed 4*	Syros. Piraeus.
22.30	*Express Athina*	Tinos. Andros. Rafina.

⑤

09.20	*Daedalus*	Naxos. Santorini. Crete (Iraklion).
09.50	*Sea Jet 2*	Paros.
10.30	*Highspeed 2/3*	Tinos. Syros. Piraeus.
11.00	*Highspeed 4*	Naxos. Paros. Piraeus.
11.50	*Sea Jet 2*	Tinos. Rafina.
12.00	*Aeolos Express II*	Tinos. Syros. Piraeus.
13.00	*Express Athina*	Tinos. Andros. Rafina.
13.30	*Superferry II*	Tinos. Andros. Rafina. Crete (Iraklion).
14.00	*Flying Cat 3*	Tinos. Rafina.
14.30	*Express Aphrodite*	Tinos. Syros. Piraeus.
14.30	*Flying Cat 4*	Naxos. Paros. Ios. Santorini.
18.30	*Sea Jet 2*	Tinos. Rafina.
18.45	*Flying Cat 3*	Syros. Kythnos. Lavrio.
20.30	*Aeolos Express II*	Syros. Piraeus.
21.30	*Aqua Jewel*	Paros. Rafina.
21.45	*Highspeed 4*	Syros. Piraeus.
22.15	*Daliana*	Ikaria (Agios Kyrikos). Fourni. Samos (Karlovassi). Samos (Vathi). Patmos. Lipsi.
23.15	*Express Athina*	Tinos. Andros. Rafina.
23.50	*Blue Star 1*	Kos. Rhodes.

⑥

06.35	*Daedalus*	Tinos. Skiathos. Thessalonika.
08.30	*Express Penelope*	Tinos. Andros. Rafina.
09.50	*Sea Jet 2*	Paros.
10.30	*Highspeed 2/3*	Tinos. Syros. Piraeus.
11.00	*Highspeed 4*	Naxos. Paros. Piraeus.
11.50	*Sea Jet 2*	Tinos. Rafina.
12.45	*Aeolos Express II*	Tinos. Syros. Piraeus.
13.00	*Express Athina*	Tinos. Andros. Rafina.
13.30	*Superferry II*	Tinos. Andros. Rafina. Crete (Iraklion).
14.00	*Flying Cat 3*	Tinos. Rafina.
14.30	*Express Aphrodite*	Tinos. Syros. Piraeus.
14.30	*Flying Cat 4*	Naxos. Paros. Ios. Santorini.
14.30	*Express Penelope*	Tinos. Rafina.
18.30	*Sea Jet 2*	Tinos. Rafina.
18.45	*Flying Cat 3*	Syros. Kythnos. Lavrio.
21.00	*Aqua Jewel*	Paros. Rafina.
21.45	*Highspeed 4*	Syros. Piraeus.

⑦

08.30	*Express Penelope*	Tinos. Andros. Rafina.
09.50	*Sea Jet 2*	Paros.
10.30	*Highspeed 2/3*	Tinos. Syros. Piraeus.
11.00	*Highspeed 4*	Naxos. Paros. Piraeus.
11.50	*Sea Jet 2*	Tinos. Rafina.
12.00	*Aeolos Express II*	Tinos. Syros. Piraeus.
12.00	*Aqua Jewel*	Paros.
13.00	*Express Athina*	Tinos. Andros. Rafina.
13.30	*Superferry II*	Tinos. Andros. Rafina. Crete (Iraklion).
13.45	*Daedalus*	Paros. Santorini. Crete (Iraklion).
14.00	*Flying Cat 3*	Tinos. Rafina.
14.30	*Express Aphrodite*	Tinos. Syros. Piraeus.
14.30	*Flying Cat 4*	Naxos. Paros. Ios. Santorini.
14.30	*Express Penelope*	Tinos. Rafina.
15.00	*Aqua Jewel*	Tinos. Andros. Rafina.
18.30	*Sea Jet 2*	Tinos. Rafina.
18.40	*Milena*	Tinos. Syros. Piraeus.
18.45	*Flying Cat 3*	Syros. Kythnos. Lavrio.
20.00	*Marina/Rodanthi*	Patmos. Leros. Kalimnos. Kos. Rhodes.
20.30	*Aeolos Express II*	Tinos. Syros. Piraeus.
21.45	*Highspeed 4*	Syros. Piraeus.

Nafplio

Argo-Saronic
p. 503

🛥 *Flying Dolphins*

② ③ ④ ⑤ ⑥ ⑦
08.00 Tolo. Porto Helio. Spetses. Ermioni. Hydra. Poros. Aegina. Piraeus.

Naxos

Cyclades Central
p. 145

①		
04.30	Express Poseidon	Ios. Santorini.
07.00	Ariadne of Naxos	Santorini.
09.45	Blue Star Naxos	Paros. Piraeus.
10.20	Aeolos Express	Paros. Piraeus.
12.00	Highspeed 4	Paros. Piraeus.
12.35	Blue Star Paros	Santorini.
13.30	Express Poseidon	Paros. Piraeus.
14.25	Panagia Ekatontapiliani	Ios. Santorini.
15.00	Express Skopelitis	Iraklia. Schinoussa. Koufonissia. Donoussa. Amorgos (Egiali). Amorgos (Katapola).
15.20	Flying Cat 4	Paros. Ios. Santorini. Crete (Iraklion).
15.30	Blue Star Ithaki	Mykonos. Tinos. Syros. Piraeus.
13.40	Flying Cat 4	Mykonos.
17.45	Blue Star Paros	Paros. Piraeus.
20.45	Highspeed 4	Mykonos. Syros. Piraeus.
21.00	Aeolos Express	Ikaria (Agios Kyrikos). Samos (Vathi).
22.50	Blue Star Naxos	Iraklia. Schinoussa. Koufonissia. Amorgos (Katapola).
23.00	Express Santorini	Ios. Santorini. Anafi.
23.00	Panagia Ekatontapiliani	Paros. Piraeus.

②		
04.30	Express Poseidon	Ios. Santorini.
09.45	Blue Star Naxos	Paros. Piraeus.
10.20	Aeolos Express	Paros. Piraeus.
11.00	Express Santorini	Paros. Piraeus.
12.00	Highspeed 4	Paros. Piraeus.
12.35	Blue Star Paros	Santorini.
13.30	Express Poseidon	Paros. Piraeus.
13.40	Flying Cat 4	Mykonos.
14.25	Panagia Ekatontapiliani	Ios. Santorini.
15.00	Express Skopelitis	Paros (Piso Livadi). Iraklia. Schinoussa. Koufonissia. Amorgos (Katapola).
15.20	Flying Cat 4	Paros. Ios. Santorini. Crete (Iraklion).
15.30	Blue Star Ithaki	Mykonos. Tinos. Syros. Piraeus.
18.05	Blue Star Paros	Paros. Piraeus.
21.00	Aeolos Express	Ikaria (Evdilos). Samos (Vathi).
23.00	Panagia Ekatontapiliani	Paros. Piraeus.
23.30	Blue Star Naxos	Ios. Santorini.

③		
04.30	Express Santorini	Ios. Santorini.
09.15	Ariadne of Naxos	Delos. Mykonos.
09.45	Blue Star Naxos	Paros. Piraeus.
10.20	Aeolos Express	Paros. Piraeus.
12.00	Highspeed 4	Paros. Piraeus.
12.35	Blue Star Paros	Santorini.
13.30	Express Santorini	Paros. Piraeus.
13.40	Flying Cat 4	Mykonos.
14.25	Panagia Ekatontapiliani	Ios. Santorini.
15.00	Express Skopelitis	Iraklia. Schinoussa. Koufonissia. Donoussa. Amorgos (Egiali). Amorgos (Katapola).
15.15	Dimitroula	Paros. Syros. Piraeus.
15.20	Flying Cat 4	Paros. Ios. Santorini. Crete (Iraklion).
15.30	Blue Star Ithaki	Mykonos. Tinos. Syros. Piraeus.
17.45	Blue Star Paros	Paros. Piraeus.
20.45	Highspeed 4	Mykonos. Syros. Piraeus.
21.00	Aeolos Express	Ikaria (Agios Kyrikos). Samos (Vathi).
21.15	Romilda	Ios. Sikinos. Folegandros. Santorini. Anafi.
22.50	Blue Star Naxos	Iraklia. Schinoussa. Koufonissia. Amorgos (Katapola).
23.00	Express Poseidon	Ios. Santorini.
23.00	Panagia Ekatontapiliani	Paros. Piraeus.

④		
01.15	Daedalus	Mykonos. Skyros. Thessalonika.
04.30	Express Santorini	Ios. Santorini.
09.00	Ariadne of Naxos	Iraklia. Koufonissia.
09.45	Blue Star Naxos	Paros. Piraeus.
10.20	Aeolos Express	Paros. Piraeus.
11.00	Express Poseidon	Paros. Piraeus.
12.00	Highspeed 4	Paros. Piraeus.
12.35	Blue Star Paros	Santorini.
13.30	Express Santorini	Paros. Piraeus.
13.40	Flying Cat 4	Mykonos.
14.25	Panagia Ekatontapiliani	Ios. Santorini.
15.00	Express Skopelitis	Paros (Piso Livadi). Iraklia. Schinoussa. Koufonissia. Amorgos (Katapola).
15.00	Romilda	Paros. Piraeus.
15.20	Flying Cat 4	Paros. Ios. Santorini. Crete (Iraklion).
15.30	Blue Star Ithaki	Mykonos. Tinos. Syros. Piraeus.
18.05	Blue Star Paros	Paros. Piraeus.
20.45	Highspeed 4	Mykonos. Syros. Piraeus.
21.00	Aeolos Express	Ikaria (Agios Kyrikos). Samos (Vathi).
21.50	Dimitroula	Donoussa. Amorgos (Katapola). Amorgos (Egiali). Astipalea.

23.00	*Panagia*	
	Ekatontapiliani	Paros. Piraeus.
23.30	*Blue Star Naxos*	Ios. Santorini.

⑤

04.30	*Express Poseidon*	Ios. Santorini.
09.45	*Blue Star Naxos*	Paros. Piraeus.
10.20	*Aeolos Express*	Paros. Piraeus.
11.00	*Daedalus*	Santorini. Crete (Iraklion).
11.30	*Dimitroula*	Paros. Piraeus.
12.00	*Highspeed 4*	Paros. Piraeus.
12.35	*Blue Star Paros*	Santorini.
13.30	*Express Poseidon*	Paros. Piraeus.
13.40	*Flying Cat 4*	Mykonos.
14.25	*Express Santorini*	Ios. Santorini.
15.00	*Express Skopelitis*	Iraklia. Schinoussa. Koufonissia. Donoussa. Amorgos (Egiali). Amorgos (Katapola).
15.20	*Flying Cat 4*	Paros. Ios. Santorini. Crete (Iraklion).
15.30	*Blue Star Ithaki*	Mykonos. Tinos. Syros. Piraeus.
17.45	*Blue Star Paros*	Paros. Piraeus.
20.45	*Highspeed 4*	Mykonos. Syros. Piraeus.
21.00	*Aeolos Express*	Ikaria (Evdilos). Samos (Vathi).
21.15	*Romilda*	Ios. Sikinos. Folegandros. Santorini. Anafi.
22.50	*Blue Star Naxos*	Koufonissia. Amorgos (Katapola).
23.00	*Express Santorini*	Paros. Piraeus.
23.00	*Panagia Ekatontapiliani*	Ios. Santorini.

⑥

04.30	*Express Poseidon*	Ios. Santorini.
07.15	*Dimitroula*	Donoussa. Amorgos (Katapola). Amorgos (Egiali). Astipalea. Kos. Nissiros. Tilos. Symi. Rhodes. Kastelorizo.
09.45	*Blue Star Naxos*	Paros. Piraeus.
10.20	*Aeolos Express*	Paros. Piraeus.
10.30	*Panagia Ekatontapiliani*	Paros. Piraeus.
12.00	*Highspeed 4*	Paros. Piraeus.
12.30	*Express Skopelitis*	Paros (Piso Livadi). Iraklia. Schinoussa. Koufonissia. Amorgos (Katapola).
12.35	*Blue Star Paros*	Santorini.
13.30	*Express Poseidon*	Paros. Piraeus.
13.40	*Flying Cat 4*	Mykonos.
14.25	*Express Santorini*	Ios. Santorini.
15.00	*Romilda*	Paros. Piraeus.
15.20	*Flying Cat 4*	Paros. Ios. Santorini. Crete (Iraklion).
15.30	*Blue Star Ithaki*	Mykonos. Tinos. Syros. Piraeus.
17.45	*Blue Star Paros*	Paros. Piraeus.
20.45	*Highspeed 4*	Mykonos. Syros. Piraeus.
21.00	*Aeolos Express*	Ikaria (Evdilos). Samos (Vathi).

Days per week:
6-7 ▬▬▬
2-3 ═══

22.35	*Blue Star Naxos*	Santorini.
23.00	*Express Santorini*	Paros. Piraeus.
23.00	*Panagia Ekatontapiliani*	Koufonissia. Amorgos (Katapola).

⑦

04.30	*Express Poseidon*	Ios. Santorini.
05.00	*Romilda*	Iraklia. Schinoussa. Koufonissia. Amorgos (Katapola). Amorgos (Egiali). Donoussa.
09.15	*Ariadne of Naxos*	Delos. Mykonos.
09.45	*Blue Star Naxos*	Paros. Piraeus.
10.20	*Aeolos Express*	Paros. Piraeus.
12.00	*Highspeed 4*	Paros. Piraeus.
12.35	*Blue Star Paros*	Santorini.
13.30	*Express Poseidon*	Paros. Piraeus.
13.45	*Romilda*	Paros. Piraeus.
14.25	*Express Santorini*	Ios. Santorini.
15.20	*Flying Cat 4*	Paros. Ios. Santorini. Crete (Iraklion).
15.30	*Blue Star Ithaki*	Mykonos. Tinos. Syros. Piraeus.
15.30	*Panagia Ekatontapiliani*	Paros. Piraeus.
13.40	*Flying Cat 4*	Mykonos.
17.45	*Blue Star Paros*	Paros. Piraeus.
20.45	*Highspeed 4*	Mykonos. Syros. Piraeus.
21.00	*Aeolos Express*	Ikaria (Agios Kyrikos). Samos (Vathi).
22.35	*Blue Star Naxos*	Santorini.
23.00	*Express Santorini*	Paros. Piraeus.
23.15	*Daliana*	Ikaria (Agios Kyrikos). Fourni. Samos (Karlovassi). Samos (Vathi). Chios.

Nea Moudania

Northern Aegean p. 453

◯
14.50 Hydrofoil Alonissos. Skopelos.
Skiathos.
Agios Konstantinos.
22.35 Hydrofoil Thessalonika.

Nea Peramos

Northern Aegean p. 453

Ⓓ 08.30 12.30 16.30 20.45
ANET Line Thassos (Skala Prinos).

Neapoli

Argo-Saronic p. 504

Ⓓ
08.30 09.45 10.45 12.00
13.45 16.45 19.00
Local Elafonissos.

Ⓓ
08.00 *Nissos Kithera* Kithera (Agia Pelagia).
17.00 *Nissos Kithera* Kithera (Agia Pelagia).

① ③
11.00 *Nissos Kithera* Kithera (Agia Pelagia). Gythio.

① ⑤ ⑥ ⑦
00.00 *Flying Dolphin* Kithera (Agia Pelagia).
Monemvassia. Piraeus.

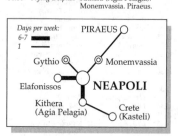

Days per week:
6-7 ▬▬▬
1 ▬▬▬

PIRAEUS ◯
Gythio ◯   ◯ Monemvassia
Elafonissos ◯
NEAPOLI
Kithera
(Agia Pelagia) ◯   ◯ Crete
(Kasteli)

Nissos

Dodecanese
p. 366

Ⓓ
07.00 Taxi boat Kos (Kardamena).
16.00 *Nissiros Express* Kos (Kardamena).

①
10.30 *Nissos Kalimnos* Tilos. Symi. Rhodes.
17.30 *SeaStar* Tilos. Rhodes.

②
00.15 *Nissos Kalimnos* Kos. Kalimnos.

③
04.15 *Dimitroula* Kos. Kalimnos.
Astipalea.
Amorgos (Egiali).
Amorgos (Katapola).
Donoussa. Naxos. Paros.
Syros.
Piraeus.
09.00 Hydrofoil Tilos. Rhodes.
20.20 Hydrofoil Kos.

④
07.00 *Patmos/Rodos* Rhodes.
10.30 *Nissos Kalimnos* Tilos. Symi. Rhodes.
17.30 *SeaStar* Tilos. Rhodes.

⑤
00.15 *Nissos Kalimnos* Kos. Kalimnos.
05.30 *Diagoras* Rhodes.
17.30 *SeaStar* Tilos. Rhodes.
18.20 *Diagoras* Kos. Piraeus.

⑥
17.00 *Dimitroula* Tilos. Symi. Rhodes.
Kastelorizo.

⑦
16.50 Hydrofoil Kos. Rhodes.

Days per week:
6-7 ▬▬▬
4-5 ▬▬▬
2-3 ▬▬▬

◯ Kalimnos
◯ Kos
NISSIROS ◯
Tilos ◯   ◯ Symi
◯ Rhodes

Odun Iskalesi

Turkey p. 568

Ⓓ x ②
00.00 TML Bozcaada.

Oinousses

Eastern Line p. 421

Ⓓ
08.00   *Inousse II*   Chios.

② ④ ⑥
16.00   Miniotis Lines   Chios.

Paros

Cyclades Central
p. 153

Ⓓ
09.45 10.30 11.30
12.30 13.30 14.30
16.00 17.30 19.00
         Antiparos Express
         Kasos Express
         Panagia Parou   Antiparos.

11.00   *Highspeed 1*   Santorini.
11.00   *Sea Jet 2*   Mykonos. Tinos. Rafina.
11.35   *Blue Star Paros*   Naxos. Santorini.
12.45   *Highspeed 4*   Piraeus.
13.00   *Flying Cat 4*   Naxos. Mykonos.
14.15   *Blue Star Ithaki*   Naxos. Mykonos.
                              Tinos. Syros. Piraeus.
15.00   *Highspeed 1*   Piraeus.
16.00   *Flying Cat 4*   Ios. Santorini.
                              Crete (Iraklion).

①
00.05   *Express Santorini*   Piraeus.
03.20   *Express Poseidon*   Naxos. Ios. Santorini.
09.00   *Romilda*   Serifos. Sifnos. Kimolos.
                              Milos.
10.45   *Blue Star Naxos*   Piraeus.
11.15   *Aeolos Express*   Piraeus.
13.25   *Panagia*
        Ekatontapiliani   Naxos. Ios. Santorini.
14.10   *Aqua Jewel*   Mykonos. Tinos.
                              Andros. Rafina.
15.00   *Express Poseidon*   Piraeus.
18.30   *Romilda*   Syros.
18.45   *Blue Star Paros*   Piraeus.
20.00   *Aeolos Express*   Naxos.
                              Ikaria (Agios Kyrikos).
                              Samos (Vathi).
20.00   *Highspeed 4*   Naxos. Mykonos. Syros.
                              Piraeus.
20.50   *Daedalus*   Mykonos. Tinos.
                              Thessalonika.
21.35   *Blue Star Naxos*   Naxos. Iraklia.
                              Schinoussa. Koufonissia.
                              Amorgos (Katapola).
21.45   *Highspeed 2/3*   Piraeus.
21.50   *Express Santorini*   Naxos. Ios. Santorini.
                              Anafi.

②
00.05   *Panagia*
        Ekatontapiliani   Piraeus.
03.20   *Express Poseidon*   Naxos. Ios. Santorini.
10.45   *Blue Star Naxos*   Piraeus.
11.15   *Aeolos Express*   Piraeus.
12.05   *Express Santorini*   Piraeus.
13.25   *Panagia*
        Ekatontapiliani   Naxos. Ios. Santorini.
14.00   *Romilda*   Serifos. Sifnos.
                              Kimolos. Milos.
14.10   *Aqua Jewel*   Mykonos. Tinos.
                              Andros. Rafina.
15.00   *Express Poseidon*   Piraeus.
19.05   *Blue Star Paros*   Piraeus.
20.00   *Aeolos Express*   Naxos. Ikaria (Evdilos).
                              Samos (Vathi).
21.45   *Highspeed 2/3*   Piraeus.
22.30   *Blue Star Naxos*   Naxos. Ios. Santorini.
23.00   *Romilda*   Syros. Piraeus.

③
00.05   *Panagia*
        Ekatontapiliani   Piraeus.
03.20   *Express Santorini*   Naxos. Ios. Santorini.
07.15   *Daedalus*   Santorini.
                              Crete (Iraklion).
10.45   *Blue Star Naxos*   Piraeus.
11.15   *Aeolos Express*   Piraeus.
13.25   *Panagia*
        Ekatontapiliani   Naxos. Ios. Santorini.
14.10   *Aqua Jewel*   Mykonos. Tinos.
                              Andros. Rafina.
15.00   *Express Santorini*   Piraeus.
16.30   *Dimitroula*   Syros. Piraeus.
18.45   *Blue Star Paros*   Piraeus.
20.00   *Aeolos Express*   Naxos.
                              Ikaria (Agios Kyrikos).
                              Samos (Vathi).
20.00   *Highspeed 4*   Naxos. Mykonos. Syros.
                              Piraeus.
20.15   *Romilda*   Naxos. Ios. Sikinos.
                              Folegandros. Santorini.
                              Anafi.
21.35   *Blue Star Naxos*   Naxos. Iraklia.
                              Schinoussa. Koufonissia.
                              Amorgos (Katapola).
21.50   *Express Poseidon*   Naxos. Ios. Santorini.

④
00.05   *Panagia*
        Ekatontapiliani   Piraeus.
03.20   *Express Santorini*   Naxos. Ios. Santorini.
10.45   *Blue Star Naxos*   Piraeus.
11.15   *Aeolos Express*   Piraeus.
12.05   *Express Poseidon*   Piraeus.
13.25   *Panagia*
        Ekatontapiliani   Naxos. Ios. Santorini.
14.10   *Aqua Jewel*   Mykonos. Tinos.
                              Andros. Rafina.
15.00   *Express Santorini*   Piraeus.
16.15   *Romilda*   Piraeus.
19.05   *Blue Star Paros*   Piraeus.
20.00   *Aeolos Express*   Naxos. Ikaria (Agios
                              Kyrikos). Samos (Vathi).

20.00	*Highspeed 4*	Naxos. Mykonos. Syros. Piraeus.
20.30	*Dimitroula*	Naxos. Donoussa. Amorgos (Katapola). Amorgos (Egiali). Astipalea.
21.45	*Highspeed 2/3*	Piraeus.
22.30	*Blue Star Naxos*	Naxos. Ios. Santorini.

⑤

00.05	*Panagia Ekatontapiliani*	Piraeus.
03.20	*Express Poseidon*	Naxos. Ios. Santorini.
04.30	*Daliana*	Syros. Piraeus.
10.45	*Blue Star Naxos*	Piraeus.
11.15	*Aeolos Express*	Piraeus.
12.40	*Dimitroula*	Piraeus.
13.20	*Express Santorini*	Naxos. Ios. Santorini.
15.00	*Express Poseidon*	Piraeus.
18.45	*Blue Star Paros*	Piraeus.
20.00	*Aeolos Express*	Naxos. Ikaria (Evdilos). Samos (Vathi).
20.00	*Highspeed 4*	Naxos. Mykonos. Syros. Piraeus.
20.15	*Romilda*	Naxos. Ios. Sikinos. Folegandros. Santorini. Anafi.
21.35	*Blue Star Naxos*	Naxos. Koufonissia. Amorgos (Katapola).
21.45	*Highspeed 2/3*	Piraeus.
22.00	*Panagia Ekatontapiliani*	Naxos. Ios. Santorini.
23.30	*Aqua Jewel*	Rafina.

PIRAEUS / Thessalonika / Rafina / Skiathos / Tinos / Samos / Mykonos / Syros / Naxos / Ikaria / **PAROS** / Kou. / Don. / Antiparos / Amorgos / Milos / Sifnos / Ira. / Sch. / Sikinos / Ios / Astipalea / Folegandros / Santorini / Rhodes / Karpathos / Crete (Iraklion)

Days per week:
6-7 ▬▬
4-5 ▬▬
2-3 ═══

⑥

00.05	*Express Santorini*	Piraeus.
03.20	*Express Poseidon*	Naxos. Ios. Santorini.
04.50	*Daedalus*	Mykonos. Tinos. Skiathos. Thessalonika.
06.00	*Dimitroula*	Naxos. Donoussa. Amorgos (Katapola). Amorgos (Egiali). Astipalea. Kos. Nissiros. Tilos. Symi. Rhodes. Kastelorizo.
10.45	*Blue Star Naxos*	Piraeus.
11.15	*Aeolos Express*	Piraeus.
12.30	*Panagia Ekatontapiliani*	Piraeus.
13.20	*Express Santorini*	Naxos. Ios. Santorini.
15.00	*Express Poseidon*	Piraeus.
16.15	*Romilda*	Piraeus.
18.45	*Blue Star Paros*	Piraeus.
20.00	*Aeolos Express*	Naxos. Ikaria (Evdilos). Samos (Vathi).
20.00	*Highspeed 4*	Naxos. Mykonos. Syros. Piraeus.
21.00	*Marina/Rodanthi*	Patmos. Leros. Kalimnos. Kos. Rhodes.
21.35	*Blue Star Naxos*	Naxos. Santorini.
21.45	*Highspeed 2/3*	Piraeus.
22.00	*Panagia Ekatontapiliani*	Naxos. Koufonissia. Amorgos (Katapola).
23.00	*Aqua Jewel*	Rafina.

⑦

00.05	*Express Santorini*	Piraeus.
03.20	*Express Poseidon*	Naxos. Ios. Santorini.
04.00	*Romilda*	Naxos. Iraklia. Schinoussa. Koufonissia. Amorgos (Katapola). Amorgos (Egiali). Donoussa.
10.45	*Blue Star Naxos*	Piraeus.
11.15	*Aeolos Express*	Piraeus.
13.20	*Express Santorini*	Naxos. Ios. Santorini.
14.10	*Aqua Jewel*	Mykonos. Tinos. Andros. Rafina.
14.45	*Romilda*	Piraeus.
15.00	*Express Poseidon*	Piraeus.
15.30	*Daedalus*	Santorini. Crete (Iraklion).
17.00	*Panagia Ekatontapiliani*	Piraeus.
18.45	*Blue Star Paros*	Piraeus.
20.00	*Aeolos Express*	Naxos. Ikaria (Agios Kyrikos). Samos (Vathi).
20.00	*Highspeed 4*	Naxos. Mykonos. Syros. Piraeus.
21.35	*Blue Star Naxos*	Naxos. Santorini.
21.45	*Highspeed 2/3*	Piraeus.
22.00	*Daliana*	Naxos. Ikaria (Agios Kyrikos). Fourni. Samos (Karlovassi). Samos (Vathi). Chios.

Paros
(Piso Livadi)

Cyclades Central
p. 157

○
00.00   Beach Boat   Naxos.

②
09.45   *Express Skopelitis*   Naxos.
15.30   *Express Skopelitis*   Iraklia. Schinoussa.
                                 Koufonissia.
                                 Amorgos (Katapola).

④
11.15   *Express Skopelitis*   Naxos.
15.30   *Express Skopelitis*   Iraklia. Schinoussa.
                                 Koufonissia.
                                 Amorgos (Katapola).

⑥
11.15   *Express Skopelitis*   Naxos.
13.00   *Express Skopelitis*   Iraklia. Schinoussa.
                                 Koufonissia.
                                 Amorgos (Katapola).

○
13.00   *Flying Cat 4*   Naxos. Mykonos.
16.00   *Flying Cat 4*   Ios. Santorini.
                              Crete (Iraklion).

Paros
(Punta)

Cyclades Central
p. 159

Ⓗ
07.00–10.00,
21.00–24.00;
ev. 30 min
10.30–20.30   *Agioi Anargiri*   Antiparos.

Paşalmanı

Turkey p. 568

① ⑥
00.00   TML   Erdek.

Patmos

Dodecanese p. 370

Ⓓ Tourist boats:
10.00   *Anna Express*   Lipsi. / Arki.
10.00   *Megalohori/*
         Patmos Express   Lipsi.
16.00   *Cassandra/*
         Hydrofoil   Samos (Pithagorio).

①
00.15   *Blue Star 1*   Syros. Piraeus.
01.00   *Marina/Rodanthi*   Piraeus.
01.45   *Marina/Rodanthi*   Leros. Kalimnos. Kos.
                               Rhodes.
08.55   Hydrofoil   Leros (Agia Marina).
                               Kalimnos. Kos.
10.00   Hydrofoil   Fourni.
                               Ikaria (Agios Kyrikos).
                               Samos (Pithagorio).
15.30   Hydrofoil   Lipsi.
                               Leros (Agia Marina).
                               Kos. Kalimnos.
16.00   Hydrofoil   Kos. Rhodes.
16.30   Hydrofoil   Samos (Pithagorio).
                               Samos (Vathi).
17.00   Hydrofoil   Leros (Agia Marina).
                               Kalimnos. Kos.
23.50   *Patmos/Rodos*   Piraeus.
23.50   *Patmos/Rodos*   Leros. Kalimnos. Kos.
                               Tilos. Symi. Rhodes.

②
08.55   Hydrofoil   Lipsi.
                               Leros (Agia Marina).
                               Kalimnos. Kos.
10.10   Hydrofoil   Samos (Pithagorio).
12.00   Miniotis Ferries   Lipsi. Arki. Agathonisi.
                               Samos (Pithagorio).
13.30   *Dodekanesos Express* Lipsi.
                               Leros (Agia Marina).
                               Kalimnos. Kos.
                               Rhodes.
15.30   Hydrofoil   Lipsi.
                               Leros (Agia Marina).
                               Kos. Kalimnos.
16.30   Hydrofoil   Samos (Pithagorio).
                               Samos (Vathi).
23.50   *Patmos/Rodos*   Piraeus.
23.50   *Patmos/Rodos*   Leros. Kalimnos. Kos.
                               Rhodes.

③
09.45   *Daliana*   Lipsi. Samos (Vathi).
                               Samos (Karlovassi).
                               Fourni.
                               Ikaria (Agios Kyrikos).
                               Mykonos. Syros.
                               Piraeus.
11.00   *Nissos Kalimnos*   Arki. Agathonisi.
                               Samos (Pithagorio).
12.15   Hydrofoil   Samos (Pithagorio).

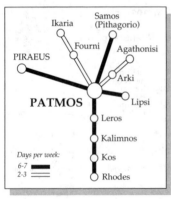

PIRAEUS
Ikaria
Samos (Pithagorio)
Fourni
Agathonisi
Arki
PATMOS
Lipsi
Leros
Kalimnos
Kos
Rhodes

Days per week:
6-7
2-3

15.00	Hydrofoil	Lipsi. Leros (Agia Marina). Kos.
18.30	*Nissos Kalimnos*	Lipsi. Leros. Kalimnos.
23.50	*Patmos/Rodos*	Piraeus.

④
02.50	*Blue Star 1*	Leros. Kos. Rhodes.
08.55	Hydrofoil	Lipsi. Leros (Agia Marina). Kalimnos. Kos.
10.10	Hydrofoil	Samos (Pithagorio).
10.15	Hydrofoil	Agathonisi. Samos (Pithagorio).
15.00	Hydrofoil	Lipsi. Leros (Agia Marina). Kalimnos. Kos.
15.30	Hydrofoil	Leros (Agia Marina). Kos. Kalimnos.
16.30	Hydrofoil	Samos (Pithagorio). Samos (Vathi).
23.50	*Patmos/Rodos*	Leros. Kalimnos. Kos. Rhodes.

⑤
01.45	*Blue Star 1*	Syros. Piraeus.
10.10	Hydrofoil	Agathonisi. Samos (Pithagorio).
10.25	Hydrofoil	Lipsi. Leros (Agia Marina). Kalimnos. Kos.
11.00	*Nissos Kalimnos*	Arki. Agathonisi. Samos (Pithagorio).
12.05	Hydrofoil	Fourni. Ikaria (Agios Kyrikos).
12.15	Hydrofoil	Samos (Pithagorio).
13.30	*Dodekanesos Express*	Lipsi. Leros (Agia Marina). Kalimnos. Kos. Rhodes.

15.30	Hydrofoil	Lipsi. Leros (Agia Marina). Kos. Kalimnos.
16.00	Hydrofoil	Kos. Rhodes.
16.30	Hydrofoil	Samos (Pithagorio). Samos (Vathi).
18.30	*Nissos Kalimnos*	Lipsi. Leros. Kalimnos.
23.50	*Patmos/Rodos*	Piraeus.

⑥
09.30	Hydrofoil	Lipsi. Leros (Agia Marina). Kalimnos. Kos.
09.45	*Daliana*	Lipsi. Samos (Vathi). Samos (Karlovassi). Fourni. Ikaria (Agios Kyrikos). Mykonos. Syros. Piraeus.
10.30	Hydrofoil	Samos (Pithagorio).
10.30	Hydrofoil	Samos (Pithagorio).
13.40	*Dodekanesos Express*	Leros (Agia Marina). Kalimnos. Kos. Rhodes.
16.30	Hydrofoil	Agathonisi. Samos (Pithagorio). Samos (Vathi).
23.45	*Diagoras*	Leros. Kalimnos. Kos. Rhodes.
23.50	*Patmos/Rodos*	Leros. Kalimnos. Kos. Rhodes.

⑦
01.30	*Marina/Rodanthi*	Leros. Kalimnos. Kos. Rhodes.
07.00	*Blue Star 1*	Leros. Kos. Rhodes.
08.55	Hydrofoil	Lipsi. Leros (Agia Marina). Kalimnos. Kos.
10.15	Hydrofoil	Ikaria (Agios Kyrikos). Samos (Pithagorio).
10.30	Hydrofoil	Samos (Pithagorio).
11.00	*Nissos Kalimnos*	Arki. Agathonisi. Samos (Pithagorio).
13.30	*Dodekanesos Express*	Lipsi. Leros (Agia Marina). Kalimnos. Kos. Rhodes.
15.30	Hydrofoil	Leros (Agia Marina). Kos. Kalimnos.
16.00	Hydrofoil	Lipsi. Leros (Agia Marina). Kalimnos. Kos.
16.30	Hydrofoil	Ikaria (Agios Kyrikos). Fourni. Samos (Pithagorio). Samos (Vathi).
18.30	*Nissos Kalimnos*	Lipsi. Leros. Kalimnos.
23.50	*Patmos/Rodos*	Piraeus.
23.50	*Patmos/Rodos*	Leros. Kalimnos. Kos. Rhodes.

Patras

Ionian Line   p. 537

International Services:

Ⓓ
14.30	Superfast Ferries	Igoumenitsa. Ancona.
17.30	ANEK Lines	Igoumenitsa. Ancona.
18.00	Minoan Lines	Igoumenitsa. Ancona.
18.00	Superfast Ferries	Igoumenitsa. Bari.
19.00	*Brindisi/Valentino*	Igoumenitsa. Brindisi.
20.00	Med Link Lines	Brindisi.
20.00	Superfast Ferries	Ancona.

Ⓐ
16.00	HML Ferries	Kefalonia (Sami). Igoumenitsa. Corfu. Brindisi.
17.00	HML Ferries	Igoumenitsa. Corfu. Brindisi.
19.00	Poseidon Lines	Igoumenitsa. Brindisi.
20.00	HML Ferries	Kefalonia (Sami). Paxi. Igoumenitsa. Corfu. Brindisi.

①
16.00	Minoan Lines	Igoumenitsa. Bari.
23.50	ANEK Lines	Igoumenitsa. Trieste.
23.55	*Blue Horizon/ Blue Sky*	Corfu. Igoumenitsa. Venice.

②
16.00	Minoan Lines	Igoumenitsa. Bari.
19.00	AK Ventouris	Bari.
24.00	Minoan Lines	Corfu. Igoumenitsa. Venice.

③
16.00	Minoan Lines	Igoumenitsa. Bari.
23.50	ANEK Lines	Igoumenitsa. Corfu. Trieste.
24.00	Minoan Lines	Corfu. Igoumenitsa. Venice.

④
16.00	Minoan Lines	Igoumenitsa. Corfu. Bari.
19.00	AK Ventouris	Bari.
23.00	*Blue Horizon/ Blue Sky*	Corfu. Igoumenitsa. Venice.
23.50	ANEK Lines	Igoumenitsa. Trieste.
24.00	Minoan Lines	Corfu. Igoumenitsa. Venice.

⑤
16.00	Minoan Lines	Igoumenitsa. Bari.
23.00	*Blue Horizon/ Blue Sky*	Corfu. Igoumenitsa. Venice.
24.00	Minoan Lines	Corfu. Igoumenitsa. Venice.

⑥
16.00	Minoan Lines	Igoumenitsa. Corfu. Bari.
24.00	Minoan Lines	Corfu. Igoumenitsa. Venice.

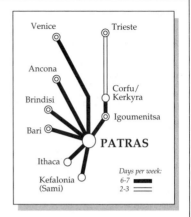

⑦
16.00	Minoan Lines	Igoumenitsa. Corfu. Bari.
19.00	AK Ventouris	Bari.
23.50	ANEK Lines	Igoumenitsa. Corfu. Trieste.
23.55	*Blue Horizon/ Blue Sky*	Corfu. Igoumenitsa. Venice.
24.00	Minoan Lines	Corfu. Igoumenitsa. Venice.

Domestic Services:

Ⓓ
12.30	*Kefalonia*	Kefalonia (Sami). Ithaca.
20.00	*Kefalonia*	Kefalonia (Sami). Ithaca.

Paxi / Paxos

Ionian Line   p. 539

Ⓓ
00.00	*Ventouris High Speed I/II*	Brindisi.

Ⓓ ex ③
07.15	Local C/F	Igoumenitsa. Corfu.

Ⓓ ex ⑦
07.30	*Pegasus* T/B	Corfu.

③
12.00	Local C/F	Igoumenitsa. Corfu.

○
06.30	HML Ferries	Igoumenitsa. Corfu. Brindisi.
07.30	HML Ferries	Kefalonia (Sami). Patras.

Piraeus

Athens & Piraeus   p. 116

Weekly updated
timetable for **Piraeus** at
greekislandhopping.com

Note:
Current weekly printed schedules are available from the central Athens and airport branches of the
NTOG/EOT. A 48-hour Saronic Gulf ferry schedule (in Greek) is posted up on the Port Police building
on the Saronic Gulf ferry quay. Saronic Gulf hydrofoil timetables are available from the quayside ticket
kiosk. International ferry information is obtained from respective agents.

International Services: (Suspended during 2003)

○
16.00	Salamis Star	Mykonos. Rhodes. Limassol. Port Said. Haifa.
19.00	Sea Harmony	Santorini. Patmos. Rhodes. Limassol. Haifa.
20.00	Princesa Cypria	Patmos. Limassol. Haifa.
19.00	Nissos Kypros	Patmos. Rhodes. Limassol. Haifa.

Domestic Services:

1. Cyclades, Crete, Dodecanese, Eastern & Northern Aegean

ⓓ
07.25	Blue Star Paros	Paros. Naxos. Santorini.
07.30	Blue Star Ithaki	Syros. Tinos. Mykonos. Paros. Naxos.
07.30	Highspeed 4	Syros. Mykonos. Naxos. Paros.
07.45	Highspeed 1	Paros. Santorini.
08.00	Express Aphrodite	Syros. Tinos. Mykonos.
16.00	Blue Star 2	Crete (Chania).
17.00	Highspeed 2/3	Syros. Mykonos. Tinos. Rafina.
20.00	Aptera/Preveli	Crete (Rethimno).
20.30	Kriti I/Kriti II	Crete (Iraklion).
21.00	Lato/Lissos	Crete (Chania).
22.00	Festos Palace/	
	Knossos Palace	Crete (Iraklion).

ⓘ
07.30	Aeolos Express II	Syros. Tinos. Mykonos.
07.30	Highspeed 2/3	Serifos. Sifnos. Milos.
08.00	Express Apollon	Kythnos. Serifos. Sifnos. Milos. Kimolos. Folegandros. Sikinos. Ios. Santorini.
08.00	Panagia	
	Ekatontapiliani	Paros. Naxos. Ios. Santorini.
15.00	Patmos/Rodos	Patmos. Leros. Kalimnos. Kos. Tilos. Symi. Rhodes.
15.30	Highspeed 2/3	Sifnos. Santorini. Paros.
16.00	Express Pegasus	Kythnos. Serifos. Sifnos. Milos.
16.00	Jet One	Kythnos. Milos. Ios. Santorini. Amorgos (Katapola).
16.00	Marina/Rodanthi	Kalimnos. Kos. Rhodes.
16.00	Milena	Tinos. Mykonos. Chios. Lesbos (Mytilini).
16.30	Aeolos Express	Syros. Paros. Naxos. Ikaria (Agios Kyrikos). Samos (Vathi).
16.30	Express Santorini	Paros. Naxos. Ios. Santorini. Anafi.
16.45	Aeolos Express II	Syros. Mykonos. Tinos.
17.00	Aeolos Kenteris	Kos. Rhodes.
17.00	Highspeed 4	Paros. Naxos. Mykonos. Syros.
17.30	Blue Star Naxos	Paros. Naxos. Iraklia. Schinoussa. Koufonissia. Amorgos (Katapola).
18.00	Mirtidiotissa	Kithera (Agia Pelagia). Antikithera. Crete (Kasteli).
19.00	Ierapetra L	Milos. Crete (Agios Nikolaos). Crete (Sitia).
19.00	Theofilos	Chios. Lesbos (Mytilini).
20.00	Blue Star 1	Syros. Kos. Rhodes.
20.00	Express Olympia	Ikaria (Evdilos). Samos (Karlovassi). Samos (Vathi).
21.00	Taxiarchis	Samos (Vathi). Chios. Lesbos (Mytilini).
22.00	Express Poseidon	Paros. Naxos. Ios. Santorini.

②
07.30	*Aeolos Express II*	Syros. Tinos. Mykonos. Amorgos (Katapola).
07.30	*Highspeed 2/3*	Serifos. Sifnos. Milos.
08.00	*Panagia Ekatontapiliani*	Paros. Naxos. Ios. Santorini.
15.00	*Patmos/Rodos*	Patmos. Leros. Kalimnos. Kos. Rhodes.
15.30	*Highspeed 2/3*	Sifnos. Santorini. Paros.
16.00	*Daliana*	Syros. Mykonos. Ikaria (Agios Kyrikos). Fourni. Samos (Karlovassi). Samos (Vathi). Patmos. Lipsi.
16.00	*Express Pegasus*	Kythnos. Serifos. Sifnos. Kimolos. Milos.
16.00	*Marina/Rodanthi*	Amorgos (Katapola). Astipalea. Kalimnos. Kos. Rhodes.
16.15	*Jet One*	Sifnos. Milos. Ios. Santorini. Crete (Iraklion).
17.00	*Aeolos Express*	Paros. Naxos. Ikaria (Evdilos). Samos (Vathi).
17.30	*Blue Star Naxos*	Syros. Paros. Naxos. Ios. Santorini.
18.00	*Aeolos Kenteris*	Chios. Lesbos (Mytilini). Limnos. Thessalonika.
18.00	*Diagoras*	Kos. Rhodes.
19.00	*Mytilene*	Chios. Lesbos (Mytilini).
22.00	*Express Santorini*	Paros. Naxos. Ios. Santorini.

③
07.30	*Aeolos Express II*	Syros. Tinos. Mykonos. Amorgos (Katapola).
07.45	*Express Apollon*	Kythnos. Serifos. Sifnos. Kimolos. Milos.
08.00	*Panagia Ekatontapiliani*	Paros. Naxos. Ios. Santorini.
15.00	*Patmos/Rodos*	Amorgos (Katapola). Astipalea. Kalimnos. Nissiros. Rhodes.
15.00	*Romilda*	Paros. Naxos. Ios. Sikinos. Folegandros. Santorini. Anafi.
16.00	*Marina/Rodanthi*	Kalimnos. Kos. Rhodes.
16.15	*Jet One*	Sifnos. Milos. Folegandros. Ios. Santorini. Amorgos (Katapola).
16.30	*Express Poseidon*	Paros. Naxos. Ios. Santorini.
17.00	*Aeolos Express*	Paros. Naxos. Ikaria (Agios Kyrikos). Samos (Vathi).
17.00	*Highspeed 4*	Paros. Naxos. Mykonos. Syros.
17.30	*Blue Star Naxos*	Paros. Naxos. Iraklia. Schinoussa. Koufonissia. Amorgos (Katapola).
19.00	*Ierapetra L*	Milos. Crete (Agios Nikolaos). Crete (Sitia).
19.00	*Theofilos*	Chios. Lesbos (Mytilini).
20.00	*Blue Star 1*	Syros. Patmos. Leros. Kos. Rhodes.
20.00	*Express Olympia*	Ikaria (Evdilos). Samos (Karlovassi). Samos (Vathi).
20.00	*Taxiarchis*	Chios.
22.00	*Express Santorini*	Paros. Naxos. Ios. Santorini.

④
07.30	*Aeolos Express II*	Syros. Tinos. Mykonos.
07.30	*Highspeed 2/3*	Serifos. Sifnos. Milos.
07.45	*Express Apollon*	Kythnos. Serifos. Sifnos. Kimolos. Milos.
08.00	*Panagia Ekatontapiliani*	Paros. Naxos. Ios. Santorini.
14.00	*Daliana*	Syros. Serifos. Sifnos. Kimolos. Milos.
15.00	*Dimitroula*	Paros. Naxos. Donoussa. Amorgos (Katapola). Amorgos (Egiali). Astipalea.
15.00	*Patmos/Rodos*	Patmos. Leros. Kalimnos. Kos. Rhodes.
15.30	*Highspeed 2/3*	Sifnos. Santorini. Paros.
16.00	*Express Pegasus*	Kythnos. Serifos. Sifnos. Milos.
16.00	*Marina/Rodanthi*	Kalimnos. Kos. Rhodes. Kastelorizo.
16.15	*Jet One*	Milos. Folegandros. Santorini. Amorgos (Katapola).
17.00	*Aeolos Express*	Paros. Naxos. Ikaria (Agios Kyrikos). Samos (Vathi).
17.00	*Aeolos Kenteris*	Kalimnos. Kos. Rhodes.
17.00	*Highspeed 4*	Paros. Naxos. Mykonos. Syros.
17.30	*Blue Star Naxos*	Syros. Paros. Naxos. Ios. Santorini.
18.00	*Diagoras*	Kos. Nissiros. Rhodes.
19.00	*Mytilene*	Chios. Lesbos (Mytilini).
19.00	*Vitsentzos Kornaros*	Milos. Crete (Agios Nikolaos). Crete (Sitia). Kassos. Karpathos (Town). Karpathos (Diafani). Chalki. Rhodes.
20.00	*Express Olympia*	Ikaria (Evdilos). Samos (Karlovassi). Samos (Vathi).
22.00	*Express Poseidon*	Paros. Naxos. Ios. Santorini.

Piraeus:

⑤

07.30	*Aeolos Express II*	Syros. Tinos. Mykonos.
07.30	*Highspeed 2/3*	Serifos. Sifnos. Milos.
08.00	*Express Santorini*	Paros. Naxos. Ios. Santorini.
12.30	*Festos Palace/*	
	Knossos Palace	Crete (Iraklion).
15.00	*Romilda*	Paros. Naxos. Ios. Sikinos. Folegandros. Santorini. Anafi.
15.30	*Highspeed 2/3*	Sifnos. Santorini. Paros.
16.00	*Daliana*	Syros. Mykonos. Ikaria (Agios Kyrikos). Fourni. Samos (Karlovassi). Samos (Vathi). Patmos. Lipsi.
16.00	*Jet One*	Milos. Ios. Santorini. Crete (Iraklion).
16.00	*Marina/Rodanthi*	Kalimnos. Kos. Rhodes.
16.30	*Aeolos Express*	Syros. Paros. Naxos. Ikaria (Evdilos). Samos (Vathi).
16.30	*Panagia*	
	Ekatontapiliani	Paros. Naxos. Ios. Santorini.
16.45	*Aeolos Express II*	Syros. Mykonos.
17.00	*Express Apollon*	Serifos. Sifnos. Milos. Kimolos.
17.00	*Highspeed 4*	Paros. Naxos. Mykonos. Syros.
17.30	*Blue Star Naxos*	Paros. Naxos. Koufonissia. Amorgos (Katapola).
18.00	*Aeolos Kenteris*	Chios. Lesbos (Mytilini).
18.00	*Mirtidiotissa*	Kithera (Agia Pelagia). Antikithera. Crete (Kasteli).
19.00	*Ierapetra L*	Milos. Crete (Agios Nikolaos). Crete (Sitia). Kassos. Karpathos (Town). Karpathos (Diafani). Chalki. Rhodes.
19.00	*Theofilos*	Chios. Lesbos (Mytilini). Limnos. Thessalonika.
20.00	*Blue Star 1*	Mykonos. Kos. Rhodes.
20.00	*Express Olympia*	Ikaria (Evdilos). Samos (Karlovassi). Samos (Vathi).
22.00	*Express Poseidon*	Paros. Naxos. Ios. Santorini.
22.00	*Taxiarchis*	Chios. Lesbos (Mytilini).
23.45	*Dimitroula*	Syros. Paros. Naxos. Donoussa. Amorgos (Katapola). Amorgos (Egiali). Astipalea. Kos. Nissiros. Tilos. Symi. Rhodes. Kastelorizo.

⑥

07.30	*Aeolos Express II*	Syros. Tinos. Mykonos.
07.30	*Highspeed 2/3*	Serifos. Sifnos. Milos.
07.45	*Express Pegasus*	Kythnos. Serifos. Sifnos. Kimolos. Milos.
08.00	*Express Santorini*	Paros. Naxos. Ios. Santorini.
12.30	*Festos Palace/*	
	Knossos Palace	Crete (Iraklion).
14.00	*Marina/Rodanthi*	Syros. Paros. Patmos. Leros. Kalimnos. Kos. Rhodes.
15.00	*Diagoras*	Patmos. Leros. Kalimnos. Kos. Rhodes.
15.00	*Patmos/Rodos*	Patmos. Leros. Kalimnos. Kos. Rhodes.
15.30	*Highspeed 2/3*	Sifnos. Santorini. Paros.
16.00	*Express Apollon*	Kythnos. Serifos. Sifnos. Milos. Kimolos. Folegandros. Sikinos. Ios. Santorini.
16.00	*Express Pegasus*	Kythnos. Serifos. Sifnos.
16.00	*Jet One*	Kythnos. Sifnos. Ios. Santorini. Amorgos (Katapola).
16.30	*Panagia*	
	Ekatontapiliani	Paros. Naxos. Koufonissia. Amorgos (Katapola).
17.00	*Aeolos Express*	Paros. Naxos. Ikaria (Evdilos). Samos (Vathi).
17.00	*Highspeed 4*	Paros. Naxos. Mykonos. Syros.
17.30	*Blue Star Naxos*	Paros. Naxos. Santorini.
18.00	*Aeolos Kenteris*	Chios. Lesbos (Mytilini).
19.00	*Mytilene*	Lesbos (Mytilini).
20.00	*Express Olympia*	Ikaria (Evdilos). Samos (Karlovassi). Samos (Vathi).
22.00	*Express Poseidon*	Paros. Naxos. Ios. Santorini.
23.30	*Romilda*	Paros. Naxos. Iraklia. Schinoussa. Koufonissia. Amorgos (Katapola). Amorgos (Egiali). Donoussa.
23.50	*Blue Star 1*	Amorgos (Katapola). Patmos. Leros. Kos. Rhodes.

⑦

07.30	*Aeolos Express II*	Syros. Tinos. Mykonos.
07.30	*Highspeed 2/3*	Serifos. Sifnos. Milos.
07.45	*Express Pegasus*	Kythnos. Serifos. Sifnos. Kimolos. Milos.

Weekly updated timetable for **Piraeus** at **greekislandhopping.com**

08.00	*Express Santorini*	Paros. Naxos. Ios. Santorini.
14.00	*Jet One*	Milos. Folegandros. Santorini. Ios.
15.00	*Marina/Rodanthi*	Syros. Mykonos. Patmos. Leros. Kalimnos. Kos. Rhodes.
15.00	*Patmos/Rodos*	Patmos. Leros. Kalimnos. Kos. Rhodes.
15.30	*Highspeed 2/3*	Sifnos. Santorini. Paros.
16.00	*Daliana*	Paros. Naxos. Ikaria (Agios Kyrikos). Fourni. Samos (Karlovassi). Samos (Vathi). Chios.
16.45	*Aeolos Express II*	Syros. Mykonos. Tinos.
17.00	*Aeolos Express*	Paros. Naxos. Ikaria (Agios Kyrikos). Samos (Vathi).
17.00	*Aeolos Kenteris*	Kalimnos. Kos. Rhodes.
17.00	*Highspeed 4*	Paros. Naxos. Mykonos. Syros.
17.30	*Blue Star Naxos*	Paros. Naxos. Santorini.
19.00	*Vitsentzos Kornaros*	Milos. Crete (Agios Nikolaos). Crete (Sitia). Kassos. Karpathos (Town). Karpathos (Diafani). Chalki. Rhodes.
21.00	*Mytilene*	Chios. Lesbos (Mytilini).
22.00	*Express Poseidon*	Paros. Naxos. Ios. Santorini.
23.45	*Romilda*	Syros. Paros. Serifos. Sifnos. Kimolos. Milos.

2. Saronic Gulf

(i). Regular Ferries & Catamarans

Ⓓ

06.30	Saronikos Ferries	Aegina (Souvala).
07.30	Saronikos Ferries	Aegina. Methana. Poros.
07.45	*Apollon Hellas*	Aegina. Methana. Poros. Hydra. Spetses. Porto Helio.
08.00	*Eftichia*	Aegina. Methana. Poros. Hydra. Ermioni.
08.00	*Elvira*	Aegina (Agia Marina).
08.00	*Georgios 2*	Aegina. Methana. Poros. Spetses. Porto Helio.
08.30	*Flying Cat 1/2*	Poros. Hydra. Spetses. Porto Helio.
09.00	*Keravnos 1/2*	Aegina. Angistri.
09.15	Saronikos Ferries	Aegina (Souvala). Aegina.
08.00	*Manaras Express*	Aegina. Angistri.
10.30	*Poseidon Hellas*	Aegina. Methana. Poros.
10.30	Saronikos Ferries	Aegina. Methana. Poros.
12.30	*Eftichia*	Aegina. Methana. Poros.
13.30	*Manaras Express*	Aegina. Angistri.
14.00	*Michael*	Aegina (Agia Marina).
14.00	Saronikos Ferries	Aegina (Souvala). Aegina.
14.15	*Nefeli*	Aegina. Methana. Poros.
14.30	*Keravnos 1/2*	Aegina. Angistri.
15.00	Saronikos Ferries	Aegina. Methana. Poros.
15.30	Saronikos Ferries	Aegina (Souvala).
18.00	Saronikos Ferries	Aegina.
18.30	*Manaras Express*	Aegina. Angistri.
18.45	*Eftichia*	Aegina. Methana. Poros. Hydra.
19.00	*Michael*	Aegina (Agia Marina).
20.00	*Poseidon Hellas*	Aegina.
20.30	*Flying Cat 1/2*	Poros. Hydra. Spetses. Porto Helio.
20.30	Saronikos Ferries	Aegina.

(ii). Hydrofoils

Ⓓ Ⓗ

06.00–19.00	Aegina (Town).
06.00–20.00	Aegina (Souvala). Aegina (Agia Marina).

Ⓓ

x 12	Poros. Hydra. Ermioni. Spetses.
08.25	Hydra. Spetses. Porto Helio.
09.00	Aegina (Town). Methana. Poros. Hydra. Ermioni. Spetses. Porto Helio.
14.30	Hydra. Spetses. Porto Helio.
16.00	Aegina (Town). Methana. Poros. Hydra. Ermioni. Spetses. Porto Helio. Tolo.

Poros

Argo-Saronic p. 506

ⓓ ev 20 min:
06.00–22.00   *Elpis I*   Galatas.

ⓓ
00.00   *Flying Cat 2*   Hydra. Spetses.
                         Porto Helio.
00.00   *Flying Cat 2*   Piraeus.
10.30   *Poseidon Hellas* Methana. Aegina. Piraeus.
10.30   *Saronikos*   Hydra. Ermioni.
10.30   *Eftichia*   Hydra. Ermioni.
                         Spetses.
10.45   Saronikos Ferries   Methana. Aegina. Piraeus.
10.50   *Apollon Hellas*   Methana. Aegina. Piraeus.
10.50   *Georgios 2*   Spetses. Porto Helio.
11.00   *Apollon Hellas*   Hydra. Spetses.
                         Porto Helio.
14.00   Saronikos Ferries   Methana. Aegina. Piraeus.
16.00   *Apollon Hellas*   Methana. Aegina. Piraeus.
16.40   *Eftichia*   Methana. Aegina. Piraeus.
17.00   *Georgios 2*   Methana. Aegina. Piraeus.
17.20   *Poseidon Hellas*   Methana. Aegina. Piraeus.
18.00   Saronikos Ferries   [⑦ 16.20]
                         Methana.
                         Aegina. Piraeus.
19.00   *Eftichia*   Methana. Aegina.
                         Piraeus.

① ② ③ ④ ⑤
06.30   Saronikos Ferries   Methana. Aegina.
                         Piraeus.

⑥ ⑦
07.00   Saronikos Ferries   Methana. Aegina.
                         Piraeus.
10.00   Saronikos Ferries   Methana. Aegina.
                         Piraeus.
19.00   Saronikos Ferries   Methana. Aegina.
                         Piraeus.

🛥 *Flying Dolphins* include:

ⓓ
x 6   Hydra.
x 7   Piraeus.
x 4   Spetses.

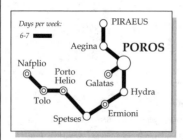

Days per week:
6-7 ▬▬▬

PIRAEUS
Aegina
POROS
Nafplio
Porto Helio   Galatas
Tolo   Hydra
Spetses   Ermioni

Port Said

Egypt p. 581

○
20.00   *Salamis Star*   Haifa. Limassol. Rhodes.
                         Santorini. Piraeus.

Porto Helio

Argo-Saronic p. 509

ⓓ
13.30   *Apollon Hellas*   Spetses. Hydra. Poros.
                         Methana. Aegina. Piraeus.

🛥 *Flying Dolphins* include:

ⓓ x 10   Hydra. Spetses.
                  Piraeus.

Princes' Islands

Turkey p. 568

ⓓ x 6
06.45–21.00   TML   İstanbul.
00.00–00.00   TML   Yalova.

Psara

Eastern Line p. 422

②
12.00   Miniotis Ferries   Chios.

④
05.00   *Saos II*   Agios Efstratios. Limnos.
                         Kavala.
12.00   Miniotis Ferries   Chios.

⑤
10.30   *Saos II*   Lavrio.

⑥
12.00   Miniotis Ferries   Chios.

○
00.00   *Nissos Limnos*   Agios Efstratios. Limnos.
                         Kavala.
00.00   *Nissos Limnos*   Rafina.

Rafina

*Weekly updated timetable for **Rafina** at greekislandhopping.com*

Athens
& Piraeus p. 122

Ⓓ

07.40	Sea Jet 2	Tinos. Mykonos. Paros.
08.00	Highspeed 2/3	Tinos. Mykonos. Tinos. Syros. Piraeus.
08.00	Evia Star	Evia (Karystos).
08.05	Superferry II	Andros. Tinos. Mykonos.
08.30	Marmari Express	Evia (Marmari).
14.15	Evia Star	Evia (Karystos).
16.00	Sea Jet 2	Tinos. Mykonos.
18.30	Evia Star	Evia (Karystos).

①

07.25	Aqua Jewel	Andros. Tinos. Mykonos. Paros.
07.45	Express Athina	Andros. Tinos. Mykonos.
12.00	Marmari Express	Evia (Marmari).
15.30	Marmari Express	Evia (Marmari).
16.30	Flying Cat 3	Tinos. Mykonos. Syros. Kythnos. Lavrio.
17.30	Express Penelope	Andros. Tinos. Mykonos.
19.00	Marmari Express	Evia (Marmari).
19.15	Superferry II	Andros.

RAFINA

Kavala
Limnos
Ag. Efstratios
Evia (Marmari)
Evia (Karystos)
Syros
Andros
Paros
Tinos
Naxos
Mykonos
Little Cyclades
Amorgos

Days per week:
6-7
2-3

②

07.25	Aqua Jewel	Andros. Tinos. Mykonos. Paros.
07.45	Express Athina	Andros. Tinos. Mykonos.
12.00	Marmari Express	Evia (Marmari).
15.30	Marmari Express	Evia (Marmari).
17.30	Express Penelope	Andros. Tinos. Mykonos.
19.00	Marmari Express	Evia (Marmari).
19.15	Superferry II	Andros.

③

07.25	Aqua Jewel	Andros. Tinos. Mykonos. Paros.
07.45	Express Athina	Andros. Tinos. Mykonos.
12.00	Marmari Express	Evia (Marmari).
15.30	Marmari Express	Evia (Marmari).
16.30	Flying Cat 3	Tinos. Mykonos. Syros. Kythnos. Lavrio.
19.00	Marmari Express	Evia (Marmari).
19.15	Superferry II	Andros.

④

07.25	Aqua Jewel	Andros. Tinos. Mykonos. Paros.
07.45	Express Penelope	Andros. Tinos. Mykonos.
12.00	Marmari Express	Evia (Marmari).
15.30	Marmari Express	Evia (Marmari).
16.30	Flying Cat 3	Tinos. Mykonos. Syros. Kythnos. Lavrio.
17.30	Express Athina	Andros. Tinos. Mykonos.
19.00	Marmari Express	Evia (Marmari).
19.15	Superferry II	Andros.

⑤

07.25	Aqua Jewel	Andros. Tinos.
07.25	Express Penelope	Andros. Tinos.
07.45	Express Athina	Andros. Tinos. Mykonos.
14.00	Marmari Express	Evia (Marmari).
16.30	Flying Cat 3	Tinos. Mykonos. Syros. Kythnos. Lavrio.
17.00	Aqua Jewel	Andros. Tinos. Mykonos. Paros.
17.00	Marmari Express	Evia (Marmari).
17.30	Express Penelope	Andros. Tinos. Mykonos.
18.30	Express Athina	Andros. Tinos. Mykonos.
19.15	Superferry II	Andros.
20.30	Marmari Express	Evia (Marmari).

⑥

07.25	Aqua Jewel	Andros. Tinos.
07.25	Express Penelope	Tinos. Mykonos.
07.45	Express Athina	Andros. Tinos. Mykonos.
12.00	Marmari Express	Evia (Marmari).

15.30	*Marmari Express*	Evia (Marmari).
16.30	*Aqua Jewel*	Andros. Tinos. Mykonos. Paros.
16.30	*Flying Cat 3*	Tinos. Mykonos. Syros. Kythnos. Lavrio.
17.30	*Express Penelope*	Andros. Tinos. Mykonos.
19.00	*Marmari Express*	Evia (Marmari).
19.15	*Superferry II*	Andros.

⑦

07.25	*Aqua Jewel*	Andros. Tinos. Mykonos. Paros.
07.25	*Express Penelope*	Tinos. Mykonos.
07.45	*Express Athina*	Andros. Tinos. Mykonos.
15.30	*Marmari Express*	Evia (Marmari).
16.30	*Flying Cat 3*	Tinos. Mykonos. Syros. Kythnos. Lavrio.
17.30	*Express Penelope*	Andros. Tinos. Mykonos.
18.30	*Express Athina*	Andros.
19.00	*Marmari Express*	Evia (Marmari).
19.15	*Superferry II*	Andros.
20.00	*Express Penelope*	Andros. Syros. Tinos. Mykonos.
22.00	*Marmari Express*	Evia (Marmari).

○

00.00	*Nissos Limnos*	Psara. Agios Efstratios. Limnos. Kavala.

Days per week:
6-7
2-3
1

Rhodes

Dodecanese p. 373

International Services:

Ⓓ

08.00	Hydrofoil	Marmaris.

Domestic Services:

Ⓓ

08.00	Hydrofoil	Kos.
09.00	*Symi II*	Symi.
17.00	Hydrofoil	Kos.
18.00	*Symi II*	Symi.

①

08.00	*Aeolos Kenteris*	Kos. Piraeus.
08.30	*Dodekanesos Express*	Kos. Kalimnos. Leros (Agia Marina).
08.30	*SeaStar*	Tilos. Nissiros.
15.00	*Patmos/Rodos*	Kos. Kalimnos. Leros. Patmos. Piraeus.
18.00	*Nissos Kalimnos*	Symi. Tilos. Nissiros. Kos. Kalimnos.
23.00	*Vitsentzos Kornaros*	Chalki. Karpathos (Diafani). Karpathos (Town). Kassos. Crete (Sitia).

②

08.30	*Dodekanesos Express*	Kos. Kalimnos. Leros (Agia Marina). Patmos. Lipsi.
08.30	*SeaStar*	Tilos.
14.00	*Dimitroula*	Kastelorizo.
15.00	*Patmos/Rodos*	Symi. Tilos. Kalimnos. Astipalea. Amorgos (Katapola). Piraeus.
18.00	*Marina/Rodanthi*	Kos. Kalimnos. Piraeus.
20.00	*Blue Star 1*	Kos. Mykonos. Piraeus.
23.45	*Dimitroula*	Symi. Tilos. Nissiros. Kos. Kalimnos. Astipalea. Amorgos (Egiali). Amorgos (Katapola). Donoussa. Naxos. Paros. Syros. Piraeus.

③

04.30	*Vitsentzos Kornaros*	Chalki. Karpathos (Diafani). Karpathos (Town). Kassos. Crete (Sitia). Crete (Agios Nikolaos). Milos. Piraeus.
07.00	*SeaStar*	Tilos.
08.30	*Dodekanesos Express*	Kastelorizo.
15.00	*Patmos/Rodos*	Kos. Kalimnos. Leros. Patmos. Piraeus.
16.00	*Marina/Rodanthi*	Kos. Kalimnos. Astipalea. Amorgos (Katapola). Piraeus.

18.00	Diagoras	Kos. Piraeus.
18.00	Hydrofoil	Tilos. Nissiros. Kos.
18.00	SeaStar	Tilos.

④

08.30	Dodekanesos Express	Kos. Kalimnos. Leros (Agia Marina).
08.30	SeaStar	Tilos. Nissiros.
11.00	Patmos/Rodos	Kos. Samos (Vathi). Thessalonika.
18.00	Marina/Rodanthi	Kos. Kalimnos. Piraeus.
18.00	Nissos Kalimnos	Symi. Tilos. Nissiros. Kos. Kalimnos.
20.00	Blue Star 1	Kos. Leros. Patmos. Syros. Piraeus.

⑤

08.00	Marina/Rodanthi	Kastelorizo.
08.30	Dodekanesos Express	Kos. Kalimnos. Leros (Agia Marina). Patmos. Lipsi.
08.30	SeaStar	Tilos. Nissiros.
15.00	Diagoras	Nissiros. Kos. Piraeus.
15.00	Patmos/Rodos	Kos. Kalimnos. Leros. Patmos. Piraeus.
18.30	Marina/Rodanthi	Kos. Kalimnos. Piraeus.
19.30	SeaStar	Tilos.

⑥

04.30	Vitsentzos Kornaros	Chalki. Karpathos (Diafani). Karpathos (Town). Kassos. Crete (Sitia). Crete (Agios Nikolaos). Milos. Piraeus.
08.30	Dodekanesos Express	Kos. Kalimnos. Leros (Agia Marina). Lipsi. Patmos.
10.00	Blue Star 1	Kos. Amorgos (Katapola). Piraeus.
18.00	Marina/Rodanthi	Kos. Kalimnos. Piraeus.
23.45	Dimitroula	Kastelorizo.

⑦

04.30	Ierapetra L	Chalki. Karpathos (Diafani). Karpathos (Town). Kassos. Crete (Sitia). Crete (Agios Nikolaos). Milos. Piraeus.
07.15	SeaStar	Tilos.
08.30	Dodekanesos Express	Kos. Kalimnos. Leros (Agia Marina). Patmos. Lipsi.
10.00	Dimitroula	Kos. Samos (Vathi). Chios. Lesbos (Mytilini). Limnos. Alexandroupolis.
15.00	Patmos/Rodos	Kos. Kalimnos. Leros. Patmos. Piraeus.
17.00	SeaStar	Tilos.
18.00	Diagoras	Kos. Piraeus.
18.00	Marina/Rodanthi	Kos. Kalimnos. Leros. Patmos. Piraeus.
18.00	Symi II	Symi.
18.30	Blue Star 1	Kos. Leros. Patmos. Syros. Piraeus.

Rhodes (Kamiros Skala)

Dodecanese p. 386

ⓓ ex ⑦

| 14.30 | Chalki/Nikos Express | Chalki. |

③ ⑦

| 09.30 | Chalki/Nikos Express | Chalki. |

Salamina / Salamis (Paloukia)

Athens & Piraeus p. 123

ⓓ ⓗ

| 06.30–21.30 | Taxi Boat | Piraeus. |

Samos (Karlovassi)

Eastern Line p. 425

①

04.50	Daliana	Samos (Vathi). Chios.
06.00	Miniotis Ferries	Fourni. Ikaria (Agios Kyrikos).
11.00	Miniotis Ferries	Samos (Vathi).
17.20	Daliana	Fourni. Ikaria (Agios Kyrikos). Piraeus.
17.30	Miniotis Ferries	Ikaria (Agios Kyrikos). Fourni.

②

04.50	Express Olympia	Samos (Vathi).
07.50	Express Olympia	Ikaria (Evdilos). Piraeus.
20.30	Miniotis Ferries	Chios.

③

| 04.00 | Daliana | Samos (Vathi). Patmos. Lipsi. |
| 17.20 | Daliana | Fourni. Ikaria (Agios Kyrikos). Mykonos. Syros. Piraeus. |

④

| 04.50 | Express Olympia | Samos (Vathi). |
| 07.50 | Express Olympia | Ikaria (Evdilos). Piraeus. |

⑤

| 04.50 | Express Olympia | Samos (Vathi). |
| 07.50 | Express Olympia | Ikaria (Evdilos). Piraeus. |

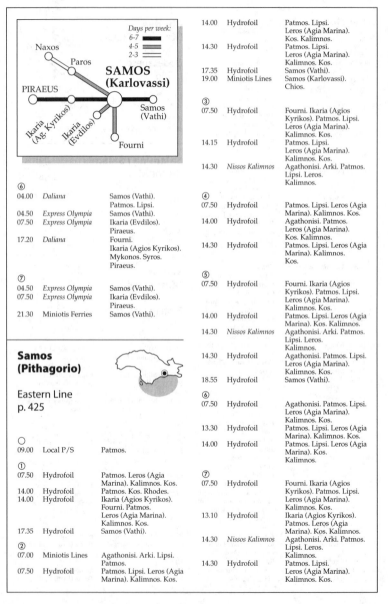

Days per week:
6-7 ▬▬▬
4-5 ▬▬▬
2-3 ▬▬▬

Naxos
Paros

**SAMOS
(Karlovassi)**

PIRAEUS

Samos
(Vathi)

Ikaria
(Ag. Kyrikos)

Ikaria
(Evdilos)

Fourni

⑥
04.00	*Daliana*	Samos (Vathi). Patmos. Lipsi.
04.50	*Express Olympia*	Samos (Vathi).
07.50	*Express Olympia*	Ikaria (Evdilos). Piraeus.
17.20	*Daliana*	Fourni. Ikaria (Agios Kyrikos). Mykonos. Syros. Piraeus.

⑦
04.50	*Express Olympia*	Samos (Vathi).
07.50	*Express Olympia*	Ikaria (Evdilos). Piraeus.
21.30	Miniotis Ferries	Samos (Vathi).

Samos (Pithagorio)

Eastern Line
p. 425

○
| 09.00 | Local P/S | Patmos. |

①
07.50	Hydrofoil	Patmos. Leros (Agia Marina). Kalimnos. Kos.
14.00	Hydrofoil	Patmos. Kos. Rhodes.
14.00	Hydrofoil	Ikaria (Agios Kyrikos). Fourni. Patmos. Leros (Agia Marina). Kalimnos. Kos.
17.35	Hydrofoil	Samos (Vathi).

②
| 07.00 | Miniotis Lines | Agathonisi. Arki. Lipsi. Patmos. |
| 07.50 | Hydrofoil | Patmos. Lipsi. Leros (Agia Marina). Kalimnos. Kos. |

14.00	Hydrofoil	Patmos. Lipsi. Leros (Agia Marina). Kos. Kalimnos.
14.30	Hydrofoil	Patmos. Lipsi. Leros (Agia Marina). Kalimnos. Kos.
17.35	Hydrofoil	Samos (Vathi).
19.00	Miniotis Lines	Samos (Karlovassi). Chios.

③
07.50	Hydrofoil	Fourni. Ikaria (Agios Kyrikos). Patmos. Lipsi. Leros (Agia Marina). Kalimnos. Kos.
14.15	Hydrofoil	Patmos. Lipsi. Leros (Agia Marina). Kalimnos. Kos.
14.30	*Nissos Kalimnos*	Agathonisi. Arki. Patmos. Lipsi. Leros. Kalimnos.

④
07.50	Hydrofoil	Patmos. Lipsi. Leros (Agia Marina). Kalimnos. Kos.
14.00	Hydrofoil	Agathonisi. Patmos. Leros (Agia Marina). Kos. Kalimnos.
14.30	Hydrofoil	Patmos. Lipsi. Leros (Agia Marina). Kalimnos. Kos.

⑤
07.50	Hydrofoil	Fourni. Ikaria (Agios Kyrikos). Patmos. Lipsi. Leros (Agia Marina). Kalimnos. Kos.
14.00	Hydrofoil	Patmos. Lipsi. Leros (Agia Marina). Kos. Kalimnos.
14.30	*Nissos Kalimnos*	Agathonisi. Arki. Patmos. Lipsi. Leros. Kalimnos.
14.30	Hydrofoil	Agathonisi. Patmos. Lipsi. Leros (Agia Marina). Kalimnos. Kos.
18.55	Hydrofoil	Samos (Vathi).

⑥
07.50	Hydrofoil	Agathonisi. Patmos. Lipsi. Leros (Agia Marina). Kalimnos. Kos.
13.30	Hydrofoil	Patmos. Lipsi. Leros (Agia Marina). Kalimnos. Kos.
14.00	Hydrofoil	Patmos. Lipsi. Leros (Agia Marina). Kos. Kalimnos.

⑦
07.50	Hydrofoil	Fourni. Ikaria (Agios Kyrikos). Patmos. Lipsi. Leros (Agia Marina). Kalimnos. Kos.
13.10	Hydrofoil	Ikaria (Agios Kyrikos). Patmos. Leros (Agia Marina). Kos. Kalimnos.
14.30	*Nissos Kalimnos*	Agathonisi. Arki. Patmos. Lipsi. Leros. Kalimnos.
14.30	Hydrofoil	Patmos. Lipsi. Leros (Agia Marina). Kalimnos. Kos.

Samos (Vathi)

Eastern Line p. 425

ⓓ

08.00	*Kapetan Giorgis*	Kuşadası.
17.00	*Fari Kaptain/Sultan I*	Kuşadası.

①

06.30	*Daliana*	Chios.
07.00	Hydrofoil	Samos (Pithagorio). Patmos. Leros (Agia Marina). Kalimnos. Kos.
07.30	*Aeolos Express*	Ikaria (Agios Kyrikos). Naxos. Paros. Piraeus.
16.00	*Daliana*	Samos (Karlovassi). Fourni. Ikaria (Agios Kyrikos). Piraeus.
16.00	Miniotis Ferries	Samos (Karlovassi). Ikaria (Agios Kyrikos). Fourni.

②

04.00	*Dimitroula*	Kos. Rhodes. Kastelorizo.
07.00	*Express Olympia*	Samos (Karlovassi). Ikaria (Evdilos). Piraeus.
07.30	*Aeolos Express*	Ikaria (Agios Kyrikos). Naxos. Paros. Piraeus.
07.50	*Taxiarchis*	Chios. Lesbos (Mytilini).

③

00.15	*Taxiarchis*	Piraeus.
06.30	*Daliana*	Patmos. Lipsi.
07.00	Hydrofoil	Samos (Pithagorio). Fourni. Ikaria (Agios Kyrikos). Patmos. Lipsi. Leros (Agia Marina). Kalimnos. Kos.
07.30	*Aeolos Express*	Ikaria (Evdilos). Naxos. Paros. Piraeus.
16.00	*Daliana*	Samos (Karlovassi). Fourni. Ikaria (Agios Kyrikos). Mykonos. Syros. Piraeus.

④

07.00	*Express Olympia*	Samos (Karlovassi). Ikaria (Evdilos). Piraeus.
07.00	Hydrofoil	Samos (Pithagorio). Patmos. Lipsi. Leros (Agia Marina). Kalimnos. Kos.
07.30	*Aeolos Express*	Ikaria (Evdilos). Naxos. Paros. Piraeus.
18.30	*Patmos/Rodos*	Thessalonika.

⑤

07.00	*Express Olympia*	Samos (Karlovassi). Ikaria (Evdilos). Piraeus.
07.00	Hydrofoil	Samos (Pithagorio). Fourni. Ikaria (Agios Kyrikos). Patmos. Lipsi. Leros (Agia Marina). Kalimnos. Kos.
07.30	*Aeolos Express*	Ikaria (Agios Kyrikos). Naxos. Paros. Piraeus.

⑥

06.30	*Daliana*	Patmos. Lipsi.
06.30	*Patmos/Rodos*	Kos. Rhodes.
07.00	*Express Olympia*	Samos (Karlovassi). Ikaria (Evdilos). Piraeus.
07.00	Hydrofoil	Samos (Pithagorio). Agathonisi. Patmos. Lipsi. Leros (Agia Marina). Kalimnos. Kos.
07.30	*Aeolos Express*	Ikaria (Agios Kyrikos). Naxos. Paros. Piraeus.
16.00	*Daliana*	Samos (Karlovassi). Fourni. Ikaria (Agios Kyrikos). Mykonos. Syros. Piraeus.

⑦

07.00	*Express Olympia*	Samos (Karlovassi). Ikaria (Evdilos). Piraeus.
07.00	Hydrofoil	Samos (Pithagorio). Fourni. Ikaria (Agios Kyrikos). Patmos. Lipsi. Leros (Agia Marina). Kalimnos. Kos.
07.30	*Aeolos Express*	Ikaria (Evdilos). Naxos. Paros. Piraeus.
18.00	*Dimitroula*	Chios. Lesbos (Mytilini). Limnos. Alexandroupolis.
23.00	Miniotis Ferries	Samos (Karlovassi).

Samothrace

Northern Aegean p. 454

①

08.00	*Niki H/F*	Alexandroupolis.
11.30	*Arsinoe/Caviros*	Alexandroupolis.
12.00	*Niki H/F*	Alexandroupolis.
19.00	*Arsinoe/Caviros*	Alexandroupolis.

②

11.00	*Niki H/F*	Alexandroupolis.
12.00	*Arsinoe/Caviros*	Alexandroupolis.
14.00	*Niki H/F*	Alexandroupolis.

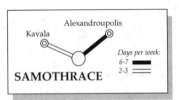

SAMOTHRACE

Alexandroupolis
Kavala

Days per week:
6-7
2-3

③		
09.00	*Arsinoe/Caviros*	Kavala.
12.30	*Niki H/F*	Alexandroupolis.
16.00	*Niki H/F*	Alexandroupolis.

④		
07.30	*Niki H/F*	Alexandroupolis.
09.00	*Arsinoe/Caviros*	Kavala.
17.30	*Niki H/F*	Alexandroupolis.
19.00	*Arsinoe/Caviros*	Alexandroupolis.

⑤		
08.00	*Niki H/F*	Alexandroupolis.
11.30	*Arsinoe/Caviros*	Kavala.
12.00	*Niki H/F*	Alexandroupolis.

⑥		
08.00	*Niki H/F*	Alexandroupolis.
09.30	*Arsinoe/Caviros*	Kavala.
11.45	*Saos II*	Alexandroupolis.
12.00	*Niki H/F*	Alexandroupolis.
16.30	*Niki H/F*	Alexandroupolis.
16.40	*Saos II*	Limnos. Agios Efstratios. Lavrio.
19.30	*Niki H/F*	Alexandroupolis.

⑦		
08.30	*Niki H/F*	Alexandroupolis.
09.00	*Arsinoe/Caviros*	Kavala.
18.20	*Niki H/F*	Alexandroupolis.
20.00	*Arsinoe/Caviros*	Alexandroupolis.

○		
08.30	*Thraki III H/F*	Alexandroupolis.
14.15	*Thraki III H/F*	Limnos.
18.00	*Thraki III H/F*	Alexandroupolis.

Santorini / Thira (Athinios)

Cyclades Central
p. 163

①		
07.30	*Blue Star Naxos*	Naxos. Paros. Piraeus.
08.45	*Jet One*	Ios. Milos. Kythnos. Piraeus.
10.00	*Express Poseidon*	Ios. Naxos. Paros. Piraeus.

11.10	*Flying Cat 4*	Ios. Paros. Naxos. Mykonos.
13.00	*Highspeed 1*	Paros. Piraeus.
15.30	*Blue Star Paros*	Naxos. Paros. Piraeus.
17.15	*Daedalus*	Paros. Mykonos. Tinos. Thessalonika.
17.30	*Flying Cat 4*	Crete (Iraklion).
19.45	*Highspeed 2/3*	Paros. Piraeus.
20.00	*Panagia Ekatontapiliani*	Ios. Naxos. Paros. Piraeus.
21.45	*Jet One*	Amorgos (Katapola).

②		
02.05	*Express Santorini*	Anafi.
08.00	*Express Santorini*	Ios. Naxos. Paros. Piraeus.
08.45	*Jet One*	Ios. Milos. Sifnos. Piraeus.
10.00	*Express Apollon*	Ios. Sikinos. Folegandros. Kimolos. Milos. Sifnos. Serifos. Kythnos. Piraeus.
10.00	*Express Poseidon*	Ios. Naxos. Paros. Piraeus.
11.10	*Flying Cat 4*	Ios. Paros. Naxos. Mykonos.
13.00	*Highspeed 1*	Paros. Piraeus.
15.30	*Blue Star Paros*	Ios. Naxos. Paros. Piraeus.
17.15	*Vergina Sky*	Crete (Rethimno).
17.30	*Flying Cat 4*	Crete (Iraklion).
19.45	*Highspeed 2/3*	Paros. Piraeus.
20.00	*Panagia Ekatontapiliani*	Ios. Naxos. Paros. Piraeus.
22.20	*Jet One*	Crete (Iraklion).

③		
07.30	*Blue Star Naxos*	Naxos. Paros. Piraeus.
09.45	*Jet One*	Ios. Folegandros. Milos. Sifnos. Piraeus.
10.00	*Express Santorini*	Ios. Naxos. Paros. Piraeus.
11.00	*Daedalus*	Crete (Iraklion).
11.10	*Flying Cat 4*	Ios. Paros. Naxos. Mykonos.
13.00	*Highspeed 1*	Paros. Piraeus.
15.30	*Blue Star Paros*	Naxos. Paros. Piraeus.
17.30	*Flying Cat 4*	Crete (Iraklion).
20.00	*Panagia Ekatontapiliani*	Ios. Naxos. Paros. Piraeus.
22.00	*Jet One*	Amorgos (Katapola).
22.15	*Daedalus*	Naxos. Mykonos. Syros. Thessalonika.

④		
04.00	*Romilda*	Anafi.
08.00	*Express Poseidon*	Ios. Naxos. Paros. Piraeus.
08.45	*Jet One*	Folegandros. Milos. Piraeus.
09.30	*Romilda*	Folegandros. Sikinos. Ios. Naxos. Paros. Piraeus.

Ferry Company Colours

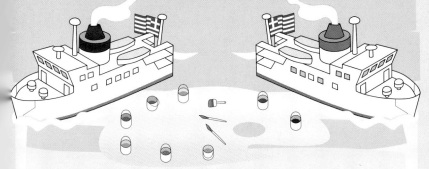

Ferry	Livery
Aeolos Express	31
Aeolos Express II	31
Aeolos Kenteris	31
Agios Andreas	26
Agios Spiridon	23
Ankara	40
Aphrodite II	27
Apollon Hellas	35
Aptera	4
Aqua Jewel	2
Aretousa	29
Ariadne Palace	29
Ariadne Palace 1	29
Arkadi	4
Arsinoe	3
Athens Express	42
Blue Horizon	10
Blue Sky	10
Blue Star 1	11
Blue Star 2	11
Blue Star Ithaki	11
Blue Star Naxos	11
Blue Star Paros	11
Brindisi	43
Chioni	28
Countess M	26
Crown M	26
Daedalus	29
Daliana	17
Dame M	26
Diagoras	13
Dimitroula	17
Duchess M	26
Eftichia	35
Egnatia II	21
Ekaterini P	14
El. Venizelos	6
Eptanisos	10
Europa Palace	29
Express Adonis	20
Express Aphrodite	20
Express Apollon	20

Ferry	Livery
Express Athina	20
Express Hermes	20
Express Olympia	20
Express Pegassos	20
Express Penelope	20
Express Poseidon	20
Express Santorini	20
Express Skopelitis	37
Fedra	20
Festos Palace	29
Grace M	26
Hellenic Spirit	4
Hercules	4
Ierapetra L	24
Ikarus	29
Iskenderun	40
JetFerry 1	17
Kapetan Alex. A	1
Kefalonia	10
Knossos Palace	29
Kriti I, II, V	4
Lato	4
Lefka Ori	4
Lissos	4
Lykomides	35
Macedon	19
Maria G	27
Marina	17
Marko Polo	22
Milena	17
Mirina Express	19
Mirtidiotissa	6
Mount Olympus	4
Mytilene	32
Nissos Kalimnos	5
Nissos Kypros	33
Olympia Palace	29
Olympic Champion	4
Panagia Ekatontapiliani	20
Pantokrator	15
Papadiamantis II	19

Ferry	Livery
Pasiphae Palace	29
Patmos	13
Penelope A	1
Polaris	42
Poseidon	16
Poseidon Hellas	35
Preveli	4
Princessa Amorosa	25
Princessa Cypria	25
Princessa Marissa	25
Prometheus	29
Proteus	41
Psara	28
Rethimno	4
Rodanthi	17
Romilda	17
Rodos	13
Salamis Star	34
Samsum	40
Santorini Sky	18
Saos II	8
Saronikos	35
Saturnus	42
Sea Harmony	33
Sea Serenade	33
Sea Symphony	33
Sophocles V	4
Superferry II	10
Superfast I–XII	38
Symi I	39
Taxiarchis	32
Thassos I–IV	7
Theofilos	32
Truva	40
Valentino	43
Vega	42
Venus	42
Vicountess M	26
Vitsentzos Kornaros	24
Zakinthos I	9
Zakinthos 2	9

Car & Passenger Ferry Liveries

International Line Only
Funnel Logo
Hull Logo

1 AGOUDIMOS LINES

2 ALPHA FERRIES

3 ΑΡΣΙΝΟΗ ΛΙΝΕΣ
ARSINOE LINES

4 *ANEK LINES*

5 ANEK SEA LINES

6 ANEN LINES

7 A. N. E. Ο.
ANE THASSOS

8 A.N.E.Σ

9 ANEZ LINES

10 *Blue Ferries*
STRINTZIS LINES

11 *Blue Star Ferries*
STRINTZIS LINES

12 D.A.N.E. SEA LINE

13 K. P. N. EUBOEA

14 FAST FERRIES

15 FEAX EXPRESS FERRIES

16 FIVE STARS LINES

17 GA FERRIES

18 GOLDEN FERRIES

19 GOUTOS LINES

20 HELLAS Ferries
HELLAS FLYING DOLPHINS

21 HML FERRIES

22 JADROLINIJA

23 KERKIRA LINES

24 LANE LINES

25 LOUIS CRUISE LINES

26 MARLINES

27 MED LINK LINES

28 MINIOTIS LINES

29 MINOAN LINES highspeed

30 MINOAN LINES

31 TELESTET
NEL LINES

32 NEL LINES

33 POSEIDON LINES

34 SALAMIS LINES

35 SARONIKOS Ferries
HELLAS FLYING DOLPHINS

36 SKYROS LINE

37 SMALL CYCLADES LINES

38 SUPERFAST

39 SYMI ANE

40 TURKISH MARITIME LINES

41 TYROGALAS

42 VENTOURIS FERRIES

43 VERGINA FERRIES

Hydrofoil Liveries

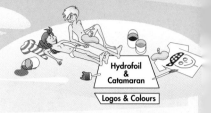

Hydrofoil & Catamaran

Logos & Colours

44
A. N. E. THASSOS
Thission Dolphin

45
BODRUM EXPRESS LINES
Bodrum Princess

46
HELLAS FLYING DOL.
Flying / Mega Dolphin I–32

47
KIRIACOULIS MARITIME
Aristea M, Georgios M Gina I, II; Mazilena I, II Samos Flying Dolphins I–IV

48
LASUMZIS
Christos L Petros L

49
NEK AE
Marina II

50
SARONIC DOLPHINS
Dolphins I–V

Catamaran Liveries

51
AEGEANJET
Jet One

52
BLUE STAR / STRINTZIS
SeaJet 2

53
DODEKANISOS SPEEDWAYS
Dodecanese Express

54
HELLAS FLYING DOLPHINS
Highspeed I, 2, 3, 4 Flying Cat I, 2, 3, 4

55
PARASKEVAS NAFTILIAKI
Keravnos 1, 2

56
SPORADES FERRIES
Express Haroulla

57
SYMI ANE
Symi II, III

58
TILOS ANE
SeaStar

59
VENTOURIS FERRIES
Ventouris High Speed I, II

10.00	Express Santorini	Ios. Naxos. Paros. Piraeus.
11.10	Flying Cat 4	Ios. Paros. Naxos. Mykonos.
13.00	Highspeed 1	Paros. Piraeus.
15.30	Blue Star Paros	Ios. Naxos. Paros. Piraeus.
17.15	Vergina Sky	Crete (Agios Nikolaos).
17.30	Flying Cat 4	Crete (Iraklion).
19.45	Highspeed 2/3	Paros. Piraeus.
20.00	Panagia Ekatontapiliani	Ios. Naxos. Paros. Piraeus.
21.05	Jet One	Amorgos (Katapola).

⑤
07.30	Blue Star Naxos	Naxos. Paros. Piraeus.
08.45	Jet One	Ios. Milos. Piraeus.
10.00	Express Poseidon	Ios. Naxos. Paros. Piraeus.
11.10	Flying Cat 4	Ios. Paros. Naxos. Mykonos.
13.00	Highspeed 1	Paros. Piraeus.
14.15	Daedalus	Crete (Iraklion).
15.30	Blue Star Paros	Naxos. Paros. Piraeus.
17.30	Flying Cat 4	Crete (Iraklion).
19.45	Highspeed 2/3	Paros. Piraeus.
20.00	Express Santorini	Ios. Naxos. Paros. Piraeus.
21.15	Jet One	Crete (Iraklion).

⑥
01.15	Daedalus	Paros. Mykonos. Tinos. Skiathos. Thessalonika.

04.00	Romilda	Anafi.
07.30	Panagia Ekatontapiliani	Ios. Naxos. Paros. Piraeus.
09.30	Romilda	Folegandros. Sikinos. Ios. Naxos. Paros. Piraeus.
09.45	Jet One	Ios. Milos. Sifnos. Kythnos. Piraeus.
10.00	Express Poseidon	Ios. Naxos. Paros. Piraeus.
11.10	Flying Cat 4	Ios. Paros. Naxos. Mykonos.
13.00	Highspeed 1	Paros. Piraeus.
15.30	Blue Star Paros	Naxos. Paros. Piraeus.
17.30	Flying Cat 4	Crete (Iraklion).
19.45	Highspeed 2/3	Paros. Piraeus.
20.00	Express Santorini	Ios. Naxos. Paros. Piraeus.
21.00	Jet One	Amorgos (Katapola).

⑦
07.30	Blue Star Naxos	Naxos. Paros. Piraeus.
10.00	Express Poseidon	Ios. Naxos. Paros. Piraeus.
11.10	Flying Cat 4	Ios. Paros. Naxos. Mykonos.
13.00	Highspeed 1	Paros. Piraeus.
15.30	Blue Star Paros	Naxos. Paros. Piraeus.
16.30	Express Apollon	Ios. Sikinos. Folegandros. Kimolos. Milos. Sifnos. Serifos. Kythnos. Piraeus.
17.30	Flying Cat 4	Crete (Iraklion).
19.15	Daedalus	Crete (Iraklion).
19.15	Jet One	Ios. Milos. Piraeus.
19.45	Highspeed 2/3	Paros. Piraeus.
20.00	Express Santorini	Ios. Naxos. Paros. Piraeus.

○
00.00	Panagia Tinou	Anafi.

PIRAEUS — Thessalonika — Skiathos — Tinos — Syros — Mykonos — Serifos — Naxos — Sifnos — Paros — Foleg. — Ios — Sikinos — SANTORINI — Milos — Anafi — Thirasia — Rhodes — Karpathos — Crete (Iraklion)

Days per week:
6-7
4-5
2-3

Santorini (Fira / Old Port)

Cyclades Central
p. 163

ⓓ
09.15	Tour Boat	Nea Kameni.
10.30	Nissos Thirassia	Nea Kameni. Thirasia (Korfos). Thirasia (Riva). Santorini (Oia).
10.30	Nissos Thirassia	Nea Kameni. Thirasia (Korfos). Thirasia (Riva). Santorini (Oia).
15.20	Tour Boat	Nea Kameni.
17.00	Nissos Thirassia	Santorini.

Schinoussa

Cyclades East p. 286

①
| 10.15 | *Express Skopelitis* | Iraklia. Naxos. |
| 17.00 | *Express Skopelitis* | Koufonissia. Donoussa. Amorgos (Egiali). Amorgos (Katapola). |

②
00.05	*Blue Star Naxos*	Koufonissia. Amorgos (Katapola).
07.45	*Express Skopelitis*	Iraklia. Paros (Piso Livadi). Naxos.
07.50	*Blue Star Naxos*	Iraklia. Naxos. Paros. Piraeus.
16.50	*Express Skopelitis*	Koufonissia. Amorgos (Katapola).

③
| 10.15 | *Express Skopelitis* | Iraklia. Naxos. |
| 17.00 | *Express Skopelitis* | Koufonissia. Donoussa. Amorgos (Egiali). Amorgos (Katapola). |

④
00.05	*Blue Star Naxos*	Koufonissia. Amorgos (Katapola).
07.45	*Express Skopelitis*	Iraklia. Paros (Piso Livadi). Naxos.
07.50	*Blue Star Naxos*	Iraklia. Naxos. Paros. Piraeus.
16.50	*Express Skopelitis*	Koufonissia. Amorgos (Katapola).

⑤
| 10.15 | *Express Skopelitis* | Iraklia. Naxos. |
| 17.00 | *Express Skopelitis* | Koufonissia. Donoussa. Amorgos (Egiali). Amorgos (Katapola). |

⑥
| 07.45 | *Express Skopelitis* | Iraklia. Paros (Piso Livadi). Naxos. |
| 14.30 | *Express Skopelitis* | Koufonissia. Amorgos (Katapola). |

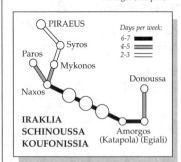

⑦
| 08.30 | *Romilda* | Koufonissia. Amorgos (Katapola). Amorgos (Egiali). Donoussa. |

Serifos

Cyclades West p. 251

①
00.20	*Express Apollon*	Kythnos. Piraeus.
09.50	*Highspeed 2/3*	Sifnos. Milos.
10.30	*Romilda*	Sifnos. Kimolos. Milos.
12.15	*Express Apollon*	Sifnos. Milos. Kimolos. Folegandros. Sikinos. Ios. Santorini.
13.05	*Highspeed 2/3*	Piraeus.
16.30	*Romilda*	Paros. Syros.
20.30	*Express Pegasus*	Sifnos. Milos.

②
01.20	*Express Pegasus*	Piraeus.
09.50	*Highspeed 2/3*	Sifnos. Milos.
13.05	*Highspeed 2/3*	Piraeus.
15.30	*Romilda*	Sifnos. Kimolos. Milos.
17.30	*Express Apollon*	Kythnos. Piraeus.
20.30	*Express Pegasus*	Sifnos. Kimolos. Milos.
21.30	*Romilda*	Paros. Syros. Piraeus.

③
01.50	*Express Pegasus*	Piraeus.
12.15	*Express Apollon*	Sifnos. Kimolos. Milos.
17.50	*Express Apollon*	Kythnos. Piraeus.

④
09.50	*Highspeed 2/3*	Sifnos. Milos.
12.15	*Express Apollon*	Sifnos. Kimolos. Milos.
13.05	*Highspeed 2/3*	Piraeus.
17.50	*Express Apollon*	Kythnos. Piraeus.
20.15	*Daliana*	Sifnos. Kimolos. Milos.
20.30	*Express Pegasus*	Sifnos. Milos.

⑤
01.20	*Express Pegasus*	Piraeus.
03.30	*Daliana*	Paros. Syros. Piraeus.
09.50	*Highspeed 2/3*	Sifnos. Milos.
13.05	*Highspeed 2/3*	Piraeus.

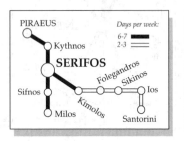

| 20.55 | *Express Apollon* | Sifnos. Milos. Kimolos. Piraeus. |

ⓖ
09.50	*Highspeed 2/3*	Sifnos. Milos.
12.15	*Express Pegasus*	Sifnos. Kimolos. Milos.
13.05	*Highspeed 2/3*	Piraeus.
17.50	*Express Pegasus*	Kythnos. Piraeus.
20.30	*Express Apollon*	Sifnos. Milos. Kimolos. Folegandros. Sikinos. Ios. Santorini.
20.30	*Express Pegasus*	Sifnos. Kythnos. Piraeus.

ⓖ
09.50	*Highspeed 2/3*	Sifnos. Milos.
12.15	*Express Pegasus*	Sifnos. Kimolos. Milos.
13.05	*Highspeed 2/3*	Piraeus.
17.50	*Express Pegasus*	Kythnos. Piraeus.

PIRAEUS — *Days per week:* 6-7, 4-5, 2-3

Kythnos — Mykonos — Paros — Serifos — Naxos — **SIFNOS** — Folegandros — Sikinos — Kimolos — Ios — Milos — Santorini

ⓔ
00.25	*Express Pegasus*	Serifos. Piraeus.
02.15	*Daliana*	Serifos. Paros. Syros. Piraeus.
10.30	*Highspeed 2/3*	Milos.
12.30	*Highspeed 2/3*	Serifos. Piraeus.
18.00	*Highspeed 2/3*	Santorini. Paros. Piraeus.
21.40	*Express Apollon*	Milos. Kimolos. Piraeus.

ⓕ
10.30	*Highspeed 2/3*	Milos.
12.30	*Highspeed 2/3*	Serifos. Piraeus.
12.45	*Jet One*	Kythnos. Piraeus.
13.10	*Express Pegasus*	Kimolos. Milos.
16.30	*Express Pegasus*	Serifos. Kythnos. Piraeus.
18.00	*Highspeed 2/3*	Santorini. Paros. Piraeus.
18.45	*Jet One*	Ios. Santorini. Amorgos (Katapola).
21.20	*Express Apollon*	Milos. Kimolos. Folegandros. Sikinos. Ios. Santorini.
21.50	*Express Pegasus*	Kythnos. Piraeus.

ⓖ
10.30	*Highspeed 2/3*	Milos.
12.30	*Highspeed 2/3*	Serifos. Piraeus.
13.10	*Express Pegasus*	Kimolos. Milos.
16.30	*Express Pegasus*	Serifos. Kythnos. Piraeus.
18.00	*Highspeed 2/3*	Santorini. Paros. Piraeus.
23.25	*Express Apollon*	Serifos. Kythnos. Piraeus.

Sifnos

Cyclades West   p. 256

ⓐ
10.30	*Highspeed 2/3*	Milos.
11.25	*Romilda*	Kimolos. Milos.
12.30	*Highspeed 2/3*	Serifos. Piraeus.
13.05	*Express Apollon*	Milos. Kimolos. Folegandros. Sikinos. Ios. Santorini.
15.35	*Romilda*	Serifos. Paros. Syros.
18.00	*Highspeed 2/3*	Santorini. Paros. Piraeus.
21.25	*Express Pegasus*	Milos.

ⓑ
00.25	*Express Pegasus*	Serifos. Piraeus.
10.30	*Highspeed 2/3*	Milos.
12.30	*Highspeed 2/3*	Serifos. Piraeus.
16.25	*Romilda*	Kimolos. Milos.
16.55	*Express Apollon*	Serifos. Kythnos. Piraeus.
18.00	*Highspeed 2/3*	Santorini. Paros. Piraeus.
20.30	*Romilda*	Serifos. Paros. Syros. Piraeus.
21.25	*Express Pegasus*	Kimolos. Milos.

ⓒ
01.00	*Express Pegasus*	Serifos. Piraeus.
13.05	*Express Apollon*	Kimolos. Milos.
13.15	*Jet One*	Piraeus.
16.55	*Express Apollon*	Serifos. Kythnos. Piraeus.

ⓓ
10.30	*Highspeed 2/3*	Milos.
12.30	*Highspeed 2/3*	Serifos. Piraeus.
13.05	*Express Apollon*	Kimolos. Milos.
16.55	*Express Apollon*	Serifos. Kythnos. Piraeus.
18.00	*Highspeed 2/3*	Santorini. Paros. Piraeus.
21.25	*Express Pegasus*	Milos.
22.30	*Daliana*	Kimolos. Milos.

Sikinos

Cyclades West
p. 259

ⓐ
| 17.45 | *Express Apollon* | Ios. Santorini. |

②   SIKINOS

②		
11.55	*Express Apollon*	Folegandros. Kimolos. Milos. Sifnos. Serifos. Kythnos. Piraeus.
③		
23.30	*Romilda*	Folegandros. Santorini. Anafi.
④		
12.50	*Romilda*	Ios. Naxos. Paros. Piraeus.
⑤		
23.30	*Romilda*	Folegandros. Santorini. Anafi.
⑥		
12.50	*Romilda*	Ios. Naxos. Paros. Piraeus.
⑦		
02.00	*Express Apollon*	Ios. Santorini.
18.20	*Express Apollon*	Folegandros. Kimolos. Milos. Sifnos. Serifos. Kythnos. Piraeus.

Skiathos

Northern Aegean
p. 454

①		
10.15	*Express Haroulla*	Skopelos. Alonissos.
14.05	*Express Haroulla*	Volos.
14.20	*JetFerry 1*	Skopelos. Alonissos.
18.20	*JetFerry 1*	Amorgos (Katapola).
20.00	*Express Haroulla*	Skopelos.

②		
10.15	*Express Haroulla*	Skopelos. Alonissos.
14.05	*Express Haroulla*	Volos.
14.20	*JetFerry 1*	Skopelos. Alonissos.
18.20	*JetFerry 1*	Amorgos (Katapola).
20.00	*Express Haroulla*	Skopelos.
21.00	*Daedalus*	Tinos. Mykonos. Paros. Santorini. Crete (Iraklion).
③		
10.15	*Express Haroulla*	Skopelos. Alonissos.
14.05	*Express Haroulla*	Volos.
14.20	*JetFerry 1*	Skopelos. Alonissos.
18.20	*JetFerry 1*	Amorgos (Katapola).
20.00	*Express Haroulla*	Skopelos.
20.00	*Milena*	Volos.
④		
04.00	*Milena*	Skopelos. Thessalonika.
10.15	*Express Haroulla*	Skopelos. Alonissos.
14.05	*Express Haroulla*	Volos.
14.20	*JetFerry 1*	Skopelos. Alonissos.
18.20	*JetFerry 1*	Amorgos (Katapola).
20.00	*Express Haroulla*	Skopelos.
⑤		
00.20	*Milena*	Agios Konstantinos.
10.15	*Express Haroulla*	Skopelos. Alonissos.
12.00	*Milena*	Skopelos.
14.00	*Milena*	Volos.
14.05	*Express Haroulla*	Volos.
17.20	*JetFerry 1*	Skopelos. Alonissos.
20.00	*Express Haroulla*	Skopelos.
22.20	*JetFerry 1*	Agios Konstantinos.
23.45	*Milena*	Limnos. Lesbos (Mytilini).

SKIATHOS

⑥		
10.15	*Express Haroulla*	Skopelos. Alonissos.
14.05	*Express Haroulla*	Volos.
14.20	*JetFerry 1*	Skopelos. Alonissos.
15.00	*Daedalus*	Thessalonika.
17.50	*JetFerry 1*	Amorgos (Katapola).
20.00	*Express Haroulla*	Skopelos.

⑦		
10.15	*Express Haroulla*	Skopelos. Alonissos.
14.05	*Express Haroulla*	Volos.
14.20	*JetFerry 1*	Skopelos. Alonissos.
17.50	*JetFerry 1*	Amorgos (Katapola).
20.00	*Express Haroulla*	Skopelos.

🐬 *Flying Dolphins* include:

⑩		
07.55	MFD Hydrofoil	Volos.
08.10	MFD Hydrofoil	Agios Konstantinos.
10.20	MFD Hydrofoil	Skopelos (Glossa).
		Skopelos. Alonissos.
11.35	MFD Hydrofoil	Skopelos (Glossa).
		Skopelos. Alonissos.
12.10	MFD Hydrofoil	Agios Konstantinos.
12.45	MFD Hydrofoil	Volos.
14.40	MFD Hydrofoil	Skopelos (Glossa).
		Skopelos. Alonissos.
15.25	MFD Hydrofoil	Volos.
15.35	MFD Hydrofoil	Skopelos.
15.50	MFD Hydrofoil	Skopelos.
16.50	MFD Hydrofoil	Volos.
17.25	MFD Hydrofoil	Agios Konstantinos.
20.50	MFD Hydrofoil	Skopelos (Glossa).
		Skopelos. Alonissos.
20.55	MFD Hydrofoil	Skopelos (Glossa).
		Skopelos. Alonissos.

Skopelos

Northern Aegean
p. 462

①		
11.30	*Express Haroulla*	Alonissos. Skiathos.
		Volos.
15.30	*JetFerry 1*	Alonissos.
17.10	*JetFerry 1*	Skiathos.
		Amorgos (Katapola).
21.30	*Express Haroulla*	Skiathos. Volos.

②		
11.30	*Express Haroulla*	Alonissos. Skiathos.
		Volos.
15.30	*JetFerry 1*	Alonissos.
17.10	*JetFerry 1*	Skiathos.
		Amorgos (Katapola).
21.30	*Express Haroulla*	Skiathos. Volos.

③		
11.30	*Express Haroulla*	Alonissos. Skiathos.
		Volos.
15.30	*JetFerry 1*	Alonissos.
17.10	*JetFerry 1*	Skiathos.
		Amorgos (Katapola).
18.30	*Milena*	Skiathos. Volos.
21.30	*Express Haroulla*	Skiathos.
		Volos.

④		
05.30	*Milena*	Thessalonika.
11.30	*Express Haroulla*	Alonissos. Skiathos.
		Volos.
15.30	*JetFerry 1*	Alonissos.
17.10	*JetFerry 1*	Skiathos.
		Amorgos (Katapola).
21.30	*Express Haroulla*	Skiathos. Volos.
23.00	*Milena*	Skiathos.
		Agios Konstantinos.

⑤		
11.30	*Express Haroulla*	Alonissos. Skiathos.
		Volos.
13.00	*Milena*	Skiathos. Volos.
18.30	*JetFerry 1*	Alonissos.
21.10	*JetFerry 1*	Skiathos.
		Agios Konstantinos.
21.30	*Express Haroulla*	Skiathos. Volos.
23.00	*Milena*	Skiathos. Limnos.
		Lesbos (Mytilini).

⑥		
11.30	*Express Haroulla*	Alonissos. Skiathos.
		Volos.
15.30	*JetFerry 1*	Alonissos.
16.40	*JetFerry 1*	Skiathos.
		Amorgos (Katapola).
21.30	*Express Haroulla*	Skiathos.
		Volos.

⑦		
11.30	*Express Haroulla*	Alonissos. Skiathos.
		Volos.
15.30	*JetFerry 1*	Alonissos.
16.40	*JetFerry 1*	Skiathos.
		Amorgos (Katapola).
21.30	*Express Haroulla*	Skiathos. Volos.

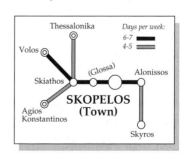

🌊 *Flying Dolphins* include:

ⓓ

07.00	MFD Hydrofoil	Skopelos (Glossa). Skiathos. Volos.
07.15	MFD Hydrofoil	Skopelos (Glossa). Skiathos. Agios Konstantinos.
11.10	MFD Hydrofoil	Alonissos.
11.30	MFD Hydrofoil	Skiathos. Agios Konstantinos.
12.10	MFD Hydrofoil	Skiathos. Volos.
12.30	MFD Hydrofoil	Alonissos.
14.30	MFD Hydrofoil	Skopelos (Glossa). Skiathos. Volos.
15.30	MFD Hydrofoil	Alonissos.
16.15	MFD Hydrofoil	Skiathos. Volos.
16.25	MFD Hydrofoil	Skopelos (Glossa). Skiathos. Agios Konstantinos.
21.45	MFD Hydrofoil	Alonissos.
21.50	MFD Hydrofoil	Alonissos.

◯

00.00	MFD Hydrofoil	Nea Moudania. Thessalonika.
00.00	MFD Hydrofoil	Skyros.

Skopelos (Glossa)

Northern Aegean
p. 464

🌊 *Flying Dolphins* include:

ⓓ

07.30	MFD Hydrofoil	Skiathos. Volos.
07.45	MFD Hydrofoil	Skiathos. Agios Konstantinos.
10.40	MFD Hydrofoil	Skopelos. Alonissos.
11.55	MFD Hydrofoil	Skopelos. Alonissos.
15.00	MFD Hydrofoil	Skopelos. Alonissos.
15.00	MFD Hydrofoil	Skiathos. Volos.
17.00	MFD Hydrofoil	Skiathos. Agios Konstantinos.
21.10	MFD Hydrofoil	Skopelos. Alonissos.
21.15	MFD Hydrofoil	Skopelos. Alonissos.

◯

00.00	MFD Ferry	Skiathos. Volos.
00.00	MFD Ferry	Skopelos. Alonissos.
00.00	MFD Ferry	Skiathos. Agios Konstantinos.

Skyros

Northern Aegean
p. 466

ⓓ ex ⑦

08.00	*Lykomides*	Evia (Kimi).
14.00	*Lykomides*	Evia (Kimi).

⑦

10.00	*Lykomides*	Evia (Kimi).
16.00	*Lykomides*	Evia (Kimi).

④

04.15	*Daedalus*	Thessalonika.

⑤

08.00	*Daedalus*	Mykonos. Naxos. Santorini. Crete (Iraklion).

Thessalonika

SKYROS

Evia (Kimi)

Tinos
Mykonos
Paros
Santorini
Crete (Iraklion)

Days per week:
6-7 ▬▬
1 ——

Spetses

Argo-Saronic   p. 509

ⓓ

x6	*Alexandros M*	Kosta.
00.00	*Flying Cat 1/2*	Porto Helio.

00.00	*Flying Cat 1/2*	Hydra. Poros. Piraeus.
10.10	*Flying Dolphin*	Porto Helio.
11.00	*Flying Dolphin*	Hydra. Poros. Piraeus.
13.00	*Apollon Hellas*	Porto Helio.
13.30	*Eftichia*	Ermioni. Hydra. Poros. Methana. Aegina. Piraeus.
14.00	*Apollon Hellas*	Hydra. Poros. Methana. Aegina. Piraeus.
14.45	*Georgios 2*	Poros. Methana. Aegina. Piraeus.
18.30	*Flying Cat 1/2*	Porto Helio.
19.20	*Flying Cat 1/2*	Hydra. Piraeus.

🜂 *Flying Dolphins*:

ⓓ x 6 Poros. Piraeus.

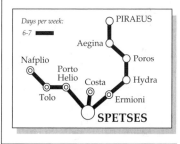

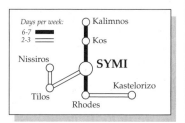

④		
14.45	*Nissos Kalimnos*	Rhodes.
20.00	*Nissos Kalimnos*	Tilos. Nissiros. Kos. Kalimnos.

⑤		
11.30	Hydrofoil	Kos.
15.40	Hydrofoil	Rhodes. Kos.

⑥		
09.00	Hydrofoil	Kos. Kalimnos. Astipalea.
11.30	Hydrofoil	Kos.
15.40	Hydrofoil	Rhodes. Kos.
19.40	Hydrofoil	Rhodes.
20.00	*Dimitroula*	Rhodes. Kastelorizo.

| ⑦ | | |
| 20.00 | *Symi II* | Rhodes. |

Symi

Dodecanese p. 387

| ⓓ | | |
| 16.00 | *Symi II* | Rhodes. |

①		
14.45	*Nissos Kalimnos*	Rhodes.
20.00	*Nissos Kalimnos*	Tilos. Nissiros. Kos. Kalimnos.

②		
07.30	*Patmos/Rodos*	Rhodes.
17.00	*Patmos/Rodos*	Tilos. Kalimnos. Astipalea. Amorgos (Katapola). Piraeus.

| ③ | | |
| 01.20 | *Dimitroula* | Tilos. Nissiros. Kos. Kalimnos. Astipalea. Amorgos (Egiali). Amorgos (Katapola). Donoussa. Naxos. Paros. Syros. Piraeus. |

Syros

Cyclades North p. 216

ⓓ		
10.15	*Highspeed 4*	Mykonos. Naxos. Paros. Piraeus.
11.35	*Highspeed 2/3*	Piraeus.
12.30	*Express Aphrodite*	Tinos. Mykonos.
16.15	*Express Aphrodite*	Piraeus.
19.45	*Highspeed 2/3*	Mykonos. Tinos. Rafina.

①		
03.30	*Blue Star 1*	Piraeus.
07.00	*Romilda*	Paros. Serifos. Sifnos. Kimolos. Milos.
10.30	*Aeolos Express II*	Tinos. Mykonos.
11.15	*Blue Star Ithaki*	Tinos. Mykonos. Paros. Naxos.
13.00	*Aeolos Express II*	Piraeus.

13.15	*Flying Cat 3*	Mykonos. Tinos. Rafina.
18.15	*Blue Star Ithaki*	Piraeus.
19.00	*Aeolos Express*	Paros. Naxos. Ikaria (Agios Kyrikos). Samos (Vathi).
19.25	*Flying Cat 3*	Kythnos. Lavrio.
19.45	*Aeolos Express II*	Mykonos. Tinos.
21.45	*Aeolos Express II*	Piraeus.
22.30	*Highspeed 4*	Piraeus.
23.20	*Blue Star 1*	Kos. Rhodes.

②
10.30	*Aeolos Express II*	Tinos. Mykonos. Amorgos (Katapola).
11.15	*Blue Star Ithaki*	Tinos. Mykonos. Paros. Naxos.
12.00	*Romilda*	Paros. Serifos. Sifnos. Kimolos. Milos.
13.15	*Flying Cat 3*	Mykonos. Tinos. Rafina.
16.45	*Aeolos Express II*	Piraeus.
18.15	*Blue Star Ithaki*	Piraeus.
21.00	*Daliana*	Mykonos. Ikaria (Agios Kyrikos). Fourni. Samos (Karlovassi). Samos (Vathi). Patmos. Lipsi.
21.10	*Blue Star Naxos*	Paros. Naxos. Ios. Santorini.

③
01.00	*Romilda*	Piraeus.
10.30	*Aeolos Express II*	Tinos. Mykonos. Amorgos (Katapola).
11.15	*Blue Star Ithaki*	Tinos. Mykonos. Paros. Naxos.
16.45	*Aeolos Express II*	Piraeus.
18.00	*Dimitroula*	Piraeus.
18.15	*Blue Star Ithaki*	Piraeus.
19.25	*Flying Cat 3*	Kythnos. Lavrio.
22.30	*Highspeed 4*	Piraeus.
23.30	*Blue Star 1*	Patmos. Leros. Kos. Rhodes.

④
00.30	*Daliana*	Piraeus.
10.30	*Aeolos Express II*	Tinos. Mykonos.
11.15	*Blue Star Ithaki*	Tinos. Mykonos. Paros. Naxos.
13.15	*Flying Cat 3*	Mykonos. Tinos. Rafina.
13.45	*Aeolos Express II*	Piraeus.
18.00	*Daliana*	Serifos. Sifnos. Kimolos. Milos.
18.15	*Blue Star Ithaki*	Piraeus.
19.25	*Flying Cat 3*	Kythnos. Lavrio.
21.10	*Blue Star Naxos*	Paros. Naxos. Ios. Santorini.
22.30	*Highspeed 4*	Piraeus.

⑤
| 05.20 | *Blue Star 1* | Piraeus. |
| 06.00 | *Daliana* | Piraeus. |

10.30	*Aeolos Express II*	Tinos. Mykonos.
11.15	*Blue Star Ithaki*	Tinos. Mykonos. Paros. Naxos.
13.00	*Aeolos Express II*	Piraeus.
13.15	*Flying Cat 3*	Mykonos. Tinos. Rafina.
18.15	*Blue Star Ithaki*	Piraeus.
19.00	*Aeolos Express*	Paros. Naxos. Ikaria (Evdilos). Samos (Vathi).
19.25	*Flying Cat 3*	Kythnos. Lavrio.
19.45	*Aeolos Express II*	Mykonos.
21.00	*Daliana*	Mykonos. Ikaria (Agios Kyrikos). Fourni. Samos (Karlovassi). Samos (Vathi). Patmos. Lipsi.
21.45	*Aeolos Express II*	Piraeus.
22.30	*Highspeed 4*	Piraeus.

⑥
04.30	*Dimitroula*	Paros. Naxos. Donoussa. Amorgos (Katapola). Amorgos (Egiali). Astipalea. Kos. Nissiros. Tilos. Symi. Rhodes. Kastelorizo.
10.30	*Aeolos Express II*	Tinos. Mykonos.
11.15	*Blue Star Ithaki*	Tinos. Mykonos. Paros. Naxos.
13.15	*Flying Cat 3*	Mykonos. Tinos. Rafina.
13.45	*Aeolos Express II*	Piraeus.
18.15	*Blue Star Ithaki*	Piraeus.
18.45	*Marina/Rodanthi*	Paros. Patmos. Leros. Kalimnos. Kos. Rhodes.
19.25	*Flying Cat 3*	Kythnos. Lavrio.
22.30	*Highspeed 4*	Piraeus.

⑦
00.30	*Daliana*	Piraeus.
10.30	*Aeolos Express II*	Tinos. Mykonos.
11.15	*Blue Star Ithaki*	Tinos. Mykonos.
		Paros.
		Naxos.
13.00	*Aeolos Express II*	Piraeus.
13.15	*Flying Cat 3*	Mykonos. Tinos.
		Rafina.
18.15	*Blue Star Ithaki*	Piraeus.
18.40	*Marina/Rodanthi*	Mykonos. Patmos.
		Leros. Kalimnos.
		Kos. Rhodes.
19.25	*Flying Cat 3*	Kythnos. Lavrio.
19.45	*Aeolos Express II*	Mykonos. Tinos.
20.30	*Milena*	Piraeus.
21.45	*Aeolos Express II*	Piraeus.
22.30	*Highspeed 4*	Piraeus.
24.00	*Express Penelope*	Tinos. Mykonos.

Thassos (Skala Prinos)

Northern Aegean
p. 470

ⓓ
06.00	07.20	12.00
14.15	16.00	18.00 19.00 Kavala.
10.30	14.30	19.00
	ANET Line	Nea Peramos.

Thassos (Town)

ⓓ
05.45	08.15	10.15 12.15
14.00	15.30	16.30 17.30
18.30	19.30	20.30 21.30
	ANET Line	Keramoti.

ⓓ x 4   Hydrofoil   Kavala.

◯
00.00   Hydrofoil   Samothrace.
                          Alexandroupolis.

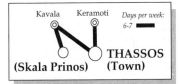

Kavala   Keramoti   *Days per week:*
                               6-7 ▬

THASSOS
(Skala Prinos) (Town)

Thessalonika

Northern Aegean
p. 473

②
15.00	*Daedalus*	Skiathos. Tinos. Mykonos.
		Paros. Santorini.
		Crete (Iraklion).

③
09.30	*Aeolos Kenteris*	Limnos.
		Lesbos (Mytilini). Chios.
		Piraeus.

④
16.00	*Milena*	Skopelos. Skiathos.
		Agios Konstantinos.
19.30	*Daedalus*	Skyros. Mykonos.
		Naxos.
		Santorini.
		Crete (Iraklion).

⑤
15.00	*Patmos/Rodos*	Samos (Vathi). Kos.
		Rhodes.

⑥
24.00	*Daedalus*	Tinos. Mykonos. Paros.
		Santorini.
		Crete (Iraklion).

⑦
01.00	*Theofilos*	Limnos.
		Lesbos (Mytilini).
		Chios. Piraeus.

◯
00.00	MFD Hydrofoil	Nea Moudania.
		Skopelos. Skiathos

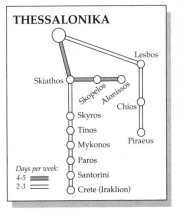

THESSALONIKA

Lesbos

Skiathos

Skopelos   Alonissos

Chios

Skyros

Tinos   Piraeus

Mykonos

Paros

Days per week:
4-5 ═══
2-3 ═══

Santorini

Crete (Iraklion)

Thirasia

Cyclades Central
p. 182

Ⓓ
16.00	*Nissos Thirassia*	Santorini (Oia). Santorini. (Old Port). Santorini.

Tilos

Dodecanese p. 393

①
12.30	*Nissos Kalimnos*	Symi. Rhodes.
14.30	*SeaStar*	Nissiros.
18.10	*SeaStar*	Rhodes.
22.25	*Nissos Kalimnos*	Nissiros. Kos. Kalimnos.

②
06.00	*Patmos/Rodos*	Symi. Rhodes.
17.00	*SeaStar*	Rhodes.
18.00	*Patmos/Rodos*	Kalimnos. Astipalea. Amorgos (Katapola). Piraeus.

③
03.00	*Dimitroula*	Nissiros. Kos. Kalimnos. Astipalea. Amorgos (Egiali). Amorgos (Katapola). Donoussa. Naxos. Paros. Syros. Piraeus.
08.30	*SeaStar*	Rhodes.
19.30	*SeaStar*	Rhodes.

④
12.30	*Nissos Kalimnos*	Symi. Rhodes.
14.30	*SeaStar*	Nissiros.
18.10	*SeaStar*	Rhodes.
22.25	*Nissos Kalimnos*	Nissiros. Kos. Kalimnos.

⑤
14.30	*SeaStar*	Nissiros.
18.10	*SeaStar*	Rhodes.

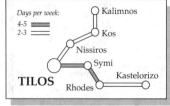

Days per week:
4-5
2-3

Kalimnos
Kos
Nissiros
Symi
Kastelorizo
TILOS
Rhodes

⑥
09.00	*SeaStar*	Rhodes.
18.15	*Dimitroula*	Symi. Rhodes. Kastelorizo.

⑦
08.50	*SeaStar*	Rhodes.
15.00	*Hydrofoil*	Rhodes. Kos.
18.30	*SeaStar*	Rhodes.

Tinos

Cyclades North
p. 220

Ⓓ
09.25	*Sea Jet 2*	Mykonos. Paros.
10.00	*Highspeed 2/3*	Mykonos. Tinos. Syros. Piraeus.
11.00	*Highspeed 2/3*	Syros. Piraeus.
11.45	*Superferry II*	Mykonos.
12.00	*Blue Star Ithaki*	Mykonos. Paros. Naxos.
12.25	*Sea Jet 2*	Rafina.
13.20	*Express Aphrodite*	Mykonos.
14.15	*Superferry II*	Andros. Rafina.
15.15	*Express Aphrodite*	Syros. Piraeus.
17.30	*Blue Star Ithaki*	Syros. Piraeus.
17.45	*Sea Jet 2*	Mykonos.
18.55	*Sea Jet 2*	Rafina.
21.00	*Highspeed 2/3*	Rafina.

①
00.45	*Express Penelope*	Mykonos.
09.15	*Express Penelope*	Andros. Rafina.
11.00	*Aeolos Express II*	Mykonos.
11.15	*Aqua Jewel*	Mykonos. Paros.
11.45	*Express Athina*	Mykonos.
12.30	*Aeolos Express II*	Syros. Piraeus.
13.45	*Express Athina*	Andros. Rafina.
14.25	*Flying Cat 3*	Rafina.
16.45	*Aqua Jewel*	Andros. Rafina.
18.20	*Flying Cat 3*	Mykonos. Syros. Kythnos. Lavrio.
21.00	*Aeolos Express II*	Syros. Piraeus.
21.30	*Express Penelope*	Mykonos.
22.00	*Milena*	Mykonos. Chios. Lesbos (Mytilini).
23.50	*Daedalus*	Thessalonika.

②
09.15	*Express Penelope*	Andros. Rafina.
11.00	*Aeolos Express II*	Mykonos. Amorgos (Katapola).
11.15	*Aqua Jewel*	Mykonos. Paros.
11.45	*Express Athina*	Mykonos.
13.45	*Express Athina*	Andros. Rafina.
14.25	*Flying Cat 3*	Rafina.
16.15	*Aeolos Express II*	Syros. Piraeus.
16.45	*Aqua Jewel*	Andros. Rafina.
21.30	*Express Penelope*	Mykonos.

③
04.30	Daedalus	Mykonos. Paros. Santorini. Crete (Iraklion).
09.15	Express Penelope	Andros. Rafina.
11.00	Aeolos Express II	Mykonos. Amorgos (Katapola).
11.15	Aqua Jewel	Mykonos. Paros.
11.45	Express Athina	Mykonos.
13.45	Express Athina	Andros. Rafina.
16.15	Aeolos Express II	Syros. Piraeus.
16.45	Aqua Jewel	Andros. Rafina.
18.20	Flying Cat 3	Mykonos. Syros. Kythnos. Lavrio.

④
09.15	Express Penelope	Andros. Rafina.
11.00	Aeolos Express II	Mykonos.
11.15	Aqua Jewel	Mykonos. Paros.
11.45	Express Penelope	Mykonos.
13.15	Aeolos Express II	Syros. Piraeus.
14.25	Flying Cat 3	Rafina.
15.15	Express Penelope	Andros. Rafina.
16.45	Aqua Jewel	Andros. Rafina.
18.20	Flying Cat 3	Mykonos. Syros. Kythnos. Lavrio.
21.30	Express Athina	Mykonos.
23.15	Express Athina	Andros. Rafina.

⑤
11.00	Aeolos Express II	Mykonos.
11.15	Aqua Jewel	Andros. Rafina.
11.30	Express Penelope	Andros. Rafina.
11.45	Express Athina	Mykonos.
12.30	Aeolos Express II	Syros. Piraeus.
13.45	Express Athina	Andros. Rafina.
14.25	Flying Cat 3	Rafina.
18.20	Flying Cat 3	Mykonos. Syros. Kythnos. Lavrio.
20.45	Aqua Jewel	Mykonos. Paros. Rafina.
21.30	Express Penelope	Mykonos.
22.30	Express Athina	Mykonos.
24.00	Express Athina	Andros. Rafina.

⑥
07.30	Daedalus	Skiathos. Thessalonika.
09.15	Express Penelope	Andros. Rafina.
10.45	Express Penelope	Mykonos.
11.00	Aeolos Express II	Mykonos.
11.15	Aqua Jewel	Andros. Rafina.
11.45	Express Athina	Mykonos.
13.15	Aeolos Express II	Syros. Piraeus.
13.45	Express Athina	Andros. Rafina.
14.25	Flying Cat 3	Rafina.
15.15	Express Penelope	Rafina.
18.20	Flying Cat 3	Mykonos. Syros. Kythnos. Lavrio.
20.15	Aqua Jewel	Mykonos. Paros. Rafina.
21.30	Express Penelope	Mykonos.

Days per week:
6-7
4-5
2-3

⑦
09.15	Express Penelope	Andros. Rafina.
10.45	Express Penelope	Mykonos.
11.00	Aeolos Express II	Mykonos.
11.15	Aqua Jewel	Mykonos. Paros.
11.45	Express Athina	Mykonos.
12.30	Aeolos Express II	Syros. Piraeus.
12.45	Daedalus	Mykonos. Paros. Santorini. Crete (Iraklion).
13.45	Express Athina	Andros. Rafina.
14.25	Flying Cat 3	Rafina.
15.15	Express Penelope	Rafina.
16.45	Aqua Jewel	Andros. Rafina.
18.20	Flying Cat 3	Mykonos. Syros. Kythnos. Lavrio.
19.30	Milena	Syros. Piraeus.
21.00	Aeolos Express II	Syros. Piraeus.
21.30	Express Penelope	Mykonos.

Trieste

Italy p. 581

② ⑤ ⑦
| 14.00 | ANEK Lines | Igoumenitsa. Patras. |

③ ⑥
| 14.00 | ANEK Lines | Corfu. Igoumenitsa. Patras. |

Venice

Italy p. 581

① ④ ⑤
15.00   Minoan Lines   Igoumenitsa. Corfu. Patras.

②
15.00   Minoan Lines   Igoumenitsa. Corfu. Patras.
19.00   *Blue Horizon/*
        Blue Sky   Igoumenitsa. Corfu. Patras.

③
19.00   *Blue Horizon/*
        Blue Sky   Igoumenitsa. Corfu. Patras.

⑥
12.00   *Blue Horizon/*
        Blue Sky   Corfu. Igoumenitsa. Patras.
15.00   Minoan Lines   Igoumenitsa. Corfu. Patras.
21.00   *Ankara*   İzmir.

⑦
12.00   *Blue Horizon/*
        Blue Sky   Corfu. Igoumenitsa. Patras.
15.00   Minoan Lines   Igoumenitsa. Corfu. Patras.

Volos

Northern Aegean p. 477

Ⓓ
09.00   MFD Hydrofoil   Skiathos. Skopelos.
                        (Glossa). Skopelos.
                        Alonissos.
13.15   MFD Hydrofoil   Skiathos. Skopelos.
                        (Glossa). Skopelos.
                        Alonissos.
14.30   MFD Hydrofoil   Skiathos. Skopelos.
19.30   MFD Hydrofoil   Skiathos. Skopelos
                        (Glossa). Skopelos.
                        Alonissos.

① ②
08.00   *Express Haroulla*   Skiathos. Skopelos.
                             Alonissos.
17.30   *Express Haroulla*   Skiathos. Skopelos.

③
08.00   *Express Haroulla*   Skiathos. Skopelos.
                             Alonissos.
17.30   *Express Haroulla*   Skiathos. Skopelos.

④
01.00   *Milena*   Skiathos. Skopelos.
                             Thessalonika.
08.00   *Express Haroulla*   Skiathos. Skopelos.
                             Alonissos.
17.30   *Express Haroulla*   Skiathos. Skopelos.

⑤
08.00   *Express Haroulla*   Skiathos. Skopelos.
                             Alonissos.
17.30   *Express Haroulla*   Skiathos. Skopelos.
19.00   *Milena*   Skopelos.
                             Skiathos.
                             Limnos.
                             Lesbos (Mytilini).

⑥
08.00   *Express Haroulla*   Skiathos. Skopelos.
                             Alonissos.
17.30   *Express Haroulla*   Skiathos. Skopelos.

⑦
08.00   *Express Haroulla*   Skiathos. Skopelos.
                             Alonissos.
17.30   *Express Haroulla*   Skiathos. Skopelos.

Zakinthos / Zante (Town)

Ionian Line
p. 542

Ⓓ
05.30   08.00   09.00   10.45   13.00   14.30
18.00   19.45
        Zakinthos I/II
        Dimitrios Miras/
        Ionis/Proteus/   Kilini.
Ⓞ
12.00   HML Ferries   Patras.
12.00   HML Ferries   Brindisi.

Zakinthos / Zante (Skinari)

Ionian Line
p. 544

Ⓓ
09.15   *Ionion Pelagos*   Kefalonia (Pessada).
19.30   *Ionion Pelagos*   Kefalonia (Pessada).

Kefalonia
(Pessada)

Days per week:
6-7

Zakinthos
(Skinari)   Kilini

ZAKINTHOS

Major Ferry Companies

Company   Livery No. (See Colour Liveries between pages 640–641)

ALPHA FERRIES   **2**
5–7 Kanare,
PIRAEUS
185 37
☎ (210) 4284001-2
Fax (210) 4284003
⊕ www.alphaferries.gr
⌂
Aqua Jewel

ANEK LINES   **4**
N. Plastria-Apokoronou,
Chania,
GREECE
☎ (28210) 27600-10
Fax (28210) 27611
⊕ www.anek.gr
⌂
*Aptera, Arkadi, El. Venizelos,
Hellenic Spirit, Hercules,
Kriti I, Kriti II,
Kriti V, Lato, Lefka Ori, Lissos,
Mount Olympos, Olympic Champion,
Preveli, Rethimno, Sophocles V.*

ANEN Lines   **6**
(20% owned by ANEK Lines)
32 Akti Possidonos & 1 Leocharous Sts
185 31 Piraeus,
GREECE
☎ (210) 4197420
⌂
Mirtidiotissa.

**BLUE STAR FERRIES /
BLUE FERRIES/
STRINTZIS**   **10, 11, 52**
26 Akti Possidonos,
185 31 Piraeus,
GREECE
☎ (210) 4225000
⊕ www.strintzis.gr
⌂
*Blue Bridge, Blue Sky,
Blue Star 1, Blue Star 2,
Blue Star Ithaki, Blue Star Naxos,
Blue Star Paros, Kefalonia,
Superferry II. C/M SeaJet 2.*

DANE SEA LINES   **12**
(DODEKANISSIAKI SHIPPING Co)
(43.5% owned by ANEK)
Parodos Amerikis,
851 00 RODOS
☎ (22410) 30930
⊕ www.helios.gr/dane
⌂
Diagoras, Patmos, Rodos.

G.A. FERRIES   **17**
**(46% owned by
Hellas Flying Dolphins)**
Akti Kondili & 2 Aitolikou,
Piraeus, GREECE
☎ (210) 4110007, 4110254
Fax (210) 4232383
⌂
*Daliana, Dimitroula, JetFerry 1,
Marina, Milena, Rodanthi, Romilda.*

HELLAS FERRIES   **20**
**(A subsiduary of
Hellas Flying Dolphins)**
2 Defteras Merachias St.
185 35 Piraeus, GREECE
☎ (210) 4283555
⊕ www.dolphins.gr
⌂
*Express Adonis, Express Aphrodite,
Express Apollon, Express Athina,
Express Dionyssos, Express Hermes,
Express Olympia, Express Penelope
Express Poseidon, Express Santorini,
Panagia Ekatontapiliani.*

HELLAS FLYING   **46, 54, 56**
DOLPHINS
(26% owned by Minoan Lines)
2 Defteras Merachias St.
185 35 Piraeus, GREECE
☎ (210) 4283555
⊕ www.dolphins.gr
⌂
*C/Ms Highspeed 1, Highspeed 2,
Highspeed 3, Highspeed 4.
H/Fs Flying Dolphin 1–32.*

LANE LINES 24
(50% owned by ANEK)
2 Loudovikou Street
185 31 Piraeus,
GREECE
☎ (210) 4274011

Ierapetra L, Vitsentzos Kornaros.

LOUIS CRUISE LINES 25
54–58 Evagoras Avenue,
P.O. Box 1301 Nicosia, CYPRUS
☎ (02) 442114

Princesa Cypria, Princesa Marissa.

MARLINES 26
38 Akti Possidonas, 18531
Piraeus, GREECE
☎ (210) 4110777
⊕ www.marlines.gr

Duchess M.

MINOAN LINES S.A. 29, 30
17, 25th August St,
712 02, Irakion, Crete, GREECE
☎ (2810) 330301
Passenger Office and Bus Terminal:
2 Vass. Kon/nou Avenue
116 35 Athens, GREECE
☎ (210) 7512356
Fax (210) 7520540
⊕ www.minoan.gr

*Aretousa, Ariadne Palace, Ariadne Palace 1
Daedalus, Europa Palace, Festos Palace,
Ikarus Palace, Knossos Palace,
N. Kazantzakis, Olympia Palace,
Pasiphae Palace, Prometheus.*

NEL LINES / 31, 32
MARITIME Co. of LESVOS S.A.
(16.5% owned by ANEK)
47 Kountouriotou Street,
811 00 Mytilini, Lesbos,
GREECE
☎ (22510) 23097, 29087

*Aeolos Express, Aeolos Express II,
Aeolos Kenteris, Mytilene,
Taxiarchis, Theofilos.*

POSEIDON LINES 33
166 73 Voula, Athens, GREECE
☎ (210) 8958923

Sea Serenade, Sea Symphony.

SALAMIS LINES 34
12 Filellinon Street, 1st Floor
185 36 Piraeus, GREECE
☎ (210) 4294325   Fax (210) 4528384

Nissos Kypros, Salamis Star.

SARONIKOS FERRIES 35
(A subsidiary of
Hellas Flying Dolphins)
2 Defteras Merachias St.
185 35 Piraeus, GREECE
☎ (210) 4283555
⊕ www.dolphins.gr

*Aegina, Afaia, Aias, Apostolos P,
Apollon Hellas, Efichia, Express Danae,
Georgios II, Hellas, Ioannis II, Nefeli,
Odysseas II, Poseidon Hellas, Saronikos.*

SPORADES FERRIES 20, 56
(A subsiduary of
Hellas Flying Dolphins)
2 Defteras Merachias St.
185 35 Piraeus, GREECE
☎ (210) 4283555
⊕ www.dolphins.gr

*Lemnos,
C/M Express Haroulla.*

SUPERFAST FERRIES 38
Amalias 30, 105 58 Athens, GREECE
☎ (210) 3313252
⊕ www.superfast.com

Superfast I–X.

VENTOURIS FERRIES 42, 59
91 Pireos Av. & Kithiron 2
185 41 Piraeus, GREECE
☎ (210) 4825815
⊕ www.ventouris.gr

*Athens Express, Polaris, Vega, Venus.
C/Ms Ventouris High Speed I–II.*

Internet Links

Greece is doing surprisingly well in getting its businesses wired into the internet revolution (though this is in part because of its comparative backwardness in other means of getting promotional messages across). Sorting the chaff from the wheat, however, can come expensive when surfing in a slow internet cafe, so it does help if you have to hand a list of some of the better sites kicking around.

Of course it is in the nature of things that sites and their links change fairly frequently. Rather than provide a list with an ever increasing number of out-of-date connections, we've opted to put the related links information on this book's web site via the *Greek Island Hopping online* '**Links Cafe**'. Hopefully, the cafe's web site content ratings will take some of the pain and a lot of the time out of surfing for information on the Greek islands.

In addition to this book's

⊕ **www.greekislandhopping.com**

site, there are a few sites with content that is deserving of particular mention:

⊕ **http://www.gnto.gr/**
National Tourist Organisation of Greece
The home page for the NTOG/EOT web site, this location has addresses of all embassies and consulates, local and foreign NTOG offices, and assorted other information. This includes museum opening times, taxi fares, long distance bus timetables from Athens (with return times), and Athens city bus schedules.

⊕ **www.gtpnet.com**
Greek Travel Pages
The main ferry timetable site—compiled by the publishers of *Greek Travel Pages* and *Greek Travel Routes* — with a semi-complete current ferry time database (small inter-island boats are often missing). The main limitations are the interface (you type in your departure and destination points and get a list of ferries and times), and the limited ability of the database to tell you what will be running next week or month.

⊕ **www.Ferries.gr**
Paleologos Shipping & Travel Agency
A run-down looking ticket agency in Crete (Iraklion)'s main street has a slow to load, but useful, ferry timetable site: links to ferry company sites are backed up by a database similar to the *Greek Travel Pages* site above.

⊕ **www.hri.org/infoxenios/english/greece.html**
InfoXenios NTOG Tourism Travel
Good overview site with pages on all the islands (complete with primitive maps and small photos). Information, however, is pretty basic, and limited to the major points of interest.

⊕ **www.islandstrolling.com/english/index.htm**

A Norwegian site that is one of the most informative going. Equipped with a nice collection of photos, info and links, it is a good example of what can happen when you get the island hopping bug really badly.

Internet Cafés

Greece is currently seeing an explosion in the numbers of internet — or cyber — cafés (in this part of the world 'internet café' is the preferred sobriquet). This rush to join in the internet revolution is driven in part because these cafés are cheap to set up, have low overheads, and are popular with locals and e-mailing tourists alike. Rates for using these facilities are surprisingly uniform (with one or two notable exceptions), though alcohol prices are usually on the high side.

Access speed is also an important issue. Any of the sites listed here will be adequate if all you want to do is send and receive e-mail (AOL subscribers will find life very easy at most of them), but if you want to seriously surf the net then expect to find life a bit slow going. This said, competition is encouraging more cafés into using fast 128Kbps ISDN lines. Note: those that don't are often not afraid to claim that they are, so don't be slow to question managers if you are surfing at a snail's pace.

The section below gives web and email addresses, times of opening, price per hour (often followed by the price for the minimum buyable on-line time). Almost all the cafés listed are located — via the net symbol: ⊕ — on the relevant city or island town map.

Amorgos

Minoa Hotel
Katapola.

⊕ NONE
E NONE
⊘ ⊕ 10.00–23.00
€ 5 per ⊕ , 30 minutes minimum.

A side room at the front of the hotel has the island's only public internet access. Not usually overwhelmed with demand, there are 4 PCs.

Athens

There are internet cafés all over the city, but the only ones likely to be of interest to island hoppers are in the city centre or at Piraeus.

City Centre:

Museum Internet Café
Patision 46, Museum, Athens, GR.

⊕ www.museumcafe.gr
E museum_netcafe@yahoo.com
⊘ ⊕ 09.30–02.30
€ 4.5 per ⊕, 1.5 for 20 minutes

The best café in the centre of Athens and very easy to find as it lies on the corner of the block just north of the National Archaeological Museum, this establishment offers a very large floor space hosting plenty of PCs (20+), lengthy opening times and refreshments. An exercise in mass surfing, it could suffer in 2003 with the temporary closure of the National Archaeological Museum.

Internet Café
22 Sofokleous, Athens, GR.

⊕ www.sofokleous.com
E sofo22@hellasnet.gr
⊘ ⊕ 10.00–22.00
€ 4.5 per ⊕

Conveniently positioned down a small mall just off Syntagma Square, this internet café is let down by its limited refreshments, smallish floor-space and 30-minute minimum online rental time. it is, however, very conviently placed. Note: take care to close the front door properly: the manager is very keen on his air-conditioning.

Piraeus:

Surf in Internet Café
Ir. Polytechneiou 42–44 & Platonos 3, Piraeus, 18535 GR.

⊕ www.surfin.gr
E surfin@harris.surfin.gr
⊘ ①–⑤ 08.00–21.00, ⑥ 08.00–15.00
€ 4.5 per ⊕

A rather swish café decorated in modernist chrome, stripped pine and buttercup yellow. Also serves as a regular café, with the usual range of drinks and a small garden.

Dios Internet
Sotiros Dios & Androutsou Pasalimani, Piraeus, 18535 GR.

⊕ NONE
E diosgr@otenet.gr
⊘ ⊕ 09.30–23.00
€ US$ 5 per ⊕

Located on 1st floor at 170 Androutsou (behind McDonald's at Pasalimani). Rather out of the way unless you are heading to Zea Marina.

Corfu

Netoikos
Kalogeretou 14, Corfu, 49100 GR.

⊕ www.netoikos.gr/internet.htm
E webmaster@netoikos.gr
⑦ ⊕ 11.00–01.00
€ 4 per ⊕, 2 for ½ ⊕

Tucked away in one of the narrow streets behind the Platia Spinada/cricket pitch this is a fairly run-of-the-mill sort of café. Refreshment prices are on the high side.

Crete (Iraklion)

Istos Cyber Café
2 Malikouti, Iraklion, Crete, 71202 GR.

⊕ www.istos.gr
E info@istos-cafe.gr
⑦ ⊕ 10.30–01.00
€ 5 per ⊕

Reasonably close to the centre, this popular café lies just inside the Old Town walls.

Netc@fe
4, 1878 St., Iraklion, Crete, GR.

⊕ www.the-netcafe.net
E —
⑦ ⊕ 10.00–24.00
€ 4.5 per ⊕

Just off the town map and more off the wall, this establishment is geared more to local gamers rather than surfing tourists.

Cyprus

Web Internet Café
Lordou Vironos no.54, Larnaca, 6030 CYPRUS.

⊕ NONE
E webcafe@webcafe.com.cy
⑦ ⊕ 10.00–03.00
€ 5 per ⊕

Located in the middle of the old town, this café has 16 PCs.

Ios

Mojo@net
Ios Town/Chora.

⊕ NONE
E NONE
⑦ ⊕ 11.00–02.00
€ 5 per ⊕

An internet café on the main 'circuit' of Ios

Town. Tends to be quiet during the day and over subscribed in the evenings. Has around 8 PCs. Action Travel has a couple of PCs at the Port.

Karpathos

Caffe Galileo Internet 2000
Pigadia, Karpathos, 85700 GR.

⊕ www.caffegalileo.gr
E caffe_galileo@yahoo.com
⑦ ○ Opening times unknown
€ 5.9 per ⊕

The only internet café on the island to date, it claims to offer the 'ultimate music and browsing experience on the web'. More rock and roll bar than café, it none-the-less has the basics needed to e-mail and surf.

Kavala

Philathlos Net Café
Royzvelt II, Kavala, 24100 GR.

⊕ www.filathlosnet.gr
E —
⑦ ⊕ 09.00–02.00
€ 4 per ⊕

A long way to come to send an email, this café is geared to the locals rather than the limited tourist traffic passing through.

Kos

Del Mare Café
Megaiou Alexandrou, Kos Town, Kos, GR.

⊕ NONE
E delmare-kos@yahoo.com
⑦ ⊕ 09.00–01.00
€ 4.5 per ⊕, 3.0 for ½ ⊕

Located close to the old harbour, this is a bar with PCs as much an internet café. Even so, it provides all that is needed in congenial, if noisy, surroundings. Closing time varies — it depends on how popular the bar is on any given night.

Lefkada/Lefkas

Internet Café
I. Gazi, Lefkada, GR.

⊕ NONE
E intercaf@lefkada.hellasnet.gr
⑦ ⊕ 10.30–14.30, 18.00–23.00
€ 3 per ⊕

An internet and games café with suspiciously low prices.

Mykonos

Angelo's Internet Café
Mykonos Town, GR.

⊕ NONE
E   mycnetcafe@otenet.gr
⑦ ⑩ 10.00–01.00
€   4.5 per ⊕

One block north of the bus station, this and other cafe a few metres away, have replaced an over expensive café (now closed). Competition ensures that prices are now reasonable. A third option — if you are camping — is *Mykonos Camping* which has internet terminal in the reception.

Naxos

Rental & Travel Center
Naxos, 84300 GR.

⊕ NONE
E   rentacar@.nax.gr
⑦ ⑩ 09.00–23.30
€   7.5 per ⊕, 4.5 for ½ ⊕

An enterprising car-rental business with an empty showroom on one of Naxos Town's main tourist squares, this establishment has branched out by filling the space with half a dozen PCs (tastefully arranged in a circle). No refreshments on offer. On the plus side, car rental is optional.

NaxosWeb
Naxos, GR.

⊕ NONE
E   webmaster@naxosweb.com
⑦ ⑩ 09.00–23.30
€   4.5 per ⊕, 2.9 for ½ ⊕

A new multi-terminal café located behind the waterfront next to the municipal showers/WCs. Boasting direct satellite high speed connections, it promises to be the fastest access point in town. This cafe should not be confused with a three-PC outlet almost opposite. There is also a bookshop with half a dozen PCs on the waterfront.

Paros

Wired Café
Main Market Street, Paros, 84400 GR.

⊕ http://parosweb.com/wiredcafe
E   wired@parosweb.com
⑦ ⑩ 10.30–14.30, 18.00–23.00
€   7.0 per ⊕, 1.75 for ¼ ⊕

Located on the main street near the kastro in Parikia, this café is the hub of the 'Wired Network' — a series of terminals around the island. Accessed via smart cards which, once purchased, can be used at any of the terminals, this is the most sophisticated network so far to appear in the Aegean. In addition to the main café, there are terminals in the ticket agency next to the OTE in Parikia, as well as at Naoussa and Punta Beach. The main café is located near a small Orthodox church, and offers devoted surfers the unique opportunity to enjoy their hobby with the combined aromas of incense and coffee wafting through the air.

MemphisNet
Parikia, Paros GR.

⊕ www.cycladesnet.gr/memphisnet
E   mphscafe@yahoo.com
⑦ ⑩ 09.00–01.00
€   4.5 per ⊕

Positioned close to the ferry quay, this useful café as much a bar as a café. Armed with a dozen PCs, it is invaluable if you want to knock off a few e-mails while waiting for a ferry.

Rhodes

Rockstyle Internet Café
7 Dimokratias, Rhodes, GR.

⊕ www.rockstyle.gr
E   admin@rockstyle.gr
⑦ ⑩ 10.00–01.00
€   4 per ⊕, 1.5 for ½ ⊕

Sited just down a side street off Dimokratias, directly opposite the main gate of the Diagoras Stadium, on the 'wrong' side of the Old City, this is a full-blown internet café. Very busy with local Greeks thanks to its low tariffs, it is worth the effort of looking out, but don't be surprised if you have to wait for access to a PC.

Rodos Internet Club
11 Iroon Politehniou St., Rhodes, 85100 GR.

⊕ www.ric.gr
E   ric@ric.gr
⑦ ⑩ 10.00–24.00
€   4.5 per ⊕, 2.75 for ½ ⊕

Located in the heart of the New Town tourist strip, this café is a more pricey tourist-orientated affair. Facilities are reasonable enough though.

Samos

Netscape Davlos
Vathi, Samos.

⊕ NONE
⑦ ⑩ 08.00–23.00

€ 4 per ⊕
On the waterfront at Vathi, near the Police station: usually empty, it isn't always open at advertised times.

Santorini/Thira

PC World
Main Square, Fira, Santorini, GR.

⊕ NONE
E PCworld@san.forthnet.gr
⑦ ⊚ 09.00–24.00
€ 4.5 per ⊕, 1.5 for ¼ ⊕

A heavily air-conditioned café that is to be found on the first floor of a building overlooking the main town square (the entrance is up a very narrow staircase), this outfit is all internet and no café. Serious surfing in silence and no socialising is the norm.

Skiathos

6th Element Net Cafe
Skiathos, GR.

⊕ -
⑦ ⊚ 10.00–24.00
€ 5.0 per ⊕

Located near the Papadiamantis Museum, this new internet cafe offers a high speed internet connection. Customers buy cards giving varying amounts of time online. The more you spend the more time you get: cost can come down to €2 per hour if you really splash out.

Internet Center
Odos Miaouli, Skiathos, GR.

⊕ www.icc-skiathos.gr
E webmaster@icc-skiathos.gr
⑦ ⊚ 10.00–23.00
€ 3.0 per ⊕

Boasting a collection of 6 PCs and 3 Sony Play-stations, this is a rather down-at-heel looking outfit more geared to keeping the local youth happy than catering to tourists. Still, it is good enough for e-mailing. There is supposed to be a second internet café near the acropolis hill on the outskirts of the town, but it is very elusive.

Skopelos

Click & Surf
Internet Café, Computers, Skopelos, GR.

⊕ www.skopelosweb.forthnet.gr
E ermis@skt.forthnet.gr
⑦ ⊚ 10.00–23.00
€ 4.5 per ⊕

A new café conveniently located on a block behind the harbour waterfront. Reasonable facilities though connections aren't the fastest.

Thassos

Larrys Internet Café
Limenaria, Thassos, 64002 GR.

⊕ www.larry.gr
E sakis@larrys.gr
⑦ ⊚ 09.00–03.00
€ 4 per ⊕

Rather out of the way, in the tourist town on the south side of the island, this café is useful in a pinch. Despite its location, most of the customers seem to be locals.

Thessalonika

Globus Internet Café
Amynta 12, Thessalonika, 54631 GR.

⊕ www.globus.gr
E globus@amynta.globus.gr
⑦ ⊚ 10.00–02.00
€ 5 per ⊕

The most central of the several internet cafés in the city, Globus is a good establishment (as much bar as café) housed in an old building near the remains of the Roman Agora, offering very competitive rates.

Volos

The Internet Channel
15 Gallias - Ag. Nikolaou, Volos, GR.

⊕ www.ichannel.gr
E info@ichannel.gr
⑦ ⊚ 10.30–14.30, 18.00–23.00
€ 7 per ⊕

Rather expensive site located near the Libo Cinema and the Fire Station (take a #3 or 4 bus from town centre): the nearest side street is Glavani.

Useful Greek

The Greek Alphabet — Transliteration

Greek Capital	Small	English Equivalent	Name	Pronounced like
A	α	A	Alpha	cat
B	β	B/V	Beta	van
Γ	γ	G	Gamma	sugar/yes
Δ	δ	D	Delta	this
E	ε	E	Epsilon	egg
Z	ζ	Z	Zeta	zoo
H	η	E	Eta	feet
Θ	θ	TH	Theta	thick
I	ι	I	Iota	feet
K	κ	K	Kappa	king
Λ	λ	L	Lamtha	long
M	μ	M	Mu	man
N	ν	N	Nu	not
Ξ	ξ	TS/KS	Tsi/Xi	box
O	ο	O	O-mikron	dot
Π	π	P	Pi	pick
P	ρ	R	Rho	red
Σ	σ, ς	S	Sigma	sit (ς only at the end of a word)
T	τ	T	Tau	tap
Y	υ	U	Upsilon	meet
Φ	φ	PH/F	Phi	fat
X	χ	CH/H	Chi	loch
Ψ	ψ	PS	Psi	lapse
Ω / Ω	ω	O	O-mega	dot

Combinations & Dipthongs

AI	αι	AI		egg
AY	αυ	AV/AF		have
EI	ει	I		seen
EY	ευ	EV/EF		ever/effort
OI	οι	I		seen
OY	ευ	OU		moon
ΓΓ	γγ	NG		go/ring
ΓΚ	γκ	G/NG		go/ring
ΜΠ	μπ	B		boat
NT	ντ	D/ND		dog/send
TZ	τζ	TS		deeds
ΤΣ	τσ	TS		deeds
YI	υι	I		seen

Greek   Pronunciation   English

Basics:

Ναι	Ne	Yes
Οχι	ochi	No
Παρακαλω	parakalo	Please
Ευχαριστω	efcharisto	Thank You
Με σoγχωρειτε	me sinkhorite	Excuse Me
Φυγετε	fiyete	Hop It!
Βοηθεια	voithia	Help!
Γεια σας	yassas (pl.)	Hello/
Γεια σου	yassoo (s.)	Goodbye
Καλημερα	Kalimera	Good morning
Καληνυχτα	Kalinihta	Good night
Συγνωμη	signomi	Sorry
Ποτε;	pote	When?
Ποσο;	posso	How much?
Που;	pu	Where?

Signs:

ΑΦΙΤΕΙΣ	Afitese	Arrivals
ΑΝΔΡΩΝ	Andron	Gentlemen
ΑΝΑΧΩΡΗΣΕΙΣ	Anachoresis	Departures
ΓΥΝΑΙΚΩΝ	Ginekon	Ladies
ΕΙΣΟΔΟΣ	Eisodos	Entrance
ΕΞΟΔΟΣ	Exodos	Exit
ΣΤΑΣΙΣ	Stasis	Bus Stop
ΤΟΥΑΛΕΤΕΣ	Toualetes	Toilets
ΦΑΡΜΑΚΕΙΟΝ	Farmakion	Pharmacy
ΞΕΝΟΔΟΧΕΙΟ	Zenodokhio	Hotel

Miscellaneous:

Αγια	Agia	Saint
Αστυνομια	Astinomia	Police Stn.
Εισιτηρια	Isitiria	Tickets
Λεωφορειο	Leoforio	Bus
Λιμανι	Limani	Port
Νησι / Νισι	Nissi	Island
Οδος	Odhos	Street
Πλατεια	Platia	Square
Πλοιο	Plio	Boat/Ferry
Σπηλαιο	Spileo	Cave
Τραινο	Treno	Train
Χωριο	Horio/Hora	Village

Numbers:

Ενας	enas	1
Δυο	deo	2
Τρεις /	Τρια	tris/tria
Τεσσερεις	tesseres	4
Πεντε	pende	5
Εξι	exi	6
Επτα	epta	7
Οκτω	okto	8
Εννεα	ennea	9
Δεκα	deka	10
Ενδεκα	andeka	11
Δωδεκα	dodeka	12
Δεκατρια	deka tria	13
Δεκατεσσερα	deka tessera	14
Εικοσι	ikosi	20
Πενηντα	peninda	50
Εκατο	ekato	100
Χιλια	chilia	1000

Days:

Δευτερα	deftera	Monday
Τριτη	triti	Tuesday
Τεταρτη	tetarti	Wednesday
Πεμπτη	pempti	Thursday
Παρασκευη	paraskevi	Friday
Ζαββατο	savato	Saturday
Κυριακη	kiriaki	Sunday
Σημερα	simera	Today
Αυριω	avrio	Tomorrow
Χθες	hthes	Yesterday

Accommodation:

Εχετε δωματια	ehete domatia	Do you have rooms?
Θελω ενα	thelo enna	I want a...
μονο	mono	single...
διπλο	thiplo	double...
δωματιο	domatio	room
για	yia	for...
δυο μερεζ	deo meres	two days
τρειζ μερεζ	tris meres	three days

Index

Abbreviations:

Al — Albania, Cy — Cyprus, Eg — Egypt, Isr — Israel, It — Italy, Leb — Lebanon,
N Cy — Northern Cyprus, Sy — Syria, Tk — Turkey.

C/F — Car Ferry, C/M — Catamaran, H/F — Hydrofoil, P/S — Passenger Ship,
T/B — Tourist Boat or Taxi Boat.

Ferry Names are listed in *Italics*.
Ferry and Island Maps are indicated by **bold** page numbers; Street/Site Maps by <u>**underlined bold**</u> numbers.

7. How many times have you visited the Greek Islands? _____

8. At what time of the year did you visit the Greek Islands with this guide?

From: _____   To: _____

9. Which islands and mainland ports did you visit and how many days did you spend at each?

Island/Port: Days:

10. How much did your Greek Island holiday cost (per person)?

   Travel to/from Greece: _____   Per day in Greece: _____

11. Which of the following age categories do you fall into?

   Under 21 ☐   21-30 ☐   31-40 ☐   41-50 ☐   Over 50 ☐

Name: _____

Address: _____

_____

E-mail: _____   Post/Zip Code: _____

Telephone: _____   Date: _____

☐ Please tick here if you do not want to receive details of products and services from Thomas Cook Publishing

Greek Island Hopping
Reader's Questionnaire

This guide is intended to be of maximum use to both new and regular island hoppers.
We are therefore interested in your views on how it could be improved. Please take a few
minutes to fill in this form and let us know how you fared with this publication.

Please send this page to:

**The Editor, Greek Island Hopping, Thomas Cook Publishing,
PO Box 227, Units 15–16, The Thomas Cook Business Park, Coningsby Road,
PETERBOROUGH, PE3 8SB, UK.**

1. What exactly did you use this guide to try to find out?

2. Have you used this guide before?
   (if YES – which edition/s?)

3. Did you use this guide more for pre-planning or for on-the-spot reference?

4. What would you like to see more of in the guide? (Please number in order
   of preference)

   Sightseeing   Expanded Island   Hotel / Rooms
   Information   Descriptions   Descriptions

   Restaurant / Bar   Other
   Descriptions

5. Are there any other changes you would like to see made to the guide?

6. Did you take any other guidebooks with you to the Greek Islands?

   (Please specify)